During the years 1946–56 the annual *Book List* of the British Society for Old Testament Study, edited by Professor H. H. Rowley, came to be widely recognized and used as an invaluable guide to current literature relating to the Old Testament and allied fields. These eleven issues, originally printed for private circulation, were collected and reissued in the volume *Eleven Years of Bible Bibliography*.

The subsequent ten issues (1957–66), edited by Professor G. W. Anderson of the University of Edinburgh, are now collected in a similar volume. Practically all the most important works on the Old Testament which have appeared during the past decade in nearly a score of languages are briefly described and appraised. The reviews for each year are grouped according to subject matter in twelve main sections; and a comprehensive author index has been provided for the entire volume, which will be found to be an indispensable tool for all who are engaged in the serious study of the Old Testament.

A DECADE OF BIBLE BIBLIOGRAPHY

A DECADE OF
BIBLE BIBLIOGRAPHY

The Book Lists of the
Society for Old Testament Study
1957–1966

Edited by
G.W. Anderson, M.A., D.D.

Professor of Old Testament Literature
and Theology, University of Edinburgh

BASIL BLACKWELL · OXFORD · 1967

Printed in Great Britain

Contents

v

Text and Versions

Exegesis and Modern Translations

Literary Criticism and Introduction

Law, Religion, and Theology

The Life and Thought of the Neighbouring Peoples

The Dead Sea Scrolls

Apocrypha and Post-Biblical Judaism

Philology and Grammar

vii

Key to Initials under Book Notices

P.R.A.	= P. R. Ackroyd		W.D.McH.	= W. D. McHardy
T.A.	= T. Aiura		J.M.	= J. Mauchline
G.W.A.	= G. W. Anderson		A.N.	= A. Neher
D.R.Ap-T.	= D. R. Ap-Thomas		C.R.N.	= C. R. North
C.K.B.	= C. K. Barrett		M.N.	= M. Noth
J.M.T.B.	= J. M. T. Barton		A.P.	= A. Parrot
W.B.	= W. Beyerlin		D.P.	= D. Patterson
M.B.	= M. Bič		A.P.	= A. Penna
M.Bl.	= M. Black		L.A.P.	= L. A. Poore
P.A.H.deB.	= P. A. H. de Boer		N.W.P.	= N. W. Porteous
J.B.	= J. Bowman		B.J.R.	= B. J. Roberts
L.H.B.	= L. H. Brockington		T.H.R.	= T. H. Robinson
F.F.B.	= F. F. Bruce		E.I.J.R.	= E. I. J. Rosenthal
M.Bu.	= M. Burdess		E.R.R.	= E. R. Rowlands
H.C.	= H. Cazelles		H.H.R.	= H. H. Rowley
R.E.C.	= R. E. Clements		E.T.R.	= E. T. Ryder
D.D	= D. Daube		J.F.A.S.	= J. F. A. Sawyer
G.H.D.	= G. H. Davies		J.N.S.	= J. N. Schofield
T.D.	= T. Donald		S.Se.	= S. Segert
H.D.	= H. Donner		N.H.S.	= N. H. Snaith
G.R.D.	= G. R. Driver		S.S.	= S. Stein
J.A.E.	= J. A. Emerton		J.W.S.	= J. W. Sweetman
C.J.G.	= C. J. Gadd		T.W.T.	= T. W. Thacker
A.G.	= A. Gelston		D.W.T.	= D. W. Thomas
G.G.	= G. Gerleman		E.U.	= E. Ullendorf
J.G.	= J. Gray		R.deV.	= R. de Vaux
E.H.	= E. Hammershaimb		G.V.	= G. Vermes
A.S.H.	= A. S. Herbert		M.W.	= M. Wallenstein
S.H.H.	= S. H. Hooke		J.W.	= J. Weingreen
A.R.J.	= A. R. Johnson		P.R.W.	= P. R. Weis
D.R.J.	= D. R. Jones		E.W.	= E. Wiesenberg
C.A.K.	= C. A. Keller		J.V.K.W.	= J.V Kinnier-Wilson
J.L.	= J. Lindblom		D.J.W.	= D. J. Wiseman
R.L.	= R. Loewe		W.Z.	= W. Zimmerli
J.Macd.	= J. Macdonald			

Editor's Preface

This volume contains the ten *Book Lists* (1957–66) of the British Society for Old Testament Study which I edited on its behalf. At the end of my term of office as editor, the Society authorized the reissue of the *Book Lists* in this form as a sequel to *Eleven Years of Bible Bibliography*, edited by Professor H. H. Rowley (The Falcon's Wing Press, 1957). My indebtedness to many colleagues is indicated in the prefaces to the several *Book Lists*. I wish also to put on record my gratitude to the publisher for accepting the volume for publication, and for the advice and help which he and his staff have readily given, and to Mr. Andrew D. H. Mayes, a research student in the Faculty of Arts in this University, for his generous assistance in the preparation of the material and the compilation of the comprehensive index of authors.

It is gratifying that the volume will appear during the Jubilee Year of the Society, since it records an important aspect of the Society's work in the furtherance of Old Testament Study.

NEW COLLEGE,   G. W. ANDERSON
UNIVERSITY OF EDINBURGH.

ix

BOOK LIST, 1957

If this edition of the *Book List* has not suffered too grievously by the change of editor, the credit is chiefly due to Professor Rowley, who, with characteristically painstaking generosity, has constantly helped me with advice, information, and the loan of books, and who has written a large number of notices at a time when, even by his own exacting standards, he was unusually busy. In expressing my gratitude to him for all his help, I wish also to thank the members of the *Book List* Panel for their loyal co-operation, Professors Bič, Cazelles, Keller, Noth, and Robinson, who, though not members of the Panel, have contributed notices, the Printer, whose courtesy and practical help have been unfailing, and Miss Gillian Unwin, who has prepared the material for the Printer. Professor de Boer has kindly provided details about works published in the Netherlands.

I regret that it has not been possible to include more Israeli books ; but I gladly acknowledge the help given by Professor Rabin in providing information, and by the Jewish Agency Department for Culture and Education in the Diaspora in supplying books.

Every effort has been made to indicate prices in the original currency wherever possible. Unfortunately, in some instances the necessary information could not be obtained. The number of gaps would have been greater but for the co-operation of the staff of B. H. Blackwell of Oxford.

The arranging of reviews in the appropriate sections sometimes presents a problem, since some books fall into more than one category. But I hope that the classification is nowhere seriously misleading. Books suitable for inclusion in school libraries are marked by an asterisk (*).

G. W. ANDERSON.

ST. MARY'S COLLEGE,
UNIVERSITY OF ST. ANDREWS.

GENERAL

Atti dell' VIII Congresso Internationale di Storia delle Religioni (Roma 17-23 Aprile, 1955). n.d. Pp. viii+500. (Sansoni, Florence. Price : 42s. 0d.)

This formal record of the Eighth Congress for the History of Religions contains an account of the business proceedings of the Congress, and summaries of the papers and discussions. Of the papers on Old Testament themes, those by Mowinckel, Kapelrud, Hempel, Coppens, Bič, de Boer, Beek, and Jansen will be published in a volume on the main theme of the Congress (Sacral Kingship) ; and that by Morgenstern will appear in book form. Some will appear, or have appeared, in learned journals. To summarize the summaries here seems pointless. G.W.A.

AVI-YONAH, M. (ed. by) : *Sepher Yerushalayim (The Book of Jerusalem) : Jerusalem, its Natural Conditions, History and Development from the Origins to the Present Day,* Vol. 1, *The Natural Conditions and the History of the City from its Origins to the Destruction of the Second Temple.* 1956. Pp. 432. (Bialik Institute and Dvir Publishing House, Jerusalem and Tel-Aviv.)

This volume, which contains contributions by a galaxy of Israeli scholars, each expert in his particular branch of study, is made up of three sections. Section I deals with Jerusalem's natural conditions, such as geography, geology, climate, flora and fauna. Section II deals with the history of the town, ranging from its origins to the destruction of the First Temple. Here we have studies about prehistoric remains ; the town before the reign of David ; history in the times of the First Temple ; cultural life ; archaeology; topography ; inscriptions ; the First Temple ; water supply of Jerusalem in ancient times. Section III is devoted to Jerusalem in the time of the Second Temple. The studies here comprise : History ; destruction of Jerusalem ; religious and cultural life ; archaeology and topography ; the Necropolis ; Hebrew and Aramaic inscriptions ; Greek inscriptions ; the ritual in the Second Temple. The volume also contains a selected up-to-date bibliography which takes cognizance of the more reputable works involved, as well as numerous maps, pictures of various archaeological finds, etc., and drawings.

The volume maintains the very high standard of the Bialik Institute in both contents and production. One is looking forward to the second volume of *SEPHER YERUSHALA-YIM* which will deal with Jerusalem from the Second Temple onwards. M.W.

Bijbels Woordenboek. 2nd ed. Parts 3 and 4. Isaias-Samaria. 1956. Cols. 769-1504. (Romen en Zonen, Roermond. Price : Fl. 10.75.)

This new and substantially revised one-volume Bible Dictionary (see *Book List,* 1955, p. 4 and 1956, p. 3) is rapidly nearing completion. A single part is now awaited to complete the work. The bibliographies are brought up to date, and the latest knowledge and research are amply utilized. H.H.R.

3

Bič, M. and Souček, J. B. (ed. by) : *Biblická Konkordance*, parts 7-9
(H-K). 1956. Pp. 80 each part. (Edice Kalich, Prague ; agents,
Artia, Ltd., 30 Smečky, Prague. Price : Kčs. 10.50 or U.S. **$1.10**
per part.)

> These three issues carry the work (on which see *Book List*,
> 1955, p. 4; 1956, p. 3) down to Kálef. It is therefore steadily
> pursuing its way towards completion, and when finished it
> will give to Czech readers an unsurpassed tool for Biblical
> study.   H.H.R.

DE Boer, P. A. H. (ed. by) :   *Volume du Congrès : Strasbourg* 1956.
(Supplements to *Vetus Testamentum*, vol. IV). 1957. Pp. 258+
6 plates+7 figures in the text. (Brill, Leiden. Price : Fl. 41).

> The only possible short review of this book, which gathers up
> the contributions of the fifteen scholars who delivered the main
> papers at the highly successful second congress of the Inter-
> national Organization of Old Testament Scholars, will be a
> list of the contents. Five are in English : the presidential
> address by G. R. Driver offers a short survey of recent and
> current linguistic work in the Semitic field ; D. Winton Thomas
> gives a careful survey of the Hebrew ḤDL ; B. Mazar (Maisler)
> makes a masterly contribution to historical geography with
> ' The Campaign of Pharaoh Shishak to Palestine '; P. W.
> Skehan confirms 135 A.D. as the terminus ad quem for the
> Qumran texts, and discusses their contribution to textual
> criticism ; while W. F. Albright has a characteristic paper on
> ' The High Place in Ancient Palestine.'
>
> The papers in French number six : J. T. Milik writes on the
> work of publishing the Dead Sea Scrolls ; and A. Diez Macho
> enumerates the important Hebrew and Aramaic biblical MSS.
> in the U.S.A. P. A. H. de Boer (who also pens a very neat and
> well-deserved tribute to the two local organizers of the Con-
> gress) comments on 2 Sam. xxiii. 1-7 ; and J. Coppens adduces
> Ugaritic parallels to Gen. xlix. G. Castellino studies the
> narratives in Gen. ii.-iv. in the light of certain Sumero-accadian
> stories ; while G. Widengren, in an illustrated paper, writes
> on Jewish-Iranian relations during the Parthian period.
>
> In German, E. Vogt adduces some very interesting and
> important evidence for the close of the Judean monarchy
> from the Wiseman Chronicles ; O. Eissfeldt stresses the
> influence of the Shilonite cult on Jerusalem ; W. Eichrodt
> discusses the validity of typological exegesis ; and, finally,
> H. Junker deals with the origin and fundamental features
> of the messianic portrait in Isa. i-xi., and particularly the
> Immanuel prophecy.
>
> This volume contains something of interest and importance
> for every *Alttestamentler* ; it is regrettable that it has to be so
> expensive.   D.R.Ap-T.

CAZELLES, H. (ed. by) : *Dictionnaire de la Bible. Supplément.* Fasc. xxix. (Midrash-Mycènes). 1957. Cols. 1281-1480. (Letouzey & Ané, Paris. Price : 22s. 3d.)

The present fascicle is the last of Volume V of the *Supplément*, and the first to be edited by H. Cazelles, who now takes the place of A. Robert, who died last year. It contains a number of important articles. There is a short study of " Milieu Biblique (le) " by the late C. F. Jean which summarizes his three volumes *Le milieu biblique de l'Ancien Testament* and adds a useful bibliography. The editor contributes two articles of value on " Moïse " and " Molok," both of which indicate clearly the present state of the questions arising from each subject. " Monnaie " by J. Babelon is an article in which no less than thirty columns of text and three pages of plates are devoted to the subject. " Murabba'at " by M. Delcor concentrates upon the two papyri that have so far been published, the letter of Bar Kokébas and the Beth Mashko document. In each case a translation and a commentary accompany the reproduction in facsimile, taken from the *Revue Biblique* for 1953. Lastly, " Musique (dans la Bible) " appears to be a very thorough treatment of the musical instruments mentioned in the Bible and of the music, by Mme. E. Gerson-Kiwi, of the research institute for Jewish music in Jerusalem.

There are short biographies of C. J. G. Montefiore, J. A. Montgomery, G. F. Moore, J. H. Moulton, S. Mowinckel, L. Murillo, and A. Musil.   J.M.T.B.

DAVIS, M. (ed. by) : *Israel : Its Role in Civilisation.* 1956. Pp. 338. (Harper & Brothers, New York : for The Seminary Israel Institute of the Jewish Theological Seminary of America. Price : $4.00.)

The purpose of the book is indicated by the four parts of which it is constituted : the role of Israel in the modern world : what history teaches : the new state : America and Israel. The first part consists of two short chapters, one by Dr. Louis Finkelstein (Chancellor of the Seminary) on the State of Israel as a spiritual force, and the other by David ben Gurion on the Spirit of the new Israel. Parts III and IV deal with the new State of Israel and its place in the modern world, but Part II is more directly within the scope of Old Testament studies. Professor W. F. Albright contributes eight pages on 'Israel—Prophetic Vision and Historical Fulfillment,' showing how the promises of the prophets have been fulfilled, though with change of emphasis. H. L. Ginsberg discusses the new light in the Graeco-Roman period provided by the Dead Sea Scrolls. Other articles by S. W. Baron, Morton Smith, S. Lieberman and C. J. Friedrich summarise the history of Israel from the Return from Babylon to the present date, and peer forward into the future. It is a volume designed to explain the new Israel to the world and to emphasise the common traditions shared by Israel and America.   N.H.S.

DORNSEIFF, F. : *Antike und Alter Orient. Interpretationen.* (Kleine Schriften, 1.) Pp. viii+444. (Koehler und Amelang, Leipzig. Price : DM. 14.50.)

This is the first of four volumes of Dornseiff's *Kleine Schriften*, which are to be published. The first part—nearly half the volume—deals with classical studies, but in the rest of the volume there is not a little of interest to Old Testament students. In one paper the Song of Songs is studied in relation to Egyptian and Greek writings, and in another study four articles which appeared in the *Zeitschrift für die alttestamentliche Wissenschaft* under the title *Antikes zum Alten Testament* are reprinted. Here there is a valuable collection of oriental and classical material illustrative of the Pentateuch. Other papers similarly deal with the books of Joshua and Judges, and one deals with theophanies in the Old Testament. The remaining studies include a review of Dussaud's *Découvertes de Ras Shamra et l'Ancien Testament*. Altogether thirty studies are collected in this volume. H.H.R.

FRIEDRICH, G. (ed. by): *Theologisches Wörterbuch zum Neuen Testament* (begun by G. Kittel). Band VI. Lieferungen 5, 6/7. 1956. Pp. 64. (Kohlhammer, Stuttgart. Price : DM. 4.60.)

In Lieferung 5 there are no articles of major importance to students of the Old Testament. (The most important section is the one on *pleroma*). Useful references to certain Hebrew words will, however, be found under *plasma* (*yeṣer*), *pleonektes* (*beṣaʿ*), *plethos* (*robh* and *hamon*, even *ʿedah*, *ʿam*, *qahal*, etc.), *pleroō* (*male*ʾ) and *plesion* (*reaʿ*).

In 6/7 there is first a brief section on ' Wealth ' and ' The Rich in the Old Testament ' by F. Hauck/Kasch. The remainder of this double Lieferung is occupied by the discussion of *pneuma* and its cognates, a discussion which is most relevant to the interests of Old Testament scholars. Baumgärtel contributes ' The Spirit in the Old Testament ' (a detailed examination of the word *ruaḥ*), ' The Spirit of God ' and the beginning of " The Spirit in Judaism.' This is continued by Bieder who among other subjects deals with ' The Spirit in Qoheleth, in Wisdom and in Hellenistic Judaism' (Philo and Josephus), while Sjöberg contributes ' The Spirit in Palestinian Judaism', dealing, e.g., with the origin of the conception of the pre-existence and immortality of the soul and with the Rabbinic view of the Spirit of God and its working. N.W.P.

GALLING, K. (ed. by) : *Die Religion in Geschichte und Gegenwart.* 3 Auflage, Band I, Lieferungen 1-4. 1956. Cols. 1-96, 97-192, 193-288, 289-384, with plates and maps. (J. C. B. Mohr. Tübingen. Subscription price : DM. 4.20 each Lieferung.)

The appearance of a new and completely revised edition of this standard work of reference is an event of major importance for all who are interested in any aspect of the study of religion.

The names of those responsible for the main groups of subjects guarantee the maintenance of the high standard associated with *R.G.G.* : and this is further borne out by the parts which have so far appeared, carrying the work down to *Anglo-katholizismus*. Of the longer articles or sections on subjects of special interest to the *Alttestamentler*, mention may be made of *Abraham* (A. Weiser), *Ackerbau in Israel* (H. W. Hertzberg), *Ägypten und die Bibel* (S. Morenz), *Altar (religions-geschichtlich*, C. H. Ratschow ; *in Israel*, K. Galling), *Amos* and *Amosbuch* (V. Maag), *Amt in Israel* (F. Horst). On a smaller scale, but valuable for their very conciseness, are the contributions on *Aaron* (F. Maass) ; *Aaronitischer Segen* and *Allerheiligstes* (K. Galling) ; *Abraham-Apokalypse*, *Abraham-Testament*, and *Adam-bücher* (R. Meyer) ; *Adonaj*, *Adonis*, *Ai*, and *Anath* (O. Eissfeldt) ; *Ahab* and *Ahas* (A. Alt) ; *Ahasver* (H. J. Schoeps) ; *Akiba* (C. H. Hunzinger) ; *Alalach*, *Amale-kiter*, and *Ammoniter* (M. Noth) ; *Amarna* and *Amenophis IV* (H. Brunner) ; and *Amraphel* (F. M. Th. Böhl).

Lief. 5/6. Cols. 385-576. (Subscription Price : DM. 8.40.)

This double Lieferung (which now takes the work down to *Arbeitsschule*) includes the articles *Antiochus IV. Epiphanes* (H. E. Stier), *Apokalyptik I. Apokalyptische Literatur, religions-geschichtlich* and *II. Jüdische Apokalyptik* (H. Ringgren), *Apokryphen des AT* (W. Baumgartner), *Aramäer* (A. Jepsen), *Aramäisches in der Bibel* (W. Baumgartner). Matters relevant to our field are also touched on in articles such as *Antike und Orient* (J. Kerschensteiner) and *Antisemitismus* (W. Holsten).
G.W.A.

HAAG, H. : (ed. by, with the collaboration of A. van den Born and others) : *Bibel-Lexikon*. Lief. 8. 1956. Cols. 1509-1784. (Benziger Verlag, Einsiedeln, Zürich and Cologne. Subscription price : Fr./DM. 11.00.)

With this issue this excellent handbook is now complete, and can be purchased bound for Fr./DM. 92.00. This final part contains articles on the Dead Sea Scrolls by Professor van der Ploeg (3 pages), and on Ugarit (3 pages, unsigned.) The short bibliographies at the end of all the principal articles are up-to-date, and the whole is a scholarly production of real value. There is an appendix on excavation in Palestine, which lists the sites excavated and their probable identifications.
H.H.R.

HAHN, H. F. : *The Old Testament in Modern Research*. 1956. Pp. xii+268. (S.C.M. Press, London. Price : 16s. 0d.)

This English edition of the work reviewed in the *Book List*, 1955, p. 7, is a photographic reprint of the American edition, which differs only in the addition of one word to its title and in being much cheaper. Its accessibility to British readers will be greatly increased by this edition, and it should be widely used. It provides a most valuable survey of scholarly work on many sides of Old Testament study since the rise of criticism, and its full references to the relevant literature will give it importance for future researchers.
H.H.R.

Hebrew Union College Annual, Vol. XXVII. 1956. Pp. 438 (+98 in Hebrew)+index. (Hebrew Union College, Cincinnati. Price : $3.00.)

Some of the 15 articles included in this volume are of very considerable length and some also of great importance. The volume opens with a most erudite disquisition by Julius Lewy on Old Assyrian Institutions, based on Hrozný's Cuneiform Inscriptions from Kültepe. This is followed by an article by S. H. Blank on Traces of Prophetic Agony in Isaiah, which, though suggestive, displays considerable subjectivity in the substance and presentation of the material. I. Lewy offers a short essay on Two Strata in the Eden Story together with a conjectural reconstruction of the basic document underlying this narrative. He assumes that the story is the amalgam of the work of separate Hebrew writers of different intellectual, moral, and religious outlook. Lewy comes to the conclusion that the original narrator was the Prophet Nathan, while the reviser was either Abiathar or one of his followers. The theory is not unattractive even to a sceptical reviewer. Julian Morgenstern contributes the first part of a weighty historical and text-critical study in which he sets out to show, on the basis of a detailed examination of the texts of Nehemiah, Lamentations, parts of Ezekiel, Obadiah and Malachi, etc., that a major catastrophe (to which Neh. i. 1-3 refers) overtook Jerusalem in 485 B.C. leading to the burning of the Second Temple and the destruction of Jerusalem and its walls by the Moabites, Ammonites, Edomites, and other neighbours of Judah. This contribution repays the closest study. L. J. Liebreich investigates Psalms 34 and 145 in the light of their key-words, in order to test the validity of the key-word-law in the composition of the Psalms postulated by M. Buber. The article is followed by an interesting *addendum* dealing with the so-called ' envelope figures ' which constitute identical or equivalent opening and closing passages in a large number of Psalms. The customary assumptions about the treatment of anthropomorphism in the LXX of Isaiah (and other parts of the O.T.) are subjected to a refreshingly original investigation by H. M. Orlinksy who reaches the conclusion that the alleged anti-anthropomorphic attitude on the part of the LXX translators is partly quite unsubstantiated and partly concerned with style and intelligibility rather than any theological prejudice. S. Sandmel contributes an article on Myths in the Gospels. E. Wiesenberg deals with the strangely related prohibitions of swine-breeding and the study of Greek which, he avers, derive their connexion from an episode during the concluding stages of the Jewish struggle against the Romans. H. Slonimsky presents an outline of the philosophy implicit in the Midrash, while A. Scheiber studies some unknown leaves from *she'eloth 'athiqoth*. E. Ashtor-Strauss discusses the policy of Saladin towards the Jews. An interesting study of the Portuguese sermons preached at *autos-da-fé* and the image of the Jew developed in these sermons is contributed by E. Glaser. F. Landsberger's article on Ritual Implements for the Sabbath contains some excellent illustrations and is a valuable contribution to the study of Jewish Art. S. S. Schwarzschild writes on the philosopher Hermann Cohen. The 98-page Hebrew part of this volume contains the exceedingly recondite *hassagoth* by R. Moses Hakohen on some books of Maimonides, according to a unique MS. in the Bodleian Library, Oxford.—Appended is an index to the HUC Annuals, vols. I-XXVI. E.U.

HOBBS, E. C. : (ed.) : *A Stubborn Faith : Papers on Old Testament and Related Subjects Presented to Honor William Andrew Irwin.* 1956. Pp. xii+170. (S.M.U. Press, Dallas 5, Texas. Price : $4.00.)
This volume is a *Festschrift* in honour of Professor W. A. Irwin, formerly of Toronto and Chicago, and latterly of Southern Methodist University, Dallas. We associate ourselves with his eleven former students in doing honour to a gifted and faithful scholar. R. J. Williams writes on ' The Fable in the Near East,' chiefly in Egypt and in Mesopotamia. In ' The Exodus and Apocalyptic,' Grace Edwards emphasises the importance of Moses and the Exodus in Hebrew thoughts and dreams of the future. E. R. Thiele returns to a former theme of his in ' The Question of Coregencies among the Hebrew Kings.' W. S. McCullough is doubtful of Mowinckel's theory concerning " The Enthronement of Yahweh " Psalms. C. F. Kraft makes considerable use of Ugaritic poetry in his essay ' Some Further Observations concerning the Strophic Structure of Hebrew Poetry ' ; he regards the existence of regular strophic structure as indisputable, but speaks in terms of couplet and triad forms. W. G. Williams links ' Jeremiah's Vision of the Almond Rod ' with Aaron's rod that budded. H. G. May deals with the diverse elements of Old Testament characters in ' Some Historical Perspectives.' H. M. Orlinsky contributes ' Notes on the Present State of the Textual Criticism of the Judaean Biblical Cave Scrolls.' R. B. Y. Scott, in ' The Service of God,' insists that the cultic service must always be secondary to the worship of the heart. W. A. Beardslee discusses chiefly Anders Nygren's *Agape and Eros* in his article entitled ' Identifying Features of Early Christianity.' Finally the editor himself comments on 'A Different Approach to the Writing of Commentaries on the Synoptic Gospels.' N.H.S.

Internationale Zeitschriftenschau für Bibelwissenschaft und Grenzgebiete, III, 1954-55, Heft 1-2. 1956. Pp. xii+232. (Patmos Verlag, Düsseldorf. Price : DM. 34 or $8.10.)
This indispensable tool of scholarship continues to offer its valuable help to all who are engaged in Biblical study and research. The present issue contains 1495 items which have appeared during the period covered, in no less than 425 periodicals. To have a classified bibliography of the articles which have appeared in so many journals, with summaries of the contents of the articles in most cases, is an inestimable

boon. There are, for instance, summaries of eighty-eight articles on the Dead Sea Scrolls, all of which appeared during the period under survey. An international team of forty-six scholars has prepared the abstracts. No scholar at work in the Biblical field should be without access to this publication.

H.H.R.

KAHLE, P. : *Opera Minora. Festgabe zum* 21 *Januar,* 1956. 1956. Pp. xviii+372, with a portrait. (Brill, Leiden. Price : £6.10s.0d.)

This collection of Dr. P. Kahle's *opera minora* is a most welcome publication, for it brings together many fugitive pieces, some not by any means easy to find and all of considerable importance, in handy form. The collection is divided into two parts, the first containing *Hebraica* (14 articles) and the second *Islamica* (9 articles). All these articles are well-known, but have still a freshness which is as stimulating as it is interesting ; and those who possess it will be glad not only on account of the valuable contents of the volume but also as a *ktema es aei*, reminding them of a great scholar, one who has taught so much to so many with unabated vigour for an immense span of years, from 1898 (when his first article appeared) till the present time. The volume is furnished also with a bibliography (from which reviews are omitted) of seven pages, listing 100 articles, a brief account of the author's work and an excellent photograph of him.

G.R.D.

KRAUS, H. J. : *Geschichte der historisch-kritischen Erforschung des Alten Testaments von der Reformation bis zur* Gegenwart. 1956. Pp. xii+478, and 8 plates. (Erziehungsverein, Neukirchen. Price : DM. 24.)

As the title indicates, this work covers much the same ground as E. G. Kraeling's *The Old Testament since the Reformation* (*Book List*, 1956, pp. 30f.) ; and it is a sign of the times, when so much that seemed assured in the attempted reconstruction of the origin and growth of the O.T. is called in question, that two such similar works should appear within a year or so of each other. The present work is wider in scope than that of Kraeling, and, on the whole, its later pages tend to leave the reader with a greater sense of direction so far as recent trends are concerned. Nevertheless the different emphases of the two writers make their works complementary, and all students of the O.T. who wish to see such a volume as *The Old Testament and Modern Study* (*Book List*, 1952, p. 8) in its historical setting should pay careful attention to both. A typical example of the many valuable features of Kraus's work may be found in the way in which he shows how the opening up of the ancient Near East through archaeological discovery has made it necessary to study the O.T. in this wider cultural setting, with results which are only now becoming generally known to demand a reassessment of the findings of the dominant school of O.T. criticism represented, for example, by the names of Graf, Kuenen and Wellhausen. The work of British scholars (e.g., A. C. Welch and H. W. Robinson) does not always receive from the author the recognition which it deserves, while our friends across the Channel may be surprised at the neglect of A. Causse ; but, despite an occasional omission of this kind, the work may be warmly recommended as a remarkably full and quite fascinating survey of the relevant literature. A.R.J.

LISOWSKY, G. : *Konkordanz zum hebräischen Alten Testament*, unter verantwortlicher Mitwirkung von L. Rost. Lieferungen 3-7. 1956. Pp. 128 each Lief. (Privileg. Württ. Bibelanstalt, Stuttgart. Price : DM. 2.60 each.)

This concordance, whose excellent features were described in the *Book List*, 1956, pp. 20f., continues to appear regularly, and will be completed during 1957, when the whole work will be available for DM. 35.00. It will form a handy concordance of the greatest value to students and others, and warm thanks are due to Professor Rost and Dr. Lisowsky for all the labour that has gone into its preparation. H.H.R.

NOTH, M. : *Gesammelte Studien zum Alten Testament* (Theologische Bücherei : Neudrucke und Berichte aus dem 20. Jahrhundert. Band 6). 1957. Pp. 306. (Chr. Kaiser Verlag, München. Price : DM. 10.)

This is a collection of studies which are republished in one volume, not because their subject-matter is closely related, but because they either were in their original form, or are even now, not easily accessible. Pride of place is given to " Die Gesetze im Pentateuch " which takes up almost half of the volume. It is concerned to trace the organization of historically conditioned laws into a co-ordinate corpus in the Pentateuch within the framework of the sacral community, until not only the Pentateuch but the Old Testament also can be described as the Law. Such a description of the Old Testament, late in its appearing and inadequate as a basis for Old Testament interpretation, illustrates how laws and regulations often outlive the institutions among which they had their *Sitz im Leben*, until a worth is claimed for them which they did not originally possess and men preserve and honour them simply because they are traditional. There is an interesting article on Old Testament covenant-making in terms of a Mari text which speaks of a peace-making by the slaughtering of the foal of an ass (cf. Pritchard, ANET, 482b) ; another discusses how it was that Jerusalem, in spite of its location west of the Jordan, was so late in coming into a positive relationship with Israelite history and examines the significance of the installation of the ark there ; while another entitled " Gott, König, Volk im Alten Testament " discusses some of the ideas of the myth-ritual school of thought and enters a caveat against the assumption that there was a generally prevailing scheme of myth and idea which Israel shared equally with the other peoples of the ancient near east. The volume contains six studies in addition to the main one

and many will find it most advantageous to have them in
one volume.   J.M.

Die Gesetze im Pentateuch was originally reviewed in *Book
List*, 1946, p. 48. *Das Geschichtsverständnis der alttestamentlichen Apokalyptik*, also included in the present volume,
was reviewed in *Book List*, 1954, p. 52.   G.W.A.

RIESENFELD, H. (ed. by) : *Svensk Exegetisk Årsbok*, xx. (1955). 1956.
Pp. 96. With supplement, *Symbolae Biblicae Upsalienses*, 15.
1956. Pp. 110. (C. W. K. Gleerup, Lund. Price : Sw. kr. 10.)

H. Ringgren contributes a very learned discussion in English
of Esther and Purim, arguing for a relation between the
Biblical story and the myths and legends connected with
the Persian New Year ceremonies, but admitting the presence
of Babylonian elements, and conceding the possibility that
the story has a historical nucleus. H. Riesenfeld writes in
Swedish on the Gospels and the historical Jesus. The annual
also contains reviews of recent literature. The Supplement
is a continuation of the translations of the Qumran texts
begun in Supplement 14. *The War of the Sons of Light* and
the *Hodayoth* are rendered into Swedish with brief introductions
and notes by H. Ringgren. The notes, which are mainly
textual and philological, are models of conciseness, and
present in convenient form a useful guide to the extensive
literature on these texts.   G.W.A.

SINOR, D. (ed. by) : *Proceedings of the Twenty-Third International
Congress of Orientalists, Cambridge, 21st-28th August, 1954.* n.d.
Pp. 422. (Royal Asiatic Society, London.)

This official record of the congress includes abstracts of most
of the papers read. Those bearing on the Old Testament
field are of varied interest. They are too condensed to summarise further here ; but those who consult the volume will
find handy references to the periodicals in which the full
texts of some of the papers may be found.   G.W.A.

SISTER, M. : *Mi-Ba'yoth ha-Siphruth ha-Miqra'ith* (in Hebrew) 1955.
Pp. 246+4 plates. (Hakibutz Hameuchad, Tel-Aviv.)

The author, known to scholars acquainted with the *Wissenschaft des Judentums* of the period immediately preceding the
advent of Hitler to power in Germany, continues here his
studies on problems of the Literature of the Bible. Among
subjects dealt with are The Story in the Bible ; Relics of War-
Poetry ; and the attitude in the time·of war of the Israelites
towards the non-belligerent population as well as towards
the captives. The author, drawing with considerable skill
on the relevant literature written mainly in European
languages, believes that some of his work may prove to be
enlightening the new Israel re-established in the Land of the
Bible.   M.W.

STEINMULLER, J. E. and SULLIVAN, K. (ed. by) : *Catholic Biblical Encyclopedia: Old and New Testaments.* 1956. Pp. xviii+1166+ xvi+680. (B. Herder, London. Price : £6.)

The New Testament section of this large work was first published in 1950. Now it has been joined in one volume with the Old Testament section, though it is possible to obtain either part separately. On almost all topics concerning the Old and New Testaments its purpose is to provide a quantity of information, though, almost needless to say, even so large a book cannot take the place of special treatises, commentaries on individual books, and so forth. The editors have been at some pains to include articles under such headings as archaeology, Ras Shamra, and the Dead Sea Scrolls. On the whole, the tendency of the work is markedly conservative, though arguments of a more critical character are usually stated when occasion arises. There are many photographs and a number of diagrams and maps. The maps are, perhaps, the weakest feature of the work. They are not very carefully drawn, and certainly cannot be compared with the excellent maps in the *Catholic Commentary on Holy Scripture* reviewed in the *Book List* for 1953, pp. 35f. J.M.T.B.

Studia theologica cura ordinum theologorum Scandinavicorum edita, Vol. IX, Fasc. i, 1955. Pp. 66. Fasc. ii, 1956. Pp. 99. (Gleerup, Lund. Price : by subscription, Sw. Kr. 12, or Sw. Kr. 8, each fascicle.)

In this notice reference is made only to those articles which have a bearing on the Old Testament field. In Fasc. i, P. Wernberg-Møller examines the Biblical material in the Manual of Discipline, indicating both echoes of Biblical phraseology and also modifications of its meaning.

In Fasc. ii, A. Ehrhardt writes on ' The Birth of the Synagogue and R. Akiba,' surveying the evidence for conflicting influences in Judaism at the end of the first and beginning of the second century. E. Sjöberg contributes a short article on ' new creation ' in the Dead Sea Scrolls. S. Mowinckel carries further the studies in Hebrew metre which he has published during the past few years in a detailed examination of the poetical form of Ecclesiasticus. G.W.A.

THOMSEN, P. : *Die Palästina-Literatur : eine internationale Bibliographie in systematischer Ordnung mit Autoren- und Sachregister,* Vol. vi, Lieferung 3. 1956. Pp. 577-832. (Akademie Verlag, Berlin. Price : DM. 28.)

This issue of the sixth volume of a work which will always be associated with the name of the late Dr. Peter Thomsen completes the volume for the years 1935-39. The two previous parts of the volume were noticed in the *Book List*, 1954, p. 15, and 1955, p. 13. Like the second part this issue was prepared by Dr. Peter Thomsen, but has been seen through the press by F. Maass and L. Rost, who have deserved well of their fellow-scholars by the immense service this work does for them.

Books and articles are covered, and there are references to reviews in important journals. Nearly 1700 items are listed in a carefully classified arrangement, covering Geography and then Syria and Palestine in modern times. Other subjects were covered in the earlier issues. There is a complete author index to the whole volume, and a brief appreciation of the late Dr. Thomsen, who conceived the work and for so many years devoted himself to it, prefaces the volume. H.H.R.

THOMSEN, P. : *Die Palästina-Literatur : eine internationale Bibliographie in systematischer Ordnung mit Autoren- und Sachregister,* Vol. A, Lieferung 1. 1957. Pp. ii+272. (Akademie Verlag, Berlin. Price : DM. 36.)

The six volumes of this well-known work hitherto issued contain the bibliography of the years 1895-1939, and the seventh volume, covering 1940-1949 is in preparation. Meanwhile the first issue of a volume covering the years 1878-1894 has appeared, to fill the gap for which no comparable work of reference existed. The material for this volume was prepared by the late Dr. Peter Thomsen, but it has been seen through the press by Professor Rost. To both the gratitude of scholars is due. This issue contains over four thousand entries, dealing with general works and history, all carefully classified. To Librarians it will be a boon, and to scholars it will be an invaluable tool. H.H.R.

EDUCATIONAL

*BROADIE, E. : *The Chosen Nation : Book Two : Kings and Prophets (David to Hosea).* 1956. Pp. 128. (Religious Education Press, Wallington, Surrey. Price : Boards, 6s. 0d. ; Limp, 5s. 0d.)

This book, which bears a commendatory preface by Professor H. H. Rowley, is the second of a series intended to help pupils in the middle forms of Grammar Schools and the upper forms of Secondary Modern Schools by supplying a background to their study of the Bible. It is written in a simple and readable style and illustrated by useful maps and diagrams. The usefulness of the book is enhanced by the well thought-out exercises appended to each of the short chapters of which it is composed. L.A.P.

*HEALING, C. A. : *The Old Testament : Its Writers and Their Messages,* 3rd ed., revised by G. T. Roberts. n.d. Pp. viii+188. (Methodist Youth Department, London. Price : 3s. 0d.)

This very succinct little compendium of elementary information, with its two useful maps, should admirably serve the needs of those who seek ' a simple and untechnical guide to the English Old Testament,' its declared purpose. The third edition, itself undated, of a work whose original date is not disclosed, it has been carefully brought up-to-date, and betrays its vintage only in its bibliography and perhaps in its general arrangement and emphasis. But this hardly detracts from its usefulness as a book of reference for beginners. M.Bu.

*HEATON, E. W. : *Everyday Life in Old Testament Times.* 1956. Pp. 240. Ills. 126. (B. T. Batsford Ltd., London. Price : 15s. 0d.)

In the preface to this excellent book Canon Heaton says that he has tried to write for all who are interested in the Old Testament, and rather unkindly adds, ' except, of course, the learned.' Whatever little learning the present writer possesses has not prevented him from enjoying to the full the spring-like freshness and unobtrusive learning of this book. An author, now dead, gave to a book about the Old Testament the title, *The Bible Comes Alive.* This is exactly what Canon Heaton, with the aid of Marjorie Quennell's admirable drawings, has done for readers, young and old, of the Old Testament. Every aspect of Hebrew life, from the beginning of Hebrew settlement in Canaan to the fall of Jerusalem, is here described vividly and faithfully, and with full knowledge of the most recent archaeological research. The chapter on Religion may give the conventionally minded a jolt when they read, ' religion is not necessarily a good thing at all,' and are told that in Old Testament times, Israel suffered not from a lack of religion, but from an excess of it, but this chapter contrives to say some very valuable things about the religion of Israel in a very short space. The book can be unreservedly recommended to all readers and teachers of the Old Testament. S.H.H.

*SMITH, J. W. D. : *God and Man in Early Israel.* 1956. Pp. vi + 122. (Methuen and Co., London. Price : 5s. 6d.)

This text-book is designed to meet the requirements of one of the " O " level syllabuses in Religious Knowledge set in the G.C.E. Examination of the Associated Examining Board. It deals with the O.T. history from Abraham to Solomon in the light of archaeological research and biblical scholarship, in which respects it is accurate and up-to-date. The biblical record is related to God's revelation of an unfolding purpose which is to culminate in Christ. The emphasis throughout is on the outstanding personalities of the story, purely critical problems being alluded to only where they bear directly on the religious teaching of the literature. The author's scholarship and religious insight should appeal to a wide audience, especially among teachers in Secondary Modern Schools. L.A.P.

ARCHAEOLOGY AND EPIGRAPHY

ALBRIGHT, W. F. : *Recent Discoveries in Bible Lands.* 1955. Pp. 136 + Chronological Table. (Biblical Colloquium, Pittsburgh, through Funk and Wagnalls Co., New York. Price : $2.00.)

The twentieth American edition of Young's *Analytical Concordance to the Bible* (1936) contained a supplement on the subject of Biblical archaeology by Professor Albright. This supplement, brought up-to-date, has been re-issued separately. The first part is largely a history of archaeological discovery in the lands of the ancient Near East. This is followed by an account in brief chapters of the most important discoveries which have a bearing on the Old and New Testaments. An inserted chronological table adds to the usefulness of the work. The whole is a clear, compact, authoritative statement, which, though brief, deserved an index. In the next revision some small alterations may be expected, e.g., ' recent ' and ' recently ' might be dropped on pages 119 and 121 and the ' Book of Lamech ' (page 130) will be renamed, while it will be noted that the British Museum is, alas, no longer the home of the Chester Beatty papyri. W.D.McH.

CANTERA, F. and MILLÁS, J. M. (ed. by) : *Las inscripciones Hebraicas de España*. 1956. Pp. xvi+476 and 36 plates. (Consejo Superior de Investigaciones Cientificas, Madrid. Price : Ps. 600.)

This is a really beautiful and scholarly edition of a new corpus of the Hebrew inscriptions that have been copied, and wherever possible photographed, in many parts of Spain. The last notable collection was made by Moïse Schwab in 1907 in his *Rapport sur les inscriptions hébraïques de l'Espagne*, who in an earlier work, published in 1904, on Hebrew inscriptions in France had ventured to say that nowhere, apart from Rome, were so many ancient inscriptions to be found as in France. In a later work he was led to change his mind and to affirm that the collections made in Spain were superior in number and age even to the French. " L'Espagne seule," he wrote, " possède sur son sol, toute la série succesive des évolutions de l'écriture, depuis le phénicien jusqu'au grec et latin, depuis l'inscription trilingue de Tortose jusqu'aux textes coufiques et néo-arabes ainsi que du judéo-rabbinique de la fin de moyen-âge, après les plus belles épitaphes hébraïques du monde entier." (*De la paléographie sémitique*, BRAH XLVIII, 1906, 464 ff.)

Since Schwab amassed his collection in 1907 the number of inscriptions known has all but doubled. Scarcely less than three hundred are collected and translated here, of which more than two-thirds are epitaphs, the remainder being inscriptions on doors, rings, amulets, dishes, and a variety of objects. There are 158 illustrations in the text and 36 full-page plates. A map of Spain showing the sites of the in-scriptions, and a series of ten indices complete a work of the greatest value for students of Hebrew epigraphy in the Christian era. J.M.T.B.

CAQUOT, A. : *Nouvelles Inscriptions Araméennes de Hatra* (III) (Extrait de la Revue *Syria*, XXXII, 1955, Fasc. 1-2.) Paris. Pp. 49-69 (With an appendix *Sur le Semeion*.) (Geuthner, Paris. Price : Fr. 400.)

M. Caquot has on two previous occasions (*Syria*, 1952 and 1953) offered interpretations of the Aramaic Inscriptions of ancient Hatra (modern *Al Hadr*). The present instalment adds a further fifteen documents, most of which are supplicatory inscriptions of the type (e.g., No. 44) : DKYR YHW BR MYN BR BLGW QDM MRN ' May there be remembered YHW son of MYN son of BLGW before our Lord.' One inscription is sepulchral and another records the names of some sculptors—altogether not an exciting collection.

M. Caquot's note on the *Semeion* discusses the possibilities of a Greek and a Semitic etymology, probes the explanation of the word as ' effigy of the Goddess Simia ' and rejects, rightly, the derivation from *šemāyā* ' heavens.' Yet, there remains an air of inconclusiveness about this appendix. E.U.

CAQUOT, A. : *Inscriptions Judéo-Arabes de Rusāfa (Sergiopolis).* (Extrait de la Revue *Syria*, XXXII, 1955, Fasc. 1-2.) Pp. 70-74 and 1 plate. (Geuthner, Paris. Price : Fr. 400.)

This offprint from *Syria* describes and translates three small inscriptions in Arabic language, but written in Hebrew characters. They are engraved partly above the opening in a wall and partly along one of its sides and are situated in the Syrian town of Rusāfa. They are dated 1413 and 1438 of the Seleucid era (=1102 and 1127, respectively) and are thus probably the oldest Judeo-Arabic inscriptions hitherto discovered in Syria.

The contents consist mainly of names, all of them attested, and refer to the Jews of Edessa. The chamber by whose entrance the inscriptions are found probably served as a place of worship (' the blessed place ') for Jewish members of caravans travelling between Edessa and Damascus. E.U.

CORSWANT, W. : *Dictionnaire d'archéologie biblique*, revised and illustrated by E. Urech, preface by A. Parrot. 1957. Pp. 324. (Delachaux et Niestlé, Neuchâtel and Paris. Price : Sw. Fr. 20.30.)

The late Professor Corswant left this work almost complete, and it has been revised, supplemented and completed since his death. Professor Parrot contributes a Preface. The title may raise expectations that the volume will not fulfil. There are no articles on the excavated sites, and there is no attempt to deal with the light shed on the history of Israel by archaeology. What the work seeks rather to do is to provide a handy book of reference on every side of the daily life of the ancient Hebrews. Its articles are very short, but it offers a useful book of reference within this limited field. Many of the entries seem to have a very tenuous connexion with archaeology, while much that the reader interested in Biblical archaeology will look for is absent. There is no article on the Dead Sea Scrolls. H.H.R.

KELLER, W. : *The Bible as History : Archaeology Confirms the Book of Books*. Translated from the German by William Neil. 1956. Pp. 430+51 plates+3 maps+76 figs. in text. (Hodder and Stoughton, London. Price : 25s. 0d.)

The popularity of this book, parts of which have been serialised in the daily press, testifies not only to the literary flair of the author, a journalist of scientific bent, but also to the skill of the translation by Dr. William Neil. The sub-title suggests the standpoint, but although only those explanations which the author accepts are mentioned, the attitude is not obscurantist or rigidly literalistic. Many of the valuable positive results of archaeology are here gathered together, but since the exact source of statements made is not given, the reader cannot control his information. There is a substantial bibliography, and two indexes add to the usefulness of the book. It will certainly have a large sale, although (perhaps in part because) the scholar would wish for a little more caution at some points. The excellent photographs deserve special mention, and so do the line drawings. D.R.Ap-T.

KRAELING, C. H. (ed. by) : *The Synagogue*. Part I of Final Report VIII on the Excavations at Dura-Europos. 1956. Pp. xviii+402, LXXVIII Plates and 124 text figures. (Yale University Press, and Oxford University Press, London. Price in U.K. : 120s. 0d.)

There are three major subjects of historical and archaeological interest concerning which the present volume provides information of the first importance. The first is the problem of the origin of the synagogue as an institution ; the second is the status of a Jewish community living in a Gentile environment ; and the third is the question of the nature and limits of Jewish iconography. With regard to the first, Professor Kraeling inclines to the view that Babylonia rather than Palestine should be regarded as ' the pioneer in, and the most significant contributor to, the development of the synagogue as a formal structure.' With regard to the second, that section of the book which deals with the history of the Jewish community at Dura throws much new light on the conditions of life of a Jewish settlement in an alien environment, and on the gradual growth of a house-synagogue. There is an interesting parallel here between the development of the earliest Christian house-churches and that of the Jewish house-synagogue. Most readers will probably turn at once to the very fine reproductions of the mural paintings which adorned the walls of the synagogue. The discovery of these paintings, together with others such as those of the Beth-Alpha synagogue, has dispelled the ancient belief that the Jews had never permitted the use of pictorial illustration of Biblical subjects. A further interest attaches to these paintings in that they offer surprising similarities with early Byzantine Christian iconography. Professor Kraeling's interpretation of the paintings as illustrating the religious thought of a Jewish community in the third century A.D. is acute and profoundly interesting. S.H.H.

MALLOWAN, M. E. L. : *Twenty-five Years of Mesopotamian Discovery* (1932-1956). Undated (1956). Pp. $80+3$ plates$+18$ figures$+1$ map. (British School of Archaeology in Iraq, London. Price : 5s. 0d.)

This booklet, written by the Director of the British School of Archaeology in Iraq to commemorate the Silver Jubilee of the School, is a handbook to the discoveries made by the School in the course of twenty-five years' work at sites in the Tigris and Euphrates valleys. The sites concerned are Arpachiyah, Chagar, Bazar, Brak, five tells in the Balikh valley, Nimrud ($=$Calah of the O.T.)—to which most space is devoted—and Balawat. The location of all these sites is clearly marked on an accompanying map, and there are eighteen illustrations. The narrative is for the most part descriptive of the discoveries—many of them of great importance—and contacts with the O.T. are noted from time to time. The influence of Mesopotamia on later ages in matters like building construction and the use of religious symbols, such as the mother goddess, the dove, and the cross, is interestingly brought out. Not only the achievements of the School are recorded. Brief indication is also given of some of the problems which remain over for solution, and which will presumably give direction to future work by the School. This handbook, which is packed with information—it is indeed a model of compression—will appeal to all who are interested in archaeology, in the growth of civilized man in Western Asia, and in the bearing of ancient problems upon the present. D.W.T.

NOTH, M. : *Die Welt des Alten Testaments. Einführung in die Grenzgebiete der alttestamentlichen Wissenschaft*, 3rd ed. (Sammlung Töpelmann, 2 Reihe : Theologische Hilfsbücher, Bd. 3). 1957. Pp. xvi$+320$ and 4 plates. (Alfred Töpelmann, Berlin. Price : DM.20.50.)

The third edition of this valuable manual on the background of O.T. study is a reprint of the second ed. (see *Book List*, 1953, pp. 46 f., and for first ed. see *Book List*, 1946, p. 16), amplified by a concise appendix (pp. 291-296) where the author notes and appraises recent excavations, researches, and publications with reference to relevant passages in his text. The worth of this work for research on the O.T. has already been proved. J.G.

PARROT, A. : *Nineveh and the Old Testament*, trans. by Beatrice Hooke. (Studies in Biblical Archaeology, 3.) 1956. Pp. 96. (S.C.M. Press, London. Price : 8s. 6d.)

This third volume in the S.C.M. Studies in Biblical Archaeology is a translation of *Ninive et l'Ancien Testament* (*Book List*, 1954, p. 20) and contains an excellent resumé of the archaeological and biblical evidence for the history of Nineveh and its relation to the Old Testament. J.N.S.

PARROT, A. : *Der Tempel von Jerusalem*, and *Golgatha und das heilige Grab*. (Bibel und Archäologie, II.) 1956. Pp. 200, with 54 illustrations in the text. (Evangelischer Verlag, Zollikon-Zürich. Price : Fr. 17.40, DM. 16.80, by subscription, Fr. 15.75, DM. 15.20.

This is a German translation of Cahiers d'Archéologie Biblique, No. 5 (cf. *Book List*, 1955, pp. 17f.) and 6, with a few additions in the notes. On the whole, the translation is very good. Only the word ' Hypogeum ' is not in accord with normal German usage. On archaeological questions, the author mostly follows L. H. Vincent, who is certainly a good guide. The inclusion of numerous photographs and of figures and plans is a welcome feature. The first part of the volume presents the various phases of the history of the Old Testament Temple.

The second contains a thorough discussion of the site of Jesus' grave, accepting the traditional identification with that in the Church of the Holy Sepulchre. This is followed by an exposition of the complicated architectural history of that Church. Finally, there is an account of the burial sites of the Greco-Roman period in the vicinity of Jerusalem, in which the view is adopted that the Jerusalem necropolis preserves traces of the primitive Christian community. Altogether, a wealth of reliable information in a single volume. M.N.

SCHAEFFER, C. F.-A. : *Reprise des Fouilles de Ras Shamra-Ugarit. Campagnes XII à XVII* (1948-1953). *Rapports Préliminaires*. 1955. Pp. 150. (Geuthner, Paris.)

A reprint of five articles published in the journal *Syria* between 1951 and 1954. In the second and third articles M. Virolleaud publishes and comments upon alphabetic texts, including alphabets, an astrological text (?), administrative and economic tablets, and two Akkadian letters and an attested deed from the palace-complex. In the fourth article he discusses deeds, letters, and economic tablets in alphabetic cuneiform, and gives notice of two alphabetic fragments of the Baal-myth and of the Akkadian legal texts now published by Nougayrol (*Mission de Ras Shamra VI*, ed. Schaeffer, 1955, cf. *Book List*, 1956, p. 15). In the first and last articles M. Schaeffer reports on field-work at Ras Shamra between 1948 and 1953. Of chief interest here is the ivory sculpture from the bed of the king and a discussion of the political situation in North Syria in the 14th and 13th centuries in the light of historical texts from the palace, which supplement the Amarna texts. J.G.

VINCENT, L. H. and STÈVE, A. M. : *Jérusalem de l'Ancien Testament. Recherches d'Archéologie et d'Histoire*. 2nd Part. *Archéologie du Temple* & 3rd Part. *Évolution historique de la Ville*. 1956. Pp. xviii+373-810+49 plates. (Gabalda, Paris. Price : Fr. 11,500.)

The first part of this immense work was reviewed in the *Book List* for 1954 (pp. 21f.). The present volume has, as its

second part, what must surely be the fullest and most scholarly
discussion of the Haram at Jerusalem, a discussion spread
over some 230 pages and divided between six chapters. Of
these latter ch. XIV is concerned with Solomon's temple, and,
after some preliminary remarks, and a few pages on the
Semitic sanctuary, discusses in detail the preparations for
building, the temple-structure (its plan, elevation, decoration
and furnishings) and Solomon's palace. Ch. XV, on Herod's
temple, considers in turn the two descriptions given by
Josephus in the *Wars* and the *Antiquities* respectively, and
comments on the date of the restoration, the preparations
made for it, and the details of the sacred enclosure, the *hieron*,
and the *naos*, on the aesthetic character of the building ;
and on the references to it in the New Testament. Ch. XVI
sets out the data on the temple as described by Ezekiel. Ch.
XVII provides a separate treatment on Herod's temple according to the Mishnah. Ch. XVIII on the *Ḥaram eš-Šerif*
as it is to-day is, as might be expected, the longest of the
chapters in this part. It is also, and this was unexpected, the
most difficult of the six chapters. It may be a surprise to some
readers to learn that, even now, not all the measurements of
the Haram and its enclosing walls can be exactly ascertained.
The third part traces the history of Jerusalem as a city from
its first beginnings down to the foundation by Hadrian of
Aelia Capitolina.

The whole work is a marvel of exact and unremitting scholarship, and it appears in its principal author's old age as a
fitting crown upon some sixty-five years of work on the
archaeology of Palestine and the Bible.   J.M.T.B.

WISEMAN, D. J. : *Chronicles of Chaldean Kings* (626-556 B.C.) *in the
British Museum.* 1956. Pp. xii+100 and 21 plates. (British
Museum, London. Price : 25s. 0d.)

Five British Museum cuneiform texts are published in this
volume. Four of them are published for the first time, while
the fifth, published by C. J. Gadd in 1923 with the title *The
Fall of Nineveh*, is re-issued with revisions. The Introduction
(pp. 1-42) contains an account of the texts, and a historical
survey of their contents—the struggle against Assyria, the
fall of Nineveh, the battle of Carchemish, the capture of
Jerusalem, and a Babylonian campaign in Western Cilicia.
A summary of the events follows (pp. 43-49), and then comes
the transliteration of the cuneiform texts, with an English
translation opposite (pp. 50-77). Some valuable additional
notes are provided (pp. 78-88), there is an appendix dealing
with some points of chronology (pp. 89-96), three maps, and
an index. Plates I-VI consist of photographs of the tablets,
and VII-XXI of the copies of the texts made by the author.
The new texts throw much fresh light on the history of the
period. The battle of Carchemish, for example, can now be
seen in truer perspective. Of quite outstanding importance
is the new and exact information supplied for the dating of
the capture of Jerusalem by Nebuchadrezzar in 597 B.C.

This event, it is now known, occurred on the second day of the month Adar (15/16 March). This volume, which does great credit to the author, has an importance out of all proportion to its size, and deserves the careful attention of all students of O.T. history which it does so much to illumine.

D.W.T.

WOOLLEY, Sir L. : *Ur Excavations*, Vol. IV. The Early Periods. 1955 (title page), 1956 (front cover). Pp. 226 and 83 plates. (British Museum, London and University of Pennsylvania Museum, Philadelphia. Price : £5. 15s.)

This volume deals with the early strata of occupation at Ur from the Ubaid Period (c. 3500 B.C.) to the end of the 2nd millennium, with appendices on graves and pottery of the various periods. The material is discussed very succinctly in relation to the cultural and political affinities of Ur, and the volume is well equipped with object-registers, photographs, plans and stratum-elevations. Of chief interest to O.T. students is a fresh discussion of the ' Flood stratum ' in its local archaeological context and in relation to other sites, particularly Kish, and its relevance to the tradition of the Flood in the literature and glyptic of the Sumerians. J.G.

WOOLLEY, Sir L. : *Ur in Chaldäa. Zwölf Jahre Ausgrabungen in Abrahams Heimat.* 1956. Pp. 248+46 plates+22 figures and plans in the text. (Brockhaus, Wiesbaden. Price : DM. 15.)

This is a German translation of *Excavations at Ur* (1954, Pub. by Ernest Benn, London). The director of the excavations which were carried out between 1922 and 1934 on the mound containing the ruins of the ancient Sumerian city of Ur here describes the course and results of that important and successful enterprise. His narrative is popularly and attractively written, the scholarly description of the discoveries being interspersed with accounts of the practical work of excavation with its difficulties, problems, and surprises, and of the thoughts, fears, and hopes of the person responsible for directing the excavation. The discoveries provide a vivid picture of the stirring history of the important city of Ur, from the earliest discernible beginnings through the early dynastic period with the famous royal cemetery of Ur and the monuments of the kings of the ' First Dynasty,' on through the age of the Sargonids to the zenith of Ur's importance under the kings of the ' Third Dynasty.' Then follows the Isin-Larsa period, with its remarkable prosperity as evidenced by the houses in the city, and the general collapse in the Kassite and Assyrian period, until the final revival in the neo-Babylonian period. The numerous plates and plans illustrate vividly the accounts in the text. The occasional references to the Old Testament tradition are not, as a rule, very happy. The German rendering is smooth and accurate.

M.N.

WRIGHT, G. E. : *Biblical Archaeology*. 1957. Pp. 288 (including 220 illustrations and 8 maps). (Westminster Press, Philadelphia and Gerald Duckworth, London. Price : 84s. 0d.)

The book studies archaeology in order to glean from it every fact that throws any light on the Bible. There is an introduction and thirteen chapters following the history from prehistoric days to the end of the New Testament period, and arranging the material to be a background to Bible history. One chapter deals with manuscript finds including the Dead Sea Scrolls. There are 220 illustrations, 8 maps and 5 indices. The material is comprehensive, reliable, and well arranged ; the book is excellently produced. It is indispensable to students of both the Old and the New Testaments. J.N.S.

HISTORY AND GEOGRAPHY

BARON, S. W. : *Histoire d'Israël : Vie sociale et religieuse*, Tome I. Des origines jusqu'au début de l'ère chrétienne. 1956. Pp. 590. (Presses Universitaires de France, Paris. Price : Fr. 1600).

This translation by V. Nikiprowetzky of the well-known work by Professor Baron of Columbia University appears in the series *Sinaï*, under the general editorship of André Chouraqui. The numerous substantial notes are relegated to the end of the book, where they occupy 200 pages. The bibliography is extensive, and reveals the endeavour to cite works in French. As is well-known, the originality of the work lies in its study of the social life of Israel ; and it does not raise questions of literary criticism. The author realized how difficult it would be to translate his work. On the whole, the translator has succeeded, though the term ' nature ' has, in French, shades of meaning which make it difficult to understand phrases like 'L'homme est appelé à surmonter graduellement la nature ' (p. 13). This has a Nietzschean ring, which must be far from the author's thought. At all events, there is much here to stimulate thought. H.C.

BRIGHT, J. : *Early Israel in Recent History Writing*. (Studies in Biblical Theology, No. 19). 1956. Pp. 128. (S.C.M. Press, London. Price : 9s. 6d.).

This is an important and valuable book. It is an enquiry into the question of how the traditions of early Israel should be investigated. In illustration of this study of *method* Dr. Bright gives convenient summaries of the views of Alt, Noth and Kaufmann, and reveals in clear but gentle light the nihilism of Noth, and the nonsequiturs of Kaufmann. The validity and soundness of this approach are further shown in a concluding chapter when positive suggestions are made. G.H.D.

*GROLLENBERG, L. H. : *Atlas of the Bible*. Translated and edited by Joyce M. H. Reid and H. H. Rowley. Foreword by W. F. Albright and H. H. Rowley. Preface by Roland de Vaux. 1956. Pp. 166+ 408 illustrations+35 maps+2 maps on end papers. (Nelson, Edinburgh. Price : 70s. 0d.)

The original Dutch edition of this superb work was reviewed in the 1955 *Book List*, p. 21, and the French translation in the 1956 *Book List*, p. 17. That it is now made available in an English edition is a major event in religious publishing. There must be very few works on the Bible which are so satisfying to so wide a range of readers. Illustrations, maps, and commentary are all first-class ; and the full index facilitates rapid reference. Much gratitude is due for the great pains taken in producing the English edition so speedily and so admirably. G.W.A.

*KRAELING, E. G. : *Bible Atlas*. 1956. Pp. 488, with numerous maps and illustrations. (Rand McNally and Co., New York. Price : $8.95.)

This new edition of the Rand McNally *Bible Atlas* (first published in 1884) is a fine achievement, sumptuously produced, with a great wealth of illustrations and excellent maps. The reader is taken systematically through Scripture, being made aware not only of the relevant localities, but also, quite unobtrusively, of the complexity of the sources. Dr. Kraeling adduces much illustrative material from the archaeological field and is always up-to-date. Of particular value is the author's personal communication of the matter from the Elephantine Papyri which he recently edited. The book, though of value to more advanced scholars, will be especially valuable in classes of Biblical Studies and in schools, particularly through its many illustrations. J.G.

PEROWNE, S. : *The Life and Times of Herod the Great*. 1956. Pp. 186+40 plates. (Hodder and Stoughton, London. Price : 21s. 0d.)

'And it is asked, how many Herods there were, as they deceive by the similarity of the name.' Many have echoed the words of Isho'dad of Merv, and many who could distinguish Herod, called ' the Great,' from the other Herods have hesitated over the title. Mr. Perowne's book is a useful introduction to the Herodian family and a most informative and stimulating biography, which though it catalogues Herod's crimes yet seeks to show his many qualities. Herod is seen as the loyal friend of Rome as well as the hated benefactor of the Jews. Only on the last page of his book does the author appear rather less than fair in his judgment. Much information has been collected. The legend of the Philistine origin of the family is quoted and evaluated. Isho'dad knew it also : ' The first Herod was a priest of the idol-temple at Ashkalon, a city of the Philistines, and this one begat Antipatros, him whom the Idumaeans made captive, and he was brought up in their customs.' Particularly useful are Mr. Perowne's sections on Herod's building programmes, where the author's familiarity with the country is evident. While the needs of the general reader are met most excellently, those of the student demand the addition of notes and index. W.D.McH.

SCHEDL, C. : *Geschichte des Alten Testaments*. Band I. *Urgeschichte und alter Orient*. 1956. Pp. xxvi+374. (Tyrolia-Verlag, Innsbruck.)

This volume, the first of a series of four on the Old Testament, deals with Gen. i.-xi. and the beginnings of mankind. It opens with a discussion of what the chapters contain, what they are trying to teach and how they reached their present form. This is followed by a survey of the nations and peoples of the world in the pre-patriarchal age, their geographical setting and their religion.

The author, a Catholic scholar, is at pains to stress the unity of the narrative and to bring out the meaning of every detail of it. Even the figures giving ages of men and duration of events are cleverly manipulated to fall into a numerical scheme which Schedl thinks was intended from the beginning—if only we knew what was meant by the scheme ! There is much useful material here, but it is presented in a rather roundabout way. L.H.B.

VAN SELMS, A. : *De Verscheurde Stad*. Undated. (1956.) Pp. 144. (Voorhoeve, Den Haag. Price : Fl. 7.90.)

" The divided city " with which this book deals is Jerusalem. The Pretoria Professor describes a recent visit paid to Old Jerusalem and the western territory of the Kingdom of Jordan. Ancient and modern questions are discussed—there is an account of the Qumran discoveries and the outline of a " natural " solution for the political problems of Israel and Jordan. The work is illustrated by a number of photographs supplied by Dr. A. van Deursen, whose name is familiar to all users of Grollenberg's *Atlas of the Bible*. F.F.B.

VRIEZEN, Th.C. : *Het Nabije Oosten in de Branding*. 1957. Pp. 263. (G. F. Callenbach N. V., Nijkerk. Price : Fl. 14.50.)

The volume is concerned with the troubles of the Near East, especially with the modern stormy waters. It contains a map of the area, 45 photographs, some modern and some of archaeological interest, and twelve pages of annotated bibliography, including books on archaeology and the Dead Sea Scrolls. Our particular interest in the book is in the evidence which the author provides that the problem of the Near East is no new problem. The Old Testament archaeology and the scrolls all tell the same story of interracial feuds, a buffer state and refugees. N.H.S.

WRIGHT, G. E. and FILSON, F. V. : *The Westminster Historical Atlas to the Bible*, with Introduction by W. F. Albright. Revised edition. 1956. Pp. 130, including 18 pp. of maps and numerous illustrations. (Westminster Press, Philadelphia. Price : $7.50.)

The new edition of this most useful work is produced in reduced format. It is characterized by expansion of paragraphs on the Hebrew Conquest and the Political History of Palestine, amounting chiefly to fuller citation of archaeological data. The most significant additions are welcome sections on the rise of Jewish Sects in Maccabean and Herodian Palestine and excavations in modern Palestine.   J.G.

TEXT AND VERSIONS

FLACK, E. E., METZGER, B. M., and others : *The Text, Canon and Principal Versions of the Bible. A brief survey of recent research extracted from the Twentieth Century Encyclopedia of Religious Knowledge.* 1956. Pp. 64. (Baker Book House, Grand Rapids, Michigan. Price : $1.50).

Recent study of the O.T. and N.T. canon and text is competently dealt with by the above-mentioned editors in four separate articles, and additional articles are provided as follows : The Dead Sea Scrolls, Millar Burrows ; Biblical and Early Christian Papyri, and N.T. Greek lectionaries, Wikgren ; the versions ancient and modern, Metzger ; LXX, Gehman ; Tatian's Harmony, Metzger ; the Bible for the Mission-field, Nida ; Annotated Bibles, Kuist ; and the Biblical Languages and lexica are dealt with in separate appendixes by Diringer, Wikgren, Flack and Gingrich respectively. The work provides the average biblical student with a concise introduction to the various topics, and a good bibliography. The over-all balance is on the whole right, but some points will no doubt receive adjustment before the next edition ; among them may be mentioned that the LXX editions need not be given twice over, the distinction between strict and paraphrastic Targums can be made, from a ' canon-history ' point of view the ' prophetic collection ' would be better envisaged as a unity (cf. Eissfeldt, *Einleitung*, p. 622), and, please, can a passing reference to the Welsh Bible be included in the section on Celtic Versions, since it is, on every count, the most important extant version in the Celtic languages, and has recently been re-issued in a standardised orthography ?   B.J.R.

GERLEMAN, G. : *Studies in the Septuagint. III. Proverbs.* (Lunds Universitets Årsskrift. N.F. Avd. 1. Bd. 52. Nr. 3.) 1956. Pp. 64. (C.W.K. Gleerup, Lund. Price : Sw. Kr. 6.50).

Professor Gerleman's first two studies in the series, Job and 2 Chronicles, appeared in 1946 (cf. *Book List*, 1947, p. 14), and this new issue follows the same pattern and ' tentatively ' confirms conclusions offered there. The Version, after scrutiny, is seen to offer but little evidence of influence by Egyptian

Wisdom, nor does the parent text show essential divergence from the MT. The numerous apparent departures are to be explained by inner-Greek taste—love of assonance, rhyme, anaphora ; hexameter metre (not iambics, *pace* Thackeray), variation of parallelism. There are also echoes of Greek influence in such matters as an occasional quotation from Homer, and more from Plato and Aristotle and others. A chapter headed ' Religion and Ethics in the LXX Proverbs ' contains a critical discussion of earlier treatments of the topic, notably by Baumgartner and Bertram, and shows that the Greek translator ' is not a mouthpiece of Jewish legalism ' but, on the contrary, produced a work largely conditioned by his Stoic background. Kaminka is wrong in urging Targumic dependence on the LXX. Likewise Thackeray is wrong in basing a *terminus a quo* in the 1st cent. B.C. on orthography. LXX Proverbs and Job emanate from an ' identical ' source, not later than mid-2nd cent. B.C. In a final note the author shows that the Sahidic translation ' renders the Greek text rather faithfully.' B.J.R.

*HERKLOTS, H. G. G. : *How Our Bible Came to Us. A Literary Pil-grimage.* 1957. Pp. 174+8 plates. (Ernest Benn, London. Price : 15s. 0d.)

This is the fourth impression of the book which was originally published in 1954 under the title *Back to the Bible* (see *Book List*, 1955, p. 42). Its continued circulation attests its popularity and usefulness ; and it is to be commended as an unusually fresh presentation. Some revision might have been attempted of the chapter on the Dead Sea Scrolls. G.W.A.

MARKS, J. H. : *Der textkritische Wert des Psalterium Hieronymi juxta Hebraeos.* 1956. Pp. 156. (Keller, Zürich. Price : DM. 15.)

The author tells us that his thesis was chosen after reading an article in the *Journal of Biblical Literature*, 69 (1950) in which C. M. Cooper claimed that the *Psalterium juxta Hebraeos* was of special importance in so far as ' it marks a stage in the history of the Hebrew text approximately half way between its early situation, as represented by the Greek Old Testament, and its final fixation in the Massoretic text.' A careful examination of the version, as it is found in Harden's edition of 1922, revealed a considerable degree of dependence on the Septuagint and the other Greek versions. One of the valuable features of this work is that Marks has drawn up a series of tables illustrating the degree of dependence on the Gallican Psalter, the *Vetus Latina*, the Septuagint, and Aquila, Symmachus, and Theodotion.

The main conclusion is that Jerome's version from the Hebrew ' auf einen Text beruht, der unserem MT im grossen und ganzen gleich war ' (p. 144). The value of the version is summed up under four heads, i.e., (1) It establishes the text of Aquila and Symmachus ; (2) It is made from a text that essentially resembles our Masoretic text ; (3) It gives us insight into

Jerome's method of translation ; and (4) It brings to light, in some manner, the Hebrew text used in the fourth century. It is regrettable that Marks has not, apparently, been able to use D. H. de Saint-Maire's critical edition of 1953, published in the *Collectanea Biblica Latina.* J.M.T.B.

WÜRTHWEIN, E. : *The Text of the Old Testament : An Introduction to Kittel-Kahle's Biblia Hebraica,* trans. by P. R. Ackroyd. 1957. Pp. xii+174, including 41 plates. (Blackwell, Oxford. Price : 17s. 6d.)

The German version appeared in 1952 (cf. *Book List,* 1953, p. 30), and three points may be made in greeting the present translation which was authorized by permission of the Priv. Württ. Bibelanstalt, Stuttgart. The first is to commend, very highly, the translator's rendering of the original ; the second is to note the useful additions of indexes and bibliography ; and third to underline the important additional material, mainly inserted in expanded footnotes, which brings the book up-to-date especially on the Dead Sea scrolls. Some minor lapses in the original have been corrected, and one or two new ones have taken their place. B.J.R.

ZIEGLER, J. : *Septuaginta. Vetus Testamentum Graecum auctoritate Societatis Litterarum Gottingensis editum Vol. XV.: Jeremias, Baruch, Threni, Epistula Ieremiae.* 1957. Pp. 504. (Vandenhoeck & Ruprecht, Göttingen. Price : DM. 63 ; bound DM. 67.)

The volume follows the well established pattern of the Göttingen Septuagint, and the editor's name is a guarantee of its excellence. Like its forerunners the edition is an absolute must for the O.T. student, and, since it is still true that the Jeremiah LXX is of first-class importance for the textualist, the edition is even more valuable than the others in the series. The text is, of course, eclectic, and based on the usual sources, mainly the texts of B and S. Among noteworthy points of introduction the following may be mentioned : Migne is set aside in favour of Ghisler for Chrysostom readings ; the text of Jerome's commentary represents the Hexaplaric recension ; there is an independence of the MT in the Catena group, and a dependence on the younger Greek translations in the Lucianic recension. Of more general interest are the editor's assessments of the major MSS. groupings and their relationship to LXX divergences from . MT ; and the treatment of the special significance of Q and its related MSS. The text is provided with a double *app. crit.,* the upper is general and the lower Hexaplaric and is demonstrably superior to Field. B.J.R.

EXEGESIS AND MODERN TRANSLATIONS

La Bible, L'Ancien Testament, Vol. I. (Bibliothèque de la Pléiade.) 1956. Pp. cxxvi+1720, including 3 maps. (Librairie Gallimard, Paris. Price : 66s. 6d.)

This book appears in a collection of World Classics, and two volumes will be devoted to the Old Testament. The first offers a new translation of the Law, the Former Prophets, Chronicles, Ezra, Nehemiah and Maccabees. Genesis to Chronicles are translated by E. Dhorme, Ezra-Nehemiah by F. Michaéli and Maccabees by A. Guillaumont. An introduction to the whole is provided by Dhorme. Three maps are included. The introduction presents clearly and simply the results of Textual, Literary and Historical Criticism, and the notes accompanying the text draw attention to these and also give valuable lexicographical and exegetical notes. The divine names (Iahvé, El-Shaddai) are used in the text, and, except for the most common, Hebrew proper names are transliterated. Where the Hebrew text is defective (e.g., I Sam. xiv. 23f., 41f.), it is restored. Sometimes the translation seems too ingenious ; one wonders whether the author of Gen. iii. 15 would intend the word-play on sh-w-p= " *écraser* " and " *viser* " in the same sentence. While the book is intended for the layman, it contains much of interest to the scholar.   A.S.H.

BRUNO, A. : *Das Hohe Lied. Das Buch Hiob. Eine rhythmische und textkritische Untersuchung nebst einer Einführung in das Hohe Lied*. 1956. Pp. 194. (Almqvist & Wiksell, Stockholm. Price : Sw. Kr. 20.)

The introduction to *Canticles*, with which this work begins, attempts to establish a dramatic interpretation of the book and to demonstrate its structural unity. The author divides it into two acts, the first of four scenes and the second of three, with a unity in time and place. The translations of both books and the notes appended to them follow the general pattern familiar from Dr. Bruno's earlier works (see *Book Lists*, 1954, pp. 45f. ; 1955, pp. 31f. ; 1956, p. 26).   G.W.A.

BUTTRICK, G. A. (ed. by) : *The Interpreter's Bible*, Vol. V (Ecclesiastes—Jeremiah). 1956. Pp. x+1142. (Abingdon-Cokesbury, New York and Nashville, and Nelson, Edinburgh. Price : $8.75, or 67s. 6d.)

This is one of the best, if not the best, of the volumes of the Interpreter's Bible yet issued. It contains the commentaries on Ecclesiastes, The Song of Songs, Isaiah and Jeremiah. The late Professor O. S. Rankin was responsible for the Introduction and Exegesis of Ecclesiastes, Professor T. J. Meek for those of the Song of Songs, Professor R. B. Y. Scott for those of Isaiah i-xxxix, Professor J. Muilenburg for those of Isaiah xl-lxvi, and Professor J. P. Hyatt for those of Jeremiah. This is a first-class team of scholars. Rankin takes the view that Ecclesiastes is a much worked-over book, which from the beginning contained elements hard to harmonize. Meek adheres in substance to the cult-liturgical view of the Song. Scott takes account of DSIa, as would be expected. Muilenburg pays much attention in his introduction to the literary structure and characteristics of Deutero-Isaiah. Hyatt rejects the Scythian background of Jeremiah's early prophecies. This is, of course, a completely inadequate account of a commentary on four books of the Old Testament, including two of its major books. There are, as in all the volumes of the series, expository sections on all the books, but they will be of less interest to readers of the *Book List*.

H.H.R.

BUTTRICK, G. A. : (ed. by) : *The Interpreter's Bible*, Vol. VI (Lamentations, Ezekiel, Daniel, Twelve Prophets.) 1956. Pp. 1144 (Abingdon Press, New York and Nashville, and Nelson, Edinburgh. Price : $8.75, or 67s. 6d.)

In so far as a volume of sixteen separate sections and twenty-three contributors can be appraised briefly it may be said that here is a valuable and compendious commentary on Lamentations, Daniel, Ezekiel and the Minor Prophets. The Hebraist, theologian, historian and expositor are all catered for and a high level of critical treatment is maintained. It is only possible to mention one or two of the books individually by way of example. The introduction and commentary on Joel, though rather long, offer a good critical handling of the problems ; that on Jonah is a thoroughly sympathetic treatment, and that on Hosea accepts the view that ch. iii. is a sequel to ch. i. and that the prophet's message can only be understood in the light of that interpretation. Ezekiel's book is regarded as edited first by the prophet himself in the thirtieth year of exile and secondly by an editor of the post-exilic period. Ezekiel is said to have returned to Jerusalem from Babylon in the year 591 shortly after the throne-chariot vision. It is claimed that " the vision of the storm, the throne chariot and the scroll form an ideological unit." This rules out the possibility of two calls. The commentator, however, does not do full justice to Ezekiel's creative genius in the ' concept of the glory of Yahweh ' for which he wrongly claims Ps. xxix. and Isa. vi. 1-3 as earlier examples. L.H.B.

CLAMER, A. : *La Sainte Bible, texte latin et traduction française d'après les textes originaux avec un commentaire exégétique et théologique.* Tome I, 2e partie. *Exode.* 1956. Pp. 304. (Letouzey & Ané, Paris. Price : 19s. 3d.)

Clamer is the general editor of the series, and he has himself undertaken the commentaries on the Pentateuch, of which this is the last to appear. The notice of *Génèse*, published in 1953 appeared in the *Book List* for 1954, pp. 32f. and praised the commentary for being " full and critical." *Exode* is, in every way, a worthy successor to the earlier commentaries, has like them a reasonably full introduction and an exegesis of the text that, while compressed, mentions most of the points that are of real importance. The discussion of the site of the Biblical Sinai is a good example of the author's careful statement of alternative theories. His knowledge of the literature is, as always, remarkably detailed and up-to-date. The absence of a map is certainly a defect, as is also the very small type in which the commentary is printed. It should be mentioned that the French text of the entire Bible with a small selection of notes has been available in one volume since 1950. J.M.T.B.

DEDEN, D. : *De Kleine Propheten uit de grondtekst vertaald en uitgelegd :
Nahum, Habakuk, Sophonias, Aggeüs, Zacharias, Malachias*
(De Boeken van het Oude Testament, Deel XII, Boek VII-XII.)
1956. Pp. 166. (J. J. Romen & Zonen, Roermond en Maaseik.
Price : Fl. 7.14 ; by subscription : Fl. 6.30.)

The second half of Volume XII of this fine series of commentaries on the O.T. covers the books of Nahum, Habakkuk,
Zephaniah, Haggai, Zechariah and Malachi, and maintains
the high standard of scholarship and lucid exposition set by
its predecessors. Each of the books is presented in a new Dutch
version from the Hebrew text. A number of familiar emendations have been admitted (e.g., in Zech. vi. 11 " the high priest
Joshua the son of Jehozadak " is replaced by " the governor
Zerubbabel the son of Shealtiel," and in verse 14 '*al kis'o* is
emended to '*al yemino*). The presence of a fragmentary alphabetic pattern is recognized in Nahum i. 2-10, but Deden wisely
declines to make this a basis for textual reconstruction. The
evidence of 1Qp Hab. is reviewed in considering the text of
Habakkuk. Hab. iii. is a genuine part of the book, the evidence
of 1Qp Hab. notwithstanding : " the totally different genre
of this chapter lent itself less well to an allegorical commentary." In most questions of introduction this conservative
position is held. Zech. ix-xiv. are dated early in the Hellenistic
period ; these chapters celebrate Yahweh's eventual world-
dominion. The " pierced " character of Zech. xii. 10 is an
eschatological figure, whose role is comparable to that of the
Ebed Yahweh. Zeph. iii. 18b-20 are typically exilic oracles ;
and ii. 11, iii. 9-10 show the influence of Deutero-Isaiah ; but
the book as a whole comes from the early part of Josiah's
reign.   F.F.B.

ELLISON, H. L. : *Ezekiel : The Man and His Message*. 1956. Pp. 144.
(Paternoster Press, London. Price : 10s. 6d.)

This is a short but useful commentary on Ezekiel, intended
for the lay student. Mr. Ellison's standpoint is, on the whole,
conservative, especially in his treatment of the last chapters.
Some of his problems, too, would have more easily solved
if he had been able to regard the book as a later collection of
Ezekiel's utterances rather than a continous book compiled
by the Prophet himself. There is a certain liberty in textual
criticism, and free use is made of earlier commentaries,
especially that of G. A. Cooke. Naturally, however, there are
points on which recent discovery and study have modified
details, and Mr. Ellison has not failed to make good use of
such as have been available to him. In quotation the R.V.
text is taken as the best for the ordinary reader, though there
is occasional reference to the R.S.V. But Mr. Ellison is a
competent Hebrew scholar, and might well have given more
original renderings. For its immediate purpose this promises
to be a useful book, and may be commended to the readers
for whom it is written.   T.H.R.

GOLDMAN, S. : *The Ten Commandments*, edited with an Introduction by Maurice Samuel. 1956. Pp. xxvi+226. (University of Chicago Press and Cambridge University Press, London. Price : $3.75 or 28s. 0d.)

This beautifully produced book, prefaced and edited by M. Samuel, is the first of the posthumous works of the late Rabbi Solomon Goldman to be published. The book is a devotional quasi-midrashic commentary on the Decalogue. The general commentary is a semi-critical introduction and this is followed by a textual commentary which expounds the Ten Command-ments themselves. There are 29 full pages of bibliography. This work is further proof of the late Rabbi's very wide reading in ancient and modern sources of all kinds, is well worth reading, and will doubtless suggest many sermons. G.H.D.

GUTBROD, K. : *Das Buch vom König. Das erste Buch Samuel*, übersetzt und ausgelegt. (Die Botschaft des Alten Testaments, 11.) 1956. Pp. viii+256. (Calwer Verlag, Stuttgart. Price : DM. 12.80.)

The critical view on which this commentary is based is that 1 Samuel is not a separate literary unity, but forms part of the Deuteronomic History, Joshua-Kings, which is to be treated as a single work. In spite of this, and in spite of the admittedly close connexion between 1 and 2 Samuel, the exposition of 1 Samuel by itself is justified on the ground that it has as its theme the nature of the kingship and its rightful holder. The translation admits a few emendations of MT, and is accom-panied, where necessary, by brief textual notes. There is a running commentary on the narrative, in which the emphasis is on the religious and theological content. Some of the suggested connexions with the New Testament appear to the reviewer to be somewhat strained. On the other hand, the relation of, e.g., 1 Sam. xv. to New Testament teaching does not seem to be adequately considered. G.W.A.

HERTZBERG, H. W. : *Die Samuelbücher*. (Das Alte Testament Deutsch, 10.) 1956. Pp. 342. (Vandenhoeck & Ruprecht, Göttingen. Price : 21s. 0d.)

For a previous volume in this series by the author, see *Book List*, 1954, p. 39. As before, the introduction is cut down to the minimum, so that the fullest possible space can be devoted to exegesis. The volume is in seven sections : I Sam. i-iii., Eli and Samuel ; I Sam. iv-vi., the fate of the Ark ; I Sam. vii-xv., Samuel and Saul ; I Sam. xvi.-II Sam. i, Saul and David ; II Sam. ii-viii., King David ; II Sam. ix-xx., con-cerning the succession ; and the supplement in II Sam. xxi-xxiv. The critical position is that there are two main strands with the six separate pieces in the supplement. N.H.S.

KRAUS, H.-J. : *Klagelieder.* (*Threni.*) (Biblischer Kommentar. Altes Testament, XX.) 1956. Pp. 88. (Verlag der Buchhandlung des Erziehungsvereins, Neukirchen. Price : DM.7 ; Subscription price : DM. 5.85.)

The commentator notes the mnemonic value of the acrostic compositions in the Book of Lamentations, but does not mention N. K. Gottwald's treatment of the matter, in which it is suggested that the alphabetic design is intended to convey the idea of totality or comprehensiveness. On ch. v, however, Kraus points out that while the alphabetic structure is not present here, the alphabetic comprehensiveness is suggested by the 22 verses (cf. Pss. xxxiii. ; ciii.). On the metre he does not reach a clearcut conclusion, but finds the views of Budde and Sievers more convincing than those of Hölscher and Mowinckel. He distinguishes three main *Gattungen* in the collection—the dirge, the community lament, and the individual lament. The particular form of dirge found here is defined more closely as " lament for the ruined sanctuary "—a *Gattung* which has Sumerian and Akkadian parallels. All five of the songs refer to the disaster of 587 B.C., and may have been composed to be sung among the ruins of the temple at a solemn ceremony of lamentation. Jerusalem suggests itself as the place of their composition ; they were probably composed by some person or persons who stood in close relation to the national priesthood or cult-prophets. In " I am the man . . . " (Lam. iii. 1) an adumbration of the passion of Christ is recognized.   F.F.B.

LE MAT, L. A. F. : *Textual Criticism and Exegesis of Psalm XXXVI. A Contribution to the Study of the Hebrew Book of Psalms.* 1957. Pp. xiv+112. (Kemink and Zoon, Utrecht. Price : Fl. 15.)

This book (in English) is a thesis for a doctorate at Utrecht. It is a detailed study of Ps. xxxvi., directed also to the understanding of the Psalter as a whole, and particularly to the meanings and significance of the titles of the psalms. Chapter I is a exegetical study of the Masoretic Text of the psalm. Chapter II is wholly concerned with the title of the psalm. ' To David ' indicates that the psalm found its way into the royal library, there to be at the disposal of the king. Dr. Le Mat does not think that there was ever a " Chief Musician's Collection," but that this title refers to the king himself as leader in pre-exilic Israel. In the third chapter the author discusses the identity of the rebel and of the evildoers. He turns against Mowinckel's theory of sorcerers, and thinks of them as enemies of the king with the rebel as their spokesman and leader. Chapter IV deals with the methods and results of previous exegetes, while Chapter V deals with the text of the psalm as found in the five ancient versions, Latin, Greek, Hebrew, Targum and Peshitta, all of which are given in parallel columns on a fly-leaf at the end. The thesis opens up debates which many have regarded as settled and closed, and is characterised by a definite freshness of viewpoint.
                                                                    N.H.S.

RIGNELL, L. G. : *A Study of Isaiah Ch.* 40-55. (Lunds Universitets Årsskrift. N. F. Avd. 1. Bd. 52. Nr. 5). 1956. Pp. 94. (Gleerup, Lund. Price : Sw. Kr. 9.50.)

The assumption of this book is that Deutero-Isaiah is a unity, though its themes are not logically or consecutively developed. The notes, except for lii. 13-liii. 12, are arranged under the chapter headings. The author's conviction is that the most important task of an exegete is to interpret the text from internal sources and he cannot imagine that Deutero-Isaiah was much influenced by Assyro-Babylonian patterns. The Servant of Yahweh is everywhere Israel, or, more specifically, that generation of Israel which lived in the exile and so made expiation for the sins of earlier generations. The forms *lāmô* and *bᵉmôṭāw* (liii. 8f.) indicate that the Servant is a group. The treatment of the text is conservative. The lexical and exegetical notes are usually stimulating, if not always convincing. For example, the pronominal subject of a verb must be determined by the context, and xlii. 1 is rendered : " Behold, Oh my servant, whom I uphold, my chosen, in whom my soul delights—I have put my spirit upon him— *mischpaṭ* is He (Yahweh) bringing to the peoples." In *v.* 2 the subject is the Servant and in *v.* 3 it is Yahweh, the bruised reed being Israel. *V.* 4 should be translated : " He (the Servant) will not faint and not be out of breath before He (the Lord) has established *mischpaṭ* on the earth." Is it possible that the prophet could be so ambiguous ?   C.R.N.

ROTH, L. : *Some Reflections on the Interpretation of Scripture.* (Claude Montefiore Lecture for 1955.) 1955. Pp. 24. (Liberal Jewish Synagogue, London. Price : 2s. 0d.)

In this stimulating lecture the author argues that the interpretation of Scripture must take into account not just words but the context of what is to be interpreted, and, further, that meaning precedes the means of expression which it uses. In the issue between Maimonides and Spinoza about context, whether it is to be so wide as to include all physics and metaphysics or to be restricted to the passage to be interpreted, he adopts a middle position ; Scripture is to be interpreted by Scripture. But Scripture is concerned with morals (Spécialité de la maison !) and we must allow Scripture to criticize Scripture. Hebrew belief in the Exodus is to find expression in moral conduct and the David who is ultimately to be remembered is the *real* David, not the *historically real* David, the man after God's own heart, an ideal which can be democratised. The appropriation of God's action in history is made by goodness in action.   N.W.P.

SEGAL, M. H.: *"Sifrē Shemū'ēl," 'arūkim ūmebō-ārîm 'im mebō' meforāt.* 1956. Pp. xii+66+416. (Kiriath Sepher, Jerusalem.)

Professor M. H. Segal, who almost 40 years ago wrote the first Hebrew commentary on Samuel along modern Western lines, presents the Hebrew reader in the present work with a new commentary on Samuel, which, although more cautious from the point of view of literary criticism (he now withdraws his support of the documentary theory), is nearer to the Western standard commentaries in method of treatment. Its scope and lay-out are very similar to those of the I.C.C. series. The general problems of composition, text and versions are dealt with in a comprehensive Introduction, while the major sections of the text are again prefaced by discussions on the historical and literary problems they present. The commentary accompanying the text consists of exegetical linguistic explanations which take into account Jewish traditional views as well as those of " the moderns," and of historical and topographical comments which embody the latest archaeological data. Full use is also made of the relevant texts of the Dead Sea documents.   P.R.W.

SNAITH, N. H. : *Amos, Hosea and Micah* (Epworth Preachers' Commentaries.) 1956. Pp. 112. (Epworth Press, London. Price : 9s. 6d.)

This is the first of the Old Testament volumes in this new series. Dr. Snaith has had Methodist preachers primarily in mind but has written a commentary that will be of value to all preachers. The comments are brief but go straight to the point and offer material for the elucidation of the message against a Christian background. The following points of interest may be mentioned. Dr. Snaith leans towards linking the Day of the Lord with the New Year Festival ; the first and third chapters of Hosea are separated and in ch. iii. " a late author is working out an allegory based on the details of Hosea's life "; and finally *chesed* is given the meaning of steadfast love.   L.H.B.

WOLFF, H. W. : *Dodekapropheton : Hosea*, Lief. 1. (Biblischer Kommentar : Altes Testament, XIV, 1). 1956. Pp. 80. (Verlag der Buchhandlung des Erziehungsvereins, Neukirchen. Price : DM. 7.00 each Lief., or by subscription DM. 5.85.)

This instalment of the O.T. Commentary edited by Martin Noth comprises a translation of the first three chapters of Hosea with a full commentary appended to each paragraph. The incidents described in these three chapters belong to the category of *memorabilia*. The woman of iii. 1 is Gomer, bought back by Hosea after her desertion of him. While the incident of iii. 1 ff. took place subsequently to the events of i. 2 ff., Hosea's first-personal narrative in iii. 1 ff. is earlier than the third-personal narrative by one of his disciples in i. 2 ff. The suggestion that in iii. 1 ff. we have simply Hosea's own account of the events of i. 2 ff. is countered by the argument that the birth of three children in quick succession (i. 3-9) is excluded by the implications of iii. 3. The description ' a wife of harlotry ' (i. 2) is to be taken neither realistically nor proleptically, nor yet figuratively in the sense of a Baal-worshipper;

it denotes an Israelite maiden ripe for marriage, who had taken part in the customary Canaanite bridal initiation-rites '; her children (even when born to her lawful husband) would by that same token be ' children of harlotry.' F.F.B.

ZIMMERLI, W. : *Ezechiel*, Lief. 3. (Biblischer Kommentar : Altes Testament, XIII, 3.) 1956. Pp. 161-240. (Verlag der Buchhandlung des Erziehungsvereins, Neukirchen. Price : DM. 7.00, or by subscription DM. 5.85.)

For the two parts of this commentary previously published, see *Book List*, 1956, p. 35. This part is marked by the same thoroughness and comprehensiveness. It contains all but the beginning of the discussion of vii., and most of viii. l-xi. 25. There is a closely reasoned critical examination of viii.-xi., with arguments for a much briefer original form. The experience described in these chapters is interpreted in terms of similar abnormal prophetic experiences, particularly 2 Kings v. 26 ; and it is held that the narrative combines memories of religious practices in Jehoiakim's reign and details drawn from reports from Palestine which reached the exiles. The topography of the vision and other details are discussed with ample reference to recent literature. The author holds that viii. 16 probably refers to a solar interpretation of Yahweh.
G.W.A.

LITERARY CRITICISM AND INTRODUCTION
(History of Interpretation, Canon, and Special Studies)

EISSFELDT, O. : *Einleitung in das Alte Testament unter Einschluss der Apokryphen und Pseudepigraphen sowie der apokryphen und pseudepigraphartigen Qumran-Schriften. Entstehungsgeschichte des Alten Testaments.* 2nd edition. 1956. Pp. xvi+956. (J. C. B. Mohr, Tübingen. Price : DM. 43, bound DM. 48.80.)

The first edition of Eissfeldt's *Einleitung* was published in 1934. Now, twenty years and more later, it appears in a revised and expanded form. The general plan of the book remains unchanged ; not only in its parts, but in many of its sections and paragraphs, the headings are as before. As the author says in his introductory statement concerning the scholarly task he has undertaken, the important new factor of wide reference which has come to the fore in the field of Old Testament scholarship since 1934, is the development of the traditio-historical approach in the work of a group of Scandinavian scholars, which has served as a valuable and necessary corrective to a too great trust in the scope and the certainty of the results of the literary-critical approach, and has come, remarkably, at a time when the evidence of arch-aeology clearly shows that the practice of writing in Palestine went back to a period centuries earlier than Wellhausen and his generation believed possible. But if, says Eissfeldt, some of the books of the Old Testament are post-exilic written records of traditions which had been handed down orally for centuries and preserve the form of the oral tradition, the same method of analysis must be applied to them as was applied when it was believed that they had been committed to written form at a much earlier date. Room has been made in the book for a discussion of Josh.-II Kings as continuing the Pentateuchal sources or as a Deuteronomic history, for an enlarged treatment of, for example, Lamentations, Daniel, Ezra-Nehemiah, and there is a special section on the writings of apocryphal and pseudepigraphical type among the Qumran scrolls ; and, of course, the various bibliographies have been brought up-to-date. This revision has increased the value of a book already held in high esteem. J.M.

FARNDALE, W. E. : *The Psalms in New Light.* 1956. Pp. 116. (Epworth Press, London. Price : 5s. 0d.)

This is an excellent non-technical book suitable for the general reader who is interested in the Psalms and wishes to know more. Dr. Farndale, having spent a lifetime in busy affairs, is now (in his ' retirement ') tutor at Cliff College, the Methodist college for lay preachers. The ' new light ' consists of all the new ideas which have latterly been associated with the study of the Psalter : Hebrew poetry, use of the Psalter in Temple and synagogue, the work of Gunkel, that of Mowinckel, evidence from Ugarit, etc. The conclusion concerns the use of the psalms by Jesus. This small book is most useful for students of all grades, and especially for the ' lay ' reader. N.H.S.

GOITEIN, S. D. : *'Omanuth ha-Sippur ba-Miqra,* (in Hebrew). 1956. Pp. 110. (Jewish Agency, Jerusalem.)

This, the 23rd publication of *'Iyyunim,* intended mainly for the teacher, gives very readable short essays on the books of Nehemiah, Ruth, Esther, Jonah and Canticles as well as on the story of the *'Aqedhah* (as related in Gen. xxii.)—with special reference to the art of story-telling in the Bible.—These essays are preceded by a more elaborate essay assessing in general terms the Biblical narrative. M.W.

HOFTIJZER, J. : *Die Verheissungen an die drei Erzväter.* 1956. Pp. viii+104. (E. J. Brill, Leiden. Fl. 10.)

This is a careful study, with ample cross reference, of the traditions of promises given to the patriarchs. The author finds that in Gen.-Numb. there are two groups of such promises—the El Shaddai (P) Gen. 17 group and the Gen. 15 group. (Both groups are *traditionsgeschichtlich* secondary in their present contexts). Other chapters deal with the Promise traditions of Deuteronomy (Exilic), and in the rest of the Old Testament.

Hoftijzer believes that the promise traditions were introduced into the Pentateuch after the Patriarchs-Joshua tradition had been established, and indeed arose when national existence was threatened.

The book is a good example of *Traditionsgeschichte*, and the
last chapter, with its thorough-going criticism of Alt, Noth
and von Rad, not only testifies to civil war in that particular
school, but also to the subjective methods employed. It is
of course possible to start from other premises and to arrive
at far less negative results.   G.H.D.

JAKUBIEC, Cz. : *Wprowadzenie do ksiag Starego Testamentu.* 1954.
Pp. 264. (" Pax," Warsaw. Price : Zl. 25.)

This work, an Introduction to the Books of the Old Testament
by a Roman Catholic scholar, fills an obvious gap in Polish
literature in this field. In the course of forty-seven chapters,
the author deals first with the divisions of the Old Testament,
then with the growth of the Canon, goes on to consider which
of the ancient forms of the text (MT, LXX, Vulgate) is nearest
the original and finally discusses the individual books. The
standpoint is strongly conservative ; but there is evidence
of a sound grasp of the problems involved. The extensive
quotations from Papal encyclicals on specific subjects of
debate should prove instructive for non-Catholic scholars.
For the benefit of readers whose interest is in religion rather
than in the technicalities of scholarship, much emphasis is
laid on the line of *Heilsgeschichte* which God has followed
throughout the vicissitudes of history.   M.B.

JOZAKI, S. : *The Secondary Passages in the Book of Amos.* (Kwansei
Gakuin University Studies, Vol. IV.) 1956. Pp. 100. (Kwansei
Gakuin University, Nishinomiya, Japan.)

The author, instructor in the Theology Department of his
university, divides the book of Amos into fifty-eight sections,
and discusses them in turn mainly from the point of view of
authenticity (i.e., are they from Amos himself, or from a later
period ?). Amos himself was active 760-750 B.C. There are
eight strata of secondary passages : the disciples' group
(shorter title ; vii. 10-17) ; Judaean editor A (four small
emendations in vi.) ; Judaean editor B (ii. 4-5 ; v. 26 ; iii.
4b and emendation in v. 6), after 621 B.C. and before the
exile ; late exilic editor (ix. 8b, 10) ; Doxologies (iv. 13 ;
v. 8 ; ix. 5-6), c. 500 B.C. ; anti-neighbour editor (i. 9-12),
fifth century ; eschatological editor (ix. 11-15), late fourth
century ; scribal works (minor glosses), early third century
(responsible for the final form of the book). We have thus a
vertical section of Hebrew-Jewish religion, and the conclusion
of the paper gives a clear and useful outline of this. N.H.S.

KAPELRUD, A. S. : *Central Ideas in Amos* (Skrifter utgitt av Det
Norske Videnskabs-Akademie i Oslo, II. Hist.-Filos. Klasse.
1956. No. 4). 1956. Pp. 86. (H. Aschehoug & Co., Oslo. Price :
Norw. kr. 8.00.)

Briefly the ideas are these : Amos, being a *noqed*, was of high
rank and was responsible for the Temple herds ; he derived
his universalism from the God El whose amalgamation with

Yahweh had taken place before the time of Amos ; he preached punishment for sins, both of Israel and the surrounding nations, sins that were both moral and social, but held out a hope for those who repented ; his literary style was so good that he must have moved in a society of high standing, this society was that of the cult personnel ; the Day of the Lord was primarily a cultic event.

Much of the evidence for these views is drawn from the Ras Shamra texts and a strong line of tradition leading up to Amos is assumed. At times the argument is tortuous and tenuous, as, for example, in the claim that i. 2-ii. 16 shows a pattern of execration that was " no invention of Amos, but . . . the old formula used by the prophets and priests in the cult when they had to convey the oracles of Yahweh to the cult audience " (p. 20). Now and again the reader gains the impression that he can never fully understand Amos because of the impenetrable complexity of the cult tradition by which alone his book, so it is implied here, can be explained.

L.H.B.

MILLER, J. W. : *Das Verhältnis Jeremias und Hesekiels sprachlich und theologisch untersucht, mit besonderer Berücksichtigung der Prosareden Jeremias* (Van Gorcum's Theol. Bibliotheek, Nr. xxviii.). 1955. Pp. x+189. (Van Gorcum and Co. Ltd., Assen. Price : Fl. 12.)

The author has written a careful, well-documented dissertation on his chosen theme, cogently argued, and with his conclusions clearly stated. It is held that Ezekiel had most probably seen and heard Jeremiah in Jerusalem before the Exile, and later had eagerly read the contents of " Baruch's Roll," which consisted of the prose speeches. It is in these speeches that Miller finds the twenty-one passages which most clearly show Ezekiel's literary dependence. Theological dependence is more difficult to prove, but a good case is made out for it, differences being put down partly to personal factors, but mainly to the changes in national circumstances in the meantime. This book should be helpful in studying some of the wider problems connected with these prophets also.

D.R.Ap-T.

ROWLEY, H. H. : *The Marriage of Hosea* (Reprinted from *Bulletin of the John Rylands Library*, xxxix., No. 1, September, 1956.) 1956. Pp. 34. (John Rylands Library, Manchester and Manchester University Press. Price : 3s. 6d.)

As one would expect, this study contains a clear presentation of the problems raised by the Biblical evidence, a comprehensive survey, copiously documented, of the wide range of solutions offered by modern scholars, and a judicious appraisal of the rival theories. Professor Rowley offers no new hypothesis, but supports the view that Hosea iii. is the sequel to i., though possibly from another source, and that both chapters are historical and refer to the same woman. He holds that Gomer was immoral before her marriage to Hosea, that Hosea was aware of this, and that iii. implies that; after leaving her husband, she had fallen into slavery from which Hosea bought her back. This lecture is an indispensable guide to one of the most intricate of Old Testament problems.   G.W.A.

WESTERMANN, C. : *Der Aufbau des Buches Hiob.* (Beiträge zur historischen Theologie, 23.) 1956. Pp. viii+116. (J. C. B. Mohr, Tübingen. Price : DM. 12.)

The thesis of this work is that the Book of Job is not concerned with the problem of the suffering of the righteous, but with man's complaint in terms of his own experience ; it is a *Daseinsvorgang.* Job's complaint is his reaction to suffering ; his question, Why must I suffer?, is primarily a question of *Existenz*, and only secondarily a subject for thought and debate. But the stuff of the Book of Job is not confined to complaint ; much of it is dialogue. But whereas the speeches of the friends are argumentative and contentious, their primary intention was to give comfort, for true comfort is not one-sided, but it is a dialogue in which the suffering person speaks out and words of comfort are given in response. Job's complaints cause his friends to abandon comfort for argument, and their arguments have the twofold effect of inducing Job to interrupt his *cris-de-coeur* to produce counter-arguments and to turn away from his friends to appeal to God and to seek comfort in Him. This dialogue of Job and his friends is set in a context of complaint (chs. iii. and xxix-xxxi.) and there is also dialogue between Job and God. But the book as a whole can be described neither as complaint nor as dialogue ; it is a drama. For this purpose the author used the living tradition of a man who had suffered, although the tradition and the complaint do not always agree. On the basis of this theory of the structure of the Book of Job, Westermann proceeds to examine the various parts of it in detail. J.M.

LAW, RELIGION, AND THEOLOGY

BERNHARDT, K.-H. : *Gott und Bild. Ein Beitrag zur Begründung und Deutung des Bildverbotes im Alten Testament.* 1956. Pp. 164. (Evangelische Verlagsanstalt, Berlin. Price : DM. 7.50.)

This is a well-documented and scholarly book which leads to conclusions in which there is little that is new. The first part of it deals with the use of images among Israel's neighbours, showing that there was no conception of a definite boundary line between the physical or material and the spiritual, that it was believed that the spirit of a dead man could enter his body again and that a demon or a god could, like a fine fluid, enter a human body or a material object and possess it. The main quality of an image was not that it should be visibly representative of a divine being in any way but that it should possess something of the spirit of that being. Objects like gryphons were believed to be not merely ornamental but the seat of a guardian spirit or demon. The

second part of the book examines the various views that
have been held concerning the origin of the prohibition of
the use of images in ancient Israel. The final part is constructive, and for the origin of Israel's prohibition of images
which he traces back to Moses and Sinai, Bernhardt lays
emphasis on the recognition by the original Israelite wilderness
amphictyony of Yahweh as a *Führergott*, on the fact that an
image would have been a dangerous rival to the ark of Yahweh,
and on the distinctive nature of Yahweh religion.   J.M.

DE BOER, P. A. H. : *Oudtestamentische Studiën*. Deel XI. *Second-
Isaiah's Message*. 1956. Pp. viii+126. (E. J. Brill, Leiden.
Price : By subscription Fl. 15 ; separately Fl. 21.)

This is a difficult book to review ; all in it concerns Isa. xl-lv.
but the whole is not closely co-ordinated. As a necessary
preliminary to the second part of his book Professor de Boer
offers a translation of these chapters, rendering, for example,
ṣedek sometimes as privilege (e.g., xlii. 6, 21 ; xlv. 8) and
hiṣdik (liii. 11) as acquire privilege, and the well-known
phrase in xlii. 6 as ' a consolidation of the people, a light
respected by the nations.' He considers the textual evidence
of the Dead Sea Isaiah scrolls but expresses reluctance to use
it for any reconstruction of MT. In Isa. li. 1 he reads the verbs
in the relative clauses as actives and makes the reference to
Yahweh not to Abraham, but whereas Yahweh could be
spoken of as ' rock ' in the sense of strength or refuge or
source of life-giving water, could it possibly be said that the
people hewed Him ? Professor de Boer states that ' Second
Isaiah's only purpose is to proclaim deliverance for the people
of Judah ; he finds no support for the missionary office of
Yahweh's people ; the *mishpaṭ* which they are to take to the
Gentiles is the sentence on them. When Yahweh thus executes
judgment and restores His people, the restored people will show
forth Yahweh's judgment in their new life, which the Gentiles
will acknowledge as wonderful salvation. This book covers in
very short compass much that is highly debatable and gives
to certain. Hebrew words and phrases meanings which will
be contested ; it is a pity that the main thesis, which is to
emphasize the redemption and restoration of Judah as the
main (and, indeed, the only) message of the Second Isaiah,
had not been worked out at much greater length.   J.M.

DE BOER, P. A. H. : *Jeremia's Twijfel*. 1957. Pp. 36. (E. J. Brill,
Leiden. Price : Fl. 1.75.)

This pamphlet contains the address delivered by Professor
de Boer as Rector Magnificus on the 382nd anniversary of
Leiden University, 8th Feb., 1957. After a sketch of the
historical situation in Jeremiah's time, he examines a few
passages where the prophet, in addressing God, expresses deep
doubt and scepticism. Jeremiah's reluctance to accept the
prophetic commission in i. 6 may be a stylistic figure ; but
he reveals his inmost misgivings in iv. 10, where he realizes

that God's word for one situation may not be His word for another ; in xii. 1-4, where he questions the righteous judgment of God in allowing the wicked to prosper ; in xv. 18, where even God seems to him "as a deceitful brook, as waters that fail," and in xx. 7-9, where he cries out that Yahweh has seduced him by leading him to prophesy falsely. The theme is treated in a manner appropriate to the occasion and the audience but it will be welcomed by everyone who is touched by the spiritual conflict of Jeremiah.   F.F.B.

BUBER, M. : *Königtum Gottes.* (Dritte, neu vermehrte Auflage.) 1956. Pp. lxiv + 222. (Lambert Schneider, Heidelberg. Price : DM. 19.80.)

It is good news for students of the Old Testament that this challenging work is available once again after an interval of some twenty years. The author tells us that he has found it unnecessary to make any considerable changes in the text, which remains substantially the same as that of the previous edition. Nevertheless in a new preface of about fourteen pages he reviews his thesis with particular reference to articles by W. F. Albright, O. Eissfeldt and A. Alt, and the notes have been revised and brought up-to-date at a number of points where the author has found this to be imperative. In this connexion the present writer must confess to finding himself even more interested in what is now omitted than in what has been added.   A.R.J.

DAKIN, D. M. : *Peace and Brotherhood in the Old Testament.* 1956. Pp. 128. (The Bannisdale Press, London. Price : 10s. 6d.)

This book ' traces those ideas of Divine Fatherhood and human brotherhood which . . . form the basis of the Christian pacifist faith.' The standpoint adopted inevitably imposes a standard of judgment on the material which, while not foreign to the Bible, is not the primary biblical standard. Jeremiah is described as the first war resister. The books of Jonah and Ruth are eloquently presented. The writer's conception of election appears to resemble that of those whom Amos denounced. We would question the statements: ' Marcion, the greatest of the Gnostics,' and ' Daniel was written to support the Maccabean revolt.' Some reference to contemporary social and religious customs would have strengthened the writer's case.   A.S.H.

DANIÉLOU, J. : *Les saints " païens " de l'Ancien Testament.* 1956. Pp. 174. (Editions du Seuil, Paris : Fr. 450.)

This small book, attractively printed in large, clear type, has a curious title, which is explained by the author in the sense that quite a number of people, mentioned in the Old Testament as worthy of praise and imitation, were neither by race nor by religion Israelites. The names that he selects for discussion are those of Abel, Enoch, Daniel, Noah, Job, Melchisedek, Lot (who is said to be " parent d'Abraham, mais étranger à son alliance ") and the Queen of Sheba. There is a thesis running through the whole booklet, namely that these " saints " who were neither Jews nor Christians " apparaissent comme l'expression du mystérieux avent du Christ dans l'âme païenne" (p. 11.). Whatever may be thought of this contention, the booklet is beautifully written and makes the most of the scanty information that can be gained from Scripture and tradition about these characters in the Old Testament. Daniélou is clearly of the opinion that he is not concerned with such exemplary pagans as Socrates or Epictetus. He prefers to limit his discussion " au solide terrain des Écritures," and this he does with charm, wisdom and charity. J.M.T.B.

DIETZFELBINGER, H. : *Gottes Weg zum Kreuz im Alten Bund. Meditationen.* 1956. Pp. 79. (Chr. Kaiser Verlag, München. Price : DM. 3.)

This is a series of 15 meditations, based on Old Testament texts, relating to the Passion and Work of Jesus Christ. The meditations fall into three groups : God and Man ; God and His People ; God and His Servant. They are not primarily Old Testament studies, but rather ' *eine existentielle Interpretation* ' in the light of the Cross of Christ. Each meditation is followed by a prayer. A.S.H.

EICHRODT, W. : *Das Gottesbild des Alten Testaments.* (Calwer Hefte zur Förderung biblischen Glaubens und christlichen Lebens, No. 1.) 1956. Pp. 24. (Calwer Verlag, Stuttgart. Price : DM. 1.20.)

This brief, popular survey of a great subject by a great scholar delineates the distinctiveness of Old Testament religion, by emphasizing the intensely personal character of the conception of God and the exclusiveness of His claim. Special attention is devoted to three aspects : moral and social life, the world of nature, and relations with other peoples. Though short, it is anything but slight ; and in practically every paragraph there are profound and stimulating observations. G.W.A.

Élie le prophéte. 2 vols. I. *Selon les Écritures et les traditions chrétiennes.* II. *Au Carmel—dans le Judaïsme et l'Islam.* (Les études carmélitaines.) 1956. Pp. 270+9 plates+3 maps ; pp. 316+13 plates. (Desclée de Brouwer, Bruges. Price : 200 Belgian francs per volume.)

These two volumes on the prophet Elijah much resemble the earlier volumes in the series *Cahiers Sioniens* on *Abraham, Père des Croyants* (1951) and *Moïse. L'homme de l'Alliance* (1955, on which cf. *Book List*, 1956, pp. 48f.). The first volume has, as its opening contribution, an essay on " Hauts Lieux Élianiques " by P. Paul-Marie de la Croix, and then prints the *Bible de Jérusalem* translations of the Old and New Testament texts on the prophet. For the passages from I Kings xvii., 1 to II Kings ii. 18 there are notes from an unpublished manuscript by R. de Vaux. There are two exegetical articles on Elijah in the Old Testament (J. Steinmann) and the New Testament (M. E. Boismard). Other articles deal with the Elijah tradition in the Greek, Syriac, and Latin writers, the cult of Elijah in the Christian church, and in Eastern tradition, and the prophet's iconography. The second volume contains a variety of articles on the Carmelite traditions and cult and on the Jewish and Islamic traditions. The two volumes are beautifully printed and delightfully illustrated. They represent one of the outstanding contributions to Old Testament hagiography. J.M.T.B.

GEISSER, W. : *Ist der Gott des Alten Testaments der Vater Jesu Christi?* (Calwer Hefte zur Förderung biblischen Glaubens und christlichen Lebens, No. 3.) 1956. Pp. 32. (Calwer Verlag, Stuttgart. Price : DM. 1.20.)

This booklet, based on an address to lay Church workers, deals with the Old Testament as part of Christian Scripture. In the three main sections, the author discusses (a) the attitude of Jesus to the Old Testament, (b) the elements in Old Testament teaching of which the value and importance are immediately evident, and those which present difficulties, and (c) the fulfilment of the Old Testament in Jesus and the Church. The booklet ends with a few simple rules for the devotional use of the Old Testament. G.W.A.

GROSS, H. : *Die Idee des ewigen und allgemeinen Weltfriedens im Alten Orient und im Alten Testament.* (Trierer Theologische Studien, 7.) 1956. Pp. xviii+186. (Paulinus Verlag, Trier. Price : 35s. 0d.)

The author of this monograph, who has already written a similar work on the idea of world dominion in the Old Testament (*Book List*, 1954, p. 63), here turns his attention to the related subject of world peace. The earlier pages are devoted to the appearance of this conception in the historical, mythological and other texts of the ancient Near East, and, in an appendix, the author even glances at the classical fields of Greece and Rome. He then proceeds to an examination of the O.T. data, particularly (a) the general terminology and its associated ideas, and (b) the realization of this ideal, with special reference to the part to be played by Yahweh Himself, by the House of David, and by the Messiah as the ideal King, the Servant of Yahweh and the Son of Man. The subject is obviously far too vast for the author to do more than touch lightly upon the issues involved ; but, like the earlier work, it may be read with profit by all who are interested in this much debated field of study. A.R.J.

GUNN, G. S. : *God in the Psalms.* 1956. Pp. xii+216. (Saint Andrew Press, Edinburgh. Price : 21s. 0d.)

This volume is based on the Cunningham Lectures delivered by the author at New College, Edinburgh. It is non-technical and is for the general reader. After a preliminary chapter on the background of the Psalter (origin, dates, timelessness, dependence, and originality), Dr. Gunn discusses in

turn a number of theological and religious issues. Under the title ' The Fringes of His Ways,' he discusses Hebrew ideas of God in Nature. Then he turns to the Divine Control of History, the Divine Conflict with Evil, and so through the Essentials and the Stresses of Personal Religion to Fulfilment in Worship. The author takes note of recent study of the Psalter, such as the work of Mowinckel, the Uppsala School, and Gunkel, and he mentions Ugarit, but he lays little stress on these matters. He deals chiefly with the text itself and his approach is definitely theological. He makes numerous references to current literature on the Psalter. The volume contains a short subject index and an index of Scripture passages, but no bibliography, since the books mentioned are listed in the preface and in the footnotes.
N.H.S.

HOOKE, S. H. : *The Siege Perilous : Essays in Biblical Anthropology and Kindred Subjects.* 1956. Pp. 264. (S.C.M. Press, London. Price : 21s. 6d.)

In this series of collected papers, originally published between the years 1930 and 1955, the author not only illustrates once again how successful he has been in his professed aim " to try and build a bridge between the three disciplines of Anthropology, Archaeology, and Biblical studies," but also enables one to trace something of the development in his thought during the quarter of a century which they cover. As one would expect, a recurrent theme is that of " patternism," particularly (a) the theory of a myth and ritual pattern, which centred in the thought of the dying and rising god and was distributed in one form or another throughout the Near East, and (b) the subsequent history of this supposed myth and ritual pattern as it affected Jewish Apocalyptic, the Mystery Religions, and primitive Christianity. The reader is constantly made aware of the wide range of the author's interests and reading ; and, while the parallels which he finds in the O.T. may occasionally seem a little strained, one is compelled to recognize anew and with gratitude the profound influence which the author has exercised and, happily, continues to exercise in the field of Biblical exegesis. A.R.J.

HOWSE, E. M. : *The Lively Oracles.* 1956. Pp. 224. (Allen & Unwin, London and Thomas Nelson, Toronto. Price : 20s. 0d.)

The author preached the twenty-one chapters of this book to tell his congregation what the Old Testament is about, and he evidently did it well, exemplifying what used to be called the ' modern approach,' and sprinkling his pages with many illustrations of biblical conditions from modern times. The author may not be quite abreast of the most modern scholarship (or, perhaps he does not agree with it) but he is certainly far ahead of many of his brethren, not to mention most congregations ; so that it is a pity that the book is quite so expensive. There seems to be a slight inconcinnity between the actual titles to chs. 8 and 15 and the Contents page. A comprehensive index adds to the book's value. D.R.Ap-T.

VAN IMSCHOOT, P. : *Théologie de L'Ancien Testament*. Tome II. *L'homme*. (Bibliothèque de Théologie. Série III. Théologie Biblique. Vol. 4). 1956. Pp. x+342. (Desclée & Cie, Tournai. Price : 23s. 6d.)

This is the second volume of a large scale work on Old Testament Theology by a Roman Catholic theologian, of which the first volume was reviewed in the *Book List* of 1955, pp. 50f. The main theme of this volume is Man, and, like the first volume, it is divided into four chapters. Chapter I deals with the origin and nature of man and discusses the various relevant terms. The author recognises the synthetic nature of Hebrew thought about man but is not prepared to accept the view that the Hebrews attributed psychical functions to the various parts of the body only by synechdoche. Chapter II deals with the life and destiny of man and discusses in detail the various passages in the Old Testament which may have a bearing on the question of a future life. Chapter III is by far the longest in the volume. Its general subject is that of the duties of man. A brief introduction deals with the moral codes in the Old Testament. The duties of man are then divided into duties towards man and duties towards God. The former are subdivided into religious duties and the cult. It is a disadvantage in this arrangement that it obscures to some extent what is surely a fact, viz., that for the best Old Testament thought the fulfilment of duty towards man is at the same time fulfilment of duty towards God. It means too that the meaning of a word like *hesed* has to be discussed in two different places. It is interesting to notice that, whereas Köhler treats the cult rather hesitantly at the end of his anthropology as man's attempt to save himself, Van Imschoot deals with the subject as part of man's duty towards God. His main subdividions are sacred places, objects, actions, times, and the distinction between clean and unclean. The section on duties towards man comprises the required attitude towards the neighbour, the scope of forgiveness, the problem of how to deal with the taking of life, respect for the neighbour's person and his property, respect for truth and for parents and all the problems of sexual morality. Chapter IV treats of the different kinds of sin, its punishment and how it may be expiated.   N.W.P.

JANSSEN, E. : *Juda in der Exilszeit. Beitrag zur Frage der Entstehung des Judentums* (Forschungen zur Religion und Literatur des Alten und Neuen Testaments, N.F., 51.) 1956. Pp. 124 (Vandenhoeck & Ruprecht, Göttingen. Price : 14s. 6d.)

This study of the state of affairs in the territory during the Babylonian exile is based on a fairly wide range of O.T. books and sections which the author assigns to the exilic and early post-exilic age. Some little attention is paid to the evidence of archaeology, especially on the extent of the destruction wrought in the land by the Babylonians. The territory of Judah was diminished by the loss of the Shephelah and the Negeb ; the remainder was parcelled out among the ' poor of the land,' to whom Nebuzaradan gave preferential treatment. The most interesting part of the study concerns the religious reaction to the disaster. While there were some who concluded that Josiah's reformation had been a great mistake, and therefore tended to revive old Canaanite cultic practices, there were others who recognized in the disaster the righteous judgment of God. Three liturgical documents emanating from the latter group in Judah are preserved in the O.T.—the Book of Lamentations ; Isa. lxiii. 7-lxiv. 11 ; Mic. vii. 7 ff. Under the impact of the disaster, and particularly of the destruction of the temple and suspension of the cultus, many turned to the formerly disregarded oracles of the prophets, which now received canonical recognition. An embryonic form of the synagogue is also traced back to Judah during the exile.   F.F.B.

JENNI, E. : *Die politischen Voraussagen der Propheten* (Abhandlungen zur Theologie des Alten und Neuen Testaments, No. 29.) 1956. Pp. 118. (Zwingli-Verlag, Zürich. Price : Sw. Fr. 14.)

The political utterances of the prophets are here examined in the light of the author's belief that prophecy is essentially eschatological in outlook and content. Only those passages, therefore, are selected for study which specifically mention nations or individuals and make some prediction about them. It is shown that where prophecy passes from what is general and eschatological to what is particular and historical in a narrow sense there are signs that the material is secondary and due to a later hand, for instance that of Baruch in the Book of Jeremiah. Such ' Historisierung ' was due to a misunderstanding of the prophet's real intention or to a desire to bring an element of potential fulfilment to prophecies that would otherwise seem only remotely capable of being fulfilled. This view of the prophets, which denies them a lively interest in people and events for their own sake as distinct from the place they have in the general eschatological pattern, seems somewhat distorted.   L.H.B.

KLEIN, W. C. : *The Psychological Pattern of Old Testament Prophecy.* 1956. Pp. viii+96. (Seabury-Western Theological Seminary, Evanston, Ill.)

Professor Klein has made a thorough study of all the modern systems of psychology and discusses them in relation to Old Testament prophecy with full use of all the technical terms of the psychologists. His study leads to the negative con- clusion that none of these systems is really satisfactory for the explanation of Old Testament prophecy, since modern techniques cannot be applied to men who are known to us from biographies so incomplete. Nevertheless, he holds that we are justified in speaking of a pattern of prophecy, since it is probable that most of the greater prophets were cast in much the same mould. So far from being men of psychological

instability, they were exceptionally stable, and the basis of their stability was their response to an inner certainty that they were called to their office. They were not men with an aptitude for prophecy, but men who with unflinching courage yielded themselves to the constraint which was laid upon them. This means that they are not to be explained in terms of mental make-up, but primarily in terms of will. For the greater prophets cannot be wholly divorced from the false prophets, as beings of a different order, since it was so hard for ordinary people to distinguish between them. The difference lay in the nature of their response to the constraint laid upon them, rather than in the realm of psychology.
H.H.R.

KOEHLER, L. : *Hebrew Man*, trans. by P. R. Ackroyd, with an appendix on Justice in the Gate, 1956. Pp. 190. (S.C.M. Press, London. Price : 12s. 6d.)

The original Swiss edition of this book (entitled *Der Hebräische Mensch*) was reviewed in the *Book List* of 1954, p. 64. It has now been translated for English readers by P. R. Ackroyd and in its new dress it deserves to win many new readers. There are various theological studies of the Old Testament Doctrine of Man available and relevant articles will be found in Hebrew Archaeologies, but never, perhaps, has anyone given us such a vivid picture of what an Ancient Hebrew must have felt and thought. The Appendix makes available in English one of the most important essays on Hebrew law, which discusses the functioning of the legal Assembly, its breakdown in the 8th century leading to the criticism of the prophets and the development of preaching which culminated in Deuteronomy. Dr. Koehler finds the model for the dialogue of the Book of Job in the speeches delivered in the legal assembly.
N.W.P.

KOOLHAAS, A. A. : *Theocratie en Monarchie in Israël* (*Theocracy and Monarchy in Israel*). *Einige opmerkingen over de verhouding van de theocratie en het Israelitische koningschap in het Oude Testament* (with summary in English). 1957. Pp. 158. (H. Veenman en Zonen, Wageningen. Price : Fl. 11.50.)

These " remarks on the relation between the theocracy and the Israelite kingship in the O.T." (to quote the sub-title) were submitted as a doctoral dissertation to Utrecht University. The author thinks that the " myth and ritual school " tends to envisage one general pattern of kingship in the Ancient Near East and to interpret the data too exclusively in terms of that pattern. But it may be suggested that the author envisages a myth and ritual school (especially when he refers to the English school of Hooke *cum suis*) which has as little real existence as he thinks the ritual pattern had. When, rather late in their history, the Israelites acquired kings, the human kingship did not replace theocracy. Saul was *nagid* over Yahweh's people ; David and his successors were regents appointed by Yahweh, Israel's true King ; the northern kings exercised a more absolute monarchy. Neither originally nor in the further development of the office did the Israelite kingship involve priestly functions, he maintains, but his rebuttal of the arguments used to show that it did is not altogether convincing. On the other hand, he rightly shows how the privileges of the people were best safeguarded when the theocratic ideals were most fully maintained.

F.F.B.

KRITZINGER, J. D. W. : *Qehal Jahwe : wat dit is en wie daaraan mag behoort.* 1957. Pp. ix+166. (Kok, Kampen. Price : Fl. 6.90.)

This Afrikaans thesis (with an English summary) was accepted by the Free University of Amsterdam for the doctorate in theology. The author approaches his two questions posed in his title by way of prolegomena to the present-day problems " What is the church?" and " Who should belong to it?" He draws a clear distinction between the *qehal Yahweh* as the " cult-assembly " and the *qehal Yisra'el* as the " assembly of the citizens." Admission to the former was dependent on circumcision and the conditions laid down in Deut. xxiii. 2-9, together with the passover stipulations of Ex. xii. 43-49 and the stipulations regarding ceremonial purity found in the Deuteronomic and Priestly codes ; but ethical conditions were emphasized as well, as is clear from Pss. xv. 1-5 and xxiv. 3-6. In Ps. xxiv. 4 *'asher lo nasa' lashshaw naphsho* is trans- lated " who does not put his faith in falseness." If the prime external condition for admission to the *qehal Yahweh* is circumcision, the ethical conditions may be summed up as " circumcision of the heart," which Yahweh himself promised to bring about (Deut. xxx. 6). The *qehal Yahweh* was both broader and narrower than ethnic Israel : the sojourner could belong to it, while the wicked Israelite was excluded from it. Yet " Israel the elect people of God was nevertheless the core around which the *qehal Yahweh* was built." F.F.B.

DE LEEUW, V. : *De Ebed Jahwe-Profetieën : historisch-kritisch onderzoek naar hun ontstaan en hun beteekenis.* 1956. Pp. xxviii+ 368. (van Gorcum, Assen. Price : Fl. 17.50.)

This full-length study of the Servant Songs covers much the same ground as C. R. North's *magnum opus* (to the first edition of which our author gratefully acknowledges his indebtedness) ; but it deals in greater detail with their interpretation in the early Christian centuries. In a review of the history of the exegesis of the Songs, from " Trito-Isaiah " down to H. H. Rowley, a separate chapter is devoted to the patristic era and the Middle Ages. We see, for example, how Thomas Aquinas and Calvin join hands with a considerable body of rabbis in maintaining an autobiographical interpretation of the Third Song. When de Leeuw comes to give his own interpretation, he prefaces it with a fresh Dutch version of of the Songs (paralleled by a French version in the French

summary of the work provided on pp. 332-356). We note that
in Isa. xlix. 3 he retains " Israel "; in lii. 15 he translates " so
will he strike many peoples with amazement "; in liii. 11 he
reads " he will see light and be satisfied." The Servant of the
Songs (unlike the servant of their context) is envisaged as an
ideal descendant of the Davidic house whose advent is
expected by the prophet in the future ; his expiatory sufferings
are depicted in the light both of his personal experiences
and of the misfortunes endured by earlier members of the
house of David. The brief account of the Qumran interpretation of the Songs (pp. 19-21) could be considerably
expanded.   F.F.B.

McKenzie, J. L. : *The Two-Edged Sword. An Interpretation of the Old
Testament.* 1956. Pp. xvi+318. (Bruce Publishing Co., Milwaukee.
Price : $4.50.)

The author of this interesting study of the Old Testament and
its theology writes in his preface :   " My excuse for doing it
is that no one else has done it." Whether or no he would find
complete agreement with him on the book's originality, he
has certainly provided something that the ordinary student
will accept as easier reading than the works of Eichrodt or
Heinisch or van Imschoot, to mention no others.   After
chapters on the books themselves and on inspiration and
revelation, he discusses the theological content of the Old
Testament under such headings as Cosmic Origins, Human
Origins, Israel and the Nations, the Hope of the Future, the
Wisdom of the Hebrews, the Mystery of Inquity, Life and
Death, the Prayer of the Hebrews, and the God of the Hebrews.
He considers, perhaps rightly, that the ordinary reader dislikes
all footnotes. Quotations from the Bible, when they do not
follow his own translations or a free paraphrase, are taken
from the version edited by Smith and Goodspeed for the
Chicago Press. A short bibliography refers his readers to
some of the best modern work on the subject.   J.M.T.B.

Martin-Achard, R. : *De la mort à la résurrection d'après l'Ancien
Testament* (Bibliothèque Théologique). 1956. Pp. 190. (Delachaux
& Niestlé, Neuchâtel & Paris. Price : Swiss Fr. 7.50.)

The author of this monograph, who is a busy French pastor,
has been led to make a careful and sympathetic examination
of the Old Testament with a view to determining how the
belief in a resurrection came into being and gradually found
acceptance in Israel. He rightly recognizes that one must
begin with the way in which the early Israelite appears to
have understood such terms as " life " and " death " vis-à-vis
the conception of Yahweh as the " Living God," and two
groups of passages are then examined in some detail, i.e.
(a) Hos. vi. 1-3, xiii. 14, Ezek. xxxvii. 1-14, Isa. liii. 10b-12,
xxv. 8, xxvi. 19, Dan. xii. 2f. ; (b) Pss. xvi. 9-11, xlix. 16,
lxxiii. 23-28, Job xix. 25-27. While consideration is also given

to the possible influence of Canaanite and Persian thought, the author finds that in origin the confidence in a resurrection springs from a realization that the life of the true believer must be of such value to the Creator that it may not be thought of as disappearing finally at death. It is impossible to do more than sketch the probable lines of development within the compass of so short a monograph, but the result is a useful piece of work which may be warmly recommended as a sound introduction to the subject.   A.R.J.

MOWINCKEL, S. : *He That Cometh*, trans. by G. W. Anderson. 1956. Pp. xvi+528. (Blackwell, Oxford. Price : 45s. 0d. Abingdon-Cokesbury, Nashville and New York. $6.50.)

This is undoubtedly the most important book on the Old Testament which has appeared during the past year. It is more than a mere translation of the Norwegian *Han som kommer*. It has been revised by the author, and references to recent literature have been added. Professor Mowinckel deals some hard blows at other scholars, and it is to be expected that he will not always secure agreement with his own positions. The chapter on the Servant of the Lord withdraws the autobiographical view which he advanced in 1921, and which has been modified in subsequent writings, and presents the view that the Servant Songs are later than Deutero-Isaiah, and that they depict a disciple of his, while maintaining that it is with justice that the Church has found in Jesus the true fulfilment of these prophecies. The reviewer finds much difficulty here. He is also surprised to find it stated with emphasis (three times on one page) that several MSS. of LXX omit ' Israel ' in Isa. xlix. 3, though Holmes and Parsons, Swete, and Ziegler, all fail to record a single MS. which omits it. No MSS. are here indicated, though decisive importance is attributed to them. It is surely imperative that we should be told what MSS. they are, so that their weight may be assessed. The chapter on the ideal of kingship in ancient Israel must be reckoned with by all subsequent writers on this subject, as must also that on the Son of Man. The dating of the ' messianic ' passages in First Isaiah is put later than by many recent writers. The book is superbly documented and it is a ' must ' for all who would be abreast of Old Testament scholarship to-day. The translation is a fine piece of work, which deserves the highest praise.   H.H.R.

MURRAY, J. : *Principles of Conduct : Aspects of Biblical Ethics.* 1957. Pp. 272. (Tyndale Press, London. Price : 15s. 0d.)

This volume is the text of the Payton Lectures delivered at the Fuller Theological Seminary, Pasadena, California, by the Professor of Systematic Theology at the Westminster Theological Seminary, Philadelphia, Pa. Professor Murray applies to the ethic of Scripture what he calls ' the biblico-theological method.' This involves, among other things, assuming that the ten commandments were in force from the time of Adam and Eve, and that many of the actions of leading figures of the Old Testament were not sub-ethical, as some of us have thought. A large part of the book is taken up with proofs of positions in which the author's premisses have involved him. Readers who do not take the author's ultra-conservative view will read with impatience ; but those who themselves favour ' the biblico-theological method ' will be edified. The appendices on Gen. vi. 1-4 and Lev. xviii. 16, 18 are examples of this. The pointing of the Hebrew leaves in many cases much to be desired. N.H.S.

NEHER, A. : *Moïse et la vocation juive* (Maîtres spirituels, 8). Undated (1956). Pp. 192. (Éditions du Seuil, Paris. Price : Fr. 350.)

This ' Pelican ' type of book is No. 8 in the series " Maîtres spirituels," and it is a very popular work dealing with the significance of Moses and of the mission of the Jew. The book is profusely illustrated, and offers an exposition of the story of Moses and Israel in the desert which is often very original and striking. The interest, however, is not mainly historical, for the Passover, the Lawgiving and the Covenant are explained as setting forth the human-mission, the universal faithfulness and the messianic solitude of the Jewish people. Here then is something like a mild Jewish typology, and so I read the book always with respect, often with profit, and sometimes with great reservation. G.H.D.

NORTH, C. R. : *The Suffering Servant in Deutero-Isaiah : An Historical and Critical Study.* 2nd edition. 1956. Pp. xii+264. (Clarendon Press, Oxford, G. Cumberlege, London. Price : 25s. 0d.)

The first edition (1948) was reviewed in the *Book List* 1949, p. 45. In the 2nd edition the bibliography has been extended by a further 34 mainly recent works, and errata have been corrected. The original $2\frac{1}{2}$ pages postscript has been extended to 20 pages giving a brief but careful appraisal of the views and interpretations expressed by Mowinckel, Nyberg, Engnell, Ringgren, Lindblom and Bentzen. The value of this study is too well-known to need further comment : the additional material increases its usefulness. In the Indexes of Authors and Subjects, a few of the entries need correction to suit the new edition. A.S.H.

ÖSTBORN, G. : *Yahweh and Baal : Studies in the Book of Hosea and Related Documents.* (Lunds Universitets Årsskrift. N.F. Avd. 1. Bd. 51. Nr. 6.) 1956. Pp. 106. (Gleerup, Lund. Price : Sw. Kr. 10.50.)

This interesting monograph emanates from that prolific school of Scandinavian Old Testament scholars to whom we already owe so many important works. The present work is a careful study of a contrast between the rival religions of Baal and Yahweh in Canaan. The main body of the evidence for the author's picture of Baalism is drawn from the oracles of the prophet Hosea, though it is supplemented by materials from other books of the Old Testament, and from external sources, such as the Ras Shamra texts and Akkadian sources. The author casts his net a little widely in his description of Baalism, and some scholars may blink at seeing the cult of Sin at Ur labelled Baalism. Some, too, may demur at the interpretation of every reference to ' king and princes ' in Hosea as meaning Baal and his attendant pantheon. The author acknowledges his debt to Nyberg's and Engnell's studies in the book of Hosea, but there is a large amount of valuable original work in his monograph. He has firmly established the thesis that the fertility cult of Baal with its accompanying ritual pattern was deeply entrenched in Israel, especially in the northern kingdom, during the period of the monarchy, and that Yahweh was generally identified with Baal where Baalism prevailed. The contrast between the materialistic aspect of the Baal cult and the spiritual character of true Yahwism as understood by those prophets who were in the Mosaic line of descent is well drawn out. In many places the author's translation of difficult and obscure passages in the Hebrew text of Hosea is determined by what he calls the *melek*-ideology which he regards as characteristic of Baalism. Some of these translations are brilliant and ingenious, but some will probably be questioned. The author's exegesis follows the traditio-historical line of criticism and is an interesting example of the findings, often illuminating, which accrue from that approach. Those scholars who cannot read Swedish will be grateful to the author for writing in English and will admire his skill in the use of a foreign tongue. There are, however, more misprints of an avoidable nature than there need be, and the English reader will hardly be able to help smiling when he sees on the fly page that the book has been published with the ' economical ' assistance of the Humanistiska Fonden. The author is to be congratulated on a valuable piece of Old Testament research, and the monograph should be read by all students interested in that field.

S.H.H.

RINGGREN, H. : *The Messiah in the Old Testament*. (Studies in Biblical Theology, No. 18.) 1956. Pp. 72. (S.C.M. Press, London. Price : 7s. 6d.)

This is a translation of the Swedish work, *Messias konungen* (see *Book List*, 1955, pp. 53f.). Slight modifications, chiefly bibliographical, have been made in the notes. As a lucid and temperate exposition of important questions in Old Testament religion, this book is highly to be commended. The translation is excellent. G.W.A.

ROSIN, H. : *The Lord is God. The Translation of the Divine Names and the Missionary Calling of the Church.* 1956. Pp. 232. (Nederlandsch Bijbelgenootschap, Amsterdam.)

In this book, the author (formerly on the staff of Djakarta Theological College) deals primarily with the translation of the divine names into the missionary languages. It argues that the NAME, YHWH, should be rigidly rendered by some synonym of *Adonai/kyrios/*LORD, while a very general designation of the " super-human " should be chosen for *'elohim*. The book is important for the Old Testament scholar in that it contains a most careful study of the meaning of the name YHWH in relation to the generic *'elohim*. The author insists that the character and function of both the NAME and the designation *'elohim* are clearly distinct and should be diligently observed. He illustrates this point from a great number of Bible passages such as Jonah, 2 Sam. vii. and 1 Chron. xvii., the Elohistic Psalter, Gen. xx., xxii., etc. Some of his interpretations are most stimulating and deserve sympathetic consideration.   C.A.K.

ROWLEY, H. H. : *Prophecy and Religion in Ancient China and Israel.* (Jordan Lectures in Comparative Religion, 1954.) 1956. Pp. 154. (University of London, The Athlone Press. Price : 21s. 0d.)

There must be few scholars who would have the necessary equipment effectively to make the comparison suggested by the title of this book ; it is a remarkable contribution to the study of Comparative Religion. The six lectures have the titles ; The Nature of Prophecy, The Prophet as Statesman, The Prophet as Reformer, The Prophet and the Golden Age, The Prophet and Worship, The Prophet and God. It is in the last two lectures that the contrasts appear most marked. Of the prophets, most use is made of the eighth century prophets, Jeremiah, and Deutero-Isaiah ; and of the Chinese sages, most references are made to Confucius, Mencius and Mo-tzŭ. The book is characteristically careful, sober and sympathetic in its appraisal of the material from both Chinese and Hebrew sources. As one reads the words of the great Chinese sages, one wonders whether China can ever completely turn its back on their teaching ; or is it that the insights gained from the study of Israel's prophets are needed for a just appreciation of China's sages ?   A.S.H.

ROWLEY, H. H. : *The Faith of Israel : Aspects of Old Testament Thought.* 1956. Pp. 220. (S.C.M. Press, London. Price : 18s. 0d.)

This is a very rich book, one of the best which Professor Rowley has yet written, and, as usual, its documentation leaves little to be desired and opens up wide fields of reading and investigation for others. Disguised by its modest title, this book virtually gives a sketch of Old Testament Theology, one more vital in character than the majority of books which treat of that subject. A discussion of the nature of revelation (in particular of the weaving together of personal and impersonal factors which is discussed at greater length in the author's *The Unity of the Bible*) and its media is followed by two chapters about the nature of God and the nature and need of man, the latter containing a helpful discussion of the perplexing features of Hebrew psychology. The chapter on individual and community discusses such matters as the relation between sin and suffering and the question of the identity of the Servant of the Lord. Here and in other parts of the book the author is able to refer the reader to fuller discussions of his own elsewhere The chapter on the good life contains a fine description of Hebrew worship as illustrated by the Psalms. A balanced discussion of the Old Testament views of death and beyond, in which Professor Rowley finds more positive features than many other scholars would accept, is followed by a concluding chapter on the Day of the Lord which contains an admirable succinct statement of the issues concerning the Messiah, the Son of Man and the Servant of the Lord. This book points the way to a more adequate conception of Old Testament Theology as involving a union of thought and practice, Israel's response to God being the test of the reality of its thought. N.W.P.

SCHARBERT, J. : *Der Schmerz in Alten Testament.* (Bonner Biblische Beiträge, 8.) 1955. Pp. 236. (Peter Hanstein Verlag, Bonn. Price : DM. 22.)

This monograph deals thoroughly with the whole question of pain in the Old Testament, pain so far as possible being isolated from the wider context of suffering. The first section discusses the numerous terms used in Hebrew to identify the various ways in which men give expression to the pain they feel. No clear distinction is possible between bodily and mental pain. The second section discusses the psychology of pain, showing what kinds of things an Israelite felt as painful, how he described painful sensations, how he reacted to them and what effect they had on his life. The questions of sympathy and of punishment are discussed. The final section treats of pain as a theological problem, first of all discussing the varying points of view expressed in the different books of the Old Testament and then going on to consider the results of the enquiry for an Old Testament theology of pain. The author shows that, while they are well aware of causal connections, the ultimate view of the Old Testament writers is that pain is due to the direct action of God. This leads him to deal with the question of judgment, of providence and of man's resistance to God's will. As sources of pain notice is taken of sympathy with the suffering of God's people and of the pious Israelite's longing for Zion. Concluding chapters discuss the effect of pain on human and on divine motivation, the significance of pain and, in an appendix, the question of God's suffering. N.W.P.

SEIERSTAD, I. P. : *Gammeltestamentlig bibelteologi*, Vols. I & II. 1956.
Pp. 1-95, 96-190. (Akademisk Forlag, Oslo. Price : Norw. kr.
19.35 each volume.)

These are the first two volumes of a Theology of the Old
Testament by a Norwegian scholar who is well-known for his
work on the prophets. Two further volumes are to be published to complete the work. About half of the first volume is
devoted to a consideration of the character and method of Old
Testament Theology, and to a survey of recent works on the
subject. After discussing the various ways of arranging the
material which others have adopted, he proposes his own :
The Old Testament message about I God, II Man, III Religious and Ethical Fellowship between God and Man. The
remainder of the two volumes is devoted to a treatment of I.
Probably III will prove to be the most important and revealing
section, since the author holds that the teaching of the Old
Testament about a God who seeks personal communion with
men gives a unity to the many phases of Old Testament religion,
links it with the New Testament, and distinguishes it from
other faiths.   G.W.A.

SMITH, C. R. : *The Bible Doctrine of Grace and Related Doctrines*.
1956. Pp. 248. (Epworth Press, London. Price : 22s. 6d.)

This is the last but one of Dr. Ryder Smith's ' Bible Doctrine '
series, and it was published soon after his death. For earlier
similar studies see *Book Lists*, 1953, p. 64 ; 1956, p. 52. This
volume follows the pattern of his previous writings on Biblical
Theology, with continuous references to Scripture passages
and virtually no references to the literature on the subject.
The word *chesed* describes righteousness on its spiritual side,
and in the Old Testament the *dominant* idea is that God shows
chesed to the faithful Hebrew. After a chapter on the Old
Testament Antecedents, the author discusses the Greek
equivalents, both in LXX and the New Testament, of all
relevant Hebrew words. The book is mostly concerned with
New Testament doctrine, but there are continual references
back into the Old Testament, notably in the chapter on
Trial, Temptation and Discipline and in the long and thorough
chapter on Election. The volume contains a great deal of
material and is therefore of value to every reader.   N.H.S.

SNAITH, N. H. : *The Inspiration and Authority of the Bible*. (A. S.
Peake Memorial Lecture, 1956.) 1956. Pp. 46. (Epworth Press,
London. Price : 3s. 6d.)

This is the first A. S. Peake Memorial Lecture, and was
delivered at the Methodist Conference in 1956. After noting
the heterogeneous character of the collection which forms
the Christian Bible, the unifying theme is found in the action
of God the Saviour. To this, the Holy Spirit in the Bible, the
Church and the individual bears witness evoking man's
response in faith. The Authority of the Bible rests on this
inner witness of the Holy Spirit.   A.S.H.

VELLAS, B. M. : *Threskeutikai Prosopikotetes tes Palaias Diathekes*, 2nd edition, Volume I, 1957. Pp. 364, 2 maps, 4 plates. (Athens).

The first edition of Professor Vellas's *Religious Personalities of the Old Testament* appeared in 1933 ; we now greet the first volume of the second and enlarged edition ; the second volume will follow soon. This volume covers the pre-exilic age ; it treats the Patriarchs, Moses, Samuel and Saul, David, and the prophets Nathan, Elijah, Amos, Hosea, Isaiah, Micah and Zephaniah. Of these Isaiah receives the fullest treatment (over 100 pages), but this treatment includes an exposition of the teaching of Isa. xl-lxvi, " whether they were written by Isaiah in the Spirit, or were arranged or written by a disciple of Isaiah's on the basis of his teaching " (p. 271). The latter alternative is that to which the author himself inclines at the end of a brief survey of " the problem of the book of Isaiah " (pp. 200-210). It is to be hoped that this book will have a wide circulation in the Greek-speaking world. It is dedicated to the Ecumenical Patriarch. F.F.B.

VOEGELIN, E. : *Order and History*, Vol. 1, *Israel and Revelation*. 1956. Pp. xxvi+534. (Louisiana State University Press, and Oxford University Press. Price : 60s. 0d.)

This book is the first volume of a work which is to be completed in six volumes. It may be gathered from the first volume that the whole work is intended to be a massive reply to the Spengler-Toynbee philosophy of history. If the author can maintain in the ensuing volumes the high level of insight and scholarship which he has displayed in the present volume, the result will be a work of first-rate importance. The author begins by examining the first manifestation of order which emerges from the mists of pre-history, namely, the cosmological order of the ancient Near East, under which head he deals with the civilizations of Mesopotamia and Egypt. The contrasts which he draws between these two great culture areas are most illuminating, and in the course of his argument he exposes the superficiality of some highly praised books on this subject. The second part of the book deals with the historical order of Israel. In this section there is much that is original and stimulating. In c. 4 of this part of the book there is a brilliant and trenchant criticism of the Spengler-Toynbee theory of civilizational cycles, for which many readers will be grateful. There is also a friendly criticism, both of ' patternism,' and of the Scandinavian traditio-historical approach to the historical traditions of Israel. The weakness of the continued exploitation of the Wellhausen position is also exposed. But the book is far more valuable for its positive and constructive approach than for its critical work, necessary as the latter is. The third part of the book has the title ' History and the Trail of Symbols,' and the author's exposition of the symbols created by the experience of Israel ' under God,' is one of the most interesting and valuable things in the book. The fourth and final section deals with Moses and the Prophets, and carries the theme up to the Suffering Servant of Deutero-Isaiah. The author seems to have read everything of importance relating to his theme in the widest sense. For the Old Testament scholar this is one of the most original and important contributions that has appeared for many years. The analytical table of contents, and the full indexes, are models of what such helps for the reader should be.   S.H.H.

WICKINGS, H. F. : *The Covenant People of God.* 1956. Pp. 192. (Independent Press, London. Price : 9s. 6d.)

This book traces in simple words the thread of God's covenant in the Bible from Moses to the New Testament, and it largely consists of a series of short notes on some of the main ideas and events of the Biblical story, each note being generally followed by a passage from Scripture. The omission of the Davidic covenant is very strange. The work represents the author's own rediscovery of the Old Testament which will surely help a number of layfolk.   G.H.D.

WILLIAMS, W. G. : *The Prophets : Pioneers to Christianity.* 1956. Pp. 224. (Abingdon Press, New York and Nashville. Price : $3.50.)

The author offers us a popular study of the background and content of the prophetic teaching as the prelude to the Christian faith. The first part deals with introductory questions, and here the author shows that he is aware of the new cultic trends in the study of prophecy. This insight is then strangely continued in the second part with an exposition of religious ideas mainly from the old Wellhausenian-evolutionary standpoint. In the third part the author gives us studies in five of the major prophets, Amos, Hosea, Isaiah, Jeremiah and Ezekiel, but here again the cultic insights of the first part are not applied. The chief merit of the work is that it does fulfil its sub-title and does succeed in setting forth " The Relevance of the Prophets for Christians To-day."
G.H.D.

ZIMMERLI, W. : *Das Alte Testament als Anrede* (Beiträge zur evangelischen Theologie, 24.) 1956. Pp. 105. (Chr. Kaiser Verlag, München. Price : DM.6.)

This consists of three lectures and two sermons. The lectures are I. Einzelerzählung und Gesamtgeschichte im Alten Testament. II. Ezechiel, ein Zeuge der Gerechtigkeit Gottes. III. Das Alte Testament in der Verkündigung der christlichen Kirche. In each of the lectures, there is a recognition of the high importance of Israel's historical Credo (e.g., Deut. xxvi. 5-9). It is this which has determined the selection of material for Israel's historiography and given it its unity. In these terms Ezekiel prophesies both the total destruction of Israel and the renewal of the covenant history in the miracle of resurrection. Because of its declaration of God Who comes to man with a summons that claims a response, the Old Testament is an essential part of the Christian proclamation of the Christ Who is God's ' Yea ' to the ancient promises.   A.S.H.

ZIMMERLI, W. and JEREMIAS, J. : *The Servant of God.* (Studies in Biblical Theology, No. 20.) 1957. Pp. 120. (S.C.M. Press, London. Price : 10s. 6d.)

The *Book List* (1953, p. 55 ; 1954, p. 6) has already noticed the substance of this widely acclaimed monograph in its original German dress as the article *Pais Theou* in *T.W.B.N.T.*, vol. V, pp. 653-713. There are four chapters, dealing with the term in I. the Old Testament, II. the LXX, III. Judaism after the LXX, IV. the New Testament. Zimmerli wrote the first two, Jeremias the latter. Both are essential for any serious study of the subject. The clarity of presentation may also be specially commended, and the rich documentation.

The general bibliographies have been arranged alphabetically, with references adjusted to English editions where available, and, most usefully, an index of scripture references is added.

D.R.Ap-T.

THE LIFE AND THOUGHT OF THE NEIGHBOURING PEOPLES

Annual of the American Schools of Oriental Research, vol. XXXI (1951-52). *The Laws of Eshnunna,* by Albrecht Goetze. 1956. Pp. 198+4 plates. (Department of Antiquities of the Government of Iraq and the American Schools of Oriental Research, New Haven. Price : $4.00.)

This edition of the Laws of Eshnunna, originally published in 1948 (in *Sumer,* IV, 63-102), is most welcome. It contains a brief introduction discussing the name of the year containing the date, which however cannot be further determined, a detailed examination of the text which is transliterated and translated and fully discussed section by section, a complete glossary, and finally the cuneiform text in autograph followed by photographs of the two tablets on which it is preserved. The editor's work is that of a pioneer and will be useful rather as a starting point for much subsequent work rather than as a definitive edition of these difficult if interesting laws. The transcription is, so far as the state of the cuneiform text permits, substantially accurate but the translation will call for revision, being in places dubious if not indeed absurd : for example the subject in § 56 is not a vicious but a mad dog ; and in § 58 ' life is in jeopardy ' is absurd, since the unfortunate victim is already dead. In fact, the translation is the work of an expert Assyriologist (whose English is sometimes strange or incorrect) while the explanation of the text often betrays itself as the work of one who is not a lawyer. His work, however, within these limits will be of great use both to Assyriologists and students of the Old Testament.

G.R.D.

CERAM, C. W. : *Narrow Pass, Black Mountain.* 1956. Pp. 284, with 48 plates. Tr. from the German by Richard and Clara Winston. (Victor Gollancz in association with Sidgwick and Jackson, London. Price : 25s. 0d.)

The volume tells the story in popular form of the discovery of the Hittite Empire and the solving of the riddle of the Hittite scripts. It is, so to speak, the missing chapter from the author's *Gods, Graves.* The Narrow Pass is the narrow passage to the ancient sanctuary across the valley from the ruins of Boghazköy, where Texier found the strange inscribed rocks of an unknown civilisation. This was in 1834: Black Mountain is Karatepe, by the Anti-Taurus mountains in south Asia Minor, where the lion stone and the statue with the Phoenician inscription was found. This led ultimately to the decipherment of hieroglyphic Hittite. The volume is ' excitingly ' written and the author has made the most of his material. A chronological table of the Hittite Empire is provided, and a full bibliography covers twenty pages. It is a fascinating story, well told. N.H.S.

DRIVER, G. R. : *Canaanite Myths and Legends* (Old Testament Studies, No. 3). 1956. Pp. xiv + 170. (T. and T. Clark, Edinburgh. Price : 25s. 0d.)

This is a treatment of the literary texts of Ras Shamra. After a description of the tablets the subject-matter is analysed, and the texts transliterated with critical apparatus, and translated with footnotes. Then follow five pages of highly condensed notes on Ugaritic philology and grammar, and the work concludes with a glossary with citation of such authorities as the writer adjudges to have made feasible suggestions. In this section and in the footnotes to his translation the author cites cognates from other Semitic languages. Here, however, in view of the problematic nature of the Ugaritic matter, more is surely demanded in a work of this scope than the simple citation of a cognate root without discussion of its actual usage apart from its place in the lexicon. On the subject of the phonetic correspondence of certain Ugaritic consonants with those of other Semitic languages it is surprising to find that, albeit with reserve (see p. 128), the author actually allows himself more liberties than he has on occasion been willing to grant to others. This, however, is admittedly difficult ground. Particularly valuable in this excellent work is the discussion on the sequence of fragments and the skilful restoration of damaged texts. J.G.

FRONZAROLI, P. : *L. 'QHT. Leggenda di Aqhat. Testo Ugaritico.* (Il Melagrano, 136-137.) 1955. Pp. 98 with 4 photographs. (Edizioni Fussi, Sansoni, Florence. Price : 6s. 0d.)

This is a small school-text of the Ugaritic poem of Aqhat, containing transliterated text and Italian translation on opposite pages (pp. 26-69), a brief introduction (pp. 9-23) and equally brief notes (pp. 73-91) and bibliography (pp. 91-94). The transliteration is accurate and the translation tolerably literal and correct, even though it tends to lean too much on Gordon and some other interpreters ; for the editor has little if anything that is fresh to offer either here or in the notes. His little book, however, is handy and trustworthy, so far as it goes, and commendably cheap, so that it will be easily accessible to students and so serve to spread the knowledge of these curious texts amongst Semitic scholars. The illustrations are well-known photographs of a broken tablet (containing a portion of Aqhat), one of the first found, and of three deities (El, Anat, Baal). G.R.D.

Moscati, S. : *Il Profilo dell'Oriente Mediterranea : Panorami di Civiltà Preclassiche*. 1956. Pp. 338. (Edizioni Radio Italiana, Turin. Price : Lire 2,500.)

Professor Moscati's pen is never still, and his publications follow hard on the heels of one another. The present work is based on a series of radio talks, and is therefore addressed to the wider public. It is a very useful work of popularization, and it is well illustrated. After a short introduction it falls into three parts, which have curious titles. ' The Elements ' deals with the Sumerians, the Babylonians and Assyrians, and the Egyptians ; ' The Catalysts ' deals with the Hittites and Hurrians, the Canaanites and Aramaeans, and the Israelites ; while ' The Synthesis ' deals with the Persians. The Philistines surprisingly get no chapter. Each chapter offers a short historical, religious, literary and cultural survey, and is followed by full documentation in the notes. H.H.R.

Moscati, S. : *I Precedessori d'Israele : Studi sulle piu genti semitiche in Siria e Palestina* (Studi Orientali pubblicati a cura della Scuola Orientale, Università di Roma, vol. IV.) 1956. Pp. 140+5 plates. (Dott. Giovanni Bardi, Tipografia del Senato. Price: Lire 3,000.)

This opuscule represents the enlarged text of a series of lectures delivered in England by Professor Moscati. It provides an outline of the ancient population of Syria and Palestine and elucidates in particular mutual relationships. Moscati holds that there is hardly any other field in the history of the Semitic peoples where so many commonplaces have been so uncritically reiterated and where conventionally accepted data have been subjected to so little precise analysis.

The author first deals with the problem of Semitic origins in that area. The weakest link in his chain of arguments here is the examination of place names. There are quite a few instances where the reader will not be entirely happy (the treatment of *Ugarit*, Egypt. *ikrit*, is a case in point : surely Hebrew *'ikkār* and South Semitic *hgr* should at least have been considered in this connection). This is followed by an account of the problem of the Canaanites and Amorites in the light of Biblical, Near Eastern, and classical sources. Moscati

arrives at the conclusion that the use of the term ' Canaanites '
for the earliest Semitic population of Syria is inaccurate,
that Canaan and Canaanites are, in fact, terms for Phoenicia
and the Phoenicians, and that they do not antedate the middle
of the second millennium. The name 'Amorites,' on the other
hand, is considered to be devoid of any ethnic connotation
and to be of purely geographical significance. Linguistically,
' Canaanite ' and 'Amorite ' are so ambiguous as to become
meaningless. The author finally suggests that in the present
case inexact terminology has falsified the entire historical
and religious framework of this area. The booklet is further
testimony to Professor Moscati's industry and command
of the subject.   E.U.

SCHMÖKEL, H. : *Geschichte des alten Vorderasiens.* (*Handbuch der
Orientalistik*, ed. by B. Spuler, Vol. II, *Keilschriftforschung und
alte Geschichte Vorderasiens*, Part 3). 1957. Pp. xii+342+10
plates+1 map. (Brill, Leiden. Price : Fl. 45.)

It may be useful to mention here those parts of the *Handbuch
der Orientalistik* which have already appeared : Vol. I,
Ägyptologie : 2nd part : Egyptian literature ; Vol. II, the
book under review ; Vol. III, Semitistik : complete ; Vol.
IV, Iranistik : 3rd part : Tocharisch ; Vol. V, Altaistik :
nil ; Vol. VI, Geschichte der Islamischen Länder : 1st part :
Die Chalifenzeit, 2nd part : Die Mongolenzeit ; Vol. VII,
Armenische und Kaukasische Sprachen : nil ; Vol. VIII,
Religion : nil.
It is thus possible, to some extent, to consider the present
volume against the background of other works already in
print in this ambitious project. The O.T. scholar will be
specially interested in vols. II and III, and it may be said
at once that this third part of vol. II (Parts 1 [language and
history of research], 2 [literature], and 4 [history from Cyrus
to Muhammad] will follow later) compares favourably with
the *Semitistik* volume (the only one so far completed) which,
despite the efforts of a galaxy of talent, remains sketchy,
uneven, and somehow unsatisfactory in its general impression.
The present historical outline of ancient Asia Minor covers the
period from about 3000 to roughly 500 B.C. ; it is a well-
integrated narrative with all the advantages of having been
written by one person. Even the inevitable weaknesses in
some parts and unevenness of competence over so wide a field
and period do not detract from this favourable assessment.
Nor are we regaled with a barren enumeration of events only,
but the author makes a serious attempt to see these events
within their historical and cultural setting. Specialists will
no doubt quarrel with individual judgments within their
own sphere of competence (e.g., the historical assessment of
Judaism and emergent Christianity on p. 291 which is neither
historically incontrovertible in its interpretation of the DS
material nor well attuned to a work of rigid scholarship),
but the over-all picture and detailed documentation inspire
confidence.

O.T. scholars will be particularly interested in the chapters dealing with Akkad, Mari and the Old Assyrian Empire (utilizing all available archaeological and other data), Hammurabi, Hittite history, Babylonia, Syria-Palestine in the 2nd millennium B.C. (including a good account of Ras Shamra-Ugarit), Phoenicia and Israel-Judah, the Aramaeans, etc. O.T. specialists may well ponder that in a work of 342 pages only 20 are allocated to the political history of Israel-Judah (religion and culture are no more than mentioned)—perhaps not an unreasonable proportion within the severely historical treatment to which the author is committed.   E.U.

THE DEAD SEA SCROLLS

ALLEGRO, J. M. : *The Dead Sea Scrolls* (Pelican Books A 376). 1956. Pp. 208+42 plates. (Penguin Books, Harmondsworth. Price : 3s. 6d.)

The story of the discovery is told with considerable charm and vividness, and current activities of scholars in Jerusalem and Qumrân are excellently described as only one who is ' inside ' can do it. But in the second half of the book the author seems to take the bit between his teeth and to rush recklessly into an interpretation of the sect that cannot but invite very serious criticism from all who study the scrolls, criticism which shows how vulnerable the author is at many points. Thus one might challenge him on his evaluation of the biblical texts and his advocacy of an ' eclectic ' O.T. text for future translations ; another might well take him up on the Messianic Banquet, or the Jubilee Calendar, and certainly on many rash conclusions which he offers on the New Testament ' parallels,' Jesus' absorption of Qumrân, the authenticity of the Gospels and the theory of the Pauline ' split.' Nevertheless, it is to Mr. Allegro's credit that he offers us in this book an over-all picture of the Qumrân community in a way which few have succeeded in doing ; and, at times at least, his basic assumption does not demand an identity of the early Church with Qumrân but reflects a common movement— a conclusion which few would deny. There are excellent plates, two maps, a bibliography and an index.   B.J.R.

AVIGAD, N. and YADIN, Y. : *A Genesis Apocryphon. A Scroll from the Wilderness of Judaea.* (Hebrew and English.) 1956. Pp. 48+40+ 14 facsimiles and photographs. (The Magnes Press of the Hebrew University and Heikhal Ha-Sefer, Jerusalem. Price : 32s. 6d.)

The volume, similar in format to previous scroll publications from the Hebrew University, contains facsimiles, transcription and translations (Hebrew and English) of five columns of the Genesis Apocryphon scroll (cols. 2, 19-22), the last of the seven major scrolls from Qumrân Cave One to be unrolled and published. In the introductory sections the editors give in outline an indication of the main contents, so far as they have been tentatively reconstructed, of the other columns

(1, 3-18). There are also preliminary discussions, some of them in considerable detail, of such matters as general content, text, orthography, linguistics, and affinities with *Jubilees* and *Enoch :* and the quality of the discussion is most lucid, interesting and cogent. In some respects this scroll may turn out to be even more illuminating than the others from Cave One, and contribute, in a way the others do not suggest, to the confusing question of what the Qumrân texts mean for the history and teaching of Jewish sectarianism. It is difficult to exaggerate the praise due to the editors and all who are responsible for this very important publication.   B.J.R.

BRUCE, F. F. : *Second Thoughts on the Dead Sea Scrolls.* 1956. Pp. 144. (Paternoster Press, London. Price : 10s. 6d.)

The ' Second Thoughts ' in the title should not be understood as having reference to any ' first thoughts ' published by the author now to be modified, but in a general sense to ' earlier estimates of the significance (of the Scrolls) which have to be revised.' It is Professor Bruce's first book on this topic, and it gives a conspectus of the scrolls and their relevance for biblical study ; as such it is most praiseworthy, and can be thoroughly recommended for general use. It is the best of its kind the reviewer has yet seen. The story of the discovery is told clearly, and Murabba'at and Mird are fitted into the picture. After an over-all description of the textual scrolls, more controversial questions are tackled, such as the Messianic hope in the scrolls, the identity of the Wicked Priest (Alexander Jannaeus), the Teacher of Righteousness (Judah ben Gedidiah?), the Man of Falsehood (Wicked Priest? or Eleazar Ben-Po'irah?), the Kitti'im (Romans), but it is necessary to add that Bruce is not adamant in his identifications. There is a convenient index and a couple of coloured photographs.   B.J.R.

BRUCE, F. F. : *The Teacher of Righteousness in the Qumran Texts.* (The Tyndale Lecture in Biblical Archaeology, 1956.) 1957. Pp. 36. (The Tyndale Press, London. Price : 2s. 0d.)

This useful survey of a much-debated complex of problems is divided into three main sections : The Teacher and the Texts ; The Teacher and His Contemporaries : The Teacher and Christianity. The author inclines to the view that the Wicked Priest was Alexander Jannaeus, and suggests that the Man of Falsehood may have been Simeon ben Shetach, but does not commit himself to any particular identification of The Teacher of Righteousness. The whole study displays sanity and balance as well as learning. A table indicating the meaning of the Sigla employed would have been a help to the less learned type of reader.   G.W.A.

FRITSCH, C. T. : *The Qumran Community : Its History and Scrolls.* 1956. Pp. 148. (Macmillan, New York. Price : $3.25.)

The first four chapters of this book deal with the excavations at Khirbet Qumran ; the history of the Sect ; the caves and the MSS. ; MSS. at Khirbet Mird and Murabba'at. Here we have the advantage of the author's visits to the area. Owing to his first-hand knowledge of the place one or two details hitherto somewhat obscure tend to become clearer. The other four chapters deal with the contents of the various MSS. and examine the relationship between the Qumran Sect and the Damascus Sect as well as with the Essenes. It is concluded that under the term Essenes (in the broadest sense as used by Josephus) the Qumran Sect is to be included. In the author's opinion the significance of the Qumran MSS. with regard to studies in the New Testament is greater than that in the Old Testament and intertestamental studies. The book, which includes a few illustrations as well as a fairly extensive bibliography, will, as is the wish of the author, interest the general reader and be of use "to the student who may wish to pursue the subject more thoroughly." M.W.

GASTER, T. H. : *The Dead Sea Scriptures in English Translation.* 1956. Pp. x+350. (Doubleday, New York. Price : $4.00, or, in paper covers, $0.95. Secker and Warburg, London. Price : 25s. 0d., or, in paper covers 10s. 6d.)
[Title of English Edition : *The Scriptures of the Dead Sea Sect in English Translation with Introduction and Notes.*]

Professor Gaster here provides a complete translation of all the non-Biblical Qumran texts so far published, including fragments of commentaries on Micah, Nahum and Psalms. There is a short introduction to the whole and special introductions to the various groups of texts translated, and the translations are accompanied by brief notes. Dr. Gaster deprecates the sensational statements that make the right teacher (not Teacher of Righteousness) the forerunner of Christ and observes that there is here no trace of any of the cardinal Christian theological concepts. He has a careful appraisal of the links of thought and phrase between the New Testament and the Scrolls, and sets this out in connection with a similarly impressive list of links with the already known intertestamental literature. He deprecates any attempt to date the right teacher, and holds that this phrase denotes an office and not a person, and therefore is applied to more than one person. The whole forms an important addition to our Scrolls literature. H.H.R.

GRAYSTONE, G. : *The Dead Sea Scrolls and the Originality of Christ.* 1956. Pp. 120. (Sheed & Ward, London. Price : 8s. 6d.)

This sober and unpretentious little book reproduces a series of articles which appeared in the *Irish Theological Quarterly* under the title : " The Dead Sea Scrolls and the New Testament." The author reviews critically some exaggerated assessments of the extent to which the Qumran discoveries have revolutionized our understanding of Christian origins—notably those propounded by Dupont-Sommer and popularized by Edmund Wilson. Even Canon Coppens' suggestion that some of the Qumran sectaries were among the early Christian converts is dismissed as unlikely, and the facts of John the Baptist's parentage are thought to render improbable the idea of others that he was at one time attracted to the sect. The practices and doctrines of the sect are outlined, and their resemblances with what we find in early Christianity are shown to be outweighed by the differences. F.F.B.

KAPELRUD, A. S. : *Dødehavsrullene. Funnene som kaster nytt lys over Bibelen og Jesu samtid.* 1956. Pp. 116+8 plates+maps on end papers. (Universitetsforlaget, Oslo. Price : 11s. 0d.)

This is a general account of the Dead Sea Scrolls, based on a University seminar course. The three main sections are : 1. The Discoveries ; 2. The Manuscripts ; 3. The Community. In the second of these, the reader is given a useful survey of the contents of the documents, portions of which are quoted in translation. The third takes up the question of the relation of the Qumran sect to contemporary Judaism. Varying views are adequately represented, with brief documentation. The presentation is competent, lucid, and eminently readable ; and the book should serve a wide public. G.W.A.

LASOR, W. S. : *Amazing Dead Sea Scrolls and the Christian Faith.* 1956. Pp. 252. (Moody Press, Chicago. Price : $3.50.)

The author has won a doctorate from the University of Southern California with a thesis (unpublished as yet), *A Reconstruction of Judaism in the Time of the Second Temple in the Light of the Published Qumran Material.* The present work is in large measure a popularization of the contents of his thesis, but he has endeavoured to show the ordinary American reader the bearing of the Qumran texts on Christianity. He has made a close study of the texts themselves, and his judgments are marked by scholarly caution and sobriety. He is not so sure as many writers are of the association of Qumran with the Essenes ; he leans rather to the view that the Qumran sect had a common origin with the Sadducees, but later parted company with them, stigmatizing them as " the house of Absalom." The reader is introduced to most of the questions raised by the discovery of these texts, and the book may safely be recommended to the public for which it is intended, although such terms as " *Vorlage* " and " Ur-Gnosticism " may not be immediately intelligible to some of them. G. R. Driver is the last man on earth to be associated with the attitude, " My mind is made up—please do not confuse me with facts," as the author does on p. 44.
F.F.B.

NIELSEN, E. : *Håndskriftfundene i Juda Ørken. Dødehavsteksterne.* 1956. Pp. 182+10 illustrations on plates+1 map. (Gad, Copenhagen. Price : 17s. 0d.)

This is an excellent, non-technical account of the Scrolls. Two chapters deal with the story of the original discoveries. The remainder of the book is concerned with the date, range, and character of the texts, the excavations at Khirbet Qumran, the character, history, and beliefs of the sect, and its relations with parties in contemporary Judaism and with Jesus and early Christianity. Though the author disclaims any attempt to make an independent contribution to the discussion, he has clearly exercised independence of judgment, and has not always been content to follow the majority opinion. But his statements are wisely cautious and temperate ; and he does not conceal from the reader the necessarily tentative nature of some theories, even when he favours them. The book is attractively written and well produced. Useful bibliographies are appended.
G.W.A.

ROBERTS, B. J. : *Sgroliau'r Môr Marw.* 1956. Pp. x+82, with 8 plates and map. (University of Wales Press, Cardiff. Price : 8s. 6d.)

In this very readable summary of the facts concerning the Dead Sea Scrolls, the author has performed a notable service to the Welsh reading public, especially by expanding the original three lectures, delivered under University College auspices before publication. There are ten chapters, beginning with the story of the discovery, and ending with the relationship of the Scrolls to the New Testament. Throughout there is evidence of the wide reading of the author in the literature of his special subject, and of his balanced judgment. We would like a larger volume on the sect itself from the same hand.
D.R.Ap-T.

ROWLEY, H. H. : *Jewish Apocalyptic and the Dead Sea Scrolls.* 1957. Pp. 36. (Athlone Press, London. Price : 4s. 0d.)

In this, the Ethel M. Wood Lecture for 1957, Professor Rowley surveys briefly the apocalyptic literature of the second and first centuries B.C. and compares with it the teaching of the Scrolls and the Zadokite work, arguing that the Scrolls have a close association with the second century documents, and that this line of evidence strengthens the case for dating the Teacher of Righteousness in the early part of that century. Both the text and the documentation of this study open up important lines of inquiry. The whole is a valuable *multum in parvo* on problems connected with the Scrolls. G.W.A.

SCHONFIELD, H. J. : *Secrets of the Dead Sea Scrolls : Studies towards their Solution.* 1956. Pp. xiii+164. (Vallentine Mitchell, London. Price : 21s. 0d.)

By means of Atbash, the book of Hagu becomes Tsoreph (*Test Book ;* cf. Dan. xii., Mal. iii.), Tahu (i.e., Taxo, ' another alias of the anonymous Teacher of Righteousness ') is Asaph

68 BOOK LIST 1957

(ben Berachiah, founder of the Asaphite guild and author of the ' Maccabean' Asaphite Psalms), and Maccabee is Yad-Shem. The Chasidim priests finally edited the text of the O.T. and established the New Covenant Party in the 2nd cent. B.C. for its elucidation. After persecution by Alcimus the Party emigrated to Damascus, where its precepts were laid down, and they became identified with the Essenes. Pseude-pigrapha were composed by members between 120 and 70 B.C., including some primary strata of the Damascus Testament (not, however, CDC, which is a later redaction), and these books became canonical. But a considerable lapse of time and a modified outlook is presupposed before the arrival of ' the End of the Days ' in which CDC and DSH and other scrolls were finally redacted in their present form at a date as late as 70 A.D. or later. It is necessary to distinguish between the original Teacher of Righteousness and the one of the End of the Days, the real hero of DSH. The marginal symbols of DSIa have relevance to the teaching of the New Covenant Party and of Judaeo-Christians ; and other features, mainly drawn from parallels with late Pseudepigrapha, make the end of the 1st cent. A.D. the only possible period for the scrolls. Earlier, 2nd cent. B.C. material, traditions and figures were used in their composition, but it is only in the setting of ' the End ' that we can really interpret the scrolls. The above is a drastic oversimplification of the treatise.

B.J.R.

VERMÈS, G. : *Discovery in the Judaean Desert. The Dead Sea Scrolls and Their Meaning.* 1956. Pp. 238. (Desclée Co., New York. Price : $5.00.)

The original French version of this book (*Les Manuscrits du Désert de Juda*, 1953), was warmly welcomed (cf. *Book List*, 1954, pp. 82f.) and this anonymous revised English version will be favourably received not only as an adequate rendering but also because it contains minor revisions and additional material ; for instance, the discussion of the Qumrân monastery has been amplified. Supplementary notes, too, give information from ' Recently Published Data.' The book should run into another edition, which might enable Father Vermès to include still further items, e.g., the mention of Demetrius in the Nahum Scroll, the significance of which will surely be discussed in the body of the book, and will possibly enable the author to omit the story of the discovery ;

B.J.R.

WILSON, E. : *Die Schriftrollen vom Toten Meer.* 1956. Pp. 134+4 plates (Winkler-Verlag, München. Price : DM. 8.80.)

This is a translation by J. Ewers of E. Wilson's *The Scrolls from the Dead Sea* (cf. *Book List*, 1956, p. 67). The translation is readable and faithful—and serves to correct some misprints in the original, though it is itself not wholly free from errors ; e.g., I have spotted K. H. Charles (for R. H.) and J. T. Teicher, (for J. L.) and sometimes Luther's text and Wilson's do not coincide in N.T. quotations. B.J.R.

APOCRYPHA AND POST-BIBLICAL JUDAISM

BIETENHARD, H. : *Soṭa (Die des Ehebruchs Verdächtige.)* Text, Über-
setzung und Erklärung nebst einem textkritischen Anhang.
(Die Mischna, ed. Rengstorf-Rost.) 1956. Pp. vii+212. (Alfred
Töpelmann, Berlin. Price : DM. 26.)

This volume on ' The Suspected Adulteress ' is far superior
to many previous ones of the series. There is a sound introduction, going into such questions as the relation between
Mishnah and Tosephta or the results to be gained for New
Testament studies ; the text with a good German translation
and a substantial commentary ; a critical apparatus ; and
several useful indices. The topic is so full of interest that
numerous investigations may start from here. The consequences of a husband renewing married intercourse with the
suspected adulteress, for instance, look quite modern (pp.
31, 83f.) ;` so do the views on the infectiousness of cowardice
(p. 137). To the speculations about delay of divine retribution
(pp. 69f.) there are illuminating parallels elsewhere, above
all, in Greek literature. The author records, without pro-
nouncing on it, Bahr and Rosenthal's theory that Soṭa is
particularly old (p. 15) ; but before accepting this, we should
ask whether it is not merely archaic (on the distinction see
the reviewer's remarks in *Tulane Law Review*, vol. 18, 1944,
pp. 367, 376). There are few defective or erroneous statements.
But, e.g., R. Judah reads ' so ' in Dt. 25.9, not simply together
with the preceding clause (p. 113), but twice, once with the
preceding clause and once with the following : a case of
absence of *hekhrea'*, adjudication. And the 32 rules of interpretation go back not to Ishmael (p. 91) but to Eliezer ben
Jose Ha-gelili. This valuable book should have a wide appeal.

D.D.

Corpus Codicum Hebraicorum Medii Aevi, redigendum curavit R.
Edelmann, pars I, *Maimonidis Commentarius in Mishnam*, Intro-
ductionem Hebraice et Britannice scripsit S. D. Sassoon, 3 vols.
Vol. I *(Zeraim et Moed)*. 1956. English Introduction, pp. 11-56
+Plates, I-LXI, Maimonides' Commentary to the Mishnah, pp.
1-416, Hebrew Introduction, pp. 11-56. (Munksgaard, Copenhagen.
Price : Dan. kr. 750.)

Maimonides wrote his classical Mishnah commentary in
Arabic, but already at the end of the 13th century it had been
rendered into Hebrew, and this translation soon gained
ascendency over the original Arabic. When the editio princeps
of the Mishnah appeared in 1492 it contained also Maimonides'
commentary in its Hebrew form, and this example was
followed by successive printers with the result that the original
Arabic text was almost completely forgotten. The Hebrew
translation, however, was known to be imperfect, some of
the original translators having been short of MSS. of the work,
others having been insufficiently familiar with Maimonides'
idiom or with the subject matter, and the edition of the
Arabic text was felt to be a desideratum of the first order.

Derenbourg, it is true, edited that part of the text apper-
taining to the last Order of the Mishnah. Of the text relating
to the remaining Orders, however, only small parts had been
edited at different times. The present edition is a reproduction
in facsimile of a MS. which but for some lacunae contains
Maimonides' commentary on the first five Orders of the
Mishnah. Moreover, Dr. Sassoon in his Introduction has
proved by an analysis of Maimonides' handwriting based on
all the available Maimonides' autographs (reproduced in the
Plates) and by other evidence that the MS. in question is
actually Maimonides' autograph. This is an exceptionally
important fact, as the MS. contains copious marginal emendations by the same hand, reflecting modifications of Maimonides'
thought in the course of time. Also, the comments are
throughout preceded by the relevant Mishnaic text. The MS.
has thus preserved for us Maimonides' text of the Mishnah.
This MS. justifies, from all aspects, its place in the series
which is to include " Hebrew (and Judeo-Arabic) manuscripts
. . . which are of particular value as literary sources or as
autographs or because they represent a particularly important
text," and the Editors fully deserve the gratitude of Talmudic
scholars in particular for making the text available. P.R.W.

FARMER, W. R. : *Maccabees, Zealots, and Josephus : An Inquiry into
Jewish Nationalism in the Greco-Roman Period.* 1956. Pp. xiv +
240. (Columbia University Press, New York. Price : $4.50.)

Dr. Farmer's thesis is that there was a positive connection,
a living continuity, between the Jewish nationalism of the
second century B.C. and that of the first century A.D. He
sets out to prove his case by a study of Jewish nationalism
in relation to the Torah and the Temple, and he seeks to show,
e.g., by reference to the observance of Hanukkah and Nicanor's
Day and by an analysis of the Scroll, *The War of the Sons of
Light against the Sons of Darkness*, that the Maccabees were
remembered during the period of the struggle with Rome.
There is much of value in this work, especially in the discussion
of Josephus' attitude to the Zealots, and Dr. Farmer makes
a convincing, if at times over-laboured, case for his main
contention.   W.D.McH.

GANDZ, S. : *The Code of Maimonides, Book Three, Treatise Eight,
Sanctification of the New Moon*, Translated from the Hebrew,
with Supplementation and an Introduction by Julian Obermann,
and an Astronomical Commentary by Otto Neugebauer. (Yale
Judaica Series, Vol. XI.) 1956. Pp. lx + 160. (Yale University
Press, New Haven and G. Cumberlege, London. Price : 30s. 0d.)

This time the publishers have brought out not an entire Book
but only a Treatise. The complete Book, which consists of
Ten Treatises, will be published later. This procedure is

justified by the peculiar nature of the present Treatise. It lists the rules followed by the court in deciding about the New Moon and the intercalation of an additional month ; it expounds the fixed calendar adopted when, about the middle of the 4th century, the court ceased to function ; and it informs us of the methods by which the court was able to predict the appearance of the new crescent.

This part of Maimonides' work sheds much light on his views concerning the nature of Jewish law and tradition, the relation between law and science and the controversy between Rabbanites and Karaites. It also of course testifies to the enormous range of his learning and a masterly use of such sources of knowledge as were then available. It is a great thing to have an authoritative rendering from the hand of Gandz, whose departure is mourned by the scholarly world. And the introduction and commentary by Obermann and Neugebauer enable even a layman to grasp the more interesting essentials.

D.D.

HAMMERSHAIMB, E., MUNCK, J., NOACK, B., SEIDELIN, P. (ed. by) : *De gammeltestamentlige Pseudepigrafer i oversaettelse med inledning og noter.* 1. Haefte, *Fjerde Ezrabog.* 1953. Pp. 1-68. 2. Haefte, *Første Enoksbog.* 1956. Pp. 69-174. (Gad, Copenhagen ; Cammermeyer, Oslo ; Gleerup, Lund. Price : 1. Dan. kr. 4.50 ; 2. Dan. kr. 8.)

These are the first two parts of a Danish edition of the apocrypha and pseudepigrapha. The books are translated into Danish, with concise textual and explanatory notes; and there are short but adequate introductions, with classified bibliographies. The whole is attractively printed and set out ; and the series, when complete, should be a great boon to Scandinavian readers.

G.W.A.

RANKIN, O. S. : *Jewish Religious Polemic of early and later centuries, a study of documents here rendered in English.* 1956. Pp. viii+256. (University Press, Edinburgh. Price : 18s. 0d.)

The purpose of this posthumously issued work of the late Professor of Old Testament Language, Literature and Theology at Edinburgh University is to show by examples from different times ranging from the early part of our era up to the 17th century the defence by Jews of their faith. To this end the editor chose for translation documents representing each of the literary categories of narrative, poetry, letters and record of debate. By his renderings he made accessible to the English reader a series of important apologetic and polemic texts to which he added introductions and notes, the whole exhibiting the high level of careful scholarship which we had come to associate with the name of this distinguished and well-loved scholar.

W.D.McH.

STRACK, H. L. and BILLERBECK, P. : *Kommentar zum Neuen Testament.* Vol. V. *Rabbinischer Index.* 1956. ed. by J. Jeremias, composed by K. Adolph. Pp. 102+xi, and a portrait of Billerbeck. (C. H. Beck, München. Price : DM. 15 ; bound DM. 18.)

The original index to Strack-Billerbeck gave only the Old Testament references ; the present volume adds the Rabbinic ones. It will greatly enhance the value of the commentary. Apart from other uses, a reader can now look up whether a striking Rabbinic text attached to one New Testament utterance is mentioned again as relevant to another. The authors have conferred a great benefit on their colleagues. A cursory check by the reviewer has disclosed no errors. The arrangement, spelling, etc., of the index are naturally conditioned by the method of quotation employed in the commentary itself. The references are grouped under eight heads : Talmud, Pseudepigrapha, Targumim, Midrashim, other Haggadic Works, Medieval Works, Prayers, and Writers (Josephus, Justin, Philo). There is an alphabetical register of all sources at the end. The authors also provide a list of errata to correct misquotations in the earlier volumes.

An index of this kind shews not only what material was available when the commentary was compiled but also what tendencies and fashions determined the choice. That the Dead Sea Scrolls should be absent is inevitable. But if the commentary were written to-day, surely many Rabbinic passages would be included for the light they throw on form as distinct from substance. An example of a different type is Mishnah Horayoth. It is poorly represented : it has long been considered as lumber (Windfuhr, 1914, ' unprofitable,' Robertson, 1952, ' abstruse '). After the experiences of the past fifty years, however, we may become interested again in such things as the distinction between ' the body,' ' the principle,' of a commandment and ' a part,' ' a detailed application,' or the Rabbinic views about the relation between a Sanhedrin proclaiming a wrong teaching and the people acting on it, with the subdivision into those who act from error and those who do not. D.D.

WALLENSTEIN, M. : *Some Unpublished Piyyuṭim from the Cairo Genizah, Reconstructed, Revocalized and Translated with Critical Notes.* 1956. Pp. xiv+124 and 14 facsimiles. (Manchester University Press. Price : 21s. 0d.)

This volume will be especially welcome to English readers for whom little on the subject of piyyuṭim (liturgical compositions) is available. Different periods in which composers of piyyuṭim wrote are specified, and the main features of their compositions are described, account being taken of their characteristic features, both external (structure, acrostic, rhyme, rhythm) and internal (contents, language, grammar). The unpublished piyyuṭim dealt with belong to the tenth century. One, from the Bodleian Library, is reproduced in facsimile. The copyist and vocalizer of it, its contents, structure, reconstruction, and vocalization, are discussed, and a translation of it is provided, with accompanying notes, which include references to a Cambridge manuscript. A British Museum manuscript is studied in a similar way. The author of the Oxford and London manuscripts is considered, and personal details about him are supplied. Some published piyyuṭim receive attention, and an attempt is made to demonstrate the identity of the author of them with the author of the Oxford and London manuscripts. The translation of the texts is faithful to the originals ; the reconstructions are carefully carried through ; and the notes are a mine of information on a large variety of topics. The work, which reveals the author's extensive knowledge of the O.T., Rabbinic literature, and the Jewish liturgy, will interest a wide circle of students since it touches so many fields— the Hebrew Bible, post-Biblical studies, Hebrew philology, grammar, vocalization, and palaeography, and hymnology. The several indices add to the usefulness of the work.

D.W.T.

PHILOLOGY AND GRAMMAR

BROCKELMANN, C. : *Hebräische Syntax*. 1956. Pp. xvi+216. Verlag der Buchhandlung des Erziehungsvereins, Neukirchen. Price : paper covers DM. 16.80 ; cloth DM. 19.50.)

This volume (the last publication of a great Semitic scholar, who died last year) presents, in a very clear way, the phenomena of Hebrew syntax. The author draws his examples not only from the O.T. and Ben Sira, but also from the Zadokite Fragments, the manuscripts from Qumran, the Moabite stone, and the Kilamuwa and Karatepe inscriptions. Up-to-date literature is cited throughout, and there is in addition a six-page bibliography. Three indices are provided : general, Hebrew words, and O.T. and other passages cited (the last covers 28 pages). Particularly interesting is the author's rejection of H. Bauer's theory of the Hebrew tenses, which has found advocates in Bergsträsser, G. R. Driver, and others. On this subject, as on some others, a longer discussion would have been welcome. The sections on the numerals and the prepositions (the latter are categorized as " old " and " new ") are especially good, and many points of interest, such as the use of emphatic *lamedh*, the way in which climatic conditions are expressed, and the occurrence of ellipse in Hebrew, receive attention. Some of the examples cited in illustration of the latter seem capable of a different explanation. While, in general, a more frequent attempt to explain some of the phenomena presented might have been looked for, the work is highly instructive, and the inclusion in it of so much fresh material and many references to syntactical uses in other Semitic languages make it a work which Hebraists will do well to have by them.   D.W.T.

CARLSON, E. L. : *Elementary Hebrew.* 1956. Pp. iii+274. (Baker Book House, Grand Rapids, Michigan. Price : $3.50.)

A welcome must be afforded to this new Hebrew Grammar, complete with Vocabularies and Index, which aims at simplifying the study of the Hebrew language by using a modified inductive method. The Preface says that " this course is divided into four quarters of study, each quarter having twenty-four lessons." The book itself has four " Parts " each having 23, 21 (followed by the paradigms), 23 and 21 lessons respectively. No doubt this discrepancy disappears during the actual teaching. The entire book covers Gen. i-xiv., and the method is to take a verse or verses of Genesis, parse each form, expound various grammatical rules, adding a numbered word list and an exercise. Every third lesson is a revision of the previous two lessons.

It is clear that there is much to be commended in this approach, especially that the Bible text is kept permanently before the student. Inevitably grammatical information on any one topic is dispersed through the book, and this is a drawback. There are also three numerical systems which give the appearance of complexity, though really they are useful and the third essential. It is a pity, too, that the Guttural verbs in the paradigms do not follow the more irregular conjugations, though the order is somewhat better than that of the present Davidson.

Dr. Carlson, one of our Associate Members, has taught the substance of this book for 23 years, and that is no small recommendation, and it is only fair that someone should test the book in teaching before a final judgment is given.

G.H.D.

KLÍMA, O. & SEGERT, S. : *Mluvnice hebrejštiny a aramejštiny* (Jazykovědné příručky a učebnice, 5.) 1956. Pp. 306. (Československá akademie věd, Prague. Price : Kčs. 20.65.)

Since then the old Hebrew Grammars in the Czech language by J. Sedláček (1893) and in Slovakian by A. Hornyánszky (1923) have been out of print for a considerable time, this new work by Klíma and Segert will be very helpful both to Biblical scholars and to philologists. In both parts of the grammar the paragraphs are numbered according to the same system, which may be applied in subsequent grammars of other Semitic languages, so that a substantial work on comparative philology may be built up. The selection and arrangement of the material indicates sound scholarship and good teaching method. M.B.

PAYNE, J. B. : *Hebrew Vocabularies, based on Harper's Hebrew Vocabularies.* 1956. Pp. iv+18. (Baker Book House, Grand Rapids 6, Michigan. Price : $1.00.)

The compiler has made available a useful and clearly lithographed compendium of all Hebrew words occurring more than ten times, classified as verbs, nouns, or particles. The two former groups are arranged in alphabetic order according to frequency, the verbs in six lists and the noun in seven. It is not obvious on what principle the particles have been ordered within their sub-sections ; some of the lines here are a little crowded, and the preposition k seems to have been omitted. It is unfortunate that only the Qal of the verb is given, even where it never actually occurs, e.g., *šāba'*, or has the meaning assigned only in a derived form, e.g., *bārak*. Only some half-dozen mistakes in pointing were noticed. For those wishing to enlarge or preserve their Hebrew vocabulary without necessarily reading a text, this book may be recommended.

D.R.Ap-T.

YATES, K. M. : *The Essentials of Biblical Hebrew,* revised by J. J. Owens. 1956. Pp. xvi+228. (Harpers, New York. Price : $5.00.)

It is claimed that this text book rests on experience with the largest Old Testament Hebrew class in the world, numbering as many as 140 students. It is simply arranged and treats the grammar systematically, in the order Article, Prepositions, Conjunction, Nouns, Pronouns, Verbs, Numerals, with syntax mainly reserved to the end. The exercises are short, and consecutive sentences are not reached until the 32nd lesson. This must be a little discouraging, but in other respects the book is admirable. Vocabularies are given at the end, together with lists of words for ' Word Drill.' H.H.R.

BOOK LIST, 1958

This issue of the *Book List* has been compiled in circumstances of peculiar difficulty. I am, therefore, the more grateful for the ready help which I have received from the members of the Panel, from Professors Bič, de Boer, Cazelles, Hammershaimb, Noth, and Robinson, Dr. Bowman, and Dr. Weis, and from the Printer, whose efficiency and courtesy have considerably lightened my task. I am also indebted to Professor Rabin and the Jewish Agency Department for Culture and Education in the Diaspora for providing me with information about, and copies of, Israeli Books, and to the staff of B. H. Blackwell, Oxford, for supplying information about publishers and prices.

Although every effort has been made to maintain consistency in the presentation of the bibliographical data, some discrepancies may be detected. But the full index ought to enable readers to trace any item without difficulty. Books suitable for inclusion in school libraries are marked by an asterisk (*).

After 31st August, 1958, all communications and copies of books for review should be sent to the Editor at 50 North Bailey, Durham.

ST. MARY'S COLLEGE,   G. W. ANDERSON.
    UNIVERSITY OF ST. ANDREWS.

GENERAL

Bič, M. and Souček, J. B. (ed. by) : *Biblická Konkordance*, parts 10-11. *Kálef-Lid*. 1957. Pp. 80 each part. (Edice Kalich, Prague ; agents, Artia, Ltd., 30 Smečky, Prague. Price : Kčs. 10.50 or U.S. $1.10 per part.)

This Concordance, which in some ways is a model for a Concordance, since it supplies fuller information than can be found in any one Concordance in any other language (see *Book List*, 1955, p. 4 ; 1956, p. 3 ; 1957, p. 4), continues to make progress. The reviewer does not read Czech, and cannot use this work in connexion with a Czech Bible, but admires the work that has gone into it, and the way it tells the reader the Hebrew and Greek words coresponding to the Czech text for every Old Testament reference, and the Greek words for the New Testament. H.H.R.

Bijbels Woordenboek, 2nd ed., Part 5. Samaritanen-Zijde. 1957. Cols. 1505-1970. (Romen en Zonen, Roermond. Price : Fl. 10.75.)

This part completes the excellent new edition of the work, which is about one fifth larger than the first edition, and which is substantially rewritten. The earlier parts have been noted in the *Book List* (1955, pp. 4f. ; 1956, p. 3 ; 1957, p. 3). It is a fine scholarly work, taking account of the latest Catholic and Protestant literature ; and the Dutch reader is fortunate in having this up-to-date and substantial one-volume Bible Dictionary to hand. H.H.R.

de Boer, P. A. H. (ed. by) : *Oudtestamentische Studiën*. Deel XII. *Studies on the Book of Genesis*. 1958. Pp. 316. (E. J. Brill, Leiden. Price : By subscription Fl. 25 ; separately Fl. 37.50.)

The present volume in this series contains contributions (mainly in English) of lengths varying from 6 pp. to 113 pp., and written by eight different Dutch scholars. A certain unity is given by the over-riding theme, but an interesting variety remains. B. Gemser singles out some noteworthy traits in the characterisation of God in Genesis, while A. van Selms has a most interesting treatment of the Canaanites in Genesis. In German, N. H. Ridderbos writes a thoughtful article supporting a *creatio ex nihilo* application of Gen. i. 1-2 ; and A. R. Hulst reaches very cautious conclusions from the use of *kol bāsār* in the P Story of the Flood. The single French article is by F. van Trigt on the significance of the Jabbok struggle in Gen. xxxii. 23-33. J. Hoftijzer contributes a few remarks on the tale of Noah's drunkenness, whereas L. A. Snijders writes at more length on the covenant with Abram (Gen. xv). The longest article is a thorough preliminary investigation by T. Jansma into Syriac Nestorian exegesis of Genesis. There is a scripture index to the whole volume, which is well up to the standard of the earlier volumes. D.R.Ap-T.

BRUCE, F. F. : *New Horizons in Biblical Studies*. 1957. Pp. 18, with 1 map. (Obtainable from The Registrar, The University, Sheffield 10.)

In his inaugural lecture as first Professor of Biblical History and Literature in the University of Sheffield, Dr. Bruce shows how new knowledge about the civilization of the ancient Near East has provided a richer context for Biblical studies and yet emphasized the distinctive character and the unity of Biblical history and literature. In brief compass he gives a telling account of the range and interest of these studies and of the material available for prosecuting them.   G.W.A.

FRIEDRICH, G. (ed. by) : *Theologisches Wörterbuch zum Neuen Testament* (begun by G. Kittel). Band VI, Lieferungen 8, 9. 1957. Pp. 128. (Kohlhammer, Stuttgart. Price : DM. 4.60 each Lieferung.)

In Lieferung 8 there is first the conclusion of the long article on *pneuma* and its cognates. Bietenhard contributes the article on *poieo* and its cognates. There is less about the corresponding Old Testament usages than one might have expected. An article on *poimen*, *poimne*, etc., by Jeremias is particularly important. Bauernfeind writes on *polemos* and has a section on the religious understanding of war in the Old Testament and in later Judaism, in which among other subjects the holy war is discussed.

Lieferung 9 begins with the conclusion of the article on *polemos*. There are comprehensive articles on *polis* and its cognates by Strathmann, on *polloi* by Jeremias (significant for Old Testament scholars), on *poneros*, *poneria*, by Harder, in which there is a discussion of the terminology in the Hebrew Old Testament, the LXX, the Dead Sea Scrolls, the Pseudepigrapha, and Josephus. The Lieferung ends with the first part of the article by Hauck and Schulz on *poreuomai* and its cognates, in which the section on the LXX and later Judaism is relevant to Old Testament interests.   N.W.P.

GALLING, K. (ed. by) : *Die Religion in Geschichte und Gegenwart*. 3. Auflage, Band I, Lieferungen 7-8, 9-10, 11-12, 13-14, 15-16, 17-19, 20-21. 1957, Cols. 577-1898, with plates and maps+Pp. XXXII. Band II, Lieferungen 22-23, 24-25. 1958. Cols. 1-352, with maps. (J. C. B. Mohr, Tübingen. Subscription price : DM. 4.20 each Lieferung.)

The successive parts of this work have appeared so rapidly that it is not practicable even to list the many articles and sections of articles which have a bearing on the O.T. In the above Lieferungen (*Arbeitsschule-Eid*) there are approximately 100, including biographical entries (from which some names which one would have expected to find are missing). The general standard is high ; and the task of compressing much information into limited space has been carried out with skill.   G.W.A.

Hebrew Union College Annual, Vol. XXVIII, 1957. Pp. 324+26 (in Hebrew)+index+VII figs. (Hebrew Union College, Cincinnati. Price : $5.00.)

LXX studies are well represented in this volume. H. M. Orlinsky contributes Chapter I and Excursus A of ' Studies in the Septuagint of the Book of Job ', an amply documented review of earlier work. His pupil, M. S. Hurwitz, examines the LXX of Isaiah xxxvi.-xxxix. in relation to i.-xxxv. and xl.-lxvi. (a note is appended on 2 Kings xviii.-xx.). Orlinsky's suggestion and guidance also underlie the contribution by A. Soffer on anthropomorphisms and anthropopathisms in the LXX of the Psalter. J. Lewy, writing on the origin and the meaning of the term ' Hebrew ', accepts the etymology suggested by the LXX rendering. J. Morgenstern continues his reconstruction of the events of 485 B.C., arguing that there is evidence of the existence and the fate of a Jewish King at that time. R. Yaron writes on two Greek words in the Brooklyn Aramaic papyri. E. Bammel investigates the historical background of 28th Adar in Megillath Ta'anith. A. Guttmann seeks to clarify the use of the terms Hillelite and Shammaite. J. J. Petuchowski discusses the implications of Rabbi Ishmael's slighting reference to Melchizedek (Nedarim 32b). J. B. Curtis writes on the Mount of Olives in Jewish and Christian tradition. F. Landsberger shows how the sacred direction of the Church was influenced by the Synagogue. R. Loewe treats of some 13th Century Christian Hebraists in England. S. Atlas presents a critical examination of Solomon Maimon's philosophy of language. The volume includes the Goldenson Lecture by J. B. Agus, a consideration of the treatment of the prophet image in modern Hebrew Literature. Finally comes a collection of Hebrew letters from Joshua (Osias) S. Schorr to Bernhard Felsenthal, edited, with a preface by E. Spicehandler. There is an index of *H.U.C.A*. I-XXVII.

G.W.A.

ILTIS, R. (ed. by) : *Jewish Studies : Essays in Honour of the Very Reverend Dr. Gustav Sicher, Chief Rabbi of Prague*. 1955. Pp. 112+portrait of Dr. Sicher. (Council of Jewish Religious Communities, Prague.)

On the occasion of Dr. Sicher's seventy-fifth birthday the Council of Jewish Communities presented to him this handsome volume, to which non-Jewish friends also contributed to express their esteem for him. R. Farkaš gives an account of Dr. Sicher's life ; and M. Bič surveys his literary output. The volume includes Dr. Sicher's own study, ' The Concept of Work in the Jewish Faith ', the scope of which may be indicated by a selection of chapter headings : ' The Study of the Torah and Work ', ' Is Work a Curse or a Blessing ?', ' Paradise, Messiah, and Work '. Other essays deal with the past and present life of Jews in Bohemia, e.g., the valuable contributions of P. Eismer (' Jews in the Literature of the Czech lands ') and of H. Volavková (' The Old-New Synagogue

—in the Steps of Josef Manes '). Many readers will be specially interested in H. Volavková's account of the State Jewish Museum in Prague and ' From the Archives of the State Jewish Museum ' by O. Muneles (120,000 items are entered in the catalogue of the Museum, some of which are extremely valuable. The archives include many precious mediaeval MSS). Earlier periods are represented by the contributions of S. Segert (' The Unity of the New Covenant—the Unity of the Brethren ') and Greta Hort (' Musil, Madian and the Mountain of the Law '). All are in English.   M.B.

Internationale Zeitschriftenschau für Bibelwissenschaft und Grenzgebiete, IV, 1955/56, Heft 1-2. 1957. Pp. xii+272. (Patmos-Verlag, Düsseldorf. Price : DM. 38 or $9.10.)

This volume contains 1,680 entries, classified on the same general plan as in former years. The arrangement and indexing of this work of reference make it a very easily used guide to the bewildering proliferation of periodical literature. One can only endorse the eulogies of earlier issues and express gratitude to the team of scholars whose exemplary industry lightens the work of others.   G.W.A.

LISOWSKY, G. : *Konkordanz zum hebräischen Alten Testament.* 1958. Pp. XVI+1672. (Privileg. Württ. Bibelanstalt, Stuttgart. Price : DM. 40.)

A comparatively small and easily handled volume, yet comprising all that can normally be expected of a concordance. Biblical Aramaic is included, and pronouns, prepositions and interjections are mentioned with their meanings, though no references are quoted. The meaning of every word is given in German, English and Latin, and there are fairly frequent grammatical notes. In the case of verbs, if the subject is not actually quoted in the text, it is supplied in a footnote ; a certain amount of space is thus saved, for the same subject may occur several times on one page. The print is necessarily small, but the reader soon grows accustomed to it. The size of the work and its price may commend it to many Bible students who would find the well-known concordances both cumbersome to handle and expensive. (For reviews of parts of this concordance previously published, see *Book Lists* : 1956, pp. 20f. ; 1957, p.11.)   T.H.R.

Mélanges bibliques rédigés en honneur de André Robert. (Travaux de l'Institut Catholique de Paris, 4.) 1957. Pp. 580+III plates. (Bloud & Gay, Paris. Price : 37s. 0d.)

Robert, who was professor of Old Testament exegesis in the Paris Institut Catholique and editor of the *Supplément au Dictionnaire de la Bible* from 1940 until his death, died on

28 May, 1955, aged 71. This collection of fifty-seven papers (thirty-one for the Old Testament and twenty-six for the New) bears the name of no editor, but the bibliography has been prepared by Joseph Trinquet. Like so many works of the kind there is no very marked unity about it, and apart from the bibliography, only a short memoir bears any direct reference to Robert himself. The two parts are entitled respectively : ' L'Ancien Testament et son Milieu ', and ' Le Nouveau Testament, son Milieu et son Exégèse '.

Among the thirty-one papers on Old Testament subjects may be mentioned W. F. Albright's 'The Refrain "and God saw $ki\ t\hat{o}b$"'; G. R. Driver's ' Problems of interpretation in the Heptateuch ' ; ' The Israelite settlement in Galilee and the wars with Jabin of Hazor ' by S. Yeivin; 'Military Rationing in Papyrus Anastasi I and the Bible ' by A. Malamat ; ' Le caractère du temple salomonien ' by H. Vincent ; ' Quelques traits essentiels de la piété des Psaumes ', by H. Ringgren, and ' Le Psaumes des Hasidim ' by J. Coppens. Qumran studies, grouped in the New Testament section include H. H. Rowley's ' The 390 years of the Zadokite Work ', and J. Van der Ploeg's ' La guerre sainte dans la "Règle de la guerre" de Qumran '. J.M.T.B.

MILLER, M. S. & J. L. : *Encyclopedia of Bible Life.* 1957. Pp. 494+ 245 ills.+14 maps. (A. & C. Black, London. Price : 40s. 0d.)

This is the first British edition of the work first published in New York (Harper) in 1944 and revised in 1955. This is a well illustrated and informative, if somewhat diffuse, picture of the various aspects of life in the Bible lands, and contains certain details to which the feminine mind seems to be particularly alert. It is quite entertaining, though there is often a tendency to vagueness and it is not up to date with archeological research nor very critical in the use of older authorities. J.G.

RIESENFELD, H. (ed. by) : *Svensk Exegetisk Årsbok*, xxi. (1956). 1957. Pp. 162. (C. W. K. Gleerup, Lund. Price : Sw. kr. 10.)

None of the articles in this issue bears directly on the Old Testament. W. D. Davies discusses the relation between the Dead Sea Scrolls and the religious vocabulary, organization, sacraments, and Messianic theology of the early Church. T. Arvedson writes on Matthew xx. 1ff. and John xxi. 15ff., C. K. Barrett on ' The Apostles in and after the New Testament ', B. Gärtner on Judas Iscariot, P. Janzon on the Nicolaitans, and S. Petri on Lutheran interpretation of John iv. 21-24. There are also reviews of recent literature. G.W.A.

RYCKMANS, G. (ed. by) : *L'Ancien Testament et l'Orient. Études pré-sentées aux VIes Journées Bibliques de Louvain* (11-13 *septembre* 1954). (Orientalia et Biblica Lovaniensia, I). 1957. Pp. 232. Publications Universitaires, Louvain. Price : B. Frs. 220 ; bound, B. Frs. 260.)

This collection of papers read at Louvain in the autumn of 1954 contains a rich diversity of material drawn from all quarters of the ancient world, and all are excellent, being the work of specialists, each in his own line. Most of them give news of new discoveries or new interpretations bearing on the Old Testament. Professor Rowley has some important criticisms to make with regard to the late Professor Torrey's theories concerning Sanballat and the Samaritan schism. Professor Driver has a long and learned article on Glosses in the Hebrew Text of the Old Testament, which is an attempt to establish principles of classification for the glosses which editors of the books of the Old Testament have claimed to find in the Masoretic text. Professor Guillaume discusses the importance of Arabic language and traditions for the inter-pretation of the Old Testament. Dr. F. M. Braun attempts to establish a relation between the religion of the Mandaeans and the Qumran sectaries. It may be remarked that his claim that the members of the Qumran community believed in the resurrection of the body rests upon a somewhat doubtful interpretation of a single passage in the Manual of Discipline. Monsignor Kissane discusses, all too briefly, the much disputed saying in the Immanuel oracle, ' Butter and honey shall he eat '. He inclines to take the *lamedh* clause as meaning ' *until* the child ', an interpretation which many scholars will hesitate to accept. Altogether the book is full of ' butter and honey ', taking that expression as meaning luxury food. S.H.H.

Studia theologica cura ordinum theologorum Scandinavicorum edita. Vol. X, fasc. i (1956), 1957. Pp. 64. Fasc. ii (1956), 1957. Pp. 128. Vol. XI, fasc. i 1957. Pp. 120. (C. W. K. Gleerup, Lund. Price : Vol. X, by subscription, Sw. kr. 12, or Sw. kr. 8 each fascicle ; Vol. XI and subsequent vols., by subscription, Sw. kr. 15, or Sw. kr. 10 each fascicle.)

To X, i L. G. Rignell contributes a study of Isaiah viii, which he treats as a unity foretelling both catastrophe and the survival of a remnant. F. Løkkegaard, in an article entitled ' The Canaanite Divine Wetnurses ', discusses the character and functions of the *ktrt* in NK and some other Ugaritic texts. The other articles are on New Testament subjects. X, ii contains no contributions on Old Testament themes. It includes an index to vols. I-X. Two of the three articles in XI are of interest to the *Alttestamentler*. B. Otzen contributes a textual study of 1QS. L. G. Rignell examines Isaiah vii, arguing that it is a unity : he identifies the '*almah* with Israel and Immanuel with the new Israel of the future. G.W.A.

TOGAN, Z. V. (ed. by) : *Proceedings of the Twenty-Second Congress of Orientalists held in Istanbul*, 1951. Vol. II, Communications. 1957. Pp. xvi+650+40 figures. (Brill, Leiden. Price : Fl. 85.)

The papers read at Istanbul in 1951 were published just before a new stream began to flow at Munich in 1957. Most of the 183 communications have been abridged : some have been published elsewhere in full. The Editor deserves praise for his tenacity in collecting all these papers and thus giving the reader a total impression of the Congress and also enabling him to read selectively *procul negotiis*.

The Old Testament section contains much of interest. E. P. Castro's paper ' Le problème de l'édition d'une nouvelle Bible hebraïque et les manuscrits hébreux en Espagne ' describes the lines on which a new edition of the Hebrew Bible is being prepared in Spain : the Ben Asher text is being used, and an extended apparatus criticus is in preparation. In ' Zur Geschichtsauffassung der Deuteronomisten ', M. Noth examines 2 Kings xxv. 27-30 and cogently defends the view that the Deuteronomistic History was written from the viewpoint that the Davidic dynasty was definitively ended. ' " Élus de Dieu " et " Élu de Dieu " dans le Commentaire d'Habacuc ' is a brilliant and impressive argument by A. Dupont-Sommer, emphasizing the messianic and priestly character of the Teacher of Righteousness. The late E. L. Sukenik's survey, ' The Present State of Research on the Dead Sea Scrolls ', is still valuable. J. Leveen examines ' The Orthography of the Hebrew Scroll of Isaiah A '. Summaries are given of H. H. Rowley, ' Moses and the Decalogue ' ; H. E. Del Medico, ' Les rouleaux de la Mer Morte et le " Manuel de Discipline " ' ; K. Galling, ' Die Politik der Perser und die Heimkehr aus Babel ' ; and E. Jacob, ' Le thème de l'Imago Dei dans l'Ancien Testament '.

Papers included in other sections are also of interest to the Alttestamentler : e.g., K. Balkan, ' Ein kurzer Bericht über die neuen Tafeln aus Kültepe ' ; C. F. A. Schaeffer, ' Découverte d'un sceau royal hittite à Ras Shamra-Ugarit ' ; V. Korošec, ' Uber die Bedeutung der Gesetzbücher von Ešnunna und von Isin für die Rechtsentwicklung in Mesopotamien und Kleinasien ' ; W. F. Albright, ' The Results of Recent American Archaeological Research in South Arabia ' ; A. F. L. Beeston, ' The Position of Women in Pre-Islamic South Arabia ' ; F. Cantera, ' Les Juifs dans l'historiographie espagnole ' ; G. R. Driver, ' Mythical Monsters in the Old Testament ' ; P. Bosch-Gimpera, ' Problèmes de l'histoire phénicienne dans l'Extrème Occident ' ; R. A. de Langhe, ' Vingt ans d'études ugaritiennes ' ; K. H. Rengstorf, ' Rabbinistische Studien in Deutschland nach 1945'; A. M. Honeyman, ' The Order of the Letters in North and South Semitic Alphabets ' (summary) ; and A. Schaade, ' Genusvertauschung in Mehri und anderen semitischen Sprachen '.

P.A.H.deB.

EDUCATIONAL

*BROADIE, E. : *The Chosen Nation : Book Three : The Prophets of Judah (Isaiah to the Exile)*. 1958. Pp. 130. (Religious Education Press, Wallington, Surrey. Price : Boards, 6s. 0d. ; Limp, 5s. 0d.)

This book, which is commended by Professor H. H. Rowley, is a sequel to *Kings and Prophets* noticed last year (p. 14). It is well designed for its purpose, and teachers will be grateful for the generous provision of exercises at the end of each of the twenty-five short chapters into which the book is divided.
L.A.P.

*BULL, N. J. : *From Prophecy to Law : Lessons on Secondary School Sections of the Agreed Syllabus*. 1958. Pp. 144. (Religious Education Press, Wallington, Surrey. Price : 6s. 6d.)

This book will prove an excellent guide to teachers in Modern Secondary Schools. In ten chapters it outlines the O.T. history and the teaching of the Law and the Prophets from the seventh to the fourth centuries. The teaching notes and the suggestions for practical class work will be found particularly useful.
L.A.P.

*HEATON, E. W. : *Hverdagsliv i det gamle Israel*, translated by G. Gersfelt in collaboration with E. Nielsen. 1957. Pp. 196+ills. 103. (Branner & Korch, Copenhagen. Price : paper covers, D. kr. 24.75 ; bound, D. kr. 29.75.)

Canon Heaton's excellent book (*Everyday Life in Old Testament Times* cf. *Book List*, 1957, p. 15), is here published in a Danish translation, which has been checked by Professor Nielsen, who has also added a few notes (e.g., on points in the standard Danish version of the Bible). Most but not all of the attractive drawings by Marjorie Quennell are included.
G.W.A.

*PFEIFFER, C. F. : *The Book of Leviticus : A Study Manual* (Shield Bible Study Series, Vol. 2). 1957. Pp. 60. (Baker Book House, Grand Rapids, Michigan. Price : $1.25.)

This is the first O.T. volume to be published in the Shield Bible Study Series of paper-bound manuals for the use of students in Colleges and Seminaries. It consists of a detailed analysis of the contents of Leviticus with a brief explanation of the meaning of each group of verses yielded by the analysis. Critical questions do not come within the scope of the series and the exposition aims at summarising the meaning of the text with an occasional Christian comment. The exposition is clear and well-written and this is a useful book of its kind.
L.A.P.

86

ARCHAEOLOGY AND EPIGRAPHY

ALBRIGHT, W. F. : *Die Bibel im Licht der Altertumsforschung. Ein Bericht über die Arbeit eines Jahrhunderts.* Preface by O. Eissfeldt. 1957. Pp. 148+chronological table. (Calwer Verlag, Stuttgart. Price : paper covers, DM. 6.80 ; bound, DM. 8.80.)

This is a translation of *Recent Discoveries in Bible Lands* (see *Book List*, 1957, pp. 15f.), felicitously introduced to the German reader by Professor Eissfeldt's Preface. The translator (D. Th. Schlatter) has added a few notes, recording, inter alia, the publication of Papyrus Bodmer II, and the unrolling of the Copper Scrolls and the Genesis Apocryphon.

The wider circulation of this compact and informative survey is to be welcomed. G.W.A.

AVI-YONAH, M., AVIGAD, N., AHARONI, Y., DUNAYEVSKY, I., GUTMAN, S. : *Masada. Survey and Excavations, 1955-1956 by the Hebrew University, Israel Exploration Society, Department of Antiquities.* 1957. Pp. 60+16 plates+22 figures and maps. (Israel Exploration Society, Jerusalem.)

The book contains a summary of the history of Masada with a careful, detailed account of the surface survey, soundings, and excavations of the palace remains in March, 1955 and 1956. The results appear to confirm the description of the palace made by Josephus as against the identifications of Schulten (*ZDPV*, 56, 1933, pp. 1-185), but there is evidence that Josephus described the fortress from outside and did not enter it. J.N.S.

BERGHE, L. V. and MUSSCHE, H. F. : *Bibliographie analytique de l'assyiologie et de l'archéologie du Proche-orient.* Vol. I, Section A, *L'archéologie*, 1954-55. 1956. Pp. 132+5 maps. (Brill, Leiden. Price : Fl. 10.)

This informative work will be found useful by all students of the ancient Near East. The first part of it consists of a general bibliography of acquisitions, both in museums and private collections, and of exhibitions. In the second part the bibliography is arranged according to regions (Turkey and Soviet Armenia ; Cyprus ; Syria and Lebanon ; Israel and Jordan ; Iraq ; Iran ; Afghanistan and Pakistan ; Saudi Arabia, Yemen, Aden, Oman, and Bahrein), and the material is grouped throughout under various headings (excavations and sites, architecture, iconography, sculpture, painting, mosaics, ceramics, seals, coins, ivories, and so on). These two parts together contain 657 items. The third part is a bibliography of reviews of publications which appeared before 1954. The bibliography ranges over a vast period, from pre-historic times to the birth of Islamic civilisation. Christian and Byzantine architecture are not included, but Graeco-Roman, Parthian and Sasanian antiquities find a place in it. There are five maps and two indices (authors and place names). A further volume, which will deal with philological material published in 1954-1956, is promised for 1957. D.W.T.

The Holy Land : New Light on the Prehistory and Early History of Israel (*Antiquity and Survival*, Vol. II, No. 2/3). 1957. Pp. 77-318, with numerous illustrations and maps. (Luctor et Emergo, N.V., The Hague. Price : paper covers, DM. 8.50 ; pasteboard, DM. 9.65).

This issue of Antiquity and Survival is devoted entirely to articles by Jewish scholars on the pre-history of Palestine and various phases of later local culture and history, including that of Israel until the Talmudic age. The articles are written from an archaeological point of view and are a valuable first-hand record of the intense archaeological activity in modern Israel. Old Testament scholars, even those not interested primarily in archaeology, will welcome particularly Dr. Yadin's report on his work at Hazor and Dr. Glueck's state-ment on his recent exploration of the Negeb. A feature of this work is the ample collection of excellent photographs.

J.G.

Judah and Jerusalem. The Twelfth Archaeological Convention (in Hebrew, with an English summary). 1957. Pp. viii + 208 + 5 plates + 12 illustrations and maps in the text + 1 folding map. (Israel Ex-ploration Society, Jerusalem.)

This volume contains 22 articles (some embodying original researches), which were originally given in the form of lectures at the Twelfth Archaeological Convention in Jerusalem, September, 1956. The articles which have a direct bearing on the Bible are : Jerusalem, ' King's Chapel ' and ' Royal City ' (B. Mazar) ; Jerusalem—in Judah or in Benjamin? (Z. Kallai-Kleinman) ; The Gibeonites, the Nethinim and the Servants of Solomon (M. Haran) ; The Negev (South) of Judah (Y. Aharoni) ; The Necropolis of Jerusalem in the Time of the Monarchy (Ruth Amiran) ; A Further Note on Nebucha-drezzar's Palestinian Campaigns (A. Malamat) ; The Growth of Jerusalem in the Israelite Period (M. Hecker) ; and Jeru-salem in Jewish-Hellenistic Thought (J. A. Seeligman). M.W.

MADER, E. : *Mambre. Die Ergebnisse der Ausgrabungen im heiligen Bezirk râmet el-ḫalîl in Südpalästina* 1926-1928. 1957. I. (Text-band) Pp. 356. II. (Tafeln) 108 Zeichnungen, 183 Photographien auf 103 Tafeln, 2 Pläne. (E. Wewel Verlag, Freiburg i. Br. Price : DM. 165.)

The MS. of the final report on the results of the excavations carried out thirty years ago was practically complete when the author died (1949). It was seen through the press by Fr. Stummer (d. 1955) and later by V. Hamp. The state of the excavations at ḥarām râmet el-ḫalîl is presented with the aid of very many diagrams, photographs, and plans. In addition to a few examples of early Bronze Age pottery, there are some rather doubtful traces of the early and middle Iron Age, fragments from a somewhat loosely defined pre-Herodian period, and above all the ruins of an incomplete *temenos* King Herod's time, a sanctuary from the reign of the Emperor

Hadrian, and, in particular, a Constantinian basilica, with later Byzantine and Arab additions. With the aid of the written records a detailed account is given of the history of Mamre and Hebron from the earliest times till the age of the Crusades. Up to the latter period, tradition rightly located Mamre at *ḥaram rāmet el-ḫalīl.* According to the author, pre-Israelite and Israelite Hebron is certainly to be found on *jebel er-rumēde.* This book must hence forward be regarded as the basic work on the topography and history of Mamre and Hebron. M.N.

PARROT, A. : *Babylone et l'Ancien Testament.* (Cahiers d'archéologie biblique, 8.) 1956. Pp. 142+viii. plates+54 figures. (Delachaux et Niestlé, Neuchâtel. Price : Swiss Fr. 6.25.)

This, the latest of Professor Parrot's useful manuals of Biblical archaeology, has all the excellent qualities of its predecessors. It is devoted to a description of the somewhat chequered history of the excavation of the site of Babylon, and of the part which that city played in the history of Israel. A certain amount of unavoidable repetition occurs, since the author has made use of material from the books on Samaria, Nineveh and Jerusalem, where the history overlaps. In illustrating and commenting on the *marru,* Marduk's ceremonial implement, whose original use was as an agricultural rather than a warlike implement, the author points out that it explains those passages in the prophets which speak of swords beaten into ploughshares, and spears into pruning-knives. But it is questionable whether Marduk's *marru* was ever anything but a spade. This useful book will soon appear in an English translation from the S.C.M. Press. S.H.H.

MAZAR (MAISLER), B. : *Beth She'arim* (in Hebrew with a summary in English), 2nd edition. 1957. Pp. x+156. (Israel Exploration Society, Jerusalem. Price : $10.)

This scholarly volume, dedicated to the late Prof. Samuel Klein of the Hebrew University, deals with the Israel Exploration Society's excavations of Beth She'arim (Sheikh Abreiq, in Arabic) a place in Lower Galilee referred to by Josephus as belonging to Berenice, daughter of Agrippa I, and in Talmudic sources referred to as a Jewish settlement in the Roman period, serving as the residence of Rabbi Judah Hannasi and the Synedrion in the second half of the second century C.E. Important data are given about the first period of the excavations performed during 1936-40, when catacombs, graves and a synagogue were found, and also about the second period of excavations which took place during 1953-55, when various finds, including over 200 Greek, Hebrew and Palmyrene inscriptions, were discovered. The book, which is delightfully produced, is enhanced by 36 plates and a great number of drawings and charts. M.W.

KENYON, K. M. : *Digging up Jericho.* 1957. Pp. 272+64 plates+18 figures. (Ernest Benn Ltd., London. Price : 30s. 0d.)

Two periods in the history of Jericho are of special interest, the earliest and the time of the Israelite entry into Palestine, and Miss Kenyon's book throws light on both as well as on the intervening age. While her conclusion about the walls in which biblical scholars are most interested is negative, for the main result of her excavations is to show that earlier judgments about the date of the collapse of the walls are erroneous, her recovery of the remains of the earliest period has pushed back the whole time-scale of human pre-history and afforded a graphic picture of life in the earliest known town. The book contains many fine illustrations. W.D.McH.

PARROT, A. : *Le musée du Louvre et la Bible* (Cahiers d'archéologie biblique, No. 9.) 1957. Pp. 166+12 plates+76 figures. (Delachaux et Niestlé, Neuchâtel & Paris. Price : Sw. frs. 7.50.)

This book gives an account of the material in the Louvre illustrative of the Old and New Testaments. It is in nine chapters (Origins, Patriarchal Age, Amarna Period, Baals and Astartes, The Israelite monarchy, Babylon, Assyria, Esther, and the New Testament), and shows the wide diversity of archaeological evidence bearing on the Bible, puts these remains into their historical and geographical setting, and shows their importance for biblical study. A valuable book which should, like the other volumes in this series, be translated into English. J.N.S.

PARROT, A. : *The Temple of Jerusalem* (Studies in Biblical Archaeology, 5.) 1957. Pp. 112+7 illustrations on plates+xxv. figures in the text. (S.C.M. Press, London. Price : 9s. 6d.)

This work, translated by B. E. Hooke from the French book published in 1954 (see *Book List*, 1955, pp. 17f.) contains forty-six pages on the Temple of Solomon, seven on the Temple of Ezekiel, nine on the Second Temple, twenty-five on Herod's Temple, a short epilogue on the present buildings in the Temple area, and an excellent bibliography ; and it is well illustrated. There is much more biblical material in it than in some of the other books in this series ; and it should be compared with G. E. Wright, *Biblical Archaeology*, pp. 136ff. It is a valuable and interesting contribution to the subject. J.N.S.

HISTORY AND GEOGRAPHY

BALY, D. : *The Geography of the Bible. A Study in Historical Geography.* 1957. Pp. xiv+304+97 illustrations+48 maps and diagrams. (Harper Brothers, New York. Price : $4.95.)

This is a thoroughly well-informed description of Palestine and Transjordan by one who has had several years' first-hand experience of the land at a time when scientific observations were being made and officially recorded, and has himself observed local phenomena with a scientific eye. The first quarter of the book is devoted to geology, but this is presented with practical good taste and with vivid graphs and excellent documentary photographs, so that, though technical, the matter is far from forbidding. Flora, fauna, weather, regional boundaries, etc., are dealt with, and the whole is an excellent presentation of the ecology of Palestinian life. The long bibliography of works old and new will be found most helpful, though a surprising omission is Dalman's monumental *Arbeit und Sitte in Palästina*.   J.G.

EHRLICH, E. L. : *Geschichte Israels von den Anfängen bis zur Zerstörung des Tempels* (70 *n. Chr.*) (Sammlung Göschen, Band 231/231a). 1958. Pp. 158+1 map. (de Gruyter, Berlin. Price : DM. 4.80.)

A highly compressed but, within its bounds, very comprehensive sketch of the history of Israel in its political and, to a certain extent, religious aspects. The main chronology is adopted from Albright, whose authority is frequently cited amongst the many—mostly post-war—books and articles to which reference is given in the footnotes, these being a most useful guide to further study on particular problems.

The arrangement is chronological, and the biblical data are given respectful, though not uncritical, attention, but not to the exclusion of the external evidence. As must now be expected, the Dead Sea Sect is considered in its period, which is placed as the century before and the half-century after the beginning of our era.

The author has a clear style, which leaves a well-defined overall picture of events in the mind. Students will consequently value this small book, both as a useful introduction, and as a valuable aid to revision. Would that it were available in English!

Everyone can find omissions from a book written to these limits, but C. J. Gadd, *The Newly Discovered Babylonian Chronicle* (or *A.N.E.T.*, p. 305) might have been cited (p. 69) with reference to Josiah, Necho and Assyria ; Grollenberg, *Atlas of the Bible* should find a place in the short general bibliography, and Samaria should appear on the sketch-map (the weakest feature). There are good general and scripture reference indexes.   D.R.Ap-T.

HITTI, P. K. : *Lebanon in History from the Earliest Times to the Present*. 1957. Pp. xx+548+20 maps and numerous illustrations. (Macmillan, London. Price : 42s. 0d.)

This is a useful, interesting, and well-informed survey of the place occupied by the area now covered by the Lebanese Republic in world history. Rather more than a third of the book covers the pre-Christian period and is of value to Old Testament scholars. It has the obvious merit of focussing attention on this comparatively small territory and is able to deal in full detail with its topography, its climate, its plant and animal life, its peoples and its political life. The author has drawn upon a wide range of knowledge and is up-to-date in archaeological matters. (One curious misprint has been allowed to remain (p. 38) : " Originally an American animal, the horse was domesticated somewhere east of the Caspian Sea ".)   L.H.B.

NOTH, M. : *The History of Israel*, translated from the second edition of *Geschichte Israels* by Stanley Godman. 1958. Pp. viii+480. (A. & C. Black, London. Price : 42s. 0d.)

The German original of this deservedly famous work will be familiar to most members of this society ; but those who are engaged in teaching will be glad to have an English version available for their classes. The translation has been made from the second German edition (*Book List*, 1955, p. 23).

A.R.J.

PARKER, R. A. and DUBBERSTEIN, W. H. : *Babylonian Chronology 626 B.C.—A.D. 75.* (Brown University Studies XIX.) 1956. Pp. xii+48. (Brown University Press, Providence, Rhode Island. Price : 20s. 0d.)

The aim of this study is to provide a brief, but thorough and complete, presentation of the data bearing upon the chronological problems of the Neo-Babylonian, Achaemenid Persian, and Seleucid periods, together with tables for the easy translation of dates from the Babylonian into the Julian calendar. The tables are intended primarily for historians, both classical and oriental. They will be useful also to Biblical students, for they enable any Biblical date in the period dealt with given in the Babylonian calendar to be translated. The present work is a revision of earlier editions which appeared in 1942 and 1946. The main features of the revision are the incorporation of numerous newly discovered intercalary months, the extension of the tables from A.D. 45 to A.D. 75, and the substitution of completely calculated dates in the tables. A slender work, but behind it lies an immense amount of detailed labour.   D.W.T.

WHITLEY, C. F. : *The Exilic Age.* 1957. Pp. 160. (Longmans, Green. Price : 16s. 0d.)

This book uses as its starting-point the great changes which took place in the Near East during the seventh and sixth centuries B.C., when the Semitic hegemony came to an end and societies dominated by a priesthood gave way to ones in which freedom of philosophical discussion, a sense of individual responsibility and an upsurge of new religious ideas were notable characteristics. The author attempts to relate the teaching of the prophets Jeremiah, Ezekiel and Second Isaiah to the changing context of the age in which they lived and to show how they represent vital aspects of the change which took place. It may be said that the attempt is particularly successful in the case of Second Isaiah, and that it might have been more effectively prosecuted if such questions as prophetic ecstasy, the date of Jeremiah's call, the identity of the foreign invaders referred to in Jer. ii.-vi., and others had been treated as irrelevant side-issues and left alone. J.M.

TEXT AND VERSIONS 93

WRIGHT, J. S. : *The Building of the Second Temple*. (Tyndale Lecture, 1952.) 1958. Pp. 20. (Tyndale Press, London. Price : 1s. 6d.)

Principal Wright here examines the evidence of Ezra, 1 Esdras, and Haggai and Zechariah. He holds that there were two foundation ceremonies (in 536 B.C. and again in 520), and, in general, argues that the account given in Ezra of the period 537—516 B.C. is not seriously at variance with Haggai and Zechariah. G.W.A.

WRIGHT, J. S. : *The Date of Ezra's Coming to Jerusalem*. (Tyndale Lecture, 1946.) 2nd Edition. 1958. Pp. 32. (Tyndale Press, London. Price : 1s. 6d.)

This is a revised edition of a useful study, previously noticed in the *Book List* (1948, p. 19). Some paragraphs have been added, taking account of criticisms of the first edition, mainly those advanced by Professor Rowley. But the author maintains his position ; and, whether or not one accepts it, one cannot but admire the clarity with which he presents it. G.W.A.

TEXT AND VERSIONS

Corpus Codicum Hebraicorum Medii Aevi, redigendum curavit R. Edelmann, Pars II, The Pre-Masoretic Bible, discovered in four manuscripts presenting a unique tradition : 1. The Codex Reuchlinianus, 2. The Parma Pentateuch, 3. The Parma Bible, 4. The London Bible. Published with a general introduction, detailed description of the MSS. and basic conclusions by Alexander Sperber. 1956. Pp. L+774 facsimiles. (Munksgaard, Copenhagen. Price : Dan. Kr. 750.)

The first volume of part 2 of this Series (cp. *Book List*, 1957, p. 69) published here is a reproduction in facsimile of the Reuchlinianus which is usually considered to be a Ben Naftali text. The Introduction does not include a 'detailed description' of the MS. nor would we infer from it that the MS. was ever discussed before (cf. *Der Bibeltext des Ben Naftali*, in P. Ķahle's *Masoreten des Westens*, II, pp. 55-60 and J. Prijs, *Über Ben Naftali-Bibelhandschriften und ihre paläographischen Besonderheiten* in *ZATW*, 1957, Pp. 171-184). The Introduction is in fact a re-statement in 157 paragraphs of Dr. Sperber's views on the history of Hebrew phonology as expressed in his well-known studies on the subject, and only those particularities of the Reuchlinianus are referred to which are relevant to his thesis. Dr. Sperber maintains that the Masora Marginalis is the consecutively running application of formerly existing general masoretic lists which were compiled on the basis of MSS. which differed in many details. The so-called ' Masoretic Bibles ', i.e., whose texts agree with their masora, justify their name not on account of preserving the traditional text but, on the contrary, because they conform to masoretic innovations. The earliest traceable stage as represented by the Palestinian Vocalization knows of no quantitative differentiation of vowels. The latter was the result of the introduction of the ultima stress, and under this influence Babylonian Vocalization evolved a separate symbol for short *a* or *e* while the Tiberian Vocalization as represented by the Reuchlinianus which used our symbols for long and short *a* and *e* promiscuously indicates short vowels by placing a distinguishing dot in the opening letter of the next syllable. The other three MSS. represent a later stage. They have symbols distinguishing between long and short vowels but retain the distinguishing dot although it lost its *raison d'être*. On the other hand, our system of punctuation logically dispensed with the distinguishing dot after the closed syllable except where it could be explained as a *dagesh lene* and after an open syllable where it was explained as a *dagesh forte*.

P.R.W.

KENYON, SIR F. : *Our Bible and the Ancient Manuscripts*. 5th edition, revised and enlarged by A. W. Adams, with an introduction by G. R. Driver. 1958. Pp. 352+XLVIII plates. (Eyre & Spottiswoode, London. Price : 42s. 0d.)

The 5th edition of this standard work makes the pre-war one and its reprints (see *Book List*, 1950, p. 30) out of date. The main additions—amounting in parts to a re-writing—have been made in ch. I, Ancient Books and Writing ; in ch. V, The Ancient Versions of the O.T. ; and in a new chapter on Revisions and Translations (in English) since 1881. But the chapters on The Hebrew O.T., The Text of the N.T., The MSS. of the N.T., and The Ancient Versions of the N.T., have all been considerably amplified, too, and the whole book has been brought abreast of modern scholarship by the addition of a phrase here, and the re-wording of a sentence there. Seventeen plates have been added ; and four of the pre-war edition's thirty-two have been replaced by others. Their reproduction is now clearer, and one or two of the captions have been corrected. The final improvements to be mentioned are the addition of an index of Biblical passages, and one inch off the height of the previous format.   D.R.Ap-T.

LAMSA, G. M. : *The Holy Bible from Ancient Eastern Manuscripts, Containing the Old and New Testaments Translated from the Peshitta, the Authorized Bible of the Church of the East*. 1957. Pp. xx+1244. (A. J. Holman Company, Philadelphia. Price : $12.50.)

The version of the New Testament in this book is a partial revision of a translation published in 1940. I dealt with this as leniently as the facts would allow in *The Bible Translator*, vol. 7, no. 2, pp. 66-72. Unfortunately the Old Testament section is disappointing also, for it contains many mistaken and misleading renderings. While it may be used to illustrate in a general way the nature of the Peshitta and the difference between the Hebrew and Syriac texts, its value for serious Old Testament studies must be regarded as limited. Of the Introduction one can but express the hope that Mr. Lamsa will live to regret it.   W.D.McH.

EXEGESIS AND MODERN TRANSLATIONS

The Apocrypha of the Old Testament. Revised Standard Version, Translated from the Greek and Latin Tongues, Being the Version Set Forth A.D. 1611, Revised A.D. 1894, Compared with the Most Ancient Authorities and Revised A.D. 1957. Pp. vi+250. (Nelson, Edinburgh. Price : 18s. 0d.)

The volume containing the Old and New Testaments in the version now regularly referred to as the R.S.V. was noticed in the 1953 *Book List* (pp. 32f.). The R.S.V. Apocrypha, uniform in appearance with the earlier work, follows similar principles of translation. Words and usages no longer familiar are replaced. While Rahlfs' text, supplemented from other sources where necessary, is the basis of the translation, the editors have felt free to resort to other texts and versions, and in particular they have scrutinized all the papyri which contain Apocrypha texts. Of their conjectural emendations some are in Rahlfs' text, e.g., I Macc. vi. 37, while others are independent introductions, e.g., I Esdras iv. 44. Sometimes an alternative interpretation might have been given, e.g., at I Macc. vi. 34 the view that the elephants were not only shown the ' juice of the grapes ' but were given it to drink. This volume is comparable to the earlier in careful scholarship and felicitous diction, and all who have shared in the production of the R.S.V. are to be congratulated on the completion of a notable addition to Bible translations. W.D.McH.

AUGÉ, R. : *Ezequiel* (La Bíblia versió dels textos originals i comentari pels monjos de Montserrat, XV-I). 1955. Pp. 430. (Monastery of Montserrat, Barcelona.)

It is perhaps a defect in the presentation of these excellent volumes of the great Montserrat Bible that nowhere is any indication given regarding the progress of the version and the titles of the volumes already published. (For the volume containing Joshua, Judges, and Ruth, cf. *Book List*, 1955, p. 39.) There is, at any rate, no change discernible in the magnificent production of the volumes, which with their large and clear type, handsome binding, and scholarly editing are among the best of their kind. They may be described as semi-popular in character, resembling in some degree the French volumes in Pirot's edition of *La Sainte Bible*.

This volume on Ezekiel has the advantage of a fairly ample preface in which the editor has found room for a full summary of the contents, a page or two on Ezekiel's physical condition, which decides that he was not a cataleptic, and a synopsis of recent views on the authorship, which takes account of the recent work by G. Fohrer, C. G. Howie, and C. J. Mullo Weir. J.M.T.B.

AUGÉ, R. : *Profetes Menors* (La Bíblia versió dels textos originals i comentari pels monjos de Montserrat, XVI). 1957. Pp. 538. (Monestir de Montserrat, Barcelona.)

This, the latest volume of the Montserrat Bible, is an excellent study of the Minor Prophets and in every way worthy of the series to which it belongs. As in all the volumes the Catalan version is based on the Hebrew text, which is corrected in what appears to be a prudent and sensible manner. The introductions, though short, manage to convey a good deal of information, e.g., on the critical approach to the book of Jonah and the arguments for regarding it as a didactic work (Cf. pages 269-272). One of the earlier commentaries that have been used in the preparation of this book is A. Van Hoonacker's *Les Douze Petits Prophètes*, still a standard work after just half-a-century since its publication. A comparison with Augé's book shows that the earlier work is still pre-eminent, though the present volume will doubtless appeal to a wider circle of readers. J.M.T.B.

BEWER, J. A. : *The Prophets in the King James Version with Introduction and Critical Notes*. 1957. Pp. viii + 664. (Eyre & Spottiswoode, London. Price : 42s. 0d.)

This volume includes all the earlier volumes of the late Dr. Bewer's Introduction and Critical Notes to all the Prophets and Daniel. See Book Lists as follows : 1950, p. 35; 1951, pp. 32f.; 1952, p. 27; 1953, p. 32; 1955, p. 30; 1956, pp. 23f. It is handsomely produced in cloth binding. G.H.D.

BRUNO, A. : *Das Buch der Zwölf : Eine rhythmische und textkritische Untersuchung*. 1957. Pp. 234. (Almqvist and Wiksell, Stockholm. Price : Sw. kr. 22.)

This is a further product of Bruno's exercise in reducing the text of the Bible to a rhythmic pattern. Like its predecessors the book consists of a German translation, in verse form, of the Hebrew text as reconstructed by the translator, followed by 38 pages of brief notes indicating the textual changes involved. For those who share Bruno's interest in poetic form this will no doubt prove a useful guide.

[Cf. *Book Lists*, 1954, pp. 45f. ; 1955, pp. 31f. ; 1956, p. 26 ; 1957, p. 29.] L.H.B.

CASSUTO, M. D. (ed. by) : *Sifre Ha-Miqra* (in Hebrew), with a commentary by A. S. Hartom. *Psalms* (4th ed., 1957. Pp. 304). *Proverbs* (2nd ed., 1955. Pp. 106). *Job* (2nd ed., 1955. Pp. 148). (Yavneh Publishing House, Tel. Aviv.)

These are reprints of books noticed in the 1955 *Book List* (pp. 32f.). These commentaries are presumably intended for use in secondary schools in Israel. They have no scholarly pretensions and do not refer the reader to the relevant learned literature. E.U.

FREY, H. : *Das Buch des Werbens Gottes um Seine Kirche : Der Prophet Hosea, übersetzt und ausgelegt* (Die Botschaft des Alten Testaments, 23/II.) 1957. Pp. xvi+318. (Calwer Verlag, Stuttgart. Price : DM. 13.80.)

This is a further volume in the series *Die Botschaft des Alten Testaments*. The author's main aim is a homiletic exposition of the message of the Book of Hosea. The translation is based on a critically edited text for which brief notes are given at the end of the volume. Many of the emendations are attractive but are difficult to find, being subordinated to the author's main purpose. The exposition of the text is suggestive but is elaborate and involved.

Chapter iii. is interpreted as being a sequel to chapter i., but both are regarded as acts of prophetic symbolism, performed deliberately and consciously by the prophet in obedience to the command of God. vi. 6 is taken to mean that God does not reject sacrifices *as such* but only the insincere sacrifices and worship that had become customary.   L.H.B.

GRINTZ, J. M. : *Sefer Yehudith : A Reconstruction of the Original Hebrew Text with Introduction, Commentary, Appendices and Indices* (in Hebrew). 1957. Pp. xii+244+2 maps. (Bialik Institute, Jerusalem.)

The author, making eclectic use of the numerous versions as given in the Brooke-McLean-Thackeray edition of the Septuagint, endeavours to give a full reconstruction of the Book of Judith in its original Hebrew. To achieve this end a careful examination is made of words and expressions of the Septuagint with special reference to their equivalents in the Hebrew Bible and in some of the earlier post-Biblical books. The book, according to the author, was most likely composed about 360 B.C., namely in the Persian Period.

The book comprises an elaborate introduction which deals with the various views propounded to date about the Book of Judith as well as with the historical, geographical and sociological-cultural backgrounds. A chapter is also devoted to the original text and its Greek translation, after which comes the Hebrew text fully vocalized with copious critical and explanatory notes. Various addenda and a fairly extensive bibliography as well as indexes and maps complete this commendable scholarly and well produced work.   M.W.

LARCHER, C. : *Le livre de Job.* 2nd edition. (La Sainte Bible traduite en français sous la direction de l'École Biblique de Jerusalem.) 1957. Pp. 170. (Les Éditions du Cerf, Paris. Price : 11s. 0d.)

The fact that a second edition is called for is evidence of its value (for 1st ed. see *Book List*, 1951, p. 33). The only part of the text which the editor is prepared to recognize as secondary is the group of Elihu speeches. He thinks that the Prologue and Epilogue contain an old story, probably still transmitted orally, but possibly written down, which the author has re-told for his purpose. The chapter on Wisdom (xxviii) he regards as having been written by the author as a kind of marginal note. It is claimed that in xix. 25-27 the author of Job expresses a faith in a momentary resurrection.

Where the translation follows an emendation, the accepted text is given in the upper footnotes. The lower footnotes are brief comments on exegetical problems.   L.H.B.

MICHAELI, F. : *Le livre de la Genèse (Chapitres 1 à 11)*. 1957. Pp. 110. (Delachaux & Niestlé, Neuchâtel & Paris. Price : Sw. frs. 2.75.)

While there can be no doubt that the material in this book is based on sound biblical scholarship, it is so presented that the layman will understand and hear for himself the Word of the Lord. It takes the form of a running commentary, and careful attention is given to difficult passages. Use is made of literary criticism ; parallels with Semitic myths are noted ; but the main purpose, that of instructing the faithful, is kept clearly in view. It includes a brief bibliography of both Catholic and Protestant books. It should be especially valuable for preachers and teachers of upper forms in schools.
A.S.H.

OSCHWALD, P. : *Le livre de Daniel*. 1957. Pp. 82. (Delachaux & Niestlé, Neuchâtel & Paris. Price : Sw. frs. 2.75.)

This presentation of the Book of Daniel has been prepared for those who have no special knowledge of the language of the Bible, to give simple exposition and to safeguard against unedifying speculation. Daniel is related to the time of Antiochus Epiphanes, but the editor has made use of ancient traditions. Its aim is to strengthen the faithful by its insistence on the faithfulness and omnipotence of God. Brief comments are given on the text of each chapter, and these are followed by reflections, mainly of a homiletical character. A.S.H.

TUR-SINAI, N. H. : *The Book of Job : a New Commentary*. 1957. Pp. lxxvi+588. (Kiryath Sepher, Jerusalem.)

This is more than a translation of Professor Tur-Sinai's earlier commentaries on Job in German and Hebrew, and it contains many new suggestions. There are innumerable ingenious and sometimes brilliant suggestions on individual texts, and the author identifies a large number of new words or new meanings to bring new light to the many difficult texts in Job. On the broader questions Professor Tur-Sinai thinks the book was composed in Aramaic and translated, sometimes not very skilfully, into Hebrew. The Elihu speeches, however, he believes to have been first composed in Hebrew by a later hand, and he finds some kinship between these speeches and the book of Ezekiel. The debate between Job and his friends is held to be older than the Prologue and Epilogue, which are thought to have replaced a lost older setting.   H.H.R.

UBACH, B. : *1 i II Dels Reis* (La Bíblia versió dels textos originals i comentari pels monjos de Montserrat, VI.) 1957. Pp. 366. (Monastery of Montserrat, Barcelona.)

This volume on I-II Kings has, it must be said, a less adequate preface than that on Ezekiel in the same series (see above, p 19). More stress might well have been laid on the characteristics in style and manner that are ably presented by C. F. Burney in his *Notes on the Hebrew Text of the Books of Kings*. The treatment of the chronology is also somewhat abbreviated. The table on p. 22 is taken from the volume by S. Garofalo in the Italian series *La Sacra Bibbia* (cf. *Book List*, 1953, p. 36).
                                                          J.M.T.B.

VAWTER, B. : *A Path Through Genesis*. 1957. Pp. x+308+12 illustrations+2 maps. (Sheed & Ward, London. Price : 18s. 0d.)

Fr. Vawter, an Associate Member, offers us a popular but careful commentary on the Book of Genesis in the form of a guide to the book. Critical and other problems are discussed in the Introduction. For the author the Book of Genesis doubtless contains errors but it teaches none. The main commentary which is a paragraph by paragraph commentary deals with Genesis in three sections containing fifteen chapters each with its appropriate title. The commentary makes use of the latest information from various sources, shows good judgement and makes a good attempt to show how reasonable and attractive the first book of the Bible can be to the modern reader.   G.H.D.

WAMBACQ, B. N. : *Jeremias, Klaagliederen/Baruch, Brief van Jeremias uit de grondtekst vertaald en uitgelegd* (De Boeken van het Oude Testament). 1957. Pp. 394. (Romen & Zonen, Roermond en Maaseik. Price : 38s. 9d.)

This is Volume X of the Dutch series, De Boeken van het Oude Testament, which is appearing under the general editorship of van den Born, Grossouw and van der Ploeg. The greater part of the volume is naturally devoted to Jeremiah, and the major problems of the book are thoroughly investigated, while the conclusions reached are generally conservative.

Jeremiah's earlier ministry was directed mainly to the inhabitants of what had been the northern kingdom, in an
attempt to bring them back to Yahweh. This helps to explain
why Josiah turned for counsel to Huldah and not to Jeremiah
in 621 B.C. It is the northerners who are addressed in x. 1-3a,
10, where Jeremiah warns them not be influenced by the
customs of the non-Israelite settlers who live among them ;
verses 3b-4a (and possibly 4b-5) were added later, by way of
impressing the same lesson on the people of Judah when they
were deported to Babylonia. Wambacq's understanding of
Jer. vii. 22 is indicated by his translation : ' I did not speak
to your fathers or command them (only) concerning burnt
offerings and sacrifices.' There is a discussion of the chronology
of the book in the light of the recently-published *Chronicles of
Chaldaean Kings* : Zedekiah's first year is reckoned as
beginning in Nisan 597 and the storming of Jerusalem is
dated in August, 587. The final publication of the book
by an ' inspired redactor ' cannot be earlier than the anti-
Babylonian oracles of chapters l.-li., which are dated shortly
before 539 B.C.

Lamentations belongs to the exilic period ; Baruch (which
consists of three independent works) was composed shortly
after 63 B.C. ; the Epistle of Jeremiah (Baruch vi.) is dated
in the reign of Artaxerxes II (404-358).   F.F.B.

WOLFF, H. W. : *Dodekapropheton : Hosea*, Lief, 2. (Biblischer Kom-
     mentar : Altes Testament, XIV, 2.) 1957. Pp. 81-160. (Verlag
     der Buchhandlung des Erziehungsvereins, Neukirchen. Price :
     DM. 7.)

The first instalment of this commentary on Hosea was noticed
in the *Book List* for 1957 (p. 35). A new German translation,
section by section, is followed by notes on the text and by a
commentary. The present instalment covers the central part
of the book, from iii. 1 to vii. 16 (the commentary reaches as
far as vii. 9). The section v. 8—vii. 16 is dated in 733 B.C.,
when Ephraim was ' oppressed, crushed in judgment ' (v.
11) by Tiglath-pileser because of the ' vanity ' (reading *shaw*'
for *saw* in v. 11b) of the alliance with Rezon. Tiglath-pileser
is the ' great king ' (dividing the words *malki rab*, v. 13),
whom they tried to placate by assassinating Pekah and re-
placing him by Hoshea. The formula of repentance in vi. 1-3
is thought to contain a mythological motif ; the cohortative
nirdephah (vi. 3) suggests ' the seeking of the absent or sleeping
god, as in 1 Kings xviii. 27 '—an unconvincing comparison.
When Wolff says that the N.T. emphasis on resurrection
on the third day (cf. 1 Cor. xv. 4) can scarcely refer back to any
other O.T. passage than Hos. vi. 2, he does not take sufficient
account of the relevance of Lev. xxiii. 9ff. to a chapter where
the theme of first fruits and harvest is so prominent as in 1
Cor. xv. In vii. 5 ' our king ' is emended to ' their king ' ;
a certain aloofness is implied. In vii. 16 ' they return, but not
(to) ' Al ' is emended to ' they return, but not to me (*'elai* or
'adai).'   F.F.B.

ZIMMERLI, W. : *Ezechiel*, Lief. 4. (Biblischer Kommentar: Altes Testament, XIII, 4.) 1957. Pp. 241-320. (Verlag der Buchhandlung des Erziehungsvereins, Neukirchen, Kr. Moers. Price : DM. 7.00, or by subscription DM. 5.85.)

For earlier parts of this commentary, see *Book List*, 1956, p. 35 ; 1957, p. 36. The present Lieferung completes the exposition of viii. 1—xl. 25 and continues as far as xiv. 14, thus including passages which have been used to support the theory that part of Ezekiel's prophetic ministry was carried out in Jerusalem. But Zimmerli argues strongly that, e.g., xii. 1-16 described acts performed in Exile. The fulness and excellence of treatment which marked the earlier parts are maintained throughout this Lieferung.   G.W.A.

LITERARY CRITICISM AND INTRODUCTION (INCLUDING HISTORY OF INTERPRETATION, CANON, AND SPECIAL STUDIES)

*ANDERSON, B. W. : *Understanding the Old Testament*. 1957. Pp. xxiv+552. (Prentice Hall, Englewood Cliffs, N.J. Price : 54s. 0d.)

This is an excellent example of the best kind of popularization. It offers a comprehensive introduction to the Old Testament, going beyond the limits of literary introduction to include the history and religion of Israel ; and running through the whole work there is a vein of theological interpretation. Arrangement and presentation are clear and stimulating. The book is profusely illustrated ; and there are some seventeen maps (mostly taken from the *Westminster Historical Atlas to the Bible* 2) and ten chronological charts. Appropriate portions of the Old Testament and Apocrypha are suggested for study together with each chapter of the book. There are references throughout to other modern works, and a useful classified bibliography at the end.   G.W.A.

BONNES, J.-P. : *David et les Psaumes* (Maîtres spirituels, 13). 1957. Pp. 192, with ills. and maps. (Éditions du Seuil, Paris. Price : Fr. 390.)

The first part of this book gives a brief sketch of the history of Israel up to the New Testament period, followed by an account of the life and achievement of David and a psychological estimate of his character. A connecting chapter, entitled ' Du juste des Psaumes à la messianité de Jésus ', leads on to the second main part, which is a study of representative Psalms. In a brief concluding section the author comments on the meaning of the Psalms for our time. The entire treatment is independent and stimulating, and enriched by references to modern literature. The majority of the illustrations are taken from medieval Psalters and Bibles.   G.W.A.

COPPENS, J. : *Moise et les Origines du Pentateuque selon M. Cazelles*
(Analecta Lovaniensia Biblica et Orientalia, Ser. II, fasc. 50.)
1956. Pp. 6 (Publications Universitaires de Louvain and Desclée
de Brouwer, Bruges. Price : B. fr. 10.)

Professor Coppens here replies to Professor Cazelles' observations in *Biblica* xxxv., the main point at issue being whether,
and how far, the latter approaches the Wellhausen position.
G.W.A.

COPPENS, J. : *La portée messianique de Psaume CX.* (Analecta Lov-
aniensia Biblica et Orientalia, Ser. III, fasc. 1.) 1955. Pp. 24.
(Publications Universitaires de Louvain and Desclée de Brouwer,
Bruges. Price : B. fr. 30.)

This is a careful study of a difficult psalm. The vexed questions
concerning the text are carefully examined. The theme is
taken to be the sacred character and functions of the king.
A pre-exilic date is supported by linquistic and other parallels
in Ugaritic literature. The possible Messianic reference is
cautiously and, with some qualification, accepted. G.W.A.

FILSON, F. V. : *Which Books Belong in the Bible? A Study of the Canon.*
1957. Pp. 174. (Westminster Press, Philadelphia. Price : $3.00.)

This is not primarily a historical study of the Canon (though
it contains much relevant historical data), but a consideration
of the questions : ' Does the Church need a Bible? Does the
Bible we have contain exactly the right books? ' Of these
questions it provides an admirably lucid discussion. The
author argues strongly for the place of the Old Testament in
the Christian Bible, but against the canonical status of the
Apocrypha, while recognizing fully the historical value of
the latter. He also discusses the canon of the New Testament
and the relation between Scripture and tradition. The book
offers much useful guidance on the interpretation of the
Bible ; and even those who (unlike the reviewer) dissent from
the author's main conclusions, will be grateful for the practical
way in which he presents the questions at issue. G.W.A.

FOHRER, G. : *Elia* (Abhandlungen zur Theologie des Alten und Neuen
Testaments, 31). 1957. Pp. 96. (Zwingli-Verlag, Zürich. Price :
DM. 12.00.)

In attempting to isolate a historical kernel in the Elijah
narrative Fohrer distinguishes two kinds of stories, those that
are based on historical fact (*Erzählungen*, e.g., the call of
Elisha) and those that are legendary (*Anekdoten*, e.g., the
ravens at the brook Cherith). He finds six of each kind. Even
the former, he maintains, have been embellished with non-
historical accretions. He rightly maintains that Elijah's
significance lies in his theological position and that he stands
midway between Moses, with whom there is much in common,
and the later individual prophets for whom he paved the way.
The final chapter is devoted to the tradition of Elijah as
forerunner.   L.H.B.

GALBIATI, E. : *La Struttura letteraria dell' Esodo: contributo allo studio dei criteri stilistici dell' A.T. e della composizione del Pentateuco.* (Schrinium theologicum, Vol. III.) 1956. Pp. 320+indexes. (Edizioni Paoline, Alba. Price : Lire 1500.)

This very careful study is concerned with the literary form of the narratives in the book of Exodus. The first part is devoted to the artistic canons of ancient oriental narrative prose. After some pages of bibliographical analysis of earlier works on the subject (Olrik, Gunkel, Jakob), the author establishes the stylistic canons which appear to govern prose works in the second millennium B.C. He discerns fifteen, e.g., dichotomy and bipartitition ; complementary repetition ; symmetry ; parallel series ; regression ; concentric symmetry. These canons are established, not only by the study of the Biblical texts but equally from examples from Egypt, the Hittites, and elsewhere. The author then devotes 150 pages to the narrative portions of the Exodus and endeavours to determine the structure of each section, emphasizing the difficulties and outlining a solution reached by the application of the canons previously established. He then examines the non-narrative sections and concludes that the literary structure of Exodus resembles the Hittite treaties. Even those who, like the reviewer, cannot accept the author's conclusions, will be impressed by the power of analysis which the book reveals.

H.C.

GESE, H. : *Der Verfassungsentwurf des Ezechiel (Kap. 40-48) traditionsgeschichtlich untersucht.* (Beiträge zur historischen Theologie.) 1957. Pp. viii+192. (J. C. B. Mohr, Tübingen. Price : DM. 23.80.)

This book is a detailed, well-documented study which subjects Ezekiel xl.-xlviii. to a thorough textual examination and literary analysis in order to substantiate the thesis that these chapters do not come from one time or from one author but have a composite origin. Evidence is found of parallel passages, of expansion of material by later hands and of dependence of some passages upon others. Chapters xl.-xlii. are regarded as basic but there are relevant, later sections, within chapters xliii.-xlviii. Chapters xliii.-xlvi. show considerable confusion of presentation, disparate passages being brought together and correlated ones, even doublets, separated. The author specifies as of great importance the sections which may be named the *nāsî* stratum, those which confine priestly status to the Zadokites and degrade the other priests to subsidiary rank and those which give the plans for the division of the land and are related to the *nāsî* stratum. Some valuable excursuses are added in an appendix. J.M.

KAUFMANN, Y. : *The Biblical Account of the Conquest of Palestine,* trans. by M. Dagut. 1957. Pp. viii+98. (Oxford University Press : Magnes Press, Jerusalem. Price : 8s. 0d.)

This book is critical of the views of Noth and Alt concerning the tribal boundaries and the city lists of the Book of Joshua, and seeks to refute the theory that they reflect the realities of the historical situation of a later epoch. That, it is said, is to confuse ethnographic with political and administrative boundaries. The Book of Joshua contains a utopian scheme of land distribution among the tribes, not a post-conquest rationalization. It is emphasised that the land of Canaan was at first conceived of as lying entirely west of the Jordan, that the Israelites conquered it from their base at Gilgal by the Jordan, destroying utterly the Canaanites, and that only after that had been accomplished was the land distributed for tribal occupation. The absence from the record in Joshua of reference to the Philistines is interpreted as another piece of evidence that the record is an ancient one which goes back to the early period of the Judges. The curious remark is made that the later Judahite editor, who made no alterations in the text of the record, was not interested in the detailed city lists of Ephraim and Judah, so that the motive for their omission ' was neither political nor religious, but, if one may say so, publisher-scribe's convenience.' J.M.

MANLEY, G. T. : *The Book of the Law. Studies in the Date of Deuteronomy.* 1957. Pp. 192. (Tyndale Press, London. Price : 12s. 6d.)

By the use of the principles of literary and historical criticism the author seeks to disprove the Graf.Wellhausen hypothesis of the date of Deuteronomy. Mosaic authorship, in the literary sense of the term, is claimed for the Code ; a Mosaic basis is claimed for the narrative material, but its authorship is assigned to one of the Settlement period. The chapter on Deuteronomy and the Prophets contains a good deal of special pleading, and is more dependent on an evolutionary hypothesis than the author appears to recognise. His use of quotations from other scholars is sometimes more clever than just. The examination of particular passages, even if the conclusions are not always convincing, deserves careful consideration. The author acknowledges his debt to authors with views differing from his own. A.S.H.

*PFEIFFER, R. H. : *The Books of the Old Testament.* 1957. Pp. xii+ 336. (Harper, New York and A. & C. Black, London. Price : 20s. 0d.)

This is an abridged and more popularly presented version of the author's *Introduction to the Old Testament,* 1941 (*Book List,* 1946, pp. 28f.), and as such makes more readily available to the Training College student and Scripture specialist in schools the material in the larger work. It is a most able and attractive presentation, but it may raise the question whether so individual a presentation (especially of the Pentateuch and the Psalter) should not carry with it a warning that there are other views. The book concludes with a concise chronological table, but the ascription of Psalms cx. and ii. to the 2nd century B.C. may cause confusion. A.S.H.

RINGGREN, H. : *Psaltarens fromhet.* 1957. Pp. 188. (Svenska Kyrkans Diakonistyrelses Bokförlag. Price : Sw. kr. 11.)

An excellent general account of the piety which the Psalter represents. The main developments in modern study of the Psalms are well outlined in an introductory section. Then nine chapters are devoted to the cult, the piety of the congregation, theocentric piety, the godly and the ungodly, piety and the conception of God, lament and confession, thanksgiving and praise, myth and history, the piety of the Law and the Messianic hope. A concluding section touches briefly on the psalmody of Israel's neighbours. The level of the book is about half way between a severely technical and a purely popular treatment. As always, Dr. Ringgren writes with clarity and moderation. He illustrates his exposition by frequent citation of the Biblical text. G.W.A.

ROBERT, A. and FEUILLET, A. : *Introduction à la Bible.* Vol. I, *Introduction générale : Ancien Testament.* 1957. Pp. xxviii+880+9 maps. (Desclée & Cie, Tournai. Price : £1 18s. 6d., cloth bound.)

The present work, which may well rank as the best of all existing French introductions by Catholic authors, is the work of ten writers, among whom may be mentioned P. Auvray, H. Cazelles, A. Gelin, and H. Lusseau. The Bishop of Strasbourg, Mgr. Jean Weber, says in his preface that it compares favourably with many of the *compendia* that were wont to summarize " brièvement, plus ou moins heureusement, le résultat des études bibliques . . . "

About a quarter of the book is taken up with a general introduction to the Bible, which deals in three sections with the inspiration and canonicity of the books of Scripture, with textual, literary and historical criticism, and with the Catholic interpretation of the books.

In the remaining three-quarters of this accomplished work there is a useful preliminary section on " Le cadre historique de la Bible " and there is a final chapter, the title of which recalls that of Professor Rowley's pocket edition on *The Growth of the Old Testament.* Among the special introductions to the individual books or groups of books quite the most striking is Cazelles' study of Pentateuchal criticism in just over a hundred pages, opening with a chapter on the literary form of the books, passing to a brief survey of criticism throughout the centuries, and continuing with chapters on the bearing of archaeological research on the literary evidence, and on the *formgeschichtliche Schule.* The final chapter on the contents and theology of the Pentateuch discusses the main characteristics of the four chief sources. The remaining books of the Bible are competently handled, there are some good illustrations and up-to-date bibliographies, and a separate sheet of maps will be of special service to those who have not access to one of the larger atlases. There are two indices, one of biblical references, and the other a fairly ample list of topics and proper names. One may look forward with pleasure to the appearance of the companion volume on the New Testament writings. J.M.T.B.

ROBINSON, P. S. : *A Layman's Guide to the Old Testament*. 1957. Pp. x+134. (S.P.C.K., London. Price : 4s. 6d.)

This is an excellent little book, intended to introduce the O.T. to intelligent adults, whose ignorance in this sphere often contrasts so startlingly with their attainments in other fields. The author believes that the need is felt, and that O.T. studies have reached a point which makes the moment ripe for such a popularisation. The discipline of selecting and interpreting in such a work is very great and no doubt scholarly readers will find disputable points of detail or emphasis. But the book is not only vividly but responsibly written and serves to show how great a measure of agreement there is indeed to-day on essentials. We wish the book a wide and interested public.
M.Bu.

SCHILLING, O. : *Das Alte Testament heute*. 1957. Pp. 68+3 plates. (Matthias-Grünewald-Verlag, Mainz. Price : DM. 3.20.)

For those with no previous knowledge, and about to begin Old Testament studies, this pamphlet provides a good introduction. After an outline of the contents of the (Vulgate) Old Testament canon, and a note on the text, a chapter is devoted to the Old Testament and Modern Knowledge. Finally the relation of the Old Testament to Christ is briefly presented. At the end of the pamphlet are a chronological table, and four photographs to illustrate the history of writing.
A.S.H.

SIMPSON, C. A. : *Composition of the Book of Judges*. 1957. Pp. x+198. (Blackwell, Oxford. Price : 42s. 0d.)

The literary analysis which Professor Simpson applied to the Hexateuch in his *The Early Traditions of Israel* he now applies to the Book of Judges and finds support in it for his theory of an original document J1 which was incorporated into, and expanded by, another and later document J2, which itself received later elaboration before it was conflated with E and received deuteronomic and post-deuteronomic editorial supplements. In xix.-xxi. he finds also material from another document which he terms C. The literary analysis is carried out with admirable thoroughness and in meticulous detail. When factual inconsistencies, stylistic differences or other scriptural passages provide clues, the definition of the source material may claim support ; but often such criteria are lacking and subjective judgment enters in. Sometimes when it is the logical inconsistency of a narrative which is used as the pointer to the presence of material from different sources, one cannot refrain from questioning the suitability of the strict application of such a category. But since Professor Simpson hopes to publish soon a similar literary analysis of the Books of Samuel and I Kings i.-xiii., fairness demands that a full evaluation of his methods should be delayed until this has appeared. To the end of the present book he appends a reply to Eissfeldt's criticisms of his *The Early Traditions of Israel*.
J.M.

WEISER, A. : *Einleitung in das Alte Testament,* 4th revised and enlarged edition. 1957. Pp. 390. (Vandenhoeck & Ruprecht, Göttingen. Price : 33s. 6d.)

The second edition of this excellent introduction was reviewed in the *Book List* for 1950, p. 46 (for the first edition, see *Book List,* 1946, p. 30.) No changes were made in the third edition. This fourth edition, however, has been revised throughout ; and the bibliographies have been brought up-to-date. The most important new feature is the survey (some 20 pages) of the Qumran material, which forms an appropriate sequel to the sections on the Apocrypha and Pseudepigrapha.

G.W.A.

*WRIGHT, G. E. and FULLER, R. H. : *The Book of the Acts of God.* 1957. Pp. 372. (Doubleday, Garden City, N.Y. Price : $4.95.)

This is a brief introduction to the Old and New Testaments written for the layman, and it directs the reader's attention throughout to the meaning of the Bible as a whole, of which the part contributed by Professor Wright and the section on the intertestamental period from Professor Fuller's pen alone concern us here. The books of the Old Testament are dealt with in the order : Tetrateuch, Deuteronomic History, Chronicler's History, Prophets, Psalms, Wisdom Literature. There is little attention to literary analysis, or the technical side of Old Testament study generally, since the purpose of the author is rather to enable the modern general reader to understand what the significance of the Bible is to him. The literature is interpreted as arising from a background of history, but less as recording history than as mediating a message, for the apprehension of which faith is as important as fact. The intertestamental period is dealt with before the New Testament is reached, and here the Dead Sea Scrolls and the community from which they came have attention. It is not quite clear why the Testament (*sic*) of the Twelve Patriarchs and 1 Enoch are dealt with, but not Jubilees or certain other inter-testamental books. The work is marked by many fine insights, and it will excellently serve those for whom it is written.

H.H.R.

LAW, RELIGION, AND THEOLOGY

ALBRIGHT, W. F. : *From the Stone Age to Christianity.* 2nd edition with a new Introduction. 1957. Pp. 432. (Johns Hopkins Press, Baltimore. Price : 40s. 0d.)

This new edition of Professor Albright's well-known work is augmented by an introduction (23 pp.) in which he surveys recent developments (including the Qumran material) in the vast field which the book covers. He records no change in his own main positions. The original edition was reviewed in the *Book List* for 1946 (p. 38). No further comment is required except to express gratification that so stimulating a work continues to be so widely used.

G.W.A.

DE BOER, P. A. H. : *De Zoon van God in het Oude Testament* (Dies-College, 1 Februari, 1958.) (Leidse Voordrachten 29.) 1958. Pp. 24. (Universitaire Pers, Leiden. Price : Fl. 1.10.)

In this lecture Professor de Boer examines the Old Testament concept ' son of God ' under four headings : (1) as used of divine beings (as in Genesis vi. 2) ; (2) as a title of the king of Israel (as in Psalm ii. 7) ; (3) as applied to the people of Israel (e.g., Exodus iv. 22) ; (4) as implied in theophoric names such as Joab, Abijah. He then considers the use of the title in the New Testament, and concludes that while in form it is derived from the Old Testament, in content·it is derived rather from the post-canonical apocalyptic literature.

F.F.B.

*CORNFORTH, G. A. E. : *Jeremiah : Studies in the Man and his Mission.* (Manuals of Fellowship. Third Series, No. 9.) 1957. Pp. 30. (Epworth Press, London. Price : 1s. 6d.)

This little work is an introduction to Jeremiah admirably designed for Bible study circles. There are six brief chapters— (1) Jeremiah : The Making of the Man ; (2) The World of Jeremiah ; (3) Jeremiah and the Meaning of Religion ; (4) Teaching about God ; (5) Jeremiah the Man ; (6) Jeremiah and the New Testament—and to each is appended a set of six to ten questions. Teachers of Scripture in school should also find it useful. F.F.B.

DANIÉLOU, J. : *Holy Pagans of the Old Testament,* translated by Felix Faber. 1957. Pp. 144. (Longmans, Green & Co., London. Price : 10s. 6d.)

This small work was noticed in the *Book List* for last year, when it appeared in its French original. It is only necessary to add that this English edition bears every mark of a good translation, made by a writer whose *nom de guerre* may itself be easily translated. J.M.T.B.

EICHRODT, W. : *Theologie des Alten Testaments.* Teil I, *Gott und Volk.* 5. Auflage. 1957. Pp. xii+362. (Ehrenfried Klotz Verlag in Stuttgart, Vandenhoeck & Ruprecht in Göttingen. Price : 26s. 0d.)

A new edition of Eichrodt's great Theology of the Old Testament is most warmly to be welcomed and it is good news to know that an English translation is in preparation. In connection with this first volume of the new edition it should be noted that the Gothic type of previous editions has been abandoned but that the general plan of the book remains unaltered. Apart from minor changes, the process of bringing the book up to date has been confined to the introduction of notes in which the author's views on certain topics which have attracted particular attention of recent years are given, e.g., on the discussions concerning the Kingship of Yahweh (Mowinckel, Engnell, Johnson, etc.) and the cult-prophets. Professor Eichrodt holds to his refusal to turn Old Testament Theology into a normative science and reasserts his belief that the subject must be treated historically and that the idea of the covenant is central. He also defines his position with reference to the view of von Rad and G. E. Wright, that Old Testament Theology is essentially based on the recital of the ' Acts of God ' in the Old Israelite cult which developed into the *Heilsgeschichte*. While recognising the value of this protest against the imposition of the categories of Dogmatic Theology on the Old Testament, Professor Eichrodt warns against the danger of undue emphasis on events and (in van Rad's case) on the application to them of the method of typology, and argues that facts can become myth if they are not linked with the inward event when the human spirit is enabled by God to bear witness and make response to the divine activity.

N.W.P.

FOHRER, G. : *Messiasfrage und Bibelverständnis* (Sammlung gemein-verständlicher Vortrage und Schriften aus dem Gebiet der Theologie und Religionsgeschichte, 213/214). 1957. Pp. 48. (J. C. B. Mohr, Tübingen. Price : DM. 3.60.)

This short study falls into two parts. In the first the author discusses the traditional Christian view of Messianic prophecy, examines briefly the interpretation of the main passages to which Messianic significance has been attributed, and sketches the history of the idea in the Biblical period. In the second part he tackles the problem of the unity of Scripture discarding the Messianic idea as an effective link between the Testaments. For this he looks to the prophetic faith, originating with Moses. In the Old Testament we find ' das Ineinander von Kerygma und Theologie '. The central and uniting theme of both Testaments he takes to be ' die Gottesherrschaft '.

G.W.A.

HANSON, A. T. : *The Wrath of the Lamb*. 1957. Pp. x + 250. (S.P.C.K., London. Price : 25s. 0d.)

The main purpose of this book is to do justice to the New Testament conception of the Wrath of God which finds its deepest expression in the Apocalypse. Since a continuity between this and the Old Testament conception is recognized, two chapters are devoted to the Wrath in the Old Testament and a third to the Inter-Testamental period. It is argued that in the earliest passages, the Wrath is neither rationalized nor moralized ; it is moralized in Deuteronomy and presented in Hosea as a strong personal reaction to sin. The most profound interpretation is to be found in Isa. lxiii. 7-lxiv. 12, where sin is both consequence and occasion of the Divine Wrath. Attempts are made, with imperfect success, by the Old Testament writers to reconcile the mercy and the wrath of God. The later writings show an impersonalizing tendency, which, with a growing eschatological presentation, prepares the way for the New Testament conception. The Old Testa-ment material must be regarded as a sketch rather than an adequate study of the subject, and the author is not always happy in his use of Old Testament terminology. A.S.H.

HEINISCH, P. : *Christus, der Erlöser im Alten Testament.* 1955. Pp. 456. (Verlag Styria, Graz. Price : S. 95.40.)

A comprehensive survey of the Messianic passages in the Old Testament, in which are included those which prophesy salvation even if they do not mention an individual Messiah. After a preliminary sketch of prediction and divination among other ancient peoples, the author discusses (a) Old Testament passages from the period before the Canonical Prophets (e.g., Genesis iii. 14, 15 ; ix. 24-27 ; Numbers xxiv. 15-19 ; Deuteronomy xviii. 15-18 ; 2 Samuel vii. 16 ; Psalms ii. ; cx. ; xxii. ; xvi.) ; (b) the earlier Canonical Prophets and Psalms xlv. and lxxii. ; (c) the Exilic Prophets ; (d) post-exilic passages. This is rounded off by a summary sketch of the intertestamental literature. Three chapters are then devoted to (a) prophecy and fulfilment ; (b) typological interpretation ; (c) the Mother of the Saviour. A brief characterization of the Biblical conception of the Messiah is followed by an outline of expectation of a deliverer in ancient oriental religions (among which, rather curiously, Vergil finds a place). Thus the work covers an extensive field, and does so with much learning. But the reviewer finds it difficult to accept the kind of Christological interpretation here advanced.

G.W.A.

HEMPEL, J. : *Das Bild in Bibel und Gottesdienst.* (Sammlung gemeinverständlicher Vorträge und Schriften aus dem Gebiet der Theologie und Religionsgeschichte, 212.) 1957. Pp. 36. (J.C.B. Mohr, Tübingen. Price : DM. 1.90, or by subscription, DM. 1.70.)

This short but attractive monograph reflects current interest in Christianity and symbolism. The study is primarily a Biblical one, for the author's aim is to provide material for discussing the presentation of religious ideas in pictorial fashion as this may affect Christian worship ; and he has in mind the part which may be played by the eye as well as the ear. The objection to the use of images in the worship of ancient Israel receives due attention, and corresponding stress is laid upon the way in which religious ideas came to be expressed for the most part in pictorial language ; but, while the author recognizes in passing the importance of prophetic symbolism, the reviewer would have liked to see more attention being paid to the realism of cultic drama in this connexion.

A.R.J.

HERKLOTS, H. G. G. : *The Ten Commandments and Modern Man.* 1958. Pp. viii+190. (Ernest Benn, London. Price : 10s. 6d.)

This is Christian Homiletics at a high level. Starting from the Biblical text, supporting it from the rest of the Bible, illustrating and illuminating it from past and present history, the relevance of the Ten Commandments is, with each in turn, brought home forcibly to the reader. In this expanded and revised form the reviewer enjoyed Canon Herklots' contribution even more than on that other occasion so graciously acknowledged in his preface. D.R.Ap-T.

KOEHLER, L. : *Old Testament Theology*, trans. by A. S. Todd. 1957. Pp. 260. (Lutterworth Press, London. Price : 35s. 0d.)

This is the first, though not the most satisfactory, of the major Old Testament theologies produced in recent years in Europe to appear in English translation. The original German edition was published in 1935 and the present translation has been made from the third revised edition of 1953. It is only necessary to recall the fact that Koehler retains the somewhat old-fashioned division of his material into the three main sections, God, Man, and Judgment and Salvation. Within these, however, the evidence of the Old Testament on a great number of themes is very conveniently grouped. Whether this is the best recipe for an Old Testament Theology is another matter. Perhaps the most serious flaw in Koehler's presentation of the subject is his curious decision to relegate his account of the cult of Israel to the end of the section on Anthropology and to describe it as ' man's expedient for his own redemption '. This is a very grave error in a book which will no doubt be largely used by students. It is unfortunate that the proof-reader has allowed a considerable number of slips in the transcription of Hebrew to escape his eye. N.W.P.

KUHL, C. : *Israels Propheten* (Dalp Taschenbücher, 324). 1956. Pp. 169+6 plates. (Francke Verlag, Berne. Price : 5s. 0d.)

A fine summary of the whole subject, comprehensive and thorough in spite of its short length. Beginning with an outline survey of prophecy in the ancient Nearer East, the book includes an account of the normal prophet and his calling, together with the *Entstehung* of the prophetic literature of the Old Testament. The individual prophets are treated in chronological order, so far as the writer finds this possible. Divergent critical and exegetical views are fairly stated and judiciously weighed, though an author is named only in a single instance ; there are no footnotes. In each case we have the prophet's background and an estimate of his place in religious history ; particularly attractive are the sympathetic studies of Hosea and II Isaiah. The closing chapters, showing how prophecy faded into apocalyptic, are an illuminating piece of work. The six plates at the end of the book are photographs of Michelangelo's pictures in the Sixtine Chapel. T.H.R.

MICHAELI, F. : *L'Ancien Testament et l'église chrétienne d'aujourd'hui*. 1957. Pp. 80. (Delachaux & Niestlé, Neuchâtel & Paris. Price : Sw. frs. 2.75.)

Although written for the younger churches, this booklet will meet a need throughout the Church, and it is good to know that it will be translated into English as well as into other languages. The Old Testament is presented as *Heilsgeschichte*, as Law whereby the sovereign Will of God operates in every domain of life, and as prophecy pointing to the manifestation of the Kingdom ; it finds its fulfilment in Jesus Christ. A restrained use of the typological (but not the allegorical) method is advocated, and some wise guidance is given at the end on reading the Old Testament both for the devotional life and for teaching purposes. It is devout, based on sound scholarship and written in simple and clear language.

A.S.H.

MORALDI, L. : *Espiazione sacrificale e riti espiatori nell' ambiente biblico e nell' Antico Testamento* (Analecta Biblica, 5). 1956. Pp. xxxii+ 304. (Pontifical Biblical Institute, Rome. Price : Lire 3.600, or S. 6.00.)

This is the fifth volume in the series *Analecta Biblica* and is the author's thesis for the doctorate in Scripture. He tells us in the introduction that it is the result of many years' work, and one can readily admire the vast amount of reading that has gone to the making of this book. It is, as the title indicates, a study of expiatory sacrifice and of rites of expiation in the nations surrounding Israel and in the Old Testament itself.

The first part contains a lengthy study, amounting to a quarter of the work, of sacrifice and expiation as they are found among the Assyrians and Babylonians, the Hittites, the Canaanites, and the Egyptians. So far as one can judge, all the best and most recent authorities have been consulted here, as well as older masterpieces such as W. Robertson Smith, *The Religion of the Semites* (unfortunately only used in the edition of 1901) and Lagrange's *Études sur les Religions Sémitiques.*

The second part comprises seven chapters, of which the first deals with sacrifice among the Semites in general and the Hebrews in particular, with sacrificial expiation in the Old Testament, and with the question of human sacrifice. Chapter II is an exegetical study of Leviticus iv. and v. ; chapter III discusses *ḥaṭṭāt* and Chapter IV *'āšām.* Perhaps the fullest study is found in chapter V, dealing with the meaning of *kipper*, summarising all the principal opinions to date, and providing sections on *kipper* as found in books other than Leviticus and Ezekiel, as it occurs in Leviticus and Ezekiel, and as it is rendered by the Septuagint and the Latin Vulgate. The author's conclusion is that, in the Old Testament, the sense is neither to cover nor to propitiate or placate, but " *una obliterazione, un cancellamento di qualche qualite inibitoria, di qualcosa di negativo* " (p. 220, sect. 2). The remaining chapters discuss the significance of blood in sacrifices of expiation, and *semikāh* or the laying-on of the hand. The author-index confuses J. Gray and G. B. Gray.

J.M.T.B.

NOTH, M. : *Amt und Berufung im Alten Testament.* Rede zum antritt des Rektorats der Rheinischen Friedrich Wilhelms-Universität zu Bonn am 9. November 1957 gehalten. 1958. Pp. 34. (Peter Hanstein Verlag, Bonn. Price : DM. 1.80.)

In this Rectoral Address, Professor Noth examines the interplay of the institutional and the inspirational in the priesthood, the monarchy, the administration of justice, and prophecy. He concludes that the distinctively Israelite element is to be sought in the experience of call and of charismatic endowment. Though brief, this masterly study combines in a remarkable way a broad view of the subject with much illuminating detail. It is usefully documented.   G.W.A.

VON RAD, G. : *Theologie des Alten Testaments.* Band I. *Die Theologie der geschichtlichen Überlieferungen Israels.* 1957. Pp. 472. (Chr. Kaiser Verlag, München. Price : 43s. 0d.)

This magnificent book which maintains the interest of the reader from the first page to the last, will be a ' must ' for all Old Testament scholars. In this first volume, which is to be followed by a second dealing with the Prophets, Professor von Rad tackles in a fresh and original way the vexed problem of how most fitly to present Old Testament Theology. Rejecting the time-honoured divisions of the subject borrowed from Dogmatic Theology and even any attempt to systematize the Old Testament material by using its own religious categories, he lays the emphasis throughout on the *Heilsgeschichte* which developed from the cultic proclamation of the *Kerygma* and not on the history of Hebrew piety. The danger of this procedure, of course, is that the *Heilsgeschichte* is not fully rooted in history and may become myth.

In the first main section there is offered a survey of the history of Yahwism and the development of Israel's sacral institutions based on the author's previous writings and those of his master, Alt, and of his colleagues Noth, Rost, Kraus, and others. Attention is drawn to the crises of Israel's history and the theological achievements which these called forth.

In the second and main section of the book von Rad proceeds, after a preliminary discussion of his own view of the nature of Old Testament Theology, to expound the various theologies which the Old Testament contains. In great detail is unfolded the message of the Hexateuch (von Rad does not, with Noth, make the division after the Tetrateuch) with brilliant studies of its components, such as the Primaeval History (Gen. i.-xi.), the Patriarchal Narratives, Deuteronomy and the Priestly writings, followed by a suggestive analysis of the traditions regarding Moses. Of outstanding interest is the section dealing with the Davidic monarchy and the remarkable literature to which it gave the impulse (especially the succession history and the royal psalms), the story of the Judges and of Saul which led up to it and the two theological histories which traced its fortunes, those of the Deuteronomist and the Chronicler. It should be noted that, in opposition to certain present tendencies, von Rad insists on the non-mythological realism with which the king is described and his fortunes recounted in the Biblical narratives. Perhaps too great an opposition is suggested between the Covenant at Horeb and the Covenant with David ; behind David was the amphictyonic authority which he took over.

The concluding sub-section is devoted to the answer of Israel to the *Heilsgeschichte*. The Psalms are dealt with from this point of view. There follows an examination of the Hebrew Conception of " righteousness ", and of the way in which Israel reacted to the trials which beset human life (the book of Job comes in here) and a treatment of the Wisdom literature which shows how it is related to Israel's cult and *Heilsgeschichte*, discusses the empirical, non-logical approach to life characteristic of Israel and leads up to the theological conception of Wisdom in Proverbs i.-ix. and the scepticism of Koheleth.

It is remarkable that there is no trace throughout the book of the typology which the author advocated some years ago.
N.W.P.

Reich Gottes nach den Urkunden der Heiligen Schrift. 1957. Pp. 364 + 4 maps. (Kösel Verlag, Munich. Price : DM. 14.80.)

This beautifully produced book is an anthology of Scripture chosen to set forth the master theme of the Kingdom of God. The anthology achieves its purpose, and short notes are interpolated to explain the gaps and to maintain the sequence of the story. The appendix includes a chronological table, index of names, list of Books of the Bible, table of contents of selected material and four maps. G.H.D.

REID, J. K. S. : *The Authority of Scripture : A Study of the Reformation and Post-Reformation Understanding of the Bible.* 1957. Pp. 286. (Methuen, London. Price : 25s. 0d.)

This book contains the most adequate treatment which has appeared for a long time of a subject of outstanding importance for the Biblical theologian. Professor Reid handles in judicious fashion the views of Luther and Calvin and makes out a good case for acquitting both of them of adherence to a hard doctrine of verbal inspiration. He shows how this doctrine came to be accepted by the Reformed Orthodoxy which followed. A long chapter is devoted to the Roman view of Scripture according to which its authority is guaranteed by the Church. There is interesting criticism of the view that the authority of Scripture is connected with the inspiration of its authors and it is cogently argued that this would lead to some strange results. There is criticism too of the theory of progressive revelation, and preference is given to the view that the promise of the Old Testament is fulfilled in the New. This masterly book closes with a study of the Theology of the Word (as in Barth and Brunner) and a persuasive argument to the effect that Scripture is to be regarded as witness to the Word of God and that, therefore, the Authority of Scripture is to be found neither in itself—the *litera scripta*—nor in the Church but in God alone. N.W.P.

SANDERS, J. A. : *Suffering as Divine Discipline in the Old Testament and Post-Biblical Judaism.* (Colgate Rochester Divinity School Bulletin, Vol. XXVIII ; Special Issue.) 1955. Pp. vi+136. (Colgate Rochester Divinity School, Rochester, 20, New York.)

This is a detailed lexical study of the use in the Old Testament of the Hebrew root *ysr* and, more briefly and without quotation of the relevant passages, of the root *ykh*. The conclusion drawn is that *mûsār* means a lesson to be learned from (a) personal or national suffering, (b) observing the suffering of others, or (c) obeying God's word as communicated by a prophet or other agent. *Mûsār*, it is taught, ought to be accepted as a call to repentance and regarded as an expression of God's love. So to accept and regard it is to grow in the knowledge of God. The use which is made of the relevant evidence in post-Biblical Judaism is very brief (16 pages).   J.M.

SLOAN, W. W. : *A Survey of the Old Testament.* 1957. Pp. 334. (Abingdon Press, New York. Price : $3.50.)

This book, described as ' a College text for Old Testament Study ', is addressed to the ' honest, serious layman ' and attempts to show how ' God Marches On ' in the thought of the Hebrew people. Interest is focussed on the story element of the Old Testament, with the result that only seven of the forty-two chapters are devoted to the post-exilic period, and three pages to Esther but only two to Job. Three pages are devoted to the Psalms, which are said to have been written mainly for private devotion. The account of the prophets is the most valuable part of the book, and is largely free from the puerilities that mar the earlier narratives. Indeed the attempt to add to the raciness of the style seriously detracts from the merits of the book for the English reader. The books recommended for further reading are almost entirely American. There is no index.   L.A.P.

DE VAUX, R. : *Les institutions de l'Ancien Testament. I. Le nomadisme et ses survivances : institutions familiales : institutions civiles.* 1958. Pp. 352. (Editions du Cerf, Paris. Price : Frs. 990.)

This is a thorough and systematic study of the institutions of Israel, social, civil, administrative, and economic. The work is prefaced by a study of nomadic society, with which the author maintains that Israel had only a relative association. The subject is studied against the background of contemporary Near Eastern societies illustrated by recent archaeology ; but it is primarily an analysis of the Biblical data. The clarity of the writer's thought and the soundness of his views on the many aspects of his subject are obviously the result of long pre-occupation with and teaching of the subject ; and the book is an excellent one both for teachers and students. A striking feature is that Père de Vaux avoids controversy with other scholars in his text and appends an excellent selective bibliography.   J.G.

VRIEZEN, TH.C. : *Geloven en Vertrouwen*. 1957. Pp. 26. (G. F. Callenbach, Nijkerk.)

Professor Vriezen, on leaving his Groningen chair to succeed A. H. Edelkoort, delivered his inaugural lecture as Professor of Old Testament Science and Israelite Religion at Utrecht on May 20, 1957, on the subject of ' Belief and Trust '. The lecture begins with some reference to the change of emphasis in Old Testament studies since the author's student days ; the centre of gravity has shifted from Egypt and Babylonia to Phoenicia, North Mesopotamia and the Judean desert. Moreover, we have the spectacle of a new and vigorous centre of biblical research in Israel, with which Vriezen has first-hand acquaintance. Reference is made to the significant work done in the schools of Cassuto, Kaufmann and Martin Buber. Special attention is paid to the latter's *Two Types of Faith*, and respectful issue is taken with Buber's characterization of Christian faith as primarily intellectual. Belief and trust are not to be divorced from each other, and the distinction which Buber discerns between the two as typical of Old and New Testament faith respectively is to be accounted for rather in terms of the difference between the Hebraic and Hellenistic environments. Basically, however, the two Testaments are at one with regard to faith : Paul links on immediately with the author of Gen. xv. 6 (' possibly a disciple of Isaiah ') in presenting faith as the way to be accounted righteous by God.

F.F.B.

VRIEZEN, TH.C. : *Theologie des Alten Testaments in Grundzügen*. n.d. (1957.) Pp. xii + 344. (Veenman & Zonen, Wageningen, and Erziehungsverein, Neukirchen. Price : DM. 20 ; bound, DM. 23.50 or Fl. 18.25 ; bound Fl. 21.50.)

This outstanding book was originally published in Dutch (see *Book List*, 1950, p. 70). It now appears in a German translation which makes it available to a wider circle of readers, and it will take its place alongside the Old Testament Theologies of Eichrodt and von Rad, which are also to appear in English, as one of the three most valuable modern treatments of the subject.

This German Edition follows the same general plan as the Dutch edition but within this framework the treatment is in many places much fuller and it is enriched by many more references to contemporary literature and current controversies. In particular, Professor Vriezen has put his mind afresh to the consideration of the problem of what an Old Testament Theology should be and has made a most stimulating contribution to its solution. None of the recent Old Testament theologies has dealt so satisfactorily with the relation of the Old Testament to the New Testament and, in consequence, Vriezen's book will be found especially helpful by those who have to expound the Old Testament and make clear its relevance to ourselves. In his treatment Vriezen stands closer to Eichrodt than von Rad but differs from the former in venturing to pass certain value judgments which Eichrodt deliberately prefers not to make within the limits set by an Old Testament theology. N.W.P.

VRIEZEN, Th.C. : *An Outline of Old Testament Theology.* 1958. Pp. VIII+390. (H. Veenman & Sons Wageningen. Price : Fl. 21.50.) (Basil Blackwell, Oxford. Price : 42s. 0d.)

The expected English translation of Professor Vriezen's outstanding work on Old Testament Theology appears just in time for notice in this year's Book List. The English version represents a more complete text of the second Dutch edition than the German does (see review above). It may be a useful guide to prospective readers to be told that, whereas von Rad's Old Testament Theology deals objectively with the various theologies in the Old Testament and whereas Eichrodt's great work is essentially a historical study, Vriezen claims that—*pace* Gabler—an Old Testament Theology ' must work with *theological standards* and must give *its own evaluation of the Old Testament message on the ground of its Christian theological starting-point.*' Vriezen considers that what Gabler was so anxious to protect from dogmatic distortion is now sufficiently covered by the science of the history of Israel's religion and that Old Testament Theology, as a branch of Biblical Theology, shoud serve as a connecting-link between Dogmatics and Historical Theology.

The first 125 pages of the book are devoted to preliminary questions regarding the nature of the Old Testament as the word of God, its spiritual structure and its use by the Church, leading up to discussion of what an Old Testament Theology should be. This is one of the most vital contributions made to the current debate, and it is indispensable for those who wish to be up-to-date in their understanding of how that debate is tending.

The second part of the book deals with the content of Old Testament Theology and is prefaced by a valuable discussion of the nature of knowledge of God in the Old Testament. The subject-matter of the Old Testament is dealt with under the headings : God—Man—the intercourse between God and Man—the intercourse between man and man—God, man and the world in the present and the future. N.W.P.

WALLACE, R. S. : *Elijah and Elisha : Expositions from the Book of Kings.* 1957. Pp. xvi+164. (Oliver & Boyd, Edinburgh. Price : 16s. 0d.)

The eighteen sermons which this book contains are based on the life and work of these two prophets as they appear in the Book of Kings, and furnish an example of sound and vigorous expository preaching. The choice of New Testament parallels is good ; no attempt is made to allegorize. The historical situation is clearly presented and the application to the twentieth century situation is unforced and convincing. The book has a well-deserved commendation by Prof. J. Barr. A.S.H.

WIÉNER, C. : *Recherches sur l'amour pour Dieu dans l'Ancien Testament. Étude d'une racine.* 1957. Pp. 88. (Letouzey et Ané, Paris. Price : Fr. 500.)

In presenting this study of the root *'hb* in the old Testament, the author rightly points out that his theme, which is that of love *towards* God, is one on which, surprisingly enough, comparatively little work has been done. Of the 89 passages examined, 52 have direct reference to Yahweh, while the remaining 37 are concerned with what the author calls ' réalités divines ', i.e., the Law, the Temple, Salvation, and the like. The author accepts the generally agreed findings of modern literary criticism in arranging his passages in chronological order ; but, for the reviewer, his conclusions seem occasionally to be governed too much by the now familiar ' evolutionary ' approach to Old Testament studies. Many readers, too, will find it difficult to follow him when he chooses to interpret the Song of Songs allegorically. Nevertheless this is a work which may be cordially recommended as one which the reviewer has read with interest and profit.   A.R.J.

THE LIFE AND THOUGHT OF THE NEIGHBOURING PEOPLES

GRAY, J. : *The Legacy of Canaan. The Ras Shamra Texts and their Relevance to the Old Testament.* (Supplements to *Vetus Testamentum,* vol. V.) 1957. Pp. x+244. (E. J. Brill, Leiden. Price : Fl. 34.)

The sub-title is an accurate indication of the scope of this fine study. The book is divided into six chapters dealing with (1) Ugarit and its records ; (2) Myths of the fertility cult ; (3) Saga and legend ; (4) The religion of Canaan (Gods, cult, and cultic personnel) ; (5) The social order ; (6) Literary and linguistic. This is followed by an excellent bibliography (the omission of a few relevant works which the reviewer has noticed may serve as an indication of the multitude of Ugaritic studies that have been produced over the past 28 years) and very full indices. Each chapter is supported by copious extracts from the Ugaritic texts in transliteration and translation together with ample philological notes. It is impossible here to do justice either to the many challenging observations or to the author's profound Semitic learning. It is obvious that on some points of detail one may reach different conclusions (especially, perhaps, in the linguistic sphere) from those canvassed by Dr. Gray, but there can be little doubt that his new book will find its place with the splendid work accomplished by C. H. Gordon, G. R. Driver, H. L. Ginsberg, U. Cassuto, and others. We have been very fortunate in the scholars who have turned to Ugaritic studies.   E.U.

KLÍMA, J. : *Zákony Chammurapiho.* (Československá akademie věd : Studie a prameny, sv. 2, sekce jazyka a literatury.) 1954. Pp. 216+8 plates+1 map. (Nakladatelství Československé akademie věd, Prague. Price : Kčs. 13.)

The author, a disciple of the great orientalist F. Hrozný, is himself a jurist and an Orientalist, known, e.g., for his earlier work, *Untersuchungen zum altbabylonischen Erbrecht,* 1940, Orientalisches Institut, Prague. In this more recent work he provides the Czech reader with an excellent translation of the laws of Hammurapi, together with a very detailed commentary. Every line is clearly the work of an expert. The work is indispensable for Old Testament scholars, and cannot be too warmly commended. M.B.

KOTALÍK, F. : *Ras Šamra-Ugarit : studie o významu a vztazích Ugaritu k prostředí a knihám starozákonním.* 1955. Pp. 160+xvi. plates+ 6, with French résumé and contents. (Česká katolická charita, Prague. Price : Kčs. 29.)

The author is Professor of Old Testament in the Catholic Theological Faculty at Leitmeritz. The content of his book is indicated by the subtitle : A Study of the Significance of Ugarit and its Connections with the Milieu and the Books of the Old Testament. First, an account is given of the original names of the city and the progress of the excavations. Then, after introductory chapters on the script and the language, the author turns to the texts, above all to the great epics. He devotes special attention to a comparison of Ugaritic literature with the Old Testament ; and, although he makes no independent contribution to the subject, the material which he has assembled is most valuable. A treatment of the Ugaritic pantheon and cult ends this short but well informed work. To each chapter an ample bibliography of relevant literature is appended. M.B.

MOSCATI, S. : *Ancient Semitic Civilizations.* 1957. Pp. 254+XXVI plates, 4 illustrations in the text, and 4 maps. (Elek Books, London. Price : 25s. 0d.)

Professor Moscati's work on this subject is already well known and has been fittingly appraised in reviews of his earlier editions in Italian, German, French (see *Book List,* 1950, p. 76 ; 1954, p. 80 ; 1956, p. 62). The new English version of this masterly conspectus of the history and culture of the Babylonians and Assyrians, the Canaanites, Hebrews, Aramaeans, Arabs, and Ethiopians, presented in fine perspective, is of great value for the general reader and scholar alike. J.G.

MOSCATI, S. : *Chi furono i Semiti?* (Atti della Accademia Nazionale dei Lincei, CCCLIV, Memorie, Ser. VIII, Vol. VIII, fasc. 1.) 1957. Pp. 52. (Accademia Nazionale dei Lincei, Rome.)

In this erudite and admirably documented monograph Professor Moscati subjects the notion of a uniform Semitic group to a searching linguistic, historical, and anthropological scrutiny. The point of departure is O. Rössler's theories about a special Libyan-Accadian affinity. Moscati arrives at the conclusion that the essential autonomy of the Semitic group remains unimpaired and that the spread of the Semites from their Arabian habitat did not occur in the form of mass invasions traceable to definite historical events, but rather as slow and prolonged movements of expansion and infiltration. E.U.

UNGER, M. F. : *Israel and the Aramaeans of Damascus (A Study in Archaeological Illumination of Bible History).* 1957. Pp. 190 (with three maps). (James Clarke, London. Price : 21s. 0d.)

The first three chapters of this volume deal with Damascus in the pre-patriarchal and patriarchal ages, the period of Egyptian control, and Damascus as a centre of Aramaean power. Chapters 4-10 treat of the period of Hebrew control ; of Damascus as a rival to, in conflict with, and as master of, Israel ; of the resurgence of Israel's power; of the decline and fall of Damascus ; and of Damascus and the last days of Israel. There are seventy pages of notes and a general index. The author has assembled a great deal of useful material, archaeological and otherwise, which he treats in a scholarly, yet generally conservative, manner. The many misprints and inconsistencies of spelling and of reference tend to mar an otherwise helpful book. D.W.T.

THE DEAD SEA SCROLLS

BRAUN, H. : *Spätjüdisch-häretischer und frühchristlicher Radikalismus. Jesus von Nazareth und die essenische Qumransekte.* Band I, *Das Spätjudentum.* Band II, *Die Synoptiker.* (Beiträge zur historischen Theologie, 24.) 1957. Pp. viii + 164 and vi + 154. (Mohr, Tübingen. Price : DM. 36.)

This work studies the teaching of the Qumran sect in relation first to normative Judaism (of which *Pirqe Aboth* is selected as a sample) and then to the teaching of Jesus preserved in the Synoptic Gospels. The Qumran sect is identified with the Essenes, on the basis of the accounts given of the latter by Philo and Josephus. To them the divine authority of the Torah was as basic and axiomatic as to normative Judaism, but its application was more thorough-going and less modified by relaxing interpretations than in the Pharisaic and rabbinic traditions. Yet even within the Essene tradition modifications may be discerned ; e.g., the Zadokite work tends to ease the rigour of the Manual of Discipline. The points of similarity between the Qumran sect and the teaching of Jesus are sufficiently numerous and significant, the author finds, to range him on the side of the sect over against traditional rabbinism, although those features which distinguish his teaching from Essenism and rabbinism alike are not over-looked. In Gospel criticism Braun is influenced by the views of Rudolf Bultmann (to whom the second volume is dedicated); this will reduce the cogency of some of his arguments for those readers who do not share Bultmann's approach. But the two volumes represent an important contribution to the compara-tive study of the Scrolls. F.F.B.

BURCHARD, C. : *Bibliographie zu den Handschriften vom Toten Meer.* (B.Z.A.W. No. 76.) 1957. Pp. xvi+118. (Töpelmann, Berlin. Price : DM.28.)

The literature on the Scrolls is well-nigh unlimited, and the flood shows no sign of abatement. Dr. Burchard has provided a most valuable list of 1556 books and articles relevant to the study of the Scrolls, in addition to references to reviews of the books. Anyone who has worked on the Scrolls knows how widely scattered the articles are, and how difficult it is to get access to them all, and those who know most of the subject will admire most the diligence which has gone into the making of this list. The author hopes in a year or two to supplement his work by an article in *Z.A.W.* or by another Beiheft. H.H.R.

DANIÉLOU, J. : *Les Manuscrits de la Mer Morte et les origines du christianisme.* 1957. Pp. 124+8 plates. (Editions de L'Orante, Paris. Price : 7s. 9d.)

This popular treatment discusses the thought-relations between the Scrolls and the New Testament. There is con-siderable affinity, though not identity, between the scrolls and John the Baptist, certain elements in the teaching of Jesus, the Gospels and the Essenes. The question of the Teacher of Righteousness takes up a considerable part of the book : he is a grand religious figure, he inaugurated a new method of Biblical interpretation, he received a revelation about the consummation of time. There are affinities with Jesus—in experience and in teaching. But the differences are fundamental : the Righteous Teacher announces the End, Jesus realises it. What was important for the former was his teaching, for the latter his saving act. The former realised his need, as a sinner, for forgiveness ; such a trait is com-pletely outside Jesus' character.

For its purpose this is a fascinating book. B.J.R.

DAVIES, A. P. : *The Meaning of the Dead Sea Scrolls.* 1957. Pp. 192+8 plates+3 maps. (Frederick Muller, London. Price : 15s. 0d.)

This is the British edition of a work published as a ' Signet Key Book ' in America in 1956. The author, who is minister of All Souls Church, Washington, D.C., gives a popular account of the discovery and contents of the Scrolls, of the excavation of Khirbet Qumran, and of the relation between these discoveries and ancient records of Essenism and Christianity. He far outruns his evidence in supposing that the bread at the communal meal of the Qumran sect represented the Messiahs of Aaron and Israel and that the wine represented their blood. His idea that New Testament scholars have ignored the significance of the discoveries is absurd : no subject has been discussed in recent years with more animation at meetings of New Testament scholars or in the pages of New Testament journals. His own account betrays the influence of a dogmatic tendency. There is indeed a fascinating affinity between the Qumran texts and Albert Schweitzer's theory of Christian origins, to which Mr. Davies leans ; but if the career of Jesus had taken the course which that theory indicates, it would have made as little impact on world history as the career of the Teacher of Righteousness made. F.F.B.

DEL MEDICO, H. E. : *L'énigme des manuscrits de la Mer Morte. Étude sur la date, la provenance et le contenu des manuscrits découverts dans la grotte I de Qumrân suivie de la traduction des principaux textes.* 1957. Pp. 592. (Librairie Plon, Paris. Price : Frs. 1350.)

A highly individual examination of the Scrolls and their background, resulting in the confirmation of the author's previous views that the Scrolls are not from a sectarian library but a Genizah ; that they are not related but heterogeneous—even individual manuscripts can be sub-divided to reveal disconnected and mutually contradictory fragments ; the Essene sect is hypothetical ; the common date for the collection is the 1st cent. A.D. A fresh translation of the documents sometimes gives the author the support he needs for his truly enigmatic treatment of the scrolls. B.J.R.

KUHN, K. G. : *Phylakterien aus Höhle 4 von Qumran* (Abhandlungen der Heidelberger Akademie der Wissenschaften, Philosophisch-Historische Klasse, Jahrgang 1957, 1. Abhandlung). 1957. Pp. 32+14 ills. on plates+11 other ills. (Carl Winter Universitäts-verlag, Heidelberg. Price : DM. 12.80.)

Four phylacteries from 4 Q are described and examined for text content and variants, form and folding, and comparison with Rabbinic instructions for Tephillin. In every case independence from the latter is established, especially in the extent and order of text. The Murabba'at phylactery, on the other hand, is true to Rabbinic injunctions. The Nash papyrus is probably not a fragment of a phylactery but was written for didactic purposes. The treatment and facsimiles are excellent. The transcription needs revision. B.J.R.

LICHT, J. : *The Thanksgiving Scroll. A Scroll from the Wilderness of Judaea. Text, Introduction, Commentary and Glossary* (In Hebrew). 1957. Pp. xvi+256+1 plate. (Bialik Institute, Jerusalem.)

This edition, which is based on Prof. E. L. Sukenik's *Ozar ha-Megilloth ha-Genuzoth* (Jerusalem, 1954), is divided into two main parts : 1. Introduction. This deals with the find in general and with the state of preservation of the Thanksgiving Scroll in particular, with its orthography and language, style and poetical construction, redaction, contents, the author and his personality, Creator and creation, man and his destiny, and the ' Community '. 2. The text. Here each hymn is prefaced by a short introduction, giving the central theme and commenting on its form. Then comes the hymn which is reconstructed and divided into lines. Below this two kinds of notes are given, one being textual and the other more general comment in which are included reasons for the many restorations of lacunae made in the text by the editor. What seemed to the editor to be direct Biblical citations are indicated in the margin. According to the editor's counting there are 32 hymns all told. Fragments 1-5 and 10 are also reproduced and explained. Addenda contain : I. Fragments 6-9, 11, 13, 15, 16, 18, 45, 47, 50, 55 and 58 ; II. " Livre des Mystéres " (IQ 27 1 I) ; III. *Pesher Tehillim* (see *P.E.Q.*, 1954, pp. 69-75), at the end of which comes a useful glossary. The book is a very valuable contribution to the study of the Scrolls for which scholars will be greatly indebted. Mosad Bialik is to be congratulated on the fine production. M.W.

MEYER, P. : *Ved Kristendommens vugge. Døde hav dokumenterne i historisk ramme.* 1957. Pp. 186. (Nyt Nordisk Forlag : Arnold Busk. Price : D. kr. 14.75.)

As the sub-title indicates, the aim of this work is to present the Dead Sea Scrolls in their historical context. Though the author is not an Old Testament specialist (he is Dr. Jur., and is Lektor in Law at Copenhagen University), he holds that he is justified in writing on the subject, since others who have previously written on it have not been specialists in all the fields required to enable authoritative pronouncements to be made. His own special competence is in the legal sphere ; and his legal knowledge has been of advantage to him in his treatment of the Manual of Discipline and its relation to CDC. Further, he has a very considerable knowledge of the Jewish people at the beginning of the Christian era. It must, on the other hand, be admitted that he is not a philologist, a theologian, or an expert in comparative religion. The weakest parts of his book are those in which he ventures on comparisons between the Dead Sea Scrolls and the New Testament. E.H.

MILIK, J. T. : *Dieci anni di scoperte nel Deserto di Giuda*. 1957. Pp. 110+17 photographs+3 maps and a plan of Qumran. (Marietti, Turin. Price : Lire 750.)

Dix ans de découvertes dans le Désert de Juda. 1957. Pp. 122+35 photographs+2 maps and a plan of Qumran. (Du Cerf, Paris. Price : Fr. 600.)

These two editions of what is substantially the same work appeared almost simultaneously. The French edition contains some supplementary pages, and in the appendix some modifications of view. The author is a member of the team engaged on the editing of the texts and he has access to unpublished information. He gives a good account of the contents of the finds, including some new information, and has an excellent chapter on the significance of the finds. Fr. Milik identifies the sect with the Essenes, and devotes an appendix to ' The Essenes and the History of the Jewish People ' .The Teacher of Righteousness is not identified, but the Wicked Priest is identified with Jonathan in the middle of the second century B.C. The migration to Damascus is placed at about 150 B.C. The importance of this little book is not to be judged by its brevity, and it is deserving of careful study. The excellent plan of the Qumran centre of the sect is very valuable.

H.H.R.

MURPHY, R. E. : *The Dead Sea Scrolls and the Bible*. 1957. (2nd printing. Originally published 1956). Pp. 122+4 plates+1 map. (Newman Press, Westminster, Md. Price : $1.50.)

In this excellent little book the Head of the Department of Semitic and Egyptian Languages and Literatures in the Catholic University of America gives a brief account of the discovery of manuscripts in the Dead Sea area up to the spring of 1956, and then considers their significance for O.T. and N.T. study respectively. The work seems to be intended chiefly for Catholic laymen, but it may confidently be recommended to the ' general reader ' of any religious persuasion or none, for there is nothing of a partisan outlook about it. The importance of the scrolls for the textual history of the O.T. books is indicated, and also for their date and literary criticism (e.g., in the relation of the *Prayer of Nabonidus* to the canonical Daniel) and for the history of Hebrew and Aramaic. In the N.T. field Fr. Murphy goes quite a long way in allowing contacts between the Qumran community and primitive Christianity ; e.g., John the Baptist ' lived in the Judean desert where Qumran is located ; he must have had some contact with them because he echoes several points that are found in their teachings ' (p. 66) ; and parallels between the Qumran literature on the one hand and St. John's Gospel and the Sermon on the Mount on the other are traced in some detail. Dupont-Sommer receives some sharp criticism.

F.F.B.

NÖTSCHER, F. : *Zur theologischen Terminologie der Qumran-Texte*. (Bonner Biblische Beiträge, 10.) 1956. Pp. 202. (Peter Hanstein Verlag, Bonn. Price : DM. 22.50.)

Professor Nötscher discusses in an introductory way the main religious terms and ideas in the scrolls under the headings Gnosis, Dualism, Light and Darkness, Eschatology ; and compares them with similar conceptions in Judaism, Mandaism, Manichaism, New Testament, Apocrypha. The treatment is readable and clear, and in every sense the book is very much worth while. It is no disparagement to say, however, that when the time comes to make a more thorough analysis of the Qumran religious teaching, this work will be listed amongst other useful introductory studies. There are a few misprints, and the Hebrew printing needs to be corrected when a suitable opportunity occurs either in a second edition or in an English translation, which would be very acceptable.

B.J.R.

RABIN, C. : *Qumran Studies* (Scripta Judaica II). 1957. Pp. xvi+ 136. (Clarendon Press, Oxford. Price : 21s. 0d.)

Professor Rabin argues that the scrolls belong not to the Essenes but the Pharisees, who, however, are the continuation of the *haburah* of the 1st cent. B.C. and not the orthodox party of Rabbinic Judaism. Amongst other features an examination of Qumran and Rabbinic texts dealing with the novitiate, communal property, common meals, rituals and other items serves to show the differences between the Rabbis and the Pharisees, and the similarities between the latter and the Qumranites.

It is a very competent piece of work, and even if some specialists might feel that Professor Rabin has not quite succeeded in presenting an overwhelming case, all scholars will accept it as a most instructive discussion of Pharisaism and Rabbinic Judaism. B.J.R.

ROWLEY, H. H. : *The Dead Sea Scrolls and the New Testament*. 1957. Pp. 32. (S.P.C.K., London. Price : 2s. 0d.)

This pamphlet contains the substance of the last of a series of four lectures delivered by the author in the University of Bristol in the spring of 1957, and it is good to see its contents made available to a wider constituency in this way. For here Professor Rowley says a few things that required to be said with all the authority attaching to such a name as his. He deals effectively with the absurd charge that New Testament scholars have, almost without exception, boycotted the whole subject of the Scrolls, and not only exposes the hollowness of the suggestion that scholars with religious commitments cannot be trusted to study the Scrolls without bias, but shows who in fact those writers are who have attempted to exploit them for propaganda purposes. But the pamphlet is only incidentally concerned with polemics; it presents a sober survey of the relations between the New Testament and the Scrolls and makes plain the extent of the gulf separating the two. The Scrolls ' throw light on the New Testament, but they do not explain it, and there is no evidence to connect Jesus or the New Testament directly with the sect.' F.F.B.

ROWLEY, H. H. : *The Teacher of Righteousness and the Dead Sea Scrolls.* (Reprinted from *Bulletin of the John Rylands Library*, vol. 40, No. 1, September, 1957.) Pp. 34. (Manchester University Press and The John Rylands Library, Manchester. Price : 3s. 6d.)

Since he published *The Zadokite Fragments and the Dead Sea Scrolls* in 1952, Professor Rowley has constantly reviewed the interpretation which he propounded there in the light of fresh evidence as it has come to light, both documentary and archaeological, but he has seen no reason to abandon his former position. In this reprint, which reproduces the text of a lecture delivered on 13th February, 1957, he restates the case for dating the Teacher of Righteousness in the Seleucid era and for identifying the Kittim of the Scrolls with the Greeks under Antiochus Epiphanes and the Wicked Priest with Menelaus. Demetrius, who according to 4QpNahum attempted to enter Jerusalem by the aid of the " seekers after smooth things ", is identified preferably with Demetrius I (cf. I. Macc. vii. 26ff.). There is hardly any relevant piece of evidence which Rowley does not take into account, and those who differ from him will be well advised to pay careful attention to his arguments. He takes issue in some detail with the interpretation which dates the material events in the first century B.C., but delivered his lecture too early to be able to treat the still later dating now favoured by G. R. Driver and C. Roth. F.F.B.

STENDAHL, K. (ed. by) : *The Scrolls and the New Testament.* 1958. Pp. xii+308. (S.C.M. Press, London. Price : 35s. 0d.)

This important addition to the mounting literature on the Qumran texts brings together fourteen essays by twelve scholars, dealing with various aspects of the relation between these texts and the early Christian documents. One contributor, K. G. Kuhn, supplies three essays (on ' The Two Messiahs of Aaron and Israel ', on ' The Lord's Supper and the Communal Meal at Qumran', and on ' New Light on Temptation, Sin, and Flesh in the New Testament ') ; the others supply one essay apiece. All but three of the essays have appeared in various periodicals ; the three new ones are by K. Stendahl (' The Scrolls and the New Testament : An Introduction and a Perspective '), W. D. Davies (' Paul and the Dead Sea Scrolls : Flesh and Spirit '), and N. N. Glatzer (' Hillel the Elder in the Light of the Dead Sea Scrolls '). The

last-mentioned is the only essay which does not bear directly
on the N.T. ; Glatzer suggests that Hillel, while adopting
some of the sect's teachings, attempted to reform Pharisaic
Judaism as an answer to the challenge of the sectarian movement. The other contributors are O. Cullmann, W. H. Brownlee, E. Vogt, K. Schubert, S. E. Johnson, B. Reicke, R. E.
Brown, and J. A. Fitzmyer. Essays which originally appeared
in other languages have been translated into English. The
contributions cannot be reviewed separately here, but they
compare from a number of standpoints the literature of two
contemporary movements both of which claimed to represent
the true Israel, voiced their claim in eschatological terms, and
supported it by a distinctive system of O.T. exegesis. If
anything could kill the charge that New Testament scholars
have boycotted the Scrolls, this volume would do so : but
those who press the charge may not be influenced by mere
evidence.   F.F.B.

WERNBERG-MØLLER, P. : *The Manual of Discipline Translated and
Annotated with an Introduction.* (Studies on the Texts of the Desert
of Judah, ed. by J. van der Ploeg, Vol. I.) 1957. Pp. 180.
(E. J. Brill, Leiden and W. B. Eerdmans, Grand Rapids, Michigan.
Price : Fl. 25.)

The main emphasis of this thorough treatment of 1QS lies
on the translation of the text and the full textual notes. It
might be felt that textual emendation has been used too
frequently, but the author conscientiously explains every
point and his arguments will carry weight with the specialist.
On the other hand, the introductory parts of the book are less
convincing, and, on the point of the dating of the sect, naïve.
But the book will find an important place on the shelves of
every student of the Scrolls.   B.J.R.

VAN DER WOUDE, A. S. : *Die Messianischen Vorstellungen der Gemeinde
von Qumrân.* (Studia Semitica Neerlandica, 3.) 1957. Pp. 276.
(Van Gorcum, Assen. Price : Fl. 17.50, or bound, Fl. 19.50.)

This is a careful and reliable study of the messianic ideas of the
Qumran sect and of the Testaments of the Twelve Patriarchs.
The main part of the book is devoted to a study of all the
passages in the texts so far published with any messianic
significance. The author finds no evidence of the resurrection
of the Teacher of Righteousness, and no evidence of the
concept of atonement through suffering. The idea of a Davidic
and a priestly head of the community standing side by side
is not a novel one with the sect, though the pre-eminence of
the priestly head is found to distinguish the thought of the
sect from orthodox Judaism.   H.H.R.

YADIN, Y. : *The Message of the Scrolls.* 1957. Pp. 192+11 plates. (Weidenfeld & Nicolson, London. Price : 21s. 0d.)

This little book gives an admirably succinct but lucid account of the Judaean Scrolls. The author, confining himself principally to those in the possession of the Hebrew University, in whose acquisition and publication both his father and he have played the principal parts, describes the discovery of the Scrolls, the caves around Qumran and the buildings there, the condition and contents of the various works, their date and the sect or group to which they seem to have belonged ; and he adds eleven excellent photographs. His views may be described as moderate and conservative for he thinks that the group were the Essenes and that the Scrolls may be referred to the last century B.C. or the first century A.D. ; but he makes no attempt to identify the Teacher of Righteousness or the Wicked Priest or any other of the persons mentioned in them. The book may be warmly commended to the general reader who wants a simple and direct account of these important documents, divested of any extravagant or sensational conjectures.   G.R.D.

APOCRYPHA AND POST-BIBLICAL JUDAISM

BARON, S. W. : *Histoire d'Israël : Vie sociale et religieuse.* Tome II. Les premiers siècles et l'ère chrétienne. (Sinaï : Collection des sources d'Israël.) 1957. Pp. 593-1320. (Presses Universitaires de France, Paris. Price : Fr. 2,000.)

This volume continues the French edition of this learned and original history of Israel (cf. *Book List,* 1957, p. 23). Although the translation has a few English touches (p. 669, 'les expectations messianiques ') it runs smoothly and gives a good impression of the candid, objective, moderate tone of the work. The arrangement is the same as that in the first volume, nearly all the notes being relegated to the end, so that the 535 pages of text are followed by more than 180 pages in small print, which are conveniently provided with headings referring to the relevant chapters. Finally comes the valuable index of more than 100 pages, covering both volumes, which provides a useful guide to a mass of unfamiliar names and of institutions.   H.C.

BARON, S. W. : *A Social and Religious History of the Jews. High Middle Ages :* Vol. III, *Heirs of Rome and Persia,* 2nd edition. 1957. Pp. x+340. Vol. IV, *Meeting of East and West,* 2nd edition. 1957. Pp. 352. Vol. V, *Religious Controls and Dissensions,* 2nd edition. 1957. Pp. 416. (Columbia University Press and Oxford University Press, London. Price : 48s. 0d. per vol. ; 120s. 0d. per set of three vols.)

These three volumes (second, revised and enlarged ed.) deal with the period comprising the years 500-1200—a period termed by the author High Middle Ages. In vol. III he discusses the position of the Jews in the pre-Islamic and the post-Islamic world as affected by Mohammed and the Chaliphate. Vol. IV discusses western Christendom and the age of Crusades and their bearing on economic transformations. Vol. V, entitled Religious Controls and Dissensions, deals with communal control, socio-religious controversies, messianic and sectarian trends, as well as with the Qaraite schism. At the end of each volume are given in small print and in a compact lay-out copious notes which occupy a very substantial part of the volume. A great variety of sources are in play in these notes—sources drawn from ancient and modern works written in various languages including Modern Hebrew and—to a lesser extent—Yiddish.

Baron's work is destined to take the honourable place which was allotted in the end of the last century and the beginning of the present century to Graetz's work and to that of Dubnow in the last generation, for it embodies a fresh and refreshing approach to Jewish history, making skilful use of hitherto untapped material.

For review of the first 2 vols., see *B.L.*, 1953, pp. 25f.

M.W.

DOTAN, A. : *Was Ben-Asher Really a Karaite?* (in Hebrew). 1957. Pp. 47. (Reprinted from *Sinai*, vol. xx, Nos. 5 & 6, August and September, 1957.)

The startling view that Ben Asher, whose Masora was considered as authoritative by Rabbinic authors and whose Bible was commended as exemplary by Maimonides who is known otherwise to have fought for the eradication of Karaite influences, was actually a Karaite, had its origin in Haskala thought. The present study is a systematic re-examination of all the evidence. The author finds the literary evidence inconclusive and shows that the colophons prove at most that Ben Asher and his father had sold their texts to Karaite personages, a practice not unparalleled, however, among Rabbinic scribes. As to the Ben Asher of Saadya Gaon's poem, he has to be identified with Saadya's Karaite opponent Samuel Ben Asher. Of the arguments which the author advances for the Rabbinism of Ben Asher, the reader will find most convincing those based on the reference to Hanuka, a festival not recognised by the Karaites, in a poem by Moses Ben Asher, and on the phrase *te'āmē sekel*, by which both Ben Asher and his father designate the Masoretic accents alluding to a Talmudic derivation based on Nehemiah viii. 8.

P.R.W.

ESH, S. : " *Der Heilige (Er sei gepriesen)* " : *zur Geschichte einer nachbiblisch-Hebräischen Gottesbezeichnung.* 1957. Pp. XVI + 86. (Brill, Leiden. Price : Fl. 12.50.)

A. Marmorstein has argued, mainly from historical and religious considerations, that the use of the phrase ' the Holy

One ' followed by the eulogy ' blessed be He ' was introduced by the Rabbis during the 3rd century A.D., and that when it is found in Tannaitic texts it must be considered a later insertion. The author of the present monograph approaches the question from a text-critical point of view, and by examining Tannaitic works which exist in critical editions finds that in about one third of all instances of the formula there is agreement of all MSS. and parallels, while in a great part of the remainder it has adequate textual support. He does not, however, present a conclusive case against Marmorstein, not so much because of the disagreeing textual evidence in the majority of instances, but mainly because of the relatively recent date of the MSS. at our disposal.

The author is on safer ground in the second part of his study. It was suggested by N. Bruel that ' the Holy One blessed be He ' goes back to an earlier ' The Holiness blessed be He '. By carefully examining the critical editions of the Tannaitic texts Dr. Esh finds, on the one hand, that there are more than a score of instances where ' the Holiness ' is used for ' God ', and, on the other, that the confusion between ' the Holiness ' and ' the Holy One ' arose from the fact that the formula always occurs in abbreviated form. Readers of the *Book List* may find special interest in the final sections of this work, where it is suggested that *(haq)qodesh* stands for ' God ' in the following instances : Isaiah xxvii. 13 ; xxxv. 8 ; xlviii. 2 ; lii. 1 ; lxii. 12 ; Jeremiah xxxi. 23 ; Zechariah ii. 16 ; viii. 3 ; Nehemiah xi. 1, 18 ; Ecclesiasticus iv. 14 ; CDC vi. 1 ; DSD ii. 21, 25 ; viii. 21 ; ix. 2.   P.R.W.

GOLDBERG, P. S. : *Karaite Liturgy and Its Relation to Synagogue Worship*. 1957. Pp. 134. (Manchester University Press, Manchester. Price : 16s. 0d.)

This succinct and useful little book is an introduction to rather than a study of the Karaite Liturgy. The comparisons between the elements of Karaite Prayer and the Rabbanite counterparts are illuminating. One feels that the book would have gained if more space had been devoted to the contents of the Liturgy itself and less to matters such as the times of Prayer, position in Prayer, modes of dress for Prayer, etc., which take up more than one third of the whole book. Valuable as such introductory information is to the non-specialist, the specialist in Karaitica will be disappointed at the narrowness of the scope of the comparison of Karaite and Rabbinic liturgical material discussed in the whole work.

Dr. Goldberg in dealing with the composition of Karaite Prayer is right in stressing the Karaite reliance on Scripture as both the authoritative and material source of their prayers ; but is he entirely justified in alleging that this militated against the clear and concise expression of the purpose of their prayers? Interesting is Chapter 13 on Paraphrases of Rabbinic Prayers found in later Karaite Liturgy. One would have appreciated the furnishing of further evidence for this.

In the final chapter (15) on Festive Wreath and Booths, Dr. Goldberg says ' There may be no historical evidence to support the Rabbis in their detailed prescriptions governing the use of this Festive Wreath ' (the Lulab). He accepts, however, that it was an old-established Jewish custom, and alleges that : ' It may thus be considered as one of the most striking innovations of Karaism that it abolished such an old-established custom.' Samaritanism never had the Lulab. It seems to the reviewer that whether one accepts that Anan made an innovation in forbidding the use of the Lulab or reverted to an earlier Jewish celebration of Hag Sukkoth without any Lulab, depends on what one thinks as to the date when Rabbinic Judaism became Normative Judaism.

The General Index could with advantage have been enlarged.
J.B.

JAUBERT, A. : *La date de la Cène. Calendrier biblique et liturgie chrétienne* (Études bibliques). 1957. Pp. 160+2 ills. (Gabalda, Paris.)

In this relatively short but important work Mlle. Jaubert takes up again and completes her earlier researches. The first part is an examination of the calendar of Jubilees, which is also that of the Qumran sect ; and this ancient priestly calendar is shown to be that of Ezekiel and of the Priestly sections of the Pentateuch. With its insistence on Wednesday and Friday, it leads us to the origins of Christian liturgy (the Didache). The second part is a patristic study. Gathering these varied materials together, the author shows how the dual character of the Palestinian calendars in the time of Christ may explain the differences which have long been noted between the Synoptics on the one hand and the Fourth Gospel on the other relating to the chronology of the Passion.
H.C.

LEVNER, J. B. : *The Legends of Israel*, translated from the Hebrew by Joel Snowman. *From the Birth to the Death of Moses.* 1956. Pp. 146. (James Clarke, London. Price : 12s. 6d.)

This book, which contains 158 legends about Moses, forms a selection from J. B. Levner's version in Biblical style of various legends drawn from the Midrashic literature. Mr. Snowman's renderings are mainly intended for young boys and girls. Their reading them may stimulate in their minds a wish to study more closely the sources upon which the legends are based.
(On the 1st vol., see *Book List* for 1948, p. 53.) M.W.

MACH, A. : *Der Zaddik in Talmud und Midrasch.* 1957. Pp. xii+246 (Brill, Leiden. Price : 51s. 6d.)

The present work is the first attempt to collect and arrange the statements found in the Talmud and in the better known Midrashim concerning the term *saddîq*, which is the most common designation for the ideal man in Rabbinic literature. The collection is almost exhaustive and the material is divided into two major groups : part I, the means by which the status of *saddîq* can be achieved and part II, the effect of such achievement in this life and the hereafter. Despite the author's efforts, however, to present a coherent account of the Rabbinic teachings on the various aspects of *saddîq*, the picture is not without inconsistencies. These are bound to occur when, on the one hand, the literature covering a millennium and representing the schools of thought of many generations is treated as a homogeneous unit and, on the other, no account is taken of the different degrees of righteousness for which *saddîq* stands in Rabbinic literature.   P.R.W.

METZGER, B. M. : *An Introduction to the Apocrypha.* 1957. Pp. xii+ 274. (Oxford University Press, New York & London. Price : $4.00 or 28s. 0d.)

Like most introductions to the Apocrypha this discusses that term and the growth of the Hebrew canon, and gives an outline of the contents of the several books. The last three chapters treat of the Apocrypha in relation to the New Testament, the Church and the arts, and here the results of the author's own studies are most evident. Professor Metzger has produced an admirable companion to the *R.S.V. Apocrypha.* He writes with a clarity and freshness which will commend his book to student and general reader alike.   W.D.McH.

POLACK, A. I. and SIMPSON, W. W. : *Jesus in the Background of History.* 1957. Pp. 160+1 map. (Cohen & West, London. Price : 16s. 0d.)

Over a third of Polack's masterly work is devoted to a description of the society into which Jesus was born and its antecedents. Then comes the life of Jesus : childhood, contact with the Baptist and early ministry, successes and opposition, decision to force the issue, Jerusalem and the end. There follow three chapters on the Teachings—Transcendental, Ethical, Practical—and a brief account of Jesus's impact on history. The author has a full grasp of the material and the appropriate methods of dealing with it. His judgment is sound, and he possesses a remarkable gift for bringing out the essentials of any development and situation. His picture of Jesus as, on the one hand, falling into a category— being an itinerant preacher-prophet with apocalyptic-Pharisaic leanings—and on the other, endowed with a unique personality is scholarly, sensitive and convincing. Written by a Jew, who does not accept Christological premises, this book will be of particular value in a world whose attitude to denominational doctrines is largely sceptical. Simpson's notes on the points where, as a Christian, he differs are most interesting.   D.D.

Sérouya, H. : *La Kabbale : ses origines, sa psychologie mystique, sa métaphysique* (Nouvelle édition revue et augmentée d'une introduction.) 1957. Pp. 534. (Grasset, Paris. Price : Fr. 1,260.)

This work falls into three major parts, the first surveys the sources, elements and literature of Jewish mysticism from the Talmudic period to the end of the 13th century, and the last part deals with the Cabbalistic movements from the 16th century onwards. It is the middle section which distinguishes this book from the many other introductions to Cabbala in European languages. The author's main interest being the place of Cabbala in philosophic thought, he examines here most of the fundamental philosophic elements in theoretical Cabbala, illustrating his theses copiously, mainly from the Zohar. This offers the non-Hebrew reader an opportunity to acquaint himself with this type of literature. The work has an interesting preliminary discussion on the psychological nature of mysticism and its predominance among the Jews, and a concluding one on the general influence of Cabbala.

P.R.W.

Schoeps, H.-J. : *Urgemeinde-Judenchristentum-Gnosis.* 1956. Pp. 88. (J. C. B. Mohr, Tübingen. Price : DM. 9.80.)

This is an interesting and well-argued defence of the author's view of the Pseudo-Clementies. (1) By isolating the oldest parts—the Ebionite Acts of the Apostles—it is possible to reconstruct the kerygma of the Christian Pharisees of the earliest Church : Jesus was the prophet foretold by Moses in Dt. xviii. 15 ; he preached the resurrection of the dead and rose himself *in humilitate*, to return at a future date *in gloria*—in accordance with Jacob's prophecy in Gn. xlix. 10 ; he abolished sacrifice, as already Moses had wanted to do, and substituted baptism as a requisite for forgiveness and entry into the Kingdom ; and as the Jews continued sacrificing and did not believe in him, he predicted the destruction of the Temple and it became necessary to proselytize the gentiles. From this teaching derives the developed Ebionite theology, where Jesus remains man and his work consists in reforming the Law. (2) Ebionite theology is anti-Gnostic, and where it uses Gnostic concepts it does so meet the enemy's arguments. Gnosis is pagan, characterized by physical dualism, a breach within the godhead, lustfulness of matter, rejection of the world and self-redemption—all of it foreign to Jews, Christians and Ebionites. What often misleads scholars is the fact that, in the NT period, Judaism contained not a few heterodox circles besides those known from Josephus, and some of their doctrines show a close similarity to Gnostic ones—yet they do not mean the same. The Ebionites draw on such heterodox doctrines, but it is they who won the battle against Marcion and Valentine. (3) In an Appendix Schoeps comments on the affinities between the Dead Sea sect and Ebionites, both *ḥasidhim*, and the latter having joined the former after 70.

D.D.

PHILOLOGY AND GRAMMAR

BERTSCH, A. : *Kurzgefasste hebräische Sprachlehre.* 1956. Pp. 218. (W. Kohlhammer, Stuttgart. Price : DM. 12.60.)

The author has sought to write an elementary Hebrew grammar for school and university which shall pay greater attention than usual to the more primitive forms from which Massoretic Hebrew is believed to derive, though reference to other Semitic languages is purposely avoided. Perhaps too little weight is laid on the principles of the actual Massoretic system for an elementary grammar.

While it may be defensible on logical grounds, the rigid separation of accidence from syntax, and the relegation of virtually all tables and paradigms to a separate section may tell against the practical convenience of the book for learners. There is little attempt at providing explanations of the syntax, and the teacher will have to supplement a good deal in class.

A praiseworthy feature is that only attested forms are quoted, and that all Hebrew sentences in the exercises can be verified by chapter and verse ; but the arrangement of the grammar often makes it necessary for the student to refer forward for some feature in his exercise, and less than half of the exercises provide for any translation *into* Hebrew. The printing and proof-reading are good, and this is a welcome essay at providing a new, up-to-date elementary Hebrew grammar.

D.R.Ap-T.

DRIVER, G. R. : *Aramaic Documents of the Fifth Century B.C. Abridged and revised edition, with help from a typescript by E. Mittwoch, W. B. Henning, H. J. Polotsky, and F. Rosenthal.* 1957. Pp. xvi+106. (Clarendon Press, Oxford. Price : 35s. 0d.)

This is a corrected and shortened form of a work which was noticed in the *Book List* for 1954 (pp. 92f.) and is now out of print. The plates and the text of the fragments in the original edition are omitted, while the appendix is cut. The Greek texts of the first edition are now given in translation, and to the glossary which remains in its full form there is subjoined an index of biblical references. While the whole work has been revised and improved, attention may be directed to Professor Henning's rewriting of the notes on Iranian terms. The change to a smaller and more convenient format and the reduced price will be welcomed by all who use this work as a text-book. W.D.McH.

HAMMERSHAIMB, E. : *Genesis : en sproglig analyse.* 1957. Pp. 86. (G. E. C. Gad, Copenhagen. Price : D. kr. 10.50.)

Professor Hammbershaimb has provided a very practical aid for students reading Genesis as their first connected Hebrew text. Grammatical forms are explained for the beginner, with appropriate references to Pedersen's Hebrew Grammar (Danish) and occasionally to Nyberg's (Swedish). But the explanations given usually provide the necessary help without necessitating recourse to any other work. Though no vocabulary is provided, the notes themselves give the meanings of words as they occur. This work will doubtless be widely used in Scandinavia. It should do much to lighten the task of both teacher and student. G.W.A.

HOLLENBERG-BUDDE : *Hebräisches Schulbuch*, 22nd. ed., edited by W. Baumgartner. 1957. Pp. 230. (Helbing and Lichtenhahn, Basel. Price : Sw. Fr. 7.80.)

The appearance of yet another edition of this work testifies to its proved usefulness since it was first published over a century ago. The four main sections consist of grammar and syntax, with paradigms ; exercises ; reading selections, with notes—there are vocalized texts from the Old Testament, and unvocalized from Tobit, Luke, Acts, the Manual of Discipline and the Hymns from Qumran, together with the Siloam inscription ; and Hebrew-German and German-Hebrew vocabularies, with a separate one for the exercises. The main essentials of Hebrew grammar and syntax are clearly presented, the exercises are well planned, the pieces for reading are judiciously selected. Misprints in the twenty-first edition have been corrected, and some small improvements have been introduced. An excellent work which deserves to be widely known D.W.T.

KÖBERT, R. : *Vocabularium Syriacum*. 1956. Pp. viii+216. (Pontificium Institutum Biblicum, Rome. Price : Lire 2,400 or $4 ; cloth, Lire 2,700 or $4.50.)

In the *Book List*, 1953 (p. 82), review of Fr. Köbert's *Textus et Paradigmata Syriaca* Professor Rowley wrote : ' A vocabulary would have added greatly to the value of the work '. The present work fills the gap most admirably. It contains the words found in the New Testament Peshitta and in commonly used chrestomathies; the meanings are given in Latin, and etymologies are added where necessary. This is a scholarly and handy companion to the editor's grammar.
W.D.McH.

MURTONEN, A. : *Materials for a non-Masoretic Hebrew Grammar. I. Liturgical Texts and Psalm Fragments Provided with the So-Called Palestinian Punctuation, edited with an introduction, partial translation, comments and plates*, with a contribution by G. J. Ormann. 1958. Pp. 126+60+5 photostats. (Akateeminen Kirjakauppa, P.O.B. 128, Helsinki. Price : Fmk. 1,600 or $5.)

The work here noticed is intended as the first of a series of studies of pre-Tiberian, non-Masoretic, Hebrew grammar, inspired by Dr. P. Kahle. It falls into two parts ; the first, by Dr. Murtonen, contains an examination of a number of

Biblical texts, chiefly extracts from the Psalms, and liturgical texts from the now well-known *genîzāh* at Cairo and a sketch of the grammar (accidence, not syntax, which hardly yields itself to such treatment) of these texts ; the second, by Dr. Ormann, contains samples of *pîyûtîm* by Yannai, printed at length, translated and furnished with variant readings and comments. Most of the matter here collected is new and extremely important, and the two authors' treatment of it is highly competent. Unfortunately, the excellence of their work is greatly impaired by its reproduction ; the text has been reproduced from typescript on so small a scale that the English part is very tiring to the eyes and much of the Hebrew part (especially the vowel signs, which are of crucial importance) more or less (sometimes quite) illegible.   G.R.D.

WEINGREEN, J. : *Classical Hebrew Composition*. 1957. Pp. viii+146. (Clarendon Press : Oxford University Press. Price : 21s. 0d.)

The aim of this book is to train students in writing Hebrew composition in the style of the O.T. Users of it are expected already to have covered the general groundwork of Hebrew grammar and to have read some O.T. Hebrew texts. Fifty pieces of prose and five of verse, written in the style of the A.V. of the O.T., are provided, the themes selected dealing with O.T. personalities and events in chronological order. The rules of Hebrew syntax are explained in accompanying notes, and points of grammar and syntax which the student has met earlier are constantly reiterated. In the English-Hebrew vocabulary the main parts of difficult nouns and verbs are given, and an index to the notes enables the student to revise more easily the rules of syntax. Teachers and students alike should be grateful for this book.   D.W.T.

YOUNG, G. D. : *Concordance of Ugaritic*. (Analecta Orientalia, 36.) 1956. Pp. viii+74. (Pontificium Institutum Biblicum, Rome. Price : Lire 1,800, $3.00.)

This useful work of reference, on the basis of the glossary in Gordon's Ugaritic Manual (*Analecta Orientalia*, 35) is a concordance to the vocabulary of the texts published until 1956, but includes words from the more recently discovered alphabetic texts communicated by Virollead in correspondence with the writer. Unfortunately there are no specific references to the latter incidences, though that will doubtless be remedied soon now that the new alphabetic texts have been published by Virollead.   J.G.

BOOK LIST, 1959

A protracted succession of severe domestic difficulties has seriously hindered the work of editing this issue of the *Book List*. In the circumstances, I have probably overlooked a considerable number of works which ought to have been included. For these omissions, and for the delay in publication, I now apologize to all concerned. I shall be glad to have my attention drawn to works which have escaped my notice, so that they may be included in the 1960 issue.

I wish to record my gratitude for the co-operation of the members of the *Book List* Panel and also to others who have helped in various ways. My colleagues, Professor C. K. Barrett, Professor T. W. Thacker, and the Revd. D. R. Jones have contributed reviews ; and bibliographical details have been supplied by Professors H. Cazelles, E. Hammershaimb, and R. de Langhe, and by the staff of B. H. Blackwell of Oxford. The Revd. A. W. Kay has generously compiled the Index. As in previous years, I am deeply indebted to the Printer for his unfailing helpfulness.

UNIVERSITY OF DURHAM.   G. W. ANDERSON.

GENERAL

von ALLMEN, J.-J. (ed. by) : *Vocabulary of the Bible*, with an introduction by H. H. Rowley. 1958. Pp. 480. (Lutterworth Press,
London. Price : 30s 0d.).

The French edition of this book was noted in Book List, 1955,
pp. 45f. The English edition was translated from the second
French edition (1956) and contains a foreword by H. H.
Rowley. Translators and publishers are to be thanked for
making available to the English public a book that is
scholarly and stimulating.   A.S.H.

BIČ, M. and SOUČEK, J. B. (ed. by) : *Biblická Konkordance*, parts
12-14. Lidé-Nedaleko. 1958. Pp. 80 each part. (Edice Kalich,
Prague ; agents, Artia Ltd., 30 Smečky, Prague. Price Kčs.
10.50, or $1.10 each part).

This Czech Concordance (on which see *Book List*, 1955, p. 4 ;
1956, p. 3 ; 1957, p. 4 ; 1958, p. 3) steadily pursues its way
towards completion, though the end is not yet in sight. Would
that it might inspire a similar English Concordance, which
would give us in a single volume more than is at present
available in one book.   H.H.R.

CAZELLES, H. (ed. by) : *Dictionnaire de la Bible. Supplément.* Fasc.
xxxi. (Mythe-Noeldeke). 1958. Cols. 257-512. (Letouzey et Ané,
Paris. Price : 19s. 0d.).

In this fascicle H. Cazelles finishes his article on Myth in the
Old Testament. Two Babylonian monarchs (Nabonidus and
Nebuchadnezzar) are the subjects of articles by P. Garelli
and M. Leibovici respectively. The article on Navigation in
antiquity is a trifle disappointing, since it does no more than
supplement the article by H. Lesetre in the original *Dictionnaire de la Bible.* It gives no help regarding the interesting
problems raised by Acts xxvii. R. Bagatti supplies an up-to-
date account of recent excavations in Nazareth, and J.
Schmitt discusses the Nazareth inscription that excited so
much interest on its publication in 1930. Nehemiah and
Ezra are treated at moderate length by A. Lefevre. J. Sey-
naeve in an article extending over nearly fifty columns deter-
mines the scriptural teaching of Cardinal Newman, more
especially on inspiration. He published in 1953 his thesis
entitled *Cardinal Newman's Doctrine of Holy Scripture* (see
Book List, 1954, pp. 71-72) of which the present article is a
summary. Nineveh as a topic has been divided among three
authors, of whom M. Rutten writes on the site and excavations,
E. Cavaignac on its history and R. Largement on its libraries.
There are short biographical notices of E. H. Naville, Eberhard
and Erwin Nestle, J. Nikel and T. Noeldeke (the last unfortunately left unfinished pending the issue of the next fascicle).
                                                             J.M.T.B.

139

Eretz Israel. Archaeological, Historical and Geographical Studies. Volume Five. Dedicated to Professor Benjamin Mazar on his Fiftieth Birthday. 1958. Pp. 259 (in Hebrew)+97 (in English)+ 26 plates+portrait+numerous drawings, maps and plans. (Israel Exploration Society and the Hebrew University, Jerusalem, with the assistance of the Bialik Institute).

This scholarly and well produced volume contains two sections, the one, comprising 36 studies, in Hebrew (with English summaries), and the other, comprising 11 studies, in English (with Hebrew summaries). The studies which have a direct bearing on the Old Testament in the Hebrew section are : ' On Some Historical References in the Bible ' (N. H. Tur-Sinai) ; ' The Bearing of Psalm 81 upon the Problem of Exodus ' (S. E. Loewenstamm) ; ' The Ark of the Covenant and the Cherubs ' (M. Haran) ; ' The Dial of Ahaz ' (Y. Yadin) ; ' Jachin and Boaz ' (S. Yeivin) ; ' " Slag " and " Tin " in the First Chapter of Isaiah ' (S. Abramski) ; ' The House of Eliakim, a Family of Royal Stewards ' (H. J. Katzenstein) ; ' *Hemmah haqqinim habba'im mehammath 'abhi bheth-rekhabh* ' (I Ch. ii. 55) (S. Talmon) ; ' The Return from Babylon, its Time and Scope ' (J. Liver) ; ' En-Dor ' (Z. Kallai-Kleinmann) ; ' Bet Dagon and Gedereth-Kidron, Eltekeh and Ekron ' (M. Naor) ; ' Tamar and the Roads to Elath ' (Y. Aharoni) ; ' The Date of the " Limes Palestinae " ' (M. Avi-Yonah) ; ' Meša (A Study of Certain Features of Old Hebrew Dialects) ' (S. Morag) ; ' Some Manifestations of Milra' Tendency in Hebrew ' (I. Yeivin). The studies with a direct bearing on the Old Testament in the English section are : ' Was the Age of Solomon without Monumental Art ?' (W. F. Albright) ; ' Indo-European and Hebrew Epic ' (C. H. Gordon) ; ' Geographical Problems ' (G. R. Driver) ; ' The Biblical Institution of Deror in the Light of Akkadian Documents ' (J. Levy) ; ' In Search of Nimrod ' (E. A. Speiser) ; 'An Unrecognized Allusion to Kings Pekah and Hoshea of Israel ' (H. L. Ginsberg).   M.W.

FOERSTER, W. and QUELL, G. : *Lord*, translated from the German with additional notes by H. P. Kingdon (Bible Key Words from Gerhard Kittel's *Theologisches Wörterbuch zum Neuen Testament*, No. VIII). 1958. Pp. xiv+122. (Adam and Charles Black, London. Price : 12s. 6d.).

This is a notable addition to the series Bible Key Words initiated by the late Professor J. R. Coates. The article in *T.W.z.N.T.* of which this is a translation is in five parts, four by W. Foerster, viz., I ' The Meaning of the word *Kyrios* '; II ' Gods and Rulers as *Kyrioi* '; IV ' " Lord " in Late Judaism ' ; and V ' *Kyrios* in the New Testament '. Section III, ' The Old Testament Name for God ', is by G. Quell. It is this last mentioned section which is of quite unusual value for Old Testament scholars, though the whole article is of very great interest. Quell's discussion of the meaning of the Tetragrammaton and the way in which it was repre-sented in Greek and of the use of the word *'adhônāi* as the usual Qerê of Yahweh in the Massoretic text provides an indispensable supplement to Baudissin's great book *Kyrios* and in part a criticism of it. Sections 9 and 10 in Quell's contribution are most important for the Biblical theologian and are full of original and challenging comments. Unfortunately the translation is not impeccable. On p. 65, e.g., *Gott der Väter* and *Vätergötter* are translated as ' God the Father ' and ' Father-gods ' !   N.W.P.

FRIEDRICH, G. (ed. by) : *Theologisches Wörterbuch zum Neuen Testament* (begun by G. Kittel). Band VI, Lieferungen 10, 11, 12, 13. 1958. Pp. 256. (Kohlhammer, Stuttgart. Price : DM. 4.60 each Lieferung).

In Lieferung 10 there is a long article by Hauck and Schulz on *pornē* and its cognates, of which the sections on Old Testament and Late Judaism are of special interest to Old Testament scholars. In the article on *potamos* by Rengstorf there is a short section on *river* in the Old Testament and at the end a long and valuable section on the River Jordan.

Lieferung 11 contains an article on *praüs* which treats briefly of '*anaw* and '*ani*. The long article on *presbys* and its cognates by Bornkamm has a section on the *elders* (*zekenim*) in the Old Testament. In the article on *pro* by Reicke there is reference to the theological bearing of the expressions *beterem* and *liphene*, while something of interest will be found in Rengstorf's article on *prothymos*.

In Lieferung 12 Stählin in his article on *prokopē* devotes space to discuss the concept of the movement of the *Heilsgeschichte* towards a goal. The article on *prosēlytos* by Kuhn, in addition to discussion of the whole subject of proselytes, has a useful treatment of the Hebrew conception of the *ger* and the *toshabh*. The article on *proskoptō*, *proskomma*, etc., gives Stählin the opportunity to treat briefly of the Hebrew analogues and in particular of the theological conception of the *mishkol*. Greeven, dealing with *proskyneo*, has a short section on the Hebrew words for ' to worship '.

Lieferung 13 begins with a section on *prosōpon* by Lohse which contains a short treatment of *panim* and also a discussion of the conception ' the face of God '. The main part of the Lieferung is occupied by a long article on *prophētēs* and its cognates by Krämer, Rendtorff, Meyer, and Friedrich which is not yet complete. The Old Testament scholar will turn to the treatment of *nabhi'* and the other Hebrew designations of the prophet by Rendtorff.   N.W.P.

GALLING, K. (ed. by) : *Die Religion in Geschichte und Gegenwart.* 3 Auflage, Band II, Lieferungen 26-42, Cols. 353-1924+Plates and maps+pp. XXXII. Band III, Lieferungen 43-54, Cols. 1-1152+Plates and maps. (J. C. B. Mohr, Tübingen. Subscription price : D.M. 4.20 each Lieferung).

The Lieferungen noted above extend from *Eiferopfer* to *Karl V* and include many articles on important Old Testament subjects. Much new material is here conveniently and reliably summarised.   G.W.A.

HEMPEL, J. and ROST, L. : *Von Ugarit nach Qumran : Beiträge zur Alttestamentlichen und altorientalischen Forschung Otto Eissfeldt zum 1 September, 1957, dargebracht von Freunden und Schülern,* herausgegeben in Zusammenarbeit mit W. F. Albright, W. Baumgartner, J. Lindblom und H. H. Rowley (B. Z. A. W. 77). 1958. Pp. 304. (Alfred Töpelmann, Berlin. Price : DM. 40).

Essays in honour of Eissfeldt's 70th birthday by a team of twenty-three international scholars are collected in this book. As the title indicates, there is no close controlling theme ; but, on the other hand, several of the present trends and interests of Old Testament scholarship are reflected in the essays. Two are based on traditio-historical investigation, one a study of the David-Michal story (Stoebe) and the other an attempt to define the period within which the idea of the Rachel and Leah tribes came into being (Mowinckel). Distrust of a too rigid literary analysis of the Pentateuch is reflected in an essay on the divine names in the Balaam stories (von Pákozdy). A study of some difficult passages in Isaiah (Driver) uses the evidence of cognate languages and the ancient versions to defend the Massoretic text where possible. Qumran is represented by two essays, one on the occurrence of a present-future tense (Meyer) and one on the identity of the sect (Rowley). An essay on lexicography (Baumgartner) also lays the Qumran material under contribution. L.H.B.

HUMBERT, P. : *Opuscules d' un hébraisant,* with a preface by W. Baumgartner. (Mémoires de l' Université de Neuchâtel, xxvi.) 1958. Pp. 228+Portrait. (Secrétariat de l' Université, Neuchâtel. Price : Sw. fr. 20).

Few volumes of papers already published are likely to receive as warm a welcome as this attractive collection of thirteen essays by Professor Humbert, ranging in date from 1924 to 1955 and in subject from linguistic studies of *hineni, hineni eleka, bara ', qana ', pa'al, zar* and *nokri, samah* and *gil,* and *'ebyon,* to interpretations of Genesis i, Psalm civ, Ruth, and Job, and a critical appraisal of Renan. Rich stores of learning are here presented with precision and grace. Professor Baumgartner contributes a biographical preface ; and a bibliography of the author's writings is appended. G.W.A.

RIESENFELD, H. (ed. by) : *Svensk exegetisk arsbok,* xxii.-xxiii. (Odeberg Festskrift.) 1958. Pp. 290 with portrait. (C. W. K. Gleerup, Lund. Price : SW. kr. 15).

This special double number is a presentation volume to Professor H. Odeberg and reflects in its contents the wide range of his learning. The contributions are arranged in the following sections : Synoptic Gospels ; Fourth Gospel ; Acts of the Apostles ; Epistles ; Extra-canonical literature and Jewish exegesis ; Old Testament. The last named contains only two : G. Gerleman on ' Struktur und Eigenart der Hebräischen Sprache ' and I. Engnell on ' Die Urmenschvorstellung und das Alte Testament '. Other essays which will be of special interest to readers of the *Book List* are: B. Noack on ' Qumran and the Book of Jubilees ' ; T. Arvedson on the *Hodayot* ; G. Lindeskog on Buber's teaching about faith ; H. Ljungman on a Sifre text bearing on Matthew xi. 18f. ; and E. Starfelt on Landau's theory about *gezera shawa*. The essays are in Swedish, Norwegian, German, and English.

G.W.A.

RIESENFELD, H. (ed. by) : *Svensk exegetisk årsbok* xxiv. 1959. Pp. 170+50 (supplement). (C. W. K. Gleerup, Lund. Price : Sw. kr. 10).

The high quality of this annual is fully maintained in this latest issue. J. H. Grønbaek writes on eschatology in the teaching of the prophets of judgement (German). Y. Yadin contributes an illustrated report on the fourth season of excavations at Hazor (English). H. Ringgren discusses *gnosis* in the Qumran texts (Swedish). W. G. Kümmel writes on future and present eschatology in the primitive church (Swedish). B. Gerhardsson gives an account of a Greek MS Lectionary in the Library of Uppsala University (German) ; and L. Cervall describes a Greek MS Lectionary of the Old Testament in Linköping Diocesan Library (French). There are reviews of important new books, and a very useful survey (to which I. Engnell contributes an introduction) of literature on the Old Testament (Swedish). The supplement (Symbolae Biblicae Upsalienses 16) contains translations into Swedish of the Gospel of Truth and the Gospel of Thomas by T. Säve-Söderbergh. G.W.A.

SCHMIDT, K. L., KLEINKNECHT, H., KUHN, K. G., VON RAD, G. : *Basileia*, translated from the German with additional notes by H. P. Kingdon (Bible Key Words from Gerhard Kittel's *Theologisches Wörterbuch zum Neuen Testament*, No. VII). 1958. Pp. xiv+62 (Adam and Charles Black, London. Price : 8s. 6d.).

In this new volume in the series Bible Key Words three of the chapters are of particular concern to Old Testament Scholars, viz., II ' *Melek* and *Malkûth* in the Old Testament ' (by G. von Rad) ; III ' *Malkûth Shāmayim* in Rabbinic Literature ' (by K. G. Kuhn) ; and ' Basileia (*tou theou*) in Hellenistic Judaism ' (by K. L. Schmidt). Brief as von Rad's contribution is, it is most useful, in anticipation of the publication in English of his *Old Testament Theology*, to have here his views on the nature of the Hebrew monarchy, on the relation between the Davidic monarchy and the Messianic hope, and on the vexed question of the Kingship of Yahweh, in discussing which he aligns himself with von Gall's criticism of Mowinckel's views which the latter in part retracted. It is useful to be reminded in Kuhn's contribution that in late Judaism there were two uncorrelated lines of thought about the Kingship of God in one of which religion was determined by nationality, while in the other man stands before God simply as an individual able to accept or reject God's Kingship by a free act of will. N.W.P.

Studia theologica cura ordinum Scandinavicorum edita. Vol. XI, fasc. ii. (1957), 1958. Pp. 72. Vol. XII, fasc. i. (1958), 1958. Pp. 108. Vol. XII, fasc. ii. (1958), 1958. Pp. 102. (C. W. K. Gleerup, Lund. Price : by subscription, Sw. kr. 15 each vol. or Sw. kr. 10 each fascicle).

XI, ii. contains an exegetical study of Isaiah i. by L. G. Rignell who claims that there is a close relation between the chapter and parts of Deuteronomy, particularly xxviii.-xxxii. J. P. Asmussen contributes an article on sacral prostitution in the Old Testament. XII i. contains nothing of direct interest to the *Alttestamentler :* but P. Winter's short study of Luke i., ii adduces many Old Testament parallels. In XII ii. there is an interesting study by F. Willesen of the *yalid* in Hebrew society.   G.W.A.

THOMAS, D. W. : *The Hebrew Bible since Claude Montefiore* (Claude Montefiore Centenary Lecture). 1958. Pp. 18 (Liberal Jewish Synagogue, London. Price : 2s. 6d.).

In this lecture the formidable task of indicating the development of the critical study of the Hebrew Bible since Montefiore's Hibbert Lectures is handled with skill and judgement. Examples are given of the wide range of external evidence now available, of the light shed on our knowledge in different departments of Old Testament study, and also of the limits and dangers of the use of such evidence. A most valuable survey.   G.W.A.

THOMSEN, P. : *Die Palästina-Literatur : eine internationale Bibliographie in systematischer Ordnung mit Autoren— und Sachregister,* ed. by O. Eissfeldt and L. Rost. Vol. A, Lieferung 2. 1958. Pp. 272. (Akademie-Verlag, Berlin. Price : DM. 36).

This is the second issue of the volume covering the years 1878-1894 (see *Book List*, 1957, p. 14), containing more than 4,500 entries in the field of History and Archaeology. The volume will be completed in a third issue, which will be devoted to Geography and kindred fields. The immense labour which the late Dr. Thomsen devoted to the compilation of these bibliographical volumes rendered a great service to scholars everywhere, and will continue to facilitate the research of others.   H.H.R.

EDUCATIONAL

*ACKROYD, P. R. : *The People of the Old Testament.* 1959. Pp. 272+ IV plates+ 27 drawings+ 5 maps. (Christophers, London. Price : 15s. 0d. ; School Edition, 12s. 6d.).

This general introduction to the Old Testament can be recommended unreservedly : it will appeal especially to the interested Sixth Former, to students in Training Colleges, and to all who want a readable, reliable, and intelligent history of the people who produced the Old Testament Scriptures. It is simply and lucidly written and is not overloaded with detail ; the critical positions adopted are cautious and conservative ; the selection of material is highly judicious ; the scholarship is impeccable and unobtrusive. After an account of the beginnings and the period of the kingdoms and before dealing with the post-exilic period the author includes a section ' Looking back and looking forward ' in which he treats of the ancient traditions of Israel in Genesis and in the account of the Exodus and of the deuteronomic history and the work of the Chronicler, an unconventional and interesting arrangement. The book is attractively produced and illustrated, and reasonably priced. L.A.P.

ARCHAEOLOGY AND EPIGRAPHY

Annual of the American Schools of Oriental Research, vol. XXXII-XXXIII (1952-4). *The Excavation at Herodian Jericho*, 1951, *conducted by the American School of Oriental Research at Jerusalem*, by James B. Pritchard, with contributions by Sherman E. Johnson and George C. Miles. 1958. Pp. xi+58+66 plates. (A.S.O.R., New Haven, Conn. Price : $7.50).

This report on one large building in the vicinity of the impressive facade and ornamental gardens feasibly associated with Herod the Great on the Wadi Qelt just west of modern Jericho is of limited scope and interest. It is suggested that the building itself, to judge by the baths and hypocaust, was most probably a bath-house with gymnasium rather than a palace or mansion. This building, on the evidence of pottery and coins, is associated with the early Herodian period, specifically with the reign of Archelaus (4 B.C.—6 A.D.). There is an earlier, Chalcolithic, stratum on the site, which was later occupied to a limited extent by the Arabs. Appendices on Arabic and Roman coins have been given respectively by G. C. Miles and S. E. Johnson. J.G.

MICHAUD, H. : *Sur la pierre et l'argile. Inscriptions hébraïques et Ancien Testament.* (Cahiers d'archéologie biblique No. 10.) 1958. Pp. 128+X plates+34 figures. (Delachaux & Niestlé, Neuchâtel & Paris. Price : Sw. frs. 5.70).

This book gives an account of the principal inscriptions in Hebrew on hard materials; papyri, the Qumran material, and coins are excluded. The book is intended to be an elementary introduction, for ordinary readers, to the bearing of some of these inscriptions on the Old Testament ; there are adequate notes, a bibliography, nineteen plates and thirty-four figures. J.N.S.

PARROT, A. : *Samaria the Capital of the Kingdom of Israel* (Studies in Biblical Archaeology, No. 7), trans. by S. H. Hooke. 1958. Pp. 144+12 plates+XXXIII figures. (S.C.M. Press, Ltd., London. Price : 10s. 6d.).

This book was originally published in 1955 (see *Book List*, 1956, p. 15). It contains a clear, concise history of the kingdom of Israel, and an account of Israelite Samaria in the light of archaeology, Samaria in the Assyrian, Babylonian, Hellenistic and Roman periods, and the relationship between Samaria and John the Baptist. It is well written, uses fully the Biblical and archaeological evidence, throws interesting light on the historical and prophetic books of the Old Testament, and gives valuable background material for Old Testament and New Testament and for the first Christian missionary enterprise. J.N.S.

PARROT, A. : *Babylon and the Old Testament* (Studies in Biblical Archaeology, No. 8), trans. by B. E. Hooke. 1958. Pp. 166+13 plates+LIV figures. (S.C.M. Press, Ltd., London. Price : 10s. 6d.).

This book was originally published in French in 1956 (see *Book List*, 1958, p. 13). It gives an interesting history of Babylon based on exploration and on Old Testament references, taking account of Wiseman's publication of the chronicles of the Chaldean kings, and reflects the author's first-hand knowledge of the site and his usual careful research. J.N.S.

*THOMAS, D. W. (ed. by) : *Documents from Old Testament Times* translated with Introductions and Notes by Members of the Society for Old Testament Study. 1958. Pp. xxvi +302. (Thomas Nelson & Sons, London. Price : 18s. 0d.).

The Scholarship of Professor Winton Thomas and his collaborators, and the enterprise of Messrs. Thomas Nelson, have most happily combined to give all readers who are interested in the background of the Old Testament a book which, if the cliché may be forgiven, is worth its weight in gold. The two splendid volumes edited by Professor James Pritchard, though far from dear for what they give, are somewhat beyond the means of most students ; but the very moderate price of this book brings it within the reach of all.

The aim of this book, published under the auspices of the Society for Old Testament Study, is, in the words of its editor, ' to meet the needs more particularly of teachers of Scripture in schools, of the clergy, and of others who are not professional scholars.' It contains a well-chosen selection of non-biblical documents illustrating the background of the history and religion of Israel. The cuneiform documents include extracts from the Epic of Creation and the Gilgamesh Epic, newly translated and annotated by Mr. Kinnier Wilson ; several historical documents, religious and commercial texts, all newly translated and annotated by competent scholars. There is a useful selection from Egyptiam texts. Dr. John Gray has translated represented extracts from the difficult Ras Shamra Texts ; and some of the most recently discovered Aramaic documents are here made available to students. The only omission, if it is not unreasonable to ask for more when so much has been given, is that Hittite texts are not represented. There is a useful chronological table, and 16 excellent illustrations. This admirably produced aid to the study of the Old Testament should, and will undoubtedly, receive a wide welcome. S.H.H.

TUFNELL, O. : *Lachish IV (Tell ed-Duweir) : The Bronze Age.* 2 volumes : text and plates. 1958. Pp. 352+20 figures (Vol. 1) ; 87 plates+9 plans (Vol. 2). (Published for the Wellcome Trust by the Oxford University Press, London. Price : £8 8s. 0d.).

This is the fourth and last full report on the excavation of Lachish undertaken, but unfortunately uncompleted, by the late J. L. Starkey, and concerns the early periods of occupation. The material from the caves in the rock-spur running N.W from the mound, which served as dwellings in the Chalcolithic and Early Bronze Ages and as tombs in the Middle Bronze Age, is published and compared with the pottery and artifacts from E. B. sites, especially from Tell Beit Mirsim, Tell Far ' a in the Wadi Ghazzeh, and Jericho. Apart from this matter, the Bronze Age at Lachish is known only from the outer defences, three levels of a temple in the Middle Bronze fosse, and from a limited sector opened at the N.E. edge of the mound. In the last sector three levels are distinguished, the remains of which are studied comparatively, the results being summarized in a chronological chart (p. 67). In addition to ample illustrations in the text, a whole volume of plates is appended, and there are various specialized studies, particularly a chapter on inscriptions by Dr. Diringer, which will primarily interest O.T. scholars. With these volumes Miss Tufnell brings her sterling work on Lachish to a worthy conclusion.

J.G.

HISTORY AND GEOGRAPHY

BAR-DEROMA, H. : *Wezeh Gevul Haares. The True Boundaries of the Holy Land according to the Sources* (in Hebrew). 1958. Pp. 30+ 808+74 plates+1 detached map. (B.E.R. Publishing, Jerusalem).

This book, the title of which is drawn from Ezek. xlvii. 15, embodies a very detailed piece of research concerning the boundaries of the Holy Land based on a wealth of Hebrew sources as well as numerous non-Hebrew sources. In it the author endeavours to present the boundaries of the country as conceived in ancient times, before they were (in the author's view) distorted through prejudice or unwillingly through ignorance. In the first of its six chapters the problem of the country's boundaries in general is dealt with, and it is shown that the boundaries mentioned in Gen. xv. 8, and no others, are those assumed by the minds of the Jews throughout the ages. In its succeeding three chapters a minute account of the southern, northern, and eastern boundaries is given, after which comes an elaborate chapter containing well over three hundred pages, which forms a full study in its own right. Apart from the reinforcement it gives to the views already expressed, it expounds the well-known *Beraitha* concerning the boundaries of the Holy Land in its various versions as recorded in the *Yerushalmi, Siphre* and *Tosephta*. The last chapter treats of the *Beraitha*, attributed to the Tannaitic Period, about the seven seas and the four rivers encompassing the country.

The book, magnificently produced, and containing four detailed indices, deserves attention for its entirely independent views which are argued with erudition. M.W.

BUIS, P. : *Josias* (Témoins de Dieu, 16) 1958. Pp. 120. (Les Éditions du Cerf, Paris. Price : Frs. 270).

In eight chapters the author sketches a mainly convincing picture of king Josiah and his times. As in the previous volumes of this popular and useful series, the narrative is straight-forward, eschews controversy and discussion (though based on modern work of all confessions), and is aimed at the

' intelligent layman '. The materials used are biblical, being mainly those in the books of Kings and Chronicles, helped out by Deuteronomy and Jeremiah. Any imaginative reconstruction is restrained, and the book may usefully be read by scholars, not least as a lesson in how to present material intelligently and intelligibly. There is a short bibliography (where the I.C.C. of Montgomery and Gehman is incorrectly cited).   D.R.Ap-T.

DU BUIT, M. : *Géographie de la Terre Sainte* 2 vols. 1958. Pp. 238 (Vol. 1)+18 maps (Vol. 2). (Éditions du Cerf, Paris. Price : Frs. 1,200).

The first volume of this useful supplement of the ' Bible de Jérusalem ' is divided into two parts. The first concerns the physical geography of Palestine and Transjordan and the influence of the regional peculiarities on the sociology of the inhabitants. The second part is devoted to historical geography. Here the author limits himself practically to the Biblical period, taking Biblical texts as the basis of his elucidation of local communications and settlements. This treatment will be of definite service to the student and explorer alike, though the larger historical range of Sir George Adam Smith's work gives a more lasting impression of the relationship of the geography of Palestine to Biblical history. A topographical index with Biblical references and brief notes of archaeological and topographical research is also most useful. Volume 2 contains 18 loose political and contour maps.   J.G.

BUSCH, F–O. : *The Five Herods*, trans. by E. W. Dickes, 1958. Pp. 192+19 illustrations+1 map. (Robert Hale, London. Price : 21s. 0d.).

This is not a textbook, for much of it is imaginative reconstruction and imaginary conversation ; it is rather a personal retelling of the story of the Herods by one who has made a serious study of their lives and times. Herr Busch has produced a most reasonable book.   W.D.McH.

JOIN-LAMBERT, M. : *Jerusalem*, trans. by C. Haldane. (Ancient Cities and Temples.) 1958, pp. 224, including 134 plates. (Elek Books, London. Price : 30s. 0d.).

The inaugural volume of a series on ancient cities and temples published in conjunction with Putnam's of New York and the Ryerson Press of Canada. It is translated by C. Haldane and sumptuously illustrated with photographs, maps, charts, and reproduced prints (the ' Seal of Jazaniah ', plate 28, is printed from the wrong side of the negative). The book contains a popular history of the city from earliest times to 1187 A.D., using evidence from the Bible, archaeology, and pilgrims' accounts, but without any critical study of the sources. It is well written and translated, and easy to read.   J.N.S.

PEROWNE, S. : *The Later Herods : The Political Background of the New Testament*. 1958. Pp. xvi+216+43 plates and 3 maps. (Hodder & Stoughton, London. Price : 25s. 0d.).

This is a sequel to the author's earlier work, *The Life and Times of Herod the Great* (Book List, 1957, pp. 24f.) but it is also quite different, for the story of the Herodian family with its dynastic rivalries and religious feuds lacks a strong central figure and is best regarded, as the sub-title indicates, as an account of the political background of the New Testament. Mr. Perowne has produced a well-written book, adorned with carefully chosen and beautifully reproduced plates.

W.D.McH.

TÄUBLER, E. : *I Biblische Studien : Die Epoche der Richter* (Herausgegeben von Hans-Jürgen Zobel). 1958. Pp. xvi+320. (J. C. B. Mohr, Tübingen. Price : DM. 33 ; bound, DM. 37).

Eugen Täubler (d. 1953) was predominantly an ancient historian, but was trained also in classical and oriental philology and archaeology ; it was only in his later years that he devoted himself to Old Testament Studies. Whereas the period of the Judges is commonly treated as a preparatory prelude to the establishment of the Israelite kingdom, Täubler maintains that it would more fitly be described as the period of the free tribes, bound together, not in any kind of *Ämterstaat*, but in what may be designated as a *Personenverbandstaat* based on kinship. This period had many literary types, but most characteristic of it was the *novelle* which in some cases received a later theocratizing form. He deals with the historical problems of his period with great care and considers the term '*ibrim-Habiru* to have designated those who lived on the *bank* (of the middle Euphrates) ; likewise he gives much attention to the geographical questions which lie in the line of his inquiries and (of importance for his own line of interpretation) he identifies the Yenoam of the last line of Menephta's inscription with the Janoha (Janoah) of Jos. xvi. 6f. which lies some seven miles south-east of Shechem. Not all his conclusions will be accepted, but he has a fresh and stimulating way of dealing with problems of interpretation which have caused much discussion ; and, when we note that he takes within his field of survey, not only the narratives of the Book of Judges, but the utterances concerning the tribes in Gen. xlix, we may concede that he has ample room in which to operate. This book will renew discussion on many subjects in a field of investigation in which the evidences are extremely difficult to control. J.M.

WELLHAUSEN, J. : *Israelitische und Jüdische Geschichte*. (9th Edition). 1958. Pp. 372. (Verlag Walter de Gruyter & Co., Berlin. Price : DM. 14.80).

The student of Israel's history will always be indebted to the analytical method of Wellhausen, but the reprinting of this *Geschichte* serves rather to remind us of the great amount of new source material and new methods of historiography that have come to us during the last fifty years. A.S.H.

TEXT AND VERSIONS

HANHART, R. and KAPPLER, W. : *Septuaginta. Vetus Testamentum Graecum auctoritate Societatis Litterarum Gottingensis editum, Vol. IX, fasc.* 2. *Maccabaeorum Liber II*. 1959. Pp. 116. (Vandenhoeck & Ruprecht, Göttingen. Price : DM. 14.50 ; by subscription, DM. 12.30).

The editor of I Macc. (published in 1936), Werner Kappler,

left behind on his death the manuscript form of his reconstructed
edition of II Macc., and the *apparatus criticus*, and this was
revised by Robert Hanhart, and is now published as the
second fascicle of volume IX of the Göttingen LXX. The
work follows the usual pattern of this extremely important
edition and, obviously, will be included in the library of every
serious Biblical student. The S.O.T.S. congratulates the
Göttingen Society on the speedy appearance of its LXX, and
on its ability to recruit a succession of very fine scholars to
take the lead in this work.   B.J.R.

HERKLOTS, H. G. G. : *How the Bible Came to Us : Its Texts and Versions.*
1959. Pp. 190+8 plates (Penguin Books, Harmondsworth, Middlesex. Price : 3s. 6d.).

This is a revised edition of the book published in 1954, under
the title *Back to the Bible*, and reviewed in *Book List*, 1955,
p. 42 (cf. 1957, p. 27). The additions are an expansion of the
chapter dealing with the Qumran Scrolls (but still giving
prominence to datings not now widely held), and an excellent
new chapter on modern translations.   D.R.J.

ROTH, C. : *The Aberdeen Codex of the Hebrew Bible.* (Aberdeen University Studies, No. 138). 1958. Pp. 38+25 plates. (Oliver & Boyd,
Edinburgh, for the University of Aberdeen. Price : 21s. 0d.).

MS 23 in the University Library, Aberdeen, is a Hebrew Bible
' of exquisite penmanship ' as Dr. Johnson described it in
1773. Written in a Sephardi hand on 388 vellum leaves it was
completed in A.D. 1494. In this well-produced, well-illustrated
book Dr. Roth provides a full introduction to the manuscript.
He concludes from its binding, calligraphy, and illuminations
that its place of origin was Naples, and he gives a very reasonable reconstruction of its genesis and early history, showing
that though the writing was done by a Spanish exile the
decoration is Christian. We commend warmly the enlightened
policy of the University of Aberdeen in providing so useful a
handbook.   W.D.McH.

SCHREINER, J. : *Septuaginta-Massora des Buches der Richter : Eine
textkritische Studie* (Anelecta Biblica 7). 1957. Pp. xii+138.
(Pontificio Istituto Biblico, Rome. Price : 5.50).

The introduction to this most valuable study contains a
brief historical survey of the ' two-fold ' Greek text of Judges
and recent modifications of the theory. Despite all pre-
dilection for Greek MSS, however, relationship must be
established with M.T., and this aim fully justifies the author's
collation in the remainder of the book. Variants are classified
under the following headings : the use of common words such
as pronouns; the Divine Name ; syntax ; plus and minus
readings ; influence of context ; changes due to content and
exegesis ; style ; errors and incidental omissions ; doublets ;
varying nuances of individual words ; scribal errors ; inner-
Greek corruption.   B.J.R.

SNAITH, N. H. (ed. by) : *Sepher Torah, Nebi' im U-Kethubim*. 1958
Pp. 1366 (The British and Foreign Bible Society, London. Price :
17s. 6d.).

All that can be reasonably expected here is a warm greeting
to the British and Foreign Bible Society's long-awaited new
edition of the Hebrew Bible by Principal Snaith. It is well
produced, printed by the Oxford University Press in an
attractive fount, on thin paper tightly bound so that the
volume is of convenient size. As is customary with the
Society's publications, the edition has no introduction, and
the serious student must still turn to the editor's announcement in *Vetus Testamentum*, VII, 2 (April, 1957) pp. 107f,
for an all-too-brief account of the edition.

The text shows paragraph divisions and the final massorah
for each book, and in both cases divergences are to be found
with BH^3. A table of Haphtaroth is added.

No doubt the edition will be critically assessed and possibly
some shortcomings pointed out. But the Society for O.T.
Study welcomes very sincerely this new edition, to replace
the rather unsatisfactory Letteris text with which too many
theological students of too many generations have tried to
work on the set texts of their degree courses.   B.J.R.

WALLENSTEIN, M. : *A Dated Tenth Century Hebrew Parchment Frag-
ment from the Cairo Genizah in the Gaster Collection in the John
Rylands Library* (Reprinted from *Bulletin of the John Rylands
Library*, vol. 40, No. 2, March, 1958.) Pp. 551-558 (Manchester
University Press and the John Rylands Library, Manchester,
Price : 2s. 6d.).

Written on both sides, the fragment contains *recto* a colophon
by a Scribe in Gaifa (N.N.E. of Cairo) ' in the year 886 '
($+ 68 = $A.D. 954) and *verso* parts of the text of Jer. i. 1-12
in two columns, supplied with Tiberian vowel and accent
marks and also Babylonian pointing, both by the same hand.
The intrinsic value of the fragment is secondary to its significance as a rare remnant of bi-vocalised texts. Dr. Wallenstein has produced a workmanlike treatment of this important
fragment, and we hope that he will make further successful
researches into the riches of the Gaster Collection now in the
John Rylands Library at Manchester.   B.J.R.

EXEGESIS AND MODERN TRANSLATIONS

ARCHER, G. L. Jr., (Translator) : *Jerome's Commentary on Daniel*.
1958. Pp. 190. (Baker Book House, Grand Rapids. Price :
$3.95).

The translator's reason for undertaking the present work is
made sufficiently clear in the first sentence of Dr. Wilbur M.
Smith's introduction. ' The most important single work produced by the Church Fathers on any of the prophetic writings
of the Old Testament, commenting upon the original Hebrew
text, and showing a complete mastery of all the literature of
the Church on the subjects touched upon to the time of

composition, is without question St. Jerome's commentary
on the Book of Daniel.' Most of the writers on Jerome's
exegetical work stress one or more of the three characteristics
that make his commentary on Daniel so precious. First, he
includes a great variety of factual information ; next, he
provides copious details about obscure phases in the history
of the ancient world ; lastly, he includes many quotations
from early writers whose works are no longer available in
their entirety.

Dr. Archer has evidently taken great pains over the version,
and a comparison with the text as printed in volume xxv.
of the Latin Migne shows that he has given us a faithful rendering. He has also included, in an appendix, his translation
of Migne's footnotes to the text. The addition of a few notes
of his own and of an index to the proper names would have
increased the usefulness of the book.   J.M.T.B.

BONHOEFFER, D. : *Creation and Fall : A Theological Interpretation of
Genesis* 1-3. Trans. by J. C. Fletcher 1959. Pp. 96. (S.C.M. Press.
Price :   8s. 6d.).

This book is the translation of the German work reviewed in
the *Book List* for 1956, pp. 41f. In its English dress it will
reach a wider circle of readers in this country and be valued
as a further revelation of a remarkably penetrating theological
mind. The warning should be issued again, however, that this
book passes beyond the limits of exegesis proper and, further,
delights in paradoxes which can scarcely have been present
to the minds of the original writers. They may well be in
order, of course, when the question of the theological appropriation of Scripture is raised, as it is in this book. A criticism
of Bonhoeffer's theological views, however, would not be in
place here.   N.W.P.

VAN DEN BORN, A. : *Koningen uit de grondtekst vertaald en uitgelegd*
(De Boeken van het Oude Testament, Deel IV, Boek II.) 1958.
Pp. 238 (J. J. Romen & Zonen, Roermond en Maaseik. Price :
Fl. 9, by subscription).

•In this commentary van den Born recognizes Kings to be the
concluding part of the work of the Deuteronomic historian.
He is not convinced that in its first form it ended with Josiah's
reformation, holding that the fall of the southern monarchy
was in the writer's mind from the outset as part of his history.
There are, he thinks, a number of even later additions ; e.g.,
1 Kings iv. 24 (Heb., v. 4), where the description of Solomon's
realm as *kol 'eber hannahar* must come from the Persian period.
He justly describes Kings as ' the first comprehensive and
synoptic history book that has come down to us from the
Ancient Near East ' (p. 11), and finds the author's unifying
principle (apart from his general Deuteronomic outlook) in
the promise of Nathan to David in 2 Sam. vii. This promise
influences the whole history, and although it seems doomed
to frustration by the fall of the Davidic monarchy, the last

incident to be recorded—the release of Jehoiachin—is intended as a token that the promise still holds good. There is a useful appendix of thirty-three translations of contemporary documents, from Shalmaneser III's account of the battle of Karkar to the list of Jehoiachin's rations.
F.F.B.

ELLISON, H. L. : *From Tragedy to Triumph. The Message of the Book of Job.* 1958. Pp. 128. (Paternoster Press, London. Price : 10s. 6d.).

The author first discusses various topics relating to the Book of Job itself. Then the text of R.V. is printed chapter by chapter, and after each chapter a page or two of general comment on the meaning of the chapter. The comments are brief, simple, and clear and would be helpful to the general reader. It is strange that as so often in popular books on Job there is no mention of Pedersen's helpful exposition. G.H.D.

GUTBROD, K. : *Das Buch vom Reich : Das Zweite Buch Samuel übersetzt und ausgelegt.* (Die Botschaft des Alten Testaments, 11/II.) 1958. Pp. 290. (Calwer Verlag, Stuttgart. Price : DM. 12.80).

Granted that a theological christological exposition of the books of the Old Testament is valid, then this commentary commends itself as a lively guide to the interpretation of 2 Samuel. The book is treated separately from 1 Samuel on the grounds that whereas the first book treats of the person of the king and the nature of kingship (see *Book List*, 1957, p. 32) the second book treats of the kingdom and its founder seen as a type and anticipation of the greater kingdom and its founder. The translation takes account of recent work on the Hebrew text and has brief footnotes when other readings and emendations have been followed. The running commentary also takes account of recent work ; but critical study is subordinated to didactic and homiletic interests.

In the opinion of the reviewer the book abounds in examples of forced exegesis and of exposition by association of ideas which show the weakness of such an approach to the interpretation of the Old Testament. We are told that the theologian can gain a much more competent conception of the significance of David's capture of Jerusalem than the historian can (p. 69) ; the death of the child born to David and Bath-sheba shows the cost of forgiveness and becomes a hinge on which to hang a homily on the vicarious death of Jesus (p. 150) ; of David's encounter with the Philistines in the valley of Rephaim (v. 17-25) Gutbrod says, ' Dies alles is freilich nur ein Modell und Zeichen für das letzte Ziel Gottes ' (p. 81).
L.H.B.

HAMMERSHAIMB, E. : *Amos fortolket.* 2nd edition. 1958. Pp. 140. (Nyt Nordisk Forlag, Arnold Busck, Copenhagen. Price : Dan. kr. 14.00).

The first edition of this valuable commentary was reveiwed in *Book List*, 1947, p. 21 (cf. *Eleven Years*, p. 83). In this new edition minor alterations and additions have been made, mainly in the footnotes, and the bibliography has been expanded ; but there is no important change in substance. The reviewer, who has found the book an admirable basis for teaching, warmly welcomes this new edition.　G.W.A.

KRAUS, H.-J. : *Psalmen*. (Biblischer Kommentar Altes Testament, XV) Lieferungen 1-5 (1958), 6 (1959). Pp. 1-480. (Verlag der Buchhandlung des Erziehungsvereins, Neukirchen, Kr. Moers. Price per Lieferung : DM. 7.00 or, by subscription, DM. 5.85).

It is no matter for surpise that for this new and attractive series of commentaries the volume on the Psalter was entrusted to Professor H. J. Kraus, who came to the fore in the field of O.T. study with his monograph on the so-called Enthronement Songs, i.e., *Die Königsherrschaft Gottes im Alten Testament* (see *Book List*, 1952, pp. 54f.) ; and it is clear from the pages already to hand that we are to have here a worthy and stimulating contribution to the study of the Psalms. The treatment of each psalm is prefaced, as a rule, with a bibliography of varying length, which takes note of special studies bearing on the psalm in question ; and this is followed by (a) a translation into German, (b) notes on the text, (c) a discussion of metrical form, literary style, and " Sitz im Leben ", and (d) a detailed exegesis of the psalm's contents. Passing reference is repeatedly made to some of the more recent literature bearing on the points under discussion, and a particularly valuable part of the commentary is the series of special studies on issues which are currently much to the fore. On the whole the author is restrained in the matter of textual criticism, and in his exegesis he normally shows himself familiar with present-day trends. With the study of the Psalter in its present highly controversial state it is unlikely that all the author's views on the more important issues will find anything like general acceptance, but there can be no reasonable doubt that in several respects this commentary carries the discussion forward along constructive lines ; and the reviewer's warm commendation is in no way tempered by the fact that in connexion with Ps. xlviii. 15 the author attributes to him a point of view which, in the work cited and elsewhere, he has been at pains to reject.
A.R.J.

RINGGREN, H. and WEISER, A. : *Das Hohe Lied, Klagelieder, Das Buch Esther*. (Das Alte Testament Deutsch, XVI, 2.) 1958. Pp. iv + 144. (Vandenhoeck und Ruprecht, Göttingen. Price : DM. 6.50, by subscription 5.60, or bound DM. 9.40, by subscription DM. 8).

In this volume, which conforms to the now well-known pattern of the series, Ringgren is responsible for the Song of Songs and Esther, and Weiser for Lamentations. The introduction to the Song of Songs is very brief, but Ringgren reviews the different interpretations of the book that have been proposed, and favours the cultic view of its origin, but thinks the origin had been forgotten before it was taken into the canon. Weiser gives a longer introduction to Lamentations, which he thinks came from the hand of a single author, and holds that chapter i was written after the surrender of Jerusalem by Jehoiachin and the others after the destruction of the city by Nebuchadrezzar. The introduction to Esther is again very brief. Here Ringgren does not rule out the possibility of a historical kernel in the book, though it is not a strictly historical work. He is more interested in the origin of the feast of Purim, which he traces to a Persian New Year feast, Mithrakāna. In *Svensk exegetisk årsbok* xx, 1956, Ringgren has a much fuller discussion of this question. The new translations of the books are accompanied by the briefest of textual notes, and followed by commentaries dealing with the thought and meaning, and not of the verse by verse kind. H.H.R.

RUDOLPH, W. : *Jeremia* (Handbuch zum Alten Testament, 12). 2nd edition. 1958. Pp. XXIV+302. (J. C. B. Mohr, Tübingen. Price : 47s. 0d.).

In this second and revised edition of his excellent commentary on Jeremiah, Professor Rudolph takes account of work published since its first appearance in 1947, (see *Book List*, 1947, p. 22 ; *Eleven Years*, p. 84), particularly the cuneiform texts published by D. J. Wiseman, thus adding to the usefulness of one of the best helps to the understanding of the prophet. G.W.A.

La Sainte Bible traduite en français sous la direction de l'École Biblique de Jérusalem.

L'Exode, by B. Couroyer. 2nd ed. revised, 1958. Pp. 182+1 map. Price : Frs. 600. *Le Lévitique*, by H. Cazelles. 2nd ed. revised, 1958. Pp. 132. Price : Frs. 420. *Les Nombres*, by H. Cazelles. 2nd ed. revised. 1958. Pp. 156+1 map. Price : Frs. 600. *Le Deutéronome*, by H. Cazelles. 2nd ed. revised. 1958. Pp. 142+1 map. Price : Frs. 465. *Le Livre de Josué*, by F-M. Abel and M. du Buit. 2nd ed. revised. 1958. Pp. 110+1 map. Price : Frs. 465. *Le Livre des Juges*. *Le Livre de Ruth*, by A. Vincent. 2nd ed. revised. 1958. Pp. 166+1 map. Price : Frs. 540. *Les Livres des Rois*, by R. de Vaux. 2nd ed. revised. 1958. Pp. 248+1 map. Price : Frs. 690. *Tobie*, by R. Pautrel. 2nd ed. revised. 1957. Pp. 64. Price : Frs. 270. *Judith*. *Esther*, by A. Barucq. 2nd ed. revised. 1959. Pp. 136. Price : Frs. 540. *Le Livre de Job*, by C. Larcher. 2nd ed. revised. 1957. Pp. 176. Price : Frs. 555. *Le Livre des Proverbes*, by H. Duesberg and P. Auvray. 2nd ed. revised. 1957. Pp. 136. Price : Frs. 465. *L'Ecclésiaste*, by R. Pautrel. 3rd ed. revised. 1958. Pp. 44. Price : Frs. 255. *Le Livre de la Sagesse*, by E. Osty. 2nd ed. revised. 1957. Pp. 116. Price : Frs. 420. *L'Ecclésiastique*, by H. Duesberg and P. Auvray. 2nd ed. revised. 1958. Pp. 240. Price : Frs. 780. *Isaïe*, by P. Auvray and J. Steinmann. 2nd ed. revised. 1957. Pp. 268. Price : Frs. 825. *Ezéchiel*, by P. Auvray. 2nd ed. revised. 1957. Pp. 196, inc. 5 figs. Price : Frs. 660. *Daniel*, by J. de Menasce. 2nd ed. revised 1958.

Pp. 108. Price : Frs. 390. *Michée, Sophonie, Nahum*, by A. George. 2nd ed. revised. 1958. Pp. 100. Price : Frs. 360. *Le Livre de Jonas*, by A. Feuillet. 2nd ed. revised. 1957. Pp. 36. Price : Frs. 150. (Les Éditions du Cerf, Paris).

These volumes of the Jerusalem Bible have all appeared in revised form. In each case the revision has been made by two or more scholars other than the original author of the particular volume. The comments of correspondents and reviewers have been taken into consideration, as well as new sources of knowledge. The amount of the revision differs in the various volumes, and in some cases is quite considerable. Some volumes have been extended by ten or more pages. Editions with abridged notes may be obtained, though not of the separate books. H.H.R.

VON UNGERN-STERNBERG, R. Freiherr : *Der Rechtsstreit Gottes mit seiner Gemeinde : Der Prophet Micha, übersetzt und ausgelegt* (Die Botschaft des Alten Testaments, 23/III). 1958. Pp. 179. (Calwer Verlag, Stuttgart. Price : DM. 9.80).

The interest of the writer of this exposition of Micah lies in the message offered by the book when it is treated as a unity and as a product of the Exile, a work which incorporated what remained (i-iii, vi-vii. 7) of the prophecies of the prophet himself. The message is regarded as of universal application and capable of being read as if it were addressed to a Christian community. For example, in discussing the prophecy addressed to Bethlehem (iv. 14–v. 5) the author says (p. 116), ' This prophecy reaches forward to the Second Coming of the Shepherd and Lord, to the time when his rule and pastoral work will be visible to the whole world '. And on the next page, ' The community at that time (i.e., the time of utterance) could do no more than hear this prophecy as applicable to its own need '. That is to say, the expositor expects his material to yield two meanings, one for the time in which it was uttered or written, and one for the Christian church at all times, including our own day.

The method followed is to offer a translation of each section (without any notes to explain emendations) and then to give a running commentary, in homiletic fashion. L.H.B.

ZIMMERLI, W. : *Ezechiel*, Lief. 5. (Biblischer Kommentar : Altes Testament, XIII, 5). 1958. Pp. 321-400. (Verlag der Buchhandlung des Erziehungsvereins, Neukirchen Kr. Moers. Price : DM. 7.00, or by subscription DM. 5.85).

This further Lieferung (cf. *Book List*, 1956, p. 35 ; 1957, p. 36 ; 1958, p. 25) carries the exposition up to the beginning of xviii, but the exposition of the great section on individual responsibility remains to be completed in the next Lieferung. Unquestionably Professor Zimmerli is giving us one of the outstanding expositions of Ezekiel. G.W.A.

LITERARY CRITICISM AND INTRODUCTION
(including History of Interpretation, Canon, and Special Studies)

AUZOU, G. : *La tradition biblique : histoire des écrits sacrés du peuple de Dieu.* 1957. Pp. 462. Éditions l'Orante, Paris. Price : 22s. 6d.

The aim of this author is to provide an account of the composition of the Bibilical writings (including the Apocrypha, much of the Pseudepigrapha, and the New Testament) in their historical relationship. He writes for students and non-expert readers, and therefore sets out to give the more or less agreed results of modern scholarship, without the complications that follow from presenting a bewildering variety of opinions. Bibliographical footnotes are reduced to a minimum and are mainly confined to available works in French. The reviewer's opinion is that he has succeeded in this objective, despite, on so large a canvas, the occasional superficiality or lack of balance. The virtues of the book are rare enough. First, it is written well, in French that is terse, economical and sometimes brilliantly felicitous. Secondly, the total presentation of entirely up-to-date scholarship is such as to create an impressive and positive synthesis. The critical approach is seen to minister everywhere to the unfolding of the story of salvation. As the reader lays down this book, he may well say : ' This has entirely vindicated both criticism and biblical truth '. Thirdly, the range of the author's scholarship is immense. He is free with the civilizations of Greece and Rome, as well as with the Near Eastern background to the Bible. Fourthly he combines with his flair for the sound critical position (exemplified in his handling of the material from Qumram), a fine spiritual penetration. This book ought to be welcomed and used far outside the Roman Communion. D.R.J.

DRIJVERS, P. : *Les Psaumes : genres littéraires et thèmes doctrinaux* (Lecto divina, 21). 1958. Pp. 226. (Les Editions du Cerf.).

This useful introduction to the Psalter is a translation of a work which originally appeared in Dutch under the title *Over de Psalmen : Een Inleiding tot hun Betekenis en Geest* (Utrecht, 1956). That which makes this introduction specially commendable is the way in which the author goes beyond the now familiar approach to the study of the Psalms in terms of their literary types in an effort to bring out the important elements in the religious faith which they reflect, notably the thought of "salvation" ; for this is wholly in line with the most recent trends in this field. Although the subject is treated from within the context of the Christian faith as taught by the Roman Catholic Church, those outside this communion should welcome the book for the author's recognition of what needs to be done. Having said as much, however, the reviewer must add that the work as a whole, is marked by leaps of thought, due in some measure to neglect of the important historical factors involved, which leave him far from satisfied with the final result. Even so, a valuable little book. A.R.J.

EISSFELDT, O. : *Die Genesis der Genesis. Vom Werdegang des ersten Buches der Bibel.* 1958. Pp. viii+86+1 map. (J. C. B. Mohr, Tübingen. Price : paper, DM. 7.40 ; bound, 9.40).

This little book is a slightly altered and expanded form in German of an article on Genesis which Professor Eissfeldt has written for the Interpreter's Dictionary of the Bible. It is an excellent example of *multum in parvo*. After a brief survey of the various types of hypothesis which have been propounded concerning the composition of the Pentateuch, Eissfeldt argues that even a documentary hypothesis must leave room for isolated fragments ; and that leads him to introduce his theory of the document L as the only way to represent the coherence of the fragments separable from the document J. He then analyses the nature of the earlier materials which were utilized by the editors of the pentateuchal documents, such as genealogical and king lists, songs and sayings, cosmological and anthropological myths, aetiological stories concerning place-names and so on. The question of the historicity of the pentateuchal narratives is discussed in cases in which it is apposite to raise it, and Eissfeldt finds most historical value in narratives concerning tribes and peoples and in cult legends. He would admit that some of the statements which he makes are highly controversial, but he has, in remarkable detail for so small a book, shown the nature of the pentateuchal problem ; and he has added a valuable bibliography.   J.M.

HYATT, J. P. : *Jeremiah, Prophet of Courage and Hope.* 1958. Pp. 128. (Abingdon Press, New York and Nashville. Price : $2.00).

The author has concentrated on Jeremiah for some fifteen years, and has now written a popular and very readable interpretation of the prophet's life and thought. The first chapter discusses prophets in general, and after a chapter on the historical background, the various prophecies are discussed in the setting of three periods of the prophet's life. Other chapters deal with the character of the prophet's life, his ideas of God, his thought concerning God and man, his hope, and finally the permanent values in the prophet's life and message. The book is to be commended to all preachers and general students.   N.H.S.

LINDBLOM, J. : *A Study on the Immanuel Section in Isa. vii. 1-ix. 6.* 1958. Pp. 58. (C. W. K. Gleerup, Lund.).

This valuable study is built on a sound introductory foundation of observations on the nature of the prophetic oracles and their transmission. There are no startling revelations, but it is good to have Lindblom's mind on a host of disputed points.

Thus, he follows Köhler in his interpretation of *sheār yāshûb* ; translates vii. 9 as : ' If you will not have trust, you will surely not stand steadfast' ; identifies the *'almâh* with the consort of Ahaz ; finds in ' curds and honey ' the symbol of abundance ; offers an interesting but not compelling interpretation of viii. 13-14 ; identifies the wonderful child of ix. 1-6 with Immanuel ; translates viii. 6 as : ' it shall surely dissolve together with Rezin and Remalyahu ' ; regards the binding and sealing of viii. 16 as metaphorical ; and so on. But the details are meant to serve a wider thesis, viz. : that, in the Syro-Ephraimitic crisis, Isaiah predicted the birth of a prince (Immanuel), who would introduce a new period of history. This period of bliss would, however, be no more than an interregnum. The disbelief of Ahaz revealed to the prophet that Judah's doom must follow the period of happiness ; and the divine purpose would then be realized through a ' remnant ', ruled by an everlasting series of Davidides. Here many will cease to follow Lindblom in attributing so clear-cut a scheme of salvation to Isaiah himself. It may be objected that he has failed to carry through his own principles of traditio-historical criticism, and has not allowed sufficiently for the handling of these oracles in the school of Isaiah up to and during the Exile. D.R.J.

MARIANI, B. : *Introductio in libros sacros Veteris Testamenti*. 1958. Pp. xiv.+646. (Casa Editrice Herder, Rome. Price : L. 3,600).

This is a work of considerable learning and of extremely conservative tendency. In fact one earlier reviewer (L. Alonso-Schökel in *Biblica*, Vol. 39, pp. 499 ff.) declares that Mariani's position is ' non valde dissimilem illi quae a sic dictis " fundamentalistis " tenetur .' The section on the Pentateuch occupies, as might be expected, about a quarter of the volume and concludes to the whole being written by Moses himself with the exception of the account of his death and some later glosses. There are many other sections in which, as in regard to the Pentateuch, the author's critical judgment does not seem to be equal to his learning. It is, at least, instructive to compare his views with those of Miller and Metzinger in their enlightened *Introductio specilis in Vetus Testamentum* (cf. *Book List*, 1946, p. 25). J.M.T.B.

PRELIPCEAN, V., NEAGA, N. and BARNA, G. : *Studiul Vechiule Testament ; Manual pentru uzul studentilor istitutelor teologice*. 1955.

Pp. 288 (Editura Istitutului biblic și de misiune ortodoxă, Bucuresti.)

Following the work of V. Tarnavschi, *Introducere în Sf. Cărti ale Testamentului Vechiu* (1928), we now have this new introduction to the Old Testament from the Rumanian Orthodox Church. It is abundantly and comprehensively informative. Great importance is attached to the views of the Fathers ; and, in general, the position of the Orthodox Church is strongly represented. The unity and Mosaic authorship of the Pentateuch are maintained, as are the unity and Isaianic authorship of the Book of Isaiah, to take but two examples. On the other hand, the author of the Books of Samuel is said to be unknown. Nevertheless, the authors of the volume are well informed about the positions of critical scholarship, and refer to them in the text, though they reject them. It is noteworthy that there is a sharp break in the literature cited, just before the first World War ; for the period between the Wars only four Western and four Eastern Orthodox books are mentioned, and for the years since the second World War nothing at all. Nor is there any reference to the Qumran Texts. But in spite of these defects, our Rumanian colleagues have produced a good and useful work.   M.B.

WATTS, J. D. W. : *Vision and Prophecy in Amos :* 1955. Faculty Lectures, Baptist Theological Seminary, Ruschlikon/ZH, Switzerland. 1958. Pp. viii+90. (E. J. Brill, Leiden. Price : Fl. 9).

This brief study of the visions and message of Amos reaches three main conclusions. First, that Amos was a regular prophet and that he carried out his prophetic task *within* the cult. That cult was a syncretistic one having Canaanite elements originating in the fertility cult and Israelite elements whose main feature was the re-establishing of the covenant between Yahweh and his people. Second, that the terms of Amos's expectation of the Day of Yahweh and the judgment attending it were directly borrowed from the language of the cult. 'Amos knew the cult of his day to be syncretistic. He therefore did not hesitate to use its valid portions in the very act of condemning those invalid parts.' (p. 67) Third, the so-called doxologies form parts of an ancient hymn to Yahweh. This last is probably the weakest part of the book, not so much in its presentation as in its resort to a very free handling of the text in order that it may say the things that the hymnic pattern demands of it.
The attempt to demonstrate Amos's attachment to the cult serves a useful purpose in examining once again the vexed question of the nature of his prophethood, although the arguments do not always carry conviction.   L.H.B.

YOUNG, E. J. : *Daniel's Vision of the Son of Man* (Tyndale Old Testament Lecture, 1958.) 1958. Pp. 28. (Tyndale Press, London. Price : 1s. 6d.).

The author argues briefly for the unity of Dan. 7, but devotes his attention mainly to verses 13f. He finds no identification in the Vision of the ' one like unto a son of man ' with ' the saints of the Most High ', and claims that it should be understood as the Messiah and quite specifically of Jesus Christ. He has taken note of recent discussions of this subject, but the theological interests that govern his argument might have been more adequately served by a better appreciation of the concept of corporate personality.   A.S.H.

LAW, RELIGION, AND THEOLOGY

ABBA, R. : *The Nature and Authority of the Bible.* 1958. Pp. xvi+334. (James Clarke & Co., London. Price : 21s. 0d.).

The author of this book offers it as his response to a suggestion that he ' should write a book about the Bible which would gather up, for the educated layman, the chief fruits of twentieth-century biblical scholarship'. It should therefore be judged with reference to its aim and it should be admitted that the educated layman will find here much that will be most helpful to him. He will learn about the history of Biblical interpretation, about the Biblical view of history and the way in which revelation comes through history, about the universalizing of the historical revelation in ' myth ', about the relation between the Testaments and about what the author calls ' differing levels of truth '. It is regrettable, therefore, that in a book which purports to gather up ' the chief fruits of twentieth-century biblical scholarship ' there should be no mention of the work of Alt, Noth, and von Rad. Eichrodt's work is described as ' epoch-making ', but the author clearly has not been able to make much use of his great book on Old Testament Theology. Vriezen's *An Outline of Old Testament Theology* doubtless appeared in English too late to be used, but the German translation was available earlier. The references to the work of Scandinavian scholars are quite inadequate. The volume contains copious quotations, often skilfully used and handsomely acknowledged. Indeed, much of what is good is based on the work of Rowley, Dodd and Richardson. What is good in this book makes one sorry to have to point out how much is lacking. There is, however, much that is well said and will be most helpful to the readers for whom the book is intended.

N.W.P.

ASENSIO, F. : *El Dios de la Luz : Avances a través del A. Testamento y contactos con el Nuevo.* (Analecta Gregoriana, Vol. XC. A 16.) 1958. Pp. 226. (Pontificia Universita Gregoriana, Rome. Price : $3.50).

The author has already contributed two volumes to the series of *Analecta Gregoriana* namely *Misericordia et Veritas* (cf. *Book List*, 1951, p. 73) and *Yahweh y su Pueblo* (cf. *Book List*, 1954, p. 56). The present study, which has many references to the work of S. Aalen, *Die Begriffe " Licht " und " Finsternis " im Alten Testament, im Spätjudentum und in Rabbinismus* (Oslo, 1951 ; cf. *Book List*, 1952, p. 47) was originally intended as a monograph on the two concepts of light and life. Eventually it was seen that the concept of Light alone would be sufficient for a single study, based mainly on the Old Testament, while concerned also with extra-biblical writings, and with the New Testament. So the work which begins with the first chapter of Genesis ends with the Apocalypse. The chapter-headings give a fair idea of the contents : Light of the world, Light in Israel ; Light in the

161

ways of Life ; and ' The Gentiles shall walk in thy light '.
As usual the author has consulted a very wide range of
literature in a variety of languages.
It is unfortunate that there are a good many misprints in
proper names, which will, no doubt, be easily corrected. Thus
on p. 8 n. 14, Gressmann is spelt with only one ' n ' and
Blackman with two. Zimmern is misspelt on p. 18, n. 47
and elsewhere. Cheyne, given correctly in the index, appears
twice in the text in the form Cheine (p. 174, n. 69, and p. 179,
n. 95). Van den Oudenrijn is spelt with a final " h " (p. 174,
n. 71). There are misprints in H. Frankfort's name and in
the title of his work *Kingship and the Gods* (p. 197, n. 194).
One has also noticed Gottesnecht (p. 199, n. 212), Proksch
(p. 201, n. 218), and G. con Rad (p. 205, n. 241).   J.M.T.B.

BALLA, E. : *Die Botschaft der Propheten*, herausgegeben von G. Fohrer.
1958. Pp. viii+484. (J. C. B. Mohr, Tübingen. Price : paper
covers, DM. 15.50 bound, DM. 19.80).

In this posthumous volume, which has been edited and seen
through the press by Professor Georg Fohrer, we have the
legacy of more than twenty years of special study on the part
of one who first made a name for himelf nearly fifty years ago
by his examination of the ' I ' of the Psalms. Much of the volume
is taken up by a translation of the most important passages
in the books of the canonical prophets, and as a rule this is
accompanied in each case by a simple exposition which is
often little more than a simple paraphrase of the original.
Although the book thus appears to be designed for the general
reader, the expert will recognize at once the careful scholarship
upon which it is based ; and here, perhaps, the most interesting feature is Balla's acceptance of the view that the
figure portrayed in the Servant Songs of Isaiah xl-lv is the
prophet himself.   A.R.J.

ELLIS, E. E. : *Paul's Use of the Old Testament*. 1957. Pp. xii.+204.
(Oliver and Boyd, Edinburgh. Price : 21s. 0d.).

The author accurately describes his own book : ' The present
study is not primarily textual . . . . . . but rather seeks the
rationale underlying the Pauline usage both in its textual
manifestation and in its theological application ' (p. 1). He
concludes that though Paul's methods sometimes recall those
of the rabbis his use of the Old Testament is determined by
that of the apostolic Church and of Jesus himself. Much use
is made of the discussion by K. Stendahl (in *The School of
St. Matthew*) of *pesher* in the Dead Sea commentary on
Habakkuk, and there is a long discussion of Pauline typology.
The book contains some useful material, but does not inspire
confidence in all its details (e.g., the question of the possessive
pronoun with ' faith ' in Hab. ii. 4 is not mentioned) ; and no
treatment of Paul's use of the Old Testament can be counted
complete which deals only with quotations and does not take
into account the background of Pauline words such as
' righteousness '.   C.K.B.

ELLISON, H. L. : *Men Spake from God : Studies in the Hebrew Prophets.* 2nd edition. 1958. Pp. 160. (Paternoster Press, London. Price : 10s. 6d.).

This appears to be a reprint of the first edition (see *Book List*, 1952, p. 53 ; *Eleven Years*, p. 424), and the book now begins to appear rather dated, for there is little evidence of the more recent developments in the study of the prophets.
                                                                    G.H.D.

FOULKES, F. : *The Acts of God. A Study of the Basis of Typology in the Old Testament* (Tyndale Old Testament Lecture, 1955). 1958. Pp. 40. (Tyndale Press, London. Price : 1s. 6d.).

The author pursues a well founded argument that typology is rightly based on the conviction that the acts of God in Israel could be repeated, and that their repetition would occur on a surpassing scale of glory and significance. He illustrates this excellent argument with a number of well chosen illustrations which command assent. Then suddenly he leaps to the conclusion (p. 35) that 'All the action of God in the Old Testament history foreshadows His unique action and revelation in Christ '. This is a conclusion which his own argument has not proved, and which is not true in the sense in which the author intends it. It is a pity that such a logical failure should mar such an attractive piece of work.   G.H.D.

GEMSER, B. : *Vragen rondom de Patriarchenreligie* (Rede naar aanleiding van de annvaarding van het ambt van Hoogleraar in de oudtestamentische vakken aan de Rijksuniversiteit te Groningen, gehouden op. 22 April, 1958). 1958. Pp. 30. (J. B. Wolters, Groningen).

For his inaugural lecture as Professor of Old Testament at Groningen the author chose to deal with some of the chief questions about the religion of the patriarchs. Following Böhl, he notes four important features of the patriarchal traditions—their distinctive presentation, their personal emphasis, their historical setting, and their religious significance—and concentrates on the fourth. The patriarchal religion, he finds, was practically monotheistic. The various divine names compounded with ' El (' El-' Elyon, ' El-Shaddai, ' El-Ro'i, ' El-' Olam, etc.) do not denote distinct local numina, but local manifestations of one and the same ' El. Similarly, the God of Abraham, the God of Isaac and the God of Jacob are not three Gods but one. Such a monetheism on the part of a family whose migration to Canaan was dictated by a religious urge is, he holds both intrinsically probable and consistent with what we know today of the Near East in patriarchal times.   F.F.B.

HEATON, E. W. : *The Old Testament Prophets.* 1958. Pp. 188. (Penguin Books, Harmondsworth. Price : 3s. 6d.).

The author has completely revised the book earlier published under the title, *His Servants the Prophets* and noted in *Book List*, 1950, p. 57 ; the revision has increased the value of a deservedly popular book. Quotations are taken from R.S.V. ; the two important chapters, " The Vocation of the People " and " Faith and Fulfilment " have been considerably re-written. Two appendixes have been added ; I sets side by side the biblical event and its prophetic interpretation—this might well be revised in a subsequent edition ; II gives some valuable guidance on further reading. It is a vigorously written and deeply sensitive study and will be gratefully received by those engaged in teaching. A.S.H.

HENRY, M.–L. : *Das Tier im religiösen Bewusstsein des alttestament-lichen Menschen* (Sammlung gemeinverständlicher Vorträge und Schriften aus dem Gebiet der Theologie und Religionsgeschichte, 220/221), 1958. Pp. 52. (J. C. B. Mohr, Tübingen. Price : 7s. 0d.).

This is an important study of the relationship between animals and man in the thought of the Old Testament, and provides material which will have to be taken into account in future expositions of the Old Testament doctrine of man, as also in histories of the religion of Israel. The author's case is strongest when dealing with the earlier evidence for a sense of the unity of all created life, and there are many significant points contributing to her cumulative argument. Its weakness lies in a tendency to read perhaps too much significance into passages which may well be imaginative poetry rather than serious theological statements. It is doubtful whether one may argue from the Old Testament that, whereas man lost his original purity, the animals retained it. There is also a failure to observe that the *final* Old Testament doctrine of man is determined by Gen. i and Ps. viii, and that, in the total picture, these crucial pictures, though unique, are meant to reinterpret the earlier conceptions. In short, the author over-estimates the *nearness* of the relationship between animals and man, and under-estimates the *distance* in Old Testament thought.

D.R.J.

HOOKE, S. H. (ed. by) : *Myth, Ritual, and Kingship : Essays on the Theory and Practice of Kingship in the Ancient Near East and in Israel.* 1958. Pp. xii+308 (Clarendon Press, Oxford. Price : 35s. 0d.).

The hypothesis of a cult-pattern related to seasonal crises in the Ancient Near East is now reviewed after 25 years by S. H. Hooke, and S. Smith, H. Fairman, O. R. Gurney, R. De Langhe, G. Widengren, A. R. Johnson, H. H. Rowley, and S. G. F. Brandon. The present tone is one of reserve, and all are disposed to emphasize local peculiarities more than was previously done. The view nearest to the original hypothesis is held by Professor Widengren in his essay on ' Early Hebrew Myths and their Interpretation ', which is most stimulating even if, in our opinion, demanding serious qualification. Widengren's study and those of Professors Johnson and Rowley on Hebrew kingship and prophecy respectively indicate that ritual characteristics of the contemporary Near East, while not explaining Hebrew institutions fully, must certainly enter into our reckoning in Hebrew studies, the influence of liturgy certainly suggesting forms in which prophetic oracles were occasionally conveyed. J.G.

LAW, RELIGION, AND THEOLOGY 165

JACOB, E. : *Theology of the Old Testament*, trans. by A. W. Heathcote and P. J. Allcock. 1958. Pp. 368. (Hodder & Stoughton, London. Price : 30s. 0d.).

> In welcoming most warmly the appearance of this Theology of the Old Testament in an English dress it is not necessary to do much more than to refer to the review of the original French edition which appeared in the *Book List* of 1956, and to express the hope that this excellent work will now find many more readers. While not on the scale of the works by Eichrodt and Von Rad and while lacking the profound understanding of the problem of Old Testament theology which is such a notable feature of Vriezen's work, Jacob's contribution must be rated high for its comprehensiveness and the clarity of its statements. The most exciting part of the book is the treatment of God's mastery of history of which a foretaste was given in Jacob's brilliant monograph *La tradition historique en Israël*. As a reliable text-book for students this book should have a long life.   N.W.P.

ROWLEY, H. H. : *The Book of Job and its Meaning* (Reprinted from the *Bulletin of the John Rylands Library*, Vol. 41, No. 1. 1958. Pp. 167-207). 1958. Pp. 44 (Manchester University Press. Price : 3s. 6d.).

> We are once more indebted to one of our most prolific first rank scholars for an admirable monograph. The bibliographical guidance is as thorough as ever, and through the maze of suggestion and hypothesis which has gathered around this subject we are directed at every step to the real points at issue. Among the facts never to be forgotten are that Job never claims to have been perfect, but that he shares with his friends the thought that merit and fortune ought to be matched ; for despite all his complaints, Job never for one moment regrets his integrity of character. It is useful to remember, too, that the book of Job is concerned less with theology than with religion ; by insisting on the existence of innocent suffering, the way is opened for communion with God even in suffering. Everyone dealing in any way with the book of Job ought to have a copy of this lecture.   D.R.Ap-T.

SCHARBERT, J. : *Solidarität in Segen und Fluch im Alten Testament und in seiner Umwelt. I. Väterfluch und Vätersegen.* (Bonner Biblische Beiträge, No. 14.) 1958. Pp. xiv.+294. (Hanstein, Bonn. Price : DM. 32.00.)

> This work is presented as the first of a trilogy, which is designed to help solve the problem of the connexion between the individual and the community in O.T. theology, and the volume under review approaches the question by studying the concepts of " curse " and " blessing " within the father-son relationship. By carefully examining these ideas (*a*) as they operated at the various levels of society, and (*b*) as they appear in the different literary sources of the O.T. (ranged in what

is currently the most widely accepted chronological sequence), the author has no difficulty in showing how careful the Biblical exegete must be to recognize that, in seeking to evaluate the significance of the individual or the influence of sin upon the life of the community, he is dealing with a world of ideas very different from those of modern Western thought. The author has read widely, and his work is enriched with much valuable material of a comparative kind from the peoples of the ancient Near East and, equally important, the Bedouin of our own day. This is an encouraging beginning to what promises to be a most useful series of studies ; and the many members of this Society who have enjoyed the friendship of the Rev. Father R. A. Dyson, S.J., will welcome the tribute which the author pays to the inspiration which he received in this connexion from his former teacher. A.R.J.

SMITH, C. R. : *The Bible Doctrine of the Hereafter.* 1958. Pp. xiv+282· (Epworth Press, London. Price : 30s. 0d.).

This is the last of the late Dr. Ryder Smith's eight books on ' The Bible Doctrine of . . . ' , and it is published posthumously through the good graces of Dr. T. F. Glasson and G. W. Anderson. It was not the author's custom to quote authorities or to indicate where his views differed from those of other scholars, but here the editors have drawn the reader's attention to cases of widely differing opinion. The volume, like its predecessors, is a careful study of all the Biblical material, both Hebrew and Septuagint. He finds only two sure references in the Hebrew Bible to a belief that the individual rises from the dead, Isa. xxvi. 19 and Dan. xii. 2. The belief appears after the time of Alexander the Great. The Greek idea of the ' immortality of the soul ' when freed from the trammels of the body, has no place in Hebrew thought. The Parousia (date and nature), is fully discussed. The author finds an unresolved dilemma in the New Testament : everlasting punishment and universalism ; though he notes that the latter is more prominent in later documents, and refers to the Church rather than to the individual. There is no New Testament evidence for a conversion in an Intermediate State. N.H.S.

STAMM, J. J. : *Der Dekalog im Lichte der neueren Forschung.* (Studientage für die Pfarrer, Heft 1.) 1958. Pp. 56. (Paul Haupt, Bern. Swiss Fr. 3.80).

This little book contains two lectures, the first reviewing in a general way recent study of the Decalogue, and the second examining the ten commandments one by one. The author is well acquainted with recent literature on this much discussed subject, and many besides the parish clerk for whom the study was written will benefit from its reading. Abundant references to the literature will be found in the footnotes. In the first part of the study special attention is given to the work of Mowinckel and of Alt. H.H.R.

STAMM, J. J. : *Der Staat Israel und die Landverheissungen der Bibel.* 1957. Pp. 45. (Gotthelf-Verlag, Zürich.)

This is an attempt to understand the rôle of Israel in the Christian scheme of salvation. The author takes his stand between the familiar Christian view which simply identifies the new Israel with the Church, and the Jewish nationalist view which regards the new state of Israel as an important element in Israel's vocation to mediate blessing to the world. Professor Stamm surveys both the Old and the New Testament passages in two masterly chapters, and has no difficulty in showing that the final Christian hope includes the conversion of Israel. But this is now connected with the *second* coming of the Messiah ; Israel no longer has a mediatorial rôle ; and the Old Testament promise of land no longer has any place. The main queries arise from New Testament exegesis.

D.R.J.

STEINER, F. : *Taboo.* 1956. Pp. 154. (Philosophical Library, New York. Price : $4.75).

Dr. Steiner died in 1952, mostly because of sufferings caused in the last war, and his lectures have been prepared for the press by Dr. Laura Bohannan with a preface by Professor Evans-Pritchard. Taboo is an element in situations in which attitudes to values are expressed in terms of danger behaviour. It has two social functions : the classification and identification of transgressions, and the institutional localization of danger. Dr. Steiner discusses the discovery of taboo, and its outworkings in Polynesia, and then proceeds to discuss in turn the work of the main writers on Taboo and kindred subjects in recent years : Robertson Smith, Snaith, Frazer, Marett, van Gennep, Radcliffe-Brown, Wundt, and Freud. This is a book to be read by all students of primitive (and not so primitive) religion, and where the author's early and lamented death has prevented him from coming to well-matured opinions, the ideas themselves are most fruitful.

N.H.S.

TERRIEN, S. : *Job : Poet of Existence.* 1957. Pp. 256. (The Bobbs-Merrill Co., Inc., Indianapolis and New York. Price : $3.75).

For a commentary on the book of Job by this author see *The Interpreter's Bible* Vol. III (*Book List*, 1955, p. 32 ; *Eleven Years* p. 665). Here Terrien distils as it were the essence of the book into eight chapters whose aim is to show its relevance, interest and importance, whether viewed from the angle of psychology, literary experiment, existentialist philosophy, modern aesthetic, or theology of crisis. But such a cursory summary, even though it paraphrases the blurb, may be doing an injustice to what is a deeply thought out and very suggestive attempt to bring out not only the literary unity and progress of the poem, broadly speaking, but also its climax in a ' theology of creative participation '. We may wonder occasionally whether the author of Job might not be startled by some of the credits he receives here, but in the hands of

Professor Terrien the book does come alive and speaks to the doubting and despairing in contemporary thought form, and with many a quotation from a wide range of modern literature.
D.R.Ap-T.

WELCH, A. C. : *Visions of the End : A Study in Daniel and Revelation*. New edition with a forward by N. W. Porteous. 1958. Pp. 260. (James Clarke, London. Price : 12. 6d.).

This work by an influential scholar and teacher makes a welcome re-appearance after being out of print for some years. Like *Kings and Prophets of Israel*, it makes one envy those who were privileged to be Welch's students.   G.W.A.

WOOD, J. D. : *The Interpretation of the Bible : a Historical Introduction* (Studies in Theology.) 1958. Pp. 184. Gerald Duckworth, London. Price : 10s. 6d.).

In this book Professor Wood seeks to set forth the theological significance of the Bible, and endeavours to do this by tracing how Biblical interpreters in successive periods of the Church have understood the Bible. Then in a final chapter he estimates the meaning of the Bible for today. The book is mainly illustrative, recapitulating familiar material and favourite quotations. An interesting book for the general reader ; a parallel to but not a substitute for Farrar's Bampton Lectures of 1885.   G.H.D.

YOUNG, E. J. : *The Study of Old Testament Theology Today*. 1958. Pp. 112. (James Clarke & Co., London. Price : 10s. 6d.).

This little book may be welcomed as the attempt of a well-known American fundamentalist to explain his view of Old Testament Theology. He declares unequivocally ' that a truly Scriptural Old Testament Theology will part company with those approaches which do not receive the Scriptures as the authoritative revelation of God ', that means with all those who do not understand the Old Testament in a strictly literal way. It is not enough to believe that the Scriptures mediate revelation. We must accept one particular view of how God reveals Himself in Scripture. Need more be said? Though von Rad is praised for his competence and the great interest of his work on Old Testament Theology, his method is pronounced unacceptable because it ' is perfectly willing to make use of a " criticism " that will lead to results which conflict with the Bible's witness to itself '. Of course Biblical critics have said many things to which Professor Young rightly objects, but it is to be hoped that he would agree that it does not follow that, because A has been guilty of x, B of y and C of z, A, B and C are guilty of x, y and z. Many of his criticisms do not touch many of the critics at all. How many responsible scholars would agree with Edmund Wilson's view of the Dead Sea Scrolls (v. pp. 45-6)? On pp. 18 and 19 there seems to be a confusion between *Geschichte* and *Urgeschichte* which does not make for clarity.   N.W.P.

THE LIFE AND THOUGHT OF
THE NEIGHBOURING PEOPLES

MOSCATI, S. (ed. by) : *Le Antiche Divinità Semitiche*. (Studi Semitici, vol. I). 1958. Pp. 148. (Centro di Studi Semitici, Università di Roma. Lire 3000=$5=35/-).

This first volume of the newly constituted Centre of Semitic Studies at Rome University is edited, introduced, and summarized by the ever active and enthusiastic proponent of Semitic Studies in Italy, Professor Sabatino Moscati. It does honour to its learned editor and to this ancient seat of Oriental Studies—formerly graced by such famous scholars as Ignazio and Michelangelo Guidi, C. A. Nallino, U. Cassuto, and others. Each of the three contributors to this volume lectured on his subject at Rome University (and the reviewer had the privilege of being present at one of those lectures) and now presents his paper in his own language, i.e., French, English, and German. Professor Moscati provides an excellent introduction (in Italian) to the general question of the ancient Semitic deities and also offers a judicious summary and evaluation of the arguments propounded by the three contributors.

Professor Jean Bottero of the Ecole des Hautes Etudes speaks about the ancient Semitic deities of Mesopotamia ; Professor M. J. Dahood of the Pontificio Istituto Biblico about those of Syria and Palestine ; and Professor W. Caskel of Cologne University about the deities of ancient Arabia. There are also indexes of divine names as well as modern scholars, both compiled by G. Garbini.

All three studies are of profound relevance to O.T. scholars, and their principal value lies in the comprehensive treatment here provided. One must not look for significant advance beyond existing studies of detail nor for startling innovations. In the absence of explicit information much of the research inevitably turns on etymological discussion of divine nomenclature. It is for this reason in particular that Caskel's contribution appears a little too concerned with chronological minutiae. Dahood should not have omitted, on p. 67, a reference to G. R. Driver's *Canaanite Myths and Legends*, or, on p. 80, to U. Cassuto's *Goddess Anath*. Caskel might with advantage have made greater use of G. Ryckmans' *Les religions arabes préislamiques* ; and, though the early Ethiopian pantheon was not expressly included (p. 14), C. Conti Rossini's important observations (*Storia d'Etiopia*, chapter VI) should have received some consideration in a treatment of ancient Arabian deities, for they throw much light on the origin of at least some Semitic gods.   E.U.

THE DEAD SEA SCROLLS

BURROWS, M. : *More Light on the Dead Sea Scrolls : New Scrolls and New Interpretations with Translations of Important Recent Discoveries*. 1958. Pp. xiv+434+1 plate. (Secker & Warburg, London. Price : 35s. 0d.).

To his earlier book *The Dead Sea Scrolls* (cf. *Book List*, 1956, p. 65) Professor Burrows has now added a sequel of the same length. He brings the story of the discoveries up to date and adds translations of documents which were published after the appearance of his earlier book (including the published parts of the Genesis Apocryphon and selected texts from Vol. I of *Discoveries in the Judaean Desert);* he reviews the most significant recent lines of interpretation of the Qumran material, and he deals with some of the questions which have been most in the public mind since the Scrolls became front-page news. The biblical scholar may feel some impatience at the amount of space devoted to the criticism of certain theories whose flimsiness is self-evident to him ; but Professor Burrows is not writing primarily for scholars (although scholars will do well to read his book) but for interested laymen who have been bombarded with contradictory accounts of the Scrolls and their meaning and may well wonder which, if any, they are to believe. For these readers Professor Burrows expounds the subject patiently and objectively, considering the light thrown by the Scrolls on Christian origins, Old Testament and New Testament studies, and so forth, and describing the history, beliefs, and organization of the Qumran community. There is a good bibliography, and since many reviewers complained that the former volume lacked an index, the index to this one does duty for both volumes. This is a worthy sequel to what was justly acclaimed as ' the most comprehensive as well as the most readable ' of popular works on the Scrolls. F.F.B.

CARMIGNAC, J. : *La Règle de la Guerre des Fils de Lumière contre les Fils de Ténèbres*. 1958. Pp. xx+288. (Letouzey et Ané, Paris. Price : Fr. 2500).

This edition of the War Scroll contains the Hebrew text of the Scroll, with a number of emendations proposed by the editor, together with a translation and commentary. Carmignac believes the Scroll was written by the Teacher of Righteousness towards the end of his life, *circa* 110 B.C., and considered it to be a liturgy, rather than an apocalyptic text. The Kittim are equated with foreign foes in general, rather than with the Macedonians or the Romans. The introduction is very brief, but the commentary is full and it takes account of most of the literature which has already grown up around this text. Succeeding scholars will gratefully learn much from Carmignac, though not all of the proposed

170

emendations and interpretations may prove acceptable, and the reviewer is doubtful about the date and authorship proposed for the Scroll. By the patient and detailed study of the text, however, the editor has made an important contribution to the ever-growing literature on the Scrolls.   H.H.R.

CROSS, F. M. : *The Ancient Library of Qumran and Modern Biblical Studies* (Haskell Lectures, 1956-57). 1958. Pp. ix + 198 + 4 plates + 1 map + plan on end-paper. (Doubleday, New York. Price : $4.50).

Dr. Cross adds another to the already long, if not over-long, list of books on the Judaean Scrolls ; yet he has something new to say. In five chapters he gives an account of the documents discovered at Qumran, of the Essenes and the people of the Scrolls, of the Essenes in relation to the ' Teacher of Righteousness ', of the text of the Old Testament as revealed in the Scrolls, and of the relation of the Essenes to the early Christian Church. He identifies the Essenes with the Covenanters without attempting to prove the identification or discussing the striking differences between the two groups ; and he assigns their beginnings to the 2nd century B.C. throwing back many (if not all) of the Scrolls to the same date on a gross over-estimate of the palaeographical evidence and a complete disregard of the inconvenient if not fatal Roman evidence. Such a date enables him to identify the Wicked Priest with Simon the Maccabee, high-priest from, 142/1-135/4 B.C. ; this is another weak point in the argument, since the number of high-priests available for the part is ample, while no suitable character for the Teacher of Righteousness is proposed or indeed can be proposed in this period, and nothing is done with Absalom and Judah. A partial solution of a problem, however, is not a solution but a hypothesis and can but remain such until it is proved. None the less, Dr. Cross makes much recent information accessible to the general reader, and even the professed student will read his book with interest and profit. It contains also four excellent photographs, a chart of Jewish scripts, and a plan (inserted as an end-piece) of the buildings at Qumran.   G.R.D.

KUHN, K. G. (ed. by, in collaboration with H. Stegemann & G. Klinzing): *Rückläufiges Hebräisches Wörterbuch : Retrograde Hebrew Lexikon.* 1958. Pp. 144. (Vandenhoeck & Ruprecht, Göttingen. Price : DM. 32).

The aim of this lexicon, which is the product of the Heidelberg Qumran research group, is to enable workers on the Qumran texts to fill in the many lacunae in them. To this end the Hebrew words, mostly unvocalized, are arranged according to the sequence of letters beginning with the end of the word. The lexicon is based upon Biblical Hebrew. It includes all the words in the Hebrew part of the O.T., proper names as well, and the vocabulary of all the published Qumran texts in

Hebrew, except the purely Biblical manuscripts, and of the Zadokite fragments. It includes further words which are unknown to Biblical Hebrew, but which occur in Ben Sira, the Siloam inscription, the Lachish ostraca, the Gezer calendar, and the published Hebrew texts from Wadi Murabba ' at, with the omission of purely Biblical fragments. Aramaic texts from Qumran, like Biblical Aramaic, are excluded, but some Aramaic words find a place. Also excluded from consideration is the Rabbinical–Talmudical vocabulary. A system of sigla makes it easy to see at once where a word occurs, so that the Qumran Hebrew vocabulary can be quickly discovered. Qumran researchers have here a very useful tool.

D.W.T.

LEANEY, A. R. C., HANSON, R. P. C., POSEN, J. : *A Guide to the Scrolls : Nottingham Studies on the Qumran Discoveries.* 1958. Pp. 128. (S.C.M. Press, London. Price : 8s. 6d.).

These studies on the Qumran discoveries have grown out of five extramural lectures given by members of the Department of Theology at Nottingham University—Dr. R. P. C. Hanson, Rabbi J. Posen, and the editor. After an editorial introduction putting the reader *au fait* with the discovery of the Qumran scrolls, their historical background, and theories of their significance, Rabbi Posen describes the scrolls and the character of the sect from which they came, Dr. Hanson considers the identification of the sects, and Mr. Leaney discusses the scrolls in relation to the New Testament and the Christian Church. Mr. Leaney's section is the longest and the most important in the book. He considers a number of suggested contacts between the thought of Qumran and various groups of New Testament books, but makes no reference to Dr. Yadin's theory of the origin of the Epistle to the Hebrews in this connection. Qumran research does not stand still, and introductions to the subject quickly become dated, but those who follow this sober and unpretentious guide will not be misled.

F.F.B.

DEL MEDICO, H. E. : *Le Mythe des Esséniens des origines à la fin du moyen âge.* 1958. Pp. 334+3 folding tables. (Librairie Plon, Paris.)

The author has frequently mentioned in his books on the Dead Sea Scrolls that the sect of the Essenes not only have nothing to do with the Qumran scrolls but also that he has serious doubts about the validity of the traditional descriptions of the sect. In the present book he elaborates his views. The Essenes were ' born ' in the mind of Philo, as the Jewish counterpart of his beloved Egyptian *Therapeutae ;* Pliny the Elder ' invents ' an Essene phalanestery for some unfortunates near the Dead Sea. Josephus' works originally contained not a single word about the Essenes or their customs. The present passages are later interpolations, going back in part to the

3rd century A.D., made by a Greek pagan who sought to amuse his fellow pagans by attributing to a *bona-fide* Jewish historian (Josephus) a paraphrase, full of satire, which had originally been composed about another set of people by St. Hippolytus. With considerable ingenuity del Medico pursues his theory further, but has to produce a second interpolation, and numerous cases of acceptance by Christian Fathers of apocryphal writings and other deceptions. He concludes, as the title of his present book says, that the whole is a myth.

B.J.R.

DEL MEDICO, H. E. : *The Riddle of the Scrolls*, trans. by H. Garner. 1958. Pp. 432+6 photographs. Burk's Publishing Co., London. Price : 25s. 0d.).

This is a translation of *L'énigme des Manuscrits de la Mer Morte* (cf. *Book List*, 1958, p. 46) and provides interesting reading for those who find themselves doubting their ability to understand the original book because of the run of its argument. The translation, which is admirably done, is the work of an esteemed former member of the Society.   B.J.R.

MARTIN, M. : *The Scribal Character of the Dead Sea Scrolls*, Vol. I. (Bibliothèque du Muséon, Vol. 44.) 1958. Pp. xxxii.+410+70+3 tables. (Publications Universitaires, Louvain. Price : B. Frs. 600).

This lengthy study provides an analysis of the mechanics of the scribal activity at Qumran and offers conclusions about the textual characteristics of the manuscripts. Part I describes the pecularities of the major Cave 1 manuscripts and the scripts (by 13 hands), paragraphing (including the mysterious horizontal marks), and orthographies. Part II is devoted to grammatical phenomena and Part III leads up to general conclusions on the historical significance of the scribal activity, and shows how mistaken most of the earlier theories (outlined quite thoroughly in the introductory parts of the book) had been. There is nothing to suggest that the Scribes reflect any deliberately Sectarian tradition, though in one *genre* of writing, which contains ' organisational ' scrolls (IQS, IQM), a clearly defined scribal style is used, which is called ' official phonetic '. Of the other three *genres*, the ' interpreted texts ' (IQpHab) is likewise ' official phonetic ', the ' acquired ' or ' adopted ' (IQH) varies from ' exclusive consonantal ' (such as that in IQIsb), via ' transitional ' (such as CD) and ' phonetic '. Biblical scrolls vary considerably in scribal tradition. Part IV of the work, which will appear as volume II, and which, according to the contents table of the present volume, will contain some 300 pages, will deal mainly with the extent and significance of the Scribes' interference with the texts. The work is very competent, and fulfils a basic and real need in the study of the Scrolls.   B.J.R.

NIELSEN, E. & OTZEN, B. (ed. by) *Dødehavsteksterne. Skrifter fra den jødiske menighed i Qumran i oversaettelse og med noter.* 1st and 2nd editions 1959. Pp. 246+1 plate. (G. E. C. Gads Forlag, Copenhagen.)

This is an attractive annotated rendering into Danish of a number of the Qumran texts. The documents selected are : 1QpHab, 1QpMic, 1QS, 1QH, 1QM, 1QSa, and 1QMyst. There are short introductions with references to other editions and important relevant literature, text-critical notes, and explanatory commentaries. The whole is admirably done. The fact that a second edition has already been called for testifies to the usefulness of the work. G.W.A.

NÖTSCHER, F. : *Gotteswege und Menschenwege in der Bibel und in Qumran* (Bonner Biblische Beiträge, 15). 1958. Pp. 134 (Peter Hanstein Verlag, Bonn. Price : DM. 14).

Professor Nötscher, who has already contributed a study of the theological terminology of the Qumran texts to this series of Beiträge (*Book List*, 1958, p. 49), pays special attention in the present study to the use of the terms ' way ', ' walk ' and so forth in an ethical and religious sense in the Old Testament (63 pages), the Qumran literature (26 pages) and the New Testament (25 pages). His bringing together of the relevant material is useful and illuminating. As for the Qumran texts, he finds that the use of the terms is more restricted in them than in the Old Testament. They lay particular emphasis on the distinction between the way of light and the way of darkness, the former being the way ordained in advance by God for the elect to follow, with special reference to their observance of his commandments in their communal life ; the latter being further described as ' the way of the people ' or ' the way of wickedness '. The ' way ' terminology of Qumran, he concludes, has as little to do with Gnosticism as has the ' way ' terminology of the Old and New Testaments. F.F.B.

VAN DER PLOEG, J. : *The Excavations at Qumran : A Survey of the Judaean Brotherhood and its Ideas,* trans. by Kevin Smyth. 1958. Pp. xii+234+14 plates+1 plan. (Longmans, Green & Co., London, London. Price : 16s. 6d.).

This excellent work is a translation of the author's *Vondsten in de Woestijn van Juda,* which was published in 1957 in the Dutch series *Prismaboeken* (comparable to our Penguins and Pelicans). It is written for the general public, not for specialists ; it is therefore accompanied by no scholarly apparatus, but the discerning reader will realize that the work is based throughout on first-class scholarship and sound judgment. The author was one of the first European scholars to see the manuscripts from Cave I which the Syrian monastery acquired in 1947 ; his account of the discovery, which forms the first chapter of his book, thus contains some original contributions to this complicated story. He summarizes for his readers the course of Jewish history from 200 B.C. to A.D. 70 ; against this historical background he then discusses the rise and fall, beliefs and practices, of the Qumran community, describes the contents of their library, and concludes with a survey of the comparisons and contrasts between the community and the early Christian Church. He holds the community to be an Essene group. The identification of the Wicked Priest with Alexander Jannaeus ' has much to be said for it, though it is not yet fully proven ' (p. 62). Something has gone wrong on p. 59 where ' Jonathan Simon (161-143 B.C.)' represents the Dutch ' Simon de Makkabeeër (142-135)'. There are fourteen plates. F.F.B.

RABIN, C. : *The Zadokite Documents : I The Admonition. II The Laws*, edited with a translation and note. 2nd revised edition. 1958. Pp. xvi+104. (Clarendon Press, Oxford. Price : 25s. 0d.).

Additions to the first edition (cf. *Book List*, 1955, p. 63) are not confined to addenda lists, but are also interspersed throughout the book, and explain the lengthened list of sigla, annotation, Index of Dead Sea Scrolls and four pages of addenda. That is, they are substantial and ubiquitous, and add to the importance of this very valuable book. Unfortunately most of the notes in the addenda of the first edition (p. 96) have disappeared completely. The texts of MSS A and B (conflated here as in the first edition) are also given separately in an appendix. Collation of published scrolls material is brought up to date, and it is regrettably unavoidable that it was impossible to include the fragments of the Documents which are now in the Scrollery in the Palestine Archaeological Museum, awaiting publication. B.J.R.

RABIN, C. and YADIN, Y. : *Aspects of the Dead Sea Scrolls*. (Scripta Hierosolymitana, IV.) 1958. Pp. x+282. (Magnes Press, Jerusalem, and O.U.P. Price : 40s. 0d.).

An important volume, consisting of ten studies. N. Avigad shows how the palaeographical situation has changed since Scrolls discussion began, since we now have the dated Bar-Cochba letters as a basis of comparison. E. Y. Kutscher has a fine study of the Aramaic of the Genesis Apocryphon. Linguistic studies on the Hebrew of the Scrolls come from M. H. Goshen-Gottstein, Ch. Rabin, and Z. Ben–hayyim. S. Talmon deals with the calendar of the sect and J. Licht with the treatise of the two Spirits in DSD. M. H. Segal argues for a second century background and origin for the War Scroll, as against Yadin's date. Y. Yadin argues that the Epistle to the Hebrews was written to people who had been influenced by Qumran circles, and D. Flusser writes on the Qumran sect and pre-Pauline Christianity. These are all significant studies, and the volume cannot be neglected by those interested in the Scrolls—at least those whose interest is scholarly, rather than popular. H.H.R.

ROTH, C. : *The Historical Background of the Dead Sea Scrolls.* 1958.
Pp. viii+88. (Blackwell, Oxford. Price : 10s. 6d.).

This fuller statement by Dr. Roth of his interpretation of the
scrolls will be widely welcomed. He identifies the Qumran
community with the Zealots, and the Teacher of Righteousness
either with their leader Menahem, son of Judas the Gaulonite,
or with his kinsman Eleazar son of Jair. It is evident that Dr.
Roth has continued to think actively about the whole question
during the writing of his book, and whereas to begin with he
had no doubt that the Teacher was Menahem, who met a
violent death at the hands of Eleazar, captain of the temple,
in the autumn of A.D. 66, he has found himself becoming
less certain on this score. ' The death of the Teacher is nowhere
stated unmistakably and categorically in the extant literature
—only his persecution, it is true with deadly intent ' (p. vii).
Accordingly he is increasingly inclined to identify the Teacher
with Eleazar son of Jair, who escaped when Menahem was
captured and killed, and lived to fight another day. But in
either case the Wicked Priest is identified with Eleazar,
captain of the temple. There are many problems raised by
this interpretation which are not satisfactorily cleared up,
and no doubt Dr. Roth will have more to say on the subject.
For example, he dates the Damascus residence of the community tentatively in the period between 4 B.C. and A.D. 6.
In that case, who was the ' Teacher of Righteousness ' of the
Zadokite work? Judas? Or his colleague Sadduk ! We hope
that Dr. Roth will return to this question.   F.F.B.

ROWLEY, H. H. : *The Dead Sea Scrolls from Qumran* (The Second Montefiore Lecture). 1958. Pp. 24 (University of Southampton. Price :
2s. 6d.).

Professor Rowley here describes the discovery, the documents,
jars, coins, and sites, discusses the chronological problems, the
character of the sect, and its relation to Christianity, giving
particular attention to some of the more recent hypotheses,
and sums up the importance of the Scrolls. A comprehensive,
closely-packed but lucid survey, which is scrupulously fair
on matters of dispute.   G.W.A.

WALLENSTEIN, M. : *The Nezer and the Submission in Suffering Hymn
from the Dead Sea Scrolls. Reconstructed, Vocalized and Translated
with Critical Notes.* 1959. Pp. XII+46+11 plates. (Nederlands
Historisch-Archaeologisch Instituut te Istanbul. Price : Fl. 15).

This monograph consists of a study of the important hymn
contained in Plates XLII and XLIII of E. L. Sukenik's
' *Ozar ha-Megilloth ha-Genuzoth.* Facsimiles of the plates are
supplied. The hymn, of over two hundred lines, is the longest
included in the ' *Ozar,* and is interesting alike for its language
and its subject matter. Its two outstanding ideas are, first,
the idea of an ever-lasting branch (*nezer*), hidden at a secret
fountain, and secondly, the idea of joy in tribulation. The

author has carried out his work of reconstruction and vocalization well, his translation is pleasingly and accurately done, and the critical notes, which cover twenty-four pages, are informative and illuminating. There are general and author indices, and an index of Biblical and other references. Students of the Hymns, indeed of the scrolls in general, will find the monograph a valuable aid to their studies.   D.W.T.

APOCRYPHA AND POST-BIBLICAL JUDAISM

ALTMANN, A. : *Tolerance and the Jewish Tradition* (Robert Waley Cohen Memorial Lecture, 1957.) n.d. (1958). Pp. 20. (Council of Christians and Jews, London, Price : 2s. 0d.).

This lecture, delivered by a great theologian, deserves a wide public. Dr. Altmann points out that the problem of tolerance can arise only where there is a vision of absolute truth, such as we find in the Bible which demands exclusive adherence to God. Yet even the Bible displays much tolerance towards those outside Israel. Rabbinic Judaism, struggling for survival, reinforces the barriers between Jews and pagans. At the same time it produces the doctrine of Noachian humanity, bringing within the kingdom all Gentiles who observe natural religion and morality. ' It would be wrong to designate this as mere tolerance. It abolishes the dichotomy.' The development was not, of course, a simple one. The author follows it through the Middle Ages (where the difference in the Jewish attitude to Islam and Christianity is of special interest) and modern times (Mendelssohn, Hermann Cohen, Benamozegh)— a masterly survey.   D.D.

BARON, S. W. : *A Social and Religious History of the Jews.* High Middle Ages (500-1200) : Vol. VI, *Laws, Homilies, and the Bible.* 2nd Edition. 1958. Pp. 486 (Price : 60s. 0d.) Vol. VII, *Hebrew Language and Letters.* 2nd edition. 1958. Pp. 322. (Price : 45s. 0d.). Vol. VIII, 2nd edition. *Philosophy and Science.* 1958. Pp. 406. (Price : 55s. 0d.) (Columbia University Press and Oxford University Press, London. Price : 140s. 0d. the set).

In these three volumes, as in the three preceding ones, vols. IV-VI (see *Book List,* 1958, pp. 52f.) we are still moving within the High Middle Ages—the period the author has chosen to term the years 500-1200. We thus have detailed accounts of many phenomena in Jewish history of this period—a period hitherto not so fully dealt with by Jewish historians.
In volume VI, the first chapter, entitled Reign of Law, assesses, among other matters the interrelation of Jewish and Muslim law, interpretation, codification and philosophy of Law. Other subjects dealt with in other chapters are homilies and histories and study of the Bible. Volume VII concerns itself with linguistic renascence ; worship—unity amidst

diversity ; and poetry and belles-lettres. The subjects of vol. VIII are : magic and mysticism ; faith and reason ; scientific exploration ; medical science and practice.

The work draws on a large number of diverse sources. Scholars will eagerly await the other volumes which will occupy themselves with the period from 1200 onwards. M.W.

HAMMERSHAIMB, E., MUNCK, J., NOACK, B., SEIDELIN, P. (ed. by) : *De gammeltestamentlige Pseudepigrafer i oversaettelse med indledning og noter.* 3. Haefte 1958. Pp. 175-316. (Gad, Copenhagen ; Cammermeyer, Oslo ; Gleerup, Lund.).

This fascicle (cf. *Book List,* 1957, p. 71) contains Jubilees (edited by B. Noack) and the Martyrdom of Isaiah (edited by E. Hammershaimb). The pattern of the earlier fascicles is followed and the same high standard maintained. G.W.A.

LEWITTES, M. : *The Code of Maimonides, Book Eight, The Book of Temple Service, Trans. from the Hebrew.* (Yale Judaica Series, Vol. XII.) 1957. Pp.XXVII+525. (Yale University Press, New Haven, and Oxford University Press, London. Price : 52s. 0d.).

This volume is worthy of its predecessors. It is the first translation into any language of this part of Maimonides' Code. Probably even now comparatively few scholars will be interested in all the nine chapters : the Temple, Vessels and Ministers of the Sanctuary, Entrance into the Sanctuary, Things Prohibited for the Altar, Manner of Sacrificing, Daily and Additional Offerings, Offerings Rendered Unfit, Service of the Day of Atonement, Trespass in regard to Sacred Objects. Yet there is much that is relevant to questions such as attract modern historians of theology : for example, the exact kinds of incorrect intention that render an offering unfit. And if in matters of substance Maimonides follows Talmudic authorities, the selection and arrangement are to a considerable extent his own, and they still await a thorough analysis. The translator has done a difficult job extremely well. One might wish his Introduction a little more extensive, though he does refer to a few notable features—perhaps the most striking being the very fact that this Book of the Temple Service should exist : the subject went on being studied and elaborated even when, in A.D. 70, it lost its practical applicability. D.D.

REIDER,·J. : *The Book of Wisdom. An English translation with Introduction and Commentary* (Dropsie College Edition : Jewish Apocryphal Literature). 1957. Pp. xii+234. (Harper, New York.) (Price : $5.00.).

Like the first volume in this series (see *Book List* 1951, p. 42) this work, also sponsored by Dropsie College, consists of a Greek text and an English translation, with introduction, commentary, and critical apparatus. Rahlfs' text is used and

the textual notes are based on his edition. The 46-page introduction covers the usual topics—contents, text, purpose,
date, authorship, language, theology and Rabbinic sources.
The views of many previous workers in the field are briefly
touched on, and the author sums up the discussion and gives
his verdict with caution and sobriety. The notes are limited
in extent but they are to the point ; their indebtedness to
earlier works, particularly those of Gregg and Goodrick, is
acknowledged.   W.D.McH.

PHILOLOGY AND GRAMMAR

DIRINGER, D. : *The Story of the Aleph Beth*, n.d. (1958). Pp. 196+
xxvii. plates. (Lincolns-Prager, London, for the World Jewish
Congress, British Section. Price : 4s. 6d. paper, 7s. 6d. cloth).

This excellent little book deals with the history of the Hebrew
script and is intended primarily for Jewish readers. It is
divided into three parts. The first part, consisting of four
chapters, gives a brief account of the origin of writing and
the creation of an alphabet with special reference to the
Near East. The second part, consisting of five chapters, is
concerned with the early Hebrew alphabet employed in
inscriptions, seals, ostraca, papyri, coins, etc. The third
part, consisting of five chapters, is devoted to the square
Hebrew alphabet : it also contains a chapter on the history
of vocalization and an interesting chapter on the modern
Hebrew alphabet and the adaptation of the Hebrew script
to other tongues. The book ends with a discussion on the
merits and demerits of the Hebrew alphabet and whether
any reforms are desirable. Twenty-seven plates giving
examples of the various types of Hebrew writing and tables
showing the development of the script are incorporated.
Dr. Diringer's book will be of interest to all lovers of Hebrew,
Jewish and non-Jewish : it will be especially valuable for
recommendation to undergraduates.   T.W.T.

HOLLADAY, W. L. : *The Root Šûbh in the Old Testament, with particular
Reference to its Usages in covenantal Contexts.* 1958. Pp. viii+192.
(E. J. Brill, Leiden. Price : Fl. 18).

This semantic study of the twelfth most frequent verb in the
Old Testament finds its central meaning to be ' having moved
in a particular direction, to move thereupon in the opposite
direction, the implication being (unless there is evidence to
the contrary) that one will arrive again at the *initial point of
departure*'. It is particularly related to the use of the root in
covenantal contexts, but this is only considered after the
general range of meanings has been considered. Attention is
given to the use of the root in cognate languages, and to its
translation in the ancient versions. The argument is accompanied by tables and statistical observations and concludes
with an index of all the occurrences of *šûbh* in the Old Testament. It is a thorough, patient study with important theological implications.   A.S.H.

KOEHLER, L. and BAUMGARTNER, W. : *Supplementum ad Lexicon in Veteris Testamenti Libros.* 1958. Pp. XI+228. (E. J. Brill, Leiden. Price : 37s. 6d.).

This Supplement to the now well known Lexicon contains tables of scripts and transcriptions, German-Hebrew and German-Aramaic glossaries—special features are the lists of botanical and zoological words and of words inferred from proper names—and a hundred pages of additions and corrections. Here more attention is paid to Middle-Hebrew and Jewish-Aramaic equivalents ; the more significant variants of the ' Babylonian ' or ' Oriental ' tradition are included ; Ugaritic, Akkadian and other inscriptional material has been brought up to date : the vocabulary of the Dead Sea documents has been utilized ; and recent literature, up to 1957, has been incorporated and the list of abbreviations extended accordingly. This is a work of major importance. It is a great convenience that it can be purchased separately. D.W.T.

REYMOND, P. : *L'eau, sa vie, et sa signification dans l'Ancien Testament* (Supplements to Vetus Testamentum, Vol. VI). 1958. Pp. xvi+ 282. (E. J. Brill, Leiden, Price : Fl. 28).

This is an interesting and intensive study, partly lexical and partly symbolical, of all the Hebrew terms and expressions which have any connection with water. How thorough the investigation has been may be seen from a glance at the 16 pages at the end of the book in which the author has given an index of all the Hebrew words relating to water, to the number of nearly 500, over 100 of which occur in the book of Job. The varied contents of the book justify the concluding words of the author, ' We have found that the theme of water in the Old Testament discloses an unsuspected wealth and a vast variety '. The task which the author has undertaken was well worth doing and has been well carried through, though one suspects that the lexicologists will be better satisfied with it than the symbologists. S.H.H.

WEINGREEN, J. : *Practical Grammar for Classical Hebrew,* 2nd edition. 1959. Pp. xii+316. (Clarendon Press : Oxford University Press. Price : 21s. 0d.).

In this second edition of Professor Weingreen's now well known and much used Hebrew Grammar, first published in 1939, no changes have been made in the presentation of the grammar, the tables of verbs, nouns and adjectives, or the exercises. The chief changes are the substitution of b, g, k, etc., for bh, gh, kh, etc , the addition of fresh footnotes and the expansion of others, and the inclusion of a brief note on the construct-genitive relation of nouns involving an adjectival idea. The changes, though not substantial, were worthwhile making, and students should be helped further by them. D.W.T.

BOOK LIST, 1960

In the preparation of this edition of the *Book List* I have had the help of the members of the Panel of reviewers appointed by the Society and also of the following scholars : Professors Bič, de Boer, Gerleman, and Hammershaimb, the Revd. D. R. Jones, Professor Noth, Mr. D. Patterson, and Professor T. W. Thacker. To all these I tender my thanks for their co-operation. In addition, I wish to thank those who have drawn my attention to works which might otherwise have escaped my notice. It is impossible for any one man to keep track of all the works published in our field ; and inevitably some works have been overlooked. But the gaps would have been more numerous but for the information supplied by colleagues. My gratitude is also due to the Printer for his patience and ready helpfulness.

The arrangement of the *Book List* corresponds to that of former years. Books suitable for inclusion in school libraries have been marked with an asterisk.

G. W. ANDERSON.

UNIVERSITY OF DURHAM.

GENERAL

BAUER, J. B. (ed.) : *Bibeltheologisches Wörterbuch*. 1959. Pp. 860. (Verlag Styria, Graz. Price : 239 sch.).

This useful and up-to-date work has already been noticed at some length by a reviewer in *Vetus Testamentum*, Vol. X, pp. 97-99, and I find myself in substantial agreement with his remarks. It is a book that may be said to correspond on a smaller scale to the doctrinal articles of the still-unfinished *Supplément* to the *Dictionnaire de la Bible*. The editor, who is an assistant professor in the Catholic theological faculty at Graz, has collected a team of forty contributors, most of them German or Austrian scholars, with four (H. Cazelles, J. Daniélou, J. de Fraine, and C. Spicq) from France or Belgium. All the articles are printed in German, and most of them show a high degree of competence. A fair sample would be the twenty-three page study of ' Kirche ' by V. Warnach of Maria Laach abbey, which has attached to it five closely printed pages of bibliography. No other book-list approaches this one in length (indeed, some of them are rather scanty) and it may be asked whether the readers of what is admittedly an *Einführung* would not be better served by a list of a few carefully selected items. The emphasis throughout is primarily on words occurring in the New Testament. Some of the articles are manifestly insufficient, even for beginners. ' Prophet ' runs to four pages, ' Knecht Gottes ' to three, and ' Menschensohn ' to a single page. The entry ' Tag des Herrn ' has beside it in brackets the word ' Sonntage '. The editor quite reasonably claims that a work of this character cannot be all-inclusive, but even so there are many omissions that cannot be supplied from the list of ' Stichworte und Verweise ' in the appendix at pp. 857-59. Possibly there may be some change of plan in a second edition, which would make an already serviceable book of even greater value.   J.M.T.B.

(BAUMGÄRTEL, F.) : *Festschrift Friedrich Baumgärtel zum 70. Geburtstag 14, Januar 1958 gewidmet von den Mitarbeitern am Kommentar zum Alten Testament (KAT) uberreicht von Johannes Herrmann.* Für den Druck herausgegeben von Leonhard Rost. (Erlanger Forschungen, A : 10) 1959. Pp. 200. (Universitätsbibliothek, Erlangen).

This *Festschrift* contains 14 essays and a Bibliography dedicated to Friedrich Baumgärtel on his 70th birthday by colleagues in *Kommentar zum Alten Testament*. The essays all have direct bearing on the Old Testament. There are two close studies of text (Isaiah xiv. 1-23 and xxiii. 1-14) and the other essays include such subjects as Ephod and Choschen, the Reform of Josiah, the chronology of Judges. Of special interest is a rather longer essay than most under the title ' Zur Frage der Wertung und der Geltung alttestamentlicher Texte ', which is a study in canonicity.   L.H.B.

BEEK, M. A. : *A Journey through the Old Testament* (with a foreword by H. H. Rowley), trans. by A. J. Pomerans. 1959. Pp. 254+8 plates+map on endpaper. (Hodder & Stoughton, London. Price : 21s. 0d.).

The Journey begins at dawn, goes along with the Forefathers, becomes an Exodus from Egypt, halts with the Judges, Kings, and Prophets in Canaan, returns from Exile, tarries with Israel's Wisdom and Songs, describes the guide book (the Bible) and ends at Bethlehem. With illustrations and maps an excellent popular introduction to the O.T.   G.H.D.

BIČ, M. and SOUČEK, J. B. (ed. by) : *Biblická Konkordance*, parts 15 and 16. *Nevadno-Oltář*. 1959. Pp. 80. (Edice Kalich, Prague ; agents, Artia Ltd., 30 Smečky, Prague. Price : Kčs 10.50 or U.S. $1.10 each part).

This great Concordance, whose special features have been noted in previous *Book Lists*, slowly pursues its way. It still has some way to go before it is complete, but when it is finished Czech readers will have an unrivalled tool for Biblical study.   H.H.R.

FRANKE, H. (ed. by) : *Akten des XXIV Internat. Orientalisten-Kongresses, München*, 1957. 1959. Pp. xii+776+Pl. XXI. (Deutsche Morgenländische Gesellschaft, Franz Steiner Verlag, Wiesbaden).

H. Bardtke : 'Aufgaben der Qumran-Forschung '; G. Bertram : ' . . . die Wiedergabe von schadad und schaddai im Griechischen '; H. Brunner : ' Gott als Retter im alten Aegypten '; C. Colpen : ' Werfen die neue Funde vom Toten Meer Licht auf das Verhältnis von iranischer und jüdischer Religion ?'; H. Ginsberg : ' The Classification of the N-W Semitic Languages '; W. von Soden : ' Tempus und Modus im Semitischen '; S. D. Goitein : ' Present State and Problems of the Philological and Historical Research on the Cairo Geniza '; A. Katsh : ' Hebraica Collections in the USSR '; B. Kienast : ' Das Personalpronomen der 2. Person im Semitischen '; W. G. Lambert : ' . . . the Babylonian " Poem of the Righteous Sufferer " ' ; G. Lanczkowski : 'Aegyptischer Prophetismus im Lichte des A.T. '; R. Largement : ' L'arbre de vie dans la religion sumérienne '; J. L. McKenzie : ' The " People of the Land " in the O.T. '; J. Schildenberger : ' Z. Textkritik v. Ps. 45 (44) '; K. Schubert : ' D. Messiaslehre i.d. Test. XII Patr. im Lichte d. Text v. Ch. Qumran '; J. D. W. Watts : ' Remarks on Hebrew Relative Clauses '; S. Zeitlin : ' The Dead Sea Scrolls '.

That is a bare list of those papers printed in full, or nearly so, which have most relevance for O.T. study. Almost 400 papers were read at the Congress ; the collection of the majority and their publication so soon in this remarkably complete *Acta*, is a further proof of the organizing genius of its secretary-editor.   D.R.Ap-T.

FRIEDRICH, G. (ed. by) : *Theologisches Wörterbuch zum Neuen Testament* (begun by G. Kittel). Band VI, Lieferungen 14, 15, 16. 1959. Band VII, Lieferung 1. 1960. Pp. 320. (Kohlhammer, Stuttgart. Price : DM. 4.60, each Lieferung).

Band VI. Lieferung 14 continues the article on *prophētēs* and, in particular, contains the long section by Friedrich on prophets in the New Testament and the shorter one by the same author on prophets in the early Church. The article on *prōtos*, etc., by Michaelis has its points of interest for Old Testament scholars.

Lieferung 15. The article on *ptōchos*, etc., by Hauck and Bammel contains a section entitled ' The Poor in the Old Testament ' followed by the treatment of the concept by the Rabbis, by Josephus and Philo, in the Inter-Testamental Literature, and a brief section on Qumran. An article on *pylē* by Jeremias is followed by one on *pȳr*, etc., by Lang which is of considerable interest.

Lieferung 16 concludes the article on *pȳr*. A few brief articles intervene and then there come articles on *rabbi*, etc., by Lohse, on *rhabdos*, etc., by Bauernfeind, on *rhaka* by Jeremias, on *rhantizō*, etc., by Hunzinger, on *rhiza* by Maurer, on *rhiptō*, etc., by Bieder, on *rhomphaia* by Michaelis and on *rhyomai* by Kasch, all of which have some relevance for Old Testament scholars.

Band VII, Lieferung 1 is mainly occupied by two long and important articles, viz., *Sabbaton* by Lohse and *Saddoukaios* by Meyer. There is also an article by Stählin on *sakkos*.

N.W.P.

GALLING, K. (ed. by) : *Die Religion in Geschichte und Gegenwart.* 3. Auflage, Band III, Lieferungen 55-63, Cols. 1153-1805+plates and maps+pp. XXXII. Band IV, Lieferungen 64-68, Cols. 1-384+plates. (J. C. B. Mohr, Tübingen. Subscription price : DM. 4.20 each Liefering).

In these Lieferungen, which bring the work up to ' Lippe,' the number of articles on or related to the O.T. is relatively small, but they include subjects of central importance. Among the longer articles mention may be made of ' Klagelieder Jeremiä ' (H. J. Kraus) ; ' Knecht Jahwes ' (H. H. Rowley) ; ' Königsbücher ' (R. Bach) ; ' Königtum Gottes ' (J. Hempel); ' Königtum, sakrales ' (W. von Soden) ; ' Krieg im AT ' (H. J. Kraus) ; ' Kultgeschichtliche Methode ' and ' Kultgeschichtliche Schule ' (parts by G. Lanczkowski and C. Westermann) ; ' Kultus ' (S. Mowinckel) ; ' Lade Jahwes ' (E. Kutsch) ; ' Leiden im AT ' (H. Donner) ; ' Levi und Leviten ' (F. Horst) ; ' Leviticus ' (G. Fohrer) ; ' Liebe im AT ' (W. Zimmerli). There are also several brief O.T. articles. The rapid progress of this new edition is most gratifying.

G.W.A.

Internationale Zeitschriftenschau für Bibelwissenschaft und Grenzgebiete, Band V. 1956/57, Heft 1-2. 1959. (Patmos-Verlag, Düsseldorf. Price : DM. 38 or $9.10).

Professor Stier and his colleagues are to be congratulated on reaching the milestone of a fifth volume of this invaluable bibliographical aid. This double Heft contains 1704 entries covering the entire Biblical field and related studies. The items are arranged according to subject ; and there are handy indexes and a clear table of contents. No serious student of Biblical problems can well dispense with this work. G.W.A.

KAPELRUD, A. S. : *Gamle byer og nye stater : Fra en reise i bibelske land.* 1958. Pp. 166+8 plates+1 plan+map on endpaper. (Universitetsforlaget, Oslo).

Professor Kapelrud has a genuine gift of popular exposition ; and in this book he gives an interesting and instructive account of a journey through Bible lands—Syria, the Holy Land itself, Iraq, Syria again, and Lebanon, and finally Egypt. As a travel book alone it makes good reading. But, of course, throughout there are observations on Biblical sites and archaeological discoveries, with an occasional side glance at the international situation. G.W.A.

LASOR, W. S. : *Great Personalities of the Old Testament : Their Lives and Times.* n.d. (1959). Pp. 192. (Fleming H. Revell Company. Westwood, N.J. Price : $3.00).

Eighteen chapters offer character sketches of 14 men and one woman (Ruth). A lively, colloquial series of Bible Class studies specially recommended for popular use. G.H.D.

PALACHE, J. L. : *Sinai en Paran. Opera Minora.* Pp. XII+136+ Portrait. (E. J. Brill, Leiden. Price : Fl. 15).

Eight essays, first published between 1916 and 1939, are here reprinted with a tribute by Dr. Max Reisel. ' Concerning Weeping in the Jewish Religion ' is in German, ' The Ebed-Jahveh Enigma in Pseudo-Isaiah ' is in English ; the remainder are in Dutch, being ' Three Passages in the Book of Job ', ' The Character of the Old Testament Narrative ', ' The Sabbath-Idea outside Judaism ', ' Gentile Customs ', ' The Significance of Mice in I Sam. 6 ', and ' The Change in Meaning of Words in Hebrew (Semitic) and other Languages '. A scripture reference adds to the usefulness of the book. Palache's theories were always ingenious and interesting, but not uniformly convincing. D.R.Ap-T.

VON RAD, G. : *Gesammelte Studien zum Alten Testament* (Theologische Bücherei : Neudrücke und Berichte aus dem 20. Jahrhundert, Band 8. Altes Testament). 1958. Pp. 312. (Chr. Kaiser Verlag, Munich. Price : by subscription, DM. 10.80 ; separately, DM. 12).

This is a handy collection of some important works by von Rad, many of which appeared in periodicals not easily accessible or in publications which are no longer available ; they have not been revised for the purpose of this re-publication. Pride of place is given in it to his ' Das formgeschichtliche Problem des Hexateuch ' which was noted in the *Book List* for 1938. Two other works of some length are ' Der Anfang der Geschichtsschreibung in alten Israel ', and ' Zelt und Lade ' which examines the significance in Israel's religious history of these two traditional features and the relation of the one to the other. The other articles which are included in the collection are short in extent but deal with interesting and often important points. ' Verheissenes Land und Jahwes Land im Hexateuch ' illustrate an interesting characteristic of the O.T. that promises, when they are fulfilled historically, are not regarded as now realised but remain as promises in a modified form or with a new meaning ; ' Es ist noch eine Ruhe vorhanden dem Volke Gottes ' investigates the theological significance of God's promise of rest to His people ; ' Das theologische Problem des alttestamentlichen Schöpfungsglaubens ' considers the relationship of the O.T. belief in Yahweh's choice and salvation of Israel with the belief in the God of Creation ; and ' " Gerechtigkeit " und " Leben " in der Kultsprache der Psalmen ' examines the doctrine in some passages of the Psalms of Yahweh as the Giver of life, as man's Portion in the land of the living and his Deliverer from death. The titles of not a few of the articles indicate their subject quite clearly, e.g., ' Die Stadt auf dem Berge ', ' Die deuteronomistische Geschichtstheologie in den Königsbüchern ', and ' Die levitische Predigt in den Büchern der Chronik ' ; but ' Das Judäische Königsritual ' has specific reference to the significance of the anointing of Solomon and Joash of Judah. This note gives an indication of the range of material offered here but does not exhaust the list. J.M.

ROWLEY, H. H. : *The Changing Pattern of Old Testament Studies.* (Peake Lecture, 1959.) 1959. Pp. 32. (Epworth Press, London. Price : 2s. 6d.).

This is a comprehensive survey of the more important changes which have taken place in Old Testament study during the past few decades. Special attention is devoted to literary criticism, the history of religion, and Old Testament and Biblical Theology. Though short, this lecture contains a remarkable range of material, skilfully arranged to give the reader a true perspective. G.W.A.

The Sacral Kingship/La regalità sacra. Contributions to the central theme of the VIIIth International Congress for the History of Religions (Rome, April, 1955). (Supplements to *Numen*, IV). Published with the help of the *Giunta Centrale per gli Studi Storici*, Rome. 1959. Pp. XVI+748+21 figs. on 8 plates. (E. J. Brill, Leiden. Price : Fl. 55).

The volume is divided into the following sections : I. Historical Introduction. Phenomenology. Psychology (pp. 1-80),

II. Non-literate Peoples (pp. 81-148), III. Far East. India. Iran (pp. 149-258), IV. Ancient Egypt (pp. 259-280), V. Israel (pp. 281-366), VI. Greece and Rome (pp. 367-434), VII. Christianity (pp. 435-632), VIII. Pre-christian Europe (pp. 633-734), and IX. Islam (pp. 735-748).

As the question of divine kingship has for long been prominent in O.T. research it is of great importance to have it treated by specialists in fields other than the O.T. as well as by O.T. scholars. One notes, however, that of Israel's neighbours Egypt is discussed in only some 20 pages ; and Babylon fares even worse, since no section is devoted to it.

In the section on Israel S. Mowinckel has written on ' General Oriental and Specific Israelite Elements in the Israelite Conception of the Sacral Kingdom' (pp. 283-293), A. S. Kapelrud on ' King David and the Sons of Saul ' (pp. 294-301), J. Hempel on ' Herrschaftsform und Ichbewusstsein ' (pp. 302-315), M. Bič on ' Das erste Buch des Psalters. Eine Thronbesteigungsfestliturgie ' (pp. 316-332), J. Coppens on ' Les apports du psaume CX (vulg. CIX) à l'idéologie royale Israélite ' (pp. 333-348), M. A. Beek on ' Hasidic Conceptions of Kingship in the Maccabean Period ' (pp. 349-355), and H. Ludin Jansen on ' The Consecration in the eighth Chapter of Testamentum Levi ' (pp. 356-365).

Each of the above-mentioned authors has contributed to the current discussion of divine kingship in old Israel, but in spite of that and the contents of the volume as a whole it may be taken as certain that the debate on that theme has not yet come to an end. E.H.

Studia theologica cura ordinum theologorum Scandinavicorum edita. Vol. XIII, fasc. i. 1959. Pp. 86. (C. W. K. Gleerup, Lund. Price : by subscription, Sw kr. 15 each vol. ; or Sw. kr. 10 each fascicle).

This fascicle contains nothing of direct interest to the *Alttestamentler*. There are three articles : ' Die Heiligen in Luthers Frühtheologie ', by L. Pinomaa ; ' Die Irrlehrer von Rm 16, 17-20 ; by W. Schmithals ; and ' Die Martha-Maria-Perikope Lukas 10, 38-42 ', by E. Laland. G.W.A.

EDUCATIONAL

ARUNDALE, R. L. : The Old Testament : Book Three : From the Exile to Herod. 1959. Pp. 88. (Thomas Nelson and Sons Ltd., London. Price : 3s. 0d.).

This is the concluding O.T. volume of a series designed for Secondary Modern Schools, to be used in conjunction with Nelson's School Bible. The work of a practising schoolmaster, it is very simply written and addressed directly to the pupil, with suggestions of ' Things to do '. The history of the period is outlined and there are short chapters on Ruth and Jonah, and Daniel is dealt with in some detail, but there is no mention of the Wisdom literature or of the Psalms. The maps and illustrations add to the interest of the book, which is well produced and very reasonably priced. L.A.P.

*HEATHECOTE, A. W. : *From the Death of Solomon to the Captivity of Judah.* (The London Divinity Series, The Old Testament—Vol. II). 1959. Pp. 140+4 plates. (James Clarke & Co. Ltd., London. Price : 6s. 0d.).

This text-book has been written to help candidates for the University of London G.C.E. examination in Religious Knowledge, presumably at the O. and A. levels. It is divided into thirty short chapters, each followed by two or three questions. The text is concise, informative, up-to-date, and based on sound scholarship. It seems well designed to fulfil its purpose. L.A.P.

*MATHEWS, H. F. : *Prophets of the King.* 1960. Pp. 164. (Epworth Press, London, Price : 7s. 6d.)

This class-reader, the second volume of a complete Bible course, for Secondary Modern Schools, deals with the history and teaching of the Hebrew prophets from the beginnings to ' the Unknown Prophet of the Exile '. The material is attractively presented, with excellent diagrams and illustrations. A distinctive feature is the explicit Christian approach and the attempt to relate the work of the prophets to life to-day by the suggestion of ' Things to talk about '. At the end of each chapter are also lists of Bible work, memory passages, and ' Things to do '. L.A.P.

*MATHEWS, H. F. : *Prophets of the King.* Teacher's Book. 1960. Pp. 136. (Epworth Press, London. Price : 8s. 6d.)

This Teacher's book has been specially written to accompany the above class-reader. It contains three introductory chapters on the teaching, the task, and the faith of the prophets, followed by a series of background notes to the chapters in the pupils' book. All teachers should find it helpful, and it will prove invaluable to non-specialist teachers. L.A.P.

ARCHAEOLOGY AND EPIGRAPHY

MONTET, P. : *L'Égypte et la Bible.* (Cahiers d'Archéologie Biblique, No. 11.) 1959. Pp. 142+VIII plates+ 21 figures in the text. (Delachaux & Niestlé, Neuchâtel. Price : Sw. frs. 6.50).

After a brief introduction, there are two sections in the first of which, called Kings and Places, the author reviews the history of the contacts between Israel and Egypt from Abraham to Jeremiah in the light of archaeology and the Bible records, and discusses 22 place and personal names mentioned in the Bible. The second part uses archaeological remains to illustrate the background of elements in the culture of Egypt referred to in the Old Testament—Egyptian affairs, Magic, Piety and Morals, and Wisdom. There is a short chronological table and a bibliography. A useful book which should, like the other volumes in the series, be translated into English. J.N.S.

*PRITCHARD, J. B. : *The Ancient Near East : An Anthology of Texts and Pictures.* 1959. Pp. 284 (text)+197 ills.+pp. 17 (index)+map on end paper. (Princeton University Press and Oxford University Press, London. Price : 40s. 0d.).

This volume is a handy abbreviation and combination of *ANET* and *ANEP*. Nearly all the translations are taken from the former volume to which references are given so that the interested reader may consult the ampler explanatory comments and the bibliographical data which it contains. Another valuable feature is the inclusion in the margin of references to the O.T. where these are apposite. The illustrations are described simply by brief captions ; and, again, the reader is referred to *ANEP* for further details. Teacher and student alike should find this a valuable addition to the other collections of source material which have been made available in recent years.   G.W.A.

PRITCHARD, J. B. : *Archaeology and the Old Testament.* 1959. Pp. xii+ 264+77 figs. (Princeton University Press and Oxford Univeristy Press, London. Price : 30s. 0d.).

In this popular and well-illustrated exposition of the archaeology of the Near East in Biblical times, much that is familiar is presented, often on all too familiar lines. There are fresh contributions, however, such as the recent American excavations at Gibeon. Many texts are cited directly from *Ancient Near Eastern Texts* (*Book List*, 1951, p. 21 ; *Eleven Years*, p. 316) edited by the author. Here independent translations are always more welcome, though in a work avowedly for the layman such would have perhaps been out of place. The historical account of exploration and excavation in Syria is well worth presenting periodically when absorption in more recent work tends to obscure the achievements and discoveries of pioneers. The writer is mindful of this pious duty.   J.G.

PRITCHARD, J. B. : *Hebrew Inscriptions and Stamps from Gibeon.* (Museum Monographs.) 1959. Pp. vi+32+12 figs. (The University Museum, University of Pennsylvania, Philadelphia. Price : $1.00).

This monograph contains a catalogue of 56 jar handle inscriptions found at el-Jib during 1956-7, discusses them and the evidence for their date. Then 80 jar handles with royal stamps are catalogued and discussed, together with 7 private seal impressions and an inscribed weight. The discoveries provide additional reason for identifying el-Jib with Biblical Gibeon, give evidence for the purpose of these jar labels, pottery stoppers, and a funnel, and supply material for the study of Hebrew proper names.   J.N.S.

*WISEMAN, D. J. : *Illustrations from Biblical Archaeology.* 1958. Pp. 112+117 ills.+map on endpaper. (Tyndale Press, London. Price : 12s. 6d.).

This presentation of the results of Near Eastern archaeology is advisedly limited in bulk. The material selected, succinctly discussed, and profusely illustrated is mainly such as relates directly to both Old and New Testaments, but material is also adduced which elucidates the general background of the Biblical history. The work follows conventional lines, though fresh and recent material is presented in text and illustrations, most notably from the Babylonian Chronicle and the early Christian period. A strange slip in proof-reading reduces Ahab's chariot-force at Qarqar to 200 chariots (p. 56). Teachers of Biblical study, particularly in schools, will find the work a useful resumé and the illustrations will be most helpful. A good selective bibliography will be appreciated by more advanced scholars. J.G.

YADIN, Y. (and others) : *Hazor I : An Account of the First Season of Excavations,* 1955. 1959. Pp. xxiv+160+CLXXXIV Plates. (Magnes Press, Jerusalem & Oxford University Press, London. Price : 168s. 0d.).

This is the first of several such volumes and is a strictly factual report of the first season's work at this most extensive site. In comparison with the general synthesis of the work of several seasons with documentary sources, which is promised, the present volume is of more value to the specialist archaeologist, the more especially as it contains new pottery types. The fact that it reports on simultaneous work in five different areas, however, gives it something of a general appeal, though each area is treated separately and the work of synthesis is left largely to the reader, who may be guided by the chronological discussion at the end of each chapter. The authors are to be congratulated on the thoroughness of their work and their prompt publication. The book is a beautiful production in the best tradition of Palestinian archaeology, and is worthy of the greatest archaeological enterprise in the new Israel. J.G.

HISTORY AND GEOGRAPHY

ALT, A. : *Kleine Schriften zur Geschichte des Volkes Israel,* III (herausgegeben von Martin Noth.) 1959. Pp. XII+496+portrait. (C. H. Beck'sche Verlagsbuchhandlung, Munich. Price : 63s. 0d.).

This volume contains a further 26 studies collected from the various journals in which they were first published and includes one unpublished paper. (For the first two volumes see *Book List,* 1954, p. 22 ; *Eleven Years,* p. 559). Once again, the majority of the studies lie in the realm of political geography. Especially noteworthy are those on Jerusalem and

Samaria, and a series of 5 studies on parts of the Negeb. Among the more general essays attention may be drawn to ' Hohe Beamte in Ugarit ', ' Menschen ohne Namen ', and ' Zelte und Hütten '.

The other studies in the volume are under the following titles : ' Der Rhythmus der Geschichte Syriens und Palästinas im Altertum,' 'Völker und Staaten Syriens im Frühen Altertum ', ' Die asiatischen Gefahrzonen in den Ächtungstexten der 11. Dynastie ', ' Herren und Herrensitze Palästinas im Anfang des Zweiten Jahrtausends v. Chr. ', ' Die Herkunft der Hyksos in Neuer Sicht ', ' Hettitische und ägyptische Herrschaftsordnung in Unterworfenen Gebieten ', ' Das Stützpunktsystem der Pharaonen an der phönikischen Küste und im syrischen Binnenland ', ' Eine neue Provinz des Keilschriftrechts ', ' Neues über Palästina aus dem Archiv Amenophis IV ', ' Die Deltaresidenz der Ramessiden ', ' Die syrische Staatenwelt vor dem Einbruch der Assyrer ', 'Archäologische Fragen zur Baugeschichte von Jerusalem und Samaria in der israelitischen Königszeit ', ' Das Taltor von Jerusalem ', ' Der Anteil des Königtums au der sozialen Entwicklung in den Reichen Israel und Juda ', ' Micha 2, 1-5 ΓΗΣ ΑΝΑΔΑΣΜΟΣ in Juda ', ' Barsama '. L.H.B.

BRIGHT, J. : *A History of Israel*. 1959. Pp. 500+4 (map index)+XVI maps. (Westminster Press, Philadelphia. Price : $7.50).

Professor Bright has given us in this history a work which combines depth of learning, liveliness of presentation, and sobriety of judgement. The book begins with an extremely useful sketch of the pre-history and early history of ancient Near Eastern civilization. This is followed by a cautious treatment of the Patriarchal Age, in which the author deliberately avoids offering any detailed reconstruction of events but provides valuable guidance to his readers by (*a*) outlining the international background of the narratives with illuminating reference to the archaeological evidence, and (*b*) indicating the subtlety of the problems which arise in any attempt at a historical evaluation of the sources. In the discussion of the Exodus and settlement (where, again, there is considerable caution in the treatment of the traditions) particular attention is given to the religion and constitution of Israel. Indeed it is one of the notable features of the whole work that considerable space is devoted to religion. The story is then carried through from the rise of the monarchy to the Maccabean Revolt, and rounded off with an appraisal of Judaism at the end of the O.T. period and a brief comment on the goal of Israel's history. Conflicting points of view are given fair treatment, e.g., in the discussion of the date of Ezra's coming to Jerusalem (the author favours 428 B.C.). The footnotes and an appended bibliography give useful but not overwhelming guidance for further reading. A very welcome feature is the inclusion of maps from the *Westminster Historical Atlas*. It may be safely prophesied that this able work will be widely used. G.W.A.

*GROLLENBERG, L. H. : *Shorter Atlas of the Bible* (translated by Mary F. Hedlund). 1959. Pp. 196 (including 174 illustrations)+9 maps. (Thomas Nelson & Sons Ltd., Edinburgh. Price : 15s. 0d.).

This lovely picture book is not just a selection of useful maps from the earlier *Atlas of the Bible* (see *Book List*, 1957, p. 24). It contains maps, illustrations, and a very concise and informative text. The text, which is entirely new, is an admirable introduction to the geography and archaeology of Palestine. There is, needless to say, great integrity of scholarship. While the book makes demands on the concentration of the readers, especially perhaps with the details of the pictures in pemmican form on the final pages, it is at the same time stimulating. The maps, slightly brighter and clearer than the rather etiolated maps of the big *Atlas* and with less over-printed legend, are, at any rate for the purpose for which they are intended, an improvement on those. And there are the superlative pictures. For the most part these have been selected from the original *Atlas* though there are subtle differences of printing and presentation which reflect immense care and thought. There are also some which are new. This applies particularly to the welcome series on Qumran. Mention should also be made of the excellent sketch maps and tables which here and there supplement the text. The translation reads well, though one sometimes gets the impression that the translator is not perhaps perfectly at home with Biblical material. The ‘ desert ’ of Judea sounds odd. Something has gone wrong on p. 109 line 6 ; and the sentence which begins the last paragraph of p. 74, ‘ The further history of Israel is based upon the facts of Exodus and alliance ’, will be meaningless or misleading, to English readers ; and it is a pity that the Biblical ‘ Covenant ’ was not recognized.

M.Bu.

*KRAELING, E. G. (ed. by) : *Rand McNally Historical Atlas of the Holy Land.* 1959. Pp. 88. (including XXII colour maps and 70 ills.) Rand McNally & Company, Chicago. Price : $2.95).

Dr. Kraeling presents a very comprehensive picture of the life and history of the ancient Near East from Mesopotamia and Egypt in the patriarchal age to the journeys of St. Paul. The work is introduced by a section on the Qumran community and continues through the various phases of Biblical history, each introduced by one page of text, an excellent district outline map, and well-chosen photographs of views and archaeological objects and plans with appropriate captions which are most comprehensive. That so much accurate information can be conveyed in such brief compass is no mean achievement. The atlas includes 22 beautiful coloured maps with contours, and a full chronological chart of the ancient East is so presented as to convey synchronisms at a glance. The one flaw in this beautiful production is the printing of the plate of the Isaiah-scroll (p. 7) upside-down.   J.G.

NOTH, M. : *The History of Israel*, second English edition, translation revised by P. R. Ackroyd. 1960. Pp. xii+488. (A. & C. Black, London. Price : 42s. 0d.).

The publication in English of Noth's great work was a welcome event (see *Book List*, 1958, p. 16). Its usefulness is considerably enhanced by the very thorough revision of the translation which Dr. Ackroyd has carried out. Many errors and infelicities in the rendering have been eliminated, misspellings have been corrected, and the index of names and subjects has been entirely remade. It is a matter for gratitude that a work of such distinction, which has been so widely used, is now available in this greatly improved English form. G.W.A.

SCHEDL, C. : *Geschichte des Alten Testament*. Band II. *Das Bundesvolk Gottes*. 1956. Pp. xvi+327. Band III. *Das goldene Zeitalter Davids*. 1959. Pp. xxviii+497. (Tyrolia—Verlag, Innsbruck, Vienna, Munich.)

These two volumes are arranged according to the same plan as the first (see *Book List*, 1957, p. 25). The second volume deals with the Patriarchal age (pp. 3—110), Moses and the Twelve Tribes (pp. 113—268), and the age of the Conquest (pp.217—317). In the third there are accounts of Samuel (pp.3—50), Saul and David's early career (pp. 53—176), the Davidic kingdom (pp.179—299), and Solomon and the disruption (pp. 303—397), to which are appended a short section on the chronology of the undivided kingdom (pp. 409—414) and a chapter on ' the golden age of Hebrew literature ', which is mainly concerned with the Psalms and Wisdom (pp. 417—491).

The author, who is a Roman Catholic scholar, adopts an extremely conservative attitude to the O.T. tradition, and presents us with what is in the main a retelling of the O.T. narrative. With literary and historical problems he is not greatly concerned. He disposes of doublets and contradictions by harmonizing them. In dealing with exegetical details or questions about the composition of the O.T. books he is usually content to give an account of critical theories and to treat them as inadequately supported by the evidence (e.g., the section on Pentateuchal criticism, II, pp. 234—268), which leads up to the suggestion that the Yahwist may be identified with Moses. His interest is mainly in the history of the times of Moses and David; the settlement and the period of the Judges are presented with astonishing brevity. He tends to explain miracles in rationalistic terms. Ancient oriental material is very extensively drawn upon wherever it has any bearing on the O.T., and there is ample documentation from modern scholarly works. It is in this latter aspect that the chief value of this comprehensive work lies. M.N.

SIMONS, J. : *The Geographical and Topographical Texts of the Old Testament : A Concise Commentary in xxxii. chapters.* 1959. Pp. xiv+536+76 (indexes), with 10 maps (in pocket) (Nederlands Instituut voor het Nabije Oosten, Leiden. Price : Fl. 110).

It is impossible to do Dr. Simons' *thesaurus* justice in a short review. The book is presented as a ' vademecum '. The author treats the names of places and countries following the sequence of the Bible, giving each name a special paragraph. In all there are 1710 paragraphs, some of them with a full discussion of ancient and modern theories, all with references to the texts. Several paragraphs contain the results of study on the sites, published here for the first time or with reference to treatments elsewhere. It is amazing how many details are packed into relatively short passages.

Dr. Simons' work can be estimated at its true worth only after long and varied use. Exegetes and archaeologists may differ about some of his conclusions but nobody will use this *magnum opus* without gratitude and respect for the painstaking and well balanced study, the result of many years of research in Palestine and in libraries and museums. An indication at the top of each page of the number of the paragraphs dealt with would have facilitated its use. The format and printing of the book are excellent, even sumptuous. I fear and regret that its price will preclude wide circulation.

P.A.H.deB.

WILLIAMSON, G. A. : *Josephus : The Jewish War. A New Translation with Introduction* (Penguin Classics, L 90). 1959. Pp. 412+3 maps. (Penguin Books, Harmondsworth. Price : 5s. 0d.).

A new translation into English of Josephus' *Bellum Judaicum* was badly needed, for Whiston is old and unsatisfactory and the Loeb edition is difficult to obtain. Mr. Williamson, who read Greats and is a classical master at Norwich, has filled the gap admirably with a version which is close enough to the original yet, as it is intended for the ordinary reader, strives to be lucid and readable. A useful appendix discusses and gives the substance of the Slavonic Additions. W.D.McH.

TEXT AND VERSIONS

KAHLE, P. E. : *The Cairo Geniza*, 2nd edition. 1959. Pp. xiv+370+10 plates. (Blackwell, Oxford. Price : 50s. 0d.).

The present work is a revised edition of Dr. Kahle's well known Schweich Lectures, delivered in 1941 and published in 1947 under the same title (see *Book List*, 1948, p. 20 ; *Eleven Years*, p. 130). Since then much water has flowed under the bridges ; and the discovery of Scrolls from caves near the N.W. end of the Dead Sea, which began in that year, has necessitated a complete rewriting of much then written.

The new matter, which partly confirms and partly compels modification of things which the author then said, appears chiefly in Chapter II, headed ' The Hebrew Text of the Bible ', which has doubled in length; three new appendices and ten plates of photographs showing Hebrew MSS with various types of vocalization have also been added. Dr. Kahle reinforces his arguments to the effect that no *Urseptuaginta* any more than an *Urtargum* ever existed and stoutly maintains that there were two traditions of Greek and Syriac translations of the Old Testament, the first Jewish and the second Christian, and finds proof of the primary Jewish attempts at translation in fragments from the caves at Qumrân. He also discusses the early attempts at vocalization exhibited in the *matres lectionis* in the Scrolls and draws attention to their close connection with the Samaritan pronunciation of Hebrew as found long afterwards. Like all that Dr. Kahle writes, this new edition is as stimulating as it is interesting, even where the reader disagrees with the conclusions (and most of them are convincingly argued) and will amply repay prolonged and careful study.

G.R.D.

SOISALON-SOININEN, I. : *Der Charakter der asterisierten Zusätze in der Septuaginta.* (Annales Academiae Scientiarum Fennicae. Ser. B. Tom. 114). 1959. Pp. 200 (Suomalainen Tiedeakatemia, Helsinki. Price : 1000 M.).

This careful and masterly analysis of the asterised passages in the Septuagint is intended to show to what extent Origen's additions modify the linguistic character of the LXX, and in what way they illuminate Origen's methods in the Hexapla. By far the greatest number of the additions deal with the techniques of translation, in order to approximate the LXX more closely to the Hebrew text, and the author devotes most of his book to this point. A second section deals with the comparatively rare additions whose use affects the meaning of the LXX ; they vary in length from single words to complete paragraphs, and are normally taken from Theodotion, Aquila and Symmachus. In a third section, proof-passages are given from Num. i. 1-20, Jos. ix-x., Ezek. xxxiv-xxxv., and finally a summary of findings. The book makes an important contribution in a rather narrow field, but also shows how the more general topic of Hexaplaric studies can be fruitfully approached.

B.J.R.

SPERBER, A. : *The Bible in Aramaic, based on Old Manuscripts and Printed Texts. Vol. I. The Pentateuch according to Targum Onkelos.* 1959. Pp. xxiii+357. (E. J. Brill, Leiden. Price : Fl. 90).

This is the first volume of Dr. Sperber's long awaited edition of the Targum. Volumes II and III will comprise the Former and Latter Prophets according to Targum Jonathan, and volume IV will contain the editor's general conclusions. Ms.Or.2363 (British Museum) is selected as the basic text, and use is made of other manuscripts with both Babylonian and Tiberian vocalization. Printed texts used are incunabula and rare sixteenth century books, and Targum quotations in the works of such authors as R. Nathan, Yonah ibn Ganah, and Rashi, are taken into account. On each page the Aramaic text is first given, and immediately below are listed the sigla of all the manuscripts and printed editions which are available to that page. The upper critical apparatus presents variants in the vocalization only, the lower one variant text readings. Great technical skill has been displayed by the printers in the arrangement of all this material on the page. There is no introduction of the kind which is normally expected in an edition of a text. A full exposition of the author's methods and views will presumably be supplied in the last volume, and until it has appeared it is hardly possible to give an adequate appreciation of his work. It is already evident, however, that the publication of this major edition of the Targum is an important event in the history of Biblical and Aramaic studies. It is expected that the three remaining volumes will be priced equally highly. The volumes are not obtainable separately.   D.W.T.

EXEGESIS AND MODERN TRANSLATIONS

AESCHIMANN, A. : *Le prophète Jérémie : Commentaire.* 1959. Pp. 248 (Delachaux & Niestlé, Neuchâtel. Price : paper, Sw. frs. 9.50 ; cloth, Sw. frs. 12.50).

The aim of the book is to put before the non-specialist reader what has been written concerning this prophet during the last century. First, there is a short life of Jeremiah, called in 626 B.C. at the age of 19, and continuing until after 587 B.C. There are five sources : A, Jeremiah's own lively oracles ; B, Baruch's roll ; Mowinckel's C source ; and (so the author) D, the six ' foreign ' chapters 46-51 ; E, Jeremiah's ' eschatological prediction ', chapters 30-33. Two hundred pages of the book consist of the whole of the text discussed in forty-four sections. Each section consists first of the notes on the text in small print, and then a useful exposition in ordinary type. Altogether a good, useful commentary.   N.H.S.

AHLSTRÖM, G. W. : *Psalm* 89. *Eine Liturgie aus dem Ritual des leidenden Königs.* 1959. Pp 228. (C. W. K. Gleerup, Lund. Price : Sw. kr. 25).

Psalm lxxxix. here receives royal treatment in more ways than one, as this is a most elaborate piece of work, in which the Masoretic text is printed in full along with that of the Peshitta, the Septuagint, and the Vulgate, while the variant readings are again reproduced in an *apparatus criticus* to the individual verses. Each verse also receives a detailed and, sometimes, a wide-ranging exposition, and the full documentation makes the whole work a valuable commentary, not merely on the psalm under discussion, but on current trends in the study of the Old Testament. The title gives sufficient indication of the author's interpretation of the psalm, which is in line with what one would expect from a disciple of Professor Engnell, and the study as a whole may be recommended as a very careful and painstaking piece of work. A.R.J.

BRUNO, A. : *Ezechiel. Eine rhythmische und textkritische Untersuchung.* 1959. Pp. 242. (Almqvist & Wiksell, Stockholm. Price : kr. 22.)

BRUNO, A. : *Sprüche, Prediger, Klagelieder, Esther, Daniel. Eine rhythmische und textkritische Untersuchung.* 1958. Pp. 240. (Almqvist & Wiksell, Stockholm. Price : Kr. 22.)

Eleven volumes of Dr. Bruno's metrical investigations have now appeared. The author's method may be illustrated by the fact that he treats the Book of Esther according to the same metrical principles as, e.g., Proverbs and Lamentations. Everywhere he is able to discern a rhythmical structure, if necessary by means of textual emendations. Dr. Bruno's work, no doubt, is the result of much painstaking research, and one cannot but regret that so much effort and enthusiasm have not served a more fruitful purpose. G.G.

DEERE, D. W. : *The Twelve Speak (Volume I), A Translation of the Books of Obadiah, Joel, Amos, Hosea and Micah, with exegetical and interpretative footnotes and an introductory section on Prophecy.* 1958. Pp. 164. (The American Press, New York. Price : $2.95).

The introductory section is devoted to a consideration of the various descriptive terms which are applied to prophets in the O.T., and of the prophetic mission and message. The translation, which aims at presenting the message of the prophets in modern and easily readable language, is generally adequate enough, but it is not always as accurate as it might be, and it is occasionally inelegant, at times even strange. The footnotes are intended to provide the kind of information and guidance which the not very advanced student needs. There are unfortunately a large number of misprints, some of them quite dreadful. The Latin language suffers conspicuously heavy casualties in this respect. So too do proper names. And it is disconcerting, to say the least, to be told that the battle of Waterloo was fought in 1515. Identifications of place names are sometimes antiquated, for example, the identification of Lachish with Tell el Hesy ; works are not infrequently cited erroneously ; and author's names are at times mis-spelt. The work is clearly a serious and sincere endeavour to further the understanding of the minor prophets among students. It is the greater pity, therefore, that it is so heavily marred by blemishes, which, with more care, could easily have been avoided. It is to be hoped that they will be fewer in the second volume. D.W.T.

EXEGESIS AND MODERN TRANSLATIONS   199

EICHRODT, W. : *Der Prophet Hesekiel Kap.* 1-18, *übersetzt und erklärt* (Das Alte Testament Deutsch, 22/1). 1959. Pp. 160. (Vandenhoeck & Ruprecht, Göttingen. Price: DM. 6; by subscription, DM. 5.10).

Although the point of view of the commentator appears in the exegesis, it is surprising that no introduction is given. The prophet is represented as one of the exiled community in Babylonia, but his book has received numerous additions and glosses. Of chap. x. only verses 2 and 7 are authentic ; and at times the text is rearranged, e.g., iii., 1a, 2, 3a, 1b, 3b. The passages treated as glosses do not appear in the translated text but are included in the textual notes. The ' thirtieth year ' is related to the prophet's age and to the ' fifth year ' of his consecration to the priesthood (cf. Num. viii. 24) ; so the exile coincided with the beginning of Ezekiel's priesthood, and the resultant disillusionment was a psychological factor in his call to prophesy. The prophet was subject to ecstasy, of which viii-xi. is an example. The ' māshāl ' is variously translated as *Spottwort, Sprichwort, Gleichnis.* In viii. 8 ḥ-t-r is translated ' sieh genau zu ' although in xii. 5 ' brich dir ein Loch durch '. For ' miphtān ', ' threshold ' is preferred, although ' podium of an idol ' is noted in the commentary. The magical activities in xiii. 17-21 are related to Babylonian sorcery. The commentary on the remaining chapters will be eagerly awaited.   A.S.H.

FREY, H. : *Das Buch des Ringens Gottes um seine Kirche : Der Prophet Amos.* (Die Botschaft des Alten Testaments ; 23/1). 1958. Pp. 202. (Calwer Verlag, Stuttgart. Price : DM. 10.80).

The series in which this book appears will indicate that this is a homiletical commentary. As such it presents the word of God through His prophet to the ongoing life of the people of God with eloquence and deep spiritual insight. It virtually ignores problems of authenticity, except for a brief note on ix. 11-15 which hardly does justice to the view that this section is a later addition. It does, however, make good use of well-tested textual emendations and re-arrangements, as also of the recent insights into Israelite cultic practices. It is a book to be warmly commended to the preacher, both for its translation of the prophet's words and for its comment.
A.S.H.

KNIGHT, G. A. F. : *Hosea* (Torch Bible Commentaries). 1960. Pp. 128. (S.C.M. Press, London. Price : 9s. 6d.).

Within the bounds set by this series the author has done his best to provide a ' constructive theological ' treatment of the book. Those who cannot wrestle with the text alone will find much help in the 28-page Introduction and in the necessarily very brief running comments on the 58 sections into which the text of Hosea is divided. The text used is the AV, with some

glances at the R.S.V. Not unnaturally brevity has led to
apparent dogmatism occasionally ; and sometimes there seems
to be a tendency to combine attractive features of mutually
exclusive theories. The text is regarded as mainly authentic,
edited by a disciple who escaped to Judah from the Assyrian
advance. Hosea was ' probably . . . a middle-class tradesman'
whose wife went wrong after marriage. Chap. xiv. may be
' a liturgy used in later years ', but no other concession to
the cultic approach is evident. J. Mauchline's commentary
in the Interpreter's Bible vol. VI might have been included
in the short bibliography. This commentary should be very
useful for the upper forms in schools and for non-specialist
university students.   D.R.Ap-T.

KRAUS, H. J. : *Psalmen* (Biblischer Kommentar, Altes Testament,
XV) Lieferungen 7-9, 1959. Pp. 481-720. (Verlag der Buchhandlung des Erziehungsvereins, Neukirchen, Kr. Moers. Price : DM. 7
each Lieferung).

Both author and publisher are to be congratulated upon the
speed with which the successive Lieferungen of this quite
massive commentary continue to appear. Those under review
bring the work down to Ps. cv., and to the merits already
noticed (*Book List*, 1959, p. 18) one may add a reference to
the way in which the author recognizes the influence of a
common tradition rather than the dependence of one psalm
upon another. Similary the author is to be commended for
reserving judgement on so live an issue as that of the exact
interpretation of the prophetic element in, say, Ps. lxxxi.
On the other hand, the reviewer fails to see just why the
eschatological aspects of the psalms which celebrate the
Kingship of Yahweh have to be of post-exilic rather than
pre-exilic origin, although here, of course, the author is
continuing along the lines laid down in an earlier work (see
Book List, 1952, pp. 54f ; *Eleven Years*, p. 425). All in all,
however, this is proving to be an attractive piece of work.
                                                        A.R.J.

LAMPARTER, H. : *Das Buch der Psalmen I. Psalm 1-72 übersetzt und
ausgelegt.* (Die Botschaft des Alten Testaments 14). 1958. Pp.
348. (Calwer Verlag, Stuttgart. Price : DM. 14.50).

There is a short introduction. Gunkel's psalm-types are
recognised, and the Coronation Psalms are mentioned, but
not with the cultic emphasis of some modern scholars. Indeed,
the author is not concerned so much with questions of Introduction or with textual problems as with the religious value
of the Psalms. This volume deals with Pss. i-lxxii. : first a
translation into German assuming emendations (e.g., ' and
with trembling kiss his feet ', ii. 11b), and then a religious
and devotional exposition from a definitely Christian point
of view. This union of devotion and scholarship is good ;
the scholarship is assumed, and the author proceeds to the
exposition forthwith.   N.H.S.

MARSH, J. : *Amos and Micah : Introduction and Commentary.* (Torch Bible Commentaries). 1959. Pp. 128. (S.C.M. Press, London. Price : 8s. 6d.).

After a brief introduction which indicates the distinctive nature of the prophetic tradition, beginning with Amos, and suggestions about the way in which the oral tradition was finally fixed in written form ' certainly not earlier than the fifth century B.C. and possibly as late as the third ; ' the two prophets are separately discussed. The ministry of Amos is given as about 760 B.C. The ending (ix. 11-15) is later than Amos, but ii. 4f. is authentic. We would have expected more attention to be given to v. 25 and to such passages as iv. 13. Although most of Micah's oracles are assigned to 712-700 and uttered in Jerusalem, some may have been addressed to Samaria before 721. Exilic and post-exilic additions are noted, e.g., i. 7 ; ii. 12 f ; iv. 1 - v. 15. The material in vii. 7-20 is treated as oracles by Micah or a later disciple in the Exile. A short bibliography is added ; the commentary by R. S. Cripps should have been referred to in the second (1955) edition and a reference to N. H. Snaith's Epworth Notes would have been helpful. The commentary will be useful to the general reader, and is based on the AV text.   A.S.H.

MUCKLE, J. Y. : *Isaiah* 1-39 (Epworth Preacher's Commentaries). 1960. Pp. xii+136. Price : 12s. 6d.

The author's aim is to provide a commentary which is both critical and homiletical. He has rightly judged that the text must be honestly explained before lessons are drawn from it, and therefore critical exegesis claims most of the space. The writing is competent ; but alas ! this book, for the most part, might have been written thirty years ago.   D.R.J.

NOTH, M. : *Das zweite Buch Mose : Exodus, übersetzt und erklärt* (Das Alte Testament Deutsch, 5.). 1959. Pp. 230. (Vandenhoeck & Ruprecht, Göttingen. Price : DM. 8.50 ; by subscription, DM. 11.80).

In this volume Noth has provided an important addition to ' Das Alte Testament Deutsch '. It is a series which gives the commentator some scope in which to work, and Noth has made splendid use of it.

With regard to his assessment of the nature of the source material in Exodus, Noth believes that the original corpus of Pentateuchal traditions was already in co-ordinated form in oral transmission before it became fixed in written form. The main themes of it were the Exodus from Egypt and the deliverance at the Red Sea (the plagues and the dealings of Moses with Pharaoh being part of a separate Passover tradition) and, secondly, the revelation of God and the covenant-making at Sinai. The law was incorporated later into the Sinai tradition, although it was closely associated with it. The Decalogue of Exod. xx. and the Book of the Covenant cannot with assurance be attributed to any particular source, but the Ritualistic Decalogue of Exod. xxxiv. is firmly embedded in J.

P assumes a dominant role in the book, its real purpose being the constitution of the divine community and the development of the cultic regulations of the Temple—a plan which caused a considerable expansion of the original Pentateuchal material and had vital significance for the post-exilic community in Jerusalem.

But in Exodus it is the work of the Yahwist which is of first importance ; that of the Elohist is comparatively insignificant; J, whose date is given as the time of David-Solomon, not only preserves traditional material but sets it in the light of a *heils-geschichtliche Theologie*. E is not clearly younger than J, but its narrative of covenant-making in Exod. xxiv. 9-11 is older than the comparative narrative in J.

P has its own characteristics. The element of the contingent in the course of historical events has no place, all being planned by God for His own purposes ; and the great importance of Sinai does not lie in the overwhelming experience of the people's encounter with God, but in the directions given to Moses for the preparation and regulation of the sanctuary.

The terminus *a quo* for the dating of P is 587 B.C. ; its probable date is just before the opening of the rebuilt Temple in 515.

J.M.

La Sainte Bible traduite en français sous la direction de l'École Biblique de Jérusalem. Jérémie. Les Lamentations. Baruch, by A. Gélin. 2nd ed. revised. 1959. Pp. 310. Price : NF. 12 . *Habaquq, Abdias, Joël*, by J. Trinquet. 2nd ed. revised. 1959. Pp. 94. Price : NF. 3.90. (Les Éditions du Cerf, Paris.)

These volumes of the Jerusalem Bible have been revised on the principles indicated in the notice of earlier volumes (see *Book List*, 1959, p. 19.)

G.W.A.

SCHNEIDER, H. : *Die Bücher Esra und Nehemia*. (Die Heilige Schrift des Alten Testamentes, IV, 2.) 1959. Pp. xvi+268+1 Map. (Peter Hanstein, Bonn. Price : DM. 24).

This excellent commentary brings to a completion the Bonner Bibel. An interval of no less than 18 years separates it from its last predecessor. This is not to be laid at the door of Dr. Schneider, but is due to the fact that three scholars to whom the task had been entrusted successively died before their work was completed. There is an excellent Introduction in which the problems of these books are carefully discussed, with a good closing section on their theology. On the question of the relative date of the work of Ezra and that of Nehemiah Dr. Schneider suspends judgement, after presenting the case for the three current views, but confesses that he inclines to hold the priority of Nehemiah. There is an original translation of the Biblical text and a full and adequate commentary stands beneath it. The book is particularly to be commended for its excellent bibliographies. A general bibliography stands at the beginning, and before the various sections of the Introduction this is supplemented by further relevant literature. H.H.R.

SZERUDA, J. : *Kzienga Psalmów* (*Das Buch der Psalmen, aus dem Hebr. übersetzt*). 1957. Pp. 144. (Brytyjskie i Zagraniczne Towarzystwo Biblijne, Warsaw).

This is a new rendering of the Psalter by the well-known Warsaw scholar. It had already appeared in 1937 as part of a new translation into Polish of the whole of the O.T. ; but during the War the work which had been begun was almost completely destroyed. This new translation varies markedly from the old translation which has been in use in the Evangelical Church since 1632 ; but the changes are unfortunately not always for the better, e.g., Ps. viii. 6 is now more accurately rendered ' Thou hast made him a little less than God ' (instead of ' angels '); but in ii. 11 ' Do homage to him ' is certainly not an improvement on ' Kiss the son ' (12). In xxiv. 6 the translator should have indicated that he has added the word ' God ' to ' Jacob '. Details in the translation will have to be revised ; but taken as a whole it is a worthy achievement. In 1960 the new rendering of the O.T. into Polish should be complete. M.B.

THEXTON, S. C. : *Isaiah* 40-66 (Epworth Preacher's Commentaries.) 1959. Pp. xiv+160. (Epworth Press, London. Price : 12s. 6d.).

This is the second of the Old Testament volumes in this series and takes its place alongside that of N. H. Snaith on *Amos, Hosea and Micah* (*Book List*, 1957, p. 35). The comments are pithy and admirably designed for their purpose — to help preachers. The author is not hesitant to recommend textual changes where there is good evidence, even if it means losing familiar phrases like ' the angel of his presence ' (lxiii. 9) of which he properly says that it ' finds no parallel in the Old Testament, and is almost a contradiction in terms ' (p. 142). At points of greater interest or difficulty, as at xlv. 5-7, where God is said to be the author of both good and evil, there are extended notes.

It would be a remarkable commentary that explained all the difficulties, but here and there one would have liked more, as on liii. 10 where the ' guilt-offering ' is lightly passed over. Doubtless this is dictated by the desire to expound the Servant Songs within the framework of their meaning for the Christian Church, but readers ought also to be able to find something about their fundamental meaning. L.H.B.

UBACH, B. : *I i II Dels Paralipomens; Esdras-Nehemias* (Versió dels textos originals i comentari pels monjos de Montserrat, VII.) 1958. Pp. 398. (Monastery of Montserrat, Barcelona).

Once again it is a pleasure to welcome a volume of this really good and readable commentary. The only regret must continue to be that it is written in Catalan, and not in Castilian or some other more familiar European language. The author, Dom Bonaventura Ubach, has written a number of excellent books, one of the earliest, *El Sinai*, being the record of his journey to Jebel Musa and the monastery of St. Catherine. The present volume devotes a great part of its space to a translation in Catalan with the Latin Vulgate in parallel columns. The introduction to the books of Chronicles covers the usual ground, but does not appear to have made use of Professor W. Rudolph's illuminating article in *Vetus Testamentum*, Vol. IV (October, 1954), pp. 401-409, or of the same writer's commentary in the H.A.T. series. Not much attention is paid in Ubach's introduction to the religious value of Chronicles. In the section on Ezra and Nehemiah, some space is devoted to van Hoonacker's theory of the chronology, which, as Ubach declares, ' succeeded in fascinating a goodly number of notable historians and interpreters '. None the less, the author agrees with Fernandez and de Vaux that the theory does not carry conviction. The notes to the text, are, as usual, somewhat brief, but give a good deal of help with the problems suggested by these books. The production, as always, is remarkably fine. J.M.T.B.

ZIMMERLI, W. : *Ezechiel.* (Biblischer Kommentar XIII.) Lieferung 6. 1959. Pp. 401-480. (Buchhandlung des Erziehungsvereins, Neukirchen Kreis Moers. Price : DM. 7).

This Lieferung completes the discussion of ch. xviii., continues with the allegorical ch. xix. (where the commentator regards 10-14 as a later expansion) and with the prophetic retrospect over Israel's history in ch. xx. (of the structure of which a very detailed examination is given), and ends with part of the discussion of the three ' sword ' oracles in ch. xxi. Linguistically, textually, and exegetically this commentary is a mine of erudition. G.W.A.

LITERARY CRITICISM AND INTRODUCTION
(including History of Interpretation, Canon, and Special Studies)

*ANDERSON, G. W. : *A Critical Introduction to the Old Testament.* (Studies in Theology No. 52.) 1959. Pp. viii+250. (Duckworth, London. Price : 12s. 6d.).

While Professor Anderson has had to cover much familiar ground and to confine himself within the limits set by the well-known series in which his Introduction appears, his treatment is always clear, fresh, and fair and full enough to convey to the reader a good survey of past and present work on the subject. He begins with a chapter on the canon, and then he treats of the individual books, or where convenient, of groups of books. Literary forms and literary history are discussed, and the book ends with a chapter under the title : The Old Testament as Christian Scripture. This up-to-date, compact compendium will be widely used and deservedly so.

W.D.McH.

BERNHARDT, K.-H. : *Die gattungsgeschichtliche Forschung am Alten Testament als exegetische Methode.* (Aufsätze und Vorträge zur Theologie und Religionswissenschaft, Heft 8.) 1959. Pp. 46. (Evangelische Verlagsanstalt, Berlin, D.D.R. Price : DM. 2.40).

The author seeks to determine the character and aim of O.T. exegesis. He rejects a ' theological ' exegesis governed by dogmatic considerations. The exegete must always be concerned to determine the meaning of the text without being influenced by such external factors. To this end the author thinks the method of *Gattungsgeschichte* and *Formgeschichte* the most appropriate, despite the difficulty, at times, of establishing agreed results and the use by difference scholars of technical terms in varying senses. Following Gunkel, he emphasizes the importance of the *history* of the various *Gattungen* and of establishing the *Sitz im Leben* of any given unit. He is critical of the attempts of the Uppsala School to discover an ' original pattern '. By his judicious choice of examples the author has made his position admirably clear.

M.B.

BEYERLIN, W. : *Die Kulttraditionen Israels in der Verkündigung des Propheten Micha.* (F.R.L.A.N.T., N.F. 54.) 1959. Pp. 103. (Vandenhoeck & Ruprecht, Göttingen. Price : DM. 10.80).

This is a doctoral dissertation of considerable merit. As dissertations are wont to do it leans somewhat heavily upon authority. In this case, as the footnotes show, Professor A. Weiser may be said to be the rock upon which the author's thesis rests. Other scholars whose names occur very frequently in the footnotes are G. von Rad, M. Noth, A. Alt, and S. Mowinckel, from which it may be seen to which school the author belongs. In his study of the oracles of the prophet Micah he puts forward the view that during the period of the prophet's activity the amphictyonic league with which Professor Noth has made us familiar was still functioning in Jerusalem. Dr. Beyerlin maintains that the prophet's denunciations and promises presuppose the existence of a feast of renewal of the Sinai covenant, such as Mowinckel has argued for in his early work *Le Décalogue*. At the feast an essential feature of the ritual was the solemn reading of the laws and prescriptions upon which the covenant at Sinai rested, and which were binding upon the members of the amphictyonic league. The prophet's appeal rests upon the assumption that those whom he is addressing are familiar with the cult-legends of the theophany at Sinai the Exodus and the taking possession of the land of Canaan, and the Davidic covenant. It is to the whole *Heilsgeschichte* annually rehearsed at the *Erneuerungsfest*, that the prophet refers when he answers the Israelite's question, ' Wherewith shall I come before the Lord ? ', with the words, ' He hath shown thee, O man, what he doth require of thee '. The monograph is an interesting piece of work and will repay careful study. But it must be borne in mind that the existence of the amphictyonic league is still open to question, and even more problematic is the view that the league was still functioning as late as the time of Hezekiah

S.H.H.

GESE, H. : *Lehre und Wirklichkeit in der alten Weisheit : Studien zu den Sprüchen Salomos und zu dem Buche Hiob.* 1958. Pp. VI+90 (J. C. B. Mohr, Tübingen. Price : DM. 9.)

This book, which is based on a *Habilitationsschrift*, is in two distinct parts. The first is a comparative study of Egyptian Wisdom literature and the Old Testament Book of Proverbs, not with the purpose of analysing the indebtedness of the latter to the former, but in order to distinguish what of form and content they have in common and, in particular, to examine the degree to which each seeks to represent the world of human experience as one of order. The author finds in both much to support his thesis, but he has to affirm that the Book of Proverbs has its own distinctive elements which do not fit into the pattern of ancient near-eastern wisdom, especially such a saying as : 'A man's mind plans his own life, but it is the Lord who directs his step '.

The second part deals with the theme of the Book of Job as it is found in certain Sumerian-Accadian literary documents and fragments, which, in the author's view, represent a distinct literary type. The format of this type he describes as *Not*, *Klage*, *Erhörung und Wiederstellung*, although minor variations occur within that framework. In the Sumerian literature nothing is said about a causal relation between sin and suffering, such as is prominently expressed in the Book of Job. The fact induces the author to try to trace the development of what he terms the *Tun-Ergehen-Zusammenhang* as a background to the Book of Job. This is a well written and significant study.

J.M.

GOTTWALD, N. K. : *A Light to the Nations : An Introduction to the Old Testament.* 1959. Pp. xxiv+616+33 maps+9 charts+45 ills. (Harper & Brothers, New York. Price : $6.50).

The purpose of the book is best defined in its author's words, ' It is nearest to a literary history, but its aim is broadly cultural and specifically theological . . . there has been an attempt to integrate the literature, history, and religion '. The author has indeed succeeded very well in counteracting the compartmentalizing consequences of so many specialist studies, so that the book should prove a boon to the student and educated layman ; as such it is warmly commended.

The glossary of basically important names and technical terms will be most useful for the beginner ; the detailed section on recommended further reading performs a service to those whose only language is English—and the meagreness of the list in some categories may suggest to other qualified authors where new contributions will be most welcome. It was a very good thought to include as an appendix standard translations of fifteen Near-Eastern texts or portions relevant to the O.T. ; and the frequent sketch maps in the text help to elucidate history and development by tying them up with the geography without seeking to usurp the functions of a Bible Atlas proper. There are good indexes, and the book is very good value for money. D.R.Ap-T.

GRANT, F. C. : *How to Read the Bible*. 1959. Pp. vi+136. (Thomas Nelson and Sons, Edinburgh. Price : 15s. 0d.).

Sound advice and useful basic information are given here to the ' ordinary ' reader of the Bible. Two opening chapters make a plea for the disciplined use of the intelligence and indicate the various kinds of approach which may be made to Scripture. Then three chapters are devoted to the O.T. (Pentateuch, Prophets and Historical Books, Poetical Books), one to Apocalyptic, one to the Apocrypha, and two to the N.T. The book ends with a discussion of the essential message of the Bible and an excellent guide for further reading. There is a freshness and lightness of touch about the writing which enhances the book's other merits. G.W.A.

GUNNEWEG, A. H. J. : *Mündliche und schriftliche Tradition der vor-exilischen Prophetenbücher als Problem der neueren Propheten-forschung*. (F.R.L.A.N.T. N.F. 55.) 1959. Pp. 128 (Vandenhoeck & Ruprecht, Gottingen. Price : DM. 11.80).

A thorough, balanced, and powerful investigation of the view of oral and written tradition which is associated mainly with Scandinavia. The work of Nyberg, Birkeland, Mowinckel, Engnell, Haldar, and Nielsen is expounded and appraised. The author affirms that in the O.T. oral tradition was the normal method of transmission, but denies that the written text we have is a direct fixation of oral tradition. He makes an important, if obvious, distinction between oral *recitation*, enrichment, etc., and oral *tradition*, and argues that writing was important from early times, so that written sources, expanded from oral tradition, have significance for the under-standing of our present documents. This amounts to a justification of the sort of literary analysis practised by e.g., Martin Noth and von Rad. He acutely uncovers some Scandinavian *non sequiturs*, and shows how Nyberg on Hosea, Engnell on Isa. vi., Birkeland on the prophets, and Nielsen on Jer. xxxvi. and Micah do not strengthen their case by their examples. His investigation of Isa., Jer., and Ezek. leads to the conclusion that these prophets all wrote or caused some of their prophecies to be written, that this was because their words were Word of God and were to have a continued life beyond the moment of their utterance, with a witness-character, but also with an objectivity of their own, ' a lasting dynamis '. All this leads ultimately to the conception of canonical Scripture. Once a nucleus of written tradition was established, it must needs gather to it other material from the always continuing oral tradition. The *Sitz im Leben* of *oral* tradition was the ' father's house ', but of the *written* the sanctuary where the prophets were cultic officials. Altogether an indispensable and notable book on its subject. D.R.J.

HENSHAW, T. : *The Latter Prophets*. 1959. Pp. 342. (George Allen & Unwin, London. Price : 30s. 0d.).

Five introductory chapters deal with the Literature, Background, Archaeology of the Prophets and with Hebrew poetry. Eighteen chapters then present the canonical prophets in their historical order from Amos to Deutero-Zechariah. Each chapter deals with the prophet, summarizes the contents of the book and estimates the abiding influence. 8 appendices gather together useful information on Israel's institutions and offer chronological tables and a selected bibliography to each chapter. A popular, stereotyped but scholarly introduction to the prophets along critical orthodox lines. G.H.D.

KAISER, O. : *Der königliche Knecht : Eine traditionsgeschichtlich-exegetische Studie über die Ebed-Jahweh-Lieder bei Deuterojesaja.* (F.R.L.A.N.T., N.F. 52.) 1959. Pp. 146. (Vandenhoeck & Ruprecht, Göttingen. Price : DM. 12.80).

No more important monograph on the Servant Songs has appeared for many years. On the assumption that the poems are to be understood in relation to their context, and that the prophet (not primarily a writer) preached his message to the worshipping community in exile, the author subjects every sentence of the poems to detailed scrutiny, seeking the traditional background of vocabulary and idea. His conclusion is that both the ' type ' of the poems, and the detailed allusions to the psalms of lament and the related thanksgivings, support his view that the poems are a prophetic answer to the laments of the exiles, to their broken faith and their prayer for return. (In this sense they are a ' prophetic liturgy '). This is the *Sitz im Leben* of the Songs. They assume the form of the *Heilsorakel* and the confession of faith of the believing community. The ' Servant ' is the Israel of the Gola, who succeeds to the role of the king, and embodies a prophetic function also. The prophet looks back beyond the monarchy to the institution of the Twelve Tribes which is to be restored, i.e., the institution which expresses the direct sovereignty of Yahweh over His people. The Gola is to perform the royal function of linking God with all Israel, of guarding justice, and further is to be witness to the honour and sovereignty of God among the nations. It is impossible in a short review to do justice to the immense labour of research that has been devoted to this impressive and richly-packed book, which, in the reviewer's opinion, has the virtue of asking the right questions, and may well point to many of the right answers.

D.R.J.

KOCH, K. : *Die Priesterschrift von Exodus 25 bis Leviticus 16. Eine überlieferungsgeschichtliche und literarkritische Untersuchung.* (F.R.L.A.N.T., N.F. 53.) 1959. Pp. 108. (Vandenhoeck & Ruprecht, Göttingen. Price : DM. 10.80).

This detailed study of the Pentateuchal source P takes its start from the work of Rendtorff (*Die Gesetze in der Priesterschrift*, 1954 ; see *Book List*, 1954, p.53 ; *Eleven Years*, p.590) and is concerned, not with the analysis of later additions to P so that its later literary history may be traced, but with its pre-history, i.e., with the ancient traditional materials, commonly orally transmitted, which form its core. The author believes that a survey of the Sinai legislation contained in Exod. xxv—Lev. xvi. shows that a collection of rituals consisting of varying numbers of regulative units, together with priestly torahs and some apodeictic laws, constituted the *Vorlage* for most of the chapters. These ritual complexes, which he details, are often set out in a distinctive literary framework, and they deal with the building of the sanctuary and cultic rites and regulations, and had their origin at an important cultic centre. They serve in P as a frame of reference for establishing and maintaining right practice. Pg., it is submitted, was derived from Jerusalem and its aim was to legitimize the cult usage there. It is a programme document. The new temple demanded new plans and practices ; the building had to be distinct from other buildings, the priests separated from other people, so that rituals for unsinning and cleansing are prominent. The author has tackled a very difficult historical, literary, and cultic study and has pursued a line which will stimulate discussion.

J.M.

MOWINCKEL, S. : *Den västorientaliska och israelitisk-judiska litteraturen.* 1959. Pp. 81+53 ills. (Extract from *Bonniers Allmänna Litteraturhistoria*, ed. by E. N. Tigerstedt. Albert Bonniers, Förlag, Stockholm).

Professor Mowinckel here gives a swift and fascinating survey of O.T. literature and its oriental background with a little of its sequel. What he has written is an outline of literary history rather than an introduction to the several books. After a brief account of Sumerian, Babylonian, and Egyptian literature, he considers the various types of literature which were produced in Israel. In place of the *multa* of larger works he has given us *multum* in a very attractive and compact form. The booklet is pleasantly illustrated. The language is Swedish.

G.W.A.

PIDOUX, G. : *Du portique à l'autel. Introduction aux Psaumes.* 1959. Pp. 150. (Delachaux & Niestlé, Neuchâtel. Price : Sw. fr. 5.00 (sewn), 8.50 (bound)).

A simple exposition of the contents of the Psalter along the now familiar lines of Gunkel and Mowinckel. The author stresses the fact that the language of the psalms is predominantly that of the cult, and regards the majority of them as pre-exilic. He writes succinctly and clearly, and has no difficulty in making his point that this kind of approach to the Psalms is of the first importance, if one is to appreciate aright the quality of Israel's worship.   A.R.J.

SMEND, R. : *Das Mosebild von Heinrich Ewald bis Martin Noth* (Beiträge zur Geschichte der Biblischen Exegese, 3.) 1959. Pp. VIII+80. (J. C. B. Mohr, Tübingen).

The effect of the literary, historical, and traditio-historical examination of the Pentateuch has been not only to bring in question the Mosaic authorship of any part of these books, but also to question the historicity of the various roles traditionally assigned to Moses, and therefore of Moses himself. This study examines and summarizes the results of such studies and approaches the problem along the lines suggested by Karl Jaspers' ' Grossen Philosophen '. In addition to the historical knowledge that derives from the critical technique, we must include ' das Ergriffensein von der Wirklichkeit ' and ' die Ordnung zur zusammenhängenden Konstruktion '. Moses is not merely a historical figure, but part of the history that we meet existentially.   A.S.H.

*WEBER, O. : *Ground Plan of the Bible.* 1959. Pp. 222. (Lutterworth Press, London. Price : 27s. 6d.).

This is an elementary introduction to the O.T. suitable for G.C.E. students. 211 pages with two columns are followed by chronological table and an Index of Biblical Ideas. 90 pages are devoted to the O.T. and the rest to the N.T. The information is slight.   G.H.D.

LAW, RELIGION, AND THEOLOGY

AALDERS, J. G. : *De Verhouding tussen het Verbondsboek van Mozes en de Codex Hammurabi* (Exegetica, Reeks 3, Deel 2.) 1959. Pp. 52. (Van Keulen, The Hague. Price : Fl. 3.95).

Aalders emphasizes in the first place that a comparison between the Book of the Covenant and the Code of Hammurabi is a comparison between two essentially incomparable entities —a divine law-code and a human one. He then sets side by side a number of pairs of specific laws in the two codes and shows how, time after time, the relation between the two parallels cannot be one of straightforward borrowing by the later from the earlier. Over against the Babylonian emphasis on the status of the parties concerned he draws attention to the Israelite emphasis on the person, and sees here a token of the divine Lawgiver's interest in individuals, especially in the underprivileged. The covenant code, he thinks, was probably based on an ancient common law, which developed out of the early ideas of right and wrong found among the peoples in that part of the world, but in its Biblical form it is the product of special revelation, reflecting a community life whose fundamental principles are mercy and love to one's neighbour. The Hammurabi code and the covenant code breathe two quite different atmospheres : ' the one breathes the spirit which is from beneath ; the other breathes the spirit which is from Above '. F.F.B.

BEAUCAMP, E. : *La Bible et le sens religieux de l'univers.* (Lectio Divina, 25.) 1959. Pp. 222. (Éditions du Cerf, Paris. Price : Frs. 930).

The title of this interesting work is, for one reader at least, by no means self-explanatory. The substance of it was presented as a thesis to the theological faculty of Lyon in February, 1953, when it bore the title : *Vision de l'univers et histoire du salut. Essai sur la théologie des réalités materielles dans l'Ancien Testament*, which attempted a reply to the question : What was the role of the material universe in the drama of our salvation, or, alternatively, what was its place in God's providential design ? Père Beaucamp's contention is that in most of the existing works on Old Testament theology it is the human problem, whether this is viewed individually or collectively, that usually commands the attention of interpreters and theologians. It is, the author suggests, unprofitable to ask what is the thought of the Bible on this issue, since the problem as such does not appear to have been considered by the Old Testament writers. It can, however, be asked : what in the concrete was the attitude of the chosen people to the universe of which they formed a part ? The matter is discussed in chapters with such titles as : From the God of History to the God of the Universe ; the universe in so far as it declares the meaning of history (i.e., in the theophanies and in creation) ; and the universe, the gift of the God of history. The author has evidently read widely and has made a good selection of passages from the Bible to illustrate his thesis. There is an index of Biblical quotations, but unfortunately, no index of the many authors to whose works references are given. J.M.T.B.

BLACKWOOD, A. W. (Jr.) : *Devotional Introduction to Job.* 1959. Pp. 166. (Baker Book House, Grand Rapids, Mich. Price : $2.95).

This is a very attractive preacher's study of the Book of Job in ten chapters following a Foreword. The spirit and approach of the author confirm the title of his work. Certainly one of the better examples of a modern homiletical treatment of the book. G.H.D.

BREKELMANS, C. H. W. : *De herem in het oude Testament*, with a summary in German. 1959. Pp. 200. (Centrale Drukkerij n.v., Nijmegen).

This book is a thesis of the R.C. university of Nijmegen. It deals with the root *herem* and the ban in Israel. The author treats at length the passages Lev. xxvii. 28f. and Num. xxi. 1-3. In Joshua Deuteronomistic influence is shown. Only Josh. vi. and vii. seem to preserve the ancient *herem* idea, a military custom. I Sam. xv. and I Kings xx. 35-42 have been influenced by the prophetic spirit. Dr. Brekelmans compares in a separate chapter the practice of the ban in the ancient Near East. This review of theories on its origin is followed by a distinctive picture of the development of the practice in Israel's and Judah's history. In his final chapter he deals with a theological problem. Yahweh's cruelty : and its solution in Church history. The author stands up for a sharp distinction between the Deuteronomistic theological interpretation and the historical facts behind this interpretation.

A valuable monograph, the result of careful exegesis of the texts, with an interesting and attractive attempt to solve some problems raised by the conservative attitude to the Bible. P.A.H.deB.

CHILDS, B. S. : *Myth and Reality in the Old Testament* (Studies in Biblical Theology, No. 27.) 1960. Pp. 112. (S.C.M. Press, London. Price : 9s. 6d.).

The author rejects other people's ' philosophical, historical, form-critical, or aesthetic definition of myth ' in favour of a ' *phenomenological* one ' (p. 16). In one chapter he deals with the re-shaping of myths by the Biblical writer in six passages ; the most difficult being Gen. vi. 1-4. The comparison of the mythical and the Biblical attitudes to time and space is very suggestive, but the statement ' the Old Testament concept of reality came into conflict with myth ' (p. 72, cf. p. 96) makes perhaps too sharp a dichotomy as it stands, since, as the author himself makes plain, much myth was assimilated by the Old Testament writers. Some doubts will also be felt about the validity of even the proposed form of Christological exegesis.

But this is a thought-provoking and important monograph with some good documentation, and indexes of authors and scripture references. We look forward to an expanded and maybe still further revised or developed presentation of the author's ideas in the light of the discussion this study is sure to evoke. D.R.Ap-T.

CONGAR, Y. M.-J. : *Le Mystère du Temple, ou l'Économie de la Présence de Dieu à sa Créature de la Genèse à l'Apocalypse.* (Lectio Divina, 22.) 1958. Pp. 346. (Les Éditions du Cerf, Paris. Price : 19s. 6d.).

Like all Congar's works this is a pleasantly written and well-documented book, which should prove as successful as his well-known *Esquisses du Mystère de l'Église* (1942, now translated into English). The sub-title gives a fair account of the contents. The Old Testament portion, occupying no more than 129 pages, considers the presence of God as manifested to the patriarchs and to the Israelties during the Exodus period, and, later, as foreshadowed in the prophecy of Nathan (II Sam. vii—I Chr. xvii.) and as realized in the construction of the temple of Solomon. A chapter on the prophets emphasizes their message of ' la Présence liée au règne de Dieu dans le coeur des hommes ' (p. 280). A series of notes makes up the fifth chapter, entitled ' Temple et Présence de Dieu dans la Piété et la Pensée Juives '. A note to this chapter deals with the problem of the exact site of the sanctuary in the temples of Solomon, Zorobabel, and Herod the Great. The New Testament section (pp. 133-275) is rounded off by a final chapter on the various aspects of the divine presence in the world. J.M.T.B.

DUBARLE, A.-M. : *Le péché originel dans l'Écriture.* (Lectio Divina 20.) 1958. Pp. 202. (Éditions du Cerf, Paris. Price : 14s. 6d.).

This volume consists of studies which have appeared in French journals between 1955 and 1957. There are three chapters dealing with the Old Testament and three with the New Testament. The first three chapters deal with the condition of humanity and original sin in Genesis and in the Wisdom Books, with considerable attention to Ben Sirach and Wisdom of Solomon—which the writer includes in ' Scripture '. The author finds the double strand everywhere : death is the common lot of man ; death is the penalty of sin. The idea of the solidarity of mankind is discussed, both with the past and in the present. The volume deals with diagnosis : we look forward to a book which deals more fully with the cure.

N.H.S.

EHRLICH, E. L. : *Kultsymbolik im Alten Testament und im nachbiblischen Judentum.* (Symbolik der Religionen, III.) 1959. Pp. 144. (Anton Hiersemann, Stuttgart. Price : DM. 26).

This monograph was originally written as an article for the *Handbuch der Symbolik,* but was subsequently included in Dr. F. Hermann's series, now in course of publication, entitled *Die Symbolik der Religionen.* Those who may be led by the title to expect a discussion of the significance and origin of the symbols used in the Israelite cult, will be disappointed. Nevertheless the book is a useful one, and may be recommended to students of the Israelite cult. It contains a full list with brief descriptions of all the places, objects, rites, seasons, and personnel, in any way connected with the cult during its whole history in Israel, including rituals observed in post-biblical Judaism. Although the notes on the various cult-items are brief, they are accurate, based on the latest anthropological and archaeological data, and supplemented by excellent foot-notes which enable the student to refer to the original sources. The book can be heartily recommended as a useful and reliable guide to the study of the Israelite and Jewish cultus. S.H.H.

FASCHER, E. : *Jesaja* 53 *in christlicher und jüdischer Sicht.* (Aufsätze und Vorträge zur Theologie und Religionswissenschaft, Heft 4.) 1958. Pp. 58. (Evangelische Verlagsanstalt, Berlin, D.D.R. Price : DM. 2.70.)

> The author of this study gives a detailed examination of the results of the work of Leo Baeck, Martin Buber, and Franz Rosenzweig. He surveys critically the different Christian and Jewish interpretations of Isa. liii through the centuries until the present day, and makes a valuable contribution, to a new understanding of Jewish-Christian relationships in the field of theology and faith. M.B.

DE FRAINE, J. : *Adam et son Lignage.* (Museum Lessianum, Section Biblique, 2.) 1959. Pp. 320. (Desclée de Brouwer, Bruges. Price : B. frs. 180).

> This is a most useful study by a well-known Jesuit scholar of the concept of ' corporate personality ' which the pioneer work of Lévy-Bruhl and the investigations of scholars like Pedersen, Eissfeldt, Wheeler Robinson and Johnson have made familiar. De Fraine distinguishes between the applications of the concept both in space and in time to the understanding of the relations between the individual and the totality, what he calls the horizontal and the vertical aspects. The ' père de famille ' is an illustration of the former aspect, the ancestor of the latter. Nine themes are worked out and illustrated from all four parts of the Canon. Six careful studies follow of what are called ' concrete applications of the notion of " corporate personality ", ' viz., Adam, the King, the Prophets, the Servant of Yahweh, the Son of Man and the ' I ' of the Psalms. It should be added that the author insists on the reality of the first man as an individual, while underlining at the same time his representative character. The concluding chapter illustrates the concept of ' corporate personality ' from the New Testament and in particular discusses the mystical Body of Christ.
>
> The author lays emphasis throughout on the importance of preserving the dialectic of the individual and the group. He criticizes the error of allowing the group to make one lose sight of the importance of the individual and the error of conceiving the relation of the individual and the group as one of causality. Its very full documentation adds greatly to the value of this book. N.W.P.

GÉLIN, A. : *The Religion of Israel,* trans. by J. R. Foster. (Faith and Fact Books, No. 16.) 1959. Pp. 112. (Burns and Oates, London. Price : 7s. 6d.).

> The title of the French original of which this is a translation is a rather better indication of its contents : *L'Ame d'Israël dans le Livre.* What is presented is not a history of Israel's religion but some of the central religious and theological themes in the O.T. After some 10 pages of historical outline

there follow discussions of the Covenant People, O.T. ethics, O.T. worship, the hope of the Kingdom of God, the missionary ideal, life after death, and Biblical man. The book is a compact systematic account of the subjects mentioned without loss of historical perspective. The translation reads smoothly. Presumably forms like *rouah* and *nefech* have survived by oversight. The quotation from Psalm cii. (ciii.) 1 (p. 91) *ma nefesh* presents the Psalmist as surprisingly bilingual.

G.W.A.

van Goudoever, J. : *Biblical Calendars*. 1959. Pp. XIV+296 (E. J. Brill, Leiden. Price : Fl. 21).

Here is a careful study of the calendar, as devised not only by the Jews of Bible times, both pre-exilic and post-exilic, but of later times. With this there is necessarily involved the matter of the lectionaries, chiefly the Reading of the Law. In the first seven chapters the dates of the observances of the feasts, festivals and fasts are discussed. Then the author turns to the discussion of dates given in Jubilees, Ezekiel, and the various apocalypses. Part Two deals with festivals in the early Christian Church, considering even the questions as to whether the Feasts of Ascension, Transfiguration and Church-Dedication depend strictly on the Calendar. In particular the length of the ministry of Jesus is discussed. The concluding section of the book deals with the feasts of the Gospels and in Acts. Here many suggestions are made, all interesting, some illuminating, and others speculative. It is a necessary book for all who are interested in ecclesiastical calendars, liturgies, and lectionaries.

N.H.S.

Henry, C. F. H. (ed. by) : *Revelation and the Bible : Contemporary Evangelical Thought*. 1959. Pp. 414. (Tyndale Press, London. Price : 17s. 6d.).

This volume consists of twenty-four essays on the theme of the divine revelation in and the inspiration of the Bible. The twenty-four writers call themselves ' evangelical conserva- tives ', which means that they all maintain the ' plenary ' or ' verbal ' theory of inspiration. Readers who accept this position will find all the essays interesting and helpful. Others will find the essays interesting, but often puzzling and some- times exasperating. There are three exceptions : two essays which deal with ' archaeological confirmation ' of the Old Testament (by D. J. Wiseman) and of the New Testament (by F. F. Bruce). In both of these essays the claims are moderate and reasonable. But the most helpful is that by N. H. Ridderbos (Amsterdam), dealing with ' Reversals in Old Testament Criticism '. This essay is a well-balanced estimate of the present position. He warns the ' conservatives ' that the changes are by no means as favourable to their point of view as they often suppose ; equally he warns the critical scholars of the excesses of some latter developments.

N.H.S.

HERBERT, A. S. : *Worship in Ancient Israel.* (Ecumenical Studies in Worship, No. 5.) 1959. Pp. 52. (Lutterworth Press, London : Price : 7s. 6d.).

The Old Testament Professor at the Selly Oak Colleges, Birmingham, has written a sound, balanced and informative study of Hebrew worship in its many aspects. There are four chapters : the basis of Israel's worship, its vocabulary, its media, and a final chapter on the aim and fulfilment of worship. The last is definitely Christian, and the key to the old inadequacy of sacrifice, altar, and priest is to be found in the Epistle to the Hebrews. The basis of Israel's worship is Israel's faith in Yahweh, Saviour and Redeemer, who demonstrated His character primarily in the rescue from Egypt. The short section on the vocabulary deals with such terms as ' bow oneself down ', ' slave-servant ' and the like. The main body of the book deals with the various types of sacrifice, the accompanying ritual recitals, cultic objects (Ark, pillars, etc.), cultic persons (king, priest, prophet) and such cultic occasions as the great feasts. Full recognition is given to recent studies of the New Year rites and ' sacral kingship ', but the author does not carry these to the excessive lengths characteristic of some protagonists. Altogether an excellent book, highly to be recommended to students.   N.H.S.

HOOKER, M. D. : *Jesus and the Servant.* 1959. Pp. xiv+230. (S.P.C.K., London. Price : 27s. 6d.).

Miss Hooker's study of the influence of the Servant concept of Deutero-Isaiah in the New Testament was originally undertaken for a master's degree at Bristol University. It is widely held that in Jesus' interpretation and fulfilment of his life-mission he was profoundly influenced by the Servant Songs, and particularly by the fourth ; Miss Hooker examines the evidence afresh and finds nothing to support this view. She concludes that there is no sure reference to the Servant Songs in any place where Jesus speaks of the meaning of his death, and that neither he nor the evangelists had the concept of the Servant or his suffering in mind. The Servant is Israel, and what Jesus did, she holds, was to fulfil Israel's world mission as prescribed throughout Deutero-Isaiah and not only in the Servant Songs. The Servant is not regarded as a distinct figure ; the Servant concept is but one aspect of the theology of suffering and redemption which emerges throughout the Biblical presentation of the history of Israel. The reviewer dissents from many of Miss Hooker's conclusions, but welcomes her re-opening of such a crucial question, and concurs heartily with Professor Barrett's testimony in his foreword to the ' unusual maturity ' of her scholarship.

F.F.B.

JEPSEN, A. : *Wissenschaft vom Alten Testament*. (Aufsátze und Vorträge, Heft 1.) 1958. Pp. 34. (Evangelische Verlagsanstalt, Berlin, D.D.R. Price : DM. 1.80).

Taking as his starting point Wellhausen's resignation from his theological chair because he could not prepare his students for the work of the ministry, the author examines the relationship between O.T. scholarship and the faith and life of the Church. He is convinced that God still speaks to the Church through the O.T. Accordingly, genuine O.T. scholarship exists only when it is carried on in a constant interchange and debate with other theological disciplines. Only in the light of the N.T. is the O.T. rightly understood. To treat it solely as a source for the history of religion is to be driven to wrong conclusions about it. This is an extremely stimulating study and warmly to be commended. M.B.

KAISER, O. : *Die mythische Bedeutung des Meeres in Ägypten, Ugarit und Israel*. (B.Z.A.W. 78.) 1959. Pp. viii+161. (Alfred Töpelmann, Berlin. Price : DM. 24).

This informative study begins with a discussion of Nun, the primeval ocean, as variously conceived in Egyptian mythological texts. Careful attention is given to the thought of the Nile and the Mediterranean in this connexion, and there is due recognition of what were thought to be Nun's beneficent and maleficent aspects. Further, both here and in a subsequent chapter where later folklore comes up for discussion, consideration is given to the evidence for influence from Phoenician sources. On the Ugaritic side there is a full discussion of the conflict between Baal and Yam. The relevant texts are reproduced in transliteration and translation, and then discussed within the context of the comparative material from the Ancient Near East. As for Israelite thought, the author deals, not only with the more obvious material concerning Creation, the Flood, and the crossing of the Red Sea, as found in the Pentateuch, the Psalter, and the works of the canonical Prophets, but also with the Paradise story (including a lengthy discussion of the meaning of *'ēd*) and such legends as that of Jacob at the Jabbok. Despite the circumscribed theme which is indicated by the title, the author touches, where necessary, on the comparative data from Mesopotamia ; and the monograph may be warmly welcomed as one which is written throughout with sympathy and understanding. A.R.J.

KNIGHT, G. A. F. : *A Christian Theology of the Old Testament*. 1959. Pp. 384. (S.C.M. Press, London. Price : 30s. 0d.).

This theology of the Old Testament is written with the presupposition ' that the Old Testament is nothing less than Christian Scripture ', but in what follows the author shows that he does not quite mean what the words quoted seem to

mean. Such an incautious statement, however, might lose the
book readers and that would be a pity.

The book is divided into four parts. Part I seeks to give
the Old Testament teaching about God on the basis of a
Biblical anthropology. The starting-point is man made in the
image of God and it is emphasised that man (*adam*) is a
plurality and is both male and female. God has revealed
himself through his association with Israel and also through
his heavenly family. Part II 'God and Creation' contains
discussion of the meaning of chaos in relation to creation, of
man as a creature capable of obedient response to God, who
has nevertheless fallen into the Chaos of sin and merited the
wrath of God. Part III 'God and Israel' is concerned with
God's revelation of himself in the history of Israel. There is a
detailed examination of certain figures through which Israel
interpreted to itself its unique relation to God. Part IV is
entitled 'The Zeal of the Lord' and discusses God's plan of
salvation for Israel. The author speaks of five 'moments' in
Israel's experience (which are paralleled in the New Testament)
—the birth of the people, its covenant marriage at Sinai, its
death in the Exile, its rebirth and the promise of a land which
will be itself redeemed. Chapter 25 examines seventeen
distinct but related elements in Israel's eschatological expectation. The book concludes with a study of the hope which
Israel came to cherish and an appendix on Israel and the
Church.

It is unfortunate that a book of such interest and originality
of treatment should be marred by a considerable number of
unguarded and even wrong-headed statements. Good ideas
tend to be run to death and one suspects an occasional hobby-
horse. There is an odd explanation of the pointing of the
tetragrammation on pp. 49 and 67, while the repeated 'post
eventu' makes one rub one's eyes.   N.W.P.

MARTIN-ACHARD, R. : *Israël et les nations. La perspective missionaire
de l'Ancien Testament.* (Cahiers Théologiques, 42.) 1959. Pp. 78.
Delachaux & Niestlé, Neuchâtel. Price : Sw. Frs. 4.50).

As the sub-title suggests, this study draws attention to those
parts of the Old Testament which emphasise Israel's divinely
appointed role *vis à vis* the nations of the world. The conversion of the nations is the work of God, and Israel is to
perform a mediatorial task by being the chosen people ; it is
to attract rather than to evangelize. The conversion of the
Gentiles belongs to the 'last chapter in the history of salvation'. Isa. xlii. 1-6 ; and xlix. 6 present, not a missionary
message in our sense of the term, but Israel's mediatorial
function. Other commonly cited 'missionary' passages yield
the same meaning ; even Jonah is universalistic rather than
missionary. Isa. xlv. 20-24 is a unit referring to the dispersed
Jews, not to the Gentiles. Somewhat surprisingly, no reference
is made to Isa. lii. 13-liii. 12. The treatment of some passages
might be questioned, but the book is stimulating and a valuable
contribution.   A.S.H.

MOTYER, J. A. : *The Revelation of the Divine Name* (Tyndale Old Testament Lecture, 1956) 1959. Pp. 32. (Tyndale Press, London. Price : 1s. 6d.).

In this lecture the interpretation of Exod. vi. 2f. is re-examined, the lecturer's contention being that what was new was not the Name Yahweh but the revelation of the content of the Name. Much careful work has gone into the discussion of the passage ; and frequent reference is made to works in English which have a bearing on the subject. But the conclusion is somewhat forced ; and it is not clear that the three factors to which the lecturer appeals at the outset (changes in Pentateuchal criticism, archaeological discovery, and criticism of the evolutionary interpretation of Israel's religion) really affect the issue.   G.W.A.

MOWINCKEL, S. : *He That Cometh*, trans. by G. W. Anderson. Reprinted 1959. Pp. xvi+528. (Blackwell, Oxford. Price : 45s. 0d. Abingdon Press, Nashville and New York. Price : $6.50).

This work, originally published in 1956 and noticed in *Book List*, 1957, p. 51, has been reprinted with several minor corrections.

NÉHER, A. : *Moses and the Vocation of the Jewish People*, trans. by I. Marinoff. (Men of Wisdom Books, 7.) 1959. Pp. 192+numerous ills. (Harper, New York. Price : $1.35. Longmans, Green & Co., London. Price : 6s. 0d.).

The French edition of this book was noticed in *Book List*, 1957, p. 52. We welcome the enterprise which has made this sensitive study available in a good English translation. The astonishingly wide range of illustrations is an appropriate accompaniment to the text. Unfortunately the part of the Hebrew text of Exod. xv. which appears on the inside of the back cover has been printed upside down.   G.W.A.

PEDERSEN, J. : *Israel : Its Life and Culture*, I-II, III-IV. 1959. Pp. X+578 and VI+796. (Branner & Korch, Copenhagen and Oxford University Press, London. Price : £3 10s. 0d. and £4).

This famous work has been issued with corrections. In I-II these are confined to a list of misprints. But in III-IV (cf. *Book List*, 1946, p. 49 ; *Eleven Years*, p. 49) some 7 pages have been added surveying relevant archaeological discoveries and recent discussion of the New Year Festival and kingship. Professor Pedersen expresses the hope that interest in the royal festival will not lead to neglect of the importance of Passover.   G.W.A.

PORÚBČAN, Š. *Il Patto nuovo in Is.* 40-66. (Analecta Biblica, 8.) 1958. Pp. xvi+334. (Pontifical Biblical Institute, Rome. Price : lire 5,400, or $9).

This learned and intensely thorough piece of work is a careful study of the notion of *berit*, first in general, throughout the first part ; then Isaiah xl-lxvi., where a careful exegetical examination is made of all the relevant chapters; and lastly in a synthetic study which deals with the idea of the new *berit* and its constitution, the content of the covenant, the stages of its realization, the covenant regarded as an institution, and individual participation in the *berit*. There is a final short section in which the idea of the covenant in Second and Third Isaiah is compared with the soteriological thought of the New Testament. The book suffers from the fact that much of it is really not very new, and it does not on the whole make interesting reading. It suffers, for example, by comparison with Professor C. R. North's fascinating volume *The Suffering Servant in Deutero-Isaiah* to which it is in some measure indebted. The author's courageous decision to write his treatise in a language that is not his own may have contributed to the impression of dullness. It is, none the less, a work of genuine scholarship and a worthy addition to the series in which it appears. J.M.T.B.

STAMM, J.-J. : *Le Décalogue à la lumière des recherches contemporains.* (Cahiers Théologiques, 43.) 1959. (Delachaux & Niestlé, Neuchâtel. Price : Sw. Frs. 3.50).

This is a French translation of *Der Dekalog im Lichte der neueren Forschung.* (See *Book List*, 1959, p. 30.) The Introduction has been modified, and some additions have been made to the text and the documentation. G.W.A.

STAMM, J. J. : *Die Gottesebenbildlichkeit des Menschen im Alten Testament.* (Theologische Studien 54.) 1959. Pp. 22. (Evangelischer Verlag, Zollikon-Zürich. Price : 4s. 0d.)

This is an interesting little essay on the problem of the interpretation of the *Imago Dei* in the Old Testament. After a brief reference to the old orthodox view and to the view, in its essence still held by many modern scholars, associated with the periods of the *Aufklärung*, Idealism, and Romanticism, Stamm draws attention to the interpretation of the *Imago* as concrete resemblance sponsored by Gunkel, Humbert, and Köhler. He then points out that Barth (in *Kirchliche Dogmatik* III. i.) agrees with Gunkel, etc., in their assertion that the *Imago* is not a quality of man and that in the Old Testament there is no knowledge of the loss of the *Imago*. The distinction between Barth and these scholars is that for them the whole man is reduced to an external appearance, whereas for Barth the whole man is a personality capable of fellowship with God. Stamm agrees with Barth's view that between God and man is an *analogia relationis*, there being an I—Thou relationship within the Godhead (deduced from Gen. i. 26) to which corresponds the relationship between man and woman. Stamm argues that agreement between these views is possible, since Old Testament thought does not sharply distinguish between the internal and the external, while in the Old Testament man is undoubtedly thought of as personality capable of fellowship with God. N.W.P.

STAMM, J.-J. and BIETENHARD, H. : *Der Weltfriede im Lichte der Bibel* 1959. Pp. 112. (Zwingli Verlag, Zürich. Price : Sw. Frs. DM. 5.80).

The first part of this work (which was written in preparation for the *evangelische Akademikertagung* held in the autumn of 1959) deals with the idea of world peace in the O.T., and is by Professor Stamm. First he discusses briefly the O.T. conception of the world, and then examines the meaning of *shālôm*. Three further sections are devoted respectively to the primeval peace, the ideal of peace in the present (with some reference to the Holy War), and the place of peace in the future hope. (A distinction is made between prophecies of the Kingdom of the Messiah and those of the Kingdom of God.) The establishment of peace means the restoration of the original peace of creation, a restoration which must be the work of God and not of man. Of this there are anticipations in the *Heilsgeschichte*. G.W.A.

STEINMANN, J. : *Le prophétisme biblique des origines à Osée.* (Lectio Divina, 23.) 1959. Pp. 260. (Éditions du Cerf, Paris. Price : Frs. 1260).

This author continues to produce small but excellent studies on the Old Testament. This particular volume is the fourth of seven books of similar size dealing with the history of Biblical prophecy. (See *Book List*, 1951, p. 52; 1953, p. 48; 1954, p. 54; *Eleven Years*, pp. 347, 501, 591). Here we have first a study of Canaanite religion before the Israelite invasion, material drawn largely from Ugaritic findings. Then the clash between the two religions, with the compromise. The author then deals with the period of the Judges (Deborah, Jotham, Samson), through the time of Saul, the reign of David (David, Gad, Nathan and Psalms xxivb., ii. and cx.), and so through Elijah, Elisha, and finishing with Amos and Hosea. Nearly half the book, as one would expect, is concerned with Amos and Hosea. The date of Amos is given as ca. 750 B.C. and that of Hosea ca. 743 B.C. French translations are provided for all passages discussed. The volume contains nothing particularly new, but the treatment throughout is sound, clear and throughly up to date. N.H.S.

STEWART, JAMES : *The Message of Job.* 1959. Pp. 140. (Independent Press, London. Price : 12s. 6d.).

It is a great loss that James Stewart did not live longer and write more, since this small volume has a liveliness, a wiseness, and an element of inspiration which reminds one of George Adam Smith and Cheyne at his best. The book has been constructed by Professor James Wood out of material left by James Stewart, much of it prepared during his last long illness. The starting point is that the author of Job was not a detached philosopher full of speculations, but was greatly concerned with the practical problems of his day. We need first to study the period of ca. 400 B.C. with its deceived and betrayed hope, a period of misery and even physical suffering for the new Israel. Why ? Were the times out of joint ? Were there secret sins not yet paid for ? Was the traditional teaching wrong ? The plan of the book deals with the poet's courage, sympathy, faith and peace. The last chapters set the drama-poem in the setting of prologue and epilogue, discuss God's confidence in man, and lastly the preacher and the book. The book is primarily for the scholar-preacher. It includes a brief memoir of the author, written by his elder daughter.
                                                          N.H.S.

THOMSON, J. G. S. S. : *The Word of the Lord in Jeremiah.* (Tyndale Old Testament Lecture, 1959.) 1959. Pp. 20. (Tyndale Press, London. Price : 1s. 6d.).

Dr. Thomson discusses the relation of the Word to the prophetic consciousness and the prophetic authority, argues that it demands a response, examines its effects in Jeremiah's experience, and its character as a criterion of judgment, considers the transition from the spoken to the written word, and emphasizes the relation of the Word to prayer.   G.W.A.

VAN VLIET, H. : *No Single Testimony. A Study on the Adoption of the Law of Deut. 19 : 15 par. into the New Testament.* (Studia Theologica Rheno-Traiectina, Vol. IV.) 1958. Pp. ix+162. (Kemink & Zoon, Utrecht. Price : Fl. 15).

The examination of the place given in the N.T. to the law requiring that two witnesses at least are necessary for the conviction of an accused party is prefaced by a comparative study in which it is maintained that no such provision appears in Greek or Roman law (before the time of Constantine, when Roman law began to be influenced by Biblical law). There was a tendency in Hellenistic and even in later Palestinian Judaism to water down the stringency of this Deuteronomic requirement. But in the N.T. it is reaffirmed in its full force, not only in explicit quotations but in the fabric of early Christian practice ; from this Dr. van Vliet concludes that the early Christians ' did not feel the necessity to be in line with contemporary Greek thinking . . . but dared to put forward also those elements of revelation that do not so easily find an echo in human reason '. An extremely well documented study.   F.F.B.

WESTERMANN, C. : *Der Schöpfungsbericht vom Anfang der Bibel* (Calwer Hefte zur Förderung biblischen Glaubens und christlichen Lebens, 30). 1960. Pp. 40. (Calwer Verlag, Stuttgart. Price : DM. 1.90).

The author makes the startling assertion that the Bible begins not with Gen. i. but with Exod. i., his point being that Genesis is a prologue to the history of the people of God. The main part of the pamphlet sets out the structure of the Priestly narrative of creation and the Yahwistic narrative of creation and the fall in such a way as to apply their theological and religious message. The results of critical scholarship are assumed but not obtruded. G.W.A.

THE LIFE AND THOUGHT OF THE NEIGHBOURING PEOPLES

AISTLEITNER, J. : *Die Mythologischen und Kultischen Texte aus Ras Schamra*. 1959. Pp. 113. (Bibliotheca Orientalis Hungarica VIII. Budapest. 25s. 0d.).

J. Aistleitner had previously contributed to Ugaritic studies by publishing, in 1954, his valuable *Untersuchungen zur Grammatik des Ugaritischen*. The present translation into German of a selection of Ugaritic texts (mainly Ba'al, Keret, and Aqht) does not, as far as the reviewer can see, constitute an advance over existing renderings, especially those by H. L. Ginsberg, C. H. Gordon, G. R. Driver, U. Cassuto, and J. Gray. In fact, in some respects there is retrogression compared with G. R. Driver's idiomatic, fluent, and philologically impeccable translation. Aistleitner also appears to have missed many studies of detail which had already elucidated individual points of difficulty.

Above all, one may doubt that the time has yet come for a translation which virtually dispenses with explanatory footnotes of a linguistic character and manages with a mere $1\frac{1}{2}$ pages of ' Sprachliche Bemerkungen '. To the uninitiated German reader the present rendering may have its uses ; to the scholar its value is unhappily limited. E.U.

GABRIELI, F. (ed. by) : *L'antica Società Beduina : La société béduine ancienne : Ancient Beduin Society : Die altbeduinische Gesellschaft*. (Studi Semitici, 2.) 1959. Pp. 156. (Centro di Studi Semitici, Istituto di Studi Orientali, Rome).

This second volume (the first was noticed on p. 33 of the 1959, *Book List*) issued by the Centre of Semitic Studies at Rome University (under the direction of Professor S. Moscati) presents a record of lectures delivered at Rome by five scholars on the subject of the ancient Bedouin society. A third volume on Semitic linguistics is already in preparation.

W. Dostal writes on the evolution of Bedouin life ; G. Dossin

on the Bedouin in the Mari texts ; M. Höfner on the Bedouin
in pre-Islamic Arabic inscriptions ; J. Henninger on ancient
Bedouin society and pre-Islamic religion. F. Gabrieli contributes a chapter on pre-Islamic Bedouin literature as well as
an epilogue.

Dostal deals with his subject exclusively from an ethnological point of view ; he is mainly concerned with a re-
definition of the term *badw* and the problems of the dromedary.
In his examination of the Mari texts Dossin throws a few
further rays of light on Bedouin society and particularly the
Hapiru and Yaminite groups. Maria Höfner subjects the
vast number of pre-Islamic inscriptions to careful scrutiny
and finds that, while most of the Safaitic and Thamudic
graffiti are of Bedouin origin, no mention is made of the
Bedouin (despite their important, if subordinate, function
in commercial activities) in the voluminous epigraphic literature of the sedentary South Arabians—until the critical times
shortly before the dissolution of the Southern city-states.
J. Henninger considers the mention of nomads in the Old
Testament and classical writers and offers a succinct characterization of Bedouin society. In his study of pre-Islamic
religion Henninger allows full weight to the pioneering work
of Robertson Smith, Wellhausen, Nöldeke, Goldziher, G.
Ryckmans and others. F. Gabrieli's paper on pre-Islamic
literature is a precious contribution to our knowledge of the
Mu'allaqat and the *Jahiliyya* period in general. His summing-
up of the entire volume contains judicious comments on and
gentle adjustments to some of the articles here collected.
Altogether a useful book to students of the Ancient Near
East.   E.U.

MOSCATI, S. : *The Face of the Ancient Orient.* 1960. Pp. xvi+328
+XXXII plates+5 figures+map. (Routledge & Kegan Paul,
London and Vallentine Mitchell, London. Price : 30s. 0d.).

This handsome volume is a translation of *Il Profilo dell' Oriente
Mediterraneo.* (See *Book List,* 1957, p. 61.) To have brought
together from so many specialist fields such a wealth of
material and to have presented the whole in so lucid and lively
manner is an enviable feat. The footnotes indicate a remarkable control of the relevant literature, references to which have
been brought up to date in this edition. The interest of the
text is matched by the beauty and clarity of the plates.
G.W.A.

MOSCATI, S. : *The Semites in Ancient History. An inquiry into the
settlement of the Bedouin and their political establishment.* 1959.
Pp. 142, including map. (University of Wales Press, Cardiff.
Price : 15s. 0d.).

This work is much more limited in scope than its title suggests.
The author discriminates between Semitic nations and the
Semitic race, limiting the latter to the Bedouin of the inner

steppes. He proceeds to consider the age-long trend of these tribesmen to the settled land of Mesopotamia, Syria-Palestine, and the more fertile lands in Southern Arabia. Useful as this study is, independent in judgement, and accurately documented, the study of Bedouin penetration, limited as it is to the bare fact of movement and settlement, stops short at the point where it is of most interest to Biblical study.

J.G.

ULLENDORFF, E. : *The Ethiopians. An Introduction to Country and People*. 1960. Pp. xvi+232+XVI plates+map. (Oxford University Press, London, Price : 30s. 0d.).

In his preface the author states that his aim is to present a balanced picture of Ethiopia to the general reader. This he has succeeded most admirably in doing. The book, which is devoted mainly to historic Abyssinia and the culture of the Semitized peoples, contains 10 chapters. The first gives a fascinating account of the exploration and study of Ethiopia and its peoples. This is followed by chapters on the geography and ethnography of Ethiopia. Subsequent chapters are devoted to history, religion and church, languages, literature, art and music, daily life and customs, and Ethiopia to-day. Each chapter is a mine of information, presented in a clear and readable fashion, on the topic with which it deals. The whole is illustrated by excellent and well chosen photographs, and is provided with a clear map. Of special interest to students of Hebrew and the Semitic languages are the masterly sections on the languages and literature of Ethiopia and the Ethiopians.

T.W.T.

THE DEAD SEA SCROLLS

BAUMBACH, G. : *Qumran und das Johannes-Evangelium*. (Aufsätze und Vorträge zur Theologie und Religionswissenschaft, Heft 6). 1958. Pp. 60. (Evangelische Verlagsanstalt, Berlin, D.D.R. Price: DM. 2.70).

This is a study of the Manual of Discipline and the Fourth Gospel against the background of Jewish Apocalyptic in which the author traces certain connections between the origins of Christianity and the Qumran sect. The dualistic tendencies in the Fourth Gospel make it the most appropriate for comparison with the Manual. Certain common features in terminology can be established. But this points not to direct influence from Qumran on the Gospel, but to a common inheritance from Apocalyptic, which produced teaching of a different stamp in the two contexts. In spite of the special character of the Qumran material, the author shows clearly its immense importance for the understanding of the beginnings of Christianity.

M.B.

BRUCE, F. F. : *Biblical Exegesis in the Qumran Texts.* (Exegetica, 3, 1.) 1959. Pp. 84. (van Keulen, The Hague. Price : Fl. 4.75).

This study is an expanded form of lectures delivered in the Free University of Amsterdam and the Universities of Utrecht and Leiden. Professor Bruce begins with an account, with illustrations, of the meaning of *pesher*, and sums up the principles of interpretation presupposed in the Qumran commentaries and the ways in which they are applied. He proceeds to discuss the situation in terms of which the Biblical texts were interpreted. There follow chapters on the Zadokite Work, Messianic Interpretation, the Servant of the Lord and the Son of Man, the Interpretation of Daniel, and the bearing on the New Testament of Biblical exegesis in the Qumran texts. The whole study is marked by sound judgement and lucid exposition. G.W.A.

DUPONT-SOMMER, A. : *Les écrits esséniens découverts près de la Mer Morte.* 1959. Pp. 446. including 4 figures. (Payot, Paris. Price : Frs. 3000).

In this latest contribution to the publisher's ' Bibliothèque Historique ' Dupont-Sommer has given us a comprehensive study of the Qumran discoveries, as definitive as the present state of the question allows. He has thought and thought again on the implications of these discoveries, and while he has not departed in essentials from the findings of his *Aperçus préliminaires* (cf. *Book List*, 1951, p. 19 ; *Eleven Years*, p. 314), he has given us a work both weightier and more cautious. In addition to a full account of the discoveries and a detailed examination of their significance, he has provided translations of the non-biblical texts from Qumran which are thus far available to the world of scholarship.

As the title of this work indicates, Dupont-Sommer continues to identify the Qumran sect with the Essenes, and he presents strong reasons for doing so. He continues to endorse Renan's statement that ' Christianity is an Essenism which largely succeeded ', and if he no longer describes Jesus as an ' astonishing reincarnation ' of the Teacher of Righteousness, he speaks of a special and unique relation between the two, while he recognizes important differences (pp. 385 f.). He continues to identify Hyrcanus II as the Wicked Priest, and to regard with favour Goossens' identification of Onias the Righteous as the Teacher of Righteousness, although he does not commit himself absolutely to it.

Among his literary judgments, we may mention Dupont-Sommer's insistence that the *Testaments of the Twelve Patriarchs* is not a Christian (or Judaeo-Christian) but a Jewish work, having close affinities with the Qumran literature, and his refusal to accept at this stage the argument from silence which infers the Christian origin of the *Similitudes of Enoch* from the fact that no part of this section of the Enoch literature has turned up so far at Qumran.

No doubt an English edition of this important work will be forthcoming before long ; we hope so. F.F.B.

HUPPENBAUER, H. W. : *Der Mensch zwischen zwei Welten. Der Dualismus der Texte von Qumran (Höhle 1) und der Damaskus-fragmente. Ein Beitrag zur Vorgeschichte des Evangeliums.* (Abhand-lungen zur Theologie des Alten und Neuen Testaments. No. 34.) 1959. Pp. 132. (Zwingli Verlag, Zürich. Price : DM. 19).

This very workmanlike and well-documented abstract of a dissertation presented to the Theological Faculty of Basel is a welcome addition to specialist works on the Scrolls. After a brief definition of dualism and of the problem of its pro-venance in the scrolls (to disclaim any further pre-occupation with this vexed question) the author examines the significance of relevant passages in the following scrolls :—Discipline, Habakkuk, Damascus, Thanksgiving, Warfare, Genesis Apocry-phon, and the ' Mystery Fragment ' from Cave 1. A synthetic survey deals with God (Creator of the good and of the wicked, the evil spirits and Belial as well), Lord of Seasons, including the present. He holds court, has His angels—He is the One God ; in the future He will be, above all, Judge. He communi-cates through the agency of angels. Evil is brought about by means of evil powers, who, however, are subservient to God. They fight against God only to implement the fact of Election. Belial has his place in the underworld (therefore, despite the Sect's monotheism, there is dualism in its creed, but there is no speculation concerning it). The anthropology of the sect is confused, often self-contradictory. There are two classes of men, good (the Sect) and evil (all others, Jews included). But all men are sinful (though there is no mention of the Fall), and deliberately guilty. God nevertheless acts graciously to His Elect, and the New Covenant enables them to fulfil God's law. Human ways of thought betray the same dualism as exists in the cosmic conflict ; human sin bespeaks an evil power, and it is man's duty to accept divine redemp-tion.

On the whole, we find in the Scrolls not one dualism but a number. All of them are ethical ; they demand the ful-filling of the Torah of God. But the dualism is also ' *physisch-metaphysisch* '. Creator and created are sharply distinguished, and man is not only ' created ' but also earthly : The spirits are a superior creation, though they also are separated from God. The separate evaluation of human and spiritual levels not on grounds of ethics but of ontology is important for the understanding of the sect's dualism, for it is complicated by the presence also of an ethical evaluation. This is conceived of not along Hellenistic lines of opposites (spirit and flesh) but by the fact of God and His acts. The dualism, consequently, is not of the usual anthropological kind. It is not absolute, and is conditioned through and through by ethical pre-conceptions. It is cosmic, but confined to this world of creatureliness. It is subservient, at all times, to the basic idea of salvation. B.J.R.

KOSMALA, H. : *Hebräer-Essener-Christen. Studien zur Vorgeschichte der frühchristlichen Verkündigung*. 1959. Pp. XII+480. (Brill, Leiden. Price : Fl. 28.00).

With this volume the publishers have launched their new series of monographs entitled *Studia Post-Biblica*, under the general editorship of P. A. H. de Boer. The *Hebräer* of the title are the people to whom the Epistle to the Hebrews was addressed. It would be well at the outset to stop and ask if the original writer and readers thought of them as Hebrews', or whether this was not rather a second-century inference from the contents of the document. Kosmala's view is that they were not (as commonly supposed) Christians of Jewish birth who were inclined to revert to Judaism, but Jews who had come so far on the way to Christianity, but had not yet come all the way ; that they were, in fact, people holding views very similar to those of the Qumran sect and other Essenes. Many of the leading themes of the Epistle to the Hebrews are illustrated from Qumran literature. The work as a a whole belongs to the field of New Testament rather than Old, but is at the same time an important contribution to Qumran studies. Much of the most fruitful early Christian evangelization, Kosmala believes, was carried out among Essene groups. He illustrates his point by some funerary inscriptions from Beth-shearim which he maintains are Essene in character. Among his sixteen appendices there is one which finds in the Biblical exegesis of CD vii. 9-21 an important source for the basic elements in the Qumran community's doctrine.

F.F.B.

KUTSCHER, E. Y. : *The Language and Linguistic Background of the Isaiah Scroll*. 1959. Pp. xii+529. Jerusalem (Magnes Press of the Hebrew University).

This monumental work is written in Hebrew and is provided with a very brief English summary which, however, covers only the first 70 pages of the author's introduction and conclusions. No such translation aid is offered for the great bulk of this book which analyses in detail problems of spelling, Aramaic elements, the influence of early and late Biblical as well as Mishnaic Hebrew, phonology and morphology, textual, questions, etc. There are appendices and no fewer than 45 pages of Addenda and Corrigenda which reflect the slow growth of the work over the past 10 years. A greater measure of integration and the elimination of some at least of the traces and stages of composition would have benefited the book in its literary character.

Kitscher sets out to demonstrate that the Isaiah scroll reflects the complicated linguistic situation prevailing in Palestine during the last pre-Christian centuries. Late Biblical Hebrew (as it appears in some of the later Hagiographa) and Mishnaic Hebrew with all their distinctions from the classical norm in morphology, vocabulary, and syntax have superseded the language of Classical Biblical Hebrew. And, above all, there was the powerful and all-pervading impact of Aramaic in its various dialectal manifestations. Few of these conclusions are either new or revolutionary, but Kutscher has brought to bear a mighty apparatus of proof and meticulous documentation on what used to be little more than an impressionistic structure. The principal criticism of his procedure is implicit in the self-imposed limitation to the Isaiah scroll. Coverage of all the Dead Sea material hitherto discovered might not have vitally affected the author's conclusions but it would at least have offered a substantially more secure basis.

Kutscher has, however, done much more than provide a linguistic study of the Isaiah scroll : he has, in fact, dealt with most of the basic problems of Hebrew grammar and Hebrew linguistic development—and in a manner that can be termed highly respectable in the light of contemporary notions of linguistic analysis. And this is no mean achievement at a time when teachers of Hebrew are notoriously hard put to place a reliable and up-to-date historical and grammatical treatment of the language in the hands of their pupils. It is at this point that a reviewer may justly be expected to say that ' no serious student of Hebrew can afford to neglect this work '—alas, it may confidently be expected that many will do so nevertheless. Translation of this 500-page book would be an unjustifiable waste, and the time has surely come to face the alternatives squarely : either *all* students of Hebrew should be expected to read modern Hebrew in the same way as students of Arabic are able to keep abreast of publications in modern Arabic—or publication in Hebrew of works of scholarship that are likely to be of universal interest ought to be abandoned.   E.U.

LASOR, W. S. : *Bibliography of the Dead Sea Scrolls*, 1948-1957. (Fuller Library Bulletin, Number 31 ; Theological Seminary Bibliographical Series, Number 2.) 1958. Pp. 92. (The Library, Fuller Theological Seminary, Pasadena, California. Price : $3.50).

This is a most valuable list of 2982 items on Qumran, arranged in three main groups: General Works, The Texts of Qumran, and the Interpretation of the Qumran Literature. There are useful cross references, a full index of authors, and a short subject index. All workers in this field will be indebted to Professor Lasor for his painstaking industry.   G.W.A.

LIVSHITS, G. M. : *Kumranskie rukopisi i ikh istoricheskoe znachenie.* 1959. Pp. 82. (Izdatel'stvo Belgosuniversiteta imeni V.I. Lenina, Minsk. Price : 5 roubles 55 kopecks.)

This little book " The Kumran manuscripts and their historical significance " is the first book on the Dead Sea Scrolls to be published in the USSR : hitherto the Russian contribution to these studies has been virtually confined to a few articles in the periodical *Vestnik Drevnei Istorii*. The author's aims

are to acquaint the Russian reader with the Dead Sea Scrolls
and to interpret them in the light of the Marxist theories of
history. (The present work, he says, is to be regarded as a
supplement to his earlier book *Klassovaya bor'ba v Iudee i
vosstaniya protiv Rima*—" Class struggle in Judaea and the
revolt against Rome "—Minsk, 1957.) He discusses the main
problems connected with the Scrolls and is particularly
interested in " the significance of the Kumran finds for the
study of the history of the origin of Christianity ". The book
is very well documented and furnished with copious notes :
the author shows a wide knowledge of Western works. His
presentation of the facts is sober, though naturally few Western
scholars will agree with most of his interpretations of them.
Be that as it may, he does an undoubted service by stressing
points which tend to be overlooked by the ' bourgeois '
scholars of the West. Professor Livshits's book is yet another
indication of the growing interest of Soviet scholars in the
history, civilisations and languages of the ancient Near East
and as such it is to be welcomed.   T.W.T.

MARTIN, M. : *The Scribal Character of the Dead Sea Scrolls.* Vol. II
   (Bibliothèque du Muséon, Vol. 45). 1958. Pp. 11+304+14*.
   (Publications Universitaires, Louvain. Price : B. Frs. 400).

The first volume was described in the 1959, *Book List* (p. 37).
The second volume deals mainly with the evidence of the
revisions of manuscripts, including those conducted by the
copyists themselves as well as those by later scribes. The
activity postulates the existence of a ' revisor-exemplar ' as
well as a parent copy. The seven scrolls are scrutinised,
according to their grouping of non-biblical, IQIsa, and IQIsb
with IQpHab. The conclusion is that hybrid texts (containing
' corrections ' from varying sources) themselves confirm the
objectivity of the scribes. There was no attempt to impose
anything like a uniform style of *matres lectionis* vocalization,
or any other convention ; and in this sense it is wrong to think
of a ' school ' of scribes at Qumrân. In a final chapter the
author discusses the significance of this conclusion and also,
in a separate article, the relevance of the whole inquiry for
the question of whether the Qumrân scrolls were produced
by a ' settlement ' (e.g., the Essenes) or were simply deposited
in the caves (e.g., *a genizah*). He is not wholly committed to
the former view, and thinks that before such a probability
can be really confirmed it is necessary to show that the parent
MSS must have had varying provenances, textually as well
as locally. This view had been suggested before the detailed
need for it had been established by Father Martin.

The volume also contains a name index, reference lists for the
two volumes, and a Table of contents.

It is difficult to over-praise this basic piece of research work.
                                                          B.J.R.

MILIK, J. T. : *Ten Years of Discovery in the Wilderness of Judaea.*
Trans. by J. Strugnell. (Studies in Biblical Theology, No. 26.)
1959. Pp. 160.+25 photographs+2 maps+1 plan. (S. C. M.
Press, London. Price : 12s. 6d.).

The Italian and French editions of this book were reviewed in
Book List, 1958, p. 48. In its new form it has been revised
and expanded. General introductions to the Scrolls are now
embarrassingly numerous ; but this is one which no student
of the subject can well afford to neglect.   G.W.A.

VAN DER PLOEG, J. : *Le Rouleau de la Guerre. Traduit et annoté avec une
Introduction.* (Studies on the Texts of the Desert of Judah, ed.
by J. van der Ploeg O.P. vol. II.) 1959. Pp. 198. (E. J. Brill,
Leiden, Price : Fl. 25).

This thorough and competent study of the Warfare Scroll
is a welcome addition to the DSS literature, and provides
particularly, a helpful treatment of this the most enigmatic
of the scrolls from Cave 1. In the first part the actual MS and
its contents are surveyed ; then the question of date and
unity of the text, its literary composition and theology are
outlined. A translation follows, column by column ; and in
the notes, matters of text, translation, emendations and
exegesis are discussed. They fill two-thirds of the book, and
the translation twenty pages.
Some of the points made by the author are : there is insufficient information to identify the warfare with that
conducted by the Romans at that period (2nd or 1st cent.
B.C.), but the readers were familiar with Hebrew warfare of
the time. The Scroll is not a unity, and it reflects different
stages in the history of the text of the Rule of Warfare :
first, there was an apocalyptic writing, then another author
wrote about a forty-year holy war, and there are further
revisions. It is an actual warfare, one of aggression, waged to
conquer the world in the name of the God of Israel. The
prophecies of Ezek., especially xxxviii.-xxxix. and xl-xlviii.
loom large in both the apocalyptic and warfare passages.
There is no talk in either of a resurrection ; everything takes
place on earth. There is no basic opposition to cultic sacrifice,
but the sect avoids the present temple because it is defiled
and its officers do not observe the proper calendar. The
victorious Kingdom of God will be governed by the High-
priest and the King-Messiah, the son of David.
The book has a bibliography and Bible index.   B.J.R.

VAN DER PLOEG, J. (and others) : *La secte de Qumrân et les origines du
Christianisme* (Recherches Bibliques, IV.) 1959. Pp. 244. (Desclée
de Brouwer, Bruges. Price : F. Frs. 18 ; B. Frs. 180).

In this volume ten scholars deal with various aspects of
Qumran study, most of the contributions having first been
delivered as communications at the ninth *Journées Bibliques*,
held at Louvain in September, 1957. Van der Ploeg presided

at the *Journées*, but his communication was published elsewhere ; in its place he has contributed to this volume a long survey of six years of Qumran study (1952-58)—57 pages of review and 17 pages of bibliography—which accounts for more than one-third of the total contents. G. Lambert writes on the Genesis Apocryphon, J. Coppens on historical allusions in that document and also on the piety of the Qumran psalmists, A. Jaubert on the Qumrán calendar, A. S. van der Woude on the Teacher of Righteousness and the two Messiahs, F. Nötscher on the ' ways ' of God and man in the Bible and the Qumran literature, O. Betz on the cultic ministry at Qumran and in early Christianity, D. Barthélemy on holiness in the Qumran sect and in the gospel, J. Schmitt on the organization of the primitive Church in the light of Qumran and L. Cerfaux on the influence of Qumran on the New Testament. Van der Woude maintains that the Qumran community preserved its expectation of two Messiahs from beginning to end ; he distinguishes the historic Teacher of Righteousness (or Expounder of the Law) from the Teacher of Righteousness (or Expounder of the Law) who is yet to come, identifying the latter with the expected Messiah of Aaron and the former with the ' prophet like unto Moses '.

F.F.B.

ROBERTS, B. J. : *The Second Isaiah Scroll from Qumran (IQIsb)*. (Reprinted from *Bulletin of the John Rylands Library*, Vol. 42, No. 1, 1959). 1959. Pp. 132-144. (Manchester University Press and the John Rylands Library, Manchester. Price : 2s. 6d.).

In comparison with the large amount of attention which IQIsa has received, IQIsb has hitherto received but little, and the reason is probably to be found in the close affinity with MT displayed by IQIsb. The main point which Professor Bleddyn Roberts makes is that it is precisely this close affinity which gives IQIsb its primary importance. Only one truly significant variant reading occurs, viz., in liii. 11, where ' *or* ' light ' is added after *yir'eh*. The many differences (in suffixes, genders, tenses, the use of *waw* and *yodh*, and such like) are, it is emphasized, capable of interpretation only because they reflect our M.T. They are indeed neither more numerous nor more significant than those of the Massoretic transmission itself. Divergences in the Cairo Genizah fragments too are noted, and a point is made of the frequent deviation in those fragments in the use of the divine names as compared with IQIsb which agrees largely with M.T. in this respect. The chief conclusion drawn in this useful and sober study is that the Massoretes did not in fact ' create ' a textform, nor was the Massoretic text something that ' emerged ' later. It existed, in much its present form at least as early as the Maccabean period. IQIsb gives implicit support to the likely existence of a pre-Massoretic ' Massoretic ' text, and thus presents a powerful challenge to the alleged ' standardization ' of the text by Aqiba. D.W.T.

SCHUBERT, K. (trans. by J. W. Doberstein) : *The Dead Sea Community : Its Origin and Teachings*, 1959. Pp. xii+178. (A. and C. Black, London. Price : 12s. 6d.).

The original German edition of this book, *Die Gemeinde vom Toten Meer*, appeared in 1958, and despite the over-abundance of ' introductions ' and ' background ' studies to the Scrolls the present translation is justified because it gives the general reader an interpretation which has not been too drastically worked out. After a brief introductory survey of the Scrolls, including a mention of Cave Four material, the author describes the teaching of the Sect, compares it with the information concerning the Essenes by Philo and Josephus, draws parallels with Rabbinic (with which the author is commendably familiar) and with New Testament features. In view of some recent outspoken condemnation of attempts to find in the Scrolls anything approaching Gnostic teaching it is interesting to read in this book a plausible statement of the case in favour of the idea, without, however, postulating anything closer than a common ' attitude to the concrete world and concrete history '. Likewise the discussion of New Testament affinities is fresh and instructive. It is necessary, however, to mention that nowhere in this book does the author discuss the question of the unity of individual Scrolls, and the point is rather crucial to some of them, e.g., the Manual of Discipline and the Warfare Scroll, because ultimately their use for the reconstruction of practice and belief may well be modified if, as is commonly urged, a composite origin may be assumed for them. The translation is pleasant, and the book is to be commended.   B.J.R.

APOCRYPHA AND POST-BIBLICAL JUDAISM

BAECK, L. : *Aus drei Jahrtausenden : Wissenschaftliche Untersuchungen und Abhandlungen zur Geschichte des jüdischen Glaubens*, mit einer Einführung von Hans Liebeschütz. 1958. Pp. VI+402. (J. C. B. Mohr Tübingen. Price : paper, DM. 17.50 ; bound, DM. 21).

This is a volume of essays which ought to have appeared in 1938, but that edition was destroyed by the Gestapo, about half a dozen surviving. The inclusion at that time of a study like Romantic Religion is a proof of amazing courage. The book ranges over a wide field : some of the essential features of Judaism, the relation in various contexts between Judaism and Christianity, and a number of smaller points. Baeck, though apt to pursue an idea without meticulous inspection of the evidence, emerges as a master of historical synthesis and theological discussion. If on occasion his approach is dated, that adds to the interest. Liebeschütz, in a sensitive introduction, describes the intellectual setting of Baeck's work.

For scholars, the book would be more valuable if complete and accurate bibliographical information were supplied. We are not told that seven of the twenty-two essays already figure (in English) in *The Pharisees and Other Essays*, 1947, and *Judaism and Christianity*, 1958; nor that most originally appeared in journals, and in what journals they appeared. And we are told that the collection is a reprint of the 1938 one though in fact two essays (' The Parisees ' and ' The Gospel as a Document of the History of the Jewish Faith ') are omitted.   D.D.

BRAUDE, W. G. : *The Midrash on Psalms*, translated from the Hebrew and Aramaic. 2 vols. (Yale Judaica Series, XIII, 1 & 2.) 1959. Pp. xxxvi+564 ; 630. (Yale University Press, New Haven & Oxford University Press, London. Price : 120s. 0d.)

The publication of Yale Judaica Series purues its stately course. This admirable translation of the Midrash on Psalms comes from a scholar whose work on the Rabbinic attitude to prose-lytizing is well known. There is a lively and illuminating introduction, and an appendix with good, brief notes. Braude comes down in favour of Buber's dating against Zunz : the main redaction of the Midrash goes back to Talmudic times. The Index of Biblical passages used in the Midrash, the Index of Rabbinic authorities quoted (the earliest are Hillel and Shammai, all are Palestinian), and the Index of Subjects will prove most helpful to a student of the work. This Midrash is homiletic, a mine of various information as to Rabbinic thought.   D.D.

BROOKES, R. S. : *A Dictionary of Judaism*. 1959. Pp. xvi+256. (Shapiro Vallentine & Co., London).

This book contains in the main :—1. A short bibliography of works suggested for further reading ; 2. A dictionary of Judaism. The following titles taken from the first two pages will give some idea of the character and scope of the work : Aaron ; Ablutions ; Abraham ; Abrogation of the Laws ; Abstinence ; Accents. Altogther useful for the uninitiated.

EMERTON, J. A. : *The Peshitta of the Wisdom of Solomon*. (Studia Post-Biblica, II). 1959. Pp. cii+38. (E. J. Brill, Leiden. Price : Fl. 18).

Mr. Emerton has here gathered together the available material for critical study of the Peshitta text of the Book of Wisdom. The text printed is that of Codex Ambrosianus published by Ceriani in 1876—1883. The critical apparatus has drawn on some 35 authorities, of which 22 are MSS of the Peshitta ranging in date from the 6th to the 19th centuries. The editor shows in his introduction that the differences between the MSS are on the whole very slight but that four groups may be distinguished. (i) The early pre-tenth-century MSS, (ii) a group of Nestorian MSS of eastern origin, (iii) a group of seventeenth century western MSS from a Maronite background, and (iv) a group of other western MSS. The edition is well printed, easy to use, and offers a careful record of the available material.   L.H.B.

GOLDIN, J. : *The Living Talmud. The Wisdom of the Fathers and Its Classical Commentaries, Selected and Translated with an Essay.* 1958. Pp. 244. (University of Chicago Press, Chicago, and Cambridge University Press, London. Price : 30s. 0d.).

There is no lack of translations of the Tractate of the Mishnah, *Abot*, and although Judah Goldin's version is generally pleasing and lucid, the scope of his work does not allow the author to indicate the numerous passages where more than one interpretation is possible. The merit of this work, however, lies in two other features. Firstly each verse of the Mishnah is followed by translated selections from the principal Jewish classical commentaries namely, the two versions of *Abot di Rabbi Natan*, and the commentaries of Aknin, Bertinoro, Rabbi David the Prince, Duran, Rabbi Jonah, Maimonides, Meiri, the *Midrash Shemuel* of Samuel ben Isaac, Nahmias and the *Machsor Vitri*. This arrangement provides an excellent and illuminating bird's-eye view of the principal medieval Jewish interpretations of the Tractate. Secondly the book contains a brief but very stimulating essay on the Talmud itself, including a number of intelligent illustrations. This book can be recommended as a stimulating introduction to Rabbinic method.   D.P.

JEREMIAS, J.: *Heiligengräber in Jesu Umwelt.* (*Mt.* 23, 29; *Lk* 11, 47.) *Eine Untersuchung zur Volksreligion der Zeit Jesu.* 1959. Pp. 156+6 plates+1 map. (Vandenhoeck & Ruprecht, Göttingen. Price : paper, DM. 15.80 ; cloth, DM. 19.80).

In his own characteristic way Professor Jeremias has taken a text from the gospels, ' Ye build the sepulchres of the prophets ' (Mt. xxiii. 29), and has built round it a most interesting and valuable study in the popular religion of Palestine in the time of Jesus. He points out that the material here collected gives us an insight into the background of the teaching of Jesus such as cannot be obtained from a study of Talmudic sources. It will probably come as a surprise to many readers to discover that popular tradition, borne witness to by the reports of early pilgrims to the Holy Land, had assigned sites to the burial places of an extraordinary number of Old Testament personages. It is curious that Jezebel should have been provided with a grave, when, according to the narrative in the book of Kings there was so little of her left to bury. Professor Jeremias has an interesting discussion of the legend that Adam and Eve were buried in the cave of Machpelah, in Hebron. On the material here gathered he also bases a strong argument for the probability that the early Christian community would not have forgotten the true site of the Lord's burial place. Professor Jeremias is always worth listening to, and in this scholarly and most interesting monograph he has added to the already large debt which students of the Scriptures owe to his labours. S.H.H.

JERVELL, J. : *Imago Dei. Gen.* 1, 26*f. im Spätjudentum, in der Gnosis und in den paulinischen Briefen.* 1960. Pp. 379. (Vandenhoeck & Ruprecht, Göttingen. Price : DM. 35).

The author is mainly concerned with tracing the influence of Gen. i. 26f. (the making of man in the image of God) on the thought of Paul, but by way of preface he considers the influence of the passage in pre-Christian Judaism, in Philo, in the rabbinical literature and in Gnosticism. In pre-Christian Judaism the prepositions before *selem* and *demuth* are no longer understood as Beth *essentiae* and Kaph *veritatis*, but (as in LXX *kata*) to denote that man is a copy of the image of God, not the image itself. Philo interprets the passage along the lines of Platonic idealism. While the rabbinical writings indicate a public interpretation of the passage which was calculated to safeguard monotheism, they contain evidence of fanciful esoteric theories, e.g., of the original man as an androgynous being. Gnosticism de-historicizes the passage and interprets it as a myth about Everyman. Paul uses it to justify his placing Christ, as the image of the invisible God, in the forefront of his message, and to find the ultimate fulfilment of the Creator's words in the glorified Church of the future, wearing the image of Christ. A valuable contribution to the history of Biblical interpretation. F.F.B.

KISCH, G. & ROEPKE, K. : *Schriften zur Geschichte der Juden : Eine Bibliographie der in Deutschland und der Schweiz, 1922-1955 erschienenen Dissertationen.* (Schriftenreihe wissenschaftlicher Abhandlungen des Leo Baeck Institute of Jews from Germany, 4.) 1959. Pp. XII+50. (J. C. B. Mohr, Tübingen).

This is as complete a list of German and Swiss doctor-dissertations written between 1922 and 1955 on the subject of Jewish history as the industry and knowledgeability of two devoted scholars can produce. There are twelve sections : Jewish literature, Biblical and Talmudic law, Theology, Social and Economic history, Position of Jews in the law of Germany and Switzerland, Statistics, Antisemitism in Germany, Jews and Judaism in literature and art, Education, Biology and Medicine, Psychology, Palestine and Israel. Kisch writes an excellent introductory survey of Jewish bibliography in the last hundred years. D.D.

ZIMMELS, H. J. : *Ashkenazim and Sephardim : Their Relations, Differences, and Problems as Reflected in the Rabbinical Responsa*, with a Foreword by the Very Rev. the Chief Rabbi, Rabbi Israel Brodie. (Jews' College Publications, New Series, No. 2.) 1958. Pp. xvi+348 (Oxford University Press, London, Price : 42s. 0d.).

This volume, the 2nd in the New Series of Jews' College Publications, is based mainly on *Responsa*—a branch of Jewish literature with which the author is well acquainted. The author has occupied himself only with *published* material. Following views expressed by other scholars, he advances three factors said to contribute to the pronounced dissimilarites which exist between the Ashkenazim and the Sephardim.

The work begins with a general historical survey of the relations between the Franco-German and Spanish Rabbinical schools. A number of distinct periods are given, the first being made up of early phenomena in ancient times, and the last comprising the years between the coming into being of the ' Wissenschaft des Judentums ' and the establishment of the state of Israel. It is the opinion of the author that in Israel ' the historical process of slowly but steadily removing the differences between the two Jewries' will be quickened.

This survey is followed by a detailed examination of a number of the more characteristic differences between the two Jewries, e.g., pronunciation ; the Hebrew characters ; liturgy ; poetry ; approach to the Biblical and Talmudical laws and customs affecting daily life ; the ' philosophy ' of each of the Jewries, etc. The concluding part gives a selection of *Responsa* dealing with actual differences which have arisen on various occasions between Ashkenazim and Sephardim.

The value of this fine piece of scholarly work would have been greatly enhanced had the author made use of some relevant *new* Cairo Genizah material of which there is a great deal as evidenced from lists and catalogues of numerous libraries in which Genizah fragments have been deposited. M.W.

PHILOLOGY AND GRAMMAR

WATTS, J. D. W. : *Lists of Words occurring frequently in the Hebrew Bible*. (Hebrew-English Edition : Seminary Edition). 1959. Pp. 32. (E. J. Brill, Leiden. Price : Fl. 3).

Most student-aids of this sort are based on the lists published by W. R. Harper in 1890 ; in the drawing up of the present one the *L.V.T.L.* has also been consulted. Three praiseworthy features, which make it the most practical classified vocabulary known to the reviewer, are its convenient 12mo format, its clearly *printed* Hebrew, well-spaced on the left page, with the meanings correspondingly numbered and on the right, so that any learner whose mother-tongue is not English could easily adapt this booklet.

In criticism, many *mil'el* accentuations are not so marked ;
but only sixteen incorrect vocalizations have been noticed.
Wrong consonants which have passed the proof-reader's eye
but not mine numbered only five. In all, this is a very handy
compendium which should prove its worth to those who buy it.

D.R.Ap-T.

PALACHE, J. L. : *Semantic Notes on the Hebrew Lexicon, translated
from the Dutch Original and edited by R. J. Zwi Werblowsky.* 1959.
Pp. XIV+78. (E. J. Brill, Leiden. Price : Fl. 15).

When the author, who was Professor of Semitic Languages and
the Exegesis of the O.T. in the University of Amsterdam,
was taken to a concentration camp, he left a draft of this work
with friends. It consisted of three small note-books in which
he had copied out a selection from the manuscript notes
which he had amassed. He took these notes with him into
captivity and continued to work at them until his death.
They were, however, never recovered, but the note-books
survived, and it is the contents of these that are here published.
The author's text has been left essentially in its original
form, but the editor has made a few changes and additions.
On the philological side the work contains some interesting
suggestions, but as the editor recognizes, it is already out of
date in some respects. Akkadian has not been fully exploited,
and no use at all has been made of Ugaritic. The main emphasis
of the work is, however, not on philology but on semantic
development, and the comparisons the author draws between
the Semitic and Indo-European languages well illustrate how
profitable this kind of study can be.   D.W.T.

BOOK LIST, 1961

As in former years, I am indebted to a number of scholars who are not members of the Book List Panel ; and I gladly record my gratitude to them : Professors Bič, de Boer, Cazelles, Hammershaimb, Mr. J. V. Kinnier Wilson, Mr. Loewe, Professor Penna, all of whom have supplied reviews, and Professor Castellino, who provided information about Italian works which might otherwise have been missed. To the members of the Panel I also express my thanks. Without their generous co-operation the *Book List* could not be produced.

Every effort has been made to cover as wide a field as possible and to ensure accuracy in the bibliographical details here recorded ; but inevitably there are gaps and errors. For these I apologize in advance.

The reviews have been classified as in former years ; but in some instances the assignment of a book to a particular section may seem rather arbitrary, if it has a bearing on more than one part of the field. Books suitable for inclusion in school libraries have been marked with an asterisk.

To the Printer I tender my sincere thanks for his unfailing helpfulness.

G. W. ANDERSON.

UNIVERSITY OF DURHAM.

GENERAL

BAUMGARTNER, W. : *Zum Alten Testament und seiner Umwelt.* 1959. Pp. viii+396. (Brill, Leiden. Price : Fl. 36).

Here is a collection of essays by Professor Baumgartner, issued by the Basel Faculty of Theology to celebrate his seventieth birthday. All save one, on ' Bibel und Volkskunde ' have appeared previously, but many will welcome their publication together in this volume. The subjects well represent the range and profundity of Professor Baumgartner's scholarship. They include a study of the nature and history of the Hebrew language in the light of modern knowledge, another on the Mandaean question, and another on the Aramaic of the book of Daniel. The Old Testament is further represented by studies on the nineteenth century treatment of Israelite prophecy, and on the Angel of Yahweh, while later Jewish literature receives attention in essays on the legend of Susanna and on the dividing sword of the Odes of Solomon xxviii. 4. Studies on Herodotus' description of Babylon and Assyria, the ancient oriental belief in the resurrection, Adonis gardens in the central Mediterranean area, and the links between Israelite and Greek sagas, carry the reader farther afield. Biographical notices on Gunkel and T. E. Lawrence and an article on American Folklore represent the way in which Professor Baumgartner regularly enlightens the readers of the *Neue Zürcher Zeitung* on what is happening in his field of scholarship. The essays are accompanied by brief hitherto unpublished notes taking account of more recent publications. There is also a bibliography of the author's works. Few readers will have ready access to all the articles collected here, and many will find this volume invaluable.

H.H.R.

BODENHEIMER, F. S. : *Animal and Man in Bible Lands.* (Collection de Travaux de l'Académie internationale d'Histoire des Sciences, 10.) 1960. Pp. VIII+232+portrait. (E. J. Brill, Leiden. Price : Fl. 36).

This translation from the Hebrew original was made by the author. It consists of three sections : an introductory discussion of methods, the formation of Palestine and its fauna in the Tertiary and Pleistocene, and early man in Palestine ; ancient zoology in the Middle East ; an account of animals and men in Palestine from the Neolithic to the end of the Iron Age (4500-3000 B.C.). It is well indexed. An excellent comprehensive scholarly work.

J.N.S.

DE BOER, P. A. H. (ed. by) : *Congress Volume, Oxford 1959.* (Supplements to Vetus Testamentum, Vol. VII.). 1960. Pp. viii+360. +5 Plates+sketch-map. (E. J. Brill, Leiden. Price : Fl. 46).

Twenty-two of the papers read at the above congress, and heard by many of our members, are preserved in this valuable

241

volume, which is printed as handsomely as were the others after Copenhagen, 1953 and Strasbourg, 1956. When it is realised that at least twelve countries are represented by the contributors to the present volume, it will be obvious how valuable a function this Organisation serves in bringing together Old Testament scholars from far and near.

Papers on almost every aspect of Old Testament study are included here. The two papers in French, by Ed. Jacob and A. Dupont-Sommer, are entitled 'Les bases théologiques de l'éthique de l'A.T.', and 'Exorcismes et guérisons dans les récits de Qoumrân'. Eight papers are in German, F. Pérez Castro on 'Das Kryptogramm. des Sefer Abischa', Victor Maag on 'Malkût Jhwh', L. Alonso-Schökel on 'Die stilistische Analyse b.d. Propheten', J. J. Stamm on 'Der Name d. Königs David', M. Noth (the new President) on 'Der Beitrag d. Archäologie z. Gesch. Israels', Hans Bardtke on a parallel to the War Scroll in a Leipzig Ms., Rudolph Meyer on the Hebrew verbal system, and Leonhard Rost on patriarchal religion.

The remaining papers are in English. J. B. Pritchard, H. M. Orlinsky and Millar Burrows deal with Gibeon, Qere and Kethib, and the R.S.V., respectively; while methodology, anthropomorphism, and the history of the ark occupy Ivan Engnell, James Barr, and Ed. Nielsen. B. Gemser continues his work on wisdom with a comparative study of 'Onch-sheshonqy, and B. Mazar follows up his brilliant Strasbourg paper on topography with an examination of the list of Levitical cities. Finally E. Hammershaimb, A. Diez Macho, Stanislav Segert and J. Strugnell maintain the interest and variety of the programme with papers on prophetical ethics, the new Palestinian targum, Hebrew metrics, and the angelic liturgy at Qumrân.

All in all, this volume offers as well-rounded and satisfying a congress-volume as could reasonably be desired, and reflects great credit on all concerned, not least on the well-loved editor—P.A.H. de Boer.

D.R.Ap-T.

BRIDGES, R. and WEIGLE, L. A. : *The Bible Word Book Concerning Obsolete or Archaic Words in the King James Version of the Bible.* 1960. Pp. 422. (Thomas Nelson & Sons, Edinburgh. Price : 36s. 0d.).

Dr. Bridges and Dean (Emeritus) Weigle present in this volume 827 articles to explain archaic or obsolete words and phrases in the K. J. version and to give equivalents from the modern versions. There is a comprehensive index of over 2,600 entries. The book is a very handy anthology to which each reader will be able to add according to his own store of knowledge.

G.H.D.

BRUCE, F. F. : *The English Bible. A History of Translations.* 1961. Pp. xiv+234+8 plates. (Lutterworth Press, London. Price : 25s. 0d.).

Professor Bruce surveys the history of translations of the Bible into English from Anglo-Saxon times to the New English Bible. On such a subject at such a time it would have been perilously easy to produce a pot-boiler. But this volume is in a very different class. The wealth of background information, of interesting and unfamiliar historical detail, of judicious citation of the sources (e.g., the choice specimens of Dean Burgon's ecclesiastical Billingsgate), and the sure grasp of the problems involved in Biblical translation, make this a book of unusual interest and quality.
G.W.A.

CAZELLES, H. (ed. by) : *Dictionnaire de la Bible. Supplément.* Fasc. xxxii. (Noeldeke-Oracle). 1959. Cols. 514-768. Fasc. xxxiii. (Oracle-Palestine). 1960. Cols. 779-1024. Fasc. xxxiv. (Palestine-Parenté). 1960. Cols. 1025-1280. (Letouzey & Ané, Paris. Price : 23s. 6d. each fasc.).

Among some twenty articles in Fasc. xxxii. one may mention those by H. Charles on ' Nomadisme ', ' Nouvel-An (Fête de)', by E. Drioton (Ancient Egypt), R. Largement (Sumerian and Accadian religion), A. Michel (Judaism) and H. Cazelles (' The new year in Israel '). ' Nouzi ' is discussed by R. J. Tournay, O.P., and there is a short memoir of the much regretted Roger T. O'Callaghan, S. J. ' Odes de Salomon ' is the work of J. Daniélou, and ' Offrande ' of J. de Fraine. E. Cothenet devotes some thirty columns to ' Onction '. G. Ryckmans writes with special knowledge of ' Ophir '.

The subject of ' Oracle et divination ', begun by A. Barucq in Fasc. xxxii. is concluded in xxxiii. The topic ' Orientales (Versions de la Bible) ' is the work of three writers of whom B. Botte deals with the versions in Arabic, Coptic and Ethiopic ; L. Leloir with those in Armenian and Georgian, and Cl. Van Puyvelde with the Syriac versions. Two other articles of some length are those by J. G. Février on ' Ostraka, Sceaux et Cachets ' and by J. M. Fenasse, on ' Palais'.

In Fasc. xxxiv. M. du Buit concludes his long article on ' Palestine ', and J. Starcky writes on ' Palmyre '. ' Papyrus bibliques ' is the work of B. Botte, and ' Pâque ' of H. Haag. Other articles are by A. George (' Parabole '), E. Cothenet (' Paradis '), A. M. Brunet (' Paralipomènes '), and W. Kornfeld (' Parenté '). J.M.T.B.

CAZELLES, H. (ed. by) : *Dictionnaire de la Bible. Supplément.* Fasc. xxxv. (Parenté-Passion). 1960. Cols. 1281-1492. (Letouzey & Ané, Paris. Price : 23s. 6d.).

There are only four articles in this fascicle, which completes the sixth volume (Mystères-Passion) of the *Supplément.*

The first of these rounds off the article on ' Parenté ' by W. Kornfeld, and is largely concerned with the juridical basis of relationship. É. Cothenet contributes an interesting study of ' Parfums ', which studies the use in the ancient East (Mesopotamia, Egypt, Arabia, and the Greco-Roman world), before approaching the Old Testament evidence for perfumes in the worship, as also in the daily life, of Israel. A. Feuillet is responsible for a ninety-column article on ' Parousie ' of which no more than a column or so is of interest to an *Alttestamentler*. Rather more than seventy columns are devoted to ' Récits de la Passion ' by X. L. Dufour.

J.M.T.B.

*CORSWANT, W. : *A Dictionary of Life in Bible Times*, completed and illustrated by E. Urech, trans. from the French by A. Heathcote, foreword by A. Parrot. 1960. Pp. xx+310+numerous ills. (Hodder & Stoughton, London. Price : 25s. 0d.).

The original French edition of this work was reviewed in the *Book List* for 1957, p. 17. The inappropriateness of the original title, there noted, has been rectified in this translation. Minor changes have also been made in the text by Dr. Heathcote, who has produced, as one would expect, a very readable rendering. The systematically classified lists of articles make this a very handy work of reference. G.W.A.

DANKER, F. W. : *Multipurpose Tools for Bible Study*. Pp. xii+290. (Concordia Publishing House, St. Louis, Miss. Price : $3.75).

This exceedingly useful manual provides the student of the Bible with a comprehensive survey of the tools which are at his disposal and a guide to their usefulness. The various chapters cover Concordances, the Nestle text of the Greek New Testament, the Hebrew Old Testament, the History of the Septuagint, the Use of the Septuagint, Hebrew Old Testament Grammars and Lexicons, Greek New Testament Grammars and Lexicons, the Use of Grammars and Lexicons, Bible Dictionaries, Bible Versions, the Use of English Bible Versions, Judaica, Archaeology, the Dead Sea Scrolls, and Commentaries and their Uses. There is here a mass of bibliographical data accompanied by discriminating comment ; and the author is to be congratulated on his success in producing an invaluable vade mecum. G.W.A.

ELTESTER, W. (ed. by) : *Judentum, Urchristentum, Kirche : Festschrift für Joachim Jeremias*. (B.Z.N.W. 26) 1960. Pp. 260. (Töpelmann, Berlin. Price : DM. 34).

Of the seventeen articles in this Festschrift for the distinguished New Testament scholar, Joachim Jeremias, on his sixtieth birthday, only three fall within the range of interest of the

Book List. There are eleven articles falling within the New Testament field, and three falling within the field of the Early Church. The three articles which stand under the heading of Judaism deal with the sonship of God in the Old Testament (Pss. ii., cx.), in Septuagint, Targum and Midrash, in Qumrân and the New Testament ; with *gilyonim* and *sifre minim* in Rabbinical literature ; and with the seven-branched candlestick and the Arch of Titus. The first of these three articles is by O. Michel and I. Betz, the second by K. G. Kuhn, and the third by W. Eltester, the editor of the volume. Readers whose interest includes the New Testament will find many valuable articles in this section, while in the third section there is an article by C. H. Hunzinger on the Gospel of Thomas.   H.H.R.

EULE, W. : *Zwei Jahrtausende Bibelbuch.* 1960. Pp. 252+112 plates +7 other ills. (Gütersloher Verlagshaus Gerd Mohn, Gütersloh. Price : DM. 24.80).

This beautifully produced and sumptuously illustrated volume surveys the history of the forms in which the Bible has been preserved and published. The opening section traces the history of manuscript reproduction over a millennium and a half ; and this is followed by an account of the impact of Gutenberg's work on the communication of the message of the Bible. A richly (and sometimes quaintly) illustrated chapter deals with the lively activity in this field during the greater part of the sixteenth century under the influence of the Reformation. The author then turns to the rich pro-ductions of the seventeenth century, the age of Pietism, the technical developments of the nineteenth century, and the interesting variety of production in our own day. This is not merely a history of technical experiments, but also in some sort a record of cultural development and of the application of craftsmanship and art to the expression of religious truth.

G.W.A.

FRIEDRICH, G. (ed. by) : *Theologisches Wörterbuch zum Neuen Testament* (begun by G. Kittel). Band VII, Lieferung 2/3, 1960. Pp. 96+ Abkürzungs-Verzeichnis, pp. 35. (Kohlhammer, Stuttgart. Price : DM. 9.20).

This double Lieferung contains a short article by Bertram on *Saleuō, salos* which has an Old Testament section ; a long and important article on *salpinx*, etc. which is not only interesting for the light it throws on Hebrew music, but for its discussion of the use in Israel and in Judaism of the trumpet and the horn in war and in the cult, and of its association with theo-phanies ; an article by Jeremias on *Samareia, Samarites, Samaritis* which, however, confines itself almost exclusively to New Testament times ; a brief article by Schweizer, Baum-gärtel and Meyer on *sarx*, etc. which should prove a most valuable addition to the already extensive literature on the subject ; and finally an article by Foerster on *satanas* which contains a section on the occurrence of the word in Qumran documents and in later Judaism (the New Testament part not yet complete).

N.W.P.

GALLING, K. (ed. by) : *Die Religion in Geschichte und Gegenwart.* 3 Auflage, Band IV. Lieferungen 69-70 (cols. 385-544+4 plates), 71-73 (cols. 545-736+4 plates), 74-75 (cols. 737-928), 76-78 (cols. 929-1152+4 plates), 79-80 (cols. 1153-1344), 81-82 (cols. 1345-1536), 83-85 (cols. 1537-1756+Pp. XXXVI). 1960. (J. C. B. Mohr, Tübingen. Subscription Price : DM. 4.20 each Lieferung).

These Lieferungen include the articles from 'Lippe' to 'Ozeanien' and bring the fourth volume to completion. Apart from a number of biographical articles, the reviewer has noted the following as of direct interest to the *Alttestamentler* : ' Literarkritische Schule ' (O. Eissfeldt), ' Märchen in der Bibel ' (W. Baumgartner), ' Magie im Alten Testament ' (K. Galling), ' Mahlzeiten, kultische ' (F. Bammel and G. Fohrer), ' Maleachibuch ' (R. Rendtorff), ' Manasse ' (R. Bach), ' Manasse-Gebet ' (W. Baumgartner), ' Manna ' (K. Galling), ' Mari ' (W. Röllig), ' Masse, Gewichte, Münzen in Israel ' (K. Galling), ' Megiddo ' (H. Gese), ' Megillot ' (H. Bardtke), ' Melchisedek ' (E. Kutsch, K. H. Rengstorf), ' Menahem ' (R. Bach), ' Mene Tekel ' (K. Galling), ' Mensch im Alten Testament ' (A. S. Kapelrud), ' Menschenopfer ' (O. Eissfeldt), ' Menschensohn ' (H.-F. Weiss), ' Mesa ' (K. Galling), ' Mesopotamien ' (F. M. Th. de Liagre Böhl), ' Messianismus ' (H. Desroche), 'Messias ' (F. M. Th. de Liagre Böhl, M. Weise, R. Meyer), ' Micha ' (R. Meyer), ' Michabuch ' (R. Meyer), ' Michael ' (E. Lohse), ' Midianiter ' (M. Noth), ' Midrasch ' (E. Gross), ' Milhama ' (C. H. Huntzinger), ' Mischna ' (E. Gross), ' Mitanni ' (A. Moortgat), ' Mizpa ' (A. Kuschke), ' Moabiter ' (M. Noth), ' Monotheismus im Alten Testament ' (F. Baumgärtel), ' Moses ' (E. Osswald), ' Mosessegen, Moseslied und Meerlied ' (H.-J. Stoebe), ' Musik : Instrumentale Musik, Gesang und Dichtung in Israel ' (C. Westermann), ' Synagogale Musik ' (I. Elbogen, K. Galling), ' Mythos und Mythologie im Alten Testament ' (S. Mowinckel), ' Nabatäer ' (M. Noth), ' Nahumbuch ' (E. Osswald), ' Namengebung im Alten Testament ' (J.-J. Stamm), ' Namenglaube im Alten Testament ' (K. Baltzer), ' Nasiräer ' (E. Jenni), ' Nathan ' (F. Maass), ' Nebuchadnezar II ' (W. von Soden), ' Nehemia ' (K. Galling), ' Nehemiabuch ' (K. Galling), ' Nimrod ' (W. von Soden), ' Ninive ' (A. Moortgat), ' Noachische Gebote ' (G. Strecker), ' Noah ' (G. Fohrer), ' Nomaden ' (G. Lanczkowski), ' Numeri ' (G. Fohrer), ' Obadjabuch ' (W. Vollborn), ' Offenbarung im Alten Testament ' (W. Eichrodt), ' Offenbarung im Judentum ' (E. L. Dietrich), ' Omri ' (R. Bach), ' Opfer im Alten Testament ' (R. Hentschke), ' Ophra ' (A. Kuschke), ' Ordination im Alten Testament und Judentum ' (E. Lohse),

' Ossuar ' (K. Galling). To a number of the articles there have been appended useful short bibliographies by W. Werbeck on the history of interpretation, in addition to the modern bibliographies supplied by the authors of the articles. G.W.A.

HORN, S. H. (with contributions by other writers) : *Seventh Day Adventist Bible Dictionary*. 1960. Pp. xxxii+1200+XXII Maps. (Review and Herald, Washington, D.C.)

Professor Horn and his collaborators have produced an excellent one volume Bible Dictionary, well illustrated and accompanied by the Rand-McNally maps. The individual articles are not signed, and while the special point of view of the Seventh Day Adventists appears in such articles as that on Sabbath, in the vast majority of the articles it does not figure. The work is written from a conservative viewpoint (e.g., the whole of Isaiah is attributed to the eighth-century prophet and the book of Job is attributed to Moses) but the volume will be found of great value to those who do not accept all its positions. In the field of archaeology especially there are entries which reflect high scholarship, and a great deal of information will be found here which is not available in the current handbooks. H.H.R.

Internationale Zeitschriftenschau für Bibelwissenschaft und Grenzgebiete. Band VI. 1958/59. Heft 1-2. 1960. Pp. 356. (Patmos-Verlag, Düsseldorf. Price : DM. 46 or $11).

This indispensable production maintains its excellent quality and enlarges its scope. The present double Heft contains 2217 entries, of which some few at the end are of books and not articles. As in former issues, the entries are admirably classified and indexed. The whole is a triumph of co-operative bibliography. G.W.A.

LIVINGSTONE, SIR R. : *The Influence of Greek and Hebraic Traditions on Western Ideals*. (Claude Montefiore Lecture, 1959.) n.d. Pp. 20. (The Liberal Jewish Synagogue, London. Price : 2s. 6d.).

In this brief survey, Sir Richard Livingstone characterizes the highest Greek religious tradition as anthropocentric, intellectual, and aristocratic, and the Hebraic tradition as theocentric, passionately moral, and invigorated by a conviction of the ultimate triumph of righteousness. Though different, the two traditions need not be opposed ; and mankind needs both. The lecture ends with an assessment of the need of the modern world (regarded as in a modified sense Hellenic) for the Hebraic tradition as represented by both Judaism and Christianity. G.W.A.

METZGER, B. M., FOREMAN, K. J., MILLER, D. G., RHODES, A. B., KELLY, B. H. : *Introduction to the Bible.* (Layman's Bible Commentaries) 1960. Pp. 172. (S.C.M. Press, London. Price : 6s. 0d.).

This paperback inaugurates the 25 volumes of the *Layman's Bible Commentaries*. The five essays are popular accounts of such themes as ' What is the Bible ?' and ' The History of the People of God '. There is inevitably some repetition in the last named essay, and the third, ' The Message '. The book is true to its title and may be thoroughly recommended ; but it is strange that not one of the authors thought of saying what the word ' Bible ' means! The reference to the use of the concordance in the last otherwise excellent article, is insufficient.

G.H.D.

MYERS, J. M., REIMHERR, O., and BREAM, H. N. (ed. by) : *Biblical Studies in Memory of H. C. Alleman* (Gettysburg Theological Studies). 1960. Pp. viii+224+portrait. (J. J. Augustin, Locust Valley, N.Y. Price : $6.00).

The first 66 pages of this volume are devoted to a very brief appreciation of Dr. Alleman, a series of devotional studies by him based on verses and phrases from the Psalter, and a bibliography of Dr. Alleman's works. The remainder consists of essays specially contributed by a number of scholars. J. Hempel follows up the thought of two of his earlier studies in a paper entitled ' Die Faktizität der Geschichte im Biblischen Denken '. G. E. Mendenhall writes on ' The Relation of the Individual to Political Society in Ancient Israel '. H. S. Gehman discusses natural law and the Old Testament. H. L. Creager examines Deutero-Isaiah's teaching about the grace of God ; and E. E. Flack contributes a study of the concept of Grace in Biblical thought as a whole. C. T. Fritsch draws out and assesses the evidence for the concept of God implied by the Greek translation of Isaiah. R. T. Stamm writes on three cardinal ideas in St. John's Gospel. In an article entitled ' The Cultus and its Significance ', J. M. Myers relates the Biblical evidence to Article XV of the Augsburg Confession.

G.W.A.

NOTH, MARTIN: *Gesammelte Studien zum Alten Testament,* Zweite, erweiterte Auflage. 1960. Sonderdrucke des Anhangs. Pp. 309-376. (Chr. Kaiser Verlag, Munich. Price : DM. 2).

Martin Noth's ' *Gesammelte Sudien zum Alten Testament* ' was noted in the *Book List* for 1957, pp. 11f. To the second edition of it which has now been published three articles have been added as a supplement. The first of these, 'Amt und Berufung im Alten Testament ' discusses the question of office as opposed to vocation in respect of priest, king and prophet in ancient Israel, and examines particularly the significance of the ceremony of anointing and what was involved in the act which was termed ' filling the hands '.

The early Judges of Israel were charismatic leaders in emergencies and held no office ; many later kings held office but had not been called to it. Noth affirms that such a call to office was distinctive of ancient Israel and was without parallel in the ancient Near East. The second article offers an analysis, in respect of form and content, of 2 Sam. vii. and, connecting it closely with the preceding chapter, says that it is concerned with King David as lord of the ark sanctuary in Jerusalem and, in its basic form, comes to us from that sanctuary. The third considers the effect of the fall of Jerusalem in 587 B.C. upon the life and thought of Israel and the extent to which their hopes of a restoration of the state of Judah survived the death of Jehoiachin in Babylon. J.M.

Die Ou Testamentiese Werkgemeenskap in Suid-Afrika. (Papers read at the 2nd meeting held at Potchefstroom, 2-5 February, 1959.) 1960. Pp. iv+64. Obtainable from the secretary, Dr. A. H. van Zyl, University of Pretoria, Pretoria, South Africa. Price : 10s. 0d.).

The Old Testament scholars of South Africa may be congratulated on forming their own Society in 1957. For their second meeting the Book of Judges was the general theme chosen, and seven of the nine papers here printed in English translation (one in summary) bear thereon. This fact gives a certain unity to the book though each participant has gone his own independent way. The general standard is to be warmly commended for a work of this kind, though there is evident need for a proof-reader more conversant with the vagaries of the English language and its spelling. D.R.Ap-T.

PARMELEE, ALICE : *All the Birds of the Bible, Their Stories, Identification and Meaning.* 1960. Pp. 280. (Lutterworth Press, London. Price : 30s. 0d.).

This is the English edition of a book published in 1959 in America ; it is well produced with 64 pictures. It retells all the Bible stories in which birds are mentioned and discusses the natural history problems involved. A foreword by Guy Emerson, ornithologist, guarantees the accuracy of the natural history ; the Biblical scholarship appears to be sound, and the book is written with an enthusiasm that makes it attractive reading. J.N.S.

RIESENFELD, H. (ed. by) : *Svensk exegetisk årsbok*, xxv. 1960. Pp. 182. (C. W. K. Gleerup, Lund. Price : Sw. kr. 10).

The only contribution to the present issue of this annual which has a direct bearing on the Old Testament is an article by G. Ahlström, entitled ' Profeten Natan och tempelbygget ', in which it is argued that Nathan represented not conservative Israelite tradition but the Jebusite interest in David's new capital, that David was dissuaded from building a temple so that the non-Jebusite Abiathar might not gain a position of commanding influence, and that Solomon's accession and his subsequent actions represent the triumph of a Jebusite party. H. Riesenfeld contributes two articles : one in English on the self-consciousness of Jesus and one in Swedish on the parables in the Synoptic and Johannine traditions. Also in Swedish are the articles by K. Stendahl on Paul and conscience and by J. Munck on Jewish Christianity in the post-apostolic age. There are also reviews of recent literature, including a section on books about the prophets, which is a sequel to the survey of books on the Old Testament begun in the previous number. To this last section, Professor Engnell again writes an introduction. It will be of interest to many readers of this *Book List* to know that a revised and enlarged edition of *Svenskt Bibliskt Uppslagsverk* (cf. *Eleven Years*, pp. 168, 457f.) is to be expected in the not too distant future. G.W.A.

ROBERT, A. and TRICOT, A. : *Guide to the Bible : An Introduction to the Study of Holy Scripture.* 2nd English ed. Vol. 1. 1960. Pp. xx+812. (Desclée Co., New York : Price : £2 18s. 8d.).

This volume, styled in French *Initiation Biblique*, with its English translations, has a rather complicated history. It first appeared, shortly before the war, in 1939, and a second French edition was published in 1948, in a revised and enlarged form. This second French edition was translated into English in 1951, and three years later (1954) came the third French edition. It is this last, now translated after a wait of six years, that was reviewed by N.H.S. in the *Book List* for 1956 (pp. 8f). He gave a list of the new matter, and his final verdict was : ' It is a most useful and comprehensive manual.' It contained about 100 pages more than the second French edition (1948), and included a new essay on inspiration by Père P. Benoit, O.P., of Jerusalem, which is one of the best things of its kind.

The present version by E. P. Arbez and M. R. P. McGuire seems to be entirely adequate, and there are many additional notes not present in the French. It is to be remarked that, whereas all the three French editions have been complete in one volume, the present book is the first of two, and includes no more than nine chapters of the original work. One of these chapters runs to over 300 pages ! J.M.T.B.

ROWLEY, H. H. (ed. by) : *The Old Testament and Modern Study : A Generation of Discovery and Research.* Essays by Members of the Society for Old Testament Study. 1961. Pp. xxxii+406. (Oxford Paperbacks. Oxford University Press. Price : 8s. 6d.).

This collection of twelve essays by members of the Society and an introduction by the editor, the whole forming an excellent survey of the results of Old Testament scholarship in the thirty years before 1951, was warmly commended when it first appeared (*Book List*, 1952, p. 8 ; *Eleven Years*, p. 379), and it has become a well-thumbed volume in most students' libraries. While the contents of the book are now so well-known as to make a notice superfluous, the appearance of this ' paper-back ' reprint prompts the hope that an even wider circle of readers will become familiar with this authoritative guide.

W.D.McH.

SCHWEIZER, E. (and others) : *Spirit of God*, trans. by A. E. Harvey. (Bible Key Words from Gerhard Kittel's *Theologisches Wörterbuch zum Neuen Testament*). 1960. Pp. xii+120. (A. & C. Black, London. Price : 15s. 0d.).

The article of which this book is a translation was noticed in the *Book Lists* for 1957 (p. 6) and 1958 (p. 4). It has, however, been abbreviated by the omission of H. Klein-knecht's discussion of *pneuma* in Greek literature and W. Bieder's survey of *pneuma* in the LXX and Hellenistic Judaism. From F. Baumgärtel's contribution on the Old Testament evidence, the lexicographical part has been left out. The omissions from the New Testament part (by E. Schweizer) are inconsiderable ; but E. Sjöberg's contribution on the rabbinic evidence has been somewhat reduced and forms part of a short section which also includes the discussions of Gnosticism and the Dead Sea Scrolls.

G.W.A.

Studia theologica cura ordinum Scandinavicorum edita. Vol. XIII, Fasc. ii, 1959. Pp. 94. Vol. XIV, Fasc. i, 1960. Pp. 114. (C. W. K. Gleerup, Lund. Price : by subscription, Sw. kr. 15 each vol. ; or Sw. kr. 10 each fascicle).

XIII, ii contains a lengthy article by Professor Mowinckel entitled ' Notes on the Psalms ', consisting of comments on metrical structure and on textual difficulties in a large number of passages. By its very nature, the article cannot well be summarized ; but it has some affinities with the author's work, *Real and Apparent Tricola in Hebrew Psalm Poetry* (A.N.V.A. II, 1957, 2), of which, unfortunately, no notice appeared in the *Book List*. The other articles in the fascicle are : ' Evangelium Veritatis and the Epistle to the Hebrews ' (S. Giversen), ' Revelation and Tradition ' (F. Fraenkel), ' Zwei Fälle von harmonisierendem Einfluss des Matthäus-Evangeliums auf das Markus-Evangelium ' (H. Sahlin).

In XIV, i S. Holm-Nielsen writes (in English) on the importance of late Jewish psalmody for the understanding of the Old Testament psalmodic tradition ; and M. Saebo contributes a form-critical study (in German) of Isaiah vii. 3-9. The fascicle also contains a discussion in German of the Hypomnemata of Hegesippus by N. Hyldahl.

G.W.A.

THOMSEN, P. : *Die Palästina-Literatur : eine internationale Biblio-graphie in systematischer Ordnung mit Autoren- und Sachregister*, ed. by O. Eissfeldt and L. Rost. Vol. A. Lieferung 3. 1960. Pp. XXII+545-905. (Akademie-Verlag, Berlin. Price : DM. 48).

The earlier parts of this volume (covering the years 1878-1894) were noticed in *Book Lists*, 1957, p. 14 and 1959, p. 8. The devotion with which Professors Eissfeldt and Rost and their helpers have made available this part of Dr. Thomsen's industrious compilation will earn the gratitude of a host of scholars. The works listed in this part cover individual places in the Holy Land, historical geography and topography (including the travel narratives of pilgrims and others), various branches of geographical study, works on Syria/Palestine in modern times, accounts of missions, and medical literature.

G.W.A.

WALKER, W. : *All the Plants of the Bible.* 1958 (5th imp. 1960). Pp. 244, including numerous ills.+1 plate. (Lutterworth Press, London. Price : 25s. 0d.).

That this work is now in its fifth edition since 1958 is an indication of its popular appeal, and it certainly is a handsome production. An average of half a page is devoted to each plant, which is introduced by a citation from Scripture and this is illustrated throughout on the opposite page. The work would have been improved by a fuller discussion of the Biblical references to the plants, and their equivalent Arabic names. The Biblical text is usually accepted uncritically and the etymology is not always to be trusted. In fact the identification of the various plants is not nearly so simple as the book suggests. The book, however, does serve its purpose as a manual for the layman interested in the Bible and is a pleasure for all to use.

J.G.

WRIGHT, G. E. and FULLER, R. H. : *The Book of the Acts of God.* 1960. Pp. 302+40 plates. (Gerald Duckworth, London. Price : 35s. 0d.).

These two famous authors set out to interpret the Bible to modern churchmen. The volume is really a comprehensive handbook to Biblical study. After some introductory chapters, Part I is devoted to the Priestly, Deuteronomic, and the Chronicler's History of Israel. Part II expounds Prophets, Psalms, and Wisdom books. Part III is intertestamental including all the main literatures and movements. Part IV is devoted to the New Testament and in 7 chapters sets forth Jesus, the earliest Church, non-Pauline, Hellenistic Christianity ; Pauline, post-Pauline and Johannine Literature. The information is reliable and helpful and the book will amply fulfil its purpose, which is to offer a religious and theological interpretation of the principal portions of the Bible.

G.H.D.

EDUCATIONAL

*BROADIE, E. : *The Chosen Nation : Book Four : The Re-Making of the Nation* (*From the Exile to the Time of Christ*) n.d. (1960). Pp. 128+4 maps and 2 diagrams. (Religious Education Press, Wallington, Surrey. Price : Boards, 6s. 6d. ; limp, 5s. 6d.).

This addition to the Pathfinder Series (it is commended by Professor Rowley) will prove a useful textbook for the upper forms of Secondary Modern Schools. It provides a simply written survey of the history and religion of the Jews from the Exile to the emergence of the Christian Church. The book is illustrated by maps and diagrams, and each chapter is followed by a selection of useful exercises.   L.A.P.

*FROST, S. B. : *The Beginning of the Promise*. 1960. Pp. xii+98. (Seraph Books, S.P.C.K., London. Price : 5s. 6d.).

This volume was originally a series of eight lectures given at a church in Ottawa. Primarily the lectures are on the Book of Genesis, but a considerable amount of general Old Testament teaching is worked in. The approach is modern, popular, and informative. Many of the illustrations are ultra-modern and most illuminating. It makes admirable reading for the Church member who is interested in learning more about the Bible. The first two chapters deal chiefly with the documentary theory of the Pentateuch, and the rest substantially with myths, legends and sagas as they are used selectively to declare the Word of God and the first ' promises '.   N.H.S.

*HEATHCOTE, A. W. : *Israel to the Time of Solomon*. (The London Divinity Series, The Old Testament, Vol. 1). 1960. Pp. 162+4 plates+3 maps. (James Clarke and Co. Ltd., London. Price : 6s. 0d.).

This first volume of the London Divinity Series is, like the second volume noticed last year, up-to-date, accurate and scholarly. Due consideration is given to the religion of the period (there is a useful chapter on the Canaanites and their religion) and reference is made to the most recent archaeological discoveries. Intended primarily for candidates for G.C.E. examinations in Divinity, and admirably fulfilling this aim, this book should appeal to other serious students as a clear and concise introduction to the subject.   L.A.P.

*HOLROYD, G. H. : *A Dramatic Old Testament Book* (1). 1960. Pp. xii+308+line drawings. (Macmillan, London. Price : 10s. 6d.).

The book is intended to cater for the first two years in the Secondary School, and covers most of the requirements of the Agreed Syllabuses. The story is taken up to the death of Solomon. It is told in plays, dramatic interludes, conversation pieces and choral speaking. Mr. Holroyd has had considerable practical experience and a dozen previous books of this type have met with considerable success. Every care has been taken to secure accuracy in historical and cultural details.

N.H.S.

LACE, O. J. : *Teaching the Old Testament.* 1960. Pp. 80. (Seabury Press, Greenwich, Conn.).

In this short but immensely useful work, to which the Dean of Christ Church writes a commendatory foreword, Miss Lace gives an illuminating survey of the material which the Old Testament provides for the teacher and the way in which it can best be handled. This is a refreshingly sane and wise little book which should be widely known and used.

G.W.A.

*MONRO, M. T. : *The Old Testament and our Times : a Short Reading Course with Subjects for Discussion.* 1960. Pp. 106. (Longmans, Green and Co., London. Price : 15s. 0d.).

This is an unusual, unconventional book, addressed to educated people who are ignorant of the O.T. and suppose that it is irrelevant to the problems of the twentieth century. Miss Monro, a Roman Catholic well acquainted with modern Biblical scholarship, aims simply at stimulating interest and discussion. In ten chapters, each followed by a list of passages to be read and of topics for discussion, she deals first with the Wisdom movement (as most easily understood by the modern mind), then with prophecy (especially Ezekiel and the Angry Young Men), then with the social revolution in Israel and Judah, and then (a particularly interesting chapter) with the revolution wrought by iron. Finally she treats the Creation stories and of Life after Death. Those who teach the O.T. to Sixth Forms will find in this book much that will contribute to the interest and liveliness of their lessons.

L.A.P.

*SMITH, J. W. D. : *Bible Background.* 1959. Pp. 74+ills. and maps. (Methuen, London. Price : 10s. 6d.).

This welcome addition to Methuen's *Outlines* (a reference library for boys and girls) will appeal to senior Grammar School pupils and also to older readers. The historical background of the people of Israel is traced from the beginnings to the revolt of Bar-Kochba, due attention being given to the archaeological evidence. The text is simple but well written and the critical approach judicious, conservative yet abreast of modern scholarship. The book is attractively produced and the text, printed in double columns, usefully illustrated by many admirably chosen photographs, diagrams, and maps.

L.A.P.

ARCHAEOLOGY AND EPIGRAPHY

Annual of the American Schools of Oriental Research, vols. XXXIV-XXXV (1954-56). *An Archaeological Study of Gibeah* (Tell el-Fûl), by Lawrence A. Sinclair. *The Excavations of the Conway High Place (Petra) and Soundings at Khirbet Ader,* by Ray L. Cleveland. 1960. Pp. 1-52+35 plates and pp. 53-98+24 plates. (American Schools of Oriental Research, New Haven. Price : $9.00).

This double vol. of the Annual is in two parts as the title suggests. In 1 the results of Albright's second campaign at Tell el-Fûl are presented and assessed at length, the review of the pottery being of particular value in the light of more recent field-work and research, which permits a much higher degree of particularization in dating, while confirming the general conclusions of Albright.

Cleveland presents an account of the excavation of the Conway high place under Albright during nine days in the winter of 1934, using more recent evidence from the Negeb, Transjordan, and Qumran to attempt a more precise dating of the Nabataean artifacts from the site. The study concludes with an interesting discussion of the sacred rock and circumambulatory with interesting analogies with Arab cult-places, with which, on the evidence known, the Conway high place has definite affinities, though the affinity which is suggested with the primitive Canaanite high places lacks the support of evidence.

The same author, after a description of the site of Ader in the Belqa, engages on a report on the soundings of the American School and the Transjordan Department of Antiquities in 1933 at Ader, where again the pottery, particularly from the Early Bronze Age, is compared with types from more extensive excavations up to date.

J.G.

BENTWICH, N. : *The New-Old Land of Israel.* 1960. Pp. 162+27 photographs (Allen and Unwin, London. Price : 18s. 0d.).

A well written, discursive description of the appeal of Palestine to a modern Jew. The book contains a popular account of recent Biblical archaeology, and the author, believing that ' the peculiar attraction of the discovery of antiquity in the land of the Bible is that it is linked with the rebirth of the Jewish nation in its historical environment ', writes from that standpoint ; the chronological table runs from 3000 B.C. to A.D. 1949. The photographs too are good.

J.N.S.

FINEGAN, JACK : *Light from the Ancient Past : The Archaeological Background of Judaism and Christianity,* 2nd edition. 1959. Pp. xxxvii+638+204 plates+6 maps+4 plans. (Princeton University Press and Oxford University Press, London. Price : 63s. 0d.).

This book, which was first published in 1946 (cf. *Book List,* 1947, pp. 7f.; *Eleven Years,* pp. 69f.), aims at giving a connected account of the archaeological background of Judaism

255

and Christianity from $c.$ 5000 B.C. to A.D. 600. In this second edition, which is 138 pages longer than the first, the structure of the book remains the same, but the results of many new excavations and further studies have been incorporated. The literature dealt with has been brought up to 1 January, 1959. The Qumran discoveries are treated at some length. Other new features include fresh translations of ancient texts and a useful section on the calendar and problems of Biblical chronology. The book is amply documented (though the literature cited could have been usefully supplemented at some points), generously illustrated, and packed with information. The author set himself an ambitious task in attempting to tell so long a story, but he has carried it out very competently.

D.W.T.

GLUECK, N. : *Rivers in the Desert : The Exploration of the Negeb : An Adventure in Archaeology.* 1959. Pp. xvi+302+26 plates. (Weidenfeld and Nicolson, London. Price : 30s. 0d.).

This further study of life between the desert and the sown from Professor Glueck, whose industry and skill have filled in the archaeological map of the Negeb and Transjordan so admirably, concerns the history of settlement in the Negeb from the Neolithic period to the Byzantine era, and has especial relevance now that the area is again opening in a limited degree to sedentary settlement made possible by the internal combustion engine and expensive modern methods of irrigation. Of particular interest is Professor Glueck's evidence for village settlements in the beginning of the Middle Bronze Age (21st-19th centuries), in the period in which he would place Abraham, the Solomonic era, with the development of the copper-beds of the Araba and the port of Ezion-geber, and the period of the Judaean monarchy, when these were still valuable assets. The statement that the Negeb was a land ' which tied continents and cultures together ' is typical of Professor Glueck's warm enthusiasm for his subject, which has engaged our admiration and sympathy for his archaeological work, but, as far as culture is concerned at this particular period, that is surely an overstatement, since on his own admission this period of the occupation of the Negeb was characterized by military occupation rather than sedentary agricultural settlement, to say nothing of cultural exchange. The Nabataean and Byzantine agricultural methods by which the Negeb was settled to the limit of its capacity, are of particular topical interest, and the impressive relics of the civilization of both powers add conviction to the author's conclusions as to the potentiality of the Negeb, though the work would have been improved had it been tempered by the scientific data which a trained geographer such as D. Baly has cited.

J.G.

MONTET, P. : *Das alte Ägypten und die Bibel*, trans. by M. Thurneysen (Bibel und Archäologie, IV). Pp. 228+VIII plates+21 ills. in the text. (Evz-Verlag, Zürich. Price : Sw. Frs. 17.60).

A translation of *L'Égypte et la Bible*, published in 1959 in the Cahiers d' Archéologie Biblique series and reviewed in the 1960 *Book List*, p. 9.

J.N.S.

JACOB, E. : *Ras-Shamra-Ugarit et l'Ancient Testament*. (Cahiers d' Archéologie biblique, No. 12.) 1960. Pp. 132+XII plates+13 drawings in the text. (Delachaux & Niestlé, Neuchâtel. Price : Sw. Frs. 7.50).

This presentation of the Ras Shamra discoveries and their relevance to the Old Testament is popular, but well-informed and accurate, and is one of the best studies in the series of which it is a part. The work is divided into three parts. The first is a general survey of the excavation and history of Ugarit, the script and language, editions and major studies of the texts, considered by the author to be most valuable to readers desiring to pursue the subject further. The second part deals summarily with the content of the myths and legends, and the third section with the relevance of these texts and others from Ras Shamra to the study of the literature, language, history, and religion of Israel. The work is, for the most part, derivative ; but excellent judgement is shown in the selection and presentation of theories, and brief, but pertinent, criticism of those rejected.

J.G.

KENYON, K. M. : *Archaeology in the Holy Land*. 1960. Pp. 326+56 Plates+66 illustrations in the text. (Ernest Benn. Price : 36s. 0d.).

By her excavation of Jericho Miss Kenyon has established herself as the foremost British authority in the field of Palestinian archaeology. Hence all students of the Old Testament and of Near Eastern archaeology have cause to be thankful for this fine book embodying, as it does, so much of the fruits of her own practical experience as a field archaeologist, together with a magisterial knowledge of all that has hitherto been accomplished in the excavation of Biblical sites in Palestine. An excellent sketch of the history of Palestine from the earliest evidence of settlement down to Hellenistic times serves as a framework for a first-hand account of the results of the excavation of all the most important Palestinian sites, together with a discussion of their bearing on the Biblical record of the history of Israel. The book is richly illustrated with excellent photographs, and the pottery diagrams constitute a complete and reliable guide to the whole range of Palestinian pottery, whose importance for dating is now generally recognized. The results of Miss Kenyon's excavations at Jericho have compelled a revision of some of

the late Professor Garstang's conclusions regarding the date of the Israelite capture of Jericho ; and Miss Kenyon has dealt with this controversial subject with restraint and caution. Her book will be for years to come an indispensable guide to the archaeology of Palestine, and withal a fascinating book to read.
S.H.H.

WRIGHT, G. E. : *An Introduction to Biblical Archaeology*. (Studies in Theology, No. 60.) 1960. Pp. 198. (Gerald Duckworth, London. Price : 12s. 6d.).

The Rev. R. Tomes has here condensed the large volume *Biblical Archaeology* by Professor Wright which appeared in 1957 (see *Book List*, 1957, p. 23). Much is omitted, including 200 photographs and figures ; material has been rearranged, and modifications and additions made to bring the work up to date, but the abridgement has been under the author's direction. The period covered is from pre-historic times to the establishment of the Christian Church in Rome and the Near East. It is a fitting addition to a notable series and will be widely read and used by teachers and students and as a general introduction to Biblical Archaeology for beginners.

J.N.S.

YADIN, Y., AHARONI, Y., AMIRAN, R., DOTHAN, T., DUNAYEVSKY, I., PERROT, J. (with a contribution by S. ANGRESS) : *Hazor II. An Account of the Second Season of Excavations, 1956.* 1960. Pp. xxiv+174+CCX plates. (Magnes Press, Jerusalem & Oxford University Press, London. Price : 178s. 6d.).

Like vol. I of the report on the excavation of Hazor (*Book List*, 1960, p. 11) this report describes results obtained in the various areas under investigation, the Israelite citadel and administrative quarter on the western eminence of the site, the lower city, which was the Canaanite residential quarter with shrines in the Late Bronze Age, being also occupied as a residential quarter by the Israelites. The strictly factual report on each of these areas is rounded out by conclusions on the relative chronology of the various strata and its relation to the history of the ancient East. Of particular interest to Old Testament scholarship is the evidence of casemate walling in the citadel in the Solomonic period, which is discussed with relation to the same feature at Bethshemesh, Gezer, and Tell Beit Mirsim in the same period ; destructions towards the end of the 9th and 8th centuries are plausibly related to the campaigns of Hazael and Tiglath-pileser respectively, and from investigations in the Canaanite city of the lower level, Dr. Yadin suggests that there is evidence of the taking of the city by Seti I, *c.* 1300 B.C., and its fall ' not later than the last third of the 13th century ', which he connects with the Israelite occupation. The volume, like its predecessor, is magnificently produced, with a large number of drawings of pottery and other objects, and photographic plates and plans.
J.G.

HISTORY AND GEOGRAPHY

BRIGHT, J. : *A History of Israel*. 1960. Pp. 500+4 (map index)+XVI maps. (S.C.M. Press, Ltd., London. Price : 40s. 0d.).

The American edition of this work was reviewed in the *Book List* for 1960, p. 12. Its appearance as the first volume in the new S.C.M. Old Testament Library gives that series an excellent send-off.   G.W.A.

JOIN-LAMBERT, M. : *Jerusalem*, trans. by H. Nyrop-Christensen with the co-operation of E. Nielsen. 1960. Pp. 116+frontispiece+134 plates. (G.E.C. Gads Forlag, Copenhagen).

The English translation of this beautiful work was noticed in *Book List*, 1959, p. 12. This translation into Danish has been made from the original French with the co-operation of Professor Eduard Nielsen, who also contributes a brief foreword. It has been executed with great care, to provide for Danish readers a text worthy to accompany the magnificent collection of photographs which the book contains. G.W.A.

KAPELRUD, A. S. : *Israel fra de eldste tider til Jesu fødsel*. 1960. Pp. 182+8 plates+maps on endpapers. (Universitetsforlaget, Oslo.)

Professor Kapelrud here devotes his expertise in lively and lucid presentation to a survey of the history of Israel from the patriarchal period to the death of Herod. Leaving out of account, as far as possible, questions of literary and religious history, he concentrates on the sequence of significant events, and guides the non-specialist reader through the period without, on the one hand, overwhelming him with the intricacies of the many problems which arise in evaluating the evidence of the sources, or, on the other, leaving him unaware that the difficulties exist. This is an eminently successful presentation of the data. Doubtless the book will have a sufficiently wide circulation for a second edition to be called for. In that event a chronological chart and a list of the plates could profitably be added.   G.W.A.

NIELSEN, E. : *Grundrids af Israels historie*, 2nd edition. 1960. Pp. 200. (G.E.C. Gads Forlag, Copenhagen).

The first edition of this work appeared in 1959, but was not noticed in the *Book List*, since it proved impossible to obtain a copy before this revised edition appeared. Only minor changes seem to have been made. The work is somewhat less popular than that by Professor Kapelrud noticed above. Indeed, it contains lectures delivered by the author in the University of Copenhagen in 1958/59, and is specifically directed to the needs of theological students, rather than to the general reader. As such, it is an admirable guide, presenting the essential data with moderation and balance, constantly referring the student back to the Biblical texts, and quoting some of the more important external sources. The period covered is from earliest times to bar Kokhba. The material is well and clearly arranged in chapters and sections, with a useful table of contents ; but there is no index. The addition of maps and a chronological chart would enhance the value of what is already a very workmanlike production.

G.W.A.

ORLINSKY, H. M. : *Ancient Israel*. 2nd edition. 1960. Pp. xii+164. (Cornell University Press and Oxford University Press, London. Price : paper covers, 14s. 0d.).

The first edition of this stimulating work was reviewed in the *Book List* for 1954 (see *Eleven Years*, p. 560). In this revised edition useful additions have been made to the bibliography to bring it up to date. As one of the most lively brief presentations of Israel's history which have appeared in the past few decades, it should continue to exercise a wide usefulness.

G.W.A.

PARMITER, G. DE C. : *King David*. 1960. Pp. 196. (Arthur Barker, London. Price : 25s. 0d.).

This is a popular biography of David. The approach is made through chapters on Israel, Samuel, and Saul. Two further chapters deal with David and Absalom. The book follows scripture very closely and is mainly story with a little evaluation. The last chapter, on Bethlehem, is the author's translation of Luke ii. 1-39.

G.H.D.

ROWLEY, H. H. : *The Teach Yourself Bible Atlas*. 1960. Pp. viii+88+ 28 plates+pp. 32 of maps. (English Universities Press, London. Price : 8s. 0d.).

This is a miracle of compression and cheapness. In eight brief chapters the author surveys the geography of Palestine, the world of the Bible, the identification of Biblical sites, archaeology and Biblical study, wandering and settlement, the rise and fall of the monarchy, from the Exile to the Advent, and the events of the first Christian Century. The photographs are admirably chosen and excellently reproduced. The maps (prepared by Messrs. George Philip and Son) are beautifully clear. The whole work is usefully indexed.

G.W.A.

DE WIT, C. : *The Date and Route of the Exodus*. (The Tyndale Biblical Archaeology Lecture, 1959). 1960. Pp. 20. (Tyndale Press, London. Price : 1s. 6d.).

Writing as an Egyptologist, Dr. De Wit re-examines the problems and argues in favour of a late date and a southern

route, while admitting that the evidence is not wholly con-
clusive. His discussion owes much to the studies by
E. Drioton and H. Cazelles.

G.W.A.

YEIVIN, S. : *Studies in the History of Israel and His Country* (in Hebrew)
1960. Pp. 368+4 maps and chronological table. (M. Newman,
Tel Aviv and Jerusalem).

In this book are assembled, in addition to a quasi-introduction
which deals with geography and strategy in the history of the
Holy Land, seventeen erudite articles containing many original
ideas. The articles, some of which were originally written in
English, were published in the last twenty-five years in various
periodicals and are grouped here under the following headings :
I. Under the Reign of the Pharaohs, which treats, among
others, subjects such as ' the vicinity of Jerusalem at the eve
of the era of the Patriarchs ' ; ' a new Egyptian source for
the history of Palestine and Syria '. II. Israel inheriting the
Country. III. The Epoch of the Kingdom. Some of the
subjects dealt with here are : The beginning of the dynasty
of David ; the date of Deuteronomy ; families and sections
in the Kingdom of Judah ; the historical background of the
Lachish letters. The work contains also a useful chronological chart, four indexes and numerous drawings and maps.

M.W.

TEXT AND VERSIONS

BLOEMENDAL, W. : *The Headings of the Psalms in the East Syrian
Church.* 1960. Pp. 94. (E. J. Brill, Leiden. Price : Fl. 20).

In this doctoral thesis submitted for the degree of D. Theol.
at Leiden the author presents the results of a study of the
titles of the Psalms in the East Syrian Psalter. His introduction summarizes previous work on the subject, and he
gives the general conclusion that those titles derive from the
commentary of Theodore of Mopsuestia. He shows that in the
form in which they have come down they betray very little
Western influence. There follow brief descriptions of the
sources used in this study. The main part of the work is a
collation based on eight MSS, selected from a large number
with Nestorian headings, and three editions, the Urmia Bible,
Urmia Psalter, and Mosul Bible. Use has been made also of
the evidence afforded by four commentaries, those of Theodore,
Denha/Gregorius, bar Hebraeus, and one anonymous work
written before 1286. The results are clearly set forth, and they
form a useful addition to the material available for the further
study of the Syriac Psalter.

W.D.McH.

CASTRO, F. P. : *Séfer Abiša'. Edicion del fragmento antiguo del rollo sagrado del Pentateuco Hebreo Samaritano de Nablus. Estudio, transcripcion, aparato critico y facsimiles* (Textos y Estudios del Seminario Filologico Cardinal Cisneros). 1960. Pp. LIV+114+ facsimiles XXIV. (Consejo Superior de Investigaciones Cientificas, Madrid. Price : ptas 450).

Dr. Castro has served Biblical scholarship well with this edition of the *Séfer Abiša'*, which has long been wanted. He prefixes a brief but informative description of the history and present state of the manuscript, showing that the late Dr. Gaster's assignment of it to the ' first century ' (B.C. or A.D.?) is out of the question, and disproving Sir A. E. Cowley's date early in the 13th century A.D. by cleverly deciphering the scribe's cryptogram ; for this almost certainly shows it to have been written by Abiša' ben Pinhas in A.D. 1085 (pp. xliii-xlvi). The manuscript now contains only Numbers xxxv-xxxvi and Deuteronomy in the Hebreo-Samaritan recension ; and much of Deuteronomy is almost illegible or missing in consequence of the bad state of the text ; but the editor gives a transcription of the text so far as it is preserved and legible, to which a full *apparatus criticus*, giving variant readings from other manuscripts, is added. The text can be checked by the photographic facsimiles of every sheet at the end of the book. Unfortunately these seem to be much reduced in scale, as the script often appears very small. How much it has been reduced cannot be made out, as the editor simply says (p. xxv, n. 40) that the size of the columns was not measured when the photographs were taken, the scale used by the photographer was not recorded, and the camera was not kept at a constant distance as the successive folios were photographed.

G.R.D.

Corpus Codicum Hebraicorum Medii Aevi, redigendum curavit R. Edelman, Pars II. The Pre-Masoretic Bible, Discovered in Four Manuscripts Representing a Unique Tradition. Vol. II. Codices Palatini. I. The Parma Pentateuch (MS. Parma no. 1849, formerly de Rossi no. 668). II. The Parma Bible (MS. Parma no. 2808, formerly de Rossi no. 2). Part I : The Pentateuch-Joshua-Judges-Books of Samuel, published by Alexander Sperber. 1959. Pp. 4+Facsimiles 1-124 (Munksgaard, Copenhagen. Price : Dan. Kr. 650).
Vol. III. Codices Palatini. II. The Parma Bible. Part II : Jeremiah-Ezekiel-Isaiah-Minor Prophets-Psalms-Proverbs-Five Rolls-Daniel-Ezra-Nehemiah-Job-Chronicles, published by Alexander Sperber. 1959. Pp. 4+Facsimiles 125-318 (Munksgaard, Copenhagen. Price : Dan. Kr. 600).

The two volumes under review appear in the series of medieval Hebrew manuscripts, which was started in 1956 under the general editorship of R. Edelman (cf. *Book List*, 1957, pp. 69f.). They form the second instalment of *The Pre-Masoretic Bible*, edited by Alexander Sperber, the first being *The Codex Reuchlinianus* (cf. *Book List*, 1958, pp. 17f.). The two volumes now published consist exclusively of facsimile plates. It would have increased their value considerably if some details had been given of the two manuscripts, all the more so as it is in vain one turns to ' The General Introduction, Detailed Description of the MSS, etc.' in the previously published volume for any such information.

According to the subtitles of the two volumes the Books of Kings are lacking. This is surely an oversight. 1 Kings i. 1-15 (as far as the final word) will be found on plate no. 124 in vol. I, and the text is continued in vol. II. Hence the Book of Jeremiah is not the first book in that volume as stated in the subtitle.

Whereas the reproduction of the Codex Reuchlinianus was so excellent that everyone could read it easily, it must be feared that the smaller size of the characters in these two volumes compels the reader to have a magnifying glass at hand. In particular, the notes are almost indecipherable. E.H.

GOODING, D. W. : *The Account of the Tabernacle. Translation and Textual Problems of the Greek Exodus.* (Texts and Studies, Contributions to Biblical and Patristic Literature, Second Series, VI.) 1959. Pp. XII+116 and diagram. (Cambridge University Press. Price : 22s. 6d.).

The author approaches the vexed question of the relation of the Greek text and M.T. of Exodus from the standpoint that divergences rest not on different texts (notably divergent in chapters xxxv—x) but on a rearrangement by a later editor. He discusses the translation of technical terms against the general Pentateuchal background, and scrutinizes those relating to the Tabernacle. He shows that the treatment of technical terms in i-xxxiv and xxv-xl follows basically similar lines, apart from xxxviii which was produced by a later editor. There is nothing to support the view, commonly held, that the second section, xxxv-xl, ' is marked by strong priestly influence, is based (unlike the Greek of the first section) on a late Hebrew text, and was translated some time later than the first Greek section ' (p. 31). Though he demonstrates a negative conclusion, the author nevertheless works towards a positive result, and it is simply unfortunate that by his modus operandi he leaves the impression of conducting a polemic on behalf of orthodoxy. The present reviewer, who had always accepted McNeile and Swete on this question, admits that Gooding has made a strong counter-attack which will at least call for further examination of the subject. B.J.R.

HANHART, R. : *Septuaginta Vetus Testamentum Graecum auctoritate Societatis Litterarum Gottingensis editum.* Vol. IX, fasc. 3. *Maccabaeorum Liber III.* 1960. Pp. 70. (Vandenhoeck & Ruprecht, Göttingen. Price : DM. 9.40 ; by subscription DM. 8).

The Göttingen Septuagint is proceeding apace, and the present editor, who was also partly responsible for II Macc. last year, works with his customary thoroughness. In the 30 pages of introduction he lists the available sources—Greek, Syriac and Armenian manuscripts, printed editions ; and he discusses the text-form of (a) the Uncials A and V and the minuscules, (b) the Lucianic recension, (c) the recension of q, and (d) a survey of the whole transmission. In a third section a brief discussion of grammatical features is included. The text is supplied with the usual comprehensive *apparatus criticus*.

B.J.R.

*LEISHMAN, T. L. : *Our Ageless Bible : From Early Manuscripts to Modern Versions*. 1960. Pp. 158. (Thomas Nelson and Sons, Edinburgh. Price : 18s. 0d.).

Originally published in 1939, this useful little book has been brought up to date and includes a final chapter on the Dead Sea Scrolls. It brings conveniently together in a concise form a lot of information about manuscripts and versions usually found in various volumes, and the material is attractively presented. The author occasionally betrays a certain critical naïveté when he departs from his own field, and English readers will find the bias both of text and bibliography rather American. Modern versions well-known on this side of the Atlantic, Rieu, Phillips, and Knox receive no mention, though earlier modern versions are covered ; and though a chapter is devoted to the R.S.V. nothing is said of the forthcoming New English Bible. The book will nevertheless be a useful addition to school and college libraries.

M.Bu.

SPERBER, A. : *The Bible in Aramaic, based on Old Manuscripts and Printed Texts. Vol. II. The Former Prophets according to Targum Jonathan*. 1959. Pp. x+331. (E. J. Brill, Leiden. Price : Fl. 90).

The first volume of this edition of the Targum was reviewed in the *Book List* for 1960 (pp. 16f.). This second volume follows the same general pattern. Ms. Or. 2210 (British Museum) is taken as the basic text. Other material used includes manuscripts with Babylonian and Tiberian vocalization, or no vocalization at all, early printed editions, Targum quotations in the works of R. Nathan, Yonah ibn Ganah, Rashi and Kimhi, and *Tosephta*, which are found in almost all the texts. The Biblical fragments with Targum from the Taylor-Schechter Collection (University Library, Cambridge), though small and poorly preserved, are of special interest since they frequently provide the only evidence available for the existence of variants.

D.W.T.

VÖÖBUS, A. : *Peschitta und Targumim des Pentateuchs. Neues Licht zur Frage der Herkunft der Peschitta aus dem altpalästinischen Targum.* 1958. Pp. 150. (Papers of the Estonian Theological Society in exile, 9, Stockholm. Price : $4.50).

Scholars differ about the relation of the Peshitta and the (Palestinian) Targum. Professor Vööbus offers a fresh treatment of the question. His ideas go in the same direction as Baumstark's, Peters' and Wohl's views. The author of this well-produced book has collected material of different kinds. His readers will in particular welcome the items from manuscripts, studied by the author in the monastery of Šarfeh (Lebanon), material unknown to most of us. He offers a treatment of editions, manuscripts of the Syriac translation, together with liturgical and patristic material and the Arabic tradition, with regard to the hymnic chapters, Exodus xv and Deuteronomy xxxii. His results support the thesis that the Peshitta of the Pentateuch (Professor Vööbus is inclined to include the other parts of the Syriac Bible) possesses in its origins and in its text-form a Targumic character, strongly influenced by the Palestinian Targum. The reviewer thinks that several questions remain open, e.g., the uncertain and surely incorrect dating of several manuscripts (p. 49 : MSS on paper from the 12th century!) ; the lack of distinction between Odes and the Bible text ; the unproved equation of Bible-quotations in the patristic literature and the Bible text.

P.A.H.deB.

EXEGESIS AND MODERN TRANSLATIONS

AUGÉ, R. : *Job.* (Versió dels textos originals i comentari pels monjos de Montserrat, IX). 1959. Pp. 378. (Monastery of Montserrat, Barcelona).

Dom Augé, who has been responsible for at least one other volume in this series of commentaries in Catalan, has produced a full and careful edition of Job with due attention to the correction of the Hebrew text, where, as so often, it is defective. In the discussion of the date perhaps too little weight is given to Dhorme's weighty arguments in favour of a date in the first half of the fifth century. It is curious that the bibliography fails to list any work later than Hölscher's edition on *Das Buch Hiob*, published in 1937, and does not mention this author's second edition, published in 1952.

J.M.T.B.

La Bible, L'Ancien Testament, Vol. II (Bibliothèque de la Pléïade). 1959. Pp. CLXXXVIII+1972., including 2 maps. (Librairie Gallimard, Paris. Price : 66s. 6d.).

Volume I of this edition was noted in *Book List*, 1957, pp. 28f. In this volume, the introduction to the whole is by É. Dhorme who also provides the translation of and notes to Jeremiah, the Twelve, Psalms, Job, Canticles, Ruth, and Lamentations ; J. Koenig translates and comments on Isaiah and Ezekiel ; F. Michaéli on Daniel and Esther ; J. Hadot on the Greek additions to Daniel (Theodotion's Text), Baruch, Jeremy, Ecclesiasticus ; A. Guillaumont on Proverbs, Ecclesiastes, additions to Esther, Tobit, Judith, Wisdom of Solomon. The volume contains a map of the Near and Middle East and one of Palestine ; M. Léturmy has compiled two indexes ; one theological and sociological, and the other historical and geographical.

Briefly we may note that of Ezekiel's foreign oracles, only those against Tyre and Egypt can confidently be assigned to the prophet and doubts are expressed about xxxviii f. Daniel is dated about 163 B.C. ; Hosea, during the reign of Jeroboam II (on p. XCVII a misprint gives the reign of Uzziah 780-716 B.C.) ; Jonah to the Hellenistic period. Use is made of the Qumran text in translating Habakkuk and Isaiah. In the Psalter, some Psalms, e.g., 1 and cx, are assigned to the Maccabean period. Job xix. 25f. is translated :

'Moi, je sais que mon défenseur est vivant
et que, le dernier sur la terre, il se
lèvera et derrière ma peau je me tiendrai
debout (nizqaphti) et de ma chair je
verrai Éloah.'

Notes, exegetical, philological, and critical at the foot of the page accompany the translation. Like the earlier volume, it contains much of value to the scholar as well as to the lay reader.

A.S.H.

BIČ, M. : *Vom Geheimnis und Wunder der Schöpfung : Eine Aus-legung von 1. Mose 1-3.* (Biblische Studien, 25.) 1959. Pp. 106. (Neukirchener Verlag der Buchhandlung des Erziehungsvereins, Neukirchen Kreis Moers. Price : DM. 5.50).

This is an interesting commentary on Genesis i-iii. in which, although the existence of two creation narratives is admitted, it is contended that in their present form these narratives are an indissoluble theological unity. To bring this out the exposition is based on a regrouping of the material in accord-ance with the themes which the author finds in various parts of the narrative. The general approach is theological ; and the exegesis includes a number of individual interpretations.

G.W.A.

VAN DEN BORN, A. : *Kronieken uit de grondtekst vertaald en uitgelegd.* (De Boeken van het Oude Testament, Deel V, Boek I.) 1960. Pp. 270. (Romen & Zonen, Roermond en Maaseik).

Here is a further instalment of this excellent Dutch Catholic edition of the Old Testament ; and van den Born, who is one of the editors of the series, presents his fourth contribution to it. As with the other volumes in the series, the commentator supplies a new translation of the Biblical text into Dutch, as well as introduction, exposition, and notes.

Van den Born concludes a discussion of the historical method and value of Chronicles by observing that it is a source of prime importance for the ideas and institutions of the post-exilic community, but that, in our assessment of the light which it throws on the pre-exilic period, we must distinguish between those elements where the Chronicler's presuppositions come to expression and those which wear a neutral aspect. But one frequently gets the impression that statements peculiar to Chronicles were based on good authority : e.g., the list of Rehoboam's fortifications in 2 Chr. xi. 5 ff., which are not on his northern frontier, as one might have expected. Van den Born maintains that Chronicles is a unity, composed about 300 B.C. ; the chief criterion for dating the work he takes to be its anti-Samaritan polemic. In an appendix 44 of the Chronicler's genealogical lists are reduced, as far as possible, to lucid tabular form. F.F.B.

CUNLIFFE-JONES, H. : *The Book of Jeremiah. Introduction and Commentary.* (Torch Bible Commentaries.) 1960. Pp. 286. (S.C.M. Press, London. Price : 15s. 0d.).

This most recent addition to the Torch Bible Commentaries will be welcomed. The introduction is well written and its value and scope are enhanced by the author's use of a fine economy of words. It lacks a section on the so-called confessions of Jeremiah, but these are not neglected in the commentary. Some discussion might have been expected of the prophet's attitude to, and possible part in, the reformation of Josiah, but this the author deemed not to be of sufficient importance for the general reader, presumably because the evidence is both exiguous and uncertain.

The commentary proper is well planned and the questions which one might expect a reader to ask receive careful attention. This can be achieved only at the cost of some very brief and even abrupt comments (e.g., an extreme example : xxxi. 7, *for the chief of the nations*, read instead ' on the top of the mountains '). But this, one imagines, is unavoidable in a volume which has to deal with a book of the size of the Book of Jeremiah and yet has to be confined within limits which make it easy for the reader to handle. J.M.

DAVIES, A. B. and G. (ed. by) : *The Story in Scripture : the Revised Standard Version of the Holy Bible in Shortened Form.* 1960. Pp. xx+292+27 plates+6 maps. (Thomas Nelson and Sons, Edinburgh. Price : 12s. 6d.).

This beautiful little book is sponsored by the Adult Education Committee of the British Council of Churches. It is no anthology for schools, with children's interests (and limitations) in mind : nor is it a ' Bible as literature ' venture. It attempts to give to the seeking adult some sense of the Bible as a whole and what it is all about.

The format is delightful ; clear type without distraction of chapters and verses. This could be misleading, for there is much judicious omission, but the passages used are indicated in an appendix (pp. 265-281) which is a monument of compression and contains some meaty and very helpful notes. There is also a short Introduction (pp. xiii-xix) tracing the guiding thread.

The Old Testament (pp. 3-96) occupies less than half the volume and the master hand is revealed in the great economy of selection and security of emphasis. Inevitably some omissions will seem regrettable, but the main purpose is throughout clearly kept in mind and the hope that the reader ' may be led to a closer study of the full text once he is able to relate individual passages to the main theme ' seems justified.

Such a reader is likely to be rather more familiar with the Gospel story. Perhaps no narrative based on a conflation of the Gospels, especially if it includes the Fourth, can escape criticism and, helpful though the brief notes in the Appendix are, such an arrangement may not wholly dispel the fog likely to invest the reader's vague familiarity with the material.

A delightful feature of the Old Testament selections is the way in which passages from the Prophets and the Psalms are given a setting in the historic narrative. Similarly, and very helpfully, carefully selected portions of the Pauline Epistles are suitably interspersed in the narrative of Acts. A chapter on ' Other Christian Writings ' containing quite brief selections from the rest of the New Testament (pp. 252-262), brings the work to a close. Would it have been too drastic to put the sections from the Fourth Gospel here?

There is still room in this neat little volume for admirably clear maps, well-chosen pictures, a very usefully compressed chronological table, and an index.

M.Bu.

EICHRODT, W. : *Der Heilige in Israel : Jesaja 1-12 übersetzt und erklärt.* (Die Botschaft des Alten Testaments 17, I.) 1960. Pp. 148. (Calwer Verlag, Stuttgart. Price : DM. 8.80).

This first part of Eichrodt's exposition of Isaiah i-xxxix. in this well-known series consists entirely of translation and commentary, the introduction having been reserved for the volume on the remaining chapters. vi. 1-13 is treated immediately after the superscription to the whole book ; but thereafter the various passages are taken in the order in which they stand in the text, with the exception of v. 25-30 and a few verses in viii. and x. (e.g., in viii. 16f. are transposed to follow 2 and 18 to follow 4). ii. 2-4 is regarded as Isaianic. There is a particularly interesting discussion of the Immanuel passage, the point of which is taken to be doom rather than promise. The entire exposition is concentrated yet eminently readable, taking full account (without detailed documentation) of critical discussion, yet essentially theological. The second volume will be eagerly awaited.   G.W.A.

ESTRADÉ, M. M. and GIRBAU, B. M. : *Tobit-Judit. Ester* (Versió dels textos originals i comentari pels monjos de Montserrat, VIII). 1960. Pp. 296. (Monastery of Montserrat, Barcelona).

Once again there is the pleasure of noticing a well-bound, beautifully printed volume from Montserrat, the joint work of Girbau, who has made the version of Esther and supplied a commentary to all three books, and Estradé who has translated Tobit and Judith. As in the earlier volumes there is a short introduction to each book, and the commentaries are compressed but adequate. The present volume acknowledges considerable use made of the edition of these books in the Bonn Bible, the work of A. Miller and J. Schildenberger, published in 1941.

The discussion of the historicity of Judith does not seem to be firm or decisive, and perhaps too much is made of the idea that what is difficult for our age may have been obvious to contemporary readers of the book.   J.M.T.B.

FOHRER, G. : *Das Buch Jesaja.* 1 Band, Kapitel 1-23. (Zürcher Bibelkommentare). 1960. Pp. viii+244. (Zwingli-Verlag, Zürich. Price : Sw. Frs. 10.80).

In this neat little volume Professor Fohrer provides a brief introduction and a useful running commentary on the text. The introduction is in the main concerned with the structure and growth of the book, and, after a brief glance at the whole of Isaiah, discusses the relation of i-xxxix to the ministry of Isaiah and the additions which may be supposed to have been made by later generations. The author is disposed to assign rather more material to this latter class than some other recent commentators and critics (e.g., ix. 1-6 ; xi. 1-9). The translation and commentary are conveniently arranged in brief sections, which afford an admirably clear guide for study. The commentary discusses the general sense and content of each section, without detailed examination of the phraseology. Altogether this is an attractive piece of work which should be widely used.   G.W.A.

FRITSCH, C. T. : *Genesis.* (Layman's Bible Commentaries.) 1960. Pp. 128. (S.C.M. Press, London ; John Knox Press, Richmond, Virginia ; Ryerson Press, Toronto. Price : 6s. 0d.).

Within the available space the author has written a most useful paper-back exposition for the non-specializing student and the layman. A moderate critical standpoint is unobtrusively upheld, typology is avoided, all Biblical statements are treated with reverence, and the emphasis throughout is on the permanent theological implications and religious values of the book. It is unlikely that any serious reader will long rest content without fuller and more positive statements on special points, but this book will give him a good preparation. The reviewer would seriously question the credibility of one sentence (p. 39), that ' the abnormal length of life ascribed to the Hebrew antediluvian heroes . . . may be due to the tremendous vitality of man right after creation '. Did the author perhaps intend this to express the view of the source?

D.R.Ap-T.

HORST, F. : *Hiob.* (Biblischer Kommentar, Altes Testament, XVI, Lieferung 1.) 1960. Pp. 80. (Verlag der Buchhandlung des Erziehungsvereins, Neukirchen, Kr. Moers. Price : DM. 7.00 each Lieferung ; or, by subscription, DM. 5.85).

This commentary follows the general pattern of its predecessors in the series. There are bibliographies which stand at the head of each passage treated, a translation of the Hebrew text into German, textual and linguistic notes, and a discussion of the literary structure and exegesis of each passage. Further literature is cited at relevant points. An introduction will presumably follow later. This first issue covers chs. i-v. 6. While all the ancient versions are taken into account, the LXX is studied in some detail. It is to be noted with pleasure that much recent philological material has been included, though the existence of a preterite tense in Hebrew seems not to be recognized. Several original emendations are proposed. A special feature of interest and value is the large extent to which extra-Biblical sources are utilised in explanation of the text. A wide range of Near Eastern material, both ancient and modern, has been drawn upon, as well as the classical authors, Rabbinic literature, and the documents from Qumran. This first issue gives every promise that the commentary, when completed, will be one which every student of the book of Job, whatever his standing, will need to consult.

D.W.T.

KAISER, O. : *Der Prophet Jesaja, Kap. 1-12 übersetzt und erklärt.* (Das Alte Testament Deutsch, 17.) 1960. Pp. XVI+126 (Vandenhoek & Ruprecht, Göttingen. Price : DM. 6.20 ; cloth DM. 9.20).

A short selection of commentaries, a wider range of general works, and a very exhaustive bibliography of recent periodical literature introduce this book, which takes the place of the volume which was to have been completed by the late Bishop Volkmar Herntrich. The bibliographical details are followed directly by the translation and commentary in alternating sections (the usual plan of the series); consequently matters which normally fall to be treated in an introductory chapter are dealt with as part of the exposition.

Where deemed necessary, the text is re-arranged (e.g., x 1-4 follows v. 8-24), 'intrusive phrases' are omitted from the translation. For such, and other, emendations adopted a footnote gives the reason or refers the reader to *BH*. The attempt is made to find the historical setting wherever possible (though here no doubt there is room for difference of opinion) and cultic festivals are suggested as the setting for certain oracles (e.g., i 2-9 ; v. 1-7) ; though the question is left open, how far Isaiah's familiarity with king and temple was due to birth or to profession.

The commentary takes account of modern views and is a workmanlike piece of exposition which will be of value for its intended circle of readers.   D.R.Ap-T.

KESSLER, W. : *Gott geht es um das Ganze. Jesaja 56-66 und Jesaja 24-27 übersetzt und ausgelegt.* (Die Botschaft des Alten Testaments, 19.) 1960. Pp. 176. (Calwer Verlag, Stuttgart. Price : DM. 9.80).

While recognizing the literary and historical problems involved, the author treats Isaiah lvi-lxvi as substantially the work of one prophet slightly earlier than Malachi. He touches very briefly and somewhat inconclusively on the relationship of these chapters to xl-lv. The introduction to xxiv-xxvii is very brief, and merely touches on the critical questions involved. Somewhat cautiously the author indicates a preference for the view that the fall of Babylon to Xerxes (485 B.C.) is referred to. It is, however, only fair to point out that the series of which this commentary forms a part is more concerned with exposition than with introduction, and to add that the exposition is competently done.   G.W.A.

KRAUS, H. J. : *Psalmen* (Biblischer Kommentar, Altes Testament, XV), Lieferungen 10, 1959, 11-13, 1960, and Einleitung, 1960. Pp. 721-994+I-LXXXVIII. (Verlag der Buchhandlung des Erziehungsvereins, Neukirchen, Kr. Moers. Price : Lieferungen 10-12, each DM. 7 ; Lieferung 13 & Einleitung, DM. 11.50).

The reviewer's high opinion of this commentary has been sufficiently expressed in earlier notices (*Book List*, 1959, p. 18, and *Book List*, 1960, p. 20) ; for in these Lieferungen, which carry the work from Ps. cv to the end of the Psalter, there is no lowering of standard. The introduction inevitably covers much familiar ground, but it does so in a characteristically fresh and stimulating way ; and the reviewer would single out as of particular value the balanced treatment of the problem of textual criticism ; the discussion of the now common approach to the study of the psalms in terms of their literary types and *Sitz im Leben ;* and the exposition of the theology of the psalms, which should make useful reading for all who are anxious to arrive at a balanced appreciation of Israel's faith and worship. The author, the general editor, and the publishers are to be congratulated on producing a commentary on the Psalms which is admirable in quality, pleasing in format, and, though costly, well worth the price.

A.R.J.

KROEZE, J. H. : *Het boek Job*. 1960. Pp. 296. (J. H. Kok, Kampen. Price : Fl. 8.75).

Kroeze became known as author of a thesis on Genesis xiv, presented at the Calvinistic University at Amsterdam in 1937. He is now professor at the Potchefstroom University in South Africa. His commentary and new translation of the book of Job does not offer a full discussion and treatment of the text. The author is preparing a more detailed commentary in another series, to be issued by the same publisher. The present book contains a clear outline of Dr. Kroeze's ideas. He dates the book in the ' Golden Age ' of Solomon and thinks that the story (i and ii), the speeches by Elihu (xxxii-xxxvii), and the poem on wisdom (xxviii) may be later dramatization and addition. Job is a historical person. The aim of the book is : a proclamation of God's sovereignty. With this volume the series ' Korte Verklaring der heilige Schrift ' (a series of 61 volumes, started in 1922) is complete. The very well produced volumes have found a warm welcome in the Netherlands, not only in the conservative circles. Dr. Kroeze's *Job* is an ornament of the series.

P.A.H.de B.

MAIER, W. A. : *The Book of Nahum : A Commentary*. 1959. Pp. 386. (Concordia Publishing House, St. Louis, Missouri. Price : $5.75).

This posthumous devotional commentary on Nahum comprises translation, introduction, commentary, and bibliography. The author favours Nahum's Judean origin and dates the book about 654 B.C., rejecting the theory of the liturgical character of the work, and defending its character as a divine revelation. The author catalogues the often mutually contradictory scholarly accounts of the book in order to reject them almost in toto. The information in the Introduction and Commentary, literary, archaeological, and historical, is exhaustive, illuminating, and careful. In the commentary there are long notes of various kinds on the Hebrew text to serve the various purposes of the author.

G.H.D.

MICHAELI, F. : *Le Livre de la Genèse*, Chapitres 12 à 50. (Collection La Bible Ouverte) 1960. Pp. 150. (Delachaux & Niestlé, Neuchâtel. Price : Sw. Frs. 4.00).

The same author's Genesis 1-11 in this series, 1957, was noted in the *Book List*, 1958, p. 22. While due attention is given to literary and historical problems, these patriarchal narratives have their place as declaring the faith of Israel, the covenant relationship, the declaration of the Promise. Thus the particular difficulties of Gen. 14 are noted, but its relationship to the subsequent cult-centre, Jerusalem, and to the sacral kingship is seen as the main purpose in its reference to Melchizedek. This little volume well serves the purpose of the series, to meet the needs of preacher, teacher, and thoughtful reader of the Bible. A.S.H.

MYERS, J. : *Hosea to Jonah* (Layman's Bible Commentaries). 1960. Pp. 176. (S.C.M. Press, London. Price : 6s. 0d.).

This book is true to its purpose and discusses these five prophetical books in terms intelligible to general readers untrained in Biblical criticism and yet at the same time having due regard to the results of modern scholarship. After a short introduction to the books there follows a fairly full summary of contents into which is woven any necessary comment on points of interest or difficulty. It is based on the text of the Revised Standard Version.

Now and again brevity results in too much compression, as in the discussion of Ashima of Samaria in Amos viii. 14. L.H.B.

PENNA, A. : *Isaia*. (La Sacra Bibbia, ed. by S. Garofalo.) 1958. Pp. 632+pp. 12 of plates). (Marietti, Rome. Price : 37s. 6d.).

Dom A. Penna, C.R.L., is one of the best Italian Biblical scholars of his time, and has already edited *Jeremia* in the same series. It appeared in 1952, and was noticed in the *Book List* for 1953, p. 36.

The Isaiah volume is one of the best of its kind, and, allowing for the absence of Hebrew types, except in the textual notes, and the inordinate amount of space taken up by a reprinting of the Vulgate Latin, is quite reasonably full. Its tone is somewhat conservative especially on the matter of authorship, and it may be felt that the author attached undue importance to the argument from the traditional inclusion in a single volume. The point of view of those with whom the author is not in agreement is stated fairly and often at some length. J.M.T.B.

STEINMANN, J. (and others) : *Josué*. (*Connaître la Bible*.) 1960. Pp. 148 with 40 ills. (Desclée de Brouwer, Bruges. Price : B.frs. 69).

This work begins with a brief introduction giving details of the background, both historical and geographical, and some account of the literary history of the book. Then follows a translation of the text printed on the left hand side of the page and a brief running commentary on the right hand side. There are forty illustrations and maps, of which some are very much to the point. The book may well serve its purpose of introducing the Bible easily to the non-expert. L.H.B.

STEINMANN, J. : *Daniel.* (*Connaître la Bible.*) 1961. Pp. 160, with 43 ills. (Desclée de Brouwer, Bruges. Price : B.frs. 69).

This is on the same plan as that on Joshua in the same series ; but, as might be expected, the commentary is much longer than the text. More illustrations have been inserted to fill up the left hand pages and avoid altering the lay-out of text on the left and commentary on the right. The approach is critical and up to date, but there is a tendency to see more symbolism than the author probably meant. For instance, the story of the three men in the furnace is spoken of as a symbol of resurrection, while the figure of the Son of Man is composite, representing both the people of Israel and the Messiah. For those who read French easily the book is an admirable introduction to the problems of the Book of Daniel.

L.H.B.

VON UNGERN-STERNBERG, R. FREIHERR, and LAMPARTER, H. : *Der Tag des Gerichtes Gottes. Die Propheten Habakuk, Zephanja, Jona, Nahum, übersetzt und ausgelegt.* (Die Botschaft des Alten Testaments, 23/IV). 1960. Pp. 240. (Calwer Verlag, Stuttgart. Price : DM. 12.80).

This volume follows the pattern of the series—a German translation in heavy type prefaces an extended and appealing exposition of the passage. In the present volume the first author deals with Habakkuk, Zephaniah, and Jonah. The combination of detailed and careful exposition with a lively style of writing is very attractive. The commentary on Jonah is followed by two long notes on the transmission of the Book of Jonah and on Mt. xii. 38-42. H. Lamparter translates and expounds Nahum in an equally attractive but more concise fashion. He adds a postcript on the theological relevance of Nahum. There is also a short bibliography for each prophet.

G.H.D.

VON WALDOW, H. E. : "*. . . Denn ich erlöse dich*"; *Eine Auslegung von Jesaja 43.* (Biblische Studien, 29). 1960. Pp. 92. (Neukirchener Verlag, Neukirchen, Kreis Moers. Price : DM. 4.90).

This is an exegetical and theological study of Isa. 43, influenced by the work of H. J. Kraus, M. Noth and G. von Rad. Five units within the chapter are distinguished : three salvation oracles, 1-3a ; 5a, 3b-7 ; 16-21 ; for which the setting is a Lamentation liturgy appointed for a specific day ; and two sentences of judgement, 8-13 ; 22-28 ; the former having as its background a Covenant Festival when Yahweh judges the world, the latter looking to a renewal of the covenant without cultic activity. Verses 14f. are not discussed because of the corrupt state of the text.

A.S.H.

LITERARY CRITICISM AND INTRODUCTION

(including History of Interpretation, Canon, and Special Studies)

BEHLER, G. M. : *Les confessions de Jérémie.* (Bible et Vie Chretienne.) 1959. Pp. 106. (Ed. de Maredsous, Paris. Price : NF. 4.80).

An admirable idea has been admirably carried out in this book in which studies of five short passages in Jeremiah have been grouped under the title indicated. It must be admitted that the fifth, dealing with the false prophets (xxiii 9-29) differs from the other four in being less directly related to the spiritual experience of the prophet. The first, xii 1-5 is ' a complaint about the prosperity of the wicked '. Jeremiah wants to argue with God about a question of justice ; and to this complaint and argument the author relates passages from the Psalms, Job, Wisdom, and even St. John. Next comes xv 10f., 15-20, ' the renewal of Jeremiah's call ' : and here the author offers felicitous textual emendations (v 11 ; p. 29). The third study is of ' the prayer of vengeance ', xvii 12-18, and the fourth of ' the conflicts in the prophet's soul ', xx 7-13 (14-18 being regarded as from a different period in the prophet's life). This is the most moving study in this collection. Without making a display of his learning, the author shows that he understands the critical problems, knows how to present the religious problems, and does not hesitate to throw light on a Biblical passage by a reference to St. Augustine or St. Catherine of Siena. His acquaintance with earlier translations of the text does not prevent him from offering his own original and individual rendering.   H.C.

BONNARD, P. E. : *Le Psautier selon Jérémie.* (Lectio Divina, 26). 1960. Pp. 282. (Les Éditions du Cerf, Paris. Price : NF. 13.50).

This charmingly written study follows up a desire expressed by the late Albert Gelin (d. 7 February, 1960) that a volume might be devoted to the contacts between Jeremiah and the Psalter. The author in his preface recognizes that one may speak of *Jérémie imitateur* as well as of *Jérémie imité*, though in his present book he concentrates upon the latter aspect. He investigates in some detail the Jeremian character of thirty-three psalms, and in his final chapter, entitled " Le Christ et le Psautier selon Jérémie ", claims that, of the eleven psalms used by Jesus in the New Testament accounts, seven are from among those showing Jeremiah's influence, and five of them are found on the Master's lips in the most poignant crises of His earthly life.

Whether one accepts all the arguments or not, this is a book that will lend an added interest to the reading of both Jeremiah and the book of Psalms.   J.M.T.B.

BRATTON, F. G. : *A History of the Bible : An Introduction to the Historical Method*. 1959. Pp. x+382 (Beacon Press, Boston. Price : $4.95). Also 1961. Pp. 288. (Robert Hale, London. Price : 21s. 0d.).

This is a popular presentation of the historical method based on recent archaeological and Biblical studies. The Bible is inspired because inspiring and contains a progressive discovery of truth. Sections are devoted to the Archaeological Backgrounds of the Old Testament, the Making of the Old Testament, the Making of the New Testament, the Transmission of the Bible, and a brief history of the Higher Criticism. It may be felt that an attempt has been made to put too much in too small a compass. No reference is made to Dr. K. Kenyon's work at Jericho ; no account is taken of recent work on the Pentateuch ; the treatment of the ' Myth, Symbol and Ritual school ' is less than adequate. The statements that Job is a philosophical tract, and that ' Epicurean and Stoic influences are mixed in Ecclesiastes ' would not command general agreement. Among books referred to in the Bibliography (pp. 359-371 or 265-277) one would have expected a reference to A. Bentzen : *Introduction to the Old Testament*.

A.S.H.

KUHL, C. : *The Prophets of Israel*, trans. by R. Ehrlich and J. P. Smith, with a Bibliography by N. W. Porteous. 1960. Pp. 200. (Oliver & Boyd, Edinburgh. Price : 16s. 0d.).

Dr. Kuhl covers the whole story of Israel's spiritual history from Moses to Daniel. He appears to agree that the canonical prophets were subject to ' ecstasy ' and quotes parallels elsewhere, though he writes as if this experience had no influence on the form in which the prophet's words have come down to us. His critical principles are those generally recognised to-day, but he goes rather far in denying individual oracles to the prophet whose name stands at the head of the book, and some of his dating looks subjective. Otherwise he shews a real power of sympathetic appreciation in his pictures of the prophets' character and place in history. The volume lacks a subject-index, but no small part of its value lies in the comprehensive bibliography supplied by Professor Porteous. The original German edition of this work was noticed in *Book List*, 1958, p. 35.

T.H.R.

KUHL, C. : *The Old Testament, Its Origins and Composition*, trans. by C. T. M. Herriott. 1960. Pp. VIII+354. (Oliver and Boyd, Edinburgh. Price : 25s. 0d.).

The original German edition of this work was reviewed in the *Book List* for 1954 (see *Eleven Years*, p. 588). In this English translation the bibliography has been brought up to date and adapted to the needs of English readers. The short section at the end on the Apocrypha has been rearranged to correspond to the order of the books in English Bibles. The notes, which in the German edition were collected together at the end, are now at the foot of the pages to which they refer. The documentation is fairly full.

G.W.A.

MACGREGOR, G. : *The Bible in the Making*. 1961. Pp. 310. (John Murray, London. Price : 30s. 0d.).

Professor Macgregor, taking a holiday, no doubt, from the philosophy of religion and the life of John Knox, has written a remarkably comprehensive account of the making and transmission of the Bible ; but the emphasis is on transmission. The short chapter, for instance, on the writing of the Old Testament is not only necessarily sketchy but somewhat out of touch with recent work. The strength of the book lies in the account which it gives of translations of the Bible into English. A great amount of interesting information has been packed into the chapters in which these translations are surveyed. There are eleven useful appendixes presenting, inter alia, lists of MSS, specimens of versions, a list of misleading words in the AV, selections from the Dead Sea Scrolls, and a survey (by E. H. Robertson) of the place of the Bible in Roman Catholicism in Western Europe to-day. Although Professor Macgregor mentions Dr. Hately Waddell's rendering of the Psalms into Scots, he seems to have missed the same scholar's equally engaging rendering of Isaiah.

G.W.A.

MÖLLER, W. : *Grundriss für alttestamentliche Einleitung*, unter Mithilfe von Pastor Lic. Hans Möller und Studienrätin Lic. Grete Möller. 1958. Pp. XII+390. (Evangelische Verlagsanstalt, Berlin. Price : DM. 14.50).

The aim of this introduction to the literary study of the Old Testament is to uphold the Mosaic authorship of the Pentateuch (up to Deut. xxxi. 23!) and similar strongly conservative positions with regard to higher, though not lower, criticism. Some may find the slightly polemical arguments convincing ; but to the reviewer it seems that few of the counter-arguments are fairly stated or really faced. Short, selective, and almost entirely German bibliographies are given for the first two sections of the (Hebrew) canon, but none at all for the third. The author's first book appeared in 1899, and he has had the assistance of a son and a daughter for many sections of this work. The paper is rather poor, and several additions should be made to the list of corrigenda.

D.R.Ap-T.

MOWINCKEL, S. : *Psalmenstudien*, 2 Bände. 1961. (Photomechanischer Nachdruck der Ausgabe Oslo, 1921-24.) Pp. 5+XXIII+528 and XVII+415. (P. Schippers, Amsterdam. Price : Fl. 92).

In this very welcome reprint Vol. I contains *Psalmenstudien* I-II and Vol. II *Psalmenstudien* III-VI. In the author's brief preface to the former he refers to later publications of his own, particularly to *Offersang og Sangoffer* (shortly to appear in an English rendering by Mr. D. R. Ap-Thomas) and to his commentary on the Psalms in *Det Gamle Teṣtamente*, IV, indicating (a) points at which he has modified his former positions (e.g., in *Psalmenstudien* I), (b) points on which his critics have misunderstood him, and (c) points at which others have drawn from his theories conclusions which he cannot share. The second volume contains some five pages of *Berichtigungen und Ergänzungen*, mainly corrections of misprints, but including some additions, such as references to other literature published about the same time as the original edition.

G.W.A.

MURPHY, R. E. : *Seven Books of Wisdom.* 1960. Pp. x + 164. (Bruce Publishing Company, Milwaukee. Price : $3.75).

This is a good example of a work written by a scholar for wide use. It offers a simple introduction for Catholic readers to the seven Wisdom books of the Confraternity Version of the Bible, i.e., it includes Psalms, Sirach, and the Wisdom of Solomon, as well as Proverbs, Job, Song of Songs, and Ecclesiastes. There is a short chapter on Hebrew Poetry and a concluding chapter on Wisdom in the Old Testament. The chapter on Psalms is much influenced by Gunkel, and treats of the Psalms according to their types. An Israelite Enthronement Festival is considered but not accepted. On the Elihu speeches the author does not commit himself as to whether they are original or secondary. The Song of Songs is interpreted in terms of human love, but a secondary allegorical meaning is allowed. The unity of Ecclesiastes is favoured. Prov. xxii. 17—xxiv. 22 is associated with the Amen-em-ope text, and the Confraternity Version even introduces the name Amen-em-ope conjecturally into the text of Prov. xxii. 19, boldly reading : ' I make known to you the words of Amen-em-ope '.

H.H.R.

NEHER, A. : *Jérémie.* 1960. Pp. XIV + 234. (Librairie Plon, Paris. Price : NF. 7.10).

An evocative essay on Jeremiah's vocation, the historical context of his mission, and the essence of his message. Neher finds that his call sprang from reflection on his descent from the de-sacralised priestly clan of Anathoth. Among the keywords for the understanding of Jeremiah's theology he recognises *rahoq—distant ;* impatient of all stereotyped ideas, the prophet insists that God cannot be found until the conventional assurance of His localised proximity has been exploded. An analysis of xxx-xxxiii, in symphonic terms is full of suggestiveness.

R.L.

PENNA, A. : *I Profeti* (" Ut unum sint," 8.) 1959. Pp. 182. (Edizione
Paoline, Rome. Price : L. 400).

Angelo Penna here shows all his considerable gifts as a
populariser in this attempt to compress into a small number of
pages the essential facts about the prophets of Israel. There
are chapters on divination in the ancient world, and, in
particular, on its occurrence in Israelite religion. A long
section deals with seers and prophets. Further chapters
discuss God's speaking to the prophets and to those outside
the prophetic circles. The message of the prophets is outlined
under five heads : God, religious worship, the moral sense,
the day of the Lord, and the Messiah. The bibliography
contains the titles of many works not written in Italian, e.g.,
Dr. J. Skinner's classic work, *Prophecy and Religion.* J.M.T.B.

ROWLEY, H. H. : *Elijah on Mount Carmel.* (Reprinted from *Bulletin
of the John Rylands Library*, Vol. 43, No. 1, 1960). 1960. Pp.
190-219. (Manchester University Press, and the John Rylands
Library, Manchester. Price : 5s. 0d.).

This brochure offers an examination of the perplexing exegetical
problems in the narrative of Elijah on Mount Carmel, together
with that extensive citation in footnotes of the relevant
literature on the subject which is so valuable a feature of
Rowley's writings. It may be noted that he rejects the interpretation of Elijah's pouring of the water on the altar as an
acted prayer for rain, saying that it was done to show his
confidence and to make his triumph more spectacular, as he
also rejects a similar interpretation of the prophet's later
crouching on the mount, regarding this act simply as the
adoption of an attitude of humble prayer. He admits that the
fire from heaven may have been a natural phenomenon, but
submits that it must have been a remarkable one to explain
the subsequent history of Ahab's reign. When, with reference
to the gibe cast at the unresponsive Baal as musing, or having
gone aside, or on a journey, or asleep and requiring to be
awakened, Rowley presents references to other deities in
respect of such acts or such circumstances, one wonders
whether this is necessary and whether the point of the gibe
was not to imply that all these were possibilities for Baal
who was not God in the true sense of the term. J.M.

ROWLEY, H. H. : *Darius the Mede and the Four World Empires in the
Book of Daniel. A Historical Study of Contemporary Theories.*
Reprint. 1959. Pp. xxxiv + 196. (University of Wales Press,
Cardiff. Price : 21s. 0d.).

The re-appearance of Professor Rowley's well-known work,
originally published in 1935, is a welcome event. Though this
is a reprint rather than a new edition, a number of minor
corrections have been made. G.W.A.

STEINMANN, J. : *Le livre de la consolation d'Israël et les prophètes du retour de l'exile.* (Lectio Divina, 28). 1960. Pp. 312. (Éditions du Cerf, Paris. Price : NF. 15.30).

This book sets Deutero-Isaiah in the context of world-history and even attempts to relate individual passages to contemporary events, somewhat in the manner of Sidney Smith's Schweich Lectures. It is in three parts, roughly in the proportions of 1 : 3 : 2. I. The Triumph and Fall of Babylon ; II. The Book of Consolation ; III. The Prophets of the Return from Exile (including much of Nehemiah). It is clear that Catholic scholars may now speak of the Second Isaiah as a sixth century prophet. The translations are free-flowing and vigorous, and include almost the whole of Isa. xl.—lv. Each section is followed by a paraphrase commentary, on the average rather longer than the passage itself. There is no evidence that Steinmann has seen Muilenburg's literary analysis of Deutero-Isaiah but it is unlikely that he would be convinced by it. The first Servant Song refers to Cyrus, the second and third to the prophet himself. In the fourth, ' Obviously, the Suffering Servant is depicted as an individual who personifies the expiatory destiny of the Israelite people, who symbolizes this prophetic people [influence of Lindblom here], which could reincarnate itself in a unique man, as it had done in the past in the persons of Moses, Jeremiah, and the Second Isaiah himself . . . Jesus, who was to represent all his people in his own person, was to show an absolute fidelity to the sense of the text '. A book which the layman can understand and the scholar use with profit.

C.R.N.

VERGOTE, J. : *Joseph en Égypte, Genèse chap. 37-50 à la lumière des études égyptologiques récentes.* (Orientalia et Biblica Lovaniensia, III). 1959. Pp. XII+220. (Publications Universitaires, Louvain. Price : B.Frs. 160).

The author studies the Joseph stories in Genesis from the standpoint of an Egyptologist ; accepting, in its main outline, the documentary theory of the Pentateuch, he attempts to show from a review of proper names, institutions, idioms, and play on words that the stories are rooted in Egyptian reality, that probably Moses was the author of the stories in their original form, and that it is possible to show the extent and approximate dates of the J and E redactions.

J.N.S.

LAW, RELIGION, AND THEOLOGY

AUZOU, G. : *La parole de Dieu : Approches du mystère des Saintes Écritures*, Édition Nouvelle. (Connaissance de la Bible, 1). 1960. Pp. 444. (Éditions de l'Orante, Paris. Price : 14.70).

It is difficult to do justice to this presentation of the Bible to the non-specialist but thoughtful and intelligent reader.

The first three chapters speak of the Bible as the Word of God, the response it claims from the reader, and its contents (pp. 13-97). The chapter that follows: Le Langage biblique (pp. 99-163) is particularly valuable for its discussion of the Biblical vocabulary—one only regrets that no consideration is given to the word *hesed*. A chapter on the nature of the Biblical revelation is followed by one on ' La Bible dans l'Église en marche ' (217-391) which is a most valuable summary. The final chapter, with its closing section, ' Le sacrement de la parole ' is a fitting conclusion to a book based on fine scholarship and deep devotion.

A.S.H.

BIARD, P. : *La Puissance de Dieu*. (Travaux de l'Institut Catholique de Paris, 7). 1960. Pp. 192+indexes. (Bloud & Gay, Paris. Price : NF. 19.80).

This study in Biblical Theology deals first with the power of God as shown in the history and election of Israel. Through the experience of Israel there is shown forth the power of God over the universe. While it still has its historical outworking, this power is revealed as wisdom. It ' reaches those deep levels of the soul where the entire destiny of man is shaped and definitely settled ' (p. 82). It is revealed as saving and redemptive, as righteous and compassionate ; and this explains the varied aspects of Messianic power.

The author then deals with the activity of Christ as the power of God, devoting four chapters to this aspect of Christology. First there is the picture in the Synoptic Gospels of ' Jesus mighty in deed and word ', then, in the Fourth Gospel, the communication of the power or gift of faith. Chapter VI is devoted to the Pauline references to the saving power of God in the resurrection of Jesus Christ. The last chapter deals with the power of Christ, through the Spirit, in the fellowship of the Church.

These are the main outlines of an admirable synthesis in which both the vocabulary of the subject and the relevant passages are studied. The reviewer would have preferred the Johannine Theology to be taken as concluding the development ; but the author had his own reasons for grouping the Gospels together and has produced an excellent study.

H.C.

BLANK, S. H. : *Prophetic Faith in Isaiah*. 1958. Pp. x+242. (A. and C. Black, London. Price : 18s. 0d.).

This book is a combination of critical dissection and religious exposition. Professor Blank finds many ' Isaiahs ' in the book of that name ; and he contrasts the historical Isaiah of the 8th century (stern, gloomy, displaying a faith ' freighted with imperatives ', prophesying rejection) with the other Isaiahs who bring a message of consolation and hope. Of the ' other Isaiahs' perhaps the most surprising is ' the Isaiah of Legend ',

who is what popular tradition made of the memory of the historical Isaiah ; and here Dr. Blank denies to the latter much of what is commonly believed to have been said by him in the Syro-Ephraimite crisis and at the time of Senna-cherib's siege of Jerusalem. This is but one instance of many critical judgements which are likely to be widely questioned. There will also be considerable dissent from some of the religious interpretations offered, e.g., the view of the fourth Servant Song as ' The Song of the Servant's Proud Destiny '. But dissent from many of Professor Blank's conclusions will be mingled with deep gratitude for a book of rare sensitiveness and integrity.
                                                              G.W.A.

BOMAN, T. : *Hebrew Thought compared with Greek*, trans. by J. L. Moreau. 1960. Pp. 224. (S.C.M. Press, London. Price : 21s. 0d.).

The first German edition of this book was reviewed in the *Book List* for 1953, pp. 50f. (*Eleven Years*, pp. 503f.). The English translation which has now appeared has been made from the second German edition still further revised by the author. Attention should specially be drawn to the author's preface to the English translation and to the new section (Chapter 3, Section E) which compares the Greek and Hebrew views of history and offers a discussion of Hebrew cosmology. The author insists that the Greek and Hebrew views of history are both legitimate for their own purposes but must be kept strictly distinct. He further argues that it is wrong to interpret Hebrew cosmological expressions visually, that indeed they are to be understood functionally and religiously. ' In short ', he says, ' what we call the cosmological ideas of the Bible are virtually the cosmological ideas of the Middle Ages ; they are neither Hebrew nor Greek, but a naive mixture of both '.

In its English dress this valuable book will now reach a much wider circle of readers than formerly and will undoubtedly stimulate discussion on the controversial issues it so ably raises.
                                                              N.W.P.

COLE, W. G. : *Sex and Love in the Bible.* 1960. Pp. xiv+448. (Hodder and Stoughton, London. Price : 21s. 0d.).

Dr. Cole is a Professor, student leader, and chaplain in America, author of *Sex in Christianity and Psychoanalysis*, and a member of a committee on marriage problems set up by the World Council of Churches. The book is colourfully (even sen-sationally) written in an attempt to discover Biblical guidance for the varied and urgent sex problems of to-day especially among youth. It was first printed in 1959 for the National Board of the Y.M.C.A. ; clear, lucid and comprehensive, it can safely and usefully be used even by troubled adolescents who have become antagonistic to moral and religious restraints on sex behaviour.
                                                              J.N.S.

CRAMER, K. : *Genesis 1-11 : Urgeschichte? Zur Problem der Geschichte im Alten Testament.* (Sammlung gemeinverständlicher Vorträge und Schriften aus dem Gebiet der Theologie und Religionsgeschichte, 224/225). 1959. Pp. 62. (J. C. B. Mohr, Tübingen. Price : DM. 4.50).

In this short but profound monograph Cramer challenges the validity and appropriateness of the term ' Urgeschichte ' as applied to Genesis i-xi, and maintains that in these chapters we have what may fitly be described as ' Geschichte ' and what is intended to be an inseparable part of the historical record which runs on to the end of II Kings. The theme is worked out by the author in a lively discussion of some recent views of history in the Old Testament ; and the chapters are expounded as embodying three components : Yahweh's action, man's responsible decision, Yahweh's zeal as manifested in judgement and renewal.

G.W.A.

DAUBE, D. : *Sin, Ignorance and Forgiveness in the Bible.* (Claude Montefiore Lecture, 1960.) 1960. Pp. ii+30. (The Liberal Jewish Synagogue, London. Price : 2s. 6d.).

Professor Daube here discusses the various biblical attitudes regarding the extent to which ignorance may be pleaded in mitigation of an offence, and as a ground of partial or full remission of the penalty. He distinguishes two kinds of ignorance—the purely factual ignorance displayed in those stories in which a king takes a patriarch's wife into his harem not knowing her to be another man's wife, and that deeper and more serious ignorance which manifests itself as moral blindness, failure to appreciate one's true well-being or the divine fitness of things. With the former he associates the case of the involuntary homicide and such an action as that of Uzzah, who steadied the ark with the best of intentions. The New Testament and patristic and rabbinical literature are also laid under contribution, and Professor Daube is disposed to regard as truly Judaic ' the notion of the defiant sinner, who goes on with his crime though he has all the relevant information, deserving forgiveness, or a measure of forgiveness, because he does not know (in the second and deeper sense)'. He finds support for this view in the closing words of the book of Jonah (an appointed lesson for the Day of Atonement), where the ' more than sixscore thousand persons that do not know ' are taken to be the men and women of Nineveh in their moral obtuseness.

F.F.B.

DROWER, E. S. : *The Secret Adam. A Study of Nasoraean Gnosis.* 1960. Pp. xvii+123. (Clarendon Press, Oxford. Price : 25s. 0d.).

The latest addition to Lady Drower's books on the Mandaeans deals with an important aspect of their esoteric *gnosis.* The ' secret Adam ' (*'adam kasia*), also called the ' first Adam ' (*'adam qadmaia*), preceded the physical Adam (*'adam pagria*) by many myriads of years, and comprised every manifestation of the Mighty Life. When united with the cosmic Eve, he was the soul and she the body, he the sky and she the earth. Through their union the physical Adam came into being. The affinities of this conception are not difficult to recognize, but in *nasirutha* (the secret lore of Mandaism) it has been developed in a characteristically gnostic direction. The volume contains much interesting information about *nasirutha* over and above what relates to the secret Adam, and concludes with the drawing of some comparisons between it and certain features of the Ebionites, Elkasaites and Sampsaeans as described in early Christian literature. The discoveries at Qumran and Nag Hammadi have re-awakened interest in these sects and in Mandaism, and Lady Drower's study of material to which she has had quite exceptional access has appeared opportunely.

F.F.B.

GUTHRIE, H. H. : *God and History in the Old Testament.* 1960. Pp. viii+180. (The Seabury Press, Greenwich, Conn. Price : $4.25).

In six clearly written chapters, the author presents the Old Testament material as a philosophy of history rather than as a book of religion. The Old Testament holds it as axiomatic that God has made himself known and in a variety of ways proceeds to answer the questions : ' *How* and *where* and *as whom* has God made himself known?'. The writers are thus concerned with the question ' What does history mean?' The main line of development is from J (10th century) through the prophets with a culmination in the New Testament. The material in E and D, though more consciously religious, tended to a crystallisation of the faith. The treatment of the Wisdom literature (in which Canticles is included because the Sages were ' interested in culture for its own sake '), probably because it does not lend itself to this treatment, is the weakest section of the book. The book ends with notes, bibliography and indexes. The book will be useful to students reading for an Honours degree in theology.

A.S.H.

HEŘMANSKÝ, S. : *Základní problémy biblické typologie. Příspěvek k biblické hermeneutice* (= *Fundamental Problems of Biblical Typology. A Contribution to Biblical Hermeneutics*). 1959. Pp. 92. (Cyclostyled.) (Ustřední církevní nakladatelství, Prague. Price : Kčs. 13).

This work, which is one of the series of text books issued by the Hus Faculty of the Czechoslovakian Church, is a noteworthy contribution to the problem of typology and its justification. There is a detailed treatment of the theme of promise and fulfilment, in which the narratives about the Exodus and about David are taken as examples and traced to their eschatological outcome ; and a special section is devoted to the New Testament interpretation of the Old.

Finally the author considers the kerygmatic character of the Biblical material. The work is soundly based and provides a reliable introduction to the subjects which it discusses.

M.B.

JAMES, E. O. : *The Ancient Gods : The History and Diffusion of Religion in the Ancient Near East and the Mediterranean.* 1960. Pp. 360+85 plates+11 line illustrations and 1 map in the text. (Weidenfeld & Nicolson, London. Price : 42s. 0d.).

This is the opening volume of the Weidenfeld and Nicolson *History of Religion*, of which Professor James himself is the general editor. Sixteen volumes in all are projected, involving ancient religions and living faiths. This particular volume deals with the history and diffusion of religion in the Ancient Near East and the Eastern Mediterranean. The author deals first with the Rise of Civilisation in the ancient Near East, and then with the emergence of religion. In turn the following subjects are discussed : The Mother-goddess and the young God, Sacral Kingship, Seasonal Festivals, the Cult of the Dead, Cosmology, Divination with Astrology and Prophecy, the Gods and the Good Life, ending with a chapter on the development and diffusion of Near Eastern deities. As we expect from the author, the approach is that of comparative religion, myth-ritual patterns, and sacral kingship. The book is well written and is an excellent example of good scholarship based on these particular premises.   N.H.S.

JOHNSON, A. R. : *The One and the Many in the Israelite Conception of God.* 2nd edition. 1961. Pp. vi+46. (University of Wales Press, Cardiff. Price : 8s. 6d.).

The reappearance of this widely used and much cited monograph (cf. *Eleven Years*, pp. 46f.) is a boon, particularly since it is now provided with a set of indexes similar to that in *Sacral Kingship in Ancient Israel.* Changes in the text and notes are inconsiderable.   G.W.A.

DE JONG, H. W. M. : *Demonische Ziekten in Babylon en Bijbel.* 1959. Pp. xvi+131. (Brill, Leiden. Price : fl. 15.00.).

This study is divided into four chapters, dealing successively with Babylonian medicine, diseases believed by the Babylonians to be brought on by demons, medicine in the Bible, and diseases brought on by demons in the Bible. The precise differentiation of classes of demons, and the ascription of various categories of disease to their respective activities, made their way in due course from Babylon into the Biblical milieu, but there they came under the powerful influence of Yahwism. Thus Saul's malady is brought on by an evil spirit *from Yahweh*, and although later on such evil spirits appear not as Yahweh's servants but as his opponents, yet even as late as the book of Tobit Asmodaeus (not a Babylonian demon, as our author reminds us) is allowed to wreak havoc only within limits, in order that people may realize the superior power of God's angel and the value of piety for a happy life. The book includes discussions of the maladies mentioned in the Psalter (where magical practices are discerned), of the disease described in the Qumran ' Prayer of Nabonidus ', of the references to demon activity in Josephus's writings, of the demon-possessions in the Gospels (where Satan is the ultimate cause of sickness ; in these narratives, and still more in those of Acts, the theological interest is seen increasingly to eclipse the therapeutic), and of Paul's thorn in the flesh (the ' messenger of Satan' in 2 Cor. xii. 7 is identified with Qeteb).

F.F.B.

JUDANT, D. : *Les Deux Israël : Essai sur le mystère du salut d'Israël selon l'économie des deux Testaments.* 1960. Pp. 245. (Éditions du Cerf : Paris. Price : NF. 10.80).

The sub-title to the present work explains the slightly ambiguous title ; and the author claims that, in a long search for any *ouvrage d'ensemble* on this topic he has found only one, Mgr. Journet's *Destinées d'Israël* (Éditions Egloff, Paris, 1945) which suffers from being mainly a commentary on Léon Bloy's ideas. Judant intends his work to be a contribution to the ecumenical movement, which may without giving offence to either side, set out clearly the problem of studying the relations between Jews and Christians. In a series of chapters with such titles as Israel's election, Israel and Jesus, the transformation of the covenant, and the universality of God's people, he appears to have succeeded. There are four appendices, of which the last assembles a number of texts and prayers that have Israel for their subject.

J.M.T.B.

KAUFMANN, Y. : *The Religion of Israel*, trans. by M. Greenberg. 1960 and 1961. Pp. xii+486. (University of Chicago Press, Chicago and George Allen & Unwin, London. Price : $7.50 and 42s. 0d.).

This is a readable (though sometimes inelegant) translation and abridgement of seven volumes of Kaufmann's important work. Kaufmann examines the nature of paganism and argues that Israelite religion was fundamentally different : from the time of Moses, even popular religion was monotheistic and free from mythology and magic, apart from temporary lapses and unimportant survivals of paganism. He next argues that, although the classical analysis of the Pentateuch into sources may be right, the Priestly Code is to be dated long before the exile. Finally, he traces the history of Israelite religion from the time of the Patriarchs (*c.* 1350 B.C.) to the exile, and discusses the teaching of the great prophets who, he thinks, committed their own prophecies to writing. The book has

full indices. Kaufmann's work has been very influential in Israel, and those who do not read Modern Hebrew will be grateful for this chance of examining his theories, which are certainly stimulating, whether or not they are found to be convincing.
J.A.E.

KRAUS, H. J. : *Le Peuple de Dieu dans l'Ancien Testament*, trans. by R. Brandt. 1960. Pp. 80. (Delachaux et Niestlé, Neuchâtel. Price : Sw. Frs. 2.75).

This is a discussion of the significance of God's call of Israel to be His people, of His obligation to them as their sovereign king, and of their obligation to Him as His subjects, an obligation that was sadly ignored. They came under the judgement of God just because they were His chosen people, but the judgement was the prelude to a second call after the pattern of the first Exodus (as in Deutero-Isaiah). Finally the sovereignty of God was fulfilled in the Christian Church which can truly be called the people of God.

It is inevitable that in so short a treatment much has to be taken for granted, but it also means that the kaleidoscopic pictures of the Old Testament are forced into a mould, for the sake of uniformity, which cannot contain them all. This leads to over-simplification, as in the claim that there were two kinds of judges in the period of the Judges, those who were simply administrators of justice (listed in Jdg. x. 1-5, xii. 7-15) and those, like Gideon and Barak, who were simply liberators in a time of political crisis.
L.H.B.

LIGIER, L. : *Péché d'Adam et Péché du monde*. (Bible-Kippur-Eucharistie, I. L'Ancien Testament). (Coll. Théologie, 43.) 1960. Pp. 320. (Aubier, Paris).

This very interesting work is the first volume of a study of the Biblical doctrine of sin. The writer has a thorough knowledge of the Biblical material, and his footnotes contain a wealth of exact references to a host of commentaries and monographs. But the book is more than a commentary on the relevant texts. The author is a master of the Old Testament material and knows how to plan his investigation taking full account of the problems relating to Israel's social, religious, and liturgical life. A number of points in this up-to-date study are open to debate, notably the interpretation of the opening chapters of Genesis ; but it is a valuable contribution to the religious interpretation of the Old Testament. Sin appears as Israel's sin, denounced by the prophets ; but it is universal, and is present in all other nations also. ' Collective defections ' account for collective sacrifices, and supremely the great Kippur liturgy. From this solidarity in evil the author passes to a study of the first sin : the Biblical texts are seen as explaining the situation of man by the historical situation of Israel, which chose the monarchy before the time decreed by God. In Job and the Wisdom books this view of the sin of man is no longer connected with the problems of the monarchy and the history of Israel. A most rewarding study, even if one does not accept all its conclusions.   H.C.

PENNA, A. : *La Religione di Israele*. Biblioteca di scienze religiose, IX, 7). 1958. Pp. 336. (Editrice Morcelliana, Brescia. Price : L. 800).

This remarkably compact work by the author of the commentaries on Isaiah and Jeremiah in *La Sacra Bibbia* (edited by S. Garofalo) divides the history of Israel's religion into six periods, i.e., patriarchal religion, the Mosaic period, the years from Joshua to Solomon, the period of the two kingdoms, the exile and restoration, and the Greco-Roman period. Written from a somewhat conservative standpoint it is a work of real learning, based upon a considerable amount of reading. The eight pages of bibliography would have been more useful to beginners if an evaluation of some of the works there listed had been attempted.   J.M.T.B.

MARTIN-ACHARD, R. : *From Death to Life. A Study of the Development of the Doctrine of the Resurrection in the Old Testament*, trans. by J. P. Smith. 1960. Pp. x+240. (Oliver and Boyd, Edinburgh. Price : 30s. 0d.).

This is a translation, smoothly made and carefully edited, of the work reviewed by the present writer in *Book List*, 1957, pp. 50f. ; and the welcome expressed on that occasion may be repeated here. In fact the reviewer is glad to think that in its English form it should serve to reinforce still more his own efforts to call attention to the valuable but strangely neglected work of von Baudissin on the significance of $\sqrt{hyh}$. In the circumstances, therefore, perhaps the reviewer may be allowed to give expression to the complaint (stifled on the previous occasion!) that he is cited (p. 200) in such a way as to appear to hold the view that the belief in the resurrection of the dead was derived from the theme of the dying and rising god. The fact is that the writer's own exposition of $\sqrt{hyh}$ was intended as the first stage in what should ultimately serve inter alia as a refutation of this view.   A.R.J.

MOWINCKEL, S. : *The Old Testament as Word of God*, trans. by R. B. Bjornard. 1960. Pp. 144. (Basil Blackwell, Oxford. Price : 15s. 0d.).

This book contains the translation of a series of lectures published in Norwegian over twenty years ago and, unfortunately, only now made available in English. Unpretentious as is the claim its author makes for it, he has succeeded, as was only to be expected from a scholar of such distinction, in making a contribution to the debate about the interpretation of the Old Testament which merits the most careful study. His plea is that the Old Testament must be regarded as a very human book and, at the same time, the medium of divine revelation, there being no conflict except on a fundamentalist theory of inspiration. Revelation is God acting in the real world of history ; but the authority of the witnesses to this does not rest on their infallibility. Their ability to see the creative work of God in history is due to faith. The Word of God can best be understood as testimony, man's testimony to God and God's testimony to Himself. God's Word is spoken into concrete situations and the whole Old Testament, not selected parts of it, is intended to teach us in all its variety God's relation to unrighteousness. It is just because the Old Testament is relevant to actual situations in the past that it can become relevant to actual situations to-day which can be seen as analogous to the situations recorded in the Old Testament. Professor Mowinckel makes a plea for the inclusion of the Apocrypha in the Protestant Canon and for the recognition that some light of divine revelation is to be found in other religions, though it remains true that the essential line of historical relevation runs through Israel.   N.W.P.

VON RAD, G. : *Theologie des Alten Testaments*. Band II. *Die Theologie der prophetischen Überlieferungen Israels*. 1960. Pp. 458. (Chr. Kaiser Verlag, München. Price : 43s. 0d.).

The eagerly awaited second volume of Gerhard von Rad's *Theologie des Alten Testaments* does not disappoint expectations, and with its predecessor takes its place as one of the most significant contributions in this generation to the interpretation of the Old Testament. This second volume continues the exposition of Israel's *Heilsgeschichte*. von Rad once more makes clear his conviction that the Old Testament itself wishes to be understood as witness to God's action in History and does not offer readily the material for constructing ' the inner history of Israel ' (Baumgärtel) or a history of Hebrew piety. The issue indicated here is actually one of the burning points of present controversy, von Rad himself and Baumgärtel being two of the main protagonists. The strength of von Rad's position is that he allows the Old Testament to speak for itself ; he may, however, not be hearing all that it says.

The volume falls into three main parts.

Part I deals with pre-exilic prophecy and with certain general considerations about prophecy, including a searching study of the nature of the prophetic experience, the subtle balance within it of obedience and freedom, the prophetic view of the word of God, of time and of history.

Part II deals chronologically with the Canonical Prophets. It is shown how the successive prophets, each in his own limited historical situation, exercised a radical criticism of the religious traditions of their people, opened up new vistas of eschatological hope, and uttered judgement or administered comfort as the situation demanded. Particularly impressive are the studies of Isaiah, Jeremiah and Deutero-Isaiah. In connection with the Book of Isaiah in particular there is an important discussion of the sacral tradition regarding Jerusalem-Zion and the concept of the New Jerusalem. It is suggested that the figure of the servant of the Lord in Deutero-Isaiah has a close connection with the expectation of a greater Moses.

A short section on Daniel and Apocalyptic concludes this section, Daniel being interpreted in the context of the Wisdom Literature.

Part III is devoted to a consideration of the relation of the Old Testament to the New. Just as throughout the Old Testament we have to do with successive actualizations, so the New Testament gives us the actualization of the Old Testament in the New. The prophets had discovered that God did not abandon His people in His judgement of them and this proved to be supremely true in Christ. From Him light is cast back upon the Old Testament *Heilsgeschichte*, and in connection with this von Rad develops his views about typology. The volume closes with a remarkable study of the meaning of the Law, arguing for the presence of a charismatic reinterpretation of it in the New Testament which can be recognized as anticipated in the prophetic criticism. N.W.P.

VON RAD, G. : *Moses*. (World Christian Books, No. 32. Second Series). n.d. Pp. 80. (Lutterworth Press, London. Price : 2s. 6d.).

After a short introduction Professor von Rad presents his sketch of the work and significance of Moses : Moses the Man ; The Call of Moses ; The First and Second Commandments ; God's Will as Made Manifest in Law ; From Promise to Fulfilment. This simple yet masterly study is an admirable approach to the understanding of the continuity of Biblical religion.

G.W.A.

DE VAUX, R. : *Les Institutions de l'Ancien Testament*. II. *Institutions militaires : institutions religieuses*. 1960. Pp. 542. (Éditions du Cerf, Paris. Price : NF. 19.50).

Since all serious students of the Old Testament and even general readers have already appreciated the worth of the first volume of this work (see *Book List*, 1958, p. 39) by a scholar so thoroughly versed in the critical study of the Old Testament and in Near Eastern archaeology alike, the second volume of the work needs no recommendation, and certainly no praise is too high for this monument of unobtrusive scholarship and that lucidity which marks the master. The present volume, in two parts, deals in the first with the military institutions of Israel in her historical development in Canaan, her armed forces, weapons, fortifications and methods of warfare. In this section there is a valuable discussion of the conception and practice of the holy war and a study of the Warfare Scroll from Qumran. The second part of the book is devoted to the cult, its sanctuaries, and particularly the Temple, its ritual and personnel, considered in their historical development. The seasonal festivals are also studied before and after the Exile, and also the sacred calendar. As in the first volume Père de Vaux publishes a selective bibliography and provides full indexes to his citations from Scripture and to the subject matter of both volumes.

The learned Dominican deserves our gratitude that he has so generously given us the fruit of his ripe scholarship and rich local experience as a field archaeologist.   J.G.

VUILLEUMIER, R. : *La tradition cultuelle d'Israël dans la prophétie d'Amos et d'Osée.* 1960. (Cahiers Théologiques, 45). Pp. 96. (Delachaux et Niestlé; Neuchâtel and Paris. Price : Sw. Frs. 4.75).

We have here a new study of the problem of the relation of Amos and Hosea to the cultus. The author holds that the usual approach to the subject is faulty, based as it is on the search for all sorts of liturgical and sacrificial elements, and then summarising. The true approach is to find first the fundamental motifs in the cultus, and then to see how the prophet fits into the general scheme. The fundamental themes of the cult are the Exodus, the Covenant, the glorious epoch of David, the final hope ; all of these are bound together in the ever-present now of the living cult, shot through with the Presence of the living, Saviour God. Here we have yet another author who is turning away from the Coronation of Yahweh theme, and the myth-ritual pattern theories. The author finds these themes deeply embedded in the works of these prophets, except for the David theme. But, if these two prophets spoke to the Northern Kingdom, one would not expect much about David, the Judean king.   N.H.S.

WESTERMANN, C. (ed. by) : *Probleme alttestamentlicher Hermeneutik : Aufsätze zum Verstehen des Alten Testaments.* (Theologische Bücherei, II). 1960. Pp. 366. (Chr. Kaiser Verlag, München. Price : DM. 14).

This volume of Essays is a must for anyone who wishes to acquaint himself with the issues in the current debate about the theological interpretation of the Old Testament. It contains a collection of the essays by various authors which have appeared on the Continent during the past ten years. In particular we are given a selection of the contributions to the now famous number of *Evangelische Theologie* (12 Jahrgang, 1952/53, Heft 1/2), viz. those by von Rad, Noth and

Zimmerli. It is unfortunate that the essay by von Rad is reprinted only in part, since the omitted parts are necessary for a complete understanding of the debate which followed. Noth's essay entitled ' Die Vergegenwärtigung des Alten Testaments in der Verkündigung ' denies the possibility of using the method of analogy in interpreting the Old Testament and, in holding this view, Noth contrasts sharply with von Rad. A difficult but very significant essay by Baumgärtel, ' Das Hermeneutische Problem des Alten Testaments ', is valuable for its statement of a point of view opposed to von Rad's typological exegesis and elaborated in Baumgärtel's earlier discussion in his book *Verheissung* (1952). Another contribution to the discussion of the problem of Typology is Eichrodt's article reprinted here : ' Ist die Typologische Exegese sachgemässe Exegese?' Bultmann's article, ' Weissagung und Erfüllung ' is also included and articles by Westermann, H. W. Wolff, Vriezen, Hesse, etc. The volume is rendered more useful by a bibliography containing the titles of many books and articles relevant to the main theme of the volume. It can be predicted that this book will stimulate much further discussion and one may hope that it will be translated into English.

N.W.P.

WILDBERGER, H. : *Jahwes Eigentumsvolk. Eine Studie zur Traditionsgeschichte und Theologie des Erwählungsgedankens.* (Abhandlungen zur Theologie des Alten und Neuen Testaments, 37). 1960. Pp. 126. Zwingli Verlag, Zürich. Price : Sw. Fr. 19.50).

Beginning from a consideration of Exodus xix 3b-8, which he holds to be the description of a cultic celebration, Wildberger traces the elements in the election formula elsewhere in the Old Testament. He then discusses (with reference to the work of Mowinckel, von Rad, and Kraus) the cultic associations of the election tradition and concludes that in the period of the Judges the Feast of Unleavened Bread was celebrated at the sanctuary and was the setting for the proclamation of election found in Exodus xix 3b-8, and that its location was Gilgal. This is followed by a study of the fusion of the election and covenant traditions. The book ends with a useful discussion of the religious and theological implications of the theme of election.

G.W.A.

WÜRTHWEIN, E. : *Die Weisheit Ägyptens und das Alte Testament.* Rede zur Rektoratsübergabe am 29. November, 1958. 1960. Pp. 18. (N. G. Elwert Verlag, Marburg).

In this clear and stimulating lecture Professor Würthwein gives a general account of ancient Oriental Wisdom and a more particular description of Egyptian Wisdom, emphasizing its

religious character. Turning to Wisdom teaching in Israel (and particularly in Proverbs), he argues that it took over a conception of the ordering of the world and of life and a conception of God, which were at variance with Israel's own religious tradition. He then presents Ecclesiastes and Job as protests against these alien elements.
                                                        G.W.A.

THE LIFE AND THOUGHT OF THE
NEIGHBOURING PEOPLES

BRONGERS, H. A. : *Oud-Oosters en Bijbels Recht*. 1960. Pp. 208. (G. F. Callenback, Nijkerk. Price : Fl. 12.90).

Dr. Brongers offers translations of laws from Sumer, Eshnunna, Babylon, Bogaz-köy, Assur and New Babylon, based on the translation and treatment of these texts by Driver and Miles, Goetze, Friedrich, Miles and Gurney, Meek, and other scholars. He adds short introductory remarks on date and character, together with a bibliography and references to Bible texts. In his final chapter he reviews the Pentateuchal laws chronologically. It is not his aim to discuss the problems of possible connection between the codes, although he offers some valuable remarks on the peculiar character of the various principles of justice. His caution with regard to the distinction between apodictic and causistic law (Alt) seems to the present reviewer a stronger point than his explanation of the fifth commandment. Theocracy was not a monopoly of ancient Israel. Other statements in the book might be disputed. This book will be useful for class work.
                                                        P.A.H.deB.

LAMBERT, W. G. : *Babylonian Wisdom Literature*. 1960. Pp. xx+358 +LXXV plates. (Clarendon Press, Oxford. Price : 90s. 0d.).

An Introductory Essay, eight chapters of texts given in transliteration and translation, critical and philological notes, and seventy-five beautifully reproduced plates of text copies, make up the contents of this volume which aims at presenting for the first time within a single cover all the currently available material relating to the Wisdom literature of ancient Mesopotamia. The eight chapters of texts are concerned respectively with the Poem of the Righteous Sufferer, The Babylonian Theodicy, Precepts and Admonitions, Preceptive Hymns, The Dialogue of Pessimism (thus reviving an old title not universally agreed), Fables or Contest Literature, Popular Sayings and Proverbs. Each chapter, which is provided with its own introduction and bibliography, improves significantly upon earlier presentations. Much is owed to the careful collating and re-analysis of texts already known, but more to an impressive accumulation of new texts diligently

sought out by the author from the collections of many archaeological museums. Throughout the whole, the marks of
exact and patient work are to be seen. In his preface the
author states that his book is addressed alike to the scholar
and the non-technical reader, and both are served well although
the scholar's share is the greater. If occasional modernisms
may be thought to detract from the quality of the translation
in places, there are happy turns of phrase as well, and one
cannot but admire both the vision of the book and the per-
severance which carried through so large an undertaking.

J.V.K.W.

SANDARS, N. K. : *The Epic of Gilgamesh, An English Version with an
Introduction.* (Penguin Classics, L 100). 1960. Pp. 128, with a
map. (Penguin Books, Harmondsworth, Middlesex. Price :
3s. 6d.).

It was a happy thought to include this most ancient of epics
in the admirable series of Penguin Classics. It first became
known to the world in 1872 when George Smith of the British
Museum announced that he had discovered an account of
the Deluge in a cuneiform tablet from the library of Asshur-
banipal. Further discoveries revealed that this was the XIth
tablet of a long epic poem describing the adventures of
Gilgamesh, an ancient king of Erech, and his friend Enkidu.
In 1928 Campbell Thompson published the *editio princeps*
of the Epic with text, transliteration, and an English verse
translation. Since then much new material has been discovered,
including fragments of the poem, showing that the age of
the Epic is far greater than that of the Assyrian version and
goes back into the third millennium B.C. Numerous English
translations have appeared in recent years, including an
excellent version by Professor Speiser in Pritchard's *Ancient
Near Eastern Texts Relating to the Old Testament.* But a cheap
and popular edition of this great poem was greatly needed,
and has now been provided by this admirable translation with
an equally admirable introduction, the work of one of our
younger English Assyriologists.

S.H.H.

ROLLA, A. : *L'Ambiente Biblico.* (Biblioteca di scienze religiose, II, 4).
1959. Pp. 182+2 maps. (Editrice Morcelliana, Brescia. Price :
L. 600).

This is a highly compressed study of the Biblical *milieu* or
setting, and is concerned with four topics, each of which has
its chapter to itself. These are the geography of the Holy
Land, Palestinian archaeology, the prehistory and history
of Palestine, and the peoples of the ancient Near East (here, as
so often, called Middle East). It is adequately indexed, but
the two maps supplied (of Central Palestine and of Southern
Palestine and Transjordan) are too small to be of much
service.

J.M.T.B.

Tocci, F. M. : *La Siria nell'età di Mari*. (Studi Semitici 3). 1960. Pp. 112+1 table+1 map. (Centro di Studi Semitici, Istituto di Studi Orientali, Rome).

The title delimits the field of inquiry. The principal source is constituted by the Mari texts, integrated occasionally with archaeological data and a few cylinder seals. The author states accurately the chronological and geographical limits : Syria in the first half of the XVIII century B.C. Syria is considered in its more or less traditional confines, with the exclusion of Palestine. The fragmentary character of the sources does not allow an organic history of the region. An account is given of the relations between the sovereigns of Mari (Yaḫdun-lim, Yasmaḫ-Addu, Zimri-lim) and of Assyria (Šamši-Addu, Išme-Dagan) with the independent or vassal princes of the more important city-states of Syria. The information furnished by the sources is discontinuous : while it abounds for some places, as, for instance, Yamḫad with its capital Aleppo and for Qatna, it is very scanty for other cities like Palmyra (Tadmor), Damascus, Alalaḫ, Hamat, Tyre, etc. A middle position is held by the cities of Carchemish and Elaḫut. The author never indulges in daring hypothesis. Analyzing the Mari texts, with the help of the specified bibliography, he distinguishes what is certain from what is merely conjectural. As to the chronology, he prefers the 'middle' one as fixed by S. Smith, which places Hammurabi in the years 1792-1750. The work of easy consultation by means of the indexes and enhanced by a chronological table and a map, may be considered complementary, in some aspects, to the larger and more organic work by Kupper on the Nomads in Mesopotamia in the Mari period. Lacking the total publication of the texts, the volume cannot, of course, claim to be final.

A.P.

van Zyl, A. H. : *The Moabites*. 1960. Pp. XII+240+1 map (+1 addendum containing the text of the Mesha inscription). (E. J. Brill, Leiden. Price : Fl. 15).

This thorough and well-documented monograph is the adaptation of the author's doctoral thesis at the University of Pretoria. After a methodical description of the sources, Hebrew, Moabite, Assyrian, Egyptian, Josephus, and Apocryphal, which often serves to indicate the limitation of the subject, the author discusses the topography of Moab, assembling the results of Glueck's topographical researches and archaeological survey. The survey of Moabite history, which follows, constitutes the body of the book and that part which is of chief value for Old Testament study, since theories old and new are carefully considered, the documentation again being very careful. The language is methodically studied

on the basis of the Mesha inscription, which is freshly reconstructed in an appendix. This also has real value for Old
Testament research. The final chapter on the religion of
Moab is scanty, but necessarily so, since the author refuses to
overdraw his evidence.
                                                                    J.G.

THE DEAD SEA SCROLLS

ALLEGRO, J. M. : *The Treasures of the Copper Scroll. The opening and
decipherment of the most mysterious of the Dead Sea Scrolls. A
unique inventory of buried teasure.* 1960. Pp. 191, including 9
plates, and 18 line drawings of maps and plans. (Routledge and
Kegan Paul, London, Price : 35s. 0d.).

Mr. Allegro graphically tells the story of the discovery and
opening of the scroll and then gives a drawn facsimile, transcription and translation of twelve columns of text, which he
divides into 61 items. After six brief chapters of discussion
he adds 323 notes to the translation. For review purposes the
middle section is best treated separately.

The textual treatment and annotation is admitted by the
author to be ' provisional ', and a perusal cannot but confirm
the need for caution. The one photograph of the scroll reproduced in the book shows that the text is virtually impossible
to decipher, and we cannot but congratulate Mr. Allegro on
his success in presenting the material and hope that better
pictures will be available for further study. Meantime, the
rendering by J. T. Milik in *Revue Biblique*, vol. 66, 1959, pp.
321-357, will be an obvious alternative to the present rendering.

Chapters 3 to 8 deal with the contents of the ' treasure ' :
silver and gold (in talents and bars), vessels made of both and
pitchers containing silver. Mr. Allegro says they came from
the Temple. The hiding places were (a) about the Dead Sea,
(b) near Jericho, and (c) Jerusalem. In the first area the
scroll's Secacah was in Wady Qumran, in the second lies Mount
Gerizim (cf. also the Madeba mosaic), in the last the Temple
area, the Tyropoeon, Hinnom, and Kidron Valleys figure
prominently. The people responsible for hiding the treasures
were the Zealots who, of course, had taken over control of
Jerusalem by A.D. 67 and who, according to Allegro, had
taken over control of Qumran some months before its destruction in 68. ' The Essenes had nothing at all to do with '
hiding the treasures or the scroll, he says. But the writer
has much more to say : some of his guesses are attractive,
others are rather over-played, but they are never dull. And
the book is excellently produced.   B.J.R.

BARDTKE, H. : *Die Handschriften am Toten Meer. Die Sekte von Qumran.*
1958. Pp. VIII+338+20 plates. (Evangelische Haupt-
Bibelgesellschaft, Berlin. Price : DM. 12.80).

This is the second volume of the author's general treatment
of the scrolls, and is complementary to the first (2nd ed. 1953).
The present work is divided into three sections : discussions
of various topics such as the history of the Qumran area, the
archaeological finds there, the manuscripts (only 1Q Isa
and the Hab. commentary having been discussed in vol. 1),
dating and the relationship of Qumran to Christendom. In
the second section fifteen Qumran texts are translated and
in the third the relevant parts of Philo and Josephus concerning the Essenes are translated.
The work covers ground which is largely familiar, but is marked
by competence and judicious assessments. It is probably one
of the most concise of the thoroughgoing treatments of the
scrolls, and will be very useful to the specialist who needs to
keep in mind an over-all view of the scrolls. B.J.R.

BENOIT, P., MILIK, J. T. and DE VAUX, R. : *Discoveries in the Judaean
Desert.* II. *Les Grottes de Murabba'at.* (2 vols.) 1961. Texte :
Pp. xvi+304 ; Planches : CVII. (Clarendon Press, Oxford
University Press, London. Price : 168s. 0d.).

This superb scholarly work, written mainly in French, comprises material discovered in the caves of Wadi Murabba'at,
chiefly in 1952. It is made up of twin volumes, the one containing the texts and the other the plates. The texts volume,
which begins with a chapter on the archaeology of the finds
by R. de Vaux, gives the history of the discoveries and discusses their significance. To this is added a special account
written in English by G. M. and Elizabeth Crowfoot about
the textiles and basketry. The second chapter, contributed
by J. T. Milik, constitutes over half of the number of the
pages of the entire volume and deals with the Hebrew and
Aramaic texts. The third and the fourth chapters, the one
concerning itself with Greek and Latin texts and the other
with Arabic texts, are by P. Benoit and A. Grohmann respectively. The plates volume begins with two plates, the
one showing Wadi Murabba'at and the other some of the
documents in the state in which they were found. These are
followed by twelve plates giving exhibits relating to the
Chalcolithic, Bronze, and Roman Periods, the exhibits of the
last by far outnumbering those of the two former. Plates
XV-XVIII which follow give samples of the various textiles
and basketry. Of the remaining plates, XIX-LXXIII contain
Hebrew and Aramaic texts ; LXXIV-CV Greek and Latin
texts ; and CVI-CVII Arabic texts.
Of direct interest to the Biblical scholar are : 1. Fragments
drawn from Gen. xxxii ; xxxiv and xxxv ; Ex. iv-vi ; Num.
xxxiv and xxxvi ; Deut. x-xii (from the last two sources the
fragments are rather small). 2. Small fragments from the
first half of Is. i 3. Complete phylacteries, containing, in the

order given in volume, Ex. xiii 1-10 ; 11-16 ; Deut. xi
13-21 ; vi 4-9. 4. A scroll of the Minor Prophets, found in
1955. This, severely damaged by the elements, contains
large and small fragments from Joel ii 20 ; ii 26-iv 16 ;
Amos i 5-ii 1 ; vii 3-viii 7 ; viii 11-ix 15 ; Obadiah ; Jonah ;
Micah ; Nahum ii 12-iii 19 ; Habakkuk ; Zephaniah ; Haggai ;
Zechariah i, 1-4. In all the four items variants compared with
the M.T. are relatively few and at that slight. Among other
papyrus objects, the palimpsest containing a message written
in archaic Hebrew script, which judging by palaeographical
and other evidence dates most likely from the eighth
century B.C., is of interest to the Hebrew scholar in general.
Much of the other material contains copious information
about the Second Jewish Revolt against Rome, and is complementary to those known from a preliminary report by
Y. Yadin of the finds made in March, 1960, in a cave near the
river Heber to the north of Massadah (See *Bulletin of the I.E.C.*
volume XXV, 1-2 1961). A bill of sale of a plot of land written
in Hebrew which begins with the words ' On the twenty-first
of Tishre of the fourth year of the Redemption of Israel '
is of chronological importance. The work ends with three
valuable indexes.

For review of *Discoveries I* see *Book List*, 1956, p. 64 ; *Eleven
Years*, p. 771.   M.W.

BETZ, O. : *Offenbarung und Schriftforschung in der Qumransekte.*
(Wissenschaftliche Untersuchungen zum Neuen Testament, 6).
1960. Pp. xii+202. (Mohr, Tübingen. Price : DM. 24.20).

The men of Qumran were earnest Bible students, but this
alone did not mark them off from their fellow-Jews. What
did mark them off was the conviction, implied in the very
terms of the community oath, that they alone possessed
the key to the understanding of the Scriptures, and that all
others were sinners against the divine law and apostates from
the covenant. The conviction that they alone possessed the
key is bound up with the belief that the key was ' revealed
to the sons of Zadok '. The interpretation as well as the text,
the *pesher* as well as the *raz*, was a matter of divine revelation ;
and the primary recipient of the interpretative revelation was
the Teacher of Righteousness, the *doresh hattorah* of CD vi.
7. He is called the *doresh hattorah* in the explanation of the
Song of the Well (Num. xxi. 17f.), and Dr. Betz draws an
illuminating parallel between this explanation and the sayings
of Moses in 1Q 22, where the Israelites are commanded to
appoint men who would explain to them and their children
all the words of the law. The Teacher of Righteousness is
viewed as belonging to this expository succession ; indeed,
according to Dr. Betz, he is presented as a second Moses, a
prophetic figure, but not the eschatological ' prophet like
Moses '. This is only one sample of the many important discussions in Dr. Betz's work. For students of Qumran exegesis
it is indispensable.   F.F.B.

Bič, M. : *Poklad v Judské poušti. Kumránské nálezy.* (= *The Treasure in the Desert of Judaea. The Qumran Discoveries*). 1960. Pp. 310 (Cyclostyled). (Ustřední církevní nakladaleství, Prague. Price : Kčs. 48).

This is the first comprehensive work on the Qumran discoveries to appear in Czech : and readers of the *Book List* may be interested to know of its existence and of its contents. Being unable to read Czech, and having got to know of this work too late to find a suitably qualified reviewer in time for this issue of the *Book List*, I simply record the following summary, which has been supplied to me. The first chapter describes the discoveries ; and to it are added sections on the finds in the time of Origen and Timotheos and on the origin and history of the Sect. The second is devoted to the Biblical texts, and to the reliability of the MT and the LXX in the light of the Qumran MSS. The third contains translations of parts of the non-Biblical documents. The last chapter consists of an account of the life and faith of the Sect, with an excursus on Sects in Judaism and some observations on the significance of the discoveries for the study of the New Testament and the origins of the Church.

G.W.A.

Brongers, H. A. : *De Rol van de Strijd.* 1960. Pp. 127. (Proost & Brandt, Amsterdam).

This little study of the Qumran *Rule of War* belongs to a series entitled ' De Handschriften van de Dode Zee in Nederlandse Vertaling '. It would be good if someone would launch a similar series in English, intended to introduce the Qumran texts to the non-specialist reader who would like to be as well-informed about them as is possible for anyone who knows no Hebrew or Aramaic. The nearest thing we have in English is Gaster's translation of *The Scriptures of the Dead Sea Sect*, but this Dutch series makes room for much fuller notes than can be accommodated in Gaster's single volume. Here a commendatory foreword by Professor Vriezen is followed by twenty pages of introduction to the *Rule of War*, a translation of the document into Dutch, and fifty-seven pages of notes on the translation. Dr. Brongers evidently thinks that the problems of the composition of the work are more complicated than some of its editors have allowed ; he cannot believe that 1QM represents an original literary unity, and in general follows van der Ploeg's view of its structure. On the date of the work he reserves judgement, partly because he does not think that the identity of the Kittim of Assur and the Kittim in Egypt can be decided on our evidence thus far. His cautious treatment of the various questions involved means that the reader will not be misled into thinking that some highly individual interpretation is the only possible one. The views of Yadin, Carmignac and others are referred to as well as those of van der Ploeg. A useful bibliography is provided at the end.

F.F.B.

BROWNLEE, W. H. : *The Text of Habakkuk in the Ancient Commentary from Qumran.* (Journal of Biblical Literature Monograph Series, Vol. XI). 1959. Pp. viii+130. (Society of Biblical Literature and Exegesis, Philadelphia. Price : $1.50).

This study was originally prepared as part of the author's contribution to the completed edition of *The Dead Sea Scrolls of St. Mark's Monastery* (of which the second fascicle, published in 1951, is the only part to have appeared). It was written substantially in its present form in 1954. Here we are presented with a careful and valuable analysis of the text of the first two chapters of Habakkuk as exhibited in 1QpHab. About 140 significant features are studied. Many of these are orthographical variants, principally *plene* spellings as against *defective* spellings of MT. The proportion of *defective* spellings is greater in the Biblical text than in the commentary ; the *Vorlage* was probably much more *defective* than is the Biblical text of 1QpHab., and the spelling was accommodated, but not consistently, to the scribe's preference for *scriptio plena*. Even more important is Brownlee's treatment of the evidence for the commentator's knowledge of substantial textual variants. He recognizes the probability that *mo'adehem* in Hab. ii. 15 is a deliberate alteration ; for the rest, it emerges quite clearly that the commentary sometimes makes use not only of the cited reading but also of a variant known to the commentator. The monograph is an important contribution to the study of the pre-Massoretic Biblical text.

F.F.B.

DUPONT-SOMMER, A. : *Die essenischen Schriften vom Toten Meer,* translated by W. W. Müller. 1960. Pp. xvi+458. (Mohr, Tübingen. Price : DM. 32, or bound 36).

This translation into German of the French work which was reviewed in the *Book List* for 1960 (p. 46) contains some additions not in the original edition. These include sections on Fragments from Cave 4 published since the French work appeared and an expansion of the appendix on the Copper Scroll. Some additional items have also been added to the bibliography. The translator has worked with the original Hebrew and Aramaic texts before him, as well as with the French translations. The high value and importance of this work was sufficiently indicated in the previous notice.

H.H.R.

HOLM-NIELSEN, S. : *Hodayot, Psalms from Qumran.* (Acta Theologica Danica. Vol. II). 1960. Pp. 366. (Universitetsforlaget Aarhus. Price : D.Kr. 50 ; bound D.Kr. 55).

This doctoral thesis contains a full discussion of the Songs of Thanksgiving : the text is in English with a five-page summary in Danish. The 18 columns of original text are divided into 19 Psalms ; and fragments of another 12, and the fragmentary manuscripts are also included. A translation of each Psalm is followed by a full annotation, a discussion of the ' Use of Scripture ' and ' concluding remarks ' ; and in the introduction and four concluding essays the author discusses the question of the unity of the Hymn scrolls, the theological conceptions, the use of the Old Testament, the literary origin and the purpose of the Songs. He is negative about the identity of the author with the Righteous Teacher, and regards the songs ' as examples of the community's liturgical prayers and songs of praise '. There is a considerable amount of important material in the book—and the writer proceeds cautiously to establish his conclusions, especially the more negative ones. But I trust he will forgive an older man for hoping he will grow out of his ultra-discursive manner of presenting a scholarly work.   B.J.R.

APOCRYPHA AND POST-BIBLICAL JUDAISM

BARON, S. W. : *A Social and Religious History of the Jews*, 2nd Edition. Index to Volumes I-VIII. 1960. Pp. xii + 164. (Columbia University Press, and Oxford University Press, London. Price : 48s. 0d.).

This volume contains (1) a chronological table of principal events and personalities ; (2) the index proper which is a faithful companion to vols. I-VIII. For a review of the first 2 vols., see *Book List*, 1953, pp. 24f ; for a review of vols. III-V, see *Book List*, 1958, pp. 52f. and for vols. VI-VIII, see *Book List*, 1959, pp. 41f.   M.W.

BRUNNER, G. : *Der Nabuchodonosor des Buches Judith. Beitrag zur Geschichte Israels nach dem Exil und des ersten Regierungsjahres Darius I.* Zweite gekürzte und erweiterte Auflage. 1959. Pp. 166. (Kommissionsverlag F. A. Günther & Sohn, Berlin.)

This book was originally published in 1940, but because of the War was little known outside Germany : and since stocks were destroyed during the defence of Berlin, a new edition has been issued, with some abbreviation, but also with additional matter, including replies to criticisms and consideration of more recent work. With much industry and in great detail the author labours to prove that Judith is not a historical romance reflecting conditions and events in the Maccabaean age, but a record of events at the end of the reign of Cambyses and the beginning of the reign of Darius. While dissenting from the general view of the book and the ingenious suggested identifications of some of the characters in Judith, the reviewer recognizes the labour which has been devoted to this amply documented study.   G.W.A.

CORRENS, D. : *Schebiit (Vom Sabbatjahr)*. Text, übersetzung, und Erklärung nebst einem textkritischen Anhang und zwei Karten. (Die Mischna, ed. Rengstorf-Rost). 1960. Pp. VIII+180+2 maps. (A. Töpelmann, Berlin. Price : DM. 28).

A worthy continuation of the series. The translation is reliable and the commentary helpful. The introduction deals helpfully with the position of the tractate in the Mishnah, the history of the Seventh Year, the agricultural year in Palestine, and the relation of the Mishnic tractate to the corresponding one in the Tosephta. There are minor errors. In 10.9 we learn that if a gentile and his children become Jews, in strict law a debt owing to the former need not, on his death, be paid to the latter, though the Rabbis strongly recommend such payment. According to the author, the reason for the absence of a strict duty is a proselyte's inferior status, ' between heathens and Israelites'. But this is wrong. It would be inexplicable on this basis why a debt to a gentile does, on his death, become payable to his heirs. The point is that the convert and his children all of them count as newly born. Hence they are no longer related. In principle, even the rules of incest do not apply—of course the Rabbis mitigated this consequence.

D.D.

GUILDING, A. : *The Fourth Gospel and Jewish Worship : A study of the relation of St. John's Gospel to the ancient Jewish lectionary system*. 1960. Pp. 248. (Clarendon Press : Oxford University Press, London. Price : 30s. 0d.).

This learned book is divided into two parts. In Part I (the shorter) the author discusses the lectionary system as it was used in Judaism in New Testament times ; in Part II she deals with the relation of the Fourth Gospel to the lectionary, and to the feasts. Part II is claimed to provide confirmation for the results of Part I, for it is argued that the sets of *sedarim* and *haphtaroth* as established in Part I reappear in the units of miracle and discourse in the gospel. In part I Dr. Guilding follows for the most part the conclusions of Büchler in maintaining a triennial cycle of Torah lections, beginning in Nisan, though she allows some weight to Mann's view that the cycle began in Tishri ; practice was perhaps not uniform throughout Jewish cicles. She holds, against Strack-Billerbeck and other authorities, that a complete set of *haphtaroth* was already established in New Testament times. Dr. Guilding's main contention, however, in Part II, is that the pattern of the Fourth Gospel is determined by the sequence of the Jewish feasts. Jewish Christians who had been ' put out of the synagogue ' were to find a series of sermons, based on Jesus' own, which would reflect the familiar *sedarim*, together with the *haphtaroth* and related Psalms. The argument is to be taken very seriously.

C.K.B.

HARDUF, D. M. : *Millon u-Maphteah le-midreshey ha-Shemoth ha-T^{e}nakhiyyim ba-'Aggadah.* (Dictionary & Key to the Exegesis of Biblical Proper Names in the Talmud and Midrash). 1960. Pp. 182. (Izreel Publishing House, Tel Aviv).

This little book is an abridged form of a London *Ph.D,*Thesis, intended for the popular market in Israel. The material is arranged lexically, not alphabetically by names ; but cross-reference is made easy by a full alphabetic index of proper names (which includes place names). This has some advantages —it spotlights, for instance, the fact that in *Numbers Rabbah* chap. 10 the word *m^{e}nuhah* is said to be synonym of *n^{e}bhu'ah* in the course of an etymology given for Manoah. The references to source material are adequate for the specialist in rabbinics, and usable, albeit perhaps with some irritation, by the non-specialist who can read Hebrew. The author has not correlated his findings with either such modern scholarly investigations of *nomina sacra* as those of Buchanan Gray or M. Noth, or with Philo, Eusebius, and Jerome. The neglect of patristic sources is particularly to be regretted, but anyone who wishes to compare them with the rabbinic ones for himself now has quite a convenient jumping-off point.   R.L.

MAYBAUM, I. : Jewish Existence. 1960. Pp. 192. (Vallentine, Mitchell, London.   Price :   21s. 0d.).

This is an interesting confession of faith of a Jewish thinker who, while welcoming the state of Israel, still regards the meta-political, religious-moral mission of Judaism as its true *raison d'être*. The ten chapters are inscribed : The Bourgeois, the *Citoyen* and the Jew ; German Hellenism and Zionism ; Political Idealism ; Jacob and Esau ; The Priesthood of the Father ; Sanctification and Spiritualisation ; Two Commandments ; ' My Sober House ' ; Christian Prayer for the Jews ; Assimilation and Separation.   D.D.

PARKES, J. : *The Foundations of Judaism and Christianity.* 1960. Pp. xvi+344. (Vallentine, Mitchell, London. Price : 42s. 0d.).

The theme of the book is that Christianity is not the only legitimate development of the Old Testament, particularly of post-exilic Judaism. The concluding sentence of the book is ' Judaism is not a substitute for Christianity, nor is its mission made unnecessary by the existence of the Christian Church '. There are incidental studies of importance, concerning which the author has good, and sometimes provocative things to say : origin of the Scriptures, the synagogue, and the new Temple. His study of the centuries of common growth and his picture of Palestine in A.D. 30

are both useful. The book should be read ; it gives a fairer picture of post-Temple Judaism than most people have, and it says some things about the development of the Christian Church which are well worth consideration.

N.H.S.

PFEIFFER, C. F. : *Between the Testaments*. 1959. Pp. 132. (Baker Book House, Grand Rapids, Michigan. Price : $2.95).

This is virtually a history of the period from the rise of Cyrus to the death of Herod. The author's interest lies in the sequence of historical events rather than in the life and literature of the Jews. It is only in the last two chapters that he departs from strict historical treatment to give a brief description of the Jewish sects and an account of the rise of Apocalyptic literature.

There are some inadequate statements, as, for instance, that ' Ezra and Nehemiah headed processions which moved around the walls in opposite directions ' (p. 47), and, ' With this (Nehemiah's second reform), both the Book of Nehemiah and the history of the Old Testament comes to a close '. (p. 48).

L.H.B.

RAVENNA, A. : *L'Ebraismo Postbiblico*. (Biblioteca di Scienze Religiose, IX, 8). 1958. Pp. 152. (Editrice Morcelliana, Brescia. Price : L. 500).

This is another useful addition to the series of booklets on non-Christian religions. In eight closely-packed chapters Ravenna discusses the history of post-biblical Judaism, Hebrew religious life, anniversaries, doctrinal tenets, the influence of mysticism, and various dissenting groups, such as the Samaritans. The final section deals shortly and objectively with religious life in the existing state of Israel.

J.M.T.B.

RUSSELL, D. S. : *Between the Testaments*. 1960. Pp. 176. (S.C.M. Press, London. Price : 12s. 6d.).

The emphasis here is on the life, thought, and literature of the Jews in the period between the Testaments rather than in the sequence of historical events as such. It is to be welcomed as a scholarly treatment within a small compass. Part I is concerned with the contrast between Judaism and Hellenism, the significance of the Jewish emphasis on the Law, the rise of the Jewish sects, including the Qumran community, and the development of Apocalyptic literature. The second part deals with the Apocalyptists and gives an account of the main elements in their writings and message.

Such few criticisms as the book may arouse are probably due to the necessary brevity of treatment, for instance, it is probably not fair to Alexander Jannaeus to say that he ' purposely flouted ritual requirements by pouring out the water libation on the ground ' (p. 33) ; it was surely the Pharisees whom he was flouting.   L.H.B.

TCHERIKOVER, V. : *Hellenistic Civilization and the Jews*, trans. by S. Applebaum. 1959. Pp. x+566. (Jewish Publication Society of America, Philadelphia. Price : $6.00).

This work comes from the late Head of the Departments of Classics and History in the Hebrew University, whose studies were concentrated from first to last on the Hellenistic age. Here we have the course of Hellenistic civilization traced from Alexander's invasion to the first century B.C., with special reference to the history of the Jews in this environment, both in Palestine and in the Diaspora. This period of Jewish history is one of unsurpassed interest, not least because of the scarcity and ambiguity of our sources ; and Tcherikover deals with the controversial issues one by one and voices his judgement on them in a way that commands respect if not always agreement. An attempt is made, for example, to clarify the history of Joseph the Tobiad and the principles which he introduced into Judaea. The roots of Antiochus's Jewish policy are examined ; Tcherikover's conclusion is that after Jason's failure to regain the high priesthood the control of Jerusalem passed to the anti-Hellenizing Jews, and Menelaus and the Hellenists were shut up in the citadel. This is why Jerusalem was treated as a hostile city. Menelaus's family is discussed fully in an appendix. All that can be said in mitigation of the Hasmoneans' destruction of centres of Greek culture is said here ; the judgements expressed by E. Meyer and E. R. Bevan are criticized. There are good accounts of Greek writers who deal with Jewish affairs, such as Hecataeus and Manetho. All this and much more combine to make this book a contribution of high importance for this phase of Jewish history.   F.F.B.

TESTUZ, M. : *Les idées religieuses du Livre des Jubilés*. 1960. Pp. 208. (Droz, Geneva and Minard, Paris. Price: Sw. Frs. 18).

For its study of the ideas of the book of Jubilees on the creation of the world, on good and bad spirits, on the two ways, on ritual and moral laws, on the calendar and on the last times, this work is to be warmly commended. More doubtful are the author's views that Jubilees was written by an Essene *circa* 110 B.C. and that it preceded the Zadokite Work by three-quarters of a century. On the calendar he dissents from the view of Mlle. Jaubert in that he maintains that the first day of the year in the calendar of Jubilees fell on Sunday, and makes the unlikely suggestion that this calendar was modified shortly after the composition of Jubilees. This does not lessen the reviewer's appreciation of the valuable material assembled here, or of the clear and well-supported examination of the ideas which are found in Jubilees.

H.H.R.

WALLENSTEIN, M. : *Hebrew MS. 6 in the John Rylands Library, with Special Reference to Two Hitherto Unknown Poems by Yehudah (Halevi?)* (Reprinted from the *Bulletin of the John Rylands Library*, vol. 43. No. 1, September, 1960). 1960. Pp. 243-272. (The John Rylands Library and the Manchester University Press, Manchester. Price : 6s. 0d.).

The Manuscript, which contains the 14th cent. Spanish Passover Haggadah, has well-known illuminated texts, and, more important, divergent Haggadoth, original commentaries on the Seder ritual and other items. The last includes some otherwise unknown hymns, and it is mainly two of these which Wallenstein discusses in his usual workmanlike manner in the present article. The text is reproduced, carefully annotated, and translated : reasons are given for attributing both (one more strongly than the other) to Jehudah Halevi, and the relevance of Jehudah's treatise *Kuzari* is much in evidence. It is as a tribute to the success of the present monograph to add that there are unpublished manuscripts of genuine Jehudah Halevi hymns in the Genizah fragments at the British Museum, and one non-Jewish reader at least would welcome a treatment of them by Meir Wallenstein.

B.J.R.

WIESENBERG, E. J. : *Abraham son of Maimonides's Commentary on Genesis and Exodus*, ed. and transl. into Hebrew. 1960. Pp. 539 + 63. (S. D. Sassoon, Letchworth, Herts. Price: 60s. 0d.).

The only MS of this Arabic commentary in Hebrew script is in Bodley, and it is here edited and translated into Hebrew for the first time. (Portions had been published before, and for Genesis Dr. Wiesenberg was able to use a translation, not published, by J. Dori.) The original and the translation are presented facing each other, the former on the left, the latter on the right. There is a thorough introduction, and the text is provided with illuminating footnotes. The whole is beautifully produced, for which thanks are due also to Rabbi Sassoon, who indeed suggested the undertaking. The MS was written at Aleppo (finished in 1375) for a grandson of the commentary's author. There are gaps ; but what we have forms an impressive specimen of medieval Spanish-Jewish Biblical exegesis. Dr. Wiesenberg has performed a major service to scholarship

D.D.

YARON, R. : *Gifts in Contemplation of Death in Jewish and Roman Law.*
1960. Pp. xiv+250. (Clarendon Press, Oxford. Price : 35s. 0d.).

A masterly historical exposition of the Jewish law concerning
dispositions in contemplation of death, a subject of particular
interest seeing that Jewish law does without a testament
proper. The bulk of the material is post-Biblical, though the
Bible and the Aramaic papyri are fully discussed. No praise
can be too high for the way in which original, penetrating ideas
are here combined with philological accuracy and a sure grip
on methodical principles. Some chapters are really exciting-
e.g., those in which it is shewn that the two Tannaitic dispositions go back one of them, *mattana*, to the Egyptian gift
meta ten teleuten, the other, *deyathiqi*, to the Greek *diatehke ;*
but that the Rabbis put these institutions to new uses, in
such a way that each fulfilled a definite purpose. The work
is exhaustive, and contains illuminating comparisons with
other systems, in particular Roman law.   D.D.

PHILOLOGY AND GRAMMAR

ENGNELL, I. : *Grammatik i gammaltestamentlig hebreiska.* (Scandinavian
University Books.) 1960. Pp. 184 (Svenska Bokförlaget/Norstedts
Stockholm. J. W. Cappelens Forlag, Oslo. Gyldendalske Boghandel/
Nordisk Forlag, Copenhagen. Akateeminen Kirjakauppa/
Akademiska Bokhandeln, Helsingfors. Price : Sw. Kr. 23.50).

More than 25 years of teaching experience in Hebrew is embodied in this Hebrew Grammar whose appearance was
occasioned by the revision of the Swedish theological curri-
culum in 1955 which seriously reduced requirements in the
reading of Hebrew texts. Consequently this grammar is
primarily intended for beginners and does not give a complete
treatment of Old Testament Hebrew.

This, however, has not deterred the author from discussing
many of the theoretical and much-debated questions within
the field of Hebrew philology in such an original way that the
book very definitely carries the stamp of the scholar as well
as that of the educationalist. This holds true, e.g., of his
conception of the nominal and the verbal sentences and
above all of his view of the highly complex problem of tenses.
Engnell is here greatly indebted to Johs. Pedersen but he goes
a step further in maintaining the absence of any tense-element
in his concept of the Hebrew ' perfect ' and ' imperfect '.
According to Engnell the difference between these two
principal forms originates in a difference in dignity, the
' perfect ' thus denoting a higher degree of dignity as compared
to the ' imperfect ' (cf. pp. 154 ff). It would be desirable,

however, if Engnell's conception of this problem could be known to a wider circle than the chosen few who can read his book in Swedish. Therefore it is to be hoped that the author will consider the possibility of publishing his views in a scientific periodical which has an international circulation.

                                                                                E.H.

HULST, A. R. (and others) : *Old Testament Translation Problems.* (Help for Translators prepared under the auspices of the United Bible Societies, Vol. 1). 1960. Pp. XVI+262. (E. J. Brill, Leiden. Price : Fl. 12.50).

This volume has been prepared under the auspices of the United Bible Societies by the committee which has made the new Dutch translation of the Old Testament. It is intended for the use of Bible translators. Presumably the translators are expected to have a good working knowledge of Hebrew, for the editor is careful to give his evidence (in transliteration) ; but for such translators much of the information given is gratuitous, for they will have it in their *Biblia Hebraica* or in the commentaries to which they must have access to take advantage of the advice : ' Cf. the commentaries '. Clearly in a book of this size only a selected number of passages could be discussed and it is not obvious how the verses for examination were chosen, for very many difficulties have been passed over ; but again the reader is referred to commentaries where the present volume gives no help. Professor Hulst has performed carefully his task of editing his committee's discussions, and it is useful to have this record. He is not responsible for the introduction.

                                                                            W.D.McH.

JEAN, C.-F. and HOFTIJZER, J. : *Dictionnaire des inscriptions sémitiques de l'Ouest.* Livr. I, II. 1960. Pp. XVI+128. (Brill, Leiden. Price : Fl. 36).

In 1954 C.-F. Jean published the first two fascicles of a work bearing the above title which was designed to include all the words in West-Semitic texts, outside the O.T. (see *Book List*, 1955, p. 72). When, at his death, the work was unfinished, J. Hoftijzer was charged with the task of completing it. The most important changes which have been introduced into this new edition are the inclusion of the most recent material and the treatment of each word entered under two heads. The grammatical and orthographical forms which are found in each language are first given, and then the translation of the word into French. These and other changes will be fully discussed by the editor in an introduction which will appear later. Later on too a supplement will be issued which will include recent literature which it was not possible to include on this occasion and also some articles which are not so recent but which have not been accessible to the editor up to the present. The two fascicles cover ' to ktb. The material is well set out, the particular languages in which the word occurs being especially clearly marked. The twelve pages of abbreviations testify to the wide field from which the material has been gleaned. If comment is aroused at some points (e.g., some dubious readings in the Lachish letters are perpetuated, and relevant literature could in some cases be curtailed, in others supplemented), Semitic students will appreciate the way in which the editor has carried out his difficult task, and they will be grateful for his ' new Lidzbarski ' which will provide them with much needed help. They will hope profoundly that it may be brought to a successful conclusion.

D.W.T.

BOOK LIST, 1962

For various reasons several members of the Book List Panel have had to undertake fewer reviews than might otherwise have been possible. The number of other scholars to whom I have had to turn for help is therefore larger than usual : Professors de Boer and Cazelles, The Revd. J. A. Emerton, Professor Hammershaimb, The Revd. D. R. Jones, Professor Lindblom, Mr. R. Loewe, Professors Neher and Noth, Professor Sweetman, Dr. Vermes, and Professor Weingreen. To them and to the regular members of the Panel I express my gratitude for their co-operation and for their patience with my importunity. I am also indebted to Mr. I. J. C. Foster, Keeper of Oriental Books in the Library of the Durham Colleges, and to Mr. C. N. Francis of the firm of B. H. Blackwell, Oxford, for supplying bibliographical data. As always I have been able to rely on the courteous and prompt help of the Printer. Without his help the editing of the *Book List* would be an even more arduous task.

The arrangement of reviews follows the pattern adopted in previous issues. Books recommended as suitable for inclusion in school libraries have been marked with an asterisk.

Experience shows that few items of information are harder to communicate than a change of address. I therefore record here (as I shall do elsewhere) that from 1st August, 1962, all review copies of books and all communications relating to the *Book List* should be addressed to me at NEW COLLEGE, EDINBURGH.

G. W. ANDERSON.

UNIVERSITY OF DURHAM.

GENERAL

BEEK, M. A. : *Auf den Wegen und Spuren des Alten Testaments*, aus dem Niederländischen übersetzt von Cola Minis. 1961. Pp. VIII+ 308. (J. C. B. Mohr, Tübingen. Price : paper, DM.24 ; cloth, DM. 28).

This is a translation of Professor Beek's *Wegen en voetsporen van het Oude Testament* (*Book List*, 1954, p. 45 ; *Eleven Years*, p. 582 ; for the English translation see *Book List*, 1960, p. 4.). Some chapters have been abbreviated, six have been omitted (those on the Book of Judges, the Song of Deborah, David as a psalmist, Jeremiah and his friends, Esther and the feast of Purim, and on history of the post-exilic period), together with the entire section on the growth and transmission of the Old Testament, and the illustrations. This vivid presentation of so much of the content of the Old Testament will doubtless continue to have a wide circulation and to stimulate the interest of the general reader.
G.W.A.

BIČ, M. and SOUČEK, J. B. (ed. by) : *Biblická Konkordance*, part 17. *Oltář-Pardus*. 1961. Pp. 80. (Edice Kalich, Prague. Price : Kčs. 10.50).

This unique concordance, whose publication has been unavoidably suspended since 1959, has now resumed its course. Its character has been noted in previous *Book Lists*. It is not merely a concordance to the Czech Bible, but it indicates by symbols the word in the original Hebrew or Greek represented by each word, and in the case of the Old Testament the word in the LXX represented.
H.H.R.

BOWMAN, J. (ed. by) : *Abr-Nahrain*. An annual under the Auspices of the Department of Semitic Studies, University of Melbourne. Vol. I (1959-1960). 1961. Pp. 80. (E. J. Brill, Leiden. Price : Fl. 12).

Articles of interest to Old Testament Scholars are : A. Guillaume : ' Hebrew and Arabic Lexicography. A comparative Study '. This contains a most valuable list of Arabic parallels not noted in Köhler-Baumgartner for Hebrew words in the Old Testament with a discussion of some of the most important. W. Culican : 'Aspects of Phoenician Settlement in the West Mediterranean ' : a careful survey of recent archaeological material from Phoenician sites indicates that settlements began in the second half of the eighth century B.C. (Carthage). F. I. Anderson : ' The Early Sumerian City-State in recent Soviet Historiography '. This draws attention to certain valuable contributions from Soviet scholars on this subject especially to sociological and political factors. J. Bowman : 'An Interesting Leningrad Samaritan Manuscript ':

313

a discussion of MS Firkovitch 1, section IV no. 19, Arabic with Samaritan Bible quotations in Hebrew, possibly fourteenth century. An examination of the 48 positive Commandments indicates the nature of Samaritan orthodoxy. The title of the publication is intended to indicate the interest in ' the regions beyond in Africa and Asia'.

A.S.H.

BULTMANN, R. and WEISER, A. : *Faith,* trans. by Dorothea M. Barton and ed. by P. R. Ackroyd. (Bible Key Words from Gerhard Kittel's *Theologisches Wörterbuch zum Neuen Testament.*) 1961. Pp. xiv+ 126. (A. & C. Black, London. Price : 12s. 6d.).

Practically the entire text of the article *pistis* from the Kittel-Friedrich *Wörterbuch* is here translated with some rearrangement of the sections, and some bibliographical additions. In his editorial preface Professor Ackroyd includes an anticipatory reference to Professor Barr's *The Semantics of Biblical Language* (Cf. this *Book List,* p. 81), which is the more appropriate in view of the latter's discussion of ' faith' and ' truth '.

G.W.A.

CAZELLES, H. and FEUILLET, A. : *Dictionnaire de la Bible. Supplément.* Fasc. xxxvi. (Pastorales—Paul.) 1961. Columns 1-256. (Letouzey & Ané, Paris. Price : 23s. 6d.).

The seventh volume of the *Supplément* to Vigouroux's *Dictionnaire* begins with the present fascicle, which, with two exceptions (one of these being a short article by G. Camps on Patmos) is devoted to introductions to St. Paul's epistles. The other exception is a notable study, running to seventy-five columns of print (81-156) by H. Cazelles, under the heading ' Patriarches '. This work is divided into sections which deal in turn with the state of the question, the Biblical and archaeological data, the archaeology of the sites traditionally associated with the patriarchs, the ethnographical data, the lives and characters of Abraham, Isaac, and Jacob as these are portrayed in Genesis, the latest information bearing upon their dates, and, finally, their religion. In Cazelles's submission the patriarchs are presented to us as persons who really lived, not as names of tribes, and their historical and geographical settings take on an increased importance when these are aligned with the data now accumulating about the movements of populations in the second millennium B.C. No separate bibliography is provided as a tail-piece to the article, but a large number of works are cited in the course of the investigation. As might be expected, this is a thorough and competent handling of the issues.

J.M.T.B.

CORNFELD, G. (ed. by) : *Adam to Daniel : An illustrated Guide to the Old Testament and its Background.* 1961. Pp. 560+many ills. (The Macmillan Company, New York. Price : $13.95).

This book has been produced in Israel by Hamikra Baolam Publishing House, Ltd. and much of its material has been drawn from Hamikra Ledorenu, an extensive Hebrew commentary on the Old Testament, shortly to be published. It is rightly described as a ' rich book ', being expensively produced and lavishly illustrated with hundreds of beautiful photographs, many in full colour, and many maps. Twenty-one chapters give a condensed, interesting, critical, well-illustrated account of Bible history from Genesis to the fifth century B.C. : two final chapters speak of the Wisdom literature and enter the Maccabean period with the book of Daniel ; the conclusion discusses the transmission of the text. The whole Bible background is seen in the light of archaeological discoveries and modern Biblical scholarship. Old Testament texts are quoted in full from the American Revised Standard Version. There is no index and, although many scholars are mentioned, there are no footnotes, documentation, or bibliography. It is an excellent library book or expensive present to gain interest in the Old Testament.

J.N.S.

EISSFELDT, O. : *Kleine Schriften*, herausgegeben von Rudolf Sellheim und Fritz Maass. Erster Band. 1962. Pp. 280. (J. C. B. Mohr, Tübingen. Price : paper, DM. 29 ; cloth, DM. 33).

This is the first of three volumes which will contain the most important of Professor Eissfeldt's articles in periodicals and composite works, arranged chronologically thus : vol. I, 1914-1931 ; vol. II, 1933-1945 ; vol. III, 1947 onwards. The 21 items here printed are : Jahve und Baal ; Zum Zehnten bei den Babyloniern ; Die Bedeutung der Märchenforschung für die Religionswissenschaft, besonders für die Wissenschaft vom Alten Testament ; Die Schichten des Hexateuch als vornehmste Quelle für den Aufriss einer israelitisch-jüdischen Kulturgeschichte ; Das Alte und das Neue Testament in ihrer Stellung zur Kultur ; Julius Wellhausen ; Christentum und Altes Testament ; Luther's "Ein Feste Burg " und der 46. Psalm ; Stammessage und Novelle in den Geschichten von Jakob und von seinen Söhnen ; Israelitische-jüdische Religionsgeschichte und alttestamentliche Theologie ; Vom Lebenswerk eines Religionshistorikers. Wolf Wilhelm von Baudissin ; Die kleinste literarische Einheit in den Erzählungsbüchern des Alten Testaments ; Jahwe-Name und Zauberwesen ; Jahwe als König ; Götternamen und Gottesvorstellungen bei den Semiten ; Der Gott Bethel ; Franz Delitzsch und Wolf Graf Baudissin ; Ezechiel als Zeuge für Sanheribs Eingriff in Palästina ; Werden, Wesen und Wert geschichtlicher Betrachtung der israelitisch-jüdisch-christlichen Religion ; Gott und Götzen im Alten Testament ; *jehūd* Jos. 19, 45 und *hē Ioudaia* 1 Makk. 4, 15=el-jehūdīje. Professor Eissfeldt's wine, whether old or new, needs no bush ; and it will be evident that this is a collection of outstanding interest and value. The editors are to be commended for the scrupulous care and precision with which they have done their work. This and the succeeding volumes will be welcomed by a wide circle of readers, but by none more warmly than by the members of our Society, of which Professor Eissfeldt has been for so long a distinguished honorary member.

G.W.A.

FRIEDRICH, G. (ed. by) : *Theologisches Wörterbuch zum Neuen Testament* (begun by G. Kittel). Band VII, Lieferung 4, 1961. Pp. 64. (Kohlhammer, Stuttgart. Price : DM. 4.60). Doppellieferung 5/6, 1961. Pp. 128. (Price : DM. 9.20).

Lieferung 4 concludes the articles on *satanas* by Foerster. Of the other articles sections of interest to Old Testament scholars will be found in that by Foerster on *sebomai* and its many cognates especially with reference to their occurrence in the LXX, in the pseudepigraphical writings in Philo and Josephus. The particular value of this Lieferung is to be found in the elaborate article by Rengstorf on *semeion* and its cognates, especially section B, pp. 207 ff. on *'oth* and *mopheth* in the Old Testament and in Judaism and on the corresponding words in the LXX, Philo and Josephus. This article runs right on into Lieferung 5/6. Later articles in Lieferung 5/6 which should be noted are those on *semeron* (Fuchs), *Sina* (Lohse), *skandalon* (Stählin) with special reference to its Hebrew equivalents, and finally the long and very important article on *Sion, Jerusalem*, etc. by Fohrer which deals with its subject from the historical and theological points of view.

N.W.P.

GALLING, K. (ed. by) : *Die Religion in Geschichte und Gegenwart.* 3. Auflage, Band V. Lieferungen 86-87 (cols. 1-192 including map), 88-89 (cols. 193-384), 90-91 (cols. 385-576), 92-94 (cols. 577-864), 95-96 (cols. 865-1056+map in colour), 97-98 (cols. 1057-1216), 99-100 (cols. 1217-1408 including map), 101-104 (cols. 1409-1726+ Pp. XXXII). 1961. (J. C. B. Mohr, Tübingen. Price : DM. 4.20 each Lieferung).

This volume contains the articles from ' Pacca ' to ' Sexual-pädagogik ', including the following, which, as their titles show, are of direct interest to the *Alttestamentler :* 'Palästina ' (K. Galling and A. Dietrich), ' Panbabylonismus ' (C.-M. Edsman), ' Paradies ' (F. M. Th. de Liagre Böhl, A. Jepsen, F. Hesse), ' Paralipomena Jeremiae ' (R. Meyer), ' Pentateuch ' (O. Plöger), ' Penuel ' (A. Kuschke), ' Peräa ' (H. W. Hertzberg), ' Petra ' (O. Plöger), ' Pharao ' (H. Brunner), ' Pharisäer ' (E. L. Dietrich), ' Philister ' (H. Donner), ' Philo von Alexandria ' (C. Colpe), ' Philo Byblius ' (O. Eissfeldt), ' Phönizier ' (M. Noth), 'Phrygien ' (H. Güterbock), ' Pithom ' (H. Brunner), ' Polyglotten ' (A. Bertholet and B. J. Roberts), ' Präexistenz :

Im AT und Judentum' (A. R. Hulst), 'Predigerbuch' (K. Galling), 'Priesterschrift' (G. Fohrer), 'Priestertum : In Israel' (R. Meyer, J. Fichtner, A. Jepsen), 'Prophetenspruch' (R. Rendtorff), 'Prostitution, kultische' (W. von Soden), 'Psalmen : Im AT' (K. Galling), 'Psalterbuch' (K. Galling), 'Pseudepigraphen des AT' (W. Baumgartner), 'Put' (R. Bach), 'Qumran' (M. Burrows, R. de Vaux, R. Meyer, K. G. Kuhn, C. H. Huntzinger), 'Rabbiner' (E. L. Dietrich), 'Rabula' (R. Abramowski and M. Black), 'Rama' (H. Gese), 'Raschi' (E. L. Rapp), 'Reich Gottes : Im antiken Judentum' (K. Galling), 'Rein und Unrein : Im AT' (R. Rendtorff), 'Reinigungen : Im AT und Judentum' (R. Rendtorff), 'Rekabiter' (H. Bardtke), 'Religionsgeschichtliche Schule' (J. Hempel), 'Responsen, rabbinische' (E. L. Dietrich), 'Richter in Israel' (K. Elliger), 'Richterbuch' (F. Maass), 'Ruthbuch' (J. Fichtner), 'Saadja' (S. Cohen), 'Sabbat' (E. Kutsch), 'Sacharja' and 'Sacharjabuch' (J. Bright), 'Sadduzäer' (E. L. Dietrich), 'Sagen und Legenden : Im AT' (E. Jacob), 'Salbung : Im AT' (E. Kutsch), 'Salomo' (A. Alt and R. Bach), 'Salomo-Psalmen' (H. Braun), 'Salomo-Weisheit' (J. Fichtner), 'Samaria' (R. Bach and C. Colpe), 'Samuel' (H. Wildberger), 'Samuelisbücher' (K. Koch), 'Sanchunjaton' (O. Eissfeldt), 'Sarepta' (H. Gese), 'Saul' (A. Alt and R. Bach), 'Schilo' (E. Jenni), 'Schma' (E. L. Dietrich), 'Schmone Esre' (E. L. Dietrich), 'Schöpfung : Im AT' (G. E. Wright), 'Schriftauslegung : Im AT' (F. Hesse) and 'Im Judentum' (E. L. Dietrich), 'Sedrach-Apokalypse' (R. Meyer), 'Segen und Fluch : Im AT' (F. Horst), 'Sektenregel' (H. Braun), 'Seleukiden' (H. E. Stier), 'Semiten' (W. von Soden), 'Semitische Sprachen' (E. Hammershaimb), 'Septuaginta-Forschung' (P. Katz), 'Septuaginta-Frömmigkeit' (G. Bertram). Many articles have sections headed 'religionsgeschichtlich', which also have relevance to the Old Testament. To the articles on books of the Bible there are appended valuable additional bibliographies on the history of interpretation, compiled by W. Werbeck. The brief biographies of modern scholars include those of at least four past Presidents of our Society. G.W.A.

(GELIN, A.) : *A la Recontre de Dieu. Mémorial Albert Gelin.* 1961. Pp. 446+portrait+2 plates. (Editions Xavier Mappus, Le Puy. Price : 28s. 6d.).

Albert Gelin, who was a Sulpician, and professor of Holy Scripture in the Catholic faculty at Lyons, was born in 1902 and died early in 1960. Some seventeen pages of bibliography testify to his remarkably fruitful career as a writer. The present volume contains a graceful tribute by M. Jourjon, and twenty-eight contributions, of which ten are concerned directly with the Old Testament and four others with cognate topics. One may call attention specially to R. de Vaux's excellent study 'Arche d'alliance et Tente de réunion', J. Coppens on the Messianic character of the ideal king in Isaiah ix. 5-6 and xi. 1-5, P. Bonnard's essay on the vocabulary of the *Miserere*, and P. Grelot on the eschatology of Wisdom and the Jewish apocalypses. But the general standard is high, and most of the contributions are, at the very least, careful assessments of the present state of knowledge.

J.M.T.B.

GLANZMAN, G. S. : *An Introductory Bibliography for the Study of Scripture.* (Woodstock Papers, No. 5.). 1961. Pp. XX+136. (The Newman Press, Westminster, Md. Price : $1.50).

This is an extremely useful guide to the main tools available for the study of Scripture. In all, 342 items are included, arranged in 21 sections. Periodicals ; Series ; Introductions to the Biblical Texts and Versions ; Biblical Texts and Ancient Versions ; English Versions ; Lexica ; Grammars ; Concordances ; Introductions to the Bible ; Commentaries in Series ; Dictionaries ; Biblical Theology ; Biblical Archaeo-logy ; Biblical Geography ; History ; Intertestamental Period ; Dead Sea Scrolls ; New Testament Apocrypha ; Rabbinical Literature ; Miscellany ; Bibliography. There are brief, discriminating comments on most of the items, and references to some of the more important reviews of them. Rapid reference is facilitated by an index of modern authors. This bibliography ought to be in the library of every theological college and in the possession of every theological student. It may be hoped, however, that in future editions a section will be added on the Religion of Israel.

G.W.A.

HARAN, M. (ed. by) : *Yehezkel Kaufmann Jubilee Volume. Studies in Bible and Jewish Religion Dedicated to Yehezkel Kaufmann on the Occasion of his Seventieth Birthday.* 1960. Pp. 114 (English section) +158 (Hebrew section)+portrait. (Magnes Press, Jerusalem).

Herein are assembled ten studies written in Hebrew and six in English in honour of Prof. Kaufmann on the occasion of his 70th birthday. By far the greater part of the studies deals with Biblical subjects—subjects near and dear to Kaufmann. The studies which have a direct bearing on the Bible in the Hebrew Section are : The South-Western Border of the Promised Land (Y.M. Grintz) ; The Symbolical Significance of the Complex of Ritual Acts Performed Inside the Israelite Shrine (M. Haran) ; The Ceremony of Bringing the First Fruits (Y. Gutmann) ; The Ransom of Half Shekel (J. Liver) ; The Northern Limit of David's Kingdom (A. Biram) ; The Historical Background of Hosea's Prophecies (H. Tadmor) ; The Dependence of Deuteronomy upon the Wisdom Literature (M. Weinfeld) ; Elucidation of Prov. ix 1 (N. H. Tur-Sinai) ; The Ban in Mari and in the Bible (A. Malamat). Those of the English Section are : Some Postulates of Biblical Criminal Law (M. Greenberg) ; Leviticus and the Critics (E. A. Speiser) ; David the Dancer (C. H. Gordon) ; Studies in Hosea i 3 (H. L. Ginsberg) ; The Date of Ezra's Mission to Jerusalem (J. Bright). All the contributions are of high scholarly quality.

M.W.

Hebrew Union College Annual, Vol. XXXII (ed. by Elias L. Epstein). 1961. Pp. 350+25 (in Hebrew+index to vols. I-XXXI. (Hebrew Union College, Cincinnati).

This volume celebrates the eightieth birthday of Dr. Julian Morgenstern (one of our Honorary Members), and contains a photograph of him and a short biographical appreciation by M. Lieberman. Unware that the volume was to be dedicated to him, Dr. Morgenstern himself submitted another of his 'Amos Studies', and so this volume, like the previous thirty-one, contains an article by him. N. Glueck discusses 'The Archaeological History of the Negev'. S. Sandmel outlines the history of the interpretation of Gen. iv. 26b. J. Lewy devotes a long article to a learned examination of some questions concerning the Amorites in Mesopotamian literature. S. H. Blank contributes 'Some Observations Concerning Biblical Prayer'. J. Lindblom writes on 'Theophanies in Holy Places in Hebrew Religion', and H. G. May on 'Individual Responsibility and Retribution'. S. Mowinckel's essay on 'The Name of the God of Moses' maintains that Exod. iii. 13-15 does not imply a previous ignorance of the Tetragrammation, and that the origin of the divine name was the cultic cry *ya-huwa* ('Oh He!'). J. Muilenburg contributes a detailed study of 'The Linguistic and Rhetorical Usages of the Particle *ki* in the Old Testament'. J. Gutmann discusses 'The "Second Commandment" and the Image in Judaism'. S. Cohen maintains that Amos vii. 14 is to be translated 'No! I am indeed a Navi (prophet), but not a Ben Navi (professional prophet)'. O. Eissfeldt detects in both the Sinai and the Balaam passages two different attitudes towards the land, the cultus and political power. M. Tsevat discusses 1 Sam. ii. 27-36. J. Coppens refutes Bonnard's contention that Pss. vi and xli are dependent on Jeremiah. L. J. Liebreich discusses 'The Impact of Nehemiah 9: 5-37 on the Liturgy of the Synagogue'. H. M. Orlinsky continues his 'Studies in the Septuagint of Job', and challenges some attempts to detect theological motives in the translation. E. R. Goodenough's article, 'The Rabbis and Jewish Art in the Greco-Roman Period', defends his view that many Jews were more deeply influenced by gentile religious symbols than has commonly been admitted. B. J. Bamberger examines some rabbinic laws concerning women of various ages ('Qetanah, Na'arah, Bogereth'). L. Finkelstein writes in Hebrew on *Baraytha debeth din shel lishkath ha-gazith.*

J.A.E.

HEMPEL, J.: *Apoxysmata. Vorarbeiten zu einer Religionsgeschichte und Theologie des Alten Testaments.* Festgabe zum 30. Juli 1961. (Beihefte zur Zeitschrift für die alttestamentliche Wissenschaft, 81). 1961. Pp. x+328+portrait. (Alfred Töpelmann, Berlin. Price : paper, DM. 45 ; cloth, DM. 48).

The present editor of *Z.A.W.*, together with his colleagues and the publisher, join in greeting Professor Hempel on his

70th birthday with this volume in which are reprinted ten of Hempel's own articles, some of which are substantial and most, if not all, of which are familiar and frequently cited. The titles are : ' Jahwegleichnisse der israelitischen Propheten ', ' Die israelitischen Anschauungen von Segen und Fluch im Lichte altorientalischer Parallelen ', ' Das theologische Problem des Hiob ', ' Vom irrenden Glauben ', ' Gott, Mensch und Tier im Alten Testament ', ' Das reformatorisch Evangelium und das Alte Testament ', ' Sünde und Offenbarung nach alt- und neutestamentlicher Anschauung ', ' Prophet und Dichter ', ' Wort Gottes und Schicksal ', ' Das Alte Testament in Religionsunterricht '. The result is a volume of outstanding importance and usefulness, particularly since the author has taken account of work done since these articles were first published.

Like Professor Eissfeldt's *Kleine Schriften* this collection will be warmly welcomed by our Society as the work of a distinguished honorary member of long standing. G.W.A.

(JUNKER, H.) : *Lex Tua Veritas*. Festschrift für Hubert Junker zur Vollendung des siebzigsten Lebensjahres am 8. August, 1961 dargeboten von Kollegen, Freunden und Schülern, herausgegeben von Heinrich Gross und Franz Mussner. 1961. Pp. XVI+320+ portrait. (Paulinus-Verlag, Trier).

The contributions to this *Festschrift* relate in the main to Old Testament exegesis, literature, and theology. F. Auer writes on ' Das Alte Testament in der Sicht des Bundesgedankens '. H. Cazelles contributes some observations on the composition of Esther. J. Coppens re-examines the interpretation of Isa. vii. 14 in the light of recent study. A. Deissler contributes a paper ' Zur Datierung und Situierung der " kosmischen Hymnen " Pss. 8 19 29 '. A Diez-Macho writes on ' El texto biblico del comentario de Habacuc de Qumran ', W. Eichrodt on ' Der Sabbat bei Hesekiel ', and H. Eising on ' Die ägyptischen Plagen '. Three contributors examine important problems connected with the opening chapters of Genesis : H. Gross on ' Die Gottebenbildlichkeit des Menschen ' (relating the theme to a wide range of Biblical material), H. Haag on ' Die Themata der Sündenfall-Geschichte ', V. Hamp on ' Die zwei ersten Verse der Bibel ', R. Mayer considers ' Iranischer Beitrag zu Problemen des Daniel- und Esther-Buches '. R. E. Murphy studies ' GRB and GBWRH in the Qumran writings ' ; and F. Nötscher writes on ' Sakrale Mahlzeiten vor Qumran '. J. van der Ploeg discusses ' Les anciens dans l'Ancien Testament '. M. Rehm re-examines ' Das Opfer der Völker nach Mal. 1, 11 '. J. Scharbert contributes a study of ' ŠLM im Alten Testament ', J. Schildenberger relates Ps. 78 (77) to the Pentateuchal sources. H. Schneider re-considers the identification of ' Die " Töchter " des Blutegels in Spr 30, 15 '. R. de Vaux writes on ' " Levites " minéens et lévites israélites '. J. Ziegler contributes ' Zur

GENERAL 321

griechischen Vorlage der Vetus Latina in der Sapientia Salomonis '. Two contributors deal with New Testament subjects :
F. Mussner, ' Die Idee der Apokatastasis in der Apostelge-
schichte ' and A. Vögtle, ' " Josias zeugte den Jechonias und
seine Brüder " (Mt. 1, 11) '. E. Haag has compiled a bibliography of Junker's writings. The production of the volume is
in every way excellent.

G.W.A.

KAPELRUD, A. S. : *Fra Israels profeter til de vise menn.* 1961. Pp. 95.
(Universitetsforlaget, Oslo. Price : Nor. kr. 4.50).

The book consists of a series of lectures given over the Norwegian
radio. Even though they are addressed to a general audience
the author's wide knowledge and individual approach to the
problems make themselves felt everywhere. The first two
chapters deal with the prophets of Israel and the individual
books of the prophets, the third chapter deals with the Books
of Ruth and Esther, the fourth chapter with ' Stjernefyrsten '
(the Prince of the Star). Here he demonstrates the religio-
historical foundation for the account of the wise men in the
New Testament. The fifth and last chapter is a very short
survey of the history of the Jews from A.D. 70 till the present
day.

E.H.

MACDONALD, J. (ed. by) : *The Annual of Leeds University Oriental
Society*, Vol. I (1958-1959). 1959. Pp. 76. (E. J. Brill, Leiden.
Price : Fl. 8).

The volume begins with an introduction by A. Guillaume and a
statement of the Foundation and Development of the Society
by J. MacDonald. Articles of interest to Old Testament
scholars are : ' The Dead Sea Habakkuk Scroll ' by F. F.
Bruce, in which the basic principles and the methods of interpretation current at Qumran are carefully analysed ; ' Some
Thoughts on Old Testament Miracles ' by C. J. Mullo Weir,
in which the distinction is made between the Biblical conception
of miracles and ours, and it is noted that while we might find a
rational explanation for some of the events and others show
evidence of heightening, remarkably little use is made in the
Old Testament of what we might describe as the miraculous :
' The Importance of Samaritan Research ' by J. Bowman, in
which the conservatism of Samaritan practice is noted
and it is suggested that it may well preserve customs
from the Biblical period on which the Old Testament is
silent ; and ' Notes on Jewish Art in the Period of the Second
Temple ' by B. Kanael, in which it is shown that the Second
Commandment did not always preclude figurative art.

A.S.H.

MACDONALD, J. (ed. by) : *The Annual of Leeds University Oriental Society*, Vol. II (1959-1961). 1961. Pp. 78. (E. J. Brill, Leiden. Price : Fl. 12).

We note the following articles that relate to Old Testament studies. B. S. J. Isserlin, ' Excavating in an Ancient Port in Israel ' : In 1960, limited excavations took place at Mikhmoret (Minet Abu Zabara) and evidence was found of buildings from the Hellenistic and Persian periods and pottery fragments of the Israelite period. P. Kahle, ' Pre-massoretic Hebrew ': this is a translation of the last chapter from *Der Bibeltext seit Franz Delitzsch*. J. MacDonald, ' The Theological Hymns of Amrah Darah ' : six hymns in A. E. Cowley, *The Samaritan Liturgy* are translated and checked by an Arabic translation in Crawford MS 11 in the John Rylands Library. The translation is accompanied by a running commentary.   A.S.H.

MULLO WEIR, C. J. (ed. by) : *Transactions of Glasgow University Oriental Society*, xviii (1959-1960). 1961. Pp. iv+80. (Oriental Society, Glasgow. Price : 15s. 0d.).

Five of the articles in this volume are of direct interest to the *Alttestamentler*. J. C. L. Gibson writes on ' Life and Society at Mari and in Old Israel ', adducing interesting parallels in customs and ceremonies and in prophecy. J. Wood contributes a study of ' The Idea of Life in the Book of Job ', and H. Anderson 'Another Perspective on the Book of Job ', relating the theological interpretation of the book to its literary structure. A. S. Tritton presents notes on some LXX renderings. J. M. Allegro provides a communication on the Copper Scroll from Qumran. There are also three papers on Islamic subjects : ' Muslim Wedding Feasts ' by J. Robson, ' Created in His Image : A Study in Islamic Theology ', by W. Montgomery Watt, and ' The Formative Stages of the Islamic Religious Orders ', by J. Spencer Trimingham. Unpretentious in format, these *Transactions* contain a surprising amount of useful material in a small compass.   G.W.A.

Die Ou Testamentiese Werkgemeenskap in Suid-Afrika : Studies on the Books of Samuel. Papers read at 3rd Meeting held at Stellenbosch, 26-28 January, 1960. n.d. (1961?). Pp. 80. (Obtainable from Professor A. H. van Zyl, University of South Africa, P.O. Box 392, Pretoria. Price : 10s. 0d.).

In the *Book List*, 1961 (p. 11) a short mention was made of the young Old Testament Society of South Africa and its praiseworthy effort in publishing the papers read at its second meeting. In the present booklet we have the fruit of the third meeting, held in 1960, this time devoted to studies on the book of Samuel. The contributions are arranged in alphabetic order of contributors, though the article by I. H. Eybers, ' Notes on the Texts of Samuel found in Qumran Cave IV ', is the longest as well as the first. It appears from a footnote that it may be a by-product of the author's doctoral thesis. The sections available for examination were, of course, not very long but permit the author to form conclusions about their relationship to the Massoretic Text. F. C. Fensham, 'A Few Aspects of Legal Practices in Samuel in Comparison with legal material from the Ancient Near East', makes some deductions about the legal basis of slave-owning in Israel, and concludes with a section on David's opposition to blood revenge. 'Some remarks on the prayer of David in 2 Sam. vii.' by C. J. Labuschagne upholds the authenticity of the prayer of David and deduces from it certain ideas concerning kingship in Israel. The same chapter is dealt with as a whole in E. S. Mulder's paper, 'The Prophecy of Nathan in 2 Sam. vii.' with a few references to the work of Rost, Alt, and Noth. 'The Cherethites and Pelethites' by L. M. Muntingh offers several interesting suggestions on this perennial problem. In a short note, J. P. Oberholzer associates 'The '*ibrim* in I Samuel' with the *habiru* or mercenaries. A. van Selms in 'The armed Forces of Israel under Saul and David' deals with the putative development of the military system from voluntary amateurism to professionalism in the early monarchy, a subject which, as the author admits, bristles with uncertainties, especially on the statistical side. Finally A. H. van Zyl, 'Israel and the Indigenous Population of Canaan according to the books of Samuel', after sifting the references to non-Israelites, proceeds to estimate the influence of these peoples and their cultures on kingship, law and religion in Israel.

We congratulate the Society on a very praiseworthy collection of papers.

D.R.Ap-T.

RABIN, C. (ed.) : *Studies in the Bible* (Scripta Hierosolymitana, VIII). 1961. Pp. 400. (Magnes Press, Jerusalem : Oxford University Press, London. Price : 60s. 0d.).

The studies contained in this volume are not united in subject or theme, but the majority are devoted to Old Testament subjects. One on the composition of the Pentateuch by M. H. Segal finds a starting-point in some acknowledged weaknesses of the documentary hypothesis and attempts to argue that the Pentateuch, 'a story of the past and a legislation for the future', is a continuous literary work which, apart from late glosses and additions which are numerous in the Book of Numbers but few in the other books, belongs to Mosaic times. Jacob Liver, writing on Korah, Dathan and Abiram, presents a good case for the thesis that the rebellion of Dathan and Abiram is basic and belonged to an early series of stories on the wilderness wanderings while the story of Korah belongs to the time of the monarchy and reveals the tension which developed between the Levites and the priests officiating at the Jerusalem temple. Yehezkel Kaufmann provides a somewhat discursive article, substantially descriptive, on the early Israelite period in Palestine, in which he discerns three phases from Joshua to the united monarchy : wars of conquest, of liberation, and of empire. N. H. Tur-Sinai offers a commentary on difficult passages in Isaiah i-xii ; some of his proposed readings and interpretations are attractive but others are highly conjectural. An article by Menahem Haran discusses the rites performed in the Tabernacle and seeks to show how those performed in the outer sanctum symbolized the satisfaction of the deity's ' needs ', while the deity's presence was symbolized in the inner sanctum. Two articles are concerned chiefly with matters of literary style : the one by E. Z. Melamed describing as the break-up of stereotyped phrases into parallel clauses what most would describe as the the use of parallel clauses to express similar or related ideas, and the other by Shemaryahu Talmon dealing with what he calls synonymous readings in the textual traditions of the Old Testament (MT, MT and Sam., and MT and Dead Sea Scrolls). A few of the articles use archaeological evidence to elucidate historical problems. Yigael Yadin examines some Hebrew weights, which he dates 7th century B.C., to clarify the forms of numeral signs in ancient Israel and uses the evidence thus produced to date the Samaria ostraca. Hayyim Tadmor identifies the Azriyau of Yaudi of the inscriptions with Azariah-Uzziah, king of Judah, and makes an assessment of the political power of that monarch. And Abraham Malamat considers the campaigns of Amenhotep II and Thutmose IV to Canaan in the light of the evidence of two Taanach letters from the former of these Pharaohs to the ruler of Taanach and the Accadian letter from Gezer. Finally, M. H. Goshen-Gottstein discusses the value of the MS. evidence for the production of a critical edition of the Peshitta, and Chaim Rabin writes an interesting linguistic and semantic study under the title of etymological miscellanea.

J.M.

RENDTORFF, R. and KOCH, K. (ed. by) : *Studien zur Theologie der alttestamentlichen Überlieferungen.* 1961. Pp. 176. (Neukirchener Verlag der Buchhandlung des Erziehungsvereins, Neukirchen Kreis Moers. Price : DM. 17.25).

This is a collection of essays presented to Professor Gerhard von Rad on his sixtieth birthday by ten of his former pupils, i.e., R. Bach, ' Bauen und Pflanzen ' ; K. Baltzer, ' Das Ende des Staates Juda und die Messias-Frage ' ; K. Koch, ' Tempelein-lassliturgien und Dekaloge ' ; K. von Rabenau, ' Das pro-phetische Zukunftswort im Buch Hesekiel ' ; R. Rendtorff, ' Geschichte und Überlieferung ' ; H. Köster, ' Die Auslegung der Abraham-Verheissung in Hebräer 6 ' ; U. Wilckens, ' Die Rechtfertigung Abrahams nach Römer 4 ' ; W. Pannenberg, ' Kerygma und Geschichte ' ; F. Merkel, ' Die biblische Urgeschichte im kirchlichen Unterricht ' ; D. Rössler, ' Die Predigt über alttestamentliche Texte '. There is also a biblio-graphy of von Rad's works, which has been compiled by von Rabenau. If there is nothing particularly exciting about these essays and one reader, at least, is left with the renewed feeling that we are in danger of having a surfeit of *Formgeschichte*, the volume is a pleasing tribute to the influence exerted upon Biblical studies as a whole by one of the most distinguished Old Testament scholars of this century.

A.R.J.

(RUDOLPH, W.) : *Verbannung und Heimkehr.* Beiträge zur Geschichte und Theologie Israels im 6. und 5. Jahrhundert v. Chr. Wilhelm Rudolph zum 70. Geburtstage dargebracht von Kollegen, Freunden und Schülern herausgegeben von Arnulf Kuschke. 1961. Pp. XII + 326 + portrait. (J. C. B. Mohr, Tübingen. Price : cloth, DM. 45).

The essays in this handsome volume are related to the two centuries of Biblical history with which Professor Rudolph's work has been specially concerned. F. Baumgärtel offers a closely packed statistical study of the divine names in Jeremiah and Ezekiel. O. Eissfeldt examines the oracles against Egypt and Babylon in Jeremiah. K. Elliger analyses the law of the sin-offering in Lev. iv f. J. Fichtner considers the exegesis of Isa. lii. 7-10 and its use in preaching. K. Galling contributes a study of ' Serubbabel und der Wiederaufbau des Tempels in Jerusalem '. H. W. Hertzberg writes on ' the rebels ' and ' the many ' in Isa. liii. F. Hesse treats the Book of Haggai in terms of recent discussion of the proper tasks of exegesis, exposition, and theological interpretation. F. Horst studies the terms *naḥālah* and *'ǎḥuzzah*. P. Humbert discusses the etymology of *to'ebah*. A. Jepsen contributes ' Berith : Ein Beitrag zur Theologie der Exilszeit '. A. Kuschke writes on the topography of Jer. xlviii. 1-8. In a detailed study, taking account of the evidence of the fragment from the 4th cave at Qumran, R. Meyer discusses the bearing of Deut. xxxii. 8f., 43 on the interpretation of the Song of Moses. Returning to a subject discussed in one of his earliest writings, S. Mowinckel re-examines the use of the first and third persons in the Ezra narrative. The only contribution in English is by N. W. Porteous, ' Jerusalem-Zion : The Growth of a Symbol '. By far the longest of the essays is G. Quell's ' Das Phänomen des Wunders im Alten Testament '. Finally, L. Rost offers some observations on the edict of Cyrus. There is also a classified bibliography of Rudolph's publications, compiled by R. Hentschke.

G.W.A.

SCHLATTER, T., GUTBROD, K., and KÜCKLICH, R. (ed. by) : *Calwer Bibellexikon,* 5th ed. 1959-1961. 1. Lieferung, Sp. 1-288 (A—Esra). 2. Lieferung, Sp. 289-576 (Esra—Jagd). 3. Lieferung, Sp. 577-864 (Jahasiel—Megiddo). 4. Lieferung, Sp. 865-1152 (Mehl—Sarg). 5. Lieferung, Sp. 1153-1444 (Sargon—Z). 64 ills. + XIV maps and plans. (Calwer Verlag, Stuttgart. Price : DM. 7.50 each Lieferung).

In this new edition the editors have been assisted by a team of 28 scholars. The articles contain all the information necessary in a work such as this, intended for general use. Space has been saved by the omission of some names which seldom occur ; and useful articles have been included on some general subjects. For the most part bibliographies have not been appended to the articles, the main exception being articles on the books of the Bible. The inclusion of only simple, black and white illustrations has undoubtedly helped to keep the price low ; but they are admirably clear and have been well chosen. The further the reviewer read in this excellent work of reference the more deeply he was impressed (in spite of weaknesses in one or two articles) by the unpretentious skill with which it has been produced. It deserves a wide circulation.

G.W.A.

Studia theologica cura ordinum Scandinavicorum edita. Vol. XIV, Fasc. ii, 1960. Pp. 72. (C. W. K. Gleerup, Lund. Price : Sw. Kr. 15 each vol. ; or Sw. Kr. 10 each fascicle).

None of the contributions to this fascicle has a direct bearing on the Old Testament. But H. Gottlieb's short article on *to haima mou tes diathekes* and O. Moe's study of ' Der Menschensohn und der Urmensch ' contain material of interest to the *Alttestamentler*. J. Munck contributes ' Bemerkungen zum koptischen Thomasevangelium ', and J. Aagaard writes on ' Revelation and Religion '.

G.W.A.

(VISCHER, W.) : *Maqqēl shâqēdh : la branche d'amandier : Hommage à Wilhelm Vischer.* 1960. Pp. 230, including 2 portraits. (Causse Graille Castelnau, Montpellier. Price : Sw. Frs. 16.50).

It is a somewhat unusual feature of this *Festschrift* that two of the contributions are portraits, one by Exposito-Farèse, the other by Lindegaard. The remainder are essays on Old Testament or Biblical themes. S. Amsler contributes a hermeneutic study, ' Texte et évènement '. J. Bright re-examines the problem of Sennacherib's campaigns in Palestine. A Caquot traces royal features in the person of Job. E. Dhorme offers some comments on Biblical demonology. W.-A. Goy submits an interpretation of Psalm lxxvii. The theme of hybris and its consequences is traced through the Old Testament in a characteristically thorough study by P. Humbert. E. Jacob comments on Hos. xii. 13 f. C. Keller contributes a study of Beatitudes in the Old Testament. A. Lacoque writes on ' Israel moderne et prophétie '. In 'Alchimie du verbe et démythisation ' D. Lys offers some interesting observations on assonance and paronomasia in the Old Testament. A. Maillot candidly entitles his essay ' Un peu de gnose sur Genèse 3 '. R. Martin-Achard provides a study of ' Sagesse de Dieu et sagesse humaine chez Ésaie '. F. Michaéli expounds the importance of Hebrew grammar for Biblical theology. H. Michaud analyses the interplay of religion and politics in Jeremiah. G. Miegge comments on the interpretations of Isa. xl. 6 offered by Calvin and Diodati.

In ' Jérémie le pharisien' A. Neher provides a Jewish counter-part to the Christian typological exegesis of which Vischer is an exponent. A. Parrot surveys ' Gestes de la prière dans le monde mésopotamien '. D. Piccard contributes interpretations of Gen. xviii. 22 f., xxii. 1-19, xxxii. 23-33. G. Pidoux discusses references in the Psalms to the right of asylum. G. von Rad writes on ' Les idées sur le temps et l'histoire en Israël et l'eschatologie des prophètes '. P. Reymond studies the narrative of Solomon's dream (1 Kings iii. 4-15). W. Zimmerli expounds the theme of the new Exodus in Ezekiel and Deutero-Isaiah.

G.W.A.

WEISER, A. : *Glaube und Geschichte im Alten Testament und andere ausgewählte Schriften.* 1961. Pp. 370. (Vandenhoeck & Ruprecht, Göttingen. Price : 52s. 6d.).

This is a most valuable volume, containing the welcome reprint of Professor Weiser's monograph *Glaube und Geschichte im Alten Testament* which originally appeared in 1931 in the series Beiträge zur Wissenschaft vom Alten und Neuen Testament. 4. Folge, Heft 4 and made a great impact then with its illuminating study of the way in which history and faith are linked together in the Old Testament, men recognizing both the irrationality of the history in which God reveals Himself and seeking so far as possible to see in it the mani-festation of the divine reason. The volume also contains a generous selection of essays by the author published between 1923 and 1955 and thus makes possible an understanding of the development of Professor Weiser's thought. Of particular importance are the three essays on the theological under-standing of the Old Testament which represent an important contribution to the current debate, emphasizing as they do that the task of interpretation is not complete till the point of commitment is reached, though this does not mean that something is read into the Old Testament which is not there. Reference should also be made to the elaborate essay dis-cussing religion and morality in Genesis and to the investigation of the place of Theophany in the Cult, a theme which has been further developed in the author's commentary on the Psalms. The concluding item in a peculiarly rich volume is a reprint of the article *Glauben im Alten Testament* in T.W.z. N.T. Vol. VI.

N.W.P.

WRIGHT, G. E. (ed. by) : *The Bible and the Ancient Near East : Essays in Honor of William Foxwell Albright.* 1960. Pp. 410+portrait. (Routledge and Kegan Paul, London. Price : 50s. 0d.).

Professor Albright has long been in the forefront of Near Eastern studies. Few have rendered such distinguished services to that field of scholarship, and few have so well deserved the honour of a Festschrift. It may be said at once that the book is worthy of the man. It contains twelve essays of outstanding interest by scholars all of whom have made their mark in the field of Near Eastern studies. It also includes in an appendix an important contribution by Professor Albright himself on the Role of the Canaanites in the History of Civilization. It is perhaps a little unusual for a scholar to contribute to his own Festschrift, but the essay is a valuable addition to the book.

Professor John Bright of Union Theological Seminary, whose *History of Israel* is well-known, opens the ball with an excellent survey of the present state of advance in the field of Old Testament literature, including a judicious estimate of the work of the Scandinavian school. Professor Wright, the editor, whose valuable work in the field of Palestinian archaeology is generally recognized, has given an excellent account of recent work which has been done in that field, especially as it relates to Professor Albright's contribution, reminding us how much remains to be done. His essay includes two valuable chronological tables. The same subject is dealt with in greater detail and with a full chronological chart in another essay by Professors Freedman and Campbell. This essay will be of special value to Old Testament students. Professor Noah Kramer has contributed an essay on the field which he has made specially his own, the field of Sumerian studies. Two competent essays deal with the important field of Egyptian studies as they relate to the history and religion of Israel, while Professor Goetze, the pioneer in the decipherment of Hittite scripts, bring us up to date in the field of Hittite and Anatolian studies. Space does not allow us to mention all the essays which form the content of this noble Festschrift, but all are of the highest value and worthy of the great scholar in whose honour they have been composed.   S.H.H.

EDUCATIONAL

LACE, O. J. : *Teaching the New Testament.* 1961. Pp. 96. (The Seabury Press, Greenwich, Conn. Price : $1.95).

Like the author's *Teaching the Old Testament* this book is a little masterpiece of succinct statement, penetrating insight, and wise judgment. When Miss Lace writes, ' " Teaching the New Testament " is the process of helping students, of whatever age, to read these earliest Christian books in the spirit in which they were written and to understand the faith to which they witness ' she gives us an apt description of her own pamphlet.   L.A.P.

*LEANEY, A. R. C. : *From Judean Caves, The Story of the Dead Sea Scrolls.* (Pathfinder Series, No. 15.) 1961. Pp. 128+9 plates+ other ills. and maps. (Religious Education Press, Wallington, Surrey. Price : boards, 8s. 0d. ; limp, 6s. 6d.).

This addition to the Pathfinder Series gives a comprehensive account of the Scrolls for pupils in the top forms of secondary modern and grammar schools. The story of the discoveries is traced from the beginning to the recent finds at Nahal Tseelim ; the historical and religious background of the Scrolls is then discussed in some detail and also the relation of the Scrolls to Judaism and Christianity. The author is a competent scholar who writes simply and sensibly, presenting the evidence fairly. He has given us an admirable survey of the whole subject, and his book is to be recommended to teachers as well as their pupils.

L.A.P.

*PATSTON, A. G. : *A Visual Old Testament* (from Abraham to Daniel). 1961. Pp. 47. (Religious Education Press, Wallington. Price : 5s. 0d.).

This book is carefully designed for junior children. It contains twenty-one short, plain accounts of Bible characters, with questions and exercises for the note-book. This is on the left-hand page. The opposite page contains efficient pictures, maps and diagrams of the type that are appreciated by the children for whom they are intended.

N.H.S.

ARCHAEOLOGY AND EPIGRAPHY

ELDER, J. : *Archaeology and the Bible. Scientific Proof of Bible History*. 1961. Pp. 192+26 plates+3 maps. (Robert Hale, London. Price : 18s. 0d.).

Dr. Elder's long service as a missionary in the Near East has familiarized him with the activities of field archaeologists and has deepened his respect for their aims and methods. His book is practically limited to the illustration of the course of the history of Israel and the origin and spread of the Gospel by the citation of the more concrete material remains of archaeology, but three useful chapters are devoted to writing and ancient MSS including the Qumran community and its writings. Originating in lectures at the instance of the American Army Advisory Group in Iran, the book has primarily a popular appeal, and, being generally well-informed, if obviously derivative, may be confidently recommended to interested laymen.

J.G.

MICHAELI, F. : *Textes de la Bible et de l'ancien Orient*. (Cahiers d'Archéologie Biblique, No. 13.) 1961. Pp. 134+12 plates (Delachaux & Niestlé, Neuchâtel. Price : 15s. 0d.).

There are five sections : The origin of the world and man ; From the Patriarchal age to the entry into Canaan ; From the Conquest to the Babylonian Exile ; The return from Exile and the Restoration; Various texts (legal, poetic, prophetic and proverbial). There is a short introduction to each group of texts, and then in parallel columns the relevant Old Testament and archaeological texts, with full references; there is a short bibliography and 12 full page plates of illustrations. A very useful addition to this series edited by A. Parrot.

J.N.S.

NOTH, M. : *Die Ursprünge des alten Israel im Lichte neuer Quellen*. (Veröffentlichungen der Arbeitsgemeinschaft für Forschung des Landes Nordrhein-Westfalen, Geisteswissenschaften, Heft 94). 1961. Pp. 42. (Westdeutscher Verlag, Köln und Opladen).

Starting from a summary consideration of the importance of personal names for the problem of Israel's origins, Noth proceeds to a discussion of the Mari texts and their many points of contact with the Old Testament, linguistic, sociological, legal, and religious. He then turns to the problem of the classification of the inhabitants of Mari within the family of Semitic peoples, and argues that they are best described as proto-Aramean. Israel's origins may be traced to a proto-Aramean environment ; but since proto-Aramean immigration was prolonged and widespread, the extra-Biblical evidence does not justify a more precise conclusion, which must be sought in Israel's own traditions. This closely reasoned and well documented study concludes with an appendix on non-Accadian words in the Mari texts.

G.W.A.

PARROT, A. : *Der Louvre und die Bibel*, trans. by Marc-René Jung (Bibel und Archäologie, V.) 1961. Pp. 178+XII Plates+76 ills. (Evz-Verlag Zürich. Price : Sw. Frs. 15.50).

Well produced, illustrated translation of M. Parrot's *Le Musée du Louvre et la Bible* (Cahiers d'Archéologie Biblique, No. 9, 1957) reviewed in *Book List*, 1958, p. 14.

J.N.S.

WHITCOMB, J. C. and MORRIS, H. M. : *The Genesis Flood : The Biblical Record and its Scientific Implications* (Foreword by J. C. McCampbell.) 1961. Pp. xxvi+518. (Presbyterian and Reformed Publishing Publishing Company, Philadelphia, Penna. Price : $8.95).

This book is an attempt to harmonize the scientific views of geology and palaeontology with the view of Biblical literalism on the origin of the earth and the question of the Flood. In the purely scientific field the writers find a point of attack in the methods of assessment of time in geological phases, and when science is at variance with their literalistic interpretation of Scripture the latter decides the question. Here, however, the variety of literary sources in Genesis and the conflicting archaeological evidence from Mesopotamia are blandly ignored.

We confess ourselves less edified and much more mystified by this attempt to demonstrate the historicity of the Flood than by the honest effort of critical and comparative scholarship to appraise the spiritual message which Hebrew thinkers conveyed through the old Mesopotamian traditions, the empiric accuracy of which is of no moment to revelation.

J.G.

YEIVIN, S. : *A Decade of Archaeology in Israel, 1948-1958.* 1960. Pp. XIV+62+Plates VII. (Nederlands Historisch-Archaeologisch Instituut in het Nabije Oosten, Istanbul).

A clear well-arranged account of excavations in Israel. 8 chapters arrange the finds chronologically from the Stone Age to the Hellenistic-Byzantine periods, and collect together the discoveries of tombs and religious buildings. The remaining chapters list the archaeological surveys, foreign expeditions, conservation of monuments, inspection of sites, museums and publications. There are 9 pages of figures and maps and 7 full-page plates containing 20 photographs. A 2-paged table of archaeological and historical periods in Israel gives the key to the symbols in which the Bronze Age becomes the Canaanite Period (EC, MC, LC.), the Iron Age is the Israelite Period (unfortunately I stands for both). In the text the Islamic Period appears to be denoted by EA (? Arabic), p. 50. The transliteration of Hebrew words is not consistent—e.g., Aviv but Gat. A very useful book especially if continued as a series.

J.N.S.

YEIVIN, S. and FEREMBACH, D. : *First Preliminary Report on the Excavations at Tel " Gat " (Tell Sheykh 'Ahmed el-'Areyny).* Seasons 1956-1958. 1961. Pp. 20 (English Text)+8 (Hebrew Text) +9 figs.+XII Plates. (Department of Antiquities, Jerusalem, Israel).

Eleven pages give a straightforward account in English of the excavations and suggest that the site is not Biblical Gath. At the other end of the book is the same account in Hebrew. Pages 12-20 contain the description and discussion in French by Denise Ferembach of human remains found at the site. The booklet is well illustrated by 12 full-page plates with titles in Hebrew and English ; there are 10 pages of plans and sketches. The author accepts the identification of Eglon with Tel Nagila and suggests that Tell Sheykh 'Ahmed el-'Areyny was an unknown Judaean town MMShT whose name is found with Hebron, Zif, Socho on royal seal impressions on jar handles in the tell.

J.N.S.

HISTORY AND GEOGRAPHY

ALT, A. : *Where Jesus Worked : Towns and Villages of Galilee studied with the help of local history*, trans. by K. Grayston from Beiträge zur biblischen landes- und Altertumskunde 68 (1949), pp. 51-72 ; republished in Kleine Schriften zur Geschichte des Volkes Israel (Munich 1953, 2nd ed. 1959). 1961. Pp. 30+map. (Epworth Press, London. Price : 3s. 6d.).

A well annotated study of the territorial history of Galilee in pre-Roman antiquity which discusses whether the sphere of the ministry of Jesus lay on both sides of the boundary in Palestine between Israel and Hellenism.
J.N.S.

MEEK, T. J. : *Hebrew Origins*. (Harper Torchbooks/The Cloister Library, TB 69). 1960. Pp. xvi+240. (Harper & Brothers, New York. Price : $1.35).

The first edition of this book appeared in 1936 and the second in 1950 (see *Book List*, 1951, p. 26; *Eleven Years*, p. 321). The latter embodied substantial changes ; but no such drastic alterations have been made in this Torch book. There are, for example, some adjustments in Egyptian chronology ; and in a new preface the author refers to more recent discoveries and literature ; but the main positions adopted are those of the second edition. It is unfortunate that, in reaffirming his belief that Joshua must antedate Moses, the author, by a curious verbal slip (p. vii) contradicts himself. Even those who differ from him on this and other points will welcome the reappearance of this stimulating book.
G.W.A.

PFEIFFER, C. F. : *The Patriarchal Age*. 1961. Pp. 128. (Baker Book House, Grand Rapids, Mich. Price : $2.95).

This book is the third of a projected series of eight books on the Old Testament. Here the author makes good use of recent excavations, especially at Nuzi and Mari, to rebuild the picture of life in patriarchal times. There are descriptions of life, politics, economics, and religion in Mesopotamia, Egypt and Canaan. The volume is based on ' the essential historicity of the Biblical record ', but it is by no means obscurantist. It is a good study of the period, making use of the most modern material.
N.H.S.

DE VAUX, R. : *Die hebräischen Patriarchen und die modernen Entdeckungen*. 1961. Pp. 110+portrait+3 maps. (Patmos-Verlag, Düsseldorf. Price : 18s. 6d.).

Père de Vaux' articles ' Les Patriarches hébreux et les découvertes modernes ' (*Reuve Biblique*, 1946, 1948, 1949) are here presented in book form, in a German translation, with a foreword by Professor Eissfeldt. They have been so widely used and cited that it is surprising that they have not been thus conveniently collected till now. Teachers and students alike will be grateful to the publishers for their enterprise and to the author for the lucidity and verve with which he presents his data.

G.W.A.

TEXT AND VERSIONS

KAHLE, P. : *Der Hebräische Bibeltext seit Franz Delitzsch*. (Franz Delitzsch-Vorlesungen, 1958.) 1961. Pp. 98+21 plates. (W. Kohlhammer Verlag, Stuttgart. Price : 36s. 6d.).

In this survey, which covers the period between the earliest part of the Delitzsch-Baer Masoretic Text (Genesis, 1869) down to the re-discovery of the Aleppo Codex and its discussion in the Jerusalem periodical *Textus*, Professor Kahle provides information and interpretation in his own inimitable manner. They range from the Babylonian and Palestinian texts to pre-Masoretic Hebrew and in between describe various texts, including *Minḥat Shai* (and Snaith's edition for the *British and Foreign Bible Society*), Mercati's Hexaplaric fragments, Origen, the *Cairo Codex of the Prophets*, Moshe ben Asher, Tiberian pointing, *B19a*, and many other features. Some of the information is already available in *The Cairo Geniza* (2nd edition) and elsewhere but Kahle never repeats himself in the same context, and the present book is as fascinating as any he has written. The plates appended to the book serve both as illustrations and works of art. No one will begrudge me this renewed opportunity of greeting Professor Kahle by sincerely congratulating him, in his advanced age, on his ever-young vigour and freshness.

B.J.R.

(Peshiṭṭa) : *List of Old Testament Peshiṭṭa Manuscripts* (Preliminary issue), edited by the Peshiṭṭa Institute, Leiden University. 1961. Pp. XII+114. (E. J. Brill, Leiden. Price : Fl. 12).

The Peshiṭṭa Institute of Leiden University has put all scholars of the Syriac Old Testament into their debt by publishing this list of available Old Testament Peshiṭṭa MSS. They are those to be used in the critical edition of the O.T. Peshiṭṭa, but there is an appendix of MSS lost, unavailable, or not to be used in the critical edition. The list is arranged under the alphabetical order of the place names of libraries where the MSS are to be found. A system of sigla has been devised which gives at a glance the age of the MS (an Arabic numeral for the century) and the contents (very roughly, by using a small letter, a, b, etc.). A third element of the siglum is the serial number of that particular MS. Full indices make for easy reference.

L.H.B.

RABIN, C. (ed. by) : *Textus. Annual of the Hebrew University Bible Project.* Vol. 1. 1960. Pp. 214. (Magnes Press, The Hebrew University, Jerusalem. Price : 50s. 0d.).

This volume is the first issue of a new annual whose aim is to be both the organ of the Hebrew University Bible Project and an international periodical for the textual study of the Hebrew Bible and the Versions. The principal task of the Bible Project is the publication of a reliable critical edition of the Hebrew Bible, based upon the codex of the Ben Asher school known as the Aleppo Codex, with full utilization of the variants recoverable from other early Hebrew manuscripts, the Versions, and Rabbinic literature. The first three articles argue the case for the adoption of the much debated Aleppo Codex as the text for the critical edition. They are by I. Ben-Zvi (with 12 pages of plates of the Còdex containing Deut. xxviii. 17-xxxiv. 12), M. H. Goshen-Gottstein, and D. S. Loewinger. G. R. Driver writes on the use of abbreviations in the M.T. A new fragment of Isaiah (xxxv. 9-xxxviii. 11, xl. 27-xlii. 21, xliii. 5-12) with Babylonian pointing is edited by A. Diez-Macho. Double readings in the M.T. are discussed by S. Talmon, and a fragment of a masoretic treatise from the Geniza is dealt with by I. Yeivin. The last-named also discusses a unique combination of accents at Ezek. xx. 31, and the volume ends with a brief report on the Bible Project. Short summaries in Hebrew of some of the articles, which are in English, are supplied ; other articles will be published in full in Hebrew elsewhere. This new venture has begun well and promises to be of major importance for the textual study of the O.T. It merits a warm welcome and every possible support.

D.W.T.

EXEGESIS AND MODERN TRANSLATIONS

BIČ, M. : *Das Buch Joel.* 1960. Pp. 112. (Evangelische Verlagsanstalt, Berlin. Price : DM. 7.20).

This commentary on Joel embodies a course of lectures which Professor Bič delivered in Halle in 1958. The Introduction is very brief, and this is followed by the author's translation of the text of Joel accompanied by a full commentary. Professor Bič reviews the variety of views on the date and unity of the book of Joel expressed by many scholars, and argues for the unity of the book and its early date. He notes its links with the Ras Shamra texts and thinks the prophet was acquainted with the mythology reflected in them. He also stresses links with the Elijah saga and with Hosea, and accordingly dates Joel in the period immediately before the time of Amos.

H.H.R.

BLACK, M. & ROWLEY, H. H. (ed. by) : *Peake's Commentary on the Bible*. 1962. Pp. xvi+1126+4+16 maps. (Thomas Nelson & Sons, Edinburgh. Price : 70s. 0d.).

The *Commentary on the Bible* edited by the late A. S. Peake was probably the best and most successful work of its kind ; but, since it was published in 1919 and the Supplement appeared in 1937, Biblical scholarship has developed so much that something more up-to-date has long been needed. This need is now fully met by the completely new work prepared under the editorship of M. Black and H. H. Rowley who had oversight of the articles on the New and Old Testaments respectively. The new *Peake's Commentary* follows a similar plan to that of the old, though paragraphs have now been numbered for ease of reference. However, it differs from the original edition in the greater importance attached to archaeology by the presence of articles on this subject by K. M. Kenyon, J. Gray, and W. F. Albright, and in the addition of essays on the English Versions of the Bible (A. Wikgren), on the Form Criticism of the Old Testament (E. T. Ryder), and on the Theology of the Old Testament (N. W. Porteous). It is impossible here to list all the contributors of general articles and of commentaries on particular books, but special mention may be made of the one scholar who has written both for the original edition and for the new one—S. H. Hooke, who is the author of an article on the Religious Institutions of Israel, the Introduction to the Pentateuch, and the commentary on Genesis. Each section has a select bibliography, and there are indexes and some good maps in colour at the end of the volume. The general scholarly quality of this book is fully as good as that of its predecessor, and it will doubtless prove to be a standard work for the specialized scholar, the theological student, and the ordinary reader for many years to come.

J.A.E.

BRILLET, G. : *Meditations on the Old Testament : the Narratives*, trans. by K. Sullivan. 1959. Pp. 240. (Desclée Company, New York. Price : $3.50).

BRILLET, G. : *Meditations on the Old Testament : the Psalms*, trans. by J. W. Saul. 1960. Pp. 244. (Desclée Company, New York).

The French originals of these books were both published in 1958, at a time when the author was in his eightieth year. Both volumes follow the same general plan of giving a few lines from the Biblical narrative or psalm with the recommendation that the whole passage should be carefully re-read. Then follow the words :—Adore, Speak to God. Finally, there are a few reflections on the contents of the passages cited. The first volume finds its subject-matter in most of the historical books from Genesis down to Second Maccabees ; the approach to the passages cited is pleasant and devotional.

It must, however, be admitted that only too often the comments made are trite and unoriginal with no real attempt to give advice on the deeper sense of the passages. As one example out of many, the account of David's treatment of Uriah the Hittite provokes the comment :—' How easily crime enters a life. Yet the way is often prepared in advance : dark, tortuous paths, and slow, gentle slopes. What is called a sudden impulse is really a long-prepared-for conclusion '. (p. 111).

J.M.T.B.

CASSUTO, U. : *A Commentary on the Book of Genesis, Part I, From Adam to Noah,* trans. by Israel Abrahams. 1961. Pp. XX+324. (Magnes Press, Jerusalem and Oxford University Press, London. Price : 40s. 0d.).

A mainly homiletical commentary on Genesis i. 1-vi. 8. It will be obvious that to cover so little ground in over 300 pages meant that a great deal of material had to be drawn in somehow. Some of it is made up of elementary remarks about Hebrew idiom, not always trustworthy, some by the accumulation of several different explanations of certain texts by former Jewish scholars, some loosely attached by association of idea. The translation of the Biblical text is made to suit the commentary, e.g., Gen. iv. 26 : ' Then men began once more to call upon the name of the Lord '. The following comment on ii. 21, ' and he closed up its place with flesh ' is typical : ' This detail is also emphasized for the sake of the beauty of the narrative, so that the reader should not picture to himself the body of Adam in a state of mutilation, with a bleeding wound ' (p. 134).

L.H.B.

DEISSLER, A. and DELCOR, M. : *La Sainte Bible.* Tome VIII (1) *Les Petits Prophètes.* 1961. Pp. 292. (Letouzey & Ané, Paris).

The excellent series of commentaries edited by A. Clamer, is now on the point of being finished with the publication of the Minor Prophets. This is the first instalment, which includes Hosea, Joel, Amos, Obadiah, and Jonah. Delcor tells us in a prefatory note that on being invited to undertake the commentary, he felt the need of a collaborator, and, after a long search, found one in the person of a German professor in the University of Freiburg in Baden. Deissler contributes commentaries on Hosea and Obadiah to the present volume ; he will be responsible for Micah, Zephaniah, Haggai and Malachi in the volume that is still to come. There is, as Delcor remarks, some difference in the method and approach of the two authors, but both make frequent use of the Hebrew text, and take great pains in the interpretation of the prophetic works. As in other volumes of the series some space is taken up by printing the Vulgate text, but the use of very small type for the commentary proper has made it possible to pack a great deal of valuable matter into less than three hundred pages. J.M.T.B.

EATON, J. H. : *Obadiah, Nahum, Habakkuk and Zephaniah : Introduction and Commentary.* (Torch Bible Commentary) 1961. Pp. 160. (S.C.M. Press, London. Price : 12s. 6d.).

A study of such a group of canonical prophets as this gives Mr. Eaton an opportunity, which he uses, to emphasize the association of prophets and priests at the great shrines in ancient Israel, and to show that such association at the temple in Jerusalem resulted in the presence in prophetic utterances of liturgical forms and the use of conceptions found in temple worship. The introduction to each book covers with a wise discretion the essential subjects, and the commentary gives a clear and coherent conception of the prophet's message without paying excessive attention to textual difficulties.

J.M.

DE FRAINE, J. : *Esdras en Nehemias uit de grondtekst vertaald en uitgelegd.* (De Boeken van het Oude Testament, Deel V, Boek II). 1961. Pp. 142. (Romen & Zonen, Roermond en Maaseik).

This commentary forms the sequel to van den Born's edition of Chronicles (*Book List*, 1961, p. 28) and displays the various features which we have come to expect in this excellent series. The date of Ezra-Nehemiah, bound up with that of Chronicles, is placed between 325 and 300 B.C. ; Albright's identification of the Chronicler with Ezra is rejected. The two books are regarded as being of high historical value. Ezra was probably the official whom the Persian government consulted on matters affecting the customs and law of the Jews (' scribe of the law of the God of heaven ') ; his Aramaic commission in Ezra vii. 12 ff., like the Aramaic documents quoted earlier in the book, is an authentic excerpt from the official archives. Even the edict reproduced in Hebrew in Ezra i. 2 ff. is treated as genuine. On the question of the time-relation between Ezra and Nehemiah, the traditional order is preferred as the most probable. The wall of Jerusalem whose ruined condition is reported in Neh. i. 3 must have been built shortly before 445 B.C. (not at the time of Ezra's mission 13 years previously) ; its demolition was probably the work of Samaritans (cf. Ezra iv. 23). ' Darius the Persian ' of Neh. xii. 22 is identified as probably Darius II ; Jaddua the priest of Neh. xii. 11 is not the contemporary of Alexander, but an earlier Jaddua.

F.F.B.

GERLEMAN, G. : *Ruth.* (Biblischer Kommentar, Altes Testament, XVIII, 1). 1960. Pp. 40. (Neukirchener Verlag der Buchhandlung des Erziehungsvereins, Neukirchen Kreis Moers. Price : DM. 3.50).

Here is a full commentary on the book of Ruth, with abundant text-critical and philological, as well as exegetical notes. The introduction is brief, but it contains a valuable section on the Peshitta of this book. The author briefly reviews the theories about the book advanced in modern critical works, and rejects the view that it has no historical basis, and also the view that the verses which trace David's genealogy from Ruth are a baseless addition to the book. He thinks it improbable that in the age when the book was written or later it would have been possible for anyone to have invented the statement that David had a Moabite ancestry unless there were an old and established tradition behind it.

H.H.R.

HORST, F. : *Hiob*. (Biblischer Kommentar, Altes Testament, XVI), Lieferung 2, 1960. Pp. 81-160. (Verlag der Buchhandlung des Erziehungsvereins, Neukirchen, Kr. Moers. Price : DM. 7 each Lieferung : or, by subscription, DM. 5.85).

The first number of this commentary was reviewed in the *Book List* for 1961 (p. 32). In this second number the commentary on chs. iv. 1-v. 27 is completed, and three further sections (chs. vi. 1-vii 21, viii. 1-22, ix. 1-x 22) are treated with the same thoroughness and wealth of detail which characterised the discussion of the earlier chapters. Here and there the meaning of a Hebrew word has been missed, and sometimes an unnecessary emendation is proposed. But all in all the author's persistent attempt to recover the text of the book of Job and its meaning can evoke only admiration. The wide use he makes of extra-Biblical material, Near-Eastern and other, continues to lend his commentary a special distinction.

D.W.T.

HOWIE, C. G. : *Ezekiel. Daniel*. (Layman's Bible Commentaries). 1962. Pp. 142. (S.C.M. Press, London ; John Knox Press, Richmond, Virginia ; The Ryerson Press, Toronto. Price : 6s. 0d.).

Two difficult books are here competently expounded within the limits imposed by the series. Ezekiel is treated as the record of the teaching of a 6th-century prophet in the Babylonian *golah* : and even xxxviii-xxxix, xl-xlviii are held to embody material from the prophet, though with modifications and editorial additions ; but the author makes his readers aware of the existence of other views. Daniel is held to be the work of a single author who drew material from many sources : the problem of its bilingual character is left open. This eminently readable little book should do much to help the ordinary layman to read and understand two books which he usually neglects.

G.W.A.

JONES, E. : *Proverbs and Ecclesiastes : Introduction and Commentary*. (Torch Bible Commentaries.) 1961. Pp. 350. (S.C.M. Press, London. Price : 18s. 0d.).

This is a most useful addition to this series. In the Introductions good illustrative material is quoted from extra-Biblical sources. The composite nature of Proverbs is noted, most of the book being regarded as pre-exilic; chapters i-ix and xxxi. 10-31, it is suggested, come possibly from the third century B.C. Ecclesiastes is assigned to about 250 B.C. The article on the concept of Wisdom will be found most helpful; that on *māshāl*, all the more that it is recognized as a key-word, somewhat less so. The text in the commentary is based on RSV; recent lexical studies have been well, though critically, used. In the treatment of Ecclesiastes, additions to the original by Sages, the Devout. and an editor are noted. The book will be particularly welcome to teachers and theological students.   A.S.H.

KALT, E. : *Herder's Commentary on the Psalms*, trans. by B. Fritz. 1961. Pp. xxii+560. (Newman Press, Westminster, Md. Price : $6.75).

Kalt was for many years professor of Biblical exegesis in the Mainz theological seminary. He was born in 1879 and died in 1943. This popular edition of the Psalms appeared in 1935, and this fact accounts for Cardinal Innitzer's preface (dated 21 March, 1935) in which he refers to ' the new Bible commentary, published at Freiburg '. Now, twenty-seven years after its first appearance, a translation has been made, which, so far as one can see, takes no account at all of any more recent work. One example among many of the failure to bring the commentary up to date might be verse 12 of Ps. ii, which is translated : ' Embrace discipline, lest at any time the Lord be angry ' on which the author comments that ' the psalmist closes with the admonition : " Kiss the Son ".' The now familiar and widely accepted correction of the text, first suggested, it seems, by Bertholet in 1908, is not mentioned. Yet, as a simple and popular commentary, Kalt's work may still be of value to many readers.   J.M.T.B.

KUIST, H. T. : *Jeremiah*. (Layman's Bible Commentaries.) 1961. Pp. 148. (S.C.M. Press, London. Price : 6s. 0d.).

The author deals with sections rather than with particular verses, though detailed explanations are provided in the more difficult instances. It is difficult to cover so large a prophetic work in so few pages, but the author does give more space to the more important passages such as xxxi (9 pages), where he links up with other Scriptural passages in both Testaments. The volume is concise ; it is non-technical, and it is well suited to the lone reader.   N.H.S.

MOWINCKEL, S. : *Salomos høysang. Gammelhebraiske kjaerlighetsdikte*. 1961. Pp. 42, including 14 ills. by Inge Rotevatn. (O. Falch, Oslo).

In this elegant little book Professor Mowinckel offers a rendering of the *Song of Songs* in rhymed verse with a short introduction in which he discusses the interpretation of the book, rejecting the allegorical and dramatic hypotheses and holding that it is a collection of love songs. This is the position adopted in the introduction to the equally charming unrhymed rendering which he published in 1919 (*Sangenes sang. Gammelhebraiske kjaerlighetssange*), but, as one would expect, the more recent introduction reflects the trend of the scholarship of the past 40 years.

G.W.A.

NOTH, M.: *Exodus: A Commentary*, trans. by J. S. Bowden. (The Old Testament Library). 1962. Pp. 284. (S.C.M. Press. Price: 40s. 0d.).

The original form of this publication in German was entitled *Das zweite Buch Mose : Exodus übersetzt und erklärt* and was volume 5 of the series *Das Alte Testament Deutsch*. Notice was taken of it in the *Book List*, 1960, pp. 21f. No comment need be made on it now, except to say that this excellent English translation of the German text by J. S. Bowden will introduce it to a wider circle of readers and give them a stimulating experience.

J.M.

(*Psalter*) *The Revised Psalter. The First Report of the Commission to Revise the Psalter appointed by the Archbishops of Canterbury and York*. Book I : Psalms 1-41. 1961. Pp. x+70. (S.P.C.K., London. Price : 3s. 6d.).

The first instalment of the new Anglican Psalter is here published and comes fully up to expectation. The revision is scrupulously scholarly, the alterations, aimed always at clarifying the sense, are as few as possible, and the wording everywhere is carefully adapted to Coverdale's style and period. The Hebrew text is accepted ; but emendation is accepted only where it is absolutely necessary (e.g., ii. 11, xviii. 30), when the evidence of the Versions is fully weighed and wherever possible given priority, but Coverdale's additional words and phrases, though retained when they may be regarded as legitimate expansions of the original text, are deleted where they are mere doublets (e.g., xv. 5, xxix. 1). Archaisms (e.g., ' leasing ', ' reins ', and so on), if they are misleading, are removed, and the tenses are freely changed in accordance with the latitude which the Hebrew verbal system is now thought to allow ; and new translations which improve the sense are freely admitted (e.g. xxix. 8, xxxiv. 10). Inverted commas are introduced to indicate direct speech ; and every new rendering is carefully geared to the musical needs of the congregation. The work may be judged eminently successful (within the limits imposed on the Revisers) in fulfilling the purpose for which it is designed (for it is not meant as an exposition of modern Biblical research), and future instalments will be awaited with eagerness.

G.R.D.

VON RAD, G. : *Genesis : A Commentary*, trans. by J. H. Marks. (The Old Testament Library). 1961. Pp. 434. (S.C.M. Press, London. Price : 50s. 0d.).

The component parts of this commentary in the German edition have been noted in *Book Lists* 1950, p. 40 ; 1952, p. 36 ; 1954, p. 41. The value of it is such that it needed to be translated and made available to the English reader. The Biblical text is given in full and is normally that of RSV with a few exceptions. It is primarily a theological commentary, but critical problems and archaeological data have not been neglected. The translator (in spite of a few awkward renderings) and the publishers deserve our gratitude for making this work available. A.S.H.

RHODES, A. B. : *Psalms*. (Layman's Bible Commentaries.) 1961. Pp. 192. (S.C.M. Press, London. Price : 6s. 0d.).

This handy-sized volume fulfils the best traditions of the series. The introduction is necessarily short, but it is adequate. The theological part of it is excellent. The author steers well between the Scylla of multifarious detail and the Charybdis of amorphous generalities. The references to background material, Canaanite, Babylonian, historical, and cultic are adequate. The author has not forgotten that he is dealing with a book essentially religious. N.H.S.

ROUTLEY, E. : *Ascent to the Cross*. (St. Giles Lectures, 1961). 1962. Pp. 94. (S.C.M. Press, London. Price : 5s. 0d.).

Dr. Routley here publishes his 1961 St. Giles' lectures in *The Living Church Books*. He employs a triple strand : a devotional exposition of Psalms 120-134, combined with their imagined use by pilgrims, including Jesus Christ, in the light of today's problems. Orders of service, intercessions, and prayers complete this quite devout book. G.H.D.

RUST, E. C. : *Judges, Ruth, I & II Samuel*. (Layman's Bible Commentaries). 1962. Pp. 152. (S.C.M. Press, London. Price : 6s. 0d.).

This is the thirteenth of the series, and the seventh so far as the Old Testament is concerned. It follows the pattern of previous volumes, wherein the text is dealt with paragraph by paragraph with careful explanation of the literary structure and the historical background. The author follows the normal pattern, but does not think the Book of Ruth a polemic against mixed marriages. Rather it is to show that ' the greatness of the House of David is neither from nor for Israel alone '. This leads to the universalist position. N.H.S.

La Sainte Bible traduite en français sous la direction de l'École Biblique de Jérusalem. Les Livres de Samuel, by R. de Vaux. 2nd ed. revised. 1961. Pp. 254. *Les Livres des Chroniques,* by H. Cazelles. 2nd ed. revised. 1961. Pp. 246. *Les Livres des Maccabées,* by F.-M. Abel and J. Starcky. 3rd ed. revised. Pp. 330+2 folding maps. (Les Editions du Cerf. Paris).

These volumes of the Jerusalem have been revised on the lines indicated in the notice in *Book List,* 1959, p. 19. That on Maccabees, originally entrusted to Abel, and brought to completion by Starcky, contains Abel's translation, Starcky's commentary, and an introduction which is their joint work. In addition to the two maps noted above there is a simple plan of Jerusalem at the time of the Maccabees.

G.W.A.

STEINMANN, J. (and others) : *Deutéronome.* (Connaître la Bible). 1961. Pp. 170+42 ills. (Desclée de Brouwer, Bruges. Price : B.Frs. 69).

STEINMANN, J. (and others) : *Les Juges* (Connaître la Bible). 1961. Pp. 150+45 ills. (Desclée de Brouwer, Bruges. Price: B.Frs. 69).

In each of these two admirable little books there is a short and useful Introduction (and, in *Deutéronome,* a final note on the influence of Deuteronomy), followed by a new translation of the text with a running commentary, in slightly different type, on the page facing, sub-headings and some adjustment of the numerous illustrations making it easy to keep level. Change of source is marked by *retraits,* the gloss or variant narrative is withdrawn a little from the margin which marks the main text, which is a help to the reader who does not want to get too much involved, though with a text as complicated as Deuteronomy it is a very rough guide. The work of a group of scholars, the scholarship is lightly carried, but there is no writing down. An adult and intelligent interest in Biblical criticism and archaeology is assumed, and great trouble is taken to place the material in perspective. The translation is alert and the books have freshness and style and at times a racy humour. The skilfully, even audaciously chosen pictures add a highly suggestive touch. This is *haute vulgarisation* indeed and it is good that we can look forward to more of the same quality.

M.Bu.

STEINMANN, J. : *Job.* Texte français, introduction et commentaires. (Connaître la Bible). 1961. Pp. 156+42 ills. (Desclée de Brouwer, Bruges. Price : B.Frs. 69).

For previous volumes in this series, see *Book List,* 1961, p. 35 (Joshua) and p. 36 (Daniel) : translation on the left-hand page, commentary and illustrations on the right-hand page. The introduction comprises 30 pages. It is competent and gives a good summary of the discussions on the date of the book, its composition and intention. The usual moderate attitude is adopted with the Elihu speeches, chapter xxviii, etc., as later additions. The last 30 pages are devotional in character. The French translation is that in *La Bible de Jérusalem*, see *Book List*, 1958, p. 21 for second edition, and *Book List*, 1951, p. 33 for first edition. N.H.S.

STEINMANN, J. (and others) : *Ézéchiel*. (Connaître la Bible). 1961. Pp. 192 with numerous ills. (Desclée de Brouwer, Bruges. Price : B. Frs. 69).

This is a brief outline commentary in a paperback, supplemented by pictures and a chronological chart. A French translation by Steinmann appears on each left-hand page, and the commentary opposite. The text follows the order of *Lectio Divina*, and in view of the irregular order a table at the end shows on what pages the oracles occur. A brief introduction precedes, and the indices and a catechism follows. The book is very attractive and offers a popular commentary on the prophet on Roman Catholic lines without any great profundity or adequate treatment of the more difficult portions of Ézéchiel. It is good value for money. G.H.D.

WEISER, A. : *Das Buch des Propheten Jeremia*. (Das Alte Testament Deutsch, Teilband 20/21). 4., neubearbeitete Auflage. 1960. Pp. 447. (Vandenhoeck & Ruprecht, Göttingen).

The two parts of the original edition of this commentary were noticed in the 1953 and 1955 issues of the *Book List* (see *Eleven Years*, pp. 494, 673). In this new edition account is taken of the contributions made to the study of the book in the intervening years, thus increasing the usefulness of one of the outstanding commentaries in this series. G.W.A.

WOLFF, H. W. : *Dodekapropheton : Hosea*. (Biblischer Kommentar : Altes Testament, XIV). Lieferungen 3 and 4 and Einleitung. 1961. Pp. 161-240, 241-322, and I-XXXII. (Verlag der Buchhandlung des Erziehungsvereins, Neukirchen, Kr. Moers. Price : DM. 7 each Lieferung and DM. 2.95 Einleitung).

These instalments complete Wolff's commentary on Hosea (for Lieferungen 1 and 2 see *Book List*, 1957, p. 35, and 1958, p. 24). Each paragraph of the text is translated afresh into German, and the translated paragraph is followed by notes on the text and a commentary, in which an attempt is made to relate the message of the prophecy to the New Testament gospel and to apply it to men and movements today. The work thus combines features of a critical commentary with those of a theological exposition. In viii. 12 the Kethibh *rubbô tôrāthî* is preferred and translated ' die Vielzahl meiner Weisungen ' ; in the context this is taken to indicate the presence in Hosea's time of a written tradition of the covenant law, which the people were evading by their concentration on the sacrificial cult, and it is inferred that the sacrificial cult played no part in this written tradition.

The exposition is designedly a contribution to 'Biblica theology' in the modern sense of that term ; special attention is therefore paid to the use made of Hosea by New Testament writers. For example, at the end of the exposition of ch. x there is a short homiletical excursus based on the 'rain of righteousness' in x. 12b and its reflection in Paul's 'fruits of righteousness' in 2 Cor. ix. 10, which carries us far beyond the immediate intention of Hosea's words.

The introductory *Lieferung* covers concisely the questions of the prophet's time, life, language, and theology, and of the transmission of his oracles. The book as we know it is viewed as comprising three bodies of tradition, themselves already complex, consisting of chaps. i-iii, iv-xi, and xii-xiv. In addition, three successive stages of redaction are distinguished, the last of these being marked by the *Heilseschatologie* of early Judaism.

F.F.B.

ZIMMERLI, W. : *Ezechiel.* (Biblischer Kommentar, Altes Testament, XIII), Lieferung 7. 1960. Pp. 481-578. (Neukirchener Verlag der Buchhandlung des Erziehungsvereins, Neukirchen Kreis Moers. Price : DM. 7).

This Lieferung, which is slightly larger than normal, brings the first volume of this very detailed commentary to a close, the end of ch. xxiv having been reached. The introductory material will not appear until the exegesis is complete ; and accordingly Professor Zimmerli's interpretation of the book and of Ezekiel's ministry is being communicated piecemeal ; but already the acuteness of the literary analysis and the depth of theological exposition make it evident that this will rank, with the very greatest commentaries on any of the prophetic books.

G.W.A.

LITERARY CRITICISM AND INTRODUCTION

(including History of Interpretation, Canon, and Special Studies)

ARENS, A. : *Die Psalmen im Gottesdienst des Alten Bundes : Eine Untersuchung zur Vorgeschichte des Christlichen Psalmengesanges.* (Trierer Theologische Studien 11). 1961. Pp. xx+228. (Paulinus-Verlag, Trier. Price : DM. 13.80).

The argument of this interesting monograph is too complex to be summarized satisfactorily in a few lines, and it must suffice to say that the author here develops the thesis that the origin of the canonical Psalter is to be found in a triennial cycle corresponding to the three-year reading of the Law in the synagogue ; and he seeks to show that this practice, which is described as a 'dialogue' between Yahweh and His people, has its roots in the great covenant festivals of the pre-exilic period. Despite the author's conservative attitude to the Old Testament records, this is a work which merits serious consideration, even though one's own conclusions may often be different from those of the author.

A.R.J.

BALTZER, K. : *Das Bundesformular*. (Wissenschaftliche Monographien zum Alten und Neuen Testament, 4). 1960. Pp. 216. (Neukirchener Verlag der Buchhandlung des Erziehungsvereins, Neukirchen Kreis Moers. Price : Ln. DM. 19.50, br. DM. 17.45).

Written by a colleague and former pupil of Professor Gerhard von Rad, this monograph clearly reveals the influence of the master. Using the Hittite material as characteristic of the state treaties of the ancient Near East, the author seeks to show that these possess a literary pattern which may be expressed in terms of a preamble, a sketch of the historical background, the general basis of agreement followed by a more specific elaboration of its terms, the invocation of the gods as witnesses and consequent curse or blessing. This material is then used as the basis for discerning a loosely corresponding *Gattung* as an established method of expressing the covenant relationship between Yahweh and Israel ; and an attempt is made to trace the continuity of this pattern, not merely as a literary device but also as an important aspect of cultic practice, from early times down through post-exilic Judaism (including the Qumran community) into early Christianity itself. Although, as it seems to the present writer, the author tends to overstate his case and one cannot but wonder if the term *Gattung* is not becoming suggestive of a strait jacket, this is a study which may be read with profit by all who are interested in arriving at a sounder appreciation of the covenant idea than that which was characteristic of the Wellhausen era.

A.R.J.

BARCLAY, W. : *The Making of the Bible* (Bible Guides No. 1). 1961. Pp. 96. Lutterworth, London ; Abingdon, New York and Nashville. Price : 5s. 0d.).

Dr. Barclay is well-known for his New Testament expositions for the non-theologically equipped reader. This book, like the rest of the series, is addressed to the same public. A section each is given to ' The Making of the Old Testament ', ' The Making of the New Testament ' and ' The Final Test ', the last being a discussion of the concept of canonicity. We would question the value in a book of this nature of including in ' Books for Further Guidance ' a number which are out of print. If a further edition is made, the date 180 B.C. for the Greek translation of Ecclesiasticus will need to be corrected.

A.S.H.

BARTH, C. : *Einführung in die Psalmen.* (Biblische Studien, 32). 1961. Pp. 92. (Neukirchener Verlag der Buchhandlung des Erziehungs- vereins, Neukirchen Kreis Moers. Price : DM. 4.90).

The author, already held in high regard for his monograph *Die Errettung vom Tode in den individuellen Klage- und Dankliedern des Alten Testamentes* (*Book List*, 1948, p. 38), here offers in an expanded form a German translation of the introduction which he wrote for a new Indonesian translation of the Psalms. Although intended for the general reader, it may be welcomed as a simple, but in many respects quite masterly, survey of the modern approach to the Psalter, involving, for example, its literary types, the world of thought which they reveal, and their place in Israel's worship.

A.R.J.

BEYERLIN, W. : *Herkunft und Geschichte der ältesten Sinaitraditionen.* 1961. Pp. 203. (J. C. B. Mohr, Tübingen. Price: DM. 27.80).

One feature of the magnificent contribution to the study of the Old Testament by Noth and von Rad which has aroused serious misgivings is their separation of the Exodus tradition from the Sinai tradition, of the election of Israel from the Covenant. It is the outstanding merit of Dr. Beyerlin's brilliant study of the Sinai perikopes (Exod. xix-xxiv, xxxiii-xxiv) that he challenges their view in a sustained argument which demands the most careful study. He subjects the relevant tests to a meticulous literary analysis followed by a traditio-historical study of their *Sitz im Leben.* A com- parison with the structure of the Hittite treaties, to which Mendenhall drew attention and which belong to a period and an area which makes them relevant, is made to throw the burden of proof on those who would deny the original link between God's acts in history and the Covenant in which He claims Israel's obedience. It is shown that not only the Decalogue (which is claimed as Mosaic) but also the other Covenant sections belonging to both J and E reflect the pattern of the Hittite treaties. Like his teacher, Professor Weiser, the author seeks to show how the Theophany was represented in the Hebrew cult. It is maintained that a constant feature of Covenant renewal ceremonies was the writing down of the demands of Yahweh and the reading of the Covenant law before the people. Cult, however, presupposes history and the author joins issue with those who would concentrate on *Heilsgeschichte* alone. This is a book which must not be over- looked by students of the early history of Israel.

N.W.P.

CASSUTO, U. : *The Documentary Hypothesis*, trans. by Israel Abrahams. 1961. Pp. XII+118. (Magnes Press, Jerusalem and Oxford University Press, London. Price : 20s. 0d.).

This is an attempt to disprove the documentary hypothesis, described in the translator's foreword as a ' masterly exposition of the Documentary Hypothesis '. The book was compiled as a course of lectures for school teachers, but the style of writing is better suited to their scholars. The author admits that there were pre-Torah traditions but says 'The Torah selected those traditions that appeared suited to its aims' p. 102. Of the divine names he says, 'the Torah chose one of the two names according to the context and intention precisely as follows', and then there follow seven rules to determine which name Torah should choose. One of these rules runs : 'The name YHWH occurs when the context depicts the Divine attributes in relatively lucid and, as it were, palpable terms . . . 'Elohim, when the portrayal is more general, superficial and hazy, leaving an impression of obscurity' (p. 31).

L.H.B.

HENRY, M.-L. *Jahwist und Priesterschrift : Zwei Glaubenszeugnisse des Alten Testaments.* (Arbeiten zur Theologie, 3). 1960. Pp. 32. (Calwer Verlag, Stuttgart. Price : DM. 3.20).

The sub-title correctly suggests the theme of this exceptionally suggestive lecture. An explanation is sought for the difference between the pessimistic element in J (belonging to the confident period of the monarchy), and the optimistic character of P (belonging to the period of Israel's deepest despair after the Exile). The answer is that J was correcting the hybris of confident Israel by presenting the questionableness of man before the divine grace ; whereas P was, in the spirit of a pastor, presenting to disillusioned Israel of the Exile the picture of the Creation that was rational and of the divine purpose that was unchanging. The details of this thesis are worked out with fascinating astuteness. But the unanswered questions are pressing. If P was, as the author assumes, a re-interpretation of J, was P thought up for this pastoral purpose? How far were older traditions used and other motives present? Is P all theology and not a witness to history at all? Surely the discipline of the study of the traditions must precede this kind of theological interpretation.

D.R.J.

KAPELRUD, A. S. : *Central Ideas in Amos.* (Reprint) 1961. Pp. 86. (Oslo University Press, Oslo. Price : 16s. 0d.).

This book originally appeared in 1956 as one of the studies published by Det Norske Videnskaps-Akademi (see *Book List*, 1957, pp. 38f.). No change appears to have been made in this reprint.

G.W.A.

*KNIGHT, G. A. F. : *Prophets of Israel (1) Isaiah.* (Bible Guides, No. 7). 1961. Pp. 96. (Lutterworth Press, London ; Abingdon Press, New York and Nashville. Price : 5s. 0d.).

This is probably the best of the author's books hitherto. In accordance with the aim of the series, it offers a guide to the main themes of the book of Isaiah (from a reasonable, critical standpoint) rather than a commentary on the conventional pattern. This will make it much easier for the ' interested layman ' to find out what the book is about and how to appreciate it when he goes back to read Isaiah himself, as he surely will, after gratefully taking his bearings from this guide. There is, first, a very brief literary-critical summary stating the still dominant theory of tripartite authorship ; and then we have four chapters dealing with the book's ' Purpose ', ' Plan ', ' Exposition ' and ' Power ', with a short excursus on ' The Little Apocalypse ' appended to Chap. 3. The Servant is equated with ' Israel ' in the first three Songs, but with God Himself in the fourth.

In a book such as this is intended to be it is requisite that the connection between the New Testament and the Old Testament prophet should be touched on, and most readers of this notice will probably feel much sympathy with the position taken up, though many will not see eye to eye with the author on every point. Only four misprints were noticed : p. 73, l. 1 ; p. 90, l. 13 ; p. 92, l. 27 ; p. 93, l. 20 ; though the assertion, on p. 4, that the RSV ' is used in quotations ' is not true of every quotation by any means, several appear to be the author's own translations. We predict a warm and appreciative reception for this little book.

D.R.Ap-T.

MÜLLER, N. : *Die liturgische Vergegenwärtigung der Psalmen. Untersuchungen zur hermeneutischen Problematik der lutherischen Propriumpsalmodie.* (Forschungen zur Geschichte und Lehre des Protestantismus, zehnte Reihe, Band XXI). 1961. Pp. 166. (Chr. Kaiser Verlag, Munich. Price : DM. 10).

The liturgy of the Lutheran Church in Germany contains a considerable number of texts taken from the Old Testament Psalms. This book faces the problems which such a use of the Old Testament raises for modern men. The author starts from modern critical study of the Psalter, particularly the *Gattungsforschung* inaugurated by Gunkel. He emphasizes the importance of the original forms and types for modern Christian liturgy. As regards the subject matter, he maintains that the original meaning of the texts and the historical-exegetical results must be respected ; but a sort of transposition into the Christian sphere is necessary, so that the old texts may be able to do service as a divine *kerygma* to us. This must be carried out without allegorizing on one hand and a wrong Christological interpretation on the other.

J.L.

PATERSON, J. : *The Wisdom of Israel.* (Bible Guides, No. 11). 1961. Pp. 96. (Lutterworth Press, London ; Abingdon Press, New York. Price : 5s. 0d.).

The series is designed to present ' the purpose, plan and power of the Scriptures '. This book, dealing with Job and Proverbs, may justly claim to have done this. The treatment is homiletic, although full recognition is made of critical scholarship, at least in so far as there is room in so short a book for a full critical approach. There are four short essays on each book dealing respectively with the purpose, plan, exposition and power of the book. L.H.B.

REVENTLOW, H. GRAF : *Das Heiligkeitsgesetz.* (Wissenschaftliche Monographien zum Alten und Neuen Testament 6). 1961. Pp. 172. (Verlag der Buchhandlung des Erziehungsvereins, Neukirchen Kreis Moers. Price : cloth, DM. 17.50 ; paper, 15).

The keynote of this detailed study of the Holiness Code is expressed in the words : ' Das Heiligkeitsgesetz ist ein gottesdienstliches Dokument. ' After a brief survey of the literary-critical study of the code which has to tackle the troublous question of the relation of it to D and P (as well as to Ezek.) and commonly arrives at the chronological order D, HC, P, which raises some serious interpretative difficulties, the author, finding a starting-point in some of the work of Klostermann, Noth, and von Rad, states the case for a *formgeschichtliche* approach to the code. In this the endeavour is made to show that, not only in its earliest form with apodictic laws, but in its developed form as we have it, it is rooted in the worship of ancient Israel and, in particular, in the covenant festival. In this festival the main elements were a hortatory prelude with an historical retrospect, the proclamation of the law, the renewal of the covenant and the utterance of blessings and cursings. The author then examines the suitability of the Holiness Code for this festival and affirms that, studied in this way, it is a test-piece of pentateuchal investigation, and can open up new possibilities of judgment on the dating of other parts of the Pentateuch, and in respect of the inter-relation of oral and written tradition can supply valuable evidence. This is a book which should be noted. J.M.

RICHTER, H. : *Studien zu Hiob. Der Aufbau des Hiobbuches dargestellt an den Gattungen des Rechtslebens.* 1959. Pp. 148. (Evangelische Verlagsanstalt, Berlin. Price : DM. 8.50).

This study, presented in 1954 as a thesis for a doctor's degree, takes its start from the work of L. Koehler on the juridicial aspects of Hebrew society (1931). The author rejects interpretations of the book of Job from wisdom or from the cult. He places its writer in the line of the prophets, trying to reclaim the people from wrong ideas to the true knowledge of Israel's God. The prophets spoke in times of apostasy ; the writer of the book of Job is acting during a period of traditional and cultic orthodoxy. He does not preach but chooses literature to attain his end. In the opinion of Dr. Richter the book is a unity from which the popular story of the chapters i, ii and xlii. 7 sqq. cannot be separated.

In the first part of this well composed book the author treats the judicial customs of Babylonia and Egypt, very shortly, and those of Israel, somewhat more amply. Several problems deserve a more detailed treatment, e.g., Ruth iv (p. 39) In the main part of the book the writer often uses extra-Biblical texts for his explanation of Job, in accordance with the place of action chosen by the writer of the drama. See, e.g., the treatment of Job xix. 23-27 with the help of an Egyptian custom (pp. 89 sqq). Job does not receive a reply from the God of his friends. Their God remains mute. God who answers Job is Jhwh, God of former days, speaking without the official cult in thunder and storm as in the days of law-giving and of Elijah (p. 121).

Dr. Richter's conclusions are often convincing and always instructive. Sometimes they are far-reaching but not con-clusive. It is a pity that the author confines himself almost completely to German literature.

P.A.H.deB.

VRIEZEN, TH.C. : *De Literatuur van Oud-Israël.* n.d. (1961). Pp. 248. (Servire, The Hague. Price : Fl. 3.95).

This handy introduction to the Old Testament originally appeared in 1948 under the title *Oud-israelitische Geschriften* and was reviewed in *Book List,* 1949, p. 36 (*Eleven Years,* p. 199). In its present form it has been extensively revised and enlarged, including the addition of a short section on the Apocrypha and Pseudepigrapha. There must be few manuals of its kind in which so much information is presented in so short a space and so readable a manner.

G.W.A.

WEISER, A. : *Introduction to the Old Testament,* trans. by D. M. Barton. 1961. Pp. xvi+492. (Darton, Longman & Todd, London. Price : 50s. 0d.).

The German editions of this Introduction were noted in *Book Lists,* 1946, p. 30, 1950, p. 46, and 1958, p. 31. A few additions, mainly notes on recent literature, have been made to the 4th edition, from which this translation has been made. The appearance of this English translation will be greatly welcomed. Each section is preceded by a well-selected bibliography ; the matter combines great learning with a sensitiveness to the life behind the literature. To the theological student the book may be especially commended for its sobriety of judgment.

A.S.H.

LAW, RELIGION, AND THEOLOGY

ACKROYD, P. R. : *Continuity : A Contribution to the Study of the Old Testament Religious Tradition.* (Inaugural Lecture in the Samuel Davidson Chair of Old Testament Studies delivered at King's College, London, 10 October, 1961). 1962. Pp. 32. (Basil Blackwell, Oxford. Price : 3s. 6d.).

Attempts to escape from the kind of criticism which seems to reduce the Old Testament to a collection of *disjecta membra*

have sometimes led to other extremes of imposing on it an
artificial unity. In this Inaugural Lecture Professor Ackroyd
seeks rather to indicate the interplay of conservatism and
innovation, the expression of new truth and fresh experience
in old forms, paying particular attention to the *confessio fidei*,
legal pattern, wisdom teaching, and prophecy, and to the
expressions of public cult and private piety. There are many
salutary and timely warnings here against the tendency to
dogmatic generalizations. A remarkable amount of material
has been packed into the lecture, which is amply and usefully
documented.

G.W.A.

AMSLER, S.: *L'Ancien Testament dans l'Église. Essai d'herméneutique
chrétienne.* (Bibliotheque théologique). 1960. Pp. 248. (Delachaux
& Niestlé, Neuchâtel).

This is a thorough and exceedingly well documented study of a
much debated subject ; and the author is to be congratulated
on the systematic way in which he has tackled it. The first
part of the book is devoted to an examination of the way in
which the New Testament writers interpret the Old Testament,
and consists of chapters dealing with Hebrews, 1 Peter, the
Fourth Gospel, the Pauline Epistles, the Acts, and the Synoptics. The second part is a consideration of the use of the Old
Testament in the Church. Three chapters are devoted to the
question *why* the Old Testament should be read in the Christian
Church and five to the question *how* it should be read. There
are detailed discussions of the relationship of text to event, of
allegorizing interpretation, historicism and symbolism, of the
Word of God and the written word, the Word of God and
event, and the Word of God and theological interpretation.
In a short notice such as this it is impossible to indicate the
wealth of material to be found here. Suffice it to say that this
is a book which should not be missed by anyone interested in
the complex problems which it discusses.

G.W.A.

VAN AS, J. J.: *Skuldbelydenis en Genadeverkondiging in die Ou Testa-
ment.* (Confession and Pardon of Sin in the Old Testament.)
With a Summary in English. 1961. Pp. iv+184. (Drukkerij
Elinkwijk, Utrecht).

This treatise on Confession and Pardon of Sin in the Old
Testament is a doctoral dissertation presented to the University
of Utrecht ; Professor Vriezen was the candidate's promoter.
It is written in Afrikaans, with a short English summary at the
end. The study begins with the Psalter, in which special
attention is paid to the penitential psalms ; in these the
suppliant takes the place of an accused party making his plea
to a judge. Next the Torah, and particularly the cult, is
examined. Because the cult is the outward expression of the
bond uniting Yahweh and His people, the important place
given in it to confession and pardon of sin is thoroughly justified,

for sin weakens the bond of union. Further light on the subject is found in the prophets, in Job, and in outstanding confessions of sin recorded throughout the Old Testament. Pardon does not follow automatically upon confession; true heart-repentance is required if man's fellowship with God is to be restored ; the restoration of such fellowship is embodied in the penitential liturgy, which finds room for God's gracious answer as well as man's confession.

F.F.B.

BERNHARDT, K.-H. : *Das Problem der altorientalischen Königsideologie im Alten Testament unter Berücksichtigung der Geschichte der Psalmexegese dargestellt und kritisch gewürdigt.* (Supplements to *Vetus Testamentum*, vol. VIII). 1961. Pp. VIII+352. (E. J. Brill, Leiden. Price : Fl. 46).

The opening pages of this work offer a short history of the different ways in which over the years the psalms have been interpreted, and this leads to a discussion of the currently popular approach to the study of the Psalter in terms of its literary types and the now familiar attempt to impose upon some, if not all, of the psalms the theory of a myth and ritual pattern, centring in the king, which was regarded as common to the ancient Near East. The remainder of the work is devoted to an examination of the attitude to kingship in Israel and a critical survey of the above-mentioned approach to the exegesis of the Psalter. To be frank, it is difficult to know what value to place upon a work in which the arguments of so many different authors are wrenched from their contexts and lumped together in such a way as to provide a convenient target for criticism. The present writer was warned early and with some indignation (by a distinguished O.T. scholar who has no axe to grind in the present connexion) that he would find his views grossly distorted ; and it must be admitted that it has been difficult to read with patience a work which, so far as one's own special studies are concerned, can only be described as a farrago of misrepresentation. However, this is not the place for detailed protest ; and there is at least some compensation in the fact that the author, through many of his other criticisms and by his general discussion of the Israelite monarchy, offers much which the knowledgeable reader will recognize as lending the reviewer admirable support. In short, if the reader is looking for a balanced survey of the problem, he will not find it here ; but with careful winnowing he should find much wheat amongst the chaff, and the author himself has provided an excellent tool for this purpose in the splendid collection of bibliographical material.

A.R.J.

BIČ, M. : *Die Propheten : Brückenbauer vom Knecht zum Sohn.* (Aufsätze und Vorträge zur Theologie und Religionswissenschaft, 10). 1959. Pp. 40. (Evangelische Verlangsanstalt, Berlin. Price : DM. 1.80).

In this booklet, written for wide circulation, the author dis-

claims any intention to offer a creative work on the Old
Testament prophets, but in a very brief study considers them
as bridge builders from Moses to Christ. After glancing at
prophecy outside Israel he notes the varieties of prophets
within Israel, and then considers (1) their lot as both conquered
and conquering (*überwundene and überwindende*), (2) their
mission and message, and (3) the Israel to which they were
sent and the New Israel to which they looked forward. From
this it will be seen that this study is written from the New
Testament standpoint. Professor Bič emphasizes the unity
of the two Testaments and the fulfilment of the Old Testament
in the New.

H.H.R.

BLANK, S. H. : *Jeremiah : Man and Prophet.* 1961. Pp. xii+260.
(Hebrew Union College Press, Cincinnati. Price : $6.50).

Professor Blank first expounds the biographical sections of
Jeremiah in their presumed chronological order. Section II
offers a study in the autobiographical sections, in which the
author goes beyond J. Skinner's well known treatment. In a
third section the themes of Jeremiah's message are set forth,
and finally the perspective of Jeremiah is explained and
evaluated. There are four additional notes, indices and a
glossary of Hebrew terms. The book is like its author and its
theme—instructive, suggestive, and deeply moving.

G.H.D.

EICHRODT, W. : *Theology of the Old Testament.* Vol. I., trans. by J.
Baker. 1961. Pp. 542. (S.C.M. Press. Price : 50s. net).

The publication of the 6th edition of Part 1 and the 4th
edition of Parts 2 and 3 of Professor Eichrodt's monumental
Theologie des Alten Testaments in 1959 and 1961 respectively
has been followed by the appearance of Vol. I of the excellent
translation by J. A. Baker. This puts within the reach of
English readers one of the most important works of modern
scholarship in the field of Old Testament study. Translated
as it is from the most recent edition it gives the reader the
advantage of having the corrections and additions which the
author felt necessary after nearly thirty years. He himself
points to his maturer views on the subjects of the kingship
and the cultic prophet which have been the centre of so much
discussion in recent years. To those, however, who were
familar with the book in its original form, the pages of greatest
interest will be the Preface to the Fifth Revised Edition, the
Preface to the English Edition and especially the excursus
on the Problem of Old Testament Theology which, it should
be noted, appears as the Preface to Vol. II (containing *Teil* 2/3)
of the recent German Edition. Professor Eichrodt reiterates
his conviction that Old Testament Theology is an historical
and not a normative science and reasserts his view that the
Covenant is the central concept by which the unity of the
Old Testament should be demonstrated. He rightly claims

that the activity of God in history must never be isolated from the response of the Old Testament community. ' It is the interior overmastering of the human spirit by God's personal invasion which in the first place brings to life the O.T. understanding of history. Here is to be found the decisive inward event, without which all external facts must become myth '. In the Excursus Eichrodt deals briefly but trenchantly with von Rad's *Theology of the Old Testament*, to the brilliance and value of which he pays a generous and well-deserved tribute. He joins issue with von Rad's depreciation of the importance of history for Old Testament Theology, with his refusal to recognize any underlying unity in the various Old Testament confessions of faith and with his typological interpretation of the Old Testament. It becomes clear that he finds in von Rad's work an existentialism like that of Bultmann which does not do full justice to what is to be found in the Old Testament and pleads himself for an historical realism and a recognition of an inner coherence of the Old and New Testaments and of the reality of a ' divine new creation in which the Old Testament salvation-history reaches its goal '.

N.W.P.

EICHRODT, W. : *Theologie des Alten Testaments.* Teil 2, *Gott und Welt* und Teil 3, *Gott und Mensch.* Vierte neubearbeitete Auflage. 1961. Pp. XVIII + 398. (Ehrenfried Klotz, Stuttgart, and Vandenhoeck & Ruprecht, Göttingen. Price : DM. 18.50 ; by subscription, 14.80 ; price of the entire work : DM. 32).

The reappearance of Parts 2 and 3 of Eichrodt's Old Testament Theology in a fourth German Edition is a most welcome event, not only because the earlier Editions were out of print but because the author has carefully revised the text in innumerable places and supplied references to recent literature, changes which make the book more useful than ever. Some of the Sections, e.g., §20, are to a very considerable extent re-written, so that possession of the new edition is highly desirable. English readers who now have Part 1 in translation will await impatiently Parts 2 and 3 in English dress. Meanwhile they have in the Excursus to Part 1 the brief criticism of von Rad's Old Testament Theology which appears in the preface to Parts 2 and 3 of the new German edition. N.W.P.

DE FRAINE, J. : *La Bible et l'Origine de l'Homme.* (Museum Lessianum, Section biblique, No. 3). 1961. Pp. 126. (Desclée de Brouwer, Bruges. Price : B. Frs. 96).

Professor Fraine states the problem of the origin of man in his preface, and then in the first chapter of this easily readable and delightful study, reviews the principal solutions and present state of the problem. The second and main chapter offers an exposition of the six principal Biblical texts (Gen. i. 26-28 ; Gen. ii. 7, 18-24 ; Eccles. xvii. 1-14 ; Rom. v. 12-19 ; Acts xvii. 26). The third chapter is concerned with the teaching of the Roman Church concerning the relevant doctrines ; original sin, monogenism, etc. A very useful volume but of most use to Roman Catholics.

G.H.D.

GLASSON, T. F. : *Greek Influence in Jewish Eschatology, with special Reference to the Apocalypses and Pseudepigraphs.* 1961. Pp. x + 90. (S.P.C.K., London. Price : 9s. 6d.).

This small, but important, book is the first of a new series comparable with the S.C.M. series of ' Studies in Biblical Theology '. The author's thesis is that too little attention has been paid to the influence of Greek thought on Jewish eschatology in the pre-Christian period, and he traces a number of lines of influence, particularly on such things as journeys to the realm of the dead, the divisions of the Underworld, resurrection, the intermediate state. In his introductory chapter he argues that it is antecedently likely that ideas which were first developed in Judaism after a century or more of Greek rule came more directly from Greece than from Iranian sources, and notes a number of writers who have recognized Greek influence on Palestinian Jewish thought. He might have included also Norman Bentwich, *Hellenism*, 1919.

H.H.R.

GRELOT, P. : *Le couple humain dans l'Écriture.* (Lectio Divina 31). 1962. Pp. 112. (Éditions du Cerf, Paris. Price : NF. 5.70).

As the author explains, this is not intended to be a complete theological treatment of the Biblical teaching on marriage. It contains three main sections : (1) the basic data of the Biblical revelation in deliberate reaction against the religious thought of the ancient orient ; (2) the development of Biblical teaching through the successive phases of the Old Testament ; (3) the final stage in the New Testament. Grelot gives a very effective account of the sacral character of sexuality in the ancient orient, together with a summary of the relevant myths and rituals. There are mythical archetypes, which reveal the relation between sexuality and the polytheism of the period. The Biblical revelation disposes of these myths. A new sacral character becomes apparent in the marriage blessed by Yahweh (Gen. i-ii). The Bible often presents the life of husband and wife as a drama, with barrenness, dissension, and infidelity ; but there is a progress towards redemption ; and in the prophetic teaching conjugal symbolism reflects faithful and fruitful love, which appears in post-exilic Judaism with its strong structure of family life. In Canticles love is seen as redeemed and saved from itself. A solid and stimulating book.

H.C.

GROS, A. : *Je suis la route. Le thème de la route dans la Bible.* (Thèmes bibliques). 1961. Pp. 152. (Desclée de Brouwer, Bruges. Price : B. Frs. 84).

> This is a small work originally presented as a thesis for a degree in theology, and has as its subtitle *La thème de la route dans la Bible.* After a chapter on the Biblical vocabulary, in which ' route ' is frequently used both in the literal and in the metaphorical senses, the author provides chapters on the historic route of God's people, and its progressive spiritualiza-tion in the later books, on the fulfilment of the term in the person of Christ and on the new route of the Christian Church. There is an index of Biblical quotations, and a bibliography containing exactly six items. It does not appear likely that this was a difficult book to compose, but the author has at least performed what Professor Saintsbury once styled ' porter's work ' in bringing together the many passages that have a bearing on his subject.   J.M.T.B.

GUTHRIE, H. H. : *God and History in the Old Testament.* 1961. Pp. viii+180. (S.P.C.K., London. Price : 17s. 6d.).

> This book was originally published in 1960 by the Seabury Press and was reviewed in *Book List*, 1961, p. 46. No changes have been made.   G.W.A.

HEATON, E. W. : *The Old Testament Prophets.* (Pelican Books A 414). Revised reprint, 1961. Pp. 188. (Penguin Books, Harmondsworth, Middlesex. Price : 3s. 6d.).

> In its original form, *His Servants the Prophets*, this book was reviewed in *Book List*, 1950, p. 57 (*Eleven Years*, p. 274) and in its revised form under its present title in *Book List*, 1959, pp. 27f.). Minor changes have been made, including additions to the bibliography. It should continue to serve as a stimulating and readable introduction to prophecy.   G.W.A.

HEBERT, G. : *When Israel Came out of Egypt.* 1961. Pp. 128. (S.C.M. Press, London. Price : 8s. 6d.).

> Father Herbert reviews in light and popular style the literary, historical, and religious problems of the events of the Exodus and the faith it engendered. Unfortunately the book takes no account of the work of Pedersen, von Rad, or Noth, though it quotes all three in other connections.   G.H.D.

HERRMANN, W. : *Das Wunder in der evangelischen Botschaft*. (Aufsätze und Vorträge zur Theologie und Religionswissenschaft, Heft 20). 1961. Pp. 32. (Evangelische Verlagsanstalt, Berlin. Price : DM. 1.80).

This short study of the interpretation of the terms ' blind ' and ' deaf ', with special reference to the opening of blind eyes and the unstoppng of deaf ears in the Gospels, begins with a consideration of the Old Testament material. It is easily established that the terms occur in the Old Testament not only in their literal sense, but also to denote spiritual insensitivity. It is this latter sense, the author argues, which gives meaning to the Gospel miracles in which the blind receive their sight and the deaf their power to hear.
F.F.B.

HOOKE, S. H. : *Alpha and Omega. A Study in the Pattern of Revelation*. 1961. Pp. xvi+304. (James Nisbet, Welwyn, Herts. Price : 21s. 0d.).

This book is the product of the Speaker's Lectures in the University of Oxford 1956-1961. Only the first part, pp. 108, is concerned with the Old Testament ; the remainder continues the subject into the New Testament. It deals with the Biblical pattern of Revelation, though the first chapter considers the culture of Mesopotamia and Egypt in which also the divine activity may be discerned. In the Old Testament we have the historical event in which the Call of God is discerned by men of faith and obedience. This leads to interpretation and re-interpretation. The section on the prophets presents them not only as vehicles of revelation but as instruments in the fulfilment of the divine purpose (the treatment of Ezekiel is particularly satisfying). A chapter is devoted to the Apocalyptists and one to Kingship as providing significant images which are to be realised in the Christ. This is a book which combines sound learning, theological insight and a warm devotional spirit.
A.S.H.

HORST, F. : *Gottes Recht : Gesammelte Studien zum Recht im Alten Testament*. Aus Anlass der Vollendung seines 65. Lebensjahres herausgegeben von Hans Walter Wolff. (Theologische Bücherei 12). 1961. Pp. 344. (Chr. Kaiser Verlag, Munich. Price : DM. 14.80).

Little more than the titles of the various articles included in this collection of studies can be given here, but these give a clear indication of the nature of the contents. Almost half of the volume is devoted to a lengthy treatise, published in 1930 under the title ' Das Privilegrecht Jahwes', on the laws of Deuteronomy 12-18. Other articles deal with Old Testament laws concerning property, theft and oaths, together with a few of a more general character, such as those entitled ' Naturrecht und Altes Testament ', ' Recht und Religion im Bereich des Alten Testaments ', ' Segen und Segenshandlungen in der

Bibel ' and ' Die Doxologien im Amosbuch '. One of notable theological interest is included, ' Der Mensch als Ebenbild Gottes ' ; it was published in English in 1950 in *Interpretation* IV. Finally, one wholly apart from the theme of the volume is given a place in the collection because it is not now readily obtainable, ' Die Formen des althebräischen Liebesliedes '.

J.M.

HUM, J. M. and CNEUDE, C. : *Guide Pastoral de Cantiques et Psaumes.* 1961. Pp. 404. Éditions du Cerf, Paris. Price : 23s. 6d.).

Little need be said about this interesting work, as it has a rather indirect bearing on Old Testament Studies. It is, in effect, a guide to the use of Psalms and Canticles for cate-chetical purposes, and, as such, should prove useful. Many of the Canticles are quite modern. References are made through-out to those that have already been recorded, and there are full indices, including one entitled ' Choix de Cantiques selon les Thèmes '. The book has been published simultaneously in nine different collections, and seems destined to have a wide circulation.

J.M.T.B.

JOHNSON, A. R. : *The Cultic Prophet in Ancient Israel.* 2nd edition. 1962. Pp. viii+92 (University of Wales Press, Cardiff. Price : 15s. 0d.).

In the new edition of this much quoted monograph slight changes have been made in the text and in the translations of Biblical passages, and extensive additions have been made to the footnotes. There are also indexes of subjects, authors, Scriptural references, and Hebrew words and phrases. In welcoming this publication we also look forward to its promised sequel, *The Cultic Prophet in the Psalter*, and to the revised editions of Professor Johnson's other monographs.

G.W.A.

KNIGHT, G. A. F. : *Law and Grace : Must a Christian Keep the Law of Moses?* 1962. Pp. 128. (S.C.M. Press, London. Price : 8s. 6d.).

This is an eloquent protest against the modern Marcionite attitude to the Torah, carefully discusses Jesus' treatment of the Law, and devotes particular attention to the concept of ' Christ, the End of the Law '. The phrase in John i:17 is well discussed. Passages from the Old Testament are some-times given in the author's translation, but the fact should have been noted since the attractive translation of Isa. xliii. 23f. will leave the reader, unacquainted with Hebrew, puzzled and doubtful. The size of the book does not always allow the author to justify some of his statements, e.g. his repudiation of the Greek conception of the soul. But these are small criticisms in a book that successfully repudiates any merely legal treatment of the Law.

A.S.H.

LINDBLOM, J. : *Prophecy in Ancient Israel.* 1962. Pp. viii + 449. (Blackwell, Oxford. Price : 45s. 0d.).

This is probably the best and most comprehensive book on Old Testament prophecy that has yet appeared in English, and it may never be surpassed. Individual prophets are not treated separately, but the studies of various aspects of prophecy are so thorough that little if anything important is overlooked.

The book begins with a most valuable account of ' ecstatic ' prophecy outside Israel, followed by a brief discussion of ' primitive ' prophecy in Israel. The greater part of the book is taken up with elaborate studies of the ' classical ' (i.e. canonical) Hebrew prophets from psychological, historical, and theological points of view, ending with a description of the religion of the prophets.

Professor Lindblom has an encyclopaedic knowledge of work done by his predecessors, and his footnotes alone are almost a work of reference. Naturally there are points on which a reader may disagree, but the views maintained are always possible.

Finally this unique work is written in faultless English ; it is difficult to realize that this is not the author's native language ; it is not even a translation from a foreign language. But this work must be read and studied to be properly appreciated. T.H.R.

LING, T. : *The Significance of Satan : New Testament Demonology and its Contemporary Relevance.* 1961. Pp. 114. (S.P.C.K., London. Price : 12s. 6d.).

The purpose of this new series is to introduce works of scholarly research on Biblical and related subjects. After a rapid account of Old Testament demonology, the author passes on to the New Testament, where he shows that Satan is there the central emphasis. He then discusses the chief features of ' the symbol of Satan '; e.g., spirit of the world, tempter, deceiver, destroyer. Next there comes a study of the relation between Satan and ' the angelic powers ', and finally, the significance of today, which concerns the Conquest of Satan, that victory over evil which is ' the constant justification of the Church's mission '. N.H.S.

MAARSINGH, B. : *Onderzoek naar de Ethiek van de Wetten in Deutero-nomium.* Inquiry into the Ethics of the Laws in Dt., with a summary in English. 1961. Pp. 184. (J. M. van Amstel, Winterswijk. Price : Fl. 8).

This inquiry into the ethical character of the laws in Deuteronomy is a doctoral dissertation presented to the University of Utrecht ; the author's promoter was Professor Vriezen. The distinctively cultic laws have been left out of the reckoning.

Attention is paid in turn to the laws protecting life, marriage, and the family, and socially weaker and underprivileged members of the community, to the laws regarding slavery, property, the kingship, and foreigners. Comparison is made between the Deuteronomic laws and those of the other codes of the Ancient Near East. The ethical standard governing the laws within the Israelite brotherhood is high. The *ger* is also treated sympathetically, and almost completely admitted into the brotherhood. The *nokhri* is outside the frontiers; his practices are abominations and must not be imitated. But there are distinctions within the *nokhrim* : Edomites and Egyptians are looked upon more leniently, Canaanites and Amalekites with the greatest hostility.

F.F.B.

MACLAURIN, E. C. B. : *The Hebrew Theocracy in the Tenth to the Sixth Centuries B.C. An Analysis of the Books of Judges, Samuel, and Kings.* 1959. Pp. x+140. (Angus and Robertson, Sydney. Price : 21s. 0d.).

The modest purpose of this monograph is 'to supply students of the development of religious thought with a collated basis for research within a limited period ' by a collation of statements in Samuel and Kings on God and His attributes, the functions and relations of king, priests, and prophets, and society in general, gathered, as the author tells us, and as is somewhat too obvious, in card-index form, together with a full table of verses and their sources and dates. The conclusions in this table are uncritically derivative, and are ignored in the main body of the text. The title characterizes the presupposition of the writer rather than the content of the book, which is rather a pedestrian concordance with practically no original discussion or fruitful comment. The evidence beyond the Old Testament, and indeed beyond Samuel and Kings and occasionally Judges, is entirely ignored. Within these narrow limits the writer has effected a useful piece of devilling rather than a book on the subject promised by the title.

J.G.

MAERTENS, T. : *C'est fête en l'honneur de Jahvé.* 1961. Pp. 224. (Desclée de Brouwer, Bruges. Price : B.Frs. 90).

Those who wish to know how to find relevance for the present day in the often avoided ritual stipulations of the O.T. may find help in these pages. The author seeks to show how the original ' literal ' meaning of the festivals of Judaism has been gradually modified and spiritualized in the life of Israel by the process of evolution until the final Christian interpretation is not only possible but obligatory—it is this concentration on the ' essential ' and 'eternal ' significance of these rites which alone makes it legitimate to impose them on Christians of a different cultural heritage.

A brief resumé of the underlying pagan festivals is followed
by a treatment of the celebration of New Moon, New Year,
Harvest, Tabernacles, First sheaf/Passover, Wheat sheaf
Pentecost, Sabbath/Sunday and other festivals. The interesting
point is made (p. 56f.) that, in Israel, pastoral festivals were
not accommodated to agricultural rites but, on the contrary,
the celebrations proper to a sedentary community were always
re-interpreted in terms of Israel's nomadic past though, unless
I mistake the author's meaning, it is surprising to have Lev.
xxiii. 43 put down as Deuteronomic.

Some of the author's ' transferences ' when, as do some others,
he adapts the Gospel narrative to the Jewish liturgical year
may raise doubts ; but the book is interesting, and the
author's theme clearly put forward for the reader to accept or
modify. One of the useful features of the book, though not its
main aim, is the assembly of information (without, however,
full documentation) which is not easily found together elsewhere. If we might play on the title, it might be said of this
book, *c'est fait en l'honneur de Jahvé*, and it is welcome.

D.R.Ap-T.

MENDENHALL, G. E. : *Recht und Bund in Israel und dem Alten Vordern
Orient.* (Theologische Studien 64). 1960. Pp. 63. (EVZ—Verlag,
Zürich. Price : Sw. Frs. 5.80).

This is the German translation, by F. Dumermuth, of a study
which first appeared in the Biblical Archaeologist, Vol. XVII,
No. 2 (1954), Pp. 26-46 and No. 3 (1954), Pp. 49-76. It was
reprinted and published by the Biblical Colloquium, Pittsburgh,
and reviewed by H.H.R. in *Book List*, 1955, p. 62. D.R.J.

MICHAELI, F. : *How to Understand the Old Testament*, trans. by M.
Senior. Key Books 10. 1961. Pp. 48 (United Society for Christian
Literature, Lutterworth, London. Price : 2s. 0d.).

This is an abridged translation of the author's *L'Ancien
Testament et l'église chrétienne d'aujourd'hui* which was noted
in *Book List*, 1958, pp. 35f. The abridgement is regrettable
and at times misleading. A.S.H.

MUILENBURG, J. : *The Way of Israel. Biblical Faith and Ethics.*
(Religious Perspectives, vol. 5). 1961 (U.S.A.), 1962 (U.K.). Pp.
158. (Harper, New York, and Routledge & Kegan Paul, London.
Price : $3.75 ; 15s. 0d.).

If it be true that *mega biblion mega kakon*, there could hardly
be a more convincing example than this book that a short
work of scholarship can display a rare degree of excellence
in the quality and richness of its thought and the literary
grace of its style. Although the grateful reader may wish
that the book had been twice as long ; yet it is perhaps also

true that the very brevity of the book is one of its supreme merits ; for the author has the gift not only of putting what he has to say in few words, but of suggesting more than he actually says and of constantly stimulating the reader to further thought. Here, in six chapters (The Way of the Word ; The Symbols of the Way ; The Beginning of the Way ; The Way of the Leaders—Lawgivers, Prophets, Wise Men ; The Way of Worship ; The Way of the Future) is a profound and sensitive presentation of the message of the Old Testament, which may be read with profit by beginner and specialist alike.

G.W.A.

PANNENBERG, W., RENDTORFF, R., RENDTORFF, T., WILCKENS, U. : *Offenbarung als Geschichte.* 1961. Pp. 131. (Vandenhoeck & Ruprecht, Göttingen. Price : DM. 10.80).

This book contains the papers read by a group of younger scholars representing different departments of theological study at a Conference in October, 1960 which dealt with the problem of revelation. Pannenberg, the systematic theologian of the group, discusses the view of revelation as the self-revelation of God and argues that this is made indirectly through history and not directly through the Name of God, or through Word, law and gospel. T. Rendtorff, as an Old Testament scholar, examines the Old Testament evidence in detail, dealing with expressions like *galah, nir'ah, nodha', kebhodh Yahweh* and *'ani Yahweh. Nir'ah* refers to theophanies often associated with a promise. *Nodha'* usually refers to God making himself known by his acts. The *kabhodh* of God has often a cultic significance but can be used with reference to God's eschatological intervention as by Ezekiel. The most important section deals with the expression ' I am the Lord ' and links up with the work of Zimmerli. God proclaims himself as the God who has acted on Israel's behalf in history. The same view is developed in the essays on the New Testament and on Church History. This is a useful contribution to the current debate on the nature of revelation. *Heilsgeschichte,* however, should have been balanced by the Covenant. We have in this book, as so often, some over-emphasis on the *Heilsgeschichte.*

N.W.P.

PARKES, J. : *The Theology of Toleration.* (Claude Montefiore Lecture, 1961). n.d. (1962). Pp. 28. (The Liberal Jewish Synagogue, London. Price : 3s. 0d.).

A liberal Christian here pleads for greater understanding with liberal Jews on the ground of a theology of divine toleration. It is difficult to know exactly what this theology is, since there is no systematic statement of it and little direct exposition of Scripture to support it. It seems to amount to a universalism of the kind : ' We shall all get there in the end ', expressed in the form : ' The toleration of God is not of different levels of truth but of different approaches to it '. It involves the rejection of the notion of final judgment and of any separation of sheep and goats, and intolerance of the ' anti-rationalist antics of Dr. Karl Barth ' who is alleged to teach that God is wholly unintelligible. The author, to whom otherwise the world of scholarship owes much, has clearly not come to terms with the ineradicable intolerance of the Old and New Testaments.

D.R.J.

PEDERSEN, J. : *Israel, III-IV. Hellighed og Guddommelighed.* 2nd edition. 1960. Pp. 614. (Branner & Korch, Copenhagen. Price : Dan.Kr. 55).

The Danish second edition of the second volume of this outstanding work is now photo-reprinted (The Danish third edition of the first volume was issued 1958, the English second edition of the whole work 1959, cf. *Book List,* 1960, p. 39). There are some minor corrections in the text. The notes, however, have been revised thoroughly and there is a new excursus on gods, king, and cult in Ras Shamra/Ugarit (as in the revised English edition).

E.H.

PFEIFFER, R. H. : *Religion in the Old Testament : The History of a Spiritual Triumph.* ed. by C. C. Forman. 1961. Pp. xii+276. (A. & C. Black, London. Price : 24s. 0d.).

For those who are already familiar with Pfeiffer's work and at the same time have a good working knowledge of the background of the Old Testament this book will come as a useful summary of Pfeiffer's ideas on Biblical religion. Familiar ideas, however, go hand in hand with unfamiliar ones, and, because the latter are sometimes presented without adequate statement as to how they are come by (due to insufficient editing?), a beginner might well be perplexed. Much of the book is sketchy and often one feels one ought to be told more. It is noteworthy that Pfeiffer attaches the greatest importance to the publication of Deuteronomy in 621. Before that the ancient Israelites ' knew nothing of a code of morality revealed by God or of a moral conscience regulating the conduct of the individual ' (p. 96). Again, ' Every mention of the covenant of Jehovah with Israel in the Bible is later than 621 ' (p. 55). There is much useful material however for those who can use the book to advantage.

L.H.B.

DE PURY, R. : *Der Exodus* (Biblische Studien, 30). 1961. Pp. 78. (Buchhandlung des Erziehungsvereins, Neukirchen. Price : DM. 4.80).

This book offers with Foreword, 23 homiletical studies in the events and institutions of the Book of Exodus. The author seeks to show the Christological significance and religious meaning of passages chosen from every part of the Book of Exodus. The studies are alive and suggestive.

G.H.D.

ROBERTSON, E. :   *The Role of the Early Hebrew Prophet.* (*Bulletin of the John Rylands Library*, Vol. 42, 1959/60). Pp. 412-431. (The John Rylands Library and Manchester University Press, Manchester).

> The prophet is presented as a man called of God to act as His intermediary particularly in situations of national emergency. After the division of the Kingdom the prophets acted as spies and subversive agents on behalf of Judah. Only when that Kingdom was destroyed did they become proclaimers of a moral and spiritual religion. The reader did not find the argument, especially as it related to the eighth-century prophets, convincing.
>
> A.S.H.

RONDELEUX, L.-J. :   *Isaïe et le prophétisme.* (Maîtres spirituels). 1961. Pp. 189+many ills. (Éditions du Seuil, Paris).

> This attractively produced and well written study of Isaiah sets him in the context of his time, and in the framework of Israel's religion and the prophetic movement, and ends with a short survey of Israel's spiritual pilgrimage after his time to the end of the prophetic movement and a brief glance at the relation of Jesus to prophecy. There are many unusual but attractive illustrations, maps of Palestine and of the Near East and a plan of Jerusalem, a chronological table, and useful, up-to-date bibliographies. A worthy addition to an excellent series.
>
> G.W.A.

ROWLEY, H. H. :   *The Faith of Israel : Aspects of Old Testament Thought* (The James Sprunt Lectures delivered at Union Theological Seminary, Richmond, Virginia, 1955.) Reprint, 1961 (paperback). Pp. 220. (S.C.M. Press, London. Price : 12s. 6d.).

> This is an unaltered reprint of the volume which originally appeared in 1956 and was reviewed in *Book List*, 1957, pp. 54f. Its many outstanding qualities are so well known that it must suffice here to wish that it will continue to be widely used.
>
> G.W.A.

SCHEEPERS, J. H. :   *Die Gees van God en die Gees van die Mens in die Ou Testament.* 1960. Pp. XVI+330. (J. H. Kok N.V., Kampen. Price : Fl. 9.50).

> It is with some diffidence that the present writer ventures to comment upon this monograph, as his reading of Afrikaans is painfully slow ; and his apology for attempting it must be the fact of his own deep interest in the subject. The following expression of opinion, therefore, is based primarily upon the excellent summary in English (pp. 304-22) and, in conjunction with this, a sampling of the main argument. The work is based upon a careful and exhaustive study of the term *rûaḥ* : notably, as used of wind ; of breath ; of an ' extra-natural '

power which may hold sway over men ; and of the spirit of Yahweh as active in the lives of men, e.g., prophets, national leaders such as judges and kings, the Messiah, and society at large. The author examines all the relevant passages of the Old Testament, and at the same time exhibits a due acquaintance with modern studies in this field ; and, while the reviewer cannot agree with some of the views expressed (e.g., the emphasis upon the idea of ' breath ' and the use of the familiar but surely inadequate description of the spirit of Yahweh in terms of ' impersonal power '), there can be no doubt that we have here an informative and stimulating work which will repay and, indeed, should receive careful consideration.

A.R.J.

SCHMIDT, W. : *Königtum Gottes in Ugarit und Israel : Zur Herkunft der Königsprädikation Jahwes* (B.Z.A.W., 80) 1961. Pp. x+90. (Verlag Alfred Töpelmann, Berlin. Price : DM. 14).

In the main this valuable study falls into two parts : (i) an examination of the Canaanite conception of ' Kingship ' as used of the gods in the Ras Shamra texts, and (ii) an attempt to show how this terminology came to be used of Yahweh by the Hebrews. While recognizing that the Jerusalem cultus played an important part in this connexion, the author rightly adds that the adoption of this idea need not have begun there but may, perhaps, be traceable also to other centres, particularly Shiloh. Although at times the argument may seem a little laboured (as in the discussion of ' Das Richtertum ', pp. 27ff.), this is probably indicative of the author's concern to be thorough ; and, despite the fact that the writer of this note is wrongly cited as holding the view that the autumnal festival was a ' Thronbesteigungsfest ' (p. 23, n.44), the monograph as a whole appears to be carefully annotated. Altogether, therefore, a promising piece of work.

A.R.J.

SMART, J. D. : *The Interpretation of Scripture*. 1961. Pp. 318. (S.C.M. Press, London. Price : 35s. 0d.).

The range of the book is wide : the essential mystery of the Scriptures, problems of interpretation such as the difficulty of subjective judgements and the place of the Church, the unity of the Bible, methods of interpretation (typology, allegory, analogy). The concept of the Image of God is treated in detail as an example of methods of interpretation. The author also discusses the inspiration and authority of the Bible, and modern tendencies especially the rebirth of Biblical theology. It is difficult to describe the author's precise aim. He looks for a new approach in interpretation, in which the divine and the human are ' married to each other ' in the text of Scripture, and so also history and theology. But all the interpreter's work is preparatory. Fundamentally the reader must be ' unconditionally open towards God '.

N.H.S.

STAMM, J. J. : *Der Staat Israel und die Landverheissungen der Bibel.* 2nd edition. 1961. Pp. 52. (Gotthelf-Verlag, Zürich and Frankfurt a.M.).

The original edition of this booklet was reviewed in *Book List*, 1959, p. 31. In this new edition the author has taken account of some of the comments of reviewers and has added references to more recent literature. A stimulating and attractive study.

G.W.A.

TAYLOR, W. M. : *Moses the Lawgiver.* 1961. Pp. 482. (Baker Book House, Grand Rapids, Mich. Price : $2.95).

Joseph the Prime Minister. 1961. Pp. 242. (Baker Book House, Grand Rapids, Mich. Price : $2.95).

These two books are two of altogether eight similar volumes which are reprints of 1886 originals. The author was for twenty years preacher at the Broadway Tabernacle, New York City. He died in 1902. Both volumes are based on the Bible text as it stands. The stories are interwoven with popular homiletical material, and the whole style and approach would doubtless have been considered quite bold seventy-odd years ago.

N.H.S.

THURIAN, M. : *The Eucharistic Memorial*, Part I. The Old Testament, trans. by J. G. Davies. (Ecumenical Studies in Worship, 7.) 1960. Pp. 118. (Lutterworth Press, London. Price : 9s. 6d.).

The object of this study is to provide a firm Biblical basis for eucharistic theology and the liturgy. It starts from the word *anamnesis*, and investigates the main Old Testament passages, sacrificial terms, and customs which throw light on its meaning. The conclusion is that, though the Old Testament conception of memorial has varied applications, it ' always indicates a sacrificial movement '. There are valuable comments on the Passover, intercession, vestments, music, images, angelic mediation, lights, etc. The interest of the book is beyond question. Its weakness is that the Biblical basis for its main positions is not firmly laid. Not only does the author betray a defective knowledge of the sacrificial system of Israel, but also he constantly oversteps the evidence. On page after page one scribbles : *non sequitur*. Devotion and science are out of step.

D.R.J.

DE VAUX, R. : *Ancient Israel. Its Life and Institutions*, trans. by J. McHugh. 1961. Pp. xxiv+592. (Darton, Longman and Todd, London. Price : 55s. 0d.).

The English translation of Père de Vaux's magisterial vols. *Les Institutions de l'Ancien Testament* (see *Book List*, 1958. p.39 and 1961, pp. 52f.) is cordially welcome inasmuch as such a lucid and positive presentation of the subject in just perspective by such a master as Père de Vaux has an appeal for students of the Old Testament at all levels. The translator is to be congratulated on a translation which loses nothing of the force and lucidity of the original.

J.G.

WESTERMANN, C. : *A Thousand Years and a Day. Our Time in the Old Testament*, trans. by S. Rudman. 1962. Pp. x+280. (S.C.M. Press, London. Price : 21s. 0d.).

The purpose of this book is indicated by its sub-title. The thousand years of Jewish history are interpreted as fulfilled in the one day of the crucifixion and exaltation of Christ. The book is addressed to the general, non-specialist reader, who wishes to understand the Bible as a whole, and let the O.T. speak to our present situation. The author deals mainly with the Law and the Prophets, and devotes only a tenth of the book to the Writings. He gives us valuable insights into the significance of the O.T. narratives, and preachers in particular will find here grist for their mill.

L.A.P.

YARON, R. : *Introduction to the Law of the Aramaic Papyri*. 1961. Pp. xiv+136. (Clarendon Press : Oxford University Press. Price : 30s. 0d.).

This brief introduction to the law of the Aramaic papyri from Egypt (both Cowley's and Kraeling's documents, with occasional reference to those edited by the reviewer, which are of a different type) is welcome ; it breaks new ground, raises many problems and throws out many interesting suggestions. The documents deal with a wide range of subjects ; but so few are there relating to any one subject, e.g., marriage or divorce, that the author's conclusions, as he admits, can often be nothing but tentative ; nonetheless, they are always well argued and clearly stated. The concluding chapter shows that the Jewish Colony in Egypt in the 5th century B.C. did not have their own law ; but, while much of their language reflected Babylonian law, they would seem rather to have followed Egyptian demotic terminology, form, and practice (although this suggestion raises the question of the extent to which Babylonian and Assyrian law may have influenced that of Egypt) ; and faint but possible traces of the influence of Graeco-Egyptian law can perhaps be detected. Nothing is known of Persian law at this time so that, although a few Persian commercial terms occur, no legal influence can be traced to this source. Finally, these documents have left some slight mark on the language of Talmudic law ; but many technical terms which seem at first sight likely to have passed from the earlier to the later law are strangely missing from it.

G.R.D.

368 BOOK LIST 1962

ZIMMERLI, W. : *Die Botschaft der Propheten Heute* (Calwer Hefte, **44**). 1961. Pp. 32. (Calwer Verlag, Stuttgart. Price : DM. 1.60).

This contains four broadcast addresses in which the author finds a parallel in the modern world, threatened with disintegration, to the conditions to which the prophetic word was originally addressed. The personal God comes into this human situation and requires whole-hearted obedience. The prophet is both revolutionary and conserver ; he looks with confidence for Him who comes.

A.S.H.

THE LIFE AND THOUGHT OF THE NEIGHBOURING PEOPLES

HOOKE, S. H. : *Babylonian and Assyrian Religion.* 1962 (reprint). Pp. xii+128. (Blackwell, Oxford. Price : 14s. 0d.).

This is a reprint of Professor S. H. Hooke's well-known book on Babylonian and Assyrian Religion, which first appeared in 1953, when it was reviewed in the *Book List*, p. 68 (*Eleven Years*, p. 521). It appears to be entirely unchanged except that it is now issued in an improved form, in which it will be doubly welcome.

G.R.D.

JONES, T. B. and SNYDER, J. W. : *Sumerian Economic Texts from the Third Ur Dynasty*. A Catalogue and Discussion of Documents from Various Collections. 1961. Pp. xx+422 (Lithographed). (University of Minnesota Press, Minneapolis, and Oxford University Press, London. Price : 80s. 0d.).

Thousands of Sumerian tablets of the time of Dynasty III of Ur are already known, and the present volume adds another 355 tablets from American collections ; these are presented in European transliteration (based on Labat's system) and not translation, which is not necessary, as the contents are usually bare lists of commodities. The editors are not Sumerologists in the strict sense but historians, and their work is geared not so much to the detailed interpretation of words and phrases as to restoring the archives to their original form and determining the nature of the agricultural, commercial and technical activities reflected in them. They also throw out hints regarding the last stage of such studies, which will be the synthesis of the whole matter with a view to producing a composite picture of the period ; but they admit that the time for this work has hardly yet come. The first part of the work (pp. 3-199) contains the text in transliteration, the second (pp. 203-344) is taken up with the commentary; the last part (pp. 347-421) contains a useful bibliography and valuable indices of names, titles and occupations and selected Sumerian

words and phrases. The whole work reproduced from typescript which is clearly reproduced (except for the loss of some
lines on two pages) although the individual texts taken alone
often have little interest, shows how much can be made out of
such documents when discussed in the mass with intelligence
and competence.
G.R.D.

KUPPER, J.-R. : *L'iconographie du dieu Amurru dans la glyptique de
la Ire dynastie babylonienne*. (Académie Royale de Belgique. Classe
des lettres et des sciences morales et politiques. Mémoires. Tome
LV, fasc. 1). 1961. Pp. 95+49 ills. on 9 plates. (Académie Royale
de Belgique, Brussels. Price : B. Frs. 80).

This fine study analyses the material relating to the god
Amurru which is available up to the time of the first dynasty
of Babylon. In the first chapter it is shown to be probable
that the frequently represented figure with the ' bâton
recourbé ' (' crooked stick ') is that of the god Amurru. In
chapter two, which is the main part of the book, the author
presents the entire range of representations on seals of the
god with the crooked stick ; but shows that there is no
uniformity of type, since posture, dress, headgear (generally
a tall cylindrical hat, but frequently the horned tiara), and
the accompanying animal (often a gazelle, it seems) vary. The
third chapter contains an investigation of the references to
the god Amurru in the texts (inscriptions on seals, literary
sources, votive inscriptions, etc.). Finally, chapter four is a
discussion of the cult of the god Amurru, in which the following
conclusions are reached : there are traces of a cult of the god
Amurru as early as the third dynasty of Ur ; representations
of the god first appear, on seals, after that dynasty and are quite
frequent during the old Babylonian period. The characteristic
' crooked stick ' cannot be interpreted with certainty. As
' Lord of the Steppe ', the god Amurru was a creation of
theological speculation in Mesopotamia, and was not imported
by alien elements ; but his cult acquired added importance
as a result of the immigration of the ' Western Semites '.
M.N.

LIVERANI, M. : *Storia di Ugarit nell'età degli Archivi politici*. (Studi
Semitici, 6.) 1962. Pp. 175. (Centro di Studi Semitici, Rome.
Price : paper, 45s. 0d. ; cloth, 52s. 0d.).

Under Professor Moscati's active guidance Rome has become a
remarkable centre of Semitic studies. The present volume is
the sixth in an excellent series of monographs (published in
quick succession), all dealing with vital subjects in the field
of Near Eastern research. It is particularly encouraging that
several of the authors are pupils of Professor Moscati who is
carrying out the Rabbinic maxim *ha'amidu talmidim harbe*—
and there are very few more important things that Orientalists
can do.

The present work is limited to a reconstruction of the political history of Ugarit, excluding cultural, social, economic, etc., aspects. Chronologically it deals with about two centuries (1380-1195 B.C.), from the age of el-Amarna to the sea-borne invasions. It is based on the yield of the international archives of the Palace of Ugarit, written in both Akkadian and Ugaritic, on archaeological evidence, and on data drawn from places outside Ras Shamra. Much of the material bearing upon the history of Ugarit is as yet unpublished, and it is therefore possible that Signor Liverani's outline will require modification in due course.

To us the great value and importance of Ugarit lie in its language, religion, society, and its role as a pivot of cultural irradiation in the world of the Eastern Mediterranean ; but its political status between the Hittites and the Egyptians was relatively subordinate. Signor Liverani has rendered an important service. May there soon be others to investigate the internal conditions of Ras Shamra society as reflected in the Ugaritic documents.

E.U.

MOSCATI, S. : *Die altsemitischen Kulturen.* 1961. Pp. 244+23 plates. (W. Kohlhammer, Stuttgart. Price : DM. 7.20).

Ten years ago Professor Moscati published his valuable *Storia e civiltà dei Semiti.* Since then it has appeared with alterations and additions in two German translations. Now, however, the immense increase of new archaeological material has made it necessary for the learned author to produce an entirely new book, and the present volume is the German translation (by Bruno Sandkühler) of his recently published *Le antiche civiltà. semitiche.* It is to be hoped that the book may soon be translated into English and appear in a paperback edition, as there is no comparable book in English which provides in a handy form such a comprehensive and authoritative survey of the whole 'field of ancient Semitic religion. A specially valuable feature of the book is the inclusion of an account of ancient Arabian and Ethiopian religion and culture. There is a full and up-to-date bibliography, a useful index, and an excellent collection of illustrations.

S.H.H.

VIEYRA, M. : *Les Assyriens.* 1961. Pp. 189+many ills. (Editions du Seuil, Paris. Price : 7s. 3d.).

This is the twenty-fourth volume of the series edited by Michel Chodkiewicz and contains an index, table of Chronology, a bibliography and fifty-two illustrations. There is a long list of misprints. The scope of the book includes an account of the archaeological rediscovery of the Assyrian civilization, a critical appreciation of the Assyrian empires, a chapter on the texts and their decipherment, a brief account of Assyrian kings, wars, gods, capital city, and finally assistance in using the Assyrian rooms at the Louvre. A useful introduction to the subject.

J.N.S.

THE DEAD SEA SCROLLS

BLACK, M. : *The Essene Problem.* (Friends of Dr. Williams' Library, Lecture No. 14. 1960). 1961. Pp. 28. (Dr. Williams' Trust, 14 Gordon Square, London, W.C.1. Price : 4s. 6d.).

Principal Black compares the Graeco-Roman description of the Essenes with the Scrolls, and scrutinizes them on three counts : (i) the Essene meal and the sacred meal of Qumran, (ii) the monastic order (mainly the question of Essene and Qumran celibacy), (iii) common ownership. In all three comparisons the divergences are substantial. Josephus describes an ' ordinary ' meal whereas Qumran is ' certainly a ritual or ceremonial meal '. Whatever is meant by Josephus ' and Philo's Essene celibacy, Qumran simply delayed marriage to a later age than usual in Judaism. Common ownership in Qumran was limited to the priestly hierarchy. On all three points Graeco-Roman sources are unreliable, and there is no room in them for a challenge to the view that the scrolls actually described the Essenes.   B.J.R.

BLACK, M. : *The Scrolls and Christian Origins : Studies in the Jewish Background of the New Testament.* 1961. Pp. x+206+16 plates. (Thomas Nelson, Edinburgh. Price : 25s. 0d.).

This book, which is based upon the Morse Lectures delivered by Principal Black in Union Theological Seminary, New York, in 1956, is the best contribution which any one author has made thus far to the important subject indicated in the title. The central thesis of the book is that there was, both in the north and south of Palestine, a longstanding strain of nonconformist Judaism with which historians for the most part have never reckoned adequately, and that this non-conformist Judaism supplies the background both of the Qumran community and of the early Church. The noncon-formist tradition goes back ultimately to such ascetic groups in early Israel as the Rechabites, the Kenites, and the Nazirites ; it survived the work of Ezra, from which normative Judaism stems, and may be recognized in the Samaritan schism and other sects whose peculiarities are recorded in rabbinical and patristic writings. More convincingly than Professor Cullmann, who links the Qumran community with the ' Hellenists ' of the New Testament, Principal Black suggests a link between the community and the ' Hebrews ' who stand over against the Hellenists. The men of Qumran, whose identity with the Essenes is accepted, represent the southern branch of Jewish nonconformity ; the origins of Christianity are to be sought in the northern branch. The comparative discussions of baptismal rites and the sacred meal ; legalism, prophetism, and apocalyptic ; Messianic expectation and related beliefs ; Essene celibacy and the ' virgins ' of 1 Cor. vii, contribute substantially to the value of this highly important study.   F.F.B.

371

BRUCE, F. F. : *Second Thoughts on the Dead Sea Scrolls* 2nd edition. 1961. Pp. 160+frontispiece. (Paternoster Press, London. Price : 12s. 6d.).

The first edition of this book was noticed in *Book List*, 1957, p. 64. Professor Bruce has slightly enlarged it and made certain other minor revisions ; but substantially this is the same book. We wish it the increasing circulation which it merits. G.W.A.

CARMIGNAC, J. and GUILBERT, P. : *Les textes de Qumran traduits et annotés. La Règle de la Communaté, La Règle de la Guerre, Les Hymnes.* 1961. Pp. 284. (Letouzey et Ané, Paris. Price : 31s. 6d.).

This is the first of two volumes in which the whole of the published scrolls is ultimately to be published in translation, with introduction and notes. Volume two will contain the Damascus Document, Biblical Commentaries, the Genesis Apocryphon, diverse fragments from Caves One and Four, and, in appendices, the relevant texts of Philo, Josephus, and Pliny. Indexes, and, presumably, a table of contents will also be included. The present, first volume is excellent.

The Rule is translated by Guilbert. A comprehensive introduction covers the usual topics of literary genre, the historical situation, theological themes, and a short bibliography. The translation is careful and readable. Annotation, reduced to a minimum, is thorough and particularly helpful in the matter of O.T. quotations.

Warfare and *Hymns* are rendered by Carmignac. In each case the introduction follows the same pattern. The *Warfare Scroll* had already been translated by the same author (cf. *Book List*, 1959, p. 34f.), and his standpoint is much the same in the present volume, though the notes accompanying the translation are fuller. The Hymns, twenty-five plus eight or nine culled from MSS fragments, are arranged editorially by the translator (thus Poem 1 comes from column XIII, 1-26 and three fragments; the second from column XIV, 1-7, plus fragments of it and of col. XIII). Carmignac, on the whole, is more venturesome than his colleague Guilbert in the matter of emendation and conjectural restoration, but this does not substantially affect the balance of his contribution. B.J.R.

DUPONT-SOMMER, A. : *The Essene Writings from Qumran*, trans. by G. Vermes. 1961. Pp. xvi+428. (Basil Blackwell, Oxford. Price : 45s. 0d.).

The first French edition of this work was reviewed in the 1960 *Book List*, p. 46 (see also the notice of the German Translation, *Book List*, 1961, p. 62), and the hope was expressed that an English edition would soon be forthcoming. Here it is, translated by Dr. G. Vermes from the second (revised and enlarged) French edition. An author is indeed fortunate when he secures a translator who not only possesses the the requisite linguistic ability for his work, but is thoroughly conversant with the subject-matter, and yet reproduces the author's views with complete fidelity, even where they clash with his own. Dr. Vermes has elsewhere given us his own views, and will no doubt have further opportunities of doing so; it is Professor Dupont-Sommer who speaks to English readers throughout the present volume. For example, in the *pesher* on Hab. ii. 15, the day of atonement on which ' he appeared before them to swallow them up ' is still, as in Dupont-Sommer's earlier discussions of the subject, the capture of Jerusalem by Pompey in 63 B.C., viewed as the Teacher of Righteousness's vengeance upon his persecutors. The Essene origin of the *Testaments of the Twelve Patriarchs* and the *Similitudes of Enoch* is still maintained. Here, then, we have an English version of all the non-biblical texts from Qumran which are accessible to date, introduced and elucidated by a scholar who has exceptional authority for the task—a magisterial work on what Père Daniélou, in words here quoted with approval, describes as ' the most sensational discovery ever made '.

F.F.B.

HEMPEL, J. : *Die Texte von Qumran in der heutigen Forschung : Weitere Mitteilungen über Text und Auslegung der am Nordwestende des Toten Meeres gefundenen hebräischen Handschriften.* (Reprinted from Nachrichten der Akademie der Wissenschaften zu Göttingen I, Philologisch-Historische Klasse, Jahrgang 1961). 1962. Pp. 281-374. (Vandenhoeck & Ruprecht, Göttingen. Price : DM. 9.80).

In 1949 Professor Hempel communicated to the Göttingen Academy ' vorläufige Mitteilungen ' on the Qumran texts. This further study is dedicated to Professor Albright on his seventieth birthday. Half of the study is devoted to a detailed and documented account of the manuscripts obtained in Caves I-XI. The second half contains three sections, dealing with (i) the significance of the discoveries for text, language and canon ; (ii) the history of the community ; (iii) the place of the community in the history of religion (in relation to Judaism and early Christianity). Hempel suggests that the copper scroll may record a plan for the concealment of the temple treasures, which was never put into execution. Of three possible datings of the rise of the Teacher of Righteousness—under Alcimus (*c.* 160 B.C.), under Simon (*c.* 140 B.C.), under Salome Alexandra, whose son Hyrcanus II would then be the ' Wicked Priest ' (*c.* 70 B.C.)—he inclines to the earliest. He sees no objection to calling the men of Qumran Essenes, if the word ' Essenes ' be understood in a sufficiently comprehensive sense. He acknowledges the resemblances betwen them and John the Baptist's movement, but thinks it unlikely that John was indebted to them or to any similar group. He thinks that the Zadokite work, as against the Manual of Discipline, is the ' rule ' for the non-monastic members of the community.

F.F.B.

JEREMIAS, J. : *Die theologische Bedeutung der Funde am Toten Meer* (Vortragsreihe der Niedersächsischen Landesregierung, zur Förderung der wissentschaftlichen Forschung in Niedersachsen, Heft 21). 1962. Pp. 28. (Vandenhoeck und Ruprecht, Göttingen. Price : DM. 2.50).

In this lecture Professor Jeremias gives a brief survey of the Qumran discoveries and then considers their significance for theology, in particular for our understanding of the New Testament. He deals with their enrichment of our knowledge of the world in which Jesus lived, the resemblances between the Qumran community and the primitive Church, and the cleavage between the men of Qumran and Jesus. This cleavage appears especially when we contrast the religious *apartheid* of the men of Qumran (who are held to be Essenes) with the call of Jesus to the sinners and outcasts of the ' highways and hedges '.

F.F.B.

MANSOOR, M. : *The Thanksgiving Hymns, translated and annotated with an Introduction.* (Studies on the Texts of the Desert of Judah, vol. III.) 1961. Pp. XII+228. (E. J. Brill, Leiden. Price : Fl. 30).

This work, a small part of which was published in the form of articles in collaboration with J. M. Baumgarten in *Journal of Biblical Literature*, is essentially eclectic. This is the more true with regard to part of the book where there was no collaboration with Baumgarten. It deals with the familiar topics peculiar to the Hymns in particular : topics which have been dealt with with more originality by a number of other writers and especially by J. Licht from whom Mansoor borrows liberally. Following these comes a translation with copious textual notes which, alas, include, as do the other parts of the book, numerous inaccuracies. This again is followed by useful Reference Tables which contain a classified and fairly extensive bibliography and four Indexes. The book on the whole is not void of some merits and the publishers are to be congratulated on the neat and handy production.

M.W.

RABIN, C. and YADIN, Y. (ed. by) : *Essays on the Dead Sea Scrolls in Memory of E. L. Sukenik* (in Hebrew). 1961. Pp. 240+portrait. (Hekhal Ha-Sefer, Jerusalem).

This volume of essays in memory of the late E. L. Sukenik, is a fitting tribute to a scholar who was the first to recognize the antiquity and the significance of the Scrolls. There are, all told, eleven highly meritorious essays, four of which (those of N. Avigad, N. A. Segal, S. Talmon, and Y. Yadin) have already appeared in English in *Aspects of the Dead Sea Scrolls* IV, Jerusalem, 1958 (see *Book List*, 1959, p. 39) and the other eight appear here for the first time in Hebrew with short English summaries. The eight contributions are : 1. The War Scroll— its Time and Authors (J. M. Grintz). It was written under the rule of the Roman Procurators by a sect greatly resembling

THE DEAD SEA SCROLLS 375

the *Stiphos* (see Josephus, B.J.XIII 4). 2. The Literary Structure of the War Scroll (C. Rabin). The War Scroll is composed of three distinct books : (*a*) The Book of the War ; (*b*) The Book of God's Time ; (*c*) The Book of Victory. 3. The Plant Eternal and the People of Divine Deliverance (J. Licht). There are two contradictory notions in the eschatology of Qumran (not realized by the Sect itself), one that only members of the Sect shall survive in the final catastrophe ; the other that the people of Israel will accept the leadership of the Sect at the End Time. 4. Remnants of a Hebrew Dialect in IQIs(a) (D. S. Loewinger). Some ' long ' and ' irregular ' forms of words are not textual variants but relics of a Hebrew dialect— relics found in other Biblical texts from Qumran and in the Massoretic Version of several Biblical books. 5. The Author of the Genesis Apocryphon knew the Book of Esther (J. Finkel). The author of the Apocryphon understood the Book of Esther, by which he was greatly influenced, in a way similar to later *Midrashim*. 6. Damascus Document VII, 9-12 (H. Kosmala). The reader will find a fuller discussion of the problems dealt with in this article in Kosmala's book entitled *Hebräer—Essener—Christen*, etc., Leiden, 1959. 7. The Baptism of John and the Dead Sea Sect (D. Flusser). John's theology of baptism is similar to that gathered from the Dead Sea Scrolls, the major difference, however, being the exclusiveness of the Sectarian rite. The difference between various concepts of ritual purity and Baptism are shown, and a line of development leading to baptism as understood by the Early Christian Church is suggested.   M.W.

RENGSTORF, K. H. : *Hirbet Qumran und die Bibliothek vom Toten Meer.* (Studia Delitzschiana, Band. 5.) 1961. Pp. 82. (S. Kohlhammer Verlag, Stuttgart. Price : DM. 9.30).

The brochure, originally the Montague Burton Lecture at Leeds, consists of some thirty pages of text and over 200 notes of a bibliographical and explanatory nature, and together they form an attractive, if not wholly convincing, case against attributing the scrolls to the Essenes and for regarding them as remnants of the official library of the Temple stored away before the fall of Jerusalem in 70 A.D. The Scrolls library needs to be regarded as a whole ; the O.T. texts reveal a process of ' correction ' towards standardisation, other texts witness to the totality of spiritual movements in Judaism between 200 B.C. and 100 A.D. Neither of these points is met by the Essene theory, and it is significant that even supporters of the theory implicitly allow this by the admission that an Essene origin cannot be postulated for each one of the scrolls simply because it was found in Qumran. But this is a drastic over-simplification of a carefully constructed argument.

B.J.R.

RINGGREN, H. : *Tro och liv enligt Döda-havsrullarna.* 1961. Pp. 202. (Diakonistyrelsens Bokförlag, Stockholm. Price : Sw. krs. 17.50).

In this book the author aims at giving in moderate compass a general survey of the religious teaching of the Dead Sea Scrolls, prefaced by a brief account of the materials available and the literary and historical problems which they raise. The bulk of the book is an exposition of theological themes ; but there are also short sections on the organization of the community and its cult, and of its relation to other religious movements. The discussion is illustrated throughout by citations from the texts in the author's own renderings, which sometimes include modifications of those which he has previously published. The entire treatment of the subject is marked by the author's gift for lucid and balanced exposition. There are useful bibliographical notes, which, though selective, concentrate on the essentials.

G.W.A.

ROWLEY, H. H. : *The Qumran Sect and Christian Origins.* (Reprinted from the *Bulletin of the John Rylands Library,* vol. 44, No. 1, September, 1961). 1961. Pp. 119-156. (The John Rylands Library and the Manchester University Press, Manchester. Price : 6s. 0d.).

With characteristically full documentation and equally characteristic fair-mindedness Professor Rowley discusses the main points of similarity which have been alleged between the Qumran Sect and the beginnings of Christianity (Messianic teaching ; legal and ritual usage ; organization ; religious terminology), and rejects the extreme views that the Dead Sea Scrolls are either all-important or unimportant for our understanding of the New Testament. As usual, he seems to be able to cram into a *parergon* what some would regard as adequate for a *magnum opus :* and readers will be grateful for his gift of compressing without distorting.

G.W.A.

SCHREIDEN, J. : *Les énigmes des manuscrits de la Mer Morte.* 1961. Pp. VI+408. (Editions Cultura. Wetteren. Price : B.Frs. 300).

The author pleads that his book should not be read ' like a novel, from beginning to end ', but consulted as a book of reference. It consists of surveys of various studies mainly of the historical controversies about the Righteous Teacher, the Wicked priest and their suggested identification. The works discussed are mainly written in French, Del Medico, Dupont-Sommer, Goossens, Vermès, Vincent, Michel, Delcor, but brief discussions are also included of Roth, Teicher, I. Levi among others. Obviously the book lacks unity and a great deal of repetition might be expected, but it was rather tiresome to find, e.g., Del Medico turning up on p. 296f. when one had imagined he had been disposed of about two hundred pages earlier. Furthermore, there are far too many lengthy quotations. On the other hand, the notes on a divergence of minor topics, such as the sign *NOUN*, Essenes in Patrologia,

Tikkun in Essene writings and Kabbala are rather slight. A translation (' literal rather than elegant ') of the Habakkuk Scroll, Manual of Discipline (*sic*), and the Damascus Document (based on Rost's edition) rounds off the volume. B.J.R.

SUTCLIFFE, E. F. : *The Monks of Qumran as Depicted in the Dead Sea Scrolls, with Translations in English.* 1960. Pp. xvi+272. (Burns and Oates, London. Price : 30s. 0d.).

This is one of the best of the many general works on the Dead Sea Scrolls, containing an account of the Scrolls and of the life and thought of the community from which they come and a translation of all the sectarian texts available at the time of its preparation. Particularly valuable is the section dealing with the manner of life of the community, while that on the relations between the sectaries and early Christianity is marked by sobriety of judgement and careful attention to the evidence. In a number of works the tendency to set the Teacher of Righteousness in the first century B.C. was very marked for a time, but now the tendency is to move back to the second century B.C. Father Sutcliffe shares this tendency, and he sets him in the middle of that century, in the time of Jonathan, who is identified with the Wicked Priest. H.H.R.

DE VAUX, R. : *L'Archéologie et les manuscrits de la Mer Morte.* (Schweich Lectures, 1959.) 1961. Pp. xvi+104+xlii plates and drawings. (Oxford University Press, London. Price : 30s. 0d.).

After a foreword by Professor Driver, Father de Vaux offers in an eminently clear and comprehensive form a statement of the current position in the presentation of the scrolls. Far from being a survey of all that has been written, he describes, as only the Director can describe, the actual examination of the site and its relevance for the interpretation of the scrolls. The first lecture deals with the ruins ; the Israelite traces, the three main periods of occupation and the later semi-occupation during 132-5 A.D. The second lecture deals with the caves, Cave 1, those of the cliffs (Caves 2, 3, 6, 11) and of the marl terrace (Caves 4, 5, 7, 8, 9, 10) and with the relation-ship of the caves with the monastery, and of the latter with the settlement at 'Ain Feshḥa. The third lecture, again mainly archaeological, discusses the date of the scrolls, and their being placed in the caves. In a lengthy discussion of the history of the community the author reconstructs strictly according to the archaeological indications wherever this is possible, but it is significant that there are questions, especially about the early phases, which must still remain open. Like-wise, for the identity of the community with the Essenes, archaeology obviously does not offer a final answer. Never-theless, though archaeology must necessarily play a supple-mentary role, its contribution is always a safeguard where speculation is rampant B.J.R.

WEISE, M. : *Kultzeiten und kultischer Bundesschluss in der " Ordens-
regel " vom Toten-Meer.* (Studia Post-Biblica, III.) 1961. Pp.
xi+126. (E. J. Brill, Leiden. Price : Fl. 18).

Two sections of the Order Scroll (IQS) come for special scrutiny:
the one, IQS i, line 18b-11, line 18 as a liturgy, and the other,
IQS ix line 26b-x line 8 as instruction for the observance of
cultic occasions and set prayers. The latter is discussed first.
Worship must follow a distinct temporal order, fixed by the
daily and annual circle of the sun. Prayers are fixed for daily
observance (dawn, nightfall), and also in three-monthly
periods ; the first of the month, and Sabbaths, New Year,
Sabbatical year, and Jubilee year are likewise named. The
structure of the whole passage shows that the author of IQS
had before him a fixed cultic order into which he inserted two
further passages consistent with it.

The former consists of the well-known section of columns 1
and 2 in which the priests, Levites and the community participate in the annual renewal of the convenant. The writer
argues that here, as in the former case, a traditional cult was
followed, and that the covenanters were not a separate
community but represented the whole of the Jewish cultic
community. We have here—the author insists—an example
of post-exilic cultic celebration, and solid ground for the
hypothesis of a cult-history development of Psalmody.
Furthermore, the manipulation of the text, e.g., in the Aaronite
blessing, has parallels in the comments of Rabbinic Judaism.

B.J.R.

APOCRYPHA AND POST-BIBLICAL JUDAISM

AVI-YONAH, M. : *Oriental Art in Roman Palestine* (Studi Semitici, 5).
1961. Pp. 104+XII Plates. (Centro di Studi Semitici, Rome).

Professor Avi-Yonah, who has made many valuable contributions to the archaeology of Israel and of the Middle East,
sums up in this short book the conclusions at which he has
arrived, after many years' study, concerning orientalizing
tendencies in Roman and Byzantine art. The subject is an
interesting and important one and has occupied the attention
of many scholars in recent years. Dr. Avi-Yonah's main thesis
is that in the late period of the Roman Empire the glyptic
art of what is now called the Middle East bears witness to a
profound revolution which had taken place in the religions of
these countries. According to him they had regained a
spirituality which they had possessed in the early period of
their development, but had lost during the struggle for political
power. The theory is supported by a careful analysis of the
archaeological evidence, and illustrated by 12 excellent plates.

S.H.H.

BROCKINGTON, L. H. : *A Critical Introduction to the Apocrypha.* (Studies in Theology, No. 61). 1961. Pp. vi+170. (Duckworth, London. Price : 12s. 6d.).

Some four years after Dr. B. M. Metzger's *An Introduction to the Apocrypha* Mr. Brockington's volume comes as a very welcome addition to the well-known 'Studies in Theology'. It is perhaps a shade less picturesque and alluring than the Metzger book ; it is not the less a clear and scholarly account of the books, which with the exceptions of I and II Esdras and the Prayer of Manasseh, are included in the Tridentine canon of Scripture and usually described as 'deuterocanonical'. Perhaps the most outstanding chapters are those on ' The Old Testament in the Apocrypha ' and ' The Merit and Worth of the Apocrypha '. All readers of the Bible, whether Catholic or Protestant, will find much of interest in the last-named chapter and will, at the very least, accept Mr. Brockingtons' description of the books as being 'marginally canonical'. The bibliography includes only one foreign work (Eissfeldt's invaluable *Einleitung*) and might well have referred to a French volume of proved value: the late Père M. J. Lagrange's *Le Judaisme avant Jésus-Christ* (Gabalda, Paris, 1931).

J.M.T.B.

CASARIL, R. : *Rabbi Siméon bar Yohaï et la Cabbale.* (Maîtres Spirituels.) 1961. Pp. 189, with many ills. (Editions du Seuil, Paris.).

This small illustrated volume offers the general reader an intelligible account of the history of Jewish mysticism. The book opens with a portrait of Siméon bar Yohaï, the stern nationalist and proud visionary of the Talmud and Midrash, the Teacher *par excellence* of the Zohar. Then, in the path traced by G. G. Scholem, the author follows the development of Kabbalistic doctrines (*Hekhaloth, Yezirah*) to their flowering in the ' democratic ' Hasidism of mediaeval Germany, and particularly in the intellectual mysticism of the Catalan Kabbalah. In this connection he lays stress on the importance and complex thought of the *Zohar*, treating it sympathetically and without undue simplification. The sixteenth-century revival at Safed, under the influence of Cordovero and Luria, is admired but considered to bear the seed of decadence because of the divorce between devotion and philosophy. Polish-Russian Hasidism, with its popular appeal and personality cult, is also found to be degenerate.

Although transcriptions such as Abboth, Kaddosh, Rimon, ghémétrie, etc., may irritate the Hebraist, this work as a whole is undoubtedly a balanced and useful first introduction to Kabbalism.

G.V.

CASPER, B. M. : *An Introduction to Jewish Bible Commentary*. (Popular Jewish Library). 1960. Pp. viii+128. (Thomas Yoseloff, London. Price : 7s. 6d.).

Rabbi Casper's short history of Jewish Bible interpretation is written from the ' orthodox ' point of view and addressed primarily to ' traditional ' Jews. The first half of the book deals with the origins of exegesis, the work of the Scribes and Targumists (though only Onkelos is considered), with the establishment of the Canon (the Apocrypha failed to come up to the standards of the Pharisees), with the Mishnah and with the Rabbinic exegetical *middoth*, and finally with the contribution of the Masoretes without which ' we should hardly be able to read the text '. The second half of the volume contains a series of portraits, among them Sa'adya (accompanied by an impassioned condemnation of Karaism) ; the great mediaeval philosophers such as Ibn Gabirol, Maimonides, etc. ; Rashi, who ably blended *peshat* with *midrash :* the clear and reasonable Ibn Ezra ; and other men of renown such as the Kimhis, Nahmanides, Abravanel and Mendelssohn. In the author's view, these worthy Bible interpreters, all convinced of the unity and divine origin of the Torah, contrast most favourably with modern critics who assume ' the right to amend the text, and to analyse . . . the books . . . according to date, place and authorship '.

G.V.

DUENSING, H. : *Verzeichnis der Personen - und der geographischen Namen in der Mischna*. Auf Grund der von Emil Schürer hinterlassenen einschlägigen Materialien bearbeitet und herausgegeben. 1960. Pp. 51. (W. Kohlhammer, Stuttgart).

This Mishnaic *Onomasticon* first appeared in 1913, based on material assembled by Schürer. It is now republished with minor additions (including the notation of the generations of the Tannaitic rabbis) and a supplementary *index geographicus*, in Dr. Duensing's 85th year. Since 1913 there have appeared both Kassovsky's Hebrew *Concordance* of the Mishnah and Danby's translation, the index to which renders this reprint superfluous for English readers. Some orthographic collation has been added, in a few cases through comparison with Dead Sea material, but mainly from Mishnaic MSS (no *Genizah* fragments). Since such alterations were being made, it is to be regretted that summary identifications of the place-names was not included, together with reference to substantiation in the *Sepher Ha-Yishub* (Hebrew), in which all the relevant material from Eusebius, etc. is assembled.

R.L.

EDELMANN, R. : *Jødisk litteratur gennem 2000 år* (Folkeuniversitetets bibliotek, kulturhistorie, Vol. 2). 1961. Pp. 116. (Rhodos, Copenhagen. Price : Dan. Kr. 9.85).

The author of this small book has earlier written an excellent book on Jewish mysticism (*Jødisk mystik*, Verdensreligionernes hovedværker under redaktion af Poul Tuxen og Aage Marcus, Copenhagen, 1954). In the present book he displays the same familiarity with many other parts of the comprehensive Jewish literature. The book starts after the Old Testament period, i.e., neither the Canonical books nor the Apocrypha and the Pseudepigrapha are taken into consideration. In brief chapters he gives a survey of the Talmudic and Rabbinic literature, Bible translations, exegesis, Hebrew linguistics, ethical and edifying literature, philosophy, mysticism, history, and many other themes. The last chapter deals with the literature in Yiddish ; and in an appendix he gives specimens of the older Hebrew literature. The present writer has only some minor objections to the book. The author ought to have extended his description and furthermore added an index of names and a bibliography. There is, however, good reason to expect that these deficiencies will be removed in a forth-coming English edition.

E.H.

HENGEL, M. : *Die Zeloten. Untersuchungen zur jüdischen Freiheits-bewegung in der Zeit von Herodes I. bis 70 nach Chr.* (Arbeiten zur Geschichte des Spätjudentums and Urchristentums, I). 1961. Pp. XIV+406. (E. J. Brill, Leiden/Köln. Price : Fl. 42).

This monograph, the first to be devoted to the Zealots, con-siders the movement founded by Judas the Galilean primarily as a religious sect, and not merely as a political party. Dr. Hengel begins by surveying and assessing his sources, in particular the works of Josephus, and studies the various names by which the sect was known among its opponents (robbers,. *sicarii*) and its own title ' Zealots '. He then sets out to reconstruct the message of its founder and, by collating the bare statements of the sources with parallel Rabbinic teachings, arrives at the following fundamentals of Zealot belief. God is the only Ruler. He desires Israel to be free. Jews must collaborate with Him in bringing about salvation and must, as a religious duty, oppose the Roman census. Dr. Hengel next enquires into the meaning of ' zeal ' (for the Law and the Temple), this being one of the main characteristics of Jewish piety between the Maccabaean uprising and the time of Bar Kokhba. He shows how, in Rabbinic sources, Phinehas (and also Elijah) typifies religious ' zeal '. As regards the character of the Zealot movement, he describes it as being eschatological and messianic. Prophecies were applied to the present time and more than one Zealot leader (e.g. Menahem or Simon bar Giora) considered himself to be the Messiah. Favourite eschatological themes were the exodus into the desert, martyrdom and religious suicide seen as voluntary self-sacrifice, and the Holy War. Finally the author examines the prehistory of the Zealot movement under Herod, together with the three phases of its history—the first ending with the death of Agrippa I, the second taking place at the time of the last Procurators, and the third during the Jewish War.

This careful and thorough work has considerably advanced our knowledge of first-century Judaism and, with it, our under-standing of the New Testament background.

G.V.

KATZ, J. : *Exclusiveness and Tolerance. Studies in Jewish-Gentile Relations in Medieval and Modern Times.* (Scripta Judaica III). 1961. Pp. xvi+200. (Clarendon Press. Oxford University Press, London. Price : 21s. 0d.).

This fine scholarly work, written by a professor of the Hebrew University, illuminates and explains the attitudes adopted by the Jews towards their gentile neighbours from the Middle Ages up to the 18th century. The author, though drawing the greater part of his data from Ashkenazi Jewry in its wider sense, and thus confining himself to Northern France and Germany in the Middle Ages and later to Germany, Poland and Lithuania, leaves the reader with a good insight into the problem of Jewish-Gentile relations as a whole. In the first part of the book which sets forth the problem and its terms of reference, subjects such as Doctrinal Difference, Economic Intercourse and the Religious Factor, Social and Religious Segregation, Juridical and Moral Controls, are dealt with. The second part, which concerns itself mainly with the tenth-fourteenth centuries, deals with the following : Apostates and Proselytes, The Martyrs, The Hasid, The Disputant, Men of Enlightenment. The last part, which concentrates on the sixteenth-eighteenth centuries, deals with Ghetto Segregation, The Attitude of Estrangement, The Development of Common Ground, Enlightenment and Toleration, The Political Application of Tolerance.

The book, which is well produced, comprises a selected bibliography and an Index.

M.W.

LERLE, E. : *Proselytenwerbung und Urchristentum.* 1960. Pp. 156. (Evangelische Verlagsanstalt, Berlin. Price : DM. 9).

In his analysis of proselytism the author reconstructs the atmosphere of animosity and polemics in which zealous Jews of the inter-Testamental period sought to persuade Gentiles to accept circumcision and the Torah and thereby enter into full membership of the Chosen People. As he plainly shows in a survey of inconclusive Jewish apologetical arguments, adult circumcision appears to have proved the greatest obstacle, being dangerous in practice and contrary to the accepted ideal of Hellenistic beauty. He also deduces, from statements ascribed to the school of Hillel, that the subsequent baptism of the proselyte was as integral a part of his initiation into the People of God as his circumcision, and he sees in this, and in the so-called theology of death and rebirth through circumcision, the Jewish foundation of Christian baptism.

The second half of the book is concerned with the Christian mission to the Gentiles which eventually, under the influence of the Hellenists and St. Paul, accorded equality of status to both Jew and Gentile in the Church independently of the Mosaic Law.

The student of Judaism may regret the absence of all mention of the atoning value of circumcision and of baptismal customs

in sectarian circles. It may also be asked why the writer of
this richly documented and scholarly work should have seen
fit to designate Christian teaching and preaching as a 'mission',
whilst attaching to similar Jewish fervour the terms 'agitation'
and 'religious propaganda'.

G.V.

MANTEL, H. : *Studies in the History of the Sanhedrin* : (Harvard Semitic
Series XVII). 1961. Pp. 374+xv. (Harvard University Press,
Cambridge, Massachusetts. Price : 62s. 0d.).

Information about the Sanhedrin emanates from two main
sources, Rabbinic and Greek. The Talmud represents the
Sanhedrin as a religious body concerned mainly with the
interpretation of the Law and, consequently, legislative in
character. At the same time it served as an educative institution, with students attending its deliberations. The accounts
in the New Testament and Josephus, however, assign to the
Sanhedrin political authority. Again, according to the Jewish
accounts, the president of the Sanhedrin was known as the
Nasi, while the Greek sources state that he was the High
Priest. Our author reconciles these apparently conflicting
accounts with the conclusion that there were two bodies known
as Sanhedrin, the one was political and presided over by the
High Priest, while the other was religious and its president
was the *Nasi*. It was only after the Destruction, i.e. after
70 A.D., that the Nasi also assumed the highest political office.

Though there is, on this theory, no contradiction between the
Rabbinic sources and the New Testament concerning the court
before which Jesus was tried, the author raises questions
concerning the circumstances of the trial and the nature of
the charges brought against him. Taking the Gospel story as
history, he accepts the view that the charges were of a political,
and not of a religious nature for, he claims, Jesus did not infringe
any religious laws in the eyes of the Pharisaic authorities.
This point vindicates the conclusion that the court which
investigated the charges was not the Great Sanhedrin, also
known as *Bet Din Haggadol*, but the political council-court.
One chapter is devoted to the office of *Nasi* and his special
duties. Apart from presiding over the Sanhedrin, he was
concerned with the proclamation of a leap year (with the
extra intercalary month), he visited distant Jewish communities
and collected funds. The title first appears in Jewish literature
along with, what appears to have been, the junior associate,
the *ab bet din*. They are known as the *Zugot* or 'pairs'. Our
author believes that the title is older than its first literary
appearance, as the senior of the 'pair', *ca.* 150 B.C. To New
Testament scholars this book will have a special appeal, in
that the Gospel accounts are placed in the Rabbinic background
of the period. The reader will be impressed by the vast host of
references from the Talmud, not only as indicating great
erudition, but also because of the author's skilful use of this
source as historical material.

J.W.

NEWMAN, J. : *The Commentary of Nahmanides on Genesis 1-6^8 : Introduction, Critical Text, Translation and Notes.* (Pretoria Oriental Series, Vol. IV). 1960. Pp. 95+76 (text)+xxv (notes). E. J. Brill, Leiden. Price : Fl. 30).

This book provides us with a critically edited text (based on manuscripts and early printed editions), conveniently printed in square Hebrew characters on the right-hand pages, while the English translation is given on the corresponding left-hand pages. Points arising out of the text and the translation are dealt with in full notes at the end of the book. Source references and variant readings are noted in footnotes. In his introductory chapter the author briefly sketches the life of Nahmanides and describes his personality and religious outlook, as reflected in the commentary.

Nahmanides' *Haḳdamah*, or preface to his commentary, is written in typical poetical style, in which biblical quotations are skilfully interwoven. In this he declares his high admiration for Rashi and his lesser regard for Ibn Ezra. His references, however, go beyond these two authorities and, in the commentary under review, he cites Onkelos several times, Maimonides twice, Saadya and Sharira once each.

Nahmanides regards the Torah as the repository of all truth, that is to say, not only religious truth, but also scientific truth. The theme of creation offers him ample scope for a discussion of his views and these are given at length in an introduction to Genesis. The Peshat, or plain sense of a line, is not sufficient for a complete understanding of all that is inherent in the text. Only those initiated into the mysteries of the Kabbalah can fully appreciate the wider range of knowledge implicit in the words. True satisfaction is to be attained only through the mystic, or Kabbalistic, interpretation of the text. Thus Nahmanides exhibits his opposition to the metaphysical approach of Maimonides, who attempted to harmonize the tenets of Judaism with reason. Of special interest is a summary of what Dr. Newman calls the Mosaic cosmogony, in which an account is given of the creation of material and spiritual elements.

This work has not a direct bearing on O.T. studies, but it will, nevertheless, be welcomed as illuminating an interesting phase in religious thinking among some mediaeval Jewish writers and as an important contribution to the golden age of the Spanish School of Bible commentators.

                                                                    J.W.

PETUCHOWSKI, J. J. : *Ever Since Sinai.* A Modern View of Torah. 1961. Pp. vii+134. (Scribe Publications, Inc., New York. Price : $2.95).

This little book is not primarily intended for serious Bible students ; but those of them to whom Judaism in the modern world poses problems may be interested to find here outlined an approach (written by a Reform Jewish Rabbi for a lay public) that retains all the dynamism of *Torah* as indispensable to Judaism, without tying it to the apron-strings of a fundamentalist position. The old God-Israel Marriage metaphor is taken as a basis and details of the ' marriage contract ' filled in—in terms that testify to a contemporary trend within Reform Judaism back towards traditionalism.

R.L.

RABINOWICZ, H. : *A Guide to Hassidism* (Popular Jewish Library). 1960. Pp. 163. (Thomas Yoseloff, London and New York. Price : 7s. 6d.).

This guide to Hasidism traces the history of the movement from the time of the Besht to the present day. It introduces the reader to the Baal Shem Tov himself, to the scholar Schneur Zalman, to the story-teller Nachman of Bratslav, and to the fierce opponent of the Hasidim, Elijah ben Solomon the Gaon of Vilna. Short studies are devoted to many others also, among them the Maggid, the Seer of Lublin, Jacob Isaac called the holy Yehudi, founder of the Pzysha school, and the pious Rabbi Simcha Bunam. Later chapters discuss Hasidism and the Hasidic way of life more generally and the book ends with an account of the present strength and activities of the movement in Israel, America, and the United Kingdom. Dr. Rabinowicz writes in a spirit of enthusiastic admiration. This does not, however, lead him to conceal some of the less commendable qualities of some of the Hasidic leaders.

G.V.

ROSENTHAL, E. I. J. : *Griechisches Erbe in der jüdischen Religionsphilosophie des Mittelalters.* (Franz Delitzsch-Vorlesungen 1957). 1960. Pp. 110. (W. Kohlhammer Verlag, Stuttgart).

In this series of lectures Dr. Rosenthal has succeeded in presenting an old problem in a new light. Without minimising the importance of the influence of Greek and Arabic philosophy on medieval Jewish thinkers, he shows that they treated fundamental questions from a religious standpoint derived from their own ancient traditional faith. They did not simply imitate Aristotle or borrow from Islam ; and it is the originality of their approach which explains their influence on medieval and modern spirituality. The confrontation of *Torah* and *Nomos*, with their theoretical and practical implications, provides the author with material for extensive discussions, which he supplements by clear and closely-packed appendices on *Eudaimonia* and the theory of prophecy. The numerous notes provide ample and up-to-date bibliographical documentation, which enhances the value of this fine study.

A.N.

ROSENTHAL, E. I. J. : *Judaism and Islam*. (Popular Jewish Library). 1961. Pp. xvi+154. (Thomas Yoseloff, New York, in conjunction with the World Jewish Congress, British Section. Price : 7s. 6d.).

Published under the auspices of the British Section of the World Jewish Congress. Here is *multum in parvo*, a well-produced survey of the whole cultural and historical field and a most useful introduction. In discussing origins much must still remain conjectural, e.g., between the Talmud and the Qur'an. Which came first, the hen or the egg? Only documentation can help here and its omission is understandable in a book of this scope and size. The survey of approximations in law and of the mediaeval inter-relations is very sound and of the latter the author has already given evidence of his learning. There is a good bibliography and index. A minor slip is noted (p. 15). The Ka'ba is the building in the S.E. corner of which the Black Stone is set.

J.W.S.

ROTH, L. : *Judaism : A Portrait*. 1960. Pp. 240. (Faber & Faber, London. Price : 25s. 0d.).

A series of essays, arranged in five groups:' The Pattern ' ; ' Composition ' ; ' Harmonies & Discords ' ; ' Groundwork ' ; ' The Outcome '. The kernel is perhaps the chapter on the ' Community of Holiness ', whose continuance, despite manifold default on the part of individuals, is underwritten by ' the remorseless determination, and the undying hope and confidence, of God ' (p. 113). The presentation is permeated by the spirit of Maimonides with all its universalistic potential (the great *responsum* to the convert who hesitated to use the liturgical formula ' Our God and the God of our fathers' is given in translation, p. 96), and the implicit as well as the explicit precedents for this approach in the earlier rabbinic literature are indicated. As always, Leon Roth is stimulating—not least where he describes *Aggada* as *Halakhah* in the making (p. 76). Even Judah Hallevi's philosophy of Judaism, based though it is on a mystique of blood and soil, is shown (p. 110f.) to hinge ultimately upon voluntary submission to the Yoke of Torah.

R.L.

SHUTT, R. J. H. : *Studies in Josephus*. 1961. Pp. x+132. (S.P.C.K., London. Price : 22s. 6d.).

It is many years since Dr. Shutt first made his name as a student of Josephus ; and we are glad to welcome this volume of studies, which must henceforth stand beside Thackeray's *Josephus, the Man and the Historian*. Some of the discussions in Thackeray's work are here carried further, especially on Josephus's use of amanuenses and literary sources. Dr. Shutt's detailed verbal and stylistic studies lead him to doubt seriously Thackeray's theory about the use of a ' Thucydidean ' assistant in Books xvii-xix of the *Antiquities* and of a ' Sophoclean ' assistant in Books xv-xvi. He realizes, however, that some alternative explanation must be given of the unusual words and phrases in Books xvii-xix, and he endeavours to provide one. He thinks it quite possible that a second edition of the *Antiquities* was published together with the *Life* some time after A.D. 100, after the death of Agrippa II, and that in this edition Josephus gives freer expression to his own assessment of Herod the Great, which would not have been politic while Agrippa was alive. Dr. Shutt finds himself unable to accept Weber's view that Josephus used a documentary source of Roman origin in the composition of the *War*, although he agrees that for such matters as the disposition of the Roman legions in A.D. 66 he would certainly be indebted to Roman information. There is an important chapter on Josephus's indebtedness to Nicolaus of Damascus, Dionysius of Halicarnassus, Polybius, and Strabo. In the discussion of Josephus's chronology it might have been observed that this has been affected by variant interpretations of Daniel's seventy heptads.

F.F.B.

STEWART, R. A.: *Rabbinic Theology: An Introductory Study*. 1961. Pp. xvi+202. (Oliver and Boyd, Edinburgh. Price: 21s. 0d.).

Under the familiar headings of a Christian theological manual (God, Messiah, Angels and Demons, Creation, Sin, Atonement, Immortality), Mr. Stewart has assembled many sayings from the haggadic portions of the Babylonian Talmud and the Midrash Rabbah, and has attempted, with their help, to give some idea of the religious thought of post-Biblical Judaism. It is to be hoped that his book, which is colourful and easy to read, will induce beginners to embark on a thorough study of Rabbinic literature.

Some pitfalls have not been avoided. For example, the alien framework in which the author has set his study has caused him to omit the characteristic Jewish themes of Sinai, Covenant, circumcision, etc. Again, by ignoring the historical perspective and by limiting his source material, he has failed to achieve a correct balance of emphasis. Nor has he sufficiently discriminated between *obiter dicta* and established traditions. On the other hand, the book not only pays close attention to New Testament connections, but it also makes a sincere effort to represent and appraise Judaism objectively. Its one weakness in this respect resides at those points where Rabbinic teaching, such as the doctrine of the ' treasury of merits ', offends too sharply the writer's evangelical Christian convictions.

A translation of selected Jewish prayers is given in an Appendix.

G.V.

STRACK, H. L. and BILLERBECK, P. : *Kommentar zum Neuen Testament aus Talmud und Midrasch.* Sechster Band. *Verzeichnis der Schrift-gelehrten. Geographisches Register*, herausgegeben von Joachim Jeremias in Verbindung mit Kurt Adolph. 1960. Pp. 198 + 3 folding tables. (C. H. Beck, Munich. Price : paper, DM. 25 ; cloth, DM. 29).

The immense amount of patient labour and the ingenuity of arrangement which must have gone into the compiling of these indexes will be amply justified by the usefulness of the result. Against the names of the various *Schriftgelehrten* there are indications of date, whether they belonged to the Tannaim or Amoraim, who quotes them and whom they quote ; and the three folding tables at the end of the book indicate their relationships. The geographical index is furnished with useful cross references, and, in the longer entries, with handy sub-divisions. This is a worthy companion to the earlier index volume, which was noticed in *Book List*, 1957, p. 72. G.W.A.

VERMES, G. : *Scripture and Tradition in Judaism : Haggadic Studies.* (Studia Post-Biblica, IV). 1961. Pp. X + 244. (E. J. Brill, Leiden. Price : Fl. 36).

This book brings together a collection of eight studies on themes in Haggadic literature and, though each study is complete in itself, they are linked together by the unifying thesis that the Midrash Haggadah can now be placed in an historical setting. The themes selected are grouped under four main headings, namely :— (1) the symbolism of words, (2) the re-written Bible, (3) Bible and tradition, and (4) theology and exegesis. Under (1) the individual themes are Pharaoh, Lebanon, and significant other words, under (2) comes the life of Abraham, under (3) is the story of Balaam, and under (4) is treated ' circumcision and Exodus iv. 22 ' and ' redemption and Genesis xxii '.

The author summarizes the conventional conclusions of scholars during the 1920's as follows :— (a) that the Targums of Onkelos and Jonathan, stemming from the 2nd Century A.D., represent the Tanaitic interpretation of the Torah and the Prophets, (b) that the Haggadah is the creation of individual teachers and the Haggadic traditions resulted from popular adoption and (c) that the Tanaitic Midrashim are the most ancient form of the Haggadah.

The author's aim is to show that these conclusions are no longer tenable and he draws upon the new knowledge which has become available since the 1920's. This is, on the one hand, the recognition of Haggadic elements in the writings of Josephus and in pseudo-Philo's ' Biblical Antiquities ' (1st Century, B.C.), and, on the other hand, the discovery of new Haggadic literature. Apart from the Cairo Genizah Targum fragments published by P. Kahle, the main new sources are the Midrashic works of the Qumran community and the Codex Neofiti, identified by A. Diez-Macho as being the first complete version of the Targum Yerushalmi. The new evidence points to pre-Tanaitic, and even pre-Christian, roots in the Midrashic process, stretching back to the post-Biblical period. It is, then, but a step to the further conclusion that ' the exegesis of the primitive Haggadah must coincide with that of the last redactors of the written Torah ' (p. 127). This book brings a stage further the consideration of the impact of Rabbinic writings on the study of the O.T. If we accept the premiss that the exposition of Biblical texts began with the circulation of these texts, then it follows that ' the first readers and commentators of the Bible were faced with the same problems of harmonization as were the later Midrashists ' (p. 127). The Haggadic process, then, is not a late Rabbinic phenomenon, but a line of tradition which developed in direct continuity with the Bible itself.

J.W.

WAGNER, S. : *Die Essener in der wissenschaftlichen Diskussion vom Ausgang des 18. bis zum Beginn des 20. Jahrhunderts : Eine wissenschaftsgeschichtliche Studie.* (B.Z.A.W. 79). 1960. Pp. XII+284. (Alfred Töpelmann, Berlin. Price : DM. 36).

A most learned and valuable survey of the history of the study of the Essenes and the theories advanced about them from the Enlightenment to the beginning of the present century. The extended bibliography of 34 pages is an indication of the thoroughness of the work. The author divides his study into four sections, dealing with the period of the Enlightenment, where the beginnings of freemasonry and the treatment of Essenism in novels and plays about Jesus are dealt with ; the middle of the nineteenth century ; the later nineteenth century ; and the end of that century and the beginnings of the twentieth. The revived interest in the Essenes which the discovery of the Dead Sea Scrolls has brought, has doubtless dictated this study, though it terminates before the discovery of the Scrolls, and so does not discuss the vexed question of the relation of the Qumran community to the Essenes.

H.H.R.

WALLENSTEIN, M. : *Four Unpublished Poems in Rylands Hebrew MS 6— One by Abraham (Ibn Ezra.)* (Reprinted from the *Bulletin of the John Rylands Library*, vol. 44, No. 1, September, 1961). 1961. Pp. 238-264. (The John Rylands Library and the Manchester University Press, Manchester. Price : 5s. 0d.).

This Hebrew manuscript, which contains a Passover Haggada, has incorporated in it eighty-two *piyyuṭim*. Seventy-three of them are recorded elsewhere and most of their composers have been identified. Two more were published by Dr. Wallenstein in 1960 (see *Book List*, 1961, p. 68), and in this present work he publishes four further poems. Each one is introduced by a discussion, reconstructed so as to indicate its external artistic features, translated, and annotated. The first, with the name Mosheh spelt acrostically, may be by Mosheh b. Naḥman or Mosheh Hacohen Ibn Chiqatilla. The second, with the name Abraham spelt acrostically, is attributed, for reasons that are given, to Abraham Ibn Ezra. It falls, however, below the standard of his best poems. The third contains favourite ideas of Yehudah Halevi, which were, however, shared also by several other well-known poets. No suggestion is made as to the authorship of the fourth poem. The translation is accurate, but suffers at times from being too literal. The critical notes contain much that is of interest and value, especially for Hebraists. We may hope that Dr. Wallenstein will in due course treat the remaining three poems in a similar way.

D.W.T.

WINTER, P. : *On the Trial of Jesus.* (Studia Judaica : Forschungen zur Wissenschaft des Judentums, Band 1). 1961. Pp. x+216. (Walter de Gruyter & Co., Berlin. Price : DM. 22).

Dr. Winter presents us with an extremely learned investigation of some of the principal aspects of the trial of Jesus. He discusses such questions as the identity of the high priest, the character of Pilate, the competence of the Sanhedrin, the Barabbas incident, the mockery of the prisoner, the inscription of the cross. All the available evidence on the successive points at issue is marshalled and evaluated. In discussing the question whether the Sanhedrin at that time had the right to execute a capital sentence or not he makes telling use of the parallel narrative of Paul's arrest and trial in Acts xxi. ff. He dismisses the statement in TJ *Sanh.* i. 1, vii. 2 that the right to inflict capital punishment was taken away from Israel 40 years before the destruction of the Temple as a later interpretation of statements in TB about the Sanhedrin's abandonment of the Hall of Hewn Stones at that time. But insufficient attention is paid to the fact that TJ claims to be quoting a *baraitha.* Dr. Winter's estimate of the historical element in the Gospels is unduly negative. He accepts the Johannine evidence that Jesus was arrested by a detachment of Roman soldiers, but other features in the Johannine passion narrative are rejected without adequate weighing of the Evangelist's claim that his narrative here is based on the testimony of an eyewitness. Indeed, so scanty is the historical element in the Gospels, according to Dr. Winter, that one wonders what historical basis he has for his affirmation on page 148 that Jesus ' was the norm of normality '. But nothing can diminish the importance of Dr. Winter's study, which must be taken into serious account by anyone who writes about the trial of Jesus in future.

F.F.B.

PHILOLOGY AND GRAMMAR

BARR, J. : *The Semantics of Biblical Language.* 1961. Pp. x+314. (Clarendon Press, Oxford. Price : 37s. 6d.).

Everyone whose business is the language and interpretation of the Bible is urged to study this able book. It has been written in the conviction that sound interpretation of the Bible is today endangered by procedures which, though they claim to be based upon a knowledge of Israelite and Greek ways of thinking, mishandle the linguistic evidence of Hebrew and Greek as they are used in the Bible. Especially characteristic of the modern attempt to relate theological thought to Biblical language is its unsystematic nature, which is due to a double failure—both to examine Greek and Hebrew as a whole, and to relate what is said about these languages to a general semantic method related to general linguistics. Current views on Hebrew morphological and syntactical phenomena are criticised, and the dangers involved in etymologizing inter- pretation, as against the semantic value of a word, are illus- trated by studies of the meanings of particular words, e.g. ' holy ', *qahal-ecclesia*, *dabhar*, ' baptism ', ' man '. Some recent linguistic arguments concerning ' faith ' and ' truth ' are examined, and also the linguistic and theological principles followed in Kittel's *Theol. Wörterbuch*. Interesting suggestions and salutary warnings abound. For example, a better approach to Biblical language and theology can be made at the sentence level (and larger linguistic complexes) than at the lexical (word unit) level. And there is the possibility of misuse of inter- pretation of words which results from ' seeing the Bible as a unity '. The views of Thorleif Boman are considered at length and come under heavy fire, as do also those of some other well- known scholars. The book is, so to say, a *praeparatio* to further, constructive, study of Biblical theology.   D.W.T.

BAUMGÄRTEL, F. : *Hebräisches Wörterbuch zur Genesis.* (Einzelwörter- bücher zum Alten Testament, 1). Dritte, ergänzte Auflage. 1961. Pp. VIII+44. (Alfred Töpelmann, Berlin. Price : DM. 1.50).

This simple Hebrew-German dictionary is intended for students beginning to read the Hebrew Bible at Genesis. It contains a table of abbreviations, 37 pages of dictionary, some notes and a register of proper names. An excellent tool for a beginner. The same sort of thing is needed in English.   G.H.D.

LEVI DELLA VIDA, G. (ed. by) : *Linguistica Semitica : Presente e Futuro. Linguistique Sémitique : Présent et Avenir. Semitic Linguistics : Present and Future. Semitische Sprachwissenschaft : Gegenwart und Zukunft.* (Studi Semitici, 4). 1961. Pp. 184. (Centro di Studi Semitici, Rome).

In May, 1961, the Centro di Studi Semitici in Rome invited six distinguished scholars to survey the present position in Semitic studies and to state the most important tasks to be under- taken in the future. This volume contains the addresses, all

391

of them of the highest quality, delivered on this occasion. Comparative Semitics is surveyed by E. Ullendorff (in English), Akkadian by W. von Soden, Arabic by A. Spitaler (both in German), Hebrew by H. Cazelles (in French), North-West Semitic and Aramaic by G. Garbini, and Ethiopic by E. Cerulli (both in Italian). A preface and a concluding summary are contributed by G. Levi Della Vida. The claims of fresh material and the need for new methods of dealing with it are everywhere stressed. Two general conclusions that emerge are that greater progress appears to have been made in the study of the structure and historical development of the individual languages than in some larger questions, such as the problem of proto-Semitic and the relationship between Semitic and Hamitic ; and that the view that Arabic has preserved better than any other Semitic language primitive elements must be considerably modified, if not given up altogether, in the light of greater knowledge today of archaic elements in Akkadian. There is an insistent call for more adequate aids—lexica, grammars, dialectical studies—for a more satisfactory classification of the Semitic languages, and for further investigation into the Semitic tense system. The full documentation provides a valuable guide to important recent research. An English edition would be very welcome.

D.W.T.

MURTONEN, A. : *Materials for a non-Masoretic Hebrew Grammar II. An Etymological Vocabulary to the Samaritan Pentateuch* (Studia Orientalia edidit Societas Orientalis Fennica, XXIV). 1960. Pp. 227. (Helsinki. Price : Fmk. 1,800).

The first volume of *Materials*, a sketch of Hebrew grammar according to the Palestinian tradition, was reviewed in the *Book List* for 1958 (pp. 59f.). Often the forms noted there appear to be closely related to the Samaritan pronunciation of Hebrew. The Samaritan vocabulary presented here is based mainly upon material drawn from modern recitation of the Pentateuch among the Samaritans, the earlier material available being supplemented by recent tape recordings. A few vocalised manuscripts too are used. The material is presented mainly in simple transcription, and the vocabulary is arranged under roots in the order of the Hebrew alphabet, except in the case of words beginning with an initial guttural which are all entered at the beginning. Meanings of words are rarely given, and references to the Pentateuch are generally only provided in the case of proper names. An interesting feature is the employment of a new terminology, especially verbal, of Hebrew grammar. The word ' etymological ' in the sub-title is not easy to justify since only little comparative etymological material is included. While not all scholars are convinced of the value of the Samaritan tradition of Hebrew pronunciation for the recovery of the pre-Massoretic form of Hebrew, additional means for the study of the subject, such as is here provided, must always be welcome. A third volume, which will deal with the grammar of Samaritan, is promised.

D.W.T.

ROSENTHAL, F. : *A Grammar of Biblical Aramaic* (Porta Linguarum Orientalium). 1961. Pp. x+100. (Otto Harrassowitz, Wiesbaden. Price : DM.10).

Clearly and concisely written, well arranged and beautifully printed, this grammar covers the usual topics, provides a short bibliography and ends with paradigms and vocabulary. Two features may be noted. This introduction does not presuppose a knowledge of Hebrew as do so many. The section on vocabulary, which is more advanced than the rest of the book, gives a useful survey of the various influences, Hebrew, Akkadian, Persian and Greek, which are to be found in Biblical Aramaic.   W.D.McH.

STEVENSON, W. B. : *Grammar of Palestinian Jewish Aramaic.* Second Edition, with an Appendix on Numerals by J. A. Emerton. 1962. Pp. 108. (Clarendon Press, Oxford. Price : 15s. 0d.).

This lithographic reprint of the late Professor Stevenson's grammar makes available once more a work too well-known to require commendation. While it contains almost too much for the beginner, for it introduces him to the dialects of the Targums, the Palestinian Talmud and Midrashim, and the Aramaic portions of the Old Testament, more advanced students find the parallel paradigms convenient for quick reference. Mr. J. A. Emerton has added a useful appendix on the numerals ; the omission of this part of the subject was a serious defect in the 1924 edition. Unfortunately the Hebrew script in the addition is but indifferently reproduced.

W.D.McH.

BOOK LIST, 1963

In the preparation of this, the seventh *Book List* which I have had the honour to edit on behalf of the Society, I have enjoyed the collaboration not only of my colleagues who are members of the *Book List* Panel, but also of the following scholars: Dr. W. Beyerlin, Professors M. Bič, P. A. H. de Boer, and H. Cazelles, Drs. R. E. Clements and H. Donner, Professors C. J. Gadd and E. Hammershaimb, Mr. R. Loewe, and Professors C. R. North, A. Parrot, and T. W. Thacker. In technical and practical matters I have been helped by Mr. C. N. Francis of the firm of B. H. Blackwell, who has provided necessary bibliographical data, Mrs. E. S. K. Paterson of the secretarial staff of New College, whose patience and accuracy have saved me an immense amount of labour, and by the Printer and his staff, whose helpfulness and care are unfailing. To all of these I tender my sincere thanks.

I also owe much to many scholars who from time to time pass on items of information or ensure that review copies of books reach me promptly. But for such ready co-operation the *Book List* could not reach its present level of usefulness. Even so, there are inevitably omissions and errors; and for these I offer my apologies. One most unfortunate error which occurred in the 1962 *Book List* calls for special mention. The review, on p. 59, of J.-R. Kupper's *L'iconographie du dieu Amurru* was written by Professor M. Noth; but by a slip for which I was unwittingly responsible, and which I much regret, my own initials were printed under it.

I have tried, wherever possible, to indicate prices in the currency of the country of publication; but this information has not always been accessible. The classification of books presents a perennial problem. Some notices might with equal appropriateness appear in more than one section. As in former years, books which are recommended for inclusion in school libraries have been marked by an asterisk.

G. W. ANDERSON.

NEW COLLEGE,
UNIVERSITY OF EDINBURGH.

GENERAL

Annual of the Swedish Theological Institute, ed. by H. Kosmala in collaboration with G. Gerleman, G. Lindeskog, and H. S. Nyberg. Vol. I. 1962. Pp. 160+1 map+1 plate. (E. J. Brill, Leiden. Price: Fl. 24).

Appropriately, this volume is dedicated to Professor Lindblom, to whose interest the Swedish Theological Institute owes so much. There is a report on the work of the school during 1961, followed by seven important articles. P. R. Ackroyd contributes a discussion of the vitality of the word of God in the Old Testament (this was read as a lecture at the Institute). G. Gerleman writes on 'Die Bildsprache des Hohenliedes und die altägyptische Kunst'. H. Kosmala re-examines the so-called ritual decalogue, which he maintains is an ancient festival calendar. S. Talmon (in a paper read at the Institute) considers DSIa as a witness to ancient exegesis of the Book of Isaiah. B. Noack discusses (also in a paper read at the Institute) the day of Pentecost in Jubilees, Qumran, and Acts. G. Lindeskog writes on 'Die Essenerfrage in Geschichte und Gegenwart'. A. Schalit examines the early Christian tradition about the origin of Herod's family.

G.W.A.

BAUER, J. B. (ed.): *Bibeltheologisches Wörterbuch* I/II. 2nd ed. 1962. Pp. 1292. (Verlag Styria, Graz. Price: S. 350).

This excellent work first appeared, in one volume, in 1959 and was noticed at some length in the *Book List* for 1960 (p. 3). The chief criticism offered was that there were many omissions from the list of key-words employed. In the present two-volume edition a serious attempt has been made to increase the number of subjects discussed so that, out of a hundred and seventy-five articles, no less than seventy have been specially written for the new issue. Though the new articles are not distinguished by any special sign, a comparison with the first edition shows that the following items are new. Abraham, Adam, Almosen, Amen, Anbetung, Antichrist, Arbeit, Barmherzigkeit, Begierde, Betrachtung, Brüder Jesu, Buch, Dekalog, Demut, Drem, Ehe, Eifer, Einfalt, Entrückung, Erbauung, Erbsünde und Erbtod, Evangelium, Fasten, Feuer, Frau, Fürbitte, Furcht, Gehorsam, Gewissen, Gleichnis, Haupt, Heil, Heilsgewissheit, Heimsuchung. (Vol. II) Herrentag, Herz, Himmelfahrt Christi, Hirt, Höllenfahrt Christi, Jungfrauengeburt, Jungfraulichkeit, Kraft, Lamm Gottes, Leib, Leidenschaft, Mächte und Gewalten, Meer, Mensch, Moses, Paradies, Passion Jesu, Primat, Rest, Ruhe, Schöpfung, Sendung, Siegel, Sohnschaft, Tag des Herren, Torheit, Trost, Vater, Verfolgung, Verklärung, Volk (Gottes), Vollkommenheit, Vollmacht, Vorherbestimmung, Wachen, Wasser. The article 'Solidarität' (1st ed., pp. 699–706) does not appear in the new edition.

J.M.T.B.

BEN-HORIN, M., WEINRYB, B. D., ZEITLIN, S. (ed. by): *Studies and Essays in honor of Abraham A. Neuman*. 1962. Pp. xiii+650+portrait. (E. J. Brill, Leiden, for the Dropsie College, Philadelphia. Price: $7.50).

This volume comprises thirty-three articles, contributed by friends and pupils of Dr. Neuman, three of which are in Hebrew and the rest in English. The articles which have a direct bearing on Biblical studies are: 1. Some Hebrew Manuscripts from Seville, by Franciso Cantera Burgos. 2. Plurima Mortis Imago, by Godfrey Rolles Driver. Here we find remarks which have arisen out of the new English translation of the Bible. 3. The YQTL–QTL (QTL–YQTL) Sequence of Identical Verbs in Biblical Hebrew and in Ugaritic, by Moshe Held. 4. S. Baer's Unpublished Targum Onkelos Text, by Abraham I. Katsh. This article is the result of an examination of a USSR. MS. 5. The Liturgical Use of Psalm 78 : 38, by Leon J. Liebreich. 6. The Tribal System of Israel and Related Groups in the Period of the Judges, by Harry M. Orlinsky. Of an indirect bearing on Biblical studies is the article Translation and Mistranslation in the Apocalypse of Baruch, by Frank Zimmermann. The volume is well produced. M.W.

BIČ, M. and SOUČEK, J. B. (ed by): *Biblická Konkordance*, Parts 18, 19, 20, and 21. Pargamén-Rozpáleni. 1962. Pp. 80 each part. (Edice Kalich, Prague. Price: Kčs. 10.50 each).

Despite many difficulties this Concordance to the Czech Bible, giving indications of the Hebrew and Greek equivalents in the Old Testament and Greek equivalents in the New Testament, slowly continues its course. H.H.R.

BOWMAN, J. (ed. by): *Abr-Nahrain*. An Annual under the Auspices of the Department of Semitic Studies, University of Melbourne. Vol. II (1960–1961). 1962. Pp. 76+2 plates. (E. J. Brill, Leiden. Price: Fl. 12).

The main article of interest to Old Testament scholars is that by A. Guillaume: 'Hebrew and Arabic Lexicography. A Comparative Study'. This continues the article in Vol. I (*Book List*, 1962, p. 3) and contains a further 200 suggested Arabic cognates to Hebrew words, a few of which are, but the great majority are not, noted in Köhler-Baumgartner's *Lexikon*. A further article is promised for the next volume. W. Ulican continues his Phoenician studies with 'Melqart Representations on Phoenician Seals' (pp. 41–54). N. Milne: 'Prophet, Priest and King and their Effects on Religion in Israel' (pp. 55–67) seems hardly aware of much recent work in this field in presenting his material to demonstrate that 'Kingship broadened the popular mind while priests and prophets fought a rearguard action against this'. A.S.H.

Catholic Biblical Quarterly (ed. by R. E. Murphy). Vol. XXV: 1. 1963. Pp. 118. (Catholic Biblical Association of America, Washington, D.C. Price: $1.50 per copy).

Although this *Book List* does not normally review quarterlies, the appearance of this special Jubilee issue of the *C.B.Q.*, devoted entirely to Old Testament subjects, merits special mention. A distinguished team of contributors have written on a wide range of subjects: Jethro, Hobab and Reuel in Early Hebrew Tradition (W. F. Albright); La Nouvelle Alliance en Jer. 31. 31–34 (J. Coppens); Biblical Criticism (P. G. Duncker); Der Aufbau der Apokalypse des Jesajabuchs (Is. 24–27) (G. Fohrer); Zur Darbietungsform der "Ich-Erzählung" im Buche Qohelet (O. Loretz); The City and Israelite Religion (R. A. F. Mackenzie); Jacob at Peniel (J. L. McKenzie); The Ancient Near Eastern Background of the Love of God in Deuteronomy (W. L. Moran); "To Know Your Might is the Root of Immortality" (Wis. 15, 3) (R. E. Murphy); The Hand of Judith (P. W. Skehan); Background and Function of the Biblical Nāśî' (E. A. Speiser). Members of our Society will wish to congratulate the Catholic Biblical Association on reaching this milestone, and the *Quarterly's* Editor on this noteworthy production. G.W.A.

CAZELLES, H. and FEUILLET, A.: *Dictionnaire de la Bible. Supplément.* Fasc. xxxvii. (Paul-Péché.) 1962. Columns 1–256. (Letouzey & Ané, Paris. Price: 31s. 0d.).

The latest fascicle of this excellent supplement to Vigouroux's now ancient *Dictionnaire* has not a great deal of special interest to an *Alttestamentler*. C. Spicq completes his study of Hebrews, and J. Cambier writes on 'Vie et Doctrine de S. Paul'. A. George has an article on 'Pauvre', considering the Old Testament use of the word in sections concerned with the vocabulary, poverty as a social factor, and the religious sense of poverty. J. Trinquet devotes a column to the life and work of A. S. Peake, and the article on 'Péché' opens with a study of sin in the Old Testament by E. Beaucamp. This is a useful, perhaps a trifle too analytical, handling of the subject. The bibliography evidently does not profess to be complete, most of the works mentioned being fairly recent. The next fascicle will have sections on the concept of sin in ancient Greece and in Judaism. J.M.T.B.

DOUGLAS, J. D. (ed. by): *The New Bible Dictionary.* 1962. Pp. xvi+1376+ XVI plates+17 maps. (Inter-Varsity Fellowship, London, Price: 45s. 0d.).

Two of the consulting Editors and about twelve other contributors to this volume are members of our Society. They have contributed to the making of a worthwhile volume. Inevitably in this one-volume work, the Dictionary is neither biographically nor topographically complete, and the 2300 articles are of uneven quality. Some articles, especially those above the initials F.F.B. those on archaeology (J.D.W.) and Palestine and Jerusalem (J.M.H.) are models. Indeed the claim of the Preface that the

Dictionary is an up-to-date handbook on archaeology is largely justified. There are distinct cracks in the belief of the Mosaic authorship of the Pentateuch (308b; 849b f; 963b). Some of the articles on Literature, e.g., Psalms, give little evidence of the new cultic approach to the Literature of the Old Testament as a whole, or of the latest movements of scholarly thought in the perpetual wrestle with O.T. problems. But by and large this is a useful and worthy volume. The indices are valuable though unfortunately there is no list of contributions by the various authors. The Biblical knowledge is fairly complete and almost always reliable, though the interpretations of the material sometimes avoid the problems or fail to face them realistically. The volume is adorned with 237 line drawings, and altogether the pictorial side of the book is excellent. The volume represents wonderful value for money, and interestingly reveals varying degrees of interpretation and standpoint within the conservative point of view. The Editors are to be congratulated on a very good piece of work, even if some of the dogmatic articles are rather extreme.

G.H.D.

ENGNELL, I. (ed. by): *Svenskt bibliskt uppslagsverk*, 2nd edition, vol. I, A–L. 1962. Pp. XI+cols. 1574. (Nordiska Uppslagsböcker, Stockholm. Price of the whole work: Sw. Kr. 290).

The first edition of the first volume of this encyclopedia was published in 1948 by Engnell and Fridrichsen as editors, the second volume in 1952 (see *Book List*, 1949, p. 5, *Eleven Years*, p. 168; and 1953, p. 4, *Eleven Years*, p. 457). Since Fridrichsen's death Engnell alone has prepared the new edition with a large team of Scandinavian Scholars as collaborators. In no other work are the results of recent Scandinavian research to be found in such a clear and brief form. All the articles have been carefully revised or, if necessary, rewritten. About a fifth of the work consists of completely new articles, e.g., those on the Dead Sea Scrolls and the Nag Hammadi texts, other articles have been greatly expanded, e.g., the articles on Hazor, Jericho, and similar localities where excavations have taken place. The selection of literature is up-to-date.

E.H.

FRIEDRICH, G. (ed. by): *Theologisches Wörterbuch zum Neuen Testament* (begun by G. Kittel). Band VII. Lieferung 7, 1962. Pp. 64 (Kohlhammer, Stuttgart. Price: DM. 4.60). Doppellieferung 8/9, 1962. Pp. 128 (Price: DM. 9.20). Lieferung 10, 1962. Pp. 64 (Price: DM. 4.60).

Lieferung 7 concludes the article on *skandalon* by G. Stählin and continues with articles on *skenos* by C. Maurer, on *skene* and its cognates by W. Michaelis (especially the discussion of the Tabernacle and of *skenopegia*, the Feast of Booths) and on *skia* by S. Schulz.

Lieferung 8/9. The article on *skorpizo* by Michel has interesting remarks on the Theophany of Sinai and the Holy War. H. Conzelmann contributes a long and important article on *skotos* and its cognates. O. Michel writes on *skythes*, F. Lang on *skolex*

GENERAL 401

and E. Lohse on *Solomon*. An article of major importance on *sophia, sophos* by U. Wilckens includes an Old Testament section by G. Fohrer. O. Michel writes on *spendo* and S. Schulz on *sperma* and its cognates.

Lieferung 10 concludes the article on *sperma* and continues with articles on *splanchnon* and its cognates by Köster, on *spoudazo* and its cognates by G. Harder, and, among other articles of lesser concern to Old Testament scholars, with a long article by J. Schneider on *stauros*.

N.W.P.

GALLING, K. (ed. by): *Die Religion in Geschichte und Gegenwart*, 3. Auflage, Band VI. Lieferungen 105–106 (cols. 1–192), 107–108 (cols. 193–384), 109–110 (cols. 385–576, including map+2 plates), 111–112 (cols. 577–767), 113–114 (cols. 769–960), 115–116 (cols. 961–1152), 117–119 (cols. 1153–1440, including 2 maps), 120–121 (cols. 1441–1632), 122–125 (cols. 1633–1970+pp. XXXVI). 1962. (J. C. B. Mohr, Tübingen. Price: DM. 4.20 each Lieferung).

Professor Galling and his collaborators are to be warmly congratulated on the completion of this, the final volume of the new *R.G.G.* Their immense task has been carried out with great expedition. In this volume the following articles or parts of articles have been noted as of direct interest to the *Alttestamentler:* Sibyllinen (F. C. Grant); Sichem (E. Kutsch); Sidon (R. Bach); Siegel (K. Galling); Silo (E. Kutsch); Simon ben Kosiba (C. H. Hunzinger); Simson (H. Gese); Sinai (O. Eissfeldt); Sintflut, religionsgeschichtlich (W. von Soden): Im AT (C. A. Keller); Sittlichkeit: Im AT (G. Fohrer): Im Judentum (E. L. Dietrich); Sodom und Gomorrha (O. Eissfeldt); Sopherim (E. L. Dietrich); Speiseverbote: Im AT und Judentum (R. Rendtorff); Stämme Israels (M. Noth); Stein, heilige (K. Galling); Stierdienst (W. von Soden); Sünde und Schuld: Im AT (Th. C. Vriezen): Im Judentum (E. Lohse); Sündenbock (E. Kutsch); Sündenvergebung: Im AT (Th. C. Vriezen); Sumerer (F. M. Th. de Liagre Böhl); Susa (W. von Soden); Susannabuch (M. Weise); Symbole, jüdische (K. Galling); Synagoge (K. Galling); Synhedrium (E. Lohse); Syrien, Geschichte (H. Donner), religionsgeschichtlich (O. Eissfeldt); Syrische Literatur (B. Spuler); Tabor (E. Kutsch); Talmud (E. L. Dietrich); Tammuz (W. Röllig); Tanit (O. Eissfeldt); Tarphon (E. Lohse); Tarsis (R. Bach); Tekoa (E. Kutsch); Tempel, religionsgeschichtlich (K. Galling): In Israel (K. Galling); Tempelgeräte in Israel (K. Galling); Teraphim (K. Elliger); Testamente der XII Patriarchen (L. Rost); Tetragramm (D. W. Thomas); Teufel: Im AT, Judentum und NT (F. Horst); Textkritik der Bibel: Altes Testament (E. Würthwein); Theophanie: Im AT (J. Hempel); Tibboniden (E. L. Rapp); Tiberias (E. Lohse); Tirza (A. Kuschke); Tod und Totenreich im AT (H. Schmid); Todesstrafe, Biblisch (F. Horst); Tora (R. Rendtorff); Tosefta (E. Gross); Totenverehrung: Im AT (H. Schmid); Tradition: Im AT (L. Rost), Im Judentum (E. Lohse); Trauerbräuche: Im AT, NT und Judentum (H. Schmid); Traum: Im AT (E. L. Ehrlich); Typologie: Im AT (F. Hesse); Ugarit (A. Kuschke, H. Donner, O. Eissfeldt); Universalismus und Partikularismus: Im AT (J. Hempel);

Uriel (E. Lohse); Urim und Tummim (K. Galling); Urmensch
(K. Rudolph); Urstand: Im AT und Judentum (Fr. Ellermeier);
Vatername Gottes: Im AT (H.-J. Kraus); Verborgenheit Gottes,
AT (H. Bandt); Verdienst: Im Judentum (E. Lohse); Vergeltung:
Im AT (F. Horst): Im Judentum (C. H. Hunzinger); Ver-
siegelung (E. Dinkler); Versöhnung: Im AT (K. Koch): Im Juden-
tum (C. H. Hunzinger);Verstockung: Im AT (F. Hesse); Vision:
Im AT (V. Maag); Völkertafel (H. Gese); Wein und Wein-
enthaltung: Im AT (R. Rendtorff); Weisheit, Weisheitsdichtung
(H. Gese); Weissagung (F. M. Th. de Liagre-Böhl); Weissagung
und Erfüllung: Im AT (F. Baumgärtel); Weltbild: Alter Orient
(F. M. Th. de Liagre Böhl): Im AT (H. W. Hertzberg) ; Wirt-
schaftsgeschichte: In Israel (K. Galling); Wort Gottes: Im AT
(W. Zimmerli); Wunder: Im AT (W. Vollborn): Im Judentum
(E. Lohse); Zadok (W. Schottroff); Zebaoth (O. Eissfeldt);
Zedekia (R. Bach); Zehnten, religionsgeschichtlich (O. Eissfeldt):
Im AT (W. Schmidt); Zeloten (E. Lohse); Zelt (E. Kutsch);
Zephanja-Apokalypse (R. Meyer); Zephanjabuch (H. Gese);
Zorn Gottes: Im AT (W. Eichrodt); Zwölfprophetenbuch (F.
Hesse). In addition, many other articles have an indirect bearing
on our field.

G.W.A.

Hebrew Union College Annual, Vol. XXXIII (ed. by Elias L. Epstein).
1962. Pp. 276+portrait+26 (in Hebrew)+index to vols. I–XXXII.
(Hebrew Union College, Cincinnati.)

In the first article of the present volume, W. Hallo attempts to
establish 'A Typology of the Royal Inscriptions of Ur'. As
historical documents and as objects of art they have a value of
their own. The literary analysis of their inscriptional *genre*
shows that they were subject to strict rules of composition,
which remained largely unchanged for a period of nearly a
thousand years, i.e., up to the time of Hammurabi. Looking
towards the west of the Mesopotamian area, we might add that
a discernible influence of their pattern (a dative phrase naming
the deity, a nominative giving the builder's or donor's name, an
accusative identifying the object built or donated, and a verb
expressing the act of construction) extends to the Palmyrenian
inscriptions of the second post-Christian century and beyond.
Julius Lewy discusses 'Old Assyrian Evidence Concerning
Kuššara and its Location' and provides interesting new material
for more comprehensive studies in the field of the early history
of Anatolia. Julian Morgenstern concludes a series of articles
on 'The Book of the Covenant', started as early as in 1928. Only
few of the more recent books on the subject are referred to.
One misses, for example, a consideration of Alt's *Ursprünge
des israelitischen Rechts*, of Cazelles' *Études sur le Code de
l'Alliance*, or of Cassuto's relevant observations in his Hebrew
Commentary on Exodus. Morgenstern holds that most of the
Covenant Laws belong to the time of Jeremiah or even Ezekiel,
but his view is unlikely to carry conviction, since — to make
only one reservation — they reflect the social conditions of a
group of half-sedentary people, who, for the time being, were
assured of their livelihood by a pastoral mode of life. M. Tsevat

offers 'A New Interpretation of I Samuel, 10:2', dealing with the topographical identification of Rachel's tomb. H. Orlinsky continues his 'Studies in the LXX of Job' with chapter IV on 'The Present State of the Greek Text of Job'. He confines himself to an examination of those seemingly corrupt readings of the LXX, which represent original Greek renderings, identical with or closely related to the masoretic text.

Articles by E. Wiesenberg, M. Harris and A. Reines comprise researches on Mishnaic, Kabbalistic and mediaeval philosophical literature, but have no direct bearing on the study of the ancient Near East or on that of the Hebrew Bible. A. Scheiber publishes a number of letters, exchanged between Schechter, Bacher, and Goldzieher. The last article by D. Jarden is written in Hebrew and offers a pointed and carefully annotated edition of hitherto unknown religious poems by the 13th-century poet Eleazar ben Jacob ha-Babhli.
S.S.

HERTZBERG, H.-W.: *Beiträge zur Traditionsgeschichte und Theologie des Alten Testaments*. 1962. Pp. 186. (Vandenhoeck & Ruprecht, Göttingen. Price: DM. 14.80).

This contains fourteen articles, thirteen of which have appeared in various journals from 1925 to 1960. The author's intimate knowledge of Palestinian geography and place-names has provided him with a powerful tool for the investigation of some Old Testament problems. If we single out certain articles for special notice, it may indicate the value of the whole collection. The paper on 'Adonibesek' (Jdg. i. 1–7) argues for the originality of the name which preserves therefore the name of a Perizzite god Bezek, after whom the place (now *chirbet ibzik*) was named. The battle appears to precede the incident in Gen. xxxiv. 30. The article 'Die Melchisedek-Traditionen' takes note of various traditions linking the king with Jerusalem, Golgotha, Gerizim, and Tabor. The Melchizedek story is seen to be the *hieros logos* of an old Canaanite sanctuary, perhaps originally at Tabor, and later transferred by Jews to Jerusalem, by Samaritans to Gerizim and by Christians to Golgotha. Deut. xxxiii. 19 may originally have been 'sacrifices of (the god) Sadik'. Again we would note the perceptive article, 'Die Nachgeschichte alttes- tamentliche Texte innerhalb des Alten Testaments', which dis- cusses the glosses, additions and omissions in the MT of Isaiah i–xxxix as furnishing a valuable insight into the use made by later Judaism of the received Word of God. We are grateful that these articles have been assembled in this form.
A.S.H.

KLEINKNECHT, H. & GUTBROD, W.: *Law*, trans. by Dorothea M. Barton and ed. by P. R. Ackroyd. (Bible Key Words from Gerhard Kittel's *Theologisches Wörterbuch zum Neuen Testament*.) 1962. Pp. xii+158. (A. & C. Black, London. Price: 15s. 0d.).

This volume conforms to the general pattern of the translations of articles from the Kittel *Wörterbuch*. There is some slight abridgement in the early part; but there are additional references to literature in the bibliography and in the footnotes.
G.W.A.

(MUILENBURG, J.): *Israel's Prophetic Heritage:* Essays in honor of James Muilenburg, ed. by B. W. Anderson and W. Harrelson. 1962. Pp. xiv+242+portrait. (Harper & Brothers, New York and S.C.M. Press Ltd., London. Price: $5 and 27s. 6d.).

The best compliment that a reviewer can pay to this notable *Festschrift* is that it is not unworthy of the great scholar and teacher in whose honour it has been produced. The title of the volume has been interpreted widely, as the subjects of the contributions show: In the Beginning (W. Eichrodt), a study of Gen. i. 1; The Prophets and the Problem of Continuity (N. W. Porteous); The Lawsuit of God: a Form-critical Study of Deuteronomy 32 (G. E. Wright); The Background of Judges 17–18 (M. Noth); The Prophetic Call of Samuel (M. Newman); The Prophet as Yahweh's Messenger (J. F. Ross); Amos and Wisdom (S. Terrien); "Rejoice not, O Israel!" (Dorothea W. Harvey); Essentials of the Theology of Isaiah (Th. C. Vriezen); Nonroyal Motifs in the Royal Eschatology (W. Harrelson); The King in the Garden of Eden: a Study of Ezekiel 28: 12–19 (H. G. May); Exodus Typology in Second Isaiah (B. W. Anderson); The Promises of Grace to David in Isaiah 55: 1–5 (Otto Eissfeldt); The Samaritan Schism in Legend and History (H. H. Rowley); Prophecy and the Prophets at Qumrân (M. Burrows). The volume ends with a list (compiled by R. L. Hicks) of the writings of Professor Muilenburg to whom, as one of our distinguished honorary members, we extend congratulations and good wishes.

G.W.A.

NÖTSCHER, F.: *Vom Alten zum Neuen Testament.* Gesammelte Aufsätze. (Bonner Biblische Beiträge, 17.) 1962. Pp. VI+250. (Peter Hanstein Verlag, Bonn. Price: DM. 32).

This is a collection of thirteen articles, all of which have previously appeared in print. Subscribers to the *Revue de Qumran* will be familiar with two of them, the more important of which is a contribution of almost fifty pages on 'Heiligkeit in den Qumran-schriften' (pp. 126–174). Others first saw the light in *Biblica*, the *Mélanges Robert*, the *Festgabe* for Cardinal Frings, and the volumes presented to H. Junker and V. Christian. Some of the articles are quite short. One of the longer essays is that in the Frings volume and is entitled: 'Vorchristliche Typen urchristlicher Ämter? Episkopos und Mebaqqer', in which, apropos of the various uses of the term 'Bishop' Dr. Nötscher reminds his readers that the words *Pamphlet*, *Gift*, and *Mist* have not quite the same meaning in English and in German (p. 192, n. 11).

J.M.T.B.

RIESENFELD, H. (ed. by): *Svensk exegetisk årsbok*, xxvi. 1961. Pp. 166. (C. W. K. Gleerup, Lund. Price: Sw. kr. 10).

This issue begins with two short studies in English on Work in the Old Testament and Work in the New Testament, by I. Engnell and B. Gärtner respectively. M. Ottoson contributes, in Swedish, a study of the military and historical geography of ancient Palestine, 'From Megiddo to Masada'. There are New

Testament articles by H. Riesenfeld, G. Lindeskog, E. Lövestam, and E. Schweizer, all of which have some indirect interest for the *Alttestamentler*, notably that by Lindeskog, 'Israel in the New Testament'. E. Larsson contributes a sketch of the history of the Uppsala Exegetiska Sällskap. Following the review articles there is a further contribution in Swedish (by A. Carlson) to the series surveying commentaries and other helps to the study of Old Testament books, this article being devoted entirely to literature on Ezekiel. Those responsible for this annual are to be congratulated for the unfailing interest, variety, and usefulness of its contents.

G.W.A.

SHEWELL-COOPER, W. E.: *Plants and Fruits of the Bible.* 1962. Pp. v+174. (Darton, Longman & Todd Ltd., London. Price: 16s. 0d.).

The Principal of a Horticultural college attempts to identify the flowers, trees, vegetables and herbs mentioned in the Bible. He discusses the weeds, diseases, and pests, and horticultural and farming operations referred to in both Testaments. There is no index but the format makes reference possible. Coloured end-papers illustrate 30 species mentioned in the book. The author has a popular style and uses his identifications to interpret Bible passages.

J.N.S.

Studia theologica cura ordinum Scandinavicorum edita. Vol. XV, Fasc. i. 1962. Pp. 1–112. Fasc. ii. 1961 (*sic*). Pp. 113–196+Index. Vol. 16, Fasc. 1. 1962. Pp. 1–108. (Aarhus University, Aarhus. Price: Vol. XV: D.kr. 20 the vol.; or D.kr. 14 each fascicle. Vol. 16 and subsequent vols. D.kr. 30 each vol.; or D.kr. 20 each fascicle).

Publication of this annual has been transferred from Gleerups of Lund to Aarhus University. This change may account for the curious (and accidental?) throwback in the dating of XV, ii., and the change of style in the numbering of the latest volume. XV, i. contains a study by S. Mowinckel of the verb *siah* and the nouns *siah* and *sihā*, an article by E. Hammershaimb entitled 'Einige Hauptgedanken in der Schrift des Propheten Micha', and a discussion (in French) by E. Nielsen of war considered as a religion and religion considered as a war (from the Song of Deborah to the Qumran War Scroll). There are also three articles, by K. H. Rengstorf, C. Spicq, and E. Bammel, on New Testament subjects. In XV, ii., the longest article is a learned and detailed study by P. Wernberg-Møller on the relationship of the Peshitta Version of Genesis to the Palestinian Targum fragments published by Kahle and to the Targum Onkelos. N. Hyldahl and J. Munck contribute articles on New Testament subjects. Vol. 16, 1 contains no articles of direct interest to the *Alttestamentler*.

G.W.A.

EDUCATIONAL

*Avi-Yonah, M. & Malamat, A. (ed. by): *Illustrated World of the Bible Library.* Vol. 1, *The Law;* Vol. 2, *The Former Prophets;* Vol. 3, *The Latter Prophets;* Vol. 4, *The Writings;* Vol. 5, *The New Testament.* [n.d.] Pp. 304; 304; 304; 296; 302+numerous ills. (McGraw-Hill Book Company, Inc., New York, Toronto, and London. Price: Vols. 1–4, £25 the set; Vol. 5, £6 10s.).

These magnificent volumes, which were originally published in Jerusalem (the first four under the title *Views of the Biblical World*), provide a most attractive educational tool for the teacher of Scripture. On each page there is a short passage from the Biblical text (following the RSV in the main), accompanied by an illustration in colour (e.g., a map, a view, a photograph of some ancient monument or document) and an interpretative comment. The work is based on up-to-date scholarship, and has been carried out by a distinguished team of scholars. Any school library which can afford this acquisition is to be envied.

G.W.A.

*Avi-Yonah, M. and Kraeling, E. G.: *Our Living Bible.* 1962. Pp. 384. (Oldbourne Press, London. Price: 70s. 0d.).

This is a condensed edition in one volume of *The Illustrated World of the Bible Library*, reviewed above. A selection of the illustrations has been made; and altogether a remarkable amount of useful material has been assembled. The commentary is based on the text of the larger work, which, in every respect except size and cost, this volume closely resembles. It may be warmly recommended as a reliable and attractive educational tool.

G.W.A.

*Hebert, G.: *The Old Testament from Within.* 1962. Pp. 154. (Oxford University Press, London. Price: 7s. 6d.).

This work is a completely revised edition of *The Bible from Within* 1950 (see *Book List*, 1951, p. 16; *Eleven Years*, p. 311). Father Hebert adopts the rôle of a *ger*, and expounds the purpose of God from Abraham to the promised Messiah, and he does this in relation to contemporary issues. It is an excellent book for all who are seeking to discover the meaning of the O.T.

G.H.D.

Mason, D. H.: *Thus Saith the Lord.* (The Christian Students' Library, No. 26.) 1962. Pp. 164. (The Christian Literature Society, Madras, for the Senate of Serampore College. Price: Rs. 2.50).

Mr. Mason has lived in India for seventeen years, working in the Mysore Diocese, now in the Church of South India. He is at present Superintendent of the Boys' Home and School at Tum-kur, Mysore State. This paperback is an introduction to the prophets of Israel, and its standard is that of the L.Th. Diploma of Serampore College. The first part of the book contains short introductions to the work of each prophet. The second part deals with the messages they proclaimed. The book is written primarily for Indian students, but it is wholly suitable for theological students generally, and is entirely safe as a guide.

N.H.S.

*WAINWRIGHT, J. A.: *God and Man in the Old Testament.* 1962. Pp. 176. (National Society and S.P.C.K., London. Price: 17s. 6d.).

This book, based on lectures given at a Teachers' Training College, will be found especially useful by teachers in secondary Modern and Grammar Schools and by Training College students who are completing courses in Divinity. A knowledge of O.T. history is presupposed, and attention is directed to the basic O.T. concepts relating to God and Man, the use of some of the key words being studied in detail. The author does not pretend to treat his subject exhaustively but he has written an attractive and stimulating book that deserves a wide welcome. L.A.P.

ARCHAEOLOGY AND EPIGRAPHY

FRANKEN, H. J.: *Heilig-Land en heilige huisjes.* 1962. Pp. 38. (E. J. Brill, Leiden. Price: Fl. 1.75).

Dr. Franken's inaugural lecture as reader in Palestinian Archaeology in the University of Leiden reviews shortly the development of the discipline *biblical antiquities* with illustrations from archaeological excavations in Palestine. He discusses methods of excavating, distinguishing between scholars mainly interested in literature, whose archaeological results are often influenced prejudicially by theories about the Bible texts, and scholars trained in the modern stratigraphical method of digging, introduced in Palestine by Miss Kenyon at Jericho, wrongly understood as the improved Reisner-Fisher method. P.A.H.deB.

GARBINI, G.: *Le origini della statuaria Sumerica.* 1962. Pp. 45, English résumé 7 pp.+28 plates and 1 map. (Università degli Studi, Rome. Price: Lire 6,000, $10).

The versatile author of this archaeological and artistic book is already known for his exposition of ancient Aramaic and for his grammar of the N.W. Semitic inscriptions. What he now presents is a study of the earliest 'Mesopotamian' sculptures of the human figure — by no means all of them necessarily to be dubbed 'Sumerian', despite the title. Indeed, this title might be criticized on another ground as well: to consider the *origini* of this sculpture would involve asking why some of the earliest stone figures of the Ancient East were produced by a people living in a stoneless country, and this might bring in the origin of the Sumerians themselves, a question now prudently avoided.

The book is illustrated with photographs from the ample collections of material in the University of Rome and also by twelve good hand-drawings which have the merit of including some less-familiar subjects. The text is clear, is very competently summarized in an English résumé, and is followed by a short bibliography. Only the paltry sketch-map at the end is unworthy of so well-constituted a book.

Dr. Garbini allows that his material has received much attention of late, but he expresses dissatisfaction with two recent works upon the subject. His own most distinctive contribution lies in emphasis upon territorial (as well as the recognized chronological) distinctions, even if a common centre of departure is ultimately postulated (p. 41). In the course of his theme he has many good observations — he is sceptical of jaunty artistic labels (pp. 11, 42); he sees that the manifestation of Babylonian figural talent was in metal rather than stone, and therefore mostly lost (p. 16); he is not above admitting that some of the early productions are simply the work of poor craftsmen (pp. 29, 43); he notices the rarity of stone figures in later Babylon and in Assyria, though the reason assigned is questionable (p. 13), and so, too, is the relevance of the head from Brak (p. 17). It may be doubted also whether the difference he detects between the earlier and the later inscriptions (p. 13) really affects the intention of those who dedicated their effigies.

C.J.G.

GRAY, J.: *Archaeology and the Old Testament World*. 1962. Pp. 256 (including 5 maps)+25 plates. (Thomas Nelson & Sons, Edinburgh. Price: 30s. 0d.).

A well-produced book in two sections: geographical and historical — The Fertile Crescent, and Israel among the Nations. The author makes good use of the results of archaeological discoveries and of his own experiences of life in the Near East to present the institutions, conventions, and beliefs which were the environment of the Old Testament. He deals with the cultural background of the Old Testament rather than its history, religion, and literature. The book is well illustrated and has a useful bibliography for each chapter.

J.N.S.

MATTHIAE, P.: *Ars Syra*, contributi alla storia dell'arte figurativa siriana nelle età del Medio e Tardo Bronzo. (Serie Archeologica 4.) 1962. Pp. 156+XXVIII plates. (Centro di Studi Semitici, Rome. Price: L.9.000, $15.00).

In this volume the author presents a study of Syrian figurative art in the Middle and Late Bronze ages. He attempts to define the nature of its development, to indicate the extent of external influence upon it, and to describe its coherence and unity. Is it the original product of an independent civilization, or the peripheral manifestation of a larger cultural unity? M. Matthiae's investigations are not confined to examples of 'Syrian' art found in Syria proper, but extend to those from Phoenicia and Palestine.

He discusses the most important examples of stone sculpture (the statue of Idrimi, the head from Jabbul), bronzes (reliefs from Simiriyan, Megiddo, Ugarit, the Orontes valley, seated deities, deities standing on animals, deities in motion with uplifted arm brandishing a characteristic weapon), ivories (Megiddo, Ras Shamra), finally *glyptics* (Beit Mirsim, Hazor, tell 'Ajjul). This inquiry shows that there was a specifically Syrian type of art, displaying, however, influences which are readily recognizable (Anatolian and Egyptian). Two main streams exist side by side: the art of the court, and a narrative type which is popular in origin. The latter came in the end to predominate over the former, which, however, survived in small-scale productions.

A.P.

NOTH, M.: *Die Welt des Alten Testaments. Einführung in die Grenz-gebiete der alttestamentliche Wissenschaft.* (Sammlung Töpelmann. Zweite Reihe: Theologische Hilfsbücher, Band 3.) Vierte, neubearbeitete Auflage. 1962. Pp. XVI+356, including 10 maps, plans, and other illustrations in the text, and one folding chronological table. (Alfred Töpelmann, Berlin. Price: DM.28).

The earlier editions of this immensely valuable work of reference were noticed in the *Book Lists* for 1946, p. 16 (*Eleven Years*, p. 16); 1953, p. 46 (*Eleven Years*, p. 499); 1957, p. 19. In the preparation of this edition full account has been taken of recent work; and in two pages of addenda reference is made to material which could not be included in the body of the work. Of the additions made in the text the most substantial is a section entitled 'Die Verkehrswege des Landes im Altertum'. The plates have been omitted, for adequate reasons.

G.W.A.

PARROT, A.: *Abraham et son Temps.* (Cahiers d'Archéologie Biblique No. 14.) 1962. Pp. 140+43 plates. (Les Éditions Delachaux et Niestlé S.A., Neuchâtel & Paris).

This latest study by the distinguished excavator of Mari maintains the high standard of Professor Parrot's archaeological studies. The Biblical account of Abraham from Ur via Harran, Shechem, and Bethel to Hebron is documented by archaeology at all localities mentioned, both by material remains and texts from Mari and Nuzu, which illustrate history and society in patriarchal times. The study ends, as Professor Parrot's study of the Tower of Babel ended, with a chapter on Abraham in iconography and in Christian typology. Interesting and feasible, if somewhat daring, is the explanation of Abraham's wandering from Ur to Harran and southwards by Aleppo and the vicinity of Qatna in the light of the information of the Mari Texts on the Beni-iamina, Semites from the south who had migrated to the north. Useful facts are also assembled on the Herodian building at Ramat el-Khalil (Mamre) and the Cave of Machpelah in Hebron. Professor Parrot's attractive book will be read with profit and pleasure by scholars and students at all stages.

J.G.

PRITCHARD, J. B.: *The Water System of Gibeon.* (Museum Monographs.) 1961. Pp. viii+24+48 figs. (The University Museum, University of Pennsylvania, Philadelphia. Price: $2.50).

A description of the water systems at el Jib discovered in the 1956-7 campaigns by the University Museum-Church Divinity School of the Pacific. There is a careful account of the objects found in the pool and tunnel, and the conclusion that the pool was probably constructed in the twelfth century B.C., the tunnel later, and the pool was probably filled in by the sixth century B.C. The discoveries are linked with references in Josh. ix. 21; II Sam. ii. 13; Jer. xli. 12.   J.N.S.

PRITCHARD, J. B.: *Gibeon — Where the Sun Stood Still.* The Discovery of the Biblical City. 1962. Pp. xx+176 incl. 9 drawings+110 ills. (Princeton University Press, Princeton, U.S.A. Price: 46s. 0d.).

In his semi-popular presentation of the results of his work of four seasons at Gibeon (el-Jib) Professor Pritchard has presented a picture of archaeological work in Palestine, of local description, and of the rôle of Gibeon in the records which is both authoritative and agreeable to the general reader. A chapter is devoted to the chief industry of Gibeon, the making of wine, storage room for 25,000 gallons of which was discovered, with many jar-handles inscribed with the name of the place and of two persons responsible for the wine or for the vessels. The water installations too, the stair-well to the water-table and the shaft under the wall to the spring outside, dated by the wall *c.* 1200, are also spectacular remains, of which the author is at no pains to conceal his justifiable pride.   J.G.

WRIGHT, G. E.: *Biblical Archaeology.* New and Revised Edition. 1962. Pp. 292, with 220 ills. and VIII maps. (Gerald Duckworth & Co. Ltd., London. Price: 50s. 0d.).

A new and revised edition of the work first published in 1957 (*Book List*, 1957, p. 23). The alterations bring the book up to date especially in view of Yadin's excavations at Hazor and Megiddo — which have caused the change of plates and the removal of the word Solomon from two of the Megiddo illustrations — and the American excavations at Shechem. The bibliographies at the end of each chapter have also been revised. The book is printed on much better paper than the first edition and this has made possible better reproduction of the many illustrations. It is a book to be commended unreservedly.

J.N.S.

HISTORY AND GEOGRAPHY

BRIGHT, J.: *Altisrael in der neueren Geschichtsschreibung.* Eine methodologische Studie. (Abhandlungen zur Theologie des Alten und Neuen Testaments, 40.) 1961. Pp. 140. (Zwingli Verlag, Zürich/Stuttgart. Price: Sw. Frs. 18.50).

This is the German translation of *Early Israel in Recent History Writing*, reviewed by G. H. D. in *Book List*, 1957, p. 23. The translation reads well and retains the freshness and vividness of the original, to which it is faithful both in details and in the general impression which it gives. Only very occasionally do misunderstandings appear (notably p. 21, lines 19 ff.). There are a few instances where foreign terms have been used (e.g., 'Dokumentenanalyse' instead of 'Quellenscheidung', 'Typus' instead of 'Gattung'). Where appropriate, references to literature have been amplified or abbreviated.   W.B.

The Cambridge Ancient History: Revised Edition of Volumes I & II.
It is good news that at last the revision of that most valuable guide and companion to historical studies has begun to appear. For the convenience of students the Cambridge University Press is issuing the revised edition in fascicles, and the following fascicles are now available:

Egypt: from the death of Ammenemes III to Seqenenre II: by William C. Hayes. Fasc. 6. Pp. 44. 6s. 0d.

Anatolia: by O. R. Gurney. Fasc. 8. Pp. 32. 3s. 6d.

The Cities of Babylonia: by C. J. Gadd. Fasc. 9. Pp. 60. 6s. 0d.

Egypt: Internal affairs from Tuthmosis I to the death of Amenophis III: by William C. Hayes. Fasc. 10, Part I. Pp. 54. 6s. 0d. *Egypt: Internal affairs from Tuthmosis I to the death of Amenophis III:* by William C. Hayes. Fasc. 10, Part II. Pp. 72. 8s. 6d.

Northern Mesopotamia and Syria: by J.-R. Kupper. Fasc. 14. Pp. 46. 6s. 0d.

A full estimate of the value of these first instalments of the revised history must, of course, await the judgement of the experts. Here it must suffice to say that to the present writer the contributions listed above fully come up to the reputations of their authors and to the standard set by the old edition of the Cambridge Ancient History. One observes the immense advances in knowledge brought about by recent archaeological researches. This is specially noticeable in the treatment of Northern Mesopotamia and Syria, where the new material from Mari has completely transformed the picture and thrown a flood of new light on what was previously an obscure period of Mesopotamian history. The same can be said about Professor Gurney's fascinating account of the rise of the Hittite empire in Anatolia, where he has made full use of his own archaeological and linguistic researches as well as those of earlier scholars to illuminate another obscure period of ancient history. Professor Gadd's unrivalled knowledge of the Sumerian civilization, set forth in a style of classical elegance, vividly recreates the life of those early Babylonian cities. The brilliant 18th dynasty of Egypt receives able treatment at the hands of Mr. W. C. Hayes, and one can only say that the whole of this first instalment of the revision offers abundant promise for what is yet to come. Nor should the due meed of praise be omitted to the labours and wise direction of the editor, Professor Sidney Smith.   S.H.H.

*MAY, H. G. (ed. by) and HAMILTON, R. W. and HUNT, G. N. S.: *Oxford Bible Atlas*. 1962. Pp. 144 including many ills.+26 maps. (Oxford University Press, London. Price: 21s. 0d.).

This excellent Bible Atlas contains a plethora of fine coloured historical and archaeological maps in contour supplemented by a brief recapitulation of the appropriate part of the Bible; each illustrated with Scriptural references. A welcome feature is the inclusion of maps of the natural regions of Palestine, hydrographical maps, and one of the vegetation of Palestine based on the modern Israeli Atlas of Israel, the last with a complete annual rainfall and temperature chart.

The atlas is introduced by a conspectus of the history of Biblical times and is rounded out by a masterly statement on Archaeology and the Bible by R. W. Hamilton, formerly of the Department of Antiquities in Palestine during the British Mandate, with 20 well-chosen illustrations. A feature which should not be overlooked is the gazetteer of 26 pp., which lists all place-names in the text and maps with their modern identifications as far as that is possible. The atlas may be cordially recommended as a useful instrument in Biblical study classes in schools and colleges and especially in adult education classes.

J.G.

SCHEDL, C.: *Geschichte des Alten Testaments*. Band IV. *Das Zeitalter der Propheten*. 1962. Pp. xix+474, incl. 4 ills.+6 maps. (Tyrolia-Verlag, Innsbruck, Vienna, Munich. Price: S. 160, DM. 27).

This volume follows the same lines as vol. I (*Book List*, 1957, p. 25) and vols. II, III (*Book List*, 1960, p. 14). The story of the prophets, from Elijah to Ezekiel, is told within the framework of the history and closely follows the Biblical narrative. Again the chief value of the book from the scholar's point of view is to be found in the material in small type and footnotes which draw upon non-Biblical material and give full references. Only very occasionally does the author get away from a strictly conservative approach, as for instance, when he allows that the Elisha stories have gathered much legendary material.

L.H.B.

TEXT AND VERSIONS

ECKER, R.: *Die arabische Job — Übersetzung des Gaon Saadja Ben Josef Al-Fajjûmî*. Ein Beitrag zur Geschichte der Übersetzung des Alten Testaments. (Studien zum Alten und Neuen Testament. Band IV.) 1962. Pp. XX+428. (Kösel-Verlag, München. Price: DM. 38).

The work here noticed is an exhaustive examination of Sa'adyah's methods of translation, based on J. & H. Derenbourg's edition of his *Version Arabe du Livre de Job* (*Oeuvres Complètes*, Vol. V; 1899) in Hebrew characters; and the author expressly excludes all reference to the problems raised by the manuscripts and the question of the authenticity of Sa'adyah's various works. Sa'adyah's work is examined in 22 sections in which such diverse problems as its relationship to the Targum, the explanations of his renderings in his commentary, his treatment of rare and unique words, his use of Arabic words similar to the Hebrew words which they are chosen to represent, doublets, expansions, abbreviated renderings, free translations, inversions, even the rendering of numbers and rhetorical questions, parallelism and paronomasia, are all included; a summary of results concludes each section, and a final *resumé* of the principles enunciated is added at the end. Almost every other word receives a comment; but whether the results thus obtained are commensurable with the labour expended on the task is another matter. Naturally, the author succeeds in explaining Sa'adyah's methods of translation and accounting for his vagaries, but the length at which he does it is excessive, and many of the notes are otiose; no one will read Sa'adyah who is not a sufficiently good Arabist to find the bulk of the solutions unaided and alone. The author, however, obviously knows his subject well; possibly then he can be induced to prepare a dictionary of Sa'adyah's works such as J. & H. Derenbourg are said to have unsuccessfully projected.

The work is very well reproduced typescript, in which both Hebrew and Arabic characters come out very well. G.R.D.

KENYON, F. G., ADAMS, A. W.: *Der Text der griechischen Bibel. Zweite überarbeitete und ergänzte Auflage.* (Göttinger Theologische Lehrbücher). 1961. Pp. 200. (Vandenhoeck & Ruprecht, Göttingen. Price: DM. 14.80).

This book is a translation of *The Text of the Greek Bible, A Student's Handbook* by the same author and reviser, and adds a table on the textual history of the New Testament by Ferdinand Hahn. The section devoted to the Septuagint covers some fifty pages. Other sections, too, have incidental items of information relevant for the O.T. textualist.

As a student's text-book for which the first requirement is clarity of treatment, the book easily scores an alpha. On the other hand, whether the basic idea of 'bringing up-to-date' a highly individual work of a past generation is a good one or not is still a moot point; the reviser's contributions are sometimes cramped by his desire to retain more than is necessary of Kenyon's presentation. It is to be hoped that now that the German translation has appeared the English version will soon be published! B.J.R.

LEHMANN, O.: *The Damascus Pentateuch and its manuscript tradition according to Ben Naphtali.* 1962. Pp. 20. (Obtainable from B. H. Blackwell, Ltd., Oxford. Price: 10s. 6d.).

The Pentateuch Codex presented here is in the David Sassoon collection, and, with the exception of Gen. i–ix. 26, and a folio containing Ex. xviii. 1–23, contains the whole of the Pentateuch, and comes from a synagogue in Damascus. Dr. Lehmann, in describing its scribal character, examines its claim to represent the Ben Naphtali tradition, and on the whole confirms it. As such, and because of its age (9th or early 10th century), it forms a highly important witness to a text-form otherwise known in the main only from two manuscripts and the Massoretic treatise by Misha'el ben Uzziel. At the same time the MS shows that the Ben Naphtali tradition is not uniform, and is not wholly either 'Eastern' or 'Western'. The discussion is an important one for the history of the Massoretic text and a welcome addition to the very small number of monographs on the subject.

The book is typewritten, and the Hebrew words (unnecessarily, one would think) entered in handwriting. The typing is not as clean as it might be for publication. As mentioned above, the book is not published by Blackwell but obtainable from them.

B.J.R.

RABIN, C. (ed. by): *Textus. Annual of the Hebrew University Bible Project.* Vol. II. 1962. Pp. 150+62 (Hebrew). (Magnes Press, The Hebrew University, Jerusalem. Price: 43s. 0d.).

This second volume fully maintains the high standard set by the first (see *Book List*, 1962, p. 24). P. E. Kahle writes on pre-Massoretic vocalisation. N. H. Snaith considers the question where the true Ben Asher text is to be found. The three scrolls of the Law which were found in the Temple court are discussed by S. Talmon. M. Goshen-Gottstein gives a full account of his search for Biblical manuscripts in America, and reports his discovery of evidence for the lost readings of the Aleppo Codex. An examination of the indefinite subject in the ancient versions leads C. Rabin to conclude that the deviations in them from the Hebrew construction do not in general necessarily point to a different *Vorlage*. J. Shunary provides the text and a translation of an Arabic *tafsir* of Judges v., and considers the identity of the translator (Saadiah?). D. N. Freedman argues that palaeo-graphical study of the oldest Qumran manuscripts shows that Massoretic spelling, as a definite orthographic system, originated in the late-third or early-second century B.C. G. E. Weil treats of the Babylonian Massoretic tradition, and adds the Babylonian Massorah according to MS. or. qu.680 (Berlin) to extracts from the first two chapters of Ecclesiastes, with commentary. I. Yeivin studies Geniza fragments of Lev. (xi. 32–xvi. 14, xvi. 15–xxiii. 10) and Num. (xxiv. 3–xxix. 36), with Babylonian vocalisa-tion, written in abbreviated form (six plates). In another article he considers the vocalisation of Qere-Kethibh in MS. Firk. 11, Arab. Heb. 147 (Leningrad). D. Flusser discusses the reading of DSIa in Isa. xlix. 17—'thy builders shall be quicker than thy destroyers'. In Isa. xiv. 31 B. Kedar-Kopfstein reads *we'ên nôḏēḏ benô'āḏāw* 'and none is fleeing among his summoned troops'. L. Lipschuetz contributes the text of Mishael b. Uzziel's treatise on the differences between Ben Asher and Ben Naphtali, with critical apparatus. Short summaries in Hebrew of the articles are supplied.

D.W.T.

SPERBER, A.: *The Bible in Aramaic, based on Old Manuscripts and Print-Texts. Vol. III. The Latter Prophets according to Targum Jonathan.* 1962. Pp. xi+505. (E. J. Brill, Leiden. Price: Fl. 100).

The first two volumes of this edition of the Targum were reviewed in the *Book List* for 1960 (pp. 16 f.) and 1961 (p. 26). The pattern of the present volume is the same as previously. There is a basic text (MS. Or. 2211 of the British Museum); and other material used consists of manuscripts with Babylonian and Tiberian vocalisation, or no vocalisation at all, printed editions, and Targum quotations from early Jewish writers. The text of the Targum of the Latter Prophets has been handed down in a most deplorable state. The proof of this assertion will be supplied in the next volume, in which the editor will return to a considera-tion of many problems to which he has hitherto made only passing reference. His conclusions on these, and, we may hope, on some other fundamental problems, will be of great interest and importance. D.W.T.

ZIEGLER, J.: *Septuaginta Vetus Testamentum Graecum auctoritate Societatis Litterarum Gottingensis editum.* Vol. XII, fasc. 1. *Sapientia Salomonis.* 1962. Pp. 168. (Vandenhoeck & Ruprecht, Göttingen. Price: paper, DM. 21, by subscription, DM. 18; cloth, DM. 25, by subscription, DM. 22).

The Göttingen Septuagint proceeds apace, and each number proves anew how greatly indebted we are to all concerned with its production. Two new features in the present volume are men-tioned by Professor Ziegler in the Preface, namely that the variants to each verse are given a separate section at the foot of the page, and that between text and notes the text witnesses are listed. Both features will facilitate the use of the edition.

Reference might also be made to the death of two dearly beloved experts connected with this volume; the one, whose passing is referred to in this volume, namely Emil Grosse-Brauckmann, for many years the Director of the LXX-Unternehmen, and the other, Peter Walters (better known by his German surname Katz) who was held in great affection in this country and whose ungrudging help and advice was greatly appreciated always. B.J.R.

EXEGESIS AND MODERN TRANSLATIONS

BARNES, O. L.: *The Song of Songs.* 1961. Pp. xxiv+20+47+7 appendices. (Progressive Printers, Ltd., Newcastle; Distributors, J. Thornton & Sons, Oxford. Price: 21s. 0d.).

This is a detailed study of the Song of Songs, with new interlinear translation, detailed notes, critical apparatus, and details of syntax and vocabulary. The format is reproduced typescript. It is an excellent example of the way in which a student should study a Hebrew text and of the kind of material he should amass.

N.H.S.

BREIT, H. & WESTERMANN, C.: *Calwer Predigthilfen* Band I, *Die alt-testamentliche Texte der dritten Reihe.* 1962. Pp. 256. (Calwer Verlag, Stuttgart. Price: DM. 15).

This book is intended to encourage and facilitate preaching from the Old Testament. With that end in view each of the twenty-one

Old Testament lessons in the third year of the Lutheran lectionary cycle has the main words of its Hebrew text parsed, and any variations from it in the Luther text noted. A few relevant commentaries are then mentioned and general and particular exegesis is given, ending with reflections and suggestions as to treatment from the pulpit. For its somewhat restricted purpose this book should prove very useful.

D.R.Ap-T.

DALGLISH, E. R.: *Psalm Fifty-One: in the Light of Ancient Near Eastern Patternism.* 1962. Pp. XIV+306. (E. J. Brill, Leiden. Price: Fl. 24).

There seems to be a tendency in Old Testament circles to take one of the psalms and use it as the basis for examining a particular literary type and, at the same time, passing comments on the vocabulary of Israel's religious faith and the ideas which are there at work. Despite occasional slips of reference and a number of misprints, the book under review may be regarded as a worthy addition to what may appropriately be described as a new literary *Gattung!* As is indicated by the extended title, Psalm li. is here studied in the light of the comparative data offered by the cultures of the ancient Near East, particularly the valuable material from the Sumero-Accadian field. The author's main argument is that in vv. 3–19 we have a penitential psalm ('probably the greatest penitential prayer ever composed'), which was written in the late pre-exilic period for use by or on behalf of the king. The latter is regarded as bearing a peculiar responsibility for the 'blood-guiltiness' of his people, and the psalm is thus virtually a plea for the continuation of the dynasty and the preservation of the nation. As is commonly recognized, vv. 20–21 were added after the fall of the monarchy in order to adapt the psalm for communal use. The author has read widely and enjoyed the specialist help of a number of distinguished scholars, notably Professor A. Falkenstein whose notes have been incorporated and thus add to the value of the book. Although one may have reservations with regard to the main argument as outlined above, the author is to be congratulated upon producing a painstaking, informative, and thought-provoking piece of work.

A.R.J.

FOHRER, G.: *Das Buch Jesaja.* 2. Band. Kapitel 24–39. (Zürcher Bibelkommentare). 1962. Pp. vi+196. (Zwingli-Verlag, Zurich and Stuttgart. Price: Sw. Frs. 10.80).

The first volume of this commentary was reviewed in *Book List*, 1961, p. 31, where, by a misprint, the chapters treated are given as '1–25' instead of '1–23'. The general features indicated in the earlier notice are again evident in this new volume. There is an admirably concise and judicious presentation of the so-called 'Isaiah Apocalypse', which is held not to be originally a unity but an artificial combination of previously independent units (prophetic liturgies and other elements) to form a 'Cantata' (Fohrer adopts Lindblom's term). Throughout the volume the exegesis is presented with enviable terseness and without distortion. Readers will await with eagerness the appearance of the remainder of this commentary.

G.W.A.

GRAHAM, J.: *With my Whole Heart.* A Devotional Commentary on Psalm 119. 1962. Pp. 56. (Darton, Longman & Todd, London. Price: 7s. 6d.).

This devotional commentary divides the Psalm into sections as in the Offices of Prime, Terce, Sext, and None, and relates the stanzas to successive phrases in the Lord's Prayer. It is an example of devotional application rather than of exegesis.

G.W.A.

HERBERT, A. S.: *Genesis 12–50. Introduction and Commentary.* (Torch Bible Commentaries.) 1962. Pp. 160. (S.C.M. Press, London. Price: 12s. 6d.).

Genesis xii.–l. contains ancient Israelite traditions of many kinds, historical, social, cultic, aetiological. Professor Herbert rightly adjudges that it is not enough, in a commentary such as this, to examine the nature and the trustworthiness of these traditions and to correlate with them any archaeological evidence which has come to light and which is related to the material circumstances of their time and place of origin. It is essential to make clear how the editors, to whom we owe the traditions in the form in which we have them now, saw in the human dealings, the events, and the circumstances which they record evidences of God's care and guidance of His people, so that they made these stories vehicles of torah. Within the limits of the space available to him, Professor Herbert has done this well, without any misguided idealization and without inclination to offer any moral justification of craft or cunning.

J.M.

HORST, F.: *Hiob.* (Biblischer Kommentar, Altes Testament, XVI, Lieferung 3.) 1962. Pp. 161–240. (Verlag der Buchhandlung des Erziehungsvereins, Neukirchen, Kreis Moers. Price: DM. 7 each Lieferung: or, by subscription, DM. 5.85).

It is a sad reflection that this third number of this distinguished commentary may well be the last, for the author died in June, 1962. Some of the commentary's chief excellencies have been mentioned in the reviews of the first two numbers (*Book List*, 1961, p. 32; 1962, p. 28). In this third number the discussion of ix. 1–x. 22 is concluded, and three further sections are fully treated (xi. 1–20, xii. 1–xiv. 22, xv. 1–35). The translation is continued as far as xvii. 16.

D.W.T.

JONES, D. R.: *Haggai, Zechariah and Malachi. Introduction and Commentary.* (Torch Bible Commentaries.) 1962. Pp. 208. (S.C.M. Press, London. Price: 15s. 0d.).

This commentary, based on the A.V. text, is of mixed value for the 'general reader' for whom the series is designed. It follows the now traditional dating for Hag., Zech. i.–viii. and Mal. but dates Zech. ix.–xiv. in the same period as Malachi. This treatment of Zech. ix.–xiv. is provocative and should probably have been put out in a different kind of commentary altogether. The author had not enough scope for the full discussion which his approach demands and he has had to draw his readers' attention again and again to the fact that he is not following the accustomed paths. Several times one comes across the phrase (in italics), *The reader is warned:* this, and the frequently repeated statements that other ways of taking passages are wrong, detracts from the value of the commentary.

In the arguments for the earlier date for the final chapters of Zechariah, and indeed elsewhere in the commentary, the meaning of the Hebrew text is strained to breaking point, as, for instance, in Zech. vi. 13, xi. 4, and xii. 10. The 'general reader' will be puzzled to be told on p. 56 'not to expect every detail to have meaning' and then on p. 57 that it is not wise to 'change MYRTLE TREES to "mountains" . . . . . . In fact, it may yield important meaning. For myrtles were a symbol of the happiness of the messianic age'.

L.H.B.

LAMPARTER, H.: *Das Buch der Sehnsucht: Das Buch Ruth, Das Hohe Lied, Die Klagelieder,* übersetzt und ausgelegt. (Die Botschaft des Alten Testaments, 16, II.) 1962. Pp. 192. (Calwer Verlag, Stuttgart. Price: DM. 12.80).

The book provides a translation of, and a running commentary on Ruth, Canticles and Lamentations. The title may be justified by the wider range of meaning of the German word than its English equivalents. Some of the more obvious textual diffi- culties are noted, but the main purpose is to provide an exegesis for homiletic purposes. Each book is provided with an intro- duction. Ruth is a *novelle* on the theme of Ps. xxxvi. 8 (7) and may come from the Solomonic period. The plain meaning of Canticles is preferred, with the recognition that human love is God's greatest earthly gift. Lamentations is by one author, possibly a disciple of Jeremiah (Baruch?). Lam. i. is associated with the first Babylonian invasion. This is followed by ii., iv., and v., closely connected with 587 B.C.; and Lam. iii. is the latest, but before 538 B.C. The whole book has a liturgical background. A brief bibliography is attached referring the reader to the standard German commentaries.

A.S.H.

LAMPARTER, H.: *Wecken will ich das Morgenrot. Ein Psalter.* 1962. Pp. 250. (Calwer Verlag, Stuttgart. Price: DM. 9.80).

Following on his Psalter, *Deine Rechte sind mein Lied* (which appeared in 1951 but is now out of print) Lamparter has pro- duced a new German rendering of all the poems in the canonical book of Psalms, one which is closer to the original Hebrew than his previous publication, and in which the form of a simple song is employed as the basic poetical pattern. Although he disowns any attempt at Christological interpretation, his Psalms read like Christian lyrics for use in the home. The brilliance of the original language is dimmed and the archaic violence of many passages is tamed. The impression is created that the Psalter could be used without alteration as a Christian prayer book. Clearly the author has not considered the problems raised by such an undertaking. This is evident when, for instance, the sharp antithesis between the type of the pious worshipper and the ungodly is presented to the reader.   H.D.

MAUCHLINE, J.: *Isaiah 1–39. Introduction and Commentary.* (Torch Bible Commentaries.) 1962. Pp. 238. (S.C.M. Press, London. Price: 15s. 0d.).

This is one of the best numbers of a series that has maintained a good standard both in clarity and in scholarship. In his introduction Principal Mauchline sketches in a few pages the book's historical background, gives an account of the prophet himself and goes on to consider the theological value of Isaiah's call. In answer to a common tendency to regard anything in the text that is universalist in its outlook or theology, or looks forward to a new era of peace and prosperity, as exilic or post-exilic the author records his own conviction as a result of further study of these chapters, that 'various passages within chapters 1–39 which speak of the new age could, in respect of the terms in which they are expressed, have arisen more easily and more suitably out of the circumstances of Isaiah's time than out of any later period' (p. 10). The commentary should be of value even to beginners in these studies, and calls for the use throughout its reading of a copy of the RSV. In the Immanuel passage in vii. 1–17, perhaps the most significant point made is that 'the child Immanuel is not himself a deliverer, but his name is a token of the deliverance which will have taken place by the time he is born' (p. 99). On p. 97 the section-reference to (verses) 10–17 seems to be a misprint for 10–11.   J.M.T.B.

MAY, H. G. & METZGER, B. M. (ed. by): *Oxford Annotated Bible.* Revised Standard Version containing the Old and New Testaments, with introductions, comments, cross references, general articles, tables of chronology and of measures and weights, and index. 1962. Pp. xxiv.+1544+12 maps+Index to maps. (Oxford University Press, New York. Price: 57s. 0d.).

It is difficult to praise too highly the amount of useful factual information compressed into this book. For the ordinary reader of the Bible who needs general and individual articles, together with tables and the excellent Oxford Bible Atlas maps all in the same volume with the full R.S.V. text and running (though naturally very brief) annotation, this book will be a godsend. The important names, institutions, and ideas annotated have an index whose print may try the eyes of those not-so-young, otherwise the whole book is very legible. Anyone desiring a copy of the RSV would be well advised to buy this volume; the extra material is worth much more than the difference in price.

D.R.Ap-T.

*NEIL, W.: *One Volume Bible Commentary.* 1962. Pp. 544+2 maps on endpapers. (Hodder and Stoughton, London. Price: 15s. 0d.).

This book may be styled the plain man's guide to the Bible as a book about God and His dealings with men. The author conducts the reader through all the books of the Bible (including the Apocrypha) in turn, 'on the assumption that the writers were primarily theologians and not anthropologists, scientists, or even historians, that the Old and New Testaments are part of one and the same revelation and that they cannot be understood apart from one another'. The book is a remarkable achievement, and in the Old Testament section the commentary on the Pentateuch is outstanding. This work is throughout based on sound scholarship, literary and critical questions being touched on only as they affect our understanding of the religion of the Bible.

L.A.P.

NOTH, M.: *Das dritte Buch Mose, Leviticus übersetzt und erklärt* (Das Alte Testament Deutsch, 6.) 1962. Pp. 182. (Vandenhoek & Ruprecht, Göttingen. Price: paper, DM. 7.50, by subscription, DM. 6.40; cloth, DM. 10.50, by subscription, DM. 8.90).

To draw attention to a new volume in this series and by this author is all that is really needed to ensure its being bought. Successive stages in the complex literary history of Leviticus are fully recognized; and the narrative section viii.–x. sets the whole book clearly in a P context, without any trace of J or E. However, only the account of the first great sacrifice, in ix., belongs to the earliest P narrative. The Code of Holiness (xvii.–xxvi.) at one time formed a separate, probably exilic, law-code. In most cases the cultic provisions of the book, including CH, preserve the actual praxis at the Jerusalem sanctuary, and belong in the main to the last years of the southern kingdom and the beginning of the exilic period.

There is perhaps less scope or need for originality of treatment here, but the closely packed commentary will be read with profit by all who wish to study the Pentateuchal complex and Israel's cultic life. This is a worthy addition to a most useful series.

D.R.Ap-T.

VAN DEN OUDENRIJN, M. A.: *Het Hooglied uit de grondtekst vertaald en uitgelegd.* (De Boeken van het Oude Testament, Deel VIII, Boek III.) 1962. Pp. 46. (Romen & Zonen, Roermond en Maaseik. Price: Fl. 2.25).

This work on the Song of Songs contains, like all the others in the same series, an introduction, new Dutch translation, exegetical notes, and an appendix presenting a textual apparatus. Over 50 textual emendations are suggested. In i. 5 'the curtains of Shalmah' (in N. Arabia) stand in parallelism with 'the tents of Kedar'; and the Shulammite of vi. 13 (vii. 1 in Hebrew) becomes the 'Shalmanite', and the words that follow are envisaged as sung in accompaniment to a Shalmanite dance, in which the singers recognize a close resemblance to a well-known dance from Trans-jordanian Mahanaim. The Song as a whole is regarded as a miscellany of independent lyrics on one and the same theme. Some of them are in dialogue form, like classical bucolic poetry; in the translation of these passages rubrics are added indicating the speakers — the 'bride', the 'bridegroom', and the maidens, who form a sort of chorus. The personal descriptions are seen to be of the same order as the Arabic *waṣf*. Forty-one separate units are distinguished throughout the Song. No evidence is found for an allegorical interpretation, but it is maintained that the Song can be understood in a mystical as well as a literal sense.

F.F.B.

PORTEOUS, N. W.: *Das Danielbuch*. (Das Alte Testament Deutsch, 23.) 1962. Pp. 146. (Vandenhoeck & Ruprecht, Göttingen. Price: paper, DM 6.50; by subscription, DM. 5.50; cloth, DM. 9.80; by subscription, DM. 8.30).

Here is an excellent and up-to-date commentary on Daniel that can be unreservedly commended. There is a good, though brief, introduction, in which especial attention is paid to the discussion of the literary affinities of Daniel. The original translation takes account of all relevant recent work, while the commentary is full and first class. The author has read and digested a considerable amount of modern literature on Daniel and brought to it his own careful and balanced judgement. His critical positions are rarely new, but in the reviewer's opinion they are sound — and sound judgement is better than novelty! On many of the problems of the book, such as the 'dismal swamp' of the seventy weeks, an incredible amount has been written, expressing an enormous variety of opinions. Professor Porteous is not concerned with the history of interpretation, and contents himself with a brief treatment of such questions, presenting his own considered view or suspending judgement where a decision between competing views cannot be made with confidence. Many years ago Professor Sidney Smith suggested that the story of Nebuchadnezzar's madness was a reflection of traditions about Nabonidus. In view of the Prayer of Nabonidus found among the Dead Sea Scrolls, Professor Porteous concludes that there is some relation here. More important than all such matters is the religious and theological value of the book, and it is his attention to this that gives Professor Porteous's commentary its special quality, and makes it a notable addition to the series for which it has been written.

H.H.R.

RIDDERBOS, N. H.: *De Psalmen opnieuw uit de Grondtekst vertaald en verklaard*, Eerste Deel, Psalm 1–41. (Korte Verklaaring der Heilige Schrift met nieuwe Vertaling.) 1962. Pp. 456. (J. H. Kok, Kampen. Price: Fl. 11.75).

Readers who are familiar with the author's early monograph on 'the workers of iniquity' in the Psalms (*Book List*, 1946, p. 36; *Eleven Years*, p. 36) will welcome this first volume of a commentary on the Psalter, here covering Pss. i–xli. The first sixty pages contain a general introduction which, on the whole, follows current lines, paying special attention to the literary types, their place in Israel's worship, and the religious faith which they reveal. An interesting feature in this connexion is a brief discussion of certain outstanding terms in the vocabulary of the Psalter which obviously has the general reader in view. In the commentary itself, as in the translation of the individual psalms, the specialist will miss what one would regard as due consideration of the many textual problems which arise; but, this aside, in the exposition of the text the author has some illuminating comments to make. Members of the Society who, like the present writer, are more liberal in their approach than Professor Ridderbos may read this work with profit, for the author, although belonging to a strongly conservative tradition, is clearly conversant with current research and by no means prepared to reject new ideas out of hand.   A.R.J.

RINGGREN, H. & ZIMMERLI, W.: *Sprüche/Prediger*. (Das Alte Testament Deutsch, Teilband 16/1.) 1962. Pp. iv+254. (Vandenhoeck & Ruprecht, Göttingen. Price: DM. 10; by subscription, DM. 8.50; or bound, DM. 13; by subscription, DM. 11).

These commentaries follow the usual pattern of the series to which they belong. The first half of this volume is devoted to Proverbs and is the work of Professor Ringgren. His comments tend to be brief and are sometimes meagre (Proverbs viii, for example, is discussed in no more than a page and a half). Professor Zimmerli, however, has written a slightly longer commentary on the much shorter book of Ecclesiastes. He believes that it was composed in Hebrew in Palestine about the middle of the third century B.C., and that there is no clear evidence of Greek influence. The last part of chapter xii (verses 9–11 and 12–14) is thought to be the work of two redactors, the former of whom may also have written the heading in i. 1 (the original Qoheleth having represented himself as king only in i. 12–ii. 26); otherwise, apart from a few minor glosses, the whole book is attributed to a single author. Qoheleth is not fundamentally sceptical about the existence of God or His control of the universe; but he challenges the claim of the sages to understand the working of the world so well, to have mastered the rules of human life, and thus to manage their own destinies. This challenge, though one-sided, is an important part of the O.T. In addition to advancing this interpretation of Ecclesiastes as a whole, Zimmerli also offers some fresh comments on particular passages. This commentary is one of the best in the series, and it repays the close attention which it demands.   J.A.E.

RUDOLPH, W.: *Das Buch Ruth, Das Hohe Lied, Die Klagelieder*. (Kommentar zum Alten Testament, Band XVII, 1–3.) 1962. Pp. 270. (Gütersloher Verlagshaus Gerd Mohn, Gütersloh. Price: DM. 51; by subscription, DM. 43).

This commentary by Rudolph provides, in the case of each of the three books he handles, an excellent, concise introduction dealing with such subjects as text, content, unity, time and place of origin, interpretation and theological value, followed by a translation of the text of the book in suitable sections with textual notes and exegesis. Fortunately the author has enough space at his disposal to enable him to tackle his job in a comprehensive and satisfactory manner. He surveys interestingly the various interpretations which have been given to the Book of Ruth (which, incidentally, he believes originated towards the later end of the period 1,000 — 700 B.C.), and reaches the conclusion that its primary purpose was not to serve as a counterblast to Ezra's prohibition of foreign marriages, or as a commendation of levirate marriage and the duties of a $g\bar{o}'el$. but to show that those who trust in Israel's God are cared for and blessed. The Song of Songs was interpreted allegorically, he affirms, not to secure its reception into the canon, but because it was already in the canon. He regards the book as a collection of individual love-songs, very tenuously strung together and of a kind sung on festival occasions among many Near-Eastern peoples. The place of origin of the Book of Lamentations he believes to have been Palestine, in the early years of Babylonian rule in that country in the 6th century B.C. This is a well-written, well-documented book which is commended. J.M.

La Sainte Bible traduit en français sous la direction de L'École Biblique de Jérusalem. La Genèse, by R. de Vaux. 2nd ed. revised. 1962. Pp. 222 + folding map. (Les Editions du Cerf, Paris. Price: NF. 8.70).

This volume, which has been revised on the lines indicated in the notice in *Book List*, 1959, p. 19, contains an introduction to the Pentateuch as well as the introduction to and commentary on Genesis. Written with Fr. de Vaux's characteristic clarity and vigour, it is a delight to read, containing the fruits of his immense erudition compressed in a masterly fashion and presented with sure judgement and penetration. G.W.A.

SCHNEIDER, H.: *Die Sprüche Salomos, Das Buch des Predigers, Das Hohelied*. (Die Heilige Schrift für das Leben erklärt: Herders Bibel-kommentar Vol. VII/1.) 1962. Pp. IX+332. (Verlag Herder, Freiburg. Price: cloth, DM. 28.50; paper, DM. 25).

This commentary is a devotional exposition of the three older Wisdom Books of the O.T.; Proverbs, Ecclesiastes, and the Song of Songs. A translation of the Hebrew is given in modern German, and there is a brief introduction to each book. The Introduction to the Song is nearly 17 pages, but the Intro-duction to Proverbs receives 8 pages, and that to Ecclesiastes just over 4. The introductions follow the usual themes, and the author's views and expositions follow traditional lines.

G.H.D.

SIEGMAN, E. F.: *The Book of Ezechiel*. Part 1, with a commentary. (Pamphlet Bible Series). 1961. Pp. 94. (Paulist Press, New York. Price: 6s. 0d.).

This is volume 30 of the series of which it forms part, and pro-vides the text of chapters i-xxiv in the new (1961) translation from the Hebrew, used by permission of the owners of the copyright, the (Catholic) Confraternity of Christian Doctrine. The printing is exceptionally good, and the divisions of the book most clearly indicated. There are no notes to the text, but the introduction (pp. 5–32) supplies much information about the book and summarizes the contents of the chapter. On the question of authorship Siegman is convinced of the traditional ascription, while allowing that 'the present arrangement of the prophecies may be due to a disciple or to some later scribe, and not to the prophet himself' (p. 8). J.M.T.B.

STEINMANN, J.: *Code Sacerdotal I, Genèse-Exode*. Texte français, introduction et commentaires. (Connaître la Bible.) 1962. Pp. 154. (Desclée de Brouwer, Bruges. Price: B.Frs. 69).

The Priestly material in Genesis and Exodus has been separated out, translated, and provided with a running commentary. The comments, exegetical and theological, are brief and much to the point. Good use is made of relevant archaeological material and among the forty-three illustrations are some excellent reproductions of Egyptian and Mesopotamian objects. The author has a gift for presenting the results of modern scholarship with clarity and in terms that stimulate the imagination. For those who wish to engage in serious Bible-study, this, like other volumes in the series, provides good basic material. The book ends with a list of the Priestly passages, a brief bibliography, and twenty-three questions relating to the text. A.S.H.

*STEINMANN, J. & HANON: *Michée, Sophonie, Joël, Nahoum, Habaqqouq*. (Connaître la Bible.) 1962. Pp. 118, including many ills. (Desclée de Brouwer, Bruges. Price: B.Frs. 69).

The series 'Connaître la Bible' promises to be a miniature Biblical encyclopaedia. Each of the small paperbacks gives the Biblical text in a careful translation, and an historical and archaeological commentary, with maps and numerous charming illustrations. The enormously enlarged locust that faces the opening section of Joel is almost a commentary in itself. The series will also include a history of Israel, a geography of Palestine and a theology of the Old and New Testament. J.M.T.B.

TURL, A.: *Praises Through Sorrow and Praises in Faith*. 1962. Pp. 107. (Mitre Press, London. Price: 8s. 6d.).

The author has rendered the Penitential Psalms and the fifth book of the Psalter into modern English verse, with scarcely ever any rhyme, but much pleasing rhythm; in fact, modern poetry at its best. He has based his rendering on the Authorised Version, and has exercised considerable freedom, so that sometimes it is more than doubtful whether he has retained the meaning of the psalmist. But the renderings make delightful reading, and they are devotionally helpful. Mr. Austin Turl has made a delightfully successful experiment. N.H.S.

VINK, J. G.: *Leviticus uit de grondtekst vertaald en uitgelegd.* (De Boeken van het Oude Testament, Deel II, Boek I.) 1962. Pp. 100. (Romen & Zonen, Roermond en Masseik. Price: Fl. 4.69).

This work follows the general lines of the series to which it belongs: an introduction is followed by a new Dutch translation and exegetical notes; then a textual apparatus is appended — in this case a very short one, for the editor suggests only sixteen emendations, and most of these are very slight. In the introduction and exegesis full account is taken of a number of recent monographs on topics relevant to Leviticus; the editor acknowledges his special indebtedness to R. Rendtorff's *Die Gesetze in der Priesterschrift* and K. Koch's *Die Priesterschrift von Exodus 25 bis Leviticus 16* for their isolation of earlier literary units (ritual texts) incorporated in the priestly legislation. But he does not follow them slavishly, and makes further suggestions of his own. For example, in the designation of the priests as 'the sons of Aaron' he sees the result of a compromise worked out (between the time of Zerubbabel and the time of Ezra) between the two great priestly families of Abiathar and Zadok. On the relation of the Holiness Code to Ezekiel he says cautiously that the contacts are so close (especially with regard to the faults of the priesthood and the court) that Ezekiel must depend on written or oral traditions either identical with, or related to, the material in Lev. xvii–xxvi.

F.F.B

WEISER, A.: *The Psalms: A Commentary*, trans. by H. Hartwell. 1962. Pp. 842. (S.C.M. Press, London. Price: 70s. 0d.).

Professor Weiser's well-known and deservedly popular commentary on the Psalter in the series *Das Alte Testament Deutsch* needs no recommendation so far as members of the Society are concerned; it is sufficient to welcome it in its English dress (based on the fifth, revised edition). A sampling of the translation suggests that this has been well done; indeed the translator's occasional notes, his substitution of the English counterparts of foreign works cited by the author, and his careful comparison of the renderings of the R.S.V., all serve to show that he has been concerned to smooth the path of the English reader. The lay-out, too, is pleasing; the divisions of the Introduction stand out more clearly than in the German edition, and the short type of note, which is there often embedded in the text, is added here to the footnotes. It is unfortunate that the price, which does not seem unreasonable in the light of current printing and binding costs, places this admirable commentary beyond the reach of those who would in some ways benefit most by having it on their shelves, i.e., clergy and ministers, who are on the look-out for a sympathetic but up-to-date exposition of the Psalter, and the average undergraduate, for whom the Introduction should prove to be a mine of information and a real stimulus to thought.

A.R.J.

WOLFF, H. W.: *Frieden ohne Ende: Eine Auslegung von Jes. 7, 1–17 und 9, 1–6.* (Biblische Studien, 35.) 1962. Pp. 94. (Buchhandlung des Erziehungsvereins, Neukirchen. Price: DM. 5).

This is a revision and expansion of an earlier study (Biblische Studien, 23), which was published in 1959 and unfortunately was not noticed in the *Book List*. To the original discussion of the Immanuel passage the exposition of ix. 1–6 is now added. The aim throughout is to present the results of technical study to non-technical readers and to demonstrate the modern relevance of the passages discussed. Extensive reference is made to recent literature relating to both passages. Wolff thinks the formulation of the Immanuel oracle is less likely to be an echo of Ugaritic phraseology than of other significant predictions, within the Old Testament, of births (e.g., Genesis xvi. 11; Judges xii. 3, 5), and in particular of the promise of a deliverer in the Holy War. The identity of the mother, he believes, was not evident to Isaiah's hearers. He holds that ix. 1–6 is probably to be regarded as coming from Isaiah of Jerusalem, though the exact occasion remains uncertain. This is a careful and penetrating exegetical study.

G.W.A.

ZIMMERLI, W.: *Ezechiel* (Biblischer Kommentar, Altes Testament, XIII.) Lieferungen 8/9, 10. 1962. Pp. 579–738, 739–818. (Neukirchener Verlag der Buchhandlung des Erziehungsvereins, Neukirchen Kreis Moers. Price: DM. 7 per Lieferung).

These new fascicles carry Professor Zimmerli's commentary from the beginning of xxv to xxxiii. 24. One of the noteworthy features of the work throughout its progress has been the thorough and detailed structural analysis of the material. This is particularly evident in the treatment of the oracles against foreign nations in xxv–xxxii. But indeed in every aspect: philological and textual comment, the application of form-critical method, the presentation of historical background, religious and theological interpretation, and documentation, Zimmerli might justifiably claim as his own the motto of the first Earl of Strafford.

G.W.A.

LITERARY CRITICISM AND INTRODUCTION
(including History of Interpretation, Canon, and Special Studies)

*ANDERSON, B. W.: *The Beginning of History.* (Bible Guides, No. 2.) 1963. Pp. 96. (Lutterworth Press, London and Abingdon Press, New York and Nashville. Price: 5s. 0d.).

The volume deals with Genesis, with a modern approach. Emphasis is laid on the fact that it is 'religious' history, and that the story of Israel is fundamentally the Story of the Acts of God. Professor Anderson shows how the northern and southern traditions are interwoven to form an introduction to the Exodus with all its covenant emphasis. A useful popular introduction, but useful also for the more advanced reader.

N.H.S.

*ANDERSON, H.: *Historians of Israel (2): 1 & 2 Chronicles, Ezra, Nehemiah.* (Bible Guides, No. 6.) 1962. Pp. 88. (Lutterworth Press, London, Abingdon Press, New York and Nashville. Price: 5s. 0d.).

This volume gives in a short space much information and exhortation. The author's approach is homiletic and he writes with enthusiasm of the religious value of these books. L.A.P.

BACH, R.: *Die Aufforderungen zur Flucht und zum Kampf im Alttestamentlichen Prophetenspruch.* (Wissenschaftliche Monographien zum Alten und Neuen Testament, 9). 1962. Pp. 112. (Verlag der Buchhandlung des Erziehungsvereins, Neukirchen Kreis Moers. Price: cloth, DM. 13.50; paper, DM. 11.25).

This book contains a *formgeschichtlich* inquiry into two types of passages in the prophetical literature of the Old Testament, particularly in the Book of Jeremiah, viz., the summons to flee from imminent disaster, and the summons to fight. These two types of literary composition, the author maintains, are not to be regarded as examples of individualistic poetic expression, but as having conventional, presumably traditional, characteristics. The inquiry into their origin and use is a difficult one to handle. The conclusion is reached that the examples of the two types found in the prophetical literature are imitations of prototypes which go back to the beginning of prophecy in Israel. So the author has to attempt to define the characteristics of the basic types, and the circumstances in which they were used. The thesis which he presents is that the summons to fight had its origin in the ancient practice of the holy war and the summons to escape from imminent disaster in the practice of the ban. The argument of this book is well presented; it will evoke careful reflection, if not always convinced consent. J.M.

BEWER, J. A.: *The Literature of the Old Testament.* Third Edition completely revised by E. G. Kraeling. 1962. Pp. xvi+ 496. (Columbia University Press, New York and London. Price: $6.00).

This is a very thorough revision of the original (First edition 1922, Second edition 1933) and takes note of much of the work that has been done in this field of recent years. This appears in the Bibliography and footnotes, in the many references to the Qumran texts, as well as in the main body of the text. Some sections, e.g., that on Deuteronomistic Historiography, have been rewritten. The chapters indicate the historical growth of the Old Testament literature rather than the Biblical order of the books, the first three chapters being devoted to pre-literary forms. The longest chapter (54 pages) is that which discusses the Psalter, and here one may feel that more attention might have been given to certain aspects of recent study. Significantly, the work of A. Johnson and A. Weiser on the Psalms is not referred to in the Bibliography. Also omitted from the Bibliography under Religion and Theology is W. Eichrodt's *Theology of the Old Testament* although those by Jacob and von Rad appear.

Four pages in an Appendix are given to notes on the Apocrypha, Pseudepigrapha, and 'Some Newly Discovered Jewish Writings' (mainly Qumran Scrolls). The book will be a valuable addition to the student's library.

A.S.H.

BRONGERS, H. A.: *De Jozefsgeschiedenis bij Joden, Christenen en Moham-medanen*. 1962. Pp. 156. (H. Veenman & Zonen, Wageningen. Price: paper, Fl. 12.50; cloth, Fl. 14.50).

The main part of this book consists of lemmata from the Biblical narrative of Joseph (Gen. xxxvii–l.) introducing quotations from Jewish, Christian, and Muslim tradition amplifying or commenting on the narrative. The Jewish sources on which Brongers draws are Philo, Josephus, Jubilees, the Testaments of the Twelve Patriarchs, the Midrashim and other rabbinic compilations, and Rashi. For Christian sources he restricts himself for the most part to Syriac material. His Muslim sources are the Qur'ān (Sura 12) and the principal commentators on it, with one or two Persian writers, notably Firdausi, who in addition to his *Shah-name* composed a poetical work on *Yusuf wa-Zulika*. For Gen. xli. 45b, Joseph's marriage with Asenath, he draws upon the rich and fascinating Asenath literature which has come down from the early Christian centuries. A closing chapter discusses the form and essence of Jewish haggada as seen in the elaborations of the Joseph story.

F.F.B.

*GUNN, G. S.: *Singers of Israel*. (Bible Guides, No. 10.) 1963. Pp. 96. (Lutterworth Press, London and Abingdon Press, New York and Nashville. Price: 5s. 0d.).

The paperbacks in this series are designed for non-theologically equipped readers who want to know what the Bible is about. They are guides, not commentaries. The volume is in four sections: the purpose, the plan, the substance and the power of the Psalter. Special attention is given to Psalms xxiii, cxxi, cxxxix, and a short essay by F. F. Bruce (one of the general editors) on 'The Pattern of the Poetry' is included. A good popular introduction.

N.H.S.

HENSHAW, T.: *The Writings*. The Third Division of the Old Testament Canon. 1963. Pp. 398. (George Allen & Unwin, London. Price: 45s. 0d.).

This is a companion to the same author's introduction, *The Latter Prophets* (*Book List*, 1960, p. 28), and follows similar lines. There are six chapters providing a general background to the history, archaeology and literature of the post-exilic age, followed by eleven chapters of detailed introduction to the contents of the third division of the Hebrew canon. A concluding summary is given for each book, and the author provides a general pre-sentation of the results of critical scholarship, without offering anything new. Bibliographical references are selective, and there are some mis-spellings of authors' names. On page 239 'Arabic' should be read as 'Aramaic'.

R.E.C.

HOLM-NIELSEN, S.: *Det gamle Testamente og det israelitisk-jødiske folks historie.* 1962. Pp. 240+3 maps. (G.E.C. Gad, Copenhagen. Price: Dan. Kr. 40).

The present book gives in condensed form an introduction to the Old Testament, a history of Israel, and a theology of the Old Testament. Although the book is not written for students of divinity, but for use in training colleges, it will be most useful for students in faculties of divinity whether they are beginners or more advanced students. The author (who is in Professor Hvidberg's chair of Old Testament exegesis in the university of Copenhagen) is always very fair in his criticism and well-balanced in his treatment of controversial subjects. He shows great knowledge of all the modern theories and gives the reader a reliable introduction to O.T. research. One might have wished that he had enlarged his bibliography to include other books than those published in the Scandinavian languages. E.H.

*KEPLER, T. S.: *Dreams of the Future. Daniel and Revelation.* (Bible Guides, No. 22.) 1963. Pp. 94. (Lutterworth Press, London; Abingdon Press, New York and Nashville. Price: 5s. 0d.).

This book provides a popular introduction to Jewish apocalyptic writing. Daniel was written in Maccabean times, and he made use of six stories and four visions to encourage the Jews to hold fast to the Faith, with the promise that on the resurrection day they will share in the blessings of the Kingdom. Like all the books which have already appeared in this twenty-two volume series, it fulfils its purpose as a sound popular introduction.

N.H.S.

LAMARCHE, P.: *Zacharie IX–XIV. Structure littéraire et Messianisme.* (Études Bibliques.) 1961. Pp. 168. (J. Gabalda & Cie, Paris. Price: NF. 27).

After a summary of the various hypotheses advanced by commentators on Deutero-Zechariah, the author indicates his method: to define the sections or literary units before establishing the text, and then to proceed to a literary analysis (some would prefer to undertake the second and third of these operations before attempting the first). He next devotes two chapters to a study of the structure of the pericopes in the two sections of the book: ix–xi and xii–xiv. He detects a number of chiastic patterns based on different themes: Israel's victory, the suppression of idolatry, and above all, in four passages, the Messianic king. He discovers literary relationships between Isaiah xl–lv. and Zechariah ix–xiv. 'The titles given by Deutero-Zechariah to the Messiah are a sort of commentary on, and a free development of, the title of Servant used by Deutero-Isaiah' (p. 147). This book is primarily a study of literary forms; and the reader will recognize that it is difficult to discover a form which is common to all the pericopes in these chapters.

Now and then the exegesis has to be very compressed; e.g., on xii. 10 (p. 80), and on the 'wisdom' of ix. 2, associated not with what precedes but with what follows. This is a stimulating book and will give rise to much discussion.

H.C.

MARTIN-ACHARD, R.: *Approche de l'Ancien Testament.* 1962. Pp. 128, including 2 maps. (Delachaux & Niestlé, Neuchâtel. Price: Sw. frs. 5.75).

This is a clearly and vividly written guide to the understanding of the Old Testament, suitable for the ordinary reader. The difficulties are fairly indicated; the setting of the Old Testament is simply described; some of the more important gains of archaeological and linguistic study are indicated; and there are useful chapters summarizing the message of the Old Testament and describing with discernment the atomistic, historical, typological, and theological methods of reading it. The book also contains five handy appendices (a chronological table, a survey of literary history, a list of important MSS., guidance on reading the Old Testament, and a brief bibliography). This is an excellent guide for the circle of readers for whom it is intended.

G.W.A.

MORIARTY, F. L.: *Introducing the Old Testament.* 1960. Pp. xi.+254. (Burns & Oates, London. Price: 21s. 0d.).

This excellent introduction could with little reserve be put into the hands of any educated person approaching the subject as a beginner. The Old Testament is presented through fifteen of its leading personalities, including 'Second Isaiah', who, while they 'differ markedly in temperament ... gifts', etc., are united by 'the pervasive presence of God'. So the approach is soundly theological, the historical background is sketched in *en route* with a sure touch, the Biblical interpretation of history is brought out, and the educational importance of liturgy as an instrument 'for keeping alive the remembrance of what Yahweh had done for his people and what he in turn expected from them'.

If we are at first surprised at the omission of Hosea and Ezra and the inclusion of Job and Qoheleth and Daniel, it is only to discover that we may perhaps best begin to learn about Hebrew wisdom and apocalyptic by means of images, and, similarly, some useful remarks on the Psalms are, with necessary safeguards, associated with the work of David. Throughout there is masterly selection. The chapter on Jeremiah, for instance, will be appreciated by anyone who has attempted to introduce this complicated material under pressure of time.

The translations appear to be the writer's own and are fresh and scholarly, with 'Yahweh' as the divine name, and there is some excellent philological exegesis. Archaeological material is effectively used, indeed the bibliography is perhaps overweighted on the archaeological side.

M.Bu.

NAPIER, B. D.: *Song of the Vineyard. A Theological Introduction to the Old Testament*. 1962. Pp. xii+388. (Harper and Brothers, New York; Hamish Hamilton, London. Price: $5.50).

The Vineyard is Israel, and the Song is God's Word to Israel, the theme of which is God's steady purpose through the ages. The volume is in four sections, which indicate the scope and method: Creation, Order out of Chaos (ending with the occupation of Canaan); Rebellion, Chaos out of Order (ending with the break-up of the Kingdom); Positive Judgment ('anticipated' in the eighth century; 'suspended' in the seventh; 'applied' in the sixth); Existence, in which, with the projection of the prophetic faith within Jewry and throughout the world, we find the meaning of Yahwism. The volume is well written, and well suited for the interested non-technical reader.   N.H.S.

PFEIFFER, C. F.: *Exile and Return*. 1962. Pp. 137. (Baker Book House, Grand Rapids, Michigan. Price: $3.50).

A further volume in a projected series of eight books on the Old Testament (see *Book List*, 1962, p. 22). Much use is made of the results of recent excavations. The attitude is conservative. Ezekiel went to Babylon in 597 B.C.; Ezra came to Jerusalem in 457 and Nehemiah 445 B.C. The books of Esther and Daniel are regarded as historical, and the problem of 'Darius the Mede' is relegated. There is much useful material in the book. N.H.S.

RENDTORFF, R.: *Gottes Geschichte: Der Anfang unseres Weges im Alten Testament* (Stundebücher, 3). 1963. Pp. 124. (Furche-Verlag, Hamburg. Price: 5s. 0d.).

This is a short introduction to the Old Testament of the type sometimes labelled 'theological'. As the sub-title shows, the aim is to indicate the religious and theological preparation for the New Testament in the Old. The five chapters are devoted to Israel's Beginnings; the Period of the Judges and the Kings; the Prophets; the Psalms; Hope and Fulfilment. Sound scholarship underlies this popular study.   G.W.A.

REVENTLOW, H. GRAF: *Wächter über Israel: Ezechiel und seine Tradition*. (Beihefte zur Zeitschrift für die Alttestamentliche Wissenschaft, 82). 1962. Pp. VIII+173. (Alfred Töpelmann, Berlin. Price: DM. 26).

This book is a *formgeschichtlich* study of the recorded utterances of the prophet Ezekiel and is very much a sequel to the author's work on the Holiness Code (*Book List*, 1962, p. 39). It seeks to show the relation, in respect of form and content, of the utterances of Ezekiel with Leviticus xxvi, and with the central Israelite revelation-tradition which found its liturgical fixation in the Covenant Festival. For the purposes of the literary analysis involved, the writer selects groups of passages to illustrate Ezekiel as *Unheilsprophet, Heilsprophet, Geschichtsprophet, Gesetzesprophet, Wächter*, and *Fremdvölkerprophet*. The result is to show a prophet who was not a religious individualist, free from legal and cultic dependence, but the bearer of an office who fulfilled that office in close connection with the tradition of the Covenant Festival, so that the very forms of expression which he used give evidence of that influence. Ezekiel's interpretation of his people's history and his hope for their future were not the product of a philosophy of history, or of a keen political insight, or of a skilful analysis of contingent historical factors. They were the expression of a word from God, whose whole concern was with *Heilsgeschichte*. This is a well-written work on a particular example of the relation of the canonical prophets to the cult; it is a notable addition to those already written on this subject.

J.M.

REVENTLOW, H. GRAF: *Gebot und Predigt im Dekalog.* 1962. Pp. 96. (Gütersloher Verlagshaus Gerd Mohn, Gütersloh. Price: DM. 11.50).

This book contains a form-critical study of the Decalogue of Exod. xx, using methods similar to those of Dr. Reventlow's earlier work on the Holiness Code (see *Book List*, 1962, p. 39). He maintains that the Decalogue was compiled from various sources (chiefly from collections of apodeictic laws), and that its setting in life was the Israelite covenant festival. Originally, he thinks, all the commandments were very brief, but some of them were expanded by preachers at the festival; the so-called Deuteronomic expressions arose in this way and are not to be attributed to a Deuteronomic literary redaction. Reventlow examines the individual commandments in detail and tries to determine their meaning and to distinguish the stages in their long process of growth. Two of his views may be specially noted: the prohibition of images is really the first commandment, whereas the reference to other gods in verse 3 (in which the verb is to be understood as an indicative) belongs to the introduction to the Decalogue; the prohibition of coveting, however, consists of two distinct apodeictic laws. Reventlow has succeeded in making a fresh and valuable contribution to the study of the Declaogue. Some of the conclusions reached by his form-critical methods, however, appear to be based on insecure foundations, and it may be doubted whether he has done full justice to the questions raised by literary criticism.

J.A.E.

REVENTLOW, H. GRAF: *Das Amt des Propheten bei Amos.* (Forschungen zur Religion und Literatur des Alten und Neuen Testaments, Heft 80). 1962. Pp. 120. (Vandenhoeck & Ruprecht, Göttingen. Price: DM. 12.80).

This is a fresh appraisal of the nature of the prophetic office, as reflected in the book of Amos. The author finds that Amos was called to his prophetic work much in the same way as David was called to be king and was 'taken from after the flock' (2 Sam. vii. 8). He became thereby a member of an institution, but had not previously been a prophet. The encounter with Amaziah is seen as a clash between two office-holders — the prophet, legitimately appointed by Yahweh, and the priest of the northern shrine appointed by a king usurping the power of

God. Though prophethood is here regarded as an institutional office the fact of divine compulsion is not lost sight of: this is made clear in the study of iii. 3–8 (pp. 24ff.).

Detailed study of further oracles from a form-critical standpoint suggests that i. 3–ii. 6 is a ritual proclamation of Yahweh's threats against non-Israelite peoples made at a covenant ceremony, that iv. 6–11 is a curse ritual and ix. 13–15 a ritual of blessing, both belonging to the same covenant background.

By taking this line the author is able to bring all the contents of the book under the umbrella of prophethood, both the prophecies of threat and those of promise, and thus he disposes of the necessity of dividing the ancient prophets into *nabi'* for oracles of promise and *writing prophet* for oracles of doom.

L.H.B.

*ROBINSON, G.: *Historians of Israel (1): 1 & 2 Samuel, 1 & 2 Kings.* (Bible Guides, No. 5). 1962. Pp. 88. (Lutterworth Press, London; Abingdon Press, New York and Nashville. Price: 5s. 0d.).

In this volume the author has admirably achieved his aim of writing not a commentary but a guide which will help the untutored reader to understand the character and content of these books.

L.A.P.

ROUTLEY, E.: *Beginning the Old Testament* (S.C.M. Paperback). 1962. Pp. 159. (S.C.M. Press, London. Price: 5s. 0d.).

The author, formerly tutor at Mansfield College, Oxford, seeks to help the general reader to an understanding of Genesis and Exodus in the light of modern scientific knowledge. He deals with the relations of the two Creation stories, both with each other and with modern nuclear theories, with the questionable actions of the patriarchs, Abraham's treatment of Hagar, and so on. Modern young people are more likely to be satisfied with the explanations than Old Testament, folklore, or ethnological students.

N.H.S.

ROWLEY, H. H.: *Hezekiah's Reform and Rebellion.* (Reprinted from the *Bulletin of the John Rylands Library*, vol. 44, No. 2, March, 1962). 1962. Pp. 395–431. (The John Rylands Library, Manchester. Price: 6s. 0d.).

Professor Rowley's critical eye is not dim, nor is his documentary force abated. Here, in the discussion of intricate problems to which a variety of solutions have been offered and where the evidence is perplexing, we find the qualities which characterize his Schweich Lectures: the dispassionate evaluation of Biblical and extra-Biblical evidence, the command of the modern literature of the subject, critical fairness to the views of others, clarity and economy in the presentation of complex data and arguments. Briefly, he maintains that having first imposed terms on and spared Jerusalem, Sennacherib (disquieted by the approach of the main Egyptian army, whose advance force he had defeated at Eltekeh) attempted to occupy Jerusalem; and that this was the occasion of Hezekiah's resistance, supported by Isaiah. He also maintains the substantial reliability of the account in II Kings of the reform. It need hardly be added that this lecture is essential reading for any serious student of the problems it handles.

G.W.A.

ROWLEY, H. H.: *The Early Prophecies of Jeremiah in their Setting*. (Reprinted from the *Bulletin of the John Rylands Library*, vol. 45, No. 1, September, 1962). 1962. Pp. 198–234. (The John Rylands Library, Manchester. Price: 6s. 0d.).

To discuss almost any aspect of Old Testament prophecy is to run the risk of being submerged in the sea of documentation. Professor Rowley, as always, breasts the waves with enviable ease. He discusses various views propounded forty years ago by Skinner (and by others before him), examining the contentions of those who have rejected those views, and concluding that Skinner's views were essentially sound. The main subjects considered are: the date of Jeremiah's call, the Scythian question, the dating of the Confessions, Jeremiah's attitude to the Reform. As in the other Rylands Lecture noticed above, Professor Rowley maintains the substantial reliability of the Biblical record.

G.W.A.

VAN RULER, A. A.: *Zechariah Speaks Today*. Studies in Zechariah Chapters i–viii. (World Christian Books: No. 43). 1962. Pp. 80. (United Society for Christian Literature, Lutterworth Press, London. Price: 2s. 6d.).

This is a translation from the Dutch of Professor van Ruler's (of Utrecht) *Het Moed voor de Wereld*. It is a paperback and it deals with the work of the prophet who flourished 520–518 B.C., together with the last two verses of the book used as a summary of the teaching of the whole. There are eighteen short chapters, and they were originally broadcast talks. They are good, popular exegesis.

N.H.S.

SEEBAS, H.: *Mose und Aaron: Sinai und Gottesberg*. (Abhandlungen zur evangelischen Theologie, Band 2). 1962. Pp. 155. (H. Bouvier & Co. Verlag, Bonn. Price: DM. 19.80).

This is a careful study of the Pentateuchal traditions relating to the call of Moses, the place of Aaron in the tradition, and the connection between Sinai and the 'Mount of God'. The author may be said to follow the school of Noth and von Rad, in that, while accepting the results of literary criticism, he uses them as a basis for a detailed analysis of the various strands of tradition revealed by literary criticism. His analysis yields some extremely interesting results, though it may be doubted whether they will be accepted without question. He finds that in the original Aaron-tradition, Aaron was the leader and priestly head of a religious community whose ideas were so similar to those characteristic of the Yahweh-religion founded by Moses, that the two could blend without difficulty. The analysis of the two strands of Sinai and the *Gottesberg* reveals that Moses is connected with Sinai, and Aaron with the Mount of God, and that 'the rod of God' originally belonged to the Aaron-tradition. An important difference between the two traditions appears in the fact that in the Moses-tradition Moses and the elders of Israel ascend the mountain and see God without suffering harm, while in the Aaron-*Gottesberg* tradition Moses ascends the mount of God alone and no one is allowed to approach the mountain. The author claims to be able to detach the *Grundquelle* (G) from the J and E Strands which it underlies. While much is highly speculative, the book also contains much that is stimulating and suggestive. It is an interesting essay in the new *traditionsgeschichtliche* method.

S.H.H.

SKLADNY, U.: *Die ältesten Spruchsammlungen in Israel*. 1962. Pp. 96. (Vandenhoeck & Ruprecht, Göttingen. Price: DM. 10.80).

This monograph (based on a Greifswald dissertation) examines four collections of maxims believed by many to be the oldest in the book of Proverbs: x–xv (A), xvi–xxii. 16 (B), xxv–xxvii (C), xxviii–xxix (D). Dr. Skladny studies not only the form of the proverbs in each of these collections but also their subject matter, paying special attention to their attitude to Yahweh and to the king, their social background (and they are found to be less individualistic than is often supposed), their contrast between the righteous or wise and the wicked or foolish, and the question whether they teach a doctrine of retribution. He arranges them (not entirely convincingly) in the chronological sequence ADBC, and argues that they are all pre-exilic. None of these collections, he maintains, teaches a doctrine of direct divine retribution, but rather an automatic causal connexion between a man's deeds or *Lebenshaltung* and what happens to him. This causal connexion has been established by Yahweh himself, and it is wrong to draw a sharp contrast between a supposedly secular and eudaemonistic wisdom literature and the other traditions in the O.T. This careful book makes a valuable contribution to the study of Israelite wisdom and its theological significance. Unfortunately, there is no index.

J.A.E.

*TOOMBS, L. E.: *Nation Making*. (Bible Guides, No. 4). 1962. Pp. 88. (Lutterworth Press, London and Abingdon Press, New York and Nashville. Price: 5s. 0d.).

The sub-title 'The Banner of the Exodus', is apt, because the volume deals with those parts of Exodus, Numbers, Joshua, and Judges, which are concerned with the deliverance from Egypt, the making of the covenant, and the fulfilment of the promises made concerning the occupation of Canaan. 'With the exodus event a radically new and transforming power has entered history', since Israel had to live henceforth under the shadow of the exodus.

N.H.S.

WEBER, O.: *Bibelkunde des Alten Testaments*, 9th ed. 1961. Pp. 380. (Furche Verlag, Hamburg. Price: DM. 21).

This work, which first appeared in 1934, is a companion to the same author's *Grundriss der Bibelkunde* (E.T., *Ground Plan of the Bible*; see *Book List*, 1960, p. 30), and contains a descriptive presentation of the contents of the Old Testament, arranged in the order of the Hebrew Bible. Matters of literary criticism and historical background are mentioned only very briefly, in accordance with the intention that the book should provide a first reader for students beginning the Old Testament. Throughout the emphasis is upon describing what the Old Testament actually contains, and commenting upon its relevance for dogmatic theology, which is where the author's chief interest lies. R.E.C.

WEISER, A.: *Samuel. Seine geschichtliche Aufgabe und religiöse Bedeutung*. Traditionsgeschichtliche Untersuchungen zu 1. Samuel 7–12. (Forschungen zur Religion und Literatur des Alten und Neuen Testaments, 81). 1961. Pp. 96. (Vandenhoeck & Ruprecht, Göttingen. Price: DM. 9.80).

In this monograph the author has reprinted articles on I Samuel vii and viii, which originally appeared in *Z. Th.K.* 56 and 57, and added an elaborate study of I Samuel ix–xii, the whole constituting a remarkable challenge to the prevalent interpretation of these chapters which contain the traditions about the founding of the monarchy in Israel. Starting from the customary literary-critical analysis into a strand of narrative favourable to the monarchy and a strand hostile to it, Weiser passes on to a traditio-historical examination of the different sections and this leads him to reject Noth's view that vii, viii, x. 17ff., and xii are the work of a Deuteronomistic editor who is critical of the monarchy. In chapter vii, he argues, we see Samuel acting as a judge in a way appropriate to the situation consequent upon the loss of the Ark and the destruction of Shiloh. He also fulfils a priestly and prophetic function, sacrificing at Mizpah and interceding for the people. Deuteronomy xxxii is adduced as illustrating the cultic background. The victory over the Philistines is legendary and anticipates the victory of David. In chapter viii we have a separate tradition in which Samuel opposes the request of the people for a king. This is quite credible and there is no need to regard it as the anachronistic anticipation of later theocratic views. The section vv. 11–17 describes not later Israelite but contemporary Canaanite monarchy. In x. 17ff. we have a credible account of the election of Saul at Mizpah, whereas the story in ix and the first part of x, is of later origin and is legendary in character, though not necessarily without an historical basis. The 'signs' in x are intended to legitimize Saul's kingship. xi contains another account of how Saul came to the front and belongs to the tradition of Gilgal. xii is not Deuteronomic and does not, as generally believed, represent Samuel's laying down of his office of judge. What we have is a covenant renewal, with Samuel taking the leading part and seeking to ensure that the monarchy will be truly Israelite in character. Weiser links up here with the important study by Muilenburg in *V.T.* ix (1959). The whole monograph deserves the closest study. N.W.P.

LAW, RELIGION, AND THEOLOGY

BÄCHLI, O.: *Israel und die Völker*. Eine Studie zum Deuteronomium. (Abhandlungen zur Theologie des Alten und Neuen Testaments, 41). 1962. Pp. 236. (Zwingli Verlag, Zürich/Stuttgart. Price: Sw.Fr. 21.50).

This fresh and interesting study is really a study in the relation of Israel to the nations as that is illustrated in the Book of Deuteronomy. The author seeks to show in what way the Deuteronomist understands that the nations endanger the life and religion of Israel; to explain which weapons the Deuteronomist brings to bear against the dangers; and to show the picture of Israel that emerges from the confrontation. Finally the author deals with the origin of Deuteronomy out of this situation. The study is original and important.

G.H.D.

BARR, J.: *Biblical Words for Time*. (Studies in Biblical Theology, 33). 1962. Pp. 174. (S.C.M. Press, London. Price: 13s. 6d.).

Professor Barr here continues his vigorous polemic against some recent tendencies in Biblical theology, which ascribe to Biblical writers a thought structure based on areas of meaning assigned to particular words. Here he selects the concept of time, and deals lustily with the alleged contrast between the Hebrew and the Greek concept of time. The main battle is directed against Marsh and Robinson for their discussions of *kairos* and *chronos* and against Cullmann for his views on *kairos* and *aiōn*; but some hard blows are also dealt out to others. Barr rightly insists that for Biblical theology Biblical statements should be relied on rather than Biblical words, and he has little difficulty in showing that *kairos* and *chronos* are often interchangeable in the New Testament. His work will have the salutary effect of checking the ready repetition of facile generalizations and driving Biblical students to a more thorough-going examination of the evidence.

H.H.R.

BISHOP, E. F. F.: *Prophets of Palestine*. The local background to the preparation of the way. 1962. Pp. 280. (Lutterworth Press, London. Price: 35s. 0d.).

Twenty-four studies of the Old Testament prophets and prophetesses from Samuel to Malachi, accepting in the main the standpoint of the *Interpreter's Bible* but illuminated by the experience of long residence in Egypt and Palestine and close contacts with their modern inhabitants. The author believes in the continuity of the 'never-changing east' and that 'the land is the best commentary on the Book'. It provides useful illustrative material for Biblical teaching.

J.N.S.

DE BOER, P. A. H.: *Gedenken und Gedächtnis in der Welt des Alten Testaments*. (Franz Delitzsch-Vorlesungen, 1960.) Pp. 76. (Kohlhammer, Stuttgart. Price: DM. 18).

This is a valuable study of the *vieldeutig* root *zkr* and its derivatives. Of the 175 or so uses of the *Qal* of the verb the AV

437

renders 'remember' 160 times. To think of a Moses or a David is of course to remember him; but how is one to 'remember' the present (Ex. xx. 8), let alone the future (Isa. xlvii. 7)? — so still the RSV. de Boer examines the parallels to both nouns and verbs from the root, the extra-Biblical uses of the root, and the post-Biblical material (the versions, ben Sira, Qumran, and Rabbinica). The general conclusion to which he comes is that the primary meaning of zkr is identical with that of the Akkadian $zakaru$, i.e., $nennen$ rather than $sich \ erinnern$, and he remarks that even the Oxford Lexicon, when it gives the primary sense as 'remember', qualifies this by adding 'usually as affecting present feeling, thought, or action'. In a concluding paragraph on $Anamnesis$ he makes a suggestion which may prove to be important, viz., that in 1 Cor. xi. 24f. the translation should be 'Machet dies (Mahl) zu meinem Erwähnungsmahl'.

C.R.N.

BRANDON, S. G. F.: $Man \ and \ his \ Destiny \ in \ the \ Great \ Religions$. An Historical and Comparative Study containing the Wilde Lectures in Natural and Comparative Religion delivered in the University of Oxford, 1954–1957. 1962. Pp. xiv+442. (Manchester University Press. Price: 45s. 0d.).

Arming himself in $robur \ et \ aes \ triplex$, Professor Brandon has essayed the Atlantean task of giving an account of the nature and destiny of man as it has been envisaged by the ten great religions of the world. These are Egyptian, Mesopotamian, Hebrew, Greek, Christianity, Islam, Iranian, Indian, Buddhism, and Chinese; with an Introduction on methodology and palaeolithic man, and a concluding chapter containing the author's impression of the crucial part, as it has appeared to him, which man's consciousness of time has played in all his many varied interpretations of his own nature and destiny.

Readers of the $Book \ List$ will be principally interested in what Professor Brandon has to say about that part of his subject which concerns Israel and Christianity. In his account of the Hebrew development of a body of beliefs about man and his destiny, Professor Brandon puts forward the view that the Yahwist account of the creation and fall of man must be regarded as a clever rebuttal of these assumptions about human destiny that inspired the mortuary cult which was deemed to be inimical to the interests of Yahwism. Not many Old Testament scholars will be inclined to admit that the existence of witchcraft in Israel affords evidence for the existence of anything like a cult of the dead.

In his treatment of Christianity Professor Brandon puts forward the view which he had already maintained in his book $The \ Fall \ of \ Jerusalem$, that the gospel of the primitive Church of Jerusalem presented Jesus as the promised Messiah who would save Israel from its heathen oppressors, and that in the future glories of his kingdom all faithful Jews would participate. The soteriological value of the death of Jesus had little importance for this Jerusalem gospel. The fully-developed Christology and soteriology of the Church of the second century were entirely due to Paul, and the triumph of the Pauline gospel over the primitive gospel of Jerusalem was due to the catastrophe of the fall of Jerusalem and the destruction of the Jerusalem Church.

Nevertheless the book is a monument of vast learning, and will provide a valuable reference book for those who pursue the comparative study of religion, a discipline of which Professor Brandon is such a brilliant exponent.

S.H.H.

CHILDS, B. S.: *Memory and Tradition in Israel.* (Studies in Biblical Theology, No. 37). 1962. Pp. 96. (S.C.M. Press, London. Price: 8s. 6d.).

The contemporary interest in the forms of Israelite worship and their influence upon the language and literature of the Old Testament here finds expression in yet another study of the root *zkr*. The author has examined all the uses of the relevant terms in the light of (*a*) what he describes as 'the Hebrew psychology of memory', and (*b*) the different implications of Yahweh's 'remembering' and Israel's 'remembering', particularly as regards the redemptive events of the nation's history. The work contains a timely, if brief, appraisal of Pedersen's treatment of Hebrew 'memory' in the light of Barr's criticism; and the work as a whole, though somewhat sketchy, offers a number of discerning comments, so that it may be recommended quite warmly as a useful introduction to an important subject. The author appears to be unaware of the fact that Lévy-Bruhl, shortly before his death, finally abandoned his theory of a 'pre-logical' mentality.

A.R.J.

Cuadernos Biblicos:

(1) GUERRA, J. SANCHEZ: *Origen y destino del hombre según la Biblia.* 1960. Pp. 73.
(2) PIGA, A.: *El Mesianismo.* 1962. Pp. 91.
(3) PIÑA, J.: *Dios es Amor.* 1960. Pp. 52.
(4) PIÑA, J.: *La Biblia es esto.* 1961. Pp. 62.
(5) SÁENZ, A.: *Palabra de Dios y Culto Litúrgico.* 1961. Pp. 52.
(6) SÁENZ, A.: *El Templo, presencia de Dios.* 1962. Pp. 43. (Ediciones Paulinas, Buenos Aires.)

The six booklets are part of a small series of pamphlets on Biblical subjects, all of them written by Jesuits of Buenos Aires. They are clearly printed and attractively produced. *El Mesianismo* is a short outline of the origin and growth of Messianic expectation, beginning with the *protoevangelium* (Gen. iii. 15) and ending with the pseudepigrapha. *Dios es amor* is mainly a study somewhat on the lines of J. Ziegler's well-known treatise *Die Liebe Gottes bei den Propheten* (Münster i.W., 1930). *Origen y destino del hombre* is a popular explanation of the first eleven chapters of Genesis. *Palabra de Dios y Culto Litúrgico* is concerned with the influence of Holy Scripture upon the liturgy of the Church. *La Biblia es esto* is a brief introduction to the Bible, with some account of individual books and of the *genres littéraires*. Finally, *El Templo* is an account of the presence of God in the Old and New Testaments, which includes chapters on the Temple as it is mentioned in the prophets, the psalms, and the New Testament writings.

J.M.T.B.

DENTAN, R. C.: *The Design of the Scriptures*. A First Reader in Biblical Theology. 1961. Pp. 276. (McGraw-Hill Publishing Co. Ltd., New York and London. Price: 39s. 0d.).

The purpose of this excellent book is to set forth the teaching of the Bible in such a way as to illustrate the organic unity of Biblical thought and the harmony of the two Testaments. It is divided into three parts — History, Doctrine, and Life (Christian conduct). Each part contains 26 short chapters, all headed by a list of readings selected from both Testaments. The book, which presupposes the 'assured results' of modern Biblical criticism, is very simply and clearly written, from a Christian standpoint. It forms an admirable introductory handbook to the study of Biblical Theology and as such should meet a felt need.

L.A.P.

DHEILLY, J.: *The Prophets*, trans. by Rachel Attwater (Faith and Fact Books, 66). 1960. Pp. 158. (Burns & Oates, London. Price: 8s. 6d.).

This book (which was originally published in French) is intended for those who are beginning their study of the prophets and it admirably fulfils that intention. It should be noted, however, that proper names and many quotations are from the Douay version, while others are from original translation. The latter might with profit have been extended; how many for instance would understand the word 'cade' in Jer. xi. 19? The book is divided into three main sections; Part I, Literary Investigation; Part II, Psychological; and Part III, Theological, the last occupying almost half the book. The main conclusions of critical scholarship are accepted (e.g., in Isaiah and Zechariah), but the closing words of the book of Amos were 'undoubtedly added by Amos in about 730 . . .' It is not clear why in the text the period of the Judges is given as ninth century. The publishers make the remarkable note that the later prophets worked from the twelfth to the ninth centuries before Christ! The book contains a number of useful chronological tables and closes with a select bibliography of Catholic and non-Catholic books.

A.S.H.

ELLIOTT, R. H.: *The Message of Genesis*. 1961. Pp. xii+210. (Broadman Press, Nashville, Tenn. Price: $4.50).

The author is head of the Old Testament Department in the new Midwestern Baptist Seminary in Kansas City, Missouri. This study is theological rather than historical or literary. The preliminary section deals with author and date: the author accepts Wellhausen's dates and documents, but says he minimized the significance of revealed religion. Part Two deals with Genesis i–xi and concerns Man's need, which involved release from his sin. These chapters are parables rather than factual history. Part Three deals with God's answer. It is summed up in election and covenant, and what the covenant people failed to do, the true Suffering Servant did.

N.H.S.

DE FRAINE, J.: *The Bible and the Origin of Man*. 1962. Pp. x+86. (Desclée Company, New York, Tournai, Paris, Rome. Price: $2.50; Belgian price: B.Frs. 125).

This little book represents the translation of the revised Dutch edition of a work originally published in Antwerp in 1956 (for the French edition cf. *Book List*, 1962, p. 44). It is of real interest as giving the views on the origin of man of a distinguished Catholic scholar who faces up to the problem of the apparent conflict between revelation and modern anthropological knowledge. He argues that the Bible is only authoritative when it makes explicit statements on its own proper subject, viz., ultimate religious truth. For anthropological information we must look to the modern scientist. Concordism, the attempted harmonization of the concepts of the Bible with scientific discoveries, is firmly rejected in agreement with most Catholic writers on the subject. The writer obviously prefers to accept the doctrine of monogenesis, i.e., the descent of all mankind from a single original pair of ancestors, but he admits that the Biblical evidence is not very clear on this point. An exegetical section of the book deals in some detail with five texts — Genesis i. 26–28; Genesis ii. 7; Genesis ii. 18–24; Romans v. 12–19; Acts xvii. 26. In discussing the fourth of these passages the author makes use of the concept of corporate personality as discussed in his book *Adam et son Lignage*. Of considerable contemporary interest is the third section of the book on the teachings of the Church.   N.W.P.

FRÖR, K.: *Biblische Hermeneutik*. Zur Schriflauslegung in Predigt und Unterricht. 1961. Pp. 397. (Chr. Kaiser Verlag, Munich. Price: DM. 23.50).

This is a rich and thoughtful book which deserves the closest attention from anyone who wishes to grapple with the ultimate problems of Biblical interpretation. The author insists that Biblical hermeneutics cannot be separated from general hermeneutics, a science associated with names like those of Schleiermacher and Dilthey. Hermeneutics has the task of interpreting tradition and actualising it in the present. Biblical interpretation is primarily carried out in a definite situation, that of the assembled congregation. Moreover within the community we have to reckon with the presence of the Risen Christ who speaks and must be heard. The writer, however, rejects Christological interpretation and advocates what he calls trinitarian interpretation. We must not separate historical and actualising exegesis and must welcome all the help that can be got from historical research. Stress is laid on the inevitability of coming to the Bible with an assumption about it, the assumption, however, being kept open to criticism. This is called the hermeneutic circle. It is also argued that the subject of knowledge must not be overlooked in the matter of interpretation; indeed the subject is necessarily involved. In interpreting any text or passage we must take the whole Canon into account at least implicitly, nor indeed should we ignore the history of interpretation. There is useful discussion of such topics as myth, typology and *Heilsgeschichte*. In particular it is insisted — and this is important in connection with present discussion — that we must not emphasise *Heilsgeschichte* to the exclusion of actual history. The *Credo*, in which the acts of God are recited, itself becomes history as an expression of the faith of real people and so part of the movement towards the consummation of history.

The second main section of the book deals more fully with some of the matters alluded to above and contains a useful sketch of the history of exegesis. It is argued that we must recognise both continuity and discontinuity in the Old Testament, both fulfilment and *krisis*.

A number of examples of exegesis are given, viz., Genesis i–xi, the patriarchal stories, the Exodus to the Conquest, the kings of Israel, the prophets, the Psalms, in the discussion of which sections of scripture the author seeks to show how the context of the Canon, including of course the New Testament is relevant to interpretation.

The concluding main section of the book deals with the New Testament and does not fall to be discussed here.   N.W.P.

*GIBLET, J. (ed. by): *The God of Israel, The God of Christians. The Great Themes of Scripture*, trans. by K. Sullivan. 1961. Pp. vii+262. (Desclée & Co., Tournai and New York. Price: B.Frs. 195 or $3.95).

The sub-title of this work is *The Great Themes of Scripture* and the subject-matter is elaborated in sixteen essays by eleven authors, among whom may be specially mentioned M. E. Boismard, X. Léon-Dufour, C. Spicq, A. Gelin, and A. Descamps. The five main divisions discuss, in turn, God's plan, God's revelation, God's demands, God's fidelity, and God's victory. If one may make a personal choice among the chapters the best appear to be 'God our Father' by M. E. Boismard, 'Men's Sin' by C. Spicq, and 'The Messias of God' by A. Gelin. It is unfortunate that there is neither a general index nor an index to the citations from Holy Scripture. The plan of the chapters is not quite uniform, since two of them have a series of notes at the end of the chapters, whereas the others have not even one footnote between them.
                                                          J.M.T.B.

GRELOT, P.: *Sens Chrétien de l'Ancien Testament*. Esquisse d'un traité dogmatique. (Bibliothèque de Théologie, Série I. Théologie Dogmatique sous la direction de P. Glorieus, A. Chavasse, Ch. Baumgartner. Vol. 3). 1962. Pp. xii+540. (Desclée & Co., Tournai. Price: NF. 33).

This massive book is of great importance for Protestant Biblical scholars who may wish to learn of the notable changes presently taking place within the Roman Catholic Church in the attitude of the scholars to the Bible.

Part I deals with the witness of the New Testament to the use made of the Old Testament by the first Christians. The changing views in Early Christianity, in the Middle Ages, in the period of the Counter-Reformation and right up to the modern period are carefully traced and it becomes evident that the author realizes how much in past interpretations of the Old Testament, even those associated with great names, may now be regarded as of a temporary character.

Part II starts by considering the relation of the Old Testament to the plan of salvation, traces the stages of that plan and discusses the relation of Christ to the Old Testament. The Old Testament is then considered as Law, as History, and as Promise and much of the discussion is of great interest and value. While much attention is devoted to the theme of prefiguration, it should be noticed that, generally speaking, the author approves of typological rather than of allegorical interpretation and warns his readers against fanciful analogies. Moreover it is made clear that Old Testament religion existed in its own right and not as a mere shadow of what was to come. It should be further noticed that full weight is given to the results of Biblical criticism and that extensive and generous use is made of the works of modern Protestant Biblical scholars.

In Part III the author seeks to show how Christian thought has to pass beyond historical criticism, legitimate as that is, and in this connection he points with approval to the works of Eichrodt and von Rad. As we might expect, there is much discussion of the so-called plenary sense of Scripture. N.W.P.

HUXTABLE, J.: *The Bible Says*. 1962. Pp. 126. (S.C.M. Press, London. Price: 8s. 6d., Book Club issue 3s. 6d.).

The Principal of New College London here discusses the question of the authority and inspiration of the Bible. He gives an account of the answers provided by Protestants and Roman Catholics, both liberal and conservative. He seeks always to be constructive even when he is dealing with modern Fundamentalism. The argument of the book is that all authority belongs to Christ. N.H.S.

HVIDBERG, F. F.: *Weeping and Laughter in the Old Testament*. A Study of Canaanite-Israelite Religion. Posthumous Edition in English. 1962. Pp. 166. (E. J. Brill, Leiden & Nyt Nordisk Forlag, Arnold Busck, Copenhagen. Price: Dan. Kr. 33.50).

In 1938 Hvidberg published the Danish original of the present study (*Graad og Latter i Det gamle Testamente. En Studie i kanaanæisk-israelitisk Religion*). It was read with the greatest interest and appreciation in all the Scandinavian countries, and it would be quite easy to point out how considerable an influence it has had on Old Testament scholarship in those countries, not least in Uppsala. Hvidberg himself had planned a translation of his book into one of the world languages, but owing to his political work he never had time to do so. After his death F. Løkkegaard, professor of Semitic philology at the University of Copenhagen, took the initiative to revise the book for publication in English. It was no easy task as Hvidberg had left no manuscript for a second edition, but only his own copy of the book with relatively few notes in the margin. The editor has done his work very carefully. It was naturally quite impossible to retain Hvidberg's translation of the Ugaritic texts owing to the progress made in the study of those texts during the intervening years. The editor has, however, altered what Hvidberg wrote only where necessary, or he has added notes in square brackets. These minor corrections and additions do not alter Hvidberg's conception of the Ras Shamra texts as cultic texts from the old Canaanite autumn festival, and still less do they cause any alteration in the main body of the work, which consists of a detailed exegesis of many O.T. passages. In this examination Hvidberg showed the influence of Canannite culture on the invading Israelites and, on the other hand, the struggle of the Old Testament prophets against the Baal religion.

Hvidberg asks the question whether the nature of Yahweh was ever so changed as to result in his death and resurrection becoming celebrated with weeping and rejoicing as that of Baal. Without denying that Yahweh's death and resurrection may have been celebrated in that way in the popular syncretism Hvidberg stresses the fact that in the Old Testament Yahweh nowhere appears as a dying and rising deity.

Many of Hvidberg's points of view are now generally accepted, but it is the hope of the present writer that his book in spite of the many years that have passed since its first appearance in Danish may have some influence outside the Scandinavian countries.

E.H.

JENNI, E.: *Die alttestamentliche Prophetie*. (Theologische Studien, Heft 67). 1962. Pp. 26. (EVZ–Verlag, Zurich. Price: Swiss frs. 2.80).

This short, semi-popular study (originally delivered as a lecture) is confessedly based on more detailed discussions by von Rad, Westermann, Wolff, and Zimmerli. It begins with a sketch of the combination of accusation and prediction of judgement on individuals in the utterances of the pre-classical prophets (II Sam. xii; I Kings xiv, xxi; II Kings i), and citation of parallels from the Mari texts illustrating the function of the prophets as *Boten*. Emphasis is laid on the radical, life-or-death character of the prophetic message in Israel, on its relation to the *Bundesrecht*, and on its application from the 8th century onwards to the entire national life. Arguments are presented against the view that the 8th-century prophets appealed for repentance: they announced radical doom and the rejection of Israel, but also predicted a radically new act of salvation in terms of the election traditions associated with the Exodus, Zion, and the Davidic house. New features in 7th- and 6th-century prophecy are touched on in the concluding paragraphs. This is a closely reasoned and clearly written study.

G.W.A.

JOCZ, J.: *The Spiritual History of Israel*. 1961 (1962). Pp. 260. (Eyre & Spottiswoode, London. Price: 25s. 0d.).

This is Professor Jocz's third volume and it worthily continues the task he has set himself of interpreting the significance of

Israel's rôle in history. Rejecting any identification of revelation with developing religious ideas and regarding it rather as encounter with the living God, he finds the unifying element amid the diversity of the Old Testament in the prophetic tradition. In this tradition he lays emphasis on the Word of God which is also act, on God's sovereignty in history, on the notable strain of universalism in the Old Testament, on election as a personal experience which, however, does not take an individual out of the context of life but points to the community, and upon the significant conflict between the moral and the cultic elements in Israel's religion. Dr. Jocz's attitude on important questions will be seen by the following quotations: 'Abraham stands for the writer's personal experience of God as a prophet' — 'The Pentateuch is . . . not constructed upon actual history but *ideal* history, though it is based upon the national tradition of the various Hebrew tribes'. The book contains many striking insights and original viewpoints. For example, he regards the shewbread as symbolizing Israel's physical dependence upon God and links it up with Deut. viii. 3 which lays stress on Israel's spiritual dependence. Issue will doubtless be taken with what he says about prophetic influence on the Psalms. The second part of the book deals with the relation between the Old Testament and the Synagogue on the one hand and the Church on the other. The book is a notable contribution to Old Testament theology and has the merit of adopting the Christian perspective without reading into the Old Testament what is not there.   N.W.P.

KAMPMANN, T.: *Das Geheimnis des Alten Testamentes*. Eine Wegweisung. 1962. Pp. 360. (Kösel-Verlag, München. Price: cloth, DM. 22.50; paper, DM. 19.80).

This is a Roman Catholic book about how to preach from the Old Testament and, whether one is able to accept all the presuppositions or not, it will be found of considerable interest and value. It is divided into two main parts. The first distinguishes preaching, which is represented correctly, as an actualising of the Bible, from Exegesis and from Dogmatics, discusses the characteristics of the Old Testament as a book of history in which God addresses Israel, claims its total surrender, and gives it a future to hope for. This is followed by a sketch of Israel's *Heilsgeschichte* and some account of the Jewish question right up to the present day. The second part of the book offers what is called a kerygma of the Book of Genesis, viz., an exposition of the book for the guidance of the preacher. The author makes skilful use of the insights furnished by modern historical criticism and makes numerous illuminating suggestions.

N.W.P.

KRAUS, H.-J.: *Gottesdienst in Israel*. Grundriss einer Geschichte des alttestamentlichen Gottesdienstes. 1962. Pp. 284. (Chr. Kaiser Verlag, Munich. Price: paper DM. 16; cloth DM. 19).

In 1954 Professor Kraus published a study of the Feast of Tabernacles under the above title. He has now expanded this to more than twice its original length, and has produced a valuable and comprehensive account of the cultic institutions of Israel. This is not a mere revision of the previous book, but an entirely new book. The first chapter contains a useful survey of the development of the study of the religious institutions of Israel from Wellhausen to von Rad. He criticizes, with fairness and restraint, the various forms which 'patternism' has taken during the last thirty years, both in England and in Scandinavian circles; he is of the opinion, not wholly justified, that studies of this type have led scholars away from the study of the Biblical text itself. He also has some penetrating criticism of von Rad's cult-legend theories. He issues a not altogether unnecessary warning to scholars against 'einer allzu raschen Usurpation von Texten, die kultischen Spuren in sich tragen'. The 2nd chapter deals with the Pentateuchal cult-calendar in great detail and is an admirable introduction to the many problems which this aspect of the cult involves. The 3rd chapter deals with the cult-officials and the sacrificial regulations. The last two chapters are occupied with the sanctuaries of Israel and their traditions. The discussion of the cultic traditions of Jerusalem contains a sharp criticism of Mowinckel's theory of an Enthronement festival of Yahweh celebrated annually in Jerusalem. This is a valuable book and it is to be hoped that it may soon be translated.

S.H.H.

KRUYSWIJK, A.: *"Geen Gesneden Beeld . . . "* (with a Summary in English). 1962. Pp. 284. (T. Wever, Franeker. Price: Fl. 13.90).

This book, a doctoral dissertation of the Free University of Amsterdam, is concerned with the prohibition of images in the O.T. It first examines the use of images elsewhere in the ancient Near East and maintains that they were regarded as objects charged with divine power which could be used by men for their own purposes. In contrast, Israel was forbidden the possession of idols, though not the representation of human or animal forms for non-religious purposes. It is argued that Israelites sometimes violated the commandment, and that Obbink was wrong in thinking that the golden calf was no more than a pedestal for the invisible Yahweh. The reason for the prohibition of images was, not that God was not pictured in human form, but that He was not to be 'drawn into the sphere of control exercised by sympathetic magic'. This discussion includes a detailed examination of Genesis i. 26. The book has an English summary of its contents, a bibliography, and an index of O.T. passages. Dr. Kruyswijk writes from a conservative point of view; but his work will be found useful by those who have a different outlook.

J.A.E.

LABUSCHAGNE, C. J.: *Die onvergelyklikheid van Jahwe in die Ou Testament* (in typescript). 1961. Pp. X+278. (Doctoral Dissertation. Pretoria).

This interesting work is a worthy addition to the contributions to Old Testament studies which have come in recent years from South Africa. The author surveys attempts to determine the *Eigenart* of Old Testament religion, and proceeds, after a brief discussion of methodology, to examine the idea of the incomparability of Yahweh as the clue to this quest. He analyses and discusses the various ways in which incomparability is expressed in the Old Testament. Next he turns to the idea of the incomparability of deities in Assyro-Babylonian, Egyptian, and (very briefly, for lack of evidence) Ugaritic religion. The fourth and fifth chapters deal with the content and origin of the idea in the Old Testament and its importance for theology. Yahweh's incomparability is seen in His actions as Saviour. The material is well presented and documented. Fortunately, it seems likely that this work will appear before long in English.   G.W.A.

LAMB, J. A.: *The Psalms in Christian Worship.* 1962. Pp. 178. (Faith Press, London. Price: 21s. 0d.).

The author is one of Scotland's leading experts on liturgy. He has provided a full account of the use of the Psalter in Jewish and Christian circles, ancient and modern, east and west. The volume is full of detailed information, and will be distinctly useful to all who wish to know how and when and where the psalms have been and are used. The book is accurate and comprehensive.   N.H.S.

LÉCUYER, J.: *Le Sacrifice de la Nouvelle Alliance.* 1962. Pp. 300. (Éditions Xavier Mappus, Le Puy. Price: NF. 21.60).

Only about a fifth of this clearly written and well documented book has direct reference to the Old Testament concept of sacrifice, which is discussed in the first three chapters. These consider in turn the covenant and the sacrifice at Sinai, the covenant sacrifice in Jewish tradition (as represented by the Targums, the Talmud, and the pseudepigraphical writings), and the Sinai sacrifice as it is envisaged in the New Testament. The first chapter is concerned with the arrival at Sinai, the completion of the covenant, the tables of the Law, and the Deuteronomic 'commentary' on the happenings at Sinai. The prophetic attitude towards the covenant is studied, as also the relations between the covenant and Jewish worship. Some use is made of the recent works by von Rad, Moraldi, and van Imschoot.   J.M.T.B.

MARTIN-ACHARD, R.: *A Light to the Nations. A Study of the Old Testament Conception of Israel's Mission to the World,* trans. by J. P. Smith. 1962. Pp. 84. (Oliver & Boyd, Edinburgh. Price: 12s. 6d.).

This is a translation of the French original, which was reviewed in the *Book List* for 1960, p. 38. Its publication in English is to be welcomed, both for the stimulus of the author's views and also for the ample documentation.   G.W.A.

MASSAUX, É. (and others): *La venue du Messie: Messianisme et Eschatologie*. 1962. Pp. 260. (Desclée de Brouwer, Bruges. Price: NF. 18).

This is the sixth, the latest and, so far, the longest volume of the collection 'Recherches Bibliques'. It contains most of the papers read at the thirteenth of the 'Journées Bibliques', held at Louvain from 28 to 30 August, 1961. In his *avant-propos*, Massaux introduces and conveniently summarizes the eleven contributions that are printed here. They include papers by P. Grelot on Messianism in the Old Testament pseudepigrapha, by H. Riesenfeld on the Messianic character of Christ's temptation; by M. Sabbe on the redaction of the transfiguration narrative; by J. Coppens on priestly Messianism as found in the New Testament writings; by A. Feuillet on 'Le Triomphe du Fils de l'homme d'après la déclaration du Christ aux Sanhédrites' and (perhaps the most considerable of all the papers) by B. Rigaux on 'La seconde venue de Jésus'. Two papers which do not strictly form part of the series are those by H. Quecke on the present state of scholarly opinion about the Gospel of Thomas, and by L. Leloir on Tatian's Diatessaron and Ephrem's commentary on it. R. de Langhe's monograph on the Messianic sense of Daniel vii was presented on the same occasion, but is to be published later.

J.M.T.B.

OSSWALD, E.: *Falsche Prophetie im Alten Testament* (Sammlung gemeinverständlicher Vorträge und Schriften aus dem Gebiet der Theologie und Religionsgeschichte, 237). 1962. Pp. 30. (J.C.B. Mohr, Tübingen. Price: DM. 2.40).

In this very useful little monograph the author surveys the numerous and varied attempts which have been made to solve the problem of false prophecy, and fellow-scholars will be grateful to her for giving so much information in a convenient form. She agrees with G. Quell in his view that the only ultimate criterion of the truth of prophecy must be a religious one, the application of which will involve decision of faith. On the other hand scientific study of the available evidence has brought to light certain marks of true prophecy which, within limits, supply useful criteria. For example, there is the test of the moral character of professing prophets and there is the fact that, as we look back on the history of Hebrew prophecy, we can see that proclamation of judgement has more often been justified by events than proclamation of salvation. As it can be shown that even the greatest prophets have on occasion made mistakes, we may have to admit that false prophecy was an ever present possibility even within true prophecy.

N.W.P.

VAN DER PLOEG, J.: *Une théologie de l'Ancien Testament est-elle possible?* (Analecta Lovaniensia Biblica et orientalia, Ser. IV, Fasc. 5). 1962. Pp. 417–434. (Publications Universitaires de Louvain; Desclée de Brouwer, Bruges. B. Frs. 25).

The author here surveys very briefly the revival of interest in Old Testament Theology and proceeds to discuss what constitutes an Old Testament Theology. The problem is raised of relating to a dogmatic scheme an undogmatic corpus such as the Old Testament, with its variety and its emphasis on right action rather than on creed. A rigorous and sympathetic historical approach must be adopted; and care must be taken to avoid importing into the Old Testament ideas foreign to it. Finally, some comments are offered on the second volume of von Rad's *Theology.*   G.W.A.

RINGGREN, H.: *Sacrifice in the Bible.* (World Christian Books, No. 42. Second Series). 1962. Pp. 80. (United Society for Christian Literature: Lutterworth Press, London. Price: 2s. 6d.).

In this handy booklet Professor Ringgren surveys the general theory of sacrifice and then proceeds to examine the various types of sacrifice in the Old Testament (the gift aspect, sacrifice as communion, expiatory sacrifices, and some special sacrifices) clearly and with appropriate citation of comparative material from Israel's environment. A further chapter is devoted to the prophetic criticism of the sacrificial system and the development of a non-sacrificial ideal of worship, including a brief reference to the Qumran sect. The closing chapter discusses the New Testament interpretation of sacrifice and high-priesthood. This is an exceedingly valuable survey of the subject at the level required by the series to which the booklet belongs. G.W.A.

SCHUSTER, H.: *Offenbarung Gottes im Alten Testament.* Ein erweiterter Vortrag. (Sammlung gemeinverständlicher Vorträge und Schriften aus dem Gebiet der Theologie und Religionsgeschichte 238/239). 1962. Pp. 60. (J.C.B. Mohr (Paul Siebeck) Tübingen. Price: DM. 4.50).

This vigorous and attractive essay on the subject of revelation in the Old Testament, starting off from the very different assessments of the Old Testament by Nietzsche and Harnack, distinguishes first a strain in it which must be described as residuary heathenism. We must not try to conceal or minimize its presence by typological or allegorical methods of which examples are given from Tertullian and W. Vischer. A contrast is then drawn between the Jewish preference for the Law as the most significant part of the Old Testament, a view which has worked itself out in a religion of observances, and the view which the author prefers and which finds revelation above all in Hebrew prophecy with its emphasis on the majesty of God and its opposition to animal sacrifice, to idol-worship and to blind nationalism. It is shown how the Old Testament points forward to the Gospel, though not in all its parts. Revelation is to be defined, not by canonicity or by invoking a theory of inspiration, but by recognizing when we are met by a challenge to which the natural man cannot respond in his own strength.   N.W.P.

STAMM, J. J.: *Der Dekalog im Lichte der neueren Forschung.* Zweite, durchgesehene und erweiterte Auflage. 1962. Pp. 64. (Verlag Paul Haupt, Bern & Stuttgart. Price: Sw. Frs. 6.80).

The first edition of this study was reviewed in *Book List*, 1959, p. 30, and the French translation in *Book List*, 1960, p. 40. Some modifications have been made in the introduction, the documentation has been brought up to date, and a number of expansions introduced into the text. The most notable of these is a discussion of the Hittite parallels adduced by Mendenhall to the Israelite covenant formulas. Account is also taken of the studies by G. Heinemann and W. Beyerlin. Stamm's summing up is eminently cautious and judicious.

G.W.A.

TAYLOR, C. L.: *Let the Psalms Speak*. 1961. Pp. x+150. (Seabury Press, Greenwich, Conn. Price: $3.00).

This was the Seabury Book for Advent 1961. It is a useful book on many psalms as the classical expression of personal religion. Full use is made of modern study, and everything is said and done to enhance the psalms in personal devotional reading and public worship. It is altogether interesting and informative particularly to those who are beginning to be interested in the psalms.

N.H.S.

VAWTER, B.: *The Conscience of Israel: Pre-exilic Prophets and Prophecy*. 1961 (1962). Pp. xii+306+2 maps. (Sheed & Ward, London. Price: 22s. 6d.).

This is a book on the pre-exilic prophets that can be recommended without reserve to student and general reader alike. It is written against a background of thorough acquaintance with modern views and with the acceptance of many of them, as, for instance, the existence of cultic prophets against whom the canonical prophets stand out as a unique phenomenon, and the probability that the latter did not utterly condemn the sacrificial system. Vawter has been able to get behind the words of the prophets to the men themselves and carries his readers with him as he sets the prophets within the historical scene and at the same time draws out their abiding relevance.

L.H.B.

VRIEZEN, TH. C.: *Jahwe en zijn Stad*. 1962. Pp. ii+26. (N.V. Noord-Hollandsche Uitgeversmaatschappij, Amsterdam. Price: 5s. 0d.).

In this lecture delivered on 31 March, 1962, before a gathering of both divisions of the Royal Dutch Academy of Sciences, Professor Vriezen discusses the place held by Jerusalem in Israel's religious life before the Exile, especially in the time of Isaiah. Jerusalem's designation as 'the holy city' is not found before the Exile, although there is pre-exilic evidence for its being called 'the city of God' or 'the city of Yahweh'. Yahweh, on the other hand, is never called 'the God of Jerusalem' — nor, in fact, is He called the God of any city (this, the author suggests, may be bound up with the fact that the formative period of Israel's religious life antedated its adoption of city life in the proper sense). There is an ambivalence in Isaiah's attitude to Jerusalem; on the one hand it cannot hope to escape the judgement of Yahweh (Isa. xxix. 1 ff.), while on the other hand it is secure because it is Yahweh's hearth and home (Isa. xxxi. 4 f., 8 f., xxxvii. 33–35). These two attitudes are not to be dated to different periods in Isaiah's career, but belong together. His whole ministry in influenced by his inaugural vision, and although he foresees desolation, it cannot be complete destruction, for the remnant in which the hope of Israel is embodied is the 'stone of sure foundation' laid by Yahweh *in Zion.* F.F.B.

WIENER, C. & COLSON, J.: *Un roi fit des noces à son fils.* Thèmes Bibliques. 1962. Pp. 176. (Desclée de Brouwer, Bruges. Price: B.Fr. 105).

The theme of the present attractive work is the metaphor of Israel as the marriage-partner of Yahweh, which is developed in the Old Testament writings and which appears again in the New Testament to designate the Church as the spouse of Christ. The imagery shows the Church as the eternal divine thought in regard to humanity. This thought is more fully realized in the Incarnation and in the Redemption wrought by Christ. The first part of the book (Les noces de Dieu) provides chapters on Hosea, Jeremiah, Ezekiel, Deutero-Isaiah, the Song of Songs, and Psalm xlv. The second part (Les noces du Christ) studies the witness of the Synoptic Gospels, St. Paul, the Fourth Gospel and the Apocalypse. J.M.T.B.

WORDEN, T.: *The Psalms are Christian Prayer.* 1961. Pp. x+220. (Geoffrey Chapman, London. Price: 18s. 0d.).

In his introduction the author develops the fuller meaning of the title chosen for his book. 'The aim of this book' (he writes) 'is to help towards the formation of this outlook or mentality, without which the Psalter cannot be used as the Christian prayer-book'. (p. viii.) But he goes on to insist that the title might be misleading in regard to the contents since 'Very little is written here about the psalms themselves'. The four chapters into which the main body of the work is divided are studies of the basic pattern of Israelite prayer, of the basic pattern of the psalms themselves, and of two of the main themes of the Psalter, i.e., the redemption of Israel and Yahweh as the conqueror of Israel's enemies. The final pages of the work give some readings from the psalms, in which the text is that of the RSV; these are followed by a general index and an index of references to the Psalter. J.M.T.B.

THE LIFE AND THOUGHT OF THE
NEIGHBOURING PEOPLES

BEEK, M. A.: *Atlas of Mesopotamia.* A survey of the history and civilisation of Mesopotamia from the Stone Age to the fall of Babylon. Trans. by D. R. Welsh, ed. by H. H. Rowley. 1962. Pp. 164+296 plates+22 maps. (Thomas Nelson & Sons Ltd., Edinburgh. Price: 70s. 0d.).

This latest of Nelson Atlases is another excellent introduction to the history, culture, and religion of Mesopotamia, solidly based on scientific excavation and the study of the multifarious documents. At all points the experience of the author, who has actually travelled extensively in the area, bears rich fruit, and the whole work is thoroughly illustrated by excellent contour maps, on which appropriate historical and archaeological notes are superimposed. The text describes the land and climate of Mesopotamia, the history of local archaeology, and the decipherment of cuneiform, and the various phases of its cultural and political history till the Persian conquest; and the study closes with a section on Mesopotamian religion and the permanent contribution of Mesopotamia to the culture of the West. Of particular value is the chapter on Mesopotamian literature. A strange omission, the only signicant one, from this excellent work is D. J. Wiseman's recent work on the Babylonian Chronicle, which accurately documents the fall of Jerusalem in 597.

J.G.

CASTELLINO, G.: *Le civiltà mesopotamiche*. n.d. (1962.) Pp. 82+folding map+11 plates. (Istituto per la collaborazione culturale, Venice & Rome. Price: Lire 1,000).

This little book, No. 4 in the series called *Le Civiltà Asiatiche*, contains a very concise account of the Sumerians, Babylonians, and Assyrians, from the earliest times to the fall of Babylon. It does not give a formal history of these peoples, even in outline, but presents brief sketches emphasizing the highlights of their history; these are arranged in three sections, dealing respectively with the Sumerians, the Semitic expansion, and their principal contributions to civilization. The illustrations are well chosen, being all well-known (including the 'ram caught in a thicket' from Ur in colour) and extremely well reproduced.

G.R.D.

GORDON, C. H.: *Before the Bible*. The Common Background of Greek and Hebrew Civilisations. 1962. Pp. 320+numerous ills. & 3 maps (one on endpaper). (Collins, London. Price: 35s. 0d.).

Professor Gordon of Ugaritic fame sets out to show that 'Greece (cannot be regarded) as the hermetically sealed Olympian miracle, nor Israel as the vacuum-packed miracle from Sinai'. While most scholars would probably agree with this proposition, few of them have acted, written, or taught accordingly. His book ought to be prescribed reading for all Old Testament scholars. If there is at times exaggeration or stress on features which are universal rather than peculiarly Mediterranean or if one facet or another is pressed rather too hard, then we should consider this the privilege of the pioneer, for the general approach may be valid even if isolated aspects should require an explanation different from that canvassed in this book.

In the 'Channels of Transmission' Gordon shows in some detail how, prior to the Amarna Age, Egyptian, Canaanite, Mesopotamian, Anatolian, Aegean, and other influences met in the Eastern Mediterranean to form an international order from whose synthesis the earliest traditions of Israel and Greece emerged. Trade, guilds, and religious shrines are, perhaps, the main links in this transmission. The Cuneiform and Egyptian Worlds are analysed in some detail, but the *pièce de résistance* is clearly the chapter on Ugarit (77 pages), the principal avenue through which Canaan and the world of the Aegean had intercourse. More argument has developed (and will continue to do so) over Gordon's interpretation of Linear A. Time as well as further documentation will tell whether the mountains in travail have brought forth a mouse or a lion.   E.U.

JIRKU, A.: *Kanaanäische Mythen und Epen aus Ras Schamra-Ugarit.* 1962. Pp. 136. (Gütersloher Verlagshaus Gerd Mohn, Gütersloh, Germany. Price: DM-West 24).

G. R. Driver has shown in his *Canaanite Myths and Legends* how the Ugaritic documents can be presented in a manner that satisfies the scholar and edifies the general reader; his edition and translation, with succinct notes and supporting vocabulary, is a model of verbal economy and of stylistic excellence. While one may, of course, expect a translation of value and competence from a scholar of Professor Jirku's rank, it is a great pity that he has not adopted Professor Driver's method and offered us a detailed linguistic justification of his reading and translation. We already possess another German translation (contrary to the assertion in the blurb; i.e., Aistleitner's rendering noticed in the *Book List* of 1960, p. 43) as well as several full or part translations in English, Hebrew, and French. The advance and progress constantly being made in Ugaritic studies require to be incorporated in a fully annotated version, without which the significance to students of Ugaritic, the Old Testament, or general Semitics is gravely impaired. This is not to say that Professor Jirku has not found a number of felicitous expressions and phrases, but their true value cannot be judged without disclosure of the philological spade-work on which they are based.   E.U.

KRAMER, S. N.: *Sumerian Mythology: A Study of Spiritual and Literary Achievement in the Third Millennium B.C.,* revised edition. 1961. Pp. xiv+130+XX plates+2 figs.+1 map. (Harper Brothers, New York. Price: $1.45).

This is a verbatim reprint of Professor Kramer's *Sumerian Mythology,* published in 1944. It now appears as a paperback volume of the Academy Library in Harper's series of Torchbooks, with four pages of supplementary notes. There are no changes in the text itself. Professor Kramer's work is too well known to need further commendation here. The American publishers are to be congratulated on making available to students in this cheap and excellent edition a work whose importance in the field of Sumerian studies has long been universally recognized.

S.H.H.

THE DEAD SEA SCROLLS

AMUSIN, I. D.: *Rukopisi Mertvogo morja* (=The Dead Sea Manuscripts). 1961. Pp. 274. (Izdatel'stvo Akademiji nauk SSSR, Moskva. Price: 1 rouble 4 kopecks).

This is the second edition of the most comprehensive Soviet book on the Qumran discoveries. It comes from the pen of the distinguished Leningrad orientalist and is published by the Moscow press of the Academy of Sciences. The author has a detailed knowledge of the present state of scholarship in the subject; but, like Livshits in the book reviewed in *Book List*, 1960, p. 49, he draws detailed conclusions from the Qumran texts about early Christianity (Chapter 5, pp. 217–258), attempting to show that Jesus is a fictitious, mythical figure. In support he cites all those western scholars who have detected any connection between the Teacher of Righteousness and the Prophet from Nazareth. The Marxist background readily explains this anti-Christian polemic; but even if one cannot follow the author here, one must recognize that his treatment of the discoveries is in general based on sound information, and welcome his work, which is already being translated into other eastern European languages. M.B.

AMUSIN, I. D.: *Rukopisy Mrtveho mora* (=The Dead Sea Manuscripts). 1962. Pp. 258. (Vydavateľstvo Osveta, Bratislava. Price: 14.90 Kčs).

This is a translation into the Slovak language of the above work. The translator is Jaroslav Čelko. The book is one of a Slovakian series on scientific atheism. The author has added a special foreword to this translation. M.B.

BAILLET, M., MILIK, J. T. and DE VAUX, R., avec une contribution de H. W. Baker: *Discoveries in the Judaean Desert of Jordan.* III. *Les 'Petites Grottes' de Qumran.* Exploration de la falaise. Les grottes 2Q, 3Q, 5Q, 6Q, 7Q, à 10Q. Le rouleau de cuivre. (2 vols.). 1962. Textes: Pp. xi+318; Planches: LXXI. (Clarendon Press, Oxford University Press, London. Price: £8 8s. 0d.).

This work, the second volume of which comprises the texts etc., in photographs begins with R. de Vaux's account of the exploration of Qumran in general and with caves 5Q – 10Q in particular, to which is added an appendix by J. T. Milik. This is followed by the texts drawn from 2Q, 3Q, 6Q, 7Q – 10Q, to which critical notes are given by M. Baillet. The greatest yield of Biblical material came from 2Q. Here small fragments from all the Pentateuch as well as from Jeremiah, Psalms, Job, Ruth, and Ben Sira (Hebrew) were found. Their deviations from the text of the MT are very small. Of some interest are those of Exodus xii. 39, where we read *gēreshûm miṣrayim*, instead of the MT's *gōreshû mimmiṣrayim*; the spelling in Ex. xviii. 21 of the plural of *me'āh*; and plural in Jer. xlvii. 4 of *'i.* 3Q yielded only fragments from Ezekiel, Psalms and Lamentation, and 6Q — from Genesis, Leviticus, Deuteronomy (?),

454

Kings (I and II), Psalms (?), Canticles and Daniel. There were only two Biblical fragments from 7Q recorded on papyrus in Greek. In 8Q were found fragments from Genesis and Psalms. The phylacteries and the *mezûzāh* which were also drawn from this cave are of special interest: the phylacteries, because they include the Ten Commandments; and the *mezûzāh*, because of the word *shadday* which is written on it in the way it is written on *mezûzôth* as known today. The texts of 5Q are introduced and explained by Milik. The Biblical texts here are from Deuteronomy, I Kings, Isaiah, Amos, Psalms, Lamentation and a tiny fragment of phylacteries.

The caves also contained a great variety of non-Biblical fragments. This is specially true with regard to 6Q and 2Q. They are, however, with one or two exceptions, very minute.

Of striking interest is the so-called Copper Scroll, which had already been discussed by scholars when a study of it appeared a few years ago by J. Allegro. The study of this scroll, brought forth from 3Q, starts with introductory remarks by R. de Vaux, followed by notes on its opening by H. Wright Baker. A translation of and commentary on the text are given by Milik. Space does not allow us to enlarge on Milik's painstaking work which exhibits great learning throughout; but it may be observed that quite a number of renderings and readings seem questionable. The volumes are, as were their preceding volumes (see *Book List*, 1956, p. 64 = *Eleven Years*, p. 771, and *Book List*, 1961, p. 59), of high scholarly merit. They include useful indexes and are excellently produced.   M.W.

BURROWS, M.: *A holttengeri Tekercsek* (=The Dead Sea Scrolls). 1961. Pp. 396. (Gondolat, Budapest, Price: 63, –Ft.).

This Hungarian translation of the world-famous work by Millar Burrows (*Book List*, 1956, p. 65) is, so far as the reviewer is aware, the only one which has appeared in any of the People's Democratic Republics. Though made from the Viking Press edition of 1958, it represents a text which has been abbreviated in places, without any indication of the justification for the omissions. On the other hand a detailed introduction by I. Hahn has been added, containing a Marxist interpretation of the Qumran discoveries (pp. 3–12). The translation was made by J. Csába and revised by G. Komoróczy, who has also supplied a translation of the Qumran texts, not dependent on Burrows's rendering, but made direct from the originals. On the whole there is a fuller selection of texts than that made by Burrows, and in places the explanations given are different from his. The bibliography includes many works which scholars in western countries will be grateful to be informed about. M.B.

DE CAEVEL, J.: *La connaissance religieuse dans les hymnes d'action de grâces de Qumrân*. (Analecta Lovaniensia Biblica et Orientalia, Ser. IV, Fasc. 6). 1962. Pp. 28. (Publications Universitaires de Louvain; Desclée de Brouwer, Bruges and Paris. Price: B.Frs. 30).

According to the *Hymns of Thanksgiving*, God alone has knowledge; man is plunged in wretchedness and ignorance. But God graciously takes the initiative in imparting knowledge to men. In spite of the absence of references to sacred scripture in the *Hymns*, de Caevel concludes that the knowledge of God in them is identical with that derived, according to other Qumran documents, from the study of the law and the prophets. This knowledge consists mainly in the mysteries of his purpose in the world and the unfolding of his will for men. The knowledge is imparted to the *maśkíl*, portrayed in terms of the Ebed Yahweh, and transmitted by him to the faithful community as a whole. Conditions for receiving this knowledge are ethical purity and possession of the spirit of God. New Testament parallels to this doctrine are traced, especially in the Fourth Gospel. The doctrine of the knowledge of God at Qumran is a remarkable but homogeneous development of Biblical tradition, and at no point involves the hypothesis of a 'gnostic' source.　　F.F.B.

CHYLIŃSKI, H.: *Wykopaliska w Qumran a pochodzenie chrześcijaństwa* (=The Excavations at Qumran and the Beginnings of Christianity). 1961. Pp. 247. (Wydawnictwo Ministerstwa Obrony Narodowej, Warszawa. Price: 11,–zl.).

This Polish work about the Qumran discoveries is only a compilation, as the author himself admits, and somewhat surprisingly, it has been published by the Ministry of Defence. There are three parts: 1. Three chapters are devoted to a description of the discoveries, the MSS, and the Community of the New Covenant (pp. 11–119). 2. A special chapter is devoted to a discussion of the bearing of the discoveries on the beginnings of Christianity (pp. 120–166). An almost unmanageable amount of material is assembled, in which, alongside theologians of all schools, there are included Marxist thinkers: a Marxist account of the origins of Christianity is given. Probably nowhere else is there to be found so full and representative a presentation of such discussions; and they will demand the full and careful attention of theologians, for the ordinary reader cannot be expected to make much of them. 3. Finally there is a translation of a selection of the texts (pp. 169–237), and a good bibliography.

M.B.

GILKES, A. N.: *The Impact of the Dead Sea Scrolls*. 1962. Pp. viii+168+ 14 ills. (Macmillan, London. Price: 15s. 0d.).

The writer, former High Master of St. Paul's School, describes his book as written 'by a layman for laymen'. In a very technical sense he may be a layman, but he exhibits a command of the subject and a capacity to form sound judgments on it which some who count themselves experts would do well to imitate. Certainly for 'laymen' who wish to have an intelligible and trustworthy survey of the story of the Scrolls from their discovery to the end of 1962 it would be difficult to recommend a better book. Mr. Gilkes has visited the sites, discussed the Scrolls and their significance with those who have made a special study of them, lectured to young people on the subject and endeavoured in every way to get his own ideas clear about it. He has been surprised to find 'how often these issues served to illuminate understanding both of the New Testament and of the Old'. One may mildly question the necessity, in a book for general readers, of giving so much space to summarizing and refuting such views as those of Dr. Del Medico. F.F.B.

MORAWE, G.: *Aufbau und Abgrenzung der Loblieder von Qumrân. Studien zur gattungsgeschichtlichen Einordnung der Hodajôth*. (Theologische Arbeiten, Band XVI). n.d. [1962?] Pp. 188. (Evangelische Verlagsanstalt, Berlin. Price: DM. 11.50).

The contents of the fragmentary Hymn Scroll from Cave 1 at Qumran have been divided into separate hymns by various editors, but there has been little unanimity on the number of hymns. This, in Morawe's view, is due to the editors' failure to establish strictly scientific criteria for the identification of individual hymns. The criteria which he himself tries to establish rise out of a 'form-critical' study of the *Hodayoth*. He classifies them as *individuelle Danklieder* or *hymnische Bekenntnislieder* according as they begin with the words *'ôdekā 'adōnāi kî* ... or with *bārûk 'attâh 'adōnāi*. But the contents of the hymns must be considered as well as their introductory formulas; and a study of their contents leads to their classification into narratives of distress, narratives of deliverance, vows, prayers, exhortations, hymnic fragments, reflective compositions and compositions in the 'wisdom' strain. After this attempt to do for the *Hodayoth* something like the service done by Gunkel for the canonical Psalter, the author distinguishes and demarcates thirty-four separate compositions in 1QH. F.F.B.

MOWRY, L.: *The Dead Sea Scrolls and the Early Church*. 1962. Pp. xi+ 260. (University of Chicago Press. Price: $6.95 or 56s. 0d.).

Professor Lucetta Mowry has been known for a number of years now as student of the relations between the Scrolls and the New Testament; her essay on 'The Dead Sea Scrolls and the Gospel of John' in *The Biblical Archaeologist* for 1954 was one of the earliest published studies on that particular subject. In this new volume she deals with several important points of comparison and contrast between what she calls 'two literatures of redemption' — in particular, with the way of redemption, the eschatological hope, and acts of devotion. She rightly attaches special importance to the outlook and influence of the founders of the two communities, recognizing the difficulty inherent in the fact that neither founder has left us direct evidence of himself. When she illustrates Jesus' combining of the figures of the Suffering Servant and the Son of Man by the combination of the Son of Man and the Elect One in the Similitudes of Enoch, it would have been well to bear in mind that Charles's suggested dating of the Similitudes (c. 94–64 B.C.) is widely contested nowadays, especially in view of the fact that every part of I Enoch has been identified in the Qumran texts *except* the Similitudes. But that is a minor point. Dr. Mowry has written an able and interesting book, and concludes that it is unlikely that in the study of Qumran-Christian connections 'we shall ever get beyond an eventual consensus of scholarly opinion, which means, in effect, a probability judgment based upon the study of the general and the particular'.

F.F.B.

VAN DER PLOEG, J.: *Le Targum de Job de la Grotte 11 de Qumran (IIQtg. Job.) Première Communication.* (Medelingen der Koninklijke Nederlandse Akademie van Wetenschappen, Afd. Letterkunde. Nieuwe Reeks, Deel 25, No. 9). Pp. 14+1 plate. (M.V. Noord-Hollandsche Uitgevers Maatschappij, Amsterdam. 1962. Price: Fl. 2.25).

The fragments of the Qumran Targum of Job have been handed over to the Royal Netherlands Academy of Science for publication and Professor van der Ploeg gives here a thorough and fascinating introduction to the important manuscript. He describes it, discusses its probable date, its linguistic features, its contribution as an early Targum to the history of Targumic writing, its textual features *vis à vis* the Hebrew text and numerous other aspects, and rounds off the study with a list (provisional) of the Biblical passages represented here. There is one facsimile and a transcription. The author's résumé states that the Targum, alongside the Genesis Apocryphon, gives an early Targumic text, and proves that Targums were in existence in the pre-Christian era; it is possibly the Targum to which Gamaliel refers, and gives the kind of language which Jesus spoke.

B.J.R.

VERMES, G.: *The Dead Sea Scrolls in English.* (Pelican Books, A551). 1962. Pp. 258. (Penguin Books, Harmondsworth. Price: 4s. 6d.).

Dr. Vermes has quickly followed up his English edition of Dupont-Sommer's translation of the Qumran texts with his own translation of them. This is an excellent piece of work, which may be commended with the utmost confidence to non-Hebraists who are interested to know what the Scrolls really say. Dr. Vermes not only gives us a trustworthy and objective translation, but one which is pleasant to read and conveys to a remarkable degree the 'flavour' of the original. It is a matter for special admiration that English is not the translator's native tongue; one would hardly believe this did one not know it for a fact! Each section of the work is prefaced by a short explanatory introduction, and the first three chapters give the reader some account of the Qumran community. Here Dr. Vermes deals with many debatable questions, but his judgment is sound and his conclusions are stated with true scholarly modesty. He thinks that the community was Essene in character. The Teacher of Righteousness is not identified, but his date is indicated by the identification of his persecutor, the Wicked Priest, with Jonathan the Hasmonaean. An appendix deals in a provisional way with the Copper Scroll.

F.F.B.

YADIN, Y.: *The Scroll of the War of the Sons of Light against the Sons of Darkness*, edited with Commentary and Introduction. Translated from the Hebrew by Batya and Chaim Rabin. 1962. Pp. xx+388+ frontispiece and 20 figs. (Oxford University Press, London. Price: 63s. 0d.).

The book is much more than a translation of the Hebrew version which appeared in 1955 (*Book List*, 1956, p. 67; *Eleven Years*, p. 774) for new materials which have appeared since that time and some modifications by the author himself have been included. It is impossible to praise too highly this exposition of what must always be one of the most enigmatic of the Dead Sea Scrolls; there is hardly any aspect which has not been included in the survey, and the treatment is balanced as well as ingenious. In Part One introductory problems include the purpose of the Scroll, the plan of the War, the Banners, Conscription, Trumpets, Weapons, Strategy, Rites, Angelology, together with a discussion of Date, Sect, and Orthography which brings the Scroll into line with other Scrolls. In Part Two we are given the text (unpointed Hebrew transcription), translation, and textual comments. The book closes with a full index of Authors, quotations (Biblical, etc.), and general. B.J.R.

APOCRYPHA AND POST-BIBLICAL JUDAISM

BUNTE, W.: *Maaserot/Maaser Scheni* (*Vom Zehnten/Vom Zweiten Zehnten*). Text, Übersetzung und Erklärung mit geschichtlichen und sprachlichen Einleitungen und textkritischen Anhängen. (Die Mischna, ed. Rengstorf and Rost.) 1962. Pp. 286. (A. Töpelmann, Berlin. Price: DM. 38).

This work is of a high standard. In his introduction the author explains the composition of the two tractates, analyses the relation between Mishna and Tosephta and gives a meticulous history of tithing. The translation is accurate, with full and valuable notes. If, occasionally, the author pronounces overconfidently on a fundamental matter, the fault lies rather with scholarship in this area in general. For example, he classes *ma'ase* pieces ('a happening', 'it once happened') as haggadic, in contradistinction to halakha (p. 5 and other places). But surely, a *ma'ase* piece which refers to a legal decision or practice may well be of halakhic character, or at least may well have been of halakhic character in the eyes of the Rabbis at some period. What a master of clear summarisation of complex matters Danby was may be seen from a comparison of his note on *Ribbui* and *Mi'ut* with that of the author under review, in connection with Maaser Sheni 5.10 (Danby, p. 82 n. 1, Bunte, p. 234, n. d 1). D.D.

GANDZ, S. and KLEIN, H. (trans. by): *The Code of Maimonides, Book Three, The Book of Seasons*, with an Appendix by Ernest Wiesenberg. (Yale Judaica Series, Vol. III). 1961. Pp. xxxiv+634. (Yale University Press, New Haven, and Oxford University Press, London. Price: $10).

The distinguished Editors of a complete, carefully annotated translation of Maimonides' *Mishneh Torah* into English are to be congratulated on having completed the greater part of their difficult task. The present volume deals with the following items: Sabbath, 'Erubh, Repose on the Day of Atonement, Repose on Festivals, Leavened and Unleavened Bread, Shofar, Booth and Palm Branch, Shekel Dues, Sanctification of the New Moon, Fasts, Purim and Hanukkah. Unfortunately, neither Dr. Gandz nor Rabbi Klein, the translators, nor Professor Obermann, the former Editor, lived to see the fruit of their work in print.

Great care has been taken to consult manuscripts and early editions, and special emphasis has been laid on an accurate though not overtechnical translation of the original into idiomatic English. An Introduction and Notes give account of the development from Biblical to Talmudic Law and of the Palestinian and Babylonian source material, on which Maimonides based his final decisions.

Dr. Wiesenberg's extensive and competent *Addenda and Corrigenda to Treatise VIII of the Book of Seasons*, which deals with the astronomical and mathematical aspects of the laws on the *Sanctification of the New Moon* and had previously been publised as a separate volume of the Yale Judaica Series, provides besides new manuscript evidence and essential improvements on earlier interpretations of the text a great deal of important and hitherto neglected subject matter for the assessment of Maimonides' place in the history of science.

Once the Great Code has appeared in its entirety, it will be an indispensable tool not only for those interested in the specific meaning of the Jewish legacy, but also for all engaged in the comparative study of medieval theology and law.   S.S.

GERHARDSSON, B.: *Memory and Manuscript: Oral Tradition and Written Transmission in Rabbinic Judaism and Early Christianity.* (Acta Seminarii Neotestamentici Upsaliensis, XXII). 1961. Pp. 380. (C. W. K. Gleerup, Lund and Ejnar Munksgaard, Copenhagen. Price: Sw. kr. 30).

This large and learned work is an elaboration of the thesis first put forward by Professor Harald Riesenfeld of Uppsala in *The Gospel History and its Beginnings* (Mowbray's, 1957). Following Riesenfeld, Dr. Gerhardsson provides a useful and necessary corrective to the theories (now grown stale) of the *Formgeschichte* School which claim that the Gospel tradition was nothing more than the written deposit of the preaching and teaching activity of the post-Resurrection church, adapted to as well as created by the needs of the expanding Christian community, both as social group and as worshipping fellowship. The author's main contention is that form-critical theories consistently ignore the important part played in the contemporary Judaism, out of which the Church came, of both oral and written tradition (Memory and Manuscript). Part I of the book is devoted to the study of the character of this tradition in the written and oral transmission of the Torah. Part II develops the thesis that there was a similar oral and written Jesus-tradition (a tradition from Jesus himself and then about

Jesus) in the primitive church, formed by the same Jewish Torah-tradition methods, prior to its eventual incorporation in the New Testament. The Evangelists 'worked on the basis of a fixed, distinct tradition from, and about Jesus — a tradition which was partly memorised and partly written down in note-books and private scrolls' (p. 335). And it is not impossible, as Dr. Riesenfeld argued, that this Jesus-tradition (as the distinctive *hieros logos* of the early church) was recited (and so preserved and also transmitted) in the course of its worship.

M.Bl.

HERTZBERG, A. (ed. by): *Judaism*. (Great Religions of Modern Man). 1961. Pp. 256. (Prentice-Hall International, London & George Braziller, Inc., New York. Price: 25s. 0d.).

This book presents methodically the meaning of Judaism in its essentials as conceived by the author, the introduction of whose work significantly begins with the assertion 'God made covenant with a particular people that it should be His priest-hood'. The chapters that follow deal with subjects such as: The people and the covenant; God is one and moral, whom man must love and serve; the teachings and commandments of the Torah; cycle of the year; the holiness of the land of Israel and the return to it from exile. The last two chapters are dedicated to doctrine and prayer, the former treating of man's dignity, responsibility, conduct, sin and repentance, suffering, death and the world to come and the Messiah, and the latter, among other matters, of the synagogue, statutory and private prayer. The book is to be recommended to all who are interested in theology in general and in views on the Jewish spirit in particular. It is well indexed and the production is pleasing.

M.W.

ISAAC, J.: *L'enseignement du mépris: vérité historique et mythes théologiques*. 1962. Pp. 196. (Editions Fasquelle, Paris. Price: NF. 9).

The author of *Jésus et Israël* (see *Book List*, 1950, p. 71; *Eleven Years*, p. 289) returns to the subject of anti-Semitism in traditional Christianity. He points out that in spite of authoritative Christian declarations that anti-Semitism is fundamentally anti-Christian, there are certain 'theological myths' which die hard and continue to foster an unconscious prejudice against the Jews: among these he singles out three for critical examination: (i) the Jews went into dispersion in A.D. 70 as a divine chastisement for their rejection of Jesus; (ii) the Jews' religion was degenerate in Jesus' time; (iii) the Jews as a nation are guilty of the crime of deicide. It is, unfortunately, too much to hope that these myths will die as a result of M. Isaac's refutation of them in the light of history; but it is reasonable to hope that historians and theologians will express themselves more accurately on these subjects than some whose careless remarks, quoted by M. Isaac, help to keep alive *l'enseignement du mépris*.

F.F.B.

SCHOLEM, G. G.: *Major Trends in Jewish Mysticism*. Paperback edition. 1961. Pp. XVI+460. (Schocken Books, New York. Price: $2.25).

This paperback edition is a reprint of the third edition (1954), with the addition of bibliographical data about recent studies in the field. The work originally appeared in 1941, and was reissued, with revisions and substantial additions, in 1946, in a second edition, of which the third is a corrected reprint. The authoritative character of this book is well known; and its availability in this new form will be widely welcomed.

G.W.A.

SCHÜRER, E.: *A History of the Jewish People in the Time of Jesus*, edited and introduced by Nahum N. Glatzer. 1962. Pp. xvii+428. (Schocken Books, New York. Price: Paper, $2.25; cloth, $4.50).

This is a reprint of the greater part of Division I of the English translation of Schürer's second edition. This translation (by John Macpherson) is now well over seventy years old, but for those who have no access to the later German editions it is still a work of great value. The reprint provides in convenient form a history of the Jews from 175 B.C. to A.D. 135. Professor Glatzer of Brandeis University has carried out a judicious abridgement of the material; he has also provided an introduction which assesses the worth of Schürer's work and indicates lines along which the study of the subject has advanced since his time, together with a useful bibliography covering the period 1900–1960.

F.F.B.

TEDESCHE, S.: *The Book of Maccabees*. n.d. (? 1962). Pp. 79 with 26 full-page coloured illustrations by Jacob Schacham. (Vallentine, Mitchell, London. Price: 30s. 0d.).

This edition of I Maccabees is prepared in Israel by Massadah — P.E.C. press, and printed by Peli — P.E.C., Ramat-Gan. The translation is by Sidney Tedesche and is used by permission of the Dropsie College, Philadelphia. It is a most elegant work of art on brown-grey tinted paper, and the illustrations are all in the heroic vein. They are essentially modern and in rich and varied colours, but are reminiscent of Greek vases, Assyrian bas-reliefs, and the Bayeux tapestry. A delightful piece of publishing.

N.H.S.

WIEDER, N.: *The Judean Scrolls and Karaism*. 1962. Pp. xii+296. (East and West Library, London. Price: 42s. 0d.).

In this book a scholar with Karaitic literature at his finger-tips brings his expertise to bear on a close examination of the Scrolls. Dr. Wieder's argumentation is throughout scrupulous, his conclusions cautious: identification of Qumranism with Karaism (or, indeed, any Jewish sect specifically named and described in ancient sources) is precluded, he holds, by the absence amongst Karaites of the dualism and ethical predestinarianism evinced by Qumranic literature. Karaism, however, was not in origin theologically homogeneous, but rather a conglomeration of elements with opposition to rabbinic Judaism and its pre-eminent position as their common factor — amongst them the descendants of the Qumran sectaries. This conclusion Wieder reaches via a most copiously documented comparison of the treatment of various topics by both the Scrolls and Karaism, gathering in *en route* most tellingly pertinent ritual survivals attested by contemporary (or quite recent) Jewish communities as remote as Kurdestan and Surinam. He deals with: *Torah and Tradition; Messianic obsession; Opponents; The Day of Atonement; Exegesis; The Book of Hegeh* (=the Bible, i.e., Reading, cf. *Miqra', Qur'an*). Many readers may find the first chapter, in which the Karaite evidence is the least prominent, the most significant study. In it Wieder considers 'Damascus' in its Qumranic context (*The Zadokite Fragment*), and is able to show from rabbinic, Judeo-Christian, New Testament, Karaite, medieval Jewish, and even Islamic sources a remarkable concord of tradition that the appearance of the Messiah was expected to occur in the area Damascus-Galilee, even as the exile had first begun in this area: Jesus' declaration *I will go before you into Galilee* is thus seen to be a distinctly self-assertive messianic gesture.

R.L.

PHILOLOGY AND GRAMMAR

BEYER, K.: *Semitische Syntax im Neuen Testament* (Band I, Satzlehre Teil 1). (Studien zur Umwelt des Neuen Testaments, Band 1). 1962. Pp. 324. (Vandenhoeck & Ruprecht, Göttingen. Price: DM. 34.80).

Hitherto the study of the New Testament documents from the point of view of Semitic influence or sources has been for the most part confined to the study of individual words or phrases in the light of Aramaic, Hebrew, or Biblical Greek, or to the attempt to find 'mistranslations' from Aramaic. In this book (which was a Göttingen doctoral dissertation) the author extends the investigation to the examination of New Testament syntax, and, in this first part, exclusively to the structure of the sentence. (The author estimates — page 17, note 2 — that this volume will represent a fifth part only of his completed work.) Semitic sentence structure prevails in the Synoptic Gospels, in the Johannine writings (where the influence is Hebrew), and in the Epistle of James. The Hebrew influence (and possible use of Hebrew sources) in the Johannine writings confirms the connection which has been traced on other grounds between John and Qumran.

M.Bl.

CLARKE, E. G.: *The Selected Questions of Ishō Bar Nūn on the Pentateuch.* Edited and Translated from MS. Cambridge Add. 2017. With a study of the relationship of Isho 'Dādh of Merv, Theodore Bar Kōnī and Ishō Bar Nūn on Genesis. (Studia Post-Biblica, V). 1962. Pp. vii+188+27 plates. (E. J. Brill, Leiden. Price: Fl. 22).

This is the Syriac text, photographically reproduced from the Cambridge Add. MS. 2017 (dated A.D. 1706) and a translation into English of the fifty-six 'questions' on the Pentateuch of a

9th-century catholicus of the Nestorian church. The questions, which would be more accurately described as 'questions and answers' of the type found among Greek and Latin as well as Syriac writers, are a kind of commentary on problems in Biblical books, the author supplying answers to questions he himself puts. Their importance is less for the student of the Old Testament than for those interested in the literary activity and exegesis of the Nestorian church during a decisive period of its history. For this reason the main part of the book is rightly given to a discussion of the relationship and editorial methods of Ishodad of Merv, Theodore bar Koni and Isho bar Nun, in which it is shown that, although they all used a common source, each used it independently and for his own purposes. W.D.McH.

GRADWOHL, R.: *Die Farben im alten Testament*. Eine Terminologische Studie. (Beihefte zur Zeitschrift für die alttestamentliche Wissenschaft, Heft 83). 1963. Pp. XIV+116. (Verlag Alfred Töpelmann, Berlin. Price: DM. 20).

The work here noticed is a dissertation for a doctorate at the University of Zürich, and is a meritorious study of a subject which has not yet been exhaustively treated. The author's method is to examine all the relevant terms under the headings of *Farbqualitäten* (pp. 3–59), and *Pigmentfarben* (pp. 60–88), which are subdivided into animal, vegetable and mineral pigments, and to bring the whole work to a conclusion with a brief summary on the development of the nomenclature of the colours in the O.T.

Each word is carefully examined in the light of every passage in which it occurs, of the renderings in the ancient versions and of its root in the cognate languages; all the matter is carefully and accurately set out, so that even if the work produces no new conclusions (which are hardly to be expected), it remains a useful storehouse of information. A few words perhaps indicating colour which ought to be included, even if such a meaning is rejected ('*āmôṣ* 'red', *ḥārûṣ* 'yellow gold', *zāraq* 'was white-haired', *sāgûr* 'red' as applied to gold), are omitted, and one or two passages are in the reviewer's opinion misinterpreted (e.g., II Kings ix. 30, since the eyes were 'not painted' but were 'set' in, i.e., framed with, black paint to enhance their brilliance, so that the verb here must be distinguished from that in Job xiii. 27; Is. lxv. 3; Job xxxviii. 14; Prov. xxiii. 31, xxxi. 21; Is. xxiv. 23; and Jer. iv. 30), one or two translations are passing strange (e.g., that oriental girls have rosy cheeks or that the bowels turn red under vehement emotion), and that the Hebrew *bûṣ* 'fine linen' and the Accadian *paṣā'u* 'to be white' are connected is extremely doubtful. Lastly, some classical knowledge would have illuminated obscure passages: the red painting of shields is analogous to the wearing of scarlet uniforms by the Spartans to terrify their enemies, and the bride's 'purple locks' (Cant. vii. 6) would have found a ready explanation, if Horace's *purpurei olores* had occurred to the author (for *purpureus* meant anything 'light-bringing', such as glossy white swans and glossy black hair, and so 'purple' as *par excellence* the glossy colour).

G.R.D.

KOOPMANS, J. J.: *Aramäische Chrestomathie*. Ausgewählte Texte (Inschriften, Ostraka und Papyri) bis zum 3. Jahrhundert n. Chr., für das Studium der aramäischen Sprache gesammelt. I. Teil: Einleitungen, Literatur und Kommentare. II. Teil: Aramäische Texte in Umschrift. 1962. Pp. 225+60. (Nederlands Instituut voor het Nabije Oosten, Leiden. Price: Fl. 35).

The scope of this book is made plain by its title. It contains seventy-one representative Aramaic texts from the KLMW documents of the 9th-century B.C. to a Dura-Europos inscription of the 3rd-century A.D.; there are also a collection of Aramaic words in the New Testament and a short list of Pehlevi ideograms (Dr. Koopmans prefers to call them logograms or Aramaeograms). The texts are reproduced in transcription, and there are brief introductions and abundant references to relevant modern literature; the bibliography is numbered 1–480, but a few numbers include more than one work. The notes discuss lexicographical and grammatical matters and suggest how Aramaic words should be vocalised, though the editor is aware of the caution with which these suggestions should be received. The book is reproduced from typescript which is unpleasing to the eye (especially where mistakes have obviously been corrected) and not always clear, but the use of this process has doubtless helped to make the price so moderate. This is a most useful book, both for teaching and as a convenient work of reference. J.A.E.

MAUCHLINE, J.: *An Introductory Hebrew Grammar with Progressive Exercises in Reading, Writing, and Pointing*, by the late A. B. Davidson, revised throughout. 25th edition. 1962. Pp. XII+314. (T. & T. Clark, Edinburgh. Price: 30s. 0d.).

This is undoubtedly a better Davidson. Professor Mauchline has made a worthwhile attempt to simplify its first forty pages, to incorporate modern knowledge and theory into explanations of form and usage (e.g., Waw Consecutive), and to improve the exercises so that beginners have longer sentences to handle and will the more readily appreciate the idiom. The printing too is of high quality, with one exception, namely that the Hebrew type has often been badly aligned with the English.

But the pruning knife could have been used to advantage. It is sometimes difficult to see the wood for the trees; explanations still tend to be involved and difficult to follow. Some things that were proper to former generations could well have been cut out, as, for instance, the printing of incorrect Hebrew forms, and the continued use of the archaic second person pronouns, 'thou', 'thee' and 'ye' in exercises.

When a new printing is called for it is to be hoped that the numerous slips in references to other parts of the grammar will be corrected. L.H.B.

MORAG, S.: *The Vocalization Systems of Arabic, Hebrew and Aramaic.* Their Phonetic and Phonemic Principles. (Janua Linguarum, Nr. XIII.) 1962. Pp. 86 incl. Tables. (Mouton & Co., 'S–Gravenhage, The Netherlands. Price: Fl. 15.0).

The series called *Janua Linguarum*, which is devoted to the investigation of problems of language in the light of modern linguistic science, has been running since 1956; the present work is numbered 13 in it, although 13 others have already appeared. Most of these are written in a form of the English language, but none of their authors has an English name; this fact, taken in connection with an extreme use of current linguistic jargon, will readily explain why so much that the authors say remains unclear; for *obscurum per obscurum* seems to be their guiding principle. Dr. Morag has much to say that is both interesting and informative; but, if he could occasionally employ a simple word or lapse into ordinary language (and much that he wants to say can be so expressed) and would introduce an occasional example, the reader would be greatly helped in penetrating his thought and so understanding a work which is breaking new ground for the ordinary Hebraist or Semitist.

G.R.D.

PEISKER, C. H.: *Hebräische Wortkunde.* 1962. Pp. 44. (Vandenhoek & Ruprecht, Göttingen. Price: DM. 4.80).

Some think it better to teach Hebrew vocabulary direct from a text, others prefer to start with a classified list. For those of the latter persuasion, whose mother tongue is German, Peisker has produced this well-printed booklet. The 934 most frequently occurring Hebrew words are printed in a single list in the alphabetical order of their root. No indication of actual frequency is given — it seems to be 'over 25' (Harper-Watts) for verbs — but the less common ('under 50'?) are starred. The student can exercise his skill in parsing in the Second Part, which consists of a list of verbal forms deriving from the stems already learnt, and arranged according to type of stem. There is a key provided whereby the analysis can be checked. The work has been carefully compiled and excellently proof-read and should prove very useful for its purpose.

D.R.Ap-T.

ROBINSON, T. H.: *Paradigms and Exercises in Syriac Grammar.* 4th ed. revised by L. H. Brockington. 1962. Pp. viii+159. (Clarendon Press, Oxford. Price: 30s. 0d.).

Every teacher of Syriac will be grateful to Mr. Brockington for the improvements he has been able to effect in what is still the only elementary text-book of the subject in English. The new edition is some ten pages longer than the last edition, a book which needs no description here as most members of the Society who read Syriac are indebted to Professor Robinson's work for much help in the initial stages of their studies. While the expansions and additions, especially those dealing with syntax, are very welcome and make the grammar even more useful, it is probable that the introduction of diacritical points on a generous scale is the feature which will have increased the value of the book most in the eyes of students and teachers alike.

W.D.McH.

RUNDGREN, F.: *Das althebräische Verbum: Abriss der Aspektlehre.* 1961. Pp. 112. (Almqvist & Wiksell, Stockholm. Price: Sw. Kr. 12).

The author of this brief introduction to the study of the Hebrew verb holds strongly that it is not possible to understand the Semitic verbal system and to provide a scientific account of it without a knowledge of the linguistic conception of aspects; and Semitists, with few exceptions, do not possess this knowledge. Their methods are accordingly faulty. In Part I of his work he presents, in twenty-five short sections, the main bases of the aspect theory, with illustrative material drawn from many languages ancient and modern, Semitic and non-Semitic (Akkadian and Turkish receive special attention); while in Part II, which consists of ten short sections, he considers the Hebrew verbal system. His plea for a wider knowledge of the aspect theory extends also to the Hamitic languages, which need to be more adequately worked out before they can be profitably used to illuminate the Hebrew verbal system. The author writes primarily as a student of linguistics who has long studied the Semitic verbal system, without himself, as he informs us, having been trained scientifically in the oriental languages with which he operates. His terminology is that of modern linguistic study, and unless the reader is prepared to familiarize himself with this terminology, if he does not already possess it, he will not appreciate fully the argument of the book. D.W.T.

SHACHTER, HAIM: *The New Universal Hebrew English Dictionary (Millôn 'Ibhrî 'Anglî Kôlēl)*, 2 vols. 2nd edition. 1962. Pp. 834. (Yavneh Publishing House, Tel-Aviv, Israel. Price: $8.00).

This dictionary gives Hebrew words, expressions, etc., drawn from the various strata of the Hebrew language, Biblical and post-Biblical. It includes a good number of the latest diversified coinages in Israel — coinages adapted to the complexities of modern life. It also gives international words (indicated by asterisks), as well as abbreviations which occur frequently in Hebrew works and especially in newspapers. The method adopted in compiling the dictionary is agreeable, and so is the print, enabling the reader to find his way about without difficulty. The great and growing number of Jewish and non-Jewish students of Modern Hebrew, and indeed any other Hebrew scholars, in the Anglo-Saxon countries, will find this dictionary of great use.

M.W.

BOOK LIST, 1964

Because of my absence in Jerusalem during much of April and May, responsibility for the final stages of proof-reading and indexing this issue of the *Book List* has been undertaken by Mrs. E. S. K. Paterson and Dr. R. E. Clements. To both of them I am indebted, not only for this but for other help in the production of this year's *Book List*. Dr. Clements, though not a member of the *Book List* Panel, has undertaken a number of reviews; and Mrs. Paterson has at every stage carried out most of the routine drudgery involved in recording bibliographical data, despatching review copies, preparing copy for the Printer, and much else. I also wish to thank for their co-operation the members of the Panel and the following other scholars: Professors P. R. Ackroyd and M. Bič, Mr. Trevor Donald, Mr. R. Loewe, Professor C. R. North, Dr. E. I. J. Rosenthal, the Rev. E. R. Rowlands, Professors S. Segert and T. W. Thacker, Dr. E. Wiesenberg, and Professor D. J. Wiseman. For bibliographical data promptly supplied I have to thank Professors P. A. H. de Boer and E. Hammershaimb, and Mr. C. N. Francis of the firm of B. H. Blackwell. Finally, and by no means merely formally, I express my sincere gratitude to the Printer and his staff.

For the guidance of readers who have a special interest in educational material, books which are recommended for inclusion in school libraries are marked by an asterisk.

G. W. ANDERSON.

NEW COLLEGE,
UNIVERSITY OF EDINBURGH.

GENERAL

ALTMANN, A. (ed. by): *Biblical and Other Studies*. (Brandeis University, Lown Judaic Institute, Studies and Texts: Volume 1). 1963. Pp. xii+266. (Harvard University Press, Cambridge, Massachusetts).

6 (out of 12) articles here directly concern the Hebrew Bible. (1) Cyrus H. Gordon, in a fairly general review of 'Hebrew Origins in the Light of Recent Discovery' puts Abraham in the Amarna age, emphasizes the value of the Nuzu documents for Biblical family law, and mentions that *Israel* is now attested in Ugaritic as the personal name of a *maryannu* warrior. (2) E. A. Speiser 'The Wife-Sister Motif in the Patriarchal Narratives' shows from Nuzu sources that under the Hurrian fratriarchal system sistership was a transferable relationship that carried legal advantages for a woman and which, when she was also wife to the adoptive 'brother', invested her marriage to him with additional prestige and status, guaranteeing the genealogical purity of her children — hence the concern of *Genesis* to assert wife/sisterhood. (3) Nahum M. Sarna 'Psalm 89: A Study in Inner Biblical Exegesis' finds it to be an adaptation of Nathan's oracle to suit the circumstances of the Syro-Ephraimite threat of 735/4 — the lament is over Ahaz, the legitimate if unworthy Davidic king, whose replacement by ben Tab'el is threatened. (4) H. L. Ginsberg 'The Quintessence of Koheleth' gives, *inter alia*, his argument that the book is a translation from an Aramaic original. (5) Robert Gordis 'Elihu the Intruder' argues for the authenticity of the Elihu speeches in Job, assigning them to the author of the main poem at a much later point in his own life. (6) M. H. Goshen-Gottstein 'The rise of the Tiberian Bible Text' offers a very detailed refutation, as urbane as it is devastating, of Kahle's whole conception of Massoretic problems: he concludes that the Aleppo Codex which is the basis of the current Jerusalem Bible project is authentically that referred to by Maimonides, who (so far from 'authorising' it) acknowledged it; and that it is the only (not just the only surviving) complete Bible codex ever prepared by Aaron b. Asher. Two further articles may interest some readers of this *Book List*: (*a*) S. Lieberam 'How Much Greek in Jewish Palestine?' (*b*) A. S. Halkin, on 'The Mediaeval Jewish Attitude Towards Hebrew'.   **R.L.**

BIČ, M. & SOUČEK, J. B. (ed. by): *Biblická Konkordance*, Parts 22 and 23. Rozpáleny-Spolu. 1963. Pp. 80 each part. (Edice Kalich, Prague. Price: Kčs. 10.50 each).

This valuable Concordance to the Czech Bible, offering the reader more help than any other single Concordance in any language known to the reviewer, since it shows not only the Hebrew original for the Old Testament and the Greek original for the New Testament, but also the Greek word used in the Old Testament, is now getting within sight of the end. Editors and users must be eagerly awaiting the completion of this great enterprise.   **H.H.R.**

472 BOOK LIST 1964

DE BOER, P. A. H. (ed. by): *Congress Volume, Bonn 1962* (Supplements to Vetus Testamentum, Vol. IX). 1963. Pp. 342+1 plate. (E. J. Brill, Leiden. Price: Fl. 46).

It is possible to do little more than list this collection of articles first read as papers to the Congress. They cover most aspects of Old Testament study; textual, literary, and traditio-historical criticism, history, religion, and relatedness to its contemporary world. The volume begins with a moving and eloquent tribute to Hermann Gunkel and his creative contributions to Old Testament study (W. Baumgartner: Zum 100. Geburtstag von Hermann Gunkel). The list of names and titles that follow will illustrate the importance of this collection. C. H. Gordon: The Mediterranean Factor in the Old Testament (those who attended the congress will observe that this differs in content though not in theme from the paper as delivered); A. Lauha: Das Schilfmeermotiv im Alten Testament; S. Herrmann: Prophetie in Israel und Ägypten — Recht und Grenze eines Vergleichs; M. Sekine: Erwägungen zur hebräischen Zeit-auffassung; G. W. Anderson: Isaiah xxiv-xxvii Reconsidered; M. Haran: The Literary Structure and Chronological framework of the Prophecies in Isa. xl-xlviii; R. E. Murphy: A Consideration of the Classification 'Wisdom Psalms'; R. Tournay: Les affinités du Ps. xlv avec le Cantique des Cantiques et leur interprétation messianique; A. Caquot; La prophétie de Nathan et ses échos lyriques; G. Rinaldi: Quelques remarques sur la politique d'Azarias (Ozias) de Juda en Philistie (2 Chron. xxvi. 6 ss.); E. Auerbach: Der Aufstieg der Priesterschaft zur Macht im Alten Israel; D. N. Freedman: The Law and the Prophets; G. E. Weil: La nouvelle édition de la Massorah (BHK iv) et l'histoire de la Massorah; J. D. Barthélemy: Les tiqquné sopherim et la critique textuelle de l'Ancien Testament; M. Mansoor: The Massoretic Text in the Light of Qumran; A. S. van der Woude: Das Hiobtargum aus Qumran Höhle XI; A. Jepsen: Von den Aufgaben der alttestamentlichen Text-kritik. The concluding sentence deserves to be quoted: the Old Testament is a work 'that speaks still today to mankind because here the speaker is also the Lord of our history.'
A.S.H.

DE BOER, P. A. H. (ed. by): *Oudtestamentische Studiën*, Deel XIII. *Studies on Psalms*. 1963. Pp. 200. (E. J. Brill, Leiden. Price: Fl. 32).

It is pleasant to record the publication of another volume in this well-known Dutch series, which thus, after an interval of five years, continues to bear witness to the enthusiasm and energy of Professor de Boer. The title of the volume should prepare the reader for the diversity of its contents, which are such that there is something here for every student of the Psalter, whatever his main interest may be. The contributors have been permitted to write in English, French, or German; and there are dis-cussions of various lexical, grammatical, and textual points (G. J. Thierry, A. S. van der Woude), an exegetical study of Psalm xv in terms of a royal psalm (J. L. Koole), of Psalm xxvi with special reference to the plea of innocence (L. A. Snijders), and of Psalm xlix with its possible thought of a future life (J. van der Ploeg), an exposition of the stylistic factor of 'repetition' (N. H. Ridderbos), an evaluation of the ethical as compared with the juridical elements in the Psalter (B. Gemser), a consideration of the psalms of vengeance and cursing (H. A. Brongers), and, indicative of the editor's wide interests, an examination of the Old Latin text of the Song of Hannah (P. A. H. de Boer). The contributions by Professors Gemser and Thierry are posthumous, and the editor pays a tribute to these scholars in a short preface. Incidentally, the appeal to Ugaritic in connexion with Ps. lxxxix. 20, which occurs on pp. 135f., was anticipated by Professor W. F. Albright some fifteen years ago.

A.R.J.

BRAUN, F. M.: *The Work of Père Lagrange*, adapted from the French by R. T. A. Murphy, O.P. 1963. Pp. xviii+306. (Bruce Publishing Co., Milwaukee. Price: $7.00).

The original French edition of this book appeared in 1944 under the title *L'Oeuvre du Père Lagrange*. It was, and remains, a selective rather than a complete account of Lagrange's life, and its chief value lies in the very full chronological bibliography of the great Dominican's publications, beginning with his thesis of 1878 for the doctorate in civil law, and ending with item 1786, his article for the 1938 volume of the *Revue biblique* (Vol. XLVII, pp. 163–183) on the Mosaic authenticity of Genesis and the documentary theory.

The chapters on Lagrange's life and work are arranged under the headings: Founder and Master, In the Light of Faith, Trials and Struggles, the Great Works, and Secret of a Full Life. To these the translator has added a sixth chapter entitled The Harvest, which helps to bridge the quarter-century that has elapsed between Lagrange's death on 10 March, 1938 and the present time. It is a pity that not all the photographs in the original work could be reproduced here. At least one photograph of the École Biblique might be added in some future edition.

J.M.T.B.

BRUCE, F. F. (ed. by): *Promise and Fulfilment*. Essays presented to Professor S. H. Hooke in celebration of his Ninetieth birthday 21st January, 1964 by Members of the Society for Old Testament Study and others. 1963. Pp. 214. (T. & T. Clark, Edinburgh. Price: 25s. 0d.).

Professor Bruce is to be congratulated upon the admirably representative team which he has gathered together on behalf of the Society in its effort to do honour to this distinguished former President, who, happily, kept to schedule and celebrated his ninetieth birthday on the 21st January, 1964; and here the reviewer must add that he, for one, cannot bring himself to refer to Professor Hooke as a nonagenarian, for this far too often carries with it a suggestion of senility which, as the delightfully characteristic frontispiece serves to show, would here be wholly out of keeping!

To cover the wide range of Professor Hooke's academic interests the editor has been forced to seek contributions from colleagues and friends outside the immediate circle of the Society, and we must all be grateful for their readiness to help. The range itself may be summed up as follows: comparative religion (S. G. F. Brandon, N. Q. King, G. Widengren); Old Testament (A. A. Anderson, G. Henton Davies, G. R. Driver, A. Guillaume, J. R. Porter, N. H. Snaith, J. Weingreen); New Testament (F. F. Bruce, A. J. B. Higgins); and, as marking, so to speak, the climax of Professor Hooke's own spiritual pilgrimage, a consideration of the rôle of imagination in divine revelation (A. M. Farrer). The volume is full of interest and a worthy tribute to one who has endeared himself to so many as both scholar and friend; and something of the way in which he has done this is sketched for the reader in the discerning personal appreciation which has been provided so very appropriately by the Dean of St. Paul's.

A.R.J.

BUTTRICK, G. A. and others (ed. by): *The Interpreter's Dictionary of the Bible: An Illustrated Encyclopedia in Four Volumes*. 1962. Pp. xxxii+876+24 maps; viii+1030; viii+978; viii+964. (Abingdon Press, New York & Nashville. Price: $45 or £18 the set).

The editors of this dictionary have drawn upon an international team of contributors, many of whom are leading experts on the subjects on which they write. The result is that many of the longer articles are of great distinction, offering valuable contributions to scholarship. Among such we may mention those of G. E. Mendenhall on Covenant and Election, K. Elliger on the Territories of the Tribes, G. von Rad on Deuteronomy, G. Henton Davies on the Ark, the Presence of God, and the Tabernacle, O. Eissfeldt on Genesis, J. Hempel on the Psalms and Old Testament Ethics, S. Mowinckel on Legend, Literature, and Tradition. Excellent surveys of modern criticism and research are given by H. H. Rowley on the History of Israel, J. Bright on the History of Hebrew Religion, and by K. Stendahl on Biblical Theology. Many other articles are of the same high standard. As often with such dictionaries there is an unevenness of quality, and some contributions disappoint. It is a pity that the articles on Abraham, Isaac, and Jacob make no attempt at an historical assessment of their subjects, so that in this regard they fall far short of the parallel contributions in the third edition of *Die Religion in Geschichte und Gegenwart*. The quality of the bibliographies is noticeably uneven, some being excellent, whilst others are scanty in the extreme. The translations seem reasonably well done, although that of Hempel's article on the Psalms reads awkwardly and betrays errors. We have places referred to as Silo and Sichem instead of Shiloh and Shechem (Vol. III, p. 947b). The volumes are attractively produced, and are not expensive for a work of such a scale. They will prove a valuable source of reference for Old Testament scholars.

R.E.C.

CAZELLES, H. & FEUILLET, A. (ed. by): *Dictionnaire de la Bible. Supplément*. Fasc. xxxviii. (Péché-Pentateuque). 1964. Tome VII, columns 481–678. (Letouzey & Ané, Paris).

In this latest fascicle S. Lyonnet continues the subject of sin in the Old Testament; here the vocabulary of the Septuagint is under close review. The same writer also contributes a long section on sin in the New Testament with special emphasis on the exegesis of Romans ch. v in respect of original sin. A somewhat unusual article deals with pilgrimages in the ancient East; later sections study pilgrimages in Israel and to the Holy Places before the period of the Crusades. 'Pella' (Khirbet Faḥil) is an up-to-date study in topography in regard to a city not mentioned in the Bible. 'Pelt' (Jean-Baptiste) is a short biography of a former Bishop of Metz, now chiefly remembered as the translator of A. Schöpfer's *Geschichte des Alten Testaments*, largely replaced by the French version of G. Ricciotti's *Storia d'Israele*. Penitence in the Old and New Testaments is considered by J. Giblet and A. M. Denis respectively. The article on the Pentateuch is by J. B. Bouhot for the patristic exegesis, and by H. Cazelles for the medieval period, modern exegesis, and the *status quaestionis* as it appears in the latest authorities.   J.M.T.B.

DEISSLER, A.: *Das Alte Testament und die neuere katholische Exegese*, für die Verkündigung und Katechese dargestellt. (Aktuelle Schriften zur Religionspädagogik 1). 1963. Pp. 127. (Verlag Herder, Freiburg. Price: DM. 7.80; by subscription, DM. 6.80).

The author tells us that, in spite of the great interest in Bible reading and sermons on the Bible, it is difficult to find a small book in German that summarizes the progress that has been achieved in Old Testament studies in recent years. In this unpretentious booklet he divides his survey into three parts, namely, the Papal encyclical *Divino afflante Spiritu* (30 Sept., 1943) as the Magna Charta of modern Catholic exegesis, the questions regarding the authorship of the individual books, and the literary *genres* exhibited in these writings. It is not quite easy to see why each book could not have been treated, as in most introductions, under a single heading, but not much, if any, confusion could result from the method adopted here, and the information is taken from the best and most progressive authors. The select bibliography is, for the most part, made up of German works by Catholic authors, with occasional reference to works in French. No English work is mentioned in the bibliography.

                                        J.M.T.B.

EISSFELDT, O.: *Kleine Schriften*, herausgegeben von Rudolf Sellheim und Fritz Maass. Zweiter Band. 1963. Pp. VIII+558+VI plates. (J. C. B. Mohr, Tübingen. Price: paper, DM. 60; cloth, DM. 65).

The first volume in this series was reviewed in *Book List*, 1962, pp. 5 f. The present volume, which has been produced with the same scrupulous care and bibliographical precision, contains the following items from the period 1933–1945 (where the subject is germane, some later essays are included): Das Datum der Belagerung von Tyrus durch Nebukadnezar; Das Berufungs-bewusstsein der Propheten als theologisches Gegenwartsproblem; Der Gott des Tabor und seine Verbreitung; Die Wanderung palästinisch-syrischer Götter nach Ost und West im zweiten vorchristlichen Jahrtausend; Ernst von Dobschütz † 20. Mai 1934. Zum Reformationstag; Der geschichtliche Hintergrund der Erzählung von Gibeas Schandtat (Richter 19–21); Neue

Zeugnisse für die Aussprache des Tetragramms als Jahwe; Nachwort; Karl Budde † am 29. Januar 1935 in Marburg; Hesekiel Kap. 16 als Geschichtsquelle; Eine Einschmelzstelle am Tempel zu Jerusalem; Hans Bauer † 6. März 1937; Hegel-Kritik und Pentateuch-Kritik. Historisch-kritische Analyse und systematisch-praktische Synthese in der Bibelforschung; Scha-memrumim "Hoher Himmel", ein Stadtteil von Gross-Sidon; Zur Frage nach dem Alter der phönizischen Geschichte des Sanchunjaton; Religionsdokument und Religionspoesie, Religionstheorie und Religionshistorie; Ras Schamra und Sanchunjaton, Philo Byblius und Eusebius von Cäsarea; Neue Götter im Alten Testament; Alfred Bertholet zum 70. Geburts-tag (9. November 1938); Linos und Alijan; Die Komposition von Exodus 1–12. Eine Rettung des Elohisten; Ba'alšamēm und Jahwe; Die Komposition der Bileam-Erzählung. Eine Nachprüfung von Rudolphs Beitrag zur Hexateuchkritik; Himmel und Erde als Bezeichnung phönizischer Landschaften; Phönizische Überlieferungen als Quelle für die Bücher 40–43 der Dionysiaca des Nonnos von Panopolis; Das Chaos in der biblischen und in der phönizischen Kosmogonie; Zum geo-graphischen Horizont der Ras-Schamra-Texte; Lade und Stierbild; Tempel und Kulte syrischer Städte in hellenistisch-römischer Zeit; Zu syrischen Tempeln und Kulten in hellenistisch-römischer Zeit; Abdalonymus und 'LNM; Zu "Abdalonymus und 'LNM"; Ruinen und Heiligtümer in Irak und Iran; Bestand und Benennung der Ras-Schamra-Texte; Die keilschriftalphabetischen Texte aus der zehnten und elften Ausgrabungskampagne in Ras Schamra; Ras Schamra: Die keilschriftalphabetischen Texte der Kampagnen 1948/51; The alphabetical cuneiform texts from Ras Shamra published in "Le Palais Royal d'Ugarit" Vol. II, 1957; Die Flügelsonne als künstlerisches Motiv und als religiöses Symbol; Mémorial Lagrange; Otto Kern † 31. Januar 1942; Wilhelm Gesenius als Archäologe; Wilhelm Gesenius und die Palästinawissenschaft; Wilhelm Gesenius 1786–1842; Neue Forschungen zum 'Ebed Jahwe-Problem; Israelitisch-philistäische Grenzverschiebungen von David bis aus die Assyrerzeit; Die Bedeutung der Funde von Ras Schamra für die Geschichte des Altertums; Mythus und Sage in den Ras-Schamra-Texten; Die Wohnsitze der Götter von Ras Schamra; Ein neuer Beleg für die Funktion der Sonnen-göttin von Arinna als Oberhaupt des hethitischen Staates; Ugaritisches 1–4; Christus-Monogramm und phönizisches "Hermes-Emblem".

G.W.A.

FRIEDRICH, G. (ed. by): *Theologisches Wörterbuch zum Neuen Testament* (begun by G. Kittel). (Band VII. Doppellieferung 11/12). 1963. Pp. 128. (Kohlhammer, Stuttgart. Price: DM. 9.20).

This double number begins with an article by G. Bertram on *stereos* and its cognates, relevant because of the LXX translation of *raqi'a* by *stereoma*. The article by W. Grundmann on *ste-phanos*, *stephanoō* deals briefly with *'aṭarah* in the Old Testament. The same author is also responsible for the article on *steko*, *histemi*, the latter verb representing a number of important Hebrew verbs. In particular attention is drawn to the linking of *histemi* in the LXX with *diatheke*, *horkos*, *logos* and *entole* which is of some theological importance. In the article by Betz on *stigma* there are interesting remarks about tattooing and other distinguishing signs in the Old Testament. The article by U. Wilckens on *stole* has a section on usage in the LXX. More important are the relevant sections of the article by K. Weiss on *stoma* and of the article by O. Bauernfeind on *strateuomenai* and its many cognates. In his article on *strepho* and its cognates G. Bertram discusses, though very briefly, the usage of *shubh* and certain other Hebrew words which correspond to this large group of Greek words in the LXX. U. Wilckens writes the concluding article, on *stulos*. Though not strictly relevant, mention should perhaps also be made of the article on *stoicheo* and its cognates, in particular of the long section on *stoicheion*.

N.W.P.

*GRANT, F. C. & ROWLEY, H. H. (ed. by): *Dictionary of the Bible*, 2nd edition (original edition by James Hastings). 1963. xvi+1060+4+16 maps. (T. & T. Clark, Edinburgh. Price: 100s. 0d.).

The fact that this book appeared just too late to be included in the 1963 *Book List* has given the reviewer the opportunity to consult it both extensively and intensively over the past year. In every way it appears to be at least as good as its predecessor. Highly skilful editing has produced a successful and harmonious blend of old and new. Some articles are unchanged, others revised, others rewritten, and others devoted to subjects (e.g., Dead Sea Scrolls, Mari, Myth and Ritual, Ras Shamra), which did not appear in the original edition. The coloured maps are beautifully clear and a delight to use. Altogether this is a triumph of scholarship, of popularization, and of editing.

G.W.A.

GREENSLADE, S. L. (ed. by): *The Cambridge History of the Bible: The West from the Reformation to the Present Day*. 1963. Pp. x+590+48 plates. (Cambridge University Press. Price: 45s. 0d.; $8.50).

Canon Greenslade has gathered a strong team of British, American, and Continental experts, and each article is written with authority and out of a full and scholarly knowledge. The Editor and Dean Weigle cover the history of English versions, and shorter accounts are given of the major European Bibles. There are chapters on the Bible in the Reformation (R. H. Bainton), the Religion of the Protestants (N. Sykes), the Bible in the Roman Catholic Church from Trent to the Present Day (F. J. Crehan, S.J.), the Bible and the Missionary (E. Fenn), and the Printed Bible (M. H. Black). Of even greater interest to members will be the chapters entitled: Biblical Scholarship (B. Hall), Criticism and Theological Use of the Bible, 1700–1950 (W. Neil), the Rise of Modern Biblical Scholarship and Recent Discussion of the Authority of the Bible (A. Richardson), and the appendices on aids to the study of the Bible (D. R. Jones). There is a useful bibliography. When the companion volume *From Jerome to the Renaissance* appears, libraries, public and private, will have an admirable work of reference covering the whole history of our Bible.

W.D.McH.

Hebrew Union College Annual, Vol. XXXIV (ed. by Elias L. Epstein). 1963. Pp. 250+40 (in Hebrew)+1 plate+portrait. (Hebrew Union College, Cincinnati).

This volume, dedicated to the memory of Dr. Julius Lewy, contains eleven articles. The articles which have a direct bearing on the Bible are: 'The "Bloody Husband" (?) (Ex. iv 24–26) Once Again' (J. Morgenstern); 'Studies in the Book of Samuel (chapter iii)' (M. Tsevat). Those having an indirect bearing are: 'A Seven Day Ritual in the Old Babylonian Cult at Larsa' (Edwin C. Kingsbury); 'Pseudo-Eupolemus' Two Greek Fragments on the Life of Abraham (Ben Zion Wacholder); 'A Suggested Interpretation of the Biblical Philosophy of History' (John Briggs Curtis). Biblical scholars may also find some interest in 'Aspects of the New Year Liturgy' (Leon J. Liebreich); 'Abrabanel on Prophecy in the Moreh Nebhukhim' (Alvin J. Reines). The other studies are: 'The Medical Profession in the Light of the Cairo Geniza Documents' (S. D. Goitein); 'Eibenschütziana' (B. Brilling); 'Two Early Jewish Polemicists on American Soil' (Judah M. Rosenthal); 'R. Moses Ha-Kohen of Lunel's Strictures of the work of Maimonides' (Samuel Atlas) (in Hebrew). At the end comes an index to H.U.C.A., vols. I-XXXIII. The articles are of a high scholarly quality.

M.W.

MACDONALD, J. (ed. by): *The Annual of Leeds University Oriental Society*, Vol. III (1961–62). 1963. Pp. 120. (E. J. Brill, Leiden. Price: Fl. 18).

Particular attention may be drawn to the following articles: G. Fohrer, The Origin, Composition and Tradition of Isaiah i-xxxix. This is a closely packed, carefully reasoned presentation. Seven Isaianic collections are distinguished, and four non-Isaianic complexes. The dates of the collections range from the end of the Syro-Ephraimite war to the post-exilic period; the whole assumed final shape by the fourth century. Certain ritual considerations determined the writing down, for the recital releases the divine power inherent in the prophetic word. N. H. Snaith in The Hebrew Root G'L(I), notes its use with God as subject chiefly in Psalms and Isa. xxxv; xl-lv; lx-lxii, and its meaning as the enforcement or restoration of a lapsed right or claim, reverting to the original owner. G. E. Weil writes on 'Un Fragment de Okhlah Palestinienne', the Cambridge Ms.heb. D.1, 12. G. Vermes discusses the Targumic versions of Gen. iv. 3–16 and finds that Onkelos is closely related to the Palestinian tradition and indicates the importance of Targumic material for New Testament study. The editor concludes the volume with a list of Samaritan studies produced by members of this School.

A.S.H.

MULLO WEIR, C. J. (ed. by): *Transactions of Glasgow University Oriental Society*, Vol. xix (1961–1962). 1963. Pp. iv+87. (Printed for the Society by E. J. Brill, Leiden. Price: 18s. 0d.).

Three of the contributions to this volume are of direct interest to the *Alttestamentler*. In 'Temple and Land', R. E. Clements offers an interesting interpretation of certain passages in the

Psalter which speak of dwelling with Yahweh. W. McKane presents a careful study of $ge'ulla$ and levirate marriage in Ruth. R. A. Stewart surveys mediaeval Hebrew interpretations of Psalm cx. H. C. Thomson writes on '*Shophet* and *Mishpat* in the Book of Judges'. H. G. Farmer contributes two articles: 'The Arabian Influence on European Music' and 'Two Genizah Fragments on Music'; and J. R. Buchanan (who has been a member of the Society since 1904) gives a sketch of the history of the Druzes to the time of Fakhr-al-Din II.

G.W.A.

NOTH, M.: *Developing Lines of Theological Thought in Germany*, trans. by J. Bright. (Fourth Annual Bibliographical Lecture). 1963. Pp. 30. (Union Theological Seminary in Virginia).

This survey, in which particular but not exclusive attention is paid to the work of German Protestant Old Testament scholars, gives a most valuable account of current trends and is admirably documented, so that the reader is enabled to see both the wood and the trees.

G.W.A.

Die Ou Testamentiese Werkgemeenskap in Suid-Afrika: Studies on the Book of Ezekiel. Papers read at 4th Meeting held at Bloemfontein, 31 January–3 February, 1961. 1961. Pp. 54. (Obtainable from Professor A. H. van Zyl, P.O. Box 185, Lynn East, Pretoria, South Africa. Price: 60 cents; 6s. 0d.).

Four South African scholars read the papers included here at the fourth meeting of their Society, held at Bloemfontein early in 1961. I. H. Eybers has a well-documented paper on 'The Book of Ezekiel and the Sect of Qumran' in the course of which he shows the prophet's influence on the vocabulary but particularly on the conception of the priesthood at Qumran. In 'The Tyre Passages in the Book of Ezekiel (Chapters 26, 27, 28: 1–19)' J. H. Kroeze gathers together some details of the history of Tyre, attempts an exegesis of the texts, and refers to some of the mythical traits present. A. van Selms speaks of the 'Literary Criticism of Ezekiel as a Theological Problem', the problem being really that of the nature or limits of inspiration. He is able to justify literary criticism on the ground that Article 3 of the Confessio Belgica differentiates between the authority of the original oral prophecy and its subsequent writing. Ezekiel is found to have delivered his prophecies originally in poetic form, orally, but later to have written them down and expanded or interpreted them in a less authoritative form. In the last article, A. H. van Zyl discusses 'Solidarity and Individualism in Ezekiel'. He finds that there is still a great deal of the 'corporate personality' concept in Ezekiel, and, though he did develop the theme of individual responsibility, this by no means began with him.

D.R.Ap-T.

Die Ou Testamentiese Werkgemeenskap in Suid-Afrika: New Light on some Old Testament Problems. Papers read at 5th Meeting held at the University of South Africa, Pretoria, 30 January–2 February, 1962. 1962. Pp. 64. (Obtainable from Professor A. H. van Zyl, P.O. Box 185, Lynn East, Pretoria, South Africa. Price: 75 cents.).

This time the South African Society for Old Testament Study has not confined itself to a single theme. I. H. Eybers begins with 'Some Light on the Canon of the Qumran Sect', in which he seeks to evaluate the quotations from, and allusions to, books of the Old Testament and Apocrypha found in the Qumran scrolls but is cautious as to the results. J. H. Kroeze puts forward 'Remarks and Questions regarding some Creation-passages in the Old Testament' in a somewhat disjointed fashion, but making some observations of value. After noting occurrences of *'amarti* in the sense of 'declare openly', 'confess (faith or guilt)', or simply 'think', C. J. Labuschagne, in an interesting short note, 'Some Remarks on the Translation and Meaning of *'amarti* in the Psalms', suggests that in at least five instances the verb means 'I wrongly or mistakenly thought'. B. J. van der Merwe in 'The Laying on of Hands in the Old Testament' comes to the conclusion that this custom was something of an innovation and, in connexion with the sacrifice, was intended to indicate the whole-hearted involvement of the giver. A. H. van Zyl studies 'Isaiah 24–27: their Date of Origin', and, after a definition of Apocalyptic, comes down against any such description being applied to these chapters. He defends their Isaianic authorship though he would find still older songs incorporated in them. Finally P. A. Verhoef in 'Some Notes on Typological Exegesis' pleads for the validity of a reasonable typological exegesis based on the revelationary character of the Bible, confined to the scheme of redemptive history but stressing the reality of the history as much as the redemption, and acknowledging the great difficulty of defining exactly what is to be regarded as typological.

D.R.Ap-T.

RIESENFELD, H. (ed. by): *Svensk exegetisk årsbok* xxvii (1962). 1963. Pp. 160. (C. W. K. Gleerup, Lund. Price: Sw. kr. 10).

In this issue Å. Sjöberg, who took part in Professor H. Lenzen's excavations at Uruk-Warka in 1962, gives a general account of that and other Sumerian cities. J. Jeremias discusses the Lord's Prayer in the light of recent research. K. H. Rengstorf writes on Paul and the earliest Christian community at Rome. E. Lövestam considers *apoluein* as a term applied to divorce. The above articles are in Swedish. In German there are the following: E. Lövestam on the title 'Son of David' in the New Testament; B. Gärtner on Paul and Barnabas at Lystra; and B. Gerhardsson on 'Die Boten Gottes und die Apostel Christi'. There are also reviews, and a useful survey by Å. Runmark, of some recent works on Jeremiah.

G.W.A.

ROWLEY, H. H.: *From Moses to Qumran.* Studies in the Old Testament. 1963. Pp. xiv+294. (Lutterworth Press, London. Price: 30s. 0d.).

This collection contains the following articles which have appeared elsewhere, mostly in journals or in volumes of essays:

The Authority of the Bible; Moses and Monotheism; The Meaning of Sacrifice in the Old Testament; Ritual and the Hebrew Prophets; The Book of Job and its Meaning; The Prophet Jeremiah and the Book of Deuteronomy; Jewish Proselyte Baptism and the Baptism of John; The Qumran Sect and Christian Origins. Although it is unlikely that any serious student of the Old Testament is unacquainted with these papers, in reissuing them Dr. Rowley has done his colleagues a service, for, quite apart from the modifications in the text and the additions to the footnotes, the convenience of having the eight essays in this form makes for ease of reference. His balanced, learned, and well-documented discussions of these major Old Testament topics will now be available to a much wider circle of readers. W.D.McH.

ROWLEY, H. H.: *Men of God. Studies in Old Testament History and Prophecy.* 1963. Pp. xii+306. (Thomas Nelson and Sons, Edinburgh. Price: 42s. 0d.).

In this volume Professor Rowley has collected eight of his John Rylands Library lectures, published originally in the Library's *Bulletin*. These lectures have all been reviewed in the *Book List* as follows: Moses and the Decalogue (in 1952), Elijah on Mount Carmel (in 1961), The Marriage of Hosea (in 1957), Hezekiah's Reform and Rebellion (in 1963), The Early Prophecies of Jeremiah in their Setting (in 1963), The Book of Ezekiel in Modern Study (in 1954), Nehemiah's Mission and its Background (in 1956), and Sanballat and the Samaritan Temple (in 1956). The text of the lectures has been modified occasionally and a few further references and additions have been made to the notes, and there are indexes of Subjects, Authors, and Texts. Students will be grateful to Professor Rowley for making more readily accessible these important and well-documented contributions to Old Testament studies. L.A.P.

*ROWLEY, H. H. (ed. by): *A Companion to the Bible*, 2nd edition (original edition edited by T. W. Manson). 1963. Pp. xii+628+6 maps. (T. & T. Clark, Edinburgh. Price: 35s. 0d.).

A notice of the first edition of this invaluable work appeared in *Book List*, 1940, p. 8. The general plan of the new edition remains much the same; but the book has been almost entirely rewritten by an almost entirely new team of contributors. In substance, scope, and approach, the articles reflect the important developments of the past quarter-century. Not the least valuable feature is the bibliographies. The maps are distinctly better than those in the original edition. It need hardly be said that the editing is impeccable. G.W.A.

Studia theologica cura ordinum theologorum Scandinavicorum edita. Vol. 16, Fasc. 2 (1962). 1963. Pp. 109–188. Vol. 17, Fasc. 1 (1963). 1963. Pp. 1–76. Vol. 17, Fasc. 2 (1963). 1963. Pp. 77–188. (Aarhus University, Aarhus. Price: D. kr. 30 each volume or D. kr. 20 each fascicle).

Vol. 16, Fasc. 2 contains two articles (both in German) of direct interest to the *Alttestamentler*. S. Granild offers a finely balanced discussion of the relation of Jeremiah and Deuteronomy; and K. T. Andersen contributes an article entitled 'Der Gott meines Vaters', which is a very useful examination of Alt's well-known hypothesis and the criticisms levelled against it. Among the contents of the other fascicles mention may be made of 'The Apocryphon of John and Genesis', by S. Giversen in Vol. 17, Fasc. 1; and in Vol. 17, Fasc. 2 of 'Are the Essenes Referred to in the Sibylline Oracles?' by B. Noack, and S. Giversen's 'Nag-Hammadi Bibliography, 1948-1963', which runs to some 46 pages.

G.W.A.

THOMAS, D. W. and MCHARDY, W. D. (ed. by): *Hebrew and Semitic Studies presented to Godfrey Rolles Driver in celebration of his seventieth birthday, 20 August, 1962.* 1963. Pp. viii+206+2 plates. (Clarendon Press, Oxford. Price: 75s. 0d.).

The essays in this volume are written in honour of one of our most distinguished members by scholars from ten different countries. W. F. Albright maintains (interestingly, but not always very convincingly) that, though the Song of Songs dates from the fifth or fourth century B.C., it contains fragments which are shown to be much older by their similarity in style and subject matter to Bronze Age texts. P. A. H. de Boer's article prints and discusses a Syro-Hexaplar text of 1 Sam. ii. 1–10 from a manuscript at Mosul. A. Díez-Macho describes some Hebrew manuscripts of a character sometimes attributed to the Ben Naphtali school; however, he thinks that they do not belong to this school and that their affinities with it are explained by a common dependence on the Palestinian tradition of pointing. A. Dupont-Sommer publishes an Aramaic letter to a certain Yedoniah which is inscribed on an ostracon from Elephantiné. C. J. Gadd's article contains part of a Sumerian lament on the fall of Ur; he believes that the book of Lamentations and other passages in the Old Testament 'are manifestly under the influence of' such texts. H. L. Ginsberg argues that the Hebrew words *peri* and *shoresh* sometimes mean 'branch' and 'stock' respectively. C. H. Gordon maintains that Abraham was a merchant-prince from a North Mesopotamian city named Ur, and that much light is thrown on the patriarchal narratives by texts of the fifteenth to the thirteenth century B.C. E. Hammershaimb examines the Hebrew use of the infinitive absolute and compares it with similar idioms in the cognate languages. S. Mowinckel defends the view that *shaḥal* is sometimes to be translated 'serpent'. C. Rabin challenges the theory that the Semitic dialects came 'into being by ethnic "waves" of emigrants from the original home of the Semites'. H. H. Rowley studies the Aramaic of the Genesis Apocryphon and concludes that the language 'is very close to that of the Aramaic parts of Daniel, though slightly later'. W. Rudolph contributes a textual and exegetical study of the prophecy about Moab in Isaiah xv-xvi, the nucleus of which comes, he thinks, from the time of Jeroboam II's attack (2 Kings xiv. 25) and is *'die älteste Schriftprophetie'* in the Old Testament. G. Ryckmans examines the office of *qayl* (which he renders *'préposé'*) in pre-Islamic South Arabia. T. W. Thacker compares the use of the verb 'to be' in Semitic languages and in Egyptian, and claims that the 'Semitic languages

can often throw light on problems of Egyptian grammar and syntax'. J. Ziegler investigates the reasons why a reviser modified the Greek version of Ecclesiasticus; he suggests that the affinity between the reviser's vocabulary and that of the New Testament and the younger Greek translations of the Old Testament helps us to date the revision. The volume ends with a bibliography of Professor Driver's many writings.
J.A.E.

WEGENER, G. S.: *6,000 Years of the Bible*, trans. by Margaret Shenfield. 1963. Pp. 352 incl. 223 ills. (Hodder and Stoughton. Price: 35s. 0d.).

This book was originally published in German in 1958. The English title may be repellent to many readers; and this attitude may be exacerbated when they find the title virtually contradicted within the book (e.g., pp. 48, 125). Beyond that, they may find in the first chapter a few statements which they adjudge to be loosely expressed or otherwise open to criticism. The book begins historically at *c.* 4,000 B.C. as the approximate date of the Flood, although surely it was not the date or place of that event, but the tradition concerning it and the interpretation put upon it which are significant for the story of the Bible.

The section of the book which deals with the Old Testament is somewhat scrappy and has little body; but thereafter the story of the Bible really begins to flow. The New Testament books and their canonization; the multiplication of Gospels of Jesus and collections of His sayings in the early Church and the assault upon it of doctrinal heresies; the versions of the Bible, the work of the mediaeval monks in making copies of it, the printed Bible; Luther, Wyclif, Tyndale and the rest; AV, RV, RSV, NEB; translation of the Bible into many tongues and distribution of it to many lands — all this and much more is here, graphically, skilfully and interestingly told and generously illustrated. An unanticipated final chapter is added for good measure, in which Count Tischendorf, modern archaeologists, vendors of manuscripts, and forgers of them are duly mentioned; and the Lachish Letters, the Oxyrhynchus Papyri, and the Dead Sea Scrolls, as well as infra-red photography and the carbon 14 test, all have their place in the crowded scene.
J.M.

WÜRTHWEIN, E. & KAISER, O. (ed. by): *Tradition und Situation*. Studien zur alttestamentlichen Prophetie. Artur Weiser zum 70. Geburtstag am 18.11.1963 dargebracht von Kollegen, Freunden und Schülern. 1963. Pp. VIII+156 incl. 1 portrait. (Vandenhoeck & Ruprecht, Göttingen. Price: DM.15).

These studies in Old Testament prophecy have been prepared as a *Festschrift* for A. Weiser's seventieth birthday by scholars who are contributors to the series of *Das Alte Testament Deutsch*. W. Beyerlin writes on the origin of the historical framework in the Book of Judges, arguing that it is pre-Deuteronomic, and goes back ultimately to the lawsuit motif in the covenant cult. W. Eichrodt examines the prophetic office of watchman from Ezekiel xxxiii, and K. Elliger studies the use and interpretation of the prophet Malachi in the preaching of the Church. K. Galling presents an interpretation of Isaiah xxi in the light of the recently discovered Nabonidus inscription from Harran, and H. W. Hertzberg raises a large question mark against the claim that intercession was an official aspect of the prophetic office. O. Kaiser examines how the words of the prophets may be understood as the Word of God, especially in the light of recent traditio-historical studies, and N. W. Porteous writes of the part played by the prophets in actualising the traditions of the covenant, and their connection with the origins of Deuteronomy. H. Ringgren examines some of the prophetic descriptions of the divine wrath, and E. Würthwein has a valuable fresh approach to bring to the prophetic criticism of the cult, arguing that it derived from a common tradition originating in a negative imitation of cultic assurances given for rites of penitence and fasting. W. Zimmerli studies the words of the two great prophets of the exile, which promise universal recognition of the reality of Yahweh. Altogether this is an attractive and stimulating collection of essays, worthily rendering honour to one to whom honour is due.

R.E.C.

ZIMMERLI, W.: *Gottes Offenbarung*. Gesammelte Aufsätze zum Alten Testament. (Theologische Bücherei: Neudrucke und Berichte aus dem 20. Jahrhundert. Band 19. Altes Testament). 1963. Pp. 336. (Chr. Kaiser Verlag, München. Price: DM. 15).

This is a valuable addition to a well-known series which makes available a collection of some of the studies of leading Old Testament scholars which are no longer easily obtainable. The main theme in the series here presented is God's self-revelation, the first three studies being entitled 'Ich bin Yahwe', 'Erkenntnis Gottes nach dem Buche Ezechiel' (the longest of the studies in the book), and 'Das Wort des göttlichen Selbsterweises (Erweiswort), eine prophetische Gattung'. The interest in Ezekiel shown in the second of these is further illustrated in three others: 'Das Gotteswort des Ezechiel', 'Die Eigenart der prophetischen Rede des Ezechiel' and ' "Leben" und "Tod" im Buche des Propheten Ezechiel'. Two others are more or less related prophetical studies, 'Der "neue Exodus" in der Verkündigung der beiden grossen Exilspropheten' and 'Zur Sprache Tritojesajas'; and with these may be mentioned 'Die Weisung des Alten Testaments zum Geschäft der Sprache'. There are included three articles on Pentateuchal subjects, which it is good to have in this context of predominantly theological studies: 'Sinaibund und Abrahambund', 'Das zweite Gebot' and 'Das Gesetz im Alten Testament'. The two which complete the selection are 'Ort und Grenze der Weisheit im Rahmen der alttestamentlichen Theologie' and 'Die Frage des Reichen nach dem ewigen Leben'. To make such a selection of articles raises embarrassing questions, but the most inaccessible ones, if they are not now outdated, should, as in this case, be given the preference.

J.M.

EDUCATIONAL

ACKROYD, P. R.: *The Old Testament Tradition* (Problems in Christian Education, No. 7). 1963. Pp. 24. (The National Society, London. Price: 1s. 6d.).

The substance of this pamphlet was originally delivered as a lecture under the title 'Recent Studies in the Old Testament

and their Bearing on Religious Education'. The meaning of the Old Testament religious tradition is exemplified with reference to the Exodus, the prophets, and the post-exilic ordering of life. Here is a suggestive and stimulating treatment of an important theme.
L.A.P.

FILTHAUT, T.: *Israel in der Christlichen Unterweisung* (Schriften zur Katechetik, Band III). 1963. Pp. 174. (Kösel-Verlag, München. Price: cloth, DM. 10.80; paper, DM. 8.80).

This symposium consists of six essays concerned with the attitude of Christians to Jews as reflected in catechetical and Biblical instruction. Its background is the Nazi persecution of the Jews and the Eichmann trial. One essay gives the detailed results of recent investigations into the attitude of pupils of secondary school age, revealing the absence of a distinctively Christian as opposed to a merely humanitarian attitude to the persecution. Other essays examine the references to the Old Testament and to the Jews in the Catechismus Romanus and the new Catholic Catechism of 1955, and deal with the subject in catechetical and Biblical teaching generally, and in the liturgy. This interesting and valuable discussion is by no means irrelevant to our own Biblical teaching; for it is doubtful whether the present emphasis on Biblical theology has deepened our pupils' understanding of the relation of Judaism to the Cross of Christ and of the Christian attitude to modern Judaism.

L.A.P.

*HILLIARD, F. H.: *Behold the Land. A Pictorial Atlas of the Bible.* 1963. Pp. 64. (George Philip and Son, Ltd., London. Price: 15s. 0d.).

This attractive and colourful volume, of which two-thirds is devoted to the Old Testament period, is an illustrated guide to the historical background of the Bible that should make a strong appeal to pupils in Secondary Modern Schools and in the lower forms of Grammar Schools. The maps are simple and graphic and like the drawings, photographs, and Biblical references, well chosen as useful aids to classroom teaching. This is a first rate book, admirably designed for its purpose, and is warmly commended.
L.A.P.

*HODGSON, C.: *Genesis in the Dock*, A Mock Trial of the first eleven chapters of Genesis. 1963. Pp. 64. (The Religious Education Press, Ltd., Wallington, Surrey. Price: 4s. 6d.).

This booklet presents a dramatic examination of the origin-stories of Genesis i-xi in the form of a mock trial, in six sessions, where the witnesses called include Old Testament Scholar, Theologian, Biblical Archaeologist, the Editor J, and the Priestly Editor. There is an appendix of questions for discussion. Sixth Form teachers, and leaders of Youth clubs and Bible classes will find here a lively and ingenious presentation of the modern understanding of these stories.
L.A.P.

*HOLROYD, G. H.: *A Dramatic Old Testament Book* (II). The History of the People of God and of His Self-Revelation to His People. 1963. Pp. xiv+306. (Macmillan, London. Price: 12s. 6d.).

The first volume appeared in 1960 (see *Book List*, 1961, p. 15). This second book is intended to cater for the third and fourth years in the Secondary School. It covers in general the requirements of the Agreed Syllabuses. In the first volume the story of Israel was taken up to the death of Solomon. This present volume completes the series, and its sub-title explains the approach: 'The History of the People of God and of His self-revelation to His People'. The book contains plays, dramatic interludes, conversation pieces, and choral speaking. There are many interesting illustrations in the text and also a time chart and map. Mr. Holroyd has himself had very considerable experience as a teacher, and he has already composed upwards of a dozen successful books of this type. N.H.S.

*JONES, C. M.: *Teaching the Bible Today*. A Book for Students and Teachers. 1963. Pp. 240. (S.C.M. Press Ltd., London. Price: 13s. 6d.).

This new paperback may be aptly described as the Bible teacher's *Vade Mecum*. The author, an experienced and skilful teacher, deals with every aspect of his subject — geography, archaeology, history, religion, theology, and problems of communication. His exposition is always clear and interesting; the non-specialist teacher will especially welcome the book, and even the experienced teacher will find here much of value and will probably gain fresh insights from reading it and may wish to keep it for reference.

L.A.P.

ARCHAEOLOGY AND EPIGRAPHY

AMIRAN, RUTH: *The Ancient Pottery of Eretz Yisrael* (in Hebrew). 1963. Pp. 366 incl. 358 photographs +101 plates. (The Bialik Institute and the Israel Exploration Society, Jerusalem).

This scholarly work, delightfully produced, is dedicated to Prof. W. F. Albright, whose influence is felt in a number of its pages. It deals with the ancient pottery of Eretz Yisrael from its beginning in the Neolithic Period to the end of the First Temple, with eleven periods. Each of these periods is discussed in a special chapter. Following, come three additional chapters, the first giving a representative group of Ammonite pottery, the second, that of Ezion Geber, and the third, pottery vessels in cultic use. The book also contains an enlightening introduction, telling about the nature of the work and the methods used in composing it; corpora of pottery; Petrie's system of sequence dating; and some notes on pottery making. Hebrew scholars who have no special knowledge of the subject, may find interest in its fascinating terminology. M.W.

DONNER, H. & RÖLLIG, W.: *Kanaanäische und Aramäische Inschriften*. (With contribution by O. Rössler). Band 1. Texte. 1962. Pp. XVI+54. (Otto Harrassowitz, Wiesbaden. Price: DM. 12).

This book promises to meet the long-felt need for an up-to-date work comparable to G. A. Cooke's *Text-Book of North-Semitic Inscriptions* of sixty years ago. This first volume prints the text of 276 Phoenician, Punic, Neo-Punic, Moabite, Hebrew, and Aramaic inscriptions; the Aramaic part has been prepared by Donner and the rest by Röllig. Two further volumes will contain translations of, and a commentary on, the selected texts. Until these volumes appear, it will not be possible to estimate the full value of the work, but already the editors and the publisher have performed a valuable service to Semitic scholarship by making available a good selection of inscriptions at a reasonable price.

J.A.E.

DUNAND, M. & DURU, R. with SEGOND, A.-M.: *Oumm el-'Amed, une ville de l'époque hellénistique aux Echelles de Tyr* (Études et Documents d'Archéologie Tome IV). 2 vols. 1962. Texte, Pp. II+248 incl. 90 figs. Atlas, CVII plates. (Librairie d'Amérique et d'Orient Adrien-Maisonneuve, Paris. Price: Paper, $39.80; cloth, $57.14).

Umm el-'Amed on the coast of Lebanon South of Tyre is known to Semitists from 16 short Phoenician inscriptions, mostly votive. These, studied afresh (ch. VIII) with relation to their accompanying sculptures (ch. VII) and in their archaeological context, will chiefly interest Semitic scholars, who will also appreciate the discussion and excellent illustration of sacred symbols from the temple of Milk-Astart, the chief feature of the site. Though traces of occupation were discovered from the 8th century there is nothing appreciable before the 5th century. From that date the site with its sanctuary flourished in the Greek and Byzantine periods. The text, which is well-illustrated by figures, is accompanied by a volume of 107 loose-leaf plates.

J.G.

FRANKEN, H. J. & FRANKEN-BATTERSHILL, C. A.: *A Primer of Old Testament Archaeology.* 1963. Pp. xiv+180+60 figs.+XXIV plates+ 1 map. (E. J. Brill, Leiden. Price: paper, Fl. 18; cloth, Fl. 22).

'This book', as the authors state, 'is written mainly for theological students and aims to put in their hands the tools for extracting relevant material from excavation reports which has direct bearing on their work of understanding and re-interpreting the Bible in the 20th century and . . . to sort out the sensational from the sound observation'. Such caution is commendable and the volume is a welcome contribution, though a somewhat negative one, which will hardly encourage the theological student who is not already interested in the minutiae of material evidence of field archaeology. Dr. Franken is obviously a disciple of Miss Kenyon in Palestinian archaeology, and both in the initial discussion of archaeological method and in the cautious reappraisal of selected material in the latter part of the book he emphasizes soil stratigraphy, placing typology in second place. While careful observation of soil strata is necessary for a just appraisal of details in a limited region, many may feel that the authors in their justifiable enthusiasm for new methods do less than justice to the progress in comparative typology of older archaeologists, of whose methods they are so critical, despite the fact that they themselves obviously make practical use of their fruitful results. Useful as this study is, it suffers through its failure to relate Palestine to the larger context of the Near East, of which it was but a province, and in its limitation in the discussion of practical problems to the Iron Age. The work would have been greatly enhanced by a section on epigraphy. The book unfortunately is marred by frequent mis-spellings, and at one point (p. 125) through careless proof-reading the sense completely breaks down. It is a pity too that the progressive work of Israeli archaeologists should receive so little notice.

J.G.

*HARRISON, R. K.: *Archaeology of the Old Testament* (Teach Yourself Books). 1963. Pp. xiv+162+12 plates+2 maps. (The English Universities Press, London. Price: 7s. 6d.).

The book follows the pattern of this series in giving an elementary introduction for non-professional students. Arranged historically, it covers Mesopotamian origins, the Patriarchal age, Israel and Egypt, the settlement in Canaan, from Monarchy to Exile, Exile and Restoration, and the Dead Sea Scrolls and the Old Testament. Notes are gathered into 39 pages at the end of the book. There is a short bibliography of works not mentioned in the notes, a short index, and 12 plates. J.N.S.

JAMME, A.: *Sabaean Inscriptions from Maḥram Bilqîs* (Mârib). (Publications of the American Formation for the Study of Man, III). 1962. Pp. xix+480 incl. 3 maps and 64 photographic plates. (The Johns Hopkins Press, Baltimore. Price: £8 0s. 0d.).

This magnificent, though expensive, volume contains the text of over three hundred Sabaean inscriptions copied by the author in the American expedition to Maḥram Bilqîs, the famous Mârib, in the Yemen in the winter of 1951–2; unfortunately, the work was prematurely cut short by unfriendly authorities, but he managed to save his copies and many photographs of the texts but, in his hurried departure, had to leave almost all the squeezes behind. Even so the volume of work done is imposing. The texts are published in transliteration, translated and furnished with ample notes. The readings are, where possible, checked by the photographs and careful notes taken at the time when they were copied. The palaeographical part of the work is completed by plates of letters (oddly numbered A–E and I–P) made from careful drawings set beside others taken from other texts published elsewhere. The contents of the inscriptions are also analyzed in order to bring together such historical and local information as can be gleaned from them; on the strength of this information the Sabaean state is estimated to have lasted from $c.$ 819 B.C. (which may be open to dispute) to $c.$ A.D. 440. Finally, admirable indices of texts and proper names as well as a bibliography of modern authors' works and an exhaustive glossary are included; this last part alone will make the work indispensable to all students of the South-Arabian inscriptions. G.R.D.

PFEIFFER, C. F.: *Ras Shamra and the Bible*. (Baker Studies in Biblical Archaeology). 1962. Pp. 74 incl. 13 ills. and 2 maps. (Baker Book House, Michigan. Price: $1.50).

Professor Pfeiffer has here produced a useful digest of Ras Shamra researches by the leading experts for popular consumption, and in so doing has done a service for interested laymen and general students as well as for the scholars whose views he so clearly communicates. He might have done a greater service had he cited his sources more fully. After an account of the excavation of Ras Shamra in rather too broad outline and with some inaccuracies he sets Ugarit in the historical context of the ancient Near East, then proceeds to his major theme, the religion, sociology, and literature of Ugarit and the value of the new discoveries for Old Testament studies. The work is unfortunately marred by inaccurate transliteration of aspirate consonants, and perhaps with respect to the general reader, is much less critical of experts' views than they themselves are.

J.G.

PRITCHARD, J. B.: *The Bronze Age Cemetery at Gibeon.* (Museum Monographs). 1963. Pp. x+182 incl. 100 figs. (The University Museum, University of Pennsylvania, Philadelphia. Price: $3.50).

This excellent description (with illustrations of the tombs and their contents) continues the technical record of the excavations at el-Jib contained in the previous publication, *The Water System of Gibeon* (see *Book List*, 1963, p. 16). The author concludes that the tombs were hewn in M.B. I., some being reused in M.B. II and L.B. A popular account of the first four seasons of work has appeared in the author's *Gibeon Where the Sun Stood Still: The Discovery of the Biblical City* (see *Book List*, 1963, p. 16).

J.N.S.

*THOMPSON, J. A.: *The Bible and Archaeology.* 1962. Pp. xxiv+468+ many ills.+9 maps+5 charts. (The Paternoster Press. Exeter. Price: 30s. 0d.).

This book contains works first published as *Archaeology and the Old Testament*, 1957, *Archaeology and the Pre-Christian Centuries*, 1958, and *Archaeology and the New Testament*, 1960. Dr. Thompson has rearranged the material and added fresh information, new maps, photographs, and references to more recent works. The book is well written and indexed. The author has practical experience in archaeology and in teaching, and holds degrees in Arts, Science, Divinity and Education together with the Ph.D. of Cambridge University.

J.N.S.

HISTORY AND GEOGRAPHY

AHARONI, Y.: *The Land of Israel in Biblical Times* (in Hebrew). 1962. Pp. 374 incl. 43 maps. (The Bialik Institute. Jerusalem Academic Press).

This book, by a lecturer of the Hebrew University, known for his geographical-archaeological studies and excavations of the 'Bar-Kokhba Caves', deals in a praiseworthy scholarly fashion with the geographical history of Eretz Israel in the Biblical Era. It makes use of the vast material about the Ancient East which has accumulated since George Adam Smith's work over seventy years ago on the same subject, dwelling, however, on historical-archaeological data rather more than on geographical descriptions. It contains forty-three illuminating maps fully bearing on the appropriate matters discussed. Towards the end come a chronological table of Eretz Israel and its neighbouring countries (Mesopotamia, Anatolia and Syria), and a list of ancient and modern names (vocalized) of settlements and their locality in the Biblical Era.

The book, which has the advantage of being written by a scholar possessing a first-hand acquaintance with the country, is well produced, as befits the high standard set by Mosad Bialik, and ends with two indexes, the one Biblical and the other geographical.

M.W.

ALBRIGHT, W. F.: *The Biblical Period from Abraham to Ezra.* (Harper Torchbooks: The Cloister Library, TB 102). 1963. Pp. 120 (paperback). (Harper and Row, New York. Price: $1.35; in U.K. 10s. 6d.).

An expansion of an essay 'The Biblical Period', first published in *The Jews: Their History, Culture, and Religion* (ed. L. Finkelstein, 1949) (see *Book List*, 1951, p. 8; *Eleven Years*, p. 303). This essay was also published separately at that time. There are ten chapters dealing in turn with every 'age' of Hebrew religion and history, and ending with the beginnings of the development of Greek culture in the near east. Considerable use is made of the results of excavations, including the author's and the recent excavations by General Yadin at Hazor. The book is thoroughly up-to-date, written in a clear and popular style for the general reader as much as for the student, and all with the author's usual brilliance and efficiency.

N.H.S.

ANATI, E.: *Palestine before the Hebrews.* A History, from the earliest arrival of man to the Conquest of Canaan. 1963. Pp. xx+454+xvii incl. many ills. and 5 maps. (Jonathan Cape, London. Price: 55s. 0d.).

We are fortunate in this definitive work from a scholar of the wide experience and breadth of vision of Dr. Anati, who is at the same time so intimately involved with the problems of the archaeology of Palestine. Palestine at the junction of two continents is a fruitful field for comparative study, and is remarkably rich in evidence of the pre-historic periods, which is Dr. Anati's proper sphere. The last quarter of his book, where he deals with the 2nd millennium, will be of special interest to students of the Old Testament. The material evidence here is carefully analyzed and constructively assembled and interpreted. The political and economic situation implied in the Amarna Tablets is well described, the author emphasizing the presence of both semi-nomadic and urban elements through the millennium with the former becoming politically active with the disintegration of Canaanite urban society in the last two centuries before the Hebrew occupation. In such a comprehensive work it is a pity that in what will be to many readers the most interesting part of the work the writer has not presented a fuller picture of Canaanite society, literature, and religion on the basis of the Ras Shamra texts, but on the subject of Canaanite religion has committed himself to the customary broad generalization which is not warranted by literary evidence outside the Old Testament. We recognize, however, that he has imposed certain limitations on himself, dealing primarily as an archaeologist with material evidence. The book is beautifully produced, with excellent and abundant illustrations and thorough documentation.

J.G.

BALY, D.: *Geographical Companion to the Bible*. 1963. Pp. 196 incl. 31 maps and diagrams+coloured maps+28 photographs. (Lutterworth Press, London. Price: 35s. 0d.).

Professor Baly's *Geography of the Bible* is already well known and appreciated (see *Book List*, 1958, p. 14), and the present volume is worthy of its predecessor. Here the subject is presented in a broader outline embracing Mesopotamia, Egypt, and Syria. The title prepares us for similar treatment of the terrain of the Christian mission. The author, however, emphasizes that St. Paul's missionary journeys were mainly by sea. He nevertheless stresses the significance of Antioch, Ephesus and Corinth at the crossroads of trade and culture. The main part of the book describes, though in less technical geological detail than in the earlier book, the structure of Palestine and Syria and peripheral regions. Professor Baly's significant contribution to his subject is in emphasizing the natural boundaries of regions of settlement not in the more obvious features of rivers, ridges, and geological faults, but rather in soil, slope, rainfall, and particular vegetation, as in the case of Asher, Ephraim, Judah, and the Philistine plain. In his interesting section on strategical geography he emphasizes the significance of basalt outcrops, scrub, and marsh as barriers, and of chalk belts with their eroded valleys as avenues of communication, leading to the canalization of international traffic in war and peace. Professor Baly's mastery of his subject and keen appreciation of its relevance to Scripture is everywhere obvious. The matter is most agreeably communicated, with liberal use of maps and geographical charts, resulting in a most handsome production.

J.G.

BEEK, M. A.: *A Short History of Israel, from Abraham to Bar Cochba*, trans. by A. J. Pomerans. 1963. Pp. x+214 incl. 7 maps+36 ills. (Hodder and Stoughton, London. Price: 21s. 0d.).

A translation of *Geschiedenis van Israël* published in 1957. It is a rapid retelling of the history of Israel in 24 chapters; it is a lively book, well written, easy to read, and offers many a refreshing insight into details of the history. It closely follows the Biblical story but at the same time makes full use of the latest archaeological material. Some readers will feel that the author has tried to cram too much into his very short book with the result that the general reader, for whom the book is intended, will sometimes be puzzled by allusions that are not explained, e.g., to the possibility that not all the Israelites were in Egypt, and to the Kenite hypothesis.

L.H.B.

BIRAM, A.: *Dibhrê Yemê Yisrā'ēl bi-Zeman ha-Miqrā' be-Misgereth Tôledhôth ha-Mizraḥ ha-Qādhûm*, 2 vols. 1964. Pp. 1–252; 253–601. (Hariali School, Haifa).

This book, accompanied by a separate cover of relevant maps, which deals with the history of Israel in the Biblical era within the framework of the history of the Ancient East, is, according to the author, intended for the pupils of the top form of Bet-ha-Sepher Hariali, a high school of considerable repute in Israel. The standard of its contents, however, is of such a quality that it may safely be used as a reference work by university students engaged in Biblical studies. Subjects such as the history of Canaan prior to the arrival of the Hebrews, scholars' views of the Biblical account of the patriarchs, and the historical background of the events in Egypt and their dating, as indeed all the other subjects embodied in the two volumes, are dealt with in a systematic and agreeable manner, embodying the results of modern Biblical scholarship. However, with an eye on the younger student, Biblical passages whenever called for are as a rule cited in full (and in many cases, in emended form), and footnotes are added explaining grammatical anomalies, etc.

It is a pity that this conscientious work by a person so distinguished for his love of harmony should have been produced in a manner incompatible with harmony; the paper, which differs from one volume to the other, is of a rather poor quality, and the size of the two volumes is not in concord. Again, the ratio of printer's errors is perhaps slightly above that usually found in books of this character.

M.W.

*BRUCE, F. F.: *Israel and the Nations: from the Exodus to the Fall of the Second Temple*. 1963. Pp. 254. (The Paternoster Press, London. Price: 16s. 0d.).

The sub-title defines the scope of this book. It is designed primarily as an aid to Scripture teachers. The main events in the history of Israel are summarized, but of necessity there is very little opportunity for detailed treatment. Yet the concise synopsis, especially of the periods from the Exile onwards, will serve as a helpful guide to both teachers and pupils who desire to acquaint themselves with current trends in the study of Israel's history. Adequate references are made to the bearing of archaeological discoveries on the Biblical narrative. The author has supplied a useful bibliography to guide those who desire to pursue a more detailed study. It is to be regretted that the patriarchal age is omitted from the study, as many teachers would have appreciated guidance on this topic.

E.R.R.

The Cambridge Ancient History: Revised Edition of Volumes I & II. Elam: c. 1600–1200 B.C.: by René Labat. Fasc. 16. Pp. 42. 6s. 0d.
The Dynasty of Agade and the Gutian Invasion: by C. J. Gadd. Fasc. 17. Pp. 54. 6s. 0d.

The Rise of Mycenaean Civilization: by Frank H. Stubbings. Fasc. 18. Pp. 38. 6s. 0d.

Persia: c. 2400–1800 B.C.: by Walther Hinz. Fasc. 19. Pp. 44. 6s. 0d.
Anatolia: c. 4000–2300 B.C.: by J. Mellaart. Fasc. 20. Pp. 54. 6s. 0d.
Persia: c. 1800–1550 B.C.: by Walther Hinz. Fasc. 21. Pp. 38. 6s. 0d.
(Cambridge University Press).

We welcome the appearance of six more fascicles of the revised edition of volumes I and II of the *Cambridge Ancient History*. On glancing through them one realizes what immense advances have been made in our knowledge of the ancient Near East since the first appearance of the *Cambridge Ancient History*. Of the authors of these six fascicles Professor Gadd is the only one who belongs to the original team of contributors; the rest have all made their reputations in recent years, and all measure up fully to the high standard set by the first edition of this great history. The advance is perhaps specially noticeable in the field of Minoan-Mycenean studies. The problem of the Elamite script still remains unsolved, as also does that of the Indus valley script. Professor Gadd's old sureness of touch remains unchanged, and we salute his unrivalled mastery in the field of Sumerian and Babylonian studies which he has made so specially his own. The two fascicles which deal with the early history of Persia contain much new information about Elamite law and religion, and the excellent fascicle on Anatolia brings us up to date on the latest theories on the Middle Helladic invaders of Greece. S.H.H.

CATTAN, L.: *Voici David.* 1963. Pp. 126. (La Colombe, Éditions du Vieux Colombier, Paris. Price: NF. 12).

A short notice cannot convey the qualities of this artistic, poetical, and almost rapturous study of David. The first chapter describes David's face and beauty, and their effect on all who knew him. The second chapter describes David's *joie de vivre* — his aptitude for living, and the exuberant quality of his royal soul. The third chapter deals with David's enemies and his own attitude to them as described in 1 and 2 Sam., and the so called Davidic Psalms. *Voici David* — the king with the harp, the servant of God, the Messianic personage. G.H.D.

*EHRLICH, E. L.: *A Concise History of Israel from the Earliest Times to the Destruction of the Temple in A.D. 70*, trans. by J. Barr. 1962. Pp. 154+map on endpaper. (Darton, Longman & Todd, London. Price: 12s. 0d.).

This work was originally reviewed in *Book List*, 1958, p. 15. It now appears in a smooth and readable translation by Professor Barr, and will doubtless be widely used as a clear and reliable introductory text-book. G.W.A.

*FARMER, L.: *Land of the Gospel.* 1963. Pp. 160 incl. 3 maps+map on endpapers+ 12 ills. (The Epworth Press and The Bible Lands Society, London. Price: 15s. 0d.).

Some years ago, when he was fortunate enough to live in Jerusalem and to be chaplain and guide to those visiting the Holy Places, the author wrote a book with the title *We Saw the Holy City*. He has now produced a smaller work that can easily be taken on a pilgrimage as a *vade-mecum* and he has arranged it very practically in the order in which the majority of pilgrimages set out at the present time i.e., from the first entry into Jordan until the time comes for the flight out of Israel, some fifteen days later. He has wisely decided not to include such places as Petra, Hazor, Jerash, and Safad in his itinerary.

The book gives a clear account of the many sites to be visited, and there are some attractive colour photographs and maps of Jerusalem, Jordan, Israel, and the walls of Zion. On the claim sometimes made for the Garden Tomb as the place of Christ's burial Farmer is frankly sceptical. He has some sensible remarks about the authenticity of the Holy Places and on the vexed subjects of commercialization of the shrines and squabbles between religious bodies. Some simple devotional reading is provided for use during pilgrimages, together with prayers to be said at the principal sites.

J.M.T.B.

HARDING, G. L.: *Baalbek*, a new guide. 1963. Pp. 70 incl. 1 map & many ills. (Khayats, Beirut; Constable, London. Price: 12s. 6d.).

This book contains chapters giving general information, history, an account of the gods and their temples, the ruins and advice to visitors to Baalbek. It is amply illustrated, with a site plan and 33 photographs. The author's name is sufficient guarantee of its accuracy.

J.N.S.

NAHON, G.: *Les Hébreux* (Le Temps Qui Court No. 32). 1963. Pp. 192 incl. many ills. (Éditions du Seuil, Paris. Price: NF. 4.90).

This is a popular history of the Hebrews viewed as the custodians of the Law of God given in its entirety to Moses on Sinai and of which some copies were taken to Babylon by priests and prophets at the time of the Exile and some stored in sacred places in Palestine such as Mizpah (p. 125). The book shows a nodding acquaintance with contemporary thought and archaeological discovery, but draws on it only if, as in the case of the copper refineries at Elath, it lends credit to the achievements of the Hebrews. The chief function of the prophets was to be heralds of universalism and of the advent of the Messianic age.

L.H.B.

NEWMAN, M. L.: *The People of the Covenant*. A Study of Israel from Moses to the Monarchy. 1962. Pp. 208. (Abingdon Press, New York and Nashville. Price: $3.75).

This book is in origin a dissertation for a doctorate and, unlike many such works when inflated for publication, is eminently successful. The author disentangles and traces the double strand running through the formative period of Hebrew history and the difficulties that defied permanent unification. He follows in detail the respective stories of J and E, reflecting cult-legends connected with cult-centres, E describing the fortunes of the Joseph-tribes with the Ark from Kadesh to Shiloh and J those of the Judah-tribes with the Tent of Meeting from the same place to Hebron, the invasion of Palestine by the Joseph-tribes in a 'holy war' led by Joshua from the east and the penetration of the Judah-tribes from the south, the Joseph-tribes with the more or less democratic Levites and the Judah-tribes with a priesthood of Kenite origin and dynastic tendencies; how the southern group with the Ark settled at Hebron, how an early attempt to set up a common centre for an 'amphictyony' of all twelve tribes at Shechem failed, how the northerners brought the Ark to Shiloh and established a centre there in Samuel's time, when the Ark played so important a part in the Philistine wars, how north and south thereafter remained separate until David established a new centre, detached both from Hebron and from Shiloh, at Jerusalem and how this new union also failed in consequence of the inherent centrifugal forces working from both sides against it and of Solomon's unfortunate policies. The author picks his way through an intricate story with commendable lucidity; he accepts much of his predecessors' work but does not shrink from criticism or actual disagreement where he finds good reasons. Not every one will agree with every detail of his, possibly oversimplified, reconstruction of the history of the period, but all will gain much from studying it.

G.R.D.

PARKES, J.: *A History of the Jewish People*. 1962. Pp. viii+254. (Quadrangle Books, Chicago. Price: $5.00).

Dr. Parkes, who has established for himself a reputation as the leading Christian historian and interpreter of Judaism, here gives in eight chapters a masterly sketch of the Jewish people from the Return from Exile to the establishment of the State of Israel. 'Encounter' is the keynote of the story, whether with Islam, Christianity, or secularism, and the tale, mostly tragic, often sordid, is unfolded by one who has made the subject peculiarly his own.

W.D.McH.

SCHUNK, K-D.: *Benjamin. Untersuchungen zur Entstehung und Geschichte eines israelitischen Stammes*. (Beihefte zur Zeitschrift für die Alttestamentliche Wissenschaft 86). 1963. Pp. 188. (Verlag Alfred Töpelmann, Berlin. Price: DM. 24).

The central, often border-land, position occupied by Benjamin among the other Israelite tribes in Palestine, its traditional, close relationship with neighbouring Joseph (Ephraim), as represented by their common descent from Jacob and Rachel, and especially the part played by it in the period from the occupation of Palestine up to the united monarchy, makes the close study of its history a matter of great importance for the understanding of the history of Israel as a whole. And the large amount of archaeological investigation which has been carried out in the territory occupied by Benjamin gives much help for such a study. Dr. Schunk gives us in this volume a very thorough piece of work which makes a full and discriminating use of all the available evidence, literary and archaeological, and shows a command of the relevant work of other scholars.

Benjamin, an incoming group of nomads or semi-nomads from the Syrian desert, made common cause with a similar group from the south country to gain a foothold in Palestine under Joshua and to expand and strengthen its acquired territory.

That other group, Ephraim, in due course gained the supremacy; but when the Benjamite Saul was later chosen king, Benjamin came into prominence again and tried to establish a common amphictyonic centre for the Israelite tribes at Gibeon. Its subsequent opposition to David is intelligible, but it was not continued against Solomon; and, in the time of the divided kingdom, when Benjamin was again border land, its attachment was to Judah rather than to Ephraim.

This book is to be commended; it is systematic, scholarly, discerning, and written with a clarity which is welcome. J.M.

SMEND, R.: *Jahwekrieg und Stämmebund.* Erwägungen zur ältesten Geschichte Israels. (F.R.L.A.N.T., 84). 1963. Pp. 100. (Vandenhoeck & Ruprecht, Göttingen. Price: DM. 9.80).

The title of this book indicates its content. Its concern is to examine the prevalence and the importance of the concept of the holy war, and the degree of realization of an amphictyonic community in pre-monarchic Israel. A survey of the narratives of the Book of Judges convinces the writer that the holy war is an active concept in them as shown by acts of consecration, sacrificial offerings, and war cries before a battle, and blessings and cursings after it. But he believes that the Judges themselves were charismatic leaders acting in a particular situation and not in the full sense amphictyonic leaders. At this early period there is seen an Israel in action and an Israel *in Potenz.* The amphictyony as an institution, it is said, required a central sanctuary and a 'judge of Israel'. This came in full in the time of Samuel. If that thesis can be sustained, it seems to rule out the suggestion that the element of the holy war was the contribution of the Rachel tribes, and the amphictyonic element of the Leah ones. Beyond that, the degree of amphictyonic cohesion of the Rachel tribes may well have depended on the prestige of Shechem and the influence of the Ark of the Covenant as a cultic symbol — two teasing problems. This is a study in the wake of Alt, Noth, and von Rad, and it is a *Habilitationsschrift* in which the candidate has attempted, with admirable patience and competence, to unravel an admittedly tangled skein. J.M.

YEIVIN, S.: *Luḥoth Chronologiyyim le-Tholedhoth Yisra'el bi-Thequphath ha-Meluchah* (in Hebrew). 1962. Pp. 21. (University of Tel-Aviv, Israel).

This stencilled brochure, especially prepared by Prof. Yeivin for his students, contains well-arranged chronological tables of the period of the Monarchy in ancient Israel based on the more 'reliable' Biblical data — tables which reasonably synchronize with those which may be obtained from parallel contemporary non-Biblical sources. M.W.

TEXT AND VERSIONS

ALBREKTSON, B.: *Studies in the Text and Theology of the Book of Lamentations* with a critical edition of the Peshitta Text (Studia Theologica Lundensia, Skrifter utgivna av Teologiska Fakulteten i Lund 21). 1963. Pp. viii+258. C. W. K. Gleerup, Lund. Price: Sw. kr. 36).

The book is in three parts. The first part is a critical edition of the Peshitta Text. The text printed is substantially that of Codex Ambrosianus published by Ceriani (1876–1883) but the editor has corrected a number of manifest errors and secondary readings. The apparatus draws on 30 other authorities, some complete MSS., others extracts only. The second part, pp. 55–213, is a textual commentary based not only on the Syriac text but also on the Hebrew and Greek. This is a careful piece of work with much helpful discussion and exegesis. After thorough study of the Syriac text the editor was led to the conclusion that its purpose was to make the text readily understandable to the ordinary reader, hence the occasional targumic touches. The third part, pp. 214–239, discusses the background and origin of the theology of Lamentations. Whereas Gottwald saw the key to Lamentations in the tension between the doctrine of retribution and the disaster of 586, Albrektson sees it in the tension between the Jerusalem tradition, centring on the Davidic kingship and incorporating the city's inviolability, and the disaster of 586. He finds that Lamentations relieves this tension by a strong leaning towards the Deuteronomic theory of divine judgement on human error.

L.H.B.

BARTHÉLEMY, D.: *Les Devanciers d'Aquila. Première publication intégrale du texte des Fragments du Dodécaprophéton trouvés dans le désert de Juda, précédée d'une étude sur les traductions et recensions Grecques de la Bible réalisées au premier siècle de notre ère sous l'influence du rabbinat palestinien:* (Supplements to *Vetus Testamentum*, Vol. X). 1963. Pp. xiv+272+2 plates. (E. J. Brill, Leiden. Price: NF. 52; by subscription, NF. 38).

It is well-known that in 1953 Father Barthélemy published his first account of the Greek MS. of the Minor Prophets from the shore of the Dead Sea which was highly significant for the early history of the Septuagint and that Professor Kahle soon afterwards published another interpretation of the MS. This triggered off a controversy which has resulted in this extremely valuable study by Barthélemy. It includes a transcription of the new MS. (and two plates of specimens from each of the two original lots), and a detailed textual study of specimen texts. It also includes general studies of the four main points which form the background to the controversy, with such items as Part I, characteristics of the group of LXX recensions implicated; Part II, some of the characteristics of certain members of the group; Part III, the new member of the group (i.e., the newly discovered fragments). Each Part is divided into chapters (18 in all), and these, in turn, into sections. The whole is a most impressive statement of a case, and, apparently, defies any future challenge. The author states in his concluding remarks that Kahle's hypothesis cannot stand up to scrutiny, but in proving this he has added immensely to our knowledge about the LXX recensions. It is impossible to over-praise this book. B.J.R.

JOHNSON, B.: *Die hexaplarische Rezension des I. Samuelbuches der Septuaginta.* (Studia Theologica Lundensia, Skrifter utgivna av Teologiska Fakulteten i Lund, No. 22). 1963. Pp. 162. (C. W. K. Gleerup, Lund. Price: Sw. Kr. 24).

This workmanlike study opens with a survey of the Hexapla, Hexaplaric material (including new discoveries), and the asterisked and obelised passages in I Sam. It then deals with the text-forms in LXX and MT, on the basis of B, and here the Version shows very few traces of a revision along Hexaplaric lines. On the other hand, Acxd + Arm do represent the Hexapla, and, of the Fathers, Eusebius. The final chapter deals with the Hexaplaric text of the last-mentioned MSS., Hexapla in the Three, the Hexapla and the Hebrew variants including those of Qumran Samuel texts, 4 Q Sam[a] and [b]. It is no adverse comment on the book to say that previously held views are on the whole predominant; the marshalling of those views, and the judicious presentation of the theme as a whole make it an important work.

B.J.R.

SIBINGA, J. S.: *The Old Testament Text of Justin Martyr. I. The Pentateuch.* 1963. Pp. 162+XXIV (Lists). (E. J. Brill, Leiden. Price: Fl. 21).

This is the first volume of a projected series which will cover the whole of the Old Testament in the writings of Justin, and it promises to be a very fruitful work. The analysis is presented in three sections of notes — readings attested twice or more, variants on which the evidence conflicts, and isolated variants. It is important to note, too, that the actual Lists are issued separately in a brochure stuck in the flap at the end of the book, and, unfortunately, might get lost. Why this section was not bound with the Notes is not clear.

Three things commend this book: the text of Justin has long needed the analysis offered here — for it is a notoriously unsatisfactory text. The importance of the Justin text has acquired fresh emphasis in view of the Greek Twelve Minor Prophets from the Scrolls and recent conflicting views on the history of the LXX. The notes by Sibinga are full of suggestive observations which lead beyond the actual analysis — thus, to choose at random, the evidence of Justin for the change which occurred in Koine Greek in the second century, the freedom with which the Divine Name was interchanged, the possible support of the LXX (and sometimes divergently by Justin) for the theory of abbreviations in the MT, the significance of Justin's texts for certain features in Gnosticism, etc.

The author stresses that it is wrong to propose or to draw general conclusions until the whole work is completed. It looks as if they will be extremely valuable.

B.J.R.

WÜRTHWEIN, E.: *Der Text des Alten Testaments. Eine Einführung in die Biblia Hebraica.* Second edition revised and enlarged. 1963. Pp. 222, incl. 48 plates. (Württembergische Bibelanstalt, Stuttgart).

The reviews of the first edition of this book (*Book List*, 1953, p. 30; *Eleven Years*, p. 483) and the English translation (*Book List*, 1957, p. 28) drew attention to its merits. The revisions in the present edition include, in the main, the addition of further material which is sometimes incorporated in the text but mainly in footnotes. There is a danger, now, of a less happy balance in the book as witness the mere mention in one footnote of the Cassuto and Snaith editions of the Massoretic text which appeared in the last few years.

B.J.R.

EXEGESIS AND MODERN TRANSLATIONS

DE BOER, P. A. H. and others (ed.): *Zoals er gezegd is over* (1) *De Schepping*, (2) *Het Paradijs*, (3) *De Vloed en de Toren*, (4) *Jozef en de Aarts-vaders*, (5) *De Uittocht*, (6) *De Woestijn* (Phoenix Bijbel Pockets, 1–6). 1962–63. Pp. 152, 154, 152, 159, 144, 167. 32 plates in each. W. de Haan, Zeist and Antwerp. Price: Hfl. 3.95 each; by subscription on 4 vols. together, Hfl. 3.50 each).

These are the first six issues in a series of 'Bible commentaries for the modern man' which will ultimately comprise 30 paper-back volumes (18 for the Old Testament and 12 for the New Testament). The first four deal with Genesis and Vols. 5 and 6 cover the rest of the Pentateuch. They differ from such English counterparts as the 'Layman's Bible Commentaries' and the Lutterworth 'Bible Guides' in two notable respects: they are provided with wisely selected illustrations, and each volume is a composite work, including essays from a variety of viewpoints on its subject-matter. These essays are written not only by Protestants and Catholics, but by Jews and Muslims as well; as the editors say, one may find here (among other things) 'what the Talmud teaches about Noah's ark, what the church fathers have to say about creation, what Calvin wrote about the prophets, what Muhammad says about Abraham, what Hegel taught about Paradise, and what Freud though about the man Moses'. In addition to Prof. de Boer, the editors are C. A. Rijk, J. Soetendorp and H. van Praag. Among other participating scholars, the best known to our members is probably Dr. Cazelles, who writes in Vol. 5 on 'Moses in the light of history'.

F.F.B.

BUIS, P. & LECLERCQ, J.: *Le Deutéronome*. (Sources Bibliques). 1963. Pp. 218+2 maps. (J. Gabalda & Cie, Paris. Price: NF. 26).

This is a very attractive commentary, based on sound scholarship but especially designed to commend the message of the Biblical book to the thoughtful Christian. Deuteronomy is seen as being the product of two main editions, the first that discovered in Josiah's reign but produced in the second half of the eighth century, the second at the end of the seventh century. Some material was added later (notably chapters xxvii, xxxii, and xxxiii) but this contained matter of a much earlier date. The aim of the book is to prepare the way for a return of independence. So the nature of the People of God, its covenant relationship, and the character of the God of Israel are declared. The com-mentary gives a translation, textual notes, and running comment. The *rib* pattern of ch. xxxii is noted; ch. xxxiii is connected with Gen. xlix and an eleventh-century date is suggested. It is a commentary that will meet a real need among priests and laity.

A.S.H.

CHASE, G. A.: *A Companion to the Revised Psalter*. 1963. Pp. xiv+122. (S.P.C.K., London. Price: 7s. 6d.).

This volume is a popular companion to *The Revised Psalter* (see pp. 39f.). It contains a short introduction to the Psalter, and follows with short notes explaining each psalm, together with an explanation of the major changes. An excellent little volume for the general reader and especially the devout worshipper.

N.H.S.

DEISSLER, A.: *Die Psalmen*, I. Teil (Ps. 1–41). (Die Welt der Bibel). 1963. Pp. 170. (Patmos-Verlag, Düsseldorf. Price: DM. 18).

This is the first volume of a new series, and it is described as a *Kleinkommentar*. The first 15 pages are an introduction to the Psalter as a whole. Technical matters are dealt with in as non-technical a way as possible. There is little emphasis on modern cult theories; but Gunkel's classification is given in full. One excellent feature is that the comments on each psalm are in four sections: A, textual matters; B, type, time, and place (*Sitz im Leben*); C, Old Testament exposition; D, what the psalm has to say for the Christian. Altogether an excellent venture, and we hope it will prosper.

N.H.S.

DRUBBEL, A.: *Numeri uit de grondtekst vertaald en uitgelegd*. (De Boeken van het Oude Testament, Deel II, Boek II). 1963. Pp. 172. (Romen & Zonen, Roermond en Maaseik. Price: Fl. 8.06).

Dr. Drubbel is a newcomer among the contributors to this distinguished Dutch Catholic series of commentaries. Like the other volumes, this one comprises introduction, fresh translation from the Hebrew, commentary, and textual appendix. The introduction includes a discussion of the literary phenomenon of a law-book interspersed with narratives — a phenomenon peculiar to Israel, as appears from a study of other ancient Near Eastern law-codes. The phenomenon is traced to the conditions of primitive Israelite society, before the age of the monarchy, in which the early fortunes and duties of the community were preserved and handed down as an interwoven whole. 'Although we cannot say precisely which fortunes and duties were the first to be preserved and handed down as a whole, the actual juxtaposition of events and laws in the Pentateuch is nevertheless a powerful proof that the first beginnings of what was later to grow into the Pentateuch must be placed in a distant past.' The census-figures of Numbers remain inexplicable to Drubbel; he rejects the view that '*eleph* means 'clan' in this context, but finds no satisfactory alternative (he does not appear to mention the theory that the figures in Numbers represent two variant reports of David's census). Throughout the commentary critical questions are touched with a very light hand.

F.F.B.

DE FRAINE, J.: *Genesis uit de grondtekst vertaald en uitgelegd*. (De Boeken van het Oude Testament, Deel I. Boek I). 1963. Pp. 340. (Romen & Zonen, Roermond en Maaseik. Price: Fl. 15.94).

Dr. de Fraine, who has already contributed the volumes on Judges-Ruth and Ezra-Nehemiah to this series, now presents us with the volume on Genesis. In addition to the features common to all parts of the series, this volume has a prefatory Introduction to the Pentateuch. The history of Pentateuchal criticism is briefly outlined; arguments for and against traditional views are set out, and special mention is made of the course of Catholic opinion on the subject, culminating in the rescript from the secretary of the Papal Biblical Commission to Cardinal Suhard of Paris in January, 1948, which treated as a matter of common acceptance the presence in the Pentateuch of material from various sources and material reflecting the later development and recension of the nuclear Mosaic law-code. Due acknowledgment is made of the part played by the leading shrines (e.g., Kadesh, Shechem, Bethel) and religious institutions (e.g., the Ark, the Aaronic priesthood) as centres round which the traditional material took shape. As for Genesis, the analysis in terms of J, E, and P (as 'layers' rather than documents) continues to be accepted. The book is regarded as composed of three parts: (a) i-iii, dealing with the cosmogony and the primal sin as two religious truths, (b) iv-xi, a collection of traditions bringing out the theology of election and serving as a link between (a) and (c), (c) xii-l, the patriarchal narratives.

F.F.B.

GAILEY, J. H.: *Micah, Nahum, Habakkuk, Zephaniah, Haggai, Zechariah, Malachi*. (The Layman's Bible Commentaries). 1962. Pp. 144; (S.C.M. Press, London; John Knox Press, Richmond, Virginia. Ryerson Press, Toronto. Price: 6s. 0d.).

The commentator is hampered in this volume by the miscellaneous character of the books with which he has to deal and the difficulty of relating most of the material to any definite period of history. He has made the best of a task rendered doubly difficult by the exigencies of space.   N.H.S.

GEMSER, B.: *Sprüche Salomos*. (Handbuch zum Alten Testament, Erste Reihe, 16) 2nd ed. 1963. Pp. 116. (J. C. B. Mohr, Tübingen. Price: DM. 15; by subscription, DM. 13.50; or bound, DM. 18.50; by subscription, DM.17).

This commentary, originally published in 1937, has been thoroughly revised and expanded so that the second edition is more than a third as long again as the first. Of the additional material, special attention may be drawn to the many notes, particularly in the *Nachtrag*, which embody the philological work of Professor G. R. Driver. By thus rewriting this book Professor Gemser has made an excellent commentary yet more useful, and the appearance of the second edition will remind the reader of the loss to Old Testament scholarship occasioned by the death of its distinguished author in November, 1962.

J.A.E.

GERLEMAN, G.: *Ruth/Das Hohelied* (*Canticum Canticorum*). (Biblischer Kommentar, Altes Testament, XVIII 2). 1963. Pp. 43–120. (Neukirchener Verlag des Erziehungsvereins, Neukirchen-Vluyn. Price: DM. 7).

This part contains the introduction to the Song of Songs and the commentary on i. 1 – ii. 7. The introduction is very full and the author gives a good survey of the history of interpretation of the Song from the Fathers through the Reformation period to modern times. He discusses the place of the Song in the Canon and in the cult, and holds that its reading at Passover is not ancient, since Theodore of Mopsuestia states that in his time it had never been read in public by Jews or Christians. There is a very useful study of the language and literary form of the Song, and an original chapter on love and beauty in the Old Testament. In the section on the date of the Song the author reaches surprising conclusions. He thinks the occasional Persian and Greek words are not indications of late origin, and holds that the humanism of the time of Solomon gives the most probable indication of its origin in the period of the early monarchy.

H.H.R.

GEYER, J.: *The Wisdom of Solomon:* Introduction and Commentary. (Torch Bible Commentaries). 1963. Pp. 128. (S.C.M. Press, London. Price: 9s. 6d.).

There is rather more Introduction than is usual in this series; the commentary begins on p. 59. This is probably all to the good, since much is needful to be said about Alexandria and the influence of Greek on Hebrew thought. There are also short essays on Wisdom, Creation, Man, Immortality, Knowledge of God, and Judgement. All are necessary and helpful to the reader who enters this new world of thought. Both here and in the commentary the standards of the series are well maintained.

N.H.S.

GRAY, J.: *I & II Kings.* A Commentary. 1964. Pp. 744+3 maps. (S.C.M. Press Ltd., London. Price: 75s. 0d.).

That a massive commentary on the books of Kings is called for so soon after J. A. Montgomery's volume (*I.C.C.*, 1951) is impressive testimony to the rapidity with which Old Testament research advances. The principal justification for a new treatment of these books is the accumulation of fresh archaeological evidence, especially from Qumran (Caves V and VI have yielded fragments of Hebrew manuscripts of Kings), Atchana, Mari, Ras Shamra, Hazor, Megiddo, Gezer, Jerusalem, and elsewhere. This material is fully used in this commentary. The introduction deals with the composition, text, and chronology of Kings, and the commentary proper consists of introductory remarks to each section of the text, the translation of the text (which is the author's own), extensive explanatory notes, and footnotes which are concerned predominantly with textual matters. A substantial bibliography is supplied, as well as three maps and useful indices. Noteworthy features of the work are the frequent references to the Ras Shamra texts; the attention that is paid to LXX readings, Lucianic included; the pursuit of the correct meanings of Hebrew words, the author himself sometimes making original suggestions; the consideration given to theological concepts; and the citation of many illuminating parallels in Arabic phraseology and in Bedouin life and custom. Major problems are discussed uniformly well. Contrary to some recent opinion the author adheres to the view that the Deuteronomic Book of Kings is a pre-exilic compilation which underwent post-exilic redaction. A smaller point of interest is his preference for 'Arabs' rather than 'ravens' in I Kings xvii. 4 (p. 339). It is on smaller, rather than larger, matters that criticism is likely to fasten. For example, Torczyner's reading 'Nedabiah' in Lachish Ostracon iii. 19 (p. 310) has long been abandoned, and some explanations of proper names that are offered are improbable (e.g., of Abishag, p. 77, and of Zimri, p. 328), even fanciful (e.g., of Shaphan and Huldah; 'mole' — the latter is a nickname given to a girl emerging from the Siloam tunnel after drawing water, p. 659). All in all, however, the commentary is a considerable achievement. It will not displace Montgomery's commentary, but will take its place as a valuable companion to it. In a book which otherwise does the author so much credit it is disconcerting to find such a large number of misprints. Most of them occur in the transliteration of Hebrew words, but there are others as well.   D.W.T.

HANSON, A. & M.: *A Commentary on the Book of Genesis*. (The Christian Students' Library, No. 29). 1963. Pp. 229. (The Christian Literature Society, Madras, for the Senate of Serampore College. Price: Rs. 4.00).

Professor and Mrs. Anthony Hanson spent many years in India, first at Dornakal and then at Bangalore. This paperback, one of a series written for Indian students of the L.Th. level of Serampore College, is suitable for theological students generally. It consists of introduction, modern but without undue emphasis on literary features; then the RSV text, section by section, with explanatory notes. It is a good and useful commentary for the ordinary reader.   N.H.S.

HERTZBERG, H. W. & BARDTKE, H.: *Der Prediger. Das Buch Esther*. (Kommentar zum Alten Testament, Band XVII, 4–5). 1963. Pp. 420. (Gütersloher Verlagshaus Gerd Mohn, Gütersloh. Price: DM. 75).

It may seem strange to find commentaries on these two Old Testament books within the same covers. Yet both are seen to be the product of Judaism at the end of the third century B.C., Qoheleth from Jerusalem, Esther from Susa. Each commentary is preceded by an introduction; then follow a translation, textual notes, and exegesis. The translation of Qoheleth is somewhat free but is intended to convey the equivalent effect of the Hebrew. Qoh. i. 2–xii. 8 is seen as a unity and is presented in twelve sections; this is followed by two epilogues, xii. 9–11 and xii. 12–14. The commentary is followed by a discussion of the theology of Qoheleth: exclusive monotheism; the transitoriness of all things terrestrial; the necessity for man to accept the present, as indeed it is, from God's hand. Esther is seen as a literary unity compounded from three previously existing traditions: a Vashti tradition, a tradition of Mordecai and Haman, and an Esther tradition (Esther probably replaced an original Hadassah in the Mordecai story). The commentary is followed by a discussion of the theological significance of the book of Esther. This is a most valuable addition to the series. A.S.H.

HONEYCUTT, R. L.: *Amos and his Message,* An expository commentary. 1963. Pp. x+182. (Broadman Press, Nashville, Tennessee. Price: $3.75).

This commentary falls between two stools, perhaps because the author tries to do too much at one time: he tries to give a commentary on the message of Amos to his own contemporaries and at the same time to give a commentary (or exposition) of the prophet's message for us today. The book shows that these two cannot readily be held in solution together. The commentary jumps about from then to now and back again in a manner that is sometimes confusing and sometimes misleading. This is unfortunate, because the author clearly has much that is useful to say about Amos and his message and is both well versed in the relevant literature, from which he frequently quotes, and well aware of the problems raised by the recorded words of the prophet.

L.H.B.

HORST, F.: *Hiob.* (Biblischer Kommentar, Altes Testament, XVI, Lieferung 4). 1963. Pp. 241–280. (Verlag der Buchhandlung des Erziehungsvereins, Neukirchen-Vluyn. Price: DM. 3.50).

When the author of this commentary died in June, 1962, it seemed that the third number might be the last to appear (see *Book List,* 1963, p. 23). Fortunately, however, the author left behind him in manuscript a continuation of the commentary as far as and including ch. xix, and it is this part of his work which now appears in this fourth (half) number. It contains critical notes and discussion of chs. xvi. l-xvii. 16 (the translation of this section was given in the previous number); translation, critical notes, and discussion of ch. xviii. 1–21; and translation and critical notes only of ch. xix. It is very welcome news that the author's pupil, Ernst Kutsch, soon to be Professor in Vienna, who saw the proofs of this number through the Press, is to undertake the completion of the commentary. With this number are issued separately a list of corrigenda to the first two numbers and a brief appreciation of Friedrich Horst and his work.

D.W.T.

KAISER, O.: *Der Prophet Jesaja, Kapitel 1–12 übersetzt und erklärt,* 2, verbesserte Auflage. (Das Alte Testament Deutsch, 17). 1963. Pp. XVI+136, incl. 1 map. (Vandenhoeck & Ruprecht, Göttingen).

The first edition of this excellent commentary was reviewed in *Book List,* 1961, p. 32. Though its general characteristics remain the same, it has been wholly revised, not only by the elimination of slips and the amplification of bibliographical references (including useful citation of commentaries by the Reformers), but also in matters of substance. The form-critical approach is given more extensive application. Professor Kaiser's treatment of the later chapters will be eagerly awaited.

G.W.A.

KELLY, B. H.: *Ezra, Nehemiah, Esther, Job.* (The Layman's Bible Commentaries). 1962. Pp. 152. (S.C.M. Press, London; John Knox Press, Richmond; Virginia; Ryerson Press, Toronto. Price: 6s. 0d.).

This volume is the best of the series: it should be, seeing it is by the general editor. He deals with Ezra-Nehemiah, Esther, and Job. Two-thirds of the volume is devoted to Job. The general modern position is taken throughout, with Ezra's date as probably the 37th year of Artaxerxes I.   N.H.S.

KENDON, F.: *Thirty-Six Psalms.* 1963. Pp. 64. (Cambridge University Press, London. Price: 25s. 0d.).

This book contains Psalms i-xxxiv and xl-xli in the version prepared by Mr. Kendon from an early draft of the *New English Bible.* Mr. Kendon's death prevented him from working through the whole Psalter, and the Syndics of the Cambridge University Press decided to publish as a separate volume the psalms which he had completed. Himself a poet, he had a sensitive feeling for the English language and the rhythms of modern speech, and the reader will regret that he did not live to give us more of this impressive rendering of the Psalter.   J.A.E.

MCKANE, W.: *I & II Samuel. Introduction and Commentary.* (Torch Bible Commentaries). 1963. Pp. 304. (S.C.M. Press, London. Price: 16s.0d.).

The commentary is based on RSV. Introductory material provides a brief but clear summary of the main views expressed as to composition and *tendenz*, while insisting on the need for relating each part to the whole. Difficulties of translation and exegesis are well presented, and restrained use is made of such emendations (especially where supported by the Versions) as are necessary to produce a meaningful text. Some good paraphrases are offered to convey the force of Hebrew idiom. Frequently the comment on a passage is followed by a longer note in which the theological intention of the passage is discussed. The commentary will be warmly welcomed by Scripture specialists in schools, and by all who are concerned to teach this (to the Western mind) often difficult material.   A.S.H.

MAYS, J. L.: *Leviticus, Numbers.* (The Layman's Bible Commentaries). 1963. Pp. 144. (S.C.M. Press, London; John Knox Press, Richmond, Virginia; Ryerson Press, Toronto. Price: 6s. 0d.).

The introduction is longer than is usual in this series; sixteen pages, containing enough history of the people and enough literary history of the traditions to make the purpose of these two books plain. The details of sacrificial rites, sanctity of people and places and things, censuses, allocation of territory, taboos and social laws — all these are carefully explained, and everything is written to show not only what was meant for Israel then, but also what it all means for us now. The volume continues the good tradition of the series in providing non-technical guides for the 'layman'.   N.H.S.

MOWINCKEL, S., KAPELRUD, A. S., & LEIVESTAD, R. (ed. by): *Det Gamle Testamente V. 2 Del.* 1963. Pp. 420. (H. Aschehoug & Co. (W. Nygaard), Oslo).

Professor Mowinckel is to be warmly congratulated on the successful completion of this massive enterprise, in the early stages of which he co-operated with S. Michelet and N. Messel. A general description of the plan and purpose of the work, and in particular of the first three volumes will be found in *Book List*, 1948, p. 9 (*Eleven Years*, p. 119). Vol. IV was noticed in *Book List*, 1956, p. 31 (*Eleven Years* p. 738). In this final volume, A. S. Kapelrud contributes the translation of and commentary on Ruth and R. Leivestad is responsible for Ecclesiastes. The late N. Messel had left MSS. on Daniel and Chronicles. These have been revised by Professor Mowinckel, who is also responsible for the rest of the volume. Corrections and minor additions to the earlier parts of the work, and a subject index to the whole have been included. Detailed comment is not possible here; but as one who has made constant use of these admirable volumes, the reviewer would pay special tribute to the excellence of introductions to the several books of the Old Testament.

G.W.A.

NAPIER, B. D.: *Exodus*. (The Layman's Bible Commentaries). 1963. Pp. 126. (S.C.M. Press, London; John Knox Press, Richmond, Virginia; The Ryerson Press, Toronto. Price: 6s. 0d.).

In this volume two and a half pages only are devoted to such technical matters as sources, etc.; and this leaves the more room for the study of the book itself, which is done section by section rather than verse by verse. A thirteenth-century Exodus is assumed. The volume is good; and the author makes full use of the new Near-Eastern material. It is far from obscurantist; but the author is rightly concerned with 'our faith in him whose love daily brings us again out of Egypt'.

N.H.S.

PHILLIPS, J. B.: *Four Prophets, Amos, Hosea, First Isaiah, Micah,* A Modern Translation from the Hebrew. 1963. Pp. xxviii+162+maps on endpapers. (Geoffrey Bles, London. Price: 15s. 0d.).

Mr. Phillips is well known for his translation of the New Testament which has proved helpful to many readers. He has now turned his attention to four Old Testament prophets: Amos, Hosea, Isaiah i-xxxv, and Micah. In the introduction, he discusses some of the difficulties of translating Hebrew and describes his methods. There is also a rather sketchy discussion of the historical background by Mr. E. H. Robertson who expresses the opinion that 'No written material of any lasting religious significance survives from the period before these eighth-century prophets', and strangely refers to 'the fall of Samaria in 732 B.C. when the whole of the North, Syria and Israel, was depopulated and organized as Assyrian provinces'. Mr. Phillips then offers a translation which is in many places certainly more comprehensible than the Authorized Version to the ordinary reader; there are also helpful brief headings to chapters and groups of verses. As a rendering of the Hebrew, however, the translation is not always so successful. Working on his own, Mr. Phillips is sometimes out of touch with recent scholarly studies of the Old Testament and Hebrew lexicography; for example (not to mention a few straight mistranslations), he seems to be unaware of the precise significance of *hesed* or that *nephesh* in Isa. v. 14 probably means 'throat'. Moreover, although a certain amount of freedom is legitimate in a translation of this kind, Mr. Phillips sometimes goes too far. It may be doubted, for instance, whether it is right, in Hosea iii. 4, to translate *teraphim* as 'wooden images' or, in Amos i. 4, 7 etc., to paraphrase *'armenoth* as 'rulers' and to omit all reference to fire; nor is Mr. Phillips always obviously right in adding words for which there is no Hebrew equivalent (e.g., 'silly' before 'dreamer' in Amos vii. 12).   J.A.E.

The Psalms, A New Translation. Translated from the Hebrew and arranged for singing to the psalmody of Joseph Gelineau. 1963. Pp. 256. (Collins, London and Glasgow. Price: 3s. 6d.).

This translation was made by a team of scholars in co-operation with *The Grail*, which has already brought out a musical edition of over fifty of these psalms. It was inspired by the French version of the Psalms in the *Bible de Jérusalem*, and, like that version, it aims especially at full literary fidelity to the Hebrew text and at the reproduction of the rhythmic structure of the poetry of the Hebrew psalms. There is a brief, but useful introduction, which includes sections on the Psalms in preaching and in prayer, and each psalm bears a descriptive heading. While in some passages the translation is in accord with recent advances in comparative Semitic philology, in many other passages it lags behind present day knowledge. In style it is often staccato, and the requirement that it should reflect the rhythmic pattern of the Hebrew seems frequently to have dictated the choice of a word or phrase which does not make for elegant English. While it can hardly be described as a poetical translation, and while too it is paraphrastic at times, it yet contains many happy renderings of the Hebrew. Both readers and singers of the Psalms (more especially the latter for whom it seems primarily designed) will derive enjoyment from this interesting experiment in the translation of Hebrew poetry.   D.W.T.

(Psalter) The Revised Psalter. The Final Report of the Commission to Revise the Psalter appointed by the Archbishops of Canterbury and York. 1963. Pp. xii+208. (S.P.C.K., London. Price: 9s. 6d.).

This is the Final Report of the Commission to revise the Psalter appointed by the Archbishops of Canterbury and York, as presented to the Convocations of the two Provinces, of which a Preliminary Report has already appeared, containing the revision of Book I of the Psalms (see *Book List*, 1962, p. 30). The Committee's terms of reference were 'to produce . . . a revision of the text of the Psalter designed to remove obscurities and serious errors of translation, yet such as to retain, as far as possible, the general character in style and rhythm of Coverdale's version and its suitability for congregational use'. The Archbishop, as chairman of the Commission, in a brief preface outlines the principles on which he and his colleagues have worked, emphasizing that its duty was 'not . . . to make a new translation but to mend an old one'. At the same time they have had before them the, as yet unfinished, drafts of the completely new translation of the Psalms now being prepared for the New English Bible; and they have also taken into account the revised translation of the Psalms in the Irish Book of Common Prayer as well as several other modern versions. The principles are these: to follow the massoretic text as basic, correcting it however when unintelligible if possible by means of the ancient versions but also conjecturally (however sparingly) when these throw no clear light on the sense, altering the vowels as required (e.g., lxxvi. 10) and even the consonants when no sense can be extracted from them (e.g., ii. 11, lviii. 7–9); to eliminate obviously impossible or absurd mistranslations (e.g., lxxii. 6, lxxiii. 9); to accept new meanings for words and phrases when comparative philology suggests or supports them (e.g., xxix. 8, lxviii. 8, lxxiv. 20, cv. 18); to remove Coverdale's additions to the Hebrew text which often but not always come from the Vulgate (e.g., xiv. 5–7, cxxxiv. 2) but on occasion to retain them if they can be regarded as 'legitimate and helpful expansions' which clarify the sense (e.g., i. 5 and cxlvii. 8, when the half-verse missing from the Hebrew text is metrically necessary). The generally used modern forms of proper names are preferred (e.g., Lebanon rather then Libanus), and archaisms are regularly replaced (e.g., 'leasing' by 'falsehood' and 'vanity' by 'folly'); but no attempt is made to eliminate phrases reflecting Hebrew modes of thought if the meaning is clear (e.g., 'to break' and 'to lift up the horn'); and for the sake of clarity inverted commas have been inserted to indicate direct oration (e.g., lxxv. 3–6).

The work has been done with all possible care; and, even if the new renderings do not always entirely hit the sense (or rather the probable sense) or are not altogether happy in catching Coverdale's rhythm, the new Psalter deserves to be warmly welcomed as a great improvement on the original work.

Finally, the Archbishop says that a Committee has been instructed to prepare a printed edition of the new translation for singing to Anglican chants and to plainsong; when this is done, one may hope that it will come into regular use in all churches and chapels.

G.R.D.

[NOTE: There has now appeared, *The Revised Psalter. The amended text as approved by the Convocations of Canterbury and York in October, 1963 with a view to legislation for its permissive use.* 1964. Pp. x+208. (S.P.C.K., London. Price: paper, 7s. 6d.; cloth, 10s. 6d.).

G.W.A.]

ROBERT, A. & TOURNAY, R.: *Le Cantique des Cantiques*, traduction et commentaire. (Études Bibliques). 1963. Pp. 464. (Librairie Lecoffre, J. Gabalda et Cie, Éditeurs, Paris. Price: NF. 78).

At the time of his death on 28 May, 1955, André Robert left behind him a bulky manuscript comprising a full-scale commentary on the Canticle, together with the first two chapters of an introduction dealing with the history of the tradition regarding the book's canonicity and the history of its interpretation. These chapters are printed on pp. 41–55 of the work as published. The manuscript was at the beginning handed over to M. André Feuillet, one of Robert's colleagues at the Institut Catholique in Paris, and was eventually edited by Père R. Tournay, O.P., of Saint Étienne, Jerusalem, who in his preface discusses the book's character, structure, date of composition and theological content, and who has added a long section on extra-Biblical parallels to the Canticle, including among other sources extracts from the article by S. H. Stephan, entitled *Modern Palestinian Parallels to the Song of Songs* (*JPOS* II, 1922, pp. 199–278). There are, at the end of the work (pp. 429–453), various notes and other additional matter contributed by Tournay.

The editor warns us on the first page of his preface that we must not look here for an exhaustive treatment of all the questions raised by the book, but any reader will realize from the start that we have here a thorough and admirably documented study, which should hold the field for some time as the leading commentary. The author's method of studying the book is well-described by himself in some lines quoted by Tournay on pp. 10–11. Briefly, like the late Mademoiselle Renée Bloch and others he regards the book as essentially a midrashic work, while he avoids the late Père Joüon's excessive appeals to symbolism and allegory. The translation is extremely clear and elegant, and one's only regret is that the cost of the book may prevent its having the circulation it deserves. J.M.T.B.

RODD, C. S.: *Psalms 1–72* (Epworth Preacher's Commentaries). 1963. Pp. 136 (The Epworth Press, London. Price: 12s. 6d.).

Within the limits set by the series, the present volume may be said to fulfil its purpose and to offer to the lay preacher a helpful commentary on these seventy-two psalms based on up-to-date exegesis. It suffers, however, from its brevity. For instance, Psalms xxiv and xlvii are both interpreted as being liturgies for the procession of the ark up Mount Zion. This is stated categorically in the comment on Ps. xxiv and qualified by 'probably' in Ps. xlvii, but in neither psalm is the reader told why they are claimed to be about the ark in procession whereas the ark is not mentioned in either psalm. L.H.B.

SNAITH, N. H.: *The Seven Psalms.* 1964. Pp. 110. (Epworth Press, London. Price: paper, 5s. 0d.; cloth, 8s. 6d.).

In this, the Methodist Lent Book for 1964, Dr. Snaith offers studies of what are traditionally known as the Penitential Psalms (vi, xxxii, xxxviii, li, cii, cxxx, cxliii). The book is a characteristic example of a *Gattung* which the author has made peculiarly his own, and which, in Gunkel's terminology, might appropriately be classified as a *Mischung*; for it contains textual and philological details, much straight exegesis, illuminating parallels from other fields of study, broad perspectives in Biblical theology, and trenchant application. G.W.A.

TERRIEN, S.: *Job*. (Commentaire de l'Ancien Testament, XIII). 1963. Pp. 278. (Delachaux & Niestlé, Neuchâtel).

This commentary in French is based on Dr. Terrien's introduction to and exegesis of Job in *The Interpreter's Bible*, vol. III (*Book List*, 1955, p. 32; *Eleven Years*, p. 665), but he has taken advantage of the opportunity to revise and expand his work in many places. He interprets Job on the lines worked out in the earlier commentary and in his more popular book, *Job: Poet of Existence* (*Book List*, 1959, p. 31). This work will be welcomed both as an excellent study of Job and as the first of an important new series of Protestant commentaries in French on the Old Testament.

J.A.E.

THOMAS, D. W.: *The Text of the Revised Psalter*. 1963. Pp. 56. (S.P.C.K., London. Price: 15s. 0d.).

This admirable little book, a model of its kind, is designed as a companion to the *Revised Psalter* (see above, under *Psalter*) issued by the Commission appointed by the Archbishops of Canterbury and York to revise Coverdale's version of the Book of Common Prayer and to bring it up to date. In it Prof. Thomas records all the readings, underlying the revised translation, which diverge from the Massoretic text, with the evidence, namely the corrected vocalization and emendations of the consonantal Hebrew text (with the evidence of the supporting versions) and in many cases the names of the scholars who have proposed them. The discerning student will also detect new suggestions which have not yet been published but which the Revisers have accepted in several places (e.g., lix. 6, lxxii. 9, cvii. 10). This brief notice may fittingly be ended with the expression of a hope that the Presses at Oxford and Cambridge will take the hint and publish a similar volume recording and explaining the amended translations in the Old Testament of the New English Bible when it appears.

G.R.D.

UNGER, M. F.: *Zechariah*. (Unger's Bible Commentary). 1963. Pp. 276. (Zondervan Publishing House, Grand Rapids, Michigan. Price: $6.95).

The whole of the Biblical book is ascribed to the one prophet, chapters i-viii to the years 520–518, and the remaining chapters to about 460 B.C. 'The prophecy abounds in far-reaching predictive allusions to the person, work, and future glory of the Coming One. ... Nowhere else in the Old Testament is there such a concentrated and rich revelation of Messianic prophecy.' The four horns of ch. i are understood as Babylon, Medo-Persia, Macedonian Greece, and Rome. The prophet 'shows indebtedness to Daniel'. A number of simple Hebrew words (e.g., *qeren*, *hinneh*, *'ish*, *na'ar*) are quoted and explained; *nosha'* in ix. 9 is rendered 'showing Himself a Saviour'. We can hardly avoid the impression that the oracles in the book of Zechariah have been forced into the mould of a pre-conceived theory.

A.S.H.

LITERARY CRITICISM AND INTRODUCTION 511

WOLFF, H. W.: *Dodekapropheton: Joel.* (Biblischer Kommentar, Altes Testament, XIV, 5). 1963. Pp. 104. (Neukirchener Verlag des Erziehungsvereins, Neukirchen-Vluyn. Price: DM. 8.75).

Having completed his commentary on Hosea in this series, Wolff now gives us Joel. The prophecy is dated in the Persian period, more particularly between 445 and 343 B.C., since on the one hand ii. 7, 9 are taken to imply that Jerusalem is now a walled city and on the other hand iii. 4 is taken to imply that the destruction of Sidon at the hands of Artaxerxes III is still future. Joel is placed at an early point in the Twelve Prophets because Amos i. 3–ii. 3 was interpreted as an amplification of the judgement of the nations proclaimed in Joel iii. 1 ff. (iv. 1 ff., Heb.). The book is treated as a literary unity; it falls into two symmetrical parts, the dividing point coming between ii. 17 and ii. 18. Within the first part, the economic disaster caused by the locust plague in ch. i is used as an illustration of the eschatological catastrophe foretold in ii. 1–11; in the second part, ii. 21–27 celebrates the relief from the economic disaster of ch. i., iii. 1–17 (iv. 1–17, Heb.) celebrates the restoration of Judah and Jerusalem after the eschatological catastrophe of ii. 1–11, and ii. 28–32 (iii. 1–5, Heb.) describes the blessings of obedience to the call to repentance in ii. 12–17. Joel's reworking of the themes of earlier prophecy is examined, as is also his progress towards apocalyptic, his influence on the New Testament, and his message for today. F.F.B.

ZIMMERLI, W.: *Ezechiel.* (Biblischer Kommentar, Altes Testament, XIII, Lieferung 11). 1963. Pp. 818-898. (Neukirchener Verlag des Erziehungsvereins, Neukirchen-Vluyn. Price: DM. 7.00).

This fascicle concludes the section on xxv. 1–xxxiii. 24 and contains xxxiv. xxxv. 1–xxxvi. 15; xxxvi. 16–38 and most of the discussion of xxxvii. 1–14. Close attention is paid to the terms used in xxxiv, and in particular to the royal terminology, with citation of ancient Near Eastern parallels, xxxv. 1-xxxvi. 16 is subjected to a characteristically close structural analysis. There is a careful examination of the form of xxxvii. 1–14 and of the relationship between the figure (1–10) and its interpretation (11–14): arguments are advanced for a date between xxx. 21 and xl. 1. As this commentary proceeds on its stately way, the reader becomes increasingly eager to read the Introduction, which will appear last, but will doubtless gather together the threads of the detailed analysis and exegesis. G.W.A.

LITERARY CRITICISM AND INTRODUCTION

(including History of Interpretation, Canon, and Special Studies)

AUZOU, G.: *Als Gott zu unseren Vätern sprach.* Geschichte der Heiligen Schriften des Gottesvolkes. 1963. Pp. 400. (Verlag Herder, Freiburg).

This attractive introduction to the Bible originally appeared in French and was reviewed in the *Book List*, 1959, p. 21. The author is a Roman Catholic who presents a critical account of the origin of the Bible in the light of its historical background.

In this edition the opportunity has been taken to bring up to date the bibliographical references in the footnotes, which serves to maintain the usefulness of the work.

                                                                    R.E.C.

CHASE, M. E.: *The Psalms for the Common Reader.* 1963. Pp. 208. (Michael Joseph, London. Price: 21s. 0d.).

The title describes the volume. It is for the interested, non-technical reader. It is in three parts plus a list of recommended books. These are modern, up-to-date and make a thoroughly good list. Parts one and two comprise half the book: what are the psalms and how should they be read? Part three consists of 40 pages of psalms in the Authorised Version and a short account of the history of Israel; Exodus *c.* 1250 B.C.; Ezra 398 B.C. Miss Chase is a novelist of repute; and this is her third popular book on the Bible.

                                                                    N.H.S.

COPPENS, J.: *Miscellannées bibliques,* XXVIII-XXXII. (Analecta Lovaniensia Biblica et Orientalia, Ser. IV, Fasc. 8). 1963. Pp. 87–122. (Descleé de Brouwer, Bruges-Paris. Price: B.Fr. 50).

With characteristic precision of language and courtesy in discussion, Canon Coppens examines views at variance with his own as they relate to Daniel vii and the Servant of the Lord. The first article discusses the treatment of Daniel vii in N. W. Porteous's commentary in ATD, with special reference to the Son of Man. To this he returns in more detail in the second article and discusses objections to the identification of the Saints of the Most High with the Heavenly Hosts. In the third the symbolic figure of the Son of Man requires no more recondite explanation than to see it as an appropriate figure for the Kingdom of God entrusted to the Heavenly Beings in collaboration with the faithful. The fourth finds no adequate evidence to support an interpretation of the Servant passages in terms of the Davidic Messiah nor to abandon his interpretation of the Son of Man symbol. The fifth offers a translation of Isa. liii. 10–12 in which 10cd is seen as a gloss and 11, with a re-pointing of two words, becomes: 'With *fear* he will be satisfied and with knowledge, and being just he will render justice to *those who serve* the great.'

                                                                    A.S.H.

CRIM, K. R.: *The Royal Psalms.* 1962. Pp. 128. (John Knox Press, Richmond, Virginia. Price: $2.75).

Although we may doubt the accuracy of the statement on the jacket of this book, that it covers 'an area that has been neglected by English-writing scholars', it is, nevertheless useful to have the relevant material collected and presented in this brief and simple form. The book consists of two roughly equal parts: first, five chapters dealing with the monarchy in ancient Israel; and second, brief expositions, based on the author's own translations of Psalms ii, xviii, xx, xxi, xlv, lxxii, lxxxix, ci, cx, cxliv, and 2 Sam. xxiii. 1–7. Psalm cxxxii is discussed in the earlier part of the book. This is a clear and readable account of the subject which will serve as a useful introduction both to the subject itself and to current trends in scholarly theory.

                                                                    G.W.A.

EISSFELDT, O.: *Einleitung in das Alte Testament unter Einschluss der Apokryphen und Pseudepigraphen sowie der apokryphen– und pseudepigraphartigen Qumrān-Schriften. Entstehungsgeschichte des Alten Testaments.* 3., neubearbeitete Auflage. 1964. Pp. XVI+1130. (J. C. B. Mohr, Tübingen. Price: paper, DM. 54; cloth, DM. 59).

The first edition of this encyclopaedic work, published in 1934, was reviewed in *Book List*, 1934, p.7. The second edition (larger by over 200 pages) appeared twenty-two years later, and was reviewed in *Book List*, 1957, pp. 36f. The third edition is over 170 pages longer still. The general plan and character of the original work have been retained; but a full account has been taken of the progress of research in all branches of the subject. A considerable part of the additional space is taken up by the formidable *Literaturnachträge*, which is impressively up-to-date. Encyclopaedic as it is in its range and documentation, the work also carries the personal stamp of one who has made his own distinctive and distinguished contributions to the subject. We congratulate our revered honorary member on the acumen, learning, and industry with which he continues to advance the study of the Old Testament and to put us all in his debt.

G.W.A.

FEY, R.: *Amos und Jesaja* — Abhängigkeit und Eigenständigkeit des Jesaja. (Wissenschaftliche Monographien zum Alten und Neuen Testament, Band 12). 1963. Pp. 160. (Neukirchener Verlag des Erziehungsvereins, Neukirchen-Vluyn. Price: DM. 15.00; cloth, DM. 17.50).

This study undertakes a detailed comparison of similar or analogous utterances of the prophets Amos and Isaiah. It argues that on the available evidence Isaiah was acquainted with about one-third of the Amos material, and the book seeks to establish the thesis that Isaiah is dependent on an Amos-*Vorlage*. Dependence, as here used, does not mean that Isaiah's work was derivative and secondary. He used subject-themes of Amos in such a way that the new material which he introduced was as notable as that which he adopted, and often more so. It is maintained that Isaiah developed and clarified what he adopted, and carried Amos's theological thought to new heights; for instance, Isaiah spoke as often as Amos concerning human sin and divine judgement, but he dwelt also upon divine salvation; righteousness for him is not an achievement of man's obedience to God's law, but a gift of God to man; and he spoke distinctively of God's holiness as both exclusive and inclusive. It is not denied that Isaiah was indebted to others (e.g., Hosea) for some of his teaching, but it is affirmed that his dependence on Amos is substantial and unmistakable. Nor is it denied that his dependence may at times have been unconscious. While impressed with the thesis as presented, and by the careful way in which the evidence is handled, one is left wondering whether, in their references, for instance, to prevailing social evils, the explanation may be, more than the writer admits, that both prophets condemned aspects of the affluent society of their day with the same degree of independence of utterance and similarity of expression which seems to characterise preachers of today in their condemnations of materialism, selfishness, or gross indulgence.

J.M.

FOHRER, G.: *Studien zum Buche Hiob*. 1963. Pp. 132. (Gütersloher Verlagshaus, Gerd Mohn. Price: DM.18).

The present work contains six essays which the author has published during the last few years (1956–62) on the various parts of the book of Job. The subjects are: the treatment of the problem of suffering, which is seen not as an abstract problem but as that of man's attitude to suffering (pp. 7–25); the composition of the book, which is regarded as a reworking and rearrangement of old material, not all of which has survived (pp. 26–43); the purpose of the book, the transformation of the legend of Job which, as preserved in the Prologue and Epilogue, can be shown to have differed considerably from the form in which it is presented in the poem itself (pp. 44–67); the form and function of the book, on which the poet is shown to have used three literary forms, of which the last is appropriated to a function quite different from its original function (pp. 68–86); the speeches of Elihu, which are treated as in themselves a unity (except for xxxvi. 27 — xxxvii. 13) but apparently (for the point is not clearly brought out) not as an integral part of the poem (pp. 87–107); and God's answer from the storm, which is taken to be an original and essential part of the work, as it has stylistic contacts with the Prologue and is implied in the Epilogue (xlii. 7), though not in its present form which shows marked signs of expansion. The author, who has read a vast amount of literature, makes a thorough examination of each problem and argues his case carefully and for the most part convincingly, but he is not endowed with the gift of lucidity, and his style is so *echtdeutsch* that he is unlikely to attract English readers. Yet his work has some importance and ought to be mastered by any one who wishes to make a serious study of Job.

G.R.D.

HARAN, M.: *Between Ri'shonôt* (*Former Prophecies*) *and Ḥadashôt* (*New Prophecies*). A literary-historical study in the group of prophecies Isaiah XL-XLVIII. 1963. Pp. 108. (The Magnes Press, The Hebrew University, Jerusalem).

This is in essence an elaboration of a lecture given by the author at the International Congress for the Study of the Old Testament at Bonn in August, 1962. The study makes pleasant reading in its Hebrew form.

M.W.

JEPSEN, A.: *Das Buch Hiob und seine Deutung*. (Aufsätze und Vorträge zur Theologie und Religionswissenschaft, Heft 28). 1963. Pp. 28. (Evangelische Verlagsanstalt, Berlin. Price: DM. 1.50).

Starting from the fact that the problems raised by the book of Job are so formidable that its entire range cannot be comprehended solely in any one way, the writer maintains that any understanding of the book will depend upon how much of its present contents is held to have originally belonged to it, and conversely, that the answer to the latter question will depend upon one's view of the message of the book. Neither literary criticism nor form criticism alone can lead to a definitive solution. Account must be taken not only of structure and form, but also of content; i.e., it is only by taking as a starting point the unity of the book as it has been transmitted that we can decide what can be established by the arguments of literary criticism and formal analysis. In the already unmanageable mass of literature on Job, Jepsen's study will serve as an admonitory and influential directive.

M.B.

KAPELRUD, A. S.: *Et folk på hjemferd.* "Trøsteprofeten" — den annen Jesaja — og hans budskap. 1964. Pp. 102. (Universitetsforlaget, Oslo).

This book (dedicated to Professor Pedersen on the occasion of his eightieth birthday) is a study of Deutero-Isaiah intended for students and non-specialists. For such readers the author performs three important services: he directs them to the actual text of Scripture; he gives them a discriminating account of recent views on problems raised by Isaiah xl-lv; and he does these things in a clear and interesting way. The main themes discussed are the structure, historical background, and provenance of the book (the author holds that there is decisive evidence that the prophet did not live in Babylonia, and that in all probability his ministry was exercised in Jerusalem), the prophet's message (emphasis is laid on the important influence on it of the autumnal festival and its enthronement motif), the Servant Songs and their literary relationship to the rest of the prophecy, the inter-pretation of the Songs, the identity of the Servant (rival views are presented with discrimination; and the concept of kingship is presented as one which combines naturally the individual and the collective), and the relationship of the Songs to the Messianic problem with a forward look at the New Testament. This is a most attractive study, which shows that a popularization need not be merely second-hand.

G.W.A.

KILIAN, R.: *Literarkritische und Formgeschichtliche Untersuchung des Heiligkeitsgesetzes.* (Bonner Biblische Beiträge, 19). 1963. Pp. XVI+186. (Peter Hanstein Verlag GMBH, Bonn. Price: DM. 24).

This volume provides a detailed analysis of Lev. xvii-xxvi, in which it attempts to distinguish the basic layer of legal material from later expansions and accretions. It maintains that three forms of laws have to be dealt with: apodictic, casuistic, and that which in form of expression is participial and is substantially parallel to, and a development of, the casuistic. The casuistic form, Dr. Kilian believes, was in use in Israel before the occupa-tion of Palestine among at least some of the component tribes which as semi-nomads had contacts with cultures which had a casuistic secular code of laws. Neither the participial nor the apodictic form was originally distinctive of, or confined in use to, Israel, being found in Egypt and, to some extent, in other parts of the ancient Near East. Dr. Kilian's method of in-vestigation is both *formgeschichtlich* and literary-critical, and gives no impression of making the evidence which he has to survey conform to any pre-conceived theory. The basic Holiness Code, as he defines it, had a 'neutral' quality until the redactor of it, Ru (*Redaktor des Urheiligkeitsgesetzes*), who was com-mentator as well as collector, left his mark upon it. This redactor's work, which was done between D and 586 B.C., was followed by that of Rh, which took place during the Exile. Later expansions are due to Priestly editing. This work of analysis is carefully done; its conclusions are not forced and are not revolutionary; and the criticism of H. Graf Reventlow's recent work on the Holiness Code as being very much a *petitio principii* is not without some justification.

J.M.

DE LANGHE, R. (ed. by): *Le Psautier. Ses origines. Ses problèmes littéraires. Son influence.* Études présentées aux XIIe Journées Bibliques (29–31 août 1960). (Orientalia et Biblica Lovaniensia IV). 1962. Pp. VI+ 454. (Editions Nauwelaerts, Louvain. Price: B.Fr. 450).

Recalling the words 'c'est bien plus beau lorsque c'est inutile', the editor (whose early death is so great a loss to Old Testament studies) of this impressive volume expresses the hope that it will be useful as well as beautiful. In a high degree it is both; it will also prove to be indispenable for serious study of the Psalter. It gives a vivid impression both of the intensity and range of contemporary Psalm study and of the outreach of such studies into other fields. Two of the contributions are of notable length and range: 'Les études récentes sur le Psautier', by J. Coppens (pp. 1–71), and 'Les psaumes de la royauté de Yahwé dans l'exégèse moderne', by E. Lipinski (pp. 133–272). Briefer contributions within the Old Testament field are 'Les genres littéraires du Psautier. Un état de la question', by A. Descamps (pp. 73–88); ' "Entmythologisierung" dans les Psaumes', by J. de Fraine (pp. 89–106), ' '*Ani* et '*Anaw* dans les psaumes', by P. van den Berghe (pp. 273–295). Two of the essays refer to the New Testament: 'L'influence des psaumes sur les annonces et les récits de la Passion et de la Resurrection dans les Évangiles', by A. Rose (pp. 297–356); and 'L'interprétation des psaumes dans les Actes des Apôtres', by J. Dupont (pp. 357–388). Qumran studies are represented by 'Psaumes, hymnes, cantiques et prières dans les manuscrits de Qumrân', by M. Baillet (pp. 389–405); and by 'Le Docteur de Justice, nouveau Moïse dans les manuscrits de Qumrân', by M. Delcor (pp. 407–423). A. Arens discusses the question, 'Hat der Psalter seinen "Sitz im Leben" in der Synagogalen Leseordnung des Pentateuch?' (pp. 107–131, an abbreviated presentation of part of his book, *Die Psalmen im Gottesdienst des Alten Bundes*, reviewed in *Book List*, 1962, pp. 34 f.). Finally, on a different theme, M. Martin contributes a study of 'The Babylonian Tradition and Targum' (pp. 425–451).

G.W.A.

LOHFINK, N.: *Das Hauptgebot.* Eine Untersuchung literarischer Einleitungsfragen zu Dtn 5–11. (Analecta Biblica Investigationes Scientificae in Res Biblicas 20). 1963. Pp. XXIV+318. (Pontificio Instituto Biblico Romae. Price: L. 4.800; $8.00).

This book, a dissertation presented at the Pontifical Biblical Institute, is a study of Deut. v–xi, of which the theme is 'Das Hauptgebot, die grundlegende und alles Einzelne umfassende Haltung Israels vor seinem Gott' (p. 112). After an introduction, including a survey of the most important work of earlier scholars, there is a lengthy investigation of words and literary forms in this part of Deuteronomy. Then comes an examination of the text and an attempted reconstruction of its literary history (including a defence of the unity and common authorship of chapters v and vi). There is also a discussion of the interchange between the singular and plural of the second person; Dr. Lohfink refuses to regard such a change as evidence for composite authorship, unless supported by other arguments, and he suggests reasons why it has taken place. Finally, there is a study of the parenetic character of these chapters. Dr. Lohfink believes that behind Deut. v–xi lie the covenantal cult and the preaching of the law; various traditions were combined by the 'Verfasser' in v. 1-vi. 25, ix. 9–19, 21, 25–29, x. 1–5, 10–18, 20–22, xi. 1–17, to which the 'Ueberarbeiter' added vii. 1–24 (25 f. ?), viii. 1–20, ix. 1–8, 22–24, xi. 18–25. At one of these stages (or perhaps later), this material was joined to xii-xxviii, and xi. 26–32 was added as a link; there were other minor additions at different times. At the end of the book are several indexes and tables listing various Deuteronomic expressions. This is a valuable contribution to the study of Deuteronomy.

J.A.E.

McCARTHY, D. J.: *Treaty and Covenant*. A Study in Form in the Ancient Oriental Documents and in the Old Testament. (Analecta Biblica, Investigationes Scientificae in Res Biblicas 21). 1963. Pp. XXIV+ 220. (Pontifical Biblical Institute, Rome. Price: L. 2.850; $4.75).

This literary genre, of Mesopotamian origin, is currently the subject of many publications, so that this analysis of the cuneiform texts with translations of the recently published treaties from Ras Shamra, Alalakh, Sfiré, and Nimrud (thus supplementing *ANET*) is to be welcomed as a well-documented general introduction to the subject. The new material in this thesis (by a student of Professor Cazelles) lies in his argument for the unbroken continuity of the basic covenant tradition from the early 2nd millennium to the 7th century B.C. (against Mendenhall and Albright); the diversity of form in which the historical prologues, stipulations, oaths and curses are presented, and in their full form traced in Deut. v-xxviii. Sections are devoted to ratification rites and to those unique ways in which Israel developed the covenant (e.g., the use of *berith*). Specific covenant terminology is only briefly mentioned. The origin of the literary form and its application to the Sinai tradition are less successfully treated.

D.J.W.

MOWINCKEL, S.: *The Psalms in Israel's Worship*, Vols. I & II, trans. by D. R. Ap-Thomas. 1962. Pp. xxiv+246 and xii+304. (Basil Blackwell, Oxford. Price: 70s. 0d. the set).

It is a privilege to extend a welcome to Professor Mowinckel's *Offersang og sangoffer* (*Book List*, 1952, p. 42; *Eleven Years*, p. 413) in its English dress. Indeed this translation is based upon so thorough a revision of the original that it may almost be regarded as a new book. To be sure, the text of some chapters remains virtually untouched; but that of others, e.g., on the so-called 'Enthronement Festival of Yahweh' and on the metre of the psalms, has been rearranged, expanded and, in part, rewritten. One whole chapter, i.e., on the Christian use of the

Psalter, has been omitted completely. The notes have been revised throughout; and. happily, most of these are now reproduced as footnotes or even in some cases (notably references to Scripture) incorporated into the text, only the longer ones being retained at the end of the work as 'Additional Notes'. The author has catered for every type of reader. The student who is beginning his Old Testament studies will have in the text of the book an exciting introduction to the Psalter. The more advanced reader, already familiar with the main lines of Professor Mowinckel's thought, will have, not only what is an almost up-to-date statement of them, but, particularly in the notes, the author's considered replies to the criticisms which have been levelled against his views and his own verdict on certain developments of these views with which he is unable to agree. Warm thanks are due to Mr. Ap-Thomas, whose fluent if, now and again perhaps, slightly colloquial translation evokes once more the admiration which the reviewer so often feels for the versatility of his Welsh-speaking colleagues and friends. He has rendered a signal service by thus making available for the English reader the views of this distinguished Norwegian scholar who must surely go down in history as one of the great creative minds in the field of Old Testament scholarship.
                                                                        A.R.J.

OSSWALD, E.: *Das Bild des Mose in der kritischen alttestamentlichen Wissenschaft seit J. Wellhausen.* (Theologische Arbeiten, Band XVIII). 1962. Pp. 370. (Evangelische Verlagsanstalt, Berlin. Price: DM. 19.50).

This work is based on the *Habilitationsarbeit* presented by the author at Jena in 1956; and she has earned our gratitude by assembling and presenting in so orderly a fashion such a wealth of material. She begins with the new literary and historical approach to the Pentateuch in the 19th century (pp. 11 ff.), passing then to Wellhausen and his disciples and opponents (pp. 40 ff.), and on to the religio-historical school (pp. 114 ff.). No critical tendency and no critic of any importance is omitted. Finally there is an account of the various forms of traditio-historical and cult-historical approach (pp. 238 ff.), and also of recent Jewish studies. The book ends with a retrospect and prospect (pp. 335 ff.) in which there are judicious suggestions about lines of future research.
                                                                        M.B.

OTZEN, B.: *Studien über Deuterosacharja.* (Acta Theologica Danica, Vol. VI). 1964. Pp. 303. (Prostant apud Munksgaard, Copenhagen. Price: D. Kr. 60).

This monograph, for which the author was awarded a doctorate at the University of Aarhus, begins with a survey of scholarly work on Zech. ix-xiv since 1620. After this introduction, the main part (pp. 35–212) of the book discusses the historical background of these prophecies in which it detects four originally independent parts. First, ix-x reflects the hopes of a restoration of the Davidic monarchy in the time of Josiah (ix. 13 refers to Greek mercenaries in the Egyptian army). Second, xi comes from a time shortly before 587; the shepherd allegory is interpreted as a somewhat unfavourable review of the monarchy since its institution. Third, xii-xiii (in which xiii. 2–6 and 7–9 are originally independent oracles) is thought to come from Judaean circles in the exilic period; xiii. 10 ff. apply to the sufferings of the nation language proper to the symbolic death of the king in the cult. Fourth, xiv is a late passage of apocalyptic character using old cultic motifs. Next there is a discussion of the literary structure of the prophecies which is sometimes critical of the views of P. Lamarche (*Book List*, 1963, pp. 35 f.), and then about forty pages of textual and exegetical notes. There are also a summary in Danish, a bibliography, and indexes. This is a clearly presented and able work (especially in its treatment of chapters ix-x) which makes a valuable contribution to the study of a very obscure part of the Old Testament.

J.A.E.

PLÖGER, O.: *Theokratie und Eschatologie* (Wissenschaftliche Monographien zum Alten und Neuen Testament, Zweiter Band). 2., durchgesehene Auflage. 1962. Pp. 142. (Verlag der Buchhandlung des Erziehungsvereins, Neukirchen Kreis Moers. Price: paper, DM. 11.25; cloth, DM. 13.50).

The first edition of this important work appeared in 1959 but unfortunately was not reviewed in the *Book List*. As the author insists, the inquiry is historical rather than theological, in spite of its title. Two questions are posed: How are we to account for the disappearance of the prophets in the latter part of the Old Testament period? and where should we look for the origins of the Hasidim? The answers are suggested in a series of discussions of the Maccabean period, the book of Daniel, the rise of Apocalyptic, Isaiah xxiv-xxvii, Zechariah xii-xiv, and Joel. The author seeks to trace lines of development from the eschatology of the prophecies of restoration to the dualistic eschatology of apocalyptic, and from the older conception of Israel and the earlier prophetic groups to the circles of the pious. Though brief, this treatise is most stimulating and merits close study.

G.W.A.

REVENTLOW, H. GRAF: *Liturgie und prophetisches Ich bei Jeremia*. 1963. Pp. 268. (Gütersloher Verlagshaus Gerd Mohn, Gütersloh. Price: DM. 38).

The presentation of Jeremiah as the prophet of individual piety needs to be modified by a recognition of his dependence on liturgical forms. The call to prophesy i. 4–10, the visions, i. 11 f, 13–16 and xxiv, follow patterns recognizable elsewhere in the Old Testament. The watchman passage in iv. 5–12 follows the form of the alarm-call; the 'enemy from the North' has no necessary historical reference, but is a cultic term deriving from the covenant-celebration. The prophet appears to have been officially recognized, especially in his work as intercessor. In these intercessions there is nothing of *individual* feeling; they are liturgical utterances. Even in the Confessions the 'I' is the representative and embodiment of the community. It should be observed that the text of the passages discussed is submitted to the most careful examination. The treatment is similar to that of the author's studies of Ezekiel and Amos (*Book List*, 1963, pp. 37 ff.). It is a fascinating and even exciting study of prophecy in general and Jeremiah in particular; it must be read together with and as complementary to Skinner's great study. It is stimulating and will, we would think, be essential reading for any study of Jeremiah.

A.S.H.

RICHTER, W.: *Traditionsgeschichtliche Untersuchungen zum Richterbuch.* (Bonner Biblische Beiträge, 18). 1963. Pp. xx+412. (Peter Hanstein Verlag, Bonn. Price: DM. 32).

This is a massive and detailed study of Judges iii-ix, presented as part of a doctoral dissertation to the Catholic Faculty of Theology at Bonn. Each section of the chapters studied is subjected to literary criticism and also to 'Gattungs'- criticism. On questions of literary criticism the author shows much independence of judgement. He is ready to recognize composite origin, but is cautious in doing so, and adopts no extreme positions. Wherever doublets have been found they are carefully examined, and in a number of cases the author denies that they are really doublets. The differences between Judg. iv and v are fully recognized, and a considerable part of the book is taken up with the study of the Song of Deborah; the full Hebrew text is given in a critical edition in an appendix. (Incidentally, it may be observed, that the author rejects the view of Albright that *zeh Sinai* in Judg. v. 5 and Ps. lxviii. 9 means 'he of Sinai'.) Following the discussion of the separate sections, chaps. iii, iv, v, vi-viii, ix, Dr. Richter takes up the question of a pre-Deuteronomic work from which these stories of Saviours were drawn. He argues for such a work, coming from the ninth century B.C., resting on older traditions, with some interpolations. In the second part of the work the author presents an examination of syntactical and stylistic questions.

H.H.R.

RINGGREN, H.: *The Faith of the Psalmists.* (S.C.M. Greenbacks). 1963. Pp. xxii+138. (S.C.M. Press, London. Price: 10s. 6d.).

This book is the author's own translation and revision of *Psaltarens fromhet*, published in 1957 (see *Book List*, 1958, p. 29). The general plan, character, and standpoint remain unchanged; but it has been deftly adapted to the needs of readers in the English-speaking countries. Some references to more recent literature have been added, and others to works available only in Scandinavian languages have been eliminated. The book may be warmly commended as an excellent introduction to the subject.

G.W.A.

SMEND, R.: *Die Bundesformel.* (Theologische Studien, Heft 68). 1963. Pp. 47. (EVZ-Verlag, Zürich. Price: Sw. Fr. 5.40).

This is a discussion of the formula: 'Yahweh the God of Israel, Israel the people of Yahweh'. Three forms, representing three stages of development, may be recognised:— 1. The most general and important, 'Yahweh *is* the God of Israel, Israel *is* the people of Yahweh'. 2. Expressions where 'the God of Israel' is in apposition to Yahweh, and 'the people of Yahweh' is in apposition to Israel. 3. A later stage suggesting meditation and

the effect of the exile makes the formula a hope for the future —
'I will be your God and you will be my people'. Particular
attention is given to Deut. xxvi. 17, 18 where uniquely the hiph'il
of *'amar* is used, with the meaning 'proclaim' and 'acclaim'.
While the first part of the formula goes back to the desert
experience, the latter is first clearly expressed at the institution
of the monarchy in l. Sam. x, the formula provides an adequate
principle of unity for an Old Testament theology yet points
beyond itself to its fulfilment in Christ Jesus.   A.S.H.

VON WALDOW, E.: *Der traditionsgeschichtliche Hintergrund der pro-
    phetischen Gerichtsreden.* (Beihefte zur Zeitschrift für die Alttesta-
    mentliche Wissenschaft 85). 1963. Pp. 54. (Verlag Alfred Töpelmann,
    Berlin. Price: DM. 10).

In this study von Waldow re-examines the prophetic oracles of
judgement, of accusation and of defence, and finds that (i) there
is no real evidence of a cultic background for them; (ii) that
there is evidence, as others have shown, that their form, but
the verbal form only, was borrowed from the language and usage
of the court of judgement; and (iii) that their content, coupled
with the fact that Yahweh appears in a dual rôle, either as
plaintiff and judge, or as defendant and judge, at one and the
same time, shows them to have a background of covenant
relationship and especially that of an annual festival of covenant
renewal.   L.H.B.

WEISER, A.: *Einleitung in das Alte Testament.* Fünfte, verbesserte und
    vermehrte Auflage. 1963. Pp. 420.   (Vandenhoeck & Ruprecht,
    Göttingen. Price: DM. 18.50).

The English translation of this Introduction was noticed in
Book List, 1962, p. 40, and previous German editions in *Book
Lists,* 1946, p. 30 (*Eleven Years,* p. 30), 1950, p. 46 (*Eleven Years,*
p. 263), and 1958, p. 31. In the present edition full account has
been taken of the work done in recent years, thus bringing the
volume up to date and adding to its proved usefulness.

                                                          G.W.A.

WEISS, M.: *The Bible and Modern Literary Theory* (in Hebrew). 1962.
    Pp. 272. (The Bialik Institute, Jerusalem).

In this book 'New Criticism' methods, used in the interpretation
of *belles lettres,* are applied with skill and fine scholarly discernment to the study of the text of the Bible. Following the teachings
of this school (in Swiss-German circles: *Werkinterpretation*),
the author takes hardly any account of philological, historical,
and sociological data, by which researchers of the last two
hundred years or so have elucidated so much of the contents
of the Bible. Instead he concentrates solely on the text, perceiving
it in its wholeness, and confining himself strictly to its intrinsic
properties; these properties, and these alone, explain the text.
Though in nature methodological, the book inevitably interprets
numerous Biblical passages. Thus, for instance, while speaking
about 'metaphor'; 'sentence'; and 'structure', appropriate Biblical

verses, especially from the Book of Psalms, are explained. The book includes a wealth of erudite notes, referring to Biblical critics of the last few generations, after which come six appendixes, constituting short studies in themselves, and a Biblical index.

M.W.

LAW, RELIGION, AND THEOLOGY

ACHTEMEIER, P. & E.: *The Old Testament Roots of Our Faith.* 1962. Pp. 158. (Abingdon Press, New York & Nashville. Price: $3.00.).

The authors are man and wife. He teaches New Testament and she teaches Old Testament in the United Church of Christ Seminary at Lancaster (Pa.). The theme of the book is that the two Testaments are essentially one. The New Testament is the culmination of an action of God which began with the call of Abraham in the eighteenth century, the promise that in a Son of Abraham all the families of the earth shall be blessed. It is a good, modern, evangelical interpretation of the Bible, with all except the last chapter dealing with the Old Testament. There is much dependence on moderns such as von Rad, and some interesting suggestions: e.g., 'image of God' is really 'image of *elohim*', divine beings.

N.H.S.

AHLSTRÖM, G. W.: *Aspects of Syncretism in Israelite Religion.* (Horae Soederblomianae, V). 1963. Pp. 98. (C. W. K. Gleerup, Lund. Price: Sw. Kr. 9).

The association of various divine names known to have a Canaanite origin with the Israelite Yahweh is evidence that there was a process of syncretism taking place in Israel as well as a vigorous repudiation of certain cult practices. The aim of this book is to examine the Old Testament evidence relating to various Canaanite cult centres which contributed to Israel's religion before the monarchy, then the Jebusite contribution, both as to cultic practice and divine names. The distinctive character of Israel's religion is not in doubt, but the inclusion within it of Canaanite elements cannot be ignored. This is a most valuable contribution distinguished alike by its careful use of the Biblical text and its mastery of related material. The treatment would suggest that it is not quite 'syncretism' which appears, but perhaps 'assimilation'.

A.S.H.

BARTHÉLEMY, D.: *Dieu et son image.* Ébauche d'une théologie biblique. 1963. Pp. 254. (Les Éditions du Cerf, Paris. Price: NF. 10.50).

This is a collection of studies, which are more in the nature of meditations on the Bible than a connected presentation of Biblical theology. They deal with man's ignorance of God and the divine action in election and redemption through which that knowledge is revealed. There is no documentation of modern theological literature and, for reasons explained in the preface, the author pays little attention to historico-critical questions.

R.E.C.

BEAUCAMP, É.: *The Bible and the Universe. Israel and the Theology of History*, trans. by D. Balhatcher. 1963. Pp. xviii+200. (Burns & Oates, London. Price: 30s. 0d.).

This is a translation of the work entitled *La Bible et le sens religieux de l'univers*, which appeared in French in 1959 and was reviewed in the *Book List* for 1960, at p. 31. The rendering seems to be, on the whole, quite competent, but, as so often, it is to be regretted that the translator cannot give much help over disputed or controversial readings. An example may be that of Job xvii. 7 (p. 154) where the author questions Dhorme's rendering, and where the translator can do no more than give the readings of the Douai and Knox editions, which, whatever may be their merits, are not versions based directly on the original text.

J.M.T.B.

BESNARD, A.–M.: *Le Mystère du Nom*. Quiconque invoquera le nom du Seigneur sera sauvé — Joël 3, 5. (Lectio Divina 35). 1962. Pp. 198+7 plates. (Les Éditions du Cerf, Paris. Price: NF. 12).

The purpose of this pleasantly written study is to investigate the significance of the name of Yahweh in the minds of dwellers in the ancient East, to comment upon the revelation of the name as described in Exodus, and to study certain formulae such as 'I am Yahweh', and 'Yahweh (Sabaoth) is his name'. A second part considers the invocation of the name, the significance in the Old Testament of invoking the name of Yahweh, and the exegesis of Joel 2:32: 'Whosoever shall call upon the name of Yahweh shall be saved'. A third part is concerned with the Christian use of the holy name, as shown in the accomplishment of Joel's prophecy on the day of Pentecost, the invocation of the name of the Lord Jesus, and prayer to the Father.

This does not strike one as a work of great originality, but it is doubtless intended chiefly for readers who are not specialists and it makes excellent use of the chief commentators. There are some interesting illustrations, notably one from the north portal of the transept in Rheims cathedral, where a statue represents Abraham as receiving into his bosom the souls of the elect.

J.M.T.B.

BRANDON, S. G. F.: *Creation Legends of the Ancient Near East*. 1963. Pp. xiv+242 incl. 5 ills.+14 plates+frontispiece. (Hodder and Stoughton, London. Price: 35s. 0d.).

In this interesting book Professor Brandon has brought together the most recent results of modern research on the Creation legends of Egypt, Mesopotamia, Israel, Greece, and Iran. He has also provided us with an original commentary on the far-reaching implications of early man's preoccupation with the problem of his own origins and of the material universe by which he found himself surrounded. One of his interesting suggestions is that Egyptian and Mesopotamian cosmogonies were not generally motivated by a desire to speculate about the beginning of things: instead they were designed to promote the interests of some sanctuary or city (p. 120f.). This would bring these creation-stories under the classification of prestige-myths. In his summing up in the Epilogue, Professor Brandon says, 'As we look back across our study of these creation legends of the ancient Near East and seek to assess their witness as a whole, it would seem that they attest most impressively man's essential consciousness of time'. This is a theme which he has more fully developed in his book *Time and Mankind.* The present book is a valuable addition to the many studies of Near Eastern mythology listed in his useful bibliography. S.H.H.

BRICHTO, H. C.: *The Problem of "Curse" in the Hebrew Bible.* (Journal of Biblical Literature Monograph Series, Volume XIII). 1963. Pp. x+232 (Photolithoprinted). (Society of Biblical Literature and Exegesis, Philadelphia. Price: $2 (post paid) from Prof. V. M. Rogers, New Brunswick Theological Seminary, New Brunswick, New Jersey).

Basing his study on the earlier work of J. Pedersen, J. Hempel, S. Mowinckel, S. Blank, S. Gevirtz, and J. Scharbert, the author investigates the terminology of the curse in the terms *'ala, 'arar, qillel* and *qbb, z'm* and *ḥrm*; their accidence, distribution, and antonyms. The author distinguishes between East-Semitic curse formulations wherein the divine agency is emphasized, and West-Semitic and Hebrew forms wherein the agent is undesignated and the automatic power of the word is all important. He discusses the connection between oath and curse, and pleads for a less magical view of the latter. Altogether a careful, competent, and helpful investigation. G.H.D.

DAUBE, D.: *The Exodus Pattern in the Bible.* (All Souls Studies, II). 1963. Pp. 94. (Faber and Faber, London. Price: 25s. 0d.).

That the great tradition of the Exodus from Egypt has served as a model for the recitals, etc., of the Biblical writers, is obvious enough. But in this study, it is suggested that the Exodus recital itself, as it appears in the various strands, has been determined by contemporary social laws and customs. The Pharaoh was flouting established social regulations in refusing to free Israel. The phrase, 'Israel is my son . . . let my son go.' is a legal claim. The group of words such as *yashab, ṣa'aq, yaṣa', halakh,* as well as the more obvious ones, have a legal connotation. The Jacob and Laban narrative is a pre-enactment of the Exodus. The Ark among the Philistines and its release reflects the same pattern. Perhaps only another great jurist could do justice to the subtlety of the argument. Your reviewer is not convinced. Surprisingly, no use is made of Exod. ix. 27, although a reference appears in a footnote. A.S.H.

DAUBE, D.: *Suddenness and Awe in Scripture* (Robert Waley Cohen Memorial Lecture, 1963). N.D. [1964] Pp. 20. (The Council of Christians and Jews, 41 Cadogan Gardens, London, S.W.3. Price: 2s. 0d.).

Professor Daube utilizes wide and deep research to present this short study of the irruption of the unexpected into human experience, with special reference to the Hebrew root *qr'*. After treating of the association of awe with the sudden, the author points out how the numinous was also recognized even early on in the regular and reliable sequence of natural events. For the extended working out of the author's theses recourse must be had to his fuller works cited in the notes; but within a very short compass we have here the thought-provoking record of what must have been a stimulating and unusual lecture.

D.R.Ap-T.

DAVIDSON, R.: *The Old Testament*. (Knowing Christianity). 1964. Pp. 240. (Hodder & Stoughton, London. Price: 12s. 6d.).

This book and the series to which it belongs is directed, not to the scholar as such, but to the general reader who wishes authoritative information about the Bible. Popular, therefore, in the best sense of the word it is intended to be and the author has succeeded to admiration in giving a truly profound exposition in simple language of what the Old Testament contains. He has an enviable gift of selecting what is significant and maintaining the interest of the reader throughout. By linking the name of God with each of the themes with which he deals, e.g., God and History, God and the Community, God and Worship, God and the troubled mind, he gives in effect a brief theology of the Old Testament, showing how it points beyond itself. 'But, if he (i.e., the Christian) is wise, he will not regard the Old Testament merely as a preparation for the New. He will turn humbly to the Old Testament knowing that Hebrew historians and prophets, priests, poets and storytellers have much to teach him.' It is to be hoped that scholars will not overlook this book which is a little masterpiece in the difficult art of getting things across without lowering the standards demanded of the scholar.

N.W.P.

DENTAN, R. C.: *Preface to Old Testament Theology*. Revised Edition. 1963. Pp. 146. (The Seabury Press, New York. Price: $3.00).

This book represents a revision of the monograph published by the Yale University Press in 1950 (see *Book List*, 1951, p. 55; *Eleven Years*, p. 350) enlarged to about twice its original size. Once more it has to be stated that the author has provided an admirable summary of the long debate about the nature and content of a theology of the Old Testament. The intervening years have enabled the author to take account of the tremendous output of the last dozen years during which the fundamental problems involved have been the subject of eager debate by many scholars and theologians. Dr. Dentan exhibits a wide range of knowledge and a sober judgement but states quite frankly that he sees no reason to change his original point of view, viz., that a theology of the Old Testament must be the systematic exposition of the normative religious ideas taught or assumed in the Old Testament Canon. In this he differs fundamentally from a view of the discipline taken by a writer like von Rad. He admits that 'sympathy, insight, and inner participation' are demanded of the student of the Old Testament and that 'an invaluable precondition for such inner participation is that the student of Old Testament theology should in some sense share the Old Testament faith — to the extent that that faith continues to form a part of the Christian religious consciousness'. It may perhaps be suggested that further thought is necessary along this line.

N.W.P.

FROST, S.: *Patriarchs and Prophets*. 1963. Pp. viii+232. (John Murray, London. Price: 25s. 0d.).

The fourteen studies in this book are of Abraham, Jacob, Joseph, Moses, Joshua, Samson, Samuel, Saul, David, Solomon, Elijah, Isaiah, Jeremiah, and Deutero-Isaiah. They are concerned to elucidate the significance of the stories or prophetic teaching for human life and conduct. The book is devotional in character, and argues that only as we begin here in our study of the Bible shall we rediscover its authority. Not all of the interpretations would command general assent. Was Joshua 'to all intents and purposes created' by the Deuteronomists? Does the description of Jeremiah as 'the first Liberal Protestant' do justice to the prophet? The book will, however, undoubtedly prove helpful to lay preachers and teachers.

A.S.H.

GRAYDON, H. (and others): *Bible Meanings* — A short theological word-book of the Bible. 1963. Pp. 80. (Oxford University Press. Price: 8s. 6d.).

The authors explain the meaning of more than 200 of the principal theological terms of the Bible. They offer a simple introduction to the central words of scripture. Most of the principal terms are included, and the book would be useful for beginners in the study of theology.

G.H.D.

HESCHEL, A. J.: *The Prophets*. 1962. Pp. xx+518. (Harper & Row, London. Price: $6.00).

This massive and enthralling book on the Hebrew Prophets represents a development of the thesis which the author put forward in the much smaller work entitled *Die Prophetie* which appeared in German in 1936. Briefly the thesis is that what was revealed to the prophets was not the divine essence but the divine *pathos*. There is a divine involvement and concern in human history, and the prophet is one who identifies himself with this concern of God in such a way that he becomes representative of man before God and that through him God can reveal *pathos* to man. Heschel seeks to demonstrate his view by a study of the eighth- and seventh-century prophets and of the Second Isaiah. As one is carried along by his argument, it becomes a matter of small importance that Heschel accepts Isaiah xxiv–xxvii as Isaianic and Isaiah lvi–lxvi as belonging to the prophecies of the Second Isaiah. There are penetrating chapters on history, chastisement, and justice, in which the tension between the will of God, and the will of man, and the paradox of God's justice and compassion are illuminatingly discussed. Other chapters seek to justify the author's view that the divine *pathos* is central to the Old Testament concept of God and contrasts sharply with the Greek view. 'The God of the prophets cares for His creatures ... He is involved in human history and is affected by human acts. ... The grandeur of God implies the capacity to experience emotion.' There is a judicious treatment of the subject of ecstasy in which it is argued that the prophet, unlike the ecstatic, is both a recipient and a participant and that he stands in a genuine dialogue relationship to God. The prophet is also compared with the poet and the impersonal nature of the poetic inspiration is set over against the subject-subject-relationship in which the prophet stands to God. It is claimed that Biblical prophecy is *sui generis* and must be distinguished from prophecy in other religions.   N.W.P.

*HOOKE, S. H.: *Middle Eastern Mythology*. 1963. Pp. 200+XVI plates. (Penguin Books, Harmondsworth. Price: 4s. 0d.).

The fact that this work has been published in the author's ninetieth year is an addition to its interest, not an excuse for any lack of merit. We would congratulate any writer on producing such a well-balanced, informative, yet comprehensible summary and interpretation of this sort, even in a field less exacting and complicated than Middle Eastern Mythology — while some of us are old-fashioned enough to prefer the epithet Near Eastern, Professor Hooke moves with the times, though even he cannot keep it up after the title!

Following a valuable introductory section on types of myth, their purpose, and their diffusion and disintegration, eight chapters acquaint us in rapid succession with some of the main myths of Mesopotamia (Sumer as well as Babylon), Egypt, Ugarit, the Hittites, the Hebrews, and then mythological elements in Jewish Apocalyptic, in the New Testament and in Christianity. Not only do we have scholarly care in description and interpretation, but a warm humanity and religious sympathy which show that there is no need for anyone to regard the ancients as half-wits or 'myth' as a dirty word. A bibliography for further reading and an index complete a most useful work of popularisation.   D.R.Ap-T.

JONES, E.: *The Cross in the Psalms*. 1963. Pp. 96. (Independent Press, London. Price: 8s. 6d.).

Various aspects of the experience and problems of suffering are here discussed as they are presented or suggested by some of the Psalms. The themes treated are: Sin and Suffering; The Divine Discipline; Suffering and the Unseen World; Suffering and Cosmic Victory; Suffering and the Silence of God; The Experience of Vicarious Suffering; Suffering and Life after Death. This is a discriminating and sensitive study, based on up-to-date scholarship, which should be of particular use to students and preachers.   G.W.A.

KRAMER, S. N. (ed. by): *Mythologies of the Ancient World*. 1961. Pp. 480. (Quadrangle Books, Chicago. Price: $7.50).

This book is a symposium, devised and edited by Professor Kramer, in which the mythologies of Egypt, Sumer and Akkad, the Hittites, Canaan, ancient Greece, India, ancient Iran, ancient

China, Japan, and ancient Mexico, are described by a team of American scholars, each of whom is a specialist in the field with which he deals. The result is a collection of material of the greatest value and interest to students of mythology. In some of the more familiar fields, such as the Egyptian, Mesopotamian, and Canaanite mythologies, the reader will be surprised at the extent to which older views have been corrected by the discovery of new material, and the deeper study of old material. It is very welcome to have such little-known ranges of mythology as those of ancient China, Japan, and Mexico, made available for the general reader. The undoubted value of this book would have been enhanced if it had included chapters on Hebrew mythology, and ancient Scandinavian mythology. Professor Kramer has rendered a great service to students of this fascinating branch of human knowledge.

S.H.H.

KRINETZKI, L.: *Der Bund Gottes mit den Menschen nach dem Alten und Neuen Testament*. (Die Welt der Bibel, Band 15). 1962. Pp. 128. (Patmos-Verlag, Düsseldorf. Price: DM. 2.88).

This handsome paperback treats of the idea of covenant in the Old and New Testaments. First the author expounds the five convenants of law (Noah, Abraham, Isaac and Jacob, Israel, Levi, and David). Then he recounts the cultic, saving (for Israel and the nations) and institutional aspects of these covenants. Deut. xxvii f. and Joshua xxiv figure as illustrations of the renewal of the desert covenant. Next he treats of the new covenant of the prophets, the covenant of freedom, and works out the programme of its realisation in the new Israel with its Davidic monarchy and Levitical Priesthood. The remaining 17 pages treat of the covenant in the N.T. The book which is well laced with copious quotations of scripture texts, is an orthodox outline, and elementary study of the idea of covenant.

G.H.D.

McKENZIE, J. L.: *Myths and Realities: Studies in Biblical Theology*. 1963. Pp. xvi+286. (The Bruce Publishing Company, Milwaukee, Wisconsin. Price: $4.75).

This volume of essays by an American Jesuit scholar is worthy of close study, proceeding, as it clearly does, from a mind of high distinction. It is divided into four parts. Part I, entitled 'Free Scholarship in the Church', is especially interesting if one wishes to understand present movements in Roman Catholic theology. Part II, entitled 'Inspiration and Revelation', begins with a study of the Word of God in the Old Testament as what the author calls dynamic and dianoetic, and it is argued that one does not need to go outside the Old Testament to understand why Jesus Christ is called the Word. In another essay the view is put forward that inspiration is social in character and the importance of the community in Israel is emphasized. Part III, entitled 'Myth and the Old Testament', contains an elaborate and up-to-date discussion of the whole problem of myth in the Old Testament which indicates the indebtedness of Israel's faith to the mythopoeic thinking of the ancient eastern world and the decisive break Israel made with it through its acceptance of the revelation of divine transcendence and its rejection of polytheism. There is a study of Genesis ii-iii and Ezekiel xxviii. 12-18 which claims for the author of the Genesis pericope a highly original handling of the mythological material at his disposal. Father McKenzie believes that the traditional story used in Genesis ii probably ended with an epithalamium which has been replaced by the story of the origin of sin contained in Genesis iii. He suggests that it would be truer to describe the opening chapters of Genesis as wisdom rather than as history. 'We shall never understand the Old Testament', he declares, 'unless we learn to read its language'. Part IV, entitled 'Messianism', contains a long essay in which the main 'Messianic' passages in the Old Testament are subjected to a sober examination. The author refuses to separate the covenant with David from the covenant with Israel and he shows how the basic Israelite ideas presupposed in the king-ideology are the Sinai Covenant and the kingship of Yahweh. The ideas associated with the kingship in Israel point forward to the realization of the universal reign of God. In the concluding essay there is a discussion of the ways in which the different themes of the Old Testament were fulfilled and, in being fulfilled, transformed in Christ.

N.W.P.

MACKENZIE, R. A. F.: *Faith and History in the Old Testament.* 1963. Pp. x+120. (Minnesota University Press, Minneapolis and Oxford University Press, London. Price: 30s. 0d.).

This is a good book. It is well written, a book to be re-read and savoured. The Bibliography and Index are slight, but Father MacKenzie has read widely and pondered deeply. There are few references to distract the reader, and hardly any footnotes. The central chapter is on 'The Problem of Myth and History'. In it the author says 'I have no wish to confuse mythology and history; I wish only to show that they are not complete opposites, and that each has in it something of the other. History is not quite as historical, and myth is not quite as mythical, as we tend to think'. This is illustrated with reference to such modern figures as Christopher Columbus and George Washington. Translations from the Old Testament are the author's own, and very good they are. The dust-cover says 'the book is intended for lay people interested in modern Bible interpretation, as well as for priests, ministers, and rabbis'. But there can be few specialists who will not find in it insights worth reflecting on at leisure.

C.R.N.

MISKOTTE, K. H.: *Wenn die Götter Schweigen. Vom Sinn des Alten Testaments.* 1963. Pp. 496. (Chr. Kaiser Verlag, München. Price: DM. 28).

This massive book is the translation into German of a work which originally appeared in Dutch in 1956. It is written in a somewhat obscure theological style which will be apt to deter any but the most determined reader. This is unfortunate, because the writer really has something challenging to say. Briefly stated his view is that modern prevalence of atheism and nihilism is the inevitable consequence of a view of religion for which God is virtually a projection of human ideas and desires. To this must be opposed the Old Testament with its revelation of the 'Name', which represents God in His absolute transcendence. The author advocates instruction in Biblical truth so as to prepare those within the Church for the reception of the preached word and he is keenly interested in exploring the relation between Christianity and general culture. A large part of the book is devoted to hermeneutical problems and the concluding section gives examples of the author's exposition of individual passages. The dominant influence of the Barthian theology is evident throughout.

N.W.P.

MORGENSTERN, J.: *The Fire upon the Altar*. 1963. Pp. 132. (E. J. Brill, Leiden. Price: Fl. 28).

In this monograph Professor Morgenstern has produced another of his fascinating forays into Old Testament wonderland. In spite of the frequent occurrence of the words 'there can be no doubt', or 'it is almost absolutely certain', the bewildered reader will often rub his eyes and wonder where fact ends and fantasy begins. The picture of a great seasonal festival at the ancient sanctuary on Carmel, attended by the king and his retinue, and all Israel, at which 'the descent of the fire from heaven was a regular and integral part of the celebration of this annual festal day', somewhat strains the imagination. But when we are told that Elijah poured white naphtha upon the stones of the altar which he had built, and by some artificial means caused the light of the sun's rays to kindle the highly inflammable liquid (p. 68), the strain becomes a little too great. The solid part of Professor Morgenstern's thesis lies in his argument that the orientation of Solomon's Temple in relation to the first rays of the rising sun upon the equinoctial New Year's Day indicates a stage in the development of the religion of Israel when the worship of Yahweh had a solar character, and that this was gradually replaced by the belief that the *kᵉbod Yahweh* had taken up its permanent abode on the ark-throne in the Temple. The author's valuable collection of the Jewish legendary material relating to the sacred fire is a most interesting part of his monograph. This very learned study is a fascinating exercise in detection.

S.H.H.

MULDER, M. J. *Ba'al in het Oude Testament*. 1962. Pp. 212. (Uitgeverij van Keulen N.V., Den Haag, Holland.)

The author sets himself to study all the Old Testament references to Baal and the Baalim, including occurrences of Baal and related terms in compound names of places and persons. He takes into account all that can be learned about Baal from non-Israelite sources, especially from the Ugaritic texts. The Old Testament writers are not concerned to provide their readers with precise information about Baal and his cult, but they provide enough to make it clear that the Biblical Baal is identical with the deity worshipped under that name at Ugarit; the author thinks that we cannot be absolutely sure whether his proper name was Hadad, Baal-shamem, or something else. He does not believe that the Baal whose worship became so popular in Israel under Ahab and Jezebel was the Tyrian deity Melqart. The plural Baalim denotes not a plurality of gods but the plurality of cult-centres of the single god Baal. The semantic development of the substantive *ba'al* in Biblical Hebrew is traced to the point where it means practically 'idol' and is replaced by the editorial *bosheth*. It is, in the author's judgement, a singular fact in the history of religions that Israel's faith in Yahweh was not merged in the Baal-cult, but that Yahweh triumphed completely over Baal. There is a French summary of the thesis, and a full bibliography.   F.F.B.

PLATH, S.: *Furcht Gottes: Der Begriff YR' im Alten Testament*. (Arbeiten zur Theologie, II Reihe, Band 2). 1963. Pp. 144. (Calwer Verlag, Stuttgart. Price: DM. 18).

This is a good sample of a doctoral thesis worked up into a book. The occurrences of the root have been systematically enumerated and classified for the whole of the Old Testament. Whether *Menschenfurcht* should include everything that is not *Gottesfurcht* is a matter of the adequateness of the chosen terminology and does not really mar the clear schematisation of the author's work, as shown in the detailed tabulation of the Contents which renders a subject index unnecessary.

The concordance work seems to have been done with care, and those seeking this kind of information will find it here ready to hand. It is interesting to note the author's remark (p. 28), that fear in the Old Testament is always of something definite and is never an anxiety state. That 'fear not' is absent from the Psalter (p. 122) is not altogether surprising, but many will question the assumption that the Psalms are to be classified as post-exilic *schlechthin*.

To restrict treatment exclusively to a single root undoubtedly results in some unbalance; but it is well that detailed work such as this should be undertaken, so that the composite picture when drawn may be correct in its constituent parts. Hebrew type is used not transliteration, and there is an index of scripture references. The book may be commended though the high price is to be regretted.   D.R.Ap-T.

PORTER, J. R.: *Moses and Monarchy. A Study in the Biblical Tradition of Moses*. 1963. Pp. 28. (Basil Blackwell, Oxford. Price: 3s. 6d.).

In this inaugural lecture, delivered on his appointment to the newly established Chair of Theology in the University of Exeter, Professor Porter gathers together in summary fashion the evidence which he finds available to support his theory that the figure of Moses as presented in the Pentateuch is modelled upon that of the Davidic king, and that the basic aim was to represent the Davidic dynasty as Moses' true successor. It is useful to have the argument for the existence of such royal traits in the portrait of Moses presented so succinctly and so forcibly; and, if the writer of this note finds much of the argument somewhat strained and unconvincing, he must add that he has also found in the reading of this short but well-documented study a real stimulus to thought.   A.R.J.

QUINN, E. C.: *The Quest of Seth for the Oil of Life.* 1962. Pp. xii+196, incl. 12 ills. (University of Chicago Press, Chicago and London. Price: $5.00).

This is a study of the legend of Seth's journey to Paradise to ask God for the oil of mercy. Mrs. Quinn does not describe each major version of the legend independently but selects six motifs — the quest for the oil, the promise of the oil, the discovery of the twigs, the twigs and the seed, Seth and the twig from Paradise, and the green tree and the dry — and traces the evolution of the legend from the *Apocalypse of Moses* to the *Legende*. The symbols and motifs are pursued back into Ugaritic and Akkadian literature and this is both the most original and the least successful part of the book. The methods of legend construction employed by mediaeval authors are admirably illustrated. T.D.

RENAUD, B.: *Je suis un Dieu jaloux.* Évolution sémantique et signification théologique de $qin^{e'}ah$. (Lectio Divina 36). 1963. Pp. 160. (Les Éditions du Cerf, Paris. Price: NF. 9.60).

In this small book the sense of the word that is commonly translated as 'zeal' or 'jealousy' is traced through the ancient traditions preserved in Exodus and Joshua, the Deuteronomic recensions, the exilic literature, and the post-exilic writings. In his final summary the author, when called upon to choose between *zèle* and *jalousie* prefers the latter, provided that all idea of pettiness and paltriness has been excluded from the word's connotation. This may not seem a very exciting conclusion, but readers who are not specialists may find some interesting details in the exegesis of the numerous passages of Scripture that are laid under contribution. J.M.T.B.

RINGGREN, H.: *Israelitische Religion* (Die Religionen der Menschheit, Band 26). 1963. Pp. xii+328+1 map. (W. Kohlhammer Verlag, Stuttgart. Price: DM. 30).

A history of Israelite religion from the Patriarchal times to the beginning of the Christian era. The author's interest lies in the period of the monarchy, and particularly in the prophets and prophetic religion, and to this period he devotes about two-thirds of the book. The book is fully informed, both from the point of view of ancient evidence, Israelite and non-Israelite, and of modern scholarship and opinion. Although the fullest use is made of non-Israelite material, largely by way of illustration, Ringgren is at pains to show that Israel was creative in her religion and did not slavishly borrow from her neighbours. The value of the book, not only for the general reader for whom it is designed, but also for the scholar, is enhanced by full documentation, and by the fact that the author records the opinions of other scholars even where they differ widely from his own. If the post-exilic period had been as fully dealt with as that of the monarchy one would have said, without reserve, that this is the most satisfactory of recent studies of Israelite religion. L.H.B.

ROWLEY, H. H.: *The Relevance of Apocalyptic*. A Study of Jewish and Christian Apocalypses from Daniel to the Revelation. New and Revised Edition. 1963. Pp. i-xii+13–240. (Lutterworth Press, London. Price: 25s. 0d.).

Professor Rowley's eminently serviceable handbook first appeared in 1944 (see *Book List*, 1946, p. 51; *Eleven Years*, p. 51). In 1947 a second edition appeared in which the chief alteration was a modification of the date accepted for the Slavonic Enoch. In the present edition the most obvious new feature is the account given of the Qumran Scrolls. But it need hardly be said that note has been taken in the text, the footnotes, and the bibliography of the work done in recent years on the entire field. In its thoroughly revised and up-to-date form the book will undoubtedly continue to be widely used. G.W.A.

SAL, M.: *Les tables de la loi. Principes et rites du judaïsme originel.* 1962. Pp. 222. (La Colombe, Éditions du Vieux Colombier, Paris. Price: NF. 15).

Rabbi Sal accepts the Mosaic authorship and the literal inerrancy of the present form of the Pentateuch but is less rigid about some other sections, e.g., he dates Ezra to the 4th century, and regards the book of Esther as embroidered history. The aim is to show that the Mosaic ordinances, ritual as well as ethical and legal, are at least abreast of modern scientific theory. Some of the author's assertions would be difficult to prove (or disprove) as when he maintains that failure to abstain from blood and from food comprising both milk and meat together lead inexorably to a lack of sensibility; it is also maintained that the Jewish race produced the prophets owing to their scrupulosity in this respect. Sound notions are not lacking in this book but its main interest here will be as an example of modern haggada.

D.R.Ap-T.

SCHREINER, J.: *Sion-Jerusalem: Jahwes Königssitz. Theologie der Heiligen Stadt im Alten Testament.* (Studien zum Alten und Neuen Testament, Band VII). 1963. Pp. 312. (Kösel-Verlag, München. Price: DM. 35).

The title gives sufficient indication of the purpose behind this work, which was accepted as an *Habilitationsschrift* by the Faculty of Theology of the University of Würzburg in 1960. It assembles and discusses, usually in the form of a running commentary, all the passages in the Old Testament which have a bearing on the subject of Mount Zion, e.g., those which deal with the removal of the Ark to this cultic centre; the building and consecration of Solomon's Temple; the significance of Mount Zion for the so-called 'Name' theology; its place in Israel's hymnology, particularly the psalms which celebrate Yahweh's Kingship; and the prestige which it acquired after the failure of Sennacherib's attack upon the holy city. The study is carried through with repeated reference to contemporary discussion of the issues involved; and, if it adds little to one's knowledge and has nothing very exciting to offer, the author's agreeable style and form of presentation give it a certain attractiveness. A.R.J.

SEGAL, J. B.: *The Hebrew Passover from the Earliest Times to A.D. 70.* (London Oriental Series Volume 12). 1963. Pp. xvi+294. (Oxford University Press, London. 42s. 0d.).

This is a book of first-rate importance. There is no aspect of the origin and early history of the Hebrew Passover which has not been subjected by Professor Segal to the most thorough examination. The book is divided into two parts: the first dealing with the primary sources, and with modern theories relating to the Passover, and the second containing the author's own hypotheses concerning the origin and development of the festival. Professor Segal has divided the primary sources into two groups which he has called respectively the Historical and the Traditional Documents. He has printed the text of these, setting out the Pentateuchal sources in columns according to the accepted source-critical analysis. He admits that the tradition has been transmitted in different documents, but doubts whether the identification of the documents is helped by using the Source hypothesis (p. 72). His criticisms on pp. 70–77 call for careful consideration. Chapter III contains a critical survey of all the modern theories of the origin and early development of the Passover, from Beer's edition of *Pesachim* (1912), onwards. This first part of the book will be of the greatest help to students. The most original and exciting part of the book consists of the author's statement of his own views in the last four chapters. He lays down his ground-plan by a comparison of the similarities of Passover and Tabernacles, and sums up the results of this comparison in the following words: 'The Passover and Tabernacles have, as we have seen, each a different relationship to the agricultural seasons; on the other hand, their relationship to the calendar is constant. The date of each is not fixed by the processes of vegetation, but by the calendar. To the Hebrews the Passover (and Tabernacles) was primarily a New Year Festival'. He goes on to point out that a calendar can only have one beginning. The Israelite calendar, he remarks, cannot have begun at both the Passover and Tabernacles in a single year, and he adds that it is generally recognized by scholars that the calendar opening was moved in the course of Israelite history from the Passover to Tabernacles — or in the opposite direction. Space will not admit of a discussion of the way in which the author develops the dichotomous nature of the Hebrew calendar, and its bearing on the development of the distinctive characteristics of Passover and Tabernacles, but it must suffice to say that Professor Segal has made a contribution of outstanding value and originality to this most important subject.

S.H.H.

VELLAS, B. M.: *Threskeutikai Prosopikotetes tes Palaias Diathekes*, 2nd, enlarged, edition, Volume II. 1963. Pp. 312. (Athens).

The first volume of the second edition of this work appeared in 1957 and was reviewed in *Book List*, 1957, p. 57. This second volume treats of Jeremiah, Nahum, Ezekiel, Daniel, Haggai, Zechariah, Malachi, Ezra, Nehemiah, and the writer of the book of Jonah. The general approach adopted is to give accounts of the historical background of each prophet and the structure, content, and religious teaching of the books. It will be noted

that Daniel is treated among the prophets, and, here, as elsewhere a generally conservative line is taken, though the historical
difficulties are discussed at some length. Reference is made
throughout to recent literature; and the book ends with some
seven pages of bibliography, the books listed being mainly in
English, French, or German. The author is to be congratulated
on the production of a work which is so clear, comprehensive,
and thorough.

G.W.A.

VRIEZEN, T. C.: *De Godsdienst van Israël*. 1963. Pp. 262. (W. de Haan,
Zeist. Price: Fl. 8.90).

A comparison of this work with one bearing the same title —
Kuenen's *Godsdienst van Israël* (1869–70) — will reveal how far
the study of Israel's religion in the Old Testament period has
progressed in the more than 90 years which separate them.
Professor Vriezen first examines the religious environment amid
which Israel's national life came into being, and emphasizes the
distinctiveness of Israel's religion: 'it bears a signature all its
own, which can with difficulty be stated in one word, since its
dominant essence is a complex magnitude' (p. 59). Its central
feature, however, is Israel's faith in Yahweh as the God who
manifested himself as liberator in an historical context; Israel's
religion accordingly has an historical and teleological stamp
and not one which is cyclic and naturalistic. The religious life
of Israel around 1000 B.C. is sketched; there follow examinations
of its earlier beginnings and its later development, the close
association of Yahwism with the monarchical state, the triumph
of Yahwism and the contribution of the great prophets, reformation and downfall, restoration and re-creation, centralization
and disintegration. It is in the pre-exilic period that the finest
flowering of Israel's religion is seen. The work has been published in the series of Palladium Paperbacks; there are several
half-tone illustrations. One may hope that, like the author's
Outline of Old Testament Theology, it will one day appear in an
English edition.

F.F.B.

WHITLEY, C. F.: *The Prophetic Achievement*. 1963. Pp. 224. (E. J. Brill,
Leiden. Price: Fl. 21).

In this brief but straightforward study of the achievement of the
pre-exilic prophets the author reaffirms the unique and formative
place they occupy in Israel's religious development. The main
teaching of the prophets may be summed up as: the ethical
nature of God, leading to monotheism, the justice of God, the
grace of God which also gives scope for repentance, and the
ultimate hope in one who will suffer vicariously for all men.
Each chapter begins with a rapid review of divergent critical
opinions through which the author steers a neutral course and
the chapter closes with a résumé of the prophetic teaching largely
by stringing together passages from the prophetic books and
letting them speak for themselves.

L.H.B.

WOLFF, H. W.: *Die Botschaft des Buches Joel.* (Theologische Existenz Heute. Neue Folge Nr. 109). 1963. Pp. 48. (Chr. Kaiser Verlag, München. Price: DM. 3).

The series in which this book appears explains its aim. It is based on the author's commentary in the Biblischer Kommentar series (see above, p. 43) and sets forth the prophet's message for the Church today. It is a call for decision and return to the proclaimed and promised mercy in a day of judgement. This is presented in four chapters:— Joel i. Unparalleled Danger; ii. 1–17 What is needed in the threatening Catastrophe; ii. 18–iii. 5 The new possibility of life; iv. 1–21 Decision for the New World. A closing chapter discusses the use made of Joel iii. 1–5 in the New Testament. Our world, like that of Joel, needs the certainty that the covenant love of God for all the helpless, in the mercy of Christ, controls the actuality of the world to come.

A.S.H.

ZIMMERLI, W.: *Das Gesetz und die Propheten* — Zum Verständnis des Alten Testaments. 1963. Pp. 154. (Vandenhoeck & Ruprecht, Göttingen. Price: DM. 4.80).

This book arose from a series of popular lectures on the Old Testament, designed for a wide audience of students. The first part of the book is an historical review of the interpretation of the law in the Old Testament since Luther, with particular attention to Wellhausen's claim that the prophets preceded the law, and to the more recent studies of Alt and von Rad. The second part is a brief examination of the place of the law in the prophets from Amos to Deutero-Isaiah. There are useful footnotes introducing the relevant modern literature, and the whole study is concise and readable.

R.E.C.

THE LIFE AND THOUGHT OF THE NEIGHBOURING PEOPLES

DONADONI, S. (ed. by): *Le Fonti Indirette della Storia Egiziana.* (Studi Semitici 7). 1963. Pp. 142. (Centro di Studi Semitici, Università di Roma. Price: Lire 3000; $5).

This book, following a previous pattern of the series in which it appears, contains essays by several authorities centering on one theme, in this case the indirect sources for ancient Egyptian history. Four essays are introduced briefly by S. Donadoni. G. Posener writes on 'L'apport des textes littéraires à la connaissance de l'histoire égyptienne', J. Černý on the 'Contribution of the Study of Unofficial and Private Documents to the History of Pharaonic Egypt', W. Helck on the 'Entwicklung der Verwaltung als Spiegelbild historischer und soziologischer Faktoren' and A. Volten on 'I testi demotici quali fonti della storia della religione egiziana'. The book ends with a synthesis by S. Donadoni. It is intended primarily for students of ancient Egypt, but all who are interested in the history of the ancient Near East will find much to interest them in it. Volten's essay on the religion of Egypt in the late period, a subject on which few Egyptologists have ventured to write, will be of value to Old Testament scholars for comparative purposes.

T.W.T.

GARCIA DE LA FUENTE, O.: *Los Dioses y el Pecado en Babilonia* (Biblioteca 'La Ciudad de Dios', 6). 1961. Pp. 212. (Real Monasterio de el Escorial Madrid).

This is a praiseworthy attempt to throw light on a subject which has not, according to the author, been fully explored hitherto, that is, the relation between the Babylonian pantheon and the idea of sin. There are chapters on the Babylonian expressions for sin; religion and sin; the moral order; consciousness of sin, and its consequences; the justice dealt out by the gods and the problem of innocent suffering; and magic, religion, and morality. It is not quite clear how far the author has a first-hand knowledge of Assyrian, but he has certainly consulted many works on his subject, and gives copious extracts from a variety of translations, including those of Gressmann, Hehn, Langdon, Landsberger, and Pritchard's *Ancient Near Eastern Texts*.　J.M.T.B.

KITCHEN, K. A.: *Suppiluliuma and the Amarna Pharaohs*, A Study in Relative Chronology (Liverpool Monographs in Archaeology and Oriental Studies 5). 1962. Pp. x+62. (Liverpool University Press. Price: 22s. 6d.).

It is thirty years since the publication of Professor Cavaignac's book *Subbiluliuma et son Temps*, which was at that time the last word on the subject. Mr. Kitchen's masterly monograph gives evidence of the immense advances which have been made in Hittite studies during the last thirty years. It is also a striking witness to the valuable contribution which the University of Liverpool has made and continues to make to the field of Egyptian and Hittite studies. The special value of this monograph lies in the use which the author has made of the Amarna Letters to illuminate the new accumulation of Hittite historical material. The last 18 pages consist of a most valuable table of synchronisms for the period covering the reign of Suppiluliuma.

S.H.H.

LAESSØE, J.: *People of Ancient Assyria, their Inscriptions and Correspondence*, trans. by F. S. Leigh-Browne. 1963. Pp. 170 incl. 4 figs.+24 plates. (Routledge & Kegan Paul, London. Price: 32s. 0d.).

Professor Laessøe describes and illustrates the written sources for Assyrian history, and in four main chapters discusses continuity and change in Mesopotamia, the phenomenon that was Assyria — oldest Assyria, Hurrian interlude, the Assyrian empire — Assyrians and Hurrians in the Zagrós, and Assyrian historiography. The book, which is well written and translated, is an attempt to assess the reputation of Assyrians from personal letters rather than from official documents.　J.N.S.

SAGGS, H. W. F.: *The Greatness that was Babylon*. A sketch of the ancient civilization of the Tigris-Euphrates valley. 1962. Pp. xix+562+93 plates (incl. 2 colour plates)+line ills. on 14 pp.+2 maps on endpapers. (Sidgwick & Jackson, London. Price: 63s. 0d.).

It is nearly 60 years since the publication of L. W. King's *The History of Babylon*, and during that interval no full-scale history of Babylon in English has appeared. An immense amount of new material relating to the culture of Babylon and Assyria has been accumulating during the last half-century, and the time was ripe for the harvest to be reaped. Now the task has been undertaken by a scholar with the necessary equipment and we have before us this magnificent volume by Dr. H. W. F. Saggs who is Reader in Akkadian at the School of Oriental and African Studies in the University of London. A glance at the Bibliography of 26 pages will show that the author has overlooked nothing of any importance relating to any aspect of his subject. He is even acquainted with the contribution of Soviet archaeologists to the problems of Mesopotamian archaeology, and points out amusingly that they have allowed their ideology to influence their archaeology. Dr. Saggs remarks that there are fashions in archaeology, and rehabilitates the theories of Professor Jacobsen of Chicago which have temporarily fallen into disfavour. He himself represents a swing of the pendulum against the widely held theory of dying and rising gods. An extremely interesting discussion of the significance of the Royal Graves at Ur provides a good example of the depth and brilliance of Dr. Saggs' scholarship. One notes with thankfulness that he is a rebel against the current fashion of the extreme proliferation of footnotes. Those he has given are few and necessary, only ten in the first hundred pages. The wealth of material unrolls in fascinating detail the manifold pattern of the greatness that was Babylon. Dr. Saggs has wisely not limited himself to the strict letter of his title, but has embraced in his survey Sumerian, Hurrian, Assyrian, and all the varied elements that go to make up the background of Babylonian civilization. Some of the magnificent illustrations are, of course, familiar, but many of them are new and of the greatest interest. It is difficult to praise too highly the scholarship which the book displays, and the skill with which the material has been presented. S.H.H.

TOOMBS, L.: *God's People among the Nations.* A Study of Religion in the Ancient Near East. (World Christian Books No. 45, Second Series). 1963. Pp. 80 incl. 2 maps. (U.S.C.L., Lutterworth Press, London. Price: 3s. 0d.).

After a preliminary account of the peoples of the Near East and their territories, we have short accounts of the surrounding peoples and their religions — Egyptians, Assyrians and Babylonians, the People of the North (Hittites, Philistines, Scythians, Medes and Persians), Canaanites including Ugarit. There is a final chapter on Israel's attitude to all these and the transformations of what they took over. The treatment is necessarily short and of a summary nature; but within the limits the author has produced a useful book for beginners. N.H.S.

THE DEAD SEA SCROLLS

CARMIGNAC, J.: *Christ and the Teacher of Righteousness:* The Evidence of the Dead Sea Scrolls, trans. by Katharine G. Pedley with a Foreword by W. F. Albright. 1962. Pp. viii+168. (Helicon Press, Baltimore and Dublin. Price: $3.95; 25s. 0d.).

Abbé Carmignac has published scholarly works on the Scrolls and has edited the *Revue de Qumran* from its beginning. In

1962 he published a popular book, *Le Docteur de Justice et Jésus-Christ*, and the *Book List* now welcomes the same book in English translation. The main purpose is to refute some of the sensational and ill-founded statements made by such people as Dupont-Sommer, Edmund Wilson, John Allegro, and others, and the manner in which this is done not only directly serves a useful purpose but also assembles a great deal of Scroll material around some relevant points of discussion. The chapter headings well demonstrate the point. Did Jesus imitate the Teacher of Righteousness? Christ and the Teacher Compared, Their Persons, Their Works and Doctrine. The Teacher of Righteousness Self-Revealed.

The translation is very effective: it is readable, and the renderings of original passages successful. Perhaps one might feel that the Foreword and the Translator's Preface are rather fulsome — good wine needs no bush. An annotated bibliography, by the translator, has the largest collection of superlatives the reviewer has ever seen; even Allegro's book has 'by far the best pictorial presentation of Qumran'!

B.J.R.

JEREMIAS, G.: *Der Lehrer der Gerechtigkeit*. (Studien zur Umwelt des Neuen Testaments, 2). 1963. Pp. 376. (Vandenhoeck und Ruprecht, Göttingen. Price: DM. 32.00).

This doctoral dissertation offers a very careful and learned study of the Teacher of Righteousness, taking account of the vast literature that has so rapidly grown up around the Scrolls, and reaching independent conclusions. Dr. Jeremias finds the materials available too scanty to make possible any secure identification of the Teacher of Righteousness, but finds a secure indication of the period in which he lived in the identification of the Wicked Priest, who is here held to be Jonathan. The Man of Lies is differentiated from the Wicked Priest, and the Kittim identified with the Romans, though probably the Kittim of the Scrolls were not contemporary with the Teacher. Some of the Hymns are believed to be from the pen of the Teacher, and they are then drawn on for the examination of the personality of the Teacher. Dr. Jeremias denies that the Teacher of Righteousness was regarded as an eschatological figure by the community, and closes the study by a comparison of the Teacher with Jesus.

H.H.R.

JONGELING, B.: *Le rouleau de la guerre des manuscrits de Qumran*. (Studia Semitica Neerlandica, No. 4). 1962. Van Gorcum & Comp. N.V., Assen. Price: Fl. 30.90).

The book presents a thorough and masterly treatment of the Warfare Scroll, and forms one of the basic books for further work on it. The Introduction deals in detail with the text of the scroll and Sukenik's transcription column by column. Then follows a translation and commentary, which naturally occupies the body of the book (some 340 pages). The annotation (generally bibliographical references) follows in about ten pages, and the bibliography in another four. The index is limited to biblical references.

The general impression left by the book as a whole is one of careful assessment of divergent views already expressed, and a judicious verdict when this is necessary. At the same time, it is not easy to discover what the author really wishes to say; he is so anxious to deal with authorities that he does not emerge as one himself except on isolated points. One additional chapter at the end of the discussion would have redeemed the failure.

B.J.R.

MEYER, R.: *Das Gebet des Nabonid. Eine in den Qumran-Handschriften wiederentdeckte Weisheitserzählung.* (Sitzungsberichte der Sächsischen Akademie der Wissenschaften zu Leipzig, Philologisch-historische Klasse, Band 107, Heft 3). 1962. Pp. 112+1 plate. (Akademie-Verlag, Berlin. Price: 12s. 6d.).

This monograph contains a study of the two Aramaic fragments of the Prayer of Nabonidus found at Qumran. With the help of Daniel iv, Professor Meyer offers a reconstruction of the story which he then compares with Harran inscriptions of Nabonidus. He suggests that the Prayer was a popular variant of one of these inscriptions and that it originated in the Jewish dispersion of North Arabia. It was probably written there (or perhaps in Babylonia) in the fifth century, and it belonged to the category of Wisdom literature. Daniel iv contains a much later form of the same (or a closely related) tradition.

J.A.E.

PFEIFFER, C. F.: *The Dead Sea Scrolls.* 1962. Pp. 120+8 ills.+1 map. (Baker Book House, Grand Rapids, Michigan. Price: $2.50).

The description REVISED printed prominently on the dust-jacket of this introduction to the Scrolls may mislead. Nine of the ten chapters which compose the book are litho-printed from the first edition which appeared in 1957. The startling difference in print at page 103 would make this point, even if the author, more modest than his publisher, had not in his preface declared that the first nine chapters are reproduced without alteration. The same may be said about the Index, for the only entry later than page 102 is 'Chronology, 103, 104', but this subject in the new edition occupies pages 115–6, after chapter 10. The additional chapter deals with Biblical Interpretation at Qumran and is a good, if brief, introduction to the Sect's attitude to and use of Scripture.

W.D.McH.

TYLOCH, W.: *Rękopisy z Qumran nad Morzem Martwym.* = Polskie Towarzystwo Religioznawcze; Rozprawy i materiały Nr. 6). 1963. Pp. 347+20 plates+1 map. (Warszawa, Państwowe Wydawnictwo Naukowe. Price: zł. 60).

The bulk of this book is made up of very faithful Polish translations of the principal manuscripts from the First Qumran Cave (1QS, 1QSa, 1QM, 1QH, 1QpHab) and of the Damascus Document, together with introductions, ample textual notes and some historical explanations. The general introduction contains an account of the history of the discoveries, a catalogue of the Qumran library, and a short synthesis of the results of scientific research into the Qumran Community; in particular, its identity with the Essenes and its influence on early Christian history are discussed. A good bibliography and an apt selection of illustrations and maps supplement this very useful publication. This serious work by Dr. Tyloch gives readers acquainted with Polish a highly objective and scientific account of the Qumran finds and the present state of the scholarly study of them. S.Se.

APOCRYPHA AND POST-BIBLICAL JUDAISM

Avi-Yonah, M.: *Geschichte der Juden im Zeitalter des Talmud.* (Studia Judaica, Vol. II). 1962. Pp. 290. (Alfred Töpelmann, Berlin. Price: DM. 38).

This volume is a revised German version of the author's *Bīmē Rōmā u-Bhiṣanṭion*, which appeared first in Jerusalem in 1946 and has had two further Hebrew editions since. After providing a brief summary of the history of the Jews from the time of the Return to that of Hadrian, Professor Avi-Yonah gives a detailed account of the political, economic, and demographic position of Palestinian Jewry after the defeat of Bar-Kokheba. There emerges before us the gradual reorganisation of Jewish religious and national life, furthered by the conciliatory attitude of the Romans to the Patriarchate and by the latter's acceptance of certain demands of the power-in-charge. The external and internal crisis of the Roman Empire brought about a deterioration of relations, still further increased by the establishment of Christian rule in Palestine and the ensuing anti-Jewish Legislation of Constantine and his successors. Temporary changes in favour of the Jews were effected under Julian the Apostate, but at the beginning of the fifth century the Church succeeded in influencing the civil authorities to dissolve the institution of the Patriarchate which, though not always without self-interest in the preservation of its privileges, had stood for nearly 300 years between Rome and Jerusalem to mitigate radical tendencies on either side. The last parts of the book deal with inter-Christian dogmatic controversies and their impact on Palestinian Jewry, the legislation of Justinian against *deuterosis*, the Persian invasion of Palestine, and the end of the Byzantine Empire. The amount of documentary evidence which the author culled from the New Testament, patristic, Tannaitic, Amoraic, and Midrashic literature, and from *novellae* and *codices* exceeds that of his predecessors, who aimed at more than a mere political history and achieved less. Especially the evaluation of Rabbinic utterances against their historical, social, and economic background is a model of proper utilization of this widely dispersed source material. It may be suggested that a new English edition of the book should include an investigation of those parts of early Palestinian Hebrew poetry, which are relevant for a still further understanding of an era that ended with the conquest of Palestine by the Arabs. S.S.

BLACK, M.: *The Son of Man Problem in Recent Research and Debate*. (*The Manson Memorial Lecture*, reprinted from the *Bulletin of the John Rylands Library*, vol. 45, No. 2, March, 1963). 1963. Pp. 305–318. (The John Rylands Library, Manchester. Price: 4s. 0d.).

Principal Black chose for the theme of his *Manson Memorial Lecture*, delivered at Manchester in November, 1962, a subject, the Son of Man, on which Professor Manson himself had written with insight and authority. Dr. Black is here concerned mainly with the reply of E. Schweizer to P. Vielhauer's revival of the arguments put forward by H. B. Sharman in 1943. If much of the importance of this paper (and it is an important contribution to the discussion of a vexed problem) is for New Testament scholarship, readers of the *Book List* will be grateful for the analysis of and emphasis on some features of Jewish eschatology.

W.D.McH.

BROCKINGTON, L. H.: *Ideas of Mediation between God and Man in the Apocrypha*. The Ethel M. Wood Lecture delivered before the University of London on 6 March, 1962. 1962. Pp. 16. (University of London, The Athlone Press. Price: 4s. 6d.).

In this study it is pointed out that mediation between God and man flows in two directions: from God to man (descending mediation) and from man to God (ascending mediation), but it is the former of these that engages the author's attention, with special reference to the Apocrypha. Four conceptions are considered: (1) help from heaven, without further definition of the manner of its bestowal; (2) help from heaven given through apparitions; (3) angels; (4) wisdom. The first conception is illustrated from I Maccabees, the second from II Maccabees. As for the third and fourth, angelic mediation (as in Tobit) belongs to popular religion, while the mediatorial portrayal of Wisdom belongs rather to the religion of the learned and cultured. This last portrayal was destined to be the most fruitful of all, although in the form in which it appears in the Apocrypha it is subject to 'the natural limitations inherent in its being feminine', since 'it is not readily conceivable that the God whom men worship as *He* should be known upon earth through a person whom they speak of as *she*'. This point may suggest to some readers further interesting considerations which lie beyond the scope of Mr. Brockington's lecture.

F.F.B.

BROWN, J. R.: *Temple and Sacrifice in Rabbinic Judaism*. (Winslow Lectures 1963). 1963. Pp. 31. (Seabury-Western Theological Seminary, Evanston, Ill. Price: $1.00).

The author discusses two matters: first, the claim by Dr. Vermes and others that the New Testament exposition of the atoning death of Christ is largely due to Jewish theology concerning the Binding of Isaac (*Aqedah*); second, the question whether the sacrificial cult ceased entirely at A.D. 70. A capable and thorough examination of the evidence.

N.H.S.

GERBER, W. E.: *Beṣa (Ei)*. Text, übersetzung und ausführliche Erklärung, Mit eingehenden geschichtlichen und sprachlichen Einleitungen und textkritischen Anhängen. (Die Mischna, ed. Rengstorf-Rost). 1963. Pp. VI+108. (Alfred Töpelmann, Berlin. Price: DM. 20).

This work consists of four main parts: 1. the Introduction which sets forth, with admirable lucidity, the essentials of the problems in the Mishnic tractate *Beṣah*; 2. the vocalised Hebrew Text of this tractate, copied from MS. Kaufmann (hardly a happy choice, it would seem), with German translation and ponderous notes (which tend, in parts, to be rather speculative); 3. an Appendix with *variae lectiones* in 4 MS. Codices, 5 tenuous Genizah fragments and the *editio princeps* of each of the 3 recensions of the Mishnah (whilst, regrettably, no notice is taken of the older MSS. of the Mishnah with Maimonides' Arabic commentary, nor of the 15th-century Yemenite *Melekheth Shelomoh* which is an indispensable tool in the textual criticism of the Mishnah); 4. Several Indices; competent, comprehensive, and very serviceable. Readers of this *Book List* will be mainly interested in the part in the Introduction on the scriptural texts that form the background to the *halakhic* data in *Beṣah*. It must be stated that Dr. Gerber's inference from Ex. xvi. 23 that baking and cooking are permitted on the Sabbath, with the resulting contradiction to Ex. xxxv. 3, is contrary not only to Talmudic tradition but also to the plain meaning of the Biblical text, in which, accordingly, baking and cooking would not have been mentioned at all. He evinces still more patently his forgetfulness of plain scriptural data (Lev. xxv. 35–39 and Num. xxix. 12, 35) in his assumption, stated no less than six times, that the *seventh* (reviewer's italics) day of Tabernacles is a *Yom Ṭob*. His translation and notes, competent on the whole, are evidently the fruit of much painstaking study. Notwithstanding occasional slips, e.g., the blunder in the mixing up of the subject and object of the verb *zikkah* in *Beṣah* V. 8a (pp. 95–96), it would be churlish to withhold from the author the recognition of the undoubted merits of his work.

E.W.

GLATZER, N. N. (ed. by): *Faith and Knowledge*. The Jew in the Medieval World. (Beacon Texts in the Judaic Tradition, Vol. II). 1963. Pp. xx+236. (Beacon Press, Boston. Price: $6.00).

In contrast to Jacob R. Marcus' comprehensive *The Jew in the Medieval World*, this source book concentrates on the fundamental spiritual problem of the Middle Ages. It includes Hasidism (18th century) and consists of representative extracts in English translation, partly made and in other passages often revised by the editor who also provides an introduction, an epilogue, and brief, essential notes. 'Faith and Knowledge' is illustrated in nineteen sections: God, The Love of God, The Faith of Israel, Man, Knowledge, The Ways of Good Life, The Community of Israel, The Sabbath, The Ways of the Mystics, The Ways of the Hasidim, The Land of Israel, Exile and Redemption. Short biographical sketches introduce the principal Jewish thinkers, commentators, and poets, and attention is rightly paid to the Liturgy of the Synagogue. Communication and interaction between Judaism, Christianity and, to a lesser degree,

Islam emerge clearly in this judicious, catholic selection. As a result, we perceive the pattern of the inner life of the Jewish communities and their spiritual leaders in the Middle Ages. 'Suggestions for further reading' help the reader to enlarge and deepen his understanding.

E.I.J.R.

HAAG, E.: *Studien zum Buche Judith.* Seine theologische Bedeutung und literarische Eigenart. (Trierer Theologische Studien, 16). 1964. Pp. XVI+134. (Paulinus Verlag, Trier. Price: DM. 13.80).

In this study the conclusion is reached that the book of Judith, though unhistorical, is a *Rettungserzählung* for which parallels are adduced in 2 Chronicles xiv. 7–14, xx. 1–30. In Judith, however, we have an entirely fictitious narration, which is designedly a typological or parabolic presentation of the history of God's people. The argument for this is worked out in a careful analysis of the book and a theological interpretation of its contents. Even if the conclusion be regarded as an over-simplification, the value of Haag's work will doubtless be found to reside primarily in his detailed scholarly scrutiny of the problems raised by the book of Judith. His treatise will be indispensable to serious students of the subject.

G.W.A.

HAMMERSHAIMB, E., MUNCK, J., NOACK, B., SEIDELIN, P. (ed. by): *De gammeltestamentlige Pseudepigrafer i oversaettelse med inledning og noter.* 4. Haefte. 1963. Pp. 317–508. (G. E. C. Gad, Copenhagen; Cammermeyer, Oslo; C. W. K. Gleerup, Lund).

For earlier fascicles of this edition of pseudepigrapha, see *Book Lists*, 1957, p. 71, and 1959, p. 42. The present fascicle contains The Assumption of Moses (B. Noack), 1 (3) Esdras (E. Hammershaimb), The Letter of Aristeas (J. Munck), and The Sibylline Oracles (B. Noack). Like its predecessors, it provides independent translations, together with introductions which are masterpieces of brief and balanced statement, concise notes, and up-to-date bibliographies. The intense and growing interest at the present time in the intertestamental period makes this Danish enterprise most opportune.

G.W.A.

JACOBS, R. L.: *Montefiore and Loewe on the Rabbis.* (Claude Montefiore Lecture, 1962). 1963. Pp. 28. (The Liberal Jewish Synagogue, London. Price: 3s. 6d.).

This is a sympathetic appreciation of the well-known *Rabbinic Anthology*, the author inclining towards Loewe rather than Montefiore. In any case there has taken place since the disasters of the thirties a steady rapprochement between orthodox and liberal Judaism.

D.D.

KAUFMANN, D.: *Meḥqārîm ba-Siphrûth ha-'Ibhrîth shel Yemê ha-Bênayîm.* 1962. Pp. 35+238. (Mosad Harav Kook, Jerusalem).

This is a translation from the German into Hebrew of eleven of David Kaufmann's studies in medieval Jewish philosophy, the greater part of which bears on works by Solomon Ibn Gabirol and Yehudah Halevi. It is now very difficult to obtain these profound studies in their original German, and Mosad Harav Kook is to be congratulated on having given them in Dr. I. Eldad's gratifying version.

M.W.

MACDONALD, J. (ed. & trans. by): *Memar Marqah*, The Teaching of Marqah. Vol. I: *The Text*, Vol. II: *The Translation*. (Beihefte zur Zeitschrift für die alttestamentliche Wissenschaft 84). 1963. Pp. XIV+XLIV+178 (Vol. I): Pp. VI+256 (Vol. II). (Verlag Alfred Töpelmann, Berlin. Price: DM.68).

This is the first complete edition of the *Memar Marqah*, one of the most important Samaritan texts; its appearance is a welcome indication of the interest which Samaritan studies, thanks largely to the work of Prof. J. Bowman, are now beginning to rouse. No one who has not worked on the Judaean Scrolls knows how frustrating the lack of satisfactory Samaritan (and Qara'ite) texts can be. Dr. Macdonald gives a concise introduction, in which he assigns the work to a date in the 2nd–4th centuries A.D.; he then discusses the manuscripts and previous attempts to edit the text, the author's use of the Samaritan Pentateuch and Targum, the Arabic translation, the importance of the work for the study of the Samaritan Aramaic dialect and of Samaritan theology as also of Christianity; and he adds some interesting remarks on the difficulties in this field of research at the present time and our future needs. The main part of the work then follows, consisting of the Samaritan text in Hebrew furnished with brief critical notes (pp. 158) and the English translation (pp. 246); both seem to be extremely well done. An index of Biblical references completes the work. The reviewer may conclude this all too brief notice by expressing a hope that the editor will persuade other young scholars to continue the task of making these and similar texts available in so convenient and admirable a form.

G.R.D.

NEUSNER, J.: *A Life of Rabban Yohanan Ben Zakkai*. Ca. 1–80 C.E. (Studia Post-Biblica VI). 1962. Pp. X+200. (E. J. Brill, Leiden. Price: Fl. 30).

The life and personality of Rabban Yohanan ben Zakkai has in the past attracted scholars in the field 'Die Wissenschaft des Judentums'. A few monographs on the subject have been produced. These are not easily accessible now. Besides, the monographs do not make use of all the Talmudic material. Dr. Neusner's monograph is at once more comprehensive (tapping as it does additional sources and incorporating also recent notes written in English and in Hebrew on the subject) and more readable. While the author's main aim is to deal with Rabban Yohanan ben Zakkai's life, he gives a fairly good picture of first-century Judaism in general.

It is a pity that the book, which is well planned and produced and includes a useful bibliography and indexes, should have faulty transliterations of some Hebrew words and contain numerous printer's errors.

M.W.

ROTH, C.: *The Sarajevo Haggadah*. 1963. Pp. 46+117 plates. (W. H. Allen, London. Price: £10 10s. 0d.).

This world-famous fourteenth-century Haggadah, the origin of which is most likely North Spain or Provence, excels in its magnificent illuminations those included in other well-known Haggadoth (the John Rylands Haggadah, for instance). It is here superbly reproduced, giving great credit to its producers. The Biblical scholar will no doubt be interested in the consistent sequence of medieval Hebrew illuminations woven round all the narrative parts of the Pentateuch, for such a full sequence is not found in any other illuminated Haggadah. Scholars concerned with the text, palaeography and vocalization of medieval Haggadoth will find here additional interest. The liturgical poems included in the Haggadah, which form no integral part of the Haggadah proper, have not been reproduced. Dr. Cecil Roth's fine introduction adds considerably to the value of this production.

M.W.

SCHOLEM, G.: *Ursprung und Anfänge der Kabbala*. (Studia Judaica: Forschungen zur Wissenschaft des Judentums, Band III). 1962. Pp. VIII+434. (Walter de Gruyter & Co., Berlin. Price: DM. 48).

The volume under review is a revised and more than double-sized version of Professor Scholem's *Reshith ha-Kabbala* which appeared in Jerusalem in 1948. Its first chapter illustrates the insensitiveness of the purely rationalistic approach to the subject by scholars like Graetz and Neumark, traces the origin of the Kabbala in Christian Europe, i.e., in the western part of the Provence, known as Languedoc, to the second part of the twelfth century and discusses pre-Kabbalistic Jewish mysticism, such as *Merkabha-* and *Hekhaloth* literature, the *Sefer Yeṣira* and the oldest testimonies about the appearance of the *Sefer Bahir*.

Its second chapter offers a detailed analysis of the literary structure of the latter, its Gnostic elements, its transformation of Talmudic concepts, and its sources.

The third chapter gives a thorough account of the individual contributions of the first Kabbalists in the Provence, their asceticism, revelations, prayer-life, and theories about the *En-sof*, the *Sefiroth*, *Middoth* and other mystical concepts occurring in this branch of literature.

The last chapter describes the transmission of these Kabbalistic ideas from the Provence to geographically and culturally nearby Gerona, their consequent development in the thirteenth century as well as the communal strife caused by their dissemination. The reviewer may perhaps draw attention to an interesting testimony of the well known Muslim Polemicist Ali b. Ahmed b. Ḥazm of Cordova who died as early as 1064 and who does not seem to be referred to in any of Professor Scholem's writings on the subject. After ridiculing the anthropomorphic tendencies of certain Talmudic Aggadhoth, Ibn Ḥazm attacks Jewish teachings of clearly Gnostic origin such as the praying to the 'small' as well as to the real God in the ten days of penitence between the New Year and the Day of Atonement (cf. I. Goldziher *Proben muhammedanischer Polemik gegen den Talmud* in Kobak's *Jeschurun*, Volume VIII, 1871, pp. 101 ff.). The very same reproaches against the Kabbalists of the thirteenth century and particularly against the *Sefer Bahir* appear in no less fierce a form in the Hebrew MS. Parma 2749 (De Rossi 155), *Milḥemeth Miṣwa* by Rabbi Meir b. Simon of Narbonne (about 1245) whom Scholem quotes frequently as one of the important antagonists of the new 'heresy'.

Henceforth the debate on the vexed problem of the source-material which forms the background to the compilation of the *Sefer Bahir* (*c.* 1160–1180) will have to take Ibn Ḥazm's statements into account.

Professor Scholem is the internationally acknowledged master in the field of Jewish mysticism and the founder of its academic discipline. Apart from experts in this special branch of study, all those interested in the history of ideas, Comparative Religion, and the phenomenology of mystic experience will read his new classic — so distinguished for its almost incredible depth of knowledge, penetrating analytical power, and lucidity and elegance of style — with rapt attention and very great benefit.

S.S.

SOETENDORP, J.: *Symbolik der jüdischen Religion*. Sitte und Brauchtum im jüdischen Leben. 1963. Pp. 208. (Gütersloher Verlagshaus, Gerd Mohn, Gütersloh. Price: DM. 28).

The author gives a brief description of laws and customs which regulate the individual and communal religious life of the Jews. Seven sub-divisions deal with circumcision, schooling, marriage and divorce ceremonies, the dietary laws, burial regulations, the liturgy, and the major and minor festivals.

Dr. Soetendorp is Rabbi of the liberal Jewish community of Amsterdam and The Hague. He can thus give due consideration to the differences prevailing between orthodox and reform usages.

As an introduction to the rhythm of modern Jewish life, the book serves a useful purpose and steers a middle course between descriptive and symbolical presentation. The scholarly merit of the book can be gauged from the small bibliography at the end of the book. The informed reader must not expect a systematic historical approach to the rites described since to do this was not the author's aim.

Dr. Bunte's German translation of the original Dutch version reads well and betrays full familiarity with both languages.

S.S.

STROBEL, A.: *Untersuchungen zum eschatologischen Verzögerungsproblem*. Auf Grund der spätjüdisch-urchristlichen Geschichte von Habakuk 2, 2 ff. (Supplements to Novum Testamentum, II). 1961. Pp. xxxi+360. (E. J. Brill, Leiden. Price: Fl. 32).

This book is primarily concerned with the problem of the delay in the coming of the *parousia* as it was faced by the early Church. The justification for its inclusion in an Old Testament *Book List* is that the discussion is based upon the consideration of the way in which Hab. ii. 2 ff. is utilized in a wide range of writings, beginning with the Qumran documents and continuing through other early Jewish writings (apocalypses characterised by affinities with the Essenes, later rabbinic writings, the Septuagint, etc.) and so to the New Testament and the writings of the Church Fathers. In the second part of the book, there are gathered further indications of the relevance of the Habakkuk passage to New Testament exegesis, as for example in Paul and in the apocalyptic parables, with the indications of its possible relationship to the development of the Christian understanding of the Passover in connection with the death and resurrection of Christ. The detailed examination of the material shows the great influence of this particular passage in the formulation of later Jewish and early Christian ideas, and the book is thus an important contribution to the study of Biblical exegesis in the vital intertestamental period and beyond. A detailed bibliography is included, but it is to be regretted that there is no index of references.

P.R.A.

WALLENSTEIN, M.: *Gaster Hebrew MS. 4 in the John Rylands Library:* A Yemenite *Tikhlal* of the Seventeenth Century. (Reprinted from the *Bulletin of the John Rylands Library*, Vol. 45, No. 2, March, 1963). 1963. Pp. 505–532. (The John Rylands Library, Manchester. Price: 5s. 0d.).

The subject of this paper is one of the 350 Hebrew codices which with 300 Samaritan MSS. and some 12,000 Hebrew and Arabic fragments, all from the Cairo Genizah, were obtained for the John Rylands Library in 1954 from the collection of the late Dr. Moses Gaster. This codex of 408 folios from the year A.D. 1637 contains a Yemenite Prayer Book, and Dr. Wallenstein, though he indicates several promising subjects for investigation, largely confined his attention to three sections of the manuscript, the first containing 17 elegies, the next a large number of *piyyûṭîm*, and the third 21 poems. One example from each section is given with translation and notes. It is greatly to be desired that the learning by which Dr. Wallenstein makes interesting these not very distinguished compositions may be applied soon to the other problems, e.g., of vocalization, raised by the manuscript.

W.D.McH.

PHILOLOGY AND GRAMMAR

AISTLEITNER, J.: *Wörterbuch der Ugaritischen Sprache* (ed. by Otto Eissfeldt). (Berichte über die Verhandlungen der Sächsischen Akademie der Wissenschaften zu Leipzig, Band, 106 Heft 3). 1963. VIII+362. (Akademie-Verlag, Berlin. Price: DM. 23).

With this posthumous dictionary of Ugaritic, Aistleitner's distinguished contributions to Ugaritic studies have come to a sad and sudden end. We are grateful to Professor Eissfeldt for having taken charge of the orphaned manuscript.

The appearance of a full dictionary of the Ugaritic language, nearly 35 years after the discovery of the first texts, is an event of great significance. Close on 3,000 roots are listed — compared with a little over 2,000 in Gordon's *Ugaritic Manual* (his *Ugaritic Textbook* is not yet available at the time of writing) and a similar number in Driver's *Canaanite Myths and Legends*. Proper names have also been included, as in the present state of our knowledge it is not always possible to distinguish between proper and common nouns with absolute certainty. The book will also serve as a concordance to the Ugaritic texts, and each entry concludes with some brief etymological and comparative observations. It is in this latter field that room for improvement remains and where future generations of Ugaritic scholars might exercise their imaginative talents.

E.U.

AUVRAY, P.: *L'hébreu biblique*. (Connaître la Bible). 1962. Pp. 98 incl. many ills. (Desclée de Brouwer, Bruges. Price: NF. 7.50).

Père Auvray has not written a grammar to teach Hebrew to elementary students of the language; rather, he seeks to help the reader of the Bible in French to understand something of the character and ways of expression of Biblical Hebrew (and also, more briefly, Modern Hebrew). He succeeds well and his book should be very helpful, though some of his remarks (especially on pp. 49 f.) on the relation of the Hebrew language to Israelite thought are open to question. The interest of the book is increased by a good selection of photographs from both the ancient and the modern world.

J.A.E.

CASTELLINO, G. R.: *The Akkadian Personal Pronouns and Verbal System in the Light of Semitic and Hamitic*. 1962. Pp. xii+166. (E. J. Brill, Leiden. Price: cloth, Fl. 24).

This book falls into two parts. The first deals with the Akkadian pronouns and is a reprint of an article published in the *Mitteilungen des Instituts für Orientforschung*, 1957, with various modifications and additions. The second deals with the Akkadian verbal system and is an essay which was awarded the Lidzbarski Gold Medal. The author uses the Cushitic languages of East Africa, Berber, Egyptian and Coptic, Hausa and various Negro-African languages, in addition to all the Semitic languages, to elucidate the problem of the origin and development of the Akkadian pronouns and verbal system. His stimulating essays lead to conclusions which will be of the greatest interest to all scholars working in the field of Semitic linguistics. The chapters on the System of 'Tenses' and the Conjugations are of special value. In general he believes that 'many problems of Semitic linguistics cannot find a satisfying and true solution unless they are viewed from a higher and wider angle' and that 'Akkadian must be considered as having *preserved* linguistic conditions together with Hamitic, while, on the other side, Western Semitic, that differs more from Hamitic, must have *diverged* from it, and therefore introduced innovations'. He thinks that Akkadian has preserved the original features of proto-Semitic more fully than Arabic.

T.W.T.

DROWER, E. S. and MACUCH, R.: *A Mandaic Dictionary*. 1963. Pp. xii+492. (Clarendon Press, Oxford. Price: £12 12s. 0d.).

The publication of this work crowns the editorial labours of Lady Drower and her collaborator, Professor Macuch of Berlin.

Based on Lidzbarski's card index and the lexicographical notes
and gleanings gathered over many years by the editors, who
have had at their disposal both published and unpublished texts,
especially the unique collection of Mandaic manuscripts gifted
by Lady Drower to the Bodleian Library, this lexicon will be an
invaluable tool for workers in many fields, New Testament,
comparative religion, folk-lore, and so on. For readers of the
Book List, who will give this dictionary its rightful and well-
earned place alongside Nöldeke's grammar, its prime importance
is in the material it affords for the study of Semitic philology.
Here is a rich quarry in which Old Testament commentators
will dig with profit, and the editor of the new edition of *Brown-
Driver-Briggs* will no doubt make full use of its resources.
Because it is unlikely that this dictionary of the Mandaic
language will be superseded and because it is impossible that a
work of this nature and magnitude could be perfect in every
detail, as the editors would be the first to agree, it may be suggested
that all users of this work should show their gratitude by sub-
mitting additions and corrections, so that these could be printed
and made available in some form by the Press.

While due credit must be paid to Professor Macuch and high
praise given to the Clarendon Press for a difficult task accomplished most admirably, our warmest tribute and most grateful
thanks must be offered to Dr. Drower, whose indefatigable
editing of Mandaic texts has earned her not only an honoured
place in the British tradition of learned ladies but also a secure
position in the larger world of scholarship, which has recently
paid its tribute in the award to her of the Lidzbarski medal.

W.D.McH.

GOSHEN-GOTTSTEIN, M. H. (ed. by): *Aramaic Bible Versions*. Comparative selections and Glossary including unpublished chapters
from the Palestinian Targum. 1963. Pp. IV+72. (The Hebrew
University Students' Printing and Publishing House, Jerusalem.
Price: 20s. 0d.).

This 70–page typed brochure (photographically reproduced)
supplements the writer's earlier *Selections from the Aramaic
Versions of the Old Testament* (Jerusalem, 1957). Originally
designed for Seminar work, it includes samples from the Palestinian Targumim (including the still unpublished Neofiti 1),
the Samaritan Pentateuch Targum and the Peshitta (printed in
Hebrew characters); the selection excludes the Palestinian
Syriac, for which the author has special plans. The glossary is
intended simply to supplement Jastrow. An explanatory introduction is in Hebrew and English. Students of the Targum will
be grateful for this new *instrumentum studiorum.*   M.Bl.

SPINOZA, B.: *Hebrew Grammar (Compendium Grammatices Linguae
Hebraeae)*. Edited and translated with an introduction by Maurice J.
Bloom. 1963. Pp. 152. (Vision Press, London. Price: 25s. 0d.).

This edition of Spinoza's Hebrew grammar which he started
late in life and never completed is a most unsatisfactory piece
of work. A comparison with the Latin edition which is mentioned in the introduction, and from which the translation was

presumably made, shows that the editor has on countless occasions not reproduced the accurate Hebrew words and forms found there, but has put in their place words and forms which are inaccurate. Many of the inaccuracies involve quite elementary points of Hebrew grammar. Moreover, the editor does not always seem to have understood Spinoza's Latin. His translation on p. 63 (bottom), for example, makes nonsense. On p. 13 there is a meaningless *tāw*, which appears to belong properly on p. 11, where a *tāw* is missing; on p. 25 the Hebrew text of Isaiah is incorrectly quoted; on p. 43 examples of passive participles are listed under active participles; and so on. The book is poorly produced — the alignment is often faulty, sometimes with serious results (see, for example, the suffixes to *bên*, pp. 65 f.), and there are blurred letters and mixed founts. The book is almost unusable, and its publication does little honour to the great Dutch philosopher. Apart from a desire to do him honour, it is difficult to think of any *raison d'être* for its publication. It is all very puzzling. D.W.T.

BOOK LIST, 1965

In the preparation of this issue of the *Book List* I have had the co-operation of the members of the *Book List* Panel. In addition I wish to acknowledge with gratitude help received from Professors T. Aiura, W. Beyerlin, and H. Cazelles, Mr. R. Loewe, the Revd. E. T. Ryder, and Dr. E. Wiesenberg, and bibliographical information supplied by the staff of New College Library and by Mr. C. N. Francis of the firm of B. H. Blackwell. My colleague, the Revd. Dr. R. E. Clements has generously given of his time to check the page proofs; Mrs. E. S. K. Paterson has devoted unremitting care to the many routine tasks which are involved in the making of the *Book List*; and, as always, the Printer and his staff have given their efficient and willing help. To all of these I extend my warm thanks.

Titles to which an asterisk is prefixed are recommended for inclusion in school libraries.

G. W. ANDERSON.

NEW COLLEGE,
UNIVERSITY OF EDINBURGH.

GENERAL

Annual of the Swedish Theological Institute, ed. by H. Kosmala in collaboration with G. Gerleman, G. Lindeskog, and H. S. Nyberg. Vol. II. 1963. Pp. 120. (E. J. Brill, Leiden. Price: Fl. 20).

In an article entitled 'Israelite Historiography', S. Mowinckel discusses contributions to the subject by Hölscher, Noth, von Rad, and Rost, and presents his own views. There are two main articles by the editor: an examination of the phrase 'at the end of the days' in the Old Testament (including LXX), the Dead Sea Scrolls, the New Testament, and the Targumim; and the first instalment of an important extended study, 'Nachfolge und Nachahmung Gottes. I. Im griechischen Denken'. A. Schalit submits 'Kritische Randbemerkungen zu Paul Winters "On the Trial of Jesus" '. At the end of the volume under the heading 'Miscellanea', there are a number of erudite short studies from the editor's pen: 'The Name of God (YHWH and HU')'; 'Agnostos Theos'; ' "Anfang, Mitte und Ende" '; 'Agros Lustrare'; 'A Cryptic Saying of Hillel'; 'The Time of the Cock-Crow'.
G.W.A.

BARDTKE, H.: *Luther und das Buch Esther* (Sammlung gemeinverständlicher Vorträge und Schriften aus dem Gebiet der Theologie und Religionsgeschichte, 240/241). 1964. Pp. 90. (J. C. B. Mohr, Tübingen. Price: DM. 4.50; by subscription, DM. 4.10).

Most accounts of the Old Testament canon contain, at least in a footnote, a citation of Luther's vigorous disparagement of Esther and II Maccabees. In the present thorough study Professor Bardtke assembles a mass of evidence, showing that Luther's attitude to Esther was not as simple as that explosive utterance might suggest. Luther's translation of Esther, his citation of it with approval or disapproval, and his use of it as a historical source in his *Supputatio annorum mundi*, are all carefully examined in a praiseworthy attempt to present fairly Luther's views and assumptions.
G.W.A.

BEGRICH, J.: *Gesammelte Studien zum Alten Testament*, ed. by W. Zimmerli. (Theologische Bücherei 21). 1964. Pp. 277. (Chr. Kaiser Verlag, München. Price: DM. 20).

This volume, designed as a sequel to the reprint of Begrich's *Studien zu Deuterojesaja* in the same series, has a short preface by the editor pointing to the particular significance of Begrich's work, and especially his concern with the examination of method in Old Testament research. The essays, the earliest being 'Mabbūl' (1928) and the latest 'Berīt' (1944), are printed virtually as they were originally, with only a few cross-references added. They include further such important studies as 'Sofēr und Mazkīr', 'Der Syrisch-Ephraimitische Krieg und seine

555

weltpolitischen Zusammenhänge', 'Das priesterliche Heilsorakel' and 'Die priesterliche Tora'. Since they are all from fairly readily accessible German periodicals, the justification for their presentation is to be seen in their providing a convenient picture of the work of an influential scholar.

P.R.A.

BETZ, O., HENGEL, M., & SCHMIDT, P.: *Abraham unser Vater: Juden und Christen im Gespräch über die Bibel*. Festschrift für Otto Michel zum 60. Geburtstag. (Institutum Judaicum, Tübingen. Arbeiten zur Geschichte des Spätjudentums und Urchristentums V). 1963. Pp. viii+504. (E. J. Brill, Leiden. Price: Fl. 52).

The three editors, with 35 other scholars, have produced this volume to celebrate the sixtieth birthday of the distinguished New Testament professor and director of the Institutum Judaicum at Tübingen. The collaboration of Jewish and Christian writers to do him honour is a specially happy feature of the *Festschrift*, and provides the explanation of its title. The majority of the contributions deal with NT subjects, but some have an Old Testament or general Jewish interest. Thus O. Betz writes on the Jewish heritage in the recently discovered Gnostic documents in Coptic; M. Buber on 'The gods of the peoples and God'; E. Fascher on 'The Charge of Atheism in Controversies between Jews, Greeks, and Christians'; A. Finkel on Jesus' sermon at Nazareth; M. Fischer on the suffering Servant of Isa. liii; D. Flusser on the Sanctus and the Gloria; R. R. Geis on the Mendelssohn family; H. Gese on the cultic singers in the Second Temple; H. Haag on the Biblical roots of the *minyan*; M. Horkheimer on the German Jews (an impressive and thought-provoking essay); G. Kretschmar on the relation between ancient Jewish and Christian art; G. Lindeskog on the trial of Jesus in Jewish-Christian debate; E. Lohse on the Messianic expectation of the Synagogue; R. Mayer on Talmudic interpretation; R. Meyer on Elijah and Ahab; H. van Oyen on Judaism and demythologizing; Basilea Schlink on Christian help to Jews; H. J. Schoeps on anti-semitism in Germany in the thirties and forties of the nineteenth century; S. Schulz on the significance of Targum studies for the Synoptic Gospel tradition; E. Stauffer on Jesus and his Bible; W. Uhsadel on the fall of Jerusalem (a sermon based on Luke xix. 41–48 preached on the approximate anniversary of the event in 1961); K. Wilhelm on Rabbi A. I. Kook and the doctrine of perpetual soul-prayer. P. Schmidt contributes a bibliography of Michel's writings.

F.F.B.

BIČ, M. & SOUČEK, J. B. (ed. by): *Biblická Konkordance*, Parts 24 and 25. Spolu-Učiniti. 1964. Pp. 80 each part. (Edice Kalich, Prague. Price: Kčs. 10.50 each).

Slowly this great Concordance to the Czech Bible wends its way to its now approaching conclusion. To show Hebrew and Greek equivalents of every Old Testament word and Greek equivalents of every New Testament word has been an immense undertaking.

H.H.R.

BRANDON, S. G. F. (ed. by): *The Saviour God.* Comparative Studies in the concept of salvation presented to Edwin Oliver James by colleagues and friends to commemorate his seventy-fifth birthday. 1963. Pp. xxii + 242 + portrait on frontispiece. (Manchester University Press. Price: 37s. 6d.).

This volume contains essays by fifteen friends and colleagues of a devoted and distinguished scholar. Professor James's wide interests and reputation are reflected in the distribution of subjects and authors. C. J. Bleeker of Amsterdam writes on Isis as Saviour Goddess; S. G. F. Brandon of Manchester on the Ritual Technique of Salvation in the Near East, dealing especially with S. Paul's borrowing from non-Jewish sources; Angelo Brelich of Rome on Politeismo e Soteriologia. F. F. Bruce of Manchester writes on 'Our God and Saviour', dealing mostly with Yahweh's past victories over Rahab, at the Exodus. Edward Conze of Wisconsin deals with 'Buddhist Saviours', J. Duchesne-Guillemin of Liège with 'Some Aspects of Anthropomorphism', H. D. Lewis of London with 'The Idea of Creation and Conceptions of Salvation', and E. G. Parrinder with 'An African Saviour God' (Ifa-Orunmila of the Yorubas). Annemarie Schimmel of Bonn discusses the veneration of the Prophet Muhammad as reflected in Sindhi poetry. Marcel Simon of Strasbourg discusses (in French) soteriology in the New Testament. Ninian Smart of Birmingham compares the work of the Buddha with that of Christ. Howard Smith of Manchester discusses Saviour Gods in Chinese Religion. Montgomery Watt of Edinburgh describes Muslim yearning for a Saviour. G. Widengren of Uppsala writes on Baptism and Enthronement in some Jewish-Christian Gnostic Documents. R. C. Zaehner of Oxford concludes the series with an essay on Salvation in the Mahabharata. N.H.S.

DHEILLY, J.: *Dictionnaire biblique.* 1964. Pp. X + 1260 + 4 tables + 9 maps. (Desclée, Tournai. Price: B.Frs. 320).

This well-printed and attractive popular work arranges a great deal of material of Scriptural interest under short articles set out in alphabetical order, with titles ranging from Aaron to Zorobabel. The short bibliography, printed at pp. vii–viii, is entirely concerned with works available in French and must be considered insufficient, even for the general reader. The articles on the separate books show a reasonable outlook on matters of higher criticism; e.g., it is clearly stated apropos of Jonah (p. 601) under *Genre littéraire*: 'Les faits rapportés ne sauraient relever du genre historique.' The book of Judith is classified as 'midrash apocalyptique' and Daniel is assigned, as regards the first part, to the end of the 3rd century, and as regards the second and the redaction of the work as a whole, to the year 167 B.C. J.M.T.B.

FRIEDRICH, G. (ed. by): *Theologisches Wörterbuch zum Neuen Testament* (begun by G. Kittel). Band VII, Doppellieferungen 13/14, 1963. Pp. 128; 15/16, 1964, Pp. 128; 17/18, 1964, Pp. 128. (Kohlhammer, Stuttgart. Price each Doppellieferung: DM. 9.20).

These three Doppellieferungen contain a considerable number of brief articles which are not of any special concern to Old

Testament scholars. It will perhaps suffice for the purposes of this review if a list is given of a few extremely full and important articles which are relevant — *synagoge* and its cognates by Schrage; *synedrion* by E. Lohse; *syniemi* and its cognates by H. Conzelmann; *synoida* and *syneidesis* by C. Maurer; *sphazo* and *sphage* by O. Michel; *sphragis* and its cognates by Fitzer; *sozo, soteria, soter* by W. Foerster and G. Fohrer; *soma* and its cognates by E. Schweizer and F. Baumgärtel. Of these articles those on *synagoge* and *sozo*, etc. will be especially eagerly welcomed. The Doppellieferung 17/18 encloses an interesting article by Cardinal Bea containing his reflections upon the great achievement which Kittel's *T.W.B.N.T.* represents.

N.W.P.

(GABRIELI, F.): *A Francesco Gabrieli*. Studi orientalistici offerti nel sessantesimo compleanno dai suoi colleghi e discepoli. (Università di Roma Studi Orientali pubblicati a Cura della Scuola Orientale, Volume V). 1964. Pp. XXVIII+360. (Scuola Orientale, Università di Roma. Price: L. 12.000).

The somewhat shapeless literary *genre* of the *Festschrift* has been put to excellent use in this tribute to one of the foremost Arabists (unhappily almost as extinct a species as the orthodox Hebraist) and *islamisants* of our day. The contributors (led by that remarkable scholar, Professor G. Levi della Vida) are all Italians, and it is perhaps a pity that Professor Gabrieli's non-Italian admirers have not been given a chance of participating in this volume. Most of the articles are concerned with Arabic and Islamic problems, but Egyptological, general Semitic, Ethiopian, and Persian subjects have not been excluded.

Readers of the *Book List* may, perhaps, be especially interested in Castellino's article on the Semitic causative which appears to manifest similar formal elements to the elative. Garbini has some interesting and, at least in part, novel things to say about the origins of the Arabic language. Rinaldi contributes a few, perhaps somewhat inconclusive, remarks on Hebrew verbs of the type medial w/y and final y. The real strength of this presentation volume lies some way outside the sphere of the Old Testament scholar, but all the articles are well written and bear witness to the breadth and quality of Italian scholarship. E.U.

Hebrew Union College Annual, Vol. XXXV (ed. by Elias L. Epstein). 1964. Pp. 274 + 35 (in Hebrew) + 5 plates + index to Vols. I-XXXIV. (Hebrew Union College, Cincinnati. Price: $6.00).

This issue of *H.U.C.A.* is dedicated to the memory of Abraham and Sarah Neumann of Philadelphia, with a special dedicatory note to their son Sidney, under the terms of whose will funds are provided for the subvention of the *Annual* and a number of other publications and of philanthropic institutions. Incidentally, one might remark on the numerous benefits our Jewish friends are able to derive from such sources.

Old Testament articles are by J. Morgenstern, 'The Cultic Setting of the "Enthronement Psalms"'; B. Z. Wacholder, 'How long did Abram Stay in Egypt?'; H. M. Orlinsky, 'Studies in the Septuagint of the Book of Job', (Chapter V of the series published in *H.U.C.A.* since 1957). Of Rabbinic importance we have: L. J. Liebreich, 'The Insertions in the Third Benediction of the Holy Day "Amidoth"'; E. Mihely, 'A Rabbinic Defense of the Election of Israel'. Later (medieval) Jewish studies are represented by S. A. Singer, 'An Introduction to *Sefer Hasidim*'; M. A. Cohen, 'Reflections on the Text and Context of the Disputation of Barcelona'; A. Cronbach, '"Manner for Manner" in Dante'; A. J. Reines, 'Abrabanel on Prophecy in the *Moreh Nebhukhim*' (in continuation of Vol. XXXIV). For the 18th–19th century we have B. Brilling, 'Eibenschütziana' (the continuation of an article in Vol. XXXIV on the controversial family of Rabbi Jonathan Eibenschütz). An article written in Hebrew by N. Allony gives a full treatment, with translation, of a treatise contained in an Arabic manuscript written in Hebrew script, T.-S. Ar. 9/5 (with two sheets of facsimiles), on the pointing and Massorah of Moshe ben Asher.

B.J.R.

*HYATT, J. P.: *The Heritage of Biblical Faith*. An Aid to Reading the Bible. 1964. Pp. 368. (The Bethany Press, Saint Louis, Missouri. Price: $4.50).

The opening words of the Preface say that 'the purpose of this book is to encourage the reading of the Bible, and to give the reader certain basic aids to understanding it as he reads'. It is based on sound scholarship but is so presented that the ordinary reader can fully understand the way in which scholarship has helped to give content of meaning for the Christian of today to the concept of revelation. A chapter is devoted to the history and literature of the Old Testament, another to the faith, and another to the Apocrypha (with four pages on the Dead Sea Scrolls). The New Testament material is similarly discussed. Other chapters discuss the Canon, the history of the English Bible, and the Authority of the Bible. An Appendix gives a few well-chosen books for further reading (especially, though not exclusively, for American readers). It will be a useful book for teachers and Training Colleges. A.S.H.

KELLER, W.: *The Bible as History in Pictures*, trans. by W. Neil. 1964. Pp. 360 incl. 329 ills. and VIII coloured plates + 2 maps on endpapers. (Hodder & Stoughton, London. Price: 42s. 0d.).

This book is quite different in plan and execution from the same author's (and translator's) *The Bible as History* (*Book List* 1957, p. 18). Much ingenuity and care have been expended in putting together a collection of reasonable scale pictures of admirable clarity to illustrate points in the Biblical narrative of the books from Genesis to Galatians — with certain omissions, but including some of the Apocrypha. Apart from short introductions to the ten chapters, letterpress is confined to annotating the illustrations after quoting the verse being illustrated (AV mostly). The book includes a brief Synoptic Chronological Table of Biblical History, a Bibliography, an Index of Bible References, and acknowledgements of Illustrations with Commentary. In this latter, useful references are given to the main archaeological campaigns at each site (though the current American dig at Shechem is not included, nor the closing date of the Kenyon Jericho excavation). Finally there is a good General Index. The translation is excellent.

D.R.Ap-T.

KLEINKNECHT, H., FICHTNER, J., STÄHLIN, G., et al.: Wrath, trans. by Dorothea M. Barton and ed. by P. R. Ackroyd. (Bible Key Words from Gerhard Kittel's Theologisches Wörterbuch zum Neuen Testament). 1964. Pp. xii+148. (A. & C. Black, London. Price: 15s. 0d.).

This is a translation of an abridged text of the article indicated by the title, the omissions being almost wholly from the section on classical antiquity. As in other volumes in this series the addition of indexes enhances the usefulness of the translation.

G.W.A.

LIEBERMAN, S., ABRAMSON, S., KUTSCHER, E. Y., & ESH, S. (ed. by): Jubilee Volume on the occasion of the Seventy-Fifth Birthday of Henoch Yalon. 1963. Pp. 370. (Kiryat Sepher Publishing House, Jerusalem).

This volume contains twelve learned contributions in honour of E. Yalon, the eminent grammarian, on the occasion of his seventy-fifth birthday. A good number of the articles deal with linguistic matters. Of direct interest to the Old Testament scholar are the following: 'Yehudah ibn Bal'am's kitāb al-Tajnîs' (S. Abramson); '(A discussion) about the Originality of the Penultimate Accent in Hebrew' (Z. Ben-Hayyim); 'A Contribution to Biblical Hebrew Lexicography' (H. L. Ginsberg). The studies are preceded by an essay dealing with the method employed by Yalon in the investigation of Hebrew (E. Y. Kutscher) and a bibliography of Yalon's publications during 1922–1963 (S. Esh).

M.W.

McCULLOUGH, W. S. (ed: by): The Seed of Wisdom. Esays in Honour of T. J. Meek. 1964. Pp. xii + 200. (University of Toronto Press. Price: 44s. 0d.).

Professor Meek's eighty-second birthday was worthily celebrated by the presentation to him of a volume of essays in his honour, all written by members of the 'Oriental Club of Toronto', of which he himself was the first president. The Society for Old Testament Study would wish to express its felicitations to Professor Meek on the occasion.

The book contains twelve papers; and although all have a historico-religious content, six (at a stretch) relate to Old Testament Studies as such. They are 'The Reign of Nebuchadnezzar' by W. G. Lambert; 'The Formal Aspect of Ancient Near Eastern Law', by R. A. F. MacKenzie, S.J.; 'Yahweh the God of the Heavens', by D. K. Andrews; 'Proto-Septuagint Studies' by J. W. Wevers; 'Zeus in the Hellenistic Age', by F. W. Beare; 'The Molten Sea of Solomon's Temple', by G. Bagnani. The paper which interested the reviewer most of all is, of course, that by Wevers (a masterly performance); and he can only hope that others will have similar satisfaction from their particular chef-d' œuvre.

B.J.R.

MALAMAT, A. & REVIV, H.: *A Bibliography of the Biblical Period (with emphasis on publications in modern Hebrew)*. 1964. Pp. 40. (Mif'al Hashichpul, Hebrew University, Jerusalem).

This handy selected bibliography is arranged in the following main sections. The Ancient Near East and its Peoples; Source Collections; Biblical Archaeology and Geography; Hebrew Epigraphy; History of Israel (a comprehensive section including works on law, custom, culture, religion, and theology); History of Israel: Premonarchial; History of Israel: the Monarchies (including works on Exile and Return); and Reference Works.

G.W.A.

OSTERLOH. E. & ENGELLAND, H. (ed. by): *Biblisch-Theologisches Handwörterbuch* zur Lutherbibel und neueren Übersetzungen, third edition, with a cross index. 1964. Pp. 752. (Vandenhoeck & Ruprecht, Göttingen. Price: DM. 52).

More than forty contributors have helped to produce this third edition of a popular Bible dictionary. It is intended for the general reader so that literary-critical and bibliographical material has been reduced to a minimum in order to present a straightforward account of major Biblical and theological subjects. Literary and historical problems are not evaded, but they are not allowed to obtrude into the work as a whole, and there is a more conservative tone than is apparent in many of the larger theological dictionaries. A good deal of important theological information is conveniently outlined; and where it is particularly relevant to the life of the church, as e.g., on baptism, the modern theological debate is described. The dictionary represents a theologian's approach to the Bible; and it should be a useful handbook for all who have to teach the Bible in Church and School. No ready equivalent is available in English. R.E.C.

Die Ou Testamentiese Werkgemeenskap in Suid-Afrika: Studies on the Psalms. Papers read at 6th Meeting held at the Potchefstroom University for C.H.E., 29–31 January, 1963. 1963. Pp. 100. (Pro Rege–Pers Boperk, Potchefstroom, S. Africa. Price: 12s. 0d.).

This collection of 8 papers is dedicated to the memory of Professor Gemser, and shows that the O.T. Society in South Africa continues to encourage research into current Biblical problems. The first essay, on 'The Credo in the O.T.' (Th. C. Vriezen) deals specifically with the views of von Rad and M. Noth and touches on the Psalms only incidentally. S. du Toit ('The Psalms and History') also criticizes the forenamed scholars, and even Bright, for seeking to judge Biblical history like ordinary history, but gives special prominence to the historical elements in the Psalter. J. J. Glueck and J. H. Kroeze deal with the Psalmheadings and recent trends in Psalm exegesis, respectively; whereas L. M. Muntingh and F. C. Fensham refer to the Canaanite/Ugaritic background to the Psalms, the former for the social concepts, and the latter specifically for Ps. xxix. I. H. Eybers studies the meaning of the stem ShPT in the Psalms; and A. H. van Zyl gives a detailed exegesis of Ps. xxiii from the standpoint that 'shepherd' = 'king'. D.R.Ap-T.

REICKE, B. & ROST, L. (ed. by): *Biblisch-historisches Handwörterbuch*. Landeskunde, Geschichte, Religion, Kultur, Literatur. Band I, A–G. 1962. Pp. i-xvi + cols. 1–616 + 1 coloured plate, 20 black and white plates and 112 drawings + 1 map in folder. Band II, H–O. 1964. Pp. i-viii + cols. 617–1360, including 1 coloured plate, 20 black and white plates and 118 drawings. (Vandenhoeck & Ruprecht, Göttingen. Subscription price: Band I, £4 7s. 6d.; Band II, £5 6s. 6d.).

The aim of this dictionary is to provide a summary of essential information dealing with the literary and historical background of the Bible. The original plan of the work was conceived by Curt Kuhl, whose death prevented his undertaking the editorial task. The articles concentrate on presenting details of the archaeological, geographical, literary, and cultural background of the Biblical text. A very large international team of scholars, of the highest academic standing, have collaborated in the work, which is to be completed in three volumes. The editors have given it a commendable uniformity; and it is well illustrated. A great deal of archaeological and historical information is concisely summarized; and useful bibliographies refer to the most important recent literature. The whole is an exceedingly factual, informative, and convenient work of reference. Of the longer articles, that of H. Kosmala on Jerusalem is particularly noteworthy.

R.E.C.

Les sagesses du Proche-Orient ancien (Bibliothèque des Centres d'Études supérieures spécialisés. Travaux du Centre d'Études supérieures spécialisé d'histoire des religions de Strasbourg). 1963. Pp. 208. (Presses Universitaires de France, Paris. Price: F.18).

The papers collected in this book were read at a colloquium held at Strasbourg in May, 1962. The essay by J. Nougayrol is concerned with Babylonian wisdom, and those by J. Leclant (which contains a bibliography of recent publications), P. Montet, A. Volten, H. Brunner, G. Posener and J. Sainte Fare Garnot, J. Vergote, and B. van de Walle discuss different aspects of the Egyptian sapiential literature. Most of these essays are of interest to the Biblical scholar because of the light they throw on the oriental background of the Old Testament, and the remaining four are devoted more particularly to Israelite wisdom literature: H. Cazelles writes on 'Les débuts de la sagesse en Israël', S. Morenz on 'Aegyptologische Beiträge zur Erforschung der Weisheitsliteratur Israëls', W. Zimmerli on 'Ort und Grenze der Weisheit im Rahmen der alttestamentlichen Theologie', and H. Gese on 'Die Krisis der Weisheit bei Koheleth'.

J.A.E.

Studia Theologica cura ordinum theologorum Scandinavicorum edita. Vol. 18, Fasc. 1 and Fasc. 2. 1964. Pp. 1–80, 81–172. (Aarhus University, Aarhus. Price: D.Kr. 30 each volume or D.Kr. 20 each fascicle).

Each of these fascicles contains one article of direct importance for the *Alttestamentler*. In Fasc. 1, J. H. Grønbaek, a promising young Danish scholar, contributes 'Juda und Amalek. Überlieferungsgeschichtliche Erwägungen zu Exodus 17, 8–16'. In Fasc. 2, A. S. Kapelrud discusses 'Some Recent Points of View on the Time and Origin of the Decalogue'. Other contributions of Biblical and allied interest are: (in Fasc. 1) 'Jacobus wider den Reichen' (B. Noack), 'Paulus abortivus (1 Kor. 15, 8)' (T. Boman), 'The Gospel of Truth and Valentinian Gnosticism' (H. Ringgren), 'St. Matthew 5, 43' (O. Linton); (in Fasc. 2) 'Einige kritische Bemerkungen zu Stauffer's Darstellungen der spätjüdischen Ketzergesetzgebung' (B. Salomonsen), 'Die Perikope vom gerasenischen Besessenen und der Plan des Markusevangeliums' (H. Sahlin).

G.W.A.

VARDAMAN, E. J. & GARRETT, J. L. (ed. by): *The Teacher's Yoke: Studies in Memory of Henry Trantham.* 1964. Pp. 320. (Baylor University Press, Waco, Texas. Price: $4.95).

Henry Trantham (1882–1962) was from 1910 to 1958 Professor of Greek at Baylor University. This memorial volume contains twenty-three contributions in archaeological, Biblical, classical, linguistic, theological, and historical studies; a few of these are related to the Old Testament field. J. P. Hyatt discusses 'The Origin of Mosaic Yahwism' and concludes from such passages as Ex. iii. 6, xv. 2, xviii. 4 that Yahweh was the patron deity of one of Moses' ancestors, who worshipped him either as *yahweh X* ('he causes X to exist') or *yahweh 'im X* ('he is with X'). W. H. Rossell writes on the military texts from Mari; E. J. Vardaman and M. Avi-Yonah write on the inscription of the twenty-four priestly courses, fragments of which were found during the excavations at Caesarea in 1962; the fragmentary evidence confirms to an astonishing extent the reconstruction of the priestly courses made by S. Klein on the basis of the *piyyuṭim* and Talmudic sources. E. J. Vardaman also deals with the history of Herodium. W. F. Albright ('Retrospect and Prospect in New Testament Archaeology') stresses (over-stresses?) the Essene element in many New Testament writings. R. G. Jones deals with 'The Manual of Discipline (1QS), Persian Religion, and the Old Testament'; in the passage about the Two Spirits in 1QS 'the determinative faith of the Old Testament has placed its stamp on some themes which are not essentially Jewish in origin' (being derivable from the Yasna).

F.F.B.

WOLFF, H. W.: *Gesammelte Studien zum Alten Testament.* (Theologische Bücherei, neudrucke und berichte aus dem 20. Jahrhundert, Band 22 Altes Testament). 1964. Pp. 384. (Chr. Kaiser Verlag, Munich. Price: DM. 19).

As the title indicates, this is a collection of articles, etc., that have appeared from 1934 to 1964. We can do little more than list the contents. 'Die Begründungen der prophetischen Heils- und Unheilssprüche' (*Z.A.W.* lii, 1934). 'Das Zitat im Prophetenspruch', the longest section in the book, is a reprint of *Beiheft* 4, 1937, to *Evangelische Theologie.* It is in five sections, in which the form of the prophetic proclamation is discussed and this is followed by an examination of the homiletic and theological implications. 'Das Thema "Umkehr" in der alttestamentlichen Prophetie' (*Zeitscrift für Theologie und Kirche* xlviii, 1951). 'Der grosse Jesreeltag (Hosea 2, 1–3)' (*Ev. Th.* xii, 1952–53), in which the passage is subjected to text-, form- and historical criticism, and exegesis, and typologically related to the New Testament. ' "Wissen um Gott" bei Hosea als Urform von Theologie (*Ev. Th.* xii). 'Hauptprobleme alttestamentlicher Prophetie' (*Ev. Th.* xv, 1955). 'Hoseas geistige Heimat' (*T.L.Z.* lxxxi, 1956). 'Zur Hermeneutik des Alten Testaments' (*Ev. Th.* xvi, 1956). 'Das Geschichtsverständnis der alttestamentlichen Prophetie' (*Ev. Th.* xx, 1960). 'Das Kerygma des deuteronomistischen Geschichtswerks' (*Z.A.W.* liii, 1961). 'Das Alte Testament und das Problem der existentialen Interpretation' (*Ev. Th.* xxiii, 1963). 'Das Kerygma des Jahwisten' (*Ev. Th.* xxiv, 1964). The collection concludes with an index of Biblical passages cited and a list of Hebrew words discussed.

A.S.H.

EDUCATIONAL

*NORTHCOTT, C.: *Bible Encyclopedia for Children*. Designed and illustrated by Denis Wrigley. 1964. Pp. 176 incl. many ills. & maps + 2 coloured maps on endpapers. (Lutterworth Press, London. Price: 21s. 0d.).

This attractively presented book contains some excellent maps and plans, but the details of the Temple are obscure, and the child who wants to know just how the house of Dagon was constructed will get little satisfaction from the dramatic drawing on p. 144. The rather stylized drawings in line and colour are at their best in depicting common objects, and where religious experience is least involved. Some of the articles are excellent, some (e.g. 'Moses') surprisingly inadequate. A frequent technique is to select some one incident associated with the subject and recount it at some length, with the relevant reference. The rather intrusive theology is evangelical and the scholarship, where discernible, conservative (see 'Daniel').

M.Bu.

ARCHAEOLOGY AND EPIGRAPHY

DONNER, H. & RÖLLIG, W.: *Kanaanäische und Aramäische Inschriften*. (With contribution by O. Rössler). Band II. Kommentar. Pp. XVI + 330. Band III. Glossare, Indizes, Tafeln. Pp. VII + 86 + XXXIV facsimiles and plates. 1964. (Otto Harrassowitz, Wiesbaden. Price: DM. 40 and 14 respectively).

Volume II contains translations of the texts printed in the first volume (reviewed in *Book List* 1964, pp. 18 f.), each accompanied by an introduction and commentary, with reference to relevant literature. The work is completed by volume III, in which are found glossaries of Canaanite and Aramaic words, and lists of names of people, gods, and places, together with further bibliographical references and four pages of corrections and additions to the earlier volumes; there are also reproductions

of some of the texts, and several photographs, and a list of the sources from which they are derived. The three volumes are a most useful piece of work, and those who teach Semitic languages in this country will regret that we still lack a similar modern book in English.
J.A.E.

HERDNER, A.: *Corpus des tablettes en cunéiformes alphabétiques découvertes à Ras-Shamra-Ugarit de 1929 à 1939.* Tome X de la Mission de Ras Shamra dirigée par C. Schaeffer. 1963. Vol. I, Texte. Pp. 339. Vol. II, Figures et Planches. Fig. 307+Pl. LXXXVIII. (Imprimerie nationale, Paris).

This long-awaited publication is the result of the patient and devoted labours of a well-known authority on the Ugaritic texts. The revision of the *editio princeps* has been most careful, and, incidentally, indicates the incomparable quality of M. Virolleaud's copies. After a comparative table of the sigla used by different authorities (Virollead, Gordon, Bauer, Eissfeldt, de Langhe, and the present corpus), Herdner gives the Semitic texts arranged thus: mythological, religious, epistolary, economic, hippiatric. Then come the Accadian texts in alphabetic script, the Hurrian texts, *varia*, and finally a general bibliography. There is no translation, but many notes on the script and on philological questions. Thus, in this work, together with *Palais royal d'Ugarit II.* (texts discovered 1939–1953) we have a collection of the alphabetic library of Ugarit, which will be completed by *Palais royal d'Ugarit V* for the texts discovered since 1954.
H.C.

KAPELRUD, A. S.: *The Ras Shamra Discoveries and the Old Testament,* trans. by G. W. Anderson. U.S. edition, 1963. Pp. 92. (Oklahoma University Press, Norman, Oklahoma. Price: $3.75). U.K. paperback edition, 1965. Pp. 88+2 maps+VIII plates. (Basil Blackwell, Oxford. Price: 14s. 0d.).

The English translation of Professor Kapelrud's *Ras Sjamra funnene og det Gamle Testament* (see *Book List* 1954, p. 18; *Eleven Years*, p. 555) will surely be welcomed as an admirable survey of the discoveries, particularly of the texts, of Ras Shamra and their significance for Old Testament study, with the characteristically clear insight, balanced judgement, and lucid style of the author, to which the translator does full justice. Note has been taken of the results of the post-war excavation of the site, and to a certain extent of new epigraphic material and of recent researches; but in his presentation of the subject as a whole the treatment remains the same as in the Norwegian edition of 1953, i.e., on such controversial matters as the author's thesis of Baal's displacement of El in the religion of Canaan, the annual significance of the Baal-myth with relation to the death and resurrection of Baal as a vegetation deity, and the assumption of a *hieros gamos* in the Canaanite New Year Festival, his position of 1953 is simply restated. Particularly welcome is the account of Mowinckel's view of the significance of the Hebrew New Year Festival in the light of the Baal-text, to the particular relevance of which the author has long been alert.
J.G.

HISTORY AND GEOGRAPHY

The Cambridge Ancient History: Revised Edition of Volumes I & II. *Egypt from the Death of Ramesses III to the End of the Twenty-first Dynasty:* by J. Černý. Fasc. 27. Pp. 60. Price: 6s. 0d. *Babylonia:* c. 2120–1800 B.C.: by C. J. Gadd. Fasc. 28. Pp. 56. Price: 6s. 0d.

It is cheering to see from the list at the back of these fascicles that already 33 fascicles of the revision have appeared or are in the press. Some of us can hardly hope to see the completion of this great work, but we can at least joyfully welcome each instalment as it comes. In the first of the two new fascicles Professor J. Černý makes his first contribution to the work of revision with a masterly account of the history of Egypt from the death of Ramesses III up to the time of the first Egyptian monarch who established friendly relations with Israel by sending his daughter to Solomon to become one of the king's wives and giving her Gezer as her dowry. In the second of the two new instalments Professor C. J. Gadd, whom age cannot wither, continues in his own inimitable way the early history of Babylonia, and gives a brilliant picture of the famous Third Dynasty of Ur and of the achievements of Ur-Nammu and his successors. For these two new chapters we are duly grateful.

S.H.H.

The Cambridge Ancient History: Revised Edition of Volumes I & II. The Early Dynastic Period in Egypt: by I. E. S. Edwards. Fasc. 25. Pp. 74. 8s. 6d.

In this excellent fascicle a modern Egyptologist of great erudition shows both how much has been done during the last half-century to illuminate the misty period of the first three dynasties of the Old Kingdom, and how much still remains to be done. In chap. VI of Vol. I of the old edition of the *Cambridge Ancient History*, Professor Eric Peet remarks that the early civilization of the Delta remains a closed book to us (p. 256), and in the new fascicle Mr. Edwards says that the early levels of the Delta remain virtually unexplored (p. 40). It is, unfortunately, doubtful whether, under the present regime, this situation may be remedied. Nevertheless, as in the previous fascicles, so in this, much new light is thrown, for instance, on the problem of the identity of Menes, and on the question of the relation between the Sumerian pictographic script, and the early Egyptian hieroglyphic script. Interesting fresh light is thrown on the origins of the practice of mummification in Egypt. This fascicle is fully up to the standard of those which have already appeared, both in scholarship and in readability.

S.H.H.

FINEGAN, J.: *Handbook of Biblical Chronology. Principles of Time Reckoning in the Ancient World and Problems of Chronology in the Bible.* 1964. Pp. xxvi + 338. (Princeton University Press, Princeton, New Jersey; Oxford University Press, London. Price: 68s. 0d.).

The author of this book has set himself the task of throwing light on the many problems of Biblical chronology; and he has done so with singular success. In the first part he explains the principles of Babylonian and Assyrian, Egyptian, Hebrew, Greek, and Roman chronology, dealing with everything connected with it: methods of indicating numbers; days, weeks, months, years; calendars; official and regnal years; eras; and finally early Christian attempts at constructing chronologies. In the second part he examines modern schemes of Biblical chronology for both the Old and the New Testaments, from Abp. Ussher's to that of Dr. E. R. Thiele. The reader, as he threads his way through the maze, soon begins to feel that he is being guided by a master of his subject and that a secure basis for the chronology of the Bible is being established, even if he does not accept every proffered solution of a problem; and, what is most important, he will understand the processes involved, inasmuch as the account is made as lucid as the subject permits. It is also supported by numerous tables, all extremely helpful. A few inaccuracies or slips may be noted. On pp. 45–7, 57 the full force of '-m-n eludes the author, although he is right as far as he goes; on p. 193 the identification of Amraphêl with Hammu-rabi ought surely to be abandoned, if only because the names are quite different; on p. 198 ll. 6–9 'this' is used with an impossible double reference (i.e., both Samaria and its destruction as implied in the preceding verb); on p. 231 the priority of Ezra over Nehemiah is accepted without comment; on p. 239, n. 2 'Strassmeier' ought to be 'Strassmaier'; on p. 245 'sceptre' is a mistranslation for 'comet'; on p. 257, l. 25 'Tishri I' is a misprint for Tishri X or the Day of Atonement (l. 20); on p. 254 the Greek *genesis* is translated 'conception' which requires proof; on pp. 258–9 the difficulty that the birth of Christ could probably not have taken place in mid-winter if shepherds were 'abiding in the field and keeping watch by night over their flock' (Luke ii. 8) is not mentioned; on p. 278 the Gr. *stoai* is translated 'cloisters' instead of 'colonnades'; and on p. 311, ll. 1–5 the arrival of Peter in Rome is said to have been motivated by a report of something that he did while there! The author wisely eschews Daniel's mysterious figures as well as the solar eclipse in the middle of a lunar month which has appeared, in spite of Dalman's convincing explanation of the occurrence, in the New English Bible (Luke xxiii. 45).

In conclusion, the work is an exhaustive study of the chronological problems of the Bible, as interesting as it is useful, and one which no historian will be able to disregard for a long time to come.   G.R.D.

GALLING, K.: *Studien zur Geschichte Israels im persischen Zeitalter.* 1964. Pp. VIII + 222. (J. C. B. Mohr, Tübingen. Price: Paper, DM. 27; cloth, DM. 32).

This is a collection of eight essays, either new or based on articles which have appeared in various places and revised to take account of more recent discovery and research. Each essay is a thorough and well-documented study of one of the many problems that belong to the post-exilic period; to each the author brings a richly informed mind and an acute judgement, and to each he makes an original contribution. There is a long and valuable study of the political changes in the period between

Nabonidus and Darius, and studies of the proclamation of Cyrus as given in Ezra i, the account of the return of the Temple vessels, and the lists of the returning exiles. Here the author reaches the conclusion that the return should be dated in 521/0 B.C. The rebuilding of the Temple under Zerubbabel and the investiture of the High Priest are studied with new insight into the significance of passages in Zechariah. An essay on Ezra and Bagoas examines the relations between these two men in the light of the later dating of Ezra's mission. The final essay is a topographical study of the Syrian and Palestinian coast in the late Persian period, accompanied by a map. The whole is a stimulating volume.

H.H.R.

HOLT, J. M.: *The Patriarchs of Israel*. 1964. Pp. vii+240. (Vanderbilt University Press, Nashville. Price: $5.95).

This carefully produced book does great credit to its author. Accepting the literary and form-critical analysis of Genesis since Gunkel and the limitations of the matter as legends related to small ethnic groups rather than as history, he examines the credibility of these in the light of the elucidation of the period 1900–1400 by archaeology in the Near East, particularly legal texts from Mesopotamia, which are more fully and critically treated than in most studies of this kind. The reader will welcome this study and the review of recent studies on the Habiru, and the whole is marked by a just appraisal of the sources with emphasis on the theological purposefulness of J and the erudition and often astonishing accuracy of P on the details of a long bygone age, and by such moderation and commendable honesty.

J.G.

JEPSEN, A. & HANHART, R.: *Untersuchungen zur israelitisch-jüdischen Chronologie*. (Beihefte zur Zeitschrift für die alttestamentliche Wissenschaft, Heft 88). 1964. Pp. VI + 96. (Verlag Alfred Töpelmann, Berlin. Price: DM. 18).

Dr. Jepsen, in the first part of this double volume, discusses recent views on the chronology of the kings of Israel and Judah. After briefly examining the works of recent writers on the subject (Mowinckel, Albright, Thiele, Schedl) and dismissing them for reasons which may be accepted as sufficient, the author takes up that of Begrich (published as *Chronologie der Könige von Israel und Juda*, 1927; Mohr, Tübingen) and accepts his conclusions, with a few modifications, on the ground that they do not demand so many unproved assumptions (e.g., co-regencies, arbitrary alternatings between spring and autumn for the New Year, ante- or post-dating the beginnings of the various reigns, incorrect synchronisms and textual corruptions). The criticisms are pointed; but whether Begrich has really said the last word is another matter. In the second part, Dr. Hanhart, starting from a Babylonian chronicle, unfortunately badly damaged (published by Sachs and Wiseman in 1958 in *Iraq* XVI, 202–11) attempts to disentangle the chronological problems set by Daniel and 1–2 Maccabees for the period with which they deal. He concludes that the author of 1 Maccabees uses the

Syro-Macedonian Seleucid era beginning in the autumn of 312 B.C. for secular and the Babylonian-Seleucid and Jewish era beginning in the spring of 311 B.C. for sacred events, but that that used by the author of 2 Maccabees is only a relative chronology, except in the three letters which bear absolute dates (xi. 16–21, 27–33, 34–38). Basing his conclusions primarily on the Babylonian chronicle (so far as it is available) and 1 Maccabees, he briefly sketches Syro-Seleucid and Jewish history for 175–134 B.C. Here his most important point is that the Temple in Jerusalem was rededicated on 14 December (before, not after and so in consequence of, the king's death), that Antiochus IV died soon afterwards, c. 14–17 December (contrary to the figures in Daniel, which put this event on 6 Siwan or 29 Tammuz, depending on the event which is taken as the *terminus a quo* of the apocalyptic figures, which are rejected as schematic) and that the news of his death reached Babylon c. 18–20 December 164 B.C. (from which his death is calculated backwards, as the part of the chronicle recording it is lost).

These two books, or rather pamphlets (for they are commend-ably concise), are important out of all proportion to their size and call for careful study by everyone interested in the extremely difficult problems of Jewish chronology; but a reviewer may justifiably protest at the undue length of the sentences (many 15 or even 18 lines long) in which the most intricate arguments are obscured and at times made almost unintelligible. G.R.D.

JOHNSTON, L.: *A History of Israel.* 1964. Pp. viii + 248 + 1 map. (Sheed and Ward, London and New York. Price: 12s. 6d.).

This is a brief, scholarly, and readable presentation of the history of Israel by a Roman Catholic scholar. Whilst treading no new paths, it is based on sound critical scholarship, and will be valuable to the student and general reader. R.E.C.

MALAMAT, A.: *Sources for Early Biblical History.* The Second Millenium B.C. In Hebrew translation. 1964. Pp. IX+387+2 tables+1 map. (The Hebrew University Press, Jerusalem, Israel).

Early last year Dr. Malamat published a small volume of 104 pages containing transliterations and texts of 18 Old-Babylonian tablets from Mari, based on the French edition of Prof. Dossin and his colleagues. The present volume is a greatly expanded edition of that work, produced with the help of 7 colleagues. It is divided into 3 main sections, which are here further sub-divided. The first, entitled 'From the land of Hebrew origins', contains the same collection of 21 texts from Mari and 2 of Yahdunim, revised and where necessary corrected and with the addition of 2 texts from Nuzi. The second section, called 'Canaan before the Israelite conquest', comprises 11 texts or extracts from texts from Egyptian sources, as well as 25 Accadian texts from Ta'annek, El-Amarna and Alalakh, and 10 texts from Ugarit. The third section on 'Canaanite during the conquest

and settlement' comprises another selection of Egyptian documents followed by 8 treaties in the Egyptian, Hittite, and Accadian languages and 2 Assyrian historical pieces. The transliteration of the Accadian texts (for the Egyptian texts are not transliterated but only translated) seems to be generally accurate and
the translations for the most part correct if not always precise;
and occasionally the reviewer finds the modern Hebrew rendering
not so clear as the ancient Accadian text! The documents are
reasonably well selected for the purpose which the editor has in
view, and the presentation of the text, though not printed but
typed (so that the necessary diacritical points and accents have
been added by hand) is fair (even though the translation of 12
lines of one text has failed to come out and is supplied on a
loose sheet, which can be pasted on to the page in the proper
place). The volume, however, raises one important question:
will anyone not acquainted with at any rate one European
language want to use such a collection? One in English, French,
or German would have an appeal which the Hebrew edition can
never have.

G.R.D.

MALAMAT, A.: *Organs of Statecraft in the Israelite Monarchy.* (*El ha'ayin*
['Back to the Sources']. Materials for Bible Study Circles. No. 41).
1964. Pp. 58. (World Jewish Bible Society and the Israel Society for
Biblical Research, Jerusalem, in co-operation with the Department
for Education and Culture in the Diaspora).

This booklet contains the text of a lecture in which the narrative
of the disruption of the kingdom is discussed with special
reference to the nature of the covenant between king and people
and to the ministers, the elders, and the 'young men' (regarded
as princes of the court) as organs of government. A parallel is
drawn from the Gilgamesh-Agga epic. It is of interest to have,
in addition, a record of the discussion which followed the
lecture and the author's replies to questions and criticisms.

G.W.A.

*PEARLMAN, M. & YANNAI, Y.: *Historical Sites in Israel.* 1964. Pp. 248
including many ills. (W. H. Allen, London. Price: 84s. 0d.).

This magnificently produced volume (to which Professor Y.
Yadin contributes a commendatory foreword), combines the
qualities of a travel guide and a non-technical handbook to the
archaeology of Israel. In accuracy of information, effectiveness
of presentation, and excellence of photographic reproduction,
it is quite first-class. The descriptions of sites and buildings are
interwoven with surveys which admirably convey the varying
phases in the history of the land.

G.W.A.

PFEIFFER, C. F.: *Egypt and the Exodus.* 1964. Pp. 96 incl. 1 map and
15 ills. (Baker Book House, Grand Rapids, Michigan. Price:
$2.95).

The book comprises a preface and ten chapters relating to the
title, with a select bibliography, index, and map of the route of
the Exodus and conquest of Canaan, and is a brief introduction

to the geography, history, and archaeology of the wilderness period. The volume is popular, attractive, and well illustrated. The information is generally reliable, with a conservative slant.

G.H.D.

*RATTEY, B. K.: *A Short History of the Hebrews from Moses to Herod the Great.* 2nd edition. 1964. Pp. 160 incl. many ills., 2 maps & Chronological table + 3 maps on endpapers. (Oxford University Press. Price: 8s. 6d.).

This popular text-book, intended for middle and upper forms of Secondary Grammar schools, and reprinted nine times since it was first published in 1931, has now been carefully and unobtrusively brought up-to-date, and given a new and attractive format, with over thirty well-chosen illustrations and maps. Here the story of Israel from Moses to Herod the Great is presented in an accurate, compressed, readable form that makes the book still one of the best and most reliable of its kind.

L.A.P.

SPEISER, E. A. (ed. by): *At the Dawn of Civilization.* A Background of Biblical History. (The World History of the Jewish People. First Series: Ancient Times). Vol. I, ed. B. Netanyahu. 1964. Pp. XVI+388 incl. many plates+4 maps. (W. H. Allen, London. Price: £5 5s. 0d.).

This monumental history of which the blurb gives notice that it may extend to 20 vols., to appear in 5 years, is introduced by a study of the various aspects, physical, historical and cultural, of the Near Eastern world. There are studies in physical environment and pre-history and on linguistic and ethnic environment. A feature of these studies is their remarkable success in presenting the subject in clear perspective and brief compass without sacrificing significant detail, and with the undoubted note of authority. Eventually the study is concentrated in the history and cultural achievement of Mesopotamia and Egypt with due respect to objective material and documentary evidence and to the relevance of each culture to the achievement of Israel. In his editorial epilogue Speiser looks forward to forthcoming studies of the history of Israel, for which the present volume is a happy augury.

J.G.

WILLIAMSON, G. A.: *The World of Josephus.* 1964. Pp. 318. (Secker & Warburg, London. Price: 36s. 0d.).

The translator of Josephus' *The Jewish War* (see *Book List* 1960, p. 15) here provides a very readable introduction to a Jew who repels many and fascinates all. The geographical world and the historical world of Josephus are described, the Jewish world into which he was born and the Roman world which he adopted and which adopted him. The story of the Jewish tragedy is traced with a fulness and balance for which the writer's earlier work had fitted him, and Josephus' standing as author and historian is evaluated against the background of the literary fashions of his day. Mr. Williamson, for long Head of the

Classical Department, King Edward VI School, Norwich, certainly makes his point that this is 'a complex but enthralling story' in which 'Jewish history, Roman history, and Christian history are inextricably intertwined'. As this book is intended for the general reader, it would be pointless to express the wish that more precise references had been given where earlier writers of the subject are cited. His reference to 'St. Dr. John Thackeray' (p. 263) is perhaps unpremeditated rather than precise.

W.D.McH.

TEXT AND VERSIONS

*KENYON, F. G.: *The Story of the Bible*. A popular account of how it came to us. New edition with a Supplementary Chapter by B. M. G. Reardon. 1964. Pp. viii + 148 + 9 ills. (John Murray, London. Price: 6s. 0d.).

This popular account of the Biblical text and versions was the most up-to-date work of its kind when it was first published in 1936 — so up-to-date, in fact, that it contained an announcement which had not had time to get into any more learned publication, the announcement that the Chester Beatty Pauline manuscript, P 46, contained not just the ten fragmentary leaves which Kenyon had edited in 1934, but 66 more. A reprint in 1946 included an additional note mentioning the Rylands fragments of the Greek Deuteronomy and the religious texts from Ugarit. The new paperback edition is enlarged by a chapter on 'Recent Developments' in which B. M. G. Reardon deals with the Qumran and Nag Hammadi texts and their significance for Biblical studies, and with the most recent and forthcoming English versions of the Bible. Some account of the Bodmer Biblical papyri might well have been included.

F.F.B.

RABIN, C. (ed. by): *Textus. Annual of the Hebrew University Bible Project*. Vol. III. 1963. Pp. viii + 170 incl. portrait + 10 (Hebrew) + 24 plates.

This volume opens with a brief tribute by B. Mazar to the late I. Ben-zevi. M. Fitzmaurice Martin believes that Codex Neofiti 1 is the work of a scribe in the employ of Elias Levita, who was acting under orders from Aegidius of Viterbo. M. Z. Kadari shows the significance of *daleth*-clauses in Targum Onkelos for the study of the Hebrew *Vorlage* of the Targum. S. Talmon writes on four fragments of the Samaritan Pentateuch. He collates them with A. von Gall's text, and in the case of Deut. xx. l-xxi. 2 also with the text of the Abisha Scroll. Other passages included are Gen. xxxi. 43-xxxii. 1; Exod. ix. 25-xi. 2; and Gen. xviii. 31-xix. 18. G. E. Weil presents two studies of the Babylonian Massorah Magna in two Bodleian manuscripts (Exod. xvi. 29-xvii. 15, xxi. 36-xxii. 22, xxiii. 23-xxiv. 12, xxv. 39-xxvi. 18), and in a Cambridge Geniza fragment of the Prophets (I Sam. xxv. 15-25, xxvi. 2-12). I. Yeivin considers a Cambridge Geniza fragment of *haftaroth* (Isa. liii. 3, lvi. 3–5; Hos. x. 6–9; Isa. xi. 8–11, lxiii. 7–9; Mic. vii. 17 f.) and other manuscripts with mixed pointing. N. Fried finds in this fragment phenomena which differ from other known *haftaroth*. A. Mirsky stresses the importance of Biblical variants in Mediaeval Hebrew poetry. M. H. Goshen-Gottstein discusses the problem of constructing a critical apparatus to the M.T. based on retroversion from different languages, especially the Greek of the Septuagint. Passages considered are Isa. v. 18, iv. 5, xlvi. 1, v. 29, xliii. 12, ix. 2, xliv. 25, xlv. 8 f., 23. Summaries of the articles in Hebrew are provided.   D.W.T.

EXEGESIS AND MODERN TRANSLATIONS

BARUCQ, A.: *Le Livre des Proverbes*. (Sources Bibliques). 1964. Pp. 268. (J. Gabalda et Cie., Paris. Price: F.35).

Père Barucq's introduction examines the place of the Wisdom literature in the life of Israel and its relation to that of other nations, and discusses the composition and principal themes of the book of Proverbs; there is also a section on the versions which, although it finds room for the Coptic, fails to describe the later Greek versions, the Peshitta, and the Targum. A French translation of Proverbs is then given, with brief notes on the Hebrew text and a fuller commentary on the subject matter; finally, there are several indexes. The book contains a surprisingly large number of misprints, the use of *daghesh* being particularly erratic.   J.A.E.

BIČ, M.: *Die Nachtgesichte des Sacharja: Eine Auslegung von Sacharja 1–6*. (Biblische Studien 42). 1964. Pp. 76. (Neukirchener Verlag des Erziehungsvereins, Neukirchen-Vluyn. Price: DM. 5).

In this short book of seven chapters the author provides exegetical studies of Zechariah's seven Night Visions and their accompanying interpretations. The modern Lutheran translation is given, but some emendations have been incorporated and are noted. A great deal of work has gone into these studies, whose simplicity is deceptive, and new suggestions at many points add still more to the book's value. Without betraying in any way the strict historical approach, the underlying contemporary and timeless message of the visions is made sufficiently clear for any attentive reader to grasp.   D.R.Ap-T.

BIČ, M.: *Das Buch Sacharja*. 1965. Pp. 182. (Evangelische Verlagsanstalt, Berlin. Price: DM. 9.80).

In a short introduction the author acquaints the reader with the main theories as to integrity, authorship, and date. Deutero-Zechariah is regarded as forming, with the book of Malachi, an anonymous collection of oracles of unascertainable provenance. Both halves of the book proclaim the same message of universalism, looking forward to an ideal, eschatological future and a priestly-royal redeemer. The Night Visions are kept to seven by taking ch. v. as a single vision, and Zechariah's dependance on written works of the pre-exilic prophets is maintained. The difficulties of text and interpretation, especially in the later chapters, are referred to, but conjectural emendations are resolutely eschewed and no attempt is made to force an historical reference when the evidence is so ambiguous. Throughout, the emphasis is on a positive exegesis, with commentary following translation section by section. A list of some hundred works dealing with Zechariah is appended and will add to the value of this useful book which provides many new insights.

D.R.Ap-t.

BLAIR, E. P.: *Deuteronomy, Joshua.* (The Layman's Bible Commentaries). 1965. Pp. 124. (S.C.M. Press, London. Price: 6s. 0d.).

Eight pages are devoted to technical matters (sources, origin, etc.) for Deuteronomy and three and a half for Joshua. The remainder of the book is commentary, section by section. The core of Deuteronomy was brought to Jerusalem by a Northern Levite some time before 622 B.C.; it stimulated and directed the reform. Moses stands behind it as Jesus behind the Fourth Gospel. Joshua is the second volume of the Deuteronomic history, with chapters xiii-xxi and xxiv probably added later. Like other books in the series, this volume is readable, reliable, and apt for its purpose.

N.H.S.

BREIT, H. & WESTERMANN, C. (ed. by): *Die alttestamentlichen Texte der Fünften Reihe.* (Calwer Predigthilfen, Band 3). 1964. Pp. 280. (Calwer Verlag, Stuttgart. Price: DM. 16).

This volume contains 20 outlines of sermon preparation compiled by the editors in collaboration with W. Rupprecht and W. Warth. These aids relate to the following passages: Gen. xi. 1–9, xxxii. 23–32; Exod. xiv., xxxii. 15–20, 30–34; Deut. vi. 4–13; 1 Sam, ii. 1–10, xvi. 1–13; 1 Kings xix. 8b–18; Isa. xi. 1–9, xxxv. 3–10, xlii. 1–8, xliii. 1–7, l. 4–9a, lxiii. 15–lxiv. 4; Jer. xx. 7–13, xxiii. 16–29; Ezek. ii. 3–8a, iii. 17–19; Amos v. 4–6, 21–24; Mal. iii. 13–20; Ps. xc. The four editors have dealt with these texts independently but in accordance with the same general approach. After (1) explanations of the Hebrew words and a consideration of the revised Luther translation there follow (2) exegesis, (3) a meditation, and (4) suggestions for homiletic presentation. In the exegetical sections the results of scholarly study are effectively applied. The observations on homiletical preparation are stimulating. To assist in further study there are short bibliographies, confined to works in German, and prefatory sections on the value of ancient and modern Bible translations.

W.B.

BURROWS, M.: *Diligently Compared. The Revised Standard Version and the King James Version of the Old Testament.* 1964. Pp. x + 278. (Nelson, New York and Toronto. Price: $6.50).

This handbook was originally conceived as a 'companion' to the Revised Standard Version of the Old Testament, but it grew into something different. For the general reader who is interested enough to ask why the Revised Standard Version differs in so many particulars from the version of 1611 Professor

Burrows gives a helpful account of the whole matter. His material is classified under three main heads: 'Changes in English without change in meaning'; 'Differences of interpretation'; 'The Hebrew and Aramaic text'. The general reader must expect to be led over some rather steep territory, but Professor Burrows is an experienced and considerate guide and leads him by the hand through the various uses of the preposition *min* and round the pitfalls of Hebrew sentence structure. By the end of the journey the reader will have received a liberal education in Old Testament text and language, in addition to having his questions answered. It might have been mentioned on p. 58 that *ḥaruṣ* (Dan. ix. 25) is now attested from 3Q 15, with the evident meaning 'water channel' or 'conduit'. And it was not only the makers of KJV who 'simply could not believe that David's sons . . . could be priests' (p 96, on 2 Sam. viii 18); the Chronicler anticipated them by 2,000 years.   F.F.B.

CASSUTO, U.: *A Commentary on the Book of Genesis*, trans. by Israel Abrahams. Part II, *From Noah to Abraham*, Genesis VI 9–XI 32, with an Appendix: a fragment of Part III. First published 1949. 1964. Pp. XIV + 386. (The Magnes Press, The Hebrew University, Jerusalem; Oxford University Press, London. Price: 57s. 0d.).

Like the commentary on i. l-vi. 8 (*Book List* 1962, p. 26) this is homiletical and expansive (vi. 9-xi. 32 in 386 pages). Embedded in it is some useful material, e.g., a detailed comparison of the Flood story with the Gilgameš Epic, or the discussion of the word *ṣōhar* (vi. 16) suggesting either 'cover' or 'window' as its meaning and preferring the latter. But it is too often spoilt by this kind of expansion: explaining the repetition in vi. 19 f. Cassuto writes, 'Above it is stated: *you shall bring into the ark*; now Noah might have queried this instruction and said: How is it possible for me to search out all the different kinds . . .? To this potential question the following answer is given: *two of every sort shall COME IN to you* — of their own accord, as the result of an inner urge that God would arouse within them. . . . In the light of this interpretation, the meaning of the word *bring* in the preceding verse is: you shall permit them to come into the ark'. (p. 70).   L.H.B.

*CUNLIFFE-JONES, H.: *Deuteronomy*. Introduction and Commentary. (Torch Bible Commentaries). 1964. Pp. 192. (SCM Press, London. Price: 7s. 6d.).

This commentary first appeared in 1951 (see *Book List* 1952, p. 31; *Eleven Years*, p. 402), and is here re-issued as a paperback with an additional preface noting recent contributions on Deuteronomy from G. E. Wright and G. von Rad.   R.E.C.

EICHHORN, D. M.: *Musings of the Old Professor — the Meaning of Koheles*. A new translation of and commentary on the Book of Ecclesiastes. 1963. Pp. 268. (Jonathan David, New York. Price: $5.95).

First published as a serial in an American magazine this work on Koheleth has Jewish readers in mind and will appeal mainly to them. It takes the form of a commentary, sometimes by verse and sometimes by paragraph, composed largely of a wealth of material drawn from Talmudic and Midrashic sources with citations also from a select number of post-Talmudic authorities, all of which as well as those of the Tannaim and Amoraim are listed in convenient tables at the end of the book. Whilst there is much of interest in the author's citations and comments they are not always judiciously presented. Certain interpretations offered are open to question and an occasional homiletical appeal in over-popular style is apt to obtrude. The author has aimed to present 'the thought and spirit of Koheles, as well as the style and meaning of his language' in a translation which he invites his readers to take on trust. Parts of it are effectively done although there is a tendency towards the free paraphrase, so that it is perhaps surprising to find at the opposite extreme the unduly literal rendering of 'vapor of vapors' for the *vanitas vanitatum*. Useful introductory paragraphs of an explanatory character are supplied at the beginning of each chapter. There is a concluding summary of Koheleth's teaching. The unity of the book is assumed and the quality as a teacher of its author well brought out, although current literature on the subject is not discussed.

E.T.R.

FOHRER, G.: *Das Buch Hiob.* (Kommentar zum Alten Testament, Band XVI). 1963. Pp. 568. (Gütersloher Verlagshaus Gerd Mohn, Gütersloh. Price: DM. 92; by subscription, DM. 78).

This new commentary (a continuation of Sellin's well-known Kommentar zum Alten Testament) on Job follows the usual model of such works. The introduction (pp. 27–68) is useful but ill-balanced: for example, it has 12–13 pages on the *Werden* of the book, including only 1 page on the date, 12 pages on its relation to tradition which include only 2 pages on style and 1 page on vocabulary and metrical forms, and 4 pages on the text and versions. The bulk of the book consists of translation and commentary (pp. 69–545), to which a brief article on the theology is appended (pp. 546–560). The bibliography is full if not exhaustive (pp. 57–68), and the indices are reasonably full (pp. 561–5). The translation, so far as a foreigner can judge, reads very well but is marred here and there by absurd renderings such as 'I will make another face' (ix. 27), 'I become bare (*kahl*) on the skin of my teeth' (xix. 20), 'a bow of bronze pierces him' (xx. 24), 'here is my sign manual' (xxxi. 35), 'his bones, which can no longer be seen, become fleshless' (xxxiii. 21), 'as the gum tastes its food' (xxiv. 3), and so on. These and similar translations are due to a hankering after tradition, retained at whatever cost in sense against modern and improved interpretation. The commentary is divided into three parts: textual and detailed in small print, general in large print. Much of this is far too long with, at times, a marked lack of clarity or even inconsistency: e.g., the note on *rešef* (pp. 148–9) is inconclusive, partly because the meaning of the root and the renderings of the ancient Versions are not brought into the discussion; or again *jemima* is explained once as 'dove' (p. 541) and once as 'sister-in-law' (p. 544). Another weakness is the disregard of the cognate languages, to which resort must be had in solving problems in another of which so little has survived, if needless emendation is to be avoided; and the only 'Egyptian' word quoted (p. 522 on xl. 15) does not exist. Also the grammatical notes contain some very dubious remarks (e.g., on iii. 3, 22, xxv. 5). Further, the editor's knowledge of natural history is at times faulty: e.g., the hippopotamus 'lets its tail hang (*hängen*) like a cedar' (xl. 17), and 'the crocodile is hunted with fish-hooks and harpoons' (xl. 31)! Much space is wasted by noting all words which occur only once or twice (e.g., on p. 527 " . . . ist hap. leg." occurs 7 times without comment and is missed once, on *ms'* which is a totally different word from that in 1 Kings vi. 7, with which it is ineptly compared), and by citing modern scholars by full Christian (where known) and surnames; even so, the name of one English scholar is wrongly spelt wherever it occurs! Briefly, this new Commentary gives much but misses much.

G.R.D.

FOHRER, G.: *Das Buch Jesaja.* 3 Band. Kapitel 40–66. (Zürcher Bibelkommentare). 1964. Pp. 286. (Zwingli-Verlag, Zürich and Stuttgart).

Professor Fohrer has contrived to pack a surprising amount of material into this short commentary and yet to maintain an enviable lucidity of style and of general presentation. He rejects as unfounded the view that the entire book of Isaiah is the product of the activity of an Isaianic school, denying in particular that there is any special affinity between Deutero-Isaiah and Isaiah of Jerusalem. He regards xl–lv not as a planned literary unity but as a collection of short passages assembled into larger groups in accordance with subject matter. Six servant passages are recognised: xlii. 1–4, xlii. 5–7, xlix. 1–6, l. 4–9, l. 10 f., lii. 13–liii. 12. These are mainly regarded as autobiographical; but some passages, notably lii. 13–liii. 12, are regarded as coming from another hand, though referring to Deutero-Isaiah. lvi–lxvi is taken to be a collection of prophecies of varying authorship and date.

G.W.A.

GUNKEL, H.: *Genesis* (Göttinger Handkommentar zum Alten Testament. I. Abteilung, Die historischen Bücher. 1 Band). 6. Auflage: Nachdruck der 3. Auflage. 1964. Pp. cxxii+510. (Vandenhoeck & Ruprecht, Göttingen. Price: DM. 45).

That new editions of Gunkel's *Genesis* are still called for is not surprising, for his influence is still strong; all libraries must possess this book and all students must have access to it. Apart from being on whiter paper than the 5th (1922) ed., and from having dropped the dedication to Harnack, the present volume differs from earlier reprints of the 3rd ed. only in the inclusion of Baumgartner's address to the Old Testament Congress at Bonn in 1962 on the hundredth anniversary of Gunkel's birth. Baumgartner describes Gunkel's career, traces the influences on his development, and estimates his importance for Biblical studies, the whole essay being enriched by personal notes and illumined by the deep feeling the writer clearly has for his teacher.

W.D.McH.

HERTZBERG, H. W.: *I & II Samuel*. A Commentary. (The Old Testament Library). Trans. by J. S. Bowden from the German *Die Samuelbücher* (Das Alte Testament Deutsch 10), 2nd revised edition 1960. 1964. Pp. 416. (S.C M. Press, London. Price: 50s. 0d.).

This excellent translation of Hertzberg's commentary follows hard upon the companion volume on I & II Kings by Professor J. Gray. It contains one statement in the preface to the English edition that is hard to understand: viz., that Caspari's 'very learned and difficult' volume published in 1925 was the only commentary on I & II Samuel issued 'since those of Karl Budde (1902) and Hugo Gressmann (1910)'. The bibliography to this volume records no less than nine commentaries on these books published between 1925 and 1956, and even so fails to mention A Médebielle's useful short commentary in the third volume of *La Sainte Bible* published by Letouzey in 1949. In this English edition the translator has had to face the issue that Hertzberg's German translation differs markedly from the text underlying the RSV. Hence it proved simpler to 'print an English equivalent of the author's German text, checked against the Hebrew and Greek, based on RSV but deviating from it wherever this is necessary for a faithful reproduction of the author's work' (p. 12). The work is not merely an admirable commentary; it also supplies a large number of critical notes on the text, in which the Hebrew is quoted in transcription.

J.M.T.B.

*JONES, D. R.: *Isaiah 56–66 and Joel*. (The Torch Bible Commentaries). 1964. Pp. 190. (SCM Press, London. Price: 16s. 0d.).

In a useful short commentary, Professor Jones shows the continuity and vitality of the prophetic tradition as it expresses itself in two sections of prophecy, both of which he dates in the period between Cyrus and Nehemiah. The dating is reasonable, if perhaps disputable at certain points; the emphasis is appropriate and enables the commentator, in showing the relevance of the material to its own time, to bring out its deeper significance.

P.R.A.

*KIDNER, D.: *The Proverbs. An Introduction and Commentary*. (Tyndale Old Testament Commentaries). 1964. Pp. 192. (Tyndale Press, London. Price: 8s. 6d.).

This is the first of a new series of Old Testament commentaries produced under the general editorship of Professor D. J. Wiseman. Mr. Kidner is conservative in his approach to Proverbs and makes every effort to retain the Massoretic Text; but he is well-informed and far from obscurantist. After an introduction and some studies of leading themes in Proverbs, he offers a commentary on the English text (though Hebrew words are often discussed) and does not forget the religious message of the book for modern readers. The English style of the commentary makes it a pleasure to read.

J.A.E.

LAMPARTER, H.: *Prophet wider Willen: Der Prophet Jeremia.* (Die Botschaft des Alten Testaments, 20). 1964. Pp. 414. (Calwer Verlag, Stuttgart. Price: DM. 18).

This commentary is on the same lines as the others in this series. There is a very brief introduction and then the text of Jeremiah is given in sections in translation and a running commentary with homiletic purpose follows each section. Within the limits set by an almost exclusively homiletic approach the translation is useful and takes account of modern interpretation. The text is arranged in the following order: i. 1–xxv. 38; xlvi-li; xxx. 1–xxxiii. 26; xxvi. 1–xxix. 32; xxxiv. 1–xlv. 5, partly after LXX, partly to bring together the parts attributable to Baruch and partly to close the prophecies of Jeremiah with oracles of promise (xxx.1–xxxiii. 26).

The author thinks the book gives no indication as to how Jeremiah regarded the Josianic reform. He thinks the enmity of the priests was due to the Temple address, but that the reason for the particular animosity of his own family and the inhabitants of his own town is not discoverable. The false handling of the scribes (viii. 8) is said to be the way their manner of life contradicted the law.

The inner life of Jeremiah could well have been given more critical attention than it has with a greater recognition of the problem of the way in which a prophet becomes aware of the word of God. L.H.B.

LESLIE, E. A.: *Isaiah:* Chronologically arranged, translated and interpreted. 1963. Pp. 288. (Abingdon Press, New York and Nashville. Price: $5.00).

The book follows similar lines to the author's treatment of Jeremiah. The dating of some passages would not command general assent and the treatment of them is usually too brief to give adequate grounds for the dating. Chapters xxiv–xxvii are described as a 3rd century Apocalypse; xxxiii as a prophetic liturgy from 160 or 162 B.C. The Servant Songs are not specifically distinguished from the rest of Deutero–Isaiah, though the last has the title 'Israel as the Suffering Servant of the Lord'. l. 4–9 is regarded as autobiographical. Translation is clear and often lively, but few would understand *leben* in vii. 15, 22, and no explanation is given. The interpretation is mainly of a homiletic character. The book will be useful to preacher and teacher.

A.S.H.

LORETZ, O.: *Gotteswort und menschliche Erfahrung.* Eine Auslegung der Bücher Jona, Rut, Hoheslied und Qohelet. 1963. Pp. 224. (Verlag Herder, Freiburg. Price: DM. 15.80).

The author provides an introduction and an exposition of each book followed by a brief chapter in each case on its special significance. The book is well and clearly written. It is founded on scholarly opinion and popularly presents the meaning and message of the books chosen. Qohelet has the longest treatment, and there are also 23 pages of more learned notes and bibliography. The reviewer found the commentary interesting and often stimulating. G.H.D.

MINN, H. R.: *The Book of Job. A Translation with Introduction and Short Notes.* 1965. Pp. x+115. (University of Auckland, N.Z. Price: 7s. 6d. paperback).

Here we have an attempt to make the book of Job understandable to students in our Biblical Studies departments. To the maturer scholar also the author's own translation is suggestive at many points. Clearly the short bibliography of under a dozen works, all in English, does not mention more than a fraction of the commentaries consulted by the author in deciding on the final form of his most successful rendering of the original into blank verse. In his Introduction the author accepts the integrity of the book; and critical questions are scarcely touched upon. The Analysis of Job merely specifies the chapters assigned by MT to each speaker; and the 8 pages of explanatory notes are necessarily very short though to the point and very useful for the non-Hebraist as far as they go. The book is reproduced from typescript, remarkably clean and legible and attractive to read. At this price, too, no one can really go wrong! D.R.Ap-T.

NORTH, C. R.: *The Second Isaiah: Introduction, Translation and Commentary to Chapters XL-LV.* 1964. Pp. xii + 290. (Clarendon Press, Oxford. Price: 35s. 0d.).

Professor North has at last followed his great monograph on the Servant Songs by his eagerly awaited commentary on Isa. xl-lv. He gives a new translation of the text, marked by great caution in emendation, followed by a full commentary. In the commentary each section is introduced by textual and philological notes, in which Hebrew script is freely used. These are followed by general comment on the section as a whole and verse by verse comments on the English translation. Here Hebrew words stand in transliteration. In this way the author aims to serve readers of more than one level. There is a good Introduction, in which the section on the theology of Second Isaiah deserves special mention. The commentary is throughout judicious and marked by many new insights and by no eccentricities. At last we have an English commentary on the Hebrew text of these chapters which may be commended without reserve.

H.H.R.

NORTH, C. R.: *Isaiah 40–55.* Introduction and Commentary. (Torch Bible Commentaries). 1964. Pp. 158. (S.C.M. Press, London. Price: 7s. 6d.).

The text of the original edition of Professor North's little masterpiece is here reprinted in paperback form, together with an appendix of 8 pages of additional notes to bring it into line with his new full-length commentary (see above). The bibliography has been revised. The first edition was reviewed in *Book List* 1953, p. 38 (*Eleven Years*, p. 491). G.W.A.

NOTH, M.: *Leviticus. A Commentary*, trans. by J. E. Anderson. (The Old Testament Library). 1965. Pp. 208. (S.C.M. Press, London. Price: 35s. 0d.).

The original work was noticed when it appeared (*Book List* 1963, p. 26). No changes have been made for this edition;

and, as said before, it remains an essential work for all students concerned with Leviticus and the meaning of the cult and its place in the life of Israel. It is remarkable to have the book published in translation so soon, but it might have been better if another eye had looked it over first, in view of the well-known difficulty of giving a precise English equivalent of the author's language. E.g., 'This is especially true of the complex chs. 8–10. Chapter 8 also begins . . . ' (p. 10) would be better rendered, 'One section in particular which does is the complex chs. 8–10. Chapter 8 does indeed begin . . . ' Again, 'A stronger coherence is displayed by chs. 11–15' (p. 11) is really 'A larger nexus is constituted by chs. 11–15'. There are other examples which may mislead; but, as a whole, the translation reads fairly smoothly and the translator has been able to cope with most of the inequalities occasioned by printing the RSV as against Noth's own translation in the German edition, which is still necessary for the scholar. D.R.Ap-T.

NOTH, M.: *Könige*, Pt. I. (Biblischer Kommentar. Altes Testament, IX. 1). 1964. Pp. 80. (Neukirchener Verlag des Erziehungsvereins, Neukirchen-Vluyn. Price: DM. 7).

The Book of *Kings* has not really had its meed of full scale commentaries during the present generation. This ensures a double welcome for the first fascicle of the present volume in the above well-known series, of which the author is himself general editor. Professor Noth has indeed already given such clear proofs of his outstanding qualifications for just this task, that our pleasure at having the first instalment is only equalled by our impatience for the remainder, including the Introduction. The present fascicle covers 1 Kings i. 1–v. 14, divided into four sections (the last not completed here). Each section gives a bibliography, a translation, lexical notes, a treatment of the form and setting of the section, and then the commentary proper by paragraphs, all in a clearly set-out form. Non-Germans, at least, will be additionally grateful that Gothic type is confined to the translation.

Space will not permit extensive comment, but it may be noted that ch. ii is regarded as mainly later additions to the continued History of Davidic Succession in ch. i. D.R.Ap-T.

The Psalms: Fides Translation. Introduction and notes by Mary Perkins Ryan. 1963. Pp. xxxvii + 306. (Fides Publishers, Notre Dame, Indiana. Price: $1.25).

This translation (originally published in 1955) has been made in accordance with the New Roman Psalter; and it aims at providing a clear, modern version that gives due attention to the requirements not only of individual reading, but also of recitation aloud and of singing. The introduction includes sections on the nature of the Psalms, their use by Christians, their poetic character, their authors and titles, the classification of them, the key-words and themes in them. The arrangement of the Psalms in the Roman and Monastic Breviaries is given in an appendix, and there is an index of first lines. The notes which accompany each Psalm, and which, like the introduction, are intended for the guidance of laymen, are largely concerned with the way Roman Catholics think of the Psalms when they pray them, and with the occasions on which they are used in their Church's year. The translation combines simplicity with dignity and generally reads very well. The use throughout of 'You' and 'Your' in addressing God is noteworthy, as is the retention of the word 'sheol'. The absence of verse numeration, if a little inconvenient, helps to give a pleasing appearance to the page.

D.W.T.

VON RAD, G.: *Das fünfte Buch Mose, Deuteronomium übersetzt und erklärt* (Das Alte Testament Deutsch, 8). 1964. Pp. 152. (Vandenhoeck & Ruprecht, Göttingen. Price: paper, DM. 6.50; by subscription, DM. 5.50; cloth, DM. 9.80; by subscription, DM. 8.30).

The format and character of this series are now well known, but the interest of this particular volume is in the name of the author. We are all conversant with the main lines of von Rad's exposition of Deuteronomy as exhibiting the form of the Covenant pattern and as containing credos and preached law. In this volume, in its brief but stimulating introduction, and in the commentary, we have the detailed application of his well known point of view to the book. In the turn of phrase, the illuminating comment, and general exposition, this famous scholar puts us further in his debt.

G.H.D.

*RICHARDSON, A.: *Genesis I-XI*. Introduction and Commentary. (Torch Bible Commentaries). 1964. Pp. 134. (S.C.M. Press, London. Price: 6s. 6d.).

This is an unchanged re-issue in paperback of the commentary which first appeared in 1953 (see *Book List* 1954, p. 42; *Eleven Years*, p. 579).

R.E.C.

RODD, C. S.: *Psalms 73-150*. (Epworth Preacher's Commentaries). 1964. Pp. 132. (The Epworth Press, London. Price: 12s. 6d.).

This brief commentary is to be welcomed as a worthy companion to that on Psalms i-lxxii (*Book List* 1964, p. 41). It is an honest attempt to give a straightforward commentary without concealing difficulties or uncertainties of interpretation (cf. Ps. cix) and offering many useful alternative translations to difficult verses. Its brevity is both a strength and a weakness. A strength in that the reader easily finds his way about and comes straight to the point. A weakness is that some assumptions need explaining. For instance, the inquiring reader will be bound to ask why the commentator is so sure that it was a prophet who spoke the words found in Psalm lxxv. 2-9.

L.H.B.

RUPPRECHT, W.: *Die Predigt über alttestamentlichen Texte in den lutherischen Kirchen Deutschlands*. (Arbeiten zur Theologie, II, Reihe, Band 1). 1962. Pp. 403. (Calwer Verlag, Stuttgart. Price: DM. 25).

This work is a dissertation in the field of practical theology written in 1958 with reference to the new lectionary of texts for use in the United Evangelical-Lutheran Church of Germany. The introduction of many texts from the *Old* Testament raised with a new urgency the special problems involved in modern preaching from the Old Testament. Rupprecht offers a historical survey as a contribution to the solution of the problems, confining himself in the main to the *Landeskirchen* of Germany. He surveys briefly the practice of the Church in early and medieval times, following this with a detailed examination of Luther's sermons on the Old Testament, and with a briefer account of the subsequent phases of Orthodoxy, Pietism, and the Aufklärung, during which there was a decline in Old Testament preaching. The 19th-century attempts to reverse this trend are discussed in the principal section of Rupprecht's thesis, which ends with a sketch of the main developments and problems of the 20th century. Since the approach is primarily historical, the importance of the work lies in the expert presentation of the historical material which the author has assembled, and which is amply documented in the notes (pp. 229–379). The author, however, does not omit to relate his findings to the modern situation. His work is clearly arranged and may be read with pleasure and profit.

W.B.

SNAITH, N. H.: *Notes on the Hebrew Text of Genesis xxii–xxv and xxvii.* 1965. Pp. 106. (Epworth Press, London. Price: 16s. 0d.).

An excellent book for beginners who have finished Davidson or Weingreen and need help with their first reading of text. The words are parsed and construed, and where necessary fully discussed — all with an economy of words. Helpful notes are given on accents and anomalous forms.

L.H.B.

VELLAS, B. M.: *To Biblion tes Routh.* Eisagoge. Metaphrasis ek tou Ebraikou. Keimenon ton O'. Scholia. (Ermeneia Palaias Diathekes, 6). 1964. Pp. 58. ("Aster" Publishing House. Athens).

In this elegantly printed short commentary, Professor Vellas provides a valuable discussion of the general problems raised by the book of Ruth, together with a textual and linguistic commentary. The date of composition is assigned to a date between Deuteronomy and Ezra/Nehemiah. The purpose of the book is held to be to present Ruth as an example of family solidarity. The last five verses are treated as a later addition. Account is taken throughout of recent discussion of the relevant problems.

G.W.A.

WOODS, J.: *Jeremiah.* (Epworth Preacher's Commentaries). 1964. Pp. 176. (The Epworth Press, London. Price: 12s. 6d.).

Like the other volumes of the series, this is essentially a preacher's commentary, with lay preachers specially in mind. It gives, in the briefest possible form, an up-to-date critical view of the prophet's writings and then goes on to show what relevance lies in them or springs out of them for modern readers. The comments show a sympathetic and penetrating appreciation of Jeremiah's work as a prophet both to his own generation and to succeeding ones. In a commentary on Jeremiah for preachers it is not surprising that the Gospel is never very far away.

L.H.B.

WRIGHT, G. E.: *Isaiah*. (The Layman's Bible Commentaries). 1965. Pp. 160. (S.C.M. Press, London. Price: 6s. 0d.).

The book fulfils well the purpose of this series to provide concise non-technical guides for the layman's personal Biblical study; I and II Isaiah each occupy approximately half the volume, each has its own introduction of about 14 pages, and each is treated quite separately. No attempt is made to show the many links in vocabulary and theology between the two sections, and although the Servant Songs are regarded as integral to the contexts, individual songs — especially lii, 13–53 — are not all integrated in the textual setting. Isaiah xl–lxvi is regarded as 'heavily eschatological'.

J.N.S.

LITERARY CRITICISM AND INTRODUCTION

BARCLAY, R. A.: *The Law Givers*. (Bible Guides, No. 3). 1964. Pp. 86. (Lutterworth Press, London; Abingdon Press, New York and Nashville. Price: 5s. 0d.).

This volume is concerned with Leviticus and Deuteronomy. There is the absolute minimum on literary origins. The author is concerned with the books as they are, not with how they came so to be. Perhaps this is wise, because of the severe limitations of space. Leviticus is the guide-book to the laws about sacrifices. Deuteronomy is the book of a mission and the missioner is Moses. The volume deals with subject after subject as they are dealt with in the books. The reader will get a good general understanding of the meaning and contents of the two books.

N.H.S.

FEUCHT, C.: *Untersuchungen zum Heiligkeitsgesetz*. (Theologische Arbeiten, XX). 1964. Pp. 257. (Evangelische Verlagsanstalt, Berlin. Price: DM. 14.80).

This monograph was prepared as a dissertation at Greifswald before the author's death in his thirtieth year in 1959. After a detailed examination of Leviticus xvii-xxvi (in which special attention is paid to the style of the laws), it is argued that xvii, part of xxiii, and xxiv do not belong to the Holiness Code; the remaining chapters are divided into H 1 (xviii-xxii and part of xxiii, together with part of Numbers xv), and H 2 (xxv-xxvi). H 1 is dated in the early decades of the seventh century B.C., while H 2 is thought to come partly (xxv) from the period 625–608 B.C. and partly (xxvi) from the time of the exile. There is a painstaking form-critical study of the laws in H, and suggestions are made about their setting in life. The last part of the work discusses the theology of H. Even though it may be doubted whether the form-critical study of literary forms will support all the conclusions drawn from it, the student of the Old Testament will profit from this careful contribution to the study of H and will regret that the author's scholarly career was cut short so early.

J.A.E.

FOHRER, G.: *Überlieferung und Geschichte des Exodus.* Eine Analyse von Ex. 1–15. (Beihefte zur Zeitschrift für die alttestamentliche Wissenschaft, 91). 1964. Pp. 125. (Verlag Alfred Töpelmann, Berlin. Price: DM. 24).

The book offers a critical analysis (almost old-fashioned in its detail) of the literary features, forms, and contents of these chapters, divided into 7 parts. Fohrer postulates a primary course of six Exodus themes. This source leads directly to a nomadic source, N (roughly Smend's J, and Eissfeld's L), found in Ex. i-iv and xi-xv, and indirectly to a second source on which J (South) and E (North) depend, lastly there is P. Each new source adds its special features. Thus the comparison of the sources enables Fohrer to trace the earlier and later materials, and behind these to point to the historical basis of the narrative. A detailed and stimulating discussion.

G.H.D.

GEVIRTZ, S.: *Patterns in the Early Poetry of Israel.* (Studies in Ancient Oriental Civilization, No. 32). 1963. Pp. X + 98. (The University of Chicago Press, London. Price: 22s. 6d.).

A study of the poetical texts from Ugarit and of Hebrew poetry has led some scholars to recognize a poetic diction common to the two literatures, more particularly specific pairs of words in fixed parallel relationship, and to conclude that the poets of ancient Syria and Palestine had available to them a body of conventionally fixed pairs of words on which they could freely draw. These literatures accordingly represent two branches of a common, Syro-Palestinian, literary tradition. More than sixty such pairs of parallel terms occur both in Hebrew and Ugaritic. Hebrew poetry contains many more pairs, and it may be assumed that, if a pair of words found in parallel relationship in the Old Testament can be shown to have been a fixed, or relatively fixed, pair for the poets of the Old Testament (even if the pair is as yet unknown elsewhere) it must nevertheless represent an element of the same, or a similar, tradition. In this present work this principle of poetic tradition is applied systematically to a group of ancient poems (1 Sam. xviii. 7; Gen. ix. 23 f., xxvii. 28 f.; Num. xxiii. 7–10; 2 Sam. i. 18–27) and much light is thrown on the understanding of the Hebrew text and its integrity, on the meanings of Hebrew words, and on the poet's craft. The author has succeeded in showing in an interesting, and frequently original way, that this type of research can produce worthwhile results when it is pursued with restraint. Only occasionally does his reconstruction of a text seem less than Hebraic, e.g., in 2 Sam. i. 19 (p. 81).

D.W.T.

HARRELSON, W.: *Interpreting the Old Testament*. 1964. Pp. xii + 530 + 4 maps on endpapers. (Holt, Rinehart and Winston, New York. Price: 60s. 0d.).

Professor Harrelson seeks to supplement the standard introductions to the Old Testament with this volume which, after a brief survey of the history of Israelite literature and the formation of the canon, takes the form of a short commentary on the whole Old Testament. The method is to provide an outline of the contents of each book, a literary analysis together with any relevant traditio-historical information, and a theological interpretation of its significance. The bibliography is full and up-to-date, and there is a table setting out the source division of the Pentateuch and a glossary of terms used in Biblical criticism and interpretation. The book is primarily suitable for theological students beginning the study of the Old Testament, and its greatest usefulness lies in its survey of modern literature which is otherwise only available in German. R.E.C.

HEMPEL, J.: *Geschichten und Geschichte im Alten Testament bis zur persischen Zeit*. 1964. Pp. 256. (Gütersloher Verlagshaus Gerd Mohn, Gütersloh. Price: DM. 34).

The intense interest in history which the Old Testament writers display, and the historical form of so much of its literature, provides Professor Hempel with his starting point. The tension between historical events and the written accounts of them presents a problem in the Old Testament. After noting the basic geographical and chronological world-view of the Old Testament historians, Hempel examines the part played by the clan-histories, the covenant, the cult, and the knowledge of sin in bringing together the various historical traditions. This leads on to the question of the formation of the historical tradition, and the motives which led to the composition of the longer histories. Hempel distinguishes a 'biographical' motive, which led to the crystallizing of traditions around certain great personalities, and a 'religious' motive, which sought to make plain how God was at work through them. There are supplementary chapters on the language of the traditions, the form and content of the written histories, and the relationship of faith to history. Footnotes provide detailed bibliographical references, and the work does not seek to support the work of any one 'school', either of theological interpretation, or of literary criticism. It represents an important contribution to the elucidation of the literary and theological problems of Israelite historiography, and supersedes many of Hempel's earlier studies on this subject.   R.E.C.

HILLERS, D. R.: *Treaty-curses and the Old Testament Prophets*. (Biblica et Orientalia, 16). 1964. Pp. XIX + 102. (Pontifical Biblical Institute, Rome. Price: L. 1.500; $2.50).

In this doctoral thesis submitted to the Johns Hopkins University the author examines the ideas and vocabulary of the curses of the Near Eastern vassal treaties, and compares them with the threats of doom pronounced by the great prophets of Israel.

He concludes that only in Isa. xxxiv. 16 and Jer. xxxiv. 18 did the prophets deliberately use expressions derived from the treaty-curses. Elsewhere they may have been influenced by this wider Near Eastern form; but the nature of the material makes certainty impossible, since 'what we have called "treaty-curses" are for the most part simply traditional maledictions which happen to occur in treaties' (pp. 86 f.). R.E.C.

HÖPFL, H. O.: *Introductio specialis in Vetus Testamentum.* 1963. Pp. xxvi + 701. (M. D'Auria, Naples. Price: £2 4s. 0d.).

This, the sixth edition of Höpfl's excellent *Introduction*, is edited by S. Bovo, and takes the place of the 5th edition edited by A. Miller and A. Metzinger, which was reviewed in *Book List* 1946, p. 25 (*Eleven Years*, p. 25). The reviewer then noted some points on which the ultra-conservative position had been abandoned, and the process has continued in the new edition, e.g., with regard to the midrashic character of Wisdom's treatment of Exodus (p. 421) and to Darius the Mede, described as *prorsus historiae ignotus et probabiliter pseudonymus.* The bibliographies and indices are excellent, and help to make this a really useful compendium. J.M.T.B.

KOCH, K.: *Was ist Formgeschichte? Neue Wege der Bibelexegese.* 1964. Pp. XIV + 260. (Neukirchener Verlag des Erziehungsvereins, Neukirchen-Vluyn. Price: Paper, DM. 17.80; cloth, DM. 20.80).

This book should receive a warm welcome. It is written to answer clearly and fully the question in the main title. Whether, by so doing, the author enhances or detracts from the mystique of this and similar much-bandied terms is for each reader to decide. In the list of works bearing on the subject frequently cited, only two books are in English (both translations), which shows how badly handicapped the English student has been, and how useful a translation of this work would be.

After explaining the theory of style analysis, what it tries to do and what it cannot, the author says some pertinent things on the literary criticism versus oral tradition debate. In the second half of the book are given examples of the method and its results when applied to specific narratives, psalms, and prophecies. In a short appendix the Beatitudes from the Sermon on the Mount are analyzed. There are indexes of *Gattungen* and of the many Scripture references. D.R.Ap-T.

KÜLLING, S. R.: *Zur Datierung der "Genesis — P — Stücke", namentlich des Kapitels Genesis XVII.* 1964. Pp. XII + 322. (J. H. Kok N.V. Kampen. Price: Fl. 12.75).

This is a doctoral thesis submitted to the Free University of Amsterdam in 1964, which endeavours to examine in as comprehensive a manner as possible, the arguments which have led scholars to date the Priestly covenant narrative of Genesis xvii in the late exilic, or post-exilic age. In the first section the author traces the development which led up to Graf's assigning a late date to the Priestly strand of the Pentateuch in 1869. This is followed by an examination of the questions of linguistic style, literary form, and general religious development which have been claimed to support this date. The inconclusiveness of such arguments is asserted, and throughout there is an extremely conservative tendency, although the major issues are well presented, and there is a comprehensive bibliography. In the third section an early date for Genesis xvii is claimed on the grounds of both form and content. A major argument for this claim is the conjectured analogy with the form of the ancient Near Eastern vassal treaties. The attempt to use such an analogy to prove a specific dating is unconvincing in view of the wide area over which such a treaty form appears, and more attention needs to be given to the development of the idea of the covenant within the Old Testament itself. The careful presentation of many details of the origin and basis of Penta-teuchal criticism, lead to the hope that the author will seek a more promising subject for his evident gifts. R.E.C.

MARGALIOTH, R.: *The Indivisible Isaiah. Evidence for the Single Author-ship of the Prophetic Book*. 1964. Pp. x + 246. (Sura Institute for Research, Jerusalem Yeshiva University, New York. Price $4.75).

This is an attempt to prove the single authorship of the present book of Isaiah by means of arguments based on vocabulary and style. The occurrences of certain designations of God, and of references to Israel and Zion, as well as some introductory formulas, are held to show a common authorship of the book. There is a limited survey of the rise of the critical view. R.E.C.

MAUCHLINE, J.: *Prophets of Israel (3). The Twelve*. (Bible Guides, No. 9). 1964. Pp. 94. (Lutterworth Press, London; Abingdon Press, New York and Nashville. Price: 5s. 0d.).

Here we have a series of short 'introductions' to the twelve so-called 'minor' prophets. In the case of each prophet, the scheme is the Purpose, the Plan, the Exposition, and the Power of the book. Conservative views are given, but the author himself adopts a modern 'critical' attitude. Like all the books in this series, it is designed to be acceptable to all. N.H.S.

MOWINCKEL, S.: *Erwägungen zur Pentateuch Quellenfrage*. 1964. Pp. 138. (Universitets Forlaget, Trondheim. Price: N.Kr. 30).

This important Pentateuchal study begins with a survey of recent work on Pentateuchal source criticism. Thereafter it examines the P material and comes to the conclusion that the author of it was not simply a redactor or collector, but a narrator and codifier of law. But his concern was with cultic rules, not with civil regulations, and, as narrator, with church history rather than political or social history. He used J as his basis, but J as modified and amplified in oral tradition. Mowinckel maintains the post-exilic date of P, and proposes Jerusalem as its place of origin.

The source J he finds to have been expanded by later additions which are less factual than the original J and show more advanced moral and religious conceptions. But Mowinckel does not find sufficient evidence in Gen.-Num. to constitute a continuous source (E) parallel to J. He affirms that alongside the written document J there continued to develop an ancient oral tradition, which became modified according to the psychological and artistic laws of tradition history and under the influence of religious, moral, and social forces. This developed material was later incorporated into J, so that we may speak of J, J^1, J^2; but Mowinckel, for the sake of clarity, prefers to speak of J and J^v (variatus).

J.M.

MOWINCKEL, S.: *Tetrateuch-Pentateuch-Hexateuch*. Die Berichte über die Landnahme in den drei altisraelitischen Geschichtswerken. (Beihefte zur Zeitschrift für die alttestamentliche Wissenschaft, 90). 1964. Pp. V +87. (Alfred Töpelmann, Berlin. Price: DM. 18).

In this book Mowinckel is not concerned with the actual occupation of Palestine by the Israelites after the wilderness period, but with what the ancient historical sources say about it. It has to be noted that the material in the Pentateuch which is often attributed to the document E he regards as a later expansion of J. The saga of J he believes to be the prototype of all later presentations of Israel's history. Where he finds ancient traditions incorporated in or attached to a historical narrative of an event (as Num. xxxii. 39–42; Josh. ii. 11 and 13, xv. 13–19, 63, xvi. 10, xvii. 12–13, 14–18), these he attributes to J. They are mostly very brief, and in style and content differ notably from their context. Jdg. i he considers to be a piece of narrative history which was originally part of a much larger unit. It does not mention Joshua as leader in the occupation of Palestine; it preserves anecdotes about eponymous clan fathers and aetiological stories about place names, and shows knowledge of the areas in which individual tribes settled. This material, too, he attributes to J. D's saga of the occupation is contained in Josh. ii–xi, in which certain anecdotes from J are incorporated. P's interest is not in the occupation of the land, but in the development of the religious institutions of the chosen community in the promised land; of this interest he finds traces in Numbers and in Josh. ii–xii and xiii–xix. The underlying assumption that each of these sources J. D, P, would be incomplete without a narrative of the Israelite occupation of Palestine in fulfilment of the promise is intelligible and plausible; but the attribution of the oldest elements of such historical traditions to J is not proved, but it is claimed to be justified since J is the earliest of these sources.

J.M.

MOWINCKEL, S.: *Studien zu dem Buche Ezra-Nehemia*. I. Die nachchronische Redaktion des Buches. Die Listen. II. Die Nehemia-Denkschrift. (Skrifter utgitt av Det Norske Videnskaps-Akademi i Oslo. II. Hist.-Filos. Klasse. Ny Serie. No. 3 & 5). 1964. Pp. 168 & 136. (Oslo University Press. Price: N.Kr.: 26.00 & 20.00).

In these two volumes Mowinckel presents an important and complicated literary study in a notoriously difficult field. He begins Vol. I by affirming that 3 Esdras goes back to a Hebrew-Aramaic source and corresponds substantially to the original form of Ezra-Nehemiah. He believes that the Nehemiah memoirs existed as an independent source long after the time of the Chronicler, and were combined with the Ezra history by a redactor belonging to a date c. 200 B.C.

Mowinckel devotes most of the space in Vol. I to a detailed examination of the various lists in Ezra-Nehemiah. He believes that some came from the Temple archives, and, for the rest, he attributes much to later redaction. And, notably, he says that the list of Ezra ii (Neh. vii) is to be dated c. 400 B.C., and makes no distinction between families which shared in the Babylonian Exile and those which had remained in the Holy Land.

The second volume deals with the Nehemiah memoirs. Mowinckel maintains that Josephus used a haggadic, embellished version of the memoirs, which sometimes can supply corrections and expansions, but at other times appears to be a secondary text. He proceeds to make a literary analysis of the memoirs, and points to additions and modifications made by a later redactor. As a piece of literature, it celebrates Nehemiah's merits and his piety, and was intended to be laid up in the Temple before God as a *monumentum aere perennius*. In a comparison of the Nehemiah memoirs with ancient oriental royal documents, Mowinckel traces a connection in style and literary *genre*, but a difference in religious content.

In an appendix concerning the Samaritan schism, Mowinckel affirms that the Samaritans wanted to remain Israelites, and that the influence of the Assyrian colonists among them has often been exaggerated. The fact that Nehemiah excluded them from the old religious association with Jerusalem conditioned the schism and made a separate temple in Samaria necessary. That temple Mowinckel believes to have been built in the time of Darius II.

J.M.

NEIL, W.: *Prophets of Israel* (2). *Jeremiah and Ezekiel*. (Bible Guides, No. 8). 1964. Pp. 96. (Lutterworth Press, London; Abingdon Press, New York and Nashville. Price: 5s. 0d.).

Like the other volumes in this series, this paperback is concerned with exposition almost wholly. Literary problems are not discussed, except where there is absolute necessity. The studies of the character and mission of the two prophets are detailed and useful. The traditional view is taken of Ezekiel: he prophesied in Babylon and had second sight. The last nine chapters are his.

N.H.S.

PAYNE, D. F.: *Genesis One Reconsidered*. (The Tyndale Old Testament Lecture, 1962). 1964. Pp. 30. (The Tyndale Press, London. Price: 2s. 0d.).

The author attempts a reappraisal of the Creation Narrative in the light of the scientific challenge, comparative religion, and literary criticism. He adopts a very conservative position, holding that the sequence of events in Genesis i and ii is dramatic rather than chronological, and emphasizing the coherence of the two chapters. He concludes that the Biblical creation story is consistent in all essentials and totally opposed to the ancient Near Eastern myths.

L.A.P.

PRIGENT, P.: *Justin et l'Ancien Testament.* L'argumentation scripturaire du traité de Justin contre toutes les hérésies comme source principale du dialogue avec Tryphon et de la première apologie. (Études Bibliques). 1964. Pp. 358. (J. Gabalda et Cie, Paris. Price: F. 54).

This is the latest volume in the *Études Bibliques,* and is the work of the author of *Les Testimonia dans le Christianisme primitif. L'Épître de Barnabe... et ses sources,* published in the series in 1961. The aim of the book is explained in the sub-title. In his effort to trace the lost work which has been so extensively used for the later writings the author makes a reasonably full analysis of the *Dialogue,* and less systematically of the *First Apology* and the treatise on the Resurrection. He wisely does not attempt any sort of textual criticism in regard to the possible sources of the lost *Syntagma.* He is right in considering that his first chapter (which runs to fifty-four pages) will prove long and difficult. In the course of his later argument he is able to throw light on Justin's treatment of such topics as Christ's pre-existence, the Virgin Birth, the Passion and Resurrection, the relations between the Old and New Testaments, and universalism.

This is a work of learning and a search pursued with enthusiasm, which will be mainly of interest to patristic scholars. J.M.T.B.

RENAUD, B.: *Structure et attaches littéraires de Michée IV–V.* (Cahiers de la Revue Biblique, 2). 1964. Pp. 126. (J. Gabalda, Paris. Price: F. 16.000).

The author, beginning from Nielsen's study of this section in his *Oral Tradition* (see *Book List* 1954, p. 52), traces a unity of structure in which iv. 1–4 corresponds to v. 8–14, iv. 6–7 to v. 6–7, and iv. 8–14 to v. 1–5. He also links ii. 12–13 with iv. 6–7. The tracing of literary connections with a whole range of Old Testament passages leads him to describe the section as 'a meeting point of the complex strands of messianism and eschatology' (p. 74). The whole is characterized as midrashic in its reading and actualization of scripture; method, style and vocabulary all point to the post-exilic period.

This interpretation represents a reaction against recent tendencies to find considerable elements of genuine Micah material in these chapters. It is an attempt to appreciate more fully the nature of the later prophetic tradition. But one may doubt whether its division of the material and exegesis are entirely satisfactory and whether the opening part of Mic. iv can be adequately discussed without examining its relationship to Mic. iii.

P.R.A.

RENCKENS, H.: *La Bible et les Origines du Monde,* quand Israel regarde le passé, apropos de la Genèse 1–3. 1964. Pp. 200. (Desclée, Tournai. Price: B.Frs. 110).

The original Dutch text of this book, entitled *Israëls visie op het verleden,* was published in 1958, and is here translated and adapted by A. de Brouwer, O.S.B. It is a useful and up-to-date study of the first three chapters of Genesis, which explains the modern attitude of critical scholarship towards these chapters, and supplies a concise bibliography of works in French, Flemish, and German. It may be criticized on the ground that the twenty-five chapters are sometimes repetitious in style, if not in content, e.g., there are no less than three on Eden under the headings 'Le Paradis', 'Encore le Paradis', and 'Le paradis terrestre'. Surely one chapter would have been sufficient? One of the later chapters is more than welcome, being entitled: 'Démolition de l'interprétation sexuelle'.   J.M.T.B.

ROBERTS, B. J.: *The Old Testament Canon: A Suggestion* (Reprinted from the *Bulletin of the John Rylands Library*, Vol. 46, No. 1, September, 1963). 1963. Pp. 164–178. (The John Rylands Library, Manchester. Price: 4s. 0d.).

Professor Roberts, in a lecture based on a paper read to the Society in 1961, presents some reflections on the nature of the tradition which leads into the formation of the Canon. He shows how Rabbinic type glosses in the Old Testament text, Aramaic Targums, and Rabbinic use of scripture reveal a continuity of use, and how the apocalyptic literature likewise witnesses to the use and authority of Biblical writings. He claims nothing new for his statement, but it usefully emphasizes the connection between the growth and stabilizing of the Canon and the life and needs of the Jewish community in the period from Ezra to Jamnia.   P.R.A.

SCHMITT, G.: *Der Landtag von Sichem*. (Arbeiten zur Theologie, I Reihe, Heft 15). 1964. Pp. 108. (Calwer Verlag, Stuttgart. Price: DM. 9.50).

This is a critical study of the form and content of Josh. xxiv, a subject which is peculiarly significant since Sellin promulgated the view that it actually related to the union of elements of Israel freshly arrived from Egypt with others who had been long settled in the land. The interest is accentuated by significant reflections of what is now recognized as the vassal treaty con-dition in this passage. After acute literary criticism the author rejects Sellin's particularist view, but concludes that the passage does relate to a decisive juncture comparatively early in the Hebrew settlement, reflecting not the incorporation of new elements in the Covenant society, but a definite giving of the law by Joshua, with emphasis on the ritual of Yahwism.   J.G.

SUNDBERG, A. C.: *The Old Testament of the Early Church*. (Harvard Theological Studies XX). 1964. Pp. x + 190. (Harvard University Press, Cambridge, Mass.; Oxford University Press, London. Price: 24s. 0d.).

The major and most important part of this work is an argument that there never was, in the days of the Second Jewish Common-wealth, an Alexandrian Canon divergent from, and more com-

prehensive than, the Palestinian Canon. The third division of
the Hebrew Bible, the Writings, was defined for the first time
at Jamnia, and at Jamnia a strict limitation was imposed on the
range of this division. Before Jamnia, both in Palestine and in
Alexandria, many more writings had been popularly regarded
as canonical. This applies also to the Church of apostolic
days; it is evident that some New Testament writers attributed
canonicity to books which were excluded at Jamnia. (But
all the documents cited for parallel references to New Testament
passages need not have been regarded as canonical by the
New Testament writers in question, any more than all the
books in the Qumran library need have been regarded as
canonical by the Qumran community.) After Jamnia, the
definitive limitation of the Hebrew Canon influenced the Church,
as may be seen from early Christian lists of Old Testament
books. As for the Samaritan Bible, this does not hark back to a
period when Jews and Samaritans alike regarded the Pentateuch
only as canonical; it represents a deliberate rejection of the
'Prophets'. Not all the arguments in this interesting study are
equally convincing, but it is an important contribution to the
literature on the Old Testament Canon.   F.F.B.

UMEN, S. & STRICKLAND, M. B.: *A Pathway to the Bible*. 1964. Pp. 276.
(Vision Press, London. Price: 30s. 0d.).

The volume is written by a Jewish rabbi and a Congregational
minister, both American; and it is 'dedicated to all freedom
loving people'. It consists of short summaries of every book
in the Old and New Testaments, without any 'attempt to interpret or theologize'. The volume is mildly modern, but with an
occasional surprise: e.g. Isa. lvi-lxvi is dated 516 B.C., but Isa.
xl-lv is *c.* 200 B.C. According to the preface the book was written
for 'our community leaders, bankers, architects . . . educators. . . .'
                                                          N.H.S.

WIJNGAARDS, J. N. M.: *The Formulas of the Deuteronomic Creed* (*Dt.*
6/20–23: 26/5–9). Excerpta ex dissertatione ad Lauream in Facultate
Theologica Pontificiae Universitatis Gregorianae. 1963. Pp. 58.
(E. J. Brill, Leiden. Price: Fl. 12).

This book, part of a thesis, complete with list of abbreviations,
and a useful and classified bibliography of ten pages, is a survey
of the Exodus and landgiving formulas. By a comparison of the
formulas throughout the Old Testament describing the Exodus
and Settlement traditions, the author claims that these traditions
belong together in a recognizable pattern which is the structural
backbone of the history of salvation. The pattern is both
ancient and covenantal, the ninety texts exhibiting the structure
appearing also in the seven literary forms in which covenants
are expressed. On these findings the author claims (*a*) that von
Rad's view of the separate origins of the Exodus-Settlement
and the Covenant traditions is unjustified, and (*b*) that this
part of Old Testament Theology is not only recital but functional
for divine land tenure. An important and original study.
                                                          G.H.D.

ZIRKER, H.: *Die kultische Vergegenwärtigung der Vergangenheit in den Psalmen.* (Bonner Biblische Beiträge, 20). 1964. Pp. XVIII+158. (Peter Hanstein Verlag, Bonn. Price: DM. 26).

A doctoral thesis devoted to a study of the Psalter with a view to determining the use made of the appeal to history in the cultic theory and practice of early Israel, but one which touches far too lightly upon the many issues involved for the present writer to regard it as anything like a satisfactory treatment of the subject.

A.R.J.

LAW, RELIGION, AND THEOLOGY

ALTMANN, P.: *Erwählungstheologie und Universalismus im Alten Testament.* (Beihefte zur Zeitschrift für die alttestamentliche Wissenschaft 92). 1964. Pp. 31. (Verlag Alfred Töpelmann, Berlin. Price: DM. 9).

In this carefully presented short study Altmann argues that a proper theology of election requires not only a relationship between Yahweh and Israel in the covenant, but a conscious universalism which relates Israel to other nations. He studies this from the Yahwist's history through to the post-exilic Judaism, and finds not a unified doctrine of election, but a continual struggle to interpret its meaning. Both nationalist separatism as well as a belief in Israel as Yahweh's representative and servant to the nations can be found under the one heading. Altogether this is a significant contribution to an important theological theme.

R.E.C.

ANDERSON, B. W. (ed. by): *The Old Testament and Christian Faith.* Essays by Rudolf Bultmann and others. 1964. (1963 in U.S.A.). Pp. xii + 272. (S.C.M. Press, London. Price: 35s. 0d.).

This extremely valuable symposium is in a sense the sequel to the volume of essays edited by C. Westermann reviewed elsewhere in this *Book List* (p. 54). The debate which these essays represent has gone on and the issues have become still clearer. An essay entitled 'The Significance of the Old Testament for the Christian Faith' published by Bultmann in 1933 is translated here; and then a representative group of scholars, American, British, and Continental, give their reactions to it. Names like Alan Richardson, Oscar Cullmann, J. M. Robinson, G. E. Wright, C. Westermann, Emil Brunner, and J. L. McKenzie (a noted Jesuit scholar) among the contributors will make it evident how important this book is. The reactions to Bultmann's essay are most varied in character and show clearly how far we are from agreement on some of the biggest issues in Old Testament interpretation. One of the most illuminating contributions in its searching criticism of Bultmann's existentialist position is that by G. E. Wright. An interesting example of the way in which the post-Bultmannians are using form-critical methods to get back to history is given by Robinson's essay 'The Historicality of Biblical Language'.

N.W.P.

LAW, RELIGION, AND THEOLOGY 595

BARTHEL, P.: *Interprétation du langage mythique et théologie biblique.*
Étude de quelques étapes de l'évolution du problème de l'interpréta-
tion des représentations d'origine et de structure mythiques de la foi
Chrétienne. 1963. Pp. 400. (E. J. Brill, Leiden. Price: Fl. 26).

Although this book hardly concerns itself directly with the Old
Testament material, it is a penetrating discussion of those movements in modern theological and philosophical thinking which
seek to interpret the Biblical material in contemporary thought
forms. It is prompted by R. Bultmann's attempt to demythologise
the Gospel and follows the developments of his work in the
various theological schools of thought and relates this to the
existentialist approach. It seeks to effect a necessary demythologisation in the interests of a kerygmatic theology without falling
into a disastrous 'demythisation'. Already in Codex Bezae at
Acts i. 9–11 a beginning had been made in the early Church,
while, even more clearly, the authors of Genesis i and ii had
effected a theological demythologisation of ancient creation
recitals to present a theology of the prophetic and creative Word
of God. Its careful analysis and exhaustive review of the recent
developments in this field will make this an indispensable tool
for the student of Biblical theology as well as the systematic
theologian.   A.S.H.

BRAUN, F. M.: *Jean le Théologien: Les grandes traditions d'Israël et
l'accord des Écritures selon le Quatrième Évangile.* (Études Bibliques).
1964. Pp. XXII + 346. (J. Gabalda, Paris. Price: F. 50).

This outstanding contribution to Biblical scholarship (a sequel
to the author's *Jean le Théologien et son Évangile dans l'Église
Ancienne*) examines (i) the Fourth Evangelist's quotations from
the Old Testament, comparing his method of quotation and
exegesis with those found in the Synoptic Gospels, (ii) his treatment of the prophetic hope (under the headings Messiah, Lamb
of God, High Priest, Unknown Christ — the last of which
includes 'Son of Man' and 'Son of God') and of the wisdom
themes (under the headings Wisdom and Logos), (iii) his
eschatology and history (in this section we are given an exposition of the Johannine presentation of the mystery of salvation, the patriarchal cycle, Moses and the Exodus, and world
redemption). Professor Braun thinks it would be going too far
to reject completely the view that John's aim was to reconcile
the primitive Christian faith with the problem of salvation
as it presented itself in the Graeco-Roman world; but he insists
that the Fourth Gospel is mainly concerned to portray Jesus
as the one in whom a wide variety of Old Testament strands
are brought together. While the volume is of more immediate
relevance to New Testament studies, it deals with a very important
phase in the history of Old Testament interpretation. Three
appendices consider the bearing on the author's thesis of (i) the
Testaments of the Twelve Patriarchs, (ii) Essenism and Her-
meticism, (iii) St. John and the Greeks.   F.F.B.

CLEMENTS, R. E.: *Prophecy and Covenant.* (Studies in Biblical Theology, 43).
1965. Pp. 136. (S.C.M. Press, London. Price: 13s. 6d.).

This study is concerned to emphasize that the canonical prophets
are to be understood in relation to the cult, and not in isolation

from it or in antipathy to it; the covenant and the choice of Jerusalem and of the House of David were of basic importance for both. From a form-critical approach it seeks to show that the teaching given in the cult was preparatory to that of the prophet, and that prophetic forms of utterance are marked by the influence of cultic forms. The fact that the canonical prophets protested strongly against a debased cult is admitted; but it is maintained that they directed their charge of infidelity and failure particularly against the people's leaders.

Dr. Clements affirms that the prophets did not introduce a new morality; they appealed to 'a long and deeply embedded tradition of morality and ethical religion'.

This study is well worked out and carefully presented and documented, but it may be said that so much care is taken to relate the canonical prophets to the law and the cult in ancient Israel that the tension which often existed between them becomes somewhat overlaid.

J.M.

DAHL, N. A.: *Das Volk Gottes.* Eine Untersuchung zum Kirchen-bewusstsein des Urchristentums. (Photostat second impression of 1st edition, Oslo 1941. First published in Skrifter utgitt av Det Norske Videnskaps-Akademi i Oslo. II. Historiskfilosofisk Klasse. 1941. No. 2). 1963. Pp. XVI + 352. (Wissenschaftliche Buchgesellschaft, Darmstadt. Price: DM. 37).

This is a photo-mechanical reprint of Dahl's important book which was originally published in Oslo in 1941 and has been out of print for many years. It was reviewed in *Book List* 1948, pp. 41 f. (*Eleven Years*, pp. 151 f.). The first part of this book is of great interest to Old Testament scholars.

N.W.P.

DAUBE, D.: *The Sudden in the Scriptures.* 1964. Pp. 86. (E. J. Brill, Leiden. Price: Fl. 14).

Professor Daube here runs quickly through all the terms expressing 'suddenness' and the like in the Old and New Testaments, examining their occurrences respectively in the Hebrew and the Greek texts, the renderings of them in the principal ancient versions, and the light thrown on them by Rabbinic usage. He shows that in the Old Testament they commonly indicate the imminence of misfortune or disaster but rather what is startling or unexpected in the New Testament. Nothing much is said that cannot be gleaned from an intelligent use of a concordance, and the philological remarks at the end are dubious and inadequate; but readers will enjoy the references to the New English Bible (New Testament), which he charges (not without justice) with negligence in translating or even omitting these words or with sacrificing accuracy of interpretation to smoothness of diction in a certain number of places.

G.R.D.

DENTAN, R. C.: *The King and His Cross.* 1965. Pp. xii + 178. (The Seabury Press, New York. Price: $3.50).

This is a popular and devotional study of those eighteen Old Testament passages, excluding Holy Week Psalms, used in

Common Prayer and Communion for Holy Week. Their meaning is discussed and their relevance and value for Christian faith assessed. Ministers of religion will find the book helpful for sermon preparation and prayer.   G.H.D.

DUBARLE, A. M.: *The Biblical Doctrine of Orginal Sin*, trans. by E. M. Stewart. 1964. Pp. 245. (Geoffrey Chapman, London. Price: 25s. 0d.).

The original French text of this book was reviewed in the *Book List* 1960, p. 33. It contained six chapters, on the human condition in the Old Testament, original sin in Genesis, in the Wisdom Literature, in the Gospel, and in the Pauline epistles, and on original sin and the justice of God. To these has now been added a seventh, on original sin in the light of modern science and Biblical studies, in which the recent emphasis on the social character of sin is reflected. Some bibliographical additions have been made to the footnotes.   H.H.R

EISSFELDT, O., HEMPEL, J., OTTEN, H. & OTTO, E.: *Religionsgeschichte des Alten Orients*. (*Handbuch der Orientalistik*, ed. by B. Spuler. Erste Abteilung, VIII Band, I Abschnitt, Lieferung I). 1964. Pp. 154. (E. J. Brill, Leiden. Price: Fl. 28).

Emerging from a multiplicity of titles, this volume proves to be the first section of the eighth volume of the *Handbuch der Orientalistik*. It contains four essays by eminent German scholars dealing with the religion of the ancient Near East. The first and longest essay is by Eberhard Otto and deals with the religion of ancient Egypt. The second is by that veteran and universally respected Old Testament scholar whose vitality remains unimpaired by the lapse of years, Otto Eissfeldt, and deals in brief compass but perfect clarity with that form of Canaanite religion revealed to us in the Ugaritic literature. The third essay deals with the religion of the Hittites, now made known to us by the decipherment of the tablets from BoghazKöi and other sites in Asia Minor. The author, Heinrich Otten is one of the group of Hittite specialists whose names he lists at the beginning of his essay, whose labours have opened up this new and exciting field of Near Eastern archaeology. The final essay deals with the religion of the Old Testament, and is by a scholar who has contributed much of the greatest value to Old Testament studies, but has recently, alas, gone from us, Johannes Hempel. Each of the essays is a valuable résumé of the latest findings in the field of which they treat respectively.   S.H.H.

GRAVES, R. & PATAI, R.: *Hebrew Myths: the Book of Genesis*. 1964. Pp. 312, incl. 3 maps. (Cassell, London. Price: 36s. 0d.).

Those who have read *King Jesus* and *The Nazarene Gospel Restored* must have wished *ne sutor supra crepidam*, in spite of the poet's eminence in many other fields. Now, with the expert guidance of Professor Patai, he has invaded the Old Testament field, and most members of the S.O.T.S. will probably echo the same proverb. In this book the author has gone through the whole of Genesis, making no distinction between the early mythological material in the first eleven chapters, the saga material in cc. xii-xxxvi, and the historical romance of Joseph. He has grouped indiscriminately side by side the Yahwist's sober treatment of the ancient traditional Hebrew myths, and the fantastic embroideries of late rabbinical and cabbalistic speculations. The uninstructed reader might well think that all this stuff, amusing as it often is, may be regarded as Hebrew myth. The book cannot be recommended as a serious study of Hebrew mythology.   S.H.H.

HEMPEL, J.: *Das Ethos des Alten Testaments.* (Beihefte zur Zeitschrift für die alttestamentliche Wissenschaft, 67). 2nd enlarged edition. 1964. Pp. XII + 343. (Verlag Alfred Töpelmann, Berlin. Price: DM. 58).

This new edition of a book published originally in 1938 and reviewed in *Book List* 1939, p. 14, is one of the last parts of the literary legacy of a very great scholar who stuck to his task to the end. The body of the book, but for a few corrections, is unchanged, but the notes are vastly increased and contain innumerable references to relevant literature appearing since 1938. The author has also taken account of the evidence of the Dead Sea Scrolls. Hempel can have missed very little relevant to his theme and these notes should prove a stimulus to further research.   N.W.P.

JOHNSON, A. R.: *The Vitality of the Individual in the Thought of Ancient Israel.* 2nd edition. 1964. Pp. xii+154. (University of Wales Press, Cardiff. Price: 18s. 0d.).

Like the other new editions of Professor Johnson's valuable monographs, this book is sure to be warmly welcomed and widely used. The increase in size is almost wholly caused by the addition of very full indexes and the expansion of the footnotes. The first edition was reviewed in *Book List* 1950, p. 59 (*Eleven Years*, p. 276).   G.W.A.

JONES, E.: *The Greatest Old Testament Words.* 1964. Pp. 128. (S.C.M. Press, London. Price: 6s. 6d.).

This provides 25 short studies of Hebrew words, or word groups, intended to help those who have little or no knowledge of Hebrew to understand the Old Testament text. As such it should fulfil a useful service. There is an obvious homiletical interest, and much of the discussion ranges beyond the strict investigation of word meanings into questions of theological and social concepts of ancient Israel.   R.E.C.

KLOPFENSTEIN, M. A.: *Die Lüge nach dem Alten Testament. Ihr Begriff, ihre Bedeutung und ihre Beurteilung.* 1964. Pp. XVI + 518. (Gotthelf-Verlag, Zürich and Frankfurt a.M. Price: Swiss Fr. 35).

This doctoral exercise examines in every detail the occurrences of the terminology, particularly *šqr*, *kzb*, and *kḥš*, giving exegeses of the passages in which these are found. In addition *rmh* and *šw*' are considered, and more briefly in the second part of the book the passages are reviewed and discussed in which lies are indicated without the terminology being employed. The areas of life and thought in which the terms appear to belong are traced; it is shown that lying creates a breach between man and God and within the life of the community — it is 'gemein-schaftswidrig'. There is much very valuable comment on particular passages and many questions are usefully raised concerning correct interpretation. It is odd that there is no reference to Barr's *Semantics* in a work which in its range touches on so many of the questions raised there. It may be wondered whether every detail of the research needed to be published; there are 110 pp. of notes and a further 50 of indexes and bibliography.   P.R.A.

KNEVELS, W.: *Die Wirklichkeit Gottes:* Ein Weg zur Überwindung der Orthodoxie und des Existentialismus. 1964. Pp. 286. (Calwer Verlag, Stuttgart. Price: paper, DM. 9; cloth, DM. 13.50).

The aim of this book is to find a way between 'the Scylla of Orthodoxy and the Charybdis of Existentialism'. It contains a careful study of the concept of Myth, of the demythologising enterprise of Bultmann, of Existentialism (*existential* and *existentiel*), and of Revelation as Salvation-event. Demythologis-ation is regarded as an unsatisfactory and unclear term. Myth is defined as the result (*Niederschlag*) of an encounter with a transcendent Power, expressed in the form of symbol and story. Thus the Transcendent has actuality; it meets man in the here and now; it works in and upon the world; what is recited is not therefore fantasy but it must necessarily be symbolic; the myth has reference to the totality of the world. So the myth, rightly understood, is a constituent ingredient of religion. The Old Testament myths of Gen. i–xi (especially i–iii), Job xxxviii–xl and Ezekiel xxviii. 11–19 are briefly discussed. This is followed by a longer discussion of the New Testament Myth, with a special section on the Resurrection of Jesus. The book is an important contribution to the modern debate, while the concluding section, a theological reflection on the faith in the divine actuality, is a moving and deeply religious statement, a *confessio fidei.*

                                            A.S.H.

KNIGHT, G. A.: *A Christian Theology of the Old Testament.* Second (Revised) Edition. 1964. Pp. 366. (S.C.M. Press, London. Price: 18s. 0d.).

This new edition of Professor Knight's book (originally pub-lished 1959. *Book List* 1960, pp. 37 f.) contains numerous small changes with certain additions, subtractions, and re-arrangements. It is, however, essentially the same book as before, as the author himself states, since he has seen no reason to change his mind on the main issues. Many of the oddities which the reviewer previously noted remain, including a curious inability to explain clearly the Massoretic pointing of the Tetragrammaton and careless transliterations from the Hebrew. The highly question-able statement about the *nephesh* of God is still there (p. 89).

The book is full of ideas and brilliant insights, but there is something wayward, unregulated, and over-ingenious about it which detracts considerably from its value. And that is a pity.

N.W.P.

KRAUS, H.-J.: *Prophetie in der Krisis*. Studien zu Texten aus dem Buch Jeremia. (Biblische Studien 43). 1964. Pp. 124. (Neukirchener Verlag des Erziehungsvereins, Neukirchen-Vluyn. Price: DM. 6.80).

A suggestive study in the phenomena of prophecy and the distinction between true and false prophets. An introductory chapter on Jeremiah and his time is followed by three detailed textual studies of Jer. xxiii, 9–32; xxvii; xxviii. There is a chapter on true and false Prophets based on I Kings xxii (showing a recognition of primary and secondary inspiration), Num. xii, 6–8 (gradations in inspiration), Mic. iii and Jer. xxiii, 14–17 (the true prophet as one who uncovers guilt). The book finishes with a sermon on Jer. xxiii. 23f.

J.N.S.

LINDBLOM, J.: *Israels religion i gammaltestamentlig tid*. 3rd edition. (Verbum Series). 1964. Pp. 284. (Diakonistyrelsens Bokförlag, Stockholm. Price: paper, Sw.Kr. 16; cloth, Sw.Kr. 21).

Earlier editions of this admirable textbook appeared in 1936 and 1953 (see *Book List* 1953, p. 58; *Eleven Years*, p. 511). The text has now been further revised and the references to literature brought up to date. It remains a model of clear and balanced presentation.

G.W.A.

LORETZ, O.: *Die Wahrheit der Bibel*. 1964. Pp. 140. (Verlag Herder, Freiburg. Price: DM. 16.80).

In eight chapters discusses the relationship between the reliability of the Scriptures and the value of the Christian revelation of God made through them. The book is well documented from a very wide range of reading and should prove useful to readers worried by the conflict between uncritical and critical orthodoxy.

J.N.S.

MACDONALD, J.: *The Theology of the Samaritans*. (New Testament Library). 1964. Pp. 480. (S.C.M. Press, London. Price: 60s. 0d.).

By this work the author puts all Biblical students in his debt and himself in the first rank of Samaritan scholars. Dr. Macdonald has in recent years produced a series of studies, many of which had a specialist appeal; now he has written a very substantial volume which appears likely to be for many years to come the standard work of reference, to which will turn not only those whose primary interest is the Samaritan community through the ages but also those whose pursuits are in the fields of Old Testament religion or New Testament origins. After an introduction on history, literature, and creed, he deals with the main articles of Samaritan theology under the heads: God and the World; Moses, Lord of the World; Life of Man in the World; Eschatology; the World to Come. He summarizes his conclusions in the final chapter entitled Samaritanism Assessed. A comparison of this publication with earlier work on the subject makes clear how important an advance this book brings. This is due not only to Dr. Macdonald's wide knowledge and careful scholarship but also to the great increase in the amount of evidence made available to the author, whose generous citation of published and unpublished material is most welcome.   W.D.McH.

MCKANE, W.: *Prophets and Wise Men.* (Studies in Biblical Theology, 44). 1965. Pp. 136. (S.C.M. Press, London. Price: 13s. 6d.).

The vocabulary of Wisdom, and the functions of Sage, Counsellor, and Scribe are examined with an industry and perspicuity worthy of the subject. Earlier treatments are carefully and critically reviewed and the Biblical passages carefully discussed. 'Old Wisdom' is seen especially as statesmanship or political wisdom and it is against this that the prophetic polemic is directed. The passages in the prophetic books relating to Wisdom are examined; Deuteronomy is understood as subjugating Wisdom to Law. In the concluding chapter an attempt (too brief perhaps) is made to see what this means in the actual historical situation of Israel and the modern world. Some of the exegesis will provoke vigorous debate; the book is to be warmly welcomed for its treatment of an important and somewhat neglected aspect of Old Testament study.   A.S.H.

MORRIS, L.: *The Biblical Doctrine of Judgment.* 1960. Pp. vi + 72. (The Tyndale Press, London. Price: 5s. 0d.).

Dr. Morris provides a short survey of the use in the Old Testament of words connected with judgement, especially *mishpat.* There is a helpful discussion of many recent interpretations of such words, and two chapters on the idea of judgement in the New Testament.   R.E.C.

NAHMANI, H. S.: *Human Rights in the Old Testament.* 1964. Pp. 146. (Joshua Chachik Publishing House, Tel Aviv, Israel).

The book is divided into two parts, the first of which deals with various aspects of social legislation in the Pentateuch, such as the weekly day of rest, the year of release, and the Jubilee Year. In the second part some sections of 'the written constitution of the theocracy during the time of Moses' are compared with the Constitution of the United States and that of Great Britain. The extensive use of modern legal terminology does not in this case contribute to the historical understanding of a literature which extends from Genesis to the First Book of Kings. In spite of the title of the book, one looks in vain for an evaluation of the writings of the literary prophets.

Although the author shows familiarity with recent work on Babylonian and Assyrian Laws, he nowhere succeeds in presenting a convincing comparative analysis of his source material. His approach is almost entirely uncritical.

Bibliographical references to the modern study of the Old Testament are restricted to a few standard works, some of which go back to the 19th century.   S.S.

PORÚBČAN, Š.: *Sin in the Old Testament*. A Soteriological Study. (Aloisiana Scritti pubblicati sotto la direzione della Pontificia Facoltà Teologica Napoletana "San Luigi", 3). 1963. Pp. XVI+632. (Herder, Rome. Price: L. 6,000).

In this long and careful study, Part I discusses the terminology, first the Hebrew of the Old Testament, then the Aramaic of the Targums and the Greek of the LXX. Then follows, in Part II, an analysis of the nature of sin, its relation to the divine holiness, the forgiveness of sin, sin and sacrifice, and the social consequences of sin. Part III examines the history of sin in the Old Testament, with sections on the New Covenant, the nations outside Israel and Original Sin. An Appendix is added on Sin in Postbiblical Judaism. The Old Testament passages are examined in detail, but sometimes emendations are accepted without acknowledgement. It is not always clear why some words are quoted without comment, e.g. (p. 42), *tummin*; and one could have wished for more consistency of translation, e.g. (pp. 29 f.), obstinacy, rebellion, and wrongdoing are not really synonyms. One would question whether 'the official meaning of the sacrifice' as a 'gift presented . . . in order to please Him and to attain, or regain' God's favour is adequate. To describe the Servant of Yahweh as a descendant of David is going beyond the evidence. This will prove an invaluable source-book for all engaged in the study of Old Testament Theology, and of Hamartiology in particular.

A.S.H.

RESCH, A.: *Der Traum im Heilsplan Gottes:* Deutung und Bedeutung des Traums im Alten Testament. 1964. Pp. XVI+152. (Verlag Herder, Freiburg).

The first section of the book (pp. 1–36) is a survey of present day psychological theories about dreams admitting the possibility of telepathic communication in certain circumstances and also of anticipatory and even pre-cognitive functions, although it is recognised that the latter is rarely demonstrable. The rest of the book examines the Biblical records of dreams and shows that some of them can be understood entirely in relation to the circumstances in which they occurred, i.e., they can be explained psychologically, but that others can only be satisfactorily explained as being caused directly by God for prophetic purposes and therefore as part of his *Heilsplan* for Israel. It is a suggestive book which deserves thorough recognition of the value of its attempt to assess the dreams in the light of modern psychological methods and theories, but it is a provocative one in that it regards all the stories of dreams as factual and is not prepared to allow any place for myth, folk-lore, fairy-tale, or legend. Nebuchadnezzar's dream in Dan. ii is regarded as actual and self-evident, the explanation in vv. 36–45 being treated as a later Maccabaean addition.

L.H.B.

ROMEO, A.: *Il Presente e il Futuro nella Rivelazione Biblica.* 1964. Pp. XXXVI+288. (Desclée, Tournai.)

In this substantial volume Romeo has assembled ten studies of dominantly Biblical interest that have appeared in various periodicals from 1929 onwards. It is claimed that they have all been revised and brought up to date. Among them may be mentioned articles on the Antithesis of the two Cities in St. Augustine's spirituality; a lengthy exegetical comment, written throughout in Latin, on 1 Cor. xv. 51; a Marian study on the Woman clothed with the sun in Rev. xii; 'Religious Collectivism and Individualism'; and Judaism in the post-exilic and later periods, a treatment which includes an account of its historical evolution and of its articles of faith. The final essay, written in French, was delivered in 1957 as a lecture to the Montreal theological faculty and is an analysis of the Papal encyclical against Modernism, *Pascendi Gregis* (8 September, 1907) to commemorate the fiftieth anniversary of its promulgation.

J.M.T.B.

ROWLEY, H. H.: *The Biblical Doctrine of Election.* 2nd impression. 1964. Pp. 184. (Lutterworth Press, London. Price: 25s. 0d.).

This book first appeared in 1950 and was reviewed in *Book List* 1951, p. 65 (*Eleven Years*, p. 360). No change has been made in this reprint.

G.W.A.

RUSSELL, D. S.: *The Method and Message of Jewish Apocalyptic.* (Old Testament Library). 1964. Pp. 464. (S.C.M. Press, London. Price: 60s. 0d.).

Here is a first-class treatment of the source and message of the apocalyptic literature of the period running roughly from 200 B.C. to A.D. 100. It consists of three parts: (1) the nature and identity of Jewish apocalyptic; (2) the method of Jewish apocalyptic; and (3) the message of Jewish apocalyptic. It brings within its scope the relevant sections of the Dead Sea Scrolls, and emphasizes the common elements and ideas running through all the apocalyptic literature, despite its great diversity. The author gives an excellent account of the development of thought among the apocalyptists, tracing it in part to Iranian influence, and emphasizes the enduring values of their message. On the psychology of apocalyptic and the problem of pseudo-nymity he expresses the most original ideas the volume contains, arguing that just as 'corporate personality' offers an explanation of the identification of an individual with the community he represents, so it offers an explanation of the self-identification of an author with an ancient worthy whose name he took and into whose school of tradition he had entered. This is by far the most notable work in English on the apocalyptic literature for a very long time.

H.H.R.

SCHEFFCZYK, L.: *Der moderne Mensch vor dem biblischen Menschenbild.* (Aktuelle Schriften zur Religionspädagogik, 4). 1964. Pp. 138. (Verlag Herder, Freiburg).

The purpose of this book is to examine the conception of man as portrayed in modern philosophy, Hegelian, Marxist, and Existentialist and in the modern novel, especially American and German, in the light of the Biblical conception, with particular reference to the Incarnation. The conception of man in the Old Testament follows conventional lines, though the reviewer would question the statement, p. 30, 'Die Entdeckung des individuellen Menschen ist ein Vorgang, der sich erst beim Propheten Jeremias abzeichnet.' And perhaps the word *Kollecktivität* is less than adequate for the Biblical sense of corporate solidarity. The book will be welcomed as a sensitive appreciation of modern philosophy and literature in their attempt to understand human nature, and the contribution that can be made by the Biblical theologian to meet the deep need of modern man implied in them. A.S.H.

SCHMID, R.: *Das Bundesopfer in Israel.* Wesen, Ursprung und Bedeutung der alttestamentlichen Schelamim. (Studien zum Alten und Neuen Testament, Band IX). 1964. Pp. 140. (Kösel-Verlag, München. Price: DM.18).

This is a careful study of the origin and meaning of the Hebrew-Jewish sacrifice known as *zebach* or *zebach-shelamim*. It is, as the title declares, a covenant-sacrifice, a meal of which the parties to the covenant partook together. It was a covenant-meal in ancient time and developed into the Covenant-meal of Israel. A thoroughly competent piece of work, involving detailed study of this particular offering both in ancient and later Israel and among neighbouring nations. N.H.S.

SCHNACKENBURG, R. & THIEME, K.: *La Bible et le Mystère de L'Église.* 1964. Pp. 202. (Desclée, Tournai. Price: B.Frs. 120).

This is a translation of a book published in German in 1962 as part of a work entitled *Mysterium Kirche in der Sicht der theologischen Disziplinen.* Schnackenburg's contribution is concerned with the nature and mystery of the Church in the New Testament, and has chapters on the development of ecclesiology in the primitive Church, on the Church's essential characteristics, and on the mystery of the Church as the people of God and the body of Christ. Thieme considers the mystery of the Church and the Christian vision of the people of the old covenant under headings such as the patriarchal covenants, the covenant of Sinai, the *Cathedra Moysis* and the renewed 'Israel of God', and the people of the old covenant at the present day. The bibliography to the first part is characteristically good and thorough. The Catholic and Protestant authors are listed separately. J.M.T.B.

SCHOFIELD, J. N.: *Introducing Old Testament Theology.* 1964. Pp. 126. (S.C.M. Press, London. Price: 9s. 6d.).

In an introductory section this book acknowledges that man can learn about the being of God only as in experience he becomes aware of God's activity in relation to himself or his environment. From an awareness of the wonder of created things, he may be led to believe in a divine creator; from an experience of spiritual renewal in himself or observation of the effects of it in others, he may be led to believe in a Saviour-God; and such beliefs in correlation may constitute a theology. So Mr. Schofield has initial chapters on *The God Who Acts* and *The God Who Speaks* (these two functions inevitably overlap). This leads to a consideration of the way in which the relation between God and man is conceived.

The final chapter considers further God's relation with man with regard to His dwelling and the mystery of His being on the one hand, and man's attitude to life and his experience of it on the other. This little book has had to be limited to basic essentials, and both in the choice and in the presentation of these the author shows a wise discretion and a skill in communication. J.M.

SNAITH, N. H.: *The Distinctive Ideas of the Old Testament*. Paperback reprint. 1964. Pp. 194. (Schocken Books, New York. Price: $1.75).

Dr. Snaith's stimulating Fernley-Hartley Lecture was originally published in 1944 and was reviewed in *Book List* 1946, p. 52 (*Eleven Years*, p. 52). Since then it has been frequently reprinted. Its appearance in this handy form will extend its usefulness still further. G.W.A.

SNAITH, N. H.: *The Distinctive Ideas of the Old Testament* (in Japanese), 1963. Pp. ix + 286. (The Board of Publication, United Church of Christ in Japan, Tokyo. Price: Y. 950).

This is a Japanese edition of Dr. Snaith's book with a slightly altered title: *The Distinctive Characteristics of the Old Testament Religion*. The translation was done by Mr. K. Hayashi, and it was further corrected by Mr. M. Shinya and Professor J. Asano, and was published with the aid of the Theological Education Fund. The author has contributed a special preface to the Japanese edition. Except for Prof. Asano's postscript and Mr. Shinya's introduction on the life and work of Dr. Snaith, it is a faithful replica of the original book, including all the footnotes and indexes. Since the form 'Yahweh' is now universally used by Japanese scholars, the word 'Jehovah' in the original work (I am using the seventh edition) is changed accordingly.' The translation is so faithful to the original that it is a little stiff in style, and ambiguous phrases occur now and then. For example, on page 132 of the original is found the following sentence, 'it is used once only of a woman loving a man', which has become, 'it is used of a woman loving a man once only'. It is also difficult to understand why the translators have chosen the phrase, 'love of covenant' for the characteristic expression of Professor Snaith, 'covenant-love'. Nevertheless, these shortcomings are few in number, and do not detract from the merit of this attempt to introduce Dr. Snaith's excellent book to a wider circle of Japanese readers. T.A.

DE VAUX, R.: *Les Sacrifices de l'Ancien Testament*. (Cahiers de la Revue Biblique 1). 1964. Pp. 110. (J. Gabalda, Paris. Price: Fr. 13). *Studies in Old Testament Sacrifice*. 1964. Pp. xii+120. (University of Wales Press, Cardiff. Price: 15s. 0d.).

The almost simultaneous publication of the French and English texts of Fr. de Vaux's Elizabeth James Lectures, delivered at

University College, Cardiff in 1961 is a notable event, providing an elaboration of what the author had already written on the subject of sacrifices in his magisterial work on Israelite institutions. The four chapters of which the book consists are devoted to (1) the Passover sacrifice, (2) holocausts and communion sacrifices, (3) human sacrifices in Israel, (4) expiatory sacrifices. The author reaffirms his views on the nomadic origin of Passover, and records briefly his dissent from the conclusions of Professor J. B. Segal, whose book appeared too late to be fully discussed. Of particular interest and importance is the discussion of human sacrifices (which are held never to have been lawful in Israel) and the meaning of sacrifices 'to Moloch': de Vaux concludes that when such sacrifices were borrowed in Israel the term *molk* was not understood, but was taken to refer to a king-god. Expiatory sacrifices are held not to have been a late institution, but to have increased in importance with the passage of time, and to have had a special place in Israelite worship because of the moralism of Yahwist religion. The book combines clarity of presentation with rich citation of comparative material and an important element of theological interpretation. It is good to have so much in so limited a compass on so complex a subject. In the French volume we welcome the first item in what should prove to be an outstanding new series: *Cahiers de la Revue Biblique.*

G.W.A.

WALLACE, R. S.: *The Ten Commandments. A Study of Ethical Freedom.* 1965. Pp. xiv + 182. (Oliver & Boyd, Edinburgh. Price: 21s. 0d.).

This book contains a homiletic exposition of the Ten Commandments for the Christian today. While it is legitimate, from a Christian point of view, to interpret the Decalogue in the light of the total revelation of God, including the New Testament as well as the Old, Dr. Wallace sometimes pays too little attention to the problems of the original meaning of the commandments. However, this does not alter the fact that the book contains much that is true and helpful.

J.A.E.

WESTERMANN, C. (ed. by): *Essays on Old Testament Interpretation.* English translation edited by J. L. Mays. 1963. Pp. 364. (S.C.M. Press, London. Price: 45s. 0d.).

The hope expressed in the review of the original German edition of this book in the *Book List* 1961, p. 53, has been fulfilled and this English translation should do much to acquaint a wider circle of readers with the debate that is in progress about the correct interpretation of the Old Testament and, in particular, about the true relation of the Old Testament to the New. The English edition has this advantage over the German that the whole of von Rad's important and provocative article on the typological interpretation of the Old Testament which originally appeared in *Evangelische Theologie* has now been reproduced. This book forms an indispensable companion volume to *The Old Testament and Christian Faith*, ed. by B. W. Anderson, reviewed in this *Book List* (p. 42).

N.W.P.

WOLFF, H. W.: *Amos' geistige Heimat.* (Wissenschaftliche Monographien zum Alten und Neuen Testament, Band 18). 1964. Pp. 70. (Neu-kirchener Verlag des Erziehungsvereins, Neukirchen-Vluyn. Price: DM. 5.80; cloth, DM. 8.50).

An excellent antidote to the still fashionable tendency to find a liturgical origin for all the Old Testament, and should be made available to English readers. After an introduction that states the problem there are three sections considering Amos' peculiar speech forms, his characteristic themes, and some related back-ground problems. The carefully reasoned conclusion is that the prophet sprang, not from a cultic milieu, but from the oral traditions of old Israelite tribal wisdom. There are five indexes.

J.N.S.

THE LIFE AND THOUGHT OF THE NEIGHBOURING PEOPLES

GRAY, J.: *The Canaanites.* (Ancient Peoples and Places, Vol. 38). 1964. Pp. 244 incl. 61 photographs, 54 line drawings & 3 maps. (Thames and Hudson, London. Price: 30s. 0d.).

Lavishly illustrated and confined to the 2nd millennium B.C., Gray's new book is in some ways a companion to his *Legacy of Canaan* (*Book List* 1958, p. 42). After an introduction which summarizes the contributions made by the Amarna tablets, the Mari archives, and the Ras Shamra texts, the author groups his material under the following heads: Habitat and History; Daily Life; Canaanite Society; Canaanite Religion; Letters and Literature; Canaanite Art. The selected bibliography gives a good picture both of the range of the subject and the quality of recent studies. Professor Gray is an experienced guide; and those who emerge from studying his book will not be perplexed.

E.U.

HEIDEL, A.: *The Gilgamesh Epic and Old Testament Parallels.* 1963. Pp. x + 270. (University of Chicago Press, London. Price: $1.95; 14s. 0d.).

This is a paperback edition of a book that was published by the late Professor Alexander Heidel in 1946. Since then several translations of the Epic have appeared, notably Speiser's in ANET. Comparison with the latter shows that some changes in the interpretation of the text have appeared since Heidel's translation was published. Nevertheless his comments and discussion of Old Testament parallels are still of value to the student. The author's conservative position is well known. He does not admit that there are any discrepancies in the Biblical account of the Flood, due to the use of different sources by the compiler of Genesis. Nor does he admit any direct borrowing from Babylonian sources by the Hebrew writer. The phototype used in this edition is small and trying to the eyes. There is no index.

S.H.H.

HINZ, W.: *Das Reich Elam*. (Urban-Bücher 82). 1964. Pp. 160 + 32 plates. (Kohlhammer Verlag, Stuttgart. Price: DM. 4.80).

This account of Elam, its country and people and rulers, is pieced together from archaeological discoveries, the rare and often still imperfectly understood Elamite inscriptions, and incidental notices in Sumerian, Babylonian, and Assyrian records; and it takes the story from the earliest traces of man in Elam, through the early local dynasties of Awan and Simash (*c.* 2600–1830 B.C.), and those of the old kingdom (*c.* 1850–1200 [?] B.C.) and of the new kingdom (*c.* 760–644 B.C.), in spite of the long gaps in the history, down to 538 B.C., when the country came under Achaemenid rule. Chapters are devoted also to the language and writing of the Elamites, their religion and law, and their arts, as well as to their place generally in history. Thus this new work forms an admirable companion to G. G. Cameron's *History of Elam* (1936), which deals mainly with political history. The book, which contains a concise bibliography, is a masterpiece of compression and skilful presentation by an author who has not only himself made many notable contributions to Elamite studies but is also fully acquainted with the work of other scholars in the same field; it is thus completely trustworthy and fully abreast of modern research.

G.R.D.

ROUX, G.: *Ancient Iraq*. 1964. Pp. 431 + frontispiece + many ills. + 5 maps. (George Allen & Unwin Ltd., London. Price: 50s. 0d.).

The author of this book has spent over twenty years in Iraq and neighbouring countries. Between 1956 and 1960 he wrote a series of articles for *Iraq Petroleum*, and this book is a revised version, substantially enlarged, and completely rewritten, of these articles. It aims at assembling all the information about ancient Iraq which laymen and students will wish to have. It tells the long story of the political, economic, and cultural history of Mesopotamia from the first traces of human presence in north-western Iraq in palaeolithic times down to the collapse of the Sumero-Akkadian civilization at the dawn of the Christian era. A full bibliography with explanatory notes is supplied, as well as chronological tables, and an index; and texts are quoted liberally throughout. The book is clearly written, up-to-date in its information, and generally accurate. The author seems to think, however, that Ethiopic is still spoken today (p. 124), and *Aram Naharaim* is said to mean 'Aram of the Rivers' (p. 227). We may wonder too why Marduk, and not Shamash, is thought to be the god represented on the Hammurabi stele (Plate 12A), and why Ezekiah appears several times for Hezekiah (p. 265).

D.W.T.

THOMPSON, J. A.: *The Ancient Near Eastern Treaties and the Old Testament*. (The Tyndale Lecture in Biblical Archaeology, 1963). 1964. Pp. 40. (The Tyndale Press, London. Price: 2s. 0d.).

This short study gives an admirable survey of the type of vassal treaty, known from Hittite and other ancient Near Eastern sources, which has been used to illustrate certain features of the covenant form in ancient Israel. It contains an extensive documentation of the sources where such a treaty form appears, and shows the similarity with certain Old Testament passages recounting the covenant between Yahweh and Israel. There is a tendency to overstress the influence of such a form on the Old Testament, and to overlook differences. Nevertheless this is an excellent and convenient guide to an important subject. R.E.C.

THE DEAD SEA SCROLLS

BARDTKE, H.: *Die Handschriftenfunde in der Wüste Juda.* 1962. Pp. 115 + 16 plates + 3 maps. (Evangelische Haupt-Bibelgesellschaft zu Berlin. Price: DM. 6.80).

Professor Bardtke is well-known for his clear, comprehensive, and sound assessments of the Scrolls, especially as published in *Theologische Literaturzeitung* over the years, and this is the third volume in his series *Handschriftfunde am Toten Meer.* It covers the finds in Murabba'at, Khirbet Mird, and other places with extra-Qumran material, and also sets in the same perspective the Israeli discoveries of 1960 and again of 1961 on their side of the Dead Sea. Two chapters are devoted to the significance of the Biblical texts, especially the text of the Twelve Minor Prophets from Cave V of Murabba'at which diverges from MT and to that of the non-Biblical texts for the history of Bar Cochba. The last section contains translations of the texts, beginning with letters from Murabba'at, legal documents, and translations of ancient documents relating to the Second Jewish Revolt (Bar Cochba) — a most useful collection. B.J.R.

BECKER, J.: *Das Heil Gottes: Heils- und Sündenbegriffe in den Qumrantexten und im Neuen Testament.* (Studien zur Umwelt des Neuen Testaments, Band 3). 1964. Pp. 302. (Vandenhoeck & Ruprecht, Göttingen. Price: DM. 32).

After a very brief treatment of the Old Testament and Jewish background, the main part of this book, 152 of its 266 pages of text, is devoted to the Qumran documents and is of special interest to Old Testament scholars. The author's method is to discuss the meaning and usage of the various terms used to describe man's salvation and the part played by God in it and to build up from the discussion a picture of the conceptions and beliefs reflected in different parts of the literature. He shows how they develop out of the Old Testament background and yet how far at some points they differ from it. The critical work is thoroughly done and makes a valuable contribution to the literature about the Qumran sect. In the final section of the book three main conceptions are taken, representative of each of the main strata of the New Testament, the kingdom of God in the Gospels, the idea of truth in the Johannine literature, and the righteousness of God in the Pauline writings. It is taken more or less for granted that the Qumran writings represent an Essene background, although it is recognized that the documents do not reflect a single, simple, and uniform body of religious thought and belief. What emerges from this study is chiefly the fact that the Qumran Community must have been one of the workshops in which some of the dominant New Testament beliefs were forged and partially moulded. The influence of the Qumran practice and belief cannot be left out of account in any study of New Testament doctrine for there are indications that there are strong echoes of both in the New Testament.

L.H.B.

BROWNLEE, W. H.: *The Meaning of the Qumrân Scrolls for the Bible with special attention to the Book of Isaiah*. The James W. Richard Lectures in Christian Religion given at the University of Virginia. 1964. Pp. xxii + 310. (Oxford University Press, New York. Price: 52s. 6d.).

The work here reviewed is based on a number of lectures which the author, who was responsible for an excellent translation of *Discipline* in 1951 (see *Book List* 1952, p. 64), gave at various places between 1957 and 1960. It falls into two parts, the one on the meaning of the Scrolls for the Bible and the second on the significance of the scroll of *Isaiah A* for the Hebrew text of the Old Testament; and six appendices are added at the end of the book. The arrangement of the matter, due to the origin of the book, presents difficulties; for no reasoned argument can be detected running through it, and much of the first part is nothing but unproved statements. For example, the wicked Priests (*sic*), mentioned in the plural number although no 'wicked priests' are named anywhere in the Scrolls, are said to be Hyrcanus I and his two sons (pp. 103–4); the Teacher of Righteousness is left unidentified beyond the statement that he fled to Damascus 'like a bird from its nest' (p. 133), although neither the Teacher nor Damascus *eo nomine* is mentioned in the *Thanksgiving Hymns* and his authorship of them is merely assumed and nowhere proved; and other evidence of prime importance, e.g., the identity of the 'house of Absalom' and of the 'house of Judah', is completely disregarded. Similarly, the Kittides are assumed to be the Romans; but the identification is nowhere proved and 'Romans', whether Republican or Imperial, is left undefined, although plenty of evidence is available to settle the point. The other part of the book is devoted to examining the light thrown by the Scrolls on the Massoretic text; here a number of good points are made, but the author's interpretation of the text will raise doubts here and there in the reader's mind. Unfortunately, although the book ostensibly deals with the importance of the Scrolls for the understanding of the Bible, while eleven chapters are devoted to the Old Testament, only two are given to the New Testament; and it can be plausibly argued that their significance for the former is considerably smaller than it is for the latter. Their use for the Old Testament is confined almost exlusively to divergent readings, their significance for the New Testament is a matter of substance. Briefly, the book is ill-balanced (if the title-page is taken at its face-value) and shows few signs of deep thought even though a certain number of valuable observations are made.

G.R.D.

THE DEAD SEA SCROLLS 611

GÄRTNER, B.: *The Temple and the Community in Qumran and the New Testament*. A Comparative Study in the Temple Symbolism of the Qumran Texts and the New Testament. (Society for New Testament Studies, Monograph Series). 1965. Pp. xii + 164. (Cambridge University Press. Price: 25s. 0d.).

The sub-title to this work serves to indicate its chief feature, viz., a symbolic rather than a literary-historical treatment. The nature of Temple and Priesthood was, above all, holy, and this also characterises the Qumran community. This makes it 'possible to trace a connexion (*sic*) between Qumran and the temple', and 'the community constituted a new temple'. A number of Qumran texts are then discussed from this stand-point. Temple symbolism in the New Testament shows parallel features with that of Qumran, and again a number of illustrative texts are examined, taken from Epistles and Gospels. A final chapter discusses the more general topic of Temple symbolism and Christology. The book is workmanlike and interesting, though possibly more suggestive than convincing.

The Society for Old Testament Study congratulates its Sister Society on launching a monograph series in addition to its now well-established *Journal*.

B.J.R.

LOHSE, E.: *Die Texte aus Qumran. Hebräisch und Deutsch mit maso-retischer Punktation, Übersetzung, Einführung und Anmerkungen*. 1964. Pp. XXIV + 294. (Kösel-Verlag, Munich. Price: DM. 36).

A pattern seems to be emerging in the presentation of the Scrolls, consisting of a general introduction, a translation, and annota-tion; and the present book fits into it. The differences found here are that the introduction is more doctrinal than historical, and the notes make quite a substantial use of cross-references — a good thing. An unusual feature, though not an isolated instance of it, is that the Hebrew transliteration is supplied with Tiberian vocalization. It has undoubtedly pushed up the price of what is at best a student text-book, and one might well question even the wisdom of pointing the text. It is an ana-chronism, and, still more serious, we do not know nearly enough about the niceties of Qumran Hebrew grammar to superimpose a vocalization of this kind on the text.

B.J.R.

LURIE, B.: *Megillath ha-Neḥosheth* (in Hebrew). 1963. Pp. VIII + 126. (Kiryath Sepher, Jerusalem).

In this scholarly book, containing an introduction followed by the Copper Scroll text fully annotated, the view is expressed that the Scroll forms a genuine list of the sacred treasures of the Holy Temple of the Bar-Kokhba era — treasures stored away in the plains of Jericho by the Jerusalem Priesthood on seeing the Roman legionaries approaching the city. The treasures, which contained vast quantities of gold and silver, came mainly from the millions (!) of Jews living in the Roman Empire and especially, in countries beyond it, Jews who had been greatly inspired by Hadrian's permission to build the Temple anew.

The author quotes twenty-eight sources, mostly Talmudical, to show that a Holy Temple of some sort was in existence in the Bar-Kokhba era — an era in which are included a few years which preceded the commencement of the rebellion. M.W.

MANSOOR, M.: *The Dead Sea Scrolls.* A College Textbook and a Study Guide. Pp. X + 210. (E. J. Brill, Leiden. Price: Fl. 14).

This students' handbook covers not only the manuscript discoveries at Qumran and the excavations at Khirbet Qumran but the discoveries at Khirbet Mird and Wadi Murabba'at and more recent discoveries associated with the Barkokhba revolt. The data are tabulated and arranged in orderly sequence, and the author endeavours to be as objective as possible, although he properly exercises his own judgement in assessing (for example) the relative probability of the various identifications suggested for the Qumran community. The student is enabled to follow him here by the summarized information about the various Jewish sects of the relevant period which he gives before proceeding to the question of identification. At the end of each section topics for study and discussion are listed, and the student is encouraged to form his own judgement on the questions that arise (on the identity of the community, for example, or on its relation to primitive Christianity) on the basis of the evidence bearing on each one. The first general inference following a discussion of the Qumran writings and Christianity is that 'the tradition behind the Gospels and the Epistles seems to be related to Qumran thought, but it is a thought taken up and radically reinterpreted in the light of Jesus'. The book concludes with a general review, topics for further study, a glossary of technical terms and proper names, a list of the main scrolls, a short bibliography, a chronological table, and an index of subjects. F.F.B.

ROWLEY, H. H.: *The Dead Sea Scrolls and the New Testament,* 2nd edition. 1964. Pp. 32. (S.P.C.K., London. Price: 3s. 6d.).

The first edition of this excellent booklet appeared in 1957 and was reviewed in *Book List* 1958, p. 49. A few additional footnotes have been added in this reprint. G.W.A.

SIEDL, S. H.: *Qumran: Eine Mönchsgemeinde im Alten Bund.* (Bibliotheca Carmelitica, Series II; Studia, Vol. 2). 1963. Pp. v + 374. (Teresianum, Rome. Price: L. 4,500; $7.00).

This work, which bears the sub-title *Studie über Serek ha-Yaḥad,* falls into three divisions. Division I deals with the designations of the Qumran community and of its individual members; Division II deals with the religious character and aims of the community; Division III deals with its organization, discipline, and rites. The author rightly emphasizes that God was central to the thought and life of the community; their whole aim was to seek after God, to know God, and to obey God. The eschatological orientation of all this is, however, inadequately stressed. Their study of the Scriptures, it is true, 'was conceived as a preparation of the way by which God comes to us' — but this coming was his coming in judgment on the world, to put an end to the age then present and to inaugurate the new age. On the discipline of the community he considers it more probable that its members were celibate, not only on practical grounds but also because only so could they avoid those temporary occasions of ceremonial impurity mentioned in Lev. xv. 18. There is a useful discussion of the procedure laid down for addressing the assembly of the many in 1QS vi. 8–13. The author evinces the utmost sympathy with the ideals of Qumran and dedicates his work 'to the men of Qumran and to all who before them and after them live for the same end: to seek God with their whole heart, soul, mind and strength'.   F.F.B.

STAUFFER, E.: *Jesus and the Wilderness Community at Qumran*, trans. by Hans Spalteholz. (Facet Books, Biblical Series, 10). 1964. Pp. xiv + 38. (Fortress Press, Philadelphia. Price: 75 cents).

This booklet translated from *Jesus und die Wüstengemeinde am Toten Meer*, which appeared in the Calwer Hefte series in 1957, is provided with a useful introduction by John Reumann, who also amplifies several of Stauffer's footnotes for the benefit of English-speaking readers. Stauffer, who dates the formative period of the Qumran community about the middle of the second century B.C. and thinks that the Essenes were most likely one of its later offshoots, considers the resemblances and contrasts between the teaching of the community and that of Jesus. Qumran was the spiritual home of John the Baptist, but not of Jesus; eight features are listed in which the community was at the opposite pole from Jesus: its 'clericalism', its ritualism, its hatred of the unrighteous, its militarism, its concern about the calendar, its pre-dilection for secret teachings, its doctrine of an Aaronic Messiah, and its repudiation of the Temple services — but more important than all these is its 'Torah piety'. 'Jesus opposed the spirit of the Wilderness sectarians just as relentlessly as he did the spirit of the Pharisees', and had he fallen into their hands, 'according to their logic and exegesis of the Torah they would have condemned to death the rebel against the Sabbath in Qumran'.

The reference to John Allegro as 'formerly of the University of Manchester' is probably (and happily) an instance of prematurely realized eschatology.   F.F.B.

APOCRYPHA AND POST-BIBLICAL JUDAISM

ANDREWS, H. T.: *An Introduction to the Apocryphal Books of the Old and New Testament*. Revised and Edited by Charles F. Pfeiffer. 1964. Pp. 142. (Baker Book House, Grand Rapids, Michigan. Price: $2.95).

This is a rapid survey of the contents and probable date of rather more than fifty different literary works: the Old Testament Apocrypha, other late Jewish literature designated in the book as 'the wider Apocrypha', including apocalyptic literature, New Testament apocryphal books, and other books, such as the Shepherd of Hermas, which had a firm place in early

Christian literature. It has been brought up-to-date by the addition of the non-Biblical material from Qumran and the texts discovered at Chenoboskion.

With all this crowded into 125 pages it is little wonder that time and again the reader finds himself asking for more information and wanting to be told how such and such a conclusion was reached. Despite its severe limitations it is useful as a descriptive catalogue of extra-Biblical material.

L.H.B.

DANIÉLOU, J.: *The Theology of Jewish Christianity*, trans. and ed. by John A. Baker. (The Development of Christian Doctrine before the Council of Nicaea, Vol. I). 1964. Pp. xvi+446. (Darton, Longman & Todd, London. Price: 45s. 0d.).

This is the first of a new series on *Dogmengeschichte*, supplying a Roman Catholic counterpart to Harnack or Loofs. This first volume, it is important to note, is not, like H. J. Schoeps's studies in the theology of Jewish Christianity, an account of Jewish Christian heresies (though the evidence of the latter is fully discussed) but a 'reconstruction' of the earliest Jewish Christian phase in the history of doctrine. The 'breakthrough', which, in the author's opinion, has made this possible, has come through the Qumran and Nag Hammadi discoveries (p. 3). Three chapters on the Literary Heritage of Jewish Christianity (Old Testament Pseudepigrapha, New Testament Apocrypha, Barnabas, Hermas, Ignatius and Clement), Heterodox Jewish Christianity and Jewish Christian Exegesis, are followed by chapters on The Trinity and Angelology, The Son of God, Theology of the Incarnation, of Redemption, the Church, Baptism and Eucharist, etc. If Daniélou's reconstruction and use of sources is legitimate, we have travelled a long way from Harnack, or, for that matter, from H. J. Schoeps. Perhaps, as with Gnosticism, an agreed definition of 'Jewish Christianity' (Jewish-Palestinian, Jewish-Hellenistic, etc.) is needed to clarify the issues.

M.Bl.

FÖRSTER, W.: *Palestinian Judaism in New Testament Times*, trans. by Gordon E. Harris. 1964. Pp. xiv+248. (Oliver & Boyd, Edinburgh. Price: 30s. 0d.).

In view of the immense additions to our knowledge of intertestamental Judaism in the last eighteen years alone, there is an urgent need for a new Schürer. This is not such a book — Schürer's *Geschichte des Jüdischen Volkes* is, in fact, at present being brought up-to-date in a new English translation — but a highly competent and well-documented German text-book which has now gone into its third German edition. The book is in three parts, I. The Historical Situation (from the Exile to the Fall of Jerusalem), II. Palestine in Jesus' Day, and III. The Religious Situation, dealing with Pharisees, Sadducees, Essenes, etc. The successive editions have meant that attention has been paid, within the limits of a text-book, to the new knowledge, in particular from Qumran. The book seeks to take account of the relevant and important rabbinical and pseudepigraphical material and to estimate, not only the extent of indebtedness of Jesus and the primitive Church to the Synagogue, but also the contribution made by the New Testament to the Judaism of the period (see especially page 223ff.). The book contains a very useful, if necessarily short and select bibliography. M.Bl.

DE KUIPER, A.: *Israel tussen Zending en Oecumene.* 1964. Pp. X + 226. (H. Veenman & Zonen, Wageningen. Price: Fl. 13.50).

This is a welcome and timely study of the problem which must be faced by the Christian Church when it seriously seeks to secure the inclusion of the Jewish people in the Church which is the new Israel. This cannot be achieved by a simple process of missonary work, for that would be to overlook the historical standing of the Jews as a chosen people before the advent of Christianity and it would have no power to heal the schism caused by that advent. It must be achieved by fuller under-standing on both sides gained by thorough-going and heart-searching conference and discussion at all levels, each being prepared to learn from the other. The book is an excellent survey of the attitude of Christians towards the Jews, both sympathetic (missionary) and hostile, throughout the centuries. As the title suggests, it sees the Jewish people not only as an object of missionary concern and zeal, but also as a theological and practical problem for the oecumenical church. L.H.B.

LEVY, I.: *The Synagogue.* Its History and Function. 1963. Pp. 152. (Vallentine, Mitchell, London. Price: 21s. 0d.).

This well-written book containing a survey of the history of the synagogue, portrays mainly the contemporary synagogue. It should appeal to the general reader. M.W.

LURIE, B.: *Megillath Ta'anith* (in Hebrew). 1964. Pp. 202. (Mosad Bialik, Jerusalem).

This book in its first part surveys views of scholars concerning this Aramaic Megillah and concludes that the dates mentioned therein do in the main bear on significant historical events which took place during the first generations of the Hasmonean era, beginning with Mattathias the High Priest and ending with Jannaeus — events which are also echoed in early Midrashim. The document, according to the author, might well have come from Jannaeus. In the second part of the book, entitled 'elucidations of the Mishnah-paragraphs of the (Ta'anith–) Scroll', each paragraph is well scrutinized and assigned to its respective event or events. M.W.

MAYER, D. G.: *Para (Die Rote Kuh).* Text, übersetzung und ausführliche Erklärung mit eingehenden geschichtlichen und sprachlichen Ein-leitungen und textkritischen Anhängen. (Die Mischna, ed. Rengstorf-Rost). 1964. Pp. VIII+164. (Verlag Alfred Töpelmann, Berlin. Price: DM. 38).

The work under notice, like its immediate predecessor in the series known as the *Giessener Mischna* (reviewed in the 1964 *Book List*, p. 75), consists of four main parts: 1. the Introduction which sets forth the essentials of the mishnic tractate Parah; 2. the vocalised Hebrew text of this tractate mainly copied from MS Kaufmann, with German Translation and Notes; 3. an

Appendix with *variae lectiones* in 4 MS Codices, (with the interesting innovation of the distinction between the hands of several copyists at work in 2 of the Codices concerned), 8 fragments in the Cambridge Taylor-Schechter Collection and the *ed. pr.* of *Parah* in 2 Mishnah recensions. (Regrettably enough, there is again no notice taken of the older MSS of the Mishnah with Maimonides' Arabic commentary; even though variants in these are easily accessible for *Parah*, as for *Tohoroth* as a whole, in the ed. published by J. Derembourg (Berlin, 1887–9) and in the numerous excerpts from a text named *Nusaḥ 'Ereṣ Yisra'el* (=Palestinian Text) in the glosses *Tosefoth Yom Ṭov* by the erudite commentator R. Yom Ṭov Lipmann Heller (1579–1654). Equally neglected are the text-critical glosses in *Melekheth Shelomoh* by Heller's contemporary the Yemenite R. Shelomoh 'Adeni, which is an indispensable tool in the textual criticism of the Mishnah); 4. several Indices; in their wonted competency, comprehensiveness and great serviceability. Readers of this *Book List* will be mainly interested in the author's treatment of the scriptural texts, Num. xix and xxxi, 19–24, which form the background to *Parah*. In his discussion of these Dr. Mayer shows himself an adherent to the old school of the documentary hypotheses. He assumes the texts concerned to be late additions to the source P. Pivotal in this *Quellenscheidung* is his claim (p. 7) that the manner of the ritual burning of the Red Heifer (Num. xix. 5b) represents a *Sonderfall im Opfersystem*. Therein he is evidently forgetful of the numerous parallels, just to this aspect of the Red Heifer, in Ex. xxix 14 (=Lev. viii. 17), Lev. iv, 11–12, 20–21 and *ibid.* xvi. 27. It is also to be noted that in his chapter on the ritual of the Red Heifer among the Qumran Covenanters, Dr. Mayer follows too credulously the speculations of J. Bowman. His translation and notes are, on the whole, competent. There are occasional slips, e.g., the misquotation of *mish-she-'alu* (instead of *ke-she-'alu*) from Tos. Parah III 5, in the Notes on the Mishnah Parah III 3c (p. 47), which in turn leads to a perverted historical perspective. Notwithstanding this and its like, the author deserves credit for the undoubted merits of his work.
E.W.

PINES, S. (trans. by): *The Guide of the Perplexed, Moses Maimonides.* With introductory essay by Leo Strauss. 1963. Pp. cxxxiv + 658. (The University of Chicago Press. Price: £5 5s.).

This is a superb translation of S. Munk's Arabic text (edited by I. Joel). It reflects a profound understanding of Maimonides's objectives; and, while it is written in excellent English, no attempt is made to simplify into easy intelligibility what is deliberately ambiguous or obscure in the original. Italic type is used to mark off phrases which, in the original, appear in Hebrew or Aramaic. Not the least valuable parts are the two introductions. Strauss discusses the nature of the work ('How to begin to study the Guide'); some of this will be familiar to readers who have followed his publications over the past thirty years (*Gesetz und Philosophie* appeared in 1935). Pines investigates 'The Philosophic Sources of the Guide' and has interesting things to say not only about the authors Maimonides draws on but also about those he does not use or uses only little; his Jewish predecessors fall in the latter class.
D.D.

SOWERS, S. G.: *The Hermeneutics of Philo and Hebrews*. A Comparison of the Interpretation of the Old Testament in Philo-Judaeus and the Epistle to the Hebrews. (Basel Studies of Theology edited by the Faculty of Theology, Basel, No. 1). 1965. Pp. 154. (EVZ-Verlag, Zürich. Price: Fr./DM. 12; $2.75).

In this dissertation, by a former pupil of Oscar Cullmann and Bo Reicke, the background and character of Philonic allegorical exegesis is outlined, with special reference to the allegorization of Temple, sacrifice, and priesthood. Such allegorization is absent from the Epistle to the Hebrews, the more strikingly so in view of its manifest Alexandrian background and Philonic affinities. It is not that the writer to the Hebrews was ignorant of this allegorization; he shows in various ways that he had received some training in it. But he denies some of the chief emphases of the allegorical exegesis, such as the eternity of the law and the universal applicability of Judaism, because his mind has become controlled by 'the common thinking and faith' of the Church; and his understanding of the history of salvation in terms of the two covenants leads him to prefer a typological to an allegorical exegesis.

F.F.B.

PHILOLOGY AND GRAMMAR

ALCALAY, R.: *The Complete English-Hebrew Dictionary*. 1962. Pp. 4270. (Massadah Press, Jerusalem. £7 7s. 0d.).

Since the appearance in 1929 of Dr. J. Kaufman's English-Hebrew Dictionary, the Hebrew language has made startlingly rapid progress, and the lack of a new dictionary abreast of the times was strongly felt for some time. This we have in the present work. The old material has been brought up-to-date and much more new material has been added.

The dictionary is noteworthy in that it gives renderings for a great number of English expressions. There are, for instance, Hebrew renderings of forty-three expressions which contain the noun 'eye' and sixty-eight which include the noun 'hand'. In many cases, besides giving the literal translation, an equivalent original Hebrew expression is offered. Here are a few felicitous renderings bearing on the Bible: 'congratulations', *sā' berākhāh* (*cf.* Ps. xxiv. 5); 'one hand washeth the other', *ṭobhîm hashshenayim min-ha'eḥādh* (*cf.* Eccles. iv. 9); 'a six-footer', *sheshay* (originally a proper noun — one of the three tall, long-necked men. *Cf.* Num. xiii. 22). Students of the Hebrew language will do well to consult this fine dictionary.

M.W.

MOSCATI, S. (ed. by): *An Introduction to the Comparative Grammar of the Semitic Languages. Phonology and Morphology*. (Porta Linguarum Orientalium, Neue Serie, VI). 1964. Pp. viii + 186. (Otto Harrassowitz, Wiesbaden. Price: DM. 28).

This book was written by Professor Moscati with the help of Professors A. Spitaler, E. Ullendorff, and W. von Soden, who suggested additions and alterations to his first draft. It is a well-informed and judicious summary of a complicated subject and will undoubtedly prove a most useful introduction to its study. There is a bibliography of fifteen pages. In a work intended as 'an elementary introduction' suitable 'for a beginners' course' (p. 1), it would have been helpful to explain more of the technical terms used (e.g., 'glottalized ejectives' on p. 23); and the writers might sometimes have been more venturesome in seeking to account for phenomena as well as listing them. However, such minor criticisms do not alter the fact that Professor Moscati and his collaborators have ably met a need that has long been felt and have earned the gratitude of all who study and teach Semitic languages. J.A.E.

NIDA, E. A.: *Toward a Science of Translating*. With special reference to principles and procedures involved in Bible translating. 1964. Pp. x + 332 incl. 47 figs. (E. J. Brill, Leiden. Price: Fl. 25).

This is an important and complex book written by a distinguished American linguist and couched in (mostly inevitable) technical terminology. It deals with the theories of meaning, the main factors in communication, the tradition of translation in the western world, the principles of correspondence in translation, translation procedures, and machine translation. The book ranges over a very wide area and does so with great learning and acumen. A bibliography of some 55 pages underlines the author's catholicity of approach and treatment.

The present reviewer is not competent to judge what precise contribution this work is likely to make to questions of Bible translation, but he has no doubt that its closely reasoned arguments and vast body of factual information will enrich the understanding and penetration of anyone interested in the theory and practice of translation — be he concerned with multilingual scribes of cuneiform tablets or the electronic equipment used in simultaneous interpretation. A word of caution: in the context of this book MT stands for machine translation and *not* for Masoretic text. E.U.

ROSENTHAL, F.: *Die aramaistische Forschung seit Th. Nöldeke's Veröffentlichungen*. 1964. Pp. XVI + 308 + 5 tables + 1 map. (E. J. Brill, Leiden. Price: Fl. 35).

The reprinting of this survey of scholarly work on the Aramaic dialects is very welcome. The original edition (1939) was reviewed in *Book List* 1940, p. 6. Its merits are so well known that no further comment is needed. J.A.E.

ULLENDORFF, E.: *The Knowledge of Languages in the Old Testament*. (Reprinted from the *Bulletin of the John Rylands Library*, Vol. 44, No. 2, March, 1962). 1962. Pp. 455-465. (The John Rylands Library, Manchester. Price: 3s. 0d.).

In this brief but interesting article, on a topic which has received less attention than it deserves, two problems receive special consideration. The first relates to 2 Kings xviii.26, and the conclusions which may be drawn from it concerning the linguistic knowledge both of the Assyrian officers and of the Jewish negotiators. The second problem is the language in which Samson and Delilah, and more broadly, Israelites and Philistines, may have conversed, and the solution is found in the probability that the Philistines spoke a Canaanite *lingua franca* (*sefath kena'an*) which was widely understood by the peoples of Canaan. Many other well-known Old Testament passages are touched upon, among them Gen. xxxi. 47; Deut. ii. 11, 20; Ezek. iii. 5f.; Neh. xiii. 24, and the article ends with a strong plea for more intensive research into Hebrew dialects, colloquialisms, and pronunciation.

D.W.T.

WASH WATTS, J.: *A Survey of Syntax in the Hebrew Old Testament.* 1964. Pp. 12 + 164. (Wm. B. Eerdmans Publishing Company, Grand Rapids, Michigan. Price: $3.95).

The original form of this work was published in 1951, and was briefly reviewed in the *Book List* 1952, p. 82 (*Eleven Years*, p. 453). In this later form the presentation of the author's views remains obscure, and the historical aspect of the problem of the Hebrew tenses receives as little attention as previously. Indeed, the author can write of *wāw* consecutive — 'we know that probably we must look to Biblical Hebrew alone for evidence bearing on an explanation' (p. 53). However, he sometimes proposes translations of Old Testament passages which should interest students. A full index of the passages treated is supplied. Surprisingly and regrettably, both *'aleph* and *'ayin* are, except in a few cases, represented in transliteration by a smooth breathing.

D.W.T.

WILCOX, M.: *The Semitisms of Acts.* 1965. Pp. xiv+206. (Clarendon Press, Oxford. Price: 50s. 0d.).

This book had its origin in research done at Edinburgh for a Ph.D., and clearly the author was fortunate to have as a supervisor Dr. Black, who had made a special study of the Aramaic background of the New Testament and produced a standard work in this field. After a historical survey of earlier investigations, Dr. Wilcox deals with the Old Testament in Acts, finding, for example, traces of Targumic tradition, and studying the evidence for an aberrant Old Testament text, the Septuagintalisms and the sources of an alternative Greek Old Testament version. Detailed treatment is given to all the Semitisms which have been found in Acts, and the author is inclined not to favour the theory of an underlying Aramaic or Hebrew document. Many other points of significance are discussed, but most of them fall just outside the Old Testament field; their importance for the textual and literary criticism of Acts and the study of early Christian tradition is clear. This is a scholarly work, well-documented, very cautious and careful. The one slip I have noted occurs at p. 89, n. 6.

W.D.McH.

BOOK LIST, 1966

In this, the tenth and last issue of the *Book List* to be produced under my editorship, the contents have been classified as in former years. It will, however, be found that several works might reasonably have been assigned to more than one section. Books suitable for inclusion in school libraries have been marked by an asterisk (*).

I should like to thank the members of the *Book List* Panel and the following other scholars who have contributed reviews to this issue: T. Aiura, M. Bič, H. Cazelles, A. Gelston, J. Macdonald, E. R. Rowlands, E. T. Ryder, J. F. A. Sawyer, R. de Vaux, and W. Zimmerli. Without the co-operation of these and other colleagues over the years my editorial burden would have been considerably heavier. I wish also to record my thanks to Mrs. E. S. K. Paterson for valuable secretarial help. The Printer and his staff have at all times rendered magnificent service. The high quality of their work is evident to all users of the *Book List*; and as Editor I am deeply grateful for their unfailing courtesy and co-operation. At various times my wife has undertaken much of the routine work. I am particularly indebted to her for many hours devoted to the preparation of the present issue for the Printer and to the reading of the proofs.

It has been a high, though arduous, honour to be responsible for this important part of the work of the Society for Old Testament Study. In thanking the Society for much encouragement and understanding, I also extend cordial good wishes to the new Editor, Professor P. R. Ackroyd.

G. W. ANDERSON.

NEW COLLEGE,
UNIVERSITY OF EDINBURGH.

GENERAL

ALBRIGHT, W F.: *History, Archaeology, and Christian Humanism.* 1964 (U.S.A.) and 1965 (U.K.). Pp. ix + 342. (McGraw-Hill Book Company, New York; A. & C. Black, London. Price: $6.95 or 35s. 0d.).

This volume is the first of a series planned to collect together many of the shorter and lesser-known articles and reviews by this distinguished scholar. It contains fifteen studies ranging over a wide variety of topics from philosophical, historical, archaeological, and more strictly Biblical subjects. Many of them have not previously appeared in print; and all have been revised and brought up to date by the author. Of special interest to Old Testament scholars are the third essay which examines the place of the Old Testament in the history of thought, and the last two which particularly concern the author's intellectual development. One is headed 'Return to Biblical Theology', and the other is an autobiographical sketch. The whole forms, a very stimulating collection.   R.E.C.

Annual of the Swedish Theological Institute, ed. by H. Kosmala in collaboration with G. Gerleman, G. Lindeskog, and H. S. Nyberg. Vol. III. 1964. Pp. 156. (E. J. Brill, Leiden. Price: Fl. 24).

Almost the entire contents of this volume are of direct interest to the *Alttestamentler.* J. Lindblom discusses afresh the meaning of the divine name as presented in Exod. iii. 14. E. Nielsen re-examines the early history of the Levites. K. Yaron contributes a study of Ezek. xxviii. 1–19, its text, literary antecedents, and mythological colouring. A. S. Kapelrud reviews the evidence for the date of the Priestly Code, concluding that, apart from minor additions and modifications, it was complete before 550 B.C. H. Kosmala continues his study of 'Nachfolge und Nachahmung Gottes' (II 'Im jüdischen Denken'), and also contributes shorter articles on 'The Parable of the Unjust Steward in the light of Qumran' and 'Mot and the Vine: The Time of the Ugaritic Fertility Rite'. B. Noack offers some comments on Or. Sib. V.156–159. J. Sawyer writes on the Qumran reading of Isaiah vi. 13. W. Wirgin contributes some observations on A. Schalit's article in Vol. I of the *Annual* on Herod's family origin. The volume is dedicated to the late Professor Mowinckel, for whose 80th birthday it was intended.

G.W.A.

BIČ, M. and SOUČEK, J. B. (ed. by): *Biblická Konkordance,* Parts 26 and 27 Učiniti-Vstáti. 1964–65. Pp. 80 each part. (Edice Kalich, Prague. Price: Kčs. 10.70 each).

This concordance to the Czech Bible, giving Hebrew and Greek equivalents in the Old Testament and Greek equivalents in the New Testament, is now within sight of the end, and should shortly be complete, giving to Czech readers a range of information greater than that of any other concordance known to the reviewer. Unhappily he is not a Czech reader.   H.H.R.

BOWMAN, J. (ed. by): *Abr-Nahrain*. An Annual published by the Department of Semitic Studies, University of Melbourne, in association with the Department of Semitic Studies, University of Sydney. Vol. IV (1963–64). 1965. Pp. X + 112 incl. 6 plates. (E. J. Brill, Leiden. Price: Fl. 18).

This volume contains five articles of which four are of interest to Old Testament scholars. Professor Guillaume contributed his promised further (and, alas, final) article on Hebrew and Arabic Lexicography. D. Leslie discusses the Chinese-Hebrew Memorial Book from the K'aifeng synagogue (to be continued in a subsequent Annual) with six plates. A. Murtonen offers a Historico-Philological Survey of the main Dead Sea Scrolls and related Documents. A. D. Crown discusses 'Aposiopesis in the Old Testament and the Hebrew Conditional Oath'. He finds reason to doubt the occurrence of aposiopesis in the Old Testament.

A.S.H.

CAZELLES, H. & FEUILLET, A. (ed. by): *Dictionnaire de la Bible. Supplément*. Fasc. xl. (Pharisiens–Philistins). 1965. Tome VII, columns 1025–1248. (Letouzey & Ané, Paris).

In this number J. Le Moyne contributes a long article on the Pharisees, of which only three columns belong to the preceding part. B. Bagatti has a well illustrated account of Phasga or Mount Nebo. Maurice Dunand, the excavator of Byblos, has an authoritative study of Phoenicia. P. Benoit writes on Philemon, and J. Murphy-O'Connor on Philippians. M. L. and H. Ellenberger make a beginning with the Philistines, a study which, in this issue, deals with the archaeological data.

J.M.T.B.

DE BOER, P. A. H. (ed. by): *Oudtestamentische Studiën namens het Oudtestamentisch Werkgezelschap in Nederland*. Deel XIV. 1965. Pp. X + 422. (E. J. Brill, Leiden. Price: Fl. 65; by subscription, Fl. 40).

The present volume of the now well-known and highly esteemed *Studiën* appears on the occasion of the 25th anniversary year of the Netherlands Society for the Study of the Old Testament; and it is accompanied by a brief account of its work by Prof. P. A. H. de Boer (pp. vii–x) and Prof. Th. C. Vriezen (pp. 397–416), to which an index of articles from the beginning of the *Studiën* is appended. All will wish to congratulate the Society and the distinguished editor of the *Studiën* on all that they have achieved.

The present volume contains eighteen articles. Three are on gramatical points (Hoftijzer, Brongers, and Hartmann); two illustrate points in the Old Testament from Assyrian historical texts (Frankena, van Leeuwen); three deal with places of divine residence (Beek, Snijders, van den Born); one is geographical (Hulst); and one archaeological (Franken); two discuss texts (Baars, de Boer); two examine the problem of Psalms xvii and xl (van der Ploeg, Ridderbos); one discusses 'The Saints of the Most High' (Brekelmans); one collects references to the Edomitic god Qaus (Vriezen); one discusses Ben-Sira (Koole); and one is devoted to the publication of a new text from Qumrân (van der Woude). All are of high excellence, and to single out individual articles for praise is as superfluous as it is embarrassing. The attention of readers may however be drawn to one or two points of special interest: such are the new explanations of 'that dwelt in the bush' (Deut. xxxiii. 16; pp. 153–61), 'the king's entry without, turned he into the house of the LORD' (2 Kings xvi. 18; pp. 214–34), Solomon's poem at the dedication of the Temple (1 Kings viii. 12f.; pp. 235–44), and of 'the roll of the book' (Ps. xl. 7; p. 301) which is perhaps illustrated by two other passages which refer to the king's coronation (2 Kings xi. 12 = 2 Chron. xxiii. 11 and Ps. ii. 7). The remarkable text from Qumrân in which Melchizedek is raised to the rank of a heavenly being ('elōhîm) deserves special mention.

In conclusion, every article is well worth reading; but the Greek accents want checking here and there, and the English idiom is at times quite un-English!

G.R.D.

FICHTNER, J.: *Gottes Weisheit: Gesammelte Studien zum Alten Testament*, ed. by K. D. Fricke. (Arbeiten zur Theologie, II. Reihe, Band 3). 1965. Pp. 162. (Calwer Verlag, Stuttgart. Price: DM. 16).

Professor Fichtner, who died in 1962, was well known for his work on the Wisdom literature, to which several of the nine articles reprinted in this volume are devoted. The first shows how that literature moved away from a tendency to ignore history and its relation to Israel's faith, and maintains that the change was due partly to such men as Isaiah who, it is argued in a second paper, was a wise man in the technical sense before his call to be a prophet. Two other papers also discuss Isaiah's teaching. A study of the significance of Job for the preacher reveals Fichtner's interest in the place of the Old Testament in the Church, which also appears in an examination of the Christian use of the Psalms as prayers, and in a discussion of the reasons for the revision of Luther's rendering of the Old Testament together with a critical evaluation of Buber's translation. The remaining two essays are concerned with the concept of 'neighbour' in the Old Testament, in Judaism, and in the New Testament, and with the ways in which heathen practices in Israel were combated either by prohibition or by adaptation. K. D. Fricke, the editor of the collection, has written a brief account of Fichtner's work, and has compiled a list of his writings and an index of scriptural references.

J.A.E.

FRIEDRICH, G. (ed. by): *Theologisches Wörterbuch zum Neuen Testament*. (begun by G. Kittel). Band VIII, Lief. 1 and 2. 1965. Pp. 64 + 64. (Kohlhammer, Stuttgart. Price: DM. 5.80 each Lief.).

Lieferung 1 contains a long article by Grundmann on *tapeinos* and its cognates, the occurrences of which in the LXX are related to their Hebrew equivalents. There are sections on the idea of 'humility' in Judaism (in Qumran, in Apocalyptic Judaism, and in Rabbinic Judaism, as well as in the New Testament). The treatment of *tasso* and its cognates by Delling is of less importance for Old Testament scholars. Of much greater consequence is the article on *telos* and its cognates, also by Delling, though one would have expected a fuller discussion of the relevant Hebrew terms. This article is continued into Lieferung 2 in which there is an important section on *teleios* with reference to Hebrew equivalents. The article on *telōnēs* by Michel is, of course, interesting for Palestinian history and economics. The article on *teras* by Rengstorf which will be continued in Lieferung 3 promises to be important theologically. N.W.P.

GALLING, K. (ed. by): *Die Religion in Geschichte und Gegenwart*, 3. Auflage, Registerband, bearbeitet von W. Werbeck. 1965. Cols. 1–1112. (J. C. B. Mohr, Tübingen. Price: £5 10s. 6d.).

This additional volume to *R.G.G.*[3] consists of three parts: (a) an index of all the contributors and their contributions, with brief biographical entries and lists of their publications brought down to the beginning of 1964 (cols. 1–272); (b) a general index of persons and subjects discussed in the articles (cols. 273–1102); (c) a list of corrections (cols. 1103–1112). The whole is an invaluable adjunct to the main work; and much gratitude is due for the painstaking and patient labour which must have been devoted to it. G.W.A.

GRINTZ, J. M. & LIVER, J. (ed. by): *Studies in the Bible.* Presented to Professor M. H. Segal by his Colleagues and Students. (Publications of the Israel Society for Biblical Research, Vol. XVII). 1964. Pp. in Hebrew 331; in English 63 + portrait on endpaper. (Kiryat Sepher, Jerusalem).

J. Liver's bibliography of the publications of Professor M. H. Segal forms the introduction to the volume under review. Some 130 items, consisting of books, articles, and important reviews, bear witness to the ability and energy of a scholar whose interests range over more than 3,000 years of Hebrew writings: Biblical and Mishnaic literature, the Dead Sea Scrolls, the Apocrypha (particularly the Hebrew text of Ben Sira), the Targumim, the history of Jewish exegesis from the Karaites to S. D. Luzatto and beyond almost up to our day. English readers will know Prof. Segal best as the author of a widely used Grammar of Mishnaic Hebrew and as a lexicographer.

The Festschrift reflects the influence he has had on colleagues and students as well as the general affection in which he is held. The Hebrew section comprises twenty-five, the English four articles. Most of the essays deal with Biblical subjects: The Tabernacle: A Graded Taboo of Holiness (M. Haran); Judges, Chapter I (J. M. Grintz); Mice in the Cities of the Philistines (N. H. Tur-Sinai); The Opening of the Stories on the Reign of Solomon (Y. Kaufmann); The Speech of Rab-Shakeh on the Wall of Jerusalem (H. M. I. Gevaryahu); Isaiah IX, 5: A Study in Eschatology (B. Uffenheimer); The Sequence of Persian Kings in Ezra and Nehemiah (J. Liver); Eschatology in the Book of Malachi (E. Margalioth). In the English section D. Winton Thomas writes on *Niṣṣabh* in Psalm XXXIX, 6, and G. R. Driver on Psalm CX: its Form, Meaning and Purpose. E. Z. Melamed, M. Z. Kadari and D. Leibel contribute, respectively articles on: Artistic Devices in Biblical Poetry, The Syntax of the Infinitive Construct in Biblical Hebrew, and Collective Plural and Distributive Plural in Feminine Nouns. Comparisons of Biblical with Ancient Near Eastern literature and cognate fields of studies are dealt with by A. Malamat: Mari and the Bible; M. Tsevat: Assyriological Notes on the First Book of Samuel; E. Ullendorff: The knowledge of Languages in the Bible; Ch. Rabin: Hittite Words in Hebrew; and S. E. Loewenstamm: Notes on the Origin of some Biblical Figures of Speech. The English section has an article by C. H. Gordon: 'Aḥadhim in the Sense of 'Pair' and its Counterparts in Ugaritic and Akkadian. As to the Apocrypha and the DSS, A. M. Habermann adds Notes on the Book of Ecclesiasticus, whilst J. Licht throws new light on Some Terms and Concepts of Ritual Purity in the Qumran Writings. Early Rabbinic literature is covered by S. Talmon: The Three Scrolls of the Law that were Found in the Temple Court; O. Komloss: Distinctive Features in the Targum of Psalms; L. Finkelstein: A Study in Early Halakhic Traditions; B. Z. Lurie: Exodus XII, 6 and its Rabbinical Interpretations. Masoretic Studies are represented by N. Allony: The Book of Sounds by Moshe ben Asher and, indirectly, by A. Mirsky, The Masorah and Medieval Hebrew Poetry. Professor J. B. Segal contributes an article on The Jews of North Mesopotamia before the Rise of the Islam to the Festschrift in honour of his father. The reviewer is certain that all members of the Society for Old Testament Study will want to associate themselves with the wish of the late Sir Leon Simon who concluded his Reminiscences of Professor M. H. Segal with the hope that he may be spared for many years to continue his scholarly work. S.S.

(HERTZBERG, H.-W.): *Gottes Wort und Gottes Land*, ed. by H. Graf Reventlow. 1965. Pp. 228. (Vandenhoeck and Ruprecht, Göttingen. Price: DM. 28).

These studies were prepared for the 70th birthday of Professor Hertzberg who has since died, a fitting memorial to his interests, in particular in problems of exegesis and of the land of the Bible. All but one of the essays are on Old Testament subjects. Of these we may note Beyerlin's discussion of the origins of the parenetic material in the Book of the Covenant; Eichrodt's of covenant and law and the relation of this to the problem of law and gospel. Eissfeldt examines the nature of two groups of Jacob narratives. Jepsen develops a discussion of ṣedeq and ṣᵉdāqā to consider the problem of divine-human relationships. Kuschke considers topographical and historical problems in the book of Joshua. Lehming has an interesting, perhaps too precise, discussion of the tent tradition. Pfeiffer examines the nature of Kohelet's faith. Reventlow finds in Deut. xii a basic apodictic law demanding the abolition of heathen sanctuaries. Rost examines the legal background to Gen. xii 10–20 and Rudolph discusses text and exegesis of Hos. iv. 15–19. Stoebe offers reflections on the problems of Old Testament theology and suggests greater unity of presentation in a threefold scheme—'origin, way, goal'. A list of Hertzberg's writings concludes the collection. P.R.A.

MACDONALD, J. (ed. by): *The Annual of the Leeds University Oriental Society*, Vol. IV (1962–63). 1964. Pp. 156. (E. J. Brill, Leiden. Price: Fl. 36).

J. M. Allegro gives photographs, translations, and notes of fragments of two pseudepigraphical documents from Qumran. In 'Problems in Judges newly discussed', G. R. Driver offers notes on forty-three difficult passages. A. Guillaume in 'The Unity of the Book of Job' draws attention to the Hebraeo-Arabic vocabulary throughout the book. This is followed by an examination of Lamentations iv. 9 which is translated: 'More fortunate were they who died by the sword than those who wasted away from hunger; For they died quickly, having eaten their fill (Arab. *daqira*) of the fruits of the field'. J. S. Harris contributes a valuable article with twelve photographs on 'An Introduction to the Study of personal Ornaments of Precious, Semi-precious and Imitation Stones used throughout Biblical History'. Two other articles, though important, are less relevant to Old Testament Studies.

A.S.H.

MAYER, L. A.: *Bibliography of the Samaritans*, ed. by D. Broadribb. (Supplements to Abr-Nahrain. Vol. I). 1964. Pp. vi + 50. (E. J. Brill, Leiden. Price: Fl. 8).

One should expect a first comprehensive bibliography of the Samaritans to be of great value, and it is regrettable that this work should be marred by many printer's errors, editorial mistakes, omissions of works which should have been included, and particularly by the complete lack of classification. The entries include articles on pre-Exilic Samaria and travel works. There is no index. Anyone wishing data on a specific subject, e.g., history, theology, will have to read through all entries. Pp. 46–49 are devoted to publications in Hebrew and Arabic. Despite the faults, the work, if used with care, can be of service to specialists.

J.McD.

Mémorial du Cinquantenaire 1914–1964. (Travaux de l'Institut Catholique de Paris 10). 1964. Pp. 148 + 2 plates. (Bloud & Gay, Paris).

This fine and well printed volume is sponsored by the École des Langues Orientales Anciennes of the Paris Catholic Institute. The preface by its most distinguished student, Cardinal Tisserant, the present Cardinal Dean of the Sacred College, is full of interesting details about past professors, whose careers and bibliographies form the second division of the book. These lists include such well known names as Louis Delaporte, Étienne Drioton, René Graffin, and Sylvian Grêbaut. The greater part of the volume is made up of articles, the first of which, by F. Graffin, gives a short history of the École. Other articles include those by J. Starcky on a Messianic text in the fourth cave at Qumran, K. Hruby on the survival of the Hebrew language in the post-exilic period, and Y. Moubarac on Christians and the Arabic language.

J.M.T.B.

NOBER, P.: *Elenchus Bibliographicus Biblicus*, vols. xlv, 1964 and xlvi, 1965. Pp. xii + 431 and xii + 630. (Pontificio Istituto Biblico, Rome).

The *Book List* does not review journals, but attention may be drawn to the bibliographical section of *Biblica*. Each issue contains about 100 pages of bibliography, arranged according to subject, and covering every side of Biblical study, with an author index at the end of the volume for the year. Titles of books and articles are listed, and the places where the reviews of volumes have appeared are noted, together with the names of the reviewers where given. In the 1964 volume there were 4197 items and in the 1965 volume 4911 items. There are no abstracts of contents of books or articles, as in *Internationale Zeitschriftenschau für Bibelwissenschaft und Grenzgebiete*, but the coverage is much wider, and anyone doing research on any Biblical subject will find it invaluable to consult this tool. The industry of Father Nober in compiling this bibliography is exemplary and he deserves the gratitude of all whom he serves so well.

H.H.R.

VON RAD, G.: *The Problem of the Hexateuch and other Essays*, trans by E. W. Trueman Dicken. 1966. Pp. xiv + 340 + portrait. (Oliver & Boyd, Edinburgh and London. Price 47s. 6d.).

This is an eminently readable translation of *Gesammelte Studien zum Alten Testament* (reviewed in *Book List* 1960, pp. 6 f.). There is one additional essay, entitled 'Some Aspects of the Old Testament World View' which appeared in *Evangelische Theologie*, 24, (1964). In it von Rad warns against the danger of 'looking at the theological problems of the Old Testament far too much from the one-sided standpoint of an historically conditioned theology'. He examines the way in which the Old Testament world-view is expressed in the prohibition of images, and proceeds to consider the relationship between that world-view (with its universalizing tendency) and Israel's particularizing understanding of history. The discussion is related particularly to Ps. xix; Job xxviii; Prov. xxviii; and Ecclus. xxiv. Principal Porteous contributes an introduction to the volume.

G.W.A.

RIESENFELD, H. (ed. by): *Svensk exegetisk årsbok*, xxviii–xxix (1963–64). 1964. Pp. 158 including portrait. (C. W. K. Gleerup, Lund. Price: Sw. kr. 15).

Only one of the articles in this double volume is directly concerned with the Old Testament: 'The Theology of the Biblical Creation Epic', by Professor M. Bič. The author seeks to show that in Gen. i. 1–vi. 4 there is a wealth of religious symbolism which is commonly overlooked; e.g., the *'ēd* of ii. 6 is a destructive flood; the 'dust' of which man was formed is a symbol of the underworld; the garments provided for man by God are suggestive of priestly vestments, etc. The remaining articles are on New Testament subjects; and there is a brief section of reviews of recent literature. The volume also includes a portrait of the late Professor Engnell and a sympathetic appreciation of his work and personality by the editor.

G.W.A.

ROST, L.: *Das kleine Credo und andere Studien zum Alten Testament.*
1965. Pp. 266. (Quelle & Meyer, Heidelberg. Price: DM. 28).

The author warns his readers from the start that most of the
present volume's contents is by no means new. In fact, only the
title page has that distinction, and some of the essays date back
to the early days of his teaching career. The chief example of
this is the longest of all the papers, that on the line of succession
to David's throne, which first appeared in 1926, while the
contribution to the Procksch *Festschrift*, on the expressions for
the Land and the People in the Old Testament, was printed in
1934. A recent (1958) essay 'Considerations regarding Burnt-
offerings in Israel' leads the author in his preface to refer to
R. de Vaux' *Les sacrifices de l'Ancien Testament*, published in
1964 and now available in English. Other essays are on primitive
history, on Noah as a wine-grower, on Hosea iv, 14 ff., and on
Zechariah iv and vii, and on the practice of varying the pasture-
land of cattle in its relation to the ancient Israelite calendar.
The copious notes provided, normally at the end of a paper, are
among the many attractive features of this splendid collection.
There is a full index of Bible texts, but no index of subjects or
persons.
                                                        J.M.T.B.

ROWLEY, H. H.: *The Servant of the Lord and other Essays on the Old
Testament.* 2nd edition, revised. 1965. Pp. xvi + 356. (Basil
Blackwell, Oxford. Price: 50s. 0d.).

This volume, noticed in the *Book List* 1953, p. 62, (*Eleven Years*,
p. 515) has long been accepted as offering authoritative studies
in some central Old Testament topics and needs no further
commendation. In this reprint of the eight essays the author
has added material to the text and notes, bringing both sections
up to date. The appearance of the book has been improved by
the use of better paper and clearer type. All students of the Old
Testament will be glad this work is once again in print.

                                                        W.D.McH.

WEISS, J. G. (ed. by): *Papers of the Institute of Jewish Studies, London.*
Vol. I. 1964. Pp. 210. (Magnes Press, Jerusalem. Distributed in
G.B., Commonwealth, and Europe by Oxford University Press.
Price: 43s. 0d.).

The publication is intended for papers which are too long for
the *Journal of Jewish Studies*, and too short for the monograph
series, *Scripta Judaica*. The present volume contains four papers:
E. E. Urbach: 'The Laws regarding slavery as a source for social
history of the period of the Second Temple, the Mishnah and
Talmud'; R. J. Zvi Werblowski: 'Faith, Hope and Trust, a study
in the concept of Bittahon'; Raphael Loewe: 'The "plain"
meaning of Scripture in early Jewish exegesis'; S. M. Stern:
'An unpublished Maqama by Al-Harizi'. All four papers are
well written, with full annotation.
                                                        B.J.R.

WELLHAUSEN, J.: *Grundrisse zum Alten Testament*, ed. by Rudolf Smend (Theologische Bücherei, Neudrucke und Berichte aus dem 20. Jahrhundert, Band 27, Altes Testament). 1965. Pp. 138. (Chr. Kaiser Verlag, Munich. Price: DM. 9).

Both the publisher and the editor are to be congratulated on making available this collection of *scripta minora* by Wellhausen. The first item is a sketch of the history of Israel, which Wellhausen had privately printed in 1880 and which is now for the first time published in German. It corresponds to the first 9 sections of the article 'Israel' which was reprinted from the *Encyclopaedia Britannica* in the English translation of the *Prolegomena to the History of Israel*. This is followed by '*Israelitisch-jüdische Geschichte*', from *Die Kultur der Gegenwart* I, 4. Two shorter studies round off the collection: the survey of the history of the study of the Old Testament which Wellhausen contributed to the 4th, 5th, and 6th editions of Bleek's *Einleitung in das Alte Testament*, and the appreciation of Ewald which Wellhausen wrote in the *Jubiläumsschrift* of the Göttingen Academy (1901).

G.W.A.

WESTERMANN, C.: *Forschung am alten Testament. Gesammelte Studien.* (Theologische Bücherei, Neudrucke und Berichte aus dem 20. Jahrhundert, 24). 1964. Pp. 359. (Chr. Kaiser Verlag, Munich Price: DM. 15.80).

Of the nine studies here published, two are new. The remainder are reprints and cover 'The Mari-Letters and Prophecy in Israel', 'The Relation of belief in Yahweh to non-Israelite religion', 'Hope in the Old Testament', a study of the Lament form, and three studies of the Psalms—one on the actualization of history, one on the collection of the psalms, and one on Ps. xc. The two new studies are substantial and important. The first deals with the Genesis narratives and contains ninety pages of close analysis and discussion of their types and their nature in an attempt to go beyond the limitations of older aetiological study and the 'historical' approaches of some American scholarship. The second is concerned with 'The Language and Structure of the prophecy of Deutero-Isaiah'; it analyses the forms of the material, after a review of recent studies, and in its setting out of the structure and content endeavours to show the relation between the prophet's use of the forms and the task which was his in a particular situation.

P.R.A.

WOLFF, H. W.: *Wegweisung. Gottes Wirken im Alten Testament.* Vorträge zum Bibelverständnis. 1965. Pp. 198. (Chr. Kaiser Verlag, Munich. Price: DM. 14.80).

This is an interesting volume of four groups of broadcast and popular lectures to student and other bodies, dealing with Bible questions: Israel and mankind, men before God, and God for us. These titles include studies in Biblical Criticism, Salvation-History and World History, Psalms, and a particularly sympathetic study of Hosea.

G.H.D.

EDUCATIONAL

*ANDERSON, G. W.: *The History and Religion of Israel.* (The New Clarendon Bible, Old Testament, Vol. I). 1966. Pp. xii+210 incl. 2 maps
and 21 ills. and chronological tables. (Oxford University Press,
London. Price: 15s. 0d.).

This first volume of the Old Testament series of the New Clarendon Bible, appearing just thirty years after its predecessor in the
original Clarendon Bible, reflects both contributions of scholarship and changes of standpoint of the intervening period. The
chief changes are that history and religion are no longer treated
separately, because they are inseparable, that the scope of the
work is extended beyond Ezra to the Maccabaean Revolt, that
the RSV replaces the RV for Biblical quotations, and that for
extra-Biblical texts frequent references are made to Winton-
Thomas's *Documents from O.T. Times* and Pritchard's *The
Ancient Near East.* The book is well planned and although the
narrative is highly compressed it reads easily and reflects the
author's mastery of his subject and sureness of judgement. This
book will appeal not only to A level and S level candidates in the
G.C.E. examinations but to students in Colleges of Education
and in Theological Colleges and indeed to all who require a short,
general but scholarly, reliable, up-to-date and attractive conspectus of the history and religion of Israel.

L.A.P.

*HEATHCOTE, A. W.: *From the Exile to Herod the Great.* (The London
Divinity Series, Book III, Old Testament). 1964. Pp. 140 including
2 maps + 3 plates. (James Clarke, London. Price: 7s. 0d.).

This textbook, intended for candidates for the G.C.E. examinations in Divinity, is carefully planned and simply and clearly
written in seventeen short chapters. Within its limits it is a
useful and accurate factual guide to the history and literature of
the post-exilic period, though the Psalter receives only a passing
mention.

L.A.P.

*HEBERT, G.: *The Old Testament from Within.* Paperback Edition. 1965.
Pp. 154. (Oxford University Press, London. Price: 7s. 6d.).

This new Oxford Paperback, written by the late Father Hebert
for non-theological readers as a guide to the 'real issues of faith
in the various stages of the Old Testament history' was first
published in 1962 and reviewed in the *Book List* 1963, p. 12.

L.A.P.

YATES, G. G.: *A Guide to the Old Testament.* 1965. Pp. 272 + 6 maps.
(Epworth Press, London. Price: 25s. 0d.).

This book has been prepared as a textbook for Methodist lay
preachers in training. It presents in straightforward form the
assured results of modern study, and is thoroughly safe as a
guide to the beginner who has no technical knowledge. The
scheme is: as short an introduction to each chapter as possible,
followed by the study of selected passages of the Bible itself.
The title is exactly and admirably accurate. The volume covers

the Old Testament period; i.e., down to the Maccabaean Revolt. It ends with a short outline of Old Testament Theology and test questions. Less than one fifth is devoted to exilic and post-exilic times.

N.H.S.

ARCHAEOLOGY AND EPIGRAPHY

Annual of the American Schools of Oriental Research, vols. XXXVI–XXXVII (1957–58), *The Excavations at Dibon (Dhibân) in Moab,* Part I: *The First Campaign,* 1950–51, by F. V. Winnett; Part II: *The Second Campaign,* 1952, by W. L. Reed. 1964. Pp. viii + 1–30 + 25 plates and pp. 37–80 + 73 plates. (American Schools of Oriental Research, New Haven. Price: $7.50).

This double volume is devoted to reports on the excavations mainly in the S.E. corner of the mound, where the Mesha stele was found and in the tombs in the Wadi Dhiban. There seems no outstanding difficulty in identifying this six-acre site with Dibon, the significance of which is documentarily attested in the fourteenth or thirteenth centuries, the reign of Mesha (fl. 840) and the Byzantine period, and these occupation periods are attested in sherds from the Late Bronze Age, the tenth century and the second century to the Arab Age. It had been hoped to amplify by stratified excavation Glueck's general findings on the basis of surface exploration, but in the limited area excavated this could not be achieved, nor was the Mesha inscription supplemented. No significant building or fortification was discovered. Excavation in such provincial areas so far from the main highways west of the watershed in Western Palestine involves difficulties through lack of the full range of comparative material and promises limited results of generally local signifi-cance. The fact of the very substantial and significant Mesha inscription, however, might in this case justify the excavation of Dhiban.

J.G.

CAMPBELL, E. F., Jr., & FREEDMAN, D. N. (ed by): *The Biblical Archae-ologist Reader,* vol. II, 1964. Pp. xx + 420 incl. 39 ills. + 7 figures + map. (Anchor Books, Doubleday, New York. Price: $1.95 or 13s. 6d.).

There are here twenty-four articles reprinted from the Quarterly Journal of the American Schools of Oriental Research. There are three sections:
I. Cities and Lands of Israel's Neighbours, with articles on Mari, Nuzu, Ugarit, Edom, Philistines, Ammonites, Aram Naharaim, Frankincense and Myrrh, Arameans, and From Qarqar to Carchemish.
II. Reports of excavations in Palestine, at Hazor, Megiddo (two articles), Samaria, Shechem (three articles), and Lachish.
III. Cities of the New Testament Period—Antioch-on-Orontes, Ephesus (two articles), Laodicea, Athens, The Apostle Paul, and the Isthmian Games.
Some of the articles have been brought up to date, and the whole is a valuable collection, forming a useful companion to Vol. I.

J.N.S.

NOTH, M.: *The Old Testament World*, trans. by Victor I. Gruhn. 1966. Pp. xxii + 404 + 10 maps and ills. (Adam & Charles Black, London. Price: 48s. 0d.).

This English translation of the 4th edition of *Die Welt des Alten Testaments* will be most welcome to scholars and students of the Old Testament at all stages and particularly to the more advanced. Giving a very comprehensive survey of the whole Old Testament background, geographical, historical, and cultural with a section on archaeological methods and results, the work concludes with a valuable discussion of the transmission of the text and methods of textual criticism and an evaluation of the versions. The author reveals his familiarity with the topography and peasant life in Palestine in the best tradition of Dalman and Alt of the famous German Archaeological Institute in Jerusalem, with which, one hears with gratification, Professor Noth is again associated. In the translation there are certain inadvertencies, e.g., p. 79 'in post-Exilic times the Edomites pressed forward from the S. against Transjordan'. On p. 225, 'the grave of Jacob in the Kidron Valley' will not be readily understood as 'the tomb of James'. On p. 247, 'Desecration Texts' for 'Execration Texts' is an obvious, but unfortunate, slip in proof reading. There are other slips, but the translator is to be congratulated that there are so few which certainly do not impair his excellent presentation of an excellent work.

For reviews of earlier editions see *Book List* 1946, p. 16 (*Eleven Years*, p. 16); 1953, p. 46 (*Eleven Years*, p. 499); 1957, p. 19; 1963, p. 15.

J.G.

WRIGHT, G. E.: *Shechem. The Biography of a Biblical City*. (The Norton Lectures of the Southern Baptist Theological Seminary). 1965. Pp. xviii + 170 incl. Table of Archaeological Periods + 113 ills. (Gerald Duckworth, London. Price: 50s. 0d.).

In his excavation of Shechem after the earlier (and, by modern standards, destructive) work of Sellin and Welter, Professor Wright has undertaken a task which would have deterred many archaeologists, and if the earlier work complicated his task in the field, his detective work on the incomplete reports of Sellin, to which he conscientiously and patiently relates his own work, does not facilitate the reading of his book. The peculiar vicissitudes of the site, too, with its artificial fillings and levellings at various stages of its history, complicate the task for archaeologist and reader alike. Nevertheless in his study of the defences, the two gateways, the building on the acropolis, which, like Sellin (*pace* Welter) he interprets as a temple, and indeed that of Baalberith, and a limited section of the lower part of the town, Professor Wright presents an intelligible picture related to the documentary history of Shechem both Biblical and extra-Biblical. His data and discussion of the Samaritan settlement and the schism are particularly valuable. The synthesis between the documentary and material evidence will occupy the critical faculties of those competent and interested in both fields, and Professor Wright's suggestions will be found as well informed as we have come to expect. There are useful appendices by the author's colleagues on specialized subjects, of which studies on

Shechem in the Amarna Tablets and the cuneiform Texts from
Shechem will probably most interest Old Testament scholars.

J.G.

HISTORY AND GEOGRAPHY

*The Cambridge Ancient History: Revised Edition of Volumes I and II.
Greece, Crete and the Aegean Islands in the Early Bronze Age*: by
J. L. Caskey. Fasc. 24. Pp. 44. (Price: 6s. 0d.).

Elam and Western Persia: c. 1200–1000 B.C.: by René Labat. Fasc.
23. Pp. 32. (Price: 3s. 6d.).

We welcome the appearance of two more fascicles of the revised
edition of the *C. A. H.* Of more immediate interest to Old
Testament students will be René Labat's masterly account of the
most brilliant period of the kingdom of Elam, 1200–1000 B.C.
It was the period during which Elam was able to take advantage
of the weakness of both Assyria and Babylon, and to establish
mastery over the whole of Sumer and Akkad. Among the spoils
of the victorious Elamite campaigns were the statues of Marduk
and Nana, of Manishtusu, and the famous stele of Hammurabi.
Professor Caskey deals with the intricate movements of population at the end of the Neolithic Period, which brought about the
settlement of new elements in Crete, Greece, and the Aegean
Islands. He records the significant finding of a cylinder seal
impression upon a jar from Lerna III, a detail which suggests
the presence of Mesopotamian influence or cultural contact.
Sir Arthur Evans had already suggested that the presence of the
bull cult in Crete pointed in the same direction.
Both these fascicles bear witness to the continuing high standard
of scholarship maintained in the revision of the great Cambridge
Ancient History.
S.H.H.

*The Cambridge Ancient History: Revised Edition of Volumes I & II.
The Struggle for the Domination of Syria (1400–1300 B.C.)*: by A.
Goetze. Fasc. 37. Pp. 64. (Price: 6s. 0d.).

Anatolia in the Old Assyrian Period: by Hildegard Lewy. Fasc. 40.
Pp. 28. (Price: 3s. 6d.).

Assyria and Babylonia c. 1200–1000 B.C.: by D. J. Wiseman. Fasc. 41.
Pp. 48. (Cambridge University Press. Price: 6s. 0d.).

Assyria and Babylonia c. 1370–1300 B.C.: by C. J. Gadd. Fasc. 42.
Pp. 36. (Price: 6s. 0d.).

The revision of the great work has taken a leap forward and we
now have four new fascicles to engage our attention. The names
of the authors range from the old and well-tried to the younger
generation, but all give us assurance of the highest quality of
scholarship. We have first Professor Goetze's account of the
tense struggle between Egypt and the Hittites for the mastery
of Syria, together with the part played by the Mitanni and the
Hurrians in that confused struggle. Our main source of information is the Tell el-Amarna Letters, which have been subjected
to a fresh and thorough scrutiny by the author. Much fresh light
is thrown on this fascinating period of history.

In fascicle 40 which will be c. XXIV of the new edition, Professor
Hildegard Lewy deals with the part played by Anatolia in the
Old Assyrian Period, ranging from the time of Sargon of Agade
up to the end of the Assyrian occupation of Kultepe. Here the
new material from Mari has been fully used by the author to
illustrate this obscure period.

The period of the next fascicle, the history of Assyria and
Babylonia during the two hundred years from 1200 to 1000 B.C.
is one which Professor Wiseman has made his own by his work
on the Babylonian Chronicles. Here one has only to compare
the author's treatment of this period with that contained in the
old edition to realise how much new light has accrued from recent
studies, and how much is due to Professor Wiseman's own
researches. This is a most interesting and important fascicle.

Lastly, in fascicle 42, Professor Gadd, to whom we already owe
so much in this field, and whom age does not weary, takes up
the story at the point where, as he says, the gloom which the
previous disturbed centuries of internecine struggle had cast
over the Near East is beginning to disperse. In his own lucid
style he tells the story of the revival of the power of Assyria
under Ashur-uballit and its consequences.   S.H.H.

*The Cambridge Ancient History: Revised Edition of Volumes I & II.
Palestine in the Time of the 19th Dynasty.* (a) *The Exodus and Wanderings*: by Otto Eissfeldt. Fasc. 31. Pp. 32. (Price: 6s. 0d.).

The Hebrew Kingdom: by Otto Eissfeldt. Fasc. 32. Pp. 80. (Price: 8s. 6d.).

Here are two more fascicles of the rapidly advancing revision
of the Cambridge Ancient History. These two will be specially
welcome to Old Testament students as they are from the pen of
the doyen of Old Testament studies, and deal with some of the
most difficult problems in the history of Israel. Professor
Eissfeldt is inclined to concede historicity to the figure of
Abraham, but is doubtful about that of Jacob and Isaac. He
gives a searching analysis of the early settlement in Canaan,
and the Egyptian sojourn. He suggests that the Joseph tribes,
together with a nucleus of Levi, constituted that part of the
Hebrew people which went down into Egypt, and experienced
the Exodus under the leadership of Moses the Levite. It is
interesting to compare Eissfeldt's treatment of this part of
Israel's history with that by Professor Rowley in his Schweich
Lectures, *From Joseph to Joshua.* Professor Eissfeldt's account
of the Hebrew Kingdom up to the split after the death of
Solomon is marked by that breadth of learning and soundness
of judgement which we have come to expect from him. S.H.H.

HORAÏN, C. M.: *L'identité des lieux de la Jordanie et de l'Arabie. Catalogue
de 931 positions indiquant les correspondances entre les dénominations
anciennes et modernes.* 1964. Pp. 71. (Gand, Chez l'auteur: Casa
Nova, P.O. Box 4134, Jerusalem, Jordan).

The place names collected in the records of pilgrims and travellers
from the Byzantine age until 1807 (Seetzen's journey) are
arranged alphabetically and identified with those in use since

1857 (Tobler's journey). Some of the identifications are correct, some are uncertain or fanciful, and no proof is given. There is only one short note on the last page of the book, according to which the identifications thus obtained seem to convince the author that the descriptions of Sinai in the records of the early pilgrims (*Peregrinatio Sylviae, Petrus Diaconus*, and *L'Anonyme de Plaisance*) all refer to the place which is wrongly called Petra, while the Sinai Peninsula, itself wrongly named, is the Ethiopia of the Biblical texts. Such novel hypotheses call for more detailed demonstration.

R.deV.

LIVER, J. (ed. by): *The Military History of the Land of Israel in Biblical Times.* (Military Historical Library). 1965. Pp. 490 + 32 plates + many ills., maps and plans. ('Maarachoth', Israel Defence Forces Publishing House).

This volume, ably edited by Jacob Liver of the University of Tel Aviv, comprises thirty two studies, fifteen directly written as contributions to this volume and the remaining seventeen having already appeared, in a modified form, in various periodicals. The studies, composed by eminent scholars, amongst them Y. Aharoni, A. Malamat, B. Mazar, Y. Yadin, and S. Yeivin, deal with wars of three periods: (a) those which took place in Canaan before the Israelite Conquest; (b) in the Land of Israel from the Conquest to the Beginning of the Monarchy; (c) under the Monarchy. This is followed by a series of articles dealing with armies, weapons, and fortifications. The volume ends with a relevant epilogue by E. Galili and includes three detailed indexes, a great number of maps, illustrations, and plates.

M.W.

NEWMAN, M. L.: *The People of the Covenant. A Study of Israel from Moses to the Monarchy.* 1965. Pp. 208. (Carey Kingsgate Press, London. Price: 25s. 0d.).

This is an English reprint of the work published in the U.S.A. in 1962 under the same title. It was reviewed in *Book List* 1964, pp. 26 f.

G.R.D.

OLMSTEAD, A. T.: *History of Palestine and Syria to the Macedonian Conquest.* 1965. (reprint). Pp. xxxiv + 664 + frontispiece + 187 ills. + 18 maps and plans + maps on front end paper. (Baker Book House, Grand Rapids, Michigan. Price: $9.95).

This is a photolithoprinted edition of the well known work originally published by Scribner's in 1931. The binding, though stout and serviceable, lacks the sumptuous appearance of the original. The format has been reduced; but the print is admirably clear. The transformation of what were originally photographic plates into ordinary illustrations has resulted in some loss of sharpness. But the volume remains a fine example of book production. In spite of all the water that has flowed under historical and archaeological bridges since 1931, the reappearance of this important work (even though it is without addition or alteration) is to be welcomed.

G.W.A.

ORLINSKY, H. M.: *The Challenge of Idolatry: The History and Tradition of Ancient Israel.* (in Japanese). 1961. Pp. vi + 245. (Kyobunkan, Tokyo. Price: Y. 400).

This is a Japanese edition of Dr. Orlinsky's book, *Ancient Israel*, reviewed in *Book List* 1954, p. 23 (*Eleven Years*, p. 560) and *Book List* 1961, p. 22. The translation was done by Prof. Masaki Kobayashi from the first edition, but he had access to the author's unpublished manuscript prepared for revision and made minor changes accordingly. There is a special preface to the Japanese edition by Dr. Orlinsky, whose life and work is introduced by the translator.

T.A.

TEXT AND VERSIONS

*AP-THOMAS, D. R.: *A Primer of Old Testament Text Criticism.* 1964. 2nd, revised edition. Pp. 50. (Basil Blackwell, Oxford. Price: 7s. 0d.).

This work, the first edition of which was reviewed in *Book List* 1948, p. 19 (*Eleven Years*, p. 129), is for students beginning the critical study of Hebrew texts. It contains all kinds of useful information about how the text has been transmitted: the canon, development of the script, how the vowel-system developed, how the text was standardized and what the Masoretes did, the kinds of errors that have crept into the text, and all the early versions. A useful, elementary book for the Old Testament class in schools and colleges.

N.H.S.

GOSHEN-GOTTSTEIN, M. H.: *The Book of Isaiah. Sample edition with Introduction.* (The Hebrew University Bible Project). 1965. Pp. 46 + 58 (in Hebrew). (Magnes Press, The Hebrew University, Jerusalem. Price: £4 10s. 0d.).

The text of four chapters of Isaiah (chs. ii, v, xi, and li) is printed in large type, reproducing the Aleppo codex, with the *massora magna* at the top of the page and *massora parva* on both side margins. The *apparatus criticus* is in four sections, which consist of: (I) The Versions, (II) The Scrolls from the Judean Desert and Rabbinic Literature, (III) Medieval Bible Manuscripts, and (IV) Spelling, vowels, and accents. The introductory matter, given in Hebrew and English, contains information which is relevant for the future use of the text as well as a presentation of the whole practice of textual criticism. The mass of information is formidable indeed, and supersedes any edition of the Hebrew Bible hitherto published. The work is contemporary both in its critical assessments and in the virtual absence of conjectural emendations. This precursor, therefore, is valuable *per se* and indispensable for the publication as a whole. It is a *must* for the Biblical scholar.

B.J.R.

MAY, H. G.: *Our English Bible in the Making: the Word of Life in Living Language*. Revised edition, 1965. Pp. 163. (Westminster Press, Philadelphia. Price: $3.95).

The first edition of this book was issued in 1952 concurrently with the publication of the Revised Standard Version. In its revised form it takes into account the further Qumran texts which have been published, the New English Bible (New Testament), the Catholic edition of the RSV, the Confraternity Version, and other translations, such as those of Phillips. It also includes a new section on the reception the RSV had during its first ten years. All of this makes a good book better, and renews the usefulness which the original edition was recognized to have (see *Book List* 1953, p. 27; *Eleven Years*, p. 480).

H.H.R.

RAHLFS, A.: *Septuaginta-Studien I–III*. 2 Auflage. Vermehrt um einen unveröffentlichten Aufsatz und eine Bibliographie mit einem Nachruf von Walter Bauer. 1965. Pp. 16 + 688 + 1 portrait. (Vandenhoeck & Ruprecht, Göttingen. Price: DM. 38).

We certainly welcome the re-publication, photomechanically processed, of Rahlfs' *Septuaginta-Studien*, *I–III*, long since unattainable and of fundamental importance for all students of the Septuagint. The three works consist of: *Studies in the Books of Kings* (1904); *The text of the LXX-Psalter, with the appendix, Greek Psalter fragments from Upper Egypt copied by W. E. Crum*, (1907); and *Lucian's recension of the Books of Kings* (1911). In addition, there is published for the first time an article by Rahlfs on the Ethiopic version. Professor J. Jeremias supplies a Foreword, and an obituary on Rahlfs, by Walter Bauer (first published in 1935 in *N.G.G. Jahresbericht*), gives a clear assessment of Rahlfs' contribution. Finally, a bibliography of Rahlfs' works, assembled by K. Hasenfuss, cannot but be of great convenience to the expert.

B.J.R.

SOISALON-SOININEN, I.: *Die Infinitive in der Septuaginta*. (Suomalaisen Tiedeakatemian Toimituksia, Annales Academiae Scientiarum Fennicae. Ser. B. Tom. 132, 1). 1965. Pp. 230. (Helsinki. Suomalainen Tiedeakatemia).

This workmanlike examination of the LXX renderings of the Hebrew Infinitive Construct falls into two main sections. Firstly, various Hebrew Infinitives, alone and with prepositions, and the corresponding Greek renderings, are classified. A subsection deals with Greek Infinitives which are not present in Hebrew. Secondly, inner-Greek variations are considered as they are reflected in different manuscripts, and, again in subsections, the evidence of canonical and apocryphal books and of Aquila, Symmachus, and Theodotion is assessed. Incidentally, other fascinating problems are discussed, e.g., the relevance of the data for the hypothesis of different translators functioning in individual books, as in Jeremiah and Ezekiel. The author works cautiously; and possibly this is reflected in the rather negative conclusions of the book as a whole; but he shows how even leading scholars of the past were too daring in presenting hypotheses on partial evidence. The book is to be highly commended for use by all Septuagint students.

B.J.R.

TALMON, S. (ed. by): *Textus. Annual of the Hebrew University Bible Project.* Vol. IV. 1964. Pp. 231 + 12 (Hebrew). (Magnes Press, The Hebrew University, Jerusalem. Price: 43s. 0d.).

This volume, dedicated to the late Professor Kahle, opens with a study by L. Lipschütz of Michael b. Uzziel's treatise (*Kitab al-Khilaf*) on the differences between Ben Asher and Ben Naphtali. G. E. Weil discusses some new fragments of the *Massora magna* of the Targum of the Pentateuch, and in a second contribution he opposes M. F. Martin's conclusion concerning the palaeographical character of Codex Neofiti 1. A. Dothan writes on the various stages in the transmission of the text of the chapter in *Diqduqe ha-Ṭeʿamim* which deal with the minor *gaʿya*, and on the evolution in the application of the minor *gaʿya*. G. R. Driver assembles further examples of abbreviations in the MT and in other texts. S. Talmon discusses aspects of the textual transmission of the Old Testament in the light of the Qumran manuscripts. P. Wernberg-Møller considers the contribution of the *Hodayot* to the textual criticism of the Old Testament and notes especially the comparatively large number of allusions to the book of Isaiah. B. Kedar-Kopfstein examines divergent Hebrew readings in Jerome's Isaiah, and concludes that in his time there existed more divergency in Hebrew Old Testament texts than is commonly supposed. Y. Ratzahbi rejects the Saadian authorship of the Arabic *tafsir* to the Song of Deborah. D. Flusser surveys all the ancient texts in which the seventh commandment precedes the sixth; both orders are well attested in the period of the Second Temple. M. H. Goshen-Gottstein lists fourteen fragments as yet unpublished of the Syrohexapla. A one-page report of the Bible Project 1960–64 is presented, and there are the usual short summaries in Hebrew of the articles.

D.W.T.

WEIL, G. E.: *Initiation à la massorah. L'introduction au Sépher Zikhronōt d'Élie Lévita.* 1964. Pp. XI + 86. (E. J. Brill, Leiden. Price: Fl. 8).

The major part of the book outlines the life story and work of Elias Levita, and the history of Massoretic development. Levita's period A.D. 1469/70 to 1541 were fateful years in the history of the textual transmission, what with the publications of the Bomberg press, the Babylonian Talmud, Levita's *Massoreth ha Massoreth*, and other works. The outline of the history of the Massorah is no less interesting, dwelling on the development of the grammarians, the Tiberian and Babylonian vocalizations, and the study of the earlier vocalic systems. The second part gives a translation of Levita's Introduction to *Sepher Zikhronōth.* The background for the present work is the larger study by Professor Weil, *Élie Lévita, humaniste et massorète,* Leiden, 1963; and its relevance for the projected fourth edition of *Biblia Hebraica* cannot be over-estimated.

B.J.R.

YADIN, Y.: *The Ben Sira Scroll from Masada*. With Introduction, Emendations and Commentary. (Trans. & Reprinted from *Eretz-Israel*, Vol. 8). 1965. Pp. 49 + 45 (Hebrew) + 9 plates. (The Israel Exploration Society and The Shrine of the Book, Jerusalem. Price: $6.00).

Scholars will be very grateful to Yadin for the prompt and erudite edition of the twenty-six leather fragments found in Masada, comprising chapters xxxix; xxvii–xliii; xxx of Ben Sira in the original Hebrew version, copied not later than 73 B.C. This copy of Ben Sira, which is the oldest of all MSS extant, confirms the view that the well-known MSS discovered in the Cairo Genizah, in spite of the many corruptions they embody, fundamentally represent the original Hebrew version. Yadin's scrutiny of the relationship which exists between the various Genizah MSS. themselves as well as between them and the *Vorlage* used by the Greek and the Syriac translators is of special importance.

M.W.

ZIEGLER, J. (ed. by): *Sapientia Jesu Filii Sirach*. (Septuaginta. Vetus Testamentum Graecum, vol. XII, 2). 1965. Pp. 368. (Vandenhoeck & Ruprecht, Göttingen. Price: Paper, DM. 58, by subscription, DM. 50; cloth, DM. 62, by subscription, DM. 54).

The first fascicle of this volume (Wisdom of Solomon) was published in 1962 (cf. *Book List* 1963, p. 21), and with the appearance of the present volume we have an idea of the immense industry and success with which Professor Ziegler manages to fulfil his task. The Society takes this opportunity of greeting Professor Ziegler, and rejoicing in his recovery after a period of indifferent health.

The text of Ecclesiasticus is a well-known challenge to LXX specialists, and the editor has duly acknowledged the fact with characteristic humility. Detailed discussions are included in the 120 pages of introduction, and the editor's dependence on the earlier critical edition of Rahlfs (cf. p. 47) is explained.

One remarkable omission must be noted. There is no reference here to the Qumrân text of Ecclus. li. 13 ff. (cf. J. A. Sanders: *The Psalms Scroll of Qumrân Cave II*, reviewed elsewhere in the present *Book List*), and it is regrettable that two such standard works should have been produced under such conditions of mutual exclusiveness.

B.J.R.

EXEGESIS AND MODERN TRANSLATIONS

BRIGHT, J.: *Jeremiah*. Introduction, Translation, and Notes. (The Anchor Bible, 21). 1965. Pp. CXLIV + 372. (Doubleday, New York. Price: $7.00).

The Introduction gives a brief but useful account of Israelite prophecy, the historical background of Jeremiah's ministry in which the traditional date is accepted, and a clear account of the 'types'—prophetical oracles in poetry, prose discourses, and biographical material, each of which has its own history of transmission. The oracles are mainly Jeremianic, the biographical material is from an intimate of the prophet (? Baruch); the prose while not the *ipsissima verra* of Jeremiah, represents his teaching as remembered by his followers. The translation seeks to convey the equivalent effect, short of paraphrase, rather than a word-for-word rendering. 'Thou', etc., are retained for direct address to Yahweh. Perhaps a translator of i.17: 'Don't lose your nerve' could have found a modern equivalent for ix.2: 'They bent their tongue like a bow'. Of the foreign oracles, only those against Egypt and Philistia can confidently be assigned to Jeremiah. Textual and exegetical notes are attached to the translation. Use is made of the versions (mainly LXX) and conjecture. This will be a useful addition to the literature in English on Jeremiah.

A.S.H.

CUNLIFFE-JONES, H.: *Jeremiah*. Introduction and Commentary. (Torch Bible Paperbacks). 1965. Pp. 288. (S.C.M. Press, London. Price: 13s. 6d.).

This is an unchanged re-issue in paperback of the commentary which was first published in 1960 (See *Book List* 1961, p. 29).

R.E.C.

DAHOOD, M.: *Psalms I (1–50)*. Introduction, Translation, and Notes. (The Anchor Bible, 16). 1966. Pp. XLVI + 330. (Doubleday, New York. Price: $6.00).

'The present work is not a commentary on the Psalms in the traditional sense of word' (p. XVII). Thus there is no systematic discussion of such questions as the form, subject-matter, purpose, and date of each psalm; and no attempt has been made to comment on every point of interest in the individual verses; moreover, many matters that would normally be discussed in the introduction have been postponed to the second volume. The primary purpose is, rather, to give 'a translation and philological commentary which utilizes the linguistic information offered by the Ras Shamra tablets' (p. XVII). Since 'A significant corollary of Ugaritic studies will be the devaluation of the ancient versions' (p. XXIV), little is said of them in the commentary. With indefatigable ingenuity and great enthusiasm, Fr. Dahood makes a large number of new suggestions; for example, he maintains (in this case, without the support of Ugaritic) that *ṣedeḳ and ṣedeḳa* can mean 'meadow' and that, where this meaning is found in Ps. v.9, xxiii.3, xxxvi.11 and several other verses of the Old Testament, there is a reference to life after death, pictured as the Elysian Fields. Fr. Dahood's suggestions are often controversial and, as he himself says, 'To claim that the present application of this new information to the biblical text is judicious in every instance would be patently absurd' (p. XLII). The application of the method in a thoroughgoing, and even extreme, way to one book may be welcomed by students of the Old Testament, because it gives them the opportunity of judging how far it is successful. Yet it may be doubted whether *The Anchor Bible* was the right place to try out the experiment, since it is intended for 'the general reader with no special formal training in biblical studies' who will be unable to understand the philological notes and who may sometimes find it difficult to distinguish between views generally accepted by scholars and opinions held, as yet, only by Fr. Dahood.

J.A.E.

DENTAN, R. C.: *I & II Kings, I & II Chronicles*. (The Layman's Bible Commentaries). 1965. Pp. 156. (S.C.M. Press, London. Price: 6s. 0d.).

Within the scope of the series this is an admirable introduction to Kings and Chronicles, generally well informed in literary criticism and historical and archaeological background, none of the major problems being omitted, but nothing distracting from the presentation of the books according to the intention of the Deuteronomic and Priestly (Levitical) historians. Kings is presented rather in the style of paraphrase in a lucid fashion apt to engage the layman and less advanced student and presenting a wealth of expository information in the most unobtrusive fashion. In Chronicles the treatment is designedly less full, the writer noting more fully adaptations of matter common to Kings, with additions and omissions for which he notes the reasons. The difference between the two works is felicitously characterized: Kings is a news-reel with commentary; Chronicles scenes in stained glass.
J.G.

FÜGLISTER, N.: *Das Psalmengebet*. 1965. Pp. 168. (Kösel-Verlag, München. Price: DM. 9.80).

This is a series of seven lectures on the devotional use of the Psalms, its main theme being that the fact that they are poetry must never be lost sight of when they are read, recited, sung or otherwise used as prayer forms. To this end the author is not concerned with textual criticism or historical exegesis—he tends to set them aside as of very secondary significance—but urges the Christian user of the Psalms to try to identify himself with the mind and mood of the *divinely* inspired author and to accept the possibility that he may never be (nor does he need to be) able to give a meaning to every phrase in itself.
L.H.B.

GERLEMAN, G.: *Ruth/Das Hohelied*. (Biblischer Kommentar, Altes Testament, XVIII, 3). 1965. Pp. 121–235. (Neukirchener Verlag des Erziehungsvereins, Neukirchen-Vluyn. Price: DM. 11.55).

With this part the commentary on Ruth and the Song of Songs (see *Book List* 1962, pp. 27 f., and 1964, pp. 33 f.) is complete. We have here the commentary on Ca. ii. 8–viii. 14. As in all the volumes of the series a full-scale commentary is supplied, each section being given in an original German translation, with full textual notes, followed by a general discussion of the form and place of the section and a verse by verse exegetical commentary. A wide range of modern literature is drawn on, and the work is both up-to-date and indispensable to students of the Song. The individual poems are interpreted as love-songs, not all wedding-songs and not a connected succession. The view that Shulammite means Shunamite is rejected, and also that the name is connected with Solomon. Instead it is suggested that it is a passive participial form with feminine ending. In iii. 10 for 'paved with love' the reading 'laid with stones' is substituted and Driver's rendering 'upholstered with leather' is unmentioned.
H.H.R.

GOLDBERG, A. M.: *Genesis–Exodus*. (Die Heilige Schrift des Alten Testaments, Band I). 1964. Pp. 212. (Verlag Herder, Freiburg. Price: by subscription, DM. 19.80).

This is the first volume of a new translation of the Old Testament into German. The book is divided as follows: Genesis, Translation, pp. 15–102 followed by a brief Introduction to the Pentateuch and then to Genesis, pp. 103–112. Brief comments on Genesis, pp. 113–123. A similar pattern follows for Exodus. The work is therefore mainly a modern and readable translation with very brief comments.   G.H.D.

GORDIS, R.: *The Book of God and Man. A Study of Job*. 1966. Pp. x + 390. (The University of Chicago Press, Chicago and London. Price: 63s. 0d.).

This exposition of Job falls into two parts, the first containing sixteen studies on various problems in and aspects of the book (pp. 1–228) and the second a translation of the text with summaries of the contents of each section (pp. 229–306), followed by a list of abbreviations and notes explaining and justifying the translation, with ample references to current literature (pp. 307–366); and the whole work is brought to a conclusion with a bibliography and indices (pp. 367–389). The author shows a deep understanding of Hebrew modes of thought and expression and makes a number of very interesting suggestions. He is convinced of the unity of the whole poem but seems to press his case too far, e.g., in defending the authenticity of the hymn on Wisdom by arguing that it is a work of the author's early days and of the speeches of Elihu by ascribing them to the same author's old age (pp. 102–3, 110–15). His arguments, too, are not always logical, e.g., that the discovery of a fragment of the Hebrew Text of Qoheleth at Qumrân proves that the work was not originally written in the Aramaic language (p. 360); it proves nothing of the sort. The references to 'pages' and 'sheets' of the original Job (pp. 93, 102) are unhappy; for books in page-form were not invented till the Christian era. The translation reads extremely well, although some of the renderings will raise doubts: e.g., *'ôn*, 'son' and *ṣēlā* 'wife' (p. 150), although one can easily see how they have been reached. Occasionally it is ungrammatical, e.g., in having 'he' where grammar requires 'him' (p. 113, l. 9 from bottom); and some of the expressions used in it are infelicitous, e.g., 'God speeches' for 'God's speeches' (*passim*), 'locales' (presumably an Americanism) and 'frightened limbs' (p. 240, l. 12). One very good point which the author makes is in drawing attention to the Hebrew habit of changing speakers without any introductory phrase to help the reader; for the failure to recognize this often puzzling practice has led to much needless emendation (see *Z.A.W.* LXXVIII 1–7). The author's outlook is Jewish, and this has enabled him to see much that others have missed; consequently the book, even though occasional blemishes may be noticed (and these may often be such only in the eyes of a hypercritical reviewer) is one which no student of Job ought to overlook.   G.R.D.

GRISPINO, J. A.: *The Old Testament of the Holy Bible in the Confraternity Edition.* 1965. Pp. xiii + 1802, incl. 23 maps, charts, and tables. (Guild Press, New York. Price: $1.50).

This is a gallant attempt to produce the Old Testament in a paperback by making all possible use of the Confraternity Version sponsored by the Episcopal Committee of the Confraternity of Christian Doctrine. Of its 1802 pages rather less than a third (538) prints the Douay text; all the remainder is taken from the new version. The sections from Genesis to Ruth, Job to Sirach, and the prophetical books are from the Confraternity version. The portions from 1 Samuel to Esther, as well as 1 and 2 Machabees, follow the Douay. Grispino has added a good deal in the way of introductory matter and notes. There are a few maps and a sketch of the Hebrew idea of the world; also a 'tree of Jesse' that is no improvement on the one in Christchurch Priory, Hants. The print is small, but quite readable.

J.M.T.B.

HEATON, E. W.: *Daniel.* (Torch Bible Paperback). 1966. Pp. 252. (S.C.M. Press, London. Price: 12s. 6d.).

This is an unchanged reprint of the commentary which first appeared in 1956. See *Book List* 1956, p. 30; *Eleven Years*, p. 737.

R.E.C.

The Holy Bible, Revised Standard Version: Old and New Testaments together with the Apocrypha of the Old Testament. With an Introduction to the Apocrypha by H. H. Rowley. 1965. Pp. x + 1068 + xii + 212. (Thomas Nelson, Edinburgh. Price: 25s. 0d.).

It is convenient to have Old Testament, New Testament and Apocrypha in one volume of medium size. This has been achieved without sacrifice of legibility, for the print is clear and the paper not too thin. The system of indicating the stressed syllable in proper names has been extended to the Apocrypha. Professor Rowley contributes nine pages of introduction on the origin and significance of the Apocrypha, which will greatly help the general reader to understand the nature of the books, the light they shed on an important period of Jewish history, and their value for the study of both the Old and New Testaments.

W.D.McH.

KISSANE, E. J.: *The Book of Psalms translated from a critically revised Hebrew text with a commentary.* 1964 (reprint). Pp. xliv + 656. (Browne & Nolan, Dublin. Price: 55s. 0d.).

This work was originally published in two volumes in 1953 (see *Book List* 1953, pp. 37 f.; *Eleven Years*, pp. 490 f.) and 1954 (see *Book List* 1955, p. 34; *Eleven Years*, p. 667) respectively. Its reissue in one volume is to be welcomed, the more so since, not withstanding inflation, it now costs five shillings less than before.

G.W.A.

KNIGHT, G. A. F.: *Deutero-Isaiah*. A Theological Commentary on Isaiah 40–55. 1965. Pp. 284. (Abingdon Press, New York and Nashville. Price: $5.50).

The Prophet is seen as a 'theological giant' of the exilic period who insists 'that the living Word of the living God began to be united with the very flesh of God's son Israel at that specific period'. The book contains a translation, exegesis, and theological interpretation. The translation is vivid though at times somewhat free; one may question, for example, xl. 6: 'All flesh is grass, and lasts no longer than the wild flowers', which seems to miss the point of *ḥesedh*, as does the comment 'the *ḥesedh* of nature is to die'. The Servant Songs are not treated separately but as an integral part of the setting in which they are found. Thus the Servant is, throughout the chapters, Israel or the Israel that is to be. The book will be welcomed for its deeply religious and often eloquent theological interpretation and will meet the needs of the non-specialist. It should be read, as indeed the author suggests, alongside a critical commentary; a selected bibliography up to 1963 is added at the end of the book.   A.S.H.

KNIGHT, G. A. F.: *Ruth and Jonah: the Gospel in the Old Testament*. (Torch Bible Paperback). Revised ed. 1966. Pp. 94. (S.C.M. Press, London. Price: 6s. 6d.).

This is a reprint in paperback, with some minor revisions, of the commentary which first appeared in 1950. (See *Book List* 1951, p. 39; *Eleven Years*, p. 334).   R.E.C.

KNIGHT, G. A. F.: *Hosea: God's Love*. (Torch Bible Paperback). 1966. Pp. 128. (S.C.M. Press, London. Price: 7s. 6d.).

This is an unchanged reprint of the commentary which first appeared in 1960. (See *Book List* 1960, pp. 19 f.).   R.E.C.

MARSH, J.: *Amos and Micah*. Introduction and Commentary. (Torch Bible Paperbacks). 1965. Pp. 128. (S.C.M. Press, London. Price: 7s. 6d.).

This is an unchanged re-issue in paperback of the commentary which first appeared in 1959. (See *Book List* 1960, p. 21).

R.E.C.

MINN, H. R.: *The Servant Songs*. Excerpts from Isaiah 42–53. Introduction, Translation and Commentary. 1966. Pp. 34. (Presbyterian Bookroom, Christchurch, New Zealand. Price: 9s. 0d.).

In this brief exposition the Servant is treated as a fluid concept and so applicable to 'the person of the Mediator of salvation arising out of Israel'. The treatment of MT is conservative, though occasional references are made to DSI, notably at liii. 11 —'In consequence of his mortal suffering he will see light'; transliteration of Hebrew words is sometimes confusing; '*aleph* and '*ayin* are not reproduced except at liii. 8. Since this is a limited edition (475 copies) it may not be available in the Northern hemisphere.   A.S.H.

MYERS, J. M.: *1 Chronicles*. Introduction, Translation, and Notes. (The Anchor Bible, 12). 1965. Pp. XCIV + 242. (Doubleday, N.Y. Price: $6.00).

II Chronicles. (The Anchor Bible, 13). 1965. Pp. XXXVI + 270. (Doubleday, N.Y. Price: $6.00).

It is a matter for satisfaction that the same author will be commenting on Ezra, Nehemiah in volume 14 of this series, and that the work of the Chronicler is thus being given unified treatment. But each volume is separate, although a much longer introduction is given in the first of these volumes, while the second provides as appendices a full analysis of the parallels to the text of both books and a set of genealogical tables. The substantial bibliography appears in both. As in other volumes of the series, the text is newly translated and it reads well. There are short, useful textual notes with many references to the literature, and sensible comments on the content. The rehabilitation of the Chronicler is here carried a stage further, and if the historical survey in the introduction is somewhat over-simplified, the appreciation of the Chronicler's theological position is a useful contribution to seeing his work for its own sake and not as a mere appendage to the earlier Old Testament historical books.

P.R.A.

MYERS, J. M.: *Ezra, Nehemiah*. Introduction, Translation, and Notes. (The Anchor Bible, 14). 1965. Pp. LXXXIV + 268. (Doubleday, New York. Price: $6.00).

This excellent volume has a valuable introduction (which includes a good historical survey of the period from the beginning of the exile and a review of modern critical work on these books) followed by an original translation of the Hebrew and Aramaic text, accompanied by brief verse by verse notes and longer notes on each of the sections into which Professor Myers divides the books. Apart from the introduction the main value of the commentary lies in these longer notes. The authenticity of the Cyrus edict is recognised, Ezra is placed after Nehemiah but in the reign of Artaxerxes I, Ezra's lawbook is held to be the completed Pentateuch, and Ezra is held to have been the author of Chronicles-Ezra-Nehemiah and to have written circa 400 B.C. While the reviewer would not subscribe to all of these positions, he pays tribute to the careful study of all the many problems attaching to these books and to the author's acquaintance with recent literature as well as the older works, and welcomes this volume as the best available English commentary on these books.

H.H.R.

PLÖGER, O.: *Das Buch Daniel*. (Kommentar zum Alten Testament, Band XVIII). 1965. Pp. 184. (Gerd Mohn, Gütersloh. Price: DM. 28).

After a brief Introduction Plöger gives an original translation, with full linguistic and textual notes, and exegetical commentary and general discussion of each section. On critical problems the author accepts the unity of the book, with but short secondary passages, apart from the prayer in ch. ix, and places its composition in the time of Antiochus IV. He finds no Messianic significance in the figure of the Son of Man, in whom he finds a representation of Israel. In the main the author presents his own interpretation of the book, with but little discussion of other views. In the reviewer's opinion the views presented are sound and reliable, and with few exceptions he shares them. In a commentary of this length he would have liked to see fuller discussion of some of the problems on which all critical scholars are not agreed.

H.H.R.

POPE, M. H.: *Job*. Introduction, Translation, and Notes. (The Anchor Bible). 1965. Pp. LXXXII + 294. (Doubleday, New York. Price: $6.00).

Every additional help towards the understanding of the book of Job is to be welcomed. Though the series to which this volume belongs is aimed at the general reader, Professor Pope has produced a commentary which theological students will find very useful, especially for the full references to modern discoveries and recent writing. The introduction is restrained and cautious, the translation is characterized by the attempt to put over to the non-Hebraist the poetic features of the original, and the notes are a judicious mixture of exegesis and technical, mainly linguistic, comment. It is no reflection on the book to say that it supplements rather than displaces the older classic commentaries.

W.D.McH.

PORTEOUS, N. W.: *Daniel: a Commentary*. (The Old Testament Library). 1965. Pp. 174. (S.C.M. Press, London. Price: 30s. 0d.).

The German edition of this book was reviewed in the *Book List* 1963, p. 27. For this English edition the translation of RSV has been substituted for the author's original translation, with the indication of significant differences in notes. The outstanding value of this commentary was recognised in the earlier review. Its scholarship is beyond reproach, though it is not primarily concerned with the minutiae of literary or historical criticism. Above all it seeks to bring out the value of the book of Daniel for the reader today, and this it does in a most excellent way.

H.H.R.

RYLAARSDAM, J. C.: *Proverbs, Ecclesiastes, Song of Solomon*. (The Layman's Bible Commentaries). 1965. Pp. 160. (S.C.M. Press, London; John Knox Press, Richmond, Virginia; Ryerson Press, Toronto. Price: 6s. 0d.).

The value of this small commentary is disproportionate to its size. Not only does it fulfil the purpose of the series as 'a concise non-technical guide', but it provides much also to interest and stimulate the more advanced reader. Problems of introduction are simply outlined with many a shrewd observation. Resourceful though unobtrusive scholarship characterizes the interpretation of the text and the application of its meaning to current situations. The distinctive emphases of each book are indicated with judgement and sensitivity, and the question of their relationship to each other is briefly considered.

E.T.R.

SCOTT, R. B. Y.: *Proverbs, Ecclesiastes*. Introduction, Translation, and Notes. (The Anchor Bible, 18). 1965. Pp. LIV + 258. (Doubleday, New York. Price: $6.00).

In accordance with the pattern of *The Anchor Bible*, which 'is aimed at the general reader with no special formal training in biblical studies', this volume contains a new translation of Proverbs and Ecclesiastes with introductions and notes; the comments are usually brief, although important passages such as Prov. viii are discussed at greater length. There is also a general introduction which examines Israel's Wisdom literature as a whole and its relation to similar literatures of other countries. The book contains much that is valuable, but attention can here be drawn only to two points of interest. First, Prov. viii is thought to contain no more than a poetic personification of wisdom; *ḳanani* in verse 22 is rendered 'possessed', and the puzzling third word of verse 30 is pointed *'omen* and understood to mean 'binding [all] together'. Secondly, although the introduction does not discuss in detail the unity of Ecclesiastes, Dr. Scott makes it plain there and in the notes that he regards it as substantially the work of one writer who sometimes quotes older proverbs; but the presence of occasional later additions is also recognized.

J.A.E.

SPEISER, E. A.: *Genesis*. Introduction, Translation, and Notes. (The Anchor Bible, 1). 1964. Pp. LXXVI + 378. (Doubleday, Garden City, New York. Price: $6.00).

The freshness, grace, and vigour of the translation in this commentary are an index to the quality of the entire work. If all the volumes of the Anchor Bible prove to be in the same class of excellence, it will indeed be a notable series. In the introduction a brief sketch is given of the sources and of the antecedent tradition. The material is assigned to the three familiar main sources, J, E, P, but without either too precise analysis or further refinement into additional sources, though a 'Residue' is recognized which cannot be assigned to any of the three. J and E are held to be distinct sources, dependent on a prior oral tradition (T). P is held to be the work of a school whose activity lasted from early till post-exilic times. In both the introduction and the commentary, expert and judicious use is made of the extra-Biblical material, particularly the Hurrian. The commentary conveys a rich store of learning with great economy and clarity of language. The entire work is a masterpiece of interpretation and a fitting crown to the scholarly labours of its lamented author.

G.W.A.

WILDBERGER, H.: *Jesaja* (Biblischer Kommentar, Altes Testament, X, Lieferung 1). 1965. Pp. 1–80. (Verlag der Buchhandlung des Erziehungsvereins, Neukirchen–Vluyn. Price: DM. 7.75).

The first fascicle of this commentary by Professor Wildberger of Zürich deals with Isa. i. 1–ii. 5. It is clearly written, balanced in judgement, and based on an extensive knowledge of the relevant literature. Among much that is interesting, several points deserve special mention. Dr. Wildberger holds, with many modern writers, that i. 2–3 shows affinities with vassal-treaties, and he does not rule out the possibility that it has a cultic background, though Isaiah is not therefore to be regarded as a cultic prophet. He also maintains that i. 11 ff. does not contain an absolute condemnation of sacrifice, and that ii. 2–5 is probably Isaianic. Old Testament scholars will look forward to further fascicles of this valuable commentary.   J.A.E.

WOLFF, H. W.: *Dodekapropheton, 1: Hosea.* (Biblischer Kommentar, Altes Testament. XIV, Lief. 1–3). Zweite, verbesserte und ergänzte Auflage. 1965. Pp. XXXII + 322. (Verlag der Buchhandlung des Erziehungsvereins, Neukirchen, Kr. Moers. Price: DM. 40.80).

The first edition of this commentary was reviewed in *Book List* 1957, p. 35; 1958, p. 24 and 1962, pp. 33 f. For this second edition numerous detailed revisions and improvements have been made and the bibliographies brought up to date.   R.E.C.

YOUNG, E. J.: *The Book of Isaiah*, Vol. i, Chapters i–xviii. (The New International Commentary on the Old Testament). 1965. Pp. xii + 534. (Eerdmans, Grand Rapids, Michigan. Price: $7.95).

Professor Young is one of the ablest and best known of conservative writers on the Old Testament. The present volume is the first of three which will contain his commentary on Isaiah in the series of Old Testament commentaries, of which he is the General Editor. It contains an original translation of the text, and a very full verse by verse and phrase by phrase commentary, with many special notes in smaller type. The brevity of the introduction is in marked contrast with the fullness of the commentary. The author maintains the unity of the entire book of Isaiah and is conservative on textual questions. This does not mean that his work is without value for readers who do not share his approach. Professor Young is a scholar who is widely acquainted with views he does not share, and his work is a *vade mecum* of views which he accepts and rejects, and few will not learn from it or fail to find it valuable for consultation. There are three appendixes, one of which is devoted to a rejection of the theory of an Enthronement Festival in Israel in the various forms that have been proposed. A fine bibliography closes the volume.   H.H.R.

ZIMMERLI, W: *Ezechiel.* (Biblischer Kommentar, Altes Testament, XIII, Lieferung 12). 1965. Pp. 899–978. (Neukirchener Verlag des Erziehungsvereins, Neukirchen–Vluyn. Price: DM. 7.75).

This fascicle begins with the closing sections of the treatment of xxxvii and ends with the first three pages of the bibliography and introduction to xl–xlviii. Thus the bulk of it is devoted to the difficult pericope on Gog. After a careful textual and structural analysis, the conclusion is reached that the earliest form of the pericope was xxxviii, 1–9 (with minor excisions); xxxix, 1–5, 17–20, and that this core of material has been expanded in such a way as to emphasize some features in it and add others. The antecedents of the pericope are traced in earlier prophecies about a foe from the north (in Jeremiah) and about the destruction of Israel's enemies and their weapons on the mountains of Israel, or more specifically on Mount Zion (in Isaiah). A survey of views about the identity of Gog ends with a cautious and qualified approval of the equation with Gyges, and thus of Magog with Lydia. On grounds of style and content Zimmerli is disposed to hold that the core of the pericope may have originated with Ezekiel himself. In its valuable surveys of earlier discussions and its painstaking and penetrating treatment of the text this fascicle is of the same high quality as those which have previously appeared and whets the appetite for what is still to come.

G.W.A.

LITERARY CRITICISM AND INTRODUCTION

(including History of Interpretation, Canon, and Special Studies)

ANDERSON, G. W.: *Enemies and Evildoers in the Book of Psalms.* (Reprinted from the Bulletin of the John Rylands Library, vol. 48, No. 1, Autumn, 1965). 1965. Pp. 18–29. (The John Rylands Library, Manchester. Price: 3s. 0d.).

In this Rylands lecture, adapted in part from lectures delivered last year in Sweden, Professor Anderson surveys certain modern interpretations of ancient Hebrew psalmody and some criticisms levelled against them. After a brief review of the work of Smend, Rahlfs, and Gunkel, Dr. Anderson devotes the greater part of his space to Mowinckel and his critics, particularly Mowinckel's own disciple, Harris Birkeland, whose researches had persuaded Mowinckel to modify his position. The study ends with a wise caution against inflexibility of approach and overstatement of results, and a hint that the lecturer will return to this theme of width of interpretation in studying enemies and evildoers in the Psalter.

W.D.McH.

BEYERLIN, W.: *Origins and History of the Oldest Sinaitic Traditions,* trans. by S. Rudman. 1965. Pp. xviii + 192. (Basil Blackwell, Oxford. Price: 37s. 6d.).

This book was originally published in German in 1961 and was reviewed in *Book List* 1962, p. 30. It was immediately recognized as a work of outstanding importance in the debate about Israel's historical and religious origins which centres round the views

of scholars like Noth and von Rad. S. Rudman has done a service by making this scholarly and indeed exciting book more widely available. Professor G. W. Anderson underlines its significance in a foreword.
N.W.P.

BLACKWOOD, A. W.. Jr.: *Ezekiel. Prophecy of Hope*. 1965. Pp. 274. (Baker Book House, Grand Rapids, Michigan. Price: $4.50).

This is a popular and lively book. After a foreword in which the author protests, and rightly, against the cavalier handling of the book in recent, especially American, scholarship, (H. H. Rowley's study in *B.J.R.L.*, September 1953, is not mentioned), the book is divided into two parts 'The Prophecy of Judgement' pp. 35–164 and 'The Prophecy of Hope' pp. 165–274. The author shows good knowledge of LXX and of the rabbinical and modern commentaries. The book stands beside, but does not replace, W. F. Lofthouse's study *Ezekiel, the Prophet of Reconstruction*, without Lofthouse's insight into the conception of idolatry, and without a proper understanding of Ezekiel's dumbness, which is here spiritually interpreted. The author appears to be aware of the textual, literary, and historical problems with which the book abounds; but inevitably the treatment is superficial, although he strikes a strongly religious note in his exposition.

G.H.D.

BOECKER, H. J.: *Redeformen des Rechtslebens im Alten Testament*. (Wissenschaftliche Monographien zum Alten und Neuen Testament, Band 14). 1964. Pp. 182. (Neukirchener Verlag des Erziehungs-vereins, Neukirchen-Vluyn. Price: cloth, D.M. 19.80; paper, DM. 17.80).

This dissertation examines the stereotyped forms of speech used in Israelite legal proceedings. It distinguishes three major groups of formal speech making. The first took place before a lawsuit was actually established, raising an accusation that a crime had been committed, seeking to avert a court case on the part of the accused, and summoning a legal assembly. The second group were speeches made before an assembled court, pressing the accusation and making a defence against it. The third group concerned the conclusion of proceedings; the passing of sentence and consequences further to this. Boecker adds a fourth section dealing with speeches in civil proceedings con-cerning family and property laws. There are useful semantic notes on YKḤ, *hôšî'â*, ZKR; and the study is particularly helpful in its examination of the use by the prophets of speech-forms rooted in Israel's legal practice.
R.E.C.

BRUNO, A.: *Alttestamentliche Texträtsel und Strophische Analyse*. Paralipomena zu den Büchern Genesis-Exodus, Josua, Richter, Samuel, Könige. Biographische Einleitung von Kurt Wilhelm. 1965. Pp. 232 + 1 portrait. (Almqvist & Wiksell, Stockholm. Price: Sw.Kr. 22).

The late Dr. Bruno's studies of the text of various books of the Old Testament have already been noticed in *Book List* 1954, pp. 45 f. (*Eleven Years*, pp. 582 f.); 1955, p. 31 (*Eleven Years*, p. 664); 1956, p. 26 (*Eleven Years*, p. 733); and 1957, p. 29. The present volume consists of a collection of various passages, almost wholly in the prose narrative in German translation arranged so far as possible to indicate the rhythm of the original according to the principles applied by Dr. Bruno, who recognizes only one heavy beat in each word. The expansions to, and omissions from, the MT which he proposes in agreement with his somewhat mechanical principle, while occasionally feasible, are generally arbitrary, especially in narrative prose. Of the various emendations, conjectural and otherwise, some are quite feasible, but in the total want of notes their value is lost.   J.G.

CARLSON, R. A.: *David, the Chosen King*. A Traditio-Historical Approach to the Second Book of Samuel, trans. by E. J. Sharpe and S. Rudman (notes). 1964. Pp. 304. (Almqvist & Wiksell, Uppsala. Price: Sw.Kr. 30).

The author of this book has provided us with a fine example of the traditio-historical approach to the Old Testament. In the introduction he gives a clear statement of the aims of this type of criticism. We are told that it 'includes the examination of the historical background of a particular tradition in its thematic, ideological and form-critical aspects, and its relation to that background'. Then the remainder of the book is an application of this method to the contents of 2 Samuel. In its present form this Biblical book is to be regarded as the work of the Deuteronomists. Their main aim in presenting the material was to bring the historical David into line with the ideal king as described in Deut. xvii. 14–20. Throughout this presentation can be detected the Deuteronomic emphasis upon obedience, disobedience, judgement, repentance, and deliverance. This is clearly brought out in Carlson's book under the headings given to the three main chapters, viz., (1) David under the blessing (a study of 2 Samuel ii–vii), (2) David under the curse (a study of 2 Samuel ix–xxiv), and (3) David and the hidden future. The text of 2 Samuel is carefully examined; and thus the book will prove valuable to the textual critic, as well as supplying a good example of traditio-historical criticism.   E.R.R.

DONNER, H.: *Israel unter den Völkern*. Die Stellung der klassischen Propheten des 8. Jahrhunderts v. Chr. zur Aussenpolitik der Könige von Israel und Juda. (Supplements to Vetus Testamentum, Vol. XI). 1964. Pp. XII + 194 incl. XX tables. (E. J. Brill, Leiden. Price: Fl. 36).

The subtitle defines the purpose of this book. It is an examination of the reaction of the Hebrew prophets to the political situations in the life of the nation. This the author does by confining himself to the study of a definite period in the history of Israel and Judah, viz., that which extends from 735 B.C. to 701 B.C. A clear and accurate review of the main events is given, but most of the book is an examination of specific oracles from the works of the eighth-century prophets. The title of the first chapter is 'The Syro-Ephraimite war', and passages from Isaiah vii, viii, x, xvii and

Hosea v, viii are considered against this background. In the second chapter, passages from Isaiah ix–x (+ v. 25–30), xxviii; Hosea vii, ix, xi, xii, and Micah i., are discussed in relation to the fall of the kingdom of Ephraim and the conquest of Samaria. The years 721–711 B.C. are called a 'Decade of revolt', and are related to passages from Isaiah xiv and xx. In the fourth chapter attention is concentrated upon the short period 705–701 B.C., which is called 'The Last Rebellion'. Selections from Isaiah i, xviii, xxii, xxx, and xxxi are examined in the light of this historical setting. Then there follows another chapter called 'Miscellanea', where other passages from Isaiah and Hosea are studied, because they may be considered as related to the historical period under consideration.

To the Hebrew prophets, the events of 735–701 B.C. were more than episodes in the history of the expansion of the new Assyrian Empire. They perceive in them the character of 'world history', history which derives its meaning and significance from Yahweh, the God of Israel. Before offering his interpretation of a passage, the author submits the text to a careful examination. At the end of the book is appended the reconstructed Hebrew text of most of the passages which have been considered.

E.R.R.

DRIJVERS, P.: *The Psalms: Their Structure and Meaning.* 1965. Pp. xiv + 270. (Herder, Freiburg. Burns & Oates, London. Price: 30s. 0d.).

Beginning with an account of the Psalter as used in Christian liturgical prayer, the author provides the general reader with an account of the origin of the Psalter in the light of modern study. The various types of psalms are described, and they are related not only to their ancient life-setting in Israel's liturgy but also to their new life-setting in the Church's liturgy; thus the enthronement psalms find their fulfilment 'in the life of the Church, in the inner loving presence of God to men of faith, in his indwelling in those living temples that are the faithful, in his real presence in the Eucharist compared to which the ark was no more than a faint shadow' (p. 182).

F.F.B.

EISSFELDT, O.: *The Old Testament. An Introduction,* including the Apocrypha and Pseudepigrapha, and also the works of similar type from Qumran. The History of the Formation of the Old Testament, trans. by P. R. Ackroyd. 1965. Pp. xxiv + 862. (Basil Blackwell, Oxford. Price: 70s. 0d.).

The contents of an Introduction may be expected to reflect dominant contemporary scholarly interests in the field of study which it introduces, be they historical, literary, liturgical, religious, theological, or other, as well as to follow traditional procedures as may be considered appropriate. But, as Professor Eissfeldt remarks, many of these interests are pursued in separate studies and published in separate books today. He takes as his main subject the growth of the canon, the history of the text and the origin of the individual books—the last of these taking by far the largest place. The result is a book of comprehensive and genuine scholarship and of well-balanced judgement, written with clarity and grace. The bibliography of the German

edition is itself comprehensive, but Peter R. Ackroyd, who has
provided this excellent English translation, has enhanced the
value of this bibliography, especially for the English reader, by
adding references to many recent publications in English. It
can be said without hesitation that this introduction will hold
a prominent place for many years to come.
A very minor point may be added. In future editions of the
book it is hoped that in the Hebrew form of the titles of certain
books and journals quoted in the Index of Abbreviations, the
Hebrew letters may be made to 'toe the line'.   J.M.

GERLEMAN, G.: *Studien zu Esther*. (Biblische Studien, 48). 1966. Pp. 48.
(Neukirchener Verlag des Erziehungsvereins, Neukirchen-Vluyn.
Price: DM. 4.20).

The most striking feature of these short studies is the detailed
comparison which Professor Gerleman makes between the
narratives of Esther and of the Exodus. In matters of style, of
personalities, and of narrative features he traces similarities, and
if some of the parallels are rather fanciful, the overall impression
is persuasive. He considers further the narrator's method and
his language, and finally assesses, more positively than many
scholars, the place of Esther in the canon. He describes the work
as a secularised presentation of the Exodus theme, believing that
the author 'knows nothing of divine guidance or divine intervention' (p. 29). It would appear appropriate to ask whether it
is not rather true that the author expresses a conviction of divine
providence in the whole narrative rather than in precise statement. The whole presentation offers easy and stimulating
reading.   P.R.A.

GOOD, E. M.: *Irony in the Old Testament*. 1965. Pp. 256. (S.P.C.K.,
London. Price: 30s. 0d.).

The author first describes irony and then discusses the satiric
irony of the Book of Jonah, the tragic irony of the life of Saul,
various ironies in Genesis, the biting irony of Isaiah, the sardonic
irony of Qoheleth and the ironies of the Book of Job. Although
there is evidence of wide reading, and of great desire and effort
to understand Old Testament irony in the light of Old Testament
faith, the treatment tends to be superficial as perhaps befits the
theme, and not always convincing.   G.H.D.

GOTTWALD, N. K.: *All the Kingdoms of the Earth*. Israelite Prophecy and
International Relations in the Ancient Near East. 1964. Pp. xv +
448. (Harper & Row, New York. Price: $7.00).

A welcome and fresh examination of prophetic political utterances especially those dealing with international relations. The
book begins with a description of the background to prophetic
activity of imperialism and international relations in the Ancient
Near East. Then the author goes on to examine minutely all
that the prophets said about Israel's contacts with the nations
and her policies towards them. This part of the book shows not

only a wide acquaintance with recent literature but a sensitive understanding of the prophetic political consciousness. The book shows very clearly that the prophets were not conscious policy makers; they were interpreters of events in the light of their self-identification with God. International relations were shaped by God and not by men. In the prophecies of Second Isaiah Gottwald sees the prophet interpreting the rise of Cyrus, the Messianic leader, as the means of releasing Israel for her world-wide task not as the head of an empire but as priest to the world.

L.H.B.

GRANT, R. M.: *A Short History of the Interpretation of the Bible.* 1965. Pp. viii + 184. (A. & C. Black, London. Price: 21s. 0d.).

This is a revised edition of a work first published in U.S.A. in 1948 under the title *The Bible in the Church*; it was reviewed by A. R. Johnson in *Book List* 1949, p. 24, (*Eleven Years*, p. 187). The principal changes come at the beginning of the book, where the author's further study of the New Testament and early Church has led to some modification of his views, and at the end, where he finds it much more difficult to sum up the contemporary state of Biblical interpretation and predict its future course than he did in 1948.

F.F.B.

GRELOT, P.: *La Bible, Parole de Dieu.* Introduction théologique à l'étude de l'Écriture Sainte. (Bibliothèque de la Théologie Dogmatique — Series I — Vol. 5). 1965. Pp. XII + 418. (Desclée, Tournai. Price: B. Fr. 330).

Those who are familiar with Grelot's excellent contributions to the second volume of *Introduction à la Bible*, on the literary and historical background to the New Testament books, will be fully aware that he is an accurate writer with a fine gift of compression. The present book provides, first, a remarkably full account of the Bible as the Word of God, of the meaning of Biblical inspiration, and of the Canon of Scripture. The second part is concerned with interpretation and deals with the senses of Scripture, and in the chapter on Biblical hermeneutics has much to say on the literal sense and on the *sensus plenior*. Having read a quantity of books that cover the same ground, it seems clear to me that this is a vast improvement on the older manuals, and has the quality of clarity that pertains to all that is best in French literature. The three indexes (of authors, of subjects, and of Biblical texts) all appear to be exact and adequate.

J.M.T.B.

INGEBRAND, S.: *Bibeltolkningens problematik. En historisk översikt.* 1965. Pp. 260. (Diakonistyrelsens Bokförlag, Stockholm. Price: Sw.kr. 22).

This is a percipient treatment of the history and the contemporary problems of Biblical interpretation. Though the bulk of the book is devoted to the historical survey, and an appropriate emphasis is laid on the importance of a historical perspective in any attempt to interpret the Bible today, there is a useful discussion of the contemporary debate. A chapter is devoted to an exposition and critique of Bultmann's views, which have not met with ready acceptance in Sweden. Appropriately, there is also an appraisal of the views and continuing influence of the late Professor Fridrichsen. A brief closing chapter reviews outstanding contemporary problems.

G.W.A.

JEREMIAS, J.: *Theophanie, Die Geschichte einer alttestamentlichen Gattung.* (Wissenschaftliche Monographien zum Alten und Neuen Testament, Band 10). 1965. Pp. VIII + 182. (Neukirchener Verlag des Erziehungsvereins, Neukirchen-Vluyn. Price: paper, DM. 18; cloth, DM. 21).

Jeremias begins with a detailed analysis of those texts which describe Yahweh's coming to his people in a theophany. He distinguishes two basic elements: the coming of Yahweh, usually associated with storm phenomena, and the confusion wrought in nature by this advent. This theophany is often connected with judgement upon the nations, but also, especially in the prophets, upon Israel. In a further section Jeremias then discusses analagous theophany descriptions from other Near Eastern literatures. He rejects the idea that in Israel the theophany tradition, as a whole, arose from the experience on Sinai, and also dismisses the view that its origin was in a regularly repeated cultic event. He finds the *Sitz im Leben* of the basic form in victory hymns of the pre-monarchic period, and traces distinct origins for each of the two basic elements. The 'confusion of nature' theme was borrowed from the surrounding nations, and the 'coming of Yahweh from his dwelling-place' arose from the unique encounter on Sinai. The victory hymns in which the theophany tradition grew up were used in the early cult, and the form was borrowed by the prophets. The conclusion does not appear convincing, particularly in its splintering of the basic tradition into two separate elements which had quite distinct origins. Both elements would appear to belong together. Nevertheless there is an immense amount of rewarding material and comment in this study, which is commendably clear and readable. It is better in its criticism of existing views than in its offer of a new one.

R.E.C.

KELLER, C-A.: *Découverte de l'Ancien Testament.* 1965. Pp. 106. (Semeur Vaudois, Lausanne).

This attractive little book consists of a collection of brief studies of nearly all the books of the Old Testament, originally published *seriatim* in the Swiss weekly, *Semeur Vaudois.* Professor Keller's aim is to bring out, first their literary quality, and then, and more particularly, the fact that this is an inspired literature, the word of the living God, reducing to a minimum 'considerations d'ordre purement scientifique'. Some of the studies are little gems, all are suggestive and stimulating. The section on the Book of Proverbs (une petite bibliothèque de pédagogie) is particularly good, perhaps however exemplifying a tendency of the author to stress the humanistic element in the Old Testament while, very slightly, deflating the prophetic element; but the book is full of meaty sayings and interesting judgements and is written with distinction and clarity of style.   M.Bu.

MARTIN-ACHARD, R.: *An Approach to the Old Testament*, trans. by J. C. G. Greig. 1965. Pp. x + 96, including 2 maps. (Oliver & Boyd, Edinburgh & London. Price: 15s. 0d.).

The French original of this book was reviewed in *Book List* 1963, p. 36. Its appearance in a competent English rendering is welcome. The bibliography has been recast to suit the needs of the English reader.   G.W.A.

NIELSEN, E.: *De ti bud: en traditionshistorisk skitse.* (Saertryk af Københavns universitets festskrift i anledning af Hans Majestaet Kongens fødselsdag 11. marts 1965). 1965. Pp. 138. (Copenhagen). = *Die Zehn Gebote: eine traditionsgeschichtliche Skizze*, trans. by H.-M. Junghans. (Acta Theologica Danica, Vol. VIII). 1965. Pp. 128. (Munksgaard, Copenhagen. Price: D.Kr. 40.00).

This valuable study of a subject which has been prominent in recent discussion is based on a course of lectures delivered at the Swedish Theological Institute in Jerusalem in 1962. Though the author has modestly described his book as a sketch and disclaims any pretensions to either exhaustive treatment or definitive solutions, anyone who follows his discussion of the related problems will have a clearer picture of the main trends in contemporary study of the Decalogue and of the issues at stake. The book demands a fuller review than is possible here; and it must suffice to indicate the main themes which the author examines. These are: the presumed ten-fold structure, its parallels, and the division into two tables; the textual and literary problems relating to the two forms of the Decalogue and the relation of these forms to their present literary settings; the form-critical problem and the question of the original form of the Decalogue; the traditio-historical problem (here it is interesting to note that the author maintains that parallels from Hittite formulas cannot legitimately be used to define the *original* situation of the Decalogue); and the region and circles from which the Decalogue emanated (priests and elders in the Northern Kingdom, possibly at Shechem, in the early period of the monarchy) and its subsequent history as a covenant document. This informative, suggestive, and balanced treatise merits close study.   G.W.A.

NYSTRÖM, S.: *Gamla Testamentet och förkunnelsen.* Prästmötesavhandling för Växjö stift. 1965. Pp. 134. (Svenska Kyrkans Diakonistyrelses Bokförlag, Stockholm. Price: Sw.Kr. 15).

Nearly thirty years ago the reviewer attended an illuminating course of lectures by Professor Lindblom on the Old Testament passages in the cycles of texts prescribed for use in the national Church of Sweden. The course was motivated by a desire to relate exegesis and homiletical practice. A similar desire has led Dr. Nyström (one of Lindblom's former students) to write the book now under review. It falls into three parts: a historical sketch of the place of the Old Testament in the context of the liturgy, with special attention to Scandinavian Lutheranism; a survey of the history of Old Testament scholarship in relation to interpretation and preaching; and an examination of various forms of the theological interpretation of the Old Testament, with particular reference to allegorical, typological, and Christological interpretation. The value of the book lies in its factual character, its useful historical surveys, and its documentation.

G.W.A.

PERLITT, L.: *Vatke und Wellhausen. Geschichtsphilosophische Voraussetzungen und historiographische Motive für die Darstellung der Religion und Geschichte Israels durch Wilhelm Vatke und Julius Wellhausen.* (Beihefte zur Zeitschrift für die alttestamentliche Wissenschaft, 94). 1965. Pp. X + 249. (Alfred Töpelmann, Berlin. Price: 77s. 0d.).

In recent times it has often been maintained (e.g., by Kraus and Pedersen) that in his presentation of the history of Israel Wellhausen was influenced by the philosophy of Hegel as mediated by Vatke. Perlitt provides a convincing demonstration that this view is untenable. He gives a careful characterization of the fundamental views on the philosophy of history held by Lessing, Herder, and Kant, and of their subsequent development, on the one hand in Hegel's system, and on the other hand in the historiography of Niebuhr, Ranke, and Mommsen (pp. 6–85). The central section of the book (pp. 86–152) is devoted to a detailed discussion of Vatke, whose hermeneutic approach is clearly expounded. The third section (pp. 153–243) is devoted to Wellhausen himself; and it is shown that his views were determined not by abstract theory but by sober examination of the text. The work is readable and carefully documented, and represents a contribution to our understanding of Vatke's approach to history as well as that of Wellhausen. W.Z.

RICHTER, W.: *Die Bearbeitungen des 'Retterbuches' in der deuteronomischen Epoche.* (Bonner Biblische Beiträge, 21). 1964. Pp. XVIII + 148. (Peter Hanstein Verlag, Bonn. Price: DM. 38).

The findings of this careful and accurate analysis of the literary structure of the various editorial strands of Judges are briefly as follows: since the framework is found only in iii. 6–viii there existed a *Retterbuch* before that framework and the final Deuteronomic editor found framework and *Retterbuch* already put together. The 'specimen' story in iii. 7–12 is very close to the framework in phrasing but shows an advance in the thought of the framework, namely a movement towards purifying the religion. The writer of this specimen was dependent on the first introduction to the book of Deuteronomy and also on some of the Deuteronomic laws, and he probably re-edited the *Retterbuch*. The 'introductions' (ii. 6–iii. 6; x. 6–16) take this religious element a stage further and agree in outlook with the main Deuteronomic writer. The author of these re-edited the book as part of the Deuteronomic history. No writer on Judges will be able to afford to neglect this work. L.H.B.

ROTH, W. M. W.: *Numerical Sayings in the Old Testament. A Form-Critical Study.* (Supplements to Vetus Testamentum, Vol. XIII). 1965. Pp. X + 104. (E. J. Brill, Leiden. Price: Fl. 24).

The work here noticed deals with the numerical saying (*middāh*), which plays so noticeable a part in the Old Testament. In the introduction, and again in the conclusion, the author deals with previous explanations of the origin and purpose of this practice; he then examines it under three main groups, with the appropriate sub-groups, namely Narrative Numerical Sayings, Reflective Numerical Sayings, and Hortative Numerical Sayings. To these he might have added Practical Numerical Devices, such as the decreasing numbers of the bullocks sacrificed as the days of the month increased (Numbers xxix. 17–34). In concluding he accepts the suggestion originally put forward by Alt, that the numerical sayings in Proverbs xxx. 15–31 are formulations of early Hebrew nature-wisdom of an encyclopaedic character; and he extends this explanation to embrace all such sayings. They are, in the author's view, a frame-pattern, i.e., a pattern which frames several items into a connected whole; its setting in life are those situations in human life when elementary items of information knowledge, or ethics, are to be grouped together as of equal importance. Briefly, whenever human reflection is at work by way of ordering and classifying, the pattern of the numerical saying offers itself as a form which most readily and adequately fixes the results of such reflection. Such sayings originated among, and were transmitted by, the wise men and the priests who were the guardians of both secular and sacred traditions. The matter is fully collected and clearly arranged by the author, and it is well illustrated from other literature, notably the Ugaritic poems.

G.R.D.

RUPPERT, L.: *Die Josephserzählung der Genesis.* Ein Beitrag zur Theologie der Pentateuchquellen. (Studien zum Alten und Neuen Testament, Band XI). Pp. 178. 1965. (Kösel-Verlag, München. Price: DM 38).

There are two basic assumptions which determine the starting-point for this study. The first is that the literary-critical approach to Pentateuchal study, in spite of the arguments adduced for J^1 and J^2, S, L, and other sources, is at least temporarily becalmed, and J, E, and P remain as generally acceptable, with no recognisable alternative in the offing. The second assumption is that the theological approach to the Bible today is a fruitful one and deserves to be pursued further. For that purpose the Joseph narratives in the Book of Genesis present an eminently suitable block of material because of their lengthy history of composition and editing.

After the introduction the book is divided into three parts. The first part gives a literary-critical and a theological analysis of all the Joseph narratives. The second part then considers the relation of these to Wisdom literature and shows that, if they originally came from that source, they are used in the J source to reveal Yahweh's guidance and salvation of undeserving Israel, so that the story of Joseph as a whole is to be interpreted as the hopeful prelude to the history of Israel. The editor of the passages from the source E sees the guidance given to Joseph as the prelude to God's guidance of Moses in the Exodus and in the wilderness, and correlates Joseph in his work with King David in his rule of the united kingdom. On the other hand, the Joseph story in the document P is in extent negligible and is part and parcel of the Jacob story; and the burial of Jacob at Hebron is regarded as the prelude to the entrance of Israel into Canaan.

Such a theological interpretation of Joseph's life and career as is given here finds explicit support of course in the Genesis narratives themselves. This book works it out systematically and correlates the interpretation which it gives with that which is also found to be applied to the history of Israel as related in the Books of Joshua, Judges, and 1 and 2 Samuel. Thus the book implicitly establishes a principle, if not the principle, on which each Pentateuchal editor chose his narrative material and the aim with which he presented it; it is a tenable and well-argued theory.

J.M.

SCHMIDT, W. H.: *Die Schöpfungsgeschichte der Priesterschrift*. (Wissenschaftliche Monographien zum Alten und Neuen Testament. Band 17). 1964. Pp. 204. (Neukirchener Verlag des Erziehungsvereins, Neukirchen-Vluyn. Price: cloth, DM. 23.50; paper, DM. 19.50).

The author's investigation into the traditions that lie behind Gen. i. 1–ii. 4a opens with a review of the critical treatment of this section of Genesis from the eighteenth century to the present day. Ancient Near Eastern parallels to Gen. i (cosmological myths and hymnic and wisdom texts) are next surveyed, and certain Old Testament texts, canonical and non-canonical, are also compared. Then follows the main part of the book, which is concerned with the analysis of the text of the Priestly account of the creation, with special reference to its formal structure, and to the relationship between *Wortbericht* (God as subject speaking) and *Tatbericht* (God as subject acting), the eight acts of creation being treated *seriatim*. Finally, the problem of the *Urtext* is discussed, and the theological working over of the traditional material is examined. A full bibliography is supplied in addition to a wealth of valuable footnotes. This is an important book, well planned, and detailed and thorough in its discussion. The author's rejection of the view that in i. 1 *reshith* is in the construct state, and his preferred translation 'wind' for *ruach* in i. 2 may be noted.

D.W.T.

WESTERMANN, C.: *The Praise of God in the Psalms*, trans. by K. R. Crim. 1965. Pp. 172. (John Knox Press, Richmond, Virginia. Price: $4.25).

The original German edition of this book was published by the Evangelische Verlagsanstalt, Berlin, in 1953, and was reviewed in *Book List* 1954, p. 55 (*Eleven Years*, p. 592). The present translation is based on the second edition (practically unaltered) which was published by Vandenhoeck & Ruprecht in 1961. The original *Sitz im Leben* of the book was the German Church struggle and the author's own experience of imprisonment; hence the element of devotional interpretation. At the more technical level, the author rejects the cult-functional and cult-historical approach of Mowinckel and others, and holds the proper complement to Gunkel's work to be the carrying on of Gunkel's own methods. To this task the bulk of the book is devoted. The author recognizes two basic psalm categories: laments, and psalms of praise, the latter being divided into 'declarative' psalms of praise (those which acknowledge specific acts of God, and which, in fact correspond to what are usually called psalms of thanksgiving) and 'descriptive' psalms of praise (those which praise God for what He is and for His acts in general). The bulk of the book consists of detailed analyses of form and content.

G.W.A.

WHYBRAY, R. N.: *Wisdom in Proverbs: the Concept of Wisdom in Proverbs 1–9.* (Studies in Biblical Theology, No. 45). 1965. Pp. 120. (S.C.M. Press, London. Price: 13s. 6d.).

This book, which is based on an Oxford D.Phil. thesis, begins with a brief discussion of the Wisdom literature in general and some problems of Proverbs i–ix in particular. These chapters are then analysed, primarily on the ground of form, and an original ten discourses are separated from later material. The discourses are compared with Egyptian literature and some substantial resemblances are noted. The rest of the monograph examines the later material and maintains that it was added in two stages. In the first stage, which reflects a 'state of affairs' that 'corresponds to the period of the great pre-exilic prophets' (p. 105), additions were made in order to 'equate the words of the Wisdom teacher with a personified Wisdom' although 'no explicit mention is made . . . of the connexion of this Wisdom with God' (p. 92). The remedying of this defect was the purpose of the second stage, in the Persian period, when further additions were made, among them viii. 22–31. The monograph contains a discussion of the principal theories of the origin of the personification of Wisdom, including a detailed refutation of Albright's attempt to find a Canaanite background. This interesting and stimulating study concludes with a bibliography and indexes.

J.A.E.

WISEMAN, D. J., MITCHELL, T. C., JOYCE, R., MARTIN, W. J., KITCHEN, K. A.: *Notes on some Problems in the Book of Daniel.* 1965. Pp. 80. (The Tyndale Press, London. Price: 8s. 6d.).

Four articles are included in this book in which on historical and linguistic grounds reasons are offered for caution in accepting a second century date for the book of Daniel. The first by D. J. Wiseman tentatively suggests reasons for the view that 'Darius the Mede' could be another name used of Cyrus the Persian, and that the argument from silence is not adequate for rejecting the accuracy of Daniel i. 1. The second article discusses the translation of Daniel's musical instruments and suggests a possible sixth century date. The third, 'The Hebrew of Daniel' and the fourth, 'The Aramaic of Daniel', both argue for the possibility of a sixth century dating. Such a study is to be welcomed, so long as it does not cause the non-specialist to draw hasty conclusions.

A.S.H.

ZOBEL, H.-J.: *Stammesspruch und Geschichte*. Die Angaben der Stammes-sprüche von Gen. 49, DTN 33 und JDC 5 über die politischen und kultischen Zustände im damaligen 'Israel'. (Beihefte zur Zeitschrift für die alttestamentliche Wissenschaft, 95). 1965. Pp. XII + 163. (Verlag Alfred Töpelmann, Berlin. Price: DM. 34).

The conclusions reached in this scholarly and well-documented investigation are, on the whole, those which have been reached by other scholars; e.g., fluctuations and changes in the tribal groupings in Israel in the period 1400–1000 B.C. (as exemplified, for instance, in Simeon, Levi, Reuben, and Gad); the fact that one or two tribes in certain cases developed by stages into a tribal group whose leadership did not remain constantly with one tribe and the evidence for more than one tribal movement into Pales-tine (e.g., Naphtali and Zebulun in the north, Ephraim and Manasseh in the central area, etc.), so that some had no tradition of enslavement in Egypt or covenant-making with Yahweh at Sinai. But collateral with all the social and political adaptations involved in these tribal associations and tensions and in tribal relations with the resident Canaanites, there was a sacral factor which was active and of great importance; Tabor and Shiloh have significant places in this respect. Add to this, says the author, a Canaanite conception of kingship in the south, contrasted with the amphictyonic leadership of the north, election theology in the south and covenant theology in the north, and a varied pattern of tradition, belief, attitude, and practice is disclosed. Finally the book tries to show the persistence of some of these differentials as significant factors during the monarchic period in Israel.   J.M.

LAW, RELIGION, AND THEOLOGY

AMSLER, S.: *David, Roi et Messie*. La tradition davidique dans l'Ancien Testament. (Cahiers Théologiques 49). 1963. Pp. 80. (Delachaux & Niestlé, Neuchâtel).

The theme of this monograph is to demonstrate how the David of history developed into the Messianic figure. First of all attention is called to the portrait of David which is given in the early traditions about him, such as the story of the Ark (1 Sam. iv-vii. 1, and 2 Sam. vi. 1–15, 17–20a), the account of the ascension of David (2 Sam. vii. 11–20; 1 Kings i-ii), and 'the last words of David' (2 Sam. xxiii. 1–7). Then there follows a discussion on the way in which these ideas have been developed in the Psalms (especially the Royal Psalms), the Prophets, and the historical writers (the Deuteronomist and Chronicler). The arguments are presented with clarity and persuasion, and will stimulate further thinking upon this theme.   E.R.R.

BARR, J.: *Old and New in Interpretation*. A Study of the Two Testaments. (The Currie Lectures delivered at Austin Presbyterian Theological Seminary, Texas, February 1964). 1966. Pp. 216. (S.C.M. Press London. Price: 30s. 0d.).

This book continues the author's argument in *The Semantics of Biblical Language* (*Book List* 1962, p. 81), and develops and expands his article 'Revelation' in *H.D.B.*, rev. ed., p. 849. He examines critically some of the recent studies in Old Testament theology, though neither van Imschoot nor Koehler are specifically discussed. He questions the centrality of the concept of history for that of revelation and indeed prefers a theology of the divine word to one based on divine action. Typology and allegory are sympathetically discussed; the presence of both in the New Testament is noted. In the chapter, 'Old and New Testaments in the Work of Salvation' he would argue for a Trinitarian rather than a Christological approach; salvation is founded in the juncture of Old and New. The Word became flesh in the Jewish humanity of the first century within the context of the scriptural heritage and interpretative processes of that time. Understanding of the Bible must come both from an appreciation of Biblical categories and from categories and concepts external to the Bible. Theology is not dependent on philosophy yet it must pay heed to philosophical discussion. The Bible belongs to the world, and not to the Church only. This is a valuable contribution to all who are engaged in the work of Old Testament hermeneutics. It will promote vigorous discussion and, no doubt, criticism. But it cannot be ignored.

A.S.H.

BLEEKER, C. J. (ed. by): *Initiation*. Contributions to the theme of the Study-Conference of the International Association for the History of Religions held at Strasbourg, September 17th to 22nd 1964. (Studies in the History of Religions (Supplements to *Numen*), X). 1965. Pp. VIII + 310. (E. J. Brill, Leiden. Price: Fl. 48).

The 28 articles contained in this volume, by scholars of many nationalities, range over a very wide field, both in space and in time. Professor Éliade opens the ball with a brilliant essay on the significance of Initiation in the modern world, and the Editor contributes a valuable essay on the general significance of Initiation. Professor Brandon deals with a theme near to his heart, the significance of Time in some ancient Initiatory Rituals. The only essay dealing directly with the Old Testament is by the French scholar A. Caquot who writes on Initiation in ancient Israel. Several essays are concerned with Baptism in the New Testament and in Qumran. Professor Widengren winds up the discussion with a characteristic essay summing up the results of the Conference. The book should be of great importance and interest to Old Testament scholars.

S.H.H.

BONHOEFFER, D.: *Creation and Temptation*. 1966. Pp. 128. (S.C.M. Press, London. Price: 10s. 6d.).

The first part of this book was originally published in 1937 as *Schöpfung und Fall* (Chr. Kaiser Verlag, München). A later edition published in 1955 was reviewed in *Book List* 1956, pp. 41 f. (*Eleven Years*, pp. 748 f.). Still later it appeared in English in 1959 (see *Book List* 1959, p. 16) and was reprinted in 1960 and 1962. It consists of a theological exposition of Genesis i–iii. The book now appears again, this time bound up with a study of temptation based on New Testament passages. Nothing written by Bonhoeffer is without interest; but what we are offered here is eisegesis rather than exegesis.

N.W.P.

CLEMENTS, R. E.: *God and Temple. The Idea of the Divine Presence in Ancient Israel*. 1965. Pp. xii+164. (Basil Blackwell, Oxford. Price: 25s. 0d.).

An interesting attempt to trace a development in the conception of Yahweh's presence in Israel as a unifying theme of the first importance for our understanding of the Bible. The main lines of this development are found (a) in the mythology associated with Solomon's Temple, which links Israel's possession of the Holy Land with Yahweh's dwelling-place on Mount Zion in terms of 'a "cultic" entitlement', (b) in the Deuteronomic Reform, which stresses, rather, the gift of the Holy Land as an historical event, and, correspondingly, replaces the earlier mythology of the Jerusalem Temple with a theology of the divine 'Name' as the means of accounting for Yahweh's presence in Israel, and (c) in the various attempts which were made in early Judaism to explain the continuing experience of Yahweh's presence despite the fall of the Temple and the disaster of the Exile. It is not surprising that the treatment of so vast a theme in so small a compass has led to many generalizations which the trained student of the Old Testament may well wish to question; but, if one is left with the strong impression that the author's argument is largely based upon a somewhat too ready acceptance of current theory, this in no way detracts from one's appreciation of his attempt to find a way through the maze of contemporary argument concerning the Old Testament, coupled as it is with evidence of wide reading, a certain independence of judgement, and a pleasingly clear style. A.R.J.

COMBLIN, J.: *Le Christ dans l'Apocalypse*. (Bibliothèque de Théologie: Théologie biblique, Série III, Vol. 6). 1965. Pp. XII + 268. (Desclée, Paris and Tournai. Price: B.Fr. 290).

This is a scholarly and well-documented study of the various figures and titles under which Christ is portrayed in the Book of Revelation, in the light of their Old Testament and Intertestamental background. The figures and titles include the Lamb, the Servant, the Coming One, the Son of Man, the Word of God, Jesus Imperator, Wisdom, the Witness, the Messiah, the Living One. The great novelty of John's Apocalypse by contrast with Jewish apocalypses in general is its identification of the two figures of Son of Man and King Messiah in the person of Jesus, an identification made possible for John by his prior identification of Jesus with the Ebed Yahweh, who is both Son of Man and King Messiah. An interesting section of this study compares the biblical Son of Man with the *maśkil* of 1QS, and suggests that Jesus' twofold fulfilment of the Son of Man ideal corresponds to the main functions predicted of the Qumran *maśkil*. F.F.B.

DULIÈRE, W. L.: *De la Dyade à l'Unité par la Triade*. 1965. Pp. 560. (Adrien Maisonneuve, Paris).

This is a learned and ingenious, but unconvincing, book which argues that in the Biblical tradition man was originally androgynous and was created by a duality of gods, one male and one female. Yahweh was later introduced as a third and ultimately became the sole deity. Evidence from Mesopotamia, Egypt, and Greece is introduced alongside statements from the Talmud and the Zohar, with abundant pictorial illustration from archaeological finds. Some remarkable equations of Hebrew words are proposed, and every word ending in -aim, -on, or -an is treated as a dual, and made to support ditheism — e.g., Jerusalem, Dagon, Nehushtan, Zion, Rephaim (with which Raiphan of LXX in Am. v. 26 is equated). Jeroboam I is held to have been a priest who was converted by tradition into a king, and is held to have set up two images in Bethel. Even the ox and the ass of the traditional pictures of the birth of Jesus are converted into a male and a female deity. Yahweh, Adrammelek, and Annamelek are treated as a trinity. It is a pity that so much learning was not devoted to a better cause. That pairs of deities were widely worshipped and may have been worshipped by Israelites under alien influence does not justify the reading of this everywhere into the Bible.   H.H.R.

FALK, Z. W.: *Hebrew Law in Biblical Times*. An Introduction. 1964. Pp. 180. (Wahrmann Books, Jerusalem, Israel. Price: $3.60).

The author describes, apparently exhaustively, the provisions of Biblical Law under ten headings: I Source; II Tribe, nation, and state; III Administration of justice; IV Crime and punishment; V Things and contracts; VI Persons; VII Family; VIII Marriage and divorce; IX Children; X Succession. The provisions of the law are in each case succinctly set out and illustrated, where possible, by Babylonian and Assyrian and occasionally by Hittite law; and Rabbinical interpretations of Biblical law are often introduced. Thus far the book will be found useful to the student who wants a clear exposition of the facts; but its utility is impaired by the uncritical use of sources. In fact, his use of these is pre-critical; everything is taken at its face value. Sweeping statements, such as that Darius promulgated laws based on the Code of Hammu-rabi and that his legislation for Egypt was a restatement of the old native rules (pp. 54 f.) will surprise any reader tolerably well-informed on the subject of ancient law; both appear to be quite unjustified amplifications of or deductions from something that Diodorus Siculus said long afterwards. Some of the author's philological remarks are extremely dubious and his English idiom is apt to be strange.   G.R.D.

GUNNEWEG, A. H. J.: *Leviten und Priester*. Hauptlinien der Traditions- bildung und Geschichte des israelitisch-jüdischen Kultpersonals. (Forschungen zur Religion und Literatur des Alten und Neuen Testaments, Heft 89). 1965. Pp. 226. (Vandenhoeck & Ruprecht, Göttingen. Price: DM. 24).

So much has been written about Israelite priests and Levites that there might appear little chance of any fresh ideas being advanced. Yet Dr. Gunneweg has succeeded in working out a new theory of the origin of the Levites in this monograph, which is based on a *Habilitationsschrift* presented at Marburg in 1962. He maintains both that there was never a secular tribe of Levi and that the word

'Levite' does not mean 'priest'; rather, the Levites were originally something like a religious order. When a man became a Levite, he severed his legal connexion with his own tribe and lived as a *ger*. The proper function of the Levites was to teach, and not to perform priestly duties, but they later laid claim to the priesthood. Gunneweg discusses the early texts dealing with the Levites, and also those mentioning Aaron and Zadok and the groups of priests associated with their names. The second part of the book examines the changes brought about by Josiah's reformation and the developments in the later period. Among the many interesting views advanced, the treatment of Ezek. xliv deserves special mention: this chapter does not, it is argued, degrade the country Levites from the priesthood, but presupposes an already existent distinction between Levites and Zadokite priests and attempts further to depress the status of the former to the advantage of the latter. The theory proposed in this monograph has its weak points and is unlikely to win general acceptance; but it is good that widely-held opinions should be challenged and tested, and Gunneweg's discussion of many passages deserves careful consideration and may be read with profit.   J.A.E.

HANSON, A. T.: *Jesus Christ in the Old Testament.* 1965. Pp. viii + 212. (S.P.C.K., London. Price: 30s. 0d.).

This is a study of Old Testament interpretation in the New Testament. Its main thesis is that the 'normative approach' of New Testament writers in interpreting the Old Testament so as to find Christ and the gospel there is not allegory nor yet typology (though typology is admittedly present) but what the author calls 'real presence'—i.e., the doctrine that Christ himself was personally active in the great events of Old Testament history. There is much in what he says; the LXX use of *Kyrios* to render Yahweh made it easy for Greek-speaking Christians to understand references to *Kyrios* as references to Jesus, whom they called *Kyrios*, and examples of this are not lacking in the NT. That Jesus was personally present with Israel at the Exodus and in the wilderness was believed by more than one New Testament writer. But Professor Hanson carries his thesis to extremes; despite his arguments to the contrary, the writer to the Hebrews does not identify Melchizedek with Jesus. If Melchizedek *resembles* the Son of God (Heb. vii. 3) and Jesus exercises his priesthood *after the order* of Melchizedek (Heb. v. 6, etc.), the relationship implied in these expressions excludes identity.

F.F.B.

HERMISSON, H.-J.: *Sprache und Ritus im altisraelitischen Kult: zur 'Spiritualisierung' der Kultbegriffe im Alten Testament.* (Wissenschaftliche Monographien zum Alten und Neuen Testament, Band 19). 1965. Pp. 166. (Neukirchener Verlag des Erziehungsvereins, Neukirchen-Vluyn. Price: paper, DM. 15.80; cloth, 18.30).

Anyone who has read von Rad's *Theology of the Old Testament* will recognize that the author of this interesting monograph is largely indebted to that scholar. There is a tendency in modern German theological circles to stress the importance of preaching,

and the '*Word*' has come to have an almost sacramental significance. In this monograph the author has devoted special
attention to the '*muthos*', the spoken element in the ritual, and,
connecting this with the 'word' of the prophet, has developed the
theme of a gradual 'spiritualization' of the cult in Israel. He
uses von Rad's conception of the Holy War to illustrate his
theme, and, also following von Rad, would find the beginnings
of the process in what he calls the *Aufklärung*, the 'enlightenment'
of the Solomonic era. The age-old discussion of the attitude of
the eighth-century prophets to the cult is worked over again in
relation to the author's main thesis. The bibliography suggests
that his reading has been entirely confined to the very considerable output of German Old Testament scholarship. W. B.
Stevenson is the only British scholar honoured by inclusion.

S.H.H.

HEYDE, H.: *Kain, der erste Jahwe-Verehrer*. 1965. Pp. 44. (Calwer
Verlag, Stuttgart. Price: DM. 4.80).

Is this the first time that Cain has been honoured by having a
special monograph devoted to him? Heyde has made an
interesting contribution, which provides, first, a translation and
exegesis of Gen. iv. 1–16, with some discussion of the early
material in the passage and of the original significance of the
narrative. A second section compares the passage with other
evidence from the Old Testament books, its most important
pages being those on the origin of Yahweh-worship, for which,
and for the connection with the Kenites, the author quotes von
Rad's *Theologie des Alten Testaments*, I, 19; = E. T. I, 9,
àpropos of the 'almost inevitable conclusion' that the Midianites
were worshippers of Yahweh before the 'Israelites' and that this
can be said 'with quite a measure of probability' of the Kenites.

J.M.T.B.

JONES, E.: *The Triumph of Job*. 1966. Pp. 126. (S.C.M. Press, London.
Price: 9s. 6d.).

It is often said that only the expert can write a book for beginners,
and the master-hand is recognisable in this excellent introduction
to the book of Job, with its lightly carried learning and its vigorous concentration on essentials.
The beginner, whether the student, dismayed to find how much
there is of Job to be 'done' in a limited time, or the general
reader, who knows that the book is a literary masterpiece but
nevertheless finds it difficult to detect any movement of thought
or any solution to what he regards as the main problem, will find
here a lamp to his feet. A few crucial readings are discussed, a
widely accepted rearrangement of chapters xxv–xxvii is suggested,
and the speeches of Elihu and the hymn to Wisdom (independent
but related to the main theme) are regarded as later additions,
possibly from the same hand as the rest. The question as to the
integrity of the Yahweh speeches is not even raised. The book of
Job is not primarily concerned with the problem of suffering
but with the character of man's relation to God. Hence the
title.

The text, like that of Job itself, would seem to be liable to hazards of transmission and for some readers the meaning could be obscured by what is surely the printer's omission of the word '*no*' on p. 76. There is a useful bibliography.
M.Bu.

DE JONGE, M.: *De toekomstverwachting in de Psalmen van Salomo*. (Openbare les gegeven bij de aanvaarding van het ambt van gewoon lector in de oud-christelijke en interestamentaire letterkunde aan de Rijksuniversiteit te Groningen op dinsdag 5 oktober 1965). 1965. Pp. 44. (E. J. Brill, Leiden. Price: Fl. 2).

In this inaugural lecture de Jonge emphasises the importance for New Testament studies of a critical reading of the later Jewish works of the intertestamental period with special reference to the Psalms of Solomon and the term 'the Anointed of the Lord' in xvii. 36 (cf. xviii. 6). He shows how present and future are knit together in the Psalmist's thought and that the 'Messiah' figure is very much subordinate to the sovereign power of God.

L.H.B.

KÄHLER, M.: *Jesus und das Alte Testament*, bearbeitet und mit einer Einleitung versehen von Ernst Kähler. (Biblische Studien, Heft 45). 1965. Pp. 87. (Neukirchener Verlag, Neukirchen-Vluyn. Price: DM. 5.45).

This essay, first published in 1907, was (as the foreword by Ernst Kähler informs) the fruit of the author's long participation in the controversy about the Christian relevance of the Old Testament which raged in Germany in the 1890's and earlier years of the present century. There, as in this country, Biblical criticism occasioned agonizing reappraisals of long-cherished beliefs. The reappraisals were probably more agonizing in Germany than elsewhere because of the publicity given to such extremists as those of the *Babel und Bibel* school. Kähler's contribution consists of fifteen theses which are defended in the light of the questions then being asked; it must have helped many readers to see how the continued acceptance of the Old Testament as canonical scripture was perfectly compatible with acceptance of the findings of reasonable critical study.
F.F.B.

KNIERIM, R.: *Die Hauptbegriffe für Sünde im Alten Testament*. 1965. Pp. 280. (Gütersloher Verlagshaus Gerd Mohn, Gütersloh. Price: DM. 48).

A common way to attempt to understand what the Old Testament means by its words for *sin* is to search out their etymology and semantic range. This method, this book maintains, is necessary and valuable, but in itself insufficient. It is necessary also to examine each word for *sin* in the context in which it is used in order to discover the nuances of meaning which thus become known.
The stems which are investigated in this volume are ḤṬ', PŠ', and 'WH. The investigation is done in detail and with patient persistence. Sometimes such a term, as originally used, has no theological significance at all (e.g., ḤṬ' means originally to miss

or to fail); but sometimes a profane use of the term is found collateral with the theological one; always it is the second which predominates in the Old Testament. To make the various nuances or shades of meaning intelligible, a problem of hermeneutics is inevitably involved, for each has to be expressed in terms of the rootage of the word in its own environment; thus ḤṬ' can mean to commit a sin, but also to have a sense of guilt or shame because of the sin committed, so that the sinner is said to be worthy of death and to depend for life upon the self-giving and suffering of an agent able to *carry away* sin.

In some aspects of this investigation the criteria for judgement are very difficult to handle. The fact that in the rhythmic passages of the Old Testament two of the three terms here examined are sometimes used in parallel leads us to conclude that distinctive meanings of individual words may not always have been held clearly in the mind of Old Testament writers. But in spite of all difficulties this work is certainly the result of assiduous application and shows keen discernment in judgement.

J.M.

LAMPARTER, H.: *Das Psalmengebet in der Christengemeinde.* (Calwer Hefte zur Förderung biblischen Glaubens und christlichen Lebens, No. 75). 1965. Pp. 44. (Calwer Verlag, Stuttgart. Price: Dm. 2.50; by subscription, DM. 2.10).

As its title indicates, this booklet has a homiletic purpose; it deals briefly with the place and form of congregational prayer and supports the argument for a fuller use of the Psalms in public and private prayer by quotations from the Psalter and references to the words and practice of Luther.

D.R.Ap-T.

LIPIŃSKI, E.: *La royauté de Yahwé dans la poésie et le culte de l'ancien Israël.* (Verhandelingen van de Koninklijke Vlaamse Academie voor Wetenschappen, Letteren en Schone Kunsten van België. Klasse der Letteren, Jahrgang XXVII, Nr. 55). 1965. Pp. 560. (Paleis der Academiën — Hertogstraat 1, Brussel. Price: B.Fr. 1.000).

This is a most important contribution to the continuing debate on the Kingship of Yahweh. After a careful review of previous work on the subject, the author presents a detailed study of the three main psalms (xciii, xcvii, xcix) which begin *Yahweh mālak*. He argues that the widely different contents and dates (e.g., Ps. xcvii is Maccabean, incorporating an older psalm from the Holy War) show that the common classification of 'Enthronement Psalms' is a fallacy. A fifth chapter reviews formulae of investiture, acclamation, homage, proclamation, and fidelity, concluding that *Yahweh mālak* belongs to the category of proclamation. The final chapter traces the development of the Israelite conception of Yahweh's kingship from His early victories in the Holy War, through His cultic enthronement at the feast of Tabernacles in Jerusalem, to the eschatological expectation of His enthronement over the whole world. The bibliography covers 42 pages and the indices 45. The printing of Hebrew in transliteration throughout is unfortunate in a work directed primarily to scholars.

A.G.

MAIER, J.: *Das altisraelitische Ladeheiligtum.* (Beihefte zur Zeitschrift für die alttestamentliche Wissenschaft, 93). 1965. Pp. X + 88, incl. 2 tables. (Verlag Alfred Töpelmann, Berlin. Price: DM. 21).

This study of the significance and function of the ark in ancient Israel presents a viewpoint which disagrees at many points with currently accepted views. The ark is traced back to Shiloh, where it served as a symbol of the political organization of a number of tribes. These were less in number than the twelve tribes of the Israelite amphictyony. In David's time the ark was used by the king as a dynastic symbol expressing the political concept of a united Israel, as found in the title Yahweh Sebaoth. This is interpreted as Yahweh of the armies (of Israel and Judah). Not until it was set in the temple in Solomon's reign did the ark gain a predominantly cultic meaning. Deuteronomy reinterpreted the ark in order to divest it of its dynastic association, and to relate it to the Horeb covenant. In the Priestly Document the ark was regarded in retrospect as an item of cult furniture. Maier has many points of interest and some useful suggestions, although his literary criticism appears rather arbitrary and far from convincing. He has not said the final word about the ark but has produced a study which further research will need to take into consideration.   R.E.C.

MARQUARDT, F. W.: *Die Bedeutung der biblischen Landverheissungen für die Christen.* (Theologische Existenz Heute, No. 116). 1964. Pp. 56. (Chr. Kaiser Verlag, München. Price: DM. 3.80).

This is an enlarged form of a paper read to a study group on Jews and Christians at an assembly of the German Evangelical Church in 1964. There are three sections. The first shows how in the Old Testament emphasis tended to shift from the whole land to Mount Zion and Jerusalem as the dwelling place of God, and how ṣedaḳah became an all-important qualification. The second section discusses the changing conceptions in the New Testament moving towards a recognition of Christ as the place of inheritance and to live 'in Christ' as the New Testament complement of ṣedaḳah. The third calls for a more realistic study of the implications of both Testaments in view of the tension raised by the revival of 'Israel' and its occupation of Palestine. L.H.B.

MILDENBERGER, F.: *Gottes Tat im Wort.* Erwägungen zur alttestamentlichen Hermeneutik als Frage nach der Einheit der Testamente. 1964. Pp. 148. (Gütersloher Verlagshaus Gerd Mohn, Gütersloh. Price: DM. 19.80).

The author presents his discussion, holding on the one hand to the conviction that the Old Testament is Holy Scripture, and on the other hand to the recognition that its material must be studied with all the critical skill appropriate to ancient documents. The Old Testament writings express the faith of the community in Yahweh, as men were moved by the Spirit of God. Israel through its *traditio* of the historical activity of Yahweh became and was maintained as Israel. Through promise and fulfilment, even through Israel's failure (cf. Ezek. xxxvi. 16–28) God's actuality is to become manifest. Empirical Israel will become Israel as it identifies itself with its *traditio* of God's historical acts. From this the line continues into the New Testament with its fulfilment of Israel in Christ. The claim of God can only be met by the Church as she acknowledges in the works of Jesus, the human expression of God's activity. This book might well be read alongside J. Barr: *Old and New in Interpretation* (reviewed above).

A.S.H.

MULDER, M. J.: *Kanaänitische Goden in het Oude Testament.* (Exegetica Oud- en Nieuw- Testamentische Studiën, 4 and 5). 1965. Pp. 112. (N.V. Voorheen van Keulen Periodieken, Den Haag. Price: Fl. 9).

This is a careful and competent study of all Old Testament references and allusions to the principal Canaanite gods and godesses — El, Baal, Ashera, Astarte, Anat, Moloch, Mot, Dagon, Kamos (Chemosh), Hadad, Rimmon, Gad and Meni, and Resheph. In each case the author gives a clear statement of the nature of the god and his worship in Canaanite religion and elsewhere and then deals fully with Old Testament references to it, including proper names (of persons). He shows that the Old Testament dependence on Canaanite religion is not substantial and is powerfully overweighted by the uniqueness of Yahwism. It is a readable book which moves quickly through its well marshalled facts with a quick eye for the salient points. It is well documented and should prove an important study on the subject.

L.H.B.

VON RAD, G.: *Old Testament Theology*, trans. by D. M. G. Stalker. Vol. I The Theology of Israel's Historical Traditions. 1962. Pp. xii + 484. Vol. II. The Theology of Israel's Prophetic Traditions. 1965. Pp. xiv + 470. (Oliver and Boyd, Edinburgh and London. Price: each volume, 45s. 0d.).

With the publication of Vol. II the translation of this extremely important work is now available for English readers and Mr. Stalker is warmly to be congratulated on the accomplishment of what must have been no easy task. The original German edition was reviewed at some length in *Book List* 1958, pp. 37 f., 1961, pp. 51 f. Since then there has been much keen debate between those who accept and those who find difficulty with von Rad's point of view. In this connection it should be noted that the author has added a most interesting postscript at the end of Vol. II of the English edition in which he seeks to make clearer some of his fundamental convictions about the right way to handle the Biblical material. This will repay reading and re-reading and will undoubtedly stimulate further discussion about the relations between the Old Testament records and history.

N.W.P.

ROBERTS, B. J.: *Sôn am Achub. Ysgrifau ar Ddiwinyddiaeth yr Hen Destament.* 1965. Pp. 94. (Gwasg Prifysgol Cymru, Caerdydd. Pris: 10s. 6d.) (University of Wales Press, Cardiff. Price: 10s. 6d.).

Welsh readers will be indebted to Professor Roberts for introducing them to the emphasis on *Heilsgeschichte* which plays such an important part in the treatment of the theology of the Old Testament. In a clear and stimulating way he demonstrates how this is proclaimed in the Creation narratives, the Worship of Israel, the Covenant Tradition, the Prophets (their words and acts), and also in the Wisdom and Apocalyptic Literature. It was the emphasis on Salvation History which stimulated the translation of the Old Testament into Greek, and the production of Apocryphal writings. The author also summarizes his own contributions to the study of the Massoretic text, and shows that the establishing and preserving of the Massoretic tradition are part of the Salvation History. The most important works on the theology of the Old Testament are evaluated, and also the author has his own original contributions to make. Among these can be mentioned his treatment of the term *Maśkil* (interpreter) in the section on the Apocalyptic Literature and the Scrolls, and the emphasis upon the contributions of the Levites in producing the Massoretic element in the transmission of the text.

E.R.R.

ROWLEY, H. H.: *Apokalyptik: ihre Form und Bedeutung zur Biblischen Zeit.* Eine Studie über jüdische und christliche Apokalypsen vom Buch Daniel bis zur Geheimen Offenbarung, 3rd edition, trans. by I. and R. Pesch. 1965. Pp. 250. (Verlagsanstalt Benziger, Einsiedeln/ Zürich.)

The third English edition of this invaluable work was reviewed in *Book List* 1964, p. 65. This rendering into German should extend still further the sphere of its usefulness.

G.W.A.

SCHARBERT, J.: *Heilsmittler im Alten Testament und im Alten Orient.* (*Quaestiones Disputatae*, Band 23/24). 1964. Pp. 346. (Herder Verlag, Freiburg. Price: DM. 26.80).

Intended originally as the second volume in a trilogy, dealing with the interconnection of individual and community in Old Testament theology (cf. *Book List* 1959, pp. 29 f.), this work, owing to the centrality of its subject in current theological discussion and the consequent desirability of its reaching a wider public, has instead been issued as a separate study in the present series. Although much consideration appropriately is here given to the sacral king, a necessary balance is preserved by attention also to other mediators such as the priest, the prophet, and those besides through whom weal or woe may befall their compatriots. In this widely ranging survey based upon extensive reading the author examines the rôle of the mediator, firstly among the peoples of the ancient Near East (Egyptian, Mesopotamian, Syro-Palestinian, and Hittite), and secondly within the various literary groupings of the Old Testament. A third and final section brings together his conclusions and includes a valuable summary, which clearly shows that what has been so carefully elaborated is but a necessary prolegomenon to a proper understanding of the function of the apostles and the other office-holders within the New Testament *ecclesia* as participation in the mediatorship of Christ.

E.T.R.

SCHARBERT, J.: *Die Propheten Israels bis 700 v. Chr.* 1965. Pp. 362, incl. 2 maps and 1 chronological table. (Verlag J. P. Bachem, Köln. Price: DM. 36).

This is a historical study of Israel's earliest prophets from Samuel to Micah, with emphasis on the contents of the prophecies, which are arranged in a chronological order. The result is a running commentary on the message of each prophet interspersed with sections on the history of the period. It is a pleasant book to read and can be recommended as a useful introduction to prophetic activity, particularly on the political side, and to prophetic teaching. The author is not always as critically objective as one would wish. Sometimes he appears to read too much into brief Biblical statements and sometimes to argue from silence. Because a song is attributed to Deborah it is assumed that she used to sing and dance on cultic occasions at Ramah and Bethel. Samuel, although leader of a group of ecstatic prophets, is not himself an ecstatic because it is said that Saul prophesied *before* Samuel (p. 43). Nathan is said to have had his visions usually at night. Again, there seems to be an over-emphasis on forms of prophetic utterance, so that because there is no set form of words to make his message a *Botenspruch* in 1 Kings xx. 22, the prophet is said to be speaking from his own mind. The story of Jonah is taken to be pre-exilic and to be comparable with the legends that attached themselves to Elijah and Elisha. The Messianic prophecies in Isaiah are treated as genuine and as applying to the birth of Hezekiah (vii. 14 included) in the first place, but also as prophesying the birth of Christ: 'Der Jesaja inspirierende Gottesgeist hat in einem tieferen Sinn bereits jene Erfüllung mitgemeint' (p. 236). Scharbert is aware of and discusses the problem of false prophets, but shows no awareness of any problem in this double application, to the present and to the indefinite future; he speaks confidently of a *sensus plenior*.

L.H.B.

SEIERSTAD, I. P.: *Die Offenbarungserlebnisse der Propheten Amos, Jesaja und Jeremia.* Eine Untersuchung der Erlebnisvorgänge unter besonderer Berücksichtigung ihrer Religiös-Sittlichen Art und Auswirkung. 2nd Edition. (The Norwegian Research Council for Science and the Humanities 1965 (Norges almenvitensapelige forskningsråd) Section: A. 586–13T). 1965. Pp. 272. (Universitetsforlaget. Price: N.kr. 48.00).

This book was originally published in 1946 in the series S. N. V. A. O., and reviewed in *Book List* 1948, p. 49 (*Eleven Years*, p. 159). It is now reprinted with a foreword (including a reply to a criticism by Professor Lindblom) and a page of corrections. The importance of the work has been widely recognised, even by those who dissent from the author's views; and its republication is to be welcomed.

G.W.A.

SMART, J. D.: *The Old Testament in Dialogue with Modern Man.* 1964. Pp. 138. (The Westminster Press, Philadelphia. Price: $3.50).

The intention of the book is to assist ministers and ordinands in the exposition of the Old Testament. The dialogue requires that man hear the divine word of judgement and salvation and make response. Particular passages discussed are Genesis i (Creation), Genesis ii f., (Human Nature and Destiny), Genesis xxi, 1 Kings xviii, Jeremiah, especially chapters vii and xxvi, and Deutero-Isaiah. The Old Testament passages are seen as relating to the condition of man in the world to-day with particular reference to the Church. The book may be welcomed as an example of the way in which contemporary Biblical scholarship may help the preacher, and through him the congregation, to know the works and word of God.   A.S.H.

WOLFF, H. W.: *Studien zum Jonabuch*. (Biblische Studien, No. 47). 1965. Pp. 130. (Neukirchener Verlag des Erziehungsvereins, Neukirchen-Vluyn).

Hans Walter Wolff is already well known for his interest in the minor prophets. Here the exegete and the preacher are both in evidence for a compressed but most lucid study of Jonah. The usual introductory subjects are discussed in six chapters, and these are followed by a translation, which groups the material in five scenes. Last come three sermons, or sets of material for sermons, the first of which is entitled 'Jonas Freiheiten und die Freiheit Gottes'.   J.M.T.B.

ZIMMERLI, W.: *The Law and the Prophets. A Study of the Meaning of the Old Testament*, trans. by R. E. Clements. 1965. Pp. 102. (Basil Blackwell, Oxford. Price: 14s. 0d.).

This really excellent and flowing translation of the author's *Das Gesetz u. d. Propheten* (see *Book List* 1964, p. 68) does at least three things: it gives a brief historical résumé of its subject in the critical writings of some representative German scholars; it traces the influence of earlier Israelite law on the teaching of the main prophets, and the development of later law in consequence; and it brings out the positive abiding values of the Old Testament message and the need for a new Christian/Jewish dialogue. Professor Zimmerli's audience at Richmond, Va., will have enjoyed these lectures, and not least the clarification of what some of his colleagues have written about the law.

D.R.Ap-T.

ZIMMERLI, W. & JEREMIAS, J.: *The Servant of God*. (Studies in Biblical Theology, No. 20). 2nd revised edition, 1965. Pp. 126. (S.C.M. Press, London. Price: paper, 18s. 0d.).

For the first edition see *Book List* 1957, p. 59. Both authors have revised their respective sections, but changes in substance are mainly in Professor Jeremias's section. The witness of the Qumran literature is now mentioned, and there have been numerous improvements of wording. The bibliography has been revised, but the 1956 edition of C. R. North, *The Suffering Servant*, and V. de Leeuw, *De Ebed Jahweh-Profetieën*, 1956 are not included. The addition of an Author Index is to be commended. This work will continue to be necessary for both Old and New Testament scholars.   D.R.Ap-T.

THE LIFE AND THOUGHT OF THE NEIGHBOURING PEOPLES

ASTOUR, M. C.: *Hellenosemitica: An Ethnic and Cultural Study in West Semitic Impact on Mycenaean Greece.* 1965. Pp. xx + 416 + 2 folding maps. (E. J. Brill, Leiden. Price: Fl. 45).

The author, a pupil of C. Virolleaud, describes his work as being, 'mutatis mutandis, . . . a posthumous vindication of Bérard's cause' defended in such works as *Les Phéniciens et l'Odyssée* (1927). Bérard took seriously the evidence for West Semitic influence on Greece in the heroic age, but his work was briefly dismissed by most of his fellow-classics, and was in any case impaired by his inadequate knowledge of Semitic languages or of pre-Phoenician Semitic literature. With the study of the Ugaritic texts and Cretan linear inscriptions (the latter study much less advanced than the former), the whole subject of 'Hellenosemitic' contacts has been reopened, notably by C. H. Gordon, who writes a foreword to this book. Astour deals with the Danaans-Danunians (whom he links with Dan/Danel), with Cadmus and the Cadmids, with Bellerophon and other Greco-Semitic healer-heroes (such as Jason, Cheiron, Asklepios), and with the evidence of archaeology and epigraphy. His arguments are not equally convincing: the Semitic origin of Cadmus may be taken as certain but one must beware of being over-impressed by such similarities as between Danaoi/Danuna and Dan/Danel/Dinah, or between Semele and Ugaritic Ṣml, the mother of eagles. Zeus's rescue of the unborn Dionysus from the womb of Semele is not a good parallel to Danel's recovery of undigested fragments of Aqhat from the stomach of Ṣml! Gordon's identification of the language of the Linear A inscriptions as Semitic is accepted, but until this identification is established (and a stronger case, *me judice*, can be made out for Luwian), it cannot be used as a basis for more far-reaching conclusions. Astour's book makes fascinating reading, and if used with proper scepticism will help to establish more certain positions on the relation between the Semitic and Hellenic worlds of the second millennium B.C.

F.F.B.

GRAY, J.: *The KRT Text in the Literature of Ras Shamra. A Social Myth of Ancient Canaan.* (Documenta et Monumenta Orientis Antiqui, V). 2nd, revised edition. 1964. Pp. xii + 88. (E. J. Brill, Leiden. Price: Fl. 20).

This widely appreciated work now appears in a second edition, more than a quarter longer than before and enriched by the recent publications of J. Nougayrol, G. R. Driver, and J. Aistleitner (but betraying no awareness of the latest views of C. Virolleaud as expressed in his *Légendes de Babylon et de Canaan*). The text has been not only extended but recast in ways indicated in the opening pages. He defines 'the major theme' with great precision as 'the legitimation of a later dynasty'. With the aid of felicitously selected texts he brings out the exact aim of the royal ideology — the maintenance of the stability of the social rather than of the natural order. The translation has been carefully revised. The commentary (pp. 31–79) is fuller

676

than that in the original edition; but in places a fuller documentation might have been supplied. It is unfortunate that on Reshef
the publications of Caquot, Simpson, and Bresciani are not
mentioned. But there can be no doubt that this second edition
will be as warmly welcomed as the first and will be a valuable
help for the Biblical scholar who, in interpreting the ancient
narratives of the Pentateuch, needs sober works such as the
volume under review bearing on the family and dynastic epics
of Canaan.

H.C.

GRAY, J.: *The Legacy of Canaan. The Ras Shamra Texts and their relevance
to the Old Testament.* (Supplements to Vetus Testamentum, Vol. V).
Second, revised edition. 1965. Pp. XII + 348. (E. J. Brill, Leiden.
Price: Fl. 52).

The first edition of this important work was noticed in the
Book List for 1958, p. 42, and this new recension equally deserves
the close attention of Old Testament scholars and Semitists alike.
Professor Gray has adhered to the arrangement of the first
edition, but the expanded bibliography testifies to the progress
in Ugaritic studies during the past eight years. It is gratifying to
record that this bibliographical material does not lie fallow in
the author's card-index but has been worked into the revised
text which has been enlarged by more than one hundred pages
compared with its predecessor. Few points of importance have
escaped the author's vigilance. The Ugaritic discoveries continue
apace and constitute the most direct and valuable source for the
documentary underpinning of the Old Testament.

E.U.

SAGGS, H. W. F.: *Everyday Life in Babylonia and Assyria.* 1965. Pp. 207
incl. 115 ills. (Batsford, London; Putnams, New York. Price:
21s. 0d.).

This well-produced and well-illustrated book, sixth in the series,
admirably fulfils its purpose of presenting, by emphasis on certain
key points, an outline of Mesopotamian life from 3000 to 300 B.C.
There are special chapters on Life at an Amorite Court, The
Scribe, Warfare, Crafts and Industries, Law, and Assyrian
religion in the seventh century. The book is popularly written,
has a good index, and for each chapter a list of books and
periodicals for further reading.

J.N.S.

SCHWANTES, S. J.: *A Short History of the Ancient Near East.* 1965.
Pp. 192, incl. 3 chronological tables, 5 maps, and many ills. (Baker
Book House, Grand Rapids, Michigan. Price: $4.95).

This photolithoprinted book contains a rapid survey of the
peoples of the Near East from the early Mesopotamian to the
Israelite period. It provides a useful introduction for beginners
in the subject. There are three synoptic chronological charts
of the empires concerned, from 2850 to 609 B.C., together with a
select bibliography and an index.

J.N.S.

VIROLLEAUD, C.: *Le Palais royal d'Ugarit*. Tome V. *Texts en cunéiformes alphabétiques des archives sud, sud-ouest et du petit palais*. (Mission de Ras Shamra, Tome XI, ed. by Schaeffer). 1965. Pp. 206. (Paris).

This work, dedicated to G. R. Driver, contains 172 more or less fragmentary texts. It needs to be noted that pp. 109–204 contain *addenda* and a second glossary. The texts vary greatly in content: mythological and liturgical fragments, letters, lists of royal servants and of men in different occupations, etc. The tablets found in an oven (thus bearing witness to the last hours of Ugarit) are arranged as numbers 59–113 and in the *addenda* as 158–170. There is a letter from the King of Tyre to the King of Ugarit, and a letter from the 'Sun' to Hammurapi, which are translations into Ugaritic, probably from Akkadian originals. New texts are expected to appear in *Ugaritica* V, increasing further the evidence at our disposal of the life and institutions of this west Semitic city, which must have closely resembled those of Jerusalem.

H.C.

THE DEAD SEA SCROLLS

AMUSIN, I. D.: *Nachodki u Mertvogo morja*. (= The Discoveries at the Dead Sea). 1964. Pp. 104. (Izdatel'stvo 'Nauka', Moskva. Price: 30 kopecks).

Since the author's book about the Dead Sea Manuscripts (*Book List* 1963, p. 60) has long been out of print, he has prepared this new account of them. The new book is written in a popular form, but is based on sound scholarship. It gives objective information about the sectarian library and about the organisation of the sect, and then follows the traces of Bar Kokhba's revolt. In an additional chapter it presents the findings of Samarian papyri from the fourth century B.C. in the region of Jericho, and the excavations at Masada. It is a very good survey. In an appendix there is a survey of literature written in Russian about the Dead Sea discoveries.

M.B.

BURCHARD, C.: *Bibliographie zu den Handschriften vom Toten Meer*, Band II. (Beihefte zur Zeitschrift für die alttestamentliche Wissenschaft, No. 89). 1965. Pp. XX + 359. (Alfred Töpelmann, Berlin. Price: DM. 84).

In the former volume (see *Book List* 1958, p. 45) Dr. Burchard listed 1556 books and articles on the Scrolls, besides reviews of books. He has now continued his work with a further 2903 entries, with references to reviews in addition. The entries are alphabetically arranged under the authors' names, with separate lists of Greek and Hebrew entries. At the end of the volume the various texts which have been brought to light are listed and the publications in which they have appeared are indicated. Of the enormous labour that has gone into this volume every user will be immediately aware, and the quite fantastic list of journals which have been combed for entries will be found most impressive. The way of the bibliographer is hard and often thankless, but he makes the way much easier for others.

H.H.R.

CROSS, F. M. & OTHERS: *Scrolls from the Wilderness of the Dead Sea.*
A guide to the exhibition, *The Dead Sea Scrolls of Jordan*, arranged
by the Smithsonian Institution in co-operation with the Government
of the Hashemite Kingdom of Jordan and the Palestine Archaeological
Museum. 1965. Pp. 36 inc. 3 ills. and 19 plates with 2 plans inside
covers. (The Trustees of the British Museum. Price: 3s. 0d.).

The bulk of this brochure consists of a description of the contents
of the various Caves of Qumran, contributed by Professor F. M.
Cross, and translations by various scholars of texts displayed in
the exhibition, which consist mainly of Cave 4 material. The
information is clear and relevant. An inset of four pages is
supplied by the British Museum, and introduces supplementary
items which have been added to the Jordanian collection,
presumably to illuminate the main exhibition. Some of the
items, however, might possibly result in confusing the ordinary
visitor rather than helping him. B.J.R.

DRIVER, G. R.: *The Judaean Scrolls. The Problem and a Solution.* 1965.
Pp. xii + 624, incl. 1 map and table of dates. (Basil Blackwell,
Oxford. Price: 70s. 0d.).

Nowhere else in the literature on the Scrolls is such a vast fund
of knowledge and information presented as in this long awaited
book. In ten sections, each with an average of six or seven
sub-sections, every aspect of the study is treated and the discussion
ranges from a rigorous scrutiny and condemnation of practically
every theory already devised to the presentation of the author's
own solution. Occasionally, scholars have come to the same
general position as Professor Driver, but no one has been
treading along his paths. The work is indeed a *tour de force*.
The author describes the discovery of the Scrolls, and the
contemporary party-formations in Judaism, and then tackles the
contents of the Scrolls. The Sons of Zadok are associated
ultimately with Balthusians in Egypt in the first century B.C.,
and their 'fourth philosophy'. By the first century A.D. they were
back in Judaea, and able to withstand opposition by virtue of
their fortifications in Qumran. As Roman attack became
imminent, the more militarist elements became extremist and
Zealot. The 'Rightful Teacher' is Menahem, who was murdered
on Mount Ophel in A.D. 66. The identification of the Zadokite
(ultimately Zealot) movement is further considered in the light
of the Calendar, ciphers and cryptograms, literary devices, and
fasts in the Scrolls. Finally, general questions of date, concealment in the caves, archaeology, palaeography, and of doctrines
and customs, contacts with New Testament and other literatures
are discussed.
The book is not likely to carry immediate conviction, especially
to the specialists who are wedded to other interpretations, but
no one will be able to refute its details without a second and even
a third reading. And certainly no one can afford not to study the
book very carefully. B.J.R.

ROTH, C.: *The Dead Sea Scrolls: A New Historical Approach.* 1965. Pp. xx + 99. (W. W. Norton, New York. Price: $4.50).

This is a reissue of the author's *The Historical Background of the Dead Sea Scrolls* (reviewed in *Book List* 1959, p. 40), with an enlarged introduction and three additional appendices, on 'The Era of the Habakkuk Commentary' (previously published in *Vetus Testamentum*, xi, 1961), 'The Zealots — a Jewish Religious Sect' (previously published in *Judaism*, viii, 1959), and 'The Characters of the Qumran Documents'. Dr. Roth is now less inclined to identify the Teacher of Righteousness, but claims that his view is rendered certain by the discovery at Masada of a document which quite indisputably came from the Qumran sect. Yadin is more cautious (cf. *Illustrated London News*, October 31st, 1964, p. 697), and it is hard to see why this new evidence is inconsistent with the view, published long before it was found, that the Qumran sect supported the rebels in the Roman war. After the destruction of the Qumran centre by the Romans, it would be natural for any Qumran sectaries who escaped to go to Masada, and to take with them such of their books as they could carry.

H.H.R.

SANDERS, J. A.: *The Psalms Scroll of Qumrân Cave 11 ($11QPs^a$)*. (Discoveries in the Judaean Desert of Jordan, IV). American Schools of Oriental Research; Palestine Archaeological Museum. 1965. Pp. xii + 100 + XVII plates. (Clarendon Press, Oxford. Price: 63s. 0d.).

The official publication of Qumran material keeps up with its timetable, and the contents of the present volume are particularly welcome, because they provide the text of the much vaunted Psalms texts of Cave 11. Whatever importance one might attach to the sectarian scrolls of Qumran, the texts are always insurpassable. In addition to Ps. cxix (9 columns, placed between Pss. cxxxii and cxxxv) there are fragments of some forty others. Of the non-Biblical material special mention must be made of the 'Syriac' non-canonical Psalms (one of them being the Hebrew text of the LXX Ps. cli with variants). All the texts are reproduced, transcribed, and translated, with full annotation. The introductory portions are workmanlike and interesting. The indexes are also helpful. The publication is worthy of the series, and we congratulate Professor Sanders on his achievement.

B.J.R.

VELLAS, B. M.: *Ek ton cheirographon tes Nekras Thalasses: To Biblion tou Polemou ton Hyion tou Photos kata ton Hyion tou Skotous.* (Phrontisteriake Bibliotheke tes Palaias Diathekes, Teuchos IV). 1965. Pp. 92. (Athens).

This is a Greek translation of the War Scroll from Qumran with introduction and notes — the notes appearing on the lower half of each page beneath the translation. The compiler of the work, who is seen to have based it especially on Ezekiel xxxviii, xxxix, and on Daniel xi. 40–xii. 3, is held to have written it before the

Roman occupation of 63 B.C. Vellas agrees that the weapons and tactics described are Roman, but points out that Roman arms were familiar in Western Asia long before Pompey. The internal evidence of the work suggests to him a date in the second century B.C., after the Hasmonean rising and the onset of internal strife in the Seleucid kingdom. The Kittim of the Scroll, he thinks, are not the Romans only but all the enemies of Israel. If the weapons and tactics are Roman, however, it is relevant that they appear to be those of the Roman army of the first century B.C., not of the second century. Vellas is inclined to regard the contents of 1QM as a unity, but considers that the publication of the material from Cave 4 must be awaited before anything more certain is said.

F.F.B.

DE WAARD, J.: *A Comparative Study of the Old Testament Text in the Dead Sea Scrolls and in the New Testament.* (Studies on the Texts of the Desert of Judah, Volume IV.) 1965. Pp. vi + 101. (E. J. Brill, Leiden. Price: Fl. 25).

The author undertakes a comparative study of Old Testament quotations in the New Testament with Biblical texts from Qumran and with Biblical quotations in non-Biblical texts from Qumran. His most interesting conclusions relate to Biblical quotations in the speeches in Acts (e.g., Deuteronomy xviii. 18 f. in Acts iii. 22 f., Hab. i. 5 in Acts xiii. 41, and Amos ix. 11 in Acts xv. 16); he has added to the arguments (already very strong) against regarding these speeches as free compositions by the author of Acts.

F.F.B.

YADIN, Y.: *The Finds from the Bar Kokhba Period in the Cave of Letters.* (Judean Desert Studies). 1963. Pp. xx + 280 incl. 21 tables and 94 figures + 108 plates. (The Israel Exploration Society, Jerusalem. Price: $20; £7 7s. 0d.).

This is the first of two volumes which will give the authentic account of the contents of the Cave of Letters discovered by the Israelis in 1953, and explored in 1960 and 1961. The cave is in the region of Engedi, and is one of two well-known sources of extremely important manuscripts from the Bar Kokhba period. The present volume consists of a detailed description of the excavation and of the vast horde of utensils and objects of all kinds discovered there. The second will provide the texts. The objects range from utensils used for ritual purposes to domestic items made of leather, wool, and linen, and provide both unique specimens and objects comparable with others found throughout the extent of the Roman Empire. The 108 Plates include some 24 colour reproductions and a textiles colour chart of 40 different shades. Of the 94 figures 4 consist of curves of infra-red spectograms and provide a challenge to most Old Testament scholars. The superb production is financed by the 'Bar Kokhba Foundation' associated with the name of Mr. Charles Clore. The second volume is avidly awaited.

B.J.R.

APOCRYPHA AND POST-BIBLICAL JUDAISM

*BELFORD, L.: *Introduction to Judaism*. (Libra Books). 1965. Pp. 128. (Darton, Longman & Todd, London. Price: 6s. 6d.).

The author has aimed at giving a thumbnail sketch of Judaism. It can be said without hesitation that he has succeeded admirably. His style is clear and succinct and he manages to cover some 3,000 years on about 130 pages. There are five chapters: God and the Covenant with Israel, the Foundations of Jewish Survival, including a survey on Mishnah and Talmud, The Making of Modern Judaism, containing brief introductions to mediaeval Jewish philosophy, Kabbalism, the Hasidim, the Reform Movement, Neo-orthodoxy, Conservative Judaism, and Zionism. The last two chapters deal with Observances and Ceremonies, and Questions about Judaism, such as what do Jews think of Jesus and of Christians; do they engage in missionary activities and how do they react to intermarriage? There are some minor errors concerning the attitude of Maimonides to 'unbelievers', Jewish or Gentile, *mezuzoth* at the doorposts of synagogues, the origin of the *Qaddish* and the small tractate Gerim which is described as a treatise of the Gemara, but none of these mars the excellence of the book which should serve very well indeed to meet the needs of Sixth-Formers and of the many who have only vague notions about the main tenets of Jewish faith and practice.

S.S.

LESHEM, H.: *The Sabbath and Festivals of Israel in Halacha, Aggadah, History, Way of Life and Folklore.* Vol. I: Sabbath, New Year, Day of Atonement (sic), Sukkot, Hanukkah and Purim. Pp. 1–334. Vol. II: Passover, Jndependence (sic) day, Pentecost, The Three Mourning Weeks, Bibliography and Index. Pp. 335–704. 1965. ('N.I.V.', Tel-Aviv).

These two volumes of short essays, referring, as occasion presents itself, to Arabic and Qaraitic sources, are packed with ingenious notes and will interest mainly students of Judaism. Biblical scholars, however, may be interested in pp. 185–186; 228–233; 300–309; 387–390; 397–401; 507–510. The work contains a fine bibliography and three indexes.

M.W.

METZGER, B. M. (ed. by): *The Oxford Annotated Apocrypha.* The Apocrypha of the Old Testament, Revised Standard Version, with introductions, comments, cross references, tables of chronology, and index. 1965. Pp. xxii + 298 + maps on endpapers. (Oxford University Press, New York. Price: 25s. 0d.).

This is a companion volume to the *Oxford Annotated Bible* (*Book List* 1963, p. 25), and is an equally good guide for those who want to see at a glance what the text is about. The notes, necessarily brief and therefore sometimes dogmatic, are adequate for the ordinary reader. The introduction, in five sections, is a straightforward statement of what the Apocrypha contains, how it has been received by different sections of the Church, and the influence it has exercised.

L.H.B.

SCHOLEM, G. G.: *On the Kabbalah and its Symbolism*, trans, by Ralph Manheim. 1965. Pp. vi+216. (Routledge and Kegan Paul, London. Price: 30s. 0d.).

This volume is a translation of the author's *Zur Kabbala und ihrer Symbolik*, published in Zürich in 1960. It contains five essays: Religious Authority and Mysticism, The Meaning of the Torah in Jewish Mysticism, Kabbalah and Myth, Tradition and New Creation in the Ritual of the Kabbalists, and The Idea of the Golem. Only the first two articles have a more direct interest for *Alt-Testamentler*. Within the framework of a short notice it is impossible to do justice to the depth of scholarship and insight which confronts the reader on every page. There are important observations on the rarity of secular mysticism and its structural difference from religious mysticism. In spite of the recognised danger of 'uncontrolled and uncontrollable deviation from traditional authority' mystics appear to remain, on the whole, faithful to their denominational legacy. Kabbalists in particular continued to live according to the rules and laws of normative Judaism. In fact they added to, rather than detracted from, them and their ideas were expressed in commentaries on the Bible — or read into it. The distinction between the literal and the spiritual meaning of Scripture is traced back to Philo whose exegetical methods were taken over by the Church Fathers, the Christian Middle Ages and also by Islamic authors. The Kabbalists added the theosophico-mystical sense (*sod*) to the *peshaṭ*, aggadic and philosophico-allegorical interpretation. Scholem is inclined to assume, with Bacher, that the combination of these four levels of exegetic endeavour owes its appearance to the influence of contemporary Christian hermeneutics in Spain. Everybody interested in the wider aspects of mysticism will read the whole book with unabated attention. A useful index concludes the volume. The translation by Manheim is excellent.

S.S.

SCHRIRE, T.: *Hebrew Amulets*. 1966. Pp. xii + 180 incl. 53 plates. (Routledge & Kegan Paul, London. Price: 50s. 0d.).

This work is the result of a painstaking study of close upon a thousand amulets. It contains an introduction which deals, amongst other things, with typical Hebrew amulets reflecting beliefs and notions stemming from Kabbalistic and Hasidic lore. Amulets having a Judaeo-Arabic and Judaeo-Christian origin are also dealt with. *Shemoth* (names) of God, of angels, and of various Biblical passages which prevail in the amulets are given special attention. It is a pity that there is no consistency in the transliteration of Hebrew words.

M.W.

SIMPSON, W. W.: *Jewish Prayer and Worship: An Introduction for Christians*. 1965. Pp. 128. (S.C.M. Press, London. Price: 9s. 6d.).

This volume is described exactly in the title and sub-title. It is a sympathetic study of the modern Jewish prayer book (the first 66 pages), and for the rest an anthology of Synagogue prayers, and translations of Jewish synagogue and home hymns. The volume fulfils its purpose admirably, and includes even the 'madrigal of numbers' found at the end of the Passover books — the one-to-thirteen hymn, and the glorious Pentecost hymn, 'Could we with ink the ocean fill'.   N.H.S.

PHILOLOGY AND GRAMMAR

BARNES, O. L.: *A New Approach to the Problem of the Hebrew Tenses and its Solution without Recourse to Waw-Consecutive.* Illustrated by New Translations of various O.T. passages with an Analysis of each Verb. 1965. Pp. v + 134 incl. 2 diagrams. (J. Thornton and Son, Oxford. Price: 10s. 0d.).

Mr. Barnes, whose study *The Song of Songs* was reviewed in *Book List* 1963, p. 21, now gives us in similar reproduced typescript his explanation of the Hebrew verbal system. Exemplifying his results by a translation and analysis of selected Old Testament passages he seeks to demonstrate that the Hebrew tenses 'mark *the time* of an action or state expressed by the Verb, and the completeness of the action or state *at that time* vividly viewed as NOW in course of fulfilment (Imperfect) or ALREADY FULFILLED *before one's eyes* (Perfect), even though the event or state realised may *actually* be in the Past or Future'. (p. 7). While Mr. Barnes's work might be characterized as description rather than explanation, it is to be welcomed as an ingenious attack on an old problem.   W.D.McH.

BLAU, J.: *The Emergence and Linguistic Background of Judaeo-Arabic.* A study of the origins of Middle Arabic. (*Scripta Judaica. V*). 1965. Pp. xx + 228. (Oxford University Press, London. Price: 75s. 0d.).

Dr. Blau, who is the author also of a *Grammar of Mediaeval Judaeo-Arabic* (Jerusalem, 1961), here examines the history and development of this dialect. The successive chapters discuss its emergence, its characteristic marks and phonetics, its various linguistic trends, its inconstancy and laxity of expression, its general and isolated patterns; and three appendices deal with the linguistic character of early Moslem 'Middle-Arabic', the integration of Hebrew elements in Judaeo-Arabic, and vestiges of *tanwîn* in the modern Arabic dialects of the Bedouin. The author's conclusions are that Middle-Arabic dialects arose in the early years of the Arab conquests, and as a consequence of them, among the lower elements of the conquered urban population but that they rapidly penetrated the upper literate classes, that the Judaeo-Arabic dialect, used by Jews addressing their fellow Jews, was a language in its own right; that it was used in both religion and secular literature and was regarded by Jews themselves as a distinct literary language which also possessed its own literary tradition; and that, apart from the Hebrew scripts, it did not differ much from the Middle-Arabic dialects of their Moslem and Christian neighbours, though more vulgar than that of the Moslem texts and in this respect nearer to the Christian forms. Unlike these last, Judaeo-Arabic texts are not found before the ninth century A.D., although Jews were probably among the first speakers of Middle-Arabic dialects; and dialectal variations can be detected in Judaeo-Arabic texts. Every peculiarity of the dialect here examined is discussed, in detail and with ample illustrations, within the historical framework of its development and within the light of the parallel dialects. The English is exceptionally good, being marred by scarcely a dozen solecisms, and other slips are commendably few. Altogether, the book is an admirable piece of work, which will be very useful to both Hebraists and Arabists who find themselves reading Judaeo-Arabic works, especially commentaries on the Old Testament and lexical compilations.   G.R.D.

DAHOOD, M.: *Ugaritic-Hebrew Philology.* Marginal Notes on Recent Publications. (Biblica et Orientalia (Sacra Scriptura Antiquitatibus Orientalibus Illustrata, 17). 1965. Pp. VIII + 90. (Pontifical Biblical Institute, Rome. Price: L. 1.200; $2.00).

Father Dahood's monograph provides a most useful supplement to Gordon's new *Ugaritic Textbook* and carries bibliographical documentation beyond 1961 when Gordon's work was consigned to the printers. He follows Gordon's numbering, and students will find it convenient to consult the two works in conjunction. Dahood, who has collected copious notes on the grammar and lexicon of Ugaritic, provides a running commentary on all sections of Gordon's masterpiece. Meanwhile there are quite a few further marginalia that might be added to both books. After 37 years of discovery and research Ugaritology shows a vitality and productivity which are likely to grow for many more years.

E.U.

GORDON, C. H.: *Ugaritic Textbook.* Grammar, Texts in transliteration, Cuneiform selections, Glossary, Indices. (Analecta Orientalia 38). 1965. Pp. XVI + 548. (Pontificium Institutum Biblicum, Rome. Price: £11).

Gordon's Ugaritic *chef-d'oeuvre* has progressed from the slim *Ugaritic Grammar* in 1940 (*Book List* 1946, p. 59; *Eleven Years*, p. 59) by way of the 1947 *Handbook* (*Book List* 1948, p. 14; *Eleven Years*, p. 124) and the 1955 *Manual* (*Book List* 1956, p. 72; *Eleven Years*, p. 779) to this massive tome of 547 pages bearing eloquent testimony to the important developments in this field of study and to the author's scholarship and toil. The printing of this complex work has extended over four years, so that (apart from some additions entered in March 1965) it reflects the position as of 1961. Much progress has been achieved since then, and some of it has been embodied in Father Mitchell Dahood's *Ugaritic-Hebrew Philology*, Rome 1965 (reviewed above). All students of Ugaritic are once again profoundly indebted to Professor Gordon.

Scholars who already possess the *Ugaritic Manual* will wish to know to what extent the *Textbook* supersedes its predecessor. Apart from revisions throughout the book, the grammatical part has been enlarged by some 35 pages, the texts in transliteration by some 60 pages (including the texts of *PRU* V), the cuneiform selections have been more than doubled, and some 700 entries have been added to the glossary. The indices have been much expanded and now include a most useful English-Ugaritic part. A select bibliography of some dimensions (beyond the rather summary bibliographical notes) would have been of great value to the student and would also have mitigated the long delay in the printing of the book by taking documentation up to 1965. However, any critical note must pale before so massive an achievement.

E.U.

GOSHEN-GOTTSTEIN, M. H.: *Hebrew and Semitic Languages. An Outline Introduction.* (In Hebrew). 1965. Pp. 28. (Devir, Tel Aviv).

Professor Goshen-Gottstein's three short articles on Aramaic, Biblical Hebrew, and the Semitic Languages, written for the *Lexicon Biblicum* (Tel Aviv, 1965), present simply and soberly the results of research there so far. Some readers will be disappointed to find that semantic problems are mentioned only as they affect questions of phonology and morphology (e.g. on p. 14). On the other hand, a brief reappraisal of the evidence for different dialects within Old Testament Hebrew (pp. 11 f.), and a tentative description of the Semitic language family based on a chronological framework (instead of the traditional geographical one) (p. 23), together with an interesting Semitic 'family tree' (p. 28), comparative tables, and up-to-date bibliographies at the end of each article, make one hope that a European translation will soon make these important little articles easily available outside Israel. The booklet ends with a plea for closer co-operation between Biblical scholars and linguists.

J.F.A.S.

HUFFMON, H. B.: *Amorite Personal Names in the Mari Texts.* A structural and lexical study. 1965. Pp. xvi + 304. (Johns Hopkins Press, Baltimore, Maryland, U.S.A. Price: $7.50 or 60s. 0d.).

The work here reviewed is a study of the personal names of the Old-Babylonian period on the tablets from Mari. These have raised the number of such names from the relatively few which T. Bauer studied in his *Ostkanaanäer* (1926) to nearly 900, forming a homogeneous and easily recognized class, clearly distinguishable from those of pure Babylonian origin. They show great consistency in spelling and inflection, as also in their structural patterns, which makes them extraordinarily valuable for any attempt to reconstruct the 'Amorite' dialect. The author studies these names under six heads according as they consist of a single verbal element, a nominal sentence, a noun qualified by another in the genitive case, three elements, hypocoristic forms, and a single nominal element. He also gives a glossary of names, of the Amorite elements comprising them, and of the names of Mesopotamian gods included in them. The work is very carefully done (except that Aistleitner's name is misspelt throughout the book) and offers a welcome summary of present knowledge of the Amorite language, even if some of the interpretations may well be doubted; but certainty is unobtainable where no context is available to control speculation.

G.R.D.

SCHOTTROFF, W.: *'Gedenken' im alten Orient und im Alten Testament. Die Wurzel zākar im semitischen Sprachkreis.* (Wissenschaftliche Monographien zum Alten und Neuen Testament, Band 15). 1964. Pp. X + 370. (Neukirchener Verlag des Erziehungsvereins, Neukirchen-Vluyn. Price: DM. 59.50).

This volume contains the fullest treatment of the root *zkr* 'remember' and its derivatives which has ever been published, and is certain to establish itself as the standard work of reference on the subject. All the available material has been assembled and is thoroughly discussed. The first part is devoted to the etymology of *zkr*, and to its occurrence in Akkadian, Canaanite (Amarna Letter 228, Lachish ostracon II, Phoenician inscriptions), Aramaic, and South Semitic (it is lacking in Ugaritic), and in Semitic proper names. The second part is concerned with the root as used of God and man in the Old Testament, with the derived stems of the verb, and with the nouns *zeker*, *zikkaron*, and *'azkarah*. There is a full bibliography and an index of passages in the Old Testament, and in non-canonical, including Qumran, literature. Of lexicographical interest is the separation of *zkr* 'remember' from *zkr* II (*zakar* 'male'), and the technical meaning 'protocol' given to *zikkaron* which is held to be of Aramaic origin.

D.W.T.

ULLENDORFF, E.: *The Challenge of Amharic.* 1965. Pp. 22. (School of Oriental and African Studies, University of London).

In this inaugural lecture of the first holder of the newly created Chair of Ethiopian Studies in the University of London, some of the main characteristics of Amharic, the official language of the Ethiopian Empire, and the difficulties which they present to western students, are admirably sketched. Among them are extreme brachylogy, the absence of indirect speech, abrupt changes of person, a tendency to concrete expressions, long periods, and inadequacy of punctuation. A literal translation of Amharic is often unintelligible. The Amharic verbal system is essentially Semitic in character, and fifty per cent of the vocabulary has a Semitic basis. The introduction of European loanwords into the language and its effect upon Amharic readers, and the services to the language which the establishment of an Amharic Language Academy might perform, are touched on. If Amharic is a difficult language, its attractiveness and charm amply reward the student of it. The challenge of Amharic is not only to linguists, but also to anthropologists, sociologists, and students of literature, to Semitists and Africanists alike. The lecture will be enjoyed by everyone who has an interest in language problems, both theoretical and practical.

D.W.T.

UNGNAD, A.: *Grammatik des Akkadischen*. (Völlig neubearbeitet von Lubor Matouš). 1964. Pp. xvi+202. (Verlag C. H. Beck, München. Price: paper, DM. 28; cloth, DM. 32).

Ungnad's *Babylonisch-assyrische Grammatik* has proved its value as an introduction to Akkadian for forty years, and a warm welcome will be accorded to this fourth edition of it, which represents a completely fresh revision of the third edition in the light of present-day knowledge. The work of W. von Soden especially has made some rearrangement of the material necessary, particularly in the treatment of the structure of Akkadian syntax. References to important articles and monographs published since von Soden's *Grundriss* appeared in 1952 are included in the footnotes. This revised edition, which retains the economy and clarity of its predecessors, will ensure a prolonged period of usefulness for the grammar, and it may serve as an admirable introduction to von Soden's more advanced work.

D.W.T.

WECHTER, P.: *Ibn Barūn's Arabic Works on Hebrew Grammar and Lexicography*. 1964. Pp. xvi + 236. (The Dropsie College for Hebrew and Cognate Learning, Philadelphia. Oxford University Press, London. Price: 60s. 0d.).

The Spanish Jew Yiṣḥāq Abū Ibrāhīm Ibn Barūn, whose writings were known to and highly regarded by his contemporaries Moses Ibn Ezra and Judah Halevi, wrote in Arabic *The Book of Comparison between the Hebrew and the Arabic Languages* at the end of the eleventh century. It is extant in fragmentary form only. The first part of it comprises a comparative grammar, and the second an alphabetically arranged lexicon of Hebrew words which have Arabic equivalents. Hitherto scholars have had to rely upon the Russian translation of this work by the late P. K. Kokovtsov. Now comes this welcome complete translation of it by the late Dr. Wechter, who has added to it introductions and voluminous notes which display wide erudition. Ibn Barūn has much to contribute to Hebrew-Arabic study, and many of his Arabic etymologies and phrases deserve inclusion in an up-to-date Hebrew lexicon.

D.W.T.

WILENSKI, M. (ed. by): *Sepher-ha-Riqmah* (in Hebrew), 2 vols. 2nd ed. 1964. Vol. I, pp. 16 + 398; Vol. II, IV plates + pp. 399–736. (The Hebrew Language Academy, Jerusalem).

Jonah ibn Janaḥ's *Kitab Al-Luma* (containing contributions to grammar proper, syntax, and Biblical hermeneutics, consultable even at the present day with great profit!), rendered into Hebrew by Yehudah ibn Tibbon who called it *Sepher ha-Riqmah*, was first edited by Michael Wilenski, collating four MSS of Tibbon's translation with the Arabic original. This edition is now very difficult to obtain. Moreover, since its appearance (Berlin 1929–31), Wilenski kept on adding copious notes in the margin of his private copy. Now, Wilenski's original edition along with these notes have been edited by David Tené in consultation with Zeev Ben-Hayyim. Scholars will be greatly indebted to them for having done their work so well and with so much erudition.

M.W.

Index of Authors

689

BÄCHLI, O., 437
BAECK, L., 233
BAGATTI, B., 624
BAGATTI, R., 139
BAGNANI, G., 560
BAILLET, M., 454, 516
BAINTON, R. H., 477
BAKER, H. W., 454
BAKER, J. A., 353, 614
BALHATCHER, D., 523
BALKAN, K., 85
BALLA, E., 162
BALTZER, K., 246, 324, 345
BALY, D., 90, 491
BAMBERGER, B. J., 319
BAMMEL, E., 81, 185, 405
BAMMEL, F., 246
BANDT, H., 402
BARCLAY, R. A., 584
BARCLAY, W., 345
BAR-DEROMA, H., 147
BARDTKE, H., 184, 242, 246 297,
    503, 555, 609
BARNA, G., 159
BARNES, O. L., 415, 684
BARON, S. W., 5, 23, 128, 177, 301
BARR, J., 242, 391, 437, 493, 663
BARRETT, C. K., 83
BARTH, C., 346
BARTHEL, P., 595
BARTHÉLEMY, J. D., 232, 472, 497,
    522
BARTON, D. M., 314, 350, 403, 560
BARUCQ, A., 155, 243, 573
BAUER, J. B., 183, 397
BAUER, W., 639
BAUERNFEIND, O., 80, 185, 477
BAUMBACH, G., 225
BAUMGÄRTEL, F., 6, 183, 245, 246,
    251, 292, 325, 391, 402, 558
BAUMGARTNER, W., 7, 135, 142,
    180, 241, 246, 317, 472, 577
BEA, A., 558
BEARDSLEE, W. A., 9
BEARE, F. W., 560
BEAUCAMP, E., 211, 399, 523
BECKER, J., 609
BEEK, M. A., 3, 184, 188, 313, 451,
    491, 624
BEESTON, A. F. L., 85
BEGRICH, J., 555
BEHLER, G. M., 275
BELFORD, L., 682
BEN-HAYYIM, Z., 175, 560, 688
BEN-HORIN, M., 398

BENOIT, P., 250, 297, 624
BENTWICH, N., 255
BEN-ZEVI, I., 334, 572
BERGHE, L. V., 87
VAN DEN BERGHE, P., 516
BERNHARDT, K.-H., 40, 205, 352
BERTHOLET, A., 316
BERTRAM, G., 184, 245, 317, 476,
    477
BERTSCH, A., 134
BESNARD, A.-M., 523
BETZ, I., 245, 477
BETZ, O., 232, 298, 556
BEWER, J. A., 96, 427
BEYER, K., 463
BEYERLIN, W., 205, 346, 483, 627,
    651
BIARD, P., 281
Bibel-Lexikon, 7
Bibeltheologisches Wörterbuch,
    183, 397
La Bible, 28, 265
Bible Encyclopaedia for Children,
    564
Bible, La Sainte (de Jérusalem),
    155, 202, 342, 423
Bible, Oxford Annotated, 419
Bible, The Holy (R.S.V.), 645
Biblická Konkordance, 4, 79, 139,
    313, 398, 471, 556, 623
Biblisch-historisches Handwörter-
    buch, 562
Biblisch-theologisches Hand-
    wörterbuch, 561
BIČ, M., 3, 4, 79, 81, 139, 184, 188,
    266, 299, 313, 334, 352, 398,
    471, 556, 573, 623, 629
BIEDER, W., 6, 185, 251
BIETENHARD, H., 69, 80, 221
Bijbels Woordenboek, 3, 79
BILLERBECK, P., 72, 388
BIRAM, A., 318, 492
BISHOP, E. F. F., 437
BJORNARD, R. B., 288
BLACK, M., 317, 335, 371, 477,
    542
BLACKWOOD, A. W., 211, 652
BLAIR, E. P., 574
BLANK, S. H., 8, 281, 319, 353
BLAU, J., 684
BLEEKER, C. J., 557, 664
BLOEMENDAL, W., 261
BLOOM, M. J., 550
BODENHEIMER, F. S., 241
BOECKER, H. J., 652